Elements of
Language
Program

Sixth Course

Elements of
Language

Sixth Course

Lee Odell

Richard Vacca

Renée Hobbs

Grammar, Usage, and Mechanics
Instructional Framework by

John E. Warriner

HOLT, RINEHART AND WINSTON

A Harcourt Classroom Education Company

Austin • New York • Orlando • Atlanta • San Francisco • Boston • Dallas • Toronto • London

STAFF CREDITS

EDITORIAL

Director
Mescal Evler

Manager of Editorial Operations
Bill Wahlgren

Executive Editor
Kristine E. Marshall

Program Editors
Marcia L. Kelley
Suzanne Thompson

Project Editor
Megan W. Truex

Writing and Editing
Jane Archer Feinstein, Rebecca Bennett, Roger Boylan, Eric Estlund, Annie Hartnett, Sean W. Henry, Jim Hynes, Kevin Lemoine, Carla C. Robinson, Errol Smith, Pam Thompson

Quality Assurance—Grammar, Mechanics, and Usage
Robert H. Hoyt
Kathryn Rogers

Copyediting
Michael Neibergall, *Copyediting Manager;* Mary Malone, *Senior Copyeditor;* Joel Bourgeois, Gabrielle Field, Suzi A. Hunn, Jane Kominek, Millicent Ondras, Theresa Reding, Désirée Reid, Kathleen Scheiner, *Copyeditors*

Project Administration
Marie Price, *Managing Editor;* Lori De La Garza, *Editorial Operations Coordinator;* Tracy DeMont, Heather Cheyne, Mark Holland, Marcus Johnson, Jill O'Neal, Joyce Rector, Janet Riley, Kelly Tankersley, *Project Administration;* Gail Coupland, Elizabeth Dickson, Ruth Hooker, Margaret Sanchez, *Word Processing*

Editorial Permissions
Janet Harrington

ART, DESIGN, AND PHOTO

Book Design
Senior Design Director
Diane Motz

Robin Bouvette, Candace Moore, *Senior Designers*
John Harrison, David Hernandez, *Designers;* Mercedes Newman, Charlie Taliaferro, *Design Associates*

Photo Studio
Lauren Eischen, Victoria Smith

Graphic Services
Kristen Darby, *Manager;*
Jane Dixon, Linda Wilbourn

Image Acquisitions
Joe London, *Director*
Elaine Tate, *Supervisor;* Erin Cone, Sunday Patterson, *Art Buyers*

Jeannie Taylor, Tim Taylor, *Photo Research Supervisors;* Rick Benavides, *Assistant Photo Researcher*

Book and Media Design
Joe Melomo, *Design Director*

Cover Design
Joe Melomo
Jane Dixon

PRODUCTION

Simira Davis, Joan Lindsay, Beth Prevelige

MANUFACTURING

Shirley Cantrell, *Senior Manufacturing Coordinator*

LEE ODELL helped establish the pedagogical framework for the composition strand of *Elements of Language*. In addition, he guided the development of the scope and sequence and pedagogical design of the Writing Workshops. Dr. Odell is Professor of Composition Theory and Research and, since 1996, Director of the Writing Program at Rensselaer Polytechnic Institute. He began his career teaching English in middle and high schools. More recently he has worked with teachers in grades K–12 to establish a program that involves students from all disciplines in writing across the curriculum and for communities outside their classrooms. Dr. Odell's most recent book (with Charles R. Cooper) is *Evaluating Writing: The Role of Teachers' Knowledge about Text, Learning, and Culture* (1999). Dr. Odell is Past Chair of the Conference on College Composition and Communication and of the NCTE's Assembly for Research.

RICHARD VACCA helped establish the conceptual basis for the reading strand of *Elements of Language*. In addition, he guided the development of the pedagogical design and the scope and sequence of skills in the Reading Workshops. Dr. Vacca is Professor of Education at Kent State University. He recently completed a term as the forty-second President of the International Reading Association. Originally a middle school and high school teacher, Dr. Vacca served as the project director of the Cleveland Writing Demonstration Project for several years. He is the co-author of *Content Area Reading; Reading and Learning to Read;* and articles and chapters related to adolescents' literacy development. In 1989, Dr. Vacca received the College Reading Association's A. B. Herr Award for Outstanding Contributions to Reading Education. Currently, he is co-chair of the IRA's Commission on Adolescent Literacy.

RENÉE HOBBS helped develop the theoretical framework for the viewing and representing strand of *Elements of Language*. She guided the development of the scope and sequence; served as the authority on terminology, definitions, and pedagogy; and directed the planning for the video series. Dr. Hobbs is Associate Professor of Communication at Babson College in Wellesley, Massachusetts, and Director of the Media Literacy Project. Active in the field of media education, Dr. Hobbs has served as Director of the Institute on Media Education, Harvard Graduate School of Education; Director of the "Know TV" Project, Discovery Networks and Time Warner Cable; and Board Member, The New York Times Newspaper in Education Program. She works actively in staff development in school districts nationwide. Dr. Hobbs has contributed articles and chapters on media, technology, and education to many publications.

JOHN E. WARRINER was a high school English teacher when he developed the original organizational structure for his classic *English Grammar and Composition* series. The approach pioneered by Mr. Warriner was distinctive, and the editorial staff of Holt, Rinehart and Winston have worked diligently to retain the unique qualities of his pedagogy. For the same reason, HRW continues to credit Mr. Warriner as an author of *Elements of Language* in recognition of his groundbreaking work. John Warriner also co-authored the *English Workshop* series and was editor of *Short Stories: Characters in Conflict*. Throughout his career, however, teaching remained Mr. Warriner's major interest, and he taught for thirty-two years in junior and senior high schools and in college.

The following teachers and students worked with HRW's editorial staff to provide models of student writing for the book.

Teachers

Karen L. Bradberry
Van Buren High School
Van Buren, Arkansas

Ann E. Dixon
DeLand High School
DeLand, Florida

Linda Elliott
Del Campo High School
Fair Oaks, California

Richard Gruss
Rockingham County High
    School
Burlington, North Carolina

Judith Mullins
Westwood High School
Austin, Texas

Victoria Reis
Western High School
Ft. Lauderdale, Florida

Linda Shepherd
Terry Parker High School
Jacksonville, Florida

Students

Colin Dietch
Rockingham County High
    School
Burlington, North Carolina

Cara Farris
Del Campo High School
Fair Oaks, California

Cody Keller
Van Buren High School
Van Buren, Arkansas

Stacey Kounelias
Westwood High School
Austin, Texas

Natalia Machuca
Western High School
Ft. Lauderdale, Florida

Billie Jean Murray
Moncks Corner High School
Moncks Corner, South Carolina

Shiven Patel
DeLand High School
DeLand, Florida

Elizabeth Shaw
Alexandria, Virginia

Carlos Williams
Terry Parker High School
Jacksonville, Florida

The following teachers participated in the pre-publication field test or review of prototype materials for the *Elements of Language* series.

Nadene Adams
Robert Gray Middle School
Portland, Oregon

Carol Alves
Apopka High School
Apopka, Florida

Susan Atkinson
O. P. Norman Junior High School
Kaufman, Texas

Sheryl L. Babione
Fremont Ross High School
Fremont, Ohio

Jane Baker
Elkins High School
Missouri City, Texas

Martha Barnard
Scarborough High School
Houston, Texas

Jennifer S. Barr
James Bowie High School
Austin, Texas

Leslie Benefield
Reed Middle School
Duncanville, Texas

Gina Birdsall
Irving High School
Irving, Texas

Sara J. Brennan
Murchison Middle School
Austin, Texas

Janelle Brinck
Leander Middle School
Leander, Texas

Geraldine K. Brooks
William B. Travis High School
Austin, Texas

Peter J. Caron
Cumberland Middle School
Cumberland, Rhode Island

Patty Cave
O. P. Norman Junior High School
Kaufman, Texas

Mary Cathyrne Coe
Pocatello High School
Pocatello, Idaho

Continued

Geri-Lee DeGennaro
Tarpon Springs High School
Tarpon Springs, Florida

Karen Dendy
Stephen F. Austin Middle School
Irving, Texas

Dianne Franz
Tarpon Springs Middle School
Tarpon Springs, Florida

Doris F. Frazier
East Millbrook Magnet Middle
    School
Raleigh, North Carolina

Shayne G. Goodrum
C. E. Jordan High School
Durham, North Carolina

Bonnie L. Hall
St. Ann School
Lansing, Illinois

Doris Ann Hall
Forest Meadow Junior High
    School
Dallas, Texas

James M. Harris
Mayfield High School
Mayfield Village, Ohio

Lynne Hoover
Fremont Ross High School
Fremont, Ohio

Patricia A. Humphreys
James Bowie High School
Austin, Texas

Jennifer L. Jones
Oliver Wendell Holmes Middle
    School
Dallas, Texas

Kathryn R. Jones
Murchison Middle School
Austin, Texas

Bonnie Just
Narbonne High School
Harbor City, California

Vincent Kimball
Patterson High School #405
Baltimore, Maryland

Nancy C. Long
MacArthur High School
Houston, Texas

Carol M. Mackey
Ft. Lauderdale Christian School
Ft. Lauderdale, Florida

Jan Jennings McCown
Johnston High School
Austin, Texas

Alice Kelly McCurdy
Rusk Middle School
Dallas, Texas

Elizabeth Morris
Northshore High School
Slidell, Louisiana

Victoria Reis
Western High School
Ft. Lauderdale, Florida

Dean Richardson
Scarborough High School
Houston, Texas

Susan M. Rogers
Freedom High School
Morganton, North Carolina

Sammy Rusk
North Mesquite High School
Mesquite, Texas

Carole B. San Miguel
James Bowie High School
Austin, Texas

Jane Saunders
William B. Travis High School
Austin, Texas

Gina Sawyer
Reed Middle School
Duncanville, Texas

Laura R. Schauermann
MacArthur High School
Houston, Texas

Stephen Shearer
MacArthur High School
Houston, Texas

Elizabeth Curry Smith
Tarpon Springs High School
Tarpon Springs, Florida

Jeannette M. Spain
Stephen F. Austin High School
Sugar Land, Texas

Carrie Speer
Northshore High School
Slidell, Louisiana

Trina Steffes
MacArthur High School
Houston, Texas

Andrea G. Freirich Stewart
Freedom High School
Morganton, North Carolina

Diana O. Torres
Johnston High School
Austin, Texas

Jan Voorhees
Whitesboro High School
Marcy, New York

Ann E. Walsh
Bedichek Middle School
Austin, Texas

Mary Jane Warden
Onahan School
Chicago, Illinois

Beth Westbrook
Covington Middle School
Austin, Texas

Char-Lene Wilkins
Morenci Area High School
Morenci, Michigan

CONTENTS IN BRIEF

CONTENTS

CHAPTER

1

Remembering People 16

Narration/Description

Harnessing Your Imagination 56

Comparing and Contrasting Media Messages 94

CHAPTER

4

Exposition

Analyzing Causal Relationships **138**

Analyzing Drama 180

Researching Literary Subjects 230

CHAPTER 7

Persuasion

Defending a Position 288

Recommending Solutions 374

CHAPTER

12

Improving Sentence Style 452

CHAPTER

13

Understanding Paragraphs and Compositions 464

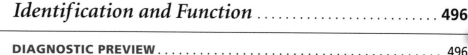

The Parts of a Sentence

CHAPTER

The Phrase

The Clause

Agreement
Subject and Verb, Pronoun and Antecedent **598**

Using Pronouns Correctly

Case Forms of Pronouns; Special Pronoun

Clear Reference

Using Verbs Correctly

Using Modifiers Correctly
Forms and Uses of Adjectives and Adverbs;
Comparison **720**

CHAPTER

22

Placement of Modifiers

CHAPTER

23

A Glossary of Usage

Common Usage Problems **754**

Capitalization

Standard Uses of Capital Letters **788**

Punctuation
End Marks and Commas **818**

Punctuation

Other Marks of Punctuation **848**

Spelling

CHAPTER

28

Song-Yuan Dynasties (13th century). Tray, brown and red lacquer with gilt background. Height, 1 in.; diameter, 9 in. #B83M9. The Avery Brundage Collection. Asian Art Museum of San Francisco.

Correcting Common Errors

CHAPTER

29

MODELS

TO OUR STUDENTS

On any given day, you probably watch TV, surf the Internet, read magazines, and listen to CDs. Each day you probably also write papers in school, send e-mails, and talk on the phone. The world of language around you is expanding rapidly. To keep up, you need to become a skilled language user. *Elements of Language* can be an important resource by helping you use language more effectively as you communicate in the twenty-first century.

Elements of Language is divided into four major parts:

PART 1 Communications shows you how to develop the skills you use to **receive** communications through **reading, listening,** and **viewing** and to **send** communications through **writing, speaking,** and **representing.**

PART 2 Sentences and Paragraphs shows you how to develop interesting, clear **sentences** and **paragraphs.**

PART 3 Grammar, Usage, and Mechanics provides instruction and practice with the **building blocks of language**—words, phrases, and clauses—so you can convey meaning clearly and correctly.

PART 4 Quick Reference Handbook is a one-stop **reference guide** to a variety of skills and concepts—in a concise, easily accessible form.

Think of *Elements of Language* as your personal communication resource. As you use this resource, remember that everything is here for a reason. For example, **boldface** type and color draw your attention to important words or ideas; **charts** present information in an easy-to-read form; and **headings** show the organization of ideas.

PART 1 chapters include the following sections:

> **Reading Workshop**—to show you how to develop and improve your reading skills

> **Writing Workshop**—to show you how to use the writing process to develop a piece of your own writing

> **Focus on Speaking and Listening** or **Focus on Viewing and Representing**—to help you master either the skills of speaking and listening or of viewing and representing

You will also encounter the following features in PART 1.

- **Mini-Lessons**—vocabulary and test-taking strategies, as well as writing or critical thinking skills
- **A Writer's Model**—a model of how you might write your own paper
- **A Student's Model**—a paper written by a real student
- **Content and Organization Guidelines for Peer and Self-Evaluation** and **Style Guidelines**—questions, tips, and techniques to help you evaluate and revise *what* you say as well as *how* you say it
- **Designing Your Writing**—pointers on how to present ideas and information visually so your readers can grasp them more easily
- **Connections to Literature** and **Connections to Life**—communication activities related to literature or to the world at large

Here are some of the features you will meet in PART 2 and PART 3.

- **Rules**—the grammar, usage, and mechanics concepts in each Part 3 chapter, numbered in each chapter
- **Exercises**—practice for skills and concepts
- **Tabs**—colored corners on the Part 3 pages that show rule numbers
- **Tips & Tricks**—easy-to-use hints about grammar, usage, and mechanics
- **Style Tips**—information about formal and informal uses of English
- **Help**—pointers to help you understand concepts and complete exercises
- **Computer Tips**—hints for using a computer to help you write better
- **Writing Applications**—activities that link grammar, usage, and mechanics skills and concepts with writing activities

Elements of Language on the Internet

At the *Elements of Language* Internet site, you can dissect the prose of professional writers, crack the codes of the advertising industry, and find out how your communication skills can help you in the real world. You can also submit your work for publication in one of our online galleries. As you move through *Elements of Language*, you will find the best online resources at **go.hrw.com**.

Let this book be your guide to developing your skill as an effective and critical language user—a communicator—in the twenty-first century.

The Authors and Editors

Communications

Introduction

READING·WRITING

READING·WRITING

READING·WRITING

READING·WRITING

READING·WRITING

Thinking About Reading and Writing

"But who shall be the master? The writer or the reader?"

—Denis Diderot, *Jacques le fataliste*

Writers communicate a message to readers. Readers, in turn, receive, understand, and respond to the writer's message. In fact, the two activities—reading and writing—are inseparable, and you have been the master of both for years. Yet because your reading and writing tasks continue to grow increasingly sophisticated, you need to keep honing your skills to meet the challenge.

Practice the Process

Yes, you still dash off notes and read fluffy magazine articles, but you probably also encounter complex essays and demanding essay prompts. Focusing on the **process,** the logical steps that underlie reading and writing, can mean the difference between progress and frustration. For each step, you can learn activities and thinking strategies to help you through any rough situation. In this chapter, you will become better acquainted with the steps you can take

- **before** you start reading or writing
- **while** you are reading someone else's ideas or expressing your own
- **after** you have put down the book or the pen

YOUR TURN 1 Analyzing the Reading and Writing Processes

- Write a paragraph discussing your ideas about a concept such as *loyalty, originality,* or *lying.* After a classmate has read your draft, explain to him or her how you approached and carried out this writing task.
- Ask a classmate to select a short nonfiction text for you to read. Then, read the text, taking note of how your mind works before, during, and after reading. Finally, explain to your classmate what you learned from the text and what you learned about your own reading process.

Reading as a Process

Long ago you learned that written symbols (letters of an alphabet) correspond to sounds and that combinations of these symbols form words representing specific things or concepts. These simple but profound principles apply to thousands of written languages around the world.

However, in order to understand many of the world's most inspired and fascinating texts—from the Hindu scripture *Rig-Veda*, dating back several thousand years, to a modern scientific treatise on the formation of the universe—you have to move far beyond these fundamental principles. Exactly how do you do that? To grasp any writer's message thoroughly, you must use thinking strategies *before*, *while*, and *after* you read.

What You Do During the Reading Process	
Before You Read: Prereading	- **Preview** the text and **make predictions** about its content, organization, and style. - **Draw upon prior knowledge,** what you already know, about the subject matter of the text. - **Determine your purpose** for reading the text. - **Focus** your attention on the text.
While You Read: Reading	- **Adjust your reading rate** based on your purpose, the level of difficulty of the text, and your prior knowledge about the subject. - **Identify** the text's **main ideas, supporting details, and organizational structure.** If the text is complex, jot down notes as you read. - **Adjust and confirm your predictions** about the text. - **Make connections** between the text and your prior knowledge and experience. - **Identify the writer's purpose** and overall **message.**
After You Read: Exploring and Extending Your Reading	- **Confirm your understanding** of the text. - **Decide whether you achieved your purpose** for reading. - **Draw conclusions and make generalizations** about the text. - **Summarize** the text's main ideas and important details. - **Evaluate** the text for accuracy, bias, and overall quality. - **Extend** your reading by using the ideas you encountered in the text.

Prereading

Getting Ready

Like musicians warming up with their instruments before a performance, effective readers warm up their minds before beginning to read a text. Use the following prereading strategies to fine-tune your mind for reading.

- **Preview** the text. Begin by examining the work's table of contents, major headings, and subheadings. Then, consider how any illustrations, photographs, diagrams, and other graphic elements contribute to the message. Skimming the introduction and a handful of paragraphs from various sections of the text will acquaint you with the writer's style and the type of vocabulary used. Look for special features, such as terms that appear in boldface or italics.

- **Make predictions** about the text's content, the writer's overall message and purpose, and his or her approach to the material. Making educated guesses about issues such as these—then adjusting your predictions as you read—will help you stay actively engaged with the reading material.

- **Make connections** to the text by considering your own **prior knowledge** about the topic. Your prior knowledge might include personal observations, recollections, past reading, and life experiences.

- **Consider your purpose** for reading. If, for example, you are about to read an instruction manual, your purpose will be obvious. Otherwise, use impressions gathered in your preview to determine your purpose. For instance, if you see that a text assigned in your history class concerns troop movements during World War II, your purpose for reading might be to acquire factual information. Knowing this prepares you to read carefully as you seek out main ideas and related details. On the other hand, if you see that another text assigned for the class is composed of letters written by those same troops, you might read for the purpose of making more personal connections and gaining insight into human nature.

- **Focus your attention** on the text you are about to read. If your mind wanders, gently steer it back on course.

> **TIP** For various reasons, you may have to read texts that do not at first interest or inspire you. When this happens, try locating an angle or approach to the subject that *does* motivate you. For example, you might become more interested in an article on India's struggle for independence from Britain if you rented and watched the award-winning film *Gandhi* before reading.

While Reading

Making Sense

During an average day you may read a dozen or more very different texts—a lunch menu, a newspaper editorial, an e-mail, an excerpt from Virginia Woolf's diaries. In all of these cases your goal remains the same: to interpret and comprehend the words before you. The following strategies will help you make sense of any written message.

- **Adjust your reading rate.** If the text is more difficult than you predicted or if you are not achieving your purpose for reading, slow down. You might even need to re-read especially complex or important passages.

- **Identify the text's main ideas.** If main ideas are not directly stated, infer them by considering ideas and details from the text in relation to what you already know. Titles, headings and subheadings, repeated and boldface terms, and organizational patterns can all provide clues about a text's main ideas.

- **Interpret and analyze details.** What insights do details, such as examples, descriptions, and facts, provide? Do these details adequately support the writer's main ideas?

- **Identify the organizational pattern** of the text. This identification will help you understand the relationships among ideas and refine your predictions. For example, if you detect an *order-of-importance* pattern in an essay, you can anticipate that paragraphs will be arranged so that the ideas the writer considers most (or least) significant come last.

- **Adjust your predictions about the text.** If your predictions now seem imprecise, rethink them, and stay flexible. Perhaps the text has even more surprises in store.

- **Make connections.** Consider how what you are reading relates to other text or media you have read, seen, or heard and how it relates to your personal experience. Does it confirm, contribute to, or contradict your prior knowledge? How?

- **Identify the writer's purpose and overall message.** Is the writer trying to persuade you of something, or is he or she simply imparting information? Identifying a writer's purpose will make you a more critical reader, one who is less susceptible to propaganda.

- **Jot down notes.** Take note of any questions you have, and watch for the answers. You might also jot down observations and comments about the text, just as if you were having a conversation with its writer. In the margin of the short passage on the next page, you can see one reader's dialogue with the writer of the text.

TIP Writers most frequently organize ideas according to *main ideas and supporting details, causes and effects, chronological order, problems and solutions, order-of-importance,* or some other logical progression of ideas.

It is usually assumed that, when we are reading, our eyes travel smoothly, without interruptions, along the lines of a page, and that, when we are reading Western writing, for instance, our eyes go from left to right. This isn't so. A century ago, the French ophthalmologist Émile Javal discovered that our eyes actually jump about the page; these jumps or saccades take place three or four times per second, at a speed of about 200 degrees per second. The speed of the eye's motion across the page—but not the motion itself—interferes with perception, and it is only during the brief pause between movements that we actually "read." Why our sense of reading is related to the continuity of the text on the page or to the scrolling of the text on the screen, assimilating entire sentences or thoughts, and not to the actual saccadic movement of the eyes, is a question which scientists have not yet been able to answer.

Analysing the cases of two clinical patients—one an aphasic[1] who could make eloquent speeches in a language that was gibberish, and the other an agnosic[2] who could use ordinary language but was incapable of imbuing it with tone or emotion—Dr. Oliver Sacks argued that "speech—natural speech—does not consist of words alone. . . . It consists of utterance—an uttering-forth of one's whole meaning with one's whole being—the understanding of which involves infinitely more than mere word-recognition." Much the same can be said of reading: following the text, the reader utters its meaning through a vastly entangled method of learned significances, social conventions, previous readings, personal experience, and private taste. . . .

Alberto Manguel, *A History of Reading*

1. **aphasic** (ə•fā´zik): one who has sustained a total or partial loss of the power to use or understand words, usually as a result of brain disease or injury.
2. **agnosic** (ag•nō´zik): one who has sustained a total or partial loss of the ability to recognize familiar objects, especially by seeing, hearing, or touching, usually as the result of brain damage.

This implies that not all writing is read from left to right.

I guess "saccade" means "jump."

This makes reading seem so mysterious.

From its context, I gather that "aphasic" means not able to use ordinary language, which corresponds with the definition given in the footnote at the bottom of the page.

We have talked about this in class—making connections to the text by relating it to what we already know or have experienced.

After Reading

Exploring and Extending

Good readers know that the reading process isn't over when they arrive at the final word of a text. They know that it is crucial to continue to explore the concepts and images they have just encountered. Here are some post-reading strategies that can transform you into a more effective reader.

- **Confirm your understanding of the text.** You have just been handed a lot of information. Strengthen your grasp of it by communicating your ideas about what you read. You might summarize a text's overall message in a paragraph or two or in a graphic organizer, or you might discuss the text's message with other readers. Jot down or discuss your personal responses as well. Consider whether the text has provoked in you any vivid or unexpected thoughts, associations, or memories. Has it agitated you or raised insistent questions in your mind?

- **Draw conclusions and make generalizations.** Combine the information in the text with your prior knowledge to draw conclusions about what you read and to make generalizations about the world at large.

- **Decide whether you achieved your purpose for reading.** How well did your understanding of the text match up with what you wanted to achieve by reading? For instance, if you read to learn a skill, do you feel confident in performing it?

- **Evaluate the text.** Did the writer communicate information effectively? Do you judge the work to be accurate, fresh, imaginative, free of bias, intelligent, and engaging? Why or why not? For instance, you might judge that the frequent use of loaded language in an editorial constitutes bias on the part of the writer and makes the text's message less credible.

- **Extend your reading.** You might respond creatively by writing a story, essay, or poem or by creating a unique work of visual or performance art relating to the text. You could also use the text as a springboard to read further in another text on the same or a related topic—or to read another work by the same author. Finally, brainstorm ways you can relate your reading to the world around you. If a text has inspired you or given you ideas about solving problems, addressing social issues, or enriching your family or community, use them.

Reflecting on the reading process helps you appreciate that reading is inseparable from writing: Meaning gets communicated only if readers and writers work together. As you take a closer look at the writing process, see how you can relate it to the reading process.

Writing as a Process

ost writers have memories of an occasion when their ideas flowed onto the page smoothly and easily. Not only did sentences seem to flow like water, but they were also, like water, crystal clear.

Of course, experienced writers know how rare this is. Most often, effective writing involves a process. The steps in this process, called a **recursive process** because it is usually necessary to repeat them several times, are like those of a spiral staircase—you must travel around and around, yet with each revolution you ascend toward your goal. Of course, each writer's process is slightly different, yet most effective writers follow the steps given in the chart below.

WHAT'S AHEAD?

In this section, you will learn about the steps of the writing process, including

- **prewriting**
- **writing**
- **revising**
- **publishing**

What You Do During the Writing Process
Before You Write: Prewriting <ul><li>**Identify your purpose** and **audience.**</li><li>**Choose a topic** and the **form** that best suits the purpose, audience, and topic you have identified.</li><li>**Formulate your thesis,** or main idea about the topic.</li><li>**Gather information** about the topic.</li><li>**Organize information** in a preliminary plan.</li></ul>
While You Write: Writing a Draft <ul><li>**Draft an introduction** that seizes your reader's attention and provides necessary background information.</li><li>**State your thesis** clearly and assertively.</li><li>**Develop body paragraphs** that elaborate on main ideas.</li><li>**Follow an organizational plan.**</li><li>**Draft a memorable conclusion** that restates your thesis and leaves the reader with something to think about.</li></ul>
After You Write: Revising <ul><li>**Evaluate** your draft.</li><li>**Revise** to improve content, organization, and style.</li></ul>
After You Write: Publishing <ul><li>**Proofread** your draft, and correct errors in spelling, punctuation, grammar, and usage.</li><li>**Share** your final draft with readers.</li><li>**Reflect** on your writing experience.</li></ul>

TIP In addition to these very general prewriting steps, many writers have more personal, individual ways of preparing themselves to write. For instance, some writers like to listen to certain music, while others choose to sit at a particular desk, or fix themselves a snack. Anything that helps you write can be incorporated into your own personal prewriting ritual.

Prewriting

Getting Ready

Before you begin writing anything, you probably spend some time preparing. You may go in search of tools such as a pen, a pencil, or a computer. In order to create a well-constructed, elegant composition, however, you will also need to collect more intangible tools—such as your thoughts. Take a look at the following strategies for collecting these less tangible—but essential—tools for writing.

■ **Identify your purpose and audience.** Before you can make any other decisions, you will need to ask yourself, "Why am I writing?" Your answer will dictate all of your subsequent choices. Setting out to review a film, for example, would be very different from setting out to win someone's heart. Your audience is closely tied to your purpose. Knowing your audience will help you decide on an approach. For instance, you would not want to take a comic **tone** in a formal situation—or with someone who does not have a very good sense of humor.

■ **Choose a topic and a form** that will help you achieve your purpose and reach your intended audience. For instance, if your purpose for writing were to win someone's heart, you probably would not want to write a research report about diesel engines. However, you might want to write a persuasive letter explaining your adorable qualities. Whatever your purpose, be sure to narrow your topic to a manageable size, one that you can thoroughly cover in your alloted space.

■ **Formulate your thesis,** or main idea about the topic. Clarifying your overall message before you begin your draft will help guide your writing.

■ **Gather information about the topic.** When you begin your draft you will want to have all the necessary information at your fingertips. Sources for such information can include books, magazines, journals, newspapers, Web sites, films, tape recordings, interviews, and your own memory. For instance, if you were writing a persuasive love letter, you might want to take a look at what philosophers and poets through the ages have had to say about love.

■ **Organize your information** by creating a preliminary plan, or outline. Use the organizational strategy best suited to your purpose and audience and to the type of information you have gathered. In the letter designed to win someone's heart, for instance, you might use comparison and contrast structure to convince the object of your affections that you are more fabulous than his or her other suitors.

TIP Throughout the prewriting stage, work **collaboratively** with peers to generate ideas, plan, and gather information.

TIP If you decide to write a poem or story, the steps of your prewriting process will differ slightly from those described here. For example, rather than formulating a thesis, you will develop a theme. Even so, you can still refer to these steps as general guidelines, making adaptations where necessary.

Making a Start

During the prewriting process, you collected all the tools you needed to begin writing. When you write a draft, you put all those tools to work to create something concrete. (You will probably write independently most of the time; sometimes, however, try drafting with peers **collaboratively.**) Below are steps and strategies that you can use to create a solid, workable first draft.

- **Introduce the piece by seizing your reader's attention** immediately. You can do this with an arresting statement, quotation, short anecdote, or detail. Then, **provide necessary background information.** For instance, you may need to summarize key pieces of historical or scientific information that help illuminate your topic.

Reference Note

For more about writing **introductions,** see pages 476 and 1066.

- **State your thesis clearly** so that your readers will know where you are headed. A strong thesis is assertive, interesting or even provocative, and specific enough to be fully discussed or proven within the length limitations of your piece.

- **Develop body paragraphs** that explain your **main ideas** and **elaborate** fully upon them. Elaboration may include facts, details, examples, anecdotes, and quotations that explain and support your main ideas. For example, rather than writing "Computers have changed the way people get and spend money" and proceeding to your next main idea, prove your statement by providing statistics, facts, or expert testimony.

- **Organize body paragraphs** so that your ideas flow smoothly and logically from one to the next. Strive also for cohesion and clarity within each paragraph by **organizing supporting details** and by using transitional words and phrases to show the relationships among ideas.

- **Conclude by restating your thesis** to provide your audience with a sense of closure. You will also want to make a vivid final impression so that your writing resonates in readers' minds even after they have finished reading.

Reference Note

For more about **writing conclusions,** see pages 486 and 1069.

> **TIP** As you make your way through the writing process, you may discover that you need to change your approach to a topic or even your thesis. **Stay flexible,** and feel free to make adjustments such as using another organizational strategy or narrowing your topic further.
>
> Also, don't worry about making each sentence or paragraph perfect before preceeding to the next one. That is why people call it a *first,* or *rough,* draft. You will have an opportunity to **edit** (evaluate, revise, and proofread) it in the final stages of the writing process.

Revising

Going Back Over Your Draft

As the French writer André Gide said, "No human masterpiece has ever been created without great labor." In other words, once your first draft has been written, there is still work to be done. Now you must take off your writer's hat, assume the persona of an editor, and mold and hone sentences and paragraphs to make your writing as effective as possible. **Editing** involves evaluating (deciding what needs fixing), revising (making changes), and proofreading (correcting grammar, punctuation, and spelling errors). Since it is difficult to focus on all three of these steps at once, many writers focus on one at a time.

TIP **Editing** collaboratively with peers can be especially helpful if you provide your peer editor with a list of questions and concerns before he or she begins. For instance, you might ask your peer editor to focus on something you have had difficulty with in the past, such as elaboration. Then, listen carefully to what your peer editor has to say; if he or she doesn't understand something, it probably needs clarification.

- **Evaluate your draft,** re-reading it at least twice—once for content and organization and once for style. Have you conveyed your ideas lucidly and with panache? Peer editors can often provide invaluable feedback.

- **Revise your draft,** based on your evaluations. Here are five strategies you can use.

  1. **Add.** Include details, illustrations, and examples; add transitions to lend coherence. For example, add a topic sentence to focus a paragraph that seems vague or an interesting detail to liven up a flat description.

  2. **Delete.** Cut any words, phrases, sentences, or even whole paragraphs that do not support your thesis—no matter how well written they might be.

  3. **Replace.** Replace vague nouns and verbs and hackneyed expressions with precise, original language.

  4. **Rearrange.** Rearrange phrases, sentences, and entire paragraphs to present a logical progression of ideas.

  5. **Elaborate.** Add sensory details, interesting facts, and clarifying examples to flesh out skeletal body paragraphs.

- **Fine-tune for style.** Go over your writing once more to make sure that it is not only functional, but also beautiful. This time focus on refining style to suit occasion, audience, and purpose. Will your words create vivid pictures in readers' minds? Does the rhythm of the sentences convey what you intend? Do ideas flow smoothly from one paragraph to the next?

TIP Set your writing aside, at least overnight, before you attempt to evaluate and revise. This will help you gain distance from your work and see it with a fresh eye.

Publishing

Going Public

After having worked hard to create an original piece of writing, you will want to see the project through to completion by polishing your work, sharing it with an audience, and reflecting on the writing process.

- **Proofread, or edit, your final draft** to catch and correct mistakes in the nuts-and-bolts part of writing—spelling, grammar and usage, punctuation, and capitalization. Be sure to adhere to the **conventions of written English,** and produce an error-free finished product. The following chart includes some of the questions you will want to consider as you proofread and tells you where you can find information about how to identify and correct any errors.

Proofreading Guidelines
1. Is every sentence complete, not a fragment or a run-on? (See page 431.)
2. Are punctuation marks used correctly? (See page 818.)
3. Are the first words of sentences, proper nouns, and adjectives capitalized? (See page 788.)
4. Does every verb agree in number with its subject? (See page 600.)
5. Are verb forms used correctly? (See page 670.) Are verb tenses used correctly? (See page 692.)
6. Are subject and object forms of personal pronouns used correctly? (See page 632.)
7. Does every pronoun agree with its antecedent in number and gender? (See page 618.) Are pronoun references clear? (See page 656.)
8. Are frequently confused words (such as *fewer* and *less, affect* and *effect*) used correctly? (See page 756.)
9. Are all words spelled correctly? (See page 889.)
10. Is the paper neat and in correct manuscript form? (See page 962.)

- **Publish your work** in one or more places. Brainstorm ways to publish your work—school newspapers, magazines, literary journals, poetry slams, and Web sites are a few of the possibilities.

■ **Reflect on your writing experience.** Even veteran authors learn something about themselves as writers, and as people, each time they write. After you have finished writing, don't miss this opportunity to grow. Here are some questions that can serve as springboards for reflection.

1. With what in this piece are you most and least satisfied? Why?
2. At what points did you glide forward with ease? At what points did you agonize? Why?
3. How might you approach the writing process differently next time?

In this chapter, you have considered reading and writing as processes. As you may already have noted, these processes are intimately related—one cannot exist without the other and they mirror one another in many ways. The following chart presents a step-by-step comparison of reading and writing.

The Reading-Writing Connection		
	The Reading Process	**The Writing Process**
Before Reading or Writing	▪ Identify your **prior knowledge** about the topic. ▪ Preview the text to identify the writer's **purpose** and **audience**. ▪ While scanning the text, **make predictions** about its content.	▪ Identify your **prior knowledge** about the topic and do **research** to deepen this knowledge. ▪ Think ahead to identify your **purpose** and **audience**. ▪ While preparing to write the piece, **make a plan** for its content.
While Reading or Writing	▪ Identify the writer's **main ideas** and seek out **supporting details**. ▪ Take **notes** on key ideas and details. You may also want to **outline** the text. ▪ Look for **transitional words and phrases** that indicate the text's **organizational pattern** and the **relationships among ideas**.	▪ Express your **main ideas** clearly and provide **supporting details**. ▪ Follow your prewriting **notes** or **outline**. ▪ Use **transitional words and phrases** that help readers follow your **organizational pattern** and understand the **relationships among ideas**.
After Reading or Writing	▪ **Evaluate** the text, considering its content, organization, and style. ▪ **Connect** the text to the real world by applying what you learned. ▪ **Reflect** on the text and your reading process. ▪ **Explore** the topic further by reading more on it or **related topics**.	▪ **Evaluate** and **revise** your work to improve its content, organization, and style. ▪ **Connect** your writing to the real world by publishing it. ▪ **Reflect** on your work and your writing process. ▪ Keep your essay in a **portfolio,** and return to it later in order to prompt new ideas for **related topics** for writing.

Choices

Choose one of the following activities to complete.

▶ WRITING

1. Two Audiences Select a topic for a research report, and identify two specific, very different audiences (such as a college history professor and a group of ten-year-old children). Then, after thinking carefully about the knowledge and abilities of each audience, explain in a brief **essay** how reports on the same topic would differ if written for the two different audiences. Consider differences in content and style.

▶ CROSSING THE CURRICULUM: SPEAKING AND LISTENING

2. Ask the Writer Identify a writer in your community—perhaps a local author or journalist. Then, prepare interview questions related to the writing process. For example, you might ask the writer where he or she seeks inspiration. Finally, set up and conduct the **interview**. If possible, audiotape or videotape the interview, too.

▶ COLLABORATIVE READING

3. Real Life With a partner, choose a short nonfiction text to read. After using prereading and reading strategies to understand the text, get together with your partner for a **discussion** of what you read. Compare your observations, questions, interpretations, and experiences of reading the text. Then, brainstorm specific ideas for connecting your reading to some aspect of your community or the world at large.

▶ LITERATURE

4. Professional Advice Locate a collection of interviews with professional writers—such as those collected in *The Paris Review*. After choosing an author that interests you, use the steps and strategies of the reading process to read the interview you've chosen. In a short **oral presentation,** report your findings to your classmates. If possible, extend the activity by reading one of the writer's works.

▶ WRITING

5. Tag Team You may have played a party game in which a group writes a **collaborative story,** each person adding another sentence until the story is complete. Try this again with a group of classmates, except this time, do the prewriting and evaluating and revising stages as a group. During the writing stage, take turns adding sentences, as in the game.

PORTFOLIO

1 Remembering People

Reading Workshop

Reading a Reflective Essay
PAGE 18

Writing Workshop

Writing a Reflective Essay
PAGE 28

Focus on Speaking and Listening

Creating an Oral History
PAGE 48

Focus on Viewing and Representing

Creating an Audio-visual Self-Reflection
PAGE 53

Reflective Essay

- The sight of a kite sailing overhead recalls the neighbor who explained to you the principles of aerodynamics when she found out that you wanted to be a pilot. She made you feel your dreams were important.

- Today you play forward for your high school ice hockey team, but once upon a time you could not even stand up on ice skates. You remember the uncle who spent hours teaching you to skate at the nearby rink.

All of us have been affected by the words and actions of other people—people who taught us something valuable about life or about ourselves. Reflect for a moment. Picture the people who have had an effect on your life.

To reflect means to contemplate. It also means to mirror, or give back, an image. A **reflective essay** does both. In a reflective essay about a person, a writer contemplates the person and then gives an image of him or her to readers. Reading and writing such essays can help us in two ways—to understand ourselves and others better, and to see how we touch one another's lives.

internet connect

go. hrw .com

GO TO: go.hrw.com
KEYWORD: EOLang 12-1

YOUR TURN 1 — Considering Reflections

With a classmate, jot down answers to these questions: What effects do people have on one another's lives? Why do you think people often talk and write about these effects? Where do you read, see, or hear people reflecting on these effects?

Reading a Reflective Essay

WHAT'S AHEAD?

In this section, you will read a reflective essay. You will also learn how to

- connect with a text
- identify expressive style

When you were a child, did you ever rummage through an attic, storage closet, or basement? What did you find there? Dad's high school yearbook? Your older sister's hockey stick? Aunt Betty's wigs? Even as a child, you probably realized that people's possessions say a lot about who those people are.

In the essay that begins on the next page, a daughter gives us an image of her mother by telling us about one of her mother's possessions. As you read Alice Walker's "My Mother's Blue Bowl," allow your own memories to flow. Do you have a possession that reminds you of someone you know or once knew? Also, notice how Walker expresses her thoughts and feelings. Does it sound as if she might be talking to a friend?

Preparing to Read

READING SKILL

Making Connections   When you first read a reflective essay, you might think, "This person's life is very different from mine. We don't have anything in common." Look again. Reflective essays sometimes describe lives that, on the surface, seem very different from our own, but if we look deeper, we usually discover shared experiences, emotions, or insights. As you read the reflective essay on the next page, draw on your own background and personal experiences to **make connections** with the text.

READING FOCUS

Expressive Style   It may seem as if the writer of a reflective essay were speaking to you from across your kitchen table. This is because reflective essays are written in expressive style. **Expressive style** conveys a writer's thoughts and feelings in his or her own unique voice. Such a voice may be the result of many different elements—diction, sentence structure, figurative and connotative language—that work together to create a style as individual as the writer. As you read "My Mother's Blue Bowl," look for places the writer's thoughts and feelings are expressed in a unique and personal way.

As you read the following essay from Alice Walker's *Anything We Love Can Be Saved,* jot down answers to the numbered active-reading questions. (Underscored words will be used in the Vocabulary Mini-Lesson on page 26.)

My Mother's Blue Bowl

by Alice Walker

Visitors to my house are often served food—soup, potatoes, rice—in a large blue stoneware bowl, noticeably chipped at the rim. It is perhaps the most precious thing I own. It was given to me by my mother in her last healthy days. The days before a massive stroke laid her low and left her almost speechless. Those days when to visit her was to be drawn into a serene cocoon of memories and present-day musings and to rest there, in temporary retreat from the rest of the world, as if still an infant, nodding and secure at her breast.

> **1. To whom does the pronoun "I" refer?**

For much of her life my mother longed, passionately longed, for a decent house. One with a yard that did not have to be cleared with an ax. One with a roof that kept out the rain. One with floors that you could not fall through. She longed for a beautiful house of wood or stone. Or of red brick, like the houses her many sisters and their husbands had. When I was thirteen she found such a house. Green-shuttered, white-walled. Breezy. With a lawn and a hedge and giant pecan trees. A porch swing. There her gardens flourished in spite of the shade, as did her youngest daughter, for whom she sacrificed her life doing hard labor in someone else's house, in order to afford peace and prettiness for her child, to whose grateful embrace she returned each night.

> **2. How would this paragraph, which contains many fragments, be different if it were written in complete sentences?**

But, curiously, the minute I left home, at seventeen, to attend college, she abandoned the dream house and moved into the projects. Into a small, tight apartment of few breezes, in which I was never to feel comfortable, but that she declared suited her "to a T." I took solace in the fact that it was at least hugged by spacious lawn on one side, and by forest, out the back door, and that its isolated position at the end of the street meant she would have a measure of privacy.

Her move into the projects—the best housing poor black people in the South ever had, she would occasionally declare, even as my father struggled to adjust to the cramped rooms and hard, unforgiving qualities of brick—was, I now understand, a step in the direction of divestiture,[1] lightening her load, permitting her worldly possessions to dwindle in significance and, well before she herself would turn to spirit, roll away from her.

She owned little, in fact. A bed, a dresser, some chairs. A set of living-room furniture. A set of kitchen furniture. A bed and wardrobe (given to her years before, when I was a teenager, by one of her more prosperous sisters). Her flowers: everywhere, inside the house and outside. Planted in anything she managed to get her green hands on, including old suitcases and abandoned shoes. She recycled everything, effortlessly. And gradually she had only a small amount of stuff—mostly stuff her children gave her: nightgowns, perfume, a microwave—to recycle or to use.

Each time I visited her I marveled at the modesty of her desires. She appeared to have hardly any, beyond a thirst for a cola or a hunger for a piece of fried chicken or fish. On every visit I noticed that more and more of what I remembered of her possessions seemed to be missing. One day I commented on this.

Taking a deep breath, sighing, and following both with a beaming big smile, which lit up her face, the room, and my heart, she said: Yes, it's all going. I don't need it anymore. If there's anything you want, take it when you leave; it might not be here when you come back.

The dishes my mother and father used daily had come from my house; I had sent them years before, when I moved from Mississippi to New York. Neither the plates nor the silver matched entirely, but it was all beautiful in her eyes. There were numerous paper items, used in the microwave, and stacks of plastic plates and cups, used by the scores of children from the neighborhood who continued throughout her life to come and go. But there was nothing there for me to want.

One day, however, looking for a jar into which to pour leftover iced tea, I found myself probing deep into the wilderness of the overstuffed, airless pantry. Into the land of the old-fashioned, the outmoded, the outdated. The humble and the obsolete. There was a smoothing iron, a churn. A butter press. And two large bowls.

One was cream and rose with a blue stripe. The other was a deep, vivid blue.

May I have this bowl, Mama, I asked, looking at her and at the blue bowl with delight.

You can have both of them, she said, barely acknowledging them, and continuing to put leftover food away.

I held the bowls on my lap for the rest of the evening, while she watched a

> **3. What do you learn about the author's mother from this list of her possessions? Does she remind you of anyone? If so, who?**

> **4. What is the effect of Walker's not using quotation marks to set off dialogue?**

---

1. **divestiture** (də•vest´ə•chər): a getting rid (of something unwanted).

TV program about cops and criminals that I found too horrifying to follow.

Before leaving the room I kissed her on the forehead and asked if I could get anything for her from the kitchen; then I went off to bed. The striped bowl I placed on a chair beside the door, so I could look at it from where I lay. The blue bowl I placed in the bed with me.

5. Has anyone ever given you something of his or hers? If so, how did you feel?

In giving me these gifts, my mother had done a number of astonishing things, in her typically offhand way. She had taught me a lesson about letting go of possessions—easily, without emphasis or regret—and she had given me a symbol of what she herself represented in my life.

For the blue bowl especially was a <u>cauldron</u> of memories. Of cold, harsh, wintry days, when my brothers and sister and I trudged home from school burdened down by the silence and frigidity of our long trek from the main road, down the hill to our shabby-looking house. More rundown than any of our classmates' houses. In winter my mother's riotous flowers would be absent, and the shack stood revealed for what it was. A gray, decaying, too small barrack meant to house the <u>itinerant</u>[2] tenant workers on a prosperous white man's farm.

Slogging through sleet and wind to the sagging front door, thankful that our house was too far from the road to be seen clearly from the school bus, I always felt a wave of embarrassment and misery. But then I would open the door. And there inside would be my mother's winter flowers: a glowing fire in the fireplace, colorful handmade quilts on all our beds, paintings and drawings of flowers and fruits and, yes, of Jesus, given to her by who knows whom—and, most of all, there in the center of the rough-hewn table, which in the tiny kitchen almost touched the rusty woodburning stove, stood the big blue bowl, full of whatever was the most tasty thing on earth.

6. Which words and phrases in this paragraph express the writer's emotions?

There was my mother herself. Glowing. Her teeth sparkling. Her eyes twinkling. As if she lived in a castle and her favorite princes and princesses had just dropped by to visit.

The blue bowl stood there, seemingly full forever, no matter how deeply or rapaciously[3] we dipped, as if it had no bottom. And she dipped up soup. Dipped up lima beans. Dipped up stew. Forked out potatoes. Spooned out rice and peas and corn. And in the light and warmth that was *Her*, we dined.

7. How does the repetition of words and phrases affect your understanding of this paragraph?

Thank you, Mama

---

2. itinerant (ī•tin´ər•ənt): traveling from place to place or on a circuit.

3. rapaciously (rə•pā´shəs•lē): greedily or voraciously.

First Thoughts on Your Reading

1. **How does the writer feel about her mother? How do you know?**

2. **Do you associate an object, like the blue bowl, with a particular person? If so, briefly describe both the object and the person, and tell why you associate them, being careful not to reveal anything too personal.**

3. **How would you describe this author's way of expressing herself? Formal or informal? Poetic or dry? Logical or emotional? Explain.**

| READING SKILL

Making Connections

Finding Common Ground   No matter what you are reading, you **make connections** with the text by drawing on your own prior knowledge, background, and experiences to create meaning. Sometimes, making connections with a text is easy; but what about when you read something about which you have no knowledge or experience? For example, if you were to read a reflective essay about a Sioux teenager undergoing a coming-of-age ritual called a "vision quest" but were not familiar with Sioux culture, the account might seem strange to you at first. To fully appreciate it, you would need to think about coming-of-age rituals you or other teens you know have undergone—like graduation ceremonies, bar or bat mitzvahs, quinceañeras, and inductions into societies and clubs. You might realize that the vision quest has much in common with a coming-of-age ritual that is more familiar to you. For example, in both a vision quest and a graduation ceremony, a young person receives something that represents knowledge or wisdom. Suddenly, by drawing on your own experience of coming-of-age rituals, you might be able to relate to and understand the account of the vision quest.

This important part of the reading process, **making connections,** not only helps you understand what you read, but also helps you understand yourself and your place in the world better. You might discover that you have a lot in common with someone who, on the surface, seems very different from you.

TIP   Making connections is a useful strategy for understanding anything you read, from a lab report to a novel. As you read a text, keep in mind any experience or prior knowledge of the subject that you may have. How does what you already know compare with or shed light on what you are reading?

Making Connections with a Text

You can use the steps in the left-hand column of the following chart to make connections with a text. Look at the right-hand column to see how one reader connected with "My Mother's Blue Bowl," by Alice Walker.

▶ **STEP 1** Consider the people, events, places, or things described in the text. Do you have knowledge or experience of similar people, events, places, or things?

Text describes how author's mother began to simplify her life by giving things away, including the blue bowl she gave the author. My Uncle Joe also doesn't put much stock in possessions—he's always giving things away to people he meets.

▶ **STEP 2** Consider the emotions, attitudes, and opinions expressed. Have you ever had similar emotions, attitudes, or opinions? How are your emotions, attitudes, and opinions similar or different?

Walker expresses her love and respect for her mother. I have similar feelings for Uncle Joe. However, while Walker admires her mother's unmaterialistic values, I have always thought Uncle Joe should be less generous, more practical.

▶ **STEP 3** Consider the writer's (or character's) background. Is your own background similar, or very different? How might this affect your understanding of the text?

Both the writer and I have experienced having little money and being considered poor. However, she is older than I and has more education and experience. Maybe her attitude toward her mother's giving things away shows that maturity.

▶ **STEP 4** Consider how the connections you have made—shared background, knowledge, experience, emotions, attitudes, or opinions—can enhance your understanding of the text and its message, and of yourself.

Even though, superficially, Walker and I are worlds apart, we have had similar experiences and feelings. Maybe I can learn from her—maybe my uncle's giving away possessions isn't just impractical and eccentric. Maybe he is wise to realize that things, although they can have sentimental value, are not so important in themselves.

Making Connections

Using the steps on the previous page, make connections with passages from "My Mother's Blue Bowl." Choose either the first or last five paragraphs of the essay with which to connect. Then, for each of the four steps, write a one- to three-sentence answer on your own paper, being careful not to reveal anything you wouldn't feel comfortable sharing with others.

| READING FOCUS

Expressive Style

Getting Personal Writers of reflective essays often use an **expressive style**—a way of writing that relates a writer's thoughts and feelings in an informal and intimate way. Because expressive writing reveals the writer's unique way of saying things, reading an essay written in an expressive style can make you feel as if you know the writer personally. The following chart gives four important elements of expressive style, as well as examples of each element.

Elements	Examples
First-person point of view	*I* remember the last night Grandpa was with us. *We* sat by the fire after dinner, and he pulled out his only treasure, a pocket watch, and gave it to *me*.
Words that express feelings, such as *love, hate, envy, overjoyed,* and *afraid*	When I slipped and fell on the newly waxed floor, I felt so *embarrassed*.
Words, phrases, and sentences that echo common speech, including sentence fragments and colloquialisms	I really didn't think sharing my answers was a good idea. *No way*. I could get *kicked out* of school for that.
Evocative language—words with strong connotations, sensory details, and figures of speech that evoke emotion or relate something in a unique and vivid way (For more about figures of speech such as similes, metaphors, and personification, see page 75.)	When he bit into the *piping hot roll* Phoebe had *baked fresh* that morning, a smile *softened* Luther's usually *stony* face.

TIP Although they are taboo in formal writing, **sentence fragments** appear frequently in essays that use expressive style. Writers use them to echo everyday speech patterns, create an informal tone, emphasize a point, repeat a theme, or convey their unique thought patterns and voice.

Follow the steps below to analyze the elements of expressive style. Note, in the right-hand column, how one reader analyzed a phrase from the following sentence of "My Mother's Blue Bowl."

> Slogging through sleet and wind to the sagging front door, thankful that our house was too far from the road to be seen clearly from the school bus, I always felt a wave of embarrassment and misery.

▶ **STEP 1** Identify expressive elements. If possible, jot some of them down on a piece of paper.

The phrase "slogging through sleet and wind to the sagging front door. . . " seems expressive—the words "slogging" and "sagging" have definite connotations.

▶ **STEP 2** Think about the effect of each element on you as a reader.

"Slogging" makes me really <u>feel</u> how hard it was to walk in the sleet; "sagging" gives me a picture of the dilapidated old door.

▶ **STEP 3** Ask yourself: "How does this element contribute to the writer's message? What purpose does it serve in the essay as a whole?"

These words seem to be used to draw a sharp contrast between the hard outside world and the warmth and beauty of Walker's mother's kitchen.

TIP   When analyzing stylistic techniques in a piece of expressive writing, keep in mind the following ways various sentence structures can be used to express a writer's feelings.

- Short choppy sentences sometimes express anger.
- Many simple sentences in succession can create a sense of monotony.
- Very long sentences can create a sense of breathlessness and can be used to express feelings that build or overwhelm.

YOUR TURN 3   **Expressive Style**

Identify in the reading selection an example of each of the elements of expressive style given in the chart on the previous page. Write a sentence or two about the effect of each of the elements of expressive style on your understanding of the writer's thoughts and feelings.

Using a Dictionary to Research Word Origins

Just as knowing about someone's ancestors can often help you understand that person, knowing about a word's origins can help you understand and remember the word. If you want to find out about a word's origins, or **etymology,** you can start by looking at its dictionary etymology, the part of a dictionary entry that explains the history of the word.

Etymologies are easy to find because they appear within brackets ([ ]) or double brackets ([[ ]]) within a dictionary entry. To explain a word's origins, etymologies use a series of abbreviations and symbols, the key to which can usually be found in the dictionary's introduction.

THINKING IT THROUGH **Using a Dictionary to Research Word Origins**

Use the following steps to research word origins in a dictionary. Refer also to one reader's responses, based on the word *gradual,* following each step.

1. After finding the word's entry in the dictionary, locate the bracketed etymology. Be aware that it may direct you to the etymology of another, related word. The bracketed etymology for "gradual" looks like this: [ML "gradualis"< L "gradus": see GRADE]. It directs me to the etymology for "grade": [Fr.< L "gradus," a step, degree, rank< "gradi," to step, walk< IE base *"ghredh"-, to stride> Goth "griths," step].

2. Consult the key in the front or back of the dictionary for the meanings of any abbreviations or symbols you do not understand. "ML" means "Medieval Latin." "Fr" means "French." "L" stands for "Latin." The < symbol stands for "derived from." "IE" stands for "Indo-European." The > symbol means "whence is derived" or "from which is derived." "Goth" is short for "Gothic."

3. Compare the current meanings of the word with its original meaning or meanings. The current meaning I know is "taking place by almost imperceptible steps or degrees." The etymology tells me that the word came from the Latin word "gradus," meaning "a step, rank or degree."

4. How does knowing the story give you a deeper understanding of the word and its usage? I've never thought of "gradual" as meaning step-by-step, but it makes sense. I bet "graduate" has similar origins.

PRACTICE

Research the origins of the following words from the reading selection.

1. cocoon
2. bed
3. flourish
4. food
5. bowl
6. muse
7. obsolete
8. cauldron
9. itinerant
10. pecan

Answering Vocabulary Questions

Just as reading a reflective essay requires you to make connections based on prior experience, vocabulary questions on many standardized tests require you to draw on your prior knowledge of words and word parts. They also require you to examine a word's context for clues about its meaning. By combining your prior knowledge with evidence from the reading passage, you can often infer the meaning of an unfamiliar word.

Take a look at the following short **reading passage** and the vocabulary question that follows it.

Carly's father complained vociferously when the umpire called her "out." I was sitting next to him at the time, and I was afraid my hearing would never recover.

1. In the passage above, the word "vociferously" most nearly means?

  A. viciously

  B. loudly

  C. bitterly

  D. forcefully

  E. respectfully

THINKING IT THROUGH   **Answering Vocabulary Questions**

Use the following steps and responses based on the question above to help you answer vocabulary questions.

▶ **STEP 1** Identify word parts—prefixes, suffixes, roots—that you recognize.

The root is "voc." Doesn't that have to do with the voice?

▶ **STEP 2** Look for context clues within the sentence. Then, look for them in the passage as a whole.

The word "vociferously" is next to "complained," so maybe it describes how the father complained. The next sentence suggests that the father complained loudly, since the person next to him "was afraid [his or her] hearing would never recover."

▶ **STEP 3** Test each reasonable answer by inserting it into the sentence.

Both answers **B** and **D** can reasonably be inserted into the sentence. Answers **A, C,** and **E** don't work as well in the sentence.

▶ **STEP 4** Be sure the answer you choose gives the meaning of the word as it is used in this particular passage. Sometimes more than one of the definitions for a word with multiple meanings will be offered among the possible answers.

I think I've heard "vociferous" used to describe intensity or forcefulness, so answer **D** is technically a correct definition. However, the context of this passage—the speaker's fear of hearing loss—supports answer **B,** "loudly." **B** is correct.

Writing a Reflective Essay

WHAT'S AHEAD?

In this workshop, you will write a reflective essay about a person. You will also learn how to

- choose a memorable person
- analyze and express the significance the person has had in your life
- decide whether to "tell" or "show"
- use colloquialisms and slang for effect
- punctuate dialogue correctly

Imagine—one day you're going through your usual routine, when out of the blue someone says or does something that changes your life forever. Has that ever happened to you? Sometimes people's words or actions are the catalyst for sudden and dramatic changes in us. Usually, however, people's effects on us are more gradual, like the effect of sunlight on a seedling. Little by little, the young plant grows toward the nourishing light.

One way to explore the effects certain people have had on our lives is by writing about those people. Have you ever written

- a diary or journal entry about someone?
- a letter to an old friend describing a new one?
- a song or poem about a special person?

If so, you have used many of the exploratory and expressive skills necessary to write a reflective essay about a significant person. In this workshop, you will practice those same skills, only this time you will have a particular purpose in mind—to express to an audience, in the form of a reflective essay, your thoughts and feelings about the effects a single person has had upon your life.

Prewriting

Consider Purpose, Audience, and Tone

Explore and Express Writers of reflective essays can have several **purposes**—to explore the complexities of human relationships, to discover and reveal something about themselves, to express themselves, to share insights, and to entertain. These writers' purposes are determined partially by the **audience** they expect to have. For instance, most people who keep diaries never expect anyone else to read them, so the purpose of the reflective writings in their diaries is self-exploration and self-expression.

The reflective essay you will write for this workshop, however, will have a wider audience than most diary entries. Consequently, your purpose will include self-exploration and self-expression, but you will also seek to entertain readers and perhaps even to share with them your insights into human relationships. How will you combine these purposes—expressing yourself while at the same time engaging readers? One way writers of reflective essays achieve this balance is by using expressive style. **Expressive style** is a way of writing particularly well suited to express a writer's unique **voice.** It includes use of first-person ("I") point of view and an informal, conversational **tone.**

Reference Note

For more about **expressive style,** see page 24 in the Reading Workshop of this chapter.

TIP   A writer's **tone** conveys the writer's attitude toward his or her audience. For example, a writer might use a formal, very polite tone in a letter to a college admissions board and a joking, playful tone in a letter to a friend. A writer's tone also conveys his or her attitude toward the subject matter. For example, a writer might use a sarcastic tone to discuss something he or she disliked and a reverential tone to discuss something for which the writer felt great respect. Diction, sentence structure, and other elements of style can all serve to create a particular tone.

   Voice, like tone, is a function of a writer's style; however, a writer's voice is unique to him or her. It is that writer's distinctive way of expressing him or herself.

THINKING IT THROUGH   **Analyzing Audience and Tone**

In order to make your reflective essay interesting, relevant, and appropriate to your audience, ask yourself the following questions. Look also at one writer's responses following each question.

▶ STEP 1 Can I predict who my audience will be? *My primary audience will consist of my classmates and English teacher, but I might also want to submit my essay to the school literary magazine.*

▶ STEP 2 What kinds of people might particularly interest my audience? With what might they relate? *I'm thinking of writing about my brother. He would be a good subject for my essay because many people either have a brother or know someone who is like a brother to them.*

▶ STEP 3 What do I feel comfortable sharing with my audience? *I feel comfortable sharing my thoughts and feelings with my teacher and classmates. I'll have to think about whether or not I want to publish them in the literary magazine for the whole school to read.*

▶ STEP 4 What tone will be appropriate for my audience and my potential subject? *Since my subject will be my brother, I think a conversational, slightly nostalgic tone would work well.*

Choose a Person

Who's Who in Your Life?
Who would make a good subject for this reflective essay? You may choose to write about someone you know well, like a family member or friend. Alternatively, you may decide to write about someone you don't know intimately but who has had a profound effect on your life nonetheless—such as the music teacher who encouraged you to learn to play the guitar. If you have trouble coming up with ideas, try the following subject-generating strategies:

- **Browse** through your old diaries, journals, scrapbooks, and letters.
- **Brainstorm** a list of people who create strong feelings in you, either positive or negative.
- **Listen** to your favorite music from years gone by. Does it bring anybody to mind?

Now that you have brainstormed a crowd of possible subjects, they may all be clamoring for your attention; you may feel overwhelmed. How do you choose just one? As you consider the possibilities, keep in mind that the subject of your reflective essay should be:

- **Significant**—Did the person change you? Did he or she teach you something about yourself or the world?
- **Knowable**—Do you have first-hand, personal experience of the person?
- **Memorable**—Do you remember enough details and anecdotes about the person to describe him or her effectively?
- **Publishable**—Do you feel comfortable sharing your descriptions of and anecdotes about this person? Will you feel comfortable sharing your thoughts and feelings about him or her with readers?

Reflect on the Person's Significance

Mirror, Mirror
In reflective essays, writers don't simply describe their subjects; they also explore their own thoughts and feelings and their subjects' significance in their lives. For example, a writer describing how his dad taught him to throw a boomerang wants to give readers a clear picture not only of his father, but also of his relationship with his father and its importance to him. He may even want readers to reflect on ways their fathers—or any loved ones—are important to them.

KEY CONCEPT

To write a truly reflective essay, you will need to look inward to discover your thoughts and feelings about your subject and how he or she has affected you. Then you will need to turn outward and consider what your experience of this person tells you about the human experience more generally and what your experience might mean to readers.

Ask yourself the following questions to help you reflect on your subject's significance. Look also at the responses on the right-hand side for an example of how one writer answered these questions.

Reflection Questions	One Writer's Responses
▶ **STEP 1** How did (or does) the person affect me emotionally? How do I feel about him or her? (Don't censor yourself. Include ambivalent feelings as well as positive ones.)	I'm protective of my little brother, and I admire how thoughtful he is. When I'm feeling blue, he cheers me up. Sometimes I get irritated when he forgets to do his chores and I end up doing them.
▶ **STEP 2** What has the person taught me about myself and my relationships with others?	Doug reminds me that my problems are not as big as I sometimes think they are and that I need other people to put things in perspective for me.
▶ **STEP 3** Has the person changed my view of human relationships in general? If so, how?	He has taught me that even small nurturing gestures can mean a lot. Because of his example, I try to be more thoughtful.

TIP Don't sentimentalize your subject. Instead, create a complex picture by revealing both strengths and weaknesses, light and shadow.

Keeping your subject's significance in mind as you write will help you as you recall key events and details. Write a sentence that clearly states your subject's significance. While this sentence may not appear in your draft, it will help guide your choices throughout the writing process. In addition, reflecting upon and articulating your subject's significance can enhance not only your essay, but also your **personal growth.** The writer who answered the questions in the chart above wrote the following sentence to help keep her subject's significance in mind.

TIP This statement of your subject's significance is like a **working thesis statement**—it could change. Your ideas about your subject will evolve and crystalize as you work through the prewriting steps and write your draft. Be open to learning more about your subject and yourself during the writing process—that's what it's all about.

> My little brother, Doug, has a special gift for nurturing that always makes me feel better.

When you begin drafting your essay, refer back to your statement often. Many writers of reflective essays *hint* at their subject's significance in the introduction of the essay, *show* that significance in the body, and *fully reveal* it in the conclusion.

Recall Key Anecdotes

Anecdotal Evidence   Now that you have analyzed *what* your subject's significance to you is, think for a minute about *how* he or she became significant. Most likely, your subject's effect on your life is the result of things he or she has said and done. Consequently, to convey the person's significance to readers, you will need to show your subject in action—saying and doing the things that have had such a profound effect on your life.

KEY CONCEPT   Needless to say, you will probably not be able to describe every word or action that has affected you. **Instead, you will need to focus on the anecdotes, or brief stories, that will most effectively convey to readers your subject's significance.** These anecdotes can be about events as dramatic as your subject rescuing you from a burning building or as everyday as your subject cooking your favorite meal.

THINKING IT THROUGH   Recalling Anecdotes

The following chart provides steps to help you recall anecdotes. Look also at one writer's responses in the right-hand column.

▶ **STEP 1** Brainstorm a list of anecdotes (brief stories) that illustrate your subject's significance. List any memories of your subject doing or saying something that has had an effect on you.

- childhood games Doug and I played that helped me survive new school
- Doug restored rosebush to health
- Doug cheered me and other girls up by giving us roses
- Doug's baseball team won championship

▶ **STEP 2** Narrow the list to no more than three anecdotes. Eliminate anecdotes that don't clearly illustrate your subject's significance to you.

I will eliminate the story about how Doug's team won the championship because it doesn't show his significance to me—his gift for nurturing and how he helps me feel better when I'm blue.

▶ **STEP 3** Check the remaining anecdotes to make sure that they are likely to engage readers, that you feel comfortable sharing them, and that you remember plenty of specific details about them. Replace any that do not meet these criteria.

The remaining three anecdotes on my list meet all of these criteria. The anecdote about Doug's giving me and the other girls roses is the most vivid, so I might begin and end with it.

Recall Details

It's All in the Details   A reflective essay comes alive when the writer includes vibrant details. There are three kinds of details you can use in your essay: narrative details, descriptive details, and sensory details.

- **Narrative details** describe actions and events.

   When the back door slammed, Mom cringed. Then, she flew to the oven to see if the cake had fallen.

- **Descriptive details** describe people, places, and objects.

   A vast crater had formed at the center of the once-smooth surface of the cake. Mom's face turned ashen. "It's ruined," she said.

- **Sensory details** are narrative or descriptive details that appeal to the senses. They help readers see, hear, feel, taste, and smell what is being described. The details in the examples above appeal to the senses of hearing (*slammed*), sight (*ashen, crater*), and touch (*once-smooth*).

   Refer to the following chart to see strategies for gathering details and examples of how one writer used these strategies.

Strategies for Gathering Details	Examples
Subject: List descriptive and sensory details associated with your subject, including your thoughts and feelings about him or her.	Doug has red, curly hair. Most of the time he moves casually and slowly. He speaks quietly.
Anecdotes: Elaborate on each of the anecdotes that you plan to include in your essay with narrative details, your thoughts and feelings, and actual dialogue.	I remember the time Doug gave me that rosebud. "Here, Maria," he said, holding it out to me. That small gesture cheered me up.
Other People: List other people who will play a part in your reflective essay. Write down descriptive, narrative, and sensory details about each person. Include actual dialogue.	Dad tried to talk Doug out of attempting to save the rosebush: "Son, look how dry that is, all in the inside there. See."
Places: List places that will appear in your reflective essay. Write down descriptive and sensory details about each place.	Doug and I set up a little hideaway inside my dingy closet.

TIP Another way to make the style and voice of your writing fresh and interesting is to include literary devices such as figures of speech. A **figure of speech** is a word or phrase that describes one thing in terms of another and that is not meant to be understood literally. For more about figures of speech, see page 75.

TIP Some of the details you remember may not be *necessary* to your essay. When you write your first draft, include only details that help convey the theme, mood, ideas, emotions, and impressions that you want to communicate about your subject.

For instance, if you are trying to create a melancholy mood, you probably won't want to mention details about the upbeat music playing on the radio. However, you will want to include details about the misty weather and the sounds of a nearby foghorn.

Showing Versus Telling

When you write your reflective essay, you can tell readers directly about your subject, or you can show them indirectly by providing narrative and descriptive details. Sometimes, telling readers something directly is the best way to convey information. For instance, you might want to tell readers that no one has had a greater effect on your life than your subject. However, you will make a bigger impression on them if you also use narrative and descriptive details to *show* readers that effect.

Look at the following examples of telling and showing. Which creates a clearer picture in your mind?

Telling: Doug would not give up on the rosebush, but worked hard to save it.

Showing: Sucking the blood from one gloveless hand, Doug marched back to the rosebush. He watered and whistled. I swear I even heard him talk to it: "Yeah, the Phillies are pretty lame, but at least there's a pro team here. . . ." He kept this up all spring. Early in June a single coral blossom blushed amid green leaves.

In the first example, the writer *tells* what Doug did. In the second, she provides narrative,

descriptive, and sensory details that *show* what he did. Notice that rather than just telling the reader that Doug talked to the rosebush, she also includes **dialogue** that shows him talking to it. In addition, in the phrase *coral blossom blushed*, the writer uses personification to show her unique vision of a rose. **Personification** is a particular kind of figurative language in which a nonhuman thing is spoken of as if it were human. Here, a rose is described as blushing, a distinctly human behavior.

Another way to *show* is by using dialogue tags. **Dialogue tags** are phrases, such as *she muttered, Jamal argued,* and *whispered Casey,* that not only identify the speaker, but also show *how* he or she is speaking.

> **TIP** Note the use of the contraction *there's* in the "showing" example at left. While contractions are rare in formal writing, they are frequently used in dialogue to reflect the way people actually speak. Contractions are also used in expressive writing in general to create an informal, conversational tone.

PRACTICE

Referring to the examples above, turn the following "telling" statements into "showing" statements by using narrative and descriptive details and figurative language. Put your answers on your own paper.

1. He loved football and went to lots of football games.

2. My dog is so cute.

3. Luci denied that she liked Michael. (Rewrite this one using dialogue.)

4. Just four days before the competition, the choir sounded rotten.

5. The meal smelled delicious.

Shape Your Reflective Essay

Follow Your Own Orders   There are two organizational patterns typically used in reflective essays—**chronological order** and **order of importance**.

Chronological order tells a series of actions or anecdotes in the order they happened—first A, then B, then C. It can be used to tell the history of the relationship between the writer and the subject. Writers sometimes insert **flashbacks** and **flash-forwards** into a chronological sequence. For instance, you may begin your reflective essay in the present, flashback to a memory of the past, and then flash-forward to some projected future at the end.

Order of importance relates anecdotes and details in order from least to most important, or vice versa. In a variation on strict order of importance, the least important anecdotes might be sandwiched between more important anecdotes. Order of importance is commonly used to relate the lessons a writer learned from a subject, beginning with the least important and saving the best for last.

Often, writers use the preceding organizational patterns in conjunction with one another. For example, the body of a reflective essay could relate, in chronological order, a few anecdotes about its subject. It could then conclude by discussing the subject's effects on the writer, moving from least to most important effects.

To plan the order of your own essay, begin by arranging anecdotes and narrative details about events in chronological order; then, experiment by rearranging them in order of importance. Which order will best convey your subject's significance to your audience? Which will ensure a coherent narrative? Arrange descriptive details according to order of importance or spatial order, and see how they fit with the order of events. You will probably end up using a combination of organizational patterns.

> **TIP** You could use **spatial order**—top to bottom, left to right, inside to outside—to organize details in a brief description of a place, thing, or person. For example, one paragraph of your essay might describe your subject from top to bottom—first her floppy mauve hat, then her long blond hair, then her stylish evening dress, and finally her heavy, black boots.

YOUR TURN 4 Focusing on Your Subject

Review each of the prewriting steps as you prepare to write your draft. Be sure to

- Choose a subject, and consider the audience, purpose, and tone of your essay. What do you want to achieve?
- Reflect on your subject's significance in your life, and state it clearly.
- Choose anecdotes that illustrate your subject's significance.
- Recall narrative and descriptive details about your subject and related anecdotes, people, and places.
- Order ideas and details effectively.

Writing

Reflective Essay

Framework

Directions and Explanations

Introduction

- Engage readers' attention.
- Supply necessary background information, including an introduction of the subject.
- Hint at the subject's significance.

Compel Readers' Attention   Draw your readers into your essay with a vivid anecdote, dramatic dialogue, or a striking statement, question, quotation, or observation.

Introduce Your Subject   You might introduce your subject to your readers by describing your first encounter with him or her or by describing an important, representative moment in your relationship.

Hint at Your Subject's Significance   Suggesting the effect your subject has had on your life will prepare your readers and help keep you focused.

Body

- Relate first anecdote that conveys subject's significance.
- Relate second anecdote, third anecdote, and so on.

Bring Your Subject to Life   Use narrative and descriptive details to bring your subject to life. Remember to include your own thoughts and feelings.

Include Dialogue   If you can't remember a person's exact words, write dialogue that conveys a sense of that person's words and the spirit of those words.

Organize Details   Arrange details coherently so that your subject's significance builds in the minds of your readers.

Conclusion

- Reflect on why this person is significant to you—and possibly to your audience.

Reveal Your Subject's Significance   After you explain why your subject is important to you personally, reflect on why your thoughts and feelings about this person might be significant to others.

YOUR TURN 5   **Writing a First Draft**

Using the framework above, write the first draft of your reflective essay. For an example of a reflective essay that uses this framework, look ahead to the Writer's Model on the next page.

A Writer's Model

The reflective essay below, which is a final draft, closely follows the framework on the previous page.

Green Thumb

At his eighth-grade graduation, my younger brother Doug presented me with a rose. I had just had a major disagreement with my boyfriend over plans for the Senior Prom. I was trying to look cheerful, but I felt like a wilted flower as I stood there congratulating three of the girls in his class: Jen, Beth, and Angelika. They looked no better than I felt. Jen was leaving the next day for Kansas, and she cried as she hugged Doug goodbye. One of the pink buds in her corsage must have come loose and fallen to the concrete while they were hugging. As the girls shuffled away toward their parents, Doug spied the flower at his feet. He leaned down with the easy grace that made him lethal on the baseball field and scooped it up. The rosebud lay there in his palm, for the taking. "Here, Maria." I couldn't help smiling. It was so typical of him to know how to make things better.

Doug knows flowers—knows what they need and when they want to be left alone. When we had moved into our current home just outside Philadelphia, a rosebush was leaning against the back fence, leafless and brittle from lack of attention. Dad was ready to dig it up and plant a new one, but Doug wouldn't let him.

"Son, look how dry that is," said Dad, breaking off a branch, "all in the inside there. See. That plant's a goner."

"Just give me a few weeks," Doug replied. He squatted next to the bush and ran his fingers over the dirt at its base.

Dad shrugged. He had enough projects with the new house to keep him busy for a few weeks. He carried the shovel back to the garage.

While the rest of us were unpacking our stuff and spending long hours behind locked bedroom doors, missing Memphis, Doug launched a rescue operation for the rosebush. I was fuming at first. How had he managed to get out of unpacking?

Armed with the garden hose and a pair of clippers, he loped out into the unmowed yard. Through my open bedroom window I heard SNIP, SNIP, SNIP. After a few minutes, the rhythm became relaxing, and my irritation faded. I caught a glimpse of Doug's red curls bobbing toward the garbage, heard the thud of a pile of thorny sticks hitting the bottom of the garbage can. Sucking the blood from one gloveless hand, Doug marched back over to the

(continued)

INTRODUCTION
Engaging opening (first anecdote)

Background information/Introduction of subject

Hint at subject's significance

BODY
Flashback (second anecdote)

Descriptive details

Dialogue

Narrative details

Writer's thoughts and feelings

Descriptive and sensory details

Narrative details

(continued)

rosebush. He watered and whistled. I swear I even heard him talk to it: "Yeah, the Phillies aren't the greatest, but at least there's a pro team here. Hang on a sec—you've got an arm trying to escape here. Let me tie it up for you." He kept this up all spring. Early in June a single coral blossom blushed amid green leaves. That was when we first knew Doug had a green thumb.

That green thumb works with people, too. It seems to heal them even when they can't heal themselves. I know, because it worked with me. When I was seven and Doug was three, our family had just moved to Chicago, and I was afraid of my new school and all the unfamiliar faces. After school, I would fly in our front door, take the stairs three at a time, and bound into Doug's room. There he would be—plump as a cherub, curls wild, and green eyes lit up, standing at the crib rail with his arms out for me. I would swoop him up, or sometimes help him climb onto my back, and we would bound downstairs like cowboy and horse, galloping through the living room, snorting and pawing, until Mom yelled that we were making the dishes rattle.

So we tried other things—like saddling up the family dog, a Great Dane named Lucky, to take Doug for a ride. We older kids weren't supposed to ride Lucky, but I figured he wouldn't notice someone so small. When Doug turned four, we made a tiny desk out of cardboard boxes and plywood and set it up in my dingy closet. We brought in a lamp, and I taught him how to add and read a few words. So long as I had him for a playmate, my new school, the girls who picked on me, and the boys who shot spit-balls into my hair didn't matter at all. My troubles faded in the light of his companionship.

Years later, when Doug gave me that rose, my troubles faded into the background once again. The fight with my boyfriend would get resolved tomorrow, and if it didn't—well, it would. I watched Doug amble over to the car.

"Dad?"

"Yeah, son?"

"Pop the trunk, will you?"

"For what?"

"Just . . . something."

I watched from a distance as three coral roses emerged from the trunk, their stems wrapped in moist paper towels and silver foil. Three. One for Jen, one for Beth, one for Angie. He slipped them behind his back and walked over to where the girls stood, clinging to each other tearfully. As always, he knew what would make things better.

Flashback (third anecdote)/Writer's feelings

Descriptive and narrative details

Writer's thoughts and feelings about subject's significance

CONCLUSION
Flash-forward (back to first anecdote)

Dialogue

Subject's significance

A Student's Model

The following is an excerpt of a reflective essay written by Stacey Kounelias, a twelfth-grade student at Westwood High School in Austin, Texas.

Growing Up Together

I remember becoming entrepreneurs on Saturdays during elementary school. I remember the "vacation" she was taking to Arizona. Recalling all of these memories made it difficult for me to realize that Michele, my best friend of eight years, was going to move away. In retrospect, I realize that no one could ever replace Michele or fulfill the same kind of friendship we had. We let our imaginations run wild. Michele's ideas made our fantasies into realities. Maybe we couldn't really travel to Mars or actually become the President of the United States for a day, but we could definitely begin our own lemonade business.

Our lemonade business would not have been as successful without each other as partners. We worked together well and we complemented each other's needs. I lived on a street with ample traffic, she owned the super deluxe markers to create our business sign reading: "MICHELE and STACEY'S LEMONADE . . . the best on the street."

Michele had all of the logistics running around in her head, and she instructed me on how to make our idea come to life: "The corner of Fathom Circle will be the best place to sell. And we definitely need to pour the juice into comic cups. Everyone has more fun using those anyway."

This business was a giant undertaking for eight-year-olds. We tried to be professional; we filled the cup to the brim; we smiled and said thank you.

The afternoon should have been exhausting because the heat pounded on us from every angle, but it wasn't because Michele engineered everything perfectly. When the day was complete and the sun hiding behind the oak tree across the street, Michele counted and recounted the net profit while I stacked the chairs, sponged off the card table and gulped down the last of the lemonade, leaving Michele the final sip. She calculated that we earned almost ten dollars. In our eyes, enough money to purchase a snack from the convenience store around the corner was a dream come true.

Engaging opening

Hint at subject's significance

Anecdote

Descriptive details

Dialogue

Narrative details

Figurative language (personification)

Narrative details

Revising

Evaluate and Revise Your Draft

Do a Double Take   Congratulations! Now that you have a draft, you are well on your way to sharing the subject of your essay with a wider world. Before you publish your essay, however, work collaboratively to revise it carefully.

▷ **First Reading: Content and Organization**   With a classmate or on your own, use the chart below to make improvements to your reflective essay. Ask yourself the questions in the first column, use the second column to help you locate trouble spots, and the third to revise.

Reflective Essay: Content and Organization Guidelines for Peer and Self-Evaluation

Evaluation Questions	▶ Tips	▶ Revision Techniques
❶ Does the introduction grab the reader's attention and provide background information, including a hint at the subject's significance?	**Bracket** any attention-grabbing sentences. **Underline** background information and **circle** the sentence(s) that hints at the subject's significance. If there are no brackets or underlined sentences, revise. If there is no circled sentence, or if the circled sentence(s) leaves nothing to be discovered, revise.	**Add** zippy dialogue, an amusing anecdote, an intriguing question, or a quotation to grab the reader's attention. **Add** background about the subject and a hint about the subject's significance. If the circled sentence does more than hint, **delete** information that reveals too much about the subject's significance too early.
❷ Does the essay include anecdotes that illustrate the subject's significance?	**Highlight** each anecdote, and then **place a check mark over** any anecdotes that clearly show the subject's significance. If there are no highlighted passages with checks, revise.	**Add** or **elaborate** on anecdotes. Use words that "show" rather than "tell," including descriptive and narrative details.
❸ Are events and details ordered effectively?	**Number** events according to chronological order or order of importance. If the numbers are not in sequence (unless you have purposely added a flashback or flash-forward or used an alternate order), revise.	**Rearrange** events to reflect chronological order or order of importance, with most important last. **Add** transitions to improve the coherence of the narrative.
❹ Does the conclusion reveal the significance of the subject?	**Draw a square** around the sentence or sentences that explain why the subject was or is significant. If there isn't a square, revise.	**Add** a statement that explains the subject's significance, and **elaborate** on it by discussing related thoughts and feelings.

ONE WRITER'S REVISIONS   Here's how one writer used the content and organization guidelines to revise some sentences that appear, in revised form, in the introduction of the reflective essay on page 37. Study the revisions, and answer the questions that follow.

> He leaned down and scooped it up. *with the easy grace that made him lethal on the baseball field/* The rosebud lay there   **add**
>
> *"Here, Maria."*
> in his palm, for the taking. I couldn't help smiling. ~~Doug always~~   **add**
>
> *It was so typical of him to/things*
> knows how to make ~~people feel~~ better.   **delete**

Analyzing the Revision Process

1. Why do you think the writer added information about *how* Doug picked up the rosebud and what he said? Why did the writer revise the last sentence?

2. What effect do the changes have on the paragraph?

YOUR TURN 6   Focusing on Content and Organization

Use the guidelines in the chart on the previous page to help you revise the content and organization of your reflective essay. Use the example revisions shown above as a model.

PEER REVIEW

Ask a classmate to read your reflective essay and to answer the following questions.

1. What part of the essay is most interesting? Why?

2. After reading the essay, did you understand its subject's significance to the writer? Why or why not?

Second Reading: Style   In your second reading, use the following style guidelines to help you use **colloquialisms**—the informal words and phrases used in everyday conversation—effectively in dialogue. After all, your purpose is to share your reflective essay with your classmates and others, and colloquialisms will help create the conversational tone that will keep them interested.

Style Guidelines

Evaluation Question	▶ Tips	▶ Revision Techniques
Are colloquialisms used in dialogue to reflect the way people actually speak, to establish setting, or to characterize people?	▶ **Bracket** all the dialogue in the essay. **Underline** any colloquialisms within the dialogue. If there are no or very few underlined words or phrases, revise.	▶ **Add** colloquialisms to dialogue. **Replace** standard language with colloquialisms that mirror actual speech, that establish setting, or that characterize.

Focus on

Word Choice

Colloquialisms

Colloquialisms are often used in reflective essays to create an **informal tone** and to convey a writer's unique **voice**. In dialogue, colloquialisms can also be used to:

- **reflect the way people actually speak, making the dialogue more realistic.** For example, in a formal essay, you might write, "They did not go," whereas in conversation, you would probably say, "They didn't go."
- **establish setting.** For example, if you were describing an experience that happened five years ago, dialogue that includes colloquialisms from that period might help readers envision the setting.
- **characterize people.** How people speak can tell readers how old they are, where they are from, and what kind of personality they have.

Remember, however, not to go overboard—a few colloquialisms go a long way.

ONE WRITER'S REVISIONS Here's how the writer of the Writer's Model on page 37 followed the style guidelines to use colloquialisms effectively in dialogue.

Dialogue is bracketed.

Colloquialism is underlined.

BEFORE REVISION

["Yes, the Philadelphia Phillies are not the best team, but at least there's a <u>pro team</u> here. Wait, please. You've got an arm trying to escape. Let me tie it up for you."]

add colloquialisms

AFTER REVISION

"Yeah, the Phillies aren't the greatest, but at least there's a pro team here. Hang on a sec—you've got an arm trying to escape here. Let me tie it up for you."

Analyzing the Revision Process

1. Which of the two versions of the dialogue seems more like how people really talk? Why?

2. What effect do the revisions have on your understanding of the person speaking?

TIP **Colloquialisms** are often meant to be understood figuratively, rather than literally. For instance, if you say someone is "in the dark"—instead of saying he or she does not know what is going on—you are not only using a colloquialism, but also a figure of speech that provides readers with a concrete image. As you can see from this example, colloquialisms can give all your expressive writing, not just dialogue, color and vividness.

YOUR TURN 7 **Using Colloquialisms**

Using the style guidelines beginning on page 41, revise your essay to include colloquialisms in dialogue.

Designing Your Writing

Using Photos   Jazz up your reflective essay with photos. Paste them in or insert them directly into your document. Certain photos can even *illuminate* your essay—they can add meaning to it rather than just illustrating what is already there. As you choose photos, keep these important points in mind:

- **Use photos that correspond closely with the subject matter** of the essay. For instance, don't use photos of your subject as a child if your essay introduces her to the reader as an adult.

- **Write a caption** for a photo if readers might not understand its connection to the text.

- **Choose photos that convey the same mood and tone as your essay.** If your essay has a nostalgic tone, for instance, you might choose black and white photos that are yellowed with age.

COMPUTER TIP

If you have access to a digital camera or have photographs stored on a disk and loaded onto a computer, you can simply insert the appropriate digital images into your document.

Here I am—at the top!

- **Choose a photo that illuminates your essay,** rather than one that simply illustrates it. For example, if your essay describes how your friend Beth helped you get over your fear of heights years ago, include a recent picture of yourself at the top of the Empire State Building. Such a photo might not illustrate something that happened within the time frame of your essay, but it would illuminate your new confidence in high places— which you couldn't have managed without Beth's help years ago.

Publishing

Proofread Your Essay

Reference Note

For more about **punctuating dialogue,** see page 862.

Polishing Your Reflection   Because you want to give readers as clear an image of your subject as possible, you will want to proofread your essay carefully to eliminate any mistakes in punctuation, grammar, and spelling. Since you have probably included dialogue in your essay, pay special attention to making sure the dialogue is punctuated correctly.

Grammar Link

Punctuating Dialogue Correctly

Reflective essays often include dialogue, which must be punctuated correctly so that readers know who is speaking. When writing dialogue:

- Begin a new paragraph each time the speaker changes.
- Enclose each speaker's words in quotation marks.
- Begin a direct quotation with a capital letter.
- When an expression identifying the speaker, a **dialogue tag,** interrupts a quoted sentence, begin the second part of the quotation with a lowercase letter.
- Set off a direct quotation from the rest of the sentence with a comma, a question mark, or an exclamation point, but not with a period.
- Place commas and periods within closing quotation marks.
- Place question marks and exclamation points inside the closing quotation marks if a quotation is a question or an exclamation. Otherwise, place them outside.

Example:
    "Son, look how dry that is," said Dad, breaking off a branch, "all in the inside there.

See. That plant's a goner."
    "Would you just give me a few weeks?" Doug pleaded.

TIP   If you quote a passage of dialogue that consists of more than one paragraph, place quotation marks at the beginning of each new paragraph but at the end of only the last paragraph in the passage.

PRACTICE

The sentences below make up a dialogue between two people. Revise the sentences, starting new paragraphs where necessary and enclosing each speaker's words in quotation marks. Put your answers on your own paper.

1. Margaret, said her sister Sylvia, you took my sweater.
2. Did not!
3. Did so. I'm going to tell Mom.
4. But I didn't take it, Margaret insisted.
5. We'll just see about that, Sylvia muttered, flouncing out of the room.

Publish Your Essay

Spread the Word   Your reflective essay tells a story only you can tell. Now it is time to share that story with other people. Here are a few ways to share your reflective essay with an audience:

- Submit your essay to a local newspaper. The magazine sections of many newspapers publish reflective essays.

- Trade essays with a classmate whom you do not know very well. After reading one another's essays, get together and discuss shared experiences, feelings, and insights.

- Create a time capsule. Put your essay in a box, along with other things, such as photos and mementos, related to yourself and your subject. Share the contents of your time capsule with a few classmates, and then seal it to be opened at a later date, such as at your five-year high school reunion. You and your classmates may be interested in ways you and your relationship with your subject have changed.

- With classmates, create a Web page about yourselves and the people who have influenced you.

- Give a copy of your essay to your subject, particularly if the essay expresses appreciation for his or her effect on your life.

TIP   If you trade essays with a classmate from another culture, consider how his or her culture and traditions are revealed in the essay. Then, you might ask your classmate how your own culture is revealed in your essay.

Reflect on Your Essay

What Did You Learn?   Use the following questions to take stock of the choices you made while writing your reflective essay. Write a short response to each question to include in your portfolio, along with your final draft.

PORTFOLIO

- Why did you choose to write about your subject?

- What did writing about him or her teach you about yourself? What did you learn about relationships or life in general?

- What were the easiest and most difficult aspects of writing this essay, as compared to other essays you have written?

- What will you do differently next time you write a reflective essay?

YOUR TURN 8   **Proofreading, Publishing, and Reflecting**

Before you turn in the final draft of your reflective essay, be sure to complete each of the proofreading, publishing, and reflecting steps.

Connections to Life

Writing a College Application Essay

If you are applying to colleges, you may have **occasion** to write a personal or reflective essay. Like the reflective essay you wrote in this chapter, a college application essay often focuses on people and experiences that are important to you and what you have learned from them. However, a college application essay has one important **purpose** that other reflective essays do not: It should persuade your **audience**—the college admissions committee—to accept you into college. Consequently, you should take special care to choose the topic and use the tone—your attitude toward the topic and toward your audience—most likely to persuade them. You need to give the committee a sense of who you are, what makes you special, and what you have to offer their school.

College applications often give you a specific writing prompt that looks a bit like these:

> Write about an interest, experience, person, or achievement that has special meaning to you.

> Discuss an issue of local, national, or international concern and its significance to you.

> Discuss the greatest challenge you have had to face.

Your first step in responding to such a prompt will be to brainstorm a list of possible topics. For example, if the prompt asks you to discuss an achievement, you might list several achievements that could serve as topics—writing a children's book, saving enough money to buy a used car, and learning to play the drums.

Once you have brainstormed possible topics, choose the topic that will best help you to achieve your purpose—to persuade college admissions officials that they should admit you to their college. To make sure your college application essay achieves its purpose, be sure your topic demonstrates your:

- **Originality** What reveals the real, unique you? Keep in mind that your audience will be reading hundreds of essays; you will want yours to stand out from the crowd.

- **Integrity** What communicates your values and shows how you treat others?

- **Creativity** What shows how your mind and imagination work—and what you are capable of?

- **Maturity** What demonstrates that you can take on responsibility or have grown from your experiences?

- **Academic ability** What reveals the academic areas in which you shine—or in which you are especially interested?

On the following page you will find one student's prewriting notes for a college application essay in response to the following prompt: *Write about your greatest achievement. Why was it important to you?* The notes show how she evaluated two brainstormed topics and chose the one most likely to convince her audience that she would make a terrific addition to their school.

Possible Topics

1. **saving enough money to buy a used car**—demonstrates maturity more than creativity or academic ability, but I could demonstrate those through how well I write about the topic; not especially original—lots of people save money and buy used cars

2. **writing a children's book about children with disabilities**—demonstrates creativity, writing ability, maturity (since I completed a project), and originality (I don't know anyone else my age who has done this). I can demonstrate my integrity by discussing my motivation for writing the book—to show that people with disabilities have the same hopes and experiences as anybody else

Once you have chosen a topic in response to the prompt, formulate a working thesis statement that expresses your main idea about the topic. The writer who made the notes above developed this thesis statement:

My greatest achievement is writing a children's book about children with disabilities because it let me combine my love of writing with my desire to help these children see themselves as capable and important.

When you have written your working thesis statement, refer to the guidelines given in the Writing Workshop of this chapter as you gather details for, plan, draft, revise, and proofread your essay. As you work, keep the following tips in mind:

- **Make sure you have answered the question** or addressed the prompt. It's easy to veer off track when you are writing about yourself.

- **Be engaging.** Use a natural (not stilted) voice and enough narrative and descriptive details to make your essay lively. To grab your reader's attention, you might begin with a quotation or a vivid scene. Remember to be concise and clear, and to use precise language.

- **Double-check your work.** Ask parents, teachers, and friends to comment on your essay: Do they think it presents a positive image? When you have a final version, edit it several times to make sure it is error-free.

YOUR TURN 9 **Writing a College Application Essay**

Write an application essay in response to an actual prompt given by a college or to one of the sample prompts given on the previous page. Use the guidelines in this section to plan the essay. Remember to keep your purpose and audience in mind as you write and to allow your individuality to shine through. In other words, be yourself.

Talk   Listen

WHAT'S AHEAD?

In this section, you will create an oral history. You will also learn how to

- **prepare for and conduct an interview**
- **prepare and edit a transcript of an interview**
- **write an introduction**

Creating an Oral History

Have you listened to an older relative tell a story about his or her youth? If so, then you have heard an oral history. Oral histories are important because they provide a personal and detailed picture of what life was like for a particular person at a particular place and time. They are also an important record of the lives of people whose viewpoints could not, until recently, be found in history books.

Choosing a Subject

Someone with a Story to Tell   An oral history can only be as interesting as the person who tells it. Good subjects for oral histories are people who have specific memories of interesting or unusual experiences to share. For example, you might have a relative, friend, or aquaintance who was a real-life "Rosie the Riveter" during World War II and remembers how attitudes toward women in the work force seemed to change overnight. To choose a subject for your oral history, try asking yourself the following questions:

- Do I have an older relative who could tell me things I have always wanted to know about my family history?
- Do I know someone who has lived through a historical event I have read about but never heard about first-hand?
- Is there a nursing home nearby where I might find someone who could tell me stories of life in my town before I or my parents were born? Is there someone who remembers how technological innovations that I take for granted changed everyday life when they first appeared?
- Do I know someone who immigrated from another country?
- Do I know a veteran who is willing to share his or her experiences?

Above all, make sure the person you pick as the subject of your oral history has had experiences that are interesting to you and will be interesting to others.

Preparing for the Interview

Can We Talk?   Before they conduct interviews, oral historians must first ask their subject's permission. This can be done in person or through a polite letter or telephone call. Use the following guidelines when you contact a potential subject for an oral history.

Contacting Your Subject
Introduce yourself and your project.
Tell the potential subject what aspect of his or her life you would like to hear about.
Give the person a chance to ask *you* questions. For example, the person might want to know where the history will be published.
Set up the interview well in advance, and agree on a specific time and place that will be convenient to the person you want to interview.
Ask in advance if you can tape the interview. Specify whether you want to videotape or audiotape. Some people are comfortable being recorded in one medium but not the other.

TIP You may find it helpful, or even necessary, to research the period or event about which your subject will speak. Knowing some background information will help you ask interesting, intelligent questions.

That's a Good Question   To conduct successful interviews, oral historians prepare questions in advance. The best interview questions are open-ended questions that get the subject talking freely. Consequently, avoid questions that can be answered *yes* or *no*, or with only a few words. Use the guidelines in the left-hand column of the following chart to help you formulate at least five interview questions. Look also at the right-hand column to see how one writer used the guidelines to formulate questions.

Guidelines	One Writer's Responses
Ask questions that focus specifically on what you want to know about the time period, event, or person.	What was it like at home after the men came back from World War II and found that their jobs had been taken by women?
Ask questions that focus on things in which your audience is likely to be interested.	How were teenagers in the 1940s affected by their mothers' joining the workforce?
Ask questions that focus on the significance of the experience or event for the person being interviewed.	Why was joining the workforce important to you at the time? Why is it important now?
Ask questions that focus on the historical or cultural significance of the person's experience.	In your opinion, how did society change as a result of the increased number of women in the workforce?

Conducting the Interview

And Now, Here's Your Host . . . Conducting an interview is a little like hosting a party—you need to make sure your guest is comfortable. A comfortable environment and a respectful and interested attitude on your part will go a long way toward helping your subject open up. In addition to making your guest comfortable, you also need to *listen actively* to his or her story. Follow these guidelines to make the most of your interview:

TIP In addition to listening actively as your subject tells his or her story, call upon your capacity for empathy. **Listening empathically**—sharing your subject's feelings—will help you better understand and connect with your subject's story. For more about **empathic listening,** see page 1033 in the Quick Reference Handbook.

- **Begin by keeping your appointment and arriving on time.** Ask your subject if he or she would like a glass of water, and if you are taping the interview, if the subject feels comfortable with the video camera or tape recorder.

- **Take careful notes while your subject speaks.** Listen for transitional words such as *then, next, afterwards, because, but,* and *despite,* which signal the sequence of events or the relationships between ideas.

- **Ask follow-up questions** if you don't understand something or if you would like more information.

- **Within a week after the interview, send a thank-you letter,** just as you would if someone had given you a gift. Later, when you have finished creating the oral history, send a copy to its subject.

Preparing the Transcript

Word for Word As soon as you can, transcribe the entire interview. A **transcription** is an exact reproduction of the interview as it happened, using the exact words that you and your subject used. You will edit this transcription later to give your oral history its final shape, but for now, write down everything that was said in the interview. You should also include emotional responses, facial expressions, and gestures—crying, laughing, smirking—by placing them within brackets where they occurred. Here is a small part of one writer's transcript of an interview:

> **Interviewer:** Mrs. Johnson, how did you get your job in the local armament factory in 1943?
>
> **Mrs. Johnson:** When my husband George went off to France, I was home with our five children. [shrugs] George put a lot of money in savings before he left. But eventually we began to run out. So I told my friend Patty Keeley that I planned to apply for a job at the factory, and she thought it was a good idea, too. So we took the bus down to the factory together, all dressed up in our high heels and silk stockings. [laughter] Boy, was the foreman surprised to see us.

Shaping an Oral History

History   To transform an interview into an oral history, you will need to shape it so that its **narrative,** or storylike, qualities emerge. To create an oral history from the raw materials of your transcript, identify its theme, the essence of your subject's story. Then, organize ideas in a way that best supports and conveys this theme.

Find the Theme   Like any other story, an oral history generally has a unifying **theme.** As you read over your transcript, you will probably find that certain ideas come up again and again. Identify these recurring ideas by highlighting or underlining them in your transcript. Knowing the theme of your oral history will help you choose the most effective organizational structure for it. Emphasize any parts of the interview that express its theme.

Reference Note

For more about **theme,** see page 68.

Organize Ideas   Oral histories usually use one of three organizational structures:

- **Question and Answer**   This structure alternates between interviewer's questions and subject's responses, and resembles a dialogue. It works well when the interviewer's presence is important.

TIP   Remember to use **ellipses** to indicate omissions and to enclose any explanatory information in brackets.

> **Interviewer's Q:** When did you begin working at the armament factory, Mrs. Johnson?
>
> **Mrs. Johnson's A:** My friend Patty and I began working there in January of 1943, just a few months after my husband went away to war.

- **Weaving**   Questions and responses are woven together in paragraph form. This structure downplays the presence of the interviewer, without eliminating it completely. Weaving works well for oral histories that consist of many short episodes rather than one long story. Ideas may be arranged chronologically or thematically.

> When I asked Mrs. Johnson when she started working at the armament factory, she replied, "My friend Patty and I began working there in January of 1943, just a few months after my husband went away to war."

- **Narrative**   The oral history is told as a straight story, as if there were no interviewer present. Events are usually given in chronological order. This structure works well for oral histories that tell one long story with narrative elements such as rising action, climax, and resolution and in which the interviewer's presence would be a distraction.

> My friend Patty and I began working there [the armament factory] in January of 1943, a few months after my husband went away to war.

Writing an Introduction

I'd Like You to Meet . . .   No matter which organizational pattern you choose, you will need to write an introduction for your oral history. The introduction should:

- **Engage the reader.** Begin your introduction with a striking statement, an intriguing question, or a startling statistic. For example, a statistic about the number of women who joined the workforce during World War II might provide an engaging opening for Mrs. Johnson's oral history.
- **Give background information.** Introduce your subject, giving his or her name and any relevant biographical information. Also, provide any background information about the time and place of your subject's story that will help your audience appreciate its significance. For instance, the introduction to Mrs. Johnson's oral history might hint at the importance of her story by characterizing her as a pioneer among American working women.

Publishing an Oral History

Share and Share Alike   When you have finished your oral history, try one of the following suggestions for sharing it with a wider audience:

- **With classmates, create a series of booklets** that contain histories on common subjects and donate the booklets to the local or school library.
- **Put your oral history on the World Wide Web.** You might also add links to sites that provide additional historical context.

YOUR TURN 10   Creating an Oral History

Follow the guidelines in this section to create and share with an audience your oral history.

Creating an Audiovisual Self-Reflection

People express themselves in all sorts of ways—through the written word, photography, painting, sculpture, dance, and music. In this section, you will combine both visual and audio elements to express yourself. You may choose to relate the story of your life so far, or you may limit yourself to describing one of your favorite activities or a single aspect of your personality. Your purpose is to reflect on your life and express yourself in a creative way, but since you will share your reflection with an audience, choose your material carefully. Include only things about yourself that you feel comfortable sharing.

WHAT'S AHEAD?

In this section, you will create an audiovisual self-reflection. You will learn how to

- **use visual images and audio elements to express yourself**
- **combine visual and audio elements effectively to communicate a specific message**

Choose Sights and Sounds

Every Picture Tells a Story Once you have chosen an aspect of yourself upon which to reflect, begin to consider how to express it. You will want to choose the **medium**—visual or audio—that best communicates each element of your self-reflection. First, consider which elements will be best expressed visually. Photographs are wonderful storytelling tools, but don't limit your self-reflection to photographs only. If you like to draw or paint, include some of your own artwork. Flip through a stack of magazines and clip pictures that depict activities you enjoy or moods you want to convey. You may want to collect a large number of images that speak to you, and then narrow them down.

TIP If you have access to a video camera, you might want to use it to create your self-reflection. Use the guidelines given here for choosing and ordering images and sounds. Your finished audiovisual self-reflection will be a videotape; who will you invite to the world premiere?

Mood Music In addition to images, use music and sound to bring your self-reflection to life. You might choose music and sounds that correspond with the images you have chosen. For instance, the recorded sound of a motorcycle engine might accompany a photograph of the motorcycle whose engine you rebuilt. Alternatively, you could use music and sound to convey an overall theme or mood. The sound of waves lapping at the shore or a particular song might convey just the mood of tranquility that you are after.

Get Yourself in Order

Life Is Art   Once you have chosen or created images, music, and sounds, arrange them in a way that will help readers understand your story. Two organizational strategies are particularly well suited to this kind of project—chronological order and thematic order.

In **chronological order,** images and corresponding sounds appear in an order that conveys the sequence of events from beginning to end. This organizational strategy would work well to depict the highlights of your life so far, or an important series of events.

In **thematic order,** images and sounds that convey the same themes are grouped together. For instance, one cluster of images and sounds might depict your family, while another might relate to your love of basketball. Before deciding on any permanent order, try several arrangements; just lay all the images out on a large surface, and experiment. At left is one student's plan for a thematic self-reflection.

"My family—that's me in the middle."

"Basketball—my true love"

> **TIP**   As you arrange images, keep the following design elements in mind.
>
> - **Color** can be used to create a mood and to emphasize elements.
> - **Lines** can be used to direct the viewer's eye and to suggest different qualities. For example, curved lines suggest gracefulness.
> - **Shapes and textures** can be used to evoke emotions, to emphasize elements, and to add interest.

Revisit Your Work

You Only Live Once   Once you finish the first "draft" of your self-reflection, reflect on and evaluate it critically to make sure you have not left out or downplayed anything important. For instance, you might suddenly realize that family meals are an important part of your life, but there are no pictures of meals in your collection. Make any necessary revisions or additions.

Once you are satisfied that your self-reflection effectively expresses the parts of yourself you want to express, paste the images onto a piece of poster board and make a tape-recorded soundtrack. If you have access to a video camera, you may also want to videotape your images sequentially and record corresponding music and sounds.

YOUR TURN 11   **Creating an Audiovisual Self-Reflection**

> Create your own audiovisual self-reflection by following the guidelines given in this workshop. Then, publish it by sending it to a friend or relative who lives out-of-state and would like to have a reminder of you, or by displaying it at a "get to know you" evening at school.

Choices

Choose one of the following activities to complete.

▶ CAREERS

1. Help Wanted Apply for the job of your dreams. Begin by creating a **help wanted ad** that describes the job. Then, write an **essay** that answers the following question: "Why are you interested in this position and what makes you qualified for it?"

▶ LITERATURE

2. The Other Side of the Story Adopt the persona (personality and voice) of a literary character, and write a **reflective essay** from his or her point of view. Focus your narrative on a single person in that character's life. For instance, you might adopt the persona of the woman to whom the speaker in Andrew Marvell's poem "To His Coy Mistress" addresses himself. Include specific details about the character's thoughts and feelings.

▶ CROSSING THE CURRICULUM: SCIENCE, HISTORY, OR ART

3. I'd Like to Thank . . . Research the life of a political figure, a great artist, or a brilliant scientist to discover who was most influential in his or her life and career. Write up your findings in the form of a **brief report** that explains the relationship between the two people.

▶ SPEAKING AND LISTENING

4. The Untold Tale In a **dramatic interpretation,** recount an important historical event from the point of view of a historical figure. For instance, step into Siegfried Sassoon's shoes and recount what it was like to fight in the trenches during World War I. Be specific. Tell us what you (as the historical figure) see, hear, and feel, and use your voice to communicate the emotions that person might have experienced.

▶ CREATIVE WRITING

5. College Application Laughter Write a **parody** of a college application essay. Parodies are imitations that use exaggeration or inappropriate subject matter to make something serious seem ridiculous. What might a wildly exaggerated college application essay say about its author? You may choose to write an instructive parody that makes a point about the college application process, or you may choose simply to amuse your audience.

PORTFOLIO

Harnessing Your Imagination

Reading Workshop

Reading a Short Story
PAGE 58

Writing Workshop

Writing a Short Story
PAGE 67

Focus on Viewing and Representing

Planning a Trailer
PAGE 90

Storytelling

- You laugh as a friend tells you tall tales about her latest exploits.
- You listen, once again, to the familiar lyrics of your favorite love song.
- Your uncle tells you about the day he first met your aunt.
- You grip the edges of your seat as you watch the latest thriller.

What do all of these scenarios have in common? In each of them, you are listening to or watching a story unfold. In stories, we visit strange lands, have adventures, consider new ideas, and find meaning in the experiences all humans share. Because stories mean so much to us, we tell them all the time; in fact, we don't seem to be able to live without them.

Of course, there are many kinds of stories—from simple anecdotes to thousand-page novels. In this chapter we will focus on the **short story,** a fictional narrative that uses literary elements such as setting, plot, and character to explore what it means to be human. These stories don't just entertain us; they are often so carefully crafted that they are things of beauty in themselves, like a painting or a sculpture.

> **internetconnect**
>
> **go.hrw.com**
>
> **GO TO:** go.hrw.com
> **KEYWORD:** EOLang 12-2

YOUR TURN 1 **Brainstorming Short Stories**

Make a list of several stories you have read, watched, or listened to recently. Then, circle the stories that you liked the most and jot down the reasons that you liked them. When you have finished, share your list with a classmate or two. Do you like similar stories for similar reasons, or are your choices different?

Reading a Short Story

Our lives are shaped by thousands of decisions. Some of them, such as what to have for lunch, do not seem very important. Others, however, such as where to go to college, which job to take, and whom to marry, will have lasting consequences. Short stories often focus on a moment of decision in the main character's life. The key to understanding people's decisions is understanding—through what they say and do—what kinds of people they are. The main character in James Joyce's short story "Eveline," on the following page, faces a decision that could change her life forever.

WHAT'S AHEAD?

In this section, you will read a short story and learn how to
■ analyze characterization
■ make inferences about characters

Preparing to Read

READING FOCUS

Characterization   When we breathlessly turn the pages of stories, it is often because we care about the characters and want to find out what happens to them. How do writers make fictional characters seem so real? The process by which a writer reveals the personality of a character is called **characterization.** In addition to telling the reader directly what a character is like, most writers also use action, dialogue, description, and the character's own thoughts and feelings to show who that character is. As you read the short story on the following pages, look for ways the author tells and shows you about the character Eveline.

READING SKILL

Making Inferences About Characters   When you meet new people, you use information about what they wear, say, and do, as well as how others react to them, to **make inferences** about them. That is, you apply your knowledge of human nature to information gathered by your senses to decide what kinds of people they are. For example, if you meet a man who smiles constantly, you might infer, based on your experience that people who smile constantly want others to like them, that the man is anxious for others to like him. You can use the same process to understand characters in short stories. As you read "Eveline," pay attention to what the main character says and does. Then, try to guess what decision Eveline will make.

Many consider the Irish writer James Joyce (1882–1941) to be one of the most brilliant writers of the twentieth century. The story you will read, "Eveline," is from his first major work, a short-story collection called *Dubliners*, published in 1914. As you read "Eveline," write down your answers to the numbered active-reading questions.

Eveline

by James Joyce

She sat at the window watching the evening invade the avenue. Her head was leaned against the window curtains and in her nostrils was the odor of dusty cretonne.[1] She was tired.

1. What does this first paragraph tell you about Eveline?

Few people passed. The man out of the last house passed on his way home; she heard his footsteps clacking along the concrete pavement and afterwards crunching on the cinder path before the new red houses. One time there used to be a field there in which they used to play every evening with other people's children. Then a man from Belfast bought the field and built houses in it—not like their little brown house but bright brick houses with shining roofs. The children of the avenue used to play together in that field—the Devines, the Waters, the Dunns, little Keogh the cripple, she and her brothers and sisters. Ernest, however, never played: he was too grown up. Her father used often to hunt them in out of the field with his blackthorn stick; but usually little Keogh used to keep *nix*[2] and call out when he saw her father coming. Still they seemed to have been rather happy then. Her father was not so bad then; and besides, her mother was alive. That was a long time ago; she and her brothers and sisters were all grown up; her mother was dead. Tizzie Dunn was dead, too, and the Waters had gone back to England. Everything changes. Now she was going to go away like the others, to leave her home.

2. What has changed? How does Eveline feel about these changes?

Home! She looked round the room, reviewing all its familiar objects which she had dusted once a week for so many years, wondering where on earth all the dust came from. Perhaps she would never see again those familiar objects from which she had never dreamed of being divided. And yet during all those years she had never found out the name of the priest whose yellowing photograph hung on the wall above the broken harmonium[3] beside the colored print of the promises made

---

1. **cretonne** (krē•tän´): heavy printed cloth used for curtains.

2. **keep nix:** serve as lookout.

3. **harmonium:** small organ.

to Blessed Margaret Mary Alacoque.[4] He had been a school friend of her father. Whenever he showed the photograph to a visitor her father used to pass it with a casual word.

"He is in Melbourne now."

She had consented to go away, to leave her home. Was that wise? She tried to weigh each side of the question. In her home anyway she had shelter and food; she had those whom she had known all her life about her. Of course she had to work hard both in the house and at business. What would they say of her in the Stores when they found out that she had run away with a fellow? Say she was a fool, perhaps; and her place would be filled up by advertisement. Miss Gavan would be glad. She had always had an edge on her, especially whenever there were people listening.

"Miss Hill, don't you see these ladies are waiting?"

"Look lively, Miss Hill, please."

She would not cry many tears at leaving the Stores.

But in her new home, in a distant unknown country, it would not be like that. Then she would be married—she, Eveline. People would treat her with respect then. She would not be treated as her mother had been. Even now, though she was over nineteen, she sometimes felt herself in danger of her father's violence. She knew it was that that had given her the palpitations. When they were growing up he had never gone for her like he used to go for Harry and Ernest, because she was a girl; but latterly he had begun to threaten her and say what he would do to her only for her dead mother's sake. And now she had nobody to protect her. Ernest was dead and Harry, who was in the church decorating business, was nearly always down somewhere in the country. Besides, the invariable squabble for money on Saturday nights had begun to weary her unspeakably. She always gave her entire wages—seven shillings[5]—and Harry always sent up what he could but the trouble was to get any money from her father. He said she used to squander the money, that she had no head, that he wasn't going to give her his hard-earned money to throw about the streets, and much more, for he was usually fairly bad of a Saturday night. In the end he would give her the money and ask her had she any intention of buying Sunday's dinner. Then she had to rush out as quickly as she could and do her marketing, holding her black leather purse tightly in her hand as she elbowed her way through the crowds and returning home late under her load of provisions. She had hard work to keep the house together and to see that the two young children who had been left to her charge went to school regularly and got

> 3. Why do you think Eveline is daydreaming about her future?

---

4. **promises . . . Alacoque:** the Lord's promises to Margaret Mary Alacoque (1647–1690), French nun who as a child suffered from self-inflicted paralysis but was miraculously cured when she dedicated herself to a holy life.

5. **seven shillings:** A shilling is a former British coin worth five pennies, or one-twentieth of a pound. Seven shillings would have been a low salary.

their meals regularly. It was hard work —a hard life—but now that she was about to leave it she did not find it a wholly undesirable life.

She was about to explore another life with Frank. Frank was very kind, manly, open-hearted. She was to go away with him by the night boat to be his wife and to live with him in Buenos Aires where he had a home waiting for her. How well she remembered the first time she had seen him: he was lodging in a house on the main road where she used to visit. It seemed a few weeks ago. He was standing at the gate, his peaked cap pushed back on his head and his hair tumbled forward over a face of bronze. Then they had come to know each other. He used to meet her outside the Stores every evening and see her home. He took her to see *The Bohemian Girl* and she felt elated as she sat in an unaccustomed part of the theater with him. He was awfully fond of music and sang a little. People knew that they were courting and, when he sang about the lass that loves a sailor, she always felt pleasantly confused. He used to call her Poppens out of fun. First of all it had been an excitement for her to have a fellow and then she had begun to like him. He had tales of distant countries. He had started as a deck boy at a pound a month on a ship of the Allan Line going out to Canada. He told her the names of the ships he had been on and the names of the different services. He had sailed through the Strait of Magellan and he told her stories of the terrible Patagonians.[6] He had fallen on his feet in Buenos Aires, he said, and had come over to the old country just for a holiday. Of course, her father had found out the affair and had forbidden her to have anything to say to him.

"I know these sailor chaps,"[7] he said.

One day he had quarreled with Frank and after that she had to meet her lover secretly.

The evening deepened in the avenue. The white of two letters in her lap grew indistinct. One was to Harry; the other was to her father. Ernest had been her favorite but she liked Harry, too. Her father was becoming old lately, she noticed; he would miss her. Sometimes he could be very nice. Not long before, when she had been laid up for a day, he had read her out a ghost story and made toast for her at the fire. Another day, when their mother was alive, they had all gone for a picnic to the Hill of Howth. She remembered her father putting on her mother's bonnet to make the children laugh.

4. How does Eveline feel about her father?

Her time was running out but she continued to sit by the window, leaning her head against the window curtain, inhaling the odor of dusty cretonne. Down far in the avenue she could hear a street organ playing. She knew the air. Strange that it should come that very night to remind her of the promise to her mother, her promise to keep the home together as long as she could. She remembered

5. Why does the writer repeat this description of Eveline?

---

6. **Patagonians:** inhabitants of the southern part of Argentina; at the time of the story, Patagonia was still a frontier area, similar to the American West of the nineteenth century.

7. **chaps:** fellows.

the last night of her mother's illness; she was again in the close dark room at the other side of the hall and outside she heard a melancholy air of Italy. The organ player had been ordered to go away and given sixpence. She remembered her father strutting back into the sickroom saying:

"Damned Italians! coming over here!"

As she mused the pitiful vision of her mother's life laid its spell on the very quick of her being—that life of commonplace sacrifices closing in final craziness. She trembled as she heard again her mother's voice saying constantly with foolish insistence:

"Derevaun Seraun![8] Derevaun Seraun!"

She stood up in a sudden impulse of terror. Escape! She must escape! Frank would save her. He would give her life, perhaps love, too. But she wanted to live. Why should she be unhappy? She had a right to happiness. Frank would take her in his arms, fold her in his arms. He would save her.

She stood among the swaying crowd in the station at the North Wall.[9] He held her hand and she knew that he was speaking to her, saying something about the passage over and over again. The station was full of soldiers with brown baggages. Through the wide doors of the sheds she caught a glimpse of the black mass of the boat, lying in beside the quay wall, with illumined portholes. She answered nothing. She felt her cheek pale and cold and, out of a maze of distress, she prayed to God to direct her, to show her what was her duty. The boat blew a long mournful whistle into the mist. If she went, tomorrow she would be on the sea with Frank, steaming towards Buenos Aires. Their passage had been booked. Could she still draw back after all he had done for her? Her distress awoke a nausea in her body and she kept moving her lips in silent fervent prayer.

> **6.** In this paragraph, how does the writer show Eveline's emotions?

> **7.** To whom does the whistle sound mournful? Why does it affect this person?

A bell clanged upon her heart. She felt him seize her hand:

"Come!"

All the seas of the world tumbled about her heart. He was drawing her into them: he would drown her. She gripped with both hands at the iron railing.

"Come!"

No! No! No! It was impossible. Her hands clutched the iron in frenzy. Amid the seas she sent a cry of anguish!

"Eveline! Evvy!"

He rushed beyond the barrier and called to her to follow. He was shouted at to go on but he still called to her. She set her white face to him, passive, like a helpless animal. Her eyes gave him no sign of love or farewell or recognition.

---

8. Derevaun Seraun: Some scholars suggest that the phrase is corrupt Irish Gaelic for "the end of song is raving madness" or "the end of pleasure is pain." Although it does appear to be based on Irish Gaelic, the phrase as it stands is gibberish.

9. North Wall: wharf that is part of Dublin Harbor.

First Thoughts on Your Reading

1. **What adjectives would you use to describe Eveline? Why?**
2. **What did you predict the ending of the story would be? What elements of Eveline's character influenced your prediction?**
3. **Name some other stories you have read or seen in a movie or on television about a young person deciding whether to leave home. How were those stories similar to "Eveline"? How were they different?**

Characterization

The Life of the Story   A short story with unrealistic characters would be like a movie with bad actors—boring. How do writers bring their characters to life? There are many techniques, but they can be divided into two types:

- **Direct characterization:** The writer *tells* readers about the character.
- **Indirect characterization:** The writer *shows* readers how the character acts, speaks, looks, thinks, and affects other characters and lets readers make their own inferences, or educated guesses, about the character.

Refer to the chart below for more information about characterization techniques. The examples are from D. H. Lawrence's story "The Rocking-Horse Winner." This story describes one woman's desire for money and the disastrous effect this has on her family, especially on her son.

Characterization Techniques	Examples
Direct: The writer tells the reader what the character is like.	"There was a woman who was beautiful, ..."
Indirect: The writer describes how the character looks, moves, or dresses.	". . . [T]he waving dark hair of the boy tossed, his eyes had a strange glare in them."
Indirect: The writer gives and describes the character's speech in dialogue (both what the character says and how he or she says it).	"'Well—I suppose,' she said slowly and bitterly, 'it's because your father has no luck.'"
Indirect: The writer reveals the character's thoughts and feelings.	". . . [S]he felt she must cover up some fault in herself. Yet what it was that she must cover up she never knew."
Indirect: The writer shows the character's effect on other characters.	"The little girls dared not speak to him."
Indirect: The writer shows the character's actions.	"And he would slash the horse on the neck. . . ."

Making Inferences About Characters

Character Clues Since writers often use indirect characterization techniques, readers of short stories must make inferences in order to understand characters. When you **make inferences,** you add what you already know about how people behave (your **prior knowledge**) to the facts given about a character in a story (the **text evidence**) to infer what sort of a person the character really is. Here is a formula for this process:

Prior Knowledge + Text Evidence = Inference

TIP Information about the character— **text evidence**—may be in the form of a description, an action taken, or a thought or piece of dialogue attributed to the character.

THINKING IT THROUGH Making Inferences About Characters

Use the steps below to make inferences about characters. Look also at one reader's responses about Eveline in Joyce's story.

▶ **STEP 1** Read the story for information about the character. I notice that Eveline thinks "now she had nobody to protect her."

▶ **STEP 2** Relate this information to your own experience. What do you know about people who are like the character in this way? My little sister hides behind me for protection when she feels vulnerable and helpless.

▶ **STEP 3** Make an inference, an educated guess, about what the character is like, but be prepared to change your opinion if you get new information. I guess that, like my little sister, Eveline thinks she needs protection because she feels vulnerable and helpless.

YOUR TURN 2 Analyzing Characterization and Making Inferences

On your own paper, create a three-column chart like the one below. In the first column, list all the indirect characterization techniques given in the chart on the previous page. In the middle column, write examples from "Eveline" of each of the techniques. Finally, in the third column, write down what you can infer from each of the examples.

Technique	Example	Inference
Indirect: The writer shows the character's effect on other characters.	"The little girls dared not speak to him."	This sentence implies that the little girls were afraid of Paul and that he must have seemed frightening or dangerous.

Using Figures of Speech as Context Clues

Short-story writers often engage their readers' imaginations by using figures of speech. A **figure of speech** is a word or phrase that describes one thing in terms of another and is not meant to be understood on a literal level. Here is a figure of speech from "Eveline":

"She sat at the window watching *the evening invade* the avenue."

Notice that this example compares two seemingly unlike things—the evening to an invader. Since figures of speech compare two things, you can use the meaning of one of the things being compared as a context clue to understand the meaning of the other.

Examples:
The hedgehog was as *hirsute* as my hairbrush. (Since a hairbrush is bristly, maybe *hirsute* means "bristly.")

He *strode* into the room like a stallion. (Since a stallion walks with long steps, maybe *strode* means "walked with long steps.")

THINKING IT THROUGH **Using Figures of Speech as Context Clues**

Take a look at the sentence below. Then, follow the steps to use the figure of speech in the sentence as a context clue.

The *obelisk* towered over us.

1. **Determine whether the phrase makes or implies a comparison. If so, it may be a figure of speech.** *The obelisk is compared to a tower.*

2. **Consider the meaning of the part of the comparison that does not contain an unfamiliar word.** *Towers are tall, narrow structures.*

3. **Guess the meaning of the unfamiliar word based on the meaning of the thing to which it is being compared.** *Maybe an obelisk is a tall, narrow structure.*

4. **Check to see that the meaning you guessed works in the sentence.** *The meaning I guessed makes sense.*

PRACTICE

Use the figures of speech in the following sentences as context clues to determine the meanings of the italicized words. Write your answers on your own paper, and then check them in a dictionary.

1. A *tonsure* wreathed the monk's head.

2. Bridget is as *tenacious* as a bulldog.

3. The ice covering the river was *opaque,* like frosted glass.

4. His *virulent* tongue poisoned every conversation.

5. His face was as *placid* as a still pond.

Answering Inference Questions

As you read a short story, you make inferences constantly—about the characters, as well as about what might happen next. You will also be called upon to use this skill to answer inference questions on the standardized tests you will take for high school graduation or acceptance to college.

Inference questions require you to read a passage and to find ideas that are implied rather than directly stated. These questions often use the word *implied* or *inferred*. Read the passage below and the practice question that follows it.

When you think about literature, what picture comes to mind? If you are like most Americans, you think of a book. In Africa, however, literature is often spoken and is sometimes accompanied by music and dance. This oral literary tradition is much more than just people telling stories to their friends. African oral artists, such as *griots, iintsomi, mbongi,* and *babala-wos,* must train for years, often with a master artist, before they are ready to perform professionally. There are even formal schools in which oral artists prepare themselves to make their living creating and reciting folk tales, epics, poetry, and other types of literature. In Africa, literature comes alive.

1. It can be *inferred* from the passage that

   A. in Africa, literature is often spoken

   B. being an African oral artist is a demanding and highly specialized profession

   C. all African oral artists sing and dance

   D. African oral artists are usually members of a royal family

   E. in Africa, literature is never written down

THINKING IT THROUGH   **Answering Inference Questions**

Use the following steps to work through inference questions.

1. **Eliminate all answers directly stated in the passage.** Answer **A** is stated in the third sentence of the passage, so it cannot be a real inference.

2. **Eliminate answers that are unsupported by the passage.** The following answers are unsupported by the passage: **C** (the passage says they *sometimes* sing and dance), **D** (the passage doesn't say anything about a royal family), and **E** (the passage says literature is *often* spoken, not always). A clue to evaluating answers **C** and **E** are the words *all* and *never*.

Words that suggest absolutes, like *all* and *never,* often indicate answers that are overstated and, therefore, incorrect.

3. **Decide which of the answers still remaining is best supported by the passage. If only one answer remains, check to make sure it is supported by the passage.** Answer **B** is the only answer that has not been eliminated. It is supported because the passage states that storytellers train for years (demanding), sometimes even going to formal schools (specialized). Answer **B** must be correct.

Writing a Short Story

When a writer sits down to write a short story, he or she has the power to create new worlds, to prompt a reader to laugh or cry or shrink in terror, and to gain and share insights into what it means to be human. How does the writer harness this power? Every short-story writer has his or her own process, but many writers follow roughly the process outlined in this chapter.

As you work through the process yourself, remember that writing a short story is not linear—you do not perform each step only once. The writing process is more like baking bread. Bread dough must rise and be punched down again and again before the bread will have the right texture. Similarly, the raw materials of your story, such as character, setting, and plot, will need to be reworked again and again until the story is effective.

WHAT'S AHEAD?

In this workshop you will write a short story. You will also learn how to

- **plot a story and imagine characters and setting**
- **write effective dialogue**
- **consider point of view and style**
- **eliminate weak modifiers**
- **use the correct sequence of tenses**

Prewriting

Consider Purpose, Audience, and Tone

A Captivated Audience   Your short story will have a **literary purpose**—it will use language creatively, or artistically, to express an idea. The idea you express is up to you, and so is the effect you want to have on your readers, or **audience.** Do you want them to laugh out loud, see the world in a new way, or wonder at life's mysteries? Take a moment to consider your readers. Whether they are your peers or the adult audience of a literary magazine, you will want to write a story that compels them to keep turning the pages.

The effect you have on readers will depend a lot on your attitude toward them and toward your subject—your **tone.** Tone comes through in your choice of words, details, and sentence structures. Your tone may be serious, ironic, or comic. Just make sure that the tone you choose is appropriate to your audience and to the subject of your story.

TIP   As you begin working on your short story, don't make choices based solely on what you think your audience will want or expect. Remember, your story should express your truth, not someone else's. Follow your instincts.

Explore Story Ideas

TIP Here are two additional suggestions to help you come up with story ideas. The first will be especially helpful if you are a visual artist, while the second might appeal to musicians and others who love music.

■ Look for images. Paintings, photographs, or mental images that intrigue or move you could set the scene for an interesting story.

■ Listen to music. What mood does the music create? Try creating a story with a similar mood.

Out of the Blue Ask a hundred writers where their ideas for short stories come from, and you will get a hundred different answers. Stories, however, often take on a life of their own, and the final draft of a story may not even include the idea that first inspired its writer. Try a couple of these suggestions to spark inspiration, but don't be surprised if your original ideas for your story change as you write.

■ **Ask yourself questions.** What might happen, for example, if a bizarre new family moved into a neighborhood much like yours? Are they space aliens? How would you know?

■ **Watch people.** If someone interests you, use your observations of that person as the springboard for creating an imaginary character. For instance, if the elderly man you see every day on the bus looks like an old sea captain, spin a tale about him and how he came to have that deep scar on his arm.

■ **See through someone else's eyes.** Have you ever wondered what the world looked like to someone very different from you? Put yourself in the place of someone unlike yourself.

When you have decided on a subject for your story, consider what your **theme,** or central idea about your subject, will be. For example, if you decide to write about coming-of-age, your story might convey the theme that growing up involves gaining not only freedom, but also responsibility. If you are not sure yet what your theme will be, allow it to unfold.

Plot Your Story

The Plot Thickens The sequence of events in a story makes up its **plot.** To keep your readers interested, the events in your story should all be related to a central **conflict**—a struggle between opposing forces. **The conflict is like the engine that powers your story.** Here are a few of the different kinds of conflicts found in short stories.

| KEY CONCEPT

Types of Conflict	Examples
External Conflict: character vs. character	Saul competes with his father for his mother's attention.
character vs. the environment	Latoya struggles to carry her little sister to safety as a fire spreads through their apartment building.
character vs. a situation	Leticia is going away to college, but her best friend is not.
Internal Conflict: character vs. himself or herself (a struggle between conflicting ideas and feelings within a character)	Mr. Kitteridge wrestles to overcome his fear of failure in order to pursue his dream of becoming a pilot.

Once you have established a conflict, you will need to think about how it builds, reaches a climax, and then resolves itself. Of course, external conflicts often trigger internal conflicts, and vice versa. Most stories feature both types of conflict. As you consider the plot of your story, jot down notes to create a plot plan you can refer to later. Here's one writer's plot plan.

Conflict	• External (character vs. a situation)—Leticia is going away to college, but her best friend, Jennifer, is not.
	• Internal (character's emotions in conflict)—Leticia's feelings of happiness, sadness, and guilt are all mixed up.
Conflict Builds	• Leticia begins spending time with Megan, who is going to college and who tries to turn Leticia against Jennifer.
	• Leticia begins to change—new clothes, new hair.
	• Leticia visits Jennifer at her job and talks about college in an insensitive way.
Climax	• Jennifer tells Leticia to leave her alone; they stop speaking.
Resolution	• Leticia realizes her insensitivity and apologizes to Jennifer; they are friends again. Leticia learns a few things about herself and about life.

THINKING IT THROUGH   **Plotting Your Story**

Ask yourself the following questions to help you plot your story.

▶ **So what's your problem?** Do you know what the conflict of your story is? If not, think about your characters. What are their concerns?

▶ **What are you going to do about it?** Now that you have a conflict, ask yourself what your character is likely to do and what consequences his or her actions are likely to have.

▶ **How bad can it get?** In life, we often try to avoid conflict. In a short story, however, it is more interesting to let the conflict escalate. Think about what crisis might result from the conflict.

▶ **Happily ever after?** Remember that the reader wants to know how the conflict is resolved and how the events of the story have affected the characters.

YOUR TURN **3**   **Hatching a Plot**

Use the guidelines on plot to create a plot plan like the one above.

TIP The events that make up the plot of a story often unfold in **chronological order,** that is, in the order that they occur. However, writers also use **flash-forward,** skipping ahead in time, or **flash-back,** skipping backward in time, to describe an event that occurred much later or much earlier than the time period in which the rest of the story is set.

Remember that you make the rules for the world of your short story, so *anything* can happen.

Imagine Characters and Setting

Get Acquainted   You probably already have some ideas about your characters. After all, to plot their actions, you must have known a little about them. However, knowing what a character is likely to do is just the first step in getting to know him or her. Think of memorable literary characters such as Shakespeare's Lady Macbeth or Mark Twain's Huck Finn. Because these characters seem almost like real people, they are called "round" characters, as opposed to "flat" characters. **Round characters** are complex, multifaceted, and **dynamic**—like real people, they grow and change over time and in response to experiences. Use the following questions and one writer's responses to help you develop characters that your readers will remember.

Questions	One Writer's Responses
How does the character act, or behave? What does this tell you about him or her?	Leticia cries when she finds out Jennifer is not going to college. This shows that Leticia cares about and depends on Jennifer.
What motivates the character? What is most important to him or her? What does the character think about (wishes, hopes, worries)?	Leticia is motivated by excitement about her future and love for her friend. Friendship is most important to her. She worries about Jennifer.
What does your character enjoy? (Even if they don't appear in your story, knowing such details will help you write.)	Leticia enjoys talking on the phone and going to the mall. She loves pizza and secretly enjoys country-western music.
What does your character look like? How does he or she move and speak?	Leticia is small, with long, dark hair. She wears jeans and T-shirts, and she moves and speaks quickly.
How does your character appear to others? Do they find him or her annoying, likable, or aloof?	Other people find Leticia a little shy. Once they get to know her, they find her kind.

TIP   **Interior monologue,** or stream of consciousness, is a style that writers use to depict the flow of thoughts, feelings, and memories that rush through a character's mind. James Joyce was among the first to experiment with this style. If you would like to use this style in your story, you can find an example of it in Joyce's story "Eveline," on page 59.

TIP   Not all modern stories feature a hero—a man or woman who kills the dragon, finds the hidden treasure, and lives happily ever after. Instead, modern stories are often about an antihero—someone more like the reader, who runs from the dragon, drops the treasure, and learns something about himself or herself in the process.

Location Is Everything!   One way for you and your reader to get to know your characters is to observe them in their natural environment. In real life, people's homes or the places they choose to spend time reveal a lot about their personalities. Similarly, the **setting** of your story—its time and place—tells a lot about your characters. Setting can also

- **contribute to the plot**, especially when the main conflict is between people and the environment. For instance, in William Golding's *Lord of the Flies,* the island setting contributes to the plot.

- **help establish the mood** of the story and prepare the reader for what will happen. If the beginning of a story describes a remote castle in a thunderstorm, the reader has a pretty good idea what will follow.

- **act as a symbol**, as in Emily Brontë's *Wuthering Heights,* in which the house of that name symbolizes Heathcliff's gloomy pride and isolation.

Use the questions and one writer's responses in the chart that follows to help you develop the setting of your story.

Questions	One Writer's Responses
What details of setting could reveal information about my characters?	Details of the high school campus could illustrate Leticia and Jennifer's friendship.
Is the conflict in my story between people and the environment? If so, what will the role of the environment be? What sort of place could fill that role?	The conflict in this story will not be between people and the environment, although the environment of the BarBQ Shack should contribute to the tension.
What sensory details about setting could contribute to my story's mood?	I can build a mood of expectation and excitement by setting the story in late summer, near the beginning of the semester.
Will the setting act as a symbol? If so, what will it symbolize?	The pile of things Leticia is planning to give away will symbolize her childhood. The BarBQ Shack will symbolize confinement and lack of opportunity.

 Imagining Characters and Setting

Using the guidelines in this section, make notes about your story's characters and setting.

TIP Remember that no matter how well you get to know your characters and settings before you write, you will undoubtedly be surprised at how they develop. New characters may arrive unexpectedly, the setting may change, and consequently, the plot may not turn out as you first imagined. These surprises are a natural, and exciting, part of the creative-writing process.

Writing Effective Dialogue

Dialogue—the actual words of the characters—in a short story should always have a purpose. Effective dialogue

- moves the plot forward by suggesting the characters' intentions and motivations
- develops character by revealing characters' thoughts and feelings and showing characters' styles of expression
- explores the theme of the story in the words the writer puts in the characters' mouths

Dialogue that is doing so many jobs must be clunky and stiff, right? On the contrary, effective dialogue must be natural. Nothing ruins a story like stilted, unrealistic dialogue. Look at the following examples to see what a difference natural-sounding dialogue can make.

Stilted: "I cannot imagine what you intend by that remark," snapped Casey.

Effective: "What do you mean?" snapped Casey.

THINKING IT THROUGH **Writing Effective Dialogue**

How can you write dialogue that seems natural? Try the following suggestions.

▶ **Let your characters speak for themselves.** Midwestern teenagers and Russian grandparents don't usually talk the same way. Choose a character's words and sentence structures carefully to fit him or her.

▶ **Forget grammar.** Try to reproduce the word choice and speech patterns you hear around you. Remember that people don't always speak in complete sentences.

▶ **Spell it like it sounds.** Sometimes, such as *ven you are tryink to reproduce zee sount* of a dialect or an accent, it is more effective to spell dialogue phonetically.

▶ **Stop making sense.** Realistic dialogue often includes non sequiturs (remarks having no bearing on what has just been said) and other nonsense.

▶ **Don't mince words.** Eliminate filler words such as *um, like, ah,* and *well* unless they are an important part of the character's way of expressing himself or herself.

PRACTICE

The following sentences make up a dialogue between two modern teenagers. Revise the dialogue to make it more natural.

1. "Are you declaring your love?" said Sophie.

2. "You have misunderstood me," said Tad.

3. "Are you trifling with my affections?"

4. "I am not trifling," said Tad.

5. "Let us go and view a film," said Sophie.

Choose a Point of View

See It My Way The vantage point, or camera angle, from which a writer tells a story is called its **point of view.** The term *point of view* refers to two separate but related ideas:

- *who* tells the story
- *how much* he or she knows

Whose Story Is This, Anyway? A story can be told from the point of view of different kinds of **narrators,** or storytellers.

- In **first-person point of view,** the narrator, usually a character in the story, addresses the reader directly but is limited to telling only what he or she knows and experiences.

- In **limited third-person point of view,** the narrator is not one of the story's characters but tells the story from the perspective of one character. This narrator does not address the reader directly and is limited to telling only what one character knows and experiences.

- In **third-person omniscient point of view,** a narrator who is not one of the characters tells the story from any vantage point. *Omniscient* means "all-knowing," and this narrator can address the reader directly and has unlimited access to any information in the world of the story, including the thoughts and feelings of any character.

Whom do you want to tell your story? To help you decide, try thinking about the narrator as someone operating a video camera to record your story, as in the following illustration.

first-person narrator

limited third-person narrator

third-person omniscient narrator

TIP Just as different people have different voices—squeaky, resonant, accented—narrators have unique **voices,** too. Imagine what Mark Twain's *The Adventures of Huckleberry Finn* would be like without Huck's distinctive voice. Before you begin writing, you may want to consider your narrator's **voice.** Does your narrator speak with an accent, use slang, have a lisp, or repeat himself or herself? Does he or she have a large vocabulary or a small one?

Refer to the following chart to see the pros and cons of each of your point-of-view options.

Point of View Pros and Cons	Examples
First-person: Makes the story personal and builds strong reader response to the narrator/character, but the narrator is limited to telling readers only what he or she knows or experiences.	"Father was in the army all through the war—the first war, I mean—so up to the age of five, I never saw much of him, and what I saw did not worry me." Frank O'Connor, "My Oedipus Complex"
Third-person limited: Gives a complete, more objective view of the action, while still making readers feel close to one character. However, the narrator is limited to telling only what that character knows or experiences and cannot address readers directly.	"His father merely walked away into his room. This was most unexpected and perplexed Nneameka. His father's silence was infinitely more menacing than a flood of threatening speech." Chinua Achebe, "Marriage Is a Private Affair"
Third-person omniscient: The narrator can address readers directly, reveal the thoughts and feelings of any character, and tell readers things that none of the characters could know, such as what is happening elsewhere. However, a narrator who comments too much on the action and gives away too much information may irritate readers.	"Now, when such a thing happens on a farm, it cannot be long before everyone hears of it. Mr. and Mrs. Farquar told their neighbors and the story was discussed from one end of the district to the other. . . . Up and down the district people were telling anecdotes, reminding each other of things that had happened to them." Doris Lessing, "No Witchcraft for Sale"

TIP If you can't decide on a point of view, just begin writing and see which point of view emerges naturally. You may find that one of your characters is determined to tell his or her side of the story.

You may already have chosen a point of view. If not, choose the one that you think will work best for your story. The most important thing to remember is that once you have chosen a point of view, you must stick with it throughout your story so that the story is cohesive. Point of view is what holds the other elements of a short story—the plot, characters, and setting—together.

Consider Style

Say It Your Way   A writer's unique way of writing is called his or her **style,** and it is a crucial part of what makes a story enjoyable and memorable. Some stories are written in such a way that readers don't notice the writer's choice of words but "see" the scene being described. In other stories, the writer's way of describing things is delightful in itself.

Show or Tell?   Remember that the least interesting way to describe your characters and setting to readers is to tell them directly.

Example:
Shana was an unusual woman who lived in a spooky house.

Instead, develop a more engaging style by showing characters in action. Use **sensory details**—details of sound, smell, sight, taste, and touch—to make your characters and setting vivid.

Example:
Shana arranged a variety of potted, flesh-eating plants on her rickety front porch, which spiders had festooned with cobwebs.

Figuratively Speaking   The use of figurative language is another way writers make their stories come alive. A **figure of speech** is a word or phrase that describes one thing in terms of another and is not meant to be understood on a literal level. By comparing two unlike things, the writer helps the reader to see something familiar in a new way. There are three basic types of figurative language: simile, metaphor, and personification.

- A **simile** compares things by using a connective word such as *like* or *as*.

Example:
The crowd surged forward like an angry sea. (A crowd of people is compared to a sea.)

- A **metaphor** compares unlike things without using a connective word such as *like* or *as*.

Example:
The bus drifted through a sea of people. (A crowd of people is compared to a sea.)

- **Personification** is a kind of metaphor in which something nonhuman is given human characteristics.

Example:
The sea murmured and sighed. (The nonhuman sea is described as murmuring and sighing, which are human behaviors.)

Metaphor, simile, and personification help readers to break away from old associations they may have with things, characters, and events, and see them as you, the writer, want them to be seen.

TIP   Since the aim of figurative language is to help readers see things in a new and unique way, avoid figures of speech that have become clichéd through overuse. For example, avoid clichés such as *heavy as lead, love is a rose*, and *like a bird in a cage*.

YOUR TURN 5   Considering Point of View and Style

Using the guidelines in these sections, determine which point of view would be most effective for your story, and consider your style options.

Short Story

Framework	**Directions and Explanations**

Beginning

- Engage readers.
- Introduce main characters and establish setting.
- Set plot in motion with event or situation that initiates conflict.

Arouse interest Open with sharp dialogue, a mood-setting description, or fast action. Remember that the point of view you establish now must remain consistent throughout your story.

Introduce characters and set the scene Use sensory details and figurative language to describe characters and setting. Include dialogue that helps to characterize.

Cause conflict Introduce the conflict quickly, and let readers know what is at stake for the main characters.

Middle

- Develop conflict and characters through actions, dialogue, description, and complications.
- Bring conflict to a climax.

Keep them on the edge of their seats Keep readers' interest by building the conflict and including complications and setbacks that keep the outcome uncertain. Develop your characters so that readers come to care what happens to them.

Create a crisis Crank up the tension until the conflict reaches a climax. Something's got to give. Make readers feel like they are actually experiencing the climax of the story by using vivid language and giving details.

End

- Move toward resolution.
- Resolve conflict, including final details.

Allow the conflict to resolve itself Once the conflict has reached its climax, move it toward resolution. Show readers how characters and situations have changed.

Tie up loose ends Resolve all the conflicts, internal and external, in the story, and let readers know what the final situation is.

YOUR TURN 6 Writing a First Draft

Review the prewriting steps before you start writing. Then, use the framework above to write the first draft of your story. Refer to the Writer's Model on the next page to see an example of a short story that follows this framework. Finally, relax and have fun.

A Writer's Model

The following short story follows the framework on the previous page.

Keep the Change

Leticia threw a blue stuffed dog on the pile of things to give away. Her dorm room wouldn't have much space, and she would only be able to take her most important things when she and her best friend, Jennifer, left for college in a couple of months. As Leticia threw her old ballerina slippers on the pile, the phone rang.

"Hey, Leticia. What are you doing?"

"I'm cleaning stuff out, trying to decide what to take. Are you taking your softball trophies?" Leticia hoped Jennifer would leave the trophies at home. They planned to room together, and Leticia didn't want their room to look too childish.

"I'm not going."

Jennifer's tone was offhand. Leticia couldn't believe what she heard. "But you have to go! You have a scholarship!"

"A scholarship won't help my dad run the store. Now that Mom's gone, he can't do it himself."

"But you're the smartest kid in the class."

"Then maybe I don't need four more years of school. Look, I called to see if you want to go to a movie tomorrow."

After Leticia hung up the phone, she curled up on her bed and cried. Now everything was ruined. Who would she tell about her professors and the boys she liked? There would be no familiar face to make her feel at home. Leticia remembered when she and Jennifer had received their letters of acceptance: Jennifer had gotten hers on a Monday, and they both practically held their breath until Leticia's came on Thursday. Leticia remembered how Jennifer had danced around and sung, "Goodbye, smoke! Goodbye, carving knife! Goodbye, scale!" Leticia had never heard Jennifer complain about her job at her father's restaurant, the BarBQ Shack, but there she was, skipping around like someone let out of prison. Leticia looked at the heap of things to give away and began crying again. It was just plain wrong that Jennifer was not going to college.

But the weeks went on, and Leticia's excitement returned as she thought about living on her own. She'd go to parties and meet all sorts of new people. And she'd study hard to prove that she was a better student than her C average in high school suggested. Then she got a phone call from Megan Greene. Leticia could hardly believe it. Megan had been the most popular girl in school!

(continued)

BEGINNING
Action and vivid description
Third-person point of view established
Main characters introduced and setting established
Dialogue

Initiating event (external conflict established)

MIDDLE
Main character developed through action, description

Figurative language

Plot complication

(continued)

Conflict developed

Megan said that since they were both going to the same college, they should get to know each other.

"I don't get it," Leticia said. "You weren't interested in getting to know me in high school."

"Oh, high school," said Megan. "That's all over now."

Megan took Leticia shopping. She showed her which things looked good on her and even whisked her off to a salon to get her floppy bangs and straight hair transformed into a sleek, flattering cut. As soon as Megan left her, Leticia started for the BarBQ Shack.

Vivid description

Leticia looked in the grimy front window and saw Jennifer helping a customer. Leticia saw the man laugh and admired the easy way Jennifer scooped up change and handed it to him. When he was gone, Leticia went in. "Ta-da!" she said. Jennifer smiled, but she seemed tired. Leticia had noticed that lately, when she dropped in to show Jennifer things she had bought for college, Jennifer didn't seem that happy to see her.

Main character and conflict developed through dialogue

"New haircut. What's the occasion?"

"Not just a new haircut! New makeup, new clothes, new me. When I get to college I want everything to be new!"

Something in Jennifer's face changed. "Then you better stop hanging out with an old, worn-out friend like me."

"Oh, Jennifer! I didn't mean that."

"But I did. Leave me alone."

"But!"

"Just go."

Characterization through description, revealing character's thoughts, and dialogue

Leticia was confused. She went home and looked at herself in her full-length mirror. Who was the fashionable young woman she saw there? Leticia's mother passed by. "Look at you, Leticia! How old are you, thirty-five?" she teased.

The next time Leticia saw Megan, she told her she and Jennifer had quarreled.

"Jennifer!" Megan said. "Do you still hang out with her?"

"Jennifer's my friend."

Inner conflict developed through dialogue

Megan set down her cup of frozen yogurt. "No, Jennifer was your friend. Look, your life is about to change. You're going to get a degree and a good job. Jennifer's going to spend her life behind that counter, just someone who hands you your change. Better break it off now."

Inner conflict developed through description and narrator revealing character's thoughts

Leticia walked down to the high school and wandered around. She needed to think. There was the bench where she and Jennifer used to talk at lunch. There was their old homeroom where Jennifer had finally made her understand algebra. Leticia remembered how large and glamorous the high school had looked to her on her first day as a freshman. Everything about her had changed since then—everything except Jennifer's friendship. Leticia caught sight of herself in the cafeteria window. As though the window were a movie screen, she saw herself prancing around the BarBQ Shack, showing off her new shoes, book bag, and hairstyle. Leticia blushed. How could she have been so insensitive?

Figurative language

The next morning Leticia waited for Jennifer at the door of the BarBQ Shack.

"I told you to stay away."

Leticia swallowed hard. "Jennifer, I'm sorry."

Jennifer opened the door and turned on the lights. They walked into the permanent sausage-and-potato-salad smell of the restaurant.

"For what?"

"For prancing around, showing off all my new stuff for college when you don't even get to go. I was so insensitive."

Jennifer turned on the cash register and punched in her code. The cash register rang and spit out a few inches of tape. Jennifer turned and looked Leticia straight in the eye. "You still don't get it, do you?"

Conflict reaches climax

"Please, Jennifer, I . . ."

"What makes you and Megan Greene think that you're better than me because you're going to college? I don't need your sympathy."

"But I thought you wanted to go," pleaded Leticia.

"I did, but then I realized there were other things I'd rather do—like help my dad run the restaurant for a while, save some money." Jennifer looked around slowly, as if taking everything in. "If you're not happy where you are, Leticia, you're not going to be happy somewhere else, regardless of what you're doing." Then Jennifer smiled, a genuine smile. "I guess I'm happy where I am."

Conflict moves toward resolution

"Jennifer, you're great. You'll never be just someone who hands you your change."

Jennifer cracked open a roll of quarters. "Leticia, no one is just someone who hands you your change."

A ray of morning sun had forced its way through the BarBQ Shack's grime-spattered windows and now illuminated the quarters as they cascaded from Jennifer's hand into the change drawer.

END
Figurative language

"I guess we all have to make our own change, in our own way," said Leticia finally.

Conflict resolved

A Student's Model

The following excerpt from the beginning of a short story written by Carlos Williams, a student from Jacksonville, Florida, follows the framework on page 76.

Aiming for the Stars

Vivid description/dynamic situation

The starship Froggie sits poised for lift-off, as steam rises from the carefully molded engines. The crew makes the final preparations for their journey. Commander Froggie sits in waiting with Lieutenant First Class B. J. by his side as if it were his millionth launch. A voice comes over the intercom, continuing the final seconds of the countdown, "five, . . . four, . . . three, . . . two, . . . one."

"Froggie! Hey, Froggie! Are you there? Do I have to call a rescue team to get you?"

Main characters introduced

"Huh? What?" said Froggie, startled from his daydream. "Oh, what's up B. J.?" he said after temporarily looking up from a pile of space dust. "I was just thinking."

"About what?" B. J. asked. "Not that crazy spaceman dream of yours!"

Internal conflict

"It's not crazy, and it's not a dream," said Froggie, slightly annoyed. "It's a real goal, as real as this ship," he

Setting

said, stomping one foot on the outside of the giant ship they were cleaning.

"C'mon Froggie. We were born to be custodians. I mean, it was programmed into your code before you were even born. You can't be anything more, not in this lifetime. Maybe in the next one you'll be born something better."

Theme

"No, that's not true! I refuse to live my entire life according to what everyone else says. It doesn't matter what someone else programmed me to be; I decide how my life turns out," said Froggie as he walked toward a ladder that was resting on the side of the gigantic cargo ship.

"Wait!" yelled B. J. as he ran over to Froggie. "I'm sorry I said that. You may be right, but even if you are, how exactly do you plan on achieving your dre . . ., I mean goal?"

"I don't exactly know right now, but I do know that 'Where there's a will, there's a way.' At least that's what my grandpa says."

B. J. nodded and leaned one arm on Froggie's shoulder as they continued toward the ladder. "Doesn't your grandpa also say that his socks are trying to eat his feet?" he asked. They both laughed as they descended to the docking platform.

"I have to use the modular waste facility, Froggie."

"The what?" questioned Froggie.

"The restroom."

"Oh, yeah, I knew that. Well, the restroom's right down the hall. Go ahead. I'll wait," said Froggie, pointing to the long, sterile-looking hallway.

B. J. took one step toward the hall, stopped, and turned as if he had just been slapped with an idea. "Why walk all the way down the hall when the cargo ship has a facility?" he said with a sly grin.

"But the ship is going to take off any minute!"

"What's wrong? You're not scared are you, Froggie?"

"Are you crazy? Let's go."

Froggie and B. J. got about halfway to the ship's restroom when they heard a voice on the intercom say, "Security lockdown initiated. All nonpersonnel key cards rejected."

"Oh no. We're locked on the ship!" B. J. exclaimed in a panic-stricken voice.

Characters developed through dialogue

Figurative language

External conflict

Conflict builds

Designing Your Writing

Using Art Illustrations Writers throughout the ages—from the eighth-century monks who illuminated the *Book of Kells* to the early Romantic poet William Blake—have understood that illustrations can enhance and even contribute to the meaning of a text. Here are some tips to help you effectively illustrate your short story.

- **Don't change your story.** Create or choose illustrations that convey the same mood and tone as your story. For example, if your story is playful in tone and has a whimsical mood, the lines, colors, shapes, and textures of your illustration should reflect that.

- **Look through your narrator's eyes.** Include illustrations that show your narrator's perspective on the action. For example, a first-person narrator who is afraid of heights might not be able to see the view from the top of a water tower, while an omniscient narrator could see not only the view from the water tower, but from above, too.

- **Don't give too much away.** Your reader's eye will immediately be drawn to an illustration, so be careful that your illustrations don't give away the outcome of the events described on that page.

Revising

Evaluate and Revise Your Story

Look Again To make your short story as wonderful as it has the potential to be, you will need to evaluate and revise it at least twice. First, use the chart below to help you evaluate and revise the content of your short story. Then, use the guidelines on the next page to revise its style.

▷ **First Reading: Content and Organization** To ensure that your short story is effective, examine your artistic choices. Use the chart below to help you revise your draft for content and organization. Ask yourself the questions in the first column, use the tips in the middle column to help you visualize necessary revisions, and use the last column to make your revisions.

Short Story: Content and Organization Guidelines for Peer and Self-Evaluation

Evaluation Questions	▶ Tips	▶ Revision Techniques
❶ Is the conflict established quickly? Do events build in logical order until the conflict reaches a climax?	▶ **Draw a horizontal line** through the middle of the first page of the story. Is the conflict established above the line? **Highlight** the climax of the story and any plot complications. If the conflict is not established quickly or does not build toward a climax, revise.	▶ Early in the story, **add** an initiating event or situation that creates conflict and sets the plot in motion. **Add** plot complications that build tension and suspense, such as setbacks that the main character must overcome.
❷ Is the main character round, or fleshed out, rather than flat?	▶ **Draw a dotted line** beneath dialogue, actions, and descriptions that tell about the character. If they don't present a full and realistic picture of the character, revise.	▶ **Add** or **elaborate** on dialogue, actions, or descriptions of the character. **Replace** dialogue, actions, or descriptions that are not consistent with the character.
❸ Do details of the setting serve a purpose in the story—developing characterization, plot, mood, or symbolism?	▶ **Bracket** each setting description in the story, and identify its purpose. If it serves no clear purpose, revise.	▶ **Add, replace,** or **elaborate** on descriptions of setting to develop characterization, plot, mood, or symbolism.
❹ Is the story told from a consistent point of view?	▶ **Underline** words that describe characters' thoughts and feelings. If the narrator could not reasonably know this information, revise.	▶ **Delete** any information that the narrator would not know. **Add** the same information retold from the narrator's point of view.
❺ Do sensory details and figures of speech enhance the vividness and style of the writing?	▶ **Circle** each sensory detail and figure of speech in your story. If these are few, revise.	▶ **Add** sensory details and figures of speech to describe actions, characters, and settings.

ONE WRITER'S REVISIONS Using the content and organization guidelines on the previous page, the writer of the model on page 77 revised content and organization in the following way. Study the revisions and answer the questions that follow.

Leticia threw a ~~stuffed animal~~ *blue dog* on the pile of things to   **add and replace**

give away. Her dorm room wouldn't have much space, and

she would only be able to take her most important things when ~~her mother secretly wished she had a room of her own as a~~   **delete and elaborate**

she ~~study.~~ Leticia and her best friend, Jennifer, ~~were leaving~~ *left* for   **replace**

in a couple of months. college ~~next year.~~

Analyzing the Revision Process

1. Why did the writer add details about the stuffed animal?
2. Why did the writer cut the information about Leticia's mother?
3. Why did the writer revise the setting by changing the amount of time before the girls left for college?

YOUR TURN 7 **Revising Content and Organization**

Use the guidelines in this section to revise your story. For help, refer to the example revisions above. Don't be afraid to make changes—it is normal to make substantial revisions to a first draft.

Second Reading: Style Have you ever read a single line that made you visualize an entire setting or situation or that evoked an emotion? That's the power of style. To achieve such a powerful style, every word you use must pack a punch. Refer to the chart below to make your writing more powerful by **eliminating weak modifiers.**

PEER REVIEW

Ask a classmate to read your story and to answer the following questions.

1. Which character was most intriguing to you? Why?
2. Did the plot of the story keep you turning the pages, and were you satisfied by the resolution of the story's conflict? Why or why not?

Style Guidelines

Evaluation Question	▶ Tip	▶ Revision Technique
Do adjectives and adverbs help readers to visualize the characters, setting, and events?	▶ **Bracket** all weak adjectives and adverbs, such as *nice, pretty, very,* and *really.*	▶ **Replace** weak adverbs and weak adjectives with vivid verbs, more precise adverbs and adjectives, or figures of speech.

Focus on

Word Choice

Eliminating Weak Modifiers

In daily conversation, we tend to use a few adverbs, such as *very, really, hardly,* and *suddenly,* and adjectives, such as *pretty, nice, mean, bad, good,* and *beautiful,* over and over again. These words carry meaning when we speak them because of our tone of voice, expression, and gestures. In writing, however, these overused words fade into the background. If you replace weak modifiers with powerful verbs, vivid adjectives and adverbs, and figures of speech, your writing will jump off the page.

ONE WRITER'S REVISIONS The writer of the Writer's Model used the style guidelines on the previous page to eliminate weak modifiers. Study the revisions, and answer the questions that follow.

Weak modifiers are bracketed.

BEFORE REVISION

She . . . [quickly] took her to a salon to get her [ugly] bangs

and straight hair transformed into a [pretty] cut.

Replace weak adverb and adjectives with powerful verb and more vivid adjectives.

AFTER REVISION

She . . . whisked her off to a salon to get her floppy bangs and straight hair transformed into a sleek, flattering cut.

Analyzing the Revision Process

1. How did the change from *quickly took her* to *whisked her off* affect your mental image of the scene?
2. How did replacing *ugly* with *floppy* and *pretty* with *sleek, flattering* affect your mental image of the character?

YOUR TURN 8 **Eliminating Weak Modifiers**

Using the guidelines above and on the previous page, eliminate any weak modifiers from your story. Then, replace the less effective modifiers with powerful verbs, vivid adjectives and adverbs, and figures of speech. Use the sample revisions as a model.

Publishing

Proofread Your Story

A Polished Presentation   Why should you proofread your story? Readers will figure out what you meant to say, right? Don't count on it. Misspelled words, incorrect punctuation, and grammatical errors can convince readers that it is not worth the time to sort through your mistakes. Even if readers do finish an error-ridden story, its impact will be ruined. As you proofread, look closely for errors in verb tense.

Reference Note
For **proofreading guidelines,** see page 13.

Grammar Link

Sequence of Tenses

Using the correct verb tenses in your short story is essential if you want your readers to be able to follow the sequence of events and understand the story's meaning. Because writers often recount events that have already happened, most short stories use the past and the past perfect tense.

■ The **past tense** is used to express an action or state of being that occurred in the past but did not continue into the present. If two things happened at approximately the same time, they are both expressed in the past tense.

Example:
Jennifer **turned** on the cash register and **punched** in her code.

■ The **past perfect tense** is used mainly to express an action or state of being that was completed in the past before some other past occurrence. It always includes the helping verb *had.*

Example:
Leticia remembered how large and glamorous the high school **had looked** to her on her first day as a freshman.

The second action described in the sentence (Leticia saw the high school) happened before the first action described (Leticia remembered seeing the high school). Consequently, the second verb is in the past perfect tense to show the sequence of events.

(For more about **verb tenses,** see page 695.)

PRACTICE

Revise the following sentences by changing any verbs that are in the wrong tense. Write your answers on your own paper. If the sentence is correct, write C.

1. When she finished her tennis lessons, she played in the tournament.

2. Jason said that *Car Chase II* was the best movie he had ever seen.

3. By the time the hurricane reached the coast, most of the residents evacuated.

4. I went fishing and then had built a campfire.

5. Anita already ordered when Cesar arrived ten minutes later.

Publish Your Story

Get the Word Out   A short story is more than just a school assignment. Your story means something to you, and it may also be meaningful to others. Try a couple of these ideas to share your work with a wider audience.

- Submit your short story to your school's literary magazine or newspaper.
- Submit your short story to a contest. Various publications hold short story contests annually. Ask a librarian to help you identify several.
- Illustrate your story, put copies of it in folders, and give them as gifts.
- Submit your short story to an online literary magazine, or put your story on a Web home page.
- Have a gathering at which you and others read original plays, stories, and poems aloud.
- Obtain the address or e-mail address of a writer you admire, and send him or her a copy of your story. You might ask the writer for feedback on the story or for general advice about writing.
- As a class, develop criteria for evaluation of a short story. Then, swap stories with a classmate, and write brief reviews of one another's stories, using the criteria that you developed.

PORTFOLIO

Reflect on Your Story

Hindsight Is 20/20   Write a short response to each of the following questions. Keep your answers in your portfolio, along with the final version of your story.

- Are you happy with the way in which you established and resolved the conflict in your story? Why or why not?
- Did your short story surprise you? For example, did one of the characters do or say something unexpected? Explain.
- What part of your story—the plot, characters, or setting—was the least satisfying to you? How might you have changed this element to make it more satisfying?
- Writing stories can become a habit. What other story ideas do you have?

YOUR TURN 9   **Proofreading, Publishing, and Reflecting on Your Story**

Proofread and polish your story; then, try a couple of the ideas above for publishing it. Finally, take time to reflect.

Answering Passage Questions

Standardized tests often ask you to write short essay responses to questions about passages of prose or poetry. These questions are designed to determine whether you can **interpret the meaning of the passage** and **analyze how the author communicates this meaning.** One of the keys to answering a question like the one above is developing a strong **thesis statement**.

The following is an example of a typical passage question.

Read the following poem carefully. Then, write a well-organized essay in which you identify the theme of the poem and discuss how the author conveys that theme. Be sure to consider imagery and point of view.

When I Have Fears
by John Keats

When I have fears that I may cease to be
Before my pen has gleaned my teeming brain,
  Before high-pilèd books, in charact'ry,[1]
Hold like rich garners the full-ripened grain;
When I behold, upon the night's starred face,
  Huge cloudy symbols of a high romance,
  And think that I may never live to trace
Their shadows, with the magic hand of chance;
  And when I feel, fair creature of an hour,
  That I shall never look upon thee more,
  Never have relish in the fairy[2] power
Of unreflecting love!—then on the shore
Of the wide world I stand alone, and think
Till Love and Fame to nothingness do sink.

1. **charact'ry:** the characters of the alphabet.
2. **fairy:** supernatural; unearthly.

THINKING IT THROUGH   **Developing a Thesis Statement**

Use the following steps and student responses based on the question above to develop a thesis statement for your own answer to a passage question.

1. Read the prompt question carefully. Then, underline the key words and phrases that tell you what literary elements to discuss. *The key words and phrases are* imagery *and* point of view.

2. Read the passage carefully, and jot down its central idea, or theme. Note its literal meaning as well as any emotional response it evokes. *The poem says that life is rich, with many things to aspire to and experience, but it is also short. It makes me feel sad.*

3. Analyze how the author conveys the theme through the literary elements mentioned in the prompt. *1. First-person point of view helps readers share speaker's consciousness of mortality. 2. Images—"full-ripened grain," "night's starred face"—emphasize the richness of life.*

4. Write a thesis that states the theme of the work, provides the title and author of the passage, and mentions the literary elements from the prompt that convey the theme. *In "When I Have Fears," John Keats uses first-person point of view and concrete images to convey his ideas about the richness and shortness of life.*

Connections to Life

Characterization in Television Sitcoms

Think about your favorite television sitcom characters. You probably feel as if you know them. You might even discuss their actions with friends, as if they were real people. Perhaps you root for them when they're involved in conflicts and feel relieved when they get through yet another crisis. If so, then they are probably round, dynamic characters, like the ones you encounter in well-written short stories. A **round character** is complex and multi-faceted, and a **dynamic character** is one who changes in response to situations.

In fact, creators of television sitcoms use many of the same **characterization** strategies that short-story writers use to create believable, engaging characters. However, since television sitcoms usually do not have narrators who can tell viewers directly what a character is like or what the character is thinking or feeling, they make use of indirect characterization strategies such as:

- showing how the character looks, moves, and dresses
- showing through dialogue how the character speaks and what he or she says (which helps show what the character is thinking and feeling)
- showing how the character behaves in various situations
- showing the character's effects on other characters

For example, creators of a sitcom might communicate to viewers that a character is feeling blue by showing her wearing old sweats and sitting on the sofa with only a gallon of ice cream for company.

Now, think about the minor characters on television sitcoms. What are they like? Often, creators of sitcoms use **flat** characters as well as round ones. These flat characters are less well developed; they may even be stereotypes. A **stereotype** is a kind of character that reflects people's broad and often unfair generalizations about what that type of person is always like. For example, people often stereotype blond women as ditzy, athletes as dumb, and children as either brats or angels. Sometimes, television and other media also contain **cultural stereotypes,** stereotyped portrayals of people from a particular culture. Like all stereotypes, these representations are one-dimensional and obviously absurd.

If they are obviously absurd, why do creators of sitcoms use stereotypes? One reason is that people find exaggerated portraits funny—stereotypes are often used for comedic effect. Another reason is that when a stereotyped character appears on the screen, no characterization is necessary—viewers automatically assume that they know what that character is like. In a television show that may last for only half an hour, using a stereotype frees creators to spend more time developing the plot and other characters.

A chart like the one on the next page may help you identify and analyze sitcom characterization. Note how the student identified characterization strategies and decided whether the characters were round and dynamic, flat, or stereotyped.

Character	Strategy	Type
Gladys, a woman in her seventies	Shows how she looks—blue hair, frumpy old coat Shows how she acts—absent-minded, grumpy Shows how she speaks—out-of-date slang and old-fashioned mannerisms	Stereotype of an elderly woman
Faye, an Asian woman in her twenties	Shows how she looks—attractive, dresses in a slightly eccentric, highly individual way Shows how she acts—assertive but also vulnerable; very independent Shows how she speaks—articulate, makes jokes and puns Shows how she matures emotionally	Round, dynamic character

In order to understand the significance of an analysis like the one above, it is helpful to reflect on your findings. Answers to questions like the ones that follow may help you see more clearly how television represents and alters reality.

■ With which characters do you most identify? Why?

■ How do flat and stereotypical characters interact with round ones?

■ What do you think is the purpose of the stereotyped characters?

■ What if the roles were reversed—the flat characters made round and the round characters flat? How would this affect the show?

(For more about **characterization,** see page 63.)

YOUR TURN 10 Analyzing Sitcom Characters

With a few classmates, analyze the characters on a popular television sitcom. Use a chart like the one above, and afterward, jot down answers to the reflection questions.

Planning a Trailer

WHAT'S AHEAD?

In this section, you will plan a trailer. You will also learn how to

- convey the sense of written words using sounds and images
- create storyboards for scenes
- organize scenes to create a dramatic effect
- make production notes

When you go to the movies, the first thing you see will probably be a **trailer,** a short clip that presents a few pivotal moments from an upcoming movie to capture viewers' attention and make them want to see the movie. What if there were trailers for books? In this section, you will plan a one-minute promotional trailer for a short story. You can choose to plan a trailer for the short story you wrote in this chapter, or any other short story you like.

Choosing Scenes

Telling Moments   What scenes from the story should be used in your trailer? It's best to include intriguing, exciting, and dramatic moments that make viewers want to read the story. However, the scenes shouldn't give too much of the plot away. For instance, if you were making a trailer for "Eveline," on page 59, you might show Eveline's father criticizing her, Eveline meeting Frank secretly, and Frank calling her name from the ship. Viewers might get the idea that she is thinking of elopement, but they wouldn't know whether she goes through with it. A trailer should include at least three scenes that are narratively and visually interesting. Choose scenes that you think can be successfully adapted for film.

Film Techniques

Adept Adaptation   Now what about the scenes themselves? How are words on a page adapted into sounds and images on a screen? Dialogue and the action of the plot are easy to adapt. However, what about a character's feelings? *Body language, lighting, camera angle, music, dialogue,* and *action* can all convey a character's feelings.

   The chart on the following page shows one person's ideas for adapting the scene from "Eveline" in which Frank calls to Eveline from the ship. Notice how the chart specifies some of the types of camera shots. After you have studied the chart, make your own chart for each of the scenes in your trailer.

Idea to be adapted	Method of adaptation
Eveline's anxiety and indecision	Camera cuts back and forth from Frank and the ship to the land. A close-up of Eveline's hands gripping the railing. Discordant music that builds to a climax.
Frank's desperation	A close-up of Frank's distorted face as he yells Eveline's name. A long shot of Frank leaning over the railing and stretching out his hand to Eveline.
The irrevocable, or final, nature of Eveline's decision	A camera shot that shows the distance of the ship from the dock. A very long shot that shows the largeness of the world and of the sea into which the ship will soon disappear.

TIP A variety of shots will make a trailer more interesting. Here are some different kinds of shots used to create different effects.

- A **close-up shot** is an extremely close shot, usually of an actor's face. This kind of shot can be used to show emotions.

- A **long shot** shows the scene from a great distance. This kind of shot can be used to set a scene or to show action.

- A **reaction shot** shows an actor reacting to another actor's dialogue or movement. This kind of shot is often used to show a character's emotions.

- A **high-angle shot** places the camera above eye level, while a **low-angle shot** places the camera below eye level. A high-angle shot can make an object appear smaller or less significant. A low-angle shot can make an object appear larger, or more significant.

- A **tracking shot** is one in which the camera moves on tracks to follow a moving subject. This kind of shot is used to show action.

Storyboards

To the Drawing Board   After finishing a planning chart for each scene in your trailer, it is time to make **storyboards**—sketches of what the scenes look like. A storyboard need not be a work of art. It just shows the placement of actors in relation to each other, objects on the set, and the camera. The order in which storyboards are arranged shows the sequence of scenes. What order will most intrigue your audience? Chronological order? Thematic order?

In **chronological order,** scenes would be arranged according to the sequence of events; while in **thematic order,** scenes would be arranged according to their theme, or central idea. Take a look at the following storyboards for scenes from "Eveline"—one depicting Eveline's familiar life at home and one depicting the dramatic final scene of the story.

A good way to decide the order of the scenes in your trailer is to arrange and rearrange your storyboards until you find the order that you think will best help you to achieve your purpose—to persuade your audience to read the story.

Production Notes

What a Production!   After your storyboards are complete and in the most effective order, you will need to write production notes to go along with the sketches. These notes should describe in detail what each scene will look and sound like. They should also include notes about costume, set design, music, the exact words of dialogue, and any voice-over narration. The following notes correspond to the second storyboard panel on the previous page.

> Long shot to include Eveline on dock and Frank waving from ship. Sea in the background—choppy. Eveline wearing long, pink crinoline skirt. She is clutching the railing of the dock; her hair blows in the wind. Frank wearing a sailor's suit. Sounds of wind and sea and of Frank calling Eveline's name.

TIP   After you have finished planning your trailer, try one of the following publishing suggestions.

- Share your trailer ideas with a few friends. Would your trailer make them want to read the story?
- Borrow a video camera, and get friends or classmates to help you videotape your trailer. Show the film to your class.
- Choose one of your storyboards, and draw or paint the scene as a movie poster. Display the poster at school or at home.

Then, reflect on your work by asking yourself the following questions.

- Which elements of the story were most difficult to adapt? Why?
- If you were to plan another trailer, what would you do differently?
- Would your trailer make *you* want to read the story?

YOUR TURN 11   Planning a Trailer

Use the process outlined in this section to plan a trailer for a short story. Then, refer to the Tip above for publishing suggestions.

Choices

Choose one of the following activities to complete.

▶ **CROSSING THE CURRICULUM: HISTORY**

1. Historical Stories Think of a historical event that captures your interest. List the event's narrative elements, such as theme, characters, setting, conflict, climax, and resolution. Then, find two or more accounts of the historical event and compare and contrast their treatment of the event's narrative elements. Does one account portray the "characters" involved as more or less heroic? Do the accounts seem to have different themes? Is the conflict depicted the same way in both? How can you explain any discrepancies? Present your findings in the form of an **oral report.**

▶ **VIEWING AND REPRESENTING**

2. Picture This Create a **comic strip** based on a short story. Remember that stories with action and dialogue work best. Try to retain the theme, mood, and tone of the story in your comic strip. For instance, you might not want to use cartoon exclamations such as "Bam!" for a short story with a serious tone and a reflective mood.

▶ **CAREERS**

3. Drama at Work Think about jobs that might make interesting subjects for a short story. Police officers and paramedics, for instance, often live through conflict, climax, and resolution. Write a **short story** about someone doing one of these jobs or a job you think you might like to have.

▶ **SPEAKING AND LISTENING**

4. Tell a Tale Prepare a **reading** of your favorite story. Think carefully about how you will present the story. What tone of voice will you use? What will you emphasize? Where will you pause? Practice reading the story a couple of times. When you are ready, you might want to offer to read the story for a group that makes recordings for the blind, at a nursing home, or for children.

▶ **MEDIA AND TECHNOLOGY**

5. Spin a Web Create a **Web home page** on which to post your own and your friends' stories. You might include a bulletin board section on which readers could post comments about the stories.

PORTFOLIO

Comparing and Contrasting Media

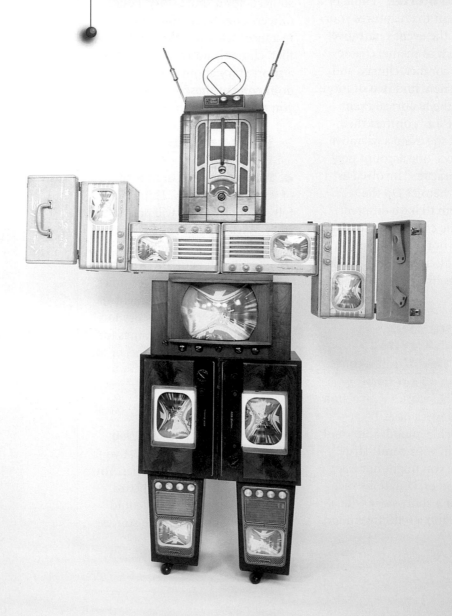

Reading Workshop

Reading a Comparison-Contrast Article
PAGE 96

Writing Workshop

Writing a Comparison-Contrast Essay
PAGE 109

Focus on Speaking and Listening

Conducting Interviews for a News Story
PAGE 133

Faced with the unfamiliar, we instinctively turn to the familiar for information and explanations: How is college (or swing music or calculus) like high school (or jazz or precalculus)? How is it different? By comparing and contrasting two or more subjects, we learn more about each of them.

GO TO: go.hrw.com
KEYWORD: EOLang 12-3

Now, think about the various media that surround us. Media news reports are such a familiar part of our lives that we sometimes tend to forget that they are different from the real thing—they are representations of reality. When you see a raging fire on a TV news report, for example, it is a painstakingly packaged version of the event, not the actual event. Everything from the camera angles to the time allotted the story has been carefully chosen by TV producers.

Furthermore, each medium represents reality a bit differently. Another way of saying this is that *the medium shapes the message.* For example, television favors visual impact, while newspapers can provide in-depth analysis. As a result of these inherent differences in the media, coverage of the same event may differ widely. These differences, in turn, profoundly affect the way we perceive the world—and each other, and even ourselves.

YOUR TURN 1 Brainstorming About Media Messages

Meet in a small group and discuss what you see as the strengths and weaknesses of various media—print (newspaper and magazines), TV, radio, and the Web. For coverage of an important event, which medium seems most dependable to you?

Reading a Comparison-Contrast Article

Where do you go to get the latest news? For years, newspapers and television news programs have competed for readers and viewers. Now this battle for an audience has moved to a new arena—the Internet. Television and print media have both adapted their products for publication on the World Wide Web. The selection you will read next, which was published in a journal for professionals in the online news industry, gives you a behind-the-scenes look at the hot competition for an audience among news cybercasters on the Internet.

Preparing to Read

READING SKILL

Main Idea and Supporting Details   News reports deluge us daily. Unless you can identify the **main idea** (the overall point the speaker or writer is trying to make) and the **supporting details** (the specific information that bears out that idea), you may find yourself at sea. Remember that the main idea is different from the **topic**—what the story is about. For instance, the topic of a news report might be a congressional election; the main idea might be that candidates spend too much of their time raising funds. (Experienced writers may not state their main idea directly. Instead, they may use an **implied** main idea—one that readers must infer from the supporting details.) Look for the writer's main idea in the article ahead.

READING FOCUS

Comparison-Contrast Structure   The two basic methods of organizing comparison-contrast articles are the block method and the point-by-point method. In the **block method,** the writer first discusses all the relevant features of one subject, and then features of the other. In the **point-by-point method,** the writer discusses one feature at a time, first for one subject and then for the other. Not all writers follow one of these methods rigidly; some use a hybrid method that combines elements of both. As you read the following article, see if you can discover how the writer organizes his material.

Kevin Featherly is a journalist and multimedia consultant. As you read his article, write down your answers to the numbered active-reading questions.

from media*info*.com

TV's Threat Gets Bigger on the Web:

How the TV Networks Are Competing with Papers

BY KEVIN FEATHERLY

In the local news market, newspapers have always gone up against local television affiliates. Now the Web is making TV an even bigger competitor for papers.

In February 1998, the fashionably late Tiffany[1] network finally joined the online news fray. With the debut of CBS.com, the network became the last of the Big Three television broadcasters to commit itself both commercially and journalistically to the World Wide Web. ABC and NBC had both been there for months, while cable news giant CNN was online before most people ever even heard the phrase "Web browser."

From the perspective of the major online newspapers, having all those networks slugging it out with them, competing 24 hours a day for a common audience on a single electronic playing field, must seem at least vaguely threatening. Television, after all, clobbers newspapers in terms of audience size and reach. [The Networks'] Web sites can be promoted instantly to millions of people at relatively low cost. Plus, there's all that talk of a coming TV-Web convergence,[2] and even the suggestion that TV Web sites might chip away at the newspaper's golden calf,[3] the classified ad.

In contrast to newspapers, TV stations dramatically improve their core services online. There are even a few people whispering that broadcasters might one day leverage[4] the Web to make a run at newspapers' primary asset, their depth and quality of news

> **1. Why does the writer think most online newspapers feel threatened by the networks' Web sites?**

---

1. **Tiffany:** here, a reference to an advertising slogan CBS once used to designate superior quality; from the name of a noted U.S. jeweler.

2. **convergence:** coming together; joining.

3. **golden calf:** source of money, greedily pursued.

4. **leverage:** use something to gain advantage or power.

coverage. A few TV sites—MSNBC on the Internet comes to mind—may already be on that path. "Of course, we are very much eager to do as many things as well as the *New York Times* or the *Washington Post* do," said Merrill Brown, editor in chief at MSNBC. "And, maybe, someday we will."

Maybe. But don't look for Douglas Feaver to lose any sleep over it. "I don't think it's a new situation," said Feaver, editor of washingtonpost.com and a 20-year *Post* veteran. "I think it's as old as competition in news." Despite its hype as a news medium, the Internet has brought about only one truly major development to the *Post*, according to Feaver—a new way to deliver his company's news content. Little else has changed. The paper still employs a squadron of some of the world's best journalists, and the networks still look to the *Post* when searching for each night's lead on-air story.

Hourly, Not Daily Deadlines

Even the Web's pressure to produce news [more quickly] doesn't really change things that much at the *Post*, Feaver contends. For years, *Post* reporters have been filing early takes of stories for the *Washington Post-New York Times* partnership in Paris, the *International Herald Tribune*, which has a much earlier deadline. "I know how to work fast," he said.

In any event, washingtonpost.com posts a new edition around midnight every day. That version contains some of the biggest breaking *Post* stories, which print readers won't see until hours later. But online readers at midnight who visit the site again at noon will often see few changes, with the exception of links to widely available Associated Press stories that are updated throughout the day. Washingtonpost.com doesn't seem to be taking the "up-to-the-minute" Web mantra totally to heart.

Feaver concedes that there are new opportunities for newspapers with video and audio, just as there are enhanced textual capabilities for broadcasters. There are new commercial opportunities online, as well. But Feaver believes this is business as usual: Newspapers have always tinkered with business strategies in changing times. Even the presence of WSC-TV, the local NBC affiliate carrying the MSNBC brand into the Washington metro area, represents more of the same old thing, Feaver said. "Channel 4 News in Washington has a very aggressive local news staff that we've competed against for years," Feaver said. "I spent 20 years in the *Post* newsroom before I came to washingtonpost.com, a large number of those years on the city desk, so I'm familiar with what the competition is that Channel 4 has to offer. I'm not seeing anything on MSNBC, by the time we get down to the Channel 4 local news product, that I haven't been watching on Channel 4 for years, in terms of competition to what we do."

2. What details support the idea that being on the Internet has not significantly changed *The Washington Post*?

3. How do Feaver's points about Channel 4 in this paragraph support the points he makes in the previous two paragraphs?

In other words, Feaver said, "I think the basic underpinning of the *Washington Post* has always been to try and deliver the best possible product, on whatever it was doing. Now, we're trying to deliver the best possible product [on the Web], and maybe we're going to deliver it a little bit earlier because of the competitive pressure, but, honestly, it's the same game. It's the same game I've been in all my life."

Papers Mimicking Print Version on Web

MSNBC is playing a different game than washingtonpost.com, Brown claims. "Mr. Feaver is a good man," said a saucy Brown. "I'm sorry he's living in the 80s." A former *Washington Post* staffer himself, Brown said newspapers are making a mistake if they are only trying to mimic their print edition online. The Web has changed the rules of news irrevocably, he contends. MSNBC.com, a site that is promoted on the air and on cable every day by three national NBC Television properties, claims a monthly audience of about 5 million people. . . . Its audience is so big that MSNBC.com claims to be the equivalent of the nation's fifth-largest daily newspaper, print or otherwise.

"The Internet is changing people's news habits dramatically," Brown said. "When news breaks, when they want up-to-the-minute stock quotes, when they want to know what their baseball team has done, . . . in any high news-interest situation, it is becoming the first place people go.

They don't wait for the morning paper. They don't wait for the Evening News with Anchor Person X. They go to the Internet."

Brown said he admires the *Washington Post*'s Web site for what it is, an online reflection of the face and voice of the newspaper. "I would not be critical of it for a moment in its core mission of putting the *Washington Post*—the newspaper—onto the Internet," Brown said. "They may feel it's their niche to provide everybody today's *Washington Post* online. That may be the right strategy for them." But it may also be a fatally limited strategy, Brown suggests. "I don't want to sound arrogant about it, but I think the *New York Times* and the *Washington Post* are actually chasing us," he said.

MSNBC, ABCNews.com, and CBS.com all seem driven by many of the same notions. Each network has fewer people to work with than the likes of the *Post*, *New York Times*, or *Los Angeles Times*, so each must take maximum advantage of the tools of their usual trade, plus the new tools made available to them by the Internet. In that spirit, each network works hard to combine the dramatic impact of TV, the immediacy of radio, the depth and integrity of newspapers, the 24-hour delivery of cable, and the community reach of their built-in local affiliation systems. "It's a wonderful opportunity," said Joshua Platt, a senior analyst for sales and marketing at CBS New Media. "What the Web offers that neither TV nor a newspaper offers is infinite space. The only thing that constrains us in how much material we can publish is the size of our servers and how

4. What point is Brown making about online newspapers?

fast we can type. And, of course, the size of our staff."

In contrast, while some newspaper companies like Knight Ridder are beginning to rethink their online strategies, many others continue to treat the Internet as just another kind of newspaper. In that sense, some argue, newspapers may be drowning in a sea of their own rich content, lulled into reasoning that by simply repackaging themselves for a computer readership, they will find equal success on the Web.

5. How is the television networks' attitude toward the Web different from the attitude of most newspapers?

"It is natural that a newspaper entering the online arena would, to a certain degree, view it as an extension of its old business," said John Pavlik, executive director for the Center for New Media at Columbia University in New York. "But I think this view will only go so far and will ultimately prove quite limiting. I view the Internet as a new medium. It requires a new form of journalism."

Papers Not Always Interactive

To be sure, newspapers are responding, by occasionally integrating multimedia and interactive elements. It is hardly uncommon now to see an online newspaper featuring sound clips or video files, usually supplied by AP, that augment important stories. Some, like the Minneapolis *Star Tribune*, even occasionally publish italicized tags at the end of stories in their print editions promoting video files available online.

This only goes part of the way, by Pavlik's reckoning. He thinks newspapers and broadcasters once operated in separate but parallel universes; now they have been pushed onto the same stage, performing before a single audience. Meanwhile, the scale of their competition has ballooned beyond anything they ever before encountered. There are now more than 3,000 newspapers online, more than 800 television stations, and more than 1,000 radio stations. There is quasi-news competition from corporate sources like Amazon.com that would not have tried to tap the information market in the past. "This level of news access changes the scale of competition and forces those involved in the business to develop new strategic thinking," Pavlik said.

6. What details support the idea that some newspapers are taking advantage of the Internet's capabilities?

Are the online TV networks further ahead of the curve in terms of this new strategic thinking than newspapers? It's possible. Right now, there are a number of similarities in the way the Big Three approach news on the Web. All have their eye on local classified-ad revenues, and each thus struggles to attract local TV affiliates to participate in Web-content partnerships. Each has achieved some success. Each network site employs a separate Internet news staff to rewrite or re-report news scripts, making the material useful to online readers; MSNBC and ABC have even gotten some TV correspondents to write for the Web.

Each uses audio and video extensively to accompany story text, a practice that will only increase as Internet bandwidth[5] improves. They all include such interactive features as instant online polls, Shockwave animations, and slide-show presentations. And, like the online newspapers, each network site engages in far-flung content and commerce pacts with outside companies like CMP Publications and Borders Books, many of which would be almost inconceivable for television networks themselves to take part in. . . .

7. How are the Big Three networks' approaches to the Web similar?

Networks Aim Locally

The networks make no bones about it. They want to use their national Web sites, and their online affiliate connections, to drill down as far into the local markets as they can. That's where the new revenue sources lie. Former CBS new media director Dean Daniels said earlier this year that if CBS could use affiliate resources to provide local garbage routes to Web users in Peoria, Illinois, and make money, they would do it.

MSNBC's Brown says he doesn't rule it out, either. "That content is already out there," MSNBC's Brown said. "The problem isn't the technology, the problem is the journalism. It's about whether there are local institutions that can actually get that done for us."

Local online garbage routes would be an example of the new form of journalism Columbia's Pavlik calls for, which he has named "contextualized journalism." (He details the concept in his

Columbia University Press book, *Journalism and New Media*.) Simply put, contextualized journalism is the use of powerful online tools—hyperlinks, multimedia, personalized features, etc.—to tell stories in unique and fresh ways that make new connections within communities.

8. How does "contextualized journalism" differ from regular newspaper journalism?

"I see it," Pavlik said, "as especially important in creating news programming that allows the reporter to make links to historical content, associations to related issues and problems, as well as other informational resources and background that can help viewers who want to drill deeper. Or go local. . . ."

With the exception of TV network-based Web sites, not many news operations have multimedia tools at their disposal. Those that do may not have a news culture that understands how best to use those tools. And since most news organizations view the Web as an extension of their main product, they don't view video and audio as terribly relevant, Pavlik said.

This suggests television networks, with their affiliate extensions into so many communities across the country, might have a big advantage over national newspapers like the *Post* and the *Times*. At last count, MSNBC had 89 online local affiliates, some of them first-class Web operations in their own right. ABC had 63 Web affiliates and CBS had 160 of them, though many of those two networks' sites remain

9. Why are local affiliates a big advantage for TV network-based Web sites?

---

5. bandwidth: capacity to carry information.

journalistically undeveloped.

Still, papers like the *Post* and *Times*, when they touch local markets at all, usually rely on Associated Press material that is widely available across the Web. That's not a great marketing advantage. Nonetheless, Pavlik cautions, don't rule out the ability of local newspapers, or even nationwide newspaper chains, to come to grips with the demands of the coming online journalism.

"I suppose networked media, especially television, might have an advantage," Pavlik said. "But newspapers have the strength of in-depth reporting and deep community roots to build upon. I think either might do well."

Whoever has the better plan, it is clear that the race to your hometown is on. Online newspapers have the obvious lead at present; most of them have been online longer than their TV counterparts, and they've got the advantage of deep content that is friendly to the Web's current text-heavy environment.

But one thing is certain: As information technology evolves and bandwidth widens, TV will pose a bigger threat. And the networks are gradually paving the way to make the most of it.

"We think inventing Web news is our mandate," said MSNBC's Brown. "This is a very large challenge that we've set for ourselves."

10. Do you think the writer has adequately supported the idea that TV-affiliated Web sites will outdo their newspaper-affiliated competitors? Why or why not?

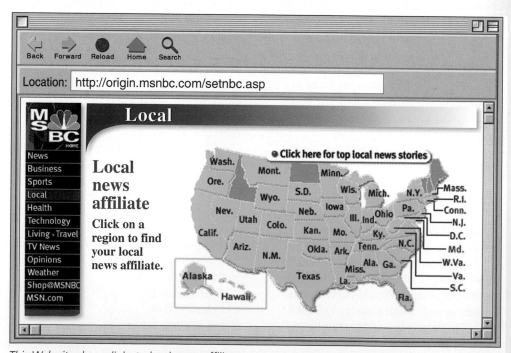

This Web site shows links to local news affiliates.

Main Idea and Supporting Details

Get the Message   Informative articles like the one you have just read are developed around a **main idea,** a central thought that controls the entire piece. To understand such articles, you need to be able to identify this controlling idea and to distinguish it from the **supporting details** that explain, prove, or elaborate on it.

In many articles the main idea is **stated directly** in a sentence or two. Often, this explicit statement appears somewhere in the opening paragraphs. In this position, it alerts you to the writer's intentions, allowing you to evaluate how effectively the rest of the article supports and explains the main idea.

Just to keep things interesting, some articles do not contain a direct statement of the main idea at all. Instead, the main idea is **implied,** or suggested. Such articles require you to **infer** (make an educated guess about) the central, controlling thought. To figure out the main idea, you should begin by identifying supporting details such as **facts, statistics, anecdotes, quotations, descriptions,** and **examples;** then, you should think about the purpose of these details or their relationship to one another within the piece. Deciding how these details are related to one another will help you infer the main idea.

Previewing an article can often help you quickly identify—or at least predict—a stated main idea. Before you read the entire piece, note the title and subtitle, headnote (if there is one), and the section headings. Then, skim the opening and closing paragraphs.

TIP   Some writers may not state a main idea until quite late in an article—even as late as in the conclusion. When you do not find the main idea stated in the first paragraph or so, you can try to predict what the writer is leading up to by analyzing each paragraph or section to identify *its* main idea and supporting details. In effect, you read along as if the main idea were implied. Then, when you do reach the main idea statement, you can confirm or modify your prediction.

Identifying the Main Idea and Supporting Details

These steps will help you identify the main idea and supporting details in informative articles.

▶ **STEP 1 Skim the article and ask yourself: "What main point does the author want me to understand?"** Then, look for a sentence within the article that is similar to your answer.

▶ **STEP 2 If you have not found a *stated* main idea, identify key details such as examples, facts, anecdotes, or statistics that can help you infer a main idea.** Keep an eye out for terms like *for example* or *also,* which often signal supporting details. With complicated or lengthy articles, it often helps to fill in a graphic organizer as you collect details. First, draw an empty circle in the middle of a sheet of paper; this is where the main idea will go. As you read each paragraph (or each section), draw a circle and in it jot the paragraph's (or section's) key detail or main idea. Draw an arrow from each surrounding circle to the central circle. Finally, fill in the central circle with an idea that sums up what all the other circled ideas suggest. Below is an example.

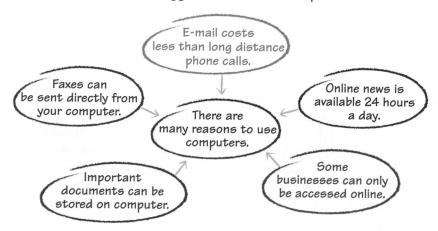

▶ **STEP 3 Re-read the article to make sure that all the supporting details actually do support the main idea you have selected.** If they do not, perhaps you have inferred the main idea too narrowly; try rephrasing it in a way that encompasses all the details you have gathered.

YOUR TURN 2 Finding Main Ideas and Supporting Details

Use the steps in Thinking It Through to identify the main idea of the Reading Selection. First, identify the main ideas in the subtitled sections. Then use those ideas to identify the main idea of the whole piece.

Analyzing Comparison-Contrast Structure

Find the Pattern Whenever you read a comparison-contrast article, look for one of these basic methods of organization:

Block method This method discusses all of the relevant features of one subject in a "block" of text, and then discusses the same features of another subject in another, separate block. ("Blocks" may be one paragraph or many.) The block method is commonly used to

- emphasize the general subject rather than each of its individual features
- present the "big picture" by discussing several features or related details together
- play down sharp individual distinctions between subjects, since one subject is not even discussed until the next "block"

Point-by-point method This method discusses one relevant feature for one subject and then the same feature for another subject, and so on. In general, the point-by-point method is used to

- emphasize a specific feature or features rather than the entire subject Writers often use this method when they are *judging* two things against a set of criteria, or standards used to evaluate the subject's features, rather than just *describing* two things completely.
- focus on a "smaller" picture, often emphasizing just a few key features
- emphasize sharp distinctions between two subjects, since the features of both subjects are discussed together

Being able to detect which method of organization an article uses will help you follow the writer's thinking and thus understand the comparison-contrast more fully. The following chart shows how an article comparing two local newspapers might be organized according to each of the two methods.

Block Method	Point-by-Point Method
Subject 1: Newspaper A Feature 1: quality of local coverage Feature 2: quality of international coverage Feature 3: clarity of sections/ organization **Subject 2: Newspaper B** Feature 1: quality of local coverage Feature 2: quality of international coverage Feature 3: clarity of sections/ organization	**Feature 1: quality of local coverage** Subject 1: Newspaper A Subject 2: Newspaper B **Feature 2: quality of international coverage** Subject 1: Newspaper A Subject 2: Newspaper B **Feature 3: clarity of sections/ organization** Subject 1: Newspaper A Subject 2: Newspaper B

TIP There is another reason, besides focus, why a writer may choose to use one method over another. Here's a hint: You are much more likely to find the point-by-point method in long articles. The block method is seldom used in long articles because most readers would find it too demanding: They would have to remember everything they read about the first subject before they started reading about the second subject.

As a reader, you should also be aware that experienced writers don't always keep strictly to one method or the other. Particularly when addressing complex subjects, they may combine the methods in various ways to create a hybrid structure. For example, a writer comparing and contrasting two different newspapers might use a structure like the one shown below to give an overview of each newspaper as well as a critique of their features.

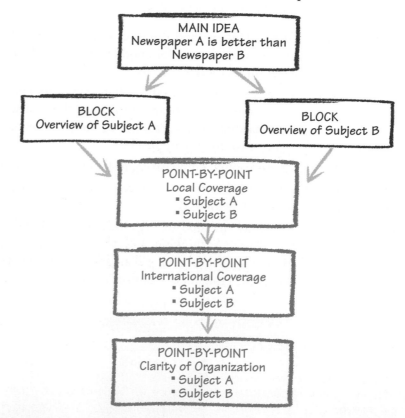

YOUR TURN 3 Analyzing Comparison-Contrast Structure

Make a structure chart like the one above for the section of the Reading Selection titled "Networks Aim Locally." Then, write a statement telling why you think the writer organized the information in this way. Prepare to discuss your chart and statement with the class.

VOCABULARY

Understanding Multiple-Meaning Words

Encountering a familiar word used in an unfamiliar way can interfere with your ability to grasp the writer's point. Look at this passage from the Reading Selection.

> "The Internet is changing people's news habits dramatically. . . . [W]hen they want up-to-the-minute **stock** quotes . . . it is becoming the first place people go. They don't wait for the morning paper."

If you look up *stock* in a dictionary, you will find the following meanings, among others: 1) the total merchandise kept by a store; 2) all the animals on a farm; 3) shares of ownership in a company; 4) the main stem of a plant; 5) the descendants of a common ancestor; and 6) the broth used as a base for soup.

In order to understand which meaning the writer intended, you must examine the surrounding words and sentences to pin down the **context** in which the word is used.

THINKING IT THROUGH **Understanding Multiple-Meaning Words**

The following steps will help you use context clues to understand which meaning the writer intends for a multiple-meaning word.

1. Re-read the sentence in which the word appears. What does it tell you about how the word is being used? *People want information about stocks to be up-to-the-minute.*

2. Look at the sentences before and after the one in which the word appears. What do they tell you about how the word is being used? *Information about stocks is considered news, and it is available in the* morning paper as well as on the Internet.

3. Read all dictionary definitions listed, as well as any sample contexts provided (bracketed examples of how the word is used), and choose the definition that fits best. *The values of shares of ownership in a corporation change many times in a day, and they are reported in the morning paper. Definition 3 must be the intended meaning.*

PRACTICE

Use the steps above to choose the intended meaning for the following boldfaced words.

1. "In February 1998, the fashionably late Tiffany network finally joined the online news **fray**." (worn spot, fight, wear away)

2. The new agreement will bring City Community College into State University's **orbit**. (range of influence, route of a planet around the sun, route of a satellite)

3. Lovers of **high** culture will rejoice at the news that Midville will soon have its own opera company. (advanced, tall, shrill)

4. Garrison's **spare** prose makes this a novel to savor. (extra, inadequate, not excessive)

5. In several of the paintings the sky has a pink **cast**. (arrangement, something thrown, tint)

Detail Questions

Without details to support main ideas, a comparison-contrast article would be little more than one writer's opinion—without proof. Many standardized tests include **detail questions,** questions that ask you to identify supporting details in a reading passage. Look at the following reading passage and question.

Community colleges are easier to get into, far less expensive, and often more convenient than universities. Each year, however, millions of high school seniors go through the grueling process of applying for admission and financial aid to attend a four-year college because these institutions offer one thing community colleges cannot—a bachelor's degree. A bachelor's degree is required for many careers and is also a prerequisite to admission to graduate programs and professional schools. Still, there are many

available jobs in fields such as health care and computer technology that require only the associate's degree granted by community colleges after two years' study. Determining which is better for you, a community college or a university, depends on your goals.

1. The passage suggests that community colleges may be more advantageous than four-year colleges because community colleges

    A. provide better preparation for jobs in health care and computer technology

    B. offer a bachelor's degree

    C. offer an associate's degree

    D. have less restrictive admissions requirements, cost less, and are located close to home

    E. offer more financial aid

THINKING IT THROUGH **Answering Detail Questions**

The following steps will help you answer detail questions.

1. **Read the question and locate the details in the passage that seem most relevant.** Two sections in the passage seem to discuss the advantages of community colleges: The first sentence and the sentence that begins "Still, there are many available jobs in fields such as health care . . ."

2. **Compare the answer choices with the relevant sections in the reading passage. Eliminate answers that do not fit.** Both relevant sections are represented in the answer choices—answers **A** and **D**.

Answer **B** is not true of community colleges and answer **C** is not an advantage over universities; answer **E** does not appear in the passage at all.

3. **Choose the remaining answer that most accurately expresses the idea in the related part of the reading passage.** Answer **A** is wrong because the passage does not address the quality of the preparation. However, Answer **D** and the related detail in the passage do express an advantage of community colleges over universities—Answer **D** is correct.

Writing a Comparison-Contrast Essay

How would you define *news?* The answer might seem obvious—news is "the most important events of the day." Still, not *all* of a day's important events are reported, only those events the media choose to report. Realistically, news is whatever the media think will attract an audience, which in turn will attract advertisers. A more useful definition of *news* might be "the presentation of events the audience will probably find important, in a way that is intended to attract an audience." A royal wedding, for example, might receive much more coverage than a famine, but that does not make the wedding more important.

In addition, media reporters, editors, and producers have different ideas about what their audiences want and what their particular medium does best. Because television is a visual medium, for example, it focuses on events with attention-grabbing images. By contrast, radio is limited to sound and therefore concentrates on news in the form of words—talk shows, interviews, speeches, and discussions. When different media cover the same event, the coverage varies a great deal. Each medium reports the story in ways that take advantage of its particular strengths, and each tries to maximize audience appeal. In this Writing Workshop, you will learn how comparing and contrasting media coverage of a single story can help you understand not only the event but also the media that covered it.

WHAT'S AHEAD?

In this workshop, you will write a comparison-contrast essay. You will also learn to

- analyze media reports
- compare and contrast media coverage of a single news event
- identify persuasion in a news story
- transform *who* and *which* clauses to phrases
- use parallel structure correctly

Prewriting

Choose an Event

What's News to You? A suitable event for your comparison and contrast essay is one that interests you and will interest your readers. You might also choose an event about which there has been some disagreement or controversy. Try at least two of the following brainstorming ideas.

Ask around   Chat with friends, relatives, and neighbors. Find out what news events interest them, and then ask yourself what you know about each event. Does the event interest you?

TIP If there is a local or national election coming up soon, it might be interesting to analyze the way the media present different candidates. Media images have a history of influencing the **democratic process**—the way people vote.

Get with the print   Read a newspaper, local or national. You may want to scan national newsmagazines as well. Remember: Not all newspapers are equally credible or news oriented. Avoid sensational tabloids that feature screaming headlines and outrageous gossipy stories.

Listen in   Attend a meeting of your city council or listen to what events people are discussing as you sit on the bus or walk through the mall. Then, look for media reports on these same topics.

Tune in   Browse the World Wide Web, listen to the news on the radio, and watch the national news on TV—all on the same day. Use a VCR or a tape recorder so that you can review the broadcasts later. Do the different media cover the same events? How do they handle them?

As you search for an event to analyze, keep the following two helpful points in mind:

- the event should be (or will be) covered in at least two different types of media

- the media coverage should be readily accessible to you. (Don't choose an event that will only be covered in obscure journals, for example, or only broadcast in France.)

When you have found several events that interest you, list them and then choose one you are interested in exploring further. Make sure that your choice is a single, concrete event. A topic such as the high cost of a college education is too general and vague for your purposes, but the announcement that a major university is dramatically lowering its tuition might prove a good subject.

Think About Purpose, Audience, and Tone

TIP Your **voice** is what makes your writing uniquely yours; your **tone** is the attitude you adopt to talk to your audience about your topic. In writing an expository essay, you should adopt a formal tone.

Get to Know Your Readers   Are your readers aware of the event on which you will focus? Do they know how news stories are gathered and reported? Your **purpose** is to *inform* your audience about the similarities and differences (or strengths and weaknesses) of two different media focused on a single event. This means you will have to familiarize your readers with the event, the coverage, and the characteristics of the media you choose. In order to communicate so much information effectively, you will need to start by analyzing your audience.

▶ **What do my readers already know about the event?** Because the event received media coverage, your audience probably knows at least something about it. You cannot assume that readers are as well informed as you are, but remember that you are not covering the event; you are covering the coverage. Include only enough of the most important facts about the event to refresh your readers' memory.

▶ **What do my readers already know about the media?** Your readers are certainly familiar with the various media, but they may never have thought about how the medium shapes the message. You will need to structure your essay clearly, define any technical terms you use, and provide concrete examples for any abstract ideas.

▶ **What effect do I want to have on my readers?** Ultimately, you want your readers to understand how differences in the media forms themselves affect the coverage an event receives. Then, your readers too will be better able to assess the media messages that bombard us all.

TIP A specific event may serve as the **occasion,** or prompt, that triggers a variety of stories related to the actual news report that tells "what happened."

For example, an approaching hurricane would be the occasion for related stories on how hurricane strength is measured. Such stories help put the event in context for the audience and examining them can help you understand the event (*your* occasion for writing).

Gather and Compare Media Forms

Is the Medium the Message? To a great extent, the medium in which an event is reported shapes the **message** the audience receives. For example, reading a newspaper report about refugees being reunited with their families, and then seeing the actual reunion on TV would have decidedly different effects—because of the media. Which report do you think would be more emotional? Which would feel more factual?

Each medium has a different set of innate characteristics; in striving to maximize its strengths and minimize its weaknesses, each medium approaches an event differently. The following chart shows the chief characteristics of television, radio, print, and the Internet.

KEY CONCEPT

Media Form	Characteristics
TV	▪ visual elements (live coverage, videotape, graphics) and audio ▪ includes various camera angles, graphics, music, connotative language, and "sound bites" (short clips featuring statements likely to be remembered easily) ▪ limited by tight time constraints; television news stories are typically less than five minutes long ▪ reaches mass audience ▪ influenced by ratings, advertisers, station owners, and network affiliation

TIP Another term for *media form* is **genre**—a French word meaning "type" or "kind." A **news genre,** then, is a type or kind of news. Genres also contain subgenres; TV news, for example, includes categories such as nightly news, newsmagazines, and documentaries.

(continued)

(continued)

TIP Of course the general characteristics of media are not the only things that distinguish them from one another. Within a single medium—print, for example—coverage may differ greatly in quality and reliability.

Also note that there are differences between the subgenres of news media: National television news is distinct from local news, for example, and weekly newsmagazines are quite different from newspapers.

TV (cont.)	• uses mostly traditional, reliable sources (authorities, eye-witnesses, and so on)
	• ability to be current
	• limited interactivity
Radio	• audio only
	• presentation includes connotative language, music, and "sound bites"
	• some time constraints, since news programs usually comprise only part of a station's format, especially when the station is devoted primarily to music, not talk
	• reaches mass audience
	• influenced by ratings, advertisers, and owners; usually more independent than TV
	• uses mostly reliable sources
	• ability to be current
	• call-in programs provide more interactivity than television, but interactive capabilities still limited
Print (both newspapers and magazines)	• visual only (text and graphics)
	• presentation includes connotative language, graphics, and quotations
	• some length constraints, so coverage often not as deep as it could be; still, print coverage not as superficial as TV or radio frequently are
	• reaches large audience, but a more limited audience than radio or TV
	• influenced by sales, advertisers, and publishers
	• uses mostly reliable sources; in turn, is the standard of reliability for other media
	• not as current as other media
	• aside from letters to the editor, limited interactivity
Internet (World Wide Web)	• audio and visual (graphics, text, and video), animation, and interactive features
	• presentation includes different camera angles, graphics, connotative language, quotations, and "sound bites"
	• no time or space constraints; users can access sites 24 hours a day and length of stories not limited by medium's form
	• audience limited to those who have access to computers and the Internet
	• some sites commercial, but many independent

Internet (World Wide Web) *(cont.)*	■ wide spectrum of sources, since anyone with the equipment may put up a site or post a message; the sites considered most reliable are those associated with other, long-established media or with government, universities, or nonprofit organizations ■ potential for up-to-the-minute coverage ■ hyperlinks and chat rooms provide immediate interactivity

Once you have pinned down your event and which two media forms you will analyze, it may be helpful to sort out the characteristics of the *particular* news reports you gather. A good way to get an initial idea of their similarities and differences is to create a Venn diagram. Look below at how one student used a Venn diagram to jot some notes about television and print coverage of U.S. Senator John Glenn's second spaceflight.

TIP For each news genre you choose, you may focus on one story or a few. The student below, for example, watched three local television broadcasts and read two print reports— from the local paper and a national magazine.

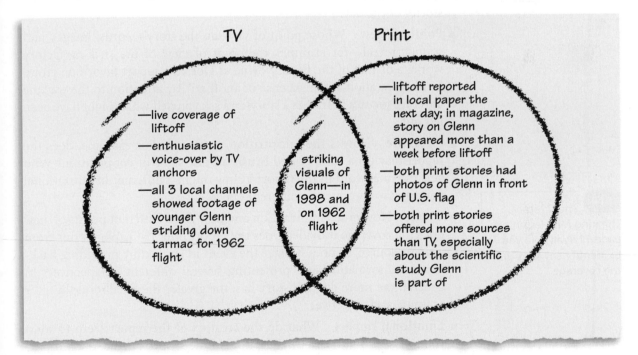

TV **Print**

—live coverage of liftoff

—enthusiastic voice-over by TV anchors

—all 3 local channels showed footage of younger Glenn striding down tarmac for 1962 flight

striking visuals of Glenn—in 1998 and on 1962 flight

—liftoff reported in local paper the next day; in magazine, story on Glenn appeared more than a week before liftoff

—both print stories had photos of Glenn in front of U.S. flag

—both print stories offered more sources than TV, especially about the scientific study Glenn is part of

YOUR TURN 4 — Choosing an Event and Media Coverage to Compare and Contrast

Review the preceding steps. As you choose an event and the types of media coverage you will compare and contrast, make sure to

■ think about your purpose, audience, and tone

■ jot some notes about how the media you have chosen are different and similar. Use a Venn diagram, if you wish.

Analyze and Compare Media Coverage

What's the Story?   In every medium, staff members carefully choose which events to cover and how to cover them. In a newspaper, for instance, editors and managing editors meet daily to decide which breaking stories they will feature on the front page and which stories will be single paragraphs or dropped altogether. To analyze the two types of media coverage you have chosen, think about how each **medium,** or form of communication, handles the elements listed below.

- **Attention-getting Techniques**   How does the report persuade you that the event is important and meaningful? Be alert for dramatic teasers (statements that build tension), images, provocative language, allusions to controversial topics, and appeals to the audience's self-interest.

- **Location**   Is the event reported as a top story? How much time and space is given to it? Where does the coverage occur in relation to other stories of the day?

- **Point of View**   Whose point of view do the story's words, images, and sounds reveal—for example, the point of view of the striking factory workers or that of the factory owners? Does the report favor one group or interpretation at the expense of another? Pay attention to the way the coverage focuses or frames a story, and ask yourself what might have been left out.

- **Structure**   How is the information organized? For example, does the report play up a conflict and brush off any signs of cooperation? Who gets the final word in the report ? How might a different organizational pattern have produced a different effect?

- **Depth**   How much information and how many different points of view does the coverage provide? Does the report offer pat explanations from a single source, or does it place the event in context by providing background information and presenting several different perspectives? In general, the more depth a story has, the greater the likelihood that it is accurate and objective.

- **Emotional Impact**   What do the creators of the report seem to want you to *feel* about the event? Take note of the reporter's tone of voice, the use of connotative language (language with emotional associations), and the kinds of visuals included.

TIP The Critical Thinking Mini-lesson on page 117 will help you to identify any **bias** in the coverage.

TIP Make sure that the information you present in your essay is **relevant** (related and important) to your purpose, which is to compare and contrast the media coverage. For example, suppose you are comparing and contrasting Web and TV coverage of the World Cup soccer championship. The amount of video (taped coverage of live action) each medium presents is relevant; a description of each team's uniforms is *not* relevant.

The following chart shows how one student used the elements on the previous page to analyze two media reports of a single event.

LOCAL TV AND NEWSPAPER COVERAGE OF THE CITY COUNCIL'S WATER-RATIONING ANNOUNCEMENT

Element	Similarities	Differences
Attention-getting Techniques	Both show pictures of parched fields and quote a council member saying, "It's going to be a long, hot, and very, very dry summer."	- Newspaper headline, "Water Watch," is in large but customary type. - TV graphic reads "DROUGHT" in large, jagged-edged type.
Location	Both run the story the day after the meeting; both give it fairly prominent coverage.	- Newspaper features story in top left column of front page (location for second most important story). - TV covers story fifth (40-second coverage).
Point of View	Both concentrate on the effect of the water rationing on the average citizen and portray the council as having no alternative.	- Newspaper points out wasteful uses of water by citizens. - TV concentrates on dry weather as cause.
Structure	Both present interviews with local farmers and water users; both end with council's warning that stricter rationing may come.	- Newspaper begins with account of city council meeting. - TV begins with question of whether the city will run out of water.
Depth	Both include views of council members, area companies, and citizens.	- Newspaper includes views of city's environmental groups. - TV includes statement by its staff meteorologist.
Emotional Impact	Both warn audience in serious language about the need for rationing, and give tips to follow. Both use the alarming word "drought" repeatedly.	- Newspaper emphasizes residents' wastefulness may be a cause of problem. - TV emphasizes the hardships of rationing.

TIP As you speculate about how and why certain media shape a story in a particular way, remember that you cannot draw very reliable conclusions on the basis of one example. Also draw on your previous knowledge of the medium, and be careful not to make absolute statements.

Once you have analyzed the media coverage, your next step is to draw conclusions about your findings: *Why* did each medium cover the story the way it did? To answer this question, you will need to sum up your analysis and combine your overall impression of the coverage with what you know about the characteristics of each medium. The student whose analysis of two media reports appears in the preceding chart drew these conclusions about how each medium shaped the message it delivered.

Local Television News Coverage

Overall impression

—sensationalistic, relatively brief, and shallow

Conclusions

—TV news is a visual medium, often pressed for time and driven by ratings.

—Sensationalistic stories and reporters who cater to viewers' needs increase ratings.

Local Newspaper Coverage

Overall impression

—thorough, more critical of residents than of businesses

Conclusions

—Newspapers have more time and space to go into detail.

—Owners and editors are often reluctant to offend advertisers, their chief source of revenue.

Identifying Persuasion in News Reports

When you read or view a news report, you should remember that it is the product of writers and other media staff who have their own points of view. You also should determine whether the report displays signs of **bias,** favoring one side in a news story over another. Be on the lookout for the following persuasive techniques, all of which reveal bias.

Loaded Language Ask yourself what *connotations,* or emotional associations, the words carry. Words with strong positive or negative connotations are known as **loaded language.** For example, a news reporter might use the negative word *brawl* to refer to a difference of opinion instead of the neutral word *discussion.* (Note: Unless they are writing signed columns or quoting someone directly, most reporters try to avoid using loaded language.)

Glittering Generalities These are words with such strongly positive connotations that they obscure the lack of support for the ideas they convey. For example, a news report might characterize someone as "a pillar of the community" without any mention of the person's contributions or accomplishments. Ask yourself whether adequate, relevant information backs up such statements.

Implications Even if a news report does not state a judgment, it may imply or suggest one. For example, a reporter might condemn with faint praise by describing a gubernatorial candidate running against a famous former general as "something of a patriot himself." Because this phrase does not use strong, unambiguous language to describe the candidate's qualifications, it implies that they are trivial compared to those of the former general. Always ask yourself whether a media report in any way hints at someone's opinion or judgment.

Symbols Visual images as well as verbal descriptions can contain emotional appeals. For example, a person wearing a T-shirt emblazoned with a dove, a symbol of peace, may or may not have peaceful intentions. Train yourself to look for symbols in news reports, and ask yourself whether words and actions align with what the symbol represents.

PRACTICE

In the brief photo description and news story that follow, find an example of each of the persuasive techniques explained above. (One example may illustrate more than one technique.) What bias do the examples suggest?

Photo Description: A bulldozer, shot from a low angle, crushes an ornate, red-carpeted staircase in an old theater.

City Razes Landmark Theater
In a crushing blow to residents working to save this elegant Central City landmark, bulldozers this morning razed the famous Witherspoon Theater on the city's south side. Peaceful protestors, who had chained themselves to the fence outside the theater to prevent the destruction of the century-old building, were forcibly removed by police. During its heyday, the landmark theater was visited by such legendary VIPs as jazz singer Ella Fitzgerald and baseball great Babe Ruth. A parking garage is to be built on the site.

Develop a Thesis

TIP The word *compare* is often used to mean both compare and contrast. For example, a test item may ask you to compare two forms of government. Usually, you are expected to point out both similarities and differences. Ask your teacher to be sure.

What's the Focus?   Your **thesis statement,** or main idea, should identify the event and the types of media coverage you will compare and contrast. It should also make clear whether you will focus on similarities, differences, or both.

In comparing and contrasting coverage of a single event, you will also be comparing and contrasting the media that broadcast the event. That is, the similarities and differences you find in the coverage of the event will to some extent reflect the inherent similarities and differences between the media. For example, you may find that the TV news coverage you watched provided less information than the print story, but that reading the print story was much less emotionally involving. Notice how each of the following examples of thesis statements addresses both the *coverage* and the *media.*

> **Focus on Differences**
> The live TV coverage of the election returns on Channels 3, 8, and 11 was much more exciting than the wrap-up in the following day's newspaper.
>
> **Focus on Similarities**
> Both TV Channels 3, 8, and 11 and the local newspaper were fair in their coverage of the recent election. In ignoring third-party candidates, however, both also demonstrated media's traditional bias in favor of business as usual.
>
> **Focus on Similarities and Differences**
> Although the TV coverage of the recent elections on Channels 3, 8, and 11 leaned more toward the sensationalistic than the newspaper coverage did, both media overlooked the most important story of the night: the solid minority turnout in support of the mayor-elect.

Organize the Structure of Your Ideas

Assemble Your Proof   You may develop some great insights into the ways each medium's inherent characteristics influenced its coverage of the event, but readers will expect you to provide plenty of well-organized support for your ideas. Make sure that all your ideas are **relevant** to your thesis; that is, that they directly relate to your main idea and its focus.

KEY CONCEPT → **The two basic methods of organizing a comparison-contrast essay are the block method and the point-by-point method.** In the **block method,** you discuss all of the relevant features of each subject separately—in a "block." In the **point-by-point method,** you discuss one relevant feature at a time, first for one subject and then the other; after one feature is covered, you move on to the next feature. The block method is often used to compare two things generally, while point-by-point is used when the writer's focus is on the specific features of two things.

For example, a writer comparing and contrasting TV and print coverage of John Glenn's second spaceflight using the *block* method would discuss the TV coverage of the flight, and then the print coverage of the flight. A writer using the *point-by-point* method would discuss one relevant feature of the TV and print coverage (such as use of images), then another feature, and so on. Whichever method you choose, be consistent about the order in which you present information. The following chart shows how the two methods work.

TIP The block method may be difficult to work with if the two subjects you are describing are complicated or your analyses are lengthy. Your readers will have to remember all of your points about the first subject as they move on to the second subject.

Block Method	Point-by-Point Method
Subject 1: TV coverage of Glenn's flight	**Feature 1:** use of past and current images
• Feature 1: use of past and current images	• Subject 1: TV coverage
• Feature 2: facts about purposes of past and current flights	• Subject 2: print coverage
• Feature 3: overall tone	
	Feature 2: facts about purposes of past and current flights
Subject 2: Print coverage of Glenn's flight	• Subject 1: TV coverage
• Feature 1: use of past and current images	• Subject 2: print coverage
• Feature 2: facts about purposes of past and current flights	**Feature 3:** overall tone
	• Subject 1: TV coverage
• Feature 3: overall tone	• Subject 2: print coverage

TIP Combinations, or hybrids, of the two methods may be used, too. The block method is commonly used to provide an overview of two subjects, followed by the point-by-point method for more specific comparisons between them.

YOUR TURN 5 **Compare Media Coverage, Write a Thesis, and Organize Ideas**

At this point in your planning, make sure to analyze the media coverage, noting the elements described on page 114; write your thesis statement; and organize your ideas using either the block or the point-by-point method.

Writing

Comparison-Contrast Essay

| **Framework** | **Directions and Explanations** |

Introduction
- Start with an interesting opener.
- Provide background information.
- Provide your thesis statement.

Pique Interest and Provide Context Begin with an attention-getting statement, question, quotation, or anecdote. Give necessary background information.

State Your Case Clearly state your main idea about the similarities and differences in the coverage of the event. Be sure to mention the *particular* articles, news programs, or Web sites you analyzed.

Body
- State the main points of comparison.
- Provide support for each point.

Explain Your Points Structure your ideas according to the **block method** or the **point-by-point method,** or a combination of the two. Aim for consistency.

Provide Support Back up each main point with *relevant* supporting details from your analysis of the coverage. Use quotations and refer to specific examples or images. Also explain any media or technical terms your readers may find unfamiliar.

Conclusion
- Summarize information and restate your thesis.
- Evaluate the relative merits of the two types of coverage, if appropriate.
- Close with a final impression.

Sum It Up Recap the support that backs up and elaborates on your thesis statement.

Speculate on Media Forms If you found one medium's coverage superior, explain why. Here is your chance to offer some thoughts about how the medium shapes the message. (Be careful, however, not to make overly broad or absolute statements.)

Offer a Final Impression Close with your conclusions about how the coverage reflected the strengths and weaknesses of the two media.

 Writing a First Draft

As you draft your comparison-contrast essay, use the framework above and the directions and explanations as a guide. The Writer's Model on the next page is a sample essay that closely follows the framework.

A Writer's Model

The following essay, which is a final draft, closely follows the framework on the previous page.

Representations of a National Hero

When U.S. Senator John Glenn soared into space aboard the space shuttle <u>Discovery</u>, a full thirty-six years after his first trip, comparisons were inevitable. The Cold War had ended, the Information Age had begun, and the astronaut-turned-senator seemed to be challenging not the Soviets but our society's notions about age. One thing had not changed, however: America's yearning for a hero. The TV cameras, always eager for a larger-than-life drama, did not disappoint the nation. Only a few voices, mostly in the print media, ventured to raise some pointed questions in the midst of all the cheers.

It was TV that originally made Glenn, the first American to orbit the earth, a living legend in black-and-white footage from his three orbits around the Earth in <u>Friendship 7</u> on February 20, 1962. Glenn's flight came at a time when Americans weren't sure they could ever catch up with the Soviets in space. On October 29, 1998, NASA's challenge was to awe an audience grown accustomed to taking even space shuttle missions for granted. If pictures are any gauge, NASA lived up to the challenge. Television reports broadcast on the three national affiliates in Cedar City captured the seventy-seven-year-old veteran striding out in his orange flight-suit just as jauntily as he had as a forty-year-old pioneer, and the TV reports unabashedly displayed Glenn's profile against a backdrop of the American flag. The youthful grin on the aging hero's face seemed to assure viewers that in America, age was no obstacle to achievement.

Print coverage was necessarily more restrained pictorially; but with space available for only a few photos, newspapers such as the <u>Cedar City Gazette</u> featured the most striking images. Among the photos were then-and-now contrasts with young Glenn in black and white and Glenn the older in full color. There were also shots of the joyful crowd at the launch site, the space shuttle poised skyward in the distance. In addition, magazines such as <u>Time</u>, taking full advantage of print's capacity for charts and the like, presented graphs tracking the space program's progress side by side with the country's progress. Other graphics offered statistics on the two flights, as well as interesting trivia. Newspaper and magazine coverage seemed more objective, more

(continued)

Attention-grabbing opening describes the event

Background

Thesis statement

Point-by-point method
First point about TV

Supporting details

First point about print

Supporting details

Elaboration of main point

(continued)

analytical than TV, its more excitable rival, but the print images were scarcely less stirring than the ones on TV.

Second point about TV

Supporting details

In their exploration of the purpose of the flights, TV coverage and print coverage differed more markedly. TV Channels 4 and 7 barely mentioned NASA's official line that the senator was the subject of research into the effects of weightlessness on the aged, burying the explanation at the end of the story. Also buried at the end of the story—and in Channel 4's case, missing altogether—was any discussion of how scientifically valid such a study was. TV producers may have been more concerned with using the story to boost their own ratings than with publicizing NASA's experiment.

Speculation on media form

Second point about print

The print media, although somewhat cautious about embracing NASA's explanation, seemed hesitant to spoil the party. The Gazette's coverage, for example, mentioned that critics had branded the event a publicity stunt not only for NASA but also for Senator Glenn. In the next breath, however, the newspaper rushed to point out that such a distinguished public servant had certainly earned a second launch. The Time reporter made an effort to explore the senator's motivations, but NASA critics were rarely named or quoted directly, only lumped together as "skeptics."

Supporting details

Third point about TV

Overall, the TV coverage of the event resembled a pep rally. Sounding grateful for the story's upbeat themes, Channel 11's anchors openly contrasted the flight with the day's disturbing or destructive events. Glenn's flight was such welcome news, in fact, that the anchors tended to falter in their professionalism. This was not TV's usual "hard-hitting" fare; it was the stuff of dreams. For one moment, on one day, TV news could live out its aspirations to be a Hollywood movie: It had the perfect script.

Supporting details

Elaboration of main point

Third point about print

If the TV coverage was a Hollywood movie, the print coverage was a Hollywood gossip columnist wanting to be the center of attention but not quite finding the stage. Though the "critics" of the flight were never named, the medium's reputation for thoroughness demanded that they be given their column inches. Nevertheless, both the Gazette and Time were filled with wide-eyed details of the flights and slightly sentimental portraits of the hero. Even if the event is a stunt, they seemed to say, it is a newsworthy one.

Supporting details

Summary of support for thesis

Final impression

All told, the two media gave their respective audiences exactly what those audiences have come to expect. Television wowed viewers with a hero inspiring his country with dazzling feats decades apart. The print media analyzed the event a bit more thoroughly, trying to stay at least slightly grounded. Nevertheless, all eyes were on the sky.

A Student's Model

The following student paper by Cara Farris, of Del Campo High School in Fair Oaks, California, closely follows the framework on page 120.

Television News vs. Radio News: Two Messages for Two Audiences

Recently a Del Campo High School student—a popular high-school cheerleader—passed away due to a rare disease known as meningococcal meningitis, a disease that can be fatal if not treated in its early stage of conception. The two main media that covered this story were the television and radio, which gave two very different presentations of the story. One focused on the disease itself, and the other focused on the personal life of the cheerleader.

The television coverage of this event consisted of formal interviews with doctors and various school administrators. These reports discussed what the disease meningococcal meningitis was, how it was contracted, if it was contagious, and how this disease could affect those in contact with the ill student. They also reported what a person should do once he or she had contracted this disease. The news reporters focused on the disease rather than the deceased student.

Radio coverage differed in a substantial way. One nearby radio station invited the student's junior varsity cheerleading squad down to its office. This interview consisted of eight girls sitting around several microphones and chatting about fond memories of their friend—her past, her personality, things she had accomplished, and the funny experiences they had with her. Also, many listeners called in to dedicate songs in her memory.

Not only was there a large difference between the formats of the two presentations but also between the time period of each different presentation. The informal interview at the radio station lasted for over an hour, unlike the two- to three-minute television presentation. In my opinion, the short television broadcast led to a less in-depth report. I believe that those who listened to the radio broadcaster got a better idea of the personality and life of the deceased student. Basically the television broadcasters focused on what the majority of the public needed to know but the radio broadcasters focused on what the young generation of listeners needed to hear.

Interesting opener

Thesis statement

Block method—first subject

Supporting details

Second subject

Supporting details

Additional comparison

Final impression

Restatement of thesis

Revising

Evaluate and Revise Your Draft

All Systems Go   Now is the time to make sure that your essay follows the style and purpose you decided on in prewriting. As you evaluate and revise your draft, work collaboratively with a peer to do at least two readings. In your first reading, focus on the content and organization, using the guidelines below. In your second reading, concentrate on the style, using the guidelines on page 126.

➤ **First Reading: Content and Organization**   In your first reading, make sure all of your paper's parts complement each other and work together. Use the following chart to evaluate and revise your essay.

Comparison-Contrast Essay: Content and Organization Guidelines for Peer and Self-Evaluation

Evaluation Questions	▶ Tips	▶ Revision Techniques
❶ Does the introduction grab the audience's attention?	**Circle** the introductory question, statement, detail, or anecdote intended to catch readers' interest. If no words are circled, revise.	**Add** a statement, detail, question, or anecdote that will capture the audience's interest. **Delete** repetitive or ineffective phrases.
❷ Does the introduction provide needed background information and contain a clear thesis statement?	**Underline** the background information. **Draw a box** around the thesis statement. Revise if either element is missing.	**Add** background information that your audience will need. **Add** a thesis statement near the end of the first paragraph or early in the second paragraph.
❸ Are the main points clearly organized?	**Number** the main points. For the block method and point-by-point method, the order of organization should be the same for both subjects, A and B. Revise if any points are out of order.	**Rearrange** your material according to one of the two methods. Be sure that you treat the ideas and the subjects in the same sequence in each section.
❹ Are the main points supported by sufficient details? Are all of the supporting details relevant to the thesis?	**Bracket** the supporting information for each main point. If any points do not have bracketed support, revise.	**Elaborate** on your main points, using facts, examples, and quotations to provide convincing support. **Delete** points that are not relevant.
❺ Does the conclusion summarize the main points in the body? Does it leave a strong final impression?	**Draw dashes** under the summary of main points in the conclusion. **Draw a wavy line** under the final impression. If either is missing, revise.	**Add** a brief summary of the support for the thesis. If appropriate, **add** an evaluation of the relative merits of the media coverage. **Add** a strong closing image or idea.

ONE WRITER'S REVISIONS Here is how one writer used the content-and-organization guidelines to revise the first paragraph of the essay on page 121. Study the revisions and answer the questions following the paragraph.

> When U.S. Senator John Glenn soared into space aboard the space shuttle <u>Discovery</u>, a full thirty-six years after his first trip, comparisons were inevitable. ~~He had flown decades earlier and was now going to fly again.~~ **[delete]** The Cold War had ended, the Information Age had begun, and the astronaut-turned-senator seemed to be challenging not the Soviets but our society's notions about age. *One thing had not changed, however: America's yearning for a hero.* **[add]** The TV cameras, always eager for a larger-than-life drama, did not disappoint the nation. Only a few voices, *mostly in the print media,* **[add]** ventured to raise some pointed questions in the midst of all the cheers.

Analyzing the Revision Process

1. Why did the writer cut a sentence?
2. What information did the writer add to the thesis statement? What is the effect of the addition?

YOUR TURN 7 — Focusing on Content and Organization

Revise the content and organization of your essay, using the guidelines on the previous page. Use the revisions above as a model.

Second Reading: Style In the second reading of your draft, focus on specific issues of style. For example, in attempting to provide your audience with all of the information they need, you may have overused adjective clauses that begin with *who, which,* or *that.*

Example:
John Glenn, *who served in the U.S. Senate for twenty-four years,* was the American astronaut *who orbited the Earth in 1962.*

PEER REVIEW

Ask a classmate to read your essay and to answer the following questions.

1. Does the essay clearly explain the event and the coverage of the event? Note any parts or sentences that are unclear.
2. What did you learn about the strengths and weaknesses of different media forms?

When you have an overdose of *who, which,* or *that* clauses, vary your sentences by changing some clauses to phrases. Use the following guidelines to vary your sentence structure.

Style Guidelines

Evaluation Question	▶ Tip	▶ Revision Technique
Have I used too many adjective clauses that begin with *who, which,* or *that*?	▶ **Underline** any *who, which,* or *that* clauses. If more than three clauses per paragraph are underlined, revise. Try to use only one adjective clause per sentence.	▶ **Change** some of the clauses to phrases, and experiment with the placement of the phrases.

Sentences

Reference Note

For more on **adjective clauses,** see page 578.

Changing Adjective Clauses to Phrases

Whenever you address an audience, one challenge is to keep the audience interested in your message. You can lose your audience by not being concise—by repeating the same sentence structure over and over. You want your sentences to flow together smoothly and to emphasize the most important ideas. You can accomplish both of these goals by sometimes changing clauses to phrases.

Adjective clauses are word groups that contain a subject and a verb and that modify a noun. Adjective clauses that begin with *who, which,* or *that* modify another noun (or pronoun) in the same sentence. Too many adjective clauses can be hard to follow in part because they separate the subject of the main clause from its verb. Look at the following example.

> Walter Cronkite, **who was once known as "the most trusted man in America,"** was one of the war correspondents **who covered the Nuremberg trials after World War II.**

Changing one of the clauses to a phrase not only shortens the sentence a bit, but it also allows you to rejoin the subject of the main clause and its verb. The revised sentence sounds much less awkward. Note that in the revised sentence, the phrase has been repositioned, too.

> **Once known as "the most trusted man in America,"** Walter Cronkite was one of the war correspondents who covered the Nuremberg trials after World War II.

ONE WRITER'S REVISIONS Here is how the writer of the model essay on page 121 used the Style Guidelines above to reduce one of her adjective clauses to a phrase. Note, in her revision, that the verb *sounded* has been changed to *sounding*, but that this change does not affect the meaning of the sentence.

BEFORE REVISION

Many Channel 11 anchors, <u>who sounded grateful for the story's</u>

<u>upbeat themes</u>, openly contrasted the flight with the day's dis-

turbing or destructive events.

Adjective clause separates subject of main clause from its verb.

AFTER REVISION

Sounding grateful for the story's upbeat themes, Channel 11's anchors openly contrasted the flight with the day's disturbing or destructive events.

Change the clause to a phrase and move it to avoid dividing the subject from the verb

---

Analyzing the Revision Process

1. How does the revision change the emphasis of the sentence?

2. What words and punctuation marks are eliminated in the revision?

YOUR TURN 8 **Focusing on Style**

Use the guidelines on page 126 to identify and correct any overuse of adjective clauses in your essay.

Designing Your Writing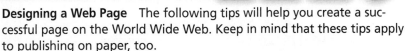

Designing a Web Page   The following tips will help you create a successful page on the World Wide Web. Keep in mind that these tips apply to publishing on paper, too.

- **Choose an attractive combination of text and graphics.** Set off your text with helpful graphics and make sure that text and graphics are balanced on the page—up and down, left and right. Use a wallpaper or background pattern that doesn't clash with your design or obscure your text.

- **Keep your pages short and well proportioned.** Long pages require your readers to do too much scrolling. Pages with too many graphics take a long time to download and may look cluttered; pages with no graphics look dull and may appear more difficult to read.

- **Arrange your page with attention to tone and theme.** If your page spoofs the media coverage of your school's disastrous football season, use bright colors and funny graphics that link to the theme. If your page analyzes the media coverage of a vanishing wilderness area, take a more understated approach, perhaps using personal photographs and graphics of the animals. (If you use graphics, photos, or video from another media source, be sure to seek permission before you include them on your page.) Look at how the following page from a NASA Web site is arranged.

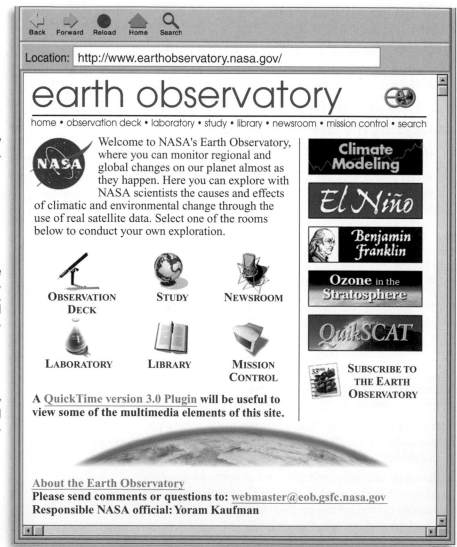

Text is short, easy to read.

Graphics are interesting, thematically related, and well balanced on the page.

Page provides many informative and helpful links.

Publishing

Proofread Your Essay

Critiquing the Critique   You have taken on the role of media critic and analyst, and your audience in turn will be analyzing *your* essay. Careless errors may make them think that your analysis is also careless. Be your own toughest critic, finding any minor—or major—mistakes *before* you publish your essay. You might also work **collaboratively** to help edit and refine the essays of your peers. As you proofread, one error you should look for is a lack of parallelism.

Reference Note

For more on **parallel structure,** see page 426.

Grammar Link

Using Parallel Structure

In a comparison-contrast essay, you want to compare and contrast ideas clearly but concisely. Using parallel structure can help to make comparisons clear. You create **parallel structure** in a sentence by using the same grammatical *form* to express two or more equal, or parallel, ideas. For example, you pair a noun with a noun, a phrase with a phrase, a clause with a clause, or an infinitive with an infinitive.

Not Parallel   Is entertainment news considered more important than reporting on sports competitions? [noun paired with gerund phrase]

Parallel   Is entertainment news considered more important than **sports news**? [noun paired with noun]

Not Parallel   Local news anchors seem more interested in complaining about the weather than to report the latest news. [gerund phrase as object of preposition paired with infinitive phrase]

Parallel   Local news anchors seem more interested **in complaining about the weather** than **in reporting the latest news.** [two gerund

phrases as objects of prepositions]

Not Parallel   To swim, running, and bicycling are good exercise. [infinitive and two gerunds]

Parallel   **Swimming, running,** and **bicycling** are good exercise. [three gerunds]

PRACTICE

On your own paper, revise each of the following sentences by putting parallel ideas in the same grammatical form. Add, delete, or replace words as necessary.

1. Several people in a recent study said that they got their news by listening to the radio or on the Web.

2. Watching the national TV newscasts is generally more informative than local TV news.

3. To know the facts and understanding the story are, surprisingly, often two different things.

4. Being able to define *news* is not only helpful in understanding a medium's presentation but also to analyze the presentation.

5. Listening critically to the news on the radio is just as important as to watch the TV news critically.

Publish Your Essay

To the Presses—or TV Screen, or Computer . . . Find an audience for your comparison-contrast essay by considering your media options. Here are some ways you can publish your essay.

TIP If you have written your essay for a general audience, try refining it for a more specific set of readers—a media watchdog group, for example. As you revise, always keep in mind what your audience already knows about the topic and what they need to know.

- Submit your essay to your school newspaper. If your school has an internal TV system, you might present your essay as a speech. If your school maintains a Web site, consider posting your essay there.

- Publish your essay in one of the media it addresses. If your essay compares Web coverage and print coverage, for example, focus on possibilities within those two media. Be sure to consider online journals as well as print publications. You might even set up your own Web page or use a desktop publishing program to print your own newsletter.

- Ask a librarian to help you find addresses and submission guidelines for several magazines that cover the media. Make sure your essay meets each publication's requirements, and then submit it.

Reflect on Your Essay

PORTFOLIO

What Have You Learned? Think about what you have learned by writing your essay. Jot short responses to the following questions.

- How did learning about the characteristics of various media help you analyze the coverage of an event?

- What was the most surprising thing you learned from comparing and contrasting coverage of a specific event?

- Consider one of the various media portrayals you analyzed. If you had been the reporter, would you have presented the story differently?

- How will you use your skills in comparing and contrasting media coverage in the future?

TIP Accumulating your essays in a portfolio will allow you the chance to review your work. As you look back, you can pinpoint your strengths and weaknesses and set writing goals for yourself.

 Proofreading, Publishing, and Reflecting

Review each of the preceding steps. Before you turn in your essay, make sure to

- proofread your essay carefully
- consider publishing options
- reflect on what you have learned while writing your essay

Connections to Life

Comparing and Contrasting Television Entertainment Genres

Thousands of years ago, Greek drama originated with ancient rituals honoring Dionysus, the god of revelry. The Greeks classified plays into two categories, comedy and tragedy. This system of classification helped shape Shakespeare's career and continues even today.

Laughter or Tears? A **tragedy,** such as Shakespeare's *Romeo and Juliet,* depicts serious and important events, and its main character comes to an unhappy or disastrous end. A **comedy,** such as Shakespeare's *A Midsummer Night's Dream,* tells a lighter story and ends happily. Tragedies and comedies may address similar themes, but because they have different purposes, they employ different techniques. A

tragedy seeks to arouse viewers' fear and pity; a comedy aims to entertain.

Examples of both genres are as close as your TV screen, in the form of "sitcoms"—or situational comedies—and nighttime dramas. (A **genre** is a type of work that has a set of identifiable characteristics; other TV genres are soap operas, mysteries, game shows, and news.) Sitcoms and nighttime dramas may take place in similar settings, and they often treat similar human experiences, but each has its own purpose and characteristics. Take a look at their similarities and differences in the following chart. Also consider whether the sitcoms and dramas you watch contain these features.

Television Genre	
Sitcoms	**Nighttime dramas**
▪ Purpose: to entertain	▪ Purpose: to entertain; to invite a thoughtful or emotional response
▪ Running time: 30 minutes, including commercials	▪ Running time: one hour, including commercials
▪ Ensemble cast (company made up of the same actors week after week): characters are usually a family or group of friends or co-workers	▪ Ensemble cast: characters are family, friends, or co-workers
▪ Two or more plots per episode; usually one main plot, one minor	▪ Many plots per episode; plots continued from one episode to the next
▪ Subject: relationships, accidents, misunderstandings, gags	▪ Subject: important, often life-and-death, decisions and conflicts
▪ Settings: limited; usually a home or workplace	▪ Settings: not as limited; often a hospital, a police department, a home, or several sites within a community
▪ Tone: light and humorous	▪ Tone: serious, with some comic relief

A Mirror to Real Life Why have these two genres—comedy and drama—survived for so long? What do they reveal about human experience? You can investigate these questions by writing a brief comparison-contrast essay on a sitcom and a nighttime drama. The following chart shows one student's early notes for a comparison-contrast of two shows, along with a thesis statement.

Characteristic	Sitcom: "Life in the Big City"	Nighttime drama: "The Cutting Edge"
Setting	• the house of a family of five	• a hospital
Characters	• usually silly or shallow, sometimes multidimensional	• complex, realistic characters with tough problems
Main Plot	• a family's teenage daughter lies about being on the swim team to impress a guy	• a teenage girl is brought to the emergency room after a serious car accident; her vital signs are low
Tone	• silly, outrageously funny	• serious, emotional, sad
Theme	• lying gets one into trouble	• reckless driving can have tragic effects
Outcome	• the guy learns the truth about the girl, but it turns out he has lied, too	• episode ends with girl in a coma; to be continued next week

Comparison-contrast thesis: In both shows, a teenage girl makes a mistake and pays a price; in the sitcom, the mistake is negligible and the price inconsequential, but in the nighttime drama, the mistake is life threatening and the potential price the ultimate one—life itself.

To gather enough information for your own essay, you will want to take more extensive notes than those shown above. For example, you should note any subplots and describe the setting and the characters more fully. Videotaping the shows you are analyzing may help you take more complete notes—you can rewind to capture things you missed in your first viewing.

YOUR TURN 10 Comparing and Contrasting Television Entertainment Genres

Compare and contrast a sitcom and a nighttime drama of your choice. Take the following steps.

- Take notes as you watch one episode from each show.
- Use a chart like the one above to compare and contrast the shows.
- Write a brief comparison-contrast essay to share with your classmates.

Conducting Interviews for a News Story

Talk   Listen

An auto racer reacts to winning the Daytona 500. A relief worker recounts efforts to ease a famine. You probably hear or read dozens of interviews like these every week. No matter what the medium—television, radio, newspaper, or the Internet—journalists rely on interviews to get facts from people in the know. A good interview may seem effortless, but it actually requires careful preparation. In this workshop, you will learn how to conduct your own interview and then use this information to prepare an interesting, credible news story.

WHAT'S AHEAD?

In this section, you will learn to
■ **prepare interview questions**
■ **conduct an interview**
■ **incorporate interview information into a news report**

Identify Sources

Who Has the Scoop? How did a local music group get its first recording contract? How does the city time the traffic lights on Main Street? What caused the fire at a local chemical plant? Here's your chance to find out. Choose an event or situation to investigate through interviews.

Once you have decided on a story, identify several people who are likely sources. Most news reports use two types of information sources, primary and secondary. Plan to use **primary sources**—people who have direct experience with the subject—to find and report the facts. You can also use **secondary sources**—people who are knowledgeable about the subject—to react to, interpret, analyze, and evaluate the event.

Make sure your sources are reliable ones. A **reliable source** is a person who knows the facts of the matter, whether firsthand or through careful study. Less reliable sources are people who may only know about the issue or event through rumor or other media reports. For example, to find out why a local community college raised its tuition, one writer decided to interview the president of the college.

Once you have a list of potential interview subjects, choose one or two people to interview. Call your interviewee(s) a couple of weeks ahead of time to schedule an appointment, and be sure to explain how long, approximately, the interview will take.

Reference Note

For more on **primary** and **secondary sources,** see page 240.

Prepare the Questions

TIP You can ask more informed, relevant questions if you research your subject and then spend some time considering the issues involved. For more on **research strategies,** see page 252.

Do Your Homework   The quality of information you get will depend on the quality of the questions you ask. To prepare for your interview, brainstorm a list of questions. Start with the basics: *Who? What? When? Where? Why?* and *How?* Then, use the list below to think of other questions.

- **What is it?** Ask for a definition of your story's subject. Ask whether it can be broken down into parts, and what other ideas, problems, or policies are related to it.

- **How does it work?** Ask whom the idea, problem, or policy affects or influences and what its consequences are likely to be.

- **What is its history?** Ask when and by whom the idea, problem, or policy was originated. What people and factors contributed to it? How has it developed over time? What alternatives are available?

- **Why is it important?** Ask whether the idea, problem, or policy makes people's lives better or worse, and how. Is it part of a larger trend? How important is it compared with similar ideas, problems, or policies?

Just as important as knowing what you want to ask is framing your questions in a way that will prompt your interviewee to provide the information you want. The following chart shows four different kinds of questions.

Types of Interview Questions		
Type of Question	**Description**	**Example**
Open Question	encourages a person to talk at length, to share feelings and impressions	"What do you feel is Central Community College's mission?"
Closed Question	can be answered with "yes" or "no" or a few words; used to obtain specific information quickly	"Has Central Community College raised its tuition by $25 per class?"
Neutral Question	promotes objectivity by giving the interviewee no hint of the answer you want	"What factors led to the decision to raise the tuition?"
Follow-up Question	probes for additional information about a previous question	"How will the tuition increase affect the college's mission?"

Plan to ask easily answered questions first, and questions calling for more complex answers later. Be sure to allow time at the end for the interviewee to clarify any earlier answers and to make additional comments.

TIP   Avoid using **leading questions,** which suggest the response you expect or desire. For example, "Didn't Central Community College raise its tuition in order to build a new basketball court?" is a leading question. Such questions bias an interview toward the interviewer's interpretation of events.

Conducting the Interview

Ask Away   Do you have your list of questions in hand and clear directions to your meeting place? Have you tested the tape or video recorder you plan to use and gathered extra pens, tapes, and batteries? If so, you are ready to go. As you conduct the interview, keep the following tips in mind.

- **Be a welcome guest.** Start by introducing yourself and thanking your interviewee for taking time to talk with you.

- **Listen well.** Maintain eye contact, nod to show that you have heard and understood, and convey interest and respect through body language. Even if you disagree with what your interviewee is saying, be courteous. After your interviewee has answered a question, briefly summarize the answer in your own words to confirm that you have understood correctly. If you have not understood, be sure to ask questions that clarify the answer.

- **Record the interview carefully.** You may choose to take notes during the interview or to make an audio or video recording. If you are making audio or video recordings, ask your interviewee's permission ahead of time and make sure you are familiar with your equipment so that you can set it up quickly and efficiently.

Let It Roll   If you are videotaping the interview, keep the following factors in mind. Camera angles and your choice of shots can affect the message you are trying to communicate.

- **Use a straight camera angle.** Do not angle the camera up or down at your interviewee. Such angles often imply an attitude about your subject: Shooting from below often suggests that your subject is powerful or authoritative, while shooting from above often indicates your subject is weak or childlike. To avoid this sort of subtle bias, film your subject from eye level.

- **Use reaction shots, if appropriate.** If you will appear on camera, have the person doing the taping capture your interaction with the interviewee, occasionally cutting back to you while you listen and nod.

> **TIP**   Also, avoid shining a bright light directly in your interviewee's eyes. Use even, medium-level light.

Presenting the Interview

Weave It In   It is a long way from an interview to a finished news story. Preparing a transcript of the interview will help you decide where to use quotes in your story and where to summarize information. Use your notes, audiotape, or videotape to produce a transcript in question-and-answer form. Look at the sample on the next page.

> **TIP**   Always write a thank-you note to anyone you interview. If possible, offer to provide a copy of the finished news story—and be sure to follow through.

Reference Note
For more on **listening,** see page 1029.

Reference Note
For more on types of **camera shots,** see page 91.

Q: What factors led to Central Community College's decision to increase its tuition?

A: Central Community College is experiencing a huge increase in the demand for its services. Not only are we called on to serve ten percent more students each semester, but those students want new programs in a variety of fields, such as computer technology. Over the past two years, we have added two new departments. Our old tuition just didn't cover the costs.

Now, you are ready to edit—to choose those parts of your interview that are important for your readers or viewers to hear. (Essential quotes are those that are especially memorable or that supply important evidence that would be less credible if it were just summarized.) As you write your news report, remember to create a context for your readers by providing any necessary background information; you should also introduce your subject (and yourself, if you are videotaping).

- For a video, write and film an introduction, or "setup." Use editing equipment (if available) to cut unimportant material or to break up a lengthy interview with your own summary or explanations.

- For an article, summarize some of the information and include only important quotations. Whether you summarize or quote, however, make sure to include answers to the *5W-How?* questions—*Who?, What?, When?, Where?, Why?,* and *How?* Compare the following paragraph from a final news story with the transcript above.

Although Central Community College's tuition increase may cause a hardship for some students, it appears to be necessary. Business is booming at CCC, with enrollment up ten percent each semester and demand for new offerings in fields such as computer technology. "Over the past two years, we have added two new departments," explains President Tomasco. "Our old tuition just didn't cover the costs."

YOUR TURN 11 **Conducting Interviews**

Use the preceding steps to conduct at least one interview and create your own news story. You may choose to write an article or produce a video. When you have completed your report, be sure to publish it by sharing it with classmates, family, or community members.

Choices

Choose one of the following activities to complete.

▶ **MEDIA AND TECHNOLOGY**

1. Whose News Do You Choose? Identify five sources of news on the Web, including sites maintained by traditional media such as newspapers and TV stations or networks. Evaluate each source on the depth and accuracy of its news as well as on the effectiveness of its use of the Web (for example, the use of links to related stories, graphics, and video clips). Rank the sites from best to worst, and present your **Five Web Sites List,** with brief descriptions of each site, to the rest of the class.

▶ **VIEWING AND REPRESENTING**

2. Home-grown News Survey Form a group with two other students. Each group member should choose a different local TV news station and, for one week, monitor the types of stories, the sequence in which they are presented, and the amount of time spent on each. As a group, decide on how each of you will categorize the stories (for example, crime news, human interest, sports, weather). Compile your statistics into **charts** or **graphs,** and present your results to the rest of the class in an **oral report.**

▶ **LITERATURE**

3. News with the Muse? Many works of literature present the reader with a particular way of looking at historical events— Shakespeare's historical plays, for example. Choose a work of fiction, poetry, or drama that recounts or responds to a historical event, and compare and contrast it with the historical record. You might also choose a famous piece of nonfiction, such as Daniel Defoe's account of the London plague of 1665. What are the facts? What is the writer's purpose, point of view, and (if applicable) bias? How does the writer's interpretation affect your understanding of the event? Post a **brief essay** on the class bulletin board.

▶ **CAREERS**

4. Nine to Five News Journalists are not the only professionals who write factual reports on events and developments. In many jobs, reports are written to explain a project's progress, to analyze a recent development, or to recommend the direction of future research. Choose a career field that interests you, and write a short **report** on a recent development in that field. Use at least two or three factual sources.

PORTFOLIO

4 Analyzing Causal Relationships

Reading Workshop

Reading a Causal Analysis
PAGE 140

Writing Workshop

Writing a Causal Analysis
PAGE 152

Focus on Speaking and Listening

Talk   Listen

Creating and Evaluating an Informative Speech
PAGE 175

"Why does the frost turn green grass brown?" "How is hail formed?" "What will happen if a river is diverted from its natural course?" Part of natural curiosity is wanting to know the causes and effects of phenomena you witness in the world around you. In answering these questions, you engage in **causal analysis,** an attempt to explain the causes and effects of events.

As a student, you probably are asked to explain causes and effects all the time. "What *caused* the Gunpowder Plot of 1605?" "What is the *effect* of multiplying both sides of an equation by the same number?" Professionals in a variety of fields also analyze causes and effects: "What *causes* the flu?" "What are the *effects* of a downturn in the U.S. stock market?"

Sometimes causes and effects are obvious; other times, events have hidden causes and effects. In this chapter you will focus on causal analysis in science. That means you will think about both natural phenomena, like lightning, and trends, like global warming, from a scientific point of view.

internet**connect**

go.
hrw
.com
GO TO: go.hrw.com
KEYWORD: EOLang 12-4

YOUR TURN 1   Brainstorming Cause-and-Effect Situations

Browse through newspapers to find current events which lend themselves to causal analysis. For example, what meteorological conditions caused the gale force of Hurricane Andrew (in 1992) and what effects did its destruction have on the economy of South Florida? List at least five situations and brainstorm the possible causes and effects for each one. Discuss your findings in a small group.

Reading a Causal Analysis

In this section, you will read a magazine article and learn how to

- identify stated and implied causes and effects
- analyze cause-and-effect structures

READING SKILL

READING FOCUS

You don't have to be a rocket scientist to have a use for causal analysis. Science-related topics are everywhere: in the news, in magazines, in the things you see and do every day. If you have ever noticed the colors of fall leaves, then you know the origins of the article you are about to read. In "The Value of Autumn Leaves," the writer examines several cause-and-effect relationships related to the changes in leaves that occur each fall.

Preparing to Read

Explicit and Implied Cause and Effect   When you read the following article, you will learn how one phenomenon can have many causes, how multiple effects can stem from one cause, and how intricate cause-and-effect chains can be. As you read, look for clue words that will help you follow an **explicit,** or overtly stated, cause-and-effect chain—words such as *reason, as a result,* and *consequently.* When clue words are not evident, use logic and your prior knowledge to figure out **implied,** or indirectly stated, causes and effects; ask yourself, "How do these things *seem* to be related?"

Cause-and-Effect Structures   Mapping the cause-and-effect relationships described in an article can help you to understand both the content and the organization of the piece. Below, you will find graphic organizers of the **three basic cause-and-effect structures**—focus on causes, focus on effects, and a causal chain.

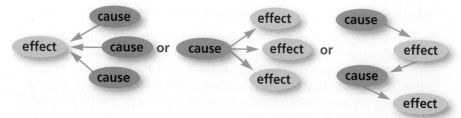

Keep these diagrams in mind when you read the following article. Also look for more complicated combinations of the three structures.

As you read, try to identify the cause-and-effect relation-ships. Also, jot down answers to the numbered active-reading questions.

from National Wildlife

The Value of Autumn Leaves

by Richard Busch   Photographs by Whit Bronaugh

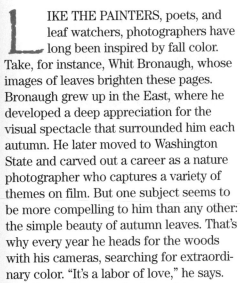

LIKE THE PAINTERS, poets, and leaf watchers, photographers have long been inspired by fall color. Take, for instance, Whit Bronaugh, whose images of leaves brighten these pages. Bronaugh grew up in the East, where he developed a deep appreciation for the visual spectacle that surrounded him each autumn. He later moved to Washington State and carved out a career as a nature photographer who captures a variety of themes on film. But one subject seems to be more compelling to him than any other: the simple beauty of autumn leaves. That's why every year he heads for the woods with his cameras, searching for extraordinary color. "It's a labor of love," he says.

He is, of course, far from alone. Getting out for the annual extravaganza is a joyful experience for millions—especially for those of us who live and work in heavily populated places where the colors are mostly those of concrete, steel, and glass. I know something about that, having lived for one period of my life in Manhattan. Every October, religiously, I would head north with my wife to Vermont to spend a weekend in the embrace of autumn.

During those outings, the sun seemed particularly brilliant, the skies intensely blue—a perfect backdrop for the hues that adorned the maples, birches, and other plants of the region. For us, the trips north were both a pilgrimage and a desperately needed escape.

Therapists explain that the positive feelings people experience in autumn are hardly exclusive to those who wander in the woods. Studies show that fall colors have a mood-elevating effect on just about anyone, anywhere. "Put people in a room decorated with certain shades of red and they immediately feel less aggression and a sense of tranquillity," says Bernard Vittone, director of the National Center for Treatment of Phobias, Anxiety, and Depression in Washington, D.C.

Like many other psychiatrists, Vittone believes a walk in the woods during autumn can be therapeutic. "We encourage our patients to take advantage of fall color," he notes. "A drive in the country makes people feel better, takes their mind off their troubles."

Autumn can also stimulate scientific

1. Why does the writer use "I" in the second paragraph?

musings: What causes leaves to change color in the first place? Where does the color come from? Does the change have a practical purpose in nature's scheme of things? And why are the colors spectacular one year, but in another just so-so?

2. What do these questions lead you to expect in the rest of the article?

Essentially, leaf colors begin to change because chlorophyll—a substance that makes them green—begins to diminish as a result of shorter days and cooler weather. As daylight shortens, the growth system in many trees begins to shut down. Tiny cells at the base of each leaf, known as the abscission layer, begin to dry out, chlorophyll dissipates,[1] and the photosynthesis process comes to a halt.

The colors that now begin to emerge are actually present in the leaves all year long; they are pigments masked by the chlorophyll during the warmer months. The yellows of such species as birch,

3. What process causes leaf colors to change?

aspen, and hickory are caused by carotene, the same pigment that gives color to corn, carrots, and egg yolks. The autumn reds and maroons in sugar maples, sumac, and other species derive from the pigment anthocyanin, formed from sugar compounds stored in the leaves. This chemical's effect on color depends on the acidity or alkalinity of the tree. Red maples, which are more acidic, turn red; ash trees, being alkaline, become purplish.

While scientists understand what causes the leaves to change color, they know virtually nothing about why they change. What role does this phenomenon play in nature's broad scheme of things?

The answer may be none at all. In his book *Leaves: Their Amazing Lives and Strange Behavior*, researcher James Poling writes: "This is both surprising and puzzling, since nature seldom wastes energy to no purpose. Yet as far as botanists can determine, the chemical energy that goes into the painting of a leaf is of no benefit at all to the plant. The colors seem merely to herald the end of a leaf's life cycle."

Caught in a whirlpool, quaking aspen leaves spin in a forest stream.

While the phenomenon of autumn foliage may not have a purpose in nature's grand scheme, falling leaves (regardless of color) do perform an important role in forest ecology. As leaves decompose, they release carbon, nitrogen, and other chemicals, providing nourishment to the soil that tree roots can assimilate[2] the following season. Falling leaves also play an important role in forest stream ecology: As the

---

1. **dissipate:** break up and scatter, disperse

2. **assimilate:** absorb, to change (food) into a form that can be used (as nourishment)

4. What role do wet leaves have in forest stream ecology?

5. What are the possible causes of sugar maple decline? What role might acid rain play?

wet leaves decompose, they are fed on by a group of aquatic insects and crustaceans called shredders—creatures including stone fly nymphs, isopods, and crane fly larvae. Shredders, in turn, are an important food source for fish. Without them, fish would have a tough time of it.

Some years, leaf watchers have a tough time of it, too. That is because fall colors can sometimes be downright dull. The reason has to do with weather. Excellent color requires excellent conditions—a stretch of mostly sunny days and cool, but not freezing, nights. Excessive rain, a prolonged period of drought, or an early freeze can each diminish autumn leaf color.

Meteorological vagaries,[3] however, are not the only threats to widespread autumn color. Since the early 1980s scientists have noted that in some areas of the country, sugar maples and some other species of trees have been declining. The result is wide swaths of dead and dying sugar maples, marring otherwise healthy forests. According to Susan Stout, a U.S. Forest Service researcher in Pennsylvania, 400,000 acres across the state's northern tier have been affected in recent years by such a blight, including about 90,000 acres of the Allegheny National Forest.

Scientists at the Environmental Resources Research Institute (ERRI) at Pennsylvania State University have found several possible causes for the sugar maple decline, including repeated attacks by pests, competition from invasive plants, and low nutrient availability. The latter

may be due in part to acid rain. "Acidification of the soil removes nutrients that are important to a tree's health," says ERRI researcher Patrick Drohan. "And to compound the situation, acid rain allows other harmful elements, such as aluminum, to increase in the soil solution, which can then become toxic to the tree's roots."

Because the problem is so complex, with so many possible causes, finding definitive answers can be tricky. "Acid rain, for instance, is a provable phenomenon," notes Drohan, "but the magnitude of its impact is hard to determine. We just don't know what role it plays in the big picture."

There is even uncertainty about the extent of the decline of sugar maples. Some woodlands that appeared to be hard hit a few years ago are now looking much better, leading some observers to suspect that much of the damage may be only a short-term problem rather than a sign of a long-range trend. One recent joint study between the United States and Canada—the North American Maple Project—concluded that in the last few years the annual mortality rate for sugar maples was "normal." Which, if so, is great news for photographers like Whit Bronaugh and leaf watchers like myself.

For those of us who eagerly await the annual autumn spectacle, there is little need for scientific explanations about what purpose changing leaf colors play in the environment. That it happens is perhaps reason enough to marvel at the power and unpredictability of nature.

---

3. **vagary:** an unexpected action

| READING SKILL

Explicit and Implied Cause-and-Effect Relationships

It's Obvious—Or Is It?   You are reading along when the clue word *cause* pops out at you. You know the clue word means that a cause and effect relationship is right there in front of you. If you notice the clue word, you probably can't miss this **explicit,** or directly stated, cause-and-effect relationship. Any of the following words can function as cause-and-effect clue words.

affect	as a result	because
consequently	determines	hence
in order	if . . . then	since

Example:
Because carotene is present, birch and aspen leaves turn yellow.

TIP While **clue words** are quite reliable, remember that sometimes these same words can have meanings and functions that are not related to causes and effects. Neither of the following sentences directly involves causes or effects:

It has been a long time *since* she went to Mexico.

They put the room back *in order.*

In this sentence, the cause-and-effect relationship is made obvious by the clue word *because:* The presence of carotene causes yellow color.

Sometimes the writer does not state the cause-and-effect relationship directly, but instead **implies,** or suggests, it. When this happens, you will have to make an **inference,** or an educated guess, about this relationship. An inference is based on information in the article and what you already know about the topic. These components can be written as a formula:

article information + prior knowledge = inference

Another way to uncover implicit cause-and-effect relationships is to look carefully at the verbs in a selection. Certain verbs are **causative verbs**—verbs that express a cause-and-effect relationship.

Example:
Excessive rain and long periods of drought can *reduce* the color of autumn leaves.

Reduce is a causative verb meaning *to lessen* or *to make less*. In the sentence on the previous page, excessive rain and drought are the causes which produce the effect of less color in autumn leaves. A cause-and-effect relationship is built into many verbs, often through a prefix suggesting motion. If you are unsure as to whether a verb is causative or not, look it up in a dictionary to see if the definition includes causing or making an effect. Here is a brief list of other causative verbs.

diminish	dissolve	emit	enlarge
expand	force	form	preserve
produce	refine	satisfy	yield

TIP Still one more way to identify cause-and-effect relationships is to look for certain **suffixes** (like the ones below) which may act as indicators of changes, causes, or effects.

Suffix	Meaning	Example
–ic	causing, producing	hypnotic
–ate	become, cause, form	aggravate
–ation	the result of something	compilation

THINKING IT THROUGH   **Implied Cause and Effect**

To figure out an implied cause or effect, you can use the steps listed below. The example responses are based on the following sentence.

An increase in the amount of carbon dioxide in the atmosphere raises worldwide temperatures.

▶ **STEP 1 Ask: "What happened?" (What's the effect?)** *Temperatures all over the world are rising.*

▶ **STEP 2 Ask: "Why?" (What's the cause?)** *The cause is an increase in the amount of carbon dioxide in the atmosphere.*

▶ **STEP 3 Ask: "What can be inferred?"** Make inferences using what is in the text and your prior knowledge. Create a chain if you can. Are there some missing causes or effects that are implied? *Carbon dioxide must play a special role in heat absorption in the atmosphere.*

▶ **STEP 4 Ask: "What direct cause-and-effect statement can be made?"** *Because of carbon dioxide's heat-absorbing properties, an increase in the amount of carbon dioxide in the atmosphere is the cause of rising worldwide temperatures.*

Read the excerpted statements from Busch's essay that appear below. Then, from the following list identify the items which apply to each statement.

- a clue word, if one exists
- a causative verb, if one exists
- an explicit or implied cause
- an explicit or implied effect

To identify implied cause-and-effect relationships, use the steps on page 145. Also, find any causative suffixes. Here is a student example.

> Acidification of the soil removes nutrients that are important to a tree's health.
>
>> **causative verb:** *removes*
>>
>> **implied cause:** *acidification of soil*
>>
>> **implied effect:** *soil loses nutrients*

1. Studies show that fall colors have a mood-elevating effect on just about anyone, anywhere.

2. A drive in the country makes people feel better, takes their mind off their troubles.

3. Essentially, leaf colors begin to change because chlorophyll—a substance that makes them green—begins to diminish as a result of shorter days and cooler weather.

4. Excellent color requires excellent conditions—a stretch of mostly sunny days and cool, but not freezing, nights.

5. Excessive rain, a prolonged period of drought, or an early freeze can each diminish autumn leaf color.

READING FOCUS

Cause-and-Effect Organizational Structures

Map It Out   A causal analysis explains the relationship between causes and effects—simple enough. However, some cause-and-effect relationships are more complex than others. One cause can have several effects, one effect can have several causes, one event can cause an effect that becomes a cause for another effect, and so forth. **The order in which these causes and effects are explained, however, is determined by the writer's focus.** Understanding that order, or organization, not to mention the content, can be easier if you use graphic organizers, or concept maps, like the ones on the next page.

Four Types of Structures   The following examples are maps of cause-and-effect structures. Each is a variation on the three basic structures you see portrayed in the margin. These combinations, or hybrids, are examples of the kinds of structures you will find most often in professional writing. Of course, writers must always portray cause-and-effect relationships accurately, but they can also choose to focus in on just one piece—or alter their organizational pattern just a bit for style, impact, or variety. (Note that in all of the following maps, causes are red, effects are blue, and effects which in turn become causes are green.)

Structure 1: Focus on Causes and Effects   In this structure, the central phenomenon is stated; then, both the causes and effects of this phenomenon are explained in the body paragraphs. A reader would map the relationships by placing the phenomenon in the middle, the identifying causes on the left, and the effects on the right.

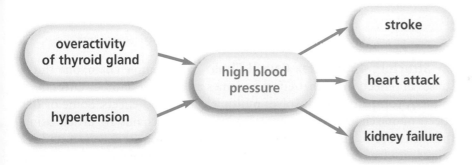

Structure 2: Focus on Sufficient Causes   In this structure, the central effect is often stated in the introduction, and *sufficient* causes are discussed in the body paragraphs. A **sufficient** cause is one that creates the effect *by itself*; sufficient causes do not act in combination—in fact, they usually have nothing to do with one another. An article about how sounds are caused by different musical instruments is an example of focusing on sufficient causes. Such an article could be mapped like this:

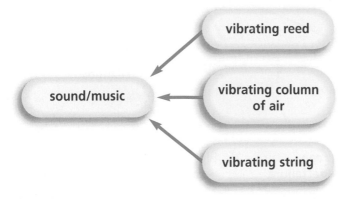

TIP Remember the three basic structures:

1. Focus on Effects

2. Focus on Causes

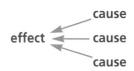

3. Causal Chain

> **Structure 3: Focus on Contributory Causes** This kind of structure is used when an effect is stated in the introduction and then a *combination* of causes are explained in the body paragraphs. A **contributory** cause helps produce an effect but cannot do so alone—it must exist with other causes, often in a specific order. For example, each of the causes in the map below *contributes* to a major forest fire, but any one of them would not create a fire by itself.

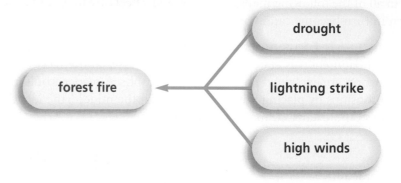

> **Structure 4: Complex Causal Chain** In a simple chain, one thing causes an effect; then, that effect becomes a cause for another effect, and so on. A complex chain involves multiple causes and effects. Some of the effects of one chain become causes leading to other chains. An article using this structure focuses on a *process,* rather than on a single effect and its causes, or vice versa. Essays with this structure often include a wide range of information or discuss a complicated system.

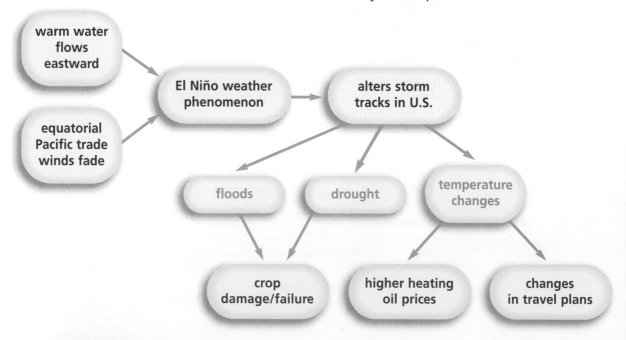

YOUR TURN 3 — Analyzing Cause-and-Effect Structures

To analyze one of the cause-and-effect structures contained in "The Value of Autumn Leaves," re-read the paragraph beginning "Some years, leaf watchers. . . ," on page 143, along with the two paragraphs following it. Copy the map below on your own paper; then, complete it to show the cause-and-effect relationships in these paragraphs. Looking back at your answers to the active-reading and post-selection questions can help.

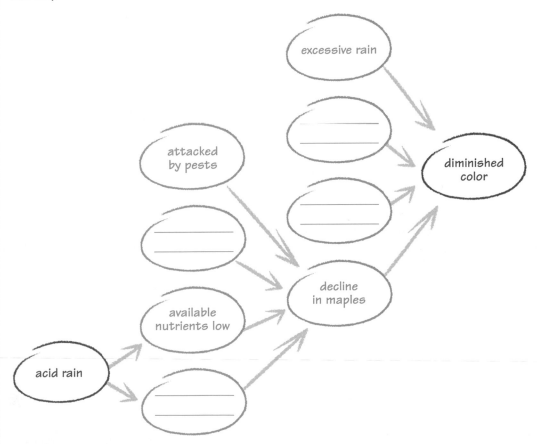

TIP Remember that the first five paragraphs of this article concentrate on people's feelings about autumn leaf color. (You can find some cause-and-effect relationships even in this introductory material.) Then, in the sixth paragraph, the writer asks scientific questions. The rest of the article answers these questions. Each answer involves its own chain, but all the answers are related to the central phenomenon—autumn leaves changing color and falling from the trees.

Cause-and-Effect Context Clues

In reading cause-and-effect articles—especially ones about science—you are bound to stumble onto words that are unfamiliar. You can often figure out the meaning of unfamiliar words by using **context clues:** the words surrounding the unfamiliar word as well as the way the word is used in the sentence. A **cause-and-effect context clue** alerts the reader to a logical relationship between the unfamiliar word and its cause or result.

THINKING IT THROUGH **Using Cause-and-Effect Context Clues**

Take a look at the example sentence and the steps below.

Many doctors believe that looking at autumn leaf colors can be **therapeutic** because it helps people take their minds off their troubles.

▶ **STEP 1 Look for standard cause-and-effect clue words.** Also look for causative verbs and suffixes. *The word because signals a reason (the cause) why the doctors think looking at the leaves is therapeutic. (I see the suffix –ic, which means causing, too.)*

▶ **STEP 2 Use the surrounding context to ask cause-and-effect questions about the unfamiliar word.** *Why do doctors suggest that their patients do something therapeutic? Why is distracting people from their troubles therapeutic?*

▶ **STEP 3 Answer your question and confirm your guess.** *A doctor tries to cure patients, or make them feel better. Therapeutic must have something to do with those activities. The dictionary confirms this guess—the word means "curative."*

PRACTICE

Use the steps above to find the meaning of the italicized words in the following sentences.

1. The beauty of fall colors is a *galvanizing* subject for Whit Bronaugh; consequently, he photographs autumn leaves every year.

2. The greening agent, chlorophyll, begins to *subside* when daylight shortens and the tree's growth system begins to shut down.

3. Autumn leaves are blown by winds, carried by streams, and decomposed by molds and insects, resulting in their complete *disintegration.*

4. Wide tracks of dead and dying sugar maples are *blighting* the otherwise healthy and beautiful forests.

5. Since decaying leaves supply nutrients to the soil that many plants can *absorb,* composted leaves make excellent mulch.

Answering Logic Questions

In nearly everything you read, details have a relationship to one another. **Logic questions** ask the reader to identify *how* details in a passage are related to one another. Clue words in a sentence or paragraph will help you answer logic questions by indicating what kind of relationship is present, whether cause-and-effect or another pattern. Example clue words include *similarly, equally* (comparison); *however, despite* (contrast); *thus, therefore* (cause/effect); and *prior, subsequently* (chronological).

Read the following **passage** and its logic question.

> Many people suppose that when a volcano erupts, lava poses the greatest threat to the surrounding environment. However, ash from the volcano creates greater havoc. In the case of the Mount St. Helens eruption, ash created innumerable problems. When the ash started

sifting to the ground, it coated and infiltrated everything. Visibility was near zero, and gusting winds created drifts of ash nearly four feet high, causing drivers to abandon their cars. The ash seeped into automobile air filters, which not only resulted in cars stalling, but also damaged engines. Because cars skidded into each other on the slick, ash-covered streets, roads were closed until the inches of slippery, dusty ash could be removed.

1. The passage relates that car engines stalled
   A. because the drivers couldn't see and slowed down too much.
   B. when the cars slid into each other.
   C. because ash clogged their air filters.
   D. after the heat from the volcano caused the car engines to overheat.
   E. despite the attempts to remove the ash.

THINKING IT THROUGH   **Answering Logic Questions**

Keep the following steps in mind as you work through the question:

1. **Locate in the passage the specific details mentioned in the question.** Then, look for clue words that show what kind of relationship the details have with other details in the passage. In the sentence about engines, the phrase *resulted in* shows a cause-and-effect relationship. Both **A** and **C** begin with *because,* a cause-and-effect clue word. Answer **E** uses the word *despite* which indicates a contrast, not cause-and-effect, so **E** is incorrect.

2. **Eliminate answers that show the correct relationship but are drawn from other parts of the passage.** The paragraph says

the ash cloud lowered visibility, not that the cars stalled because they went too slowly. The sliding accidents were due to slick roads, not stalled engines. Answers **A** and **B** are incorrect.

3. **Eliminate answer choices that are not relevant.** The passage did not mention cars overheating, so answer **D** is incorrect. By process of elimination, the answer is **C**.

4. **Make sure the remaining answer restates the sentence from the passage.** Answer **C** is correct.

Writing a Causal Analysis

WHAT'S AHEAD?

In this workshop you will write a causal analysis on a science topic. You will also learn how to

- **analyze causes and effects**
- **use maps to organize causes and effects**
- **use inductive thinking**
- **vary sentence length**
- **use logical tense sequences**

Sometimes people demand explanations—and you have to supply them. Suppose you work part-time for an outdoor sign company. After several upset customers complain about rusting signs, your boss says, "Go check out all signs installed this year. Why are some rusting and others not? Write it up for Thursday."

Sometimes *you* want explanations—and your teachers want papers. Suppose your favorite swimming spot was a foul-smelling, gray-watered disappointment last summer. What happened? When your science teacher says, "Investigate something that matters to you," you have a ready-made topic.

To write either report, for work or for school, you would engage in causal analysis of a scientific problem—the kind of thinking and writing this part of the chapter will guide you to do.

Prewriting

Choose and Narrow a Topic

What's Happening?   Things change. You can count on it. One way to begin choosing a topic is to consider changes that interest or puzzle you. When you want to ask *Why?* (seeking causes) or *Now what?* (seeking effects) about an event, phenomenon, or trend, you are homing in on a causal analysis topic. To search for topics, try these suggestions:

- **Look around you.** Remember that science is not all test tubes and labs. Almost every aspect of our lives, from exercise to memory to oil spills, is open to scientific analysis.

- **Scan the science sections** of newspapers and magazines (print or online), and pay attention to the headlines that startle you. What are you *drawn* to read about—health, wildlife, astronomy?

> **TIP** Some changes are distinct phenomena occurring at a particular time, such as a famine after a flood. Other changes are part of long-range trends that involve changes in something over time, such as the current trend toward eating healthful foods.

- **Take stock of local and personal interests** that make you ask *Why has this happened?* or *What will result?* For a few days, keep a record of what you talk about with people. Are you wondering why fog came in overnight? Is your aunt upset that a high-tech coal plant is proposed for the city?

Can You Handle It? In narrowing a cause-effect topic for a brief essay, think about the topic itself, as well as whether you will cover causes, effects, or both. To deal with damage to the Earth's marine life, you could write a book, but probably not a manageable paper. There are just too many elements—from pollution to climate changes, from minnows to whales—to cover. Focusing on causes alone (or on effects alone) still would be too broad. Focusing on a topic such as damage to coral reefs is more manageable—you could tackle both causes and effects, if you'd like.

TIP You might work collaboratively in a small group to narrow your topic. Be sure to make relevant contributions to the discussion about each group member's topic—not just your own.

Identify Your Thesis

Decision Time Now you need a **thesis,** or **main idea,** to guide your research and writing. **In a causal analysis essay, your thesis statement tells readers (and you) about both your topic *and* your focus: causes, effects, or causes and effects.**

 **KEY CONCEPT**

Say that you want to explain the possible extinction of African elephants. You might write a thesis statement that focuses on causes of extinction, its effects, or on its causes and its effects. Some specific examples of thesis statements follow:

Focus on Causes	The lucrative worldwide ivory market may lead to the extinction of African elephants.
Focus on Effects	If African elephants become extinct, an ecosystem will be altered forever.
Focus on Causes and Effects	Among other factors, commerce threatens African elephants with extinction, a loss that would disrupt an entire ecosystem forever.

Something to Go On Think of your first thesis statement as a draft. You can, and probably will, change it as you write, because

- you may not yet have enough information to write a sharply focused thesis statement
- as you learn more, you may even change your focus. Causes, for example, may seem much more interesting than effects.

■ you may discover hidden, or indirect, causes or effects

Although you may refocus it later, a **preliminary thesis** will give you something at which to aim.

Think About Purpose, Audience, Occasion, and Tone

What's It to Them?   Your fundamental **purpose** in writing a scientific causal analysis is to *explain* something to someone. When you explain something, you try to clarify it and supply evidence that supports what you say. An explanation is not valid without sound support, such as facts. Yet who **(audience)** is reading your explanation, and in what circumstances **(occasion),** may have an impact on what and how **(tone)** you write. Thus, **purpose, audience, occasion,** and **tone** are intimately tied in this essay.

TIP Even though in this chapter you are writing an expository essay explaining causes and effects, you can also use cause-and-effect relationships to elaborate your ideas in a **persuasive** essay. For example, you could describe the effects of acid rain in an argument for reducing air pollution.

TIP Avoid details or language that shout "Bias!" Look, for example, at this sentence: "Because of the destruction they cause, divers must stay away from coral reefs no matter how pretty the reefs may be." A sentence like this one overstates the facts and does not consider the research that shows damaging factors other than divers.

THINKING IT THROUGH   Analyzing Audience, Occasion, and Tone

In planning your essay, ask yourself the following questions:

▶ **STEP 1 Who is my audience, and are they listening?** At the least, your audience includes your teacher and your classmates. Even for this familiar group, however, your paper could be written for a timely **occasion;** that is, it might be written to explain or respond to a recent event in the wider world. Coral reefs, for example, are intriguing in themselves, but what if you live in a beach town and a developer has just applied for a permit to build a huge seaside resort? The threat to your town's ecology becomes an occasion for writing. Whatever your topic, thinking about occasion may lead you to other receptive readers: local newspaper readers, city council members, or an Internet newsgroup. If so, try to imagine their perspectives.

▶ **STEP 2 What does my audience already know about this topic? What background or technical information do I need to provide?** For an audience of classmates, use yourself as a gauge for technical background and terms. If you did not know the composition of coral or the meaning of *eutrophication,* then your audience probably does not either.

▶ **STEP 3 What details, approach, and tone will interest my audience? What could turn them off?** Your thinking about purpose, audience, and occasion comes out in the **voice** and **tone** of your writing. No scientific explanation has to be dry. The beauty of coral could capture any reader—as could the comparison of coral reefs to rain forests. Think hard about what your audience *cares* about, and respect the science.

Gather Information

The Hard Truth Before your information dig even starts, this section will help you scout out the ground. Look at the key words of your assignment: *Causal. Analysis. Science.* You need hard facts. Where can you find them? When you do find information, you will need to apply some critical thinking. What questions will you ask? You need to ensure that what you tell readers is scientifically accurate. How will you know?

Identifying Sources Science begins with theories and hypotheses; it leaps forward when they are proven through tests, exploration, or meticulous examination. For this paper, you will need the facts scientists have accumulated through these careful, objective processes. Consider these outside sources:

- **Print Sources** Magazines about science (*Popular Science, Scientific American, Nature, Discover*); books on your specific topic; reference books, both general and specialized (almanacs, encyclopedias, science yearbooks)
- **Cyber Sources** World Wide Web sites (especially those of government, universities, and scientific and professional organizations such as NASA, National Oceanographic and Atmospheric Administration, American Medical Association); online magazines, journals, and reference works
- **Experts** College faculty; local professionals (nutritionists, engineers, dentists, and so on); city and county employees and officials (agricultural agents, utility chiefs, and so on)

While consulting outside sources and experts is necessary, do not overlook your personal experience and knowledge. What you know firsthand about your topic can give your writing **authenticity** and **immediacy.**

COMPUTER TIP

When using a **computer-based card catalogue** or other database to find source listings, use mixed key words or advanced searching language to limit or focus your search. Also, try adding the words *cause* or *effect* to topic key words.

TIP Remember that if you use someone else's *words* or *ideas* without giving that person credit, you are guilty of **plagiarism.** Ask your teacher what style of documentation you should use. Two common styles are the APA (American Psychological Association) and the MLA (Modern Language Association). For more on **documentation,** see page 268.

No Stone Unturned To write a thesis statement, you will have already thought about at least one main cause or effect of your topic. Now you will investigate more thoroughly, using a process that you can picture as a back-and-forth motion: from your own ideas to those you find during research and back again, refining your understanding as you go.

Before you even try to get into the experts' heads, though, look into your own. Think of as many possible causes and effects as you can. Don't ignore any. Your purpose is to present a full explanation, but when you omit

TIP Remember to think about both **sufficient causes** (one cause alone is enough to create an effect) and **contributory causes** (several causes working together create an effect).

TIP It may help to map your answers to the questions in the chart. Think about the causal relationships; then, start with a simple cluster diagram, using as many arrows as needed to indicate causes and effects. For example:

boats
storms → damaged reefs
pollution

a cause or effect, readers may suspect your fairness. For example, if you do not mention that storms damage coral reefs (because, you figure, people cannot control nature), you have nevertheless left out a very real cause.

Some basic questions will help you explore causes and effects, as you will see in the following student notes. (You may ask these questions more than once while thinking, gathering information, and rethinking. Also, remember that natural phenomena and trends do not always have crystal-clear explanations; even experts speculate and disagree.) In the notes below, notice how the student explores causes and effects separately.

TOPIC: DYING CORAL REEFS

Exploring Causes	Ideas, Information
1. What are the obvious causes?	Damage from boats, storms Land development (how? why?) Snorkeling?
2. Is one cause (or several) more important than others?	Storms devastating. Human damage can be heavy; <u>preventable</u>
3. What cause is most recent?	Modern chemicals, sewage, etc.
4. Could some causes be long past, or hidden (not obvious)? Did a cause start a "snowball" effect?	Coral once a building material Tourism—good for an area's economy, bad for its reefs
5. Do all the causes merit mention or elaboration?	Coral for building no longer a threat (no need to dwell on it)
Exploring Effects	**Ideas, Information**
1. What are the obvious results?	Coral is dead (and sea animals that produce it). Beautiful, natural barrier gone.
2. What will this mean—or what are less obvious effects, especially in the future?	Marine life in reefs threatened. Fishing poorer. Beach erosion.
3. Are there hidden effects?	Medical benefits lost because coral contains important compounds.

Your exploring may lead you along a **cause-and-effect chain.** A result of one action may start, or cause, something else. When a reef dies, for example, then the fish near the shore disappear. Then, fishing lines come up empty. Then, people go hungry. So that you don't miss a link, ask "*Then what?*" for every effect.

TIP When you create a causal analysis, make sure you avoid an error in thinking called **false cause and effect.** You cannot assume that a cause-and-effect relationship exists between two events on the basis of sequence alone. Just because B *follows* A does not mean B was *caused* by A. You must establish a valid, or reasonable, connection.

> **False Cause and Effect:** My computer printer stopped working the day after I installed a new spreadsheet program. The new program must have caused the printer breakdown.

The only connection between installing a new program and a total printer failure is the sequence, or timing, of the events. When you think about it, several causes are more probable—the fact that you dropped the printer last week, perhaps, or that the printer is ten years old. To avoid a false cause-and-effect relationship, you must show logically *how* one event caused another.

Something You Can Count On   Have you ever heard the phrase, "Because I said so"? When you are judging the truth of something, that assertion probably doesn't satisfy you. Readers feel the same way. **To accept your explanation of a situation's causes and effects, your audience needs believable support: evidence that is sufficient, accurate, and reliable.**

 KEY CONCEPT

Sufficient Evidence   One way to judge how much evidence you require for a point is to keep your audience in mind. An audience that does not know your topic at all will need more evidence than a more knowledgeable one. Any audience, though, needs enough facts, examples, or statistics to *understand* your points and see them as *solid.* A rule of thumb: Avoid burying your audience in evidence; instead, select what is most relevant or strongest.

TIP Jot down support as you accumulate it. This will help you clarify ideas and formulate questions. Your notes may even lead you to discover what you still need to learn about your topic.

Accurate Evidence   Be accurate when you quote sources, both in words and numbers. A mistake may be innocent—such as reversing the calories in a gram of fat (nine) and in a gram of complex carbohydrate (four)— but readers who detect an error may question everything you say.

Reliable Evidence   You must be a skeptical, critical researcher. Never assume that just because a "fact" is published, it is correct. After all, even the most reputable newspapers and network news programs have issued retractions and corrections because of unreliable sources. Follow these guidelines.

TIP Note source titles and page numbers beside each piece of evidence for easy reference when you are writing. (For more on **sources** and **citations,** see pages 268–269.)

- **Be particularly wary of tabloid newspapers and TV shows.** They may cover serious topics, but their intent is entertainment, not balanced reporting of science.

- **Look hard at small presses and newsletters.** Always ask, "Who is publishing this information—and why? Do they have a political or philosophical bias?"

- **Remember that Web sites are supervised only by those who create them.** You may find what looks like scientific data on "N. Barry's Little-Known Health Facts" site, but check it against data on a reputable site such as the National Center for Disease Control.

- **Pay attention to dates.** Because science changes, timeliness of information is one critical gauge; newer sources may be more reliable.

- **Examine, and provide, credentials** for any authority you quote. A neighbor who has fished commercially for fifteen years can provide useful facts about net fishing, but for larger issues of marine biology, readers will want to hear from a scientist or state marine official.

Everything in Its Place   After gathering your support, you may want to chart what you have found for each cause and/or effect. Here is one entry in a writer's chart.

Cause	Evidence
Development along coast kills coral.	• Chemical nutrients from sewage, fertilizer, and fossil fuel promote algae that smother coral. • Nearly 90% of coral in heavily populated South Florida is dead or dying. • Tourism: more resorts, waste disposal; snorkelers wanting coral souvenirs • Fishing: fishing using cyanide kills coral & big fish that eat algae. Boats and anchors break coral.

YOUR TURN 4   **Choosing a Topic, Analyzing Causes and Effects, and Gathering Information**

Use these prewriting steps to focus and research your topic. Be sure to choose a specific topic; think about your purpose and your audience; write a thesis statement; and explore possible causes and effects before researching, and again as you gather information.

Test Your Thesis

It's Elementary Scientists test their hypotheses by examining and drawing conclusions from evidence. When writing a causal analysis essay, you test your thesis in the same way. After you gather and examine evidence, make a **generalization**—a broad but accurate statement—about the causes or effects of a situation based on that evidence. Moving from specific evidence to a generalization is called **induction.** For example, suppose you think that students' use of backpacks causes health problems (your thesis). To gather information, you observe and talk to students, interview a physician, and do some reading. You collect the following evidence.

- Most students at your school use backpacks to carry books.

- More students wear the packs slung over one shoulder than on the back.

- An orthopedist says that heavy backpacks, or those worn improperly on one shoulder, can cause neck, shoulder, and back pain, and permanently damage a growing spine.

- A state government health Web site says that a backpack should not weigh more than about fifteen percent of a child's body weight and that lifting and carrying even twenty pounds improperly is dangerous.

With this evidence you might formulate the following generalization:

> Students who carry heavy backpacks on one shoulder are at risk for significant muscle or skeletal problems.

Note how this statement is a refinement of the thesis above. Your original thesis statement perhaps will change after you have done research. Sometimes, the generalization you draw from the evidence you gather will be *completely* different from your original thesis. If this happens, scratch your old thesis and start again with the generalization as your new one.

TIP **Induction** and **deduction** are both valid ways of reasoning. Induction uses specific instances to form a generalization about them. Deduction applies a general rule to a specific instance in order to draw a conclusion about it.

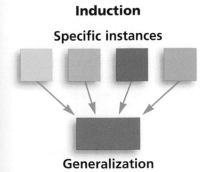

Induction

Specific instances

Generalization

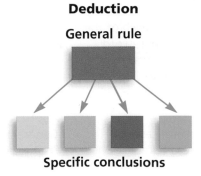

Deduction

General rule

Specific conclusions

MINI-LESSON CRITICAL THINKING

Evaluating Generalizations

You must always check generalizations—both those others make and your own—to see if they are valid, or reasonable. If yours are not valid, readers will suspect your entire essay.

How can you tell if a generalization is valid? Sometimes you must look at the evidence the generalization is based on, and sometimes you must look at the generalization itself.

THINKING IT THROUGH Making Valid Generalizations

Use these criteria to check the validity of generalizations that you make by induction.

1. **Does enough evidence support the generalization?** The broader your generalization, the more evidence you need (and the more different kinds of evidence). Also, a few instances of a phenomenon or a few personal reports are insufficient to make a valid generalization.

2. **Does the evidence come from a trustworthy source?** You and other students are trustworthy sources about backpack use at your school. However, for medical information about risks, your sources should be health experts. Always ask "Who is an expert about this?"

3. **Does all the evidence lead to the same generalization?** You cannot ignore contradictory evidence or evidence pointing to another conclusion.

4. **Is the generalization stated as an absolute, or is it tailored or qualified to fit the evidence you've gathered?** Beware all-or-nothing generalizations that you cannot support. (Words like *most* and *some* can often help you avoid unprovable absolutes.)

PRACTICE

Analyze the validity of the generalization below by carefully examining the evidence on which it is based. Write answers to each of the four criteria questions above. Then, reword the generalization in the way that *you* think most accurately reflects the evidence. Be ready to explain your answers.

Evidence:
A newspaper reports that several cases of unpasteurized apple cider were taken off the shelves at a store because illness had been traced to that product. An encyclopedia entry on *pasteurization,* the process of heating food to certain temperatures for specific periods of time in order to kill bacteria, states that almost all milk sold in the U.S. is pasteurized. A boy down the street got sick after a breakfast which included freshly-squeezed orange juice.

Generalization:
Fruit juices are unsafe for human consumption unless they are pasteurized.

Organize Your Information

Getting the Picture   Diagramming, or mapping, is an excellent way to see causal relationships and to organize information. The following graphic organizers show you the basic patterns that cause-and-effect essays can follow. Remember that these graphic organizers are of causes and effects alone. They do not include background information or discussion of a situation or phenomenon that you will include in your essay's introduction.

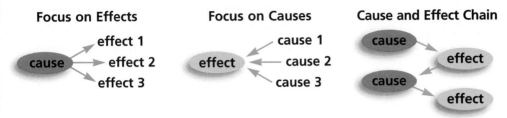

Every topic and thesis will be slightly different and may even *combine* standard causal patterns. The writer below not only focused on both causes and effects but also found cause-effect chains. Notice how mapping can help clarify and categorize information, too.

Focus on Causes and Effects

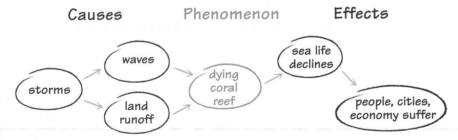

TIP   In **chronological order,** or the order of events in time, causes come before effects. In an essay, however, you may choose to give readers effects first. You might also choose to present multiple causes in **order of importance** (most important to least important, or least to most), instead of in time sequence.

YOUR TURN 5   Testing Your Thesis and Organizing Your Causal Analysis

Based on your research, confirm or adjust your original thesis. Afterward, diagram a logical presentation of your causes, effects, or both. If you prefer, create an outline instead of, or along with, a diagram.

Reference Note
For more on **outlining,** see page 1074.

Writing

Causal Analysis

Framework

Directions and Explanations

Introduction

- Pique the reader's interest.
- Establish the situation or topic.
- Present the thesis statement.

Grab Your Reader's Attention   Begin with a thought-provoking question or statistic to intrigue readers.

Set Up Your Topic   Provide background information (including technical definitions) to prepare readers for the causal relationships you will explain.

State Your Thesis   Provide a clear statement of the focus of your analysis: causes, effects, or both.

Body

- State and support with evidence the first cause or effect.
- State and support with evidence the second cause or effect, and so on.

Organize Clearly   Whether you present causes and effects in chronological order or in order of importance, make sure the relationships are explicit by using signal words and transitions. This will ensure that the logical progression of your thoughts is clearly understood.

Make Your Case   Use evidence to support each cause and effect. Cite your references—readers will want to see for themselves your authoritative sources. (See page 268 for citing evidence in an essay.)

Conclusion

- Reinforce the thesis.
- Tie the ideas together with a summary.
- Leave the reader with a final thought.

Finish Strongly   As you summarize your explanation, refer to your introduction to help readers remember where and why you began.

Offer a Prediction   If possible, predict future changes or discuss the larger implications of the trend or phenomenon. If you feel that your audience can prevent harmful effects, issue a final call to action.

 YOUR TURN 6 Writing Your First Draft

Using the framework as a guide, write the first draft of your essay. Read the Writer's Model that follows to see an example of a causal analysis built upon the framework.

A Writer's Model

The following essay, which is a final draft, closely follows the framework on the previous page.

The Killing of the Coral Reefs

Are coral reefs "the forgotten rain forests of the sea"? When biologist Clive Wilkinson chose that subtitle for a book on the world's coral reefs, he made a dramatic point. People protest the damage done to tropical rain forests and their rich resources; yet coral reefs, an equally vital resource, suffer similar damage. Some causes are natural, but human action causes most coral reef destruction—a problem with serious consequences for life on earth.

Snorkelers diving near coral reefs delight in seeing beautifully colored rock. In reality, they are looking at the protective shells—the homes—of small animals called corals. Coral reefs are limestone growths on the sea floor, sometimes hundreds of miles long and usually five to ten thousand years old, formed out of calcium carbonate excreted by these tiny meat-eaters. When scientists speak of coral reefs dying, they are not only referring to the deaths of the coral animals, but also to the deaths of millions of other sea creatures and plants that depend directly on the reefs.

Because coral reefs need sunlight to live, they exist in shallow water around land masses. As shoreline barriers, reefs are vulnerable to two destructive forces: storms and freshwater storm runoff. A hurricane's or typhoon's waves can tear away large chunks of reef. Also, heavy rains drain from adjacent land, carrying sediment that can literally smother a reef. Obviously, these natural threats cannot be prevented; however, people can control human threats, such as development along coastlines.

The most important hazard of development is eutrophication, the buildup of nutrients in the water. The nutrients—such as chemicals found in raw sewage, fertilizer, and pesticides—cause the abnormal growth of algae that cover and choke the corals. According to Dr. Stephanie Vogt, a marine researcher at Florida Coastal Laboratories, reefs all over the world are shifting from a high dominance of coral to a high dominance of algae. She says that as a result of tremendous population growth, some ninety percent of the coral reefs in South Florida are dead or dying. Experts at a 1992 International Coral Reef Symposium estimated that seventy percent of all coral will be dead by the year 2050, if present trends continue (Wilkinson 1).

(continued)

Margin notes:

INTRODUCTION:
Provocative question

Topic established
Thesis (causes and effects)

BODY

Background: defining terms

Background

Causes 1 and 2

Support

Defining terms

Cause 3

Support

(continued)

Cause 4
Support

Cause 5
Support
Causal chain

While eutrophication is the primary human danger to coral reefs, tourism and fishing contribute, too. Tourists not only require more land development—they also want coral souvenirs. Careless scuba divers and snorkelers cause significant damage to reefs, as do fishers who disregard marine ecology. In some parts of the world, people fish by dumping cyanide poison directly onto the reefs. The poison only stuns large fish, which are caught live, but it kills corals. Even if poison is not used, the disappearance of large fish jeopardizes reefs because the fish help keep algae in check. Furthermore, boat anchors and accidental boat groundings cause considerable reef damage.

Effect 1
Effect 2
Support

Ironically, Vogt notes, when fish vanish from the destroyed reefs, one result is lost fishing jobs—and suffering families. Also, dead coral hurts coastal settlements in general, because the reefs filter sea water, produce sand to replenish eroded beaches, and provide some protection from waves and storm surges.

Effect 3
Support

With all that the world stands to lose if coral reefs disappear, the most important effect may be the loss of medicinal benefits. For two decades medical scientists have been studying the organisms found in coral reefs, and already they have found chemical compounds that fight inflammation, viruses, bacteria, and cancer. If the reefs continue to deteriorate, some future medical and pharmaceutical discoveries will be impossible.

CONCLUSION

Return to thesis

Fortunately, coral recovers quickly when causes of destruction stop, a fact that explains why reefs have persisted through natural cycles of storms. Even so, human-made stress and damage will need strong measures to stop them. Like groups fighting to preserve the rain forests, coral reef organizations have begun campaigns to stop harmful practices. Anyone who has seen a brilliant coral reef, or fished in its riches, instinctively feels awe. People must now understand that this great treasure is in human hands. We can destroy coral reefs or save them.

Works Consulted

Hinrichsen, Don, "Coral Reefs in Crisis" *Bioscience* 47 October 1997: 554–5.

Levin, Ted, "To Save a Reef" *National Wildlife* February 1999: 36–42.

Vogt, Stephanie, interview by author, tape recording, Florida Coastal Marine Laboratories, Miami, Fla. 18 November 2000.

Wilkinson, Clive R. "Book of the Year (1998): Coral Reefs: The Forgotten Rain Forests of the Sea." *Britannica Online.* Accessed 12 October <2000 http://www.eb.com:180/ cgi-bin/g?DocF=boy/98/L02836.html>.

The following student essay was written by Cody Keller, a student at Van Buren High School in Van Buren, Arkansas. Pay careful attention to the writer's use of anecdotal evidence. Do you find this evidence convincing?

Playing Favorites: It Is All in Our Heads

"You never get a second chance to make a first impression." That was the slogan used in a commercial for a deodorant or toothpaste several years ago, and it highlights the weight that the all-important first impression carries. The resulting opinion frequently relies on characteristics such as looks, dress, or financial status. This snap judgment leads to the formation of favorites and non-favorites. Preferential treatment, or playing favorites, is a prevalent form of injustice because it occurs in all venues—at school, at work, even among friends and family. The roots of favoritism can be found in studying functions of the human brain, and its dastardly results can be observed practically everywhere.

Why do people pick favorites? The process begins with a physiological action. Nestled in the center of the human brain is a little structure called the amygdala, so named because it resembles an almond in size and shape. This little bundle of neurons plays a key role in processing memory, but new research suggests that it does much more. World-renowned brain experts Antonio Damasio and Ralph Adolphs, with the assistance of their research team, now conclude that the amygdala matches first impressions of people with the knowledge of past experiences (Motluk 5), thus equipping humans with the ability to make judgments about others. The direct result of this ability is our choosing favorites and non-favorites, such as people and things we like, dislike, trust, and distrust.

The activity of the amygdala causes our brain to store images and memories in correlation to positive or negative emotional responses. Imagine a person is looking for a new pet, so he pays a visit to the local animal shelter. He starts to choose a hearty, medium-sized mutt, but changes his mind when the animal barks. The sound awakens a memory of a ferocious mongrel that terrified him as a youngster. The whole decision-making process described here occurs in a flash, and the person probably is not fully

(continued)

INTRODUCTION
Attention-grabbing quotation

Setting up the topic

Thesis: cause of favoritism and its effects

BODY
Cause: physiological action

Supporting evidence

Effect 1

Support by anecdotal evidence

(continued)

aware why he so quickly developed an aversion for an animal that seemed adorable two seconds before. This is only one example, and the result here is rather harmless, as the person could find another pet that he finds more agreeable.

Effect 2

However, there are more harmful effects. How many times do people let a weak first impression keep them from getting to know another person better? Everybody has done it at some time; most could also admit to being duped by someone who oozed with charisma at the onset of an introduction, but proved later to be far less pleasant. This phenomenon certainly happens frequently enough in the realm of politics. It is time to elect a president of the student government. Candidate number one decides to promote herself as a bubbly champion of the people with goals of improving both cafeteria food and student parking. Her opponent is a less gregarious member of the class who stammers when he speaks but who has a reputation for working hard and living up to his word. Candidate number one wins the election by a landslide.

Support by anecdotal evidence

Effect 3

Favoritism's other effects can be seen anywhere one chooses to look. Favoritism of some kind will decide who gets into this prestigious college, who receives that incredible scholarship, or even who gets the only A in the toughest English teacher's advanced writing course. Someone once said, "It's not what you know; it's who you know." The more of life one experiences, the more truth that statement holds.

CONCLUSION Summary

How are we to stop favoritism? Humans are creatures that rely on their senses to provide them with information about their environment; sensory details perceived in the moments of a first impression cause our brains to approve of people and situations, or to give them the "no" vote. What has been previously known as intuition is really the work of neural structures in the brain. In the end, awareness is the key to keeping our brain's mechanisms in check. Rather than accepting preferences as "natural," individuals should monitor their responses' seeming favorites and non-favorites to prevent further injustice to fellow citizens of the world.

Strong finish: reader awareness and call to action

Work Cited

Motluk, Alison. "He Looked Shifty." <u>New Scientist</u> June 1998: 5.

Revising

Evaluate and Revise Your Draft

Giving It the Twice Over   To refine your draft, you will have to read it carefully at least twice. The first time, you should evaluate and revise for content and organization, using the guidelines that follow. The second time through, use the suggestions on page 168 to revise for sentence style.

▷ **First Reading: Content and Organization**   The tips in the middle column of the chart below will help you answer the questions in the first column of the chart. To revise, use the suggestions in the third column.

Causal Analysis: Content and Organization Guidelines for Peer and Self-Evaluation		
Evaluation Questions	▶ **Tips**	▶ **Revision Techniques**
❶ Will the introduction quickly grab readers' attention? Does it contain necessary terms and background material?	▶ **Circle** information that will pique your readers' curiosity and supply them with the terms and background they need. If you find none, revise. If you find information that is not necessary to the introduction, revise.	▶ **Add** an example or quotation about your topic that makes readers think. **Add** information your readers need to understand the terms and origins of your topic. **Delete** excess information (you may be able to use it in the body of your paper).
❷ Can readers identify a thesis that gives a clear focus: causes, effects, or both?	▶ **Highlight** the thesis. If you do not see one, or if your thesis is incomplete or lacks focus, revise.	▶ **Add** a thesis statement near the beginning of the paper. Make sure your focus is clear and complete on causes, effects, or both.
❸ Are causes or effects supported with evidence (facts, statistics, and examples)?	▶ **Underline** supporting details. If you do not see any, revise.	▶ **Add** evidence to support each cause and effect. **Elaborate** on existing support with additional examples, statistics, or facts.
❹ Are the causes or effects organized in a way that is clear and easy to follow? Are the causal chains obvious?	▶ **Bracket** each cause discussed; **put parentheses around** each effect. If there aren't several of either, or if chains are difficult to follow, revise. **Check** your text against your prewriting graphic organizers.	▶ **Rearrange** causes or effects to show clear chronological order or order of importance. **Add** missing causes or effects to your chain; **add** signal words or transitions to clearly reveal order and causal relationships.
❺ Does the conclusion create a clear closing?	▶ **Draw a wavy line under** the sentence that restates the thesis. **Highlight** any summary or closing statements. Revise if you see none.	▶ **Add** a sentence that restates the thesis. **Add** a summary or some comments about the future.

ONE WRITER'S REVISIONS   Here's how one writer used the content and organization guidelines to revise a paragraph in the essay on page 163. Study the revisions and answer the questions that follow the paragraph.

add

rearrange
add

add
delete

> *Are coral reefs*
> ∧ ∧ When writer Clive Wilkinson chose "the forgotten rain forests of the sea" ~~as a~~ *that* subtitle for a book on the world's coral reefs, he made a dramatic point. People protest the damage done to tropical rain forests and their rich resources; yet coral reefs, *an equally vital resource,* ~~made up of the protective shells of small animals called corals,~~ suffer similar damage. Some causes are natural, but human action causes most coral reef destruction—a problem with serious consequences for life on earth.

PEER REVIEW

Ask a classmate to answer the following questions after he or she has read your paper.

1. What would you like the writer to tell you more about? Where would you have liked more explanation?

2. Did you see enough evidence? Did you trust the writer's sources and generalizations? Why, or why not?

Analyzing the Revision Process

1. Why did the writer revise the first sentence in this introductory paragraph?

2. Why is some of the information in the second sentence deleted?

3. On what does the thesis focus—causes, effects, or both?

YOUR TURN 7   Focusing on Content and Organization

Revise the content and organization of your essay using the guidelines on page 167. For sample editing marks, see the revisions above.

Second Reading: Style   In your first reading, you dealt with the content of your essay and how you organized it. In the second reading, you will focus your attention on *style*, or how you express yourself. One part of style that is easy to assess is sentence length. In cause-effect writing, you may need fairly long sentences to explain that a cause leads directly to an effect. Short sentences, though, are good for emphasizing a point. Too many of either kind can detract from the interest of your paper. Make sure you keep your readers' attention by varying the length of your sentences. Use the following style guideline to help you.

Evaluation Question	▶ Tip	▶ Revision Technique
Does your essay have too many short sentences?	▶ **Underline** sentences of ten or fewer words. If you find two short sentences together, see if they can be revised.	▶ **Combine** short sentences into longer ones by placing the less important idea in an adverbial subordinate clause.

Sentences

Varied Sentence Length

Too many short sentences make for monotonous reading and for disconnected ideas—a problem when you want readers to see how causes relate to effects.

ONE WRITER'S REVISIONS   Using the style guideline above, the writer of the essay on page 163 revised some sentences to vary length. Study the revision and answer the questions below.

BEFORE REVISION

Coral reefs need sunlight to live. They exist in shallow water around land masses.

two short sentences

AFTER REVISION

Because coral reefs need sunlight to live, they exist in shallow water around land masses.

combined using an adverbial clause

Analyzing the Revision Process

1. How did the writer relate ideas by combining sentences?
2. What is another way to combine these two sentences?

YOUR TURN 8   **Focusing on Sentence Length**

Revise your essay to vary sentence length. Use the style guideline and the sample revisions above to eliminate short choppy sentences.

Designing Your Writing

N ow is
the time
for all
good men to
come to the aid

Using Flowcharts *Flowchart* is another word for the maps of cause-and-effect chains shown on page 147. A flowchart visually illustrates a process or sequence. Just as maps help you to plan your essay, flowcharts help readers quickly grasp your explanation. If you discuss causal chains in your essay, a flowchart can be used to illustrate a particular chain you wish to emphasize. Follow these pointers to create a flowchart.

- **Use boxes, circles, or other simple shapes to represent causes or effects;** make sure arrows indicate the correct direction of movement from one event to another.

- **Use labels that identify the events or steps** and place them inside the shapes that represent them; if necessary for clarity, give the entire flowchart a title.

- **Organize the shapes so that movement flows from left to right or top to bottom.**

- **Whether you draw a chart or create it with computer graphics software, be sure to refer to the chart in your essay.**

- **Place the flowchart near the spot in the text that explains it.**

   For example, the writer of the model essay could have summarized and emphasized the effects of dying coral reefs by including the following text and flowchart.

The final effect of dying coral reefs will be human suffering. As the following chart shows, whether the loss is new medicine, sound shorelines, or plentiful marine life, the real losers are people, who need nature to live.

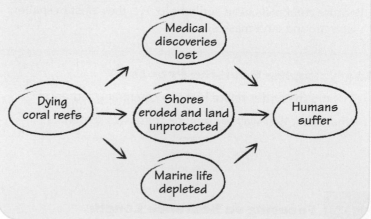

Publishing

Proofread Your Essay

Minding Your *p*'s and *q*'s   Before you prepare a final copy of your essay, you need to make sure it is free of errors in grammar, usage, and punctuation. In a cause-and-effect essay, you should be especially careful to use verb tenses correctly; doing so will enable you to show the correct sequence of events accurately.

Reference Note

For more on **verb tenses,** see page 668.

Unnecessary Shifts in Verb Tense

Unnecessary or careless shifts in verb tense can confuse readers about when events occurred. For example, you should not carelessly shift from the present tense to the past or from the past tense to the future.

Unnecessary Shift	Development **is** a primary danger, but tourism and fishing **contributed,** too. [Because all three of the dangers exist at the same time, the verbs must be written in the same tense.]
Consistent	Development **is** a primary danger, but tourism and fishing **contribute,** too. [Both verbs are in present tense.]

or

Development **was** a primary danger, but tourism and fishing **contributed,** too. [Both verbs are in past tense; this is correct only if the dangers no longer exist.]

Unnecessary shifts in verb tense also occur when a writer changes the form of two or more verbs that should be parallel. The result of such a shift is an inconsistent verb tense.

Unnecessary Shift	Every year, he **has been taking** photographs of autumn leaves and **enjoyed** a career as a nature photographer. [Both verb forms should be in the same tense for parallelism.]
Consistent	Every year, he **has been taking** photographs of autumn leaves and **enjoying** a career as a nature photographer. [Both verb forms match and are parallel with one another.]

PRACTICE

In each sentence, change the tense of the boldface verb to create a clear relationship in time between it and the underlined verb. Some sentences may have more than one correct answer. Be ready to explain your revisions. Write your answers on your own paper.

1. As the rains <u>flood</u> the fields, the crops **washed** away.

2. When the scientist **drops** the chemical into the reagent, the liquid <u>became</u> cloudy.

3. After the bell <u>rings</u>, the pigeons **ate** the corn.

4. Because few environmental protection laws <u>were enacted</u> in Eastern Europe, many lakes **are contaminating.**

5. The Hubble telescope <u>has transmitted</u> data to the earth and **leads** scientists to new discoveries about the universe.

Publish Your Essay

Spread the Word   Here are some suggestions about how you might publish your essay.

TIP   Before you publish your essay, double-check to make sure it is legible and adheres to the conventions of punctuation and capitalization.

- Attach your paper to an e-mail message and send it to an expert on your topic, especially one you consulted in your research. Ask for a response. (You might give it to your science teacher, too.)

- Post your paper to a Usenet newsgroup that focuses on your topic or on science in general. For example, if you wrote on global warming, you might send it to a physical science newsgroup.

- If your essay relates to a local event or community interest, submit it to the school or city newspaper for publication. For example, readers in your area might benefit from your analysis of oak wilt—its causes and its economic effects on your neighborhoods.

- If your subject is one that calls for action, use your essay to create a brochure and then ask permission to post it on public bulletin boards or make it available in other public places. For example, if you wrote about the effects of lawn fertilizer runoff, you might ask to put your brochure in an information rack at a local grocery store.

Reflect on Your Essay

PORTFOLIO

Stepping Back, Moving Forward   You have just created something. Take a few minutes now to reflect on your essay. Reflection helps you grasp how much you have accomplished—how much you learned about your topic *and* about your writing process. Write brief answers to the following questions and include them in your portfolio with your final copy.

- What led you to your topic? Was the process deliberate or accidental? Explain.

- What would you do differently if you wrote again on this topic? How would you refine your topic for a more specific audience?

- What did you learn about mapping and organizing causes and effects?

- What did you learn about research or writing that might help you in another kind of essay?

YOUR TURN 9   Proofreading, Publishing, and Reflecting

Proofread your essay carefully, paying special attention to verbs that establish a sequence. Then, think about how you would publish your paper. Finally, answer the reflection questions listed above.

Writing a Ballad

Causes and effects often create a **narrative;** one thing causes another to happen or sets a chain of events in motion, and presto—you have a story. The story is the most prominent part of a narrative verse form called a **ballad.** Popular since the Middle Ages and still written today, ballads are songs that usually tell tragic or sensational stories—stories in which strong emotions such as love, jealousy, or greed lead to treachery, death, or ruin. Take a different spin on causes and effects by writing a ballad of your own.

The Story's the Thing
A story always involves some kind of conflict, a problem or mystery to be solved. For your own ballad, you can begin by jotting down a conflict and its causes and effects. Consider focusing on events that lead up to the conflict (causes), or those that unwind toward the resolution of the conflict (effects). You do not have to include everything—ballads typically are short on details and force the hearer or reader to fill in gaps in the story.

Give It Form—Make It Sing
Because ballads were once committed to memory and sung rather than written down, they usually have simple four-line stanzas with a rhythm and rhyme scheme that aids memory. The rhyme scheme in ballad form is either an *abab* or *abcb* pattern. The typical ballad rhythm, or meter, takes the form of four stresses (or beats) in the first and third lines, and three stresses in the second and fourth lines. To transform your story into a ballad, you must use stanzas and make the events "sing" with rhyme and a steady beat.

The Stuff of Ballad
Their roots in the oral tradition give ballads such characteristics as dialogue and repetition. These traits are not necessarily found in every ballad, but they are common enough to be considered typical of the ballad form.

- **Repetition** A **refrain** is a phrase, sentence, or series of lines that repeats, sometimes throughout the entire ballad. Some ballads feature **incremental repetition,** which means each repetition of a line varies slightly. This device helps build suspense and creates emphasis.

- **Dialogue** The story in a ballad is often revealed as characters speak to one another in a stylized way; rather than using natural speech patterns, often, the dialogue takes the form of **questions and answers.** This device keeps the story moving without using sections of lengthy description.

An Example for Us All
Read the ballad on the next page in which a mysterious man with sinister intentions encourages a young woman to wade in a pool. Study the annotations in order to use this ballad later as a model for the poem you write. Note: In the ballad's first three stanzas (which are omitted here), the mysterious man's harp music puts everyone to sleep except for the King's daughter, whom he takes to Wearie's Well.

The Water o' Wearie's Well

Dialogue and repetition—
this stanza is a refrain.

Rhyme scheme—*abcb*,
(*well* and *befall* are near
rhymes)

Conflict/problem—
she senses danger.

Rhythm—note the pattern
of stresses, or beats,
marked in this stanza.

Crisis—he threatens
to drown her; note that
the ballad does not
state why.

Sensational end—tragedy
is averted as the heroine
tricks her assailant.

"'Wide[1] in, wide in, my lady fair,
   No harm shall thee befall;
Oft times I've watered my steed
   Wi the waters o' Wearie's Well.'

The first step that she stepped in
   She stepped to the knee;
And sighing says this lady fair,
   'This water's nae[2] for me.'

'Wide ín, wide ín, my lady faír,
   No harm shall thée befáll;
Oft times I've watered my steed
   Wi the waters o' Wearie's Well.'

[In alternating verses the princess steps in gradually as the man
entreats her to wade in farther. He then declares . . .]

'Seven king's daughters I've drowned there,
   In the water o' Wearie's Well,
And I'll make you the eight o' them,
   And ring the common bell.[3]

[When he leans down to kiss the princess, she hurls him into
the water. She repeats his words—note the variation.]

'Since seven king's daughters ye've drowned there,
   In the water o' Wearie's Well,
I'll make you bridegroom to them a'[4],
   An ring the bell mysell.'

1. **Wide:** wade

2. **nae:** not

3. **"The common bell":** a reference to the ritual ringing of
the church bell whenever
someone dies.

4. **a':** all

YOUR TURN 10 Writing a Narrative Poem

Write a ballad of your own. Be sure you use the ballad stanza and an
intriguing or suspenseful narrative. After writing the ballads, you and
your classmates can read or recite them to the class.

Creating and Evaluating an Informative Speech

A scientist makes a presentation about the causes and effects of global warming. A teacher lectures on the effects of the Treaty of Versailles. A counselor explains to your class what you can do to get good results on a college entrance test. What do these people have in common? Each is making an **informative speech.** That is, each speaker is conveying information to an audience so that the listeners will understand and remember it. You never know when you might need this skill yourself. When your boss asks you to make a report to your co-workers, or when your college professor gives you a book to speak about in class, you will need to give an informative speech.

WHAT'S AHEAD?

In this section, you will make an informative speech. You will also learn how to

- **present a thesis statement and support it**
- **structure your speech**
- **use verbal and non-verbal skills effectively**
- **evaluate informative speeches**

Speak to Inform

Make a Plan The topic you chose for your cause-and-effect essay might also be a good topic for your speech. If you want to start with something new, however, think about your interests. For example, if you are interested in computers, you could consider explaining some aspect of the Internet. Next, give your topic a focus by writing a thesis statement. Your **thesis statement** gives your audience the most important idea in the speech and guides its development. (Since speeches are often shorter and more tightly focused than papers, a precise thesis will help you narrow your ideas.) Naturally, your thesis statement belongs at the beginning of your speech, after any material you include to create interest in your topic. On the next page, see how one student thought about topic and thesis.

TIP Chances are good that you will need to discover additional facts, even on a topic you already know well. The traditional methods for conducting research will work just as well for your informative speech as they do for the papers you write.

Reference Note

For more on **conducting research,** see page 248.

Subject area	the Internet
Topic	the origins of the Internet
General purpose and task	to inform in a formal speech
Specific purpose	to explain two major innovations that were necessary to the beginning of the Internet
Thesis statement	Two early innovations that made the Internet possible are the packet switching theory and the open-architecture networking idea.

TIP Choose your words carefully to suit your **task** (the purpose your speech is meant to accomplish) and the **occasion** (the time, place, setting, and context in which the speech will be delivered). For instance, if your task is to fulfill an assignment and your occasion is a formal classroom presentation, you will want to use formal, exact language.

Seeing the People Before You   Unlike the audience for your essay, the **audience** for your speech will be people that you can see and hear. Create a mental picture of who will actually listen to your speech. Think about what they already know about the topic, and ask yourself which aspects of the topic will interest them most. Adapt your language and information to meet your audience's expectations and the needs of the **occasion.** For example, you should use standard English, and if you are speaking to an audience that is unfamiliar with the **technical language** of the Internet, you may need to define terms that Internet users already understand. Finally, to create **credibility**—to make yourself appear authoritative to your audience—say a few words about your background in relation to your topic. With these techniques, you can gain your audience's confidence and goodwill.

Put It Together   Your speech will be organized much like an essay, with an introduction, body, and conclusion. Use the following ideas to give your speech the elements it needs.

In the **introduction,** begin with

■ a startling statement or anecdote

■ a question to arouse interest

■ a brief quotation that makes the audience want to hear more

■ nonverbal materials like a picture or music

In the **body** of your speech,

■ support your points, but spare the details that will obscure your message

■ provide clear transitions from one idea to the next

■ use mnemonic devices—repetition, carefully used, can help listeners' memories. The **rhetorical strategy** of parallelism, the repetition of phrases or sentences, sets up familiar patterns an audience can remember.

TIP Spice up your speech with **rhetorical questions** such as "Where will the Internet go from here?" These questions are not meant to be answered by the audience. They are used to add force and interest to your speech and to clarify the material that follows. For instance, the example question above might introduce your speculations about the future of the Internet.

- build up to the most important and/or interesting points you have to make

In the **conclusion,** remember to

- return to your thesis
- summarize your main points
- provide a reason or ask a question that will lead the audience to apply the information to their own lives

To Inform and Project   How you decide to deliver your speech will have an effect on how you prepare it. If you plan to **read** the speech or **memorize** it word for word, write it out in full. If you plan to give an **extemporaneous** speech with some preparation but not memorized or fully written out, prepare good note cards so you do not leave anything out. Simply reading your speech may seem like the easiest option, but it is the least enjoyable method for your audience. An extemporaneous speech allows you to adjust your tone and emphasis to your listeners' reactions. In any case, you will have to limit your speech to your allotted time.

You will also want to keep in mind some techniques that will keep your audience's attention. The following chart has techniques, both verbal and nonverbal, you can use to grab and hold your listeners' attention.

Verbal Tips

- **Get excited.** The more enthusiasm you show for your topic, the more likely your audience will listen to what you say.
- **The rain in Spain.** Speak clearly and not too informally. Pronounce words fully and correctly. Clear speech is the first step to ensuring your audience understands you.
- **Voice control.** Use variety and emphasis. You can vary your volume, rate of speech, pitch, and tone of voice to emphasize key points and to make your speech more interesting. No one wants to listen to a monotone.

Nonverbal Tips

- **The eyes have it.** Use eye contact with your listeners to give them the impression you are talking *with* them and not *at* them.
- **Sign language.** Your hands and body can be important tools in giving a speech. If you have five points to make, for example, hold up a finger for each point.
- **Stand and deliver.** Stand or sit up straight while giving your speech. While you want to avoid rocking back and forth or making other kinds of distracting movements, you can still lean forward to emphasize a point.
- **Step Right Up.** Some physical movement can help to hold and recapture the audience's attention. If you are using a podium, move away from it to recapture your listener's waning attention. If you are speaking without a podium, take a step toward your audience to signal an important point is coming up.
- **Face to face.** Facial expressions can keep your audience listening. Relax enough so that your facial expressions naturally parallel what you are saying. A frown or raised eyebrow can emphasize your message. A blank face is as dull as a monotone.

TIP You can also use **audiovisual materials** and demonstrations to get your points across. Some specific examples include charts, diagrams, photos, cassette recordings, graphs, maps, video clips, and computer-generated slides. If you decide to use such materials, keep time limits in mind and be careful to choose something that truly helps clarify a point.

Listen to and Evaluate Speeches

TIP Even with a well-developed and well-rehearsed speech, unexpected events, stage fright, and distractions can interfere with your delivery. To be prepared, think in advance about how you will stay composed, and take a deep breath, whatever happens.

Make a Little List After you have put together all of the elements of your speech, practice delivering it a few times. Use the evaluation checklist below to assess the different aspects of your speech. If you have access to a video recorder, tape yourself giving the speech and watch the tape for ways to improve. You can also ask one or more classmates to watch you practice your speech. Remind them that they should provide specific reasons for their answers on the checklist and suggestions for improvement. Be prepared to do the same for them in return. Finally, use the **feedback** you get from your teacher and peers to **set goals** for future presentations.

Organization
- Did the introduction create interest?
- Were the thesis and each of the main ideas obvious to listeners?
- Did the speaker use transitions?
- Did the conclusion summarize the main ideas, provide a sense of completion, and encourage further interest?

Content
- Did the speaker appear to have a command of the topic?
- Was the speech appropriate to the audience's knowledge and interests?
- Did the speaker use the conventions of oral language—word choice, grammar, and diction—effectively?
- Were there enough, too few, or too many details to support main ideas?
- Were audiovisual materials used well?
- Did the speaker provide the means for the listeners to understand and remember the main ideas (mnemonic devices)?

Delivery
- Did the speaker seem relaxed and confident?
- Did the speaker show enthusiasm?
- Did the speaker make eye contact?
- Were facial expressions and gestures natural and appropriate?
- Was the speaker easy to understand? Did he or she speak clearly and pronounce words correctly?

YOUR TURN 11 **Preparing, Delivering, and Evaluating an Informative Speech**

Review the steps outlined above to prepare and deliver an informative speech. Use the evaluation checklist to critique your speech and your classmates' speeches. Use this feedback to set goals for future speeches.

Choices

Choose one of the following activities to complete.

▶ CAREERS

1. A Job to Do Talk to classmates and others you know with after-school jobs. What effects do these jobs have on their lives? Write a brief **case study** on the effects of after-school jobs based on the information you gather. Give a copy to your guidance counselor.

▶ CROSSING THE CURRICULUM: HISTORY

2. Special Effects Investigate the causes and/or effects of an invention, such as wireless telephones, the World Wide Web, or voice-recognition software. Don't rely solely on personal observation or the observations of friends. Instead, consult experts in reference sources or through interviews. Give a short **oral report** informing your class of your findings.

▶ VIEWING AND REPRESENTING

3. Moving Images Analyze a current issue of a national news magazine to see how its illustrations affect you. Ask yourself, "Why did the editors choose this image or this diagram to illustrate an article? Does the picture create an emotional effect?" Choose one article and its images, then write a brief **analysis** of the effects of those images.

▶ SPEAKING AND LISTENING

4. Chain, Chain, Chain There are cause-and-effect chains all around you. Create an **informative speech** about the causes and effects of a local issue that is currently in the news. How will the new bridge affect traffic patterns? Why did a new industry decide to move to the area? Why is a new school needed, and what effect will it have on local taxes? Mapping your issue's causes and effects will help make them more clear to yourself and your listeners. Create a **concept map** on poster board and use it to illustrate your informative speech.

▶ LITERATURE

5. Rhyme and Reason Even poetry has causes and effects. You may be able to map a cause and effect chain in a narrative poem, or you can trace the effects of certain poetic devices in a poem. Examine a poem you find powerful, and make notes about how the rhyme scheme, meter, alliteration, or imagery affect you as a reader or listener. Share your thoughts on causes and effects in poetry in a **short paper.**

PORTFOLIO

Analyzing Drama

Reading Workshop

Reading a Literary Analysis of a Drama
PAGE 182

Writing Workshop

Writing a Literary Analysis of a Drama
PAGE 196

Focus on Viewing and Representing

Evaluating a Film Version of a Drama
PAGE 220

Focus on Speaking and Listening

Creating and Evaluating a Dramatic Reading
PAGE 224

The lights go down. The curtain goes up. Onstage someone speaks, and suddenly you find yourself in another time and place—agonizing with John Proctor, pitying Oedipus, or growing furious with Lady Macbeth.

For more than 2,500 years, drama has worked its magic, and for almost as long, readers and playgoers have analyzed various aspects of dramatic performance to learn what makes plays soar or fall flat. Though your first responses to a play are usually informal ("I know *exactly* how Macduff feels"), with reflection you—as a reader or viewer—can develop a more rigorous study of a play. In a **literary analysis,** you study the elements of drama that work together to make up the whole. Literary analyses are borne of close, thoughtful readings (and re-readings) that assess specific literary elements, such as character, setting, plot, symbol, imagery, and theme. A literary analysis of a play can also take into account theatrical elements, such as props, costumes, and movement.

internet connect

go. hrw .com
GO TO: go.hrw.com
KEYWORD: EOLang 12-5

YOUR TURN 1   Analyzing Plays

Working with a partner, discuss a time when someone else's analysis affected your response to and understanding of a movie, play, book, television show, or CD. Did the commentary reveal symbols or characterizations you might not have noticed otherwise? Were you prepared to see beyond the plot, hear musical complexities, or think about symbolism?

Reading a Literary Analysis of a Drama

**WHAT'S
AHEAD?**

In this section you will
read a literary analysis
of a drama. You will
also

■ learn to paraphrase

■ learn to recognize
general statements
and supporting
literary evidence

Dialogue is the most important (and obvious) element in almost
all plays. However, many playwrights also pack their scripts with
descriptions and instructions, hoping to shape the productions eventually
presented on various stages. Play scripts contain the playwright's vision
about everything from the tone of an actor's voice to the exact shade of
light that should fall on her skin. As you read the following literary analysis,
think about the aspects of a play that are *not* the words themselves.

Preparing to Read

| READING SKILL

Paraphrasing   When you **paraphrase,** you use your own words to
restate someone else's ideas. You paraphrase, for instance, when you pass
along a complicated telephone message or tell a friend about a speech you
heard on television. Paraphrasing helps you check your understanding of
something you have read or heard. In a literary analysis, writers use paraphrasing to discuss someone else's ideas when direct quotation is impossible or inappropriate. In the following essay, Richard Hornby uses
paraphrasing to retell parts of George Bernard Shaw's play, *Pygmalion*.

| READING FOCUS

Supporting Details from Literary Sources   When writers analyze a work of literature—drama, fiction, nonfiction, or poetry—they support their ideas by quoting or paraphrasing the literary work itself (**the
primary source**) and by citing what other people have written or said about
the work (**secondary sources**). These two types of **literary evidence** help
critical writers substantiate their analysis of a literary work such as a
drama. Writers cannot, however, let material from primary or secondary
sources stand alone. They must elaborate upon the evidence. This elaboration should explain to you, the critical reader, how their evidence supports their ideas. As you read the following analysis, notice how Richard
Hornby uses literary evidence to support his ideas.

Below, theater professor Richard Hornby discusses some virtues of British playwright Bernard Shaw's *Pygmalion.* Shaw's play (which was the basis for the musical *My Fair Lady*) tells the story of Eliza Doolittle, a street vendor in late-nineteenth-century London who becomes Professor Henry Higgins's student. Higgins, a phonetics expert, bets his friend Colonel Pickering that he can transform Eliza from a lowborn girl with a cockney accent to a young woman who could pass for an aristocrat. Other characters Hornby refers to are Higgins's mother, Eliza's father, and Freddy Eynsford Hill, an aristocratic young man who falls in love with Eliza. As you read, jot down answers to the active-reading questions. (The parenthetical citations indicate page and act numbers where the quotations appear in the edition of *Pygmalion* used for this essay. Information about the edition appears on the Works Cited list at the end of the essay.)

Beyond the Verbal in PYGMALION

Richard Hornby

Any criticism of Shaw's plays today should take into account their continuing vitality in the theater. While some literary critics remain suspicious of Shaw, there can be no doubt that audiences love him as much as ever. He consistently ranks among the ten most frequently performed playwrights in university theaters; there are regular professional productions of his plays in every major theater capital in the world; there is even a permanent Shaw Festival performing in Canada every summer.

1. How does the writer show that his topic is relevant?

One reason for Shaw's theatrical success, of course, is his brilliance with language, which is acknowledged even by his detractors. The speeches in his plays have wit and rhetorical force even when they are dead wrong, as when Don Juan in *Man and Superman* predicts a drastic decline in population. But can linguistic[1] skill alone account for Shaw's lasting popularity? In an age when other playwrights seem to have no interest in language, when television has

---

1. linguistic: having to do with words or the nature and structure of human languages.

coarsened and debased speech, when (in contrast with those of Shaw's day) politicians and preachers and advertisers affect an inarticulate, ungrammatical "naturalness," it seems odd that audiences would be much interested in any strongly verbal play. . . .

It seems, therefore, that there is something operating in Shaw's plays beyond the purely verbal or literary, which helps to account for their success. I wish to suggest that this is his dramaturgical[2] skill, his use of performance elements, which is just as valuable as his linguistic skill. In this way, Shaw can be considered "our contemporary." The visual and aural effects in Shaw's best plays are not merely decorative; instead, they convey meanings. The painting of the Assumption of the Virgin in *Candida,* for example, or the Turkish bath in *Misalliance,* or the wonderful room designed like a ship in *Heartbreak House,* all make precise, ironical comments that are as important in performance as anything that is said in words. Contemporary dramatic theorists are becoming ever more aware that performance itself is a kind of language, that things like actions, setting, costumes, and properties can signify concepts to which the audience can strongly respond. Shaw is fully aware of the non-verbal possibilities of the theater, filling the performance elements with meanings that are not mere afterthoughts but that are central to his plays.

> **2. Based on this paragraph, how would you define *performance elements*?**

I should like to examine Shaw's dramaturgy in some detail in one of his finest plays, *Pygmalion,* which is also one of his most popular (especially if one includes the successful film and musical versions). Consider the opening act, which takes place in Covent Garden, London, in front of St. Paul's Church, "not Wren's cathedral but Inigo Jones's church" (Shaw 9; 1). Covent Garden was, until quite recently, the principal marketplace in London for fruits and vegetables—and flowers, which is why Eliza is selling violets there. Shaw's decision to place his opening scene in this location, however, reflects more than this need for a realistic motivation. The contrast between market and church, between a place of commerce and a place of the spirit, immediately sets up a conflict that is to pervade the entire play: between the outer and the inner life, the artificial role and the living person. As several critics have noted, it is the Bergsonian[3] contrast

> **3. Which performance element does Hornby discuss here? What does he believe it signifies?**

---

2. **dramaturgical** (dra´ mə·tər´ji·kəl´): having to do with play writing and the art of the theater.

3. **Bergsonian:** Henri Bergson (1859–1941), a French philosopher, wrote about the principle called *vitalism.* According to vitalism, the nature of living bodies cannot be entirely explained by science. Instead, living bodies have an internal feature, a soul or degree of consciousness, that shapes their development. This theory contrasts with the theory of *mechanism,* in which all nature is made up of predictable mechanical processes that can be explained by scientific laws.

4. Why does Hornby cite Eric Bentley's work on *Pygmalion* in footnote four?

between the mechanical and the vital.[4] In a reversal of the original Pygmalion story,[5] Higgins takes a live girl and turns her into a statue—i.e., a duchess in externals only; Eliza then comes back to life, fully transformed into an independent woman, reaffirming the Pygmalion/Galatea story after all. In the process of demonstrating this, Shaw is examining the nature of role-playing in society, the way in which social roles conflict with our true, spiritual selves.

It is raining as the play begins, and people are rushing to the portico of the church for shelter. The contrast between the gloomy outer world of commerce, and the vital refuge of the church, is thus emotionally heightened for the audience. Throughout the opening act, Shaw enhances the spiritual or vital aspect of the play through lighting and sound effects. For example, the "blinding flash of lightning, followed instantly by a rattling peal of thunder" (Shaw 10; 1), which accompany Freddy's running into Eliza, suggest a divine intervention orchestrating their meeting. (In the same vein, Higgins says that Eliza has "a soul and the divine gift of articulate speech" [18; 1]). In addition, there are the sounds of the church clock, which chimes twice during the action; the second time, Higgins hears in it "the voice of God" (19; 1). In contrast to these sounds suggesting the spiritual side of the play, there are the harsh sounds of "cab whistles blowing frantically in all directions" (9; 1), including the one that Higgins uses, which the bystander takes to be a police whistle. The whistles suggest the nonspiritual, mechanical aspect of the play's underlying dichotomy.[6]

5. In this paragraph, Hornby quotes descriptive details from the primary source, the play itself. What idea do these details support?

In costuming, the sogginess of the scene is further underlined by Freddy's and Pickering's umbrellas and soaked trousers. Eliza is described as "not at all a romantic figure" (Shaw 10; 1), dirty with shabby clothes. Of course, we shall eventually learn that this sordid exterior is not her true self, that she has (at least potentially) a very different inner self. The same kind of dichotomy operates with Freddy and the Eynsford Hills, who are elegantly dressed in evening clothes, yet turn out to be rather silly people—especially Freddy.

6. The writer chooses to paraphrase in this paragraph; elsewhere he quotes directly. Why might he do this?

---

4. In *Bernard Shaw: 1856–1950* (New York: New Directions, 1957), p. 119, Eric Bentley describes how the contrast between the mechanical and the vital in *Pygmalion* makes audiences laugh. Specifically, he says that the funniest scene in the play is in Act III, where Eliza "appears in upper-class company behaving like an imperfectly functioning mechanical doll." Charles A. Berst makes extensive use of Bergson's ideas in *Bernard Shaw and the Art of Drama* (Urbana: University of Illinois, 1973), where he cites other critics who also describe Shaw's plays in terms of contrasts.

5. **Pygmalion story:** According to Greek legend, Pygmalion, king of Cyprus, fell in love with a statue. Granting Pygmalion's request, the goddess of love brought the statue—Galatea—to life.

6. **dichotomy** (dī·kät´ə·mē): a division into two contradictory parts or principles.

Shaw uses costuming, a literal external, to stand for the external life, the role that society artificially places upon us.

Finally, there are two dominant kinds of properties in the scene: first, money, which is mentioned no less than seventeen times, and physically produced three times, the last when Higgins dramatically throws a handful of money into Eliza's basket. Second, flowers, sold by Eliza, which, as result of her collision with Freddy, are trampled in the mud—like Eliza herself, a cockney flower trampled by society. To our prop list, we should also add Higgins's notebook, in which he reduces people to mere sounds via the phonetic representations of their speech. The notebook, like the money, stands for the external, mechanical life, while the flowers, a vital, organic image, stand for the internal.

The other two settings of the play, Higgins's laboratory and Mrs. Higgins's drawing room, reflect the nature of the individuals who inhabit them, in an obvious contrast. The laboratory is loaded with scientific equipment, including "a life-size image of half a human head, shewing in section the vocal organs" (Shaw 22; 2), which (as with the notebook) expresses Higgins's mechanistic handling of human beings. In this room, Higgins experiments on people in his unfeeling way; he says that he has taught "the best looking women in the world. . . . They might as well be blocks of wood" (37; 2). The sectioned human head that the audience sees is a literal representation of this apt metaphor.

7. According to Hornby, what does the reader learn about Higgins from his laboratory?

On the walls of the laboratory, Shaw tells us, there are engravings: "mostly Piranesis and mezzotint[7] portraits" (22; 2). Since Piranesi did architectural engravings, these are again images that suggest a mechanical attitude. The stage directions also specify that there are "*no paintings*" (22; 2).

Mrs. Higgins's drawing room, on the other hand, is specifically described as "very unlike her son's room in Wimpole Street" (Shaw 53; 3). Decorated in the anti-industrial, esthetic style of William Morris and Edward Burne-Jones,[8] it definitely contains oil paintings, including a portrait of Mrs. Higgins in her youth, in "one of the beautiful Rossettian[9] costumes" (53; 3). The windows are open (in contrast with those of Higgins's lab), "giving access to a balcony

8. What main point do these quotations support? How does Hornby elaborate, or restate, that point within the paragraph?

---

7. **mezzotint:** a method of engraving that involves burnishing a copper or steel plate and scraping areas to create shadows and light.

8. **William Morris** (1834–1896) and **Edward Burne-Jones** (1833–1898): Members of the Aesthetic Movement in England, 1850–c.1890, who resented the ugly factories and cheaply made goods which resulted from the Industrial Revolution. Morris and Burne-Jones produced designs for tapestries, wallpaper, furniture, and stained glass.

9. **Rossettian:** Dante Gabriel Rossetti (1828–1882) was an English poet, painter, and founding member of the Pre-Raphaelite Brotherhood. His most easily recognized works are portraits of women in brightly colored flowing robes.

with flowers in pots" (53; 3), which recall the flowers that Eliza was selling in Act I. Similarly, there is "an Elizabethan chair roughly carved in the style of Inigo Jones" (53; 3), recalling St. Paul's church in Covent Garden, designed by Jones, which was also seen in the first act. In contrast with Higgins's cold, sterile laboratory, this drawing room suggests warmth, beauty, vitality. The dominant human image, the painting of the young Mrs. Higgins in a beautiful costume, contrasts with the wooden, sectioned head. In this drawing room, Mrs. Higgins chides her son and Pickering for turning Eliza into a mechanical "live doll" (65; 3), a verbal image which recalls that sectioned head yet again.

The two contrasting rooms, then, express the same kind of dichotomy as the two contrasting parts of the setting of the opening act. The rooms are not only appropriate to the characters who live in them and the events that take place there, but also, taken together, make a strong visual statement of the fundamental conflict in the play. What the audience *sees* speaks as loudly as what it *hears*.

Shaw continues to use costume in an expressive way throughout the play. Higgins, for example, is "dressed in a professional-looking black frock-coat with a white linen collar and black silk tie" (Shaw 22; 2), which is not only appropriate to his profession but expressive of his austere nature. For the characters in the play who are more or less fixed, like Higgins, Pickering, Mrs. Higgins, and Mrs. Pearce, Shaw's costume descriptions are usually brief, as here with Higgins, or nonexistent, because there is no conflict between clothing and self. With the two characters who change during the course of the play, however, Shaw's costume descriptions are extensive and explicit, reflecting again the dichotomy that lies at the core of the play. None of their costumes seems quite appropriate to the wearer; Eliza's garish "hat with three ostrich feathers, orange, sky-blue, and red" is expressive of her longing for elegance, but is belied by the generally bedraggled, filthy clothing she wears with it (24; 2). Yet later on, when she is "exquisitely dressed" (58; 3), her attire is hardly appropriate either; her clothing, an external along with her elegant speech, has turned her into a lifeless, mechanical doll. Doolittle, her father, in his first appearance is "clad in the costume of his profession, including a hat with a black brim covering his neck and shoulders" (40–41; 2), yet he does not really practice his profession, and certainly seems far too clever for it. On the other hand, his final appearance "resplendently dressed as for a fashionable wedding. . . . A flower in his button-hole, a dazzling silk hat, and patent leather shoes" is hardly right either, since he is no gentleman by a long shot (87; 5). With Eliza and Doolittle, costuming is an incongruous, outer thing only, a mechanical overlay that contrasts ludicrously with their actual selves. So unsuitable and incorrect is Eliza's initial costume, in fact, that Mrs. Pearce actually burns it.

9. What evidence does the writer give to show that Shaw's use of costumes is meaningful?

The major costuming of *Pygmalion*, then, usually is a "mechanical" rather than "vital" aspect of the play. In this regard, it is appropriate that in the climactic confrontation between Eliza and Higgins, she throws a pair of *slippers* at him, pieces of costuming that again stand for the external, mechanical life that he has created for her, but which she is rejecting. It is in this scene that she slips back into her natural, ungrammatical way of speaking: "I'm nothing to you—not so much as them slippers" (Shaw 77; 4). Higgins instantly corrects her with "Those slippers" (77; 4), a hilariously incongruous, mechanical remark, which once again shows him to be clinging to externals. . . .[10]

In this regard, we should look again at the rich opening scene. The scenic elements artfully establish the metatheatrical[11] ambiance of the play. St. Paul's Covent Garden is shaped like a Greek temple, which recalls the temples that stood behind ancient Greek theaters. (Shaw, with his strong sense of the theatrical tradition, "the long line from Aeschylus to me," plus his knowledge of the Greeks via his friend Gilbert Murray, must surely have been aware of this.) Inigo Jones, its architect, was himself a stage designer. It is in the heart of the theater district, and has long been known as a theater church; many theater figures have attended it over the years, and some, such as William Wycherley, Charles Macklin, and Ellen Terry, are interred there. The Eynsford Hills have just come from the theater, which is mentioned twice. Most of this would have been perfectly clear to the original London audience, who were after all watching the play in a theater not far from St. Paul's.

> **10. Hornby has already written about the opening scene. Why does he return to it?**

> **11. Why does Shaw set the opening of his play in the theater district, in Hornby's view?**

The metatheatrical elements, then, establish for the audience from the outset that they are seeing a play about theater, not in the literal sense of a play like Pinero's *Trelawny of the Wells*, but in the broader sense of a play like *Hamlet*. That is, Shaw is depicting not some particular theater, but a whole world that is theatricalized, in which people play roles that have often been artificially, and cruelly, forced upon them. Shaw's theater reflects his society, but that society is, in turn, a form of theater. Shaw in *Pygmalion* ironically uses the theater to expose this fact, turning the stage against its audience—who, like the Eynsford Hills, will rush out into the street after the final curtain in their elegant evening clothes, indifferent to the fate of the thousands of Elizas who are struggling there.

Works Cited

Bentley, Eric. *Bernard Shaw: 1856–1950.* New York: New Directions, 1957.

Shaw, George Bernard. *Pygmalion and Other Plays.* Intro. by Alan S. Downer. New York: Dodd, Mead & Co., 1967.

---

10. In the next two paragraphs, omitted in this excerpt, Hornby discusses the language of the play and points out that the play involves role-playing on two levels. Not only, as in all plays, do the actors play roles, but the *characters* play roles as well. He notes that *Pygmalion* is metatheatrical, meaning it is a piece of theater about theater, and that it examines the nature and structures of theater.

11. metatheatrical: having to do with the workings or underpinnings of theater.

Paraphrasing

Say It Again   A **paraphrase** is a restatement of ideas in different words. Paraphrases often include an element of interpretation, and are usually about the same length as the texts they are restating. A paraphrase should not be confused with a **summary,** which is shorter than the original text because it retells only the most important information. Good readers often paraphrase as a way of understanding what they are reading. As you read, ask yourself: What is the writer saying here?

Actually, you paraphrase every day without thinking much about it. For example, you use your own words to describe fascinating details about insects you learned on a science program; you retell a story heard from a friend without quoting the friend's words exactly. You may also confirm your understanding of what someone else has said by using your own words to repeat instructions or ideas.

Moreover, paraphrasing is an invaluable tool for students and others who analyze literature. Paraphrasing allows a reader or writer to discuss and interpret aspects of a play (or another work) without quoting line after line of dialogue. A paraphrase of a dramatic scene usually replaces characters' speeches with narration or indirect quotations. The chart below shows how one student paraphrased a scene from Oscar Wilde's *The Importance of Being Earnest.* (The play hinges on cases of mistaken identity. The character Jack, for example, masquerades as Ernest.)

Reference Note

For more about how to write a **summary,** see page 238.

TIP Writers also paraphrase the ideas of other writers in order to add clarity or support to their own analyses.

The Importance of Being Earnest	Student Paraphrase
Gwendolen. . . . The moment Algernon first mentioned to me that he had a friend called Ernest, I knew I was destined to love you. **Jack.** You really love me, Gwendolen? **Gwendolen.** Passionately!	Believing that Jack's name is actually Ernest, Gwendolen tells him (Jack) that she began to fall in love with him when she first heard his name (Ernest) from Algernon. Jack is thrilled to learn that Gwendolen apparently loves him. Concerned

(continued)

(continued)

> **Jack.** Darling! You don't know how happy you've made me.
>
> **Gwendolen.** My own Ernest!
>
> **Jack.** But you don't really mean to say that you couldn't love me if my name wasn't Ernest?
>
> **Gwendolen.** But your name is Ernest.
>
> **Jack.** Yes, I know it is. But supposing it was something else? Do you mean to say you couldn't love me then?
>
> that she loves him for a false name and identity, Jack asks if she would love him if his name were different. When she protests that his name is Ernest, Jack presses her and asks again, because he fears that she will no longer love him when she finds out his real name.

TIP Paraphrase rather than quote when you need to explain aspects of the literary work in your own words. Quote directly when you need the exact dialogue or a vivid detail to make your point.

THINKING IT THROUGH — Paraphrasing

The student who wrote the paraphrase above followed four basic steps.

▶ **STEP 1** Read the entire passage to determine its overall meaning. Look up any words that are unfamiliar. *This is a love scene between Jack and Gwendolen. They discuss the importance of his name, which Gwendolen thinks is Ernest.*

▶ **STEP 2** Determine how the passage fits with the sections before and after it. Keep the overall meaning in mind as you skim the surrounding text. *This scene comes shortly after the audience has learned that "Ernest's" name is really Jack. It comes right before Jack asks Gwendolen to marry him.*

▶ **STEP 3** Ask yourself: What is happening? What are the characters saying? *Gwendolen thinks that Jack's name is Ernest, so she feels comfortable explaining that she fell in love with him because of his name. Jack worries that she will stop loving him when she discovers his real name and asks if she could love him if his name weren't Ernest.*

▶ **STEP 4** Write the paraphrase in your own words, using complete sentences. Make sure that your paraphrase expresses the same ideas as the original, but do not copy the author's language. *I haven't left out anything important, and I have explained emotions implied in the scene. I have followed the scene but I haven't quoted it directly.*

YOUR TURN 2 — Paraphrasing

Using the steps above, paraphrase the tenth paragraph in Richard Hornby's essay. It begins with the phrase, "Mrs. Higgins's drawing room," on page 186.

Supporting Details from Literary Sources

Right from the Source   Film critics who appear on television often support their opinions and interpretations by showing film clips. After making a statement such as, "The special effects in this movie are first-rate," a critic may show an impressive clip (from the primary source, the movie) of a clash between a pair of cyber warriors. As viewers watch the futuristic soldiers grapple, the critic elaborates: "This battle scene makes you squirm in your seat—you feel like hiding so you don't get in the way!" Depending on how viewers evaluate this evidence, they might agree or disagree with the critic's initial assessment.

When people analyze a work of literature, they cannot show film clips of events or characters. Instead, they gather **supporting details from literary sources,** or **literary evidence.** Most often, writers of literary analyses use details from a **primary source**—the literary work being interpreted. However, they may also include details from **secondary sources,** frequently books and articles about (or in some way related to) the work. Remember that an interpretation in this kind of source is not a fact. Rather, it is another critic's idea about a literary work. Thus, it can be challenged by the reader or by a later critic.

Reference Note
For more on **secondary sources,** see page 240.

Be on the Lookout   As you read critically, think about what the writer is saying—that is, critically analyze the analysis. Whenever you read a literary analysis, ask these questions:

- **What general statements, or claims, does the writer make about the work?** You will find at least one general statement in every paragraph, sometimes more. For example, in paragraph six (beginning on page 185), Hornby says, "Shaw uses costuming, a literal external, to stand for the external life, the role that society artificially places upon us."

- **How does the writer support each major point?** Writers back up their major points with three kinds of support: direct quotations, paraphrases, and summaries. This literary evidence may come from either the work itself (the primary source) or from what someone else has written about the work (a secondary source). In paragraph six, Hornby uses all three kinds of literary evidence to support his major point that Shaw uses costuming to stand for the external life.

Direct quotation	"Eliza is described as 'not at all a romantic figure' (Shaw 10; 1)"
Paraphrase	"dirty with shabby clothes"
Summary	"The same kind of dichotomy operates with Freddy and the Eynsford Hills, who are elegantly dressed in evening clothes, yet turn out to be rather silly people. . . ."

TIP   It is important to remember that a writer's interpretation of a work of literature is not necessarily the only interpretation possible. Every reader brings a unique personality and store of knowledge and experience to a work of literature.

Every reader, therefore, perceives a work's **ambiguities, nuances, and complexities**—those things in a work of literature that lend themselves to a variety of interpretations—differently. As a critical reader, you are, therefore, free to challenge any writer's interpretation, as others are free to challenge yours.

TIP Discussing your interpretation and analysis with other students will help you clarify your own understanding. When offering feedback in these discussions, though, be sure you respect others' viewpoints and be open to differing interpretations.

Overpowering Evidence   Whenever you read a piece of literary criticism, stop to think: Do I agree with the writer's analysis and interpretation? Do I understand the text better after having read the writer's analysis? (You can really judge a literary analysis only when you have read and understood the work the writer discusses.) Ask yourself these questions about the evidence:

- Does the writer present at least two pieces of literary evidence to support each major point?
- Does each piece of literary evidence directly support the writer's interpretation, rather than restate it or distract from it?

Building Expectations   In order to understand literary analyses, you need to recognize exactly when the writer is citing literary evidence. Usually a writer introduces a supporting detail before actually presenting it. After presenting the detail, the writer goes on to elaborate or explain how it supports his or her analysis.

Example:

introduction   paraphrase
In this drawing room, Mrs. Higgins chides her son and Pickering for

quotation
turning Eliza into a mechanical "live doll" (65; 3), a verbal image which

elaboration
recalls that sectioned head yet again.

To visualize this three-part structure, you might try to imagine a literary-evidence "sandwich."

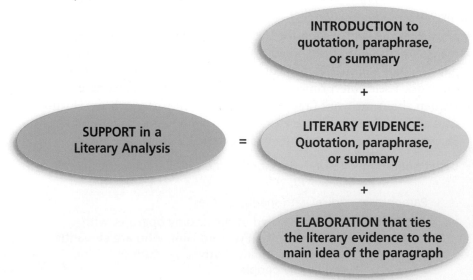

SUPPORT in a Literary Analysis

=

INTRODUCTION to quotation, paraphrase, or summary

+

LITERARY EVIDENCE: Quotation, paraphrase, or summary

+

ELABORATION that ties the literary evidence to the main idea of the paragraph

TIP As a reader, remember that literary evidence will not always be obvious, nor will it always appear as a direct quotation. In fact, writers can include a specific detail from a work in three ways.

- They can mention, without quoting, the detail in their own words.
- They can quote a key word or phrase within one of their own sentences.
- They can directly quote an important sentence or series of sentences.

Now, take a look at how one reader identifies Richard Hornby's use of literary evidence in the eighth paragraph (page 186), where Hornby discusses how Shaw uses setting to convey information about a character. You should find two literary-evidence sandwiches in this paragraph.

The other two settings of the play, Higgins's laboratory and Mrs. Higgins's drawing room, reflect the nature of the individuals who inhabit them, in an obvious contrast.	Main idea (topic sentence)
The laboratory is loaded with scientific equipment, including "a life-size image of half a human head, shewing in section the vocal organs" (Shaw 22; 2),	Introduction Quotation
which (as with the notebook) expresses Higgins's mechanistic handling of human beings.	Elaboration
In this room, Higgins experiments on people in his unfeeling way; he says that he has taught	Introduction
"the best looking women in the world. . . . They might as well be blocks of wood" (37; 2).	Quotation
The sectioned human head that the audience sees is a literal representation of this apt metaphor.	Elaboration

TIP In the paragraph above, notice that Hornby writes about Henry Higgins in the **literary present tense.** This form is based on the idea that characters and events in literature are timeless and ongoing. Henry Higgins was the same for your grandfather as he is to you and will be to your grandchildren.

YOUR TURN 3   Identifying Literary Evidence

With a partner, go back and carefully re-read three body paragraphs from Hornby's essay. On your own paper, identify and label the main ideas of each paragraph and the literary evidence Hornby gives to support them.

Prefixes and Suffixes

Many words are combinations of prefixes or suffixes and root words. A **prefix** precedes the root word and changes its meaning. A **suffix** is attached to the end of the root word, slightly altering its meaning and often changing its part of speech. For example, Richard Hornby adds the suffix *–ical* to the noun root *theater* to turn the word into an adjective. You can strengthen your vocabulary quickly by familiarizing yourself with common prefixes and suffixes.

Among the common prefixes are *de–*, meaning "down," "from," or "down from," as in *depression*; *re–*, meaning "back(ward)" or "again," as in *review*; *inter–*, meaning "between" or "among," as in *intercontinental*; *contra–*, meaning "against" or "opposed to," as in *contradict*. Common suffixes include *–ent*, *–ar*, *–er*, *–ist*, all meaning "person who," as in *student*, *scholar*, *worker*, and *scientist*; *–ance*, *–ery*, meaning "act of," as in *maintenance* and *discovery*; and *–cy*, or *–ty*, meaning "state of," as in *democracy* and *enormity*.

(For more information on prefixes, suffixes, and common roots, see pages 1009–1012.)

THINKING IT THROUGH Using Prefixes and Suffixes

To strengthen your vocabulary by understanding prefixes and suffixes, follow the steps below. Also look at how one student figured out the meaning of the word *interlinear*.

1. **Separate the prefix or suffix of the word from the root with a long dash.** inter—linear

2. **Associate the prefix or suffix with a familiar word.** Often you can connect the meaning of a word part to a word you know that uses the same part. Inter—linear is like inter-state.

3. **Write down everything you know about the familiar word.** My family drove on Interstate Highway 10 through Texas, New Mexico, and Arizona. Interstate must mean "between states."

4. **Now, use what you have discovered to make an educated guess about the unfamiliar word.** If "interstate means between states, "interlinear" must mean between lines.

PRACTICE

Using the steps above, write definitions for the following words. Then, look up the words in a dictionary to check the accuracy of your definitions.

1. interpersonal
2. novelty
3. malcontent
4. leniency
5. antagonist
6. contraindicated
7. degenerative
8. recapitulate
9. connivance
10. loiterer

Sentence-Completion Questions

As you examine the supporting details in a literary analysis, you sharpen your ability to recognize logical relationships. This skill is crucial to answering the **sentence-completion** questions that commonly appear on standardized tests. A sentence-completion question shows you only part of a sentence. Based on the content and structure of that part, you choose the appropriate word or words to complete the sentence.

Most sentence completion items will have **clue words** that hint at a logical relationship between the part of the sentence you have and the correct answer. The chart below shows clue words and the relationships they suggest.

Relationship	Clue Words
contrast	though, however, nevertheless, but, yet, although, despite
comparison	similarly, like, just as . . . so

example	such as, for example
cause and effect	because (of), as a result
chronological	previously, prior to, after, before, earlier, then, later, next, first

On a standardized test, a typical sentence completion question looks like this:

1. Although the weather forecast predicted a severe ice storm, school administrators were _____ to cancel classes.

    A. eager

    B. reluctant

    C. motivated

    D. persuaded

    E. relieved

THINKING IT THROUGH **Answering Sentence-Completion Questions**

Keep the following steps in mind as you work through a sentence-completion question.

1. **Look for clue words that indicate a relationship between ideas.** Although indicates that the meaning of the first part of the sentence contrasts with the second part. We expect administrators to cancel classes for an ice storm, so the missing word should contradict that expectation.

2. **Eliminate obviously incorrect choices.** A, C, D, and E do not show the contradictory

relationship suggested by although. All of these choices suggest that school administrators want to cancel classes.

3. **Try out the remaining answer(s) in the sentence.** Make sure the sentence makes sense. If it does not, try a different answer. Here, only **B** satisfies the contradictory relationship suggested by the clue word *although*.

Writing a Literary Analysis of a Drama

WHAT'S AHEAD?

In this workshop you will write a literary analysis of a drama. You will also learn how to

- analyze literary elements in a play
- develop a thesis statement
- use literary evidence to support your analysis
- introduce quotations into your text
- use the literary present tense correctly

Reading a play critically is like doing detective work. The playwright drops clues about the meaning—a symbol here, some characterization there. As a reader, you pick up these clues and use them to find the themes of the play. However, not even the best detective picks up all the rich meanings of a play in a single reading. You can get so caught up in the characters and plot that you cannot always explain why a play made you feel one way or another. Analysis helps you form an explanation and then go beyond feelings. Analysis brings you a deeper understanding of the meaning of the play, as you bring your imagination, life experiences, and analytical skills to bear on the literary text.

After you have finished the detective work, it is time to present your case in a **literary analysis** using the evidence you have found. Writing a literary analysis of a drama not only helps you clarify your understanding of how the various elements of a play work together to create its total effect, but also allows you to share your interpretation with readers.

Prewriting

Select a Play

The Play's the Thing   If your teacher has not already assigned a text for your literary analysis, begin by thinking about plays that made an impression on you when you saw them. You may also wish to read plays that are completely new to you. Focus on works whose basic characteristics fit your interests. For instance, do you prefer comedies or tragedies, melodramas or farces? Are you more interested in contemporary or historical characters and settings? To make a good choice, you might also

- **Scan the table of contents of your literature textbook** for familiar titles or something new and intriguing to you.

- **Ask friends, teachers, or family members for recommendations.** People who know you well may be able to identify a particular play that you might enjoy.
- **Speak to librarians or knowledgeable bookstore clerks** who can help you find anthologies of plays from many eras and geographical regions. They can also point you toward reviews of plays in magazines, newspapers, or on the Internet, which might pique your interest in a single play.

TIP Read an entire play once before deciding to use it as a subject for your literary analysis. You will be able to concentrate on analysis in your second reading if you already know the plot and characters well.

Think About Audience, Purpose, and Tone

What's Your Motivation? Though dramatists may write with a variety of purposes in mind—expressing a vision of the world, entertaining, or even persuading people about a political or social cause—your **purpose** in writing a literary analysis is set: to explain your interpretation of a literary work.

To achieve this purpose, you need to adopt an authoritative **voice** and **style** and establish an appropriate **tone** for your **audience.** Since the primary audience for your literary analysis is your teacher, using a formal tone is best. Unless your teacher specifies that first-person pronouns (such as *I* and *we*) are acceptable in this expository work, avoid them by using the third person exclusively (*he, she,* and *they*).

Find a Focus for the Analysis

Take Note of This To understand a good play, you need to read it more than once and take notes so that you will remember what you have drawn from the play. Read with a pencil in hand, and use these suggestions to look for and think about important details in a play.

- **Read stage directions** to find descriptions of characters, props, costumes, and sets.
- **Notice lines of dialogue** that reveal characterization.
- **Jot down observations about literary elements**—such as setting, conflict, or figurative language—that impress you.
- **Look for patterns** and repetition of literary elements.

TIP If you cannot write notes in your book, use slips of paper or self-sticking notes to flag pages, or keep a list of page numbers in a **learning log.**

During a second reading you can narrow your focus to find a suitable topic for your literary analysis. Most good topics relate to the author's use of literary elements. Use the chart on the next page to review how literary elements function in dramatic literature. Asking yourself questions like the ones in the right-hand column can help you decide which elements to use as the focus of your literary analysis.

Element	Analysis Questions
Character—a person (or occasionally an animal) in a play	Does one character grab your attention? What is interesting or special about him or her? How does the character speak, look, move, and behave? What motivates the character to behave in certain ways? How does he or she change during the play? Do these changes relate to any important themes in the play?
Conflict—a struggle between opposing forces in a character or in the play	What conflicts drive the characters? Are they internal (within a character) or external (between one character and some outer force) or both? How are these conflicts resolved? What is the play's primary conflict, and how is it resolved?
Imagery—language that appeals to the senses, often the sense of sight	What images does the language make you see? To what other senses does the language of the play appeal? Is there repetition or a pattern of imagery in the play?
Plot—the events of a play arranged in a particular sequence	Is the plot predictable or surprising? Are details of the plot believable? Are events presented in strict chronological order? Does the author juxtapose—put side-by-side—or otherwise order events in a meaningful way?
Setting—the time and place of the play	When and where does the play take place? Does the setting suggest a distinctive tone or mood? Does it affect the characters in any way? Is the setting somehow connected to the theme?
Symbol—a person, place, thing, or event in a play that has both a literal meaning and a larger meaning	Do any of the people, places, objects, or events in this play stand for something beyond themselves? If so, what do they represent?
Theme—an underlying idea or insight revealed by the play	What ideas about people—or life in general—does the play address or illustrate? Does the play illuminate human problems, relationships, or growth? How does the playwright use other dramatic elements—such as character, conflict, or setting—to express his or her themes?

Make notes about any passages in the text that help you answer these questions or stimulate your thinking about the play. Not all of your notes will end up directing you to a topic, but from them a topic will emerge. The following chart shows one student's reading notes about a passage from Act 3, Scene 2 of William Shakespeare's *Macbeth*, in which Macbeth has just rejoined Lady Macbeth after ordering the murders of Banquo and his son, Fleance. Macbeth fears Banquo suspects him of killing King Duncan. He also wants to prevent the witches' prophecy—that Banquo would father a line of kings—from coming to pass. In this passage, the student has noticed several details concerning the characters of Macbeth and Lady Macbeth.

LITERARY READING: NOTES FOR A LITERARY ANALYSIS

Play's Dialogue	Notes and Questions

LADY MACBETH. Come on.
  Gentle my lord, sleek o'er your
    rugged looks;
  Be bright and jovial among your
    guests tonight.
MACBETH. So shall I, love; and so, I
    pray, be you:
  Let your remembrance apply to
    Banquo;
  Present him eminence, both with eye
    and tongue:
  Unsafe the while, that we must lave
  Our honors in these flattering streams
  And make our faces vizards to our
    hearts,
  Disguising what they are.
LADY MACBETH. You must leave this.
 	
MACBETH. O, full of scorpions is my
    mind, dear wife!
  Thou know'st that Banquo, and his
    Fleance, lives.
LADY MACBETH. But in them nature's
    copy's not eterne.
MACBETH. There's comfort yet; they are
    assailable.
	Lady Macbeth tells her husband to put a "fair" face over his "foul" disposition. This picks up the "fair is foul, and foul is fair" theme. Reveals a lot about Lady M's character and about M's reactions to having killed King Duncan.
	
	Macbeth tells his wife that she must flatter Banquo. M doesn't feel safe as long as he and Lady M must hide their real feelings under flattery (more of the "fair is foul" theme).
	
	Lady M tells M to relax and not worry so much.
	In Act 1 M is compared to an eagle and to a lion. Now he says he has scorpions in his brain. Is there a pattern of images here?
	Possible topic: What kinds of animal images does Shakespeare use to describe M at different points in the play? How do they relate to changes in his character?

Develop a Thesis Statement

KEY CONCEPT

What Do You Want to Say? **Your thesis is your main idea about a topic—the principal point you want readers to take away from your literary analysis.** Since a thesis is usually stated in the introductory paragraph, readers can use it as a compass to guide them through the essay. Moreover, reminding yourself about your thesis can help you stay on course during the writing process.

To formulate a thesis that states your interpretation of some aspect of the play, review your notes on the play and ask yourself the following questions:

■ **Do any literary elements stand out as more interesting or important than others?**

TIP When you are thinking up a thesis statement, it may help to use this formula:

topic + your idea about it = thesis

- **Do some of the details have qualities in common? Do certain details create a pattern?**
- **How do the details connect to the play's overall meaning?**
- **How do these particular details help develop the themes of the play?**

Choose at least one literary element that relates to a theme in the play and that stands out in your notes. Draft a sentence that states your idea, or conclusion, about the effects or purposes of the elements you have chosen to examine. Here is an example of such a thesis statement. The topic is underlined once; the writer's conclusion about the topic is underlined twice.

> The animal images in *Macbeth* symbolize Macbeth's transition from brave soldier to cornered tyrant by emphasizing how his overreaching ambition leads to his destruction.

This thesis statement describes the relationship between symbolism and the theme of the destructive power of uncontrolled ambition. The thesis also gives readers an indication of the evidence (animal imagery) they can expect to see as the analysis develops.

> **TIP** When you start writing your essay, you might begin thinking of a **title.** Remember, the title should be a clue to your thesis and should not be a complete sentence. "The Role of Animal Imagery in *Macbeth*" is a good title for an essay with this example thesis.

Gather Support

KEY CONCEPT

Every Last Detail   **A literary analysis is an interpretation of a work that must be validated, or proven sound, by supporting evidence.** You will need to gather **literary evidence** from your **primary source** (the play you are analyzing). This evidence takes the form of *direct quotations from the text, paraphrases of a passage or a dramatic scene,* and *summaries of events.* You might also seek evidence or background information in one or more **secondary sources**—*books and articles written about the play, the playwright,* or *the time period in which the play was written or set.* Use the basic method outlined on the next page to gather and consider supporting evidence from the primary source.

As you develop ideas for your literary analysis, you can also learn from other writers' interpretations of the play. You may borrow information from sources to support your thesis, as long as you provide documentation that credits their authors. If you do not cite the sources for others' ideas and information, you will be guilty of plagiarism, a serious academic offense.

Reference Note

To find secondary sources, follow standard research practices. Remember to document any secondary sources that you use and to include them in the *Works Cited* list. For more information on **research,** see page 248. For more information on **documenting sources,** see page 268.

To gather and record evidence for your analysis, follow these steps.

▶ **STEP 1 Use your reading notes to identify specific details and quotations from the play that support your thesis.** You may need to return to the play to find additional material. *At one point, Macbeth says his brain is full of scorpions; later he compares himself to a bear chained to a stake.*

▶ **STEP 2 Copy direct quotations exactly.** If the play is written as poetry, use slash marks to show line endings. List the act, scene, and line numbers (in that order) where each quotation appears. Typically, act, scene, and line numbers are written as you see in the following parenthetical notes. *"O, full of scorpions is my mind, dear wife! / Thou know'st that Banquo, and his Fleance, lives" (3.2.36–37). "They have tied me to a stake; I cannot fly, / But bearlike I must fight the course" (5.7.1–2).*

▶ **STEP 3 Make sure that each piece of evidence is specific and that it clearly supports the thesis.** *Speech about scorpions in the mind—M's guilty conscience about Duncan's murder and worry about Banquo's power. Chained bear—M must fight or surrender.*

Don't Leave It Alone   Because you have particular knowledge and life experiences, you make unique inferences while reading a text. A character's speech may mean one thing to you and something different to another reader; therefore, in your literary analysis you need to do more than merely present quotations and other details in support of your thesis. You must also **elaborate,** or comment, on the evidence you include by explaining its meaning and tying it to your thesis statement. The chart below shows how one writer fleshed out her first notes.

TIP   When you take quotations or other details from a primary or secondary source, you must credit the author of that text by providing a **parenthetical citation.** A parenthetical citation includes the author's last name and the page number of the source of the information. Be sure to keep track of this information as you gather evidence.

A classic work like one of Shakespeare's plays has usually been published in so many editions that citations give act, scene, and line numbers. No citation of a specific edition is required.

Reference Note

For more on how to use **parenthetical citations,** see page 269.

Specific Evidence	My Comments
"O, full of scorpions is my mind, dear wife! / Thou know'st that Banquo, and his Fleance, lives." (Macbeth, 3.2.36–37)	When Macbeth complains about scorpions in his mind, he is already on his way to destruction. Scorpions symbolize Macbeth's fear of Banquo, guilt about killing Duncan, and general loss of perspective.

Evaluating Supporting Evidence

Not all evidence is truly supporting evidence, so you need to evaluate each piece of evidence to make sure it backs up the point you are making in your literary analysis. Valid supporting evidence should be

- **specific**—it should refer to the controlling idea of the thesis, not simply restate the thesis or summarize the play
- **relevant**—there must be a clear and direct relationship between the piece of evidence and the idea it supports

Read the thesis statement below, and study the examples of invalid and valid supporting evidence.

Thesis Statement: Although at the beginning of the play, Lady Macbeth is a strong and calculating character, guilt causes her to deteriorate into a haunted shadow.

Invalid: She does not seem to know what is going on around her. [This interpretive statement is true but too general. The writer needs to include specific details that show Lady Macbeth feeling guilty.]

Invalid: Lady Macbeth is an apparently strong character whose weaknesses are exposed by the guilt she feels. [This is an insightful statement, but it simply restates the thesis.]

Valid: In her sleep, Lady Macbeth wanders around the castle, trying to clean imaginary blood off her hands. [This evidence connects to the thesis by giving a specific detail from the play that shows Lady Macbeth's deterioration. With elaboration it would properly support the thesis.]

Valid: As Lady Macbeth walks around the castle in her sleep, she wonders whether the smell of blood on her hand can ever be wiped away. [This evidence connects to the thesis by giving a specific detail that shows the guilt that has caused her deterioration.]

PRACTICE

After reading the thesis statement, identify on your own paper which numbered items truly support the statement. Also explain why you think any items are invalid pieces of supporting evidence.

Thesis Statement: Eventually Eliza Doolittle demonstrates that, although Henry Higgins has passed her off as a member of proper society, she is a cockney girl at heart.

1. Though Higgins has taught her to speak with an upper-class accent, he has obviously not changed what is inside her.

2. Mrs. Higgins chastises her son, saying, "[You are] playing with your live doll."

3. Eliza helps Higgins win his bet with Pickering: He succeeds in passing her off as a lady in society.

4. Eliza becomes engaged to Freddy, a young man with an upper-class background but no money.

5. Eliza, who is angry, hurls the slippers Higgins had bought for her and says ungrammatically, "I'm nothing to you—not so much as them slippers."

Organize Your Support

Making Arrangements After gathering your evidence, you will need to arrange it in an appropriate **order,** or **logical progression.** For example, since the writer of the analysis of *Macbeth* was tracing changes that occurred in a character over time, she chose to organize her ideas in **chronological order.** Depending on the nature of your thesis, you might choose to organize your evidence according to

- **causes and effects:** This order would work for an analysis tracing the causes of Macbeth's downfall.

- **comparisons and contrasts:** This would be the best order for an analysis comparing the characters Macbeth and Macduff.

- **order of importance:** This order would be a good choice for an analysis of the reasons Macbeth turns to murder as a way to power.

Make an informal plan showing the way in which you intend to develop your ideas. The chart below shows the chronological organization the writer used in the essay on animal imagery in *Macbeth*.

Thesis: The animal images in <u>Macbeth</u> symbolize Macbeth's transition from brave soldier to cornered tyrant by emphasizing how his overreaching ambition leads to his destruction.	
First major point and supporting detail	At the beginning of the play, Macbeth is a courageous warrior who shows strength and an ability to lead. The captain describes Macbeth as an eagle and a lion (1.2.34–35).
Second major point and supporting detail	After killing Duncan, Macbeth experiences fear, guilt, and loss of perspective as he begins his descent to ruin. Macbeth says his mind is "full of scorpions" (3.2.36).
Third major point and supporting detail	In the end, Macbeth is headed toward destruction and becomes a cornered, desperate tyrant. Macbeth compares himself to a bear chained to a stake (5.7.1–2).

 YOUR TURN 4   Choosing a Topic and Organizing Ideas

Use the information on the previous pages as guidelines to help you choose a play to analyze; think about audience, purpose, and tone; find a focus for your literary analysis; develop a thesis statement; and gather and organize support for your thesis.

After you have completed each of these tasks, you should have everything in place to begin writing your literary analysis.

Writing

Literary Analysis

Framework	Directions and Explanations

Introduction
- Identify the literary work's title and author.
- Supply background information or a brief summary of the work.
- Provide a clear thesis statement.

Give Important Background Information   Include the name of the play and playwright early in your introductory paragraph. To refresh your readers' memories of the play—or perhaps to help them understand your interpretation without having to read the play—briefly summarize the play's major action and important themes.

State Your Thesis   A clear and concise thesis statement will anchor your paper's organization and indicate how you will support your ideas with textual evidence.

Body
- State major points supporting your thesis.
- Provide evidence (details from the primary source and possibly from secondary sources) that supports each major point.

Support Your Thesis   Clearly state the major points that support your thesis, using a least one paragraph for each major point. Be sure to connect each major point to your thesis.

Offer Literary Evidence   First, state each piece of literary evidence—quotations, paraphrases, and summaries—you use to support your major points. Then, elaborate on the evidence by thoroughly explaining *how* the literary evidence supports each major point.

Conclusion
- Summarize your major points and restate your thesis.

Pull It All Together   Remind readers of your thesis in a new way, and provide some fresh insight, if possible. You might comment on how your thesis relates to the playwright's theme, to life, or to theater as an art form.

YOUR TURN 5   Writing a First Draft

The Writer's Model and the Student's Model on the following pages were written with the Framework as a guide. After you have read these two models, use this Framework to help you write a first draft of your own literary analysis.

A Writer's Model

The following essay closely follows the Framework on the previous page.

From Noble Eagle to Bear at Bay: Animal Images in
The Tragedy of Macbeth

INTRODUCTION
Identification of the play's title and author

Brief summary of the plot

William Shakespeare's Macbeth is the story of a great man's fall from grace. At the beginning of the play, Macbeth is a loyal supporter of Scotland's King Duncan, but greed for power causes him to kill the king and take the crown for himself. Once he is king, Macbeth is paranoid about losing power, so he kills many more people. When the Scottish nobles see his cruelty, they rally around Macduff and Duncan's son Malcolm to overthrow Macbeth. The animal images in Macbeth symbolize Macbeth's transition from brave soldier to cornered tyrant by emphasizing how his overreaching ambition leads to his destruction.

Thesis statement

BODY
First major point

Macbeth begins the play as a courageous warrior and politically powerful leader as revealed through two images of strong animals. In Act 1, before Macbeth even appears on stage, a captain uses animal imagery to describe him to King Duncan. The images come during a description of how a Norwegian lord had launched a fresh assault on Macbeth and Banquo, who were already exhausted from fighting. When the king asks if Macbeth and Banquo were "dismayed" by the attack (1.2.34), the captain replies, "Yes / As sparrows eagles, or the hare the lion" (1.2.35), which essentially means, "No, they were not dismayed." In this comparison, Macbeth and Banquo are the eagles and the lion, and by contrast, the Norwegian forces are the sparrows and hare. The implication is that Macbeth and Banquo are skilled and effective predators, or warriors, who are not intimidated by the Norwegian forces, their natural prey. These particular animal images have additional associations that contribute to the reader's sense of Macbeth's character. The eagle's ability to soar above the earth makes the eagle seem to have perspective and nobility. The lion, too, is a noble beast known as "king of the jungle" because it possesses the kind of power and grandeur associated with leaders. Thus, these images suggest that in addition to being an effective and honored warrior, noble Macbeth is a clear thinker with the presence of a leader.

Literary evidence from the primary source that supports the first major point

Elaboration— explanation of how evidence supports major point

Shakespeare's choice of images in relationship to Macbeth begin to reflect a baseness and ugliness as Macbeth chooses the

Second major point

(continued)

path to evil. The image of scorpions, associated with Macbeth after the murder of Duncan, symbolizes Macbeth's fear, guilt, and loss of perspective. After killing the king, Macbeth fears that the witches have "placed a fruitless crown" upon his head (3.1.61), that he has defiled his mind and given up his immortal soul for the sake of Banquo's sons; the witches had prophesied that Banquo "shalt get kings, though [he] be none" (1.3.67). To prevent Banquo's children from gaining power, Macbeth hires men to kill Banquo and his son, Fleance. Before Banquo's murder, Macbeth tells Lady Macbeth, "O, full of scorpions is my mind, dear wife! / Thou know'st that Banquo, and his Fleance, lives" (3.2.36–37). The image of scorpions stinging Macbeth's brain emphasizes how fear of Banquo plagues him. Further, since Macbeth's statement comes right after his speech about the "torture of the mind" he has suffered since killing Duncan (3.2.21), the stinging scorpions seem to extend that torture, suggesting that Macbeth feels guilty about arranging another murder. Finally, the scorpion is an appropriate symbol for Macbeth at this point in the play because unlike the eagle, which views the world from above, the scorpion has no perspective; it crawls on the ground and stings anything it perceives to be a threat. Macbeth acts the same way. He has lost his ability to distinguish between real dangers and imagined ones, and he kills anyone he perceives to be a threat to his kingship, including Banquo. He goes so far as to order the murder of Macduff's innocent wife and children after the witches' apparition has assured him that "none of woman born" can harm him (4.1.80).

In the final act, Macbeth hurtles toward ruin; the animal image in this act confirms the state of desperation to which he has been reduced. When Macbeth suspects the end is near, he compares himself to a chained bear that is under attack: "They have tied me to a stake; I cannot fly, / But bearlike I must fight the course" (5.7.1–2). While the image of a bear might conjure some of the strength and nobility Macbeth possessed at the beginning of the play, the image is essentially negative. The chained bear cannot expect to escape or kill its attackers; therefore, it must fight until it dies. At this point in the play, Macbeth feels fate catching up to him. Originally he had thought he would stay in power for a long time, since an apparition had told him "Macbeth shall never vanquished be until / Great Birnam Wood to high Dunsinane Hill / Shall come against him" (4.1.92–94); however, in Act 5, Scene 5, when he hears that Birnam Wood is moving, he realizes that he has misunderstood the prophecy. In

Literary evidence

Elaboration— explanation of how the quotation supports the major point

Third major point

Literary evidence
Elaboration

Summary

Scene 7, Macbeth is resigned to the fact that he will be conquered, but he is also resolved to face it as a fighter—bound and desperate, but battling until the very end. In this scene he kills young Siward. In the next scene he clings to his tenuous belief that no man who was born to a woman can harm him. When Macduff tells him the circumstances of his coming into the world, Macbeth loses heart and refuses to fight, but when Macduff threatens to make him the monster in a sideshow, he fights on until Macduff kills him. In this way, Macbeth resembles the chained bear who struggles to fight off attacking dogs until they destroy him.

By tracing the animal images in <u>Macbeth</u>, readers discover a pattern that reflects the downward spiral of the tragic hero. At the beginning of the play, Macbeth is a powerful bird of prey or noble lion. After he kills Duncan, he becomes a poisonous arachnid, and finally he is a trapped bear, held at bay and then killed. Each successive image marks a transition in Macbeth's character. Together the images create a pattern that emphasizes one of the major themes in <u>Macbeth</u>: overreaching ambition and greed for power can destroy a person's best qualities and lead to a tragic end.

Elaboration—
explanation of how
evidence supports
major point

CONCLUSION
Restatement of thesis

**Summary of major
points**

**Comment on theme
in the play**

In the following essay, student Colin Dietsch from Rockingham County Senior High School in Burlington, North Carolina, explores the theme of another Shakespearean play.

The Alteration of Desires in William Shakespeare's
A Midsummer Night's Dream

"There is no greater calamity than lavish desires."
Lao-tze

Interesting opener

Title and author identified

Background provided

According to Buddhist doctrine, all suffering begins with desire. Dramatic works often use the emotion of desire to create conflict. In William Shakespeare's A Midsummer Night's Dream, the desires of several characters give rise to the central conflicts of the work: Theseus anxiously desires to consummate his marriage to Hippolyta, the Amazon queen; Demetrius wants to marry Hermia; Hermia, however, would rather marry Lysander, whose desire is to marry Hermia; Helena wants to marry Demetrius; and the fairy king Oberon wants Titania to give him the changeling boy in her possession. In the end, only Hermia and Lysander's desire is fully realized. The other characters attain contentment in the end, but only after their desires have been somewhat modified or completely transformed.

Thesis statement

First major point

Theseus expresses a desire for time to move faster, so that he will not have to wait to consummate his marriage to Hippolyta. In the play's opening scene, he articulates his impatience to be married to Hippolyta:

Supporting Block Quotation

> Now fair Hippolyta, our nuptial hour
> Draws on apace. Four happy days bring in
> Another moon; but, O, methinks how slow
> This old moon wanes! She lingers my desires,
> Like to a stepdame or a dowager,
> Long withering out a young man's revenue.
>
> (1.1.1–6)

Elaboration of supporting quotation

He compares himself to a young man awaiting an inheritance, straining against the shackles of time. Theseus' desire to speed up consummation remains unfulfilled. He is forced to wait for his much-anticipated wedding night. Hippolyta encourages him to moderate his desire by urging him to exhibit patience and by telling him their wedding is not as distant as it seems: "Four days will quickly steep themselves in night / Four nights will quickly dream away the time. . . ." (1.1.7–8). Theseus takes Hippolyta's advice. He moderates his passion for immediate gratification so that he may triumphantly say, in the final act, "Joy, gentle friends, joy and fresh days of love / Accompany your hearts" (5.1.29–30).

Second major point

Demetrius is another character who attains contentment only through the alteration of his desire, this time through the magical meddling of the fairy population. Demetrius is anxious to wed Hermia, but is hindered by Hermia's love for Lysander. Demetrius urges Hermia to submit to her father and asks Lysander to abandon his pursuit of Hermia: "Relent, sweet Hermia, and Lysander, yield / Thy crazèd title to my certain right" (1.1.91–92). Another obstacle to Demetrius' plans is Helena's constant pursuit of him. Demetrius achieves happiness only after Puck, the supernatural trickster, uses a love potion to remove his desire for Hermia and make him fall in love with Helena instead. "I wot not by what power / (But by some power it is) my love to Hermia / Melted as the snow . . ." (4.1.163–165).

Support of second major point with a quotation with elaboration

Second major point reiterated

A third character who can find happiness only through changing his desires is Oberon. Oberon does "but beg a little changeling boy, / To be my henchman . . ." (2.1.120–121). Titania, however, refuses to give Oberon the boy. Consequently, she becomes the victim of Oberon and Puck's practical joke. Oberon is happy in the end, but not because Titania submits to his will and turns over the changeling child; the king of the fairies finds his happiness in knowing that Titania has been humiliated. He offers her amends: "Come, my queen, take hands with me. . . . / Now thou and I are new in amity" (4.1.84–86). The changeling boy is not mentioned in their reconciliation. Oberon's original desire has been supplanted by a new one.

Third major point
Supporting quotation

Continued support of third major point

"In this world there are only two tragedies," Oscar Wilde said. "One is not getting what one wants, and the other is getting it." In A Midsummer Night's Dream Hermia and Lysander are the only two characters who attain happiness by getting what they want. Theseus and Oberon enjoy happiness because they moderate their desires. Demetrius, too, achieves happiness, but only through the magical intervention of Puck.

Interesting quotation and restatement of thesis

Summation of major points

Revising

Evaluate and Revise Your Draft

Check and Check Again   To do a thorough revision, collaborate with a classmate to read your literary analysis at least twice. First, concentrate on finding ways to strengthen the essay's content and organization; then, focus on improving its style.

First Reading: Content and Organization   The chart below can help you review the first draft of a literary analysis. Read and answer the questions in the first column, and use the tips in the middle column to identify places in your draft that need revision. Finally, make the changes suggested in the last column.

Analyzing Drama: Content and Organization Guidelines for Peer and Self-Evaluation

Evaluation Questions	▶ Tips	▶ Revision Techniques
❶ Does the introduction contain the author's name, the title of the play, and necessary background information?	▶ **Underline** the author's name and the play's title. **Bracket** any background. Revise if the name, title, or background is missing.	▶ **Add** the name of the author or title of the play. **Add** a brief summary to help readers understand the analysis.
❷ Does the introduction include a thesis statement?	▶ **Highlight** the thesis statement. If you cannot find one, revise.	▶ **Add** a sentence stating the thesis of the literary analysis.
❸ Are there at least two major points to support the thesis, with evidence from the play to prove them?	▶ **Place a star** beside each of the major points and any quotations, paraphrases, or summaries of the text. If there aren't at least two major points with supporting details from the play, revise.	▶ **Add** a major point with support. **Add** quotations, paraphrases, and summaries as necessary. **Elaborate** on the major point by explaining the supporting details. **Delete** any points that do not support the thesis.
❹ Are the major points and supporting evidence organized in an appropriate way?	▶ **Draw a jagged line under** each major point. If the order does not make sense, revise.	▶ **Reorder** points so that they appear in a logical progression, either in chronological order, order of importance, or another order.
❺ Does the conclusion summarize the thesis and bring the essay to a satisfying close?	▶ **Highlight** the sentence or sentences that restate the thesis statement. **Draw a box** around the sentence that closes the essay.	▶ **Add** a sentence that rephrases the main idea of the essay. If the last sentence does not clearly wrap things up, **replace** it with a clincher that elaborates on the thesis statement.

ONE WRITER'S REVISIONS Here is how the author of the Writer's Model used the guidelines on page 210 to revise the concluding paragraph of the essay on *Macbeth*. Review these revisions before answering the questions that follow the paragraph.

> *By tracing the animal images in <u>Macbeth</u>, readers discover a pattern that reflects the downward spiral of the tragic hero.* ∧ At the beginning of the play, Macbeth is a powerful bird of prey or noble lion. After he kills Duncan, he becomes a poisonous arachnid, and finally he is a trapped bear, *held at bay and then killed.* ∧ Each successive image marks a transition in Macbeth's character.

add

elaborate

Analyzing the Revision Process

1. How does the sentence added at the beginning of the paragraph help the reader?

2. How does the writer elaborate on the second sentence? How does this revision improve the conclusion?

YOUR TURN 6 **Focusing On Content and Organization**

Using the chart on page 210 as a guide, revise the content and organization of your literary analysis. The example above models some of the revision techniques you can apply to your analysis.

PEER REVIEW

After exchanging papers with a classmate, read his or her literary analysis and answer the questions below.

1. Which part of the literary analysis is the most effective? Why?

2. What did you learn about the play that you did not know before?

Second Reading: Style In your first reading you looked at *what* your paper says and *how* that content is organized. Now you need to refine the style of your paper. In order to achieve your purpose of informing your audience, pay special attention to how smoothly you integrated short supporting quotations into your paragraphs; otherwise you might lose your audience's interest. The following guideline will help you.

Style Guideline

Evaluation Question	▶ Tips	▶ Revision Techniques
❶ Have short quotations been correctly integrated, or worked, into sentences?	▶ **Draw a box** around each quotation. Check to see that short quotations have been worked into the sentences. If they have not, revise.	▶ **Add** clauses and **change** the words so that quotations are smoothly integrated into grammatically correct sentences.

Focus on Sentences

Integrating Quotations

When writing your literary analysis, you may shift between providing interpretation and quoting characters, the playwright, or critics. When you use a brief quotation within your own writing, you must place the quoted words carefully so that the entire sentence reads smoothly. Look at the following sentence for an example.

> Further, since Macbeth's statement comes right after his speech about the "torture of the mind" he has suffered since killing Duncan (3.2.21), the stinging scorpions seem to extend that torture, suggesting that Macbeth feels guilty about arranging another murder.

TIP If you quote more than one line of poetry or verse dialogue, you must use **slashes** to indicate where each line ends.

ONE WRITER'S REVISIONS Here is how the writer of the literary analysis on page 205 used the guideline on the previous page to integrate a quotation into the essay about Macbeth.

BEFORE REVISION

In Act 1, before Macbeth even appears on stage, a captain uses animal imagery to describe him to King Duncan. The images come during a description of how a Norwegian lord had launched a fresh assault on Macbeth and Banquo, who were already exhausted from fighting. The king asks if Macbeth and Banquo were "dismayed" by the attack (1.2.34). The captain replies as follows:

> CAPTAIN. Yes;
>   As sparrows eagles, or the hare the lion. (1.2.34–35)

In other words, "No, they were not dismayed."

Short quotation is not integrated into the text

AFTER REVISION

In Act 1, before Macbeth even appears on stage, a captain uses animal imagery to describe him to King Duncan. The images come during a description of how a Norwegian lord had launched a fresh assault on Macbeth and Banquo, who were already exhausted from fighting. When the king asks if Macbeth and Banquo were "dismayed" by the attack (1.2.34), the captain replies, "Yes; / As sparrows eagles, or the hare the lion" (1.2.35), which essentially means, "No, they were not dismayed."

Clauses help integrate quotations into the structure of the sentence

---

Analyzing the Revision Process

1. Why did the writer add clauses and integrate the quotation into the passage?

2. How do the additions and changes clarify the quotations for the reader?

 Focusing On Style

Using the Style Guideline on page 211, revise the style of your literary analysis. Be sure that short quotations are integrated smoothly into grammatically correct sentences in your essay.

Designing Your Writing

Quotations from Plays   Carefully selected quotations strengthen every literary analysis, but they should not overwhelm the writer's own inter-pretations and explanations. You should keep your quotations brief and to the point by using only the part of a passage that relates directly to the idea you wish to support. The Modern Language Association of America (or MLA) has established rules for the use of quotations in essays. As you prepare your literary analysis, review the important rules listed below.

Short Quotations (up to three lines of poetry or four lines of prose)

- Enclose direct quotations in quotation marks.
- Integrate short quotations into the sentences of the essay.
- Place quoted material at the beginning, middle, or end of a sentence.
- Reproduce quoted phrases exactly. Do not make changes to spelling, capitalization, or punctuation. At times, it is necessary to insert a bracketed explanatory phrase within a quotation, but no aspect of the quoted passage should be changed.
- Divide a quotation with your own words, if necessary.
- Place the act, scene, and line reference of a quotation (and the author's name, if necessary) in parentheses after the closing quotation marks.
- Place sentence punctuation, such as a period or question mark, after the parenthetical reference.

Example:

> The final turning point for Macbeth comes as he prepares for battle saying, "I have almost forgot the taste of fears" (5.5.9), and ends the scene doubting the word of the apparitions.

Block Quotations

In addition to the general rules about using quotations, there are some special rules that apply to longer quotations. If you quote more than three lines of poetry or four lines of prose from a play, you will need to use block quotations. A block quotation sets the quoted passage off from the rest of the text, making it easy to read. Note the following rules:

- Introduce a quotation of more than three lines, or quoted dialogue, with a colon.
- Indent the quotation ten spaces (one inch) from the left margin.
- Use double-spacing and omit quotation marks at the beginning and end of the passage.
- When quoting dialogue from a play, the quotation should begin with the name of the first character who speaks. Spell the character's name in capital letters, place a period after it, and then begin the dialogue on the same line. The next character's words should follow in the same format. If a character's speech runs more than one line, indent any additional lines another three spaces.
- When quoting verse dialogue—such as the majority of the speeches in Shakespeare's plays—maintain the author's line breaks exactly. If your quotation begins in the middle of a line, position the partial line as it is in the original; do not start it at the left margin.
- Insert end punctuation after the last line of the quotation. Then, add the source documentation in parentheses.

TIP Because of limited space, the example at right is not double-spaced or fully indented. Be sure to follow the guidelines your teacher recommends for formatting block quotations.

> When he hears of Lady Macbeth's death, Macbeth meditates briefly on the meaninglessness of life:
>
> MACBETH.   Out, out, brief candle!
>   Life's but a walking shadow, a poor player
>   That struts and frets his hour upon the stage
>   And then is heard no more. It is a tale
>   Told by an idiot, full of sound and fury,
>   Signifying nothing. (5.5.23–28)

Publishing

Proofread Your Essay

Perfect Opportunity   Writers often hurry to get their ideas down on paper. Not surprisingly, first drafts usually contain many mistakes—and often these mistakes are carried over into subsequent drafts. Consequently, it is vital that you check your essay to make sure you have followed the **conventions of written language,** the generally accepted rules for spelling, punctuation, and grammar, before submitting the essay to your teacher. In proofreading a literary analysis of a drama, you should take special care to see that you have correctly used the literary present tense wherever it is appropriate.

| COMPUTER TIP

You find yourself using the same proper nouns over and over—such as the names of the playwright, characters, or title. If you are using a computer, add these words to the dictionary in your word processor.

Grammar Link

Using the Literary Present Tense

When writing about literature, writers need to use the **literary present tense** to discuss events in a literary work, regardless of how long ago the work was written. The literary present tense essentially reminds readers that literary characters live eternally between the covers of books. Use the literary present tense to summarize plots and to paraphrase what characters do and say, as in the following sentence:

In a soliloquy in Act 5, Macbeth *ponders* the brevity of life.

The verb *ponders* is in the literary present tense. Though Shakespeare has been dead for centuries and the action in his play takes place in the eleventh century, a critical writer still discusses the characters in *Macbeth* as if they were living in the present. Here are a few exceptions to the rule about using the literary present tense.

■ When quoting directly from a literary work, do not change the author's use of the past and future tenses.

■ Preserve the past tense when characters talk about the past and the future tense when characters talk about the future.

PRACTICE

On your own paper, rewrite the following sentences so that appropriate verbs are in the literary present tense. If you believe that a sentence is correct as written, write C.

1. Banquo and Fleance entered the stage with a torch just after the murderers appeared.

2. Macbeth and Lady Macbeth argued heatedly before he finally resolved to go ahead with the murder of Duncan.

3. Lady Macbeth said that she "heard the owl scream and the crickets cry."

4. Macbeth tells his wife that two people in Duncan's chamber awakened each other.

5. Shakespeare indicated that Macduff and Lennox knock nine times at the gate before finally being allowed to enter by the porter.

TIP Before you publish, make sure your essay has an appropriate **title.** Many literary analyses use a combination title separated by a colon; the first half is catchy or inviting, and the second is more straightforward. Look back at the title of the Writer's Model.

Publish Your Literary Analysis

Spread the Word Here are some possible ways to share your literary analysis of a drama with more readers.

- Submit the essay to your school's literary magazine.
- With classmates, create a Web page with links that lead to a variety of literary analyses. Create additional links to connect your paper to sites related to the play you analyzed.
- Enter your essay in a contest, such as one sponsored by your school, local library, or an arts organization.
- Submit your essay to one of the many online literary magazines published by high school students.

PORTFOLIO

Reflect on Your Literary Analysis

Big Questions What do you think you learned from writing a literary analysis of a drama? Writing short answers to the questions below will help you reflect on the experience.

- How does analyzing a play help you understand it better?
- Did analyzing the play give you a greater appreciation of the art of the playwright? How?
- Which was more challenging for you—reading the play and formulating your interpretations or drafting your ideas? How might you make this process smoother next time?
- What have you learned about analyzing and writing an analysis that will help you with other types of writing?

YOUR TURN 8 Proofreading, Publishing, and Reflecting

Review the guidelines outlined on the last few pages. Before you submit your paper, be sure to

- proofread carefully, paying special attention to your use of quotations and of the literary present tense
- choose an appropriate place to publish your essay
- reflect on your literary analysis of a drama by answering questions about the process of writing it

Answering Open-ended Essay Questions

Even students who feel comfortable reading a literary passage and answering a series of questions about it sometimes feel less confident about responding to an open-ended essay question. Here are a few examples of such test prompts:

- Discuss the role of setting in a novel or play.

- Discuss a novel or play in which a character's strengths turn out to be his or her weaknesses, or vice versa.

- Discuss a play or novel in which one character acts as a foil for a second character.

Because questions like these allow students considerable freedom, they can be intimidating. You might wonder how you can narrow the focus of the essay into something manageable. Since open-ended essay questions appear on classroom tests as well as on national examinations, it is a good idea to make basic preparations to answer them skillfully.

Open-ended questions allow you to choose and discuss works you know well. Behind each of the example questions above—and, in fact, almost all open-ended essay questions—lie two general inquiries:

- What does a literary work mean?

- How does the author of the work use literary devices to convey that meaning?

Think of the test prompt as a springboard for developing a thesis statement about the work you choose to discuss.

THINKING IT THROUGH Developing a Thesis

These steps will help you form a thesis in response to an open-ended essay question like the one in the right-hand column below.

▶ **STEP 1 Read the prompt question carefully and bracket words and phrases that tell the type of work and the topic you should write about. Underline words and phrases that tell the goal of your essay.**

▶ **STEP 2 Choose a work that suits the prompt.**

▶ **STEP 3 Use the underlined and bracketed material to create a thesis.** Be sure to include the title of the work, the author's name, specific information to show how the work fits the prompt, and specific information to let readers know what literary element you will address.

"Choose a [novel or play] in which there is a [discrepancy between the tone and the content]. Write an essay in which you demonstrate this discrepancy and explain how it contributes to the meaning of the work. Avoid plot summary."

The Importance of Being Earnest by Oscar Wilde

In the play *The Importance of Being Earnest*, Oscar Wilde achieves biting comedy by contrasting the formal tone used by the characters with the triviality of their actions and ideas.

Writing a Dramatic Scene

In this chapter you have focused on analyzing how literary elements—such as plot, characterization, and theme—create meaning in a drama. Now here's your chance to be the playwright instead of the critic, to use your knowledge to create your own dramatic scene.

Unpacking the Toolkit While writers of novels often include detailed descriptions of people and situations, playwrights usually provide only brief notes about setting and costume, as well as the characters' feelings and gestures. These notes appear in the **stage directions,** which indicate how actors should look, move, or read certain lines, and **set directions,** which set the scene in a certain time and place (*a barren hilltop at night; 1502 Summer Lane*). The rest of the play consists of action and the literary device of **dialogue,** or the exact words the characters speak.

Because dramas are meant to be performed rather than read, action and dialogue are the primary means of revealing important information about **characters** and advancing the **plot.** From characters' words, the audience learns what these characters feel and think. The audience may hear one character describe another, and then judge for themselves whether that character fits the description. The audience also hears what **conflicts,** or problems, characters face. Seeing how characters respond to those conflicts illuminates what kinds of people they are or what they value. The play's **theme,** or main idea, eventually becomes clear through the interplay of words and actions. As you prepare to write

your own scene, put yourself in a dramatist's shoes and think about *how* you can use literary elements to communicate your ideas. (It may be helpful to review the list of common literary elements on page 198.)

Starting Point The core of all good drama—as well as all good comedy—is **conflict.** One way to begin planning your dramatic scene is to think about a situation that contains conflict—or about two or more characters whose contrasting needs create a conflict. To sharpen the conflict in your own mind, clarify what each character *wants* or *needs.* You can also draw some inspiration from the world around you:

- **Look and listen to people around you.** How do they interact? Is there some conflict between them, whether important or humorously trivial, that you might use as the core of your scene? Can you borrow some of their characteristics—how they laugh or walk or twirl their hair?

- **Use yourself as a subject.** What personal experiences offer the dramatic tension you need? What obstacles have you overcome?

- **Let your imagination roam.** Set your scene in the distant future—or a thousand years ago. Put your characters in the most ridiculous situation you can imagine.

A Prime Example After reading the following excerpt of a scene from *The Importance of Being Earnest*, think about how Oscar Wilde used literary elements. Since the play is a **farce,**

or highly exaggerated comedy, pay special attention to how the dialogue pokes fun at the manners of the very rich. In the beginning of the excerpt, Lane, Algernon's butler, announces Jack, who is posing as a witty gentleman named Ernest; Jack's pretense accounts for the discrepancy between the name used in the stage directions and the one used in the actual dialogue.

Morning room in ALGERNON's flat on Half-Moon Street. The room is luxuriously and artistically furnished. The sound of a piano is heard in the adjoining room. . . .
[*Enter LANE.*]
LANE. Mr. Ernest Worthing.
[*Enter JACK. LANE goes out.*]
ALGERNON. How are you, my dear Ernest? What brings you up to town?
JACK. Oh, pleasure, pleasure! What else should bring one anywhere? Eating as usual, I see, Algy!
ALGERNON (*stiffly*). I believe it is customary in good society to take some slight refreshment at five o'clock. Where have you been since last Thursday?
JACK (*sitting down on the sofa*). In the country.
ALGERNON. What on earth do you do there?
JACK (*pulling off his gloves*). When one is in town, one amuses oneself. When one is in the country, one amuses other people. It is excessively boring.
ALGERNON. And who are the people you amuse?
JACK (*airily*). Oh, neighbors, neighbors.
ALGERNON. Got nice neighbors in your part of Shropshire?
JACK. Perfectly horrid! Never speak to one of them.

The **set directions** explain how the stage should appear; note how sound of piano is used to set the scene, too.

Stage directions appear in brackets preceding a character's name when they are used to note an entrance or exit.

The tone of voice suggested in stage directions can tell you about a **character's** emotions—or about his or her thoughts or intentions.

In **dialogue**, literary devices like figures of speech as well as the connotations of words can communicate a great deal about the character's personality.

The contrasts and **conflicts** between Jack and Algernon hinted at in this excerpt are at the root of the play's plot; later, the two characters will find out that they are brothers.

YOUR TURN 9   Writing a Dramatic Scene

Write your own dramatic scene, paying special attention to plot, characters, dialogue, stage directions, and set directions. Remember to build your scene around a core conflict; the outcome should at least be hinted at by the end of the scene. Polish your scene before staging it for your classmates.

Evaluating a Film Version of a Drama

WHAT'S AHEAD?

In this section you will evaluate a film version of a drama. You will also

- determine criteria to evaluate a film adaptation

- analyze the differences between a drama and a film

- consider how these differences contribute to a film's meaning

Romeo and Juliet. My Fair Lady. Dancing at Lughnasa. What do these three movies have in common? Each began as a script for a stage play; when they were adapted for film, each script underwent many changes. That's because theater and film are distinct media that use unique techniques to achieve their effects. **Theater,** for example, involves a three-dimensional stage on which live performers move and speak under lights before a live audience, but theater can never be wholly realistic. **Films** are projected with light onto a two-dimensional screen but can show an audience *actual* places—whether a Peruvian mountain, or a castle in Scotland. Film directors alter plays in order to convey personal visions or to appeal to certain audiences. It is little wonder that film adaptations often look and feel radically different from the plays that inspired them.

In this workshop you will be comparing and contrasting the script of a play to a film made from that play. Your main task is to consider how the differences shape the film's meaning and impact. Remember that your evaluation (like your literary analysis of a drama) will convey your own ideas about the merits and shortcomings of the film.

Choose a Film

TIP If you do not have access to a VCR, ask your teacher or librarian to arrange for you to use one of the school's.

On with the Show Your first task is to select a film that has been adapted from a stage play. Over the past few decades, many of Shakespeare's plays have been filmed—*Romeo and Juliet, Much Ado About Nothing, Henry V,* and *Hamlet,* for example. Instead you might prefer more modern works, such as *Blithe Spirit, The Elephant Man,* or *The Glass Menagerie.* If you have trouble choosing a film adaptation, try one of these suggestions:

- Browse in a video store for familiar play titles or for the credit line, "Based upon the play by . . ."

- Read film reviews in newspapers and magazines.
- Ask a teacher or parent for a recommendation.

Identify Criteria

Setting the Standard   In order to evaluate a film adaptation of a play, you must know exactly what you will be judging. The literary elements used by playwrights—**character, dialogue, conflict, plot, setting, theme,** and **symbolism**—are used by filmmakers, as well. Yet film versions of plays contain elements like varying **camera techniques** and **editing** that are unique to the medium of film. The questions below can help you clarify the ways literary elements and film techniques are used in a film adaptation. These will be some of your main **criteria** for evaluating the film.

Reference Note

For more information about **types of film shots,** see page 91.

Literary Element or Film Technique	Questions
character	Have characters been eliminated, added, combined, or otherwise changed? Do film techniques reveal characters' personalities clearly and thoroughly, or does characterization take a back seat to cinematic effects?
conflict	How are the conflicts presented? Do scenes involving conflict rely on distinctive camera techniques or editing?
plot	Have scenes been added, cut, or rearranged? Have significant events been altered? Why?
setting	Has the setting been changed or updated? If so, what is the effect of the change? Is the setting presented realistically or symbolically?
theme	Does the film convey the same ideas as the play? If not, how are they different? How does the film convey meaning aside from dialogue and action?
camera techniques	What types of shots are used—long shots, medium shots, close-ups? How frequently does the director have the camera move, and how often does he or she keep it stationary? What do camera shots express or evoke that a stage performance might not?
editing	Do most scenes contain a small number of shots that last a long time, or many briefer shots? Do scenes jump quickly from one to the next, or do they dissolve slowly?
casting	Who plays the lead and supporting roles? Do the actors seem well cast? Why or why not? How might a different actor in the same role affect the film's meaning or quality?
sound effects and musical score	What kinds of sound effects are included? Are they different from what might be used in a theatrical production of the play? Does the film contain music? If so, how does it affect your responses to the narrative?
visual effects	Are there special visual effects? If so, do they enhance or distract you from the drama? Does the cinematographer use light and shadow in unusual ways?

If you have certain criteria in mind that are not listed in the chart on the previous page, jot them down; also, note any questions that will help you determine how the film fulfills these criteria.

Analyze the Film

A Critical Eye   Before you begin your evaluation, read (or re-read) the original play. Though you may be tempted to skip this step, reading the play gives you a basis for comparison; otherwise, you would have no idea what the film omits, adds, or changes.

Then, view the film as actively as possible. Try to predict how scenes will be played, and pay special attention when the film departs from the script of the stage play. Consult your criteria, and take notes about interesting treatments of characters, conflicts, themes, or other literary elements. Since it is a good idea to view the film twice before writing your evaluation, you might try one of these viewings with the play script open in front of you. Below is a chart in which one viewer recorded observations while comparing a scene from Shakespeare's play to a filmed version of *Hamlet*.

The Players' Scene in Act 3, Scene 2 of Shakespeare's *Hamlet*	The Players' Scene in Franco Zeffirelli's film *Hamlet* (1990)
The actors pantomime the story before enacting it with words.	The film version alternates between pantomime and words.
The original version has more than 100 lines.	Both the players' and the audience's speeches are cut down drastically. The audience hears the plot and background of the play-within-a-film through a voice-over. Most of Ophelia's lines are cut, too; instead, Hamlet delivers part of his "Get thee to a nunnery" speech from Act III, Scene i. Ophelia looks ill and upset after hearing it.
In the original stage directions, there is no indication of the characters' nonverbal reactions to the play.	When the player king "dies," King Claudius stands up, looking horrified. Reaction shots show Hamlet and Gertrude. Claudius drops his glass and staggers toward the stage, clutching his ear. He points at the crown and poison, which are held by the actor who "poisoned" the king. He laughs, turns around in a circle, and then staggers outside yelling for light.
Although the script indicates the presence of kettle drums and trumpets during this scene, there is no prescribed music in the play.	Trumpets, drums, and woodwinds play throughout the scene. The music changes to a minor key when Gonzago steps onstage with the poison. It becomes slow and dramatic as the king stumbles forward; the notes rise higher and higher as if they are building toward some climax.

Narrow the Scope and Evaluate the Film

Now, for the Envelope   After carefully viewing and reviewing the film, you can study your notes and begin to form an opinion about the relative success or failure of the adaptation. Which parts of the film were as good as (or better, or worse than) the play? Why? As you consider your reasons, look for evidence in specific passages of the film.

As you review your notes, formulate a thesis that expresses your opinion in a concise way. To lead yourself toward a thesis, you might answer questions such as,

- How did I respond to the filmed scene, as compared to the scene in the original text?

- What accounts for my response?

- What advantages—or what unforeseen problems—do the techniques of film offer in this scene? Are certain effects achieved in the film that cannot be achieved on stage or in a script alone?

Avoid a thesis that merely states a preference for one dramatic form over another. For instance, in the chart below, a student expresses admiration for a film adaptation of *Hamlet* without saying outright, "I prefer this to reading the play." The left-hand box in the chart shows notes she made during and after watching the film.

TIP Of course, you cannot hope to do justice to every aspect of the film in one brief paper. It is best to limit the scope of your evaluation to one important scene, section, or characteristic of the film.

Analysis of Details	Thesis
By cutting the pantomime and a great deal of dialogue, Zeffirelli focuses our attention on Claudius's guilty responses. When Claudius rises while watching the actors, the reaction shots of Hamlet and Gertrude (which are not present in the script) show the oddity of this behavior and connect it with Claudius's guilt. When Claudius staggers toward the stage holding his ear, it seems as if he has been poisoned like the character onstage. The music plays more slowly and dramatically as the king stumbles forward, and the rising notes make the scene build toward a climax.	In Zeffirelli's film version of Hamlet, the edited dialogue, reaction shots, score, and symbolic gestures from the actors heighten the drama and significance of the scene in which King Claudius sees his crime represented on stage.

YOUR TURN 10 **Evaluating a Film Version of a Drama**

Choose a film version of a drama, and identify criteria to guide your evaluation of it. After re-reading the play, view the film twice and take careful notes on your observations. Finally, select one major scene or aspect of the film and write an evaluation of how effectively it reimagines the play. Present your evaluation as an oral report to the class.

WHAT'S AHEAD?

In this section, you will learn how to

■ select and analyze a dramatic scene for oral interpretation

■ prepare, present, and evaluate a reading of the text

Creating and Evaluating a Dramatic Reading

A dramatic reading is a way of revealing a literary work by performing it for an audience. For both the performer and the listener, the literary work has a different impact when spoken aloud than it does when read on the page. Good dramatic readings do not happen spontaneously, however. Instead, you study the text and prepare by experimenting with voice, facial expressions, and gestures. The result is a dramatic scene that lives and breathes, as it was meant to do.

Select a Dramatic Text

A Likely Story   Only if you are truly engaged and inspired by a dramatic text will you be able to lift it off the page in a unique way. It is important, therefore, to make your choice based not only on your knowledge of literature, but also on your interests. Of course, many scenes in plays contain several characters, and this presents nearly insurmountable problems for a single reader. A scene with one or two characters will be more manageable. As you enact first one character and then another, you will need to vary the pitch and rate of your voice and use different body language. As you search through pieces of dramatic literature, you might also consider the following factors.

> **TIP**   **Readers' theater** is a form of dramatic reading that lends itself to plays with many characters. Each of several readers handles one or more parts. Readers might stand or sit in a circle or line up facing an audience. Readers' theater tends to highlight the conflict and characterizations in a piece of dramatic literature.

■ **Universal Appeal**   Look for a text that has relevance for many—if not all—human beings. Literary works dealing with themes such as life and death, love, personal identity, and nature will have meaning and interest for most people.

■ **Ideas and Insights**   Good literature offers unique ideas or perceptions of life. Look for a text that encourages you (and your listeners) to come to a fresh understanding of some aspect of the world.

■ **Emotional Appeal**   A text that appeals to the audience's emotions, as well as to their intellects, is a good choice.

■ **Aptness for the Occasion and the Audience**   The content and tone of the dramatic text must fit the occasion—a performance in a classroom.

- **Length** Rather than perform a long scene, you might wish to focus on a shorter passage that can stand on its own. Try to identify a natural or dramatic starting and ending place for such an excerpt.

TIP Choose a work that has technical and stylistic quality—one containing precise, vivid language and clearly expressed ideas. Well-written texts are the most satisfying to read aloud.

Analyze the Text

A Closer Look You must have a thorough understanding of a dramatic text before you can interpret it for others. The following suggestions will help you get to the bottom of the text before voicing an interpretation.

- Look up the **pronunciations** and **definitions** of unfamiliar words to ensure a smooth oral delivery. Find **explanatory information** about any proper nouns or adjectives that you don't understand.

- State the **conflict** of the scene in a single sentence. Imagine yourself as each character, and reflect on how you view this conflict.

- Analyze the **characters' development.** What **motivates** characters to speak or act as they do in the passage? As each character, ask yourself, "What do I want or need in this scene?" Take time to reflect on what each character thinks and feels about the other characters in the scene.

- Analyze the text to determine the best way to effectively communicate important literary elements such as **rhyme, imagery, figurative language,** and **irony.**

- Does the passage have an overall **mood**? If so, you will need to convey it in your reading. Pay close attention to the writer's **syntax,** including both the **connotations** and **denotations** of words.

- **Paraphrase** each line of the scene to make sure you understand the meanings and implications in every sentence.

Create and Rehearse Your Dramatic Reading

A Crafted Performance Your goal is to use your voice and your body to express the words and behavior of every character in your dramatic text. You will need to practice the scene many times from the point of view of each character. Repeatedly ask yourself what the character might be thinking or feeling at any given point—why does he or she say each line in this particular way?

After examining the scene as the characters, look for the scene's overall shape. Thinking about conflict will help you detect this shape. Does the passage begin calmly and rise gradually in intensity? Does it begin with explicit conflict and resolve itself? Is there an emotional peak somewhere in the middle of the scene? After you determine the shape of your scene, keep this information in mind as you make physical and verbal adjustments. Take a look at the following guidelines about vocal delivery.

TIP Vocal projection (the volume and force of the voice) is especially important in large rooms, theaters, or auditoriums that lack public-address systems. Practice projecting your voice so that it can be heard even in the back of such a room.

- By **stressing** a word or by using **pauses,** you can emphasize a word or phrase.

- Vary the **pitch** and **tone** of your voice to reflect characters' feelings or intentions. Often a rising inflection indicates uncertainty, for instance, whereas a falling inflection conveys a stronger, more definite attitude.

- Your **rate of speaking** affects both the mood of the scene and the meaning of your words. Often a slower rate signals thoughtfulness, hesitation, or deliberateness; a quicker delivery can suggest excitement, nervousness, anger, or joy.

Listen to yourself as you rehearse, and experiment with different ways of expressing yourself nonverbally as well as with your voice. What facial expressions or gestures naturally evolve in your rehearsal? It can be productive to record some of your rehearsals on video- or audiotape. As you review such a tape to evaluate your performance, try to strike a balance between being too harsh and too easy on yourself.

Road Signs in the Text As you put together your reading, remember that many clues to meaning lie embedded in the text. For instance, marks of punctuation are like road signs that can help you negotiate your way through a speech. (This is especially true of Shakespeare's texts.) The following chart shows some techniques for translating punctuation into meaningful expression and behavior.

Punctuation Appearing in the Selection	Oral Technique Used in Interpreting the Selection	Marks Made to Prepare the Reading Manuscript
Commas, semicolons, colons, dashes, and periods	These marks suggest pauses; the length of the pause is increasingly longer with each item in this list.	Use a slash (/) to indicate short pauses and a double slash (//) for longer pauses.
Words in parentheses	Pause and speak more softly.	Mark parentheses with a circle.
Italicized words	Place more stress on the words or use a louder volume.	Underscore italicized words.
Question marks	Use a rising inflection. Rhetorical questions require a flatter inflection.	Draw an arrow with a rising curve. For a rhetorical question, use a flat arrow.
Especially significant words, phrases, or lines	Make adjustments to pitch, volume, or rate to emphasize meaning.	Mark specific word groups with underscore for emphasis, or use an arrow with a falling curve.

TIP Analysis, or careful interpretation, is a recursive activity. In other words, it is an ongoing process throughout each step of preparing and delivering a dramatic reading. Analysis is especially important when considering how to emphasize meaningful word groups, such as phrases and clauses, in a variety of ways.

A Reading Map   Even if you plan to perform your dramatic reading from memory, it is a good idea to create a marked manuscript of the script. On a double-spaced copy of the scene, you can write notes and make marks that help you recall how to communicate lines or parts of lines. The chart on the previous page shows you some ways to mark a manuscript. Other possible markings include

- circles and connecting lines (or marginal brackets) to link repeated words, parallel constructions, or rhymes; when rhyming words are not next to each other, you might also highlight them
- phonetic spellings, for words you might trip over
- concise marginal notes about the passage's tone or meaning

Here is an example—from Act 1, Scene 2 of Shakespeare's *Twelfth Night*—of how one reader marked a part of a script.

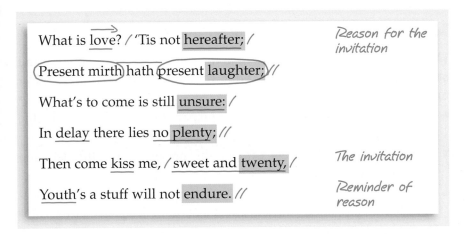

Introduce and Perform Your Dramatic Reading

First Things First   Before you perform your dramatic reading, you need to introduce it. A brief introduction not only piques the interest of your audience, but also gives them background information to help them understand and enjoy the reading. As long as you are brief, include some or all of the following elements in your introduction.

- Identify the author and title of the selection.
- Give your reasons for choosing the particular play and passage.
- Provide background information about the author or the selection.
- If you are reading an excerpt, briefly review the action that precedes the passage and introduce any characters involved.
- Describe the setting.

Loose and Confident   Make it your goal to be as relaxed and confident as you can be while giving your dramatic reading. One method of helping yourself feel positive is to remind yourself that virtually *every* performer, amateur and professional, feels nervous before "taking the stage." Accept your own nervousness; keep reminding yourself of all the careful preparation and rehearsal you have gone through, and keep your attention on the text you know so well.

During your introduction, try to make **eye contact** with all sections of your audience. If possible, look at individuals, but you must at least glance at general groups of people. As you deliver your reading, keep your eyes up and focused in the near or middle distance if you are enacting a character talking to another character. If you are delivering a soliloquy, you can look just over the heads of your audience. In general, try to make your audience feel involved in your presentation.

TIP   If possible, attend a professional dramatic reading. Many community theaters and bookstores offer such readings. Alternatively, watch for upcoming readings on television. When you listen to a dramatic reading, keep in mind the criteria listed in the bullets at right. Try to analyze, evaluate, and critique the reading. Then, share your critique with classmates.

Listen to and Evaluate a Dramatic Reading

Thinking It Over   Here are some questions that will help you (and others) analyze, evaluate, and critique your (and your classmates') dramatic reading.

- Does the introduction help a listener prepare for—or understand—the reading?
- Does the reader accurately express the personalities, attitudes, and behavior of all characters?
- Does the reader use stresses and pauses to emphasize important words and to stress the effect of artistic elements such as character development, rhyme, and imagery?
- Does the reader's voice indicate the connections between ideas?
- Does the reader vary pitch, tone, and rate of speaking in ways that convey the text's meanings and moods?
- What is my overall reaction to this dramatic reading?

Use the feedback you get from your teacher and peers to help you set your goals for any future oral presentations.

YOUR TURN 11   Preparing and Delivering a Dramatic Reading

Review the steps outlined above to prepare and deliver a dramatic reading. Use the evaluation checklist to critique your reading and classmates' readings.

Choices

Choose one of the following activities to complete.

▶ CAREERS

1. Thumbs Up, Thumbs Down!
With a classmate, attend a performance of a play both of you have read. Take notes about ways the actors and director have developed key literary elements, including character, conflict, plot, setting, and themes. Then, acting as professional critics, write a **collaborative review.** In your review, explain whether or not the production was successful in presenting the play's literary elements and why. You might even present opposite opinions about the production's quality.

▶ CROSSING THE CURRICULUM: HISTORY

2. Bounce Back in Time
Using a magazine, book, or textbook, read and analyze an article on some historical topic. Consider the writer's thesis and the kinds of evidence he or she provides to support this main idea. Then, give a short **oral presentation** in which you compare and contrast the way a thesis and supporting details function in a historical article and in a literary analysis of a drama.

▶ SPEAKING AND LISTENING

3. Page to Stage During a rehearsal of a school play, follow along in a script and listen to how the voices of the actors lift the words off the page. Take notes on your observations. If a scene is rehearsed several times, listen for variations in the way certain lines are delivered. How do the actors use their faces and bodies to convey aspects of the script? How do they use silence to communicate? After rehearsals, write a **critique** that evaluates the actors' performances.

▶ MEDIA AND TECHNOLOGY

4. World's Newest Home Videos With a small group of your classmates, select a scene from a play (or use the dramatic scene you created on page 219 of the Writing Workshop), adapt it for the screen, and create a **videotape** of it. Write a **script** that includes directions for the camera as well as for the actors. As director, one group member can prepare the actors and consult with the camera person about when to shoot, how to focus and move, and when to stop. If possible, show the videotaped performance to your class.

PORTFOLIO

6 Researching Literary Subjects

The Brontë Sisters

I have the heart and stomach of a king

King Arthur and Guinevere

...not of an age, but for all time.

... my arms and legs were strongly fastened ...

Mother, did I ever tell you? I AM LUCKY!

Reading Workshop

Reading a Literary Research Article
PAGE 232

Writing Workshop

Writing a Literary Research Paper
PAGE 244

Focus on Viewing and Representing

Researching a Film
PAGE 283

Knowledge, someone once said, is power. The more knowledge you have of a particular subject, the more you are the master of that subject. Think about these examples.

- Wall Street stockbrokerage firms research companies before recommending stocks to their customers.

- Biologists, chemists, and medical doctors continually research diseases to acquire knowledge of ways to prevent or cure them.

- Agronomists engage in research to gain the knowledge that will allow them to develop or improve crops to feed an expanding population.

People who do **literary research** explore works of literature to illuminate those works for themselves and others. For example, if research reveals that Romantic poet John Keats nursed his brother Tom as he lay dying of tuberculosis, a disease Keats himself later died of, you might see Keats's poems in a different light.

> **internet connect**
>
> **go.hrw.com**
>
> **GO TO:** go.hrw.com
> **KEYWORD:** EOLang 12-6

YOUR TURN 1

Brainstorming About Literary Research

In a small group, list titles of poems, stories, and novels that group members have recently read. Then, brainstorm for information that you would like to know about the selection or its author. For example, you might want to know what kinds of clothes people wore or what people did for entertainment at the time the work was created. Discuss how this information would add to the enjoyment, understanding, and appreciation of the literature. Share your findings with the class.

Reading a Literary Research Article

WHAT'S AHEAD?

In this section, you will read a literary research article and learn to

■ summarize what you read

■ identify primary and secondary sources

Authors have the power to create worlds. However, most authors do not create their worlds from scratch; they build them up from bits and pieces gathered from research and personal experience. Discovering the kinds of experiences that influence authors is one aspect of literary research. In the excerpt that follows, you will read Alison Sulloway's interpretation of her research into the personal experiences that influenced Jane Austen's writing, particularly her portraits of "exiled and imprisoned" women. Sulloway also did extensive research on English attitudes toward women and women's roles in the late eighteenth and early nineteenth centuries.

Preparing to Read

READING SKILL

Summarizing Sometimes, the enormous amount of information contained in researched books and articles can be overwhelming. An effective reader is one who understands the essence of a reading passage and can jot down a summary for review or study at a later time. A **summary** is a short restatement of the most important parts of any reading passage: the main ideas and the most important supporting details. As you read the following excerpt, try to identify both.

READING FOCUS

Primary and Secondary Sources Most sources of information can be divided into two categories—primary and secondary. Literary scholars make use of both. A source that provides firsthand information, such as a letter, interview, personal remembrance, or literary work, is called a **primary source.** A **secondary source** provides information that is at least once removed from the original source, such as a biography, an article from a magazine or encyclopedia, or a CD-ROM. Secondary sources usually interpret the information given by primary sources. As you read Alison Sulloway's excerpt, notice how she uses both kinds of sources to provide insight into Jane Austen's writings.

In the following excerpt, Alison Sulloway examines the influences family circumstances had on Jane Austen's novels. The letters *E* and *P*, which appear in parenthetical citations, refer to two of Austen's novels, *Emma* (1816) and *Persuasion* (1818), respectively. The abbreviation *MW* refers to a volume of Austen's minor works. As you read, jot down answers to the active-reading questions.

FROM

Jane Austen and the Province of Womanhood

BY ALISON SULLOWAY

By the time she was sixteen, [Jane Austen] had already learned how to treat women's limited choices without comic hyperbole.[1] Such phrases as "hopelessness of sorrow," "tho' all were her relations, she had no friends," "her separation from her sister," and "she usually wrote in depressed spirits" all suggest far more than a taste for fictional sorrow. This grief is pervasive,[2] and it is personal (MW 195).

> **1. What may be the source for the quotations in this sentence? Why do you think the author includes them?**

These grieving women are early Austenian examples of female exile; but there are just as many early and unfinished examples of female incarceration[3] in the women's quarters of an estate. Annis Pratt calls the feminine ghetto a "tarnished enclosure," within which women lacked "the basic element of authenticity," the liberty "to come and go" as men did, and "the right to make decisions about one's own time, work, and other activities" (5). Priscilla Wakefield[4] described the same predicament from personal experience: "Feminine action is contracted by numberless difficulties, that are no impediments of masculine exertion" (9). Knightley's

---

1. **hyperbole** (hī•pʉr´bə•lē): deliberate exaggeration for effect.
2. **pervasive** (pər•vā´siv): spread throughout.
3. **incarceration** (in•kär•´sər•ā´shən): imprisonment.
4. **Priscilla Wakefield:** a contemporary of Austen who described conditions for women at that time.

comment that "there is nobody hereabouts to attach [Emma];[5] and she goes so seldom from home" (*E* 41), anticipates Lady Russell's internal monologue about Anne Elliot's[6] isolation: "Anne had been too little from home, too little seen. Her spirits were not high. A larger society would improve them" (*P* 15). Mary Hays harshly summed up this feminine deprivation as systematic and ubiquitous:[7]

> In matters of great and important concern, women are generally soon taught to understand, that they ought to have, and can claim to have, no weight whatever. They then naturally think that the lesser ones, mere family matters, of ornament or fashion, may be left to them; but even here they are mistaken and misinformed; for their share in the management of home, and domestic concerns, lies entirely at the mercy of husbands, who except they are more than human, will rather be guided [by] their own caprice,[8] than by the exact rules of equity.

Since "the wife is acknowledged to be, even in domestic concerns, the upper servant of her husband only . . . the iron hand of authority lies desperately heavy, in even the trifles of life" (Hays 87–88).

Austen had apparently never experienced "the iron hand of authority" which Hays describes as a common feminine fate. But as a young woman who had barely reached her majority,[9] Austen did indeed suffer from the exasperating knowledge that she "ought to have, and can claim to have, no weight whatsoever [*sic*]." Enforced incarceration or enforced exile was always a personal problem for her. She was neither summarily expelled from one estate nor kept a virtual prisoner in one, according to the fate of Fanny Price,[10] Catherine Morland,[11] the Dashwood sisters,[12] Emma Woodhouse, and Anne Elliot. But all her adult life she

2. According to Sulloway, what problem do the characters Emma and Anne Elliot exemplify?

3. Why do you think the author includes this quotation?

4. What comparison between Austen's life and the lives of the characters in her novels does Sulloway make here?

---

5. **Emma:** the main character in the Austen novel of the same name; the character Knightley eventually becomes Emma's fiancé.

6. **Anne Elliot:** the main character in Austen's *Persuasion;* Lady Russell is another character.

7. **ubiquitous** (yoo•bik´wə•təs): seemingly present in all places at the same time.

8. **caprice** (kə•prēs´): sudden, impulsive change in the way one acts.

9. **majority** (mə•jôr´ə•tē): full legal age with full legal rights and responsibilities.

10. **Fanny Price:** a character in Austen's *Mansfield Park;* as a girl, Fanny must leave her parents' home to live with an uncle and aunt.

11. **Catherine Morland:** a character in Austen's *Northanger Abbey.*

12. **the Dashwood sisters:** characters in Austen's *Sense and Sensibility.*

suffered shifts of residence—from Steventon to Bath to Southampton to Chawton, or to the bedside of a sick relative. These shifts were always initiated for someone else's benefit, and they gave "no weight whatever" to Austen's own health, her publishing deadlines, or a rare visit already planned to some friends who loved her for her own sake.

Austen's rueful jokes at her helplessness began early and continued throughout her life. She enjoyed writing to her sister, her nieces, or her friends that she had intended to mount the box herself and direct the horses to carry her to them, since they, too, were as helpless about coming to see her as she was to go to them, but, as she frequently bemoaned, some malign fate intervened or was sure to intervene. Once she wrote Cassandra[13] four letters over a period of a month, complaining that one after the other of her five brothers refused to fetch her home after there was no more need of her services where she was, and where she had clearly worn out her welcome. She jokingly compared herself to Frances Burney's Camilla Tyrold,[14] whose irresponsible brother and heir to the family goods had locked his sisters in a summer house for hours by running off with the ladder, which was the only method of entrance or exit. Austen was particularly exasperated with her brother Frank, who would neither sanction her return by stagecoach nor come for her himself. After applying once or twice again to all her brothers, including her host, the rich Edward, Austen wrote in satirical exasperation: "My father will be so good as to fetch home his prodigal daughter . . . unless he wishes me to walk the Hospitals,[15] enter at the Temple,[16] or mount Guard at St. James."[17] Her final comment about her eventual return was ironically despairing: "the time of its taking place is so very uncertain that I should be waiting for *Dead-men's Shoes*" (*Letters* 9–18).[18]

In Austen's threat to become a physician, a barrister,[19] or a member of the

> **5. Does the source of the information in this paragraph—Austen's letters—provide reliable evidence about her life? Why or why not?**

---

13. **Cassandra:** Austen's sister.

14. **Frances Burney:** (1752–1840) English novelist; Camilla Tyrold is one of her characters.

15. **walk the Hospitals:** study to become a physician.

16. **enter at the Temple:** become a lawyer. The Inner and Middle Temples were two of the four English institutions responsible for legal education.

17. **mount Guard at St. James:** become a palace guard. Yeomen of the Guard who are the personal bodyguards of the English monarch. St. James is the name of a royal palace in London.

18. *Dead-men's Shoes:* Since custom dictated that Austen could not travel unless accompanied by a male member of her family, she feared her father and her brothers might die before coming to take her home. Thus, she might be waiting for the sound of "Dead-men's shoes."

19. **barrister:** There are two types of lawyers in England: barristers and solicitors. Barristers are the type who do trial work.

6. What does the author indicate by spelling the word *he* in capital letters?

household cavalry,[20] there are some quietly bitter allusions to what *HE* can do and she cannot. And her ominous reference to "Dead-men's Shoes" suggests how enormous the strain must have been to subdue constant anger and frustration over constant indifference to her needs.

Austen's yearly allowance of £20[21] partially explains why she joked so often about forbidden male professions that would have eased her constant niggling anxieties about money. Her correspondence is filled with ironic remarks about what profession she or some other woman had adopted or should adopt: the "science" of music, "the study of Medecine" (*sic*), of the navy, the law, or English history, "The Civil & Military—Religion— Constitution— Learning & Learned Men—Arts and Science— Commerce, Coins & Shipping—& Manners." She ironically included those whom she considered history's martyrs, such as Mary, Queen of Scots.[22] Nor did she ignore women's primary disenfranchisement upon which all the others rested: she even cracked a joke about voting for a candidate who was seeking a constituency so that he could stand for Parliament[23] (*Letters* 50, 40, 89, 223).

7. What can you infer is the "primary disenfranchisement" —the primary activity from which women were excluded?

Austen's father died in 1805, and soon Austen began to dwell on legacies and particularly on those who received them and those who did not—namely, herself, her sister, and her widowed mother. Various relatives and prominent people already reasonably wealthy were inheriting even more funds than they needed to function most comfortably, whereas the Austen widow and the spinsters were counting not pounds, as they estimated the cost of food, clothing, pens, writing paper, tips, and presents to tenants and the extended family, but pence; and saving not yards, but inches of fabrics for refurbishing shoddy dresses, underslips, caps, and bonnets. Austen wrote with her particular brand of tart yet wistful irony: "Indeed, I do not know where we are to get our Legacy—but we will keep a sharp look-out" (*Letters* 207; Hodge 99). "The rich," she once said mockingly to Cassandra, "are always respectable," as the poor are not (*Letters* 195).

8. How might Sulloway have found out about inheritance laws in England during the early nineteenth century?

---

20. **household cavalry:** another reference to the monarch's personal bodyguards.

21. **£20:** twenty pounds. A pound is the standard unit of English money. In Jane Austen's *Pride and Prejudice*, the Bennets—the main character's family, seven in all—have an income of £2000 a year. Another character, Mr. Bingley, has £4000 all for himself, while Mr. Darcy is considered wealthy with £10,000.

22. **Mary, Queen of Scots:** Tried and executed for high treason by her cousin Queen Elizabeth of England, Mary was considered a martyr by many, especially her fellow Roman Catholics.

23. **stand for Parliament:** run for election to a seat in the House of Commons.

Austen's open contempt for her brother James and his wife, Mary, at least in her letters, does not make pleasant reading, but the sources of her grief and anger against them are even more unpleasant. Their worst offense to this affectionate aunt was that they treated their daughters with all the varieties of hostility and contempt that Fanny Price's two families inflicted on her. And their indifference to the plight of James's mother and sisters is contemptible. They flaunted their new carriage and pair,[24] their trips, and their plentiful servants, while the little band of women who were now classified with "the genteel poor," scrimped and hoped for tips and presents from wealthy relatives. Mary complained of everybody's housekeeping except her own, and James infuriated his fiction-writing sister by visiting the three women whenever he became bored with his wife, and by behaving in a boorish fashion, slamming doors, and demanding instant service as a male right.

9. What is the main idea of this paragraph?

James must have been a rather unpleasant man even as a young curate.[25] When Mr. Austen relinquished his ecclesiastical[26] living in favor of James and then retired to Bath, James coolly bargained for all the household goods at Steventon, for the books, pictures, and silverware, in exactly the same cheap and contemptuous way as did the John Dashwoods in *Sense and Sensibility*. The cruelest "melancholy disproportion" of all was that Austen's precious piano and her equally precious books, which she had been able to purchase out of her annual allowance of £20, all had to be sold, not only to finance her father's retirement in the city of Bath, which she hated, but even more bitter, to help James's acquisition of the Steventon living from which she was now being expelled. Austen wrote Cassandra with understandable rancor that even Mr. Austen's tractable and sweet-going little mare had now deserted him, to trot over and pay permanent court to the crown prince of the Steventon rectory, before Mr. Austen and his family of women had even removed to Bath. Yet James had but recently "bought a new horse; & Mary [had] got a new maid." The pictures, the flatware, and other household goods went to James, while Mr. Austen was frantically "doing all in his power to increase his Income by raising his Tythes" (*Letters* 75, 101–103, 126). When Austen remarked, "The whole World is in a conspiracy to enrich one part of our family at the expense of another" (*Letters* 133), she was expressing the very economic underpinnings of *Sense and Sensibility*, especially the monstrous chapter where John and Fanny Dashwood defraud his mother and three penniless sisters of the funds and goods which his father— and theirs—had designated for them.

10. What comparison is the author making between Austen's life and the lives of the Dashwoods in *Sense and Sensibility*?

24. **pair:** two matched horses trained to pull a carriage.

25. **curate:** a clergyman who assists a higher ranking clergyman such as a vicar or rector.

26. **ecclesiastical:** having to do with the church or the clergy.

READING SKILL

Summarizing

A Reader's Digest   When you **summarize,** you restate the essential ideas of a text in an abbreviated form. A good summary of a reading passage shows that you have digested—or thought about and understood—what you have read. (Actually, it is impossible to write a good summary if you have not completely understood what you have read.) As a critical reader you should always be on the lookout for the main idea and major supporting details of passages. Taking a few minutes to jot down a summary can solidify your understanding of what you read and save you the time it would take to re-read an entire passage later. Instead of re-reading, you can jog your memory by referring to your summary.

Inclusion and Exclusion   Because a summary is a condensed version of a reading passage, it includes only main ideas and major supporting details. A summary excludes descriptions, examples, and other minor details. The number of main ideas and major supporting details you include in a summary depends on the length and complexity of the passage you are summarizing. If you were summarizing a scholarly work like the excerpt in the Reading Selection, you would probably want to summarize one paragraph at a time because most of the paragraphs may be quite long and complex.

One effective way to summarize is to think of summarizing as plugging in the parts of a formula like the one below.

Summary = Main Idea + Major Supporting Details

Reference Note

For more on **paraphrasing,** see page 190.

TIP   A **paraphrase** differs from a summary in that a paraphrase is usually about the same length as the original source. A paraphrase omits no details.

A careful reader might summarize the last paragraph of the Reading Selection like this.

> The unjust treatment of Jane Austen and her sister and mother by her brother, which is paralleled in *Sense and Sensibility* [**main idea**], is clearly demonstrated when Jane's piano and books are sold for the benefit of her father and brother [**major supporting detail**] and when her brother bargains for and gets all the household goods [**major supporting detail**].

TIP Writers of non-fiction often will summarize their main points in the final paragraph of a chapter or article. As an active reader, learn to identify such summarizing statements. The reading selection about Jane Austen's works does not offer a final summary because it is an excerpt from a book.

THINKING IT THROUGH   Summarizing

Keep in mind that a summary gives you the essentials of a reading passage. To create a summary, follow the steps below.

▶ **STEP 1 Review the text and identify the main idea.** The main idea of each paragraph—the topic sentence—is often located at the beginning or end of a paragraph. If you cannot locate a topic sentence, you must infer the main idea by applying your knowledge and experience to all the details in the paragraph. In a longer passage, review each paragraph, being careful to note repeated ideas and key words.

▶ **STEP 2 Look for the major supporting details in the passage.** Major supporting details refer directly to the main idea. Without such details the passage would make little, if any, sense. Minor details, on the other hand, serve only to elaborate the major supporting details and should be excluded from a summary. Be sure to jot down important names, dates, statistics, and places, but leave out examples and descriptions.

▶ **STEP 3 Use a formula such as the one on the previous page to write the summary.** Labeling the parts of your summary as you write allows you to see that you have included the essentials. When possible, condense details into broader categories; for example, if it is not important to mention *Emma* and *Persuasion* individually, use the term "Austen's novels" for both.

▶ **STEP 4 Check your summary.** Does what you have written provide a clear and concise understanding of the passage so that you will not have to re-read it? Have you omitted any important details? (Check to make sure that you've included the title and author when appropriate.)

Reference Note

For more on **making inferences,** see page 66.

YOUR TURN 2   Summarizing

Working with a partner, use the steps above to write a summary of the fourth paragraph of the excerpt by Alison Sulloway, the paragraph beginning, "Austen's rueful jokes . . ." on page 235.

Primary and Secondary Sources as Support

Go Straight to the Source   Literary scholars want to add to what is already known about their topics; they see little point in doing research that simply restates the findings of others. Therefore, scholars seek out as much primary source material as possible. A **primary source** is firsthand, original information that has not been filtered through another scholar's interpretation. Primary sources such as letters, diaries, interviews, contemporary maps, artifacts, statistics, legal documents, and the works of literature themselves are all open to continual exploration for new information and ideas about authors and their works.

A **secondary source** is secondhand information derived from primary sources and even from other secondary sources. Even the most knowledgeable scholars watch documentaries, elicit expert opinions, and research articles from encyclopedias, CD-ROMs, newspapers, and magazines. They use these secondary sources to fill in the "big picture"—to provide background information about the historical, sociological, and economic context of a literary work and to acknowledge the work of earlier scholars. Still, a critical reader of literary scholarship should be aware that scholars who rely heavily on secondary sources might not have anything original to say about their subjects.

The middle column of the following chart shows primary and secondary sources that you may encounter when reading literary research. The right-hand column describes the unique qualities of each type of source.

> **TIP** Another type of source is called a **tertiary** source, a third-level source. This is a digest of or commentary on secondary sources, such as *The Book Review Digest*. Generally, you should *avoid* using tertiary sources. It is always best to get as close to the facts as you can.

Source	Types	Unique Qualities
Primary	• literary works	• allow the reader to draw conclusions
	• diaries, journals, autobiographies, letters, and speeches	• provide direct insight into the mind of the writer
	• historical documents	• provide insight into the historical context
Secondary	• books of literary criticism	• allow the reader to share the insights of other scholars
	• scholarly journals, biographies, histories, documentary films	• give the reader an overview of the subject
	• reviews	• lead the reader to other primary and secondary sources
	• CD-ROMs, the World Wide Web	• can provide very recent information

The relative numbers and types of primary and secondary sources a reader encounters in the writings of literary scholars depend primarily upon the topic; however, a critical reader should understand that the soundest literary research generally draws from both. For example, in a study of Romantic poet John Keats (1795–1821), a literary scholar would undoubtedly make use of Keats's extensive correspondence, as well as the texts of his poems. Besides these primary sources, the scholar might consult secondary sources by reputable scholars—a biography of the poet and books and articles by critics, for example.

As a careful reader, you should check to see that scholars take a critical view of both their primary and secondary sources. The fact that a source asserts the truth of certain information does not automatically make that information true. The author of a diary might, for example, write a version of an event that would cast him or her in the best possible light rather than give an objective account of the facts. Similarly, the writer of a biography of a poet might have a political or religious bias that leads him or her to mischaracterize a particular aspect of the poet's work. Consequently, if literary scholars are completely uncritical of their sources, you have to question their conclusions.

YOUR TURN 3 — Identifying Primary and Secondary Sources

Working in groups of three or four, look back through the Reading Selection and make separate lists of the primary and secondary sources Alison Sulloway studied. Which type does Sulloway use the most? Discuss the reasons Sulloway might have chosen to use these sources. Be prepared to share your conclusions with the class.

"And what's the story behind the story?"

MINI-LESSON VOCABULARY

Word Roots Related to Communication

Because literary scholars often discuss how authors communicate their ideas, such scholars frequently use words that describe or relate to communication. Learning the meanings of the roots of these words will give you the key to unlocking the meanings of an entire family of words derived from these same roots. In addition, a familiarity with these word roots will help you in answering vocabulary questions on standardized tests. Here is a list of some roots that relate to communication.

- *–dict–*: to say, to assert (dictate, diction)
- *–loc–, –loq–*: to speak, talk (eloquent)
- *–logue–*: to speak or to write (prologue)
- *–mand–, –mend–*: to order, entrust (command)
- *–nom–, –nym–*: to name (nominate, homonym)
- *–rog–*: to ask, to question (interrogate)
- *–voc–, –vok–*: to call (invoke)

THINKING IT THROUGH   Using Word Roots Related to Communication

Look at the boldface word in this excerpt from *Jane Austen and the Province of Womanhood.* Then, use the steps following it to discover the word's meaning.

"[The passage from *Emma*] anticipates Lady Russell's internal **monologue** about Anne Elliot's isolation. . . ."

1. **Identify a familiar root within an unfamiliar word.** The *–logue* in *monologue* means "to speak."

2. **Check other word parts for familiar prefixes and/or suffixes.** The *mono–* in *monologue* means "one."

3. **Combine the meanings of the word parts to provide a tentative definition.** The word might mean "speaking to oneself."

4. **See if the meaning you have given the word makes sense in the sentence. Then, check your dictionary to confirm the accuracy of your definition.** "[The passage from *Emma*] anticipates Lady Russell's internal [speaking to herself] about Anne Elliot's isolation. . . ." The definition seems to work. A dictionary confirms that *monologue* is "a speech by one person."

PRACTICE

Use the steps above to help you determine the meaning of the italicized word in each of the sentences below.

1. The poet's *diction* made the scene she was describing come to life.

2. The scholar thought of his research project as his *vocation*.

3. To say that the author was *eloquent* would be an understatement.

4. At the beginning of the epic, the poet *invoked* the Muse, asking for inspiration and guidance.

5. The author has an irritating habit of packing many *homonyms* into a passage.

Answering Main-Idea Questions

As an active reader, you have learned to identify an author's **main ideas** when reading nonfiction such as literary research. This identification skill can also help you on standardized tests, which frequently include questions about the main idea of a passage. Take a look at the following reading passage and the main-idea question that follows it.

A Renaissance dictionary defines tragedy as "a lofty kind of Poetry and representing personages of great state and matter of much trouble, a great broil or stir: it beginneth prosperously, it endeth unfortunately or doubtfully, contrary to a comedy. . . ." Broadly speaking, Shakespeare's tragedies follow this pattern, except for *Hamlet,* where the hero is not "prosperous" at the beginning. For instance, at the start of the play Othello is newly married to Desdemona; Lear is almost a demigod giving away kingdoms; Macbeth has conquered on the battlefield and been elevated in rank. . . . And each of these tragic heroes "endeth unfortunately."

1. Which of the following statements best describes the main idea of the passage?

   A. *Hamlet* is not a tragedy.

   B. During the Renaissance, the definition of *tragedy* was different than it is today.

   C. Othello, King Lear, and Macbeth are considered "tragic heroes."

   D. Except for Hamlet, Shakespeare's tragedies conform precisely to the Renaissance definition of *tragedy.*

   E. Hamlet differs from Shakespeare's other tragedies in that the hero is not "prosperous" at the beginning of the play.

THINKING IT THROUGH   **Answering Main-Idea Questions**

To determine the best answer to a main-idea question on a standardized reading test, use the following steps.

1. **Read the entire passage slowly and carefully before answering a main-idea question.** Sometimes, it helps to look at the first and last sentences of the passage for a topic sentence that directly states the main idea.

2. **Consider each answer carefully. Eliminate answers that describe only a part of the passage, overstate the case, or distort the meaning of the passage.** For example, **A** can be excluded immediately because the passage does refer to *Hamlet* as a tragedy. **B** may be eliminated because the passage does not give the modern definition of a tragedy. **C** and **E** can be rejected because they describe details of the reading passage, not its main idea.

3. **Re-read the remaining answer choices to determine which is correct.** Only **D** has not been eliminated. It is correct because it encompasses the major points in the passage.

Writing a Literary Research Paper

WHAT'S AHEAD?

In this section you will write a formal research paper on a literary topic. You will learn how to

- **develop a research topic**
- **gather support for your topic**
- **draw conclusions about research**
- **introduce quotations**
- **punctuate quotations correctly**

To what extent were Lord Byron's heroes reflections of their author? How did Virginia Woolf's family influence her fiction? How close was Charles Dickens to depicting actual conditions in London in the 1800s? Questions such as these are the beginnings of literary research. Literary research involves a study not only of works of literature but also of works that illuminate the literature. By researching such works, you can expand your understanding of the literary work, its author, and the culture that produced it. Furthermore, although research about literature may seem very specialized, the skills you will learn in this workshop are applicable to any research project you might tackle.

Prewriting

Develop a Research Topic

Make It Click Writing a literary research paper gives you the opportunity to delve deeply into a literary subject. The research process is labor-intensive, but it can be exciting if your topic is one that interests you—one that clicks. This special topic may not immediately come to mind. Consider the following possibilities:

- **Focus on an author.** Why do you feel drawn to an author? Are you curious about the life of an author because he or she seems eccentric? To what extent did the author's life affect his or her work? Can you trace a particular idea through several works by the author?

- **Focus on a work.** Does the setting of a work seem particularly significant to you? Are you fascinated by the similarities or differences between two characters in a story, novel, or drama? Does the imagery in a certain poem seem especially important?

Once you have focused upon a work or an author, decide upon the approach you want to take in your research. Look at the following list of possible approaches for suggestions.

- **Biographical:** Look at the connections between an author's life and his or her writing. For example, you could find out how the friendship between Romantic poets Samuel Taylor Coleridge (1772–1834) and William Wordsworth (1770–1850) affected their writing. Alternatively, you could research the connection between D. H. Lawrence's (1885–1930) "The Rocking-Horse Winner" and his friendship with Lady Cynthia Asquith.

- **Historical:** Find out about the historical context of an author's life or of the setting of a poem or story. For example, you could research the nineteenth-century liberal causes that influenced the poems of Elizabeth Barrett Browning (1806–1861), or you could investigate conditions in colonial Burma, the setting of George Orwell's (1903–1950) "Shooting an Elephant."

- **Cultural:** Research the characteristics of a culture depicted in a work of literature. For example, you could examine the attitudes toward women that existed in Chaucer's time and that found their way into his work. You could also delve into the influence of nineteenth-century scientific discoveries and theories on the work of Victorian poet Alfred, Lord Tennyson (1809–1892).

- **Psychological:** Investigate how scientific knowledge about mental characteristics and human behavior is reflected in literature. For example, you might research the influence of modern ideas about psychology on Virginia Woolf's (1882–1941) stream-of-consciousness narrative technique. Similarly, you could research the effect of modern psychology on Joseph Conrad's (1857–1924) *The Secret Sharer.*

- **Literary:** Investigate an author's (or a work's) use of an element or elements of literature—plot, character, theme, symbol, point of view, and so on. For example, you could research the theme of optimism and hope in the poems of Romantic poet Percy Bysshe Shelley (1792–1822). Likewise, you could investigate the characteristics of the hero in Mary Shelley's (1797–1851) *Frankenstein.*

To get started, think about several literary topics that arouse your curiosity. You may find that as you get further into your research you will want to modify your topic or change it completely. No matter what topic you choose, however, you will need to focus it.

TIP You may want to work collaboratively with two or three other students to discuss the approach you might take in your research. Talking about your approach will help you reflect on and examine your ideas, and having others respond to your approach will help you clarify your thoughts.

Reference Note

For more on **literary analysis,** see Chapter 5, beginning on page 180.

Focus Your Research

Biting off Just the Right Amount   Once you have an author or a work and an approach in mind, you will need to narrow your topic so that you can cover it adequately in a research paper. The cultural aspects of Geoffrey Chaucer's *The Canterbury Tales,* for example, might be a good topic for a book, but it is much too broad for a research paper. **A good method for narrowing a topic is to keep challenging yourself to be more specific.** Here is an example of how one student narrowed a topic.

Subject:	Geoffrey Chaucer
What about Chaucer?	—Chaucer's late fourteenth-century masterpiece, *The Canterbury Tales*
What about Chaucer's *The Canterbury Tales?*	—the women in Chaucer's *The Canterbury Tales*
What about the women in Chaucer's *The Canterbury Tales?*	—how the women in Chaucer's *The Canterbury Tales* reflect the times
Limited topic:	—how the complex women characters in Chaucer's *The Canterbury Tales* reflect conflicting ideas about women's role in society at that time

After you have focused your potential topic, you should evaluate its appropriateness as a topic for a research paper. A topic that sounds interesting will not necessarily work well as the topic of a research paper. Look at your narrowed topic, and test its suitability by asking yourself the questions below.

1. **Is enough information available on the topic—at least five good sources, including books, articles, and nonprint sources?** Beware of topics that are too obscure, such as "the influence of the Crimean War on the work of Victorian poet Christina Rossetti."

2. **Is the topic objective?** Reporting on personal experiences or preferences is inappropriate. You should not, for example, write a paper titled "My Favorite Poems." You could, however, research and write a paper titled "Family Influences on the Poetry of Emily Brontë."

3. **Is the topic unique and interesting or does it simply repackage other people's ideas?** If your topic is a common paper topic (the witches in Shakespeare's *Macbeth*), how can you approach it in an original way? If it seems dry (Romantic poet John Keats's training as a doctor), how can you make it appealing to your readers?

4. Does the topic involve *literary* research? The research you do should enrich your understanding of a literary subject. Research that leads you to a scientific description of Lord Byron's clubfoot would probably not enrich your understanding of Byron's poetry. However, research that reveals how Byron's clubfoot affected his attitude toward himself might well enrich your understanding of his poetry.

Consider Purpose, Audience, and Tone

To Whom It May Concern   Once you have a suitable, focused topic, you are ready to think about three equally important factors that will influence your research paper: purpose, audience, and tone.

Purpose   Your **purpose,** or reason for writing this paper, is to interest readers in and inform them about the topic you have chosen. You will not, however, just compile an orderly list of facts and expert opinions. Instead, you will add the information you gather in your research to your personal insights to create an original **synthesis,** or combination, of information which you will then pass along to your readers. You will want to take your readers beyond what they already know, so look for surprising details or an unusual twist to old information.

Audience   Your readers, or **audience,** will usually be your teacher and your classmates, but also consider others who may be interested in your topic. Whoever your readers are, they are looking for information that gives them a better understanding of the topic. You should assume that they are familiar with the literature with which you are dealing; you should not, therefore, summarize the literature for them. You will, however, need to provide them with any background necessary to understand your specific topic.

Tone   People have distinctive voices when they write just as they do when they speak. **Voice** in writing is the unique sound and rhythm a writer adopts to talk to his or her readers. Like your speaking voice, your writing voice can express many different attitudes and feelings, or **tones.** The typical academic report, like the ones required in school, and the typical professional report, like the ones required in the business world, are formal in tone. To establish a formal tone in your research report,

- **use a style that is serious but not stuffy.** Avoid using slang, exclamation marks, or flowery descriptions. Use precise language and aim to communicate ideas concisely.

- **be objective.** Avoid the first-person pronouns *I, me,* or *my.* The use of *I* is appropriate in many kinds of writing, but not in a formal research report.

Make a Research Plan

Look Before You Leap   You will save yourself a great deal of time if you do some preliminary planning before beginning the information-gathering part of your research. You have already chosen a topic that arouses your curiosity, one about which you have questions. These questions can give your research some direction. You might want to brainstorm or use the *5W-How?* questions to discover some new avenues of research. The questions below could initiate research on Chaucer's depiction of women, the topic of the Writer's Model on page 259.

- **Who** are some of the women characters Chaucer created?
- **What** personalities do Chaucer's women characters have?
- **When** did medieval women become involved in business and commerce?
- **Where** did medieval women work? **Where** did they spend their leisure time?
- **Why** were women restricted in their activities?
- **How** did men treat women during Chaucer's time?

Get an Overview and Find Sources

The Big Picture   Begin your research with a general look at, or overview of, your topic. Try one or a combination of the following sources to construct an overview. Not only will you find valuable background information, but you also may get leads on additional sources.

- In encyclopedias or other general reference books, read one or two articles about your topic, or if the topic is highly limited, about related topics. For example, you would not find an article on the influence of Sigmund Freud on twentieth-century fiction in a general reference book. You would, however, find articles on Sigmund Freud and on modern literature, both of which are general topics.

- Check a World Wide Web site by inserting your author's name in a keyword search. Besides providing information you might use, such a site might provide links to other sites.

- Interview an expert (a teacher, professor, librarian, parent, or neighbor) on your topic. Such a person might be able to direct you to research materials that would prove extremely useful.

Reference Note

For more on **primary** and **secondary** **sources,** see page 232.

Source Hunting   Once you have an adequate overview of your topic, you are ready to look for specific sources of information. All sources can be classified as either primary or secondary. A **primary source** provides firsthand, original information. It may be a letter, speech, literary work, eyewitness testimony, personal remembrance, or autobiography. A **secondary source** contains secondhand, or indirect, information. An encyclopedia, an expert's opinion, a magazine article, and a biography are all secondary sources—someone's interpretation, analysis, or opinion of primary sources. Good researchers try to draw information from both primary and secondary sources, for each type has its advantages. Primary sources present you with original material that you can interpret for yourself. Secondary sources present you with the perspectives of others who have studied your topic.

Of course, in your search for information, you will want to explore both print and nonprint sources.

INFORMATION RESOURCES	
Library	
Source	**What to Look For**
Card catalog or online catalog	Books, records, audiotapes, and videotapes (Print and audio-visual listings are in separate catalogs in some libraries.)
Readers' Guide to Periodical Literature or online periodical indexes	Magazines and some journal articles indexed by subject and author
Indexes to newspapers, essays, and articles	Articles from major newspapers, such as *The New York Times;* possibly local newspapers (Newspapers are frequently on microfilm.)
Specialized reference books and CD-ROMs	Encyclopedias of special subjects, such as *Contemporary Authors, 20th Century Authors;* almanacs; biographical references like *Current Biography*
Microfilm or microfiche and online databases	Indexes to major newspapers; back issues of some newspapers and magazines
Community	
Source	**What to Look For**
World Wide Web and online services	Articles, interviews, bibliographies, pictures, videos, and sound recordings
Museums, historical societies, and government offices	Exhibits, records, and experts
Schools and colleges	Libraries, experts, exhibits, special collections, and records
Television and radio, video stores	Documentary and instructional programs and videos

Reference Note

For more on using **library resources,** whether online card catalogs, electronic databases, or the Internet, see page 984 of the Quick Reference Handbook.

COMPUTER TIP

If you have access to a computer and know specifically what you want to find on the World Wide Web, you can make your search more efficient by using combinations of **keywords.** For example, instead of sifting through excessive information as a result of using the keyword *medieval,* try using two keywords—*medieval* and *Chaucer.* Look for instructions on advanced searching strategies on the first screen of your search engine.

TIP The World Wide Web can provide an almost limitless source of information. You might find a Web site devoted entirely to information about a specific author or specific works of literature. There are, for instance, sites on Jane Austen, on Joyce's novel *Ulysses,* and on the Brontë sisters. Some sites may provide you with e-mail addresses of other people interested in the topic. Sometimes, the most valuable aspect of a Web site is that it leads you to other sources of information. When you find a Web page that seems useful, create a bookmark for that page. **Bookmarks** save time by allowing you to access the page again without going through a new search or typing in a long Web address.

Evaluate Your Sources

The Wheat from the Chaff   Because so many sources are available, you may have difficulty knowing which ones to use. To evaluate the sources you find, apply the 4R test.

TIP Be aware that information you receive from Web sites is not held to the same standards that most books and magazine articles are. Consequently, it is even more important to evaulate sources on the World Wide Web than print materials. For more on **evaluating Web sites,** see page 282.

1. **Relevant?**   The source must contain information *directly* related to your topic. You can check the table of contents and index of a book and skim articles. Videotapes and audiotapes sometimes provide a written summary; for some books, useful summaries and excerpts of reviews will appear in *Book Review Digest.*

2. **Recent?**   Always use sources that are as current as possible. Even in the slow-changing field of literary research, you should read the most recent publications. They will often show you, in their bibliographies, which older sources of information are still important.

3. **Reliable?**   The source must be accurate. Generally, a respected scholar or a respected newspaper or periodical, such as *The Washington Post* or *Smithsonian,* will provide trustworthy information. If in doubt about a source, consult a librarian or expert; also, look for the authors most often quoted on the topic or listed in the bibliographies of other sources.

4. **Representative?**   If your topic is controversial, find sources with information and opinions supporting both sides. Even if you finally draw a conclusion that one side's position is stronger, examine and present the opposing viewpoints.

Note Sources

Keep an Address Book   Just as you have consulted references cited in secondary works, readers of your research paper may want to consult *your* sources for additional information on your topic. In a *Works Cited* list at the end of your report, you will need to provide precise details about every source you have used. For this reason, always carefully record information about sources *as you use them.* Otherwise, you may find yourself running back to the library or making a hasty, last-minute phone call to track down source information. Use the following suggestions to help you record your sources.

- **Make a *source card,* or *bibliography card,* for every source you use.** You may keep your list on 3" x 5" index cards, in a computer file, or simply on several pages of a notebook.

- **Number your sources.** Assign each source a number. Then you can write the number, rather than author and title, when you are taking notes from a given source.

- **Record all publishing information.** Take down everything you might need for your *Works Cited* list, such as title and subtitle, an editor or translator, volume number, city, publisher, original publication date, and revised edition date. (Look at the sample entries on page 272 to see exactly what kinds of information will be required.)

- **Note the call number or location of the source.** This information will save you time if you must go back to a source later.

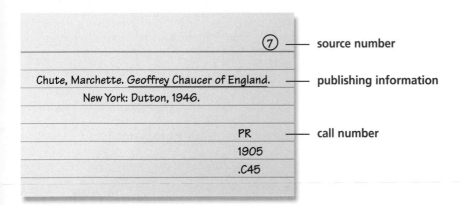

(7) —— source number

Chute, Marchette. Geoffrey Chaucer of England. —— publishing information
New York: Dutton, 1946.

PR —— call number
1905
.C45

TIP The format for recording source information shown in this chapter is that of the **Modern Language Association of America (MLA).** Your teacher may want you to follow a different format. The formats suggested by *The Chicago Manual of Style* and the **American Psychological Association (APA)** are two popular alternatives to MLA style. Whatever system you use, pay close attention to the information required and the style (capitalization, indentation, and so on) and punctuation used.

YOUR TURN 4 Focusing on a Topic and Finding Sources

Look back over the prewriting steps in the preceding pages of this workshop. Be sure you have everything in order to begin your research: a topic that is focused and suitable for a literary research project, a plan that includes research questions that you hope to answer, and ideas for sources to use. When you have found several sources, be sure to evaluate them and prepare source cards.

Research and Take Notes

A Great Leap Forward Now you are ready to leap into the major phase of your research project—the search for specific information. As you examine your source material, you will take notes on the facts, examples, and opinions pertinent to your topic. There are three ways to record this information: **summarizing, paraphrasing,** and **quoting directly.**

Note-Taking Strategies	
A **summary** is a brief restatement of main ideas and important details.	**Use:** to note general ideas about your topic that do not require detailed discussion, such as an alternative viewpoint **Example:** You might summarize a discussion of Chaucer's treatment of men, even if you are focusing on his treatment of women.
A **paraphrase** is a restatement that retains more details than a summary and is about the same length as the original.	**Use:** to include pertinent details, such as names, dates, and statistics **Example:** You might paraphrase a description of the place of nuns in medieval society.
A **direct quotation** is the exact words of an author or speaker and is always enclosed in quotation marks.	**Use:** to note ideas that are especially well phrased, to be sure of technical accuracy, and to refer to passages from works of literature **Example:** You might quote passages directly from *The Canterbury Tales* in which the Wife of Bath expresses her attitudes on marriage.

Here are some specific guidelines for creating **note cards.**

Guidelines for Note Cards
1. **Use a separate note card, sheet of paper, or computer file for each source and for each main idea.** Having separate records for each source and each main idea will make sorting and grouping your notes easier.
2. **Write the source number in the upper right-hand corner and the page number(s) at the bottom of the note card.** Both numbers are essential for correct documentation. The source number gives you access to the publication data on your corresponding source card. The page number(s) must be supplied if you use the information in your paper.
3. **Write a label at the top of the card showing the main idea.** The labels will let you see content at a glance and are useful in preparing your working outline.
4. **Re-read the note to make sure you understand it.** Decipher any abbreviations or note-taking shortcuts that might be unclear when you are writing your paper.

Below is an excerpt from "Chaucer's Discussion of Marriage," by George Lyman Kittredge. Following the passage, you will find an example of a note card summarizing the information.

> We are prone to read and study *The Canterbury Tales* as if each tale were an isolated unit and to pay scant attention to what we call the connecting links—those bits of lively narrative and dialogue that bind the whole together. Yet Chaucer's plan is clear enough. Structurally regarded, *The Canterbury Tales* is a kind of Human Comedy. From this point of view, the Pilgrims are the *Dramatis personae,* and their stories are only speeches that are somewhat longer than common, entertaining in and for themselves (to be sure), but primarily significant, in each case, because they illustrate the speaker's character and opinions, or show the relations of the travelers to one another in the progressive action of the Pilgrimage. In other words, we ought not merely to consider the general appropriateness of each tale to the character of the teller: we should also inquire whether the tale is not determined, to some extent, by the circumstances—by the situation at the moment, by something that another Pilgrim has said or done, by the turn of a discussion already under way. (130)

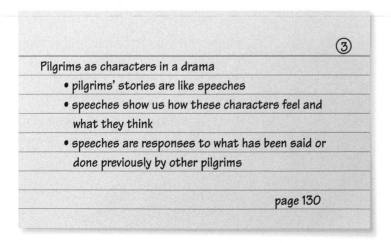

③   source number

Pilgrims as characters in a drama
- pilgrims' stories are like speeches
- speeches show us how these characters feel and what they think
- speeches are responses to what has been said or done previously by other pilgrims

page 130

Drawing Conclusions About Literary Research

As a researcher, you will have to draw **conclusions**—judgments, decisions, or opinions— about information in many of the primary and secondary sources that you read.

THINKING IT THROUGH **Drawing Conclusions**

Use the following steps to draw conclusions. The sample responses are based on information one student writer found on women in the Middle Ages.

1. **Examine *all* the information in the text.** Women were little valued during most of the Middle Ages.

   During the fourteenth century, women of the middle class were involved in business and finance.

   In the late 1300s, Christine de Pisan, who lived in France, wrote about the poor treatment of women by men.

2. **Relate information in the text to prior knowledge.** Apply what you know already from your other reading and from your own experience to the text. *People often talk about topics they wonder about* rather than topics about which they are absolutely sure.

   Chaucer's pilgrims talk about marriage as much or more than anything else. In fact, a group of tales is traditionally called the "Marriage Group."

3. **State your conclusions in precise language.** You may need to use a qualifying word or phrase like *probably* or *might be* to make your conclusion valid. *Chaucer probably wrote a great deal about marriage because people of his time were uncertain about women's roles in society and marriage.*

PRACTICE

Using the information from the steps above and from the following passage, draw conclusions about the numbered items below.

In 1040, the historical Macbeth defeated King Duncan in battle and ascended the throne of Scotland. Unlike Shakespeare's Macbeth, for seventeen years, the historical Macbeth was an able and just king. Shakespeare's source for *Macbeth* was a history written by Raphael Holinshed, who describes Macbeth as a courageous man whose wife was ambitious and whose faith in witches was too strong. According to Holinshed, Macbeth was guilty of numerous murders but was a satisfactory king.

1. The relationship between plays and history
2. Shakespeare's sources for plots of his plays
3. Macbeth's wife's attitude about power
4. Holinshed's criteria for satisfactory kings

Writing a Thesis Statement

Assert Yourself   Your **thesis statement** is a sentence or two identify-ing the main idea that you intend to explain or prove in your paper. **Like drawing a conclusion, writing a thesis statement is an act of *synthesis*, reviewing and pulling together all your information to state what your paper will say about your topic.** An effective thesis statement is

KEY CONCEPT

- **specific** Your thesis should serve to focus your entire paper. A vague or general thesis will lead to an unfocused, meandering paper.

- **assertive** Do not be afraid to state your ideas confidently.

- **arguable** If your thesis states something that everyone is likely to agree upon, your paper may lack energy and interest.

- **unique** Your thesis should make an original assertion about your subject.

Of course, any thesis statement you write at this point will be preliminary; it may change as you draft and revise the paper. As you can see from the examples below, the distance between a suitably narrow topic and a thesis statement is not great.

> **Topic:** The ways in which complex women characters in Chaucer's *The Canterbury Tales* reflect conflicting views of women's role in society
>
> **Thesis:** Chaucer portrays the changing role of women in four-teenth-century English society by creating characters like the Prioress, the Wife of Bath, and the Old Woman in the Wife of Bath's tale.
>
> **Topic:** Similarities in the lives of English novelist Jane Austen and American poet Emily Dickinson
>
> **Thesis:** Startling parallels exist between the lives of English novel-ist Jane Austen and American poet Emily Dickinson.
>
> **Topic:** The influence of John Keats's chronic illness on his poetry
>
> **Thesis:** John Keats's chronic illness influenced his treatment of the theme of death in his poetry.
>
> **Topic:** The effect of the French Revolution on William Wordsworth's views of poetry
>
> **Thesis:** The French Revolution affected William Wordsworth's ideas about the proper subject matter for poetry.

TIP Often, thesis statements include more than a topic; they also provide readers with a clue about the paper's organization. The first example at left, for instance, sug-gests the order in which the writer will discuss the characters named: first, the Prioress, fol-lowed by the Wife of Bath, and so on.

TIP Remember that you can always refine your thesis statement as you draft your essay. Ideas often become clearer as you write.

Make an Outline

Mapping the Territory   With your thesis statement as a guide, you are ready to organize the mass of information that you have collected. If you have labeled your note cards (or single sheets of paper or computer files), you can sort the notes into sets by main idea. You might find that your note cards can also be arranged in subsets. Some notes may turn out to be useless. That's to be expected. Because you have your notes on cards (or on separate sheets of paper, or in computer files), you can discard any that aren't useful, and then arrange and rearrange the ones you plan to use until you have them in the order you want. Look at the following chart to see definitions and examples of some organizational patterns.

Organizational Patterns	
Pattern	**Example of use**
chronological—events are arranged in the order in which they occurred	to discuss the events in an author's life
order of importance—ideas are arranged according to their importance, often with most important ideas last	to organize main ideas about an author's work, saving the most important point for last
logical order—ideas are grouped according to logical relationships, such as cause-effect and comparison-contrast	to discuss the effects on his or her work of an event in an author's life; to compare two works by the same author

COMPUTER TIP

If you use a computer to write your research paper, consider using a stand-alone outlining program or your word-processing program's outline feature to organize your notes into an outline.

Organizing your notes paves the way for your outline—a plan for your research paper. An **informal outline,** which allows you to organize ideas without arranging them into outline form with numbers and letters, may be all that you need. Strategies for creating informal outlines include **clustering** and **mapping.** Here is an example of clustering.

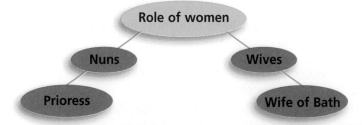

Your teacher, however, may require a final, **formal outline** to serve as a table of contents for the finished paper. This outline must follow standard outline format, as shown in the partial outline on the next page. Note that the introduction and conclusion are excluded from this model outline.

Chaucer's Female Characters: A Reflection of Change

I. The Prioress: Spiritual Concerns and Worldly Concerns

   A. Appearance
      1. Fine forehead
         a. Pride in forehead
         b. Supposed to be hidden by nuns of the time
      2. Jewelry
         a. Green-beaded rosary
         b. Gold brooch with motto

   B. Interests/pleasures
      1. French language
      2. Aristocratic manners
      3. Animals
         a. Kept dogs
         b. Feeds from table

   C. Nuns in the Middle Ages
      1. Not always a spiritual calling
         a. An alternative to marriage
         b. Fee often required of aristocratic parents
      2. Prohibitions of the church ignored
         a. Pets
         b. Leaving convent

II. The Wife of Bath: Dominance and Dependence

   A. Independence
      1. Weaver by trade
      2. Travels show a certain wealth
      3. Clothing denotes status

   B. Views on Marriage

TIP Although the process for writing a research paper might seem structured and linear, it is actually quite flexible and recursive. At any point in the process, you can stop and go back to an earlier stage. For example, when writing your outline, you may find that one or several of your main ideas lack support; consequently, you may need to retrace your steps— find additional sources and take more notes.

TIP The **title** of your paper should describe the contents of your paper clearly and concisely. You can also use **subheadings** within a research paper to make it easier to follow. The subheads, which often are written in boldface type, can be taken from the major points in your outline. Notice how the writer used subheadings in the model on page 259.

YOUR TURN 5 **Researching, Writing a Thesis Statement, and Making an Outline**

Look back over the steps in the preceding sections of this workshop and begin planning your research paper. Be sure to

- take notes to gather enough information to develop and support your thesis
- develop a thesis statement that sets forth your focus and purpose
- make an outline that logically organizes your paper

Writing

The Literary Research Paper

Framework	Directions and Explanations

Introduction

- Hook your readers.
- Provide necessary background.
- Include your thesis statement.

Body

- Develop the first idea that supports your thesis.
- Develop the second idea and so on.

Conclusion

- Restate your thesis.
- End with some final insights into your research.
- Create a *Works Cited* list.

Use a title page and formal outline if appropiate Follow your teacher's instructions.

Grab your readers' attention right away Use a vivid scene, interesting detail, or striking quotation.

Include background information Provide readers with enough background about the literary work and your topic to make your paper understandable.

State your thesis Clearly state your main idea about your research; incorporate it smoothly into the introduction.

Present your research Be certain that you support each major point about your thesis with evidence from a variety of sources, both primary and secondary. Be sure to cite your sources.

Organize your ideas Make sure to present your ideas in a way that is coherent and shows a logical progression.

Return readers to the purpose of your research Smoothly integrate into the conclusion a restatement of your thesis. Add any final insights.

Provide an alphabetically arranged list with complete publication information for each source you used The list should appear on a separate page (or pages) at the end of your paper.

YOUR TURN 6 Writing a First Draft

Before you write, look at the Writer's Model that follows. Throughout the model you will see source information in parentheses. A complete list of these sources appears on page 264. Then, gather all your materials, and using the framework above as a guide, write a first draft. Refer to page 268 for information on incorporating quotations.

A Writer's Model

The following literary research paper, which is a final draft, closely follows the framework on the previous page.

Chaucer's Female Characters: A Reflection of Change

    In the Prologue to Geoffrey Chaucer's *The Canterbury Tales*, the Prioress wears, attached to her rosary, a gold brooch inscribed with the motto *"Amor Vincit Omnia"* (Chaucer 25). Would a nun who chose "Love Conquers All" as a motto mean spiritual love or romantic love? Does Chaucer intend his ambiguous Prioress to represent nuns in general in the last half of the fourteenth century? Later in the Prologue, Chaucer introduces the independent and gregarious Wife of Bath, proud widow of five husbands. Does Chaucer intend the Wife to represent wives in general?

    Chaucer, "one of the most wonderful observers in the whole of English literature" (Power 94), often knew the people he observed "better than they knew themselves" (Chute 240). He reports everything with accuracy—even if what he sees contains contradictions. The last half of the fourteenth century, when he (and his characters) lived, was, after all, a time of contradictions, a time of dramatic and upsetting transition (Thompson and Johnson 863). Most of the traditional relationships of society were changing, and "the times were filled with war, plague, suffering, and anger" (Bishop 334). Amid all this upheaval, the fact that the relation of women to society was also changing should not be surprising. Chaucer reflects the social changes taking place for women by creating complex, often inconsistent female characters who echo the contradictions of the times.

The Prioress: Spiritual Concerns and Worldly Concerns

    The Prioress, also known as Madame Eglantine, is introduced in the General Prologue both as a woman of the Church and also as a vain woman with worldly interests. She has a "well-shaped head, / Almost a span across the brows" of which she is obviously proud (Chaucer 25). Madame Eglantine evidently does not hesitate to show off one of her finest features, even though, as Eileen Power points out, "The nuns were supposed to wear their veils pinned tightly down to their eyebrows, so that their foreheads were completely hidden" (89). The Prioress has "a set of beads, the gaudies tricked in green," from which hangs the gold brooch that ambiguously proclaims her faith in the power of love (Chaucer 25). She is obviously able to appreciate the world's

(continued)

Title not set in quotation marks

INTRODUCTION

Quotation from *The Canterbury Tales*, a primary source

Attention-grabbing questions

Quotations woven into sentence

Background information

Source by two authors cited

Transition to thesis

Thesis statement

BODY (Subhead taken from outline) Development of first main idea

Slash indicating change of line in quoted passage of poetry Author of quotation named in text

(continued)

beauties and to enhance and take pride in her own.

Specific examples

Her interests range further than devotion to God and singing "the service" (Chaucer 24). She is able to speak good French, and she has the perfect manners of an aristocratic lady. In addition, she has a tender sympathy for animals, perhaps stronger than her sympathy for people, of which Chaucer makes no mention (Schoeck 249). She keeps several dogs that she feeds from the table "roasted flesh, or milk and fine white bread" (Chaucer 25). In all these ways, she indulges her taste in the pleasures of the world rather than living the life of self-denial that one might expect of a nun.

How does Chaucer's picture match the lives of nuns at this time? Morris Bishop comments that in the late Middle Ages nuns often entered convents not because of a spiritual calling but because they were "surplus or unmarriageable daughters of the noble and bourgeois classes." He calls the convents "aristocratic spinsters' clubs" (174). They were aristocratic because, although it was not formally required, it was understood that a payment to the convent was necessary before a girl would be accepted as a novitiate (Gies and Gies, Women 64). It is no wonder, under these conditions of admission, that many of the nuns were not devoted to a spiritual life and were openly rebellious toward the restrictions that the Church tried to impose on them.

Among the Church's prohibitions were pets, which the bishops believed interfered with discipline. Such a ruling, however, did not rid the convent of animals (Power 90). Like Chaucer's Prioress, the nuns enjoyed their pets. Another unpopular rule was the restriction against leaving the convent, even for the purpose of going on pilgrimages (Schoeck 246). In 1300, a Papal Bull, a special decree or edict from the Pope, was published that ordered that nuns be confined in the convents except under the most exceptional of circumstances. In response, the nuns of one convent chased the bishop who brought the order to the gate of the nunnery and "when he was riding away . . . threw the Bull at his head, screaming that they would never obey it" (Power 93). In this situation we see women who seem to be devoted to the Church but seem to be also strongly interested in worldly affairs, the same contradiction that exists in Chaucer's Prioress.

The Wife of Bath: Dominance and Dependence

For the Wife of Bath, the conflict is between a desire for dominance and a desire for a strong husband; she wants power, but she also wants a conventional marriage relationship

Margin notes (left column):

Specific examples

Conclusion drawn from research

Transition provided by question
Source named in text

More than one title in *Works Cited* list

Specific examples

Ellipsis within quotation

Subhead taken from outline

Development of second main idea

(Patterson 142). Chaucer describes her in the Prologue as an independent woman, yet always refers to her, as she always refers to herself, as a "Wife" (Patterson 136). She has had five husbands, and she says, in introducing her tale, "Welcome the sixth, whenever he appears" (Chaucer 218).

One word quotation

The Wife of Bath is represented as a woman with money and a position of respect in society. She is a weaver by trade and has had wealth enough to travel three times to Jerusalem and through Italy and France. She makes her social position obvious by her clothing, especially the kerchiefs she wears as a headdress, which "weighed a good ten pound, / The ones she wore on Sunday" (Chaucer 34). Such clothes denoted status (Carroll). Although she wants to be admired and respected for her money and position, she does not want to "change the system" (Patterson 142). She wants to be a wife. This woman's desire is understandable when she is considered within her historical context.

No page numbers needed for online source

In the two centuries before Chaucer, conditions for women had been oppressive and unchangeable (Thompson and Johnson 322). Women were expected both by custom and by law to be subservient to their husbands and were valued in some cases for little else than their ability to bear children (Thompson and Johnson 322) and do menial work (Bishop 37). One commentary familiar to men of the Middle Ages proposed that if God had intended women to be equal to men, Eve would have been derived from Adam's head instead of his rib (Coulton 190). The men of the time accepted this reasoning as valid, agreeing "that women were inferior beings" (Rowling 72).

Specific examples from multiple sources

Meanwhile, many women, like the Wife of Bath, wanted such attitudes to change but did not advocate complete independence. She makes a case for power over men within the home, an end to men's control, particularly economic control, of women, but not for independence from men. She understands that in marriage "sovereignty is synonymous with economic control"; she also understands that by achieving economic independence, she gains "independence of spirit, the freedom to give freely" (Carruthers). Once she secures "sovereignty in wedlock," she is "as kind to him / As any wife from Denmark to the rim / Of India, and as true" (Chaucer 237).

The Wife of Bath's desire to live a married life brings to light an issue for women of the times—the right to remarry. Speaking at length on this issue, the Wife of Bath argues that women should be free to have as many husbands as they please, but she does not argue in favor of having several spouses at the

Summary of primary source

(continued)

(continued)

same time (Chaucer 215, 218). She is arguing against the Church's "attempt to impose absolute monogamy," to allow women, in other words, only one marriage during their lifetimes (Duby 11). The Wife of Bath, in defense of her own multiple marriages, cites Saint Paul's reasoning that each of several consecutive husbands was as legitimate as the first (Miller 425):

Block quotation

> I can't keep continent for years and years.
> No sooner than one husband's dead and gone
> Some other Christian man shall take me on,
> For then, so says the Apostle, I am free
> To wed, O' God's name, where it pleases me.
> (Chaucer 218)

Paraphrase of secondary source

She wants freedom to remarry but not freedom from marriage, a desire that represents the times. In fact, Chaucer's mother and grandmother were both married three times, and such remarriages were not unusual in medieval London (Chute 22).

Several sources used as support

Although during much of the Middle Ages, women "did not count" (Chute 71), women during Chaucer's time, at least in the urban areas, had made progress. Women like the Wife of Bath could be in "business for themselves and were considered legally capable of controlling funds for their business and of answering for that business in borough court" (Sheehan 32). Moreover, a woman could work with her husband, and "when a man die[d] his widow carrie[d] on the trade" (Gies and Gies, Life 53). Although their status was changing dramatically (Bishop 37), women were paid less for doing the same work as their husbands (Gies and Gies, Women 181), and within marriages husbands still expected the same compliance that seemed "natural" to the medieval male (Kittredge 143).

Indirect quotation

Connection with thesis

Like so much of what was happening at this time, there was an incongruity between the conditions that actually existed and the conventional wisdom of the past. Women seemed to be gaining independence, yet they could not escape the lingering social conventions associated with marriage. Georges Duby says that women were almost nonexistent in a social sense unless they had husbands (98). Women like the Wife of Bath were, therefore, seeking a more equitable relationship with their husbands, not complete independence.

The Queen: Power by Permission

In the "Wife of Bath's Tale," Chaucer depicts a conflict in the power afforded women. One of the main characters in this tale, the queen, is modeled on the chivalric ideal; she is a "lady" and an object of tribute. However, her role is complicated when she is given the power to judge a man. The king, after hearing the pleas of the queen and the other ladies of the court, "gave the queen the case / And granted her his [the guilty knight's] life, and she could choose / Whether to show him mercy or refuse" (Chaucer 240).

Development of third main idea

Square brackets indicate alteration for clarity

Although there were, of course, several female rulers who reigned during the Middle Ages—Empress Matilda of England, Eleanor of Aquitaine in France, Queen Blanche of France, Countess Jeanne of Flanders, Blanche of Champagne in France, among others (Gies and Gies, Life 54)—there was, in general, a feeling that a man of whatever social position was nobler and more virtuous than a woman. Therefore, a woman could no more judge a man than a subject could judge a king (Tuchman 214).

Transitional words *although* and *therefore* show relationships between sentences within paragraph

Women of the times, however, were gaining power. Noble women often took on the responsibilities of their noble husbands. When noblemen were absent "on crusade, at the wars, or in the courts," their wives were called upon to maintain not only the household but also all the business of the manor (Rowling 84). Even women of the middle class were known to wield power within their homes (Bishop 221). Again, Chaucer's characters reflect the social issues of the times.

Reference to thesis

The Old Woman: Private Self and Public Self

Another important character in "The Wife of Bath's Tale" is the Old Woman. Chaucer (through the Wife of Bath) describes her as physically repulsive and of low social status, being both poor and of common birth. In her long sermon to the knight, the Old Woman preaches that beauty, noble birth, and youth are invalid criteria for determining a woman's value. Inner value, she argues, is more important than appearance or social position (Chaucer 245–50). That a woman could be valued for her personal qualities was, as a general idea, foreign to medieval literature and probably to medieval men. However, as women started to see that they should be valued, they necessarily shifted their place in relation to a male-dominated society. In the character of the Old Woman in "The Wife of Bath's Tale," Chaucer reveals the difference between a woman's exterior image and her interior quality, thus raising yet another aspect of the problem of a woman's place in an era of change.

Development of fourth main idea

Summary of primary source

In the prologue to one of Chaucer's earlier works, a dream-vision poem called *The Legend of Good Women,* the god of love is angry with Chaucer for having written earlier about stereo-

CONCLUSION

(continued)

(continued)

Online source, encyclopedia article; no page numbers needed

Restatement of thesis Conclusion about idea expressed in thesis

typically bad women who had betrayed men. So Chaucer must now write about stereotypically good women (Lumiansky). In *The Canterbury Tales*, written a decade later, Chaucer creates women who escape the stereotypical mold, women who are real people. They mirror the contradictory times in which they lived. Chaucer observed the way in which women's place in society was changing and carefully recorded his observations. In the Prioress, the Wife of Bath, the queen, and the Old Woman, Chaucer focuses our attention on women whose complexity parallels the complexity of the times. There is nothing simple about these characters, and perhaps that is why they are still fresh and alive after six hundred years.

TIP Research papers and their *Works Cited* lists are normally double-spaced. Because of limited space on these pages, A Writer's Model and A Student's Model are single-spaced. The *Elements of Language* Internet site provides a model of a research paper in the double-spaced format. To see this interactive model, go to **go.hrw.com** and enter the keyword **EOLang 12-6.**

Works Cited

Bishop, Morris. The Middle Ages. New York: American Heritage P, 1970.

Carroll, Sharon. "Women's Clothing in the Middle Ages." Millersville U. 10 May 1999 <http://www.millersv.edu/~english/homepage/duncan/medfem/cloth.html>.

Carruthers, Mary. "The Wife of Bath and the Painting of Lions." Geoffrey Chaucer Page. Harvard U. 10 May 1999 <http://icg.fas.harvard.edu/~chaucer/canttales/wbpro/carruth.htm>.

Chaucer, Geoffrey. The Canterbury Tales. Trans. Nevill Cogill. 4th ed. New York: Penguin Classics, 1977.

Chute, Marchette. Geoffrey Chaucer of England. New York: Dutton, 1946.

Coulton, G. G. Chaucer and His England. London: Methuen, 1963.

Duby, Georges. Love and Marriage in the Middle Ages. Trans. Jane Dunnett. Chicago: U of Chicago P, 1994.

Gies, Joseph, and Frances Gies. Life in a Medieval City. New York: Harper, 1969.

---. Women in the Middle Ages. New York: Harper, 1978.

Kittredge, George Lyman. "Chaucer's Discussion of Marriage." Schoeck, Richard J., and Jerome Taylor, eds. Chaucer Criticism. Notre Dame: U of Notre Dame P, 1960. 130–159.

Lumiansky, R. M. "Chaucer, Geoffrey." Encyclopaedia Britannica Online. 10 May 1999. <http://www.eb.com:180>.

Miller, Robert P., ed. Chaucer: Sources and Backgrounds. New York: Oxford UP, 1977.

Patterson, Lee. "'Experience woot well it is nought so': Marriage and the Pursuit of Happiness in the Wife of Bath's Prologue and Tale." Geoffrey Chaucer: The Wife of Bath. Ed. Peter G. Beidler. Case Studies in Contemporary Criticism. Boston: Bedford Books of St. Martin's Press, 1996. 133–54.

Power, Eileen. Medieval People. New York: Barnes, 1968.

Rowling, Marjorie. Life in Medieval Times. New York: Capricorn, 1973.

Schoeck, Richard J. "Chaucer's Prioress: Mercy and Tender Heart." Schoeck, Richard J., and Jerome Taylor, eds. Chaucer Criticism. Notre Dame: U of Notre Dame P, 1960. 245–258.

Sheehan, Michael M. "The Wife of Bath and Her Four Sisters: Reflections on a Woman's Life in the Age of Chaucer." Medievalia et Humanistica. Ed. Paul M. Clogan. New Ser. 13. Totowa, NJ: Rowman & Allanheld, 1985. 23–42.

Thompson, James Westfall, and Edgar Nathaniel Johnson. An Introduction to Medieval Europe 300–1500. New York: Norton, 1937.

Tuchman, Barbara W. A Distant Mirror: The Calamitous 14th Century. New York: Ballantine, 1978.

TIP Your teacher may want you to begin your *Works Cited* list on a new page. Be sure to find out what your teacher prefers.

TIP In the *Works Cited* list of a research paper on a classic work of literature like *The Canterbury Tales,* you are likely to encounter sources that are quite old. Older sources should be used if scholars researching and writing today consider them classic works of scholarship. To find out whether a source is classic or simply outdated, check to see whether it is cited by recent works on the subject. For research reports in fields such as science, you should find the most recent sources available.

A Student's Model

The following is an excerpt from a literary research paper by Natalia Machuca of Western High School in Ft. Lauderdale, Florida.

<table>
<tr><td>

INTRODUCTION

Attention-grabbing quotation

Background information

Thesis

BODY
First main idea

Second main idea

Information added to quotation for clarity

</td><td>

The Importance of Guinevere in Arthurian Legend

According to Arthurian legend, Guinevere came to Arthur during the joyful spring of the year that followed the king's victories. This "lily of the west," tall with shining brown hair floating loosely around her shoulders, was considered the only maiden worthy of Arthur. She "had the composure proper to a queen, with a glance of peculiar sweetness and a becoming modesty . . ." (The Fall of Camelot 37–38). Guinevere was supposed to be "the prize of peace and the promise of fair weather after the storm" (The Fall of Camelot 37), yet she is often blamed as a main cause for the fall of Camelot. King Arthur's loving yet deceitful wife is a complex and important character, one of the principal forces driving the action in Arthurian legend.

Guinevere's importance in Arthurian legend is apparent from the very beginning. Although her origins and parentage are not clear, her father (whoever he was) was so overjoyed by the union of his daughter to the High King of Camelot that he sent a hundred knights for Arthur's service. He also sent "an enormous table, constructed in Uther Pendragon's time" in the shape of a perfect circle. This wedding gift becomes one of the most powerful symbols of Arthurian legend: a perfectly round table which not only symbolized the nobility of the knights that Arthur was gathering, but also represented equality throughout Camelot (The Fall of Camelot 37).

Guinevere is also an important influence on the relationship between Arthur and Merlin. During the festivities that followed the wedding ceremony, Merlin's mood undergoes a noticeable change and his look turns grave. He says, "Guinevere brings Arthur sorrow, and she is here by his choice" (The Fall of Camelot 39). However, Merlin feels no responsibility; he had "warned the king covertly that [Guinevere] was not wholesome for him to take to wife, for he warned him that Launcelot should love her, and she him again" (Malory 44). Arthur forgets the role Merlin has played in his life and ignores his warnings, believing Guinevere to be the most "valiant and fairest lady . . . living" (Malory 44).

</td></tr>
</table>

When Sir Launcelot of the Lake joins King Arthur's Knights of the Round Table, Guinevere's importance in Arthurian legend becomes even greater. Launcelot becomes Arthur's greatest knight, "for in all tournaments and jousts and deeds of arms, both for life and death, he passed all other knights" (Malory 99). As Merlin had foreseen, however, Launcelot falls in love with Guinevere, and Guinevere holds "him in great favour above all other knights" (Malory 119). When Arthur leaves Camelot to search for the Holy Grail, "the highest spiritual pursuit" ("The Holy Grail"), Guinevere is left alone in Camelot for many years. It is during these years that the sinful relationship between Launcelot and Guinevere becomes the most significant part of Arthurian legend, more important even than Arthur's quest for the Holy Grail. Many stories exist which detail the ways in which Guinevere tried to hide her relationship with Launcelot from the court, and especially from Arthur. According to one story from French romance, one of the ways she tried to keep her sinful relationship secret was by having her sister Gwenhwyvach, who was Guinevere's exact double, take her place at court from time to time ("Guinevere" 127).

Of course, Guinevere plays a central role in one of the most dramatic stories in Arthurian legend. According to Malory, the relationship between Guinevere and Launcelot is discovered by Mordred, King Arthur's illegitimate son, and Sir Agravaine. King Arthur, deeply influenced by Mordred, condemns Guinevere to be burned at the stake (Malory 500). Launcelot and his kinsmen rescue her (Malory 502). Malory does not mention Guinevere again until after Arthur's death, when he says that she joined a nunnery at Almesbury (Malory 527).

Works Cited

The Enchanted World: The Fall of Camelot. Alexandria, Virginia: Time–Life Books, 1986.

"Guinevere." The Illustrated Encyclopedia of Arthurian Legends. 1991. Barnes & Noble Inc., 1995.

"The Holy Grail." The Camelot Project at the University of Rochester. Online. 1 Oct. 1999. <http://www.lib. rochester.edu/camelot/grlmenu.htm>.

Malory, Sir Thomas. Le Morte D'Arthur. New York: Gramercy Books, 1995.

Third main idea

Fourth main idea

Reference Note

For more on **integrating quotations,** see page 212.

Incorporate Quotations

The Well-Turned Phrase   Because you want your paper to reflect *your* research, you will want to summarize or paraphrase much of the information from your secondary sources. However, using direct quotations from authorities adds credibility and variety to your paper. Sometimes you might want to quote a passage because it expresses a thought in a memorable fashion. Follow the guidelines below to use quotations effectively in your research paper.

- **Use ellipsis points (three spaced periods) to show where you have omitted sections from quoted material.** You may want to alter a quotation to shorten it or to make it fit grammatically into your text. If so, you must use ellipsis points for words deleted within a sentence or for any deletion that suggests a partial sentence from the source is a complete sentence.

     The men of the time accepted this reasoning as valid, agreeing "theoretically at least . . . that women were inferior beings" (Rowling 72).

- **Use a slash to indicate line breaks in verse quoted within the text.** Use a space on each side of the slash (/).

     The Prioress's forehead was "fair of spread, / Almost a span across the brows" (Chaucer 23).

- **Use square brackets to surround any letters or words you might need to add to a quotation to make its meaning clear.**

     The king, after hearing the pleas of the queen and the other ladies of the court, "gave the queen the case / And granted her his [the guilty knight's] life" (Chaucer 240).

- **Set off longer quotations as "blocks."** For prose quotations of four lines or more or for verse quotations of more than three lines, start a new line, indent the entire quotation ten spaces from the left margin, continue to double-space, and do not use quotation marks. See the block quotation in the Writer's Model on page 262.

Document Sources

Give Credit Where Credit Is Due   Giving credit to your sources is an essential part of writing a literary research paper. When you cite sources within your paper and include a *Works Cited* list at the end of your paper, you are providing your readers with **documentation.** How can you tell whether to give credit or not? The following guidelines will help you.

Guidelines for Crediting Sources
Credit the source of each direct quotation (unless it is very widely known, such as Shakespeare's "Shall I compare thee to a summer's day?").
Credit the source of any data from studies, surveys, polls, and other sources of unique or little-known information. Doing so lends credibility to your paper.
Credit any original theory, opinion, or conclusion that is not your own. You must not present another person's ideas as your own, even if you are paraphrasing them.
Do not credit common, or general, knowledge—information that appears in standard reference works or several sources. For example, you would not need to document that Chaucer wrote *The Canterbury Tales* because that is common knowledge.
Do not credit facts that appear in standard reference works or several sources. For example, you would not need to document that Chaucer died in 1400 because most reference books give that information.

The Best Policy   Using someone else's words or ideas without giving proper credit—even if you do so unintentionally—is called **plagiarism.** Plagiarism is dishonest. It is considered intellectual stealing—a serious academic offense. Therefore, the best policy is to be scrupulous about crediting not only direct quotations but also restatements of the original ideas of others. Do not use another person's phrases or exact sentence structure unless you enclose the material in quotation marks. When in doubt about whether to give credit, do so.

Using Parenthetical Citations   When you read the Writer's Model on page 259, you probably noticed the source references in parentheses. These **parenthetical citations** give the reader just enough information to find the full source listing on the *Works Cited* page. Often, only the author's last name and the page numbers are required, but here are some exceptions to that rule.

- A nonprint source such as a Web page or videotape will not have a page number.
- A print source of fewer than two pages (such as a one-page letter or a pamphlet) will not require a page number.
- If you name the author in your introduction of the quotation, you need give only the page number (for print sources of more than one page) in parentheses:

> Georges Duby says that women were almost nonexistent in a social sense unless they had husbands (98).

- If the author has more than one work in the *Works Cited* list, you will also have to give a short form of the title so readers will know which work you are citing:

> Those who did not carry on work of their own worked with their husbands and often took over the husband's business if the husband died (Gies and Gies, Life 53).

Because the correct form for parenthetical citations varies according to the source, sometimes you will need to refer to guidelines for correct form. The following chart defines and illustrates the basic forms of parenthetical citations.

Basic Content and Form for Parenthetical Citations	
These examples assume that the author or work has not already been named in a sentence introducing the source's information.	
Sources with One Author	
Author's last name and a page reference (if any)	(Patterson 135)
Separate Passages in a Single Source	
Author's last name and page references (if any)	(Olson 88, 90–91)
Sources with More Than One Author	
All authors' last names; if over three, first author's last name and *et al.* (Note that there is no comma when *et al.* is used.)	(Hill and Thomas 24) (Anderson *et al.* 313)
Multivolume Sources	
Author's last name plus volume and page	(Prucha 2: 214–15)
Sources with a Title Only	
Full title (if short) or a shortened version and page	(World Almanac 809)
Literary Sources Published in Many Editions	
As above, but cited by division references (act, scene, canto, book, chapter, part, and line numbers) in place of page references	(Shakespeare, Tempest 3.2.51–52)
Indirect Sources	
Abbreviation *qtd. in* [quoted in] before the source	(qtd. in Blamires 297)
More Than One Source in the Same Citation	
Citations separated with semicolons	(Schoeck 247; Duby 97)

TIP For documentation purposes *The MLA Handbook for Writers of Research Papers* lists standard abbreviations of certain literary and religious works. For example, *LLL* stands for *Love's Labour's Lost,* by William Shakespeare.

In addition to the rules for the content and form of citations, there are rules about placement. The following chart provides guidelines. Refer to the Writer's Model for additional examples.

Placement of Citations

1. Put the citation close to the information it documents, but try not to interrupt sentences. Instead, place it at the end of a sentence or at another point of punctuation.

2. Place the citation before the last punctuation mark of the sentence, clause, or phrase you are documenting.

> In addition, she has a tender interest in animals, perhaps stronger than her sympathy for people (Schoeck 249).

3. For a direct quotation that ends a sentence, place the citation after the quotation mark but before the end punctuation mark.

> The men of the time accepted this reasoning as valid, agreeing "theoretically at least— . . . that women were inferior beings" (Rowling 72).

4. For a block quotation (indented), place the citation two spaces after the final punctuation mark or on the following line, if necessary. See page 262.

TIP Your teacher may want you to use a documentation style different from the parenthetical citation system just discussed. The other common system uses **footnotes** or **endnotes.** Footnotes and endnotes are identical except that a footnote is placed at the bottom of the page upon which the source information is used, while endnotes are listed all together at the end of the report.

Each note is numbered, and a corresponding number appears in the body of your report. The first note for a source gives full information; following notes are shortened. If your teacher requests footnotes or endnotes, you will need additional guidelines and examples of form.

Number in body of paper:

> Chaucer is spoken of as "one of the most wonderful observers in the whole of English literature."[2]

Note (full form):

> [2] Eileen Power, Medieval People. (New York: Barnes, 1968) 94.

Listing Works Cited As its name indicates, the **Works Cited** list contains all the sources, print and nonprint, that you credit in your report. If you referred to only print material, your list would be titled **Bibliography;** if you listed all the sources you consulted—whether you cited them or not—your list would be called **Works Consulted.** As your teacher will probably prefer a *Works Cited* list, the following chart offers guidelines.

Guidelines for Preparing the List of *Works Cited*

1. **Center the heading *Works Cited* on a separate page.**
2. **Begin each entry on a separate line.** Position the first line of the entry even with the left margin, and indent all other lines five spaces. Double-space all entries.
3. **Alphabetize the sources by authors' last names.** If there is no author, alphabetize by title, ignoring the words *A, An,* or *The* and using the first letter of the next word.
4. **If you use two or more sources by the same author, include the author's name only in the first entry.** For all other entries, add three hyphens where the author's name would normally be, followed by a period (---.).

The following sample entries, in MLA style, are a reference for preparing your *Works Cited* list. Notice that you include page numbers only for articles in periodicals or for other works that are part of a whole work, such as one essay in a book of essays.

Sample Entries for List of *Works Cited*

Standard Reference Works

Note: When an author or editor is credited in a standard reference work, that person's name is written first. Otherwise, the title of the book or article appears first. Page and volume numbers are not needed if the work alphabetizes entries. For common reference works, the edition year is sufficient publication information.

Print Encyclopedia Article

Lumiansky, R. M. "Chaucer, Geoffrey." The New Encyclopaedia
  Britannica: Macropaedia. 15th ed. 1987.

"Canterbury Cathedral." Academic American Encyclopedia. 1996 ed.

Article in a Biographical Reference Book

"Chaucer, Geoffrey." British Authors Before 1800: A Biographical
  Dictionary. 1961 ed.

Books

Note: Use shortened forms of publishers' names. For the words *University* and *Press,* use *U* and *P.*

One Author

Knapp, Peggy. Chaucer and the Social Contest. New York: Routledge, 1990.

Two Authors

Allen, Judson Boyce, and Theresa Anne Moritz. A Distinction of Stories: The Medieval Unity of Chaucer's Fair Chain of Narratives for Canterbury. Columbus: Ohio State UP, 1981.

Three Authors

Klibansky, Raymond, Erwin Panofsky, and Fritz Saxl. Saturn and Melancholy: Studies in the History of Natural Philosophy, Religion, and Art. London: Nelson, 1964.

Four or More Authors

Davis, Norman, et. al. A Chaucer Glossary. Oxford: Oxford UP, 1979.

No Author Shown

An Exhibition of Fifteenth Century Manuscripts and Books in Honor of the Six Hundredth Anniversary of the Birth of Geoffrey Chaucer (1340–1400). Chicago: U of Chicago P, 1941.

Editor of a Collection of Writings

Miller, Robert P., ed. Chaucer: Sources and Backgrounds. New York: Oxford UP, 1977.

Two or Three Editors

Bryan, W. F., and Germaine Dempster, eds. Sources and Analogues of Chaucer's Canterbury Tales. Chicago: U of Chicago P, 1941.

Bibliography Published as a Book

Lagorio, Valerie Marie, and Ritamary Bradley. The 14th-Century English Mystics: A Comprehensive Annotated Bibliography. New York: Garland, 1981.

Unpublished Thesis or Dissertation

Lee, Chong-kyung. "To Pursue a Life of Perfection: Distinctive Forms of Female Monastic Life in the Early Middle Ages." Diss. U of Texas, 1997.

Selections Within Books

From a Book of Works by One Author

Woolf, Virginia. The Common Reader. New York: Harcourt, 1925.

From a Book of Works by Several Authors

Donaldson, E. Talbot. "Chaucer the Pilgrim." Chaucer Criticism: The Canterbury Tales. Eds. Richard J. Schoeck and Jerome Taylor. Notre Dame: U of Notre Dame P, 1965. 1–13.

(continued)

(continued)

Introduction, Preface, Foreword, or Afterword

Hieatt, A. Kent, and Constance Hieatt. Introduction. The Canterbury Tales. By Geoffrey Chaucer. Eds. A. Kent Hieatt and Constance Hieatt. New York: Bantam, 1981. ix–xxiv.

Articles from Magazines, Newspapers, and Journals

From a Weekly Magazine

Hughes, Robert. "Blazing Exceptions to Nature." Time 30 Nov. 1987: 94–96.

From a Monthly or Quarterly Magazine

Huneycutt, Lois. "Medieval Queenship." History Today June 1989: 16–23.

No Author Shown

"What Educated Women Want." Newsweek 13 June 1966: 68–75.

From a Scholarly Journal

Green, Richard Firth. "Women in Chaucer's Audience." The Chaucer Review 18–2 (1983): 146–54.

From a Daily Newspaper, with a Byline (Line Identifying the Writer)

Cobham, Rosemary. "Surprise and the Woman." Christian Science Monitor 2 Apr. 1955: 24.

From a Daily Newspaper, without a Byline

"20th-Century Tools Analyzing Chaucer's 14th-Century Tome." Fort Worth Star-Telegram 27 Aug. 1998, final morning ed.

Unsigned Editorial from a Daily Newspaper, No City in Paper's Title

"Woman's Hour." Editorial. Christian Science Monitor 16 July 1998: 16.

Other Sources

Personal Interview

Landow, Charles. Personal interview. 20 Oct. 2000.

Telephone Interview

Barnes, Elaine. Telephone interview. 17 Aug. 2000.

Published Interview with Title

Midgeley, Abigail. "Men Always Made the Big Decisions." Generations: A Century of Women Speak About Their Lives. By Myriam Miedzian and Alisa Malinovich. New York: Atlantic Monthly P, 1997. 241–45.

Broadcast or Recorded Interview with Title

Campbell, Joseph. "Love and the Goddess." The Power of Myth. Prod. Joan Konner and Alvin H. Perlmutter. Videocassette. Mystic Fire, 1988.

Published Letter

Paston, Margaret. "To Her Husband, John Paston." 14 Dec. 1441. Letter in Women's Lives in Medieval Europe: A Sourcebook. Ed. Emilie Amt. New York: Routledge, 1993. 170–71.

Personal Letter or E-Mail Message

Grau, Katherine. Letter to the author. 22 Jan. 2000.

Rodholm, Kai. E-mail to the author. 9 July 1999.

Sound Recording

Dyson, George. The Canterbury Pilgrims. Perf. Yvonne Kenny, Robert Tear, and Stephen Roberts. London Symphony Chorus. Cond. Malcolm Hicks. London Symphony Orch. Cond. Richard Hickox. Chandos, 1997.

Film or Video Recording

Note: Always include the title, director (if known), distributor, and year. You may include the producer. For video recordings, add a description of the medium (*Videotape* or *Videocassette*) before the distributor's name.

"The Wife of Bath" by Geoffrey Chaucer. Videocassette. Films for the Humanities and Sciences, 1996.

Material Accessed Through the Internet

"Courtly Love." Geoffrey Chaucer Page. Harvard U. 25 Jan. 1999. <http://icg.fas.harvard.edu/~chaucer/special/lifemann/love>.

Article from a CD-ROM Reference Work

Miller, Robert P. "Chaucer, Geoffrey." The 1998 Grolier's Multimedia Encyclopedia. CD-ROM. Danbury: Grolier Interactive Inc., 1998.

Full-Text Magazine, Newspaper, or Journal Article from a CD-ROM Database

"Middle Ages." History Today Apr. 1998: 51. MAS FullTEXT Select Version 5.0. CD-ROM. EBSCO Publishing, 1996.

YOUR TURN 7 Documenting Sources

Following the guidelines in the preceding section of the workshop, correctly insert the parenthetical citations in your paper. Then, prepare a *Works Cited* list of the sources you credited in your paper.

Revising

Evaluate and Revise Your Draft

The Best It Can Be   Successful revision can make a merely acceptable paper into one that is superior. Do not try to revise every aspect of your draft at one time. Work collaboratively with a peer to look at content and organization first; then, focus on style.

> **First Reading: Content and Organization**   The following chart can help you determine whether you have clearly communicated the thesis of your research paper. Alone or working collaboratively with a partner, use the tips in the middle column to help you answer the questions in the first column. Then, if necessary, revise your paper by incorporating the changes recommended in the last column.

Literary Research Paper: Content and Organization Guidelines for Peer and Self-Evaluation		
Evaluation Questions	**Tips**	**Revision Techniques**
❶ Does the introduction hook the reader's attention, give background information, and clearly state the thesis?	▶ **Circle** the hook, **underline** background information, and **bracket** the thesis statement. If any of these elements are missing, revise.	▶ **Add** a quotation or interesting detail to your first sentence. **Add or elaborate** on necessary background. **Add** a sentence or two stating the thesis.
❷ Do all key ideas and specific details relate directly to and support the thesis? Are facts and ideas stated mainly in the writer's own words?	▶ With a colored marker, **highlight** the main ideas, **check** details for each, and revise any that do not support the thesis. **Star** sentences containing direct quotations. If more than half the sentences are starred, revise.	▶ **Replace** or **delete** ideas and details that do not support the thesis. **Add** paraphrasing and summaries to replace unnecessary direct quotations.
❸ Is the report sufficiently developed with a variety of primary and secondary sources?	▶ **Write** the number **1** by primary source material and the number **2** by secondary source material. If you do not see a mixture, revise.	▶ **Add** facts, examples, opinions, and quotations from primary or secondary sources so your essay reflects more than one type of source.
❹ Are sources credited when necessary?	▶ **Place check marks** by direct quotations and any other material from outside sources. If sources are not documented, revise.	▶ **Add** necessary documentation.
❺ Does the conclusion restate the thesis?	▶ **Bracket** the restatement of the thesis. Revise if this is missing.	▶ **Add** a sentence or two that returns the reader to the purpose of the research.

ONE WRITER'S REVISIONS Notice how this writer used the content and organization guidelines to revise some sentences which appear, in revised form, in the research paper on page 259.

> Chaucer, "one of the most wonderful observers in the whole of
>
> English literature" (Power 94), ~~is known as the father of English~~   **delete**
>
> ~~poetry. He~~ often knew the people he observed "better than they
>
> *(Chute 240).*
>
> knew themselves." ⁁ He reports everything with accuracy. The last   **add**
>
> *⌐—even if what he sees contains contradictions*   **elaborate**
>
> half of the fourteenth century, when he (and his characters) lived,
>
> *a time of contradictions, a time of dramatic and upsetting transition*   **paraphrase/elaborate**
>
> was, after all, ⁁ ~~a transitional period from a medieval to a modern~~
>
> ~~world"~~ (Thompson and Johnson 863).

Analyzing the Revision Process

1. Why did the writer delete information from the first sentence?

2. Why was it necessary for the writer to add the parenthetical citation to the first sentence?

3. Why did the writer replace information in the last sentence?

YOUR TURN 8   Focusing on Content and Organization

Using the guidelines in the chart on page 276, revise your paper for content and organization. Refer to the example revisions above as a model.

PEER REVIEW

Ask a classmate to read your paper and to answer the following questions:

1. What part of the writer's literary research paper was most interesting to you? Why?

2. Which part would you have liked the writer to discuss further?

▷ **Second Reading: Style**   An important aspect of style in research papers is the introduction of quoted material in a clear and unobtrusive manner. Follow the guidelines below to revise this aspect of your paper.

Style Guidelines

Evaluation Question	▶ Tip	▶ Revision Technique
Are quotations introduced so that they fit smoothly into the paper?	▶ **Bracket** the quotations in your paper. If there is not an introduction for each quotation or if the quotation does not read like a part of the sentence, revise.	▶ **Add** an introductory phrase, an assertion—an interpretive statement or declaration—with a colon, or use an assertion within which a quotation is placed.

Focus on Sentences

Introducing Quotations

Quotations add interest, variety, and credibility to your paper, but they should not disrupt the flow of the reading or sound like a grocery list. Your goal is to introduce your quotations gracefully so that the reader does not hesitate or stumble. Here are three effective ways to introduce quotations into your paper.

- **With an introductory phrase:**

  According to Chaucer, "She certainly was very entertaining, / Pleasant and friendly in her ways . . ." (Chaucer 29).

- **With a statement that gives an interpretation followed by a colon:**

  Chaucer's description of the Prioress suggests that she is more interested in her physical appearance than in her spiritual purity: "Her veil was gathered in a seemly way, / Her nose was elegant, her eyes glass-grey;" (Chaucer 29).

- **With an interpretive assertion into which a quotation is worked:**

  The Prioress, who "used to weep if she but saw a mouse / Caught in a trap," demonstrates no parallel sympathy for her fellow man (Chaucer 29).

ONE WRITER'S REVISIONS Here is how the writer of the research paper on page 259 used the guidelines above to evaluate and revise the introductions to several quotations.

Quotations are bracketed

BEFORE REVISION

["Women did not count."] That is what one writer said was the state of women during much of the Middle Ages (Chute 71). Nevertheless, during Chaucer's time, at least in urban areas, women had made progress. Women like the Wife of Bath had some rights. ["[T]hey were sometimes in business for themselves and were considered legally capable of controlling funds for their business and of answering for that business in borough court"] (Sheehan 32).

AFTER REVISION

   Although during much of the Middle Ages, women "did not count" (Chute 71), women during Chaucer's time, at least in the urban areas, had made progress. Women like the Wife of Bath could be in "business for themselves and were considered legally capable of controlling funds for their business and of answering for that business in borough court" (Sheehan 32).

Use introductory phrase

Work quoted material into assertion

Analyzing the Revision Process

1. What is the most obvious difference in the two passages? What accounts for this difference?

2. Which of the two passages reads more smoothly? Why?

YOUR TURN 9 Focusing on Style

Re-read your paper, looking for places where you could make stylistic revisions. Pay special attention to the way you have incorporated the quoted material into your text. Use the style guidelines on page 277 and the sample revision above as a model.

Designing Your Writing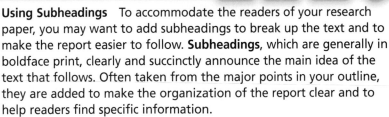

Using Subheadings   To accommodate the readers of your research paper, you may want to add subheadings to break up the text and to make the report easier to follow. **Subheadings**, which are generally in boldface print, clearly and succinctly announce the main idea of the text that follows. Often taken from the major points in your outline, they are added to make the organization of the report clear and to help readers find specific information.

   An example of a paragraph beginning with a subheading is given below. Although the subheading is written in bold type and is flush with the left-hand margin, other designs are possible.

TIP   To find the design that best communicates your information, experiment with typeface, location, and size—keeping within the limits of what is acceptable in a formal, academic report.

The Prioress: Spiritual Concerns and Worldly Concerns

   The Prioress, also known as Madame Eglantine, is introduced in the General Prologue both as a woman of the Church and also as a vain woman of worldly interests.

Publishing

Proofread Your Essay

Reference Note

For more on **punctuating quotations,** see page 859.

Polish the Prose Proofreading is vital to writing. Any mechanical errors in your paper—mistakes in capitalization, spelling, punctuation, grammar, and usage—will distract your readers, preventing them from paying attention to the strength of your ideas. Because your research paper probably includes quotations, be sure to check that they are correctly punctuated.

Grammar Link

Punctuating Quotations Correctly

Refer to these rules as you check the punctuation of the quotations in your paper.

1. **Always use quotation marks to enclose a person's exact words.**

   She has had five husbands and she says, in introducing her tale, **"**Welcome the sixth, whenever he appears**"** (Chaucer 218).

2. **Commas and periods are usually placed inside quotation marks** (unless the quotation is immediately followed by a parenthetical citation).

   One code of instruction of the Middle Ages states, "Running and trotting, your own heart will tell you, are not becoming in a lady**,**" and the lady of the castle had the responsibility of enforcing the rule (Rowling 84).

3. **Semicolons and colons are usually placed outside the closing quotation marks.**

   The women's nobleman husbands were frequently absent "on crusade, at the wars, or in the courts"**;** at these times the wives were called upon to maintain not only the household but also all the business of the manor (Rowling 84).

4. **Use single quotation marks to enclose a quotation within a quotation.**

Power gives the Wife of Bath credit for influencing dress among Chaucer's nuns: ". . . she certainly introduced hats **'**as broad as is a buckler or a targe**'** and scarlet stockings into some nunneries" (88).

PRACTICE

Use the rules above to punctuate the following sentences correctly. Enclose the underlined passages in quotation marks, and position other punctuation correctly in relation to the quotation marks.

1. Chaucer describes the Manciple as a man who <u>was never rash / Whether he bought on credit or paid cash.</u>

2. Chaucer describes the Prioress as eating <u>daintily</u>; this detail shows her aristocratic manners.

3. Chaucer also says that she <u>took great pains to behave in a well- / bred fashion</u> (9).

4. Singing of love occupies the Pardoner as he rides along; Chaucer reports <u>he sang,</u> "Come hither, love, to me," <u>and the Summoner accompanied him powerfully.</u>

5. The Host asks three people by name to <u>draw a lot before we go any further:</u> the Knight, the Prioress, and the Clerk.

Publish Your Essay

Share the Wealth (of Knowledge)   In your research paper, you have collected a great deal of information and given it an interpretation that may be of interest to other readers. Brainstorm with the class about imaginative publishing ideas, and consider these possibilities:

- Collect the papers in a class anthology, and place it in a special section of the school library.
- Submit your paper to a student magazine that focuses on your topic.
- Save your literary research project as a writing sample to submit for a college or job application.
- If the topic is one that would be of interest to students in lower grades, offer your paper to a teacher who teaches a related subject.
- If your school has a Web site, or you know of a Web site on a topic related to your paper, submit the paper to the creators of the site for possible inclusion.
- If you know a friend or relative who would be interested in the topic you have written about, bind the paper with some illustrations and a copy of the primary literary text you used, and send it to the person as a gift.

Reflect on Your Essay

Consider the Road You've Traveled   Responding to the following questions will help you to think about what this research project has meant to you and what you have learned about yourself as a writer. Keep your answers in your portfolio, along with a final version of your research paper.

PORTFOLIO

- What did I discover about my choice of topic? Did this topic hold my interest throughout the project? Why or why not?
- What additional research questions would I like to answer if I were to continue researching this topic?
- What mistakes did I make in my research procedures? How could I avoid making the same mistakes again?
- What did I enjoy about this project? Of what part am I proudest? Why?

YOUR TURN 10   **Proofreading, Publishing, and Reflecting**

Following the guidelines in this workshop, prepare your paper for final presentation by proofreading it carefully. After preparing a clean, professional-looking paper, think of publishing possibilities. Finally, reflect upon the writing experience.

Connections to Life

Evaluating Web Sources

Besides researching literary subjects, you might turn to the World Wide Web to explore travel options, to plan a purchase, to hunt for a job, or to investigate a topic of interest. The problem you face, no matter what your purpose, is how to evaluate the source.

Useful or Useless?   Earlier in this chapter, you learned to use the **4 R test** to evaluate print and nonprint sources used in research. Similarly, Web sites must be evaluated; in fact, it is more important to look closely at a Web site's information because most sites go through no review process prior to their Web "publication." On the Web, anyone can be published, and no standards of quality exist. So how can you determine whether a particular Web site is useful or useless? Use the following criteria to help you make your evaluation. The student responses are based on a Web site titled "Women Writers of the Middle Ages." This site contains a collection of bibliographies that could be used to find information for a research paper on women characters in Chaucer.

- **Accuracy: Are sources listed for verification? Does the information match other sources?** The bibliographies were credited—the one I used most was from the U. of Iowa.

- **Authority: Is the author or publisher qualified to write on this topic?** People cited in the hypertext articles were noted authorities.

- **Coverage: Is the information applicable and complete?** The extensive bibliographies were valuable. There was a wealth of material with links to other sites.

- **Currency: Is the information up-to-date? When was the site last revised?** The last update of the University of Iowa bibliography was Feb. 18, 1997. This seems reasonably current. Other parts of the site did not have updates listed.

- **Objectivity: Are affiliations clear and biases clearly stated?** It is an educational site produced by Millersville University. It has no obvious bias.

- **Stability: Will the site remain on the Web?** It will probably remain on the Web because it is maintained by university faculty and students who have a lasting interest in the subject matter the site covers.

- **User-friendliness: Can you easily navigate the site? Is it logically organized?** One link I tried resulted in an unexpected return to the home page, but it was always easy to see what was available and how to get to it.

YOUR TURN 11   Evaluating Web Sites

Alone or in a small group, write an evaluation of a Web site you used in preparing your research report or a site dealing with a topic of interest to you. Use the criteria listed above. Be prepared to share your results.

Researching a Film

In writing your literary research paper, you gathered factual information to support your thesis. You tried to be objective—to present an accurate, unbiased view of the subject matter. Similarly, when a novel, or other fictional work, is adapted for the screen, filmmakers often use research to re-create the setting and other aspects of the work as accurately as possible. To do so, they must research things like the dress styles, the speech patterns, and the social and cultural customs of the time and place they wish to portray.

WHAT'S AHEAD?

In this section, you will learn how important research is to filmmaking. You will also

■ view a film adapted from a fictional work

■ find sources of research to test the film adaptation's accuracy and realism

Film's Use of Research

Who Finds out What? In filmmaking, the director is not the only one who needs to do research to ensure accuracy. For example, to adapt Jane Austen's novel *Persuasion* for the screen, set designers not only read her novel for clues about the decorations and furniture, but also investigated typical, nineteenth-century furnishings for houses similar to the ones described in Austen's novel. In addition, choreographers studied dance forms; musicians reviewed music and instruments that the characters mention and play; and screenwriters researched speech patterns and social and cultural customs and attitudes in order to add authenticity to their script.

Bring on the Popcorn To discover the many ways research is used in the development of a film, first select and view a film adapted from a classic novel or other fictional work. You might be surprised at how many novels have been made (and often remade several times) into films. One favorite story for filmmakers is Robert Louis Stevenson's *The Strange Case of Dr. Jekyll and Mr. Hyde*. Perhaps because of its universal theme—the battle within a person between good and evil—the story has been filmed a surprising number of times, each version revealing both similar and different interpretations of the historical costumes and customs. Filmmakers have also chosen to film classic works by other well-known British authors, such as Shakespeare, Jane Austen, Thomas Hardy, W. Somerset Maugham, E. M. Forster, and Virginia Woolf.

To find film adaptations of novels or other works of fiction, use the following suggestions.

- **Look in a film or video guide for films with the same title as the work.** Usually the filmmaker will title the film with the same title as the novel; for example, Thomas Hardy's *Tess of the d'Urbervilles* had the same title in the 1998 film version made for television. Likewise, Kenneth Branagh's 1989 film *Henry V* has the same title as Shakespeare's play. There are exceptions, of course. One 1963 film version of *The Strange Case of Dr. Jekyll and Mr. Hyde* was filmed as a comedy and is titled *The Nutty Professor,* which itself has been remade.

- **Ask a video librarian for suggestions.** The librarian may steer you to the films of a particular director. Some producers and directors—Ismail Merchant and James Ivory, for example—have specialized in filming nineteenth century novels, such as *A Room with A View* and *Howards End.* The librarian can also suggest less well-known adaptations that may be of interest to you.

- **Surf the Internet for Web pages devoted to film adaptations of literary works.** Type in the author or title of the fictional work you have chosen and follow the hyperlinks for information on possible film versions of the work. For example, using "Thomas Hardy" or *"Tess of the d'Urbervilles"* as keywords will lead you to film Web pages, which sometimes list credits, ratings, and film highlights. Some Web pages also include complete screenplays.

Through the Viewfinder   As you view the film you have chosen, look at the many details the filmmakers have selected to make their version of the work as authentic as possible. For example, in the film version of Jane Austen's *Persuasion,* the central female characters wear hats—special elaborate ones for outdoors or for visiting friends, and smaller, daintier ones for indoors. The costumer for the film probably had to research hat styles of the period in order to re-create realistic costumes for the actresses playing the nineteenth-century characters of the novel.

If you were interested in learning more about the kinds of hats fashionable in that era or the reasons why women wore such hats, then you could do research yourself. Obviously, you could read the novel. However, novels, no matter how rich with details of dress styles, often do not provide as much specific description as a costumer would need in order to design hats for several characters. In addition to reading the novel, you would need to find pictures or drawings of English fashions in the early nineteenth century in both print and nonprint sources. Your research would validate the choices made by the costumer or would lead you to speculate on the reasons for the changes the costumers and filmmakers had made.

The following chart shows you how one student researched various elements in the 1995 film *Persuasion*, directed by Roger Mitchell for the BBC (British TV). The left-hand column identifies some of the researched elements considered part of the *mise-en-scène*—a French term meaning the effect created in film by the setting, props, and general environment of the scene. The middle column lists a few of the details the student noticed. The right-hand column shows the sources the student used to verify the historical accuracy of the filmmaker's choices.

Element from Film	Examples	Possible Research Sources
Setting (time and place); locations (exteriors, landscapes, and interiors of houses)	Early nineteenth century (characters mention Bonaparte and Trafalgar); English countryside and Bath, a resort town on the coast; interiors of houses loaded with furniture, wall decorations, and knickknacks	Map of England for place names, political history books and history of furniture design, picture books of English country houses and gardens, photographs and paintings of English countryside, catalogs of old china patterns
Costumes and hairstyles for men and women; for upper social class and working class	Women's hairstyles: upswept and elaborate, always covered by hats; lace-trimmed, long dresses with velvet cloaks, shawls, cloth purses; small earrings and pearls. Men's clothing: waistcoats, gloves and tall hats. Lower classes wore dull colors, coarse jackets	Museums' collections of antique clothing, social history books, interview with high school drama teacher about costume design
Cultural elements, including transportation, dance, food, entertainment	Six-horse carriage for wealthy; poorer status shown by one-horse cart; intricately patterned dances, not with partners; ham and bread; music as entertainment (pianoforte and spinet piano)—weekly concerts and recitals	Pictures and paintings of carriages and horses, interviews with dance historians, recipe books, recordings of period music with instruments from that era, online databases
Class or economic structures	A suitor's prospects: someone to recommend them, or good social connections. Women: economic status from husband; had none themselves. Lower classes were servants, workers. Upper class: plenty of leisure time	Academic studies on English class structures and the economic status of the various classes; sociology books on marriage and family life in nineteenth-century England

(continued)

Gender roles or professions	"Gentlemen" inherited money; their work—managing their possessions Women ("Ladies") did not work	Encyclopedias or online databases; biographies or autobiographies; histories of certain professions, such as sea captains, or lawyers
Dating customs or rituals of friendship	Dances, courteous and witty talk, presenting cards, taking tea with friends	Other novels from the same time period; BBC television productions; etiquette books; autobiographies

TIP Remember that filmmakers have the difficult task of representing relationships, abstract ideas, and cultural traditions in concrete ways. If you notice that a key element from the literary work is missing from the film, it may help to think about how you would have portrayed it yourself.

Now for the Big Picture As a result of your research, you may find that the filmmakers have changed various details. Sometimes this is because the filmmakers had to fill in details that are not specifically described in the literary work. For example, when filmmakers adapt a scene from a novel, they must show every detail of setting in that scene; whereas a novelist might have included only the most important elements. In other instances, filmmakers intentionally change elements of the literary work they are adapting for artistic reasons. For example, director Kenneth Branagh set his adaptation of *Hamlet* in the nineteenth century. Your research discoveries might lead you to speculate on the purposes and results of the filmmakers' additions or changes. Consider the following questions.

- Does the difference between the film adaptation and the original work affect your understanding and enjoyment of the story? If so, how?

- Were departures from historical accuracy necessary to make the world of the film appeal to a popular audience? Why or why not? Alternately, do you think the changes were made for artistic purposes? Explain.

YOUR TURN 12 **Researching a Film**

Choose and view a film adaptation of a classic work of fiction. Then, fill out a chart similar to the one that begins on page 285, including elements that probably required research, such as setting. Provide specific examples from the film, and then research their accuracy. Be sure to list your sources. Afterward, jot a few notes about how faithful the film was to the period. If it was not accurate, identify possible purposes for any discrepancies. Be prepared to share the results of your research with your classmates.

Choices

Choose one of the following activities to complete.

▶ **CAREERS**

1. Literary Work Find a recent work of fiction in which a character has a career that interests you. Read the literary work, making notes about facets of the career that are mentioned: preparation, daily routine, and positive and negative aspects. You might make inferences about such things as stress level, based on the behavior of the character. Check this information against a reliable source about the career: a book, an interview with a person now working in this career, or an Internet site. Deliver an **oral report** to the class on the career and the reliability of the information in the work of fiction.

▶ **SPEAKING AND LISTENING**

2. Writers' Craft Research is an essential activity for writers in many different professional fields, including science, medicine, history, journalism, and economics. With a small group of classmates, investigate how writers use research and compose their writings. Have each member of the group interview a professional in a different field. Ask what sources the professionals use, how they evaluate their sources, and what form their writing takes. Then,

have a **group discussion** about your findings.

▶ **CROSSING THE CURRICULUM: ART**

3. Recording on Canvas Find and carefully examine two paintings titled *La Belle Dame Sans Merci,* one by Sir Frank Dicksee and the other by Frank Cadogan Cowper. Then, study the poem "La Belle Dame Sans Merci" by John Keats. In a short **essay,** compare the poem to each of the two paintings. Which artist's depiction best captures Keats's poem? Why do you think so? Be as specific as you can. As an alternate choice, follow the above directions for two paintings titled *The Lady of Shalott,* one by James William Waterhouse and the other by William Holman Hunt, and the poem of the same name by Alfred, Lord Tennyson.

▶ **LITERATURE**

4. In Context Research the life of a poet whose work you enjoy reading, and choose one of his or her poems. Prepare a three- to four-minute **oral interpretation** in which you read the poem aloud and then talk about aspects of the poet's life that might have influenced his or her writing of the poem.

PORTFOLIO

7 Defending a Position

GLOBAL REACH.

LOCAL TOUCH.

connect @ the library

Reading Workshop

Reading a Persuasive Essay
PAGE 290

Writing Workshop

Writing a Persuasive Essay
PAGE 301

Focus on Viewing and Representing

Analyzing Persuasion in Media Messages
PAGE 322

Focus on Speaking and Listening

Making a Persuasive Speech
PAGE 325

As you open your front door, a flier advertising pizza drifts to the floor. You go inside, flop onto the sofa, toss the balled-up flier into the trash, and turn on the television. On the screen, a politician gives reasons why you should vote for him. A few minutes later, your older brother walks in, and you launch into a vigorous attempt to get him to lend you his car for the evening. He replies that he just read an editorial in the newspaper arguing that people under the age of eighteen shouldn't be allowed to drive. Indignant, you storm back to your room with your assigned reading for history class—Dr. Martin Luther King, Jr.'s "I Have A Dream" speech.

What do the pizza flier, the campaign advertisement, your pleas to your brother, the editorial, and King's speech all have in common? They are all examples of **persuasion**—attempts to convince people to believe something or to do something. Persuasion surrounds you. Magazine and newspaper articles, television and radio advertisements, online catalogs, and billboards all use persuasion to move (and sometimes manipulate) people. How do *you* use persuasion? How is it used *on* you?

GO TO: go.hrw.com
KEYWORD: EOLang 12-7

YOUR TURN 1 — Brainstorming About Persuasion

With three or four classmates, list examples of persuasion you have encountered recently. What do these different examples of persuasion have in common? What do they try to get you to believe or do? Which ones were most persuasive and why? Take notes during your discussion, and be prepared to share them with the class.

Reading a Persuasive Essay

WHAT'S AHEAD?

In this section, you will read a persuasive essay. You will also learn how to

■ recognize logical, emotional, and ethical appeals

■ identify point of view and detect bias

Do you believe everything you read? Of course not. Whether or not you are persuaded by a piece of writing probably depends on your answers to the following questions:

■ Does it make sense?

■ How does it make me feel?

■ Do I trust that the writer is fair, trustworthy, and knowledgeable?

In "Homegrown Varieties," the persuasive essay that starts on the next page, Russell A. Mittermeier argues that exploring Earth's life forms is every bit as worthwhile as searching for life on other planets. Is his argument convincing? You decide.

Preparing to Read

READING FOCUS

Logical, Emotional, and Ethical Appeals   When you read persuasive writing, you may encounter three different types of appeals designed to win you over to the writer's position or to convince you to do something.

■ **Logical appeals** speak to your ability to reason, or think clearly.

■ **Emotional appeals** target your feelings.

■ **Ethical appeals** convey the writer's integrity and knowledge and call on your sense of right and wrong.

As you read "Homegrown Varieties," look for places where the writer appeals to your mind, your heart, and your conscience.

READING SKILL

Identifying Point of View and Bias   Regardless of the subject he or she chooses to write about, every writer will have a unique **point of view**—an attitude or opinion shaped by the writer's background and values. Some writers also display a **bias**—a preference, inclination, or preconception that prevents them from being impartial. As you read "Homegrown Varieties," consider the writer's background and his attitude toward his subject. Try to see whether you can detect any bias.

As you read the following persuasive essay, jot down answers to the numbered active-reading questions.

from Newsweek

Homegrown Varieties

by Russell A. Mittermeier
President of Conservation International

My colleagues and I just discovered a distinctive new monkey species between the Rio Madeira and the Rio Tapajós in Brazil's central Amazon. In the process, we may have located two or three other monkeys and a tree porcupine previously unknown to science. The latest monkey is the seventh new primate found in Brazil alone since 1990, and others crop up on a regular basis in different regions of the tropics. Scientists working in Madagascar discover a new frog or chameleon species just about every month. Entomologists fogging the canopy of rain-forest trees uncover so many new beetle species there isn't enough museum space to house them all. And as we finally explore more of the deep-sea ocean trenches, we are finding creatures that don't even fit within the definition of plant or animal.

Meanwhile, all eyes are turned toward a couple of rocks called Yogi and Barnacle Bill on a planet 120 million miles away. Having been raised on a heavy diet of Edgar Rice Burroughs's wonderful adventure novels based on Mars, Venus, and points beyond (yes, he did write a lot more than Tarzan tales), I, too, share a fascination with what might exist in the far reaches of outer space. . . . I fully appreciate the public's fascination with the possibility of extraterrestrial life. But there was something about all the fuss over the latest surveys of rocks on Mars that bothered me. At first I couldn't pinpoint exactly what it was. Then it became clear: The justification for spending millions of dollars to send

1. What do these first two sentences suggest to you about the writer's background?

2. Why do you think the writer mentions his interest in space exploration?

probes to these planets is much the same as that used by field biologists surveying the flora and fauna in poorly documented ecosystems on Earth.

Tree porcupine

On Mars we *might* have located fossils of one-celled organisms that resemble the earliest forms of life on Earth several billion years ago. On Jupiter's moon Europa, under two miles of ice, there *appears* to be water where life might *possibly* exist. This interplanetary biodiversity, if it exists, would be quite interesting. But what about the vast, yet undiscovered variety of life that exists on this planet?

Today's sophisticated technology enables us to launch space probes, and computers can cram millions of bits of information onto tiny silicon chips. But we languish in the Dark Ages when it comes to understanding the diversity of life on Earth. Harvard University professor, biologist, and author Edward O. Wilson estimates that scientists have thus far described between 1.4 million and 1.8 million species of plants, animals, and microorganisms. Yet the total number of species could run from 10 million to 30 million to 100 million or more (I believe the 100 million figure). We don't know to within one and perhaps two orders of magnitude[1] how many forms of life share this planet with us. If we look at the complex ecological interactions among this vast array of life forms, we are probably an additional two or three orders of magnitude off in our lack of knowledge. And we're even more ignorant about the potential values these biological resources hold for humans.

This planet's intricate web of life is what we earthlings ultimately depend upon for our own survival as a species. This diversity provides us with the basics for living, as sources of food, clothing, shelter, medicine, and recreation. The onslaught of destructive forces

3. Why do you think the writer has emphasized the italicized words?

4. Why do you think the writer includes these facts?

5. What do you think the phrase *onslaught of destructive forces* refers to, and why do you think the writer used those particular words?

---

1. **order of magnitude:** a range of measurable quantities extending from a given value to ten times that value. For example, 100 is one order of magnitude greater than 10; 1,000 is two orders of magnitude greater than 10.

on the planet's living resources means that we will probably never know just exactly how many and what kinds of other life forms share the planet with us.

I have seen the medicine men and women in Suriname's jungles cure fevers and infections by directly applying healing plants to their patients. This knowledge is now sought by pharmaceutical companies to help develop drugs in the laboratory. One such drug, Vincristine, was originally created from alkaloids of the rosy periwinkle, a small plant native to Madagascar. When the young daughter of a colleague of mine was diagnosed with a rare blood-related cancer several years ago, this drug helped save her. In the course of pursuing lemurs through Madagascar's rain forests, I've come across many wild species of coffee, some of which could one day be critical for the survival of one of the world's largest agricultural commodities. In general, the key role played by uncultivated relatives of our most important crop species in maintaining genetic diversity and resistance to disease is well-known. The examples of our dependence on other forms of life are almost endless.

The latest Martian probe is said to have cost $260 million, a truly low figure for such endeavors, especially when compared with what was spent in the 1960s and 1970s. To put that figure in perspective, however, it is more than a full year of government spending on biodiversity research on our entire planet.

All the attention and hoopla surrounding the Mars expedition would be less troublesome to me if exploration of other planets in our solar system were couched in terms of astronomy, physics, or chemistry. To justify this expense in order to find new species in outer space, while our own world faces the most severe extinction spasms in the past 65 million years, seems a bit disingenuous. Based on some current biological estimates, in the 211 days it took for *Pathfinder* to make the journey to Mars, more than 20,000 rainforest species might have become extinct. During that same amount of time, by one estimate, more than 20 million acres of tropical forests were destroyed, wiping out some of the most diverse habitats on the planet.

Don't get me wrong. I am not against space research. I take as much delight as any other casual observer in seeing the diminutive *Sojourner* stumbling around the rocks of Mars. But let's be reasonable. If we are going to spend another $260 million in the name of extraterrestrial life, let's spend at least as much on conserving and cataloging living species on this planet. After all, Earth is still the only place in the entire universe where we know with certainty that life exists.

6. What effect do you think the writer intended this anecdote about his friend's daughter to have on readers?

7. In this paragraph, how does the writer appeal to his readers' sense of fairness?

8. What does the writer seem to want his readers to believe and to do?

READING FOCUS

Logical, Emotional, and Ethical Appeals

A Hard Sell   What does it take to persuade you? Could a writer win you over just by stating an opinion such as the one below?

> **Opinion:** Penalties for oil spills should be more severe.

Even if you happened to agree with the opinion, you would probably expect the writer to explain *why* you should believe as she does. To provide such an explanation, the writer would probably use one or more of the three types of persuasive appeals—**logical appeals, emotional appeals,** and **ethical appeals.**

What Do You Think?   Appeals to reason, or clear thinking, are called **logical appeals.** They provide **reasons** that explain why a writer holds a particular opinion on an issue.

> **Reason:** Oil spills damage the environment.

Logical appeals also provide **evidence,** or proof, to back up each reason. Here are three basic forms of evidence.

- **Facts** are statements that can be proved by testing, personal experience, or verification from reliable sources. Factual statements can be thought of as **data**—information from which conclusions can be drawn. Data often consist of examples and **statistics,** or numerical information.

> **Evidence:** A recent study of the effects of oil spills in the Caribbean found that coral organisms were severely harmed.

- **Expert testimony** consists of statements by people who are recognized authorities on an issue.

> **Evidence:** In her book *Silent Spring*, Rachel Carson, marine biologist and environmentalist, wrote, ". . . pollution is for the most part irrecoverable; the chain of evil it initiates not only in the world that must support life but in living tissues is for the most part irreversible."

- **Factual anecdotes,** brief stories often based on personal experiences, may also be used as logical appeals.

> **Evidence:** After the oil spill, I took a walk on the beach, where thousands of otters and birds lay dying because their protective fur and feathers were covered with oil.

When you read logical appeals, you must read critically, evaluating whether they are sound.

How Do You Feel? In addition to appealing to your reasoning ability, persuasive writers also use **emotional appeals** to tug at your heartstrings. For example, read the following anecdote—another version of the one you read above—about an Alaskan oil spill. How does it make you feel?

> After the oil spill, I took a walk on the beach. To my horror, I found the sand littered with thousands of otters and birds, slowly freezing to death because their protective fur and feathers were drenched with the black, foul-smelling oil.

Notice how the writer brings the facts to frightening life by describing the fur and feathers of creatures *drenched* (not just *covered*) with *black, foul-smelling oil* (not just *oil*) and *slowly freezing to death* (not just *dying*).

As this example shows, certain words carry with them strong **connotations**—positive or negative feelings or associations. Because highly connotative language can create such powerful effects—shocking, enraging, or saddening readers—it is sometimes called **loaded language.** In addition to connotative language, writers can use striking anecdotes and descriptions of highly charged situations, such as those endangering children, to appeal to your emotions. When you are reading, be alert to a writer's use of these emotional appeals, and take care not to let your emotions overwhelm your ability to reason.

Whom Can You Trust? A writer uses **ethical appeals** to convince readers that he or she is fair, knowledgeable, and trustworthy and to appeal to readers' ethical or moral convictions. In one type of ethical appeal, a writer tries to show that he or she has considered both sides of an issue. This is called **conceding a point,** or acknowledging an opposing argument. For example, the writer urging harsher penalties for oil spills might try to win over opponents with the statement below.

> While safeguarding our environment, we must also ensure that the world's oil supply, so vital to the global economy, is not interrupted.

Another type of ethical appeal attempts to engage readers' **values** by framing an argument in moral terms. For example, the writer might appeal to

> **TIP** One way to understand logical, emotional, and ethical appeals is to consider the questions given as subheadings in this section:
>
> - What do you think? (logical)
> - How do you feel? (emotional)
> - Whom can you trust? (ethical)

the reader's sense of right and wrong by concluding with the following statement.

> We do not own the earth. We are only its caretakers, and we should be held accountable for the damage we do.

Finally, writers can capitalize on who they are in an effort to get readers to trust them. For example, a writer arguing for stiffer penalties for oil spills might enhance her credibility by mentioning that she is a marine biologist who has seen and studied the damage that oil spills cause.

THINKING IT THROUGH   Identifying Persuasive Appeals

Use the following steps to help you identify logical, emotional, and ethical appeals.

▶ **STEP 1 Look for reasons and evidence (facts, expert testimony, and factual anecdotes).** An appeal that contains these elements is usually a **logical appeal.**

▶ **STEP 2 Look for connotative or loaded language, anecdotes that evoke emotion, and descriptions of highly charged situations** (such as those endangering children or animals). These elements usually signal an **emotional appeal.**

▶ **STEP 3 Look for statements that acknowledge other points of view, that speak to the reader's sense of right and wrong, or that enhance the writer's credibility.** These are usually **ethical appeals.**

TIP Effective persuasive essays do not usually rely on a single type of appeal. Instead, they often use a combination of logical, emotional, and ethical appeals. In fact, one sentence may represent a combination of appeals. For example, a factual statement might include highly connotative language, thus making it both a logical and an emotional appeal.

YOUR TURN 2   Identifying Logical, Emotional, and Ethical Appeals

With a group of three or four classmates, identify one logical appeal, one emotional appeal, and one ethical appeal in "Homegrown Varieties." As a group, write a brief explanation of how you arrived at each identification. Be prepared to share your responses with the class.

Identifying Point of View and Bias

Whose Side Are You On, Anyway?   A writer's **point of view,** or opinion about his or her subject, is affected by the writer's background, interests, and values. To understand how important point of view is in persuasion, imagine how different "Homegrown Varieties" might be if it had been written by a NASA official, rather than by the president of an organization concerned with conserving the earth's plant and animal resources.

As you read persuasive writing, keep in mind that the writer's goal is to convince you to believe or act in a certain way. To avoid being manipulated, or unknowingly influenced, you need to be able to recognize the writer's point of view. You also need to be able to detect whether the writer's argument is **biased**—overly partial toward a particular viewpoint.

In some cases, you can determine the writer's point of view from biographical information provided in an introduction or byline, as in "Homegrown Varieties," or from information about the writer disclosed further along in the text. In most cases, though, you will need to infer, or make an educated guess about, the writer's point of view by examining his or her logical, emotional, and ethical appeals. Bias, while it may be easier to spot, must also be inferred from evidence in the text.

THINKING IT THROUGH   Identifying Point of View and Bias

Use the following steps to identify a writer's point of view and any bias the writer might have. Look also at the example responses shown in the right-hand column. They are based on the following passage.

> I have worked as a research scientist at NASA for the past twenty years, and I can say without a doubt that more money should be allocated for research in outer space. I realize that research of animal and plant life on our own planet is important, but I can't agree with those stodgy scientists who maintain that such research is more important than research of, say, Mars. Recent studies show evidence of primitive life forms on Mars; who knows what we might learn from studying such life forms? The possibilities are, like space itself, infinite.

▶ **STEP 1 Consider the writer's background, experience, and circumstances in life. How might the writer's experience and circumstances shape his or her opinion?**

Because the writer is a research scientist at NASA, he or she might be predisposed to support spending on research in space. Funding for such research could increase the writer's job security, resources, and even his or her salary.

▶ **STEP 2 Identify any connotative or loaded language or descriptions of highly charged situations.** What attitude toward his or her subject, or **tone**, does the writer's use of language reveal? Does the writer describe situations that trigger strong emotional responses in people?

The word "stodgy," used to describe people who hold the opposing viewpoint, has negative connotations; its use suggests that the writer views those with opposing viewpoints as backward.

▶ **STEP 3 Consider how fairly the writer discusses opposing points of view.** Does the writer concede any points? Does he or she acknowledge opposing points of view at all?

The writer concedes that researching our own planet is worthwhile.

▶ **STEP 4 Evaluate the writer's logical appeals.** Are they sound, or does the writer seem to rely on propaganda techniques, such as name-calling? Are reasons supported by convincing evidence?

The writer's statement about the importance of space research is convincing because it is supported by recent, relevant evidence about the possibility of life on Mars. However, the writer's description of opponents as "stodgy" verges on name-calling.

▶ **STEP 5 After considering all these factors, write a short statement explaining the writer's point of view and identifying any biases he or she might have.**

He or she writes from the point of view of a scientist and, in particular, one who does research on outer space. Although the writer has a definite point of view, he or she does not seem overly biased. The writer uses connotative but not loaded language and acknowledges opposing viewpoints.

YOUR TURN 3 **Identifying Point of View and Bias**

With three or four classmates, use the steps on the previous page and above to identify the point of view of the writer of "Homegrown Varieties" and to detect any biases he might have. Write your response on a separate sheet of paper, and be prepared to share your group's response with the class.

Understanding Denotation and Connotation

Speak, babble, chat, gossip, converse, discuss—all are related in meaning to the word *talk*. That is, they have a related **denotation**—an explicit definition, as given in a dictionary. However, some of the words—*babble* and *gossip*, for example—also have particularly strong **connotations**—emotions and associations that become attached to words through everyday usage. Highly connotative language, or language that evokes very strong emotions, is sometimes called **loaded language.**

Use of connotative and loaded language can be a powerful weapon in persuasion. For example, a politician might disparage other people's criticism of his or her behavior by describing that criticism as *mere gossip*. Consequently, critical readers pay careful attention to the connotations of the words a writer or speaker chooses.

THINKING IT THROUGH **Understanding Connotations**

The following steps and example responses will help you understand the use of connotative language in a persuasive sentence like the one below.

> Greedy developers are dumping filth into our creeks and streams, poisoning wildlife.

1. **Underline any words in the sentence that have strong connotations** (words that evoke an emotional response, either positive or negative). Greedy developers are dumping filth into our creeks and streams, poisoning wildlife.

2. **List the underlined words, and write their connotations** beside them. Then, decide whether the connotations are positive or negative.

greedy—connotes grasping, very negative; dumping—connotes carelessness, negative; filth—connotes something disgusting, dangerous, very negative; poisoning— connotes evil intent, negative

3. **Review your findings, and draw conclusions about the writer's use of connotative language.** Does it reveal his or her point of view? The writer clearly has a negative view of developers.

PRACTICE

As you read the following paragraph, use the steps above to analyze how the connotative language in the paragraph conveys its writer's point of view. Then, write a sentence or two explaining your results.

Through their community service, young people will become not just better citizens but patriots. As they selflessly serve others across this great nation, they will learn to see beyond their own petty concerns to the good of the people. They will savor the rewards of self-sacrifice cherished by Americans since the time of the Founding Fathers.

Answering Tone Questions

A writer's **tone**—the attitude toward the subject matter and audience conveyed by his or her language—can subtly sway readers' attitudes. Consequently, when reading persuasive writing, pay close attention to the writer's tone; it is often a big clue to identifying his or her point of view. Knowing how to identify a writer's tone also comes in handy when taking standardized tests, such as the SAT and the Advanced Placement Tests in English. These tests often include questions that ask you to identify the tone of a passage. Take a look at the following short passage and the tone question that follows it.

> Every teenager has been told that driving is a privilege, not a right; yet few seem to understand what this means. As I drive to the office each morning, young people frequently streak past me at high speeds, heedless of the havoc they might wreak. For example, they change lanes without signaling or even looking, assuming that everyone else will make way for them. It is high time for these teens to get the message—reckless driving can have dire consequences.

1. Which of the following best describes the writer's tone in this passage?

   A. undecided

   B. enraged

   C. neutral

   D. indignant

   E. amused

THINKING IT THROUGH **Answering Tone Questions**

The following steps and example responses (in the right-hand column) will help you answer questions that ask you to identify the tone of a reading passage.

▶ **STEP 1 Look at the writer's diction (word choice).** In particular, identify any connotative words the writer uses. Determine what the connotations suggest about the writer's attitude toward the subject.

"Streak," "heedless," "havoc," "reckless," and "dire" have negative connotations and suggest that the writer's attitude toward the subject—teenage drivers—is negative.

▶ **STEP 2 Read all the answer choices, and eliminate those that are clearly inconsistent** with what the diction suggests about the writer's tone.

Answers **A** and **C** are incorrect because the writer clearly has a definite point of view and is promoting a specific position. **E** is also incorrect—the writer seems very serious.

▶ **STEP 3 Examine the remaining answer choices, and choose the one that best describes the tone of the passage.** (Beware of answer choices that exaggerate the writer's attitude.)

The negative connotations of the words suggest that the writer has a negative attitude toward the subject, but "enraged" (answer **B**) seems like an exaggeration. Answer **D**, "indignant," best describes the writer's tone.

Writing a Persuasive Essay

"**M**y mind's made up," declares a bumper sticker, "don't confuse me with the facts." When facts alone are not enough to win others over to your way of seeing things, what does it take? It takes the art of persuasion. People—from kings and queens to great scientists and artists to ordinary citizens—have been using this art for over a thousand years.

In this Writing Workshop, you will learn to use the art of persuasion to write an essay defending your position on an issue that is important to you. As you develop and refine your essay, you will build a repertoire of skills you can draw on throughout your personal, academic, and professional life—whether you are talking a friend into giving you his front-row tickets to the game, convincing a college admissions board to admit you to a university, or persuading your boss to give you a raise.

WHAT'S AHEAD?

In this workshop, you will write a persuasive essay. You will also learn how to

- **choose an issue and identify your position on it**
- **develop support for your position and identify opposing positions**
- **avoid logical fallacies**
- **use repetition for persuasive effect**
- **correct dangling modifiers**

Prewriting

Choose an Issue

If It Were Up to Me . . .   What changes would you make if you were in charge of your school, your town, your state, your country, or even the world?

You may already have an issue in mind; perhaps a specific incident has stirred you and given you an **occasion**—a real-life reason or impetus—to want to write persuasively. For example, if your city council decided to pass an ordinance against skateboarding on city sidewalks and you opposed such an ordinance, you would have an occasion to write an editorial expressing your opposition. If you do not have a topic in mind, use the ideas on the next page to help you choose an issue that really matters to you.

- **Watch or listen to the news and read the newspaper for a few days.** Is there an issue that inspires you to write? Read the editorial page of the newspaper. Has someone written an editorial about an issue that intrigues you?
- **Consider what is important to you.** What raises your hackles and makes your blood boil? Is there an issue about which you have strong opinions or beliefs?
- **Think locally.** Look around. Is there something in your school or community that you would like to see done or changed?

When you have brainstormed several possible topics about which to write, use the following questions to evaluate each one. Ask yourself:

- **Is it really an issue,** or just a personal preference? For instance, the opinion that rock music is better than country and western music is a personal preference that would be difficult to support.

- **Is it arguable?** Do or could reasonable people disagree on the issue? For instance, few people would argue that day-care centers should not be free of materials that might be hazardous.

- **Is it specific?** Narrow your topic enough that it can be argued successfully within the length limitations of your essay, and decide upon a specific belief or action you want readers to embrace. For instance, if you chose to write in favor of equal access for people with disabilities, you would need to narrow that topic to something more manageable and specific, such as purchasing adaptive equipment to ensure equal access for people with disabilities at your school.

Identify Your Thesis

Make a Statement   The **thesis statement** of a persuasive essay, sometimes called a **position statement** or **proposition,** states the writer's opinion or position on the issue. Here are some examples:

The government should finance political advertising.

The local animal shelter must change its policy of euthanizing stray dogs and cats.

Vote in favor of the proposition to fund construction of an art museum in Monroe.

People must fight ageism in their communities now.

As you can see from the last two examples, position statements may also include a call to action, in which the writer states what he or she wants readers to do.

As soon as you have chosen an issue, write a sentence or two in which you state your position on it. Writing a working position statement now will help you stay on track as you gather support for your argument.

TIP You may not have a definite position on your issue yet. That is fine, as long as you believe that the issue is important. Your position will evolve as you gather information about the issue and write your essay.

YOUR TURN 4 **Taking a Stand**

Use the guidelines on the previous page to choose an issue that is important to you and to state your position on the issue.

Think About Purpose, Audience, Tone, and Voice

Don't Preach to the Choir In order to succeed in your **purpose**—to persuade your **audience**—you will need to know something about that audience. Some readers may not know much about the issue you have chosen; others may have in-depth knowledge of it. Some may have already formed an opinion on the issue—perhaps an opinion that is different from yours. What will it take to convince them?

Hit the Right Note In persuasion, it is not just *what* you say, but *how* you say it. Think of how a spoken request to shut the door can evoke widely different responses—from willing compliance to anger—depending on how the request is made. Similarly, the **tone** of your essay—the attitude you take toward your topic and toward readers—can draw readers to your side or stiffen their opposition. Depending on your issue and your audience, you could strike a light, humorous note or sound a serious, dramatic one. Whatever tone you take, though, remember to let your **voice**—your particular way of expressing yourself—animate and personalize your writing.

TIP While the tone of newspaper and magazine editorials is usually informal and conversational, the tone of persuasive essays written in academic settings is usually more formal. Remember, however, that formal does not mean a stuffy or stilted style. Taking an overly formal or pompous tone with readers is almost certain to alienate rather than persuade them.

THINKING IT THROUGH **Analyzing Your Audience**

The following questions will help you analyze your audience and develop an appropriate, convincing argument. The responses in the right-hand column show how the writer of a persuasive essay about ageism used the questions to analyze a potential audience.

1. **Who will make up my audience?** Consider age, interests, education, values, and geographical location.

I'm planning on submitting my essay to the editorial page of a national magazine. My readers will be U.S. residents with a wide range of interests and education levels. Many will probably value equal rights.

2. What does my prospective audience know about the issue? If you suspect your readers are not well informed about your issue, you will need to give them enough background information to understand your argument.

Most readers probably have at least some awareness of ageism in our society but don't know specifics about laws and hiring practices.

3. How does my audience feel about the issue? Convincing people who are undecided or who are sympathetic to your position on an issue is very different from persuading those who strongly disagree.

Some may feel strongly that ageism is wrong, while others may be ambivalent because they don't think it will affect them personally. A few people may believe that ageism isn't really a problem—these people will be the hardest to convince.

4. What are the opposing arguments? To persuade those who disagree with you, you will need to anticipate and answer opposing arguments.

Some readers may be concerned that eliminating ageism would limit employment or educational opportunities for younger people. One way I can answer this concern is by pointing out that every young person will someday be old.

TIP While persuasive essays use a combination of appeals to persuade readers, **formal arguments** rely solely on logic to prove or explain. In addition to being strictly logical, formal arguments must also be impartial, taking all available evidence into consideration. Research reports, business proposals, scientific reports, and some school essays require formal argument.

Develop Support for Your Position

Increase Your Appeal   Once you have chosen an issue, written a position statement, and considered your audience, purpose, tone, and voice, you are ready to develop support for your position. Support for effective persuasive writing usually consists of a combination of three types of appeals.

- **Logical appeals** speak to the reader's ability to think by presenting **reasons** backed by **evidence**—facts, factual anecdotes, and expert testimony. **Facts** are statements that can be proved by testing, personal experience, or verification from reliable sources; they include examples and statistics. **Factual anecdotes** are brief, true stories, often based on personal experience. **Expert testimony** consists of statements by people who are recognized authorities on an issue. Logical appeals should form the backbone of your persuasive essay, providing a structure upon which the other types of appeals can rest. As you develop your logical appeals, be sure to avoid **logical fallacies,** or errors in reasoning. Look ahead to page 309 for more about logical fallacies.

- **Emotional appeals** stir readers' feelings with descriptive details, connotative language, and anecdotes that evoke emotions. **Analogies** (comparisons between two things) and other **rhetorical devices,** such as repetition, can also be used to appeal to readers' emotions.
- **Ethical appeals** establish that the writer is fair and knowledgeable or call upon the reader's sense of right and wrong. Ethical appeals include discussion of the writer's authority to speak on the subject, concessions to opposing points of view, reasonable language, and statements about values.

Reference Note

For more information about **logical, emotional,** and **ethical appeals,** see page 294.

Be Reasonable As you prepare to draft your essay, you will want to gather as much support as possible. Then you can choose only the most effective support to include in your essay. Begin by brainstorming reasons others should believe or act as you suggest in your position statement. To generate reasons to support your position, ask yourself:

- What **values** will people be upholding by acting or believing as I suggest?
- What are the **benefits** of believing or acting as I suggest?
- What are the **drawbacks** of *not* believing or acting as I suggest?

Develop at least three reasons to support your position, and provide at least two forms of evidence to back up each reason. Look at the following visual representation of the relationship between evidence, reasons, and your position.

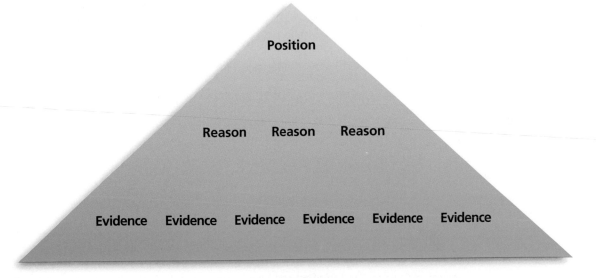

TIP If you have trouble generating reasons, you can also try the T.H.E.M.E.S. strategy. See if you can generate reasons related to **T**ime, **H**ealth, **E**ducation, **M**oney, the **E**nvironment, and **S**afety.

The chart below shows how the writer of the persuasive essay on ageism developed some logical, emotional, and ethical appeals to support her position. **Note that the types of appeals sometimes overlap.** For example, a factual anecdote (logical appeal) might be told using connotative language (emotional appeal) that also calls on the reader's sense of right and wrong (ethical appeal).

LOGICAL, EMOTIONAL, AND ETHICAL APPEALS

Position Statement: People must fight ageism in their communities now.

Reasons	Evidence
Many older Americans are able to make significant contributions to the community through work and volunteer positions.	**—Expert testimony:** Joyce Gioa of Herman Group, a management consulting firm, says that older workers want jobs in which they can make a difference. (logical appeal and ethical appeal, since making a difference is viewed as virtuous) **—Examples:** Retired doctors serve uninsured patients at thirty-nine Reach Out clinics. Retired military people and defense workers staff a boot-camp-style school for troubled teens. (logical appeal and emotional appeal, since the plight of the uninsured and of troubled teens appeals to people's emotions)
In addition to the contributions they are making to the larger world, many older Americans are proving invaluable at home.	**—Statistic:** According to Jack Rosenthal, writing for "The New York Times Magazine," March 9, 1997, grandparents are raising 3.4 million children, and 6 million families depend on grandparents for primary child care. (logical appeal) **—Anecdote:** An African saying points out that, "It takes a whole village to raise a child," and older people are a natural part of that village. (emotional and ethical appeals)
Older Americans who are no longer able to work or volunteer can make other kinds of contributions.	**—Examples:** Less-active people can contribute by mentoring, role modeling, and offering love and wisdom. (logical appeal and emotional appeal, since the word "love" appeals to the emotions)

TIP As you gather evidence to support your position, make sure that any **outside sources** you use are reliable and not unfairly biased. Because your logical appeals can be compromised by inaccurate evidence, check facts and expert opinions in more than one source. In addition, make sure to document any sources, such as books or newspaper articles, that you use. You will need to give credit to these sources either in the body of your essay, as attributions, or in parenthetical citations. For more information about **documenting sources,** see page 268.

Identify Opposing Positions

Know Your Opponent   The real challenge in persuasion is winning over those who hold opposing positions. Instead of ignoring their views, make a point of addressing them in your essay by presenting your responses, or **refutations.** You do not have to refute every possible opposing argument. Instead, choose one or two of the strongest ones and devote your energy to defusing them effectively.

If you find that one of the opposing arguments does have merit, by all means acknowledge its worth. This is called conceding a point. When you concede a point, you establish your credibility by showing that you are fair and reasonable—an effective ethical appeal.

Here is how the writer of a persuasive essay on ageism addressed an opposing position.

 KEY CONCEPT

Opposing Position	Refutations and Concessions
Many older people can't contribute to society because they have disabilities that make it difficult for them to work or stay active.	**Refutation:** The National Long-Term Care Survey, begun in 1982 by Duke University's Center for Demographic Studies, shows that fewer older people are becoming disabled. (logical appeal) **Concession:** Some older people do have physical challenges, but those that face such challenges need only a little help to remain active. (logical appeal) Often a ride and a steadying arm are all it takes for these elders to stay involved. (emotional appeal)

TIP Collaborate with a classmate to identify opposing positions. It is often especially helpful to collaborate with someone whose views are very different from your own. **Listening respectfully** to opposing viewpoints will help you to refute them effectively.

Organize Your Support

Battle Plans   In order to defend a position, a military general must have more than armies—he or she must have a battle plan. Likewise, in order to muster the best possible argument for your position, you will need to have a plan for organizing your support. You already know that you must support your position with at least three reasons and that each reason must be backed up with at least two pieces of evidence, but how will you order your reasons and evidence? Here are four basic strategies for organizing support:

- **Order of Importance:** Begin or end with the strongest reason.

   To convince readers to vote for a new airport, you might start with your most important reason, safety.

TIP Use the following criteria to identify your strongest reason.

- Which reason can be backed up with the most evidence?

- Which reason can be backed up with logical, emotional, *and* ethical appeals?

- Which reason is most relevant to readers' lives?

Revising

Evaluate and Revise Your Draft

Get a Second Opinion Your argument may seem airtight to you, but will it hold water with readers who have other opinions? Read your essay at least twice—first for content and organization, and then for style.

➤ **First Reading: Content and Organization** Use the guidelines below to evaluate and revise the content and organization of your persuasive essay. Ask yourself the questions in the first column. Use the tips in the middle column to help you determine whether revisions are necessary. Then, if necessary, use the techniques in the third column to revise.

Persuasive Essay: Content and Organization Guidelines for Peer and Self-Evaluation

Evaluation Questions	▶ Tips	▶ Revision Techniques
❶ Does the introduction grab the reader's attention and state the writer's position clearly and assertively?	▶ **Highlight** the attention grabber in the introduction. **Underline** the position statement. If there are no highlighted or underlined sentences, revise.	▶ **Add** an interesting fact or statistic, a relevant quotation, or an anecdote. **Add** a sentence that states the writer's position clearly and assertively.
❷ For support, are there at least three reasons given and at least two pieces of evidence for each reason?	▶ **Mark** each reason with an *R* and each piece of evidence with an *E*. If there are not at least three *R*'s and six *E*'s, revise.	▶ **Add** reasons backed by evidence. **Elaborate** on existing reasons by supplying additional evidence.
❸ Does the essay contain appropriate emotional and ethical appeals?	▶ **Mark** each emotional appeal *EM* and each ethical appeal *ETH*. Revise if either or both are missing.	▶ **Add** details and anecdotes with emotional impact. **Replace** neutral words with connotative language. **Add** statements that establish your credibility or that appeal to the reader's sense of right and wrong.
❹ Does the essay answer opposing positions, either conceding or refuting them?	▶ **Bracket** each opposing point mentioned in the essay. If there are no bracketed sentences, revise.	▶ **Add** mention of one or two of the strongest opposing positions, and either concede or refute each with a logical, emotional, or ethical appeal.
❺ Is the essay organized clearly and logically?	▶ **Number** the main idea of each paragraph. Then, read the ideas in order. If the ideas do not flow logically, revise.	▶ **Rearrange** reasons to show logical relationships among ideas, using order of importance, cause and effect, comparison and contrast, or problem-solution.

Identify Opposing Positions

Know Your Opponent   The real challenge in persuasion is winning over those who hold opposing positions. Instead of ignoring their views, make a point of addressing them in your essay by presenting your responses, or **refutations.** You do not have to refute every possible opposing argument. Instead, choose one or two of the strongest ones and devote your energy to defusing them effectively.

If you find that one of the opposing arguments does have merit, by all means acknowledge its worth. This is called conceding a point. When you concede a point, you establish your credibility by showing that you are fair and reasonable—an effective ethical appeal.

Here is how the writer of a persuasive essay on ageism addressed an opposing position.

 KEY CONCEPT

Opposing Position	Refutations and Concessions
Many older people can't contribute to society because they have disabilities that make it difficult for them to work or stay active.	**Refutation:** The National Long-Term Care Survey, begun in 1982 by Duke University's Center for Demographic Studies, shows that fewer older people are becoming disabled. (logical appeal) **Concession:** Some older people do have physical challenges, but those that face such challenges need only a little help to remain active. (logical appeal) Often a ride and a steadying arm are all it takes for these elders to stay involved. (emotional appeal)

Organize Your Support

Battle Plans   In order to defend a position, a military general must have more than armies—he or she must have a battle plan. Likewise, in order to muster the best possible argument for your position, you will need to have a plan for organizing your support. You already know that you must support your position with at least three reasons and that each reason must be backed up with at least two pieces of evidence, but how will you order your reasons and evidence? Here are four basic strategies for organizing support:

- **Order of Importance:** Begin or end with the strongest reason.

  To convince readers to vote for a new airport, you might start with your most important reason, safety.

TIP   **Collaborate** with a classmate to identify opposing positions. It is often especially helpful to collaborate with someone whose views are very different from your own. **Listening respectfully** to opposing viewpoints will help you to refute them effectively.

TIP   Use the following criteria to identify your strongest reason.

- Which reason can be backed up with the most evidence?

- Which reason can be backed up with logical, emotional, *and* ethical appeals?

- Which reason is most relevant to readers' lives?

- **Cause and Effect:** Propose or oppose a course of action by describing a cause-and-effect chain.

  To convince readers to support harsher penalties for oil spills, you might begin with the initial event—the release of oil into water—and continue with the effects of the spill on fish, on the animals that depend on the fish for their food supply, and on the people who depend on the animals for their livelihoods.

- **Comparison and Contrast:** Present opposing positions and concessions or refutations by using comparison and contrast. You might present all the opposing arguments first and then all your concessions or refutations, or you might present and either refute or concede the opposing positions one by one.

  To convince readers to vote for one political candidate instead of another, you might compare and contrast your candidate's record, experience, and positions with those of her opponent.

- **Problem-Solution:** Begin by describing the problem, and then describe the solution you are trying to convince readers to adopt.

  To convince readers to vote for legislation designed to combat ageism, begin by describing the seriousness of the problem—ageism. Then, discuss why the new legislation would help solve the problem.

Many persuasive essays use a combination of organizational structures. For instance, your plan might be to order reasons according to importance, with your second strongest reason first and with your strongest reason bringing up the rear. You might then either concede or refute opposing positions in an alternating, comparison-and-contrast pattern. Emotional and ethical appeals could be made in conjunction with logical appeals throughout the essay. Regardless of which organizational structure you use, make sure there is a **logical progression** of ideas—or that each idea relates closely to the idea it follows.

YOUR TURN 5 — Developing and Organizing Your Support

Use the guidelines in this section to gather support, including logical, emotional, and ethical appeals. Be sure to develop at least three reasons to support your position and at least two pieces of evidence to back up each reason. Next, identify and either concede or refute opposing positions. Then, draw up a preliminary plan for organizing support within your essay.

CRITICAL THINKING

Avoiding Logical Fallacies

You will want to be sure to avoid logical fallacies in your persuasive writing. **Logical fallacies** are statements that look like reasons but are actually *errors* in reasoning. The following chart describes different kinds of logical fallacies.

Fallacy	Example	Tip
Hasty Generalization: a conclusion based on insufficient evidence or a conclusion that ignores exceptions	All cheerleaders are happy, energetic people.	Hasty generalizations often include absolutes like *all, never, none,* and *always.* They can often be corrected by replacing absolutes with qualifiers like *often, many,* and *some.*
Attacking the Person: a criticism of those who support an opposing position rather than a discussion of the issue itself	Only crass, materialistic people are in favor of bulldozing the forest to build a new mall.	Avoid name-calling or attacking individuals or groups who hold opposing positions. Focus instead on developing convincing support for your position.
False Testimony: the testimony of someone who is not an authority on the issue	Laura Smith (a veterinarian) says that gnawing bones is good for people's teeth.	Cite the testimony of authorities on the issue, not experts in other fields or people who merely hold strong opinions.
Circular Reasoning: a "reason" that simply restates, rather than supports, a position	The school parking lot should be expanded because it should be bigger.	Check to make sure reasons explain why your position on the issue is valid.
Either-Or Reasoning: an assumption that an issue has only two possible sides	If the sales tax is not lowered, our economy will collapse.	Avoid black-and-white thinking. Remember that there are usually many choices or positions that fall between the extremes.
Non Sequitur: the presentation of unrelated statements or ideas as logically connected	Due to an increase in the number of rock concerts, crime in our city is skyrocketing.	Make sure that each logical relationship you have stated or implied is valid.

PRACTICE

Identify the type of logical fallacy in each of the following sentences. If a sentence has logical reasoning, write C, for correct.

1. Development of woodlands is never good.

2. Either we build a new wing, or education in our school will come to a standstill.

3. People who oppose building a new stadium do not care about our school.

4. According to singer Jane Haney, the depletion of the ozone layer threatens the entire human race.

5. Pet populations are exploding as a result of the global climate change.

Writing

Persuasive Essay

Framework	**Directions and Explanations**

Introduction
- Capture readers' attention.
- Provide background information.
- State your position.

Attract Attention   Focus readers' attention on your issue by beginning with an interesting fact or statistic, a meaningful quotation, or a relevant anecdote.

Fill in the Background   Give readers any information they will need to follow your argument.

Make a Statement   State your position clearly and assertively. If you don't sound sure of your position, your readers will not have much confidence in it either.

Body
- Support your position.
- Concede or refute opposing positions.

Build Your Case   Support your position with a well-organized combination of logical, emotional, and ethical appeals. Make sure your support includes at least three reasons and that each reason is supported by at least two pieces of evidence.

Look at Both Sides   Put yourself in the place of an intelligent, well-meaning person who disagrees with your position. What are the person's arguments? Concede or refute the strongest of those arguments.

Conclusion
- Restate your position.
- Call readers to take action, if appropriate.

End with a Bang   Restate your position forcefully so that readers will remember it.

Get Readers Involved   If there is something readers can do about your issue, direct them to do it. Your essay may spur them to action.

YOUR TURN 6   Writing a First Draft

Using the framework above and referring to the Writer's Model on the next page, write the first draft of your persuasive essay. Remember to:
- Think about your purpose, audience, tone, and voice.
- Develop and organize your support.
- Avoid logical fallacies.

This persuasive essay, which is a final draft, closely follows the framework on the previous page.

Do Not Count Seniors Out

What picture do the words *senior citizen, elderly,* and *old* bring to mind? Do they conjure up the image of a man in a wheelchair, wasting away in a nursing home, or a frail woman, gazing vacantly from a front-porch rocker? In the United States, *old* is too often a dirty word. Yet everyone will be old someday. Ageism—discrimination against older people—must be stopped now, or people may find themselves unwelcome in their jobs and communities. They may be relegated to rocking chairs just when they have the most to offer.

Thousands of older Americans have been the victims of ageism. Although the Age Discrimination in Employment Act, passed in 1967, bans age as a criterion for hiring, firing, salary decisions, and retirement, the law offers insufficient protection. A study by the Fair Employment Council in Greater Washington, for example, showed that older job applicants were still discriminated against one in four times. Many companies routinely maximize profits by firing, laying off, or buying out their oldest and best-paid workers and replacing them with younger, less well paid employees. As these facts show, the Age Discrimination in Employment Act has not been enough to curb ageism. Like other prejudices, ageism lives in stereotypes of older people as frail and incompetent.

However, these stereotypes just aren't valid. The National Long-Term Care Survey, begun in 1982 by Duke University's Center for Demographic Studies, shows that fewer older people are becoming disabled. Medical advances enable people to overcome ailments that were once disabling. Consequently, many older Americans have their health and energy to burn.

What are they doing with all that energy? Many are making significant contributions to their communities, their country, or the world. Some older people stay active in the workplace, where they gravitate, according to Joyce Gioa of the Herman Group, a management consulting firm, toward work that allows them to make a difference. Others choose to volunteer their time—and these volunteers are not just baking cookies and stuffing envelopes. Increasingly, they are doing important, high-profile work that improves the quality of life here and abroad. Members

INTRODUCTION
Attention-getting opening

Position statement

Emotional appeal

BODY
Background

Logical appeal
Fact

Logical appeal

Expert testimony

(continued)

(continued)

Examples

of the Executive Service Corps provide consulting services for nonprofit agencies. Retired doctors serve uninsured patients at thirty-nine Reach Out clinics. Retired military people and defense workers staff a boot-camp-style school for troubled teens.

Logical appeal

In addition to the contributions they are making to the larger world, many older Americans are proving invaluable at home. In a society in which many families experience divorce and many more depend on two incomes to subsist, grandparents are taking up the slack when it comes to child-rearing. According to Jack Rosenthal, writing for *The New York Times Magazine* (March 9, 1997), grandparents are raising 3.4 million children, and 6 million families depend on grandparents for primary child care. "It takes a whole village to raise a child," goes an African saying, and older people are a natural part of that village.

Statistics

Emotional appeal

Conceding a point

Of course, not all older people are robust and physically active. Some are ill and face physical challenges, but they can still contribute to society. These less-active people can make less tangible though equally valuable contributions by simply passing on their stories, wisdom, and love to members of the younger generation. Disabled nursing home residents can act as role models, mentors, and sources of love and guidance for children. In a society in which it seems that many young people feel lost, it would be a shame to overlook such contributions.

Logical appeal

Emotional appeal
Examples

Emotional and
ethical appeals

Ethical appeal

In fact, it would not only be a shame—it would be just plain wrong. Discrimination on the basis of age flies in the face of the values upon which the United States was founded. As a country that prides itself on championing equal rights for everyone, we need to realize that "everyone" means people over the age of sixty-five, as well. Let people be judged on the basis of their abilities and their characters rather than on the basis of something as arbitrary as how many years ago they were born.

CONCLUSION

The population of the United States is aging. As David Gergen points out in *U.S. News & World Report* (April 27, 1998), one in five people in the United States will soon be over sixty-five. If they—and all Americans in years to come—are not to suffer, ageism must not be tolerated. Society's ideas about what it means to get old must evolve, and the minds, hearts, and experiences of older Americans must not be allowed to go to waste. The words *old, elderly,* or *senior* might then conjure up the image of seventy-seven-year-old Senator John Glenn soaring into space aboard the space shuttle *Discovery*.

Restatement of
position
Call to action

Emotional appeal

A Student's Model

The following excerpt from an editorial, a type of persuasive essay, was written by Elizabeth Shaw, a student from Alexandria, Virginia. Because she wrote the editorial for a national magazine, the writer uses an informal tone, including the first-person ("I") point of view.

Is This What Life's About?

My alarm starts to ring at 6:30 A.M. In a few minutes I'm awake enough to find the OFF switch. After a few more moments hiding under the blankets, I slide out of bed and into the bathroom. Most mornings, I look into the mirror and see puffy eyes and colorless cheeks. As I wash my face, I promise that I will get more sleep, but I know I'll be up late again tonight. . . . I'm not the only high school student losing sleep; others are taking so many advanced courses that they dream of nights with only a few hours of homework. Why do we do this to ourselves?

We're not addicted to stress and not all of us are over-achievers. The numerous teens who push themselves academically have their own personal justifications, but nearly every high school student who works into the early morning hours is after one thing: acceptance to a "good" college.

Pressure to attend a prestigious university comes from everywhere. School administrators, guidance counselors and parents make it seem as if my life will be over unless I get into a good college. If I want to get a decent job, make money and generally succeed in having a happy life, I'd better attend an illustrious school. . . .

But what happens if, in spite of all my efforts, I am not accepted by any well-known school? In talking with adults, I've learned that it doesn't really matter what college you attend. People often end up pursuing careers completely different from what they studied in school. More than not attending a good school, adults seem to regret not enjoying high school for what it was—the last years of adolescence. When I look at my classmates, I see people who sometimes worry too much about achievements they can list. There is plenty of time to work as an adult, but childhood is short. Overworking as teenagers might get us into good colleges, but what sort of memories will it make?

Attention-grabbing anecdote

Thesis

Logical appeal
Expert testimony

Emotional appeal

Revising

Evaluate and Revise Your Draft

Get a Second Opinion Your argument may seem airtight to you, but will it hold water with readers who have other opinions? Read your essay at least twice—first for content and organization, and then for style.

▷ **First Reading: Content and Organization** Use the guidelines below to evaluate and revise the content and organization of your persuasive essay. Ask yourself the questions in the first column. Use the tips in the middle column to help you determine whether revisions are necessary. Then, if necessary, use the techniques in the third column to revise.

Persuasive Essay: Content and Organization Guidelines for Peer and Self-Evaluation

Evaluation Questions	▶ Tips	▶ Revision Techniques
❶ Does the introduction grab the reader's attention and state the writer's position clearly and assertively?	▶ **Highlight** the attention grabber in the introduction. **Underline** the position statement. If there are no highlighted or underlined sentences, revise.	▶ **Add** an interesting fact or statistic, a relevant quotation, or an anecdote. **Add** a sentence that states the writer's position clearly and assertively.
❷ For support, are there at least three reasons given and at least two pieces of evidence for each reason?	▶ **Mark** each reason with an *R* and each piece of evidence with an *E*. If there are not at least three *R*'s and six *E*'s, revise.	▶ **Add** reasons backed by evidence. **Elaborate** on existing reasons by supplying additional evidence.
❸ Does the essay contain appropriate emotional and ethical appeals?	▶ **Mark** each emotional appeal *EM* and each ethical appeal *ETH.* Revise if either or both are missing.	▶ **Add** details and anecdotes with emotional impact. **Replace** neutral words with connotative language. **Add** statements that establish your credibility or that appeal to the reader's sense of right and wrong.
❹ Does the essay answer opposing positions, either conceding or refuting them?	▶ **Bracket** each opposing point mentioned in the essay. If there are no bracketed sentences, revise.	▶ **Add** mention of one or two of the strongest opposing positions, and either concede or refute each with a logical, emotional, or ethical appeal.
❺ Is the essay organized clearly and logically?	▶ **Number** the main idea of each paragraph. Then, read the ideas in order. If the ideas do not flow logically, revise.	▶ **Rearrange** reasons to show logical relationships among ideas, using order of importance, cause and effect, comparison and contrast, or problem-solution.

ONE WRITER'S REVISIONS Here is how one writer used the content and organization guidelines to revise part of the persuasive essay on page 311. Study the revisions and then answer the questions that follow.

> In the United States, *old* is too often a dirty word. Yet everyone will be old someday. Ageism—discrimination against older people— ~~probably ought to~~ must be stopped now, or people may find themselves unwelcome in their jobs and communities. They may be relegated to rocking chairs just when they have the most to offer.

delete and replace

add

Analyzing the Revision Process

1. Why did the writer delete the word *probably* and replace *ought to* with *must*? What effect do these revisions have?

2. How does the addition of the last sentence strengthen the writer's argument?

YOUR TURN 7 **Focusing on Content and Organization**

Use the guidelines on the previous page to evaluate and revise the content and organization of your persuasive essay. Use the example revisions shown above as a model.

PEER REVIEW

Ask a classmate to read your persuasive essay and to answer the following questions.

1. Which appeals did you find most convincing? least convincing? Why?

2. Did the conclusion clearly restate the writer's position? Did it persuade you to act?

> **Second Reading: Style** The language in which you dress your ideas—your style—can persuade readers or put them off. An important element of style in persuasion is a rhetorical device called **repetition.** By repeating words and phrases, you can emphasize your most important points and make them memorable to readers.

Style Guidelines

Evaluation Question	▶ Tip	▶ Revision Technique
Are any words and phrases repeated to emphasize important points?	▶ **Draw boxes around** the essay's most important points. **Place check marks** over words or phrases that are repeated within these boxes. If there are no check marks, revise.	▶ **Repeat** words and phrases to emphasize important points.

Word Choice

Using Repetition for Persuasive Effect

In persuasive writing, the way you use language—your style—can make or break your argument. **Repetition** of words and phrases is both an element of style and a **rhetorical device** that can prove especially effective in persuasion. Look at the following famous example of repetition used for persuasive impact.

> "We shall not flag or fail. We shall go on to the end, we shall fight in France, we shall fight on the seas and oceans, we shall fight with growing strength and growing confidence in the air, we shall defend our island whatever the cost may be, we shall fight on the beaches, we shall fight on the landing grounds, we shall fight in the fields and in the streets, we shall fight in the hills; we shall never surrender."
>
> Sir Winston Churchill

As you can see from this example, repetition can be used to serve a variety of purposes.

■ to emphasize ideas (Repetition of *we* emphasizes the idea of a group effort.)

■ to unify ideas (Repetition of *fight* shows a unity of purpose in many situations.)

■ to establish a rhythm (Repetition of constructions, such as *we shall,* creates a rhythmic sound.)

■ to make a message memorable (Repetition of words and phrases acts as a mnemonic device, helping an audience to remember a message.)

ONE WRITER'S REVISIONS Here is how the writer of the Writer's Model on page 311 followed the style guidelines to use repetition for persuasive effect. Study the revisions, and answer the questions that follow.

BEFORE REVISION

> If they—and all Americans in years to come—are not to suffer, ageism must not be tolerated. Society's ideas about what it means to get old need to evolve, and the minds, hearts, and experiences of older Americans should not be allowed to go to waste.

There are no check marks.

AFTER REVISION

If they—and all Americans in years to come—are not to suffer, ageism must not be tolerated. Society's ideas about what it means to get old must evolve, and the minds, hearts, and experiences of older Americans must not be allowed to go to waste.

repeat the word *must*

Analyzing the Revision Process

1. Why do you think the writer revised the passage so that the word *must* is repeated? Why do you think the writer chose to use repetition in this particular part of the essay—the conclusion—rather than elsewhere?

2. Which version makes a stronger emotional appeal? Why do you think so?

YOUR TURN 8 Using Repetition for Persuasive Effect

Using the guidelines on the previous page and the model above, revise the style of your persuasive essay by repeating words and phrases for persuasive effect. Use repetition to emphasize ideas, unify ideas, establish a rhythm, and make your message memorable.

Many graphics programs can help you design diagrams, such as pie charts, on a computer. For ideas and instructions, consult the manual for the graphics program you use.

Designing Your Writing

Using Pie Charts Statistics, or numerical information, often provided as evidence in persuasive writing, can be represented visually using a pie chart. Pie charts are useful for showing percentages, or parts of a whole. Use the following steps to create a pie chart.

- **Draw a circle to represent the whole, and then draw lines that divide the circle into wedges,** like the wedge-shaped pieces of a pie. The size of each wedge should be proportional to the amount of the whole that the wedge represents.

- **Arrange the wedges in a way that best shows readers the sizes of the wedges relative to one another.** For example, place the largest wedge at the twelve o'clock position and proceed clockwise, arranging the remaining wedges in descending order of size.

- **Label the pie and each of its wedges to show clearly what each represents.** Often, as in the example below, pie charts include a key that is color coded to show what each section of the pie represents. If you use color in your chart, use it strategically to support your persuasive purpose. For example, use red for the wedge of the pie you want to stand out. In addition, the percentage that each wedge represents is often written inside the wedge.

- **Insert a pie chart into your essay at its point of use**—that is, as close as possible to the point it illustrates. However, it is usually best not to interrupt a paragraph. Alternately, you could place the pie chart in the margin or on a separate page at the end of your essay.

- **Write a sentence or two directing readers to the chart** and explaining its relationship to your thesis and how it supports the point you are trying to make.

Below is a simple pie chart that might be used to illustrate a persuasive essay in support of the addition of vegetarian meals to a school cafeteria lunch menu.

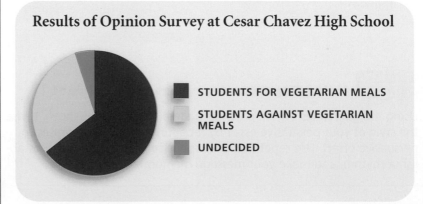

Results of Opinion Survey at Cesar Chavez High School

- STUDENTS FOR VEGETARIAN MEALS
- STUDENTS AGAINST VEGETARIAN MEALS
- UNDECIDED

Proofread Your Essay

Do Not Confuse the Issue   To maintain your carefully established credibility, proofread your persuasive essay thoroughly to correct errors, such as dangling modifiers, that can confuse readers and muddy your message.

Reference Note

For more about **dangling modifiers,** see page 746.

Grammar Link

Correcting Dangling Modifiers

A **dangling modifier** is a word, phrase, or clause that does not sensibly, or reasonably, modify any word or group of words in a sentence.

Dangling	**Having recognized the magnitude of the problem,** new child-care options must be found. [Did new child-care options recognize the magnitude of the problem?]

There are three ways to correct dangling modifiers:

■ Add a word that the dangling modifier can sensibly modify.

Correct	Having recognized the magnitude of the problem, we must find new child-care options.

■ Add words to the modifier to make its meaning clear.

Correct	Now that the magnitude of the problem has been recognized, new child-care options must be found.

■ Reword the sentence.

Correct	Since we have recognized the magnitude of the problem, we realize that new child-care options must be found.

PRACTICE

Revise the sentences below to correct the dangling modifiers. If a sentence is correct, write C. Put your answers on your own paper.

1. Concentrating on the money needed to run a campaign, issues are sometimes secondary.

2. Knowing that some of the working poor are homeless, the minimum wage should be raised.

3. One of the richest nations in the world, we must ensure that nobody goes hungry.

4. To compete in the world market, education must become a priority.

5. Concerned with homelessness, the protest was well attended.

6. The town decided to fine pet-owners, barking until all hours of the night.

7. Having converged on the town for the competition, guitars were played furiously.

8. A deadly disease, doctors from around the world battled to save the sick.

9. The teachers, including Hemingway and Steinbeck, taught American literature.

10. In Medieval Europe, a hierarchical relationship between teachers and students prevailed.

Publish Your Essay

Move Minds   No matter how persuasive your essay is, it cannot move people to action if no one reads it. Try one or more of these publishing ideas to get your point across to readers.

- **Submit your essay to the editorial section of your school, community, or town newspaper.**
- **Find a Web site created by a group that is concerned with your issue.** Then, submit your essay for publication on the group's Web site. For example, the writer of the model on page 311 might submit her essay to the Web site of the American Association of Retired Persons (AARP) or another group concerned with issues related to aging.
- **Arrange to read your essay to community groups concerned with your issue.** For instance, if your essay addresses the need to preserve a local wilderness area, ask to read it at a city council meeting or at the board meeting of a company that plans to develop the area.
- **Read your essay on your local public radio station or on a public-access television program.**

TIP   If you wrote your essay for a general audience and now wish to publish it for a more specific audience, you may need to refine your essay a bit. Keep in mind what the new audience knows about the topic and what it will take to convince them.

Before you publish your essay, be sure your manuscript is neat and legible. For **manuscript guidelines,** see page 962.

PORTFOLIO

Reflect on Your Essay

In Retrospect   Use the following questions to reflect on the choices you made in the process of writing your persuasive essay. Write a short response to each question, and include your responses in your portfolio, along with the final draft of your essay.

- Did your position on your issue change as you gathered information and wrote your essay? If so, how did you adjust the essay?
- Which type of appeal—logical, emotional, or ethical—do you think you used most effectively? Why do you think so?
- What did you learn about the power of persuasion by writing this essay?
- What might you do differently the next time you write a persuasive essay? Why?

YOUR TURN 9   Proofreading, Publishing, and Reflecting

Proofread your essay carefully, looking especially for dangling modifiers. Then, find a way to publish your essay. Finally, reflect on your writing process by answering the questions above.

Creating a Parody

You Have Got to Be Kidding

A **parody** is an imitation of something—an imitation designed to amuse and sometimes also to instruct or to persuade. Parodies have a long tradition in Western literature. For example, Alexander Pope's *The Rape of the Lock* parodies epic poems, such as the *Iliad*, and Shakespeare's "Sonnet 130" parodies the exaggerated metaphors often used by poets to describe the women they loved.

Today, parodies take many different forms—from cartoons to television skits to online magazines. In all of these different media, however, parodies share some common characteristics.

- **Parodies make fun of a particular form,** such as the sonnet, the television sitcom, or the political advertisement.
- **Parodies imitate the form** closely enough that it is clearly recognizable.
- **Parodies distort elements of the original form for comic effect.**

Sharpen Your Wit and Take Aim

Creators of parodies often take aim at things in society that they find ridiculous or in need of reform. Look around you. You might find many things worthy of being parodied—perhaps an advertisement, a literary form, a genre of television show or movie, or a recent trend in fashion. To parody one of these things, you would need to mimic its form, distorting one or more elements for humorous effect. For example, if you choose to parody an advertisement, you might use the form of an advertisement, including advertising techniques, but distort it by choosing an unusual product to advertise—a lotion that causes baldness, perhaps. Alternatively, you might advertise a typical product, but use unusual persuasive techniques to promote it, such as making wildly exaggerated claims about the product or discussing the negative aspects of the product in the advertisement. Just be sure to choose a form that your audience will recognize so that they understand your parody.

YOUR TURN 10   Creating a Parody

Use the suggestions above to create a parody. The form of your parody will depend upon what you choose to parody. For example, if you choose to parody a literary form, your parody will be written; if you choose a particular kind of television show, you might create a short skit; and if you choose a printed advertisement, your parody might consist of text and pictures. When you have finished, share your parody with classmates by reading it aloud, performing it, or displaying it where others can enjoy it.

Analyzing Persuasion in Media Messages

WHAT'S AHEAD?

In this section, you will analyze persuasion in media messages. You will also learn how to

- recognize persuasive techniques in advertising
- evaluate advertising

Take a moment to consider each of the following questions about persuasion in the media.

- When was the last time a media message, such as an advertisement, persuaded you to do something—buy a product, see a movie, or favor a candidate?

- How did the message achieve its persuasive purpose? How do you feel about having been persuaded?

- Is it possible that, at times, you have been persuaded by media messages without realizing it?

Answering questions like these will help you understand how persuasion in the media (particularly in advertising) works on you and will allow you to become a more critical media consumer—rather than one who is very susceptible to persuasion.

Persuasive Techniques in the Media

Have I Got a Deal For You!   Advertisements use many of the same techniques used in other forms of persuasion. However, unlike persuasive articles and editorials, which often rely primarily on logical appeals, advertisements tend to rely heavily on persuasive techniques (including emotional appeals) that do not include reasoned, or logical, arguments. Advertisements sometimes also include **logical fallacies**—reasons that seem logical but are actually errors in reasoning. For example, an advertisement might include a non sequitur, such as "Peace and love can save the world, and everyone should drink Brand X soda." This is an error in reasoning because there is no logical relationship between drinking Brand X soda and saving the world with peace and love. The chart on the next page gives definitions of a few persuasive techniques (also called **propaganda devices**) along with examples of how they are commonly used in advertising.

Reference Note

For more about **logical fallacies,** see page 309.

Common Persuasive Techniques in Advertising

Techniques	Examples
Glittering generalities associate a thing being promoted with words having strongly positive connotations; glittering generalities are used to persuade people to believe something without considering why they should believe it.	A candidate for political office says, "If elected, I will serve my country, the home of the brave and the land of the free, with honor and integrity." (The words *the home of the brave and the land of the free* have strongly positive connotations because they are associated with the national anthem.)
Symbols associate valued abstract qualities, such as prosperity, with a thing being advertised.	An advertisement for a car pictures a running cheetah in the background. (The car is associated with a cheetah, which symbolizes speed and freedom.)
Bandwagon appeals suggest that you should do something, such as buy a product, because everyone else is doing it.	A jeans advertisement boasts, "Brand X is America's bestselling brand of jeans." (By stating that Brand X is the bestselling brand, the advertisement suggests that everyone else is buying Brand X, so you should, too.)
Veiled threats hint that something bad will happen to you if you don't buy a certain product, vote for a particular candidate, and so on.	A TV commercial shows a man lost in a remote part of a distant country; meanwhile, a solemn narrator says, "If he had been carrying a Brand X travel guide, he wouldn't be lost now. Don't make the same mistake—buy only Brand X travel guides." (The scenario suggests a threat—that people who don't use Brand X travel guides become lost in dangerous places.)
Snob appeals play on people's desire to be better than others.	A man in a chef's hat asserts, "Tofu burgers—created for the discriminating burger connoisseur." (The chef's hat and the words *discriminating* and *connoisseur* imply that people with superior taste like the product.)

Buyer Beware   To be a critical reader, listener, and viewer of advertising, you should know not only how to analyze it, but also how to evaluate it—that is, to determine if it uses persuasive techniques responsibly. To evaluate an advertisement, ask yourself the following questions.

- **Does the advertisement provide audiences with information to help them make good decisions?** Whether it is promoting a particular car or a particular political candidate, a responsible advertisement gives consumers and voters information they need to make informed choices.

- **Does the advertisement promote products to audiences unlikely to be able to use them wisely?** For example, an advertisement for a product that children could not safely use should not be aimed at children.

- **What values and beliefs does the advertisement promote?** Are these values and beliefs consistent with your own? For example, if an advertisement suggests the belief that all men should act according to a particular definition of masculinity (play football, for instance), you should ask yourself whether or not you hold that same belief.

Hidden Persuasive Messages?   While the persuasive purpose of advertisements is usually obvious, there are many other types of media messages that persuade in less obvious ways. The stated or primary purpose of these messages may be to inform or to entertain, but closer examination often reveals that they also have an underlying, or secondary, agenda—to persuade.

Consider the nightly news. Its primary purpose is usually to inform viewers of current events. Yet **press releases**—statements prepared for release to the news media by the public relations departments of government entities, private corporations, and others with special interests— provide journalists with some of the news they report on nightly news programs. For example, a manufacturer might provide reporters at a local television station with a press release detailing its relocation to the area. Such a press release would indeed provide information, but it might also promote the private interests of the manufacturer by effectively giving it free advertising time on the news.

When reading, viewing, or listening to media messages, stay alert to underlying persuasive purposes. Ask yourself:

- **What is the source of the information given in this media message?** Consider where the information may have come from—is it the result of investigative journalism or simply a press release or prepared statement written by parties that may benefit from its being in the media?

- **Does the message make use of nonlogical persuasive techniques? For example, are emotional appeals, such as highly connotative language, used?** If so, what are these techniques and appeals trying to persuade the audience to believe or do?

Reference Note

For more about **point of view** and **bias,** see page 297.

- **Is the message impartial, or does it appear to be biased toward a particular point of view?** Are both sides of the issue presented? If not, should they be? What persuasive purpose might be served by presentation of only one side of the issue?

YOUR TURN 11   Analyzing Persuasion in Media Messages

With two or three classmates, choose two media messages—one advertisement and one message whose primary purpose is to inform or to entertain. (For example, you might choose a printed advertisement and a story from a television newsmagazine.) Use the chart on page 323 to analyze the persuasive techniques each message uses. Then, use the questions on page 323 and above to analyze and evaluate the messages. Finally, write one or two paragraphs summarizing your group's findings, and be prepared to share your findings with your class.

Making a Persuasive Speech

Talk   Listen

"The world will little note, nor long remember what we say here,"
Abraham Lincoln modestly—but mistakenly—observed in his
now-famous speech, the "Gettysburg Address." As Lincoln's memorable
speech illustrates, the power of the spoken word should not be underesti-
mated. That power is especially evident in persuasive speeches, which can
change people's minds and inspire them to act. As you develop and
deliver your own persuasive speech, you will see for yourself just how
powerful the spoken word can be.

**WHAT'S
AHEAD?**

In this section, you will
learn how to make a
persuasive speech. You
will also learn how to

■ consider the audi-
ence for a persuasive
speech

■ use verbal and non-
verbal speaking
strategies

Speaking Persuasively

Adopt a Cause   What is a good topic for a persuasive speech? You may
want to speak about the issue you wrote about in the Writing Workshop
for this chapter, or you may have an **occasion,** or real-life reason, to write
a persuasive speech on another issue. If not, here are some ideas to help
you choose a topic for your persuasive speech.

■ **Attend a city council or school board meeting.** Does one of the issues
discussed interest you? For example, your town might be considering the
adoption of a law that requires bicyclists to wear helmets. If you use a
bike for transportation, you might want to express your opinion about
the possible adoption of this new law.

■ **Ask family members and friends what issues concern them.** The best
topics for persuasive speeches are issues that are currently on people's
minds. For instance, you might discover from talking to students at your
high school that many of them feel strongly about the new helmet law.

■ **Keep your eyes peeled for an occasion to give a persuasive speech** on an
issue. For example, if you know that an upcoming town meeting will
focus on the helmet law, plan a speech to be delivered at that meeting.

■ **Respond to a persuasive speech you have recently heard and with
which you disagree.** For example, you might deliver a rebuttal to the
mayor's speech in favor of the helmet law.

To Whom Am I Speaking?   People who deliver persuasive speeches usually have a very specific **audience** in mind—the group of people to whom they plan to deliver the speech at a particular place and time. For example, Abraham Lincoln knew before he delivered the "Gettysburg Address" that he would be delivering it at the site of the Battle of Gettysburg, in Pennsylvania. He also knew that the occasion for his speech was a ceremony to dedicate part of the battlefield as a cemetery for those who lost their lives in the Civil War. His audience, he knew, would consist partially of military officers for whom the battlefield probably held special meaning. Thus, not surprisingly, he alluded to the actual site several times during the speech, saying, "We are met on a great battlefield. . . ."

Before you compose your speech, be sure you consider who your audience will be. You may already know exactly to whom you will be speaking—perhaps you will deliver your speech to classmates, for example. However, if you are not sure who your audience will be, you can ask yourself the following questions. The sample responses are based on the issue of whether or not to adopt a law requiring bicyclists to wear helmets.

TIP   To win the trust of an audience, make reassuring ethical appeals; to convince a skeptical audience, develop strong logical appeals; and to inspire a sympathetic audience to action, create compelling emotional appeals. However, when using these rhetorical strategies, be sure not to exaggerate or twist information or evidence. It is unethical to mislead your audience. Instead, make sure that your speech is informed, accurate, and completely truthful.

Who is affected by the issue?	The helmet law most affects people who use bicycles as their primary means of transportation. However, it also affects people who cycle for pleasure and the police officers who will have to enforce the law.
To what organizations might the people affected belong?	Bike riders might belong to the Metro Cycling Club or to the Bicycle Commuters Association.
What occasion might be appropriate for addressing members of these organizations or other affected people?	A meeting of the Metro Cycling Club might be a good forum for the speech, especially if traffic police were also invited.
What tone, or attitude toward the audience and the subject matter, best suits this occasion—extremely formal, jocular, vehement?	A friendly tone would be appropriate for this casual meeting, but I shouldn't be too informal because that might imply that I don't take the issue seriously.

Developing Your Persuasive Appeal   Composing a persuasive speech is much like writing a persuasive essay. You need to state your position, or **thesis,** and **reasons,** or claims, very clearly and then develop a variety of persuasive appeals—including logical, emotional, and ethical appeals—to support them. As you do so, remember to keep your audience in mind. What **rhetorical strategies** will be most likely to persuade them? What kinds of reasons and evidence will they find most convincing? See page 304 for guidance in developing a variety of persuasive appeals and valid evidence to support your points, claims, and arguments. Remember also to grab your audience's attention immediately (in the first few seconds of the speech), to provide necessary background information, and to conclude by restating your position and calling your audience to action.

TIP   To find valid, accurate evidence, or proofs, to support your claims, you may need to do some research. See page 248 for more about finding useful, **reliable sources.**

Stand and Deliver   Once you have developed a persuasive argument, how will you deliver it to your audience? The following chart gives three common methods for preparing and delivering speeches and some advantages and disadvantages of each.

Methods of Delivery	Advantages and Disadvantages
A **manuscript speech** is completely written out and then read to the audience.	This method helps you avoid the risk of making errors or leaving out important points. It also allows you to plan word choice and other elements of composition. However, if you use this method, be careful not to bury your nose in your manuscript—thereby failing to make contact with your audience, and boring them.
A **memorized speech** is written out completely and recited word-for-word.	This method has the same advantages as the manuscript method, but also has the added advantage of allowing you to focus more on delivery.
An **extemporaneous speech** is carefully outlined and rehearsed, but neither written down word-for-word, nor memorized. However, extemporaneous speakers do sometimes prepare and refer to notecards.	Because the speech is not composed in advance, you can interact with the audience and adapt the speech accordingly. As a result, you may seem more spontaneous and responsive to the audience's concerns. However, this method leaves more room for error.

TIP   Of course, even if you deliver a manuscript or memorized speech, you can still improvise. Allow inspiration to strike, and respond spontaneously to your audience as necessary. Abraham Lincoln, for example, wrote and revised his "Gettysburg Address" before speaking. He held the revised manuscript of the speech in his hand as he delivered the speech but was inspired to change some phrases and to add others as he spoke.

Language: More Than Words   Engaging speakers use their voices and bodies to express themselves. In persuasive speaking, the tone of your voice and the way you carry yourself can mean the difference between success and failure. Here are some verbal and nonverbal speaking strategies to help you win over your audience.

- **Speak clearly.** Deliver your speech at a steady rate and loudly enough so that everyone in the audience can hear and understand you.
- **Carefully vary your pitch.** The highness or lowness of your voice can be used to express your feelings about what you are saying. This can be an effective part of a spoken emotional appeal.
- **Pause for effect.** Pausing for a moment is a good way to emphasize an important point.
- **Use natural gestures.** Use the same natural gestures you would when talking to a friend.
- **Make eye contact.** As you speak, look directly at individuals throughout your audience—the idea is to give everyone the impression that you are speaking to him or her personally.

Practice Makes Perfect Knowing your speech well is the best cure for nervousness. Practice delivering the speech until you feel comfortable. Then, present your speech to a friend or classmate and ask him or her to **analyze** and **evaluate** your speech by answering each of the following questions. Use these same criteria to critique your peers' presentations.

- How did the speaker grab your attention right away?
- What was the speaker's position or thesis?
- What support did the speaker give for his or her claims? Which supports were logical appeals, emotional appeals, and ethical appeals?
- What verbal and nonverbal techniques—such as varying pitch, pausing, using natural gestures, and making eye contact—did the speaker use?
- Did the speaker succeed in persuading you to share his or her opinion or to take action on the issue? Why or why not?

Use your peers' **critique** to help you revise your speech and to help you develop stronger speaking skills for the future.

TIP What should you do about distractions and unexpected interruptions? If the distraction is ongoing, such as a noisy air conditioner, first acknowledge it in some way. (This can be an opportunity for you to connect with your audience.) Thereafter, ignore the distraction. However, if it is a short interruption, such as an announcement over the intercom, pause until it ends.

YOUR TURN 12 Making a Persuasive Speech

Use the preceding guidelines to prepare and deliver a persuasive speech. Make sure that you

- consider the audience to whom you will speak
- develop your persuasive appeals and practice your speech
- use effective verbal and nonverbal strategies
- analyze and evaluate your own and others' persuasive speeches

7 Choices

Choose one of the following activities to complete.

▶ **CAREERS**

1. Know Your Business
Imagine that you are a recruiter for a corporation. Design and write a **pamphlet** targeted at high school seniors to convince them to begin a career with your corporation. Consider your audience. What job duties and benefits would interest most seniors? Remember that pamphlets use visuals, as well as words, to persuade.

▶ **ART**

2. Worth a Thousand Words
Design and create a **poster** that uses visual images to persuade viewers to take action on an issue. For example, you might try to persuade people to recycle or to vote for a particular candidate for class office. You can use some text on your poster, but don't rely on words to make your case. Instead, try to persuade your viewers using photographs, a drawing, a painting, or a collage.

▶ **CROSSING THE CURRICULUM: MATHEMATICS**

3. Go by the Numbers Choose an issue currently under debate at your school—such as the dress code or the election of class officers—and take a position on it.

Design a **questionnaire** about the issue and have as many students as possible complete it. Tabulate the data from the completed questionnaires and use the results to argue for your position.

▶ **MEDIA AND TECHNOLOGY**

4. Mount a Campaign Plan an **advertising campaign** for a new, imaginary product. Plan how best to use different media—television, radio, newspapers, magazines, billboards, and the Web—to increase sales. Share plans for your ad campaign with classmates. Ask them whether they think your campaign would be successful, and why or why not.

▶ **CROSSING THE CURRICULUM: HISTORY**

5. Time Tourist Think of a historical event that involved conflict between people with differing opinions. Then, write a short **speech** in which you attempt to persuade the people involved to follow a course of action different from the one they actually (historically) did follow. For example, you might attempt to dissuade Henry VIII from executing Sir Thomas More.

PORTFOLIO

8 Reviewing a Documentary

Reading Workshop

Reading a Review of a Documentary
PAGE 332

Writing Workshop

Writing a Review of a Documentary
PAGE 343

Focus on Viewing and Representing

Creating an Investigative Documentary
PAGE 367

Three stars, two thumbs up, a bomb, or a blockbuster? Many people turn to reviewers to help them decide which films to see. After all, nobody wants to spend a chunk of change and waste a few hours of time watching a bad movie. A film reviewer's job is to provide reliable evaluations of films so that consumers can make informed decisions. Consequently, competent film reviewers do not let their personal preferences determine their opinions. Instead, they measure films against certain generally accepted standards, or **criteria for evaluation**.

A type of film that is often held to especially high standards is the documentary. Why? **Documentaries**—nonfiction films or television specials that consist of analysis and carefully selected and creatively arranged information—are intended to do more than simply entertain. Like nonfiction books, documentaries also aim to inform.

In addition, many documentaries interpret reality creatively and, thus, have an artistic purpose. Still others have a persuasive purpose, aiming to raise awareness of an issue or to bring about social change. In fact, the documentary offers such variation in both subject matter and approach that many experts consider it the highest form of filmmaking.

YOUR TURN 1 Brainstorming About Reviews

With three or four classmates, brainstorm a list of film reviews you have recently read, seen, or heard in different media—print, television, radio, and the Web. Which reviews persuaded you either to see or not to see a film? Why?

Reading a Review of a Documentary

WHAT'S AHEAD?

In this section, you will read a review of a documentary. You will also learn how to

- **distinguish between fact and opinion**
- **identify criteria for evaluation**

Reading reviews of documentaries can help you make wise decisions about how to spend your time, but only if you do your part by reading critically. When you read a review, you need to sort fact from opinion—to distinguish objective, provable evidence from the writer's subjective viewpoint. You also need to identify the writer's criteria for evaluation—if you know the standards a reviewer is using to judge something, you will be better able to gauge the reliability of the review. In the review on the next page, you will read one reviewer's evaluation of Ken Burns's landmark documentary, *The Civil War*, which was originally broadcast in nine segments on public television.

Preparing to Read

READING SKILL

Distinguishing Between Fact and Opinion   Reliable reviewers don't simply pull their **opinions**—personal viewpoints or positions—out of a hat. They base them on evidence in the form of **facts,** pieces of information that can be proven correct. To determine whether a reviewer's opinions are **valid**—that is, whether they are based on concrete evidence— you will need to distinguish fact from opinion. As you read the review on the next page, see if you can identify the writer's view of the documentary. Does she wholeheartedly recommend it, discourage readers from seeing it, or recommend it with some reservations? On what does she seem to base her views?

READING FOCUS

Criteria for Evaluation   Competent reviewers base their evaluations of documentaries not on their personal preferences, but on generally accepted **criteria**—the standards by which a thing is judged. People use criteria to make evaluations all the time. For example, surfers use criteria such as water depth and wave height and shape to decide where to begin their rides. You may use criteria to decide what CD to buy or which novel to read. Try to determine what criteria the writer of the following review might have used to evaluate the documentary *The Civil War.*

The following review of Ken Burns's *The Civil War* appeared in *American Historical Review,* a journal for professional historians. As you read the review, jot down answers to the numbered active-reading questions.

from American Historical Review

THE CIVIL WAR

by Ellen Carol DuBois

What is there to say about a twelve-hour documentary that draws the largest audience in the annals of public television *and* takes as its subject not body building or rap music but American history? In an age in which the consciousness of visual images has virtually replaced traditional literacy and in which historical ignorance is endemic,[1] Ken Burns's *The Civil War* seems like an achievement beyond cavil.[2] It is difficult to find anyone who watched it who was not moved by its images and details, if occasionally overwhelmed by its length. Unless, of course, you talk to American historians, especially those of us trained in precisely the social historical methods on which Burns so successfully draws. Burns uses modern historical techniques, at the level of detail and anecdote, to create an accessible, human-scale account of the Civil War. But when it comes to historical interpretation, to the process by which details coalesce to make events meaningful, *The Civil War* is vintage nineteenth century.

At the level of technique—both filmic and historical—*The Civil War* is very well done and extremely effective. To unify the story across its nine segments and many smaller fragments, Burns has established a series of

---

1. **endemic:** native to a particular region, constantly present.

2. **cavil:** an insignificant objection.

> **1. Why does this writer think that American historians might have a different view of the documentary than others?**

2. Can the statement in the first sentence of this paragraph be proved, or does it reflect the writer's opinion? Why do you think so?

historical characters, ranging from the Union Private Elisha Hunt Rhodes[3] to Mary Chesnut[4] and Frederick Douglass[5] to President Lincoln and General Lee, through whom we experience the war. Their words are read by celebrities, whose familiar voices help us recognize the character each time he or she appears and bridge the distance between the past and the present. Other aspects of the soundtrack, for which Burns was personally responsible, are also notable, particularly the repeated and constant sound of the guns. Like all good television, you can take your eyes from the screen for several minutes at a time and still follow the action. The influence of modern social history has led Burns to tell his story largely from the viewpoint of the common soldier, and the audience cannot help but be impressed with the intelligence, the independence, the experience, and the sheer power of expression that history evokes from such men. Through just such devices of the filmmaker and historian, Burns is able to make the experience of great events imaginable to his audience. Is this not what the social-historical revolution in our discipline has been all about?

The problem with *The Civil War* is the particular meaning the filmmaker chooses to draw from his material, which only becomes apparent in the course of many hours of viewing. To begin with, Burns never acknowledges that a historical event, certainly one of such epochal[6] significance, will of necessity be interpreted, not only in different but in conflicting ways. Contrast this, for instance, to *Berkeley in the Sixties*[7] (1990), in which participants and observers are constantly haggling over different assessments of the subject. For all its length and magnitude, *The Civil War* contains appallingly few interpretive voices. Even when we are introduced to conflicting perspectives, most notably, those of Shelby Foote[8] and Barbara Fields,[9] the

3. What specific filmmaking and historical techniques are discussed in this paragraph?

4. Why does the writer think historical events might be subject to conflicting interpretations? Do you agree? Why?

---

3. **Elisha Hunt Rhodes:** a Union soldier whose Civil War diary and letters are published in *All for the Union: The Civil War Diary and Letters of Elisha Hunt Rhodes.*

4. **Mary Chesnut:** a white Southern woman who kept a diary throughout the Civil War.

5. **Frederick Douglass:** a former slave and the most important advocate for African-American civil rights in the 1800s.

6. **epochal:** highly important.

7. *Berkeley in the Sixties:* a documentary film by Mark Kitchell.

8. **Shelby Foote:** the author of *The Civil War: A Narrative,* as well as other novels about the Civil War.

9. **Barbara Fields:** professor of history and author of *Slavery and Freedom on the Middle Ground: Maryland During the Nineteenth Century.*

filmmaker obscures rather than high-lights the debate between them.

Yet, more than any other event in American history, the Civil War has been and will continue to be subjected to reinterpretation. Our attitudes as a people toward our racial differences and about whatever war the United States has most recently fought end-lessly reshape what we think about the Civil War. Somewhere between the fourth and fifth episodes of my view-ing, the U.S. military began its carpet-bombing of Iraq, and the sounds of Civil War guns that permeate the soundtrack took on new and appalling power for me. Suddenly, I saw the Civil War in terms of a question I had never before asked of it: "What tran-scendent political goals are worth what amount of human suffering?" *The Civil War* does little to teach its audience this sec-ond and equally cru-cial principle of social history, that historical meaning is found in a con-stant dialogue between the present and the past.

Not that *The Civil War* lacks an interpretive perspective. Interpre-tively, *The Civil War* is as much Shelby Foote's movie as it is Ken Burns's. Foote is a charming and witty raconteur,[10] full of amusing Civil War anecdotes well told. His Civil War is the tale of the invasion and defeat of the South, an episode in American his-tory that is ultimately tragic and a tragedy that is overwhelmingly Southern. The presence of Barbara Fields, who is extraordinarily com-posed and effective before the camera, is obviously intended to offset whatever discom-fort we might feel at being guided through these events by a white man with a mel-lifluous[11] southern accent, but the balance between the two is superficial at best. The other Civil War, the Civil War as "glory," as the battle to abolish slavery, gets remarkably short shrift.

Common soldiers are carefully individualized; we learn many names, hear many voices, are told many per-sonal stories. But not a single man or woman who had been enslaved is brought to life in the entire nine episodes. Indeed, Frederick Douglass (whose oratorical powers are strongly evoked by Morgan Freeman's reading) is the only significant black character. The slaves are a vague suffering col-lectivity, a dusky Greek chorus who suffer under the lash but whose actions, resistance, and individual humanity are largely missing. Without them, *The Civil War* conveys little to the audience about the reality of slav-ery and does little to help them to appreciate its demise. As the war

5. Why does the reviewer think historical mean-ing is found in "a constant dia-logue between the present and the past"? Do you agree?

6. What does the reviewer seem to think of Burns's presen-tation of Foote and Fields? What historical perspective is not represented?

---

10. raconteur: storyteller.

11. mellifluous: smooth and sweet.

nears its end, Burns spends much more time lamenting the fall of Richmond than applauding the 13th Amendment.[12] Someone who did not know the process by which slavery came to an end could not learn it from this account. There is not a word about Reconstruction; we learn more about reunions of Civil War veterans than about the prolonged political battle which the defeat of the South set in motion and through which its consequences for whites and blacks alike were eventually determined.

The Civil War is luxuriant on military detail and very thin on political context. Each major battle is separately portrayed, the character of its generals dissected, and its battlefields, now quiet and reflective, filmed in long, beautiful shots; this is the visual version of the approach taken by generations of Civil War buffs, for whom reenacting battles is a beloved hobby. Missing are the truly decisive *political* battles, which determined what the armies of the North and South brought to each of their physical confrontations. It is never made clear, for instance, that George McClellan's infamous reluctance[13] to take the Army of the Potomac into battle reflected his political sympathies or that the

Confederate army was weakened by the periodic, large-scale desertions of soldiers who could not afford slaves to harvest their crops.

For Burns, what seems to determine the outcome of the war is something more elusive and universal: "manliness," that combination of battlefield comradeship and idealization of wife and family that turns men into soldiers. "Manliness" is an important if subtle theme of *The Civil War* to which Burns brings great feeling but little understanding. The final episode of the first segment—frequently cited in advertising leaders—is a memorable letter in which a soldier pledges his undying love to his wife and predicts his own battlefield death. The music that plays behind this episode literally haunts the rest of *The Civil War.* Despite many aspects of the film that indict the carnage of war, this aspect of Burns's approach casts a fundamentally romantic character over the conflict and also works ultimately to reconcile North and South. We are left, for all the evocative details, compelling characters, and battlefield drama, with a healing sense of a common national experience of civil war, rather than of a nation divided over a fundamental issue—racial equality—about which we can still be said to be at war.

> **7. How is the first statement in this paragraph related to the preceding paragraph?**

> **8. Why do you think the writer included these historical details?**

> **9. How does the reviewer support her opinion that "manliness" is an important theme?**

---

12. **13th Amendment:** the amendment abolishing slavery, ratified on December 6, 1865.

13. **infamous reluctance:** McClellan, commander of the Northern army, hesitated to invade the South.

Distinguishing Between Fact and Opinion

Sorting It Out All reviews contain two vital elements: facts and opinions. Often it is relatively simple to tell the difference between a **fact** (a piece of information that *can be proven true* through testing or verification from reliable sources) and an **opinion** (someone's personal viewpoint or position that *cannot* be proven true with hard evidence). For instance, compare these two very different statements.

> **Fact:** The documentary provided a look at ancient Egyptian artifacts that had been buried beneath the sand for nearly two thousand years.
>
> **Opinion:** The documentary was fascinating.

The first statement above is clearly factual because it contains objective, verifiable information, while the second is a subjective personal response. Some statements, however, are harder to identify because they include a mixture of fact *and* opinion.

> **Fact and Opinion:** The documentary provided a fascinating look at ancient Egyptian artifacts that had been buried beneath the sand for nearly two thousand years.

As you can see from this last example, the addition of a single adjective—in this case, the word *fascinating*—can turn an otherwise completely factual statement into a statement that mixes fact and opinion.

When you read a film review, or any other type of review, keep in mind that persuasion as well as evaluation is at work. Being able to distinguish facts from opinions will allow you to decide whether a reviewer's overall opinion is well supported and reliable.

TIP Not all opinions are created equal. For instance, whose opinion about a film would you be more likely to trust—the opinion of someone who had recently seen the film or the opinion of someone who had never seen it? An **informed opinion** is one that is based on knowledge or personal experience.

You can use the following steps to distinguish between facts and opinions. The related examples show how one student used these strategies, underlining key words and phrases, to analyze a review of the documentary titled *When We Were Kings.*

TIP Do not assume that a statement is a fact just because it contains a phrase such as *the fact is* or *as a matter of fact,* as in the following sentence.

The fact is, this movie is great.

Instead, ask yourself if the statement can be proven true.

1. **Look for opinion signal phrases.** Phrases such as "I think," "I believe," and "in my view" often signal opinions. <u>In my opinion,</u> *When We Were Kings is both informative and entertaining.*

2. **Look for words that have strong connotations,** either positive or negative. Loaded language, which appeals to readers' emotions, rather than their ability to reason, often expresses an opinion. *When We Were Kings is an <u>inspiring</u> film about a real <u>American hero,</u> Muhammad Ali.*

3. **Look for the use of the words** *should* **and** *must,* which usually express an opinion. *This is a film that all boxing fans <u>should</u> see and that many not interested in the sport will also enjoy.*

4. **Look for descriptive words—** primarily adjectives and adverbs. Descriptive language often states or implies a value judgment—an opinion. *Footage of Ali shows him at his <u>charming, charismatic, elo-quent,</u> and tactically <u>brilliant</u> best.*

5. **Ask yourself if a statement could be proved through testing, observation, or verification in a reliable source.** If so, it is factual. *When We Were Kings is a documentary about the boxing match between Muhammad Ali and George Foreman that was held in Zaire in 1974.*

6. **Look for opinions buried within otherwise factual statements.** *The film is made up of <u>skillfully edited</u> interviews and observational and news footage, and includes music by James Brown and B. B. King, among others.*

YOUR TURN 2 **Distinguishing Between Fact and Opinion**

Use the steps above to identify three facts and three opinions from the reading selection on page 333. Are each of the opinions you identified valid—supported with concrete evidence? Compare your findings with those of a classmate. Do the two of you agree on which statements are facts and which are opinions?

Criteria for Evaluation

Measure for Measure As you probably know from experience, two people can watch the same film and come away with very different responses to it. For this reason, reviewers are expected to base their evaluations not on their personal preferences, but on certain generally accepted **criteria for evaluation**—the standards by which something is judged to have value. Many people's criteria for evaluating a car, for example, might include good gas mileage and reliability, while criteria for an action-adventure movie might include an exciting plot and spectacular stunts. The following standards are generally accepted as criteria for evaluating documentaries.

READING FOCUS

TIP Criteria for evaluation sometimes vary because the concerns, interests, and ideas of evaluators vary. For instance, a painter might put a great deal of stock in whether a documentary about butterflies is visually pleasing, while a scientist might be more concerned that it provide certain facts about butterflies.

- The documentary makes a contribution to a field of knowledge or to society in general.

- The documentary provides accurate and comprehensive information from authoritative sources.

- The information is presented in a way that is accessible and engaging.

- The audio and visual components work in concert to create a certain effect, whether dramatic, provocative, or comedic.

- The documentary is cohesive—that is, each element (music, images, narration) contributes to the film's main idea or theme.

TIP Even though there are generally accepted criteria for evaluation of documentaries, some criteria will vary since documentaries differ greatly in form and content. For example, a documentary might consist almost entirely of interviews with ordinary people and so the criterion that information should come from "authoritative sources" might not apply. Conversely, additional **specialized criteria** may be needed to evaluate specific types of documentaries. For instance, a historical documentary might be expected to offer a variety of interpretations of a historical event, while one about baseball might be evaluated according to how well it captures the essence of the game.

To evaluate a documentary, a reviewer analyzes its visual and audio elements, looking for evidence from the documentary in order to decide whether it meets his or her criteria. The reviewer then forms an overall opinion. In the review itself, however, the reviewer's criteria are rarely stated outright; instead, they are **implied.** As a result, readers must use evidence from the review to **infer,** or make an educated guess about, the criteria the reviewer has used. For example, if a review cites dramatic tension as a reason for a positive evaluation of a film, a reader might infer that good storytelling was one of the reviewer's criteria.

TIP Since professional reviewers often base their evaluations on their audience's expectations, you can also **infer criteria** by asking yourself some questions about the publication in which the review appears:

■ What might readers of this publication want and expect (to be entertained or informed, thought-provoking observations or inspiration)?

■ Is the publication aimed at experts in a particular field or at a mainstream audience?

Answers to such questions will tell you something about the audience the reviewer wants to reach, and in turn, about the criteria the reviewer has used.

In the following chart, one student uses supporting evidence from the review on page 333 to infer the relationship between three common documentary criteria and the reviewer's corresponding evaluations.

Criteria	Evaluations	Supporting Evidence
The information is presented in a way that is accessible and engaging.	Yes, the reviewer thinks that the documentary appeals to a wide audience and is entertaining.	"Burns uses modern historical techniques . . . to create an accessible, human-scale account of the Civil War." *The Civil War* drew "the largest audience in the annals of public television."
The documentary provides accurate and comprehensive information from authoritative sources.	No, the reviewer doesn't think that the documentary provides *comprehensive* information—important points of view are absent.	". . . *The Civil War* contains appallingly few interpretive voices." "[N]ot a single man or woman who had been enslaved is brought to life in the entire nine episodes."
The audio and visual components work in concert to create a certain effect, whether dramatic, provocative, or comedic.	Yes, the reviewer thinks that the audio and visual components combine to create a powerful dramatic effect.	"It is difficult to find anyone who watched it who was not moved by its images and details. . . ." "Other aspects of the soundtrack . . . are also notable, particularly the repeated and constant sound of the guns."

YOUR TURN 3 Identifying Criteria for Evaluation

Work with a classmate to identify the criteria used in the review of *The Civil War* on page 333. Then, compare these criteria to the ones given on page 339. Do the two sets of criteria differ, and if so, how?

Using Sight-Related Word Roots

Because film is a visual medium, film reviews often include words related to sight, such as *spectacular* and *visionary*. Each of these words stems from one of two Latin verbs:

- *specere*, meaning "to look at"
- *videre*, meaning "to see"

These ancient words live on in English as **roots**—the foundations upon which words are built. The ability to recognize word roots is a powerful vocabulary-building tool. If you can recognize a root in an unfamiliar word, you can often make an educated guess about the word's meaning. The following words from the reading selection are just a few of the many English words that have grown from the roots –*spec*– and –*vis*–: *aspect, perspective, television,* and *visual.*

THINKING IT THROUGH **Using Sight-Related Roots**

The following steps will help you decipher the meanings of unfamiliar words containing the roots –*spec*– and –*vis*–. The example responses are based on the sentence below, in which the vocabulary word is boldface.

> The **prospects** for the film's success at the box office are quite good.

1. **Identify the root and its meaning.** The root of "prospects" is "–spec–", which means "to look at."

2. **Identify any prefixes or suffixes and their meanings.** The prefix in "prospects" is "pro–," which here means "forward."

3. **Based on the meaning of the root and any prefixes and suffixes together with any context clues, make an educated guess about the meaning of the unfamiliar word.** "Pro–" ("forward") plus "–spec–" ("to look at") must mean something about looking forward, maybe into the future.

4. **Check to see if the meaning you guessed makes sense in the sentence.** My guess makes sense because the sentence seems to be a prediction about how the film will do in the future.

PRACTICE

Use the steps above to guess the meanings of the italicized words below. Confirm your guesses in a dictionary.

1. In his new documentary, the director takes an *introspective* look at his own creative process.

2. Few would have been imaginative enough to *envision* a full-length documentary about a contest to win a new pickup truck.

3. The filmmakers *speculated* that the rare species might be extinct within the decade.

4. Central University will present a *retrospective* of Ms. Brown's documentaries from the past twenty years.

5. The film included many close-ups of the people's unique *visages*.

Questions About Rhetoric

To persuade readers to accept their opinions of films, reviewers often employ **rhetorical devices,** or methods for using language effectively to make or reinforce a point.

- An **argument by analogy** suggests a parallel between two subjects or situations in order to make a point.

- An **appeal to authority** involves citing the opinion of someone who is considered an authority, or very knowledgeable, and who agrees with the writer.

- An **illustrative anecdote** is a brief story that illustrates the writer's point.

- An **example** is a particular case that supports the writer's point.

- A **simile** or **metaphor** is a figure of speech that compares two unlike things.

- A **historical allusion** refers to a person, thing, or event from history.

Many standardized tests ask you to examine how a writer uses rhetorical devices in a passage. Such questions, called **rhetoric questions,** ask *how* a passage communicates meaning, not *what* the passage means. Here is an example rhetoric question:

> *Optical Yellow,* Orson Smith's documentary about the manufacture of tennis balls, is about as interesting as yesterday's chewing gum. Smith's unending shots of the assembly line may be designed to let the viewer feel the mind-numbing monotony of the factory, but they have the unpleasant effect of numbing the viewer's mind, as well. Those who expect *Optical Yellow* to follow in the tradition of *On the Line,* the classic portrait of factory life, will be sorely disappointed. No wonder critics everywhere have panned this film.

1. Each of the following rhetorical devices is used to reinforce the main idea in the passage *except*:
   A. appeal to authority
   B. simile or metaphor
   C. illustrative anecdote
   D. example
   E. historical allusion

THINKING IT THROUGH **Answering Questions About Rhetoric**

Use the steps below to answer rhetoric questions.

1. **Read the question and the passage carefully, and identify the writer's main idea.** In this case, the writer thinks that *Optical Yellow* is not an effective film.

2. **Identify *how* the writer supports this idea. What rhetorical devices are used?** The first sentence uses a **simile** to describe how boring the film is; the second gives an **example** of an ineffective film technique used. The third sentence **alludes** to a classic documentary, and the last sentence cites critics, or **authorities.**

3. **Re-read the question and the answer choices, and select the best answer.** The correct answer is **(C)** *illustrative anecdote* because it is the only rhetorical device given as an answer choice that is *not* used in the passage.

Writing a Review of a Documentary

When was the last time you voiced your opinion about some form of media—a movie, book, television show, or compact disc? Did you praise or criticize it? Upon what did you base your evaluation? Who listened to what you had to say?

You probably make such informal reviews every day. After all, half the fun of reading a book, listening to a new CD, or seeing a movie is hashing over your opinion of it with your friends. In this workshop, you will reach a wider audience for your opinion by writing a review of a **documentary**—a nonfiction film or television special that consists of carefully selected and creatively arranged information and analysis.

While all documentaries are considered nonfiction—that is, grounded in reality—many documentaries interpret reality creatively and, thus, have an artistic purpose. Still others have a persuasive purpose, aiming to raise awareness of an issue or to bring about social change. Often, all of these purposes—informative, artistic, and persuasive—are at work simultaneously. Therefore, it is especially important to watch documentaries (as opposed to fictional films) with a critical eye.

WHAT'S AHEAD?

In this workshop, you will write a review of a documentary. You will also learn how to

- **analyze the audience for a review**
- **develop specialized criteria**
- **use criteria to make an evaluation**
- **eliminate clutter from your sentences**
- **correct sentence fragments**

Prewriting

Choose a Documentary to Review

Everyone's a Critic If you have recently seen a documentary you would like to write about, you already have an **occasion,** or real-life reason, to write a review. If not, try one or more of these suggestions for choosing a documentary to review:

- **Brainstorm a list of documentaries you have seen or heard of,** and choose the one that you have the strongest opinion about, either positive or negative.

TIP For this work-shop, steer clear of tele-vision docudramas, such as *The Day Lincoln Was Shot*. **Docudramas** are a hybrid form that mixes (and too often mixes up) fact and fiction. You will also want to avoid "schlockudramas," sensational films consist-ing of live footage cob-bled together under titles such as *Rampaging Rhinoceros IV*.

- **Browse through your local library or video store,** and borrow or rent the documentary that most intrigues you. (Most video stores have a sec-tion devoted to documentaries.)

- **Review one of the year's Oscar nominees for best documentary film.** Do you agree that it is Oscar material? (Consider reviewing nominees and winners from previous years, too. For example, you might review director Matthew Diamond's *Dancemaker*, a 1999 Academy Award nominee about modern dance choreographer Paul Taylor.)

- **Check a movie guide for a list of critically acclaimed "classic" docu-mentaries,** and review one of these. For example, you might consider Robert Flaherty's *Nanook of the North*, a pioneer documentary about the daily life of Eskimos.

- **Try to locate a documentary on a topic about which you are particu-larly knowledgeable.** You will be able to offer an informed, authoritative opinion of such a film. For example, if you are an expert on entomology, you might enjoy reviewing *Microcosmos* by Claude Nuridsany and Marie Perennou, while baseball players might be well qualified to review Ken Burns's *Baseball*.

Consider Purpose, Audience, and Tone

TIP Because most reviews are published in newspapers and popular magazines, reviewers generally take a fairly informal, conversational **tone.** Unless you are planning to submit your review to an academic journal or some other publication in which the writing is very formal, you will probably want to do the same. No mat-ter what tone you use, allow your unique **voice** to flavor your writing.

Aim to Please   When you write a review of a documentary, your **pur-pose** is twofold:

- to **evaluate** the documentary

- to **persuade** your audience that your evaluation is valid and that they should either see or avoid the documentary

Identifying your potential **audience,** the people who will read your review, can help you choose effective methods of persuasion. Historians, for example, might respond to this statement about a documentary on the internment of Japanese Americans during World War II:

Children of the Camps makes a significant contribution to our understanding of a little-known chapter of American history.

A general audience, however, might respond better to this statement:

Children of the Camps provides a compelling, child's-eye view of what it was like to be a Japanese American during World War II.

Understanding your audience can also help you settle on an appropriate **tone**—the attitude you take toward your subject and your readers. For example, if you reviewed a documentary on snowboarding for a magazine geared toward young adults, an informal, "insider's" tone might strike just the right note with the magazine's readership. Whereas, if you reviewed the film for a national newspaper, a more formal tone might be appropriate.

To analyze your audience, ask yourself the following questions. The responses to the questions show how the writer of a review of the documentary film *Hoop Dreams* analyzed her audience.

1. **Who will read my review? What are their ages, interests, values, and attitudes toward the subject of the documentary?** I plan to submit my review of *Hoop Dreams* to the magazine *Crash*, whose readership consists of teenaged and adult sports fans. They will be automatically interested in the basketball aspect of the film, but I will have to work harder to convince them that the insights about society are also interesting.

2. **What does my audience know about the subject of the documentary or about the documentary itself? What information will they want and need?** Most of my readers are knowledgeable about basketball, and they may have heard of this critically-acclaimed documentary. They will probably want to know whether the film focuses more on the sport or on the boys and their families. They will be interested in what the film reveals about how the "sports machine" operates.

3. **What tone and level of language will be most appropriate, and therefore most persuasive, to my audience?** The magazine's readers are accustomed to articles with an informal tone, and they are probably familiar with specialized terms, such as "technical foul."

TIP Working collaboratively with other students may help you analyze your audience more effectively. You can help one another plan the approach and tone your reviews will take.

View and Take Notes

Show Time! Once you have a sense of your audience, you are ready to watch the documentary. Watch it once just to form a general impression. Then, watch it a second time and jot down notes. **The more extensive your notes, the more information you will have to draw on when you draft your review.** Here are some note-taking guidelines.

- **Identify the main idea or theme.** Is this idea or theme clearly expressed, or is it jumbled? Why do you think so?

- **Identify the organizational structure.** Does the documentary tell a story in chronological order, present information thematically, or arrange ideas to suggest logical relationships among them (cause and effect, problem and solution, comparison and contrast)?

- **Make note of the type of information conveyed and the manner in which it is presented.** Does the documentary make a contribution to your understanding of its subject? Is information presented in a way that is clear and accessible?

KEY CONCEPT

Reference Note

For more about **analyzing organizational structures,** see page 1000 in the Quick Reference Handbook; for more about **thematic order,** see page 54.

Reference Note

For more about **point of view** and **bias,** see page 297.

TIP The word *review* is derived from the Latin word *revidere,* meaning "to see again." As this suggests, to make an accurate appraisal you may need to watch your documentary more than twice, especially when considering its more technical aspects. If you are using a VCR, make liberal use of the rewind and pause buttons.

■ **Make note of scenes during which you are especially bored or especially interested.** What makes these scenes either boring or interesting?

■ **Identify the documentary's point of view and any bias.** What points of view are represented? If the documentary deals with a controversial issue, is voice-over narration objective, or does the narrator express opinions about the issue? Does the documentary seem biased, presenting only one side of an issue or portraying people, groups, or ideas in an unfair light?

■ **Consider both visual and audio elements.** What is the effect of the various visual and audio elements? Do they complement or conflict with one another? Do they contribute to or detract from the documentary's message or theme? Below are some of the various visual and audio elements found in documentaries. Consider any that are present in the documentary you are reviewing.

Visual Elements	Audio Elements
action sequences—shots of people and objects in motion	informal conversations
shots of people and things	interviews
shots of places	music
stills of art, documents, or photographs	narration (either on camera or voice-over—the words of an off-screen speaker)
animation	sound effects, including background noise

Here are one student's notes, based on the film *Hoop Dreams.*

—**Theme:** With hard work and a dream, people can succeed against overwhelming odds.

—**Organization:** Chronological story about five years in the lives of two teenagers. Film also uses comparison and contrast structure—compares and contrasts lives of two boys.

—**Types of information:** Valuable information about the lives of less-privileged, urban youth and the "sports machine." The film presents the information by telling an interesting story that is not dry or boring.

—**Point of view:** Narrator does not give opinions, just the facts viewers need to be able to keep up with what is going on. Viewers draw own conclusions. I didn't detect any bias.

—**Visual elements:** *Some images are dark or overexposed, like a home movie. This adds to the film's message because it reminds me I'm watching real people, not actors on a set.*

—**Audio elements:** *Mostly real sounds from environment; music used occasionally to heighten mood.*

YOUR TURN 4 | **Selecting, Viewing, and Taking Notes on a Documentary**

Use the guidelines in this section to select, view, and take notes on a documentary.

Use Criteria to Evaluate a Documentary

Setting the Standards Reviews are useful because good reviewers base their evaluations not solely on their personal preferences, but on widely accepted standards. **These standards, or criteria for evaluation, describe the qualities a thing must have in order to be judged an excellent example of its type.** Among the generally accepted criteria for evaluating a documentary are the following:

KEY CONCEPT

- **The documentary makes a contribution to a field of knowledge, to the viewer's understanding, or to society in general.**

- **The documentary provides accurate and comprehensive information from authoritative sources.**

- **The information is presented in a way that is accessible and engaging.**

- **The audio and visual components work in concert to create an effect.**

- **The documentary is cohesive—that is, each element (music, images, narration) contributes to its main idea or theme.**

TIP Another thing you should consider as you evaluate your documentary is how its representation of its subject affects your perception of the subject and of reality in general. Does this effect seem positive or negative? Why?

To use criteria to evaluate a documentary, a reviewer analyzes its visual and audio elements to decide whether it meets the criteria. The reviewer then weighs the evidence and forms an overall opinion.

Of course, because documentaries vary so widely, these general criteria are not applicable to every documentary. For example, *Koyaanisqatsi*, a groundbreaking documentary by Godfrey Reggio, consists exclusively of images and music and does not convey information in the traditional sense. Conversely, in addition to the general criteria above, some reviewers use additional, more specific criteria, depending on the type of documentary being reviewed. For example, criteria for a documentary about a highly charged political issue might include the requirement that the documentary present a balanced view of the issue.

Developing Specialized Criteria

Since documentaries vary so widely, the criteria used to evaluate them will also vary. Often, additional **specialized criteria** are needed to evaluate specific types of documentaries. For instance, a documentary on physics might be expected to offer up-to-the-minute facts and theories, while one about a fascinating person might be evaluated according to how well it captures the essence of his or her eccentric personality.

THINKING IT THROUGH **Developing Specialized Criteria**

Use the following steps to develop specialized criteria for the documentary you are reviewing.

1. **Classify your documentary according to type.** Does it focus on a particular subject or field of knowledge, such as science, history, sports, or music? Does it focus on a controversial issue? Is it biographical, telling a story about someone's life?

2. **Brainstorm a list of characteristics that you think a documentary of this type should have. These characteristics are your specialized criteria.** What do you value or expect from a work of this type?

For example, in a film on a particular artist, you might expect to see examples of his or her artwork.

3. **Eliminate any criteria based solely on personal preference.** For example, you might think that any documentary on guitar players should focus on Eric Clapton. However, if the walls of your room are plastered with posters of Clapton, you might ask yourself whether this criterion is based solely on personal preference.

PRACTICE

Using the steps above, work with a partner to develop at least one specialized criterion for each of the documentaries described below. A documentary

1. about the causes of World War I

2. about a recently developed scientific theory

3. about a controversial issue that divides the country

4. about the day-to-day life of a homeless family

5. about the history of rock and roll

6. about the art of glass blowing

7. about a mountain-climbing expedition

8. about a pop musician's career

9. about the game of lacrosse

10. about a typical teenager's life today

JIM BORGMAN reprinted with special permission of King Features Syndicate, Inc.

Here Comes the Judge Now that you have taken detailed notes on your chosen documentary, you are ready to see how well it meets the criteria for evaluation given on page 347, as well as any additional criteria specific to the particular kind of documentary you are reviewing. A good way to develop specific criteria is to ask yourself what the documentary sets out to accomplish. For instance, a documentary about a pop musician might give you an overview of the musician's career. Consequently, you would evaluate this documentary to make sure it covered the musician's early years as well as her later success. The purpose of a documentary about a recently developed scientific theory might be to make this theory accessible to the public. You would evaluate this film for clarity and accuracy. The criteria you choose to use and the degree to which the film meets the criteria—completely, partially, or not at all—is up to you to decide.

The following chart will help you use criteria to evaluate your documentary. The left-hand column lists the criteria and questions designed to help you decide whether your documentary meets each of the criteria. The right-hand column shows how the writer of a review of *Hoop Dreams* used the questions to evaluate whether the film met the criteria.

TIP To persuade your audience that your evaluation is reliable, you need to use at least three criteria for evaluation.

Criteria and Questions	Sample Responses
The documentary makes a contribution to a field of knowledge or to society in general. Did the documentary give you new information about or insight into its subject? Did it change your way of looking at the subject or at some aspect of society?	*Hoop Dreams* gave me insight into the lives of inner-city kids and into how the "sports machine" operates. It changed my way of looking at pro sports and at what it means to succeed.

(continued)

The documentary provides accurate and comprehensive information from authoritative sources. Does it present information from experts, from the people most closely affected by the issue, or from other reliable sources? Does the information seem complete—are all sides of an issue presented?	*Hoop Dreams* presents the perspectives of all those most closely involved—the kids and their families, the coaches, and school officials. It shows both the potential for exploitation and the opportunities offered by the sports machine.
The information is presented in a way that is effective and engaging. Do you understand what is happening and why? Is the main idea of the documentary clear? Does it hold your interest? How?	*Hoop Dreams* moves quickly, but the sequence of events is clear. Lots of different people appear on screen, but it is always clear who they are. I was fascinated by the stories that unfolded about the lives of the boys, and the exciting footage of basketball helped keep my attention.
The audio and visual components work in concert to create an effect. What visual elements are used—action shots, stills, close-ups? What audio elements are used—music, sound effects, background noise, informal conversations? What is the relationship between the audio and visual elements? Do they add to or detract from the documentary's message?	In *Hoop Dreams*, the audio and visual elements give the film the power of real life. The narration is minimal, and mood music is used sparingly. This is effective because it makes you feel as if you are right there watching real events unfold.
The documentary is cohesive—that is, each element (music, images, narration, etc.) contributes to its main idea and theme. Do all the sounds, images, and words relate directly to the subject and contribute to the message?	Every scene in *Hoop Dreams* relates directly to the boys' struggle to succeed. As the film progresses, their basketball games take on more significance not only for them, but also for the viewer.

State Your Opinion

Call It Like You See It   Once you have measured your documentary against the criteria for evaluation, you will need to weigh the results to come up with your overall opinion. To formulate an overall opinion, consider the extent to which your documentary meets your criteria. Does it meet most of the criteria or few? Does it shine so brightly in one area that any weak spots are eclipsed? Form your opinion carefully, and then state it in one sentence. This sentence will serve as the **thesis,** or opinion statement, of your review. Your **opinion statement** should

■ state your overall opinion clearly and assertively.

■ directly or indirectly attempt to persuade readers to either see the documentary or to avoid it.

Here are some sample opinion statements.

> See *Hoop Dreams,* a moving, intimate portrait of two boys' struggle to fulfill their individual potential.

Optical Yellow is a failure as social commentary and as entertainment—this documentary about the manufacture of tennis balls should stay in the can.

Although *Skate* is worth seeing for its fast-paced action and incredible skateboard tricks, if you are over sixteen, be sure to bring a translator.

When you write your opinion statement, remember that your purpose is to persuade, not put off, your audience. Be clear and forceful, while at the same time showing respect for the material you are reviewing and for those who hold different opinions.

> **TIP** As you gather evidence to support your opinion, you may need to revise and refine your opinion statement to reflect any new insights or reevaluations.

> **TIP** In your opinion statement, avoid **tired, overused modifiers** such as *best, worst, good,* and *bad.* Instead, use precise, vivid modifiers that express your unique point of view. For example, rather than *good,* you might describe a documentary as *hilarious, insightful, fascinating, heart-warming,* or *provocative.*

Gather and Organize Support

Why Do You Say That? On its own, your opinion is unlikely to convince anyone. Readers expect reviewers to support their opinions with **criteria-based reasons.** Reviewers must then produce evidence to show that those reasons are well-grounded. **Evidence** can be examples, quotations, and descriptions of scenes and filmic techniques from the documentary. You can also offer your personal responses as evidence—if you were moved, amused, inspired, or angered by what you saw, try to figure out why and communicate this to your readers. The following chart shows how the reviewer of *Hoop Dreams* gathered reasons and evidence to support her opinion (given at the bottom of the previous page).

Criteria	Criteria-based Reasons	Evidence
The documentary provides accurate and comprehensive information from authoritative sources.	*Hoop Dreams* shows what life is actually like for two inner-city, African American teenagers.	The film follows the two teenagers for five years and includes intimate footage of their lives at home, at school, and on the basketball court.

(continued)

> **TIP** To gather supporting reasons and evidence, you might try looking back at your responses to the criteria-related questions on pages 349–350, as well as reviewing your original notes on the film.

(continued)

The audio and visual components work in concert to create an effect.	The film's power is in its restraint—it does not go overboard.	The film uses mood music sparingly and judiciously. The commentary never comes between the viewer and the story.
The information is presented in a way that is accessible and engaging.	The film is fun to watch.	Watching *Hoop Dreams* is like watching a basketball game—you can't wait to see how it will turn out.
The documentary makes a contribution to a field of knowledge or to society in general.	The film is an important social commentary.	*Hoop Dreams* makes a significant contribution to our understanding of what life is actually like for promising young athletes.

Reference Note

For more about the three types of **persuasive appeals,** see page 294.

The support given in the chart above—reasons and evidence—makes **logical appeals** (appeals to clear thinking, the mind). You will also want to include both **ethical appeals** (appeals to shared morals and values, the conscience) and **emotional appeals** (appeals to feelings, the heart) in your review. Here are examples of these types of **persuasive appeals.**

> **Ethical appeal:** *Hoop Dreams* is an important film because it takes a steady, unflinching look at a reality most Americans prefer to avoid. (appeals to readers' sense of fairness and value placed on honesty)

> **Emotional appeal:** Its heroes are heroes in the classic sense—human beings with extraordinary ability who overcome both external adversity and their own shortcomings. (appeals to emotions by using connotative language such as *heroes* and by describing a situation that inspires feelings of admiration and sympathy)

For an effective review, develop at least three criteria-based reasons and at least two pieces of evidence to support each reason. Be sure each reason is tied to a criterion and that each piece of related evidence really supports the reason, as in the following diagram.

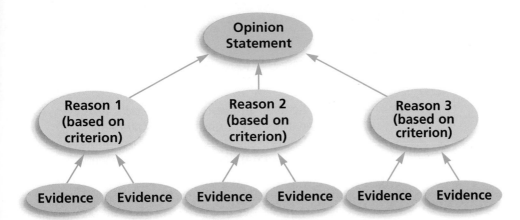

Make a Reason Sandwich Once you have gathered your support, you can begin thinking about how to organize it. One simple and effective strategy is to discuss one criterion-based evaluation, or reason, per paragraph. You might then organize your body paragraphs according to **order of importance,** beginning and ending with your strongest reasons and sandwiching weaker reasons in between. If your reasons are related chronologically or thematically, you may choose another type of order. However you choose to organize your review, make sure to lead readers through a **logical progression** of ideas.

Here is how the reviewer of *Hoop Dreams* organized support.

—first body paragraph: film makes contribution to society
—second body paragraph: background on film's success
—third body paragraph: film is engaging and accessible
—fourth body paragraph: visual and audio elements contribute to the message

TIP To identify your strongest reasons, ask yourself the following questions.

- Which reason is supported by the most **evidence** from the documentary?
- Which reasons are most likely to convince my readers? For instance, are my readers more concerned that a documentary be interesting or that it provide accurate information?

YOUR TURN 5 **Using Criteria to Evaluate a Documentary**

Review the prewriting steps to make sure you have everything in place for drafting your review. Make sure to base your evaluations on appropriate criteria, state your opinion clearly and assertively, and develop criteria-based reasons and evidence to support your opinion.

Writing

Review of a Documentary

Framework

Introduction
- Hook your readers.
- Provide background information.
- State your opinion.

Body
- Give first criterion-based reason and evidence.
- Give second criterion-based reason and evidence, and so on.

Conclusion
- Restate your opinion.
- Urge readers either to see or to avoid the documentary.
- Offer a concluding thought that goes beyond the thesis.

Directions and Explanations

Spark Readers' Interest Pique readers' attention with an arresting or unexpected statement, a metaphor or a simile, or an interesting quotation, perhaps from the documentary being reviewed.

Fill Readers In Do not forget to give your readers all the background information they will need to understand your review, including the title and director of the documentary and a brief summary of its subject.

Be Opinionated Do not be afraid to state your opinion forcefully. Remember, your purpose is not only to evaluate, but also to persuade.

Include Specifics Make sure that you provide evidence from the documentary, including reference to specific visual and audio elements, to support each criterion-based evaluation.

Call Yourself to Order Beginning and ending with your strongest reasons can ensure that you make a good first impression and leave a lasting one.

Echo Yourself Echo your opinion, rather than restating it word for word. You can do this by repeating a key word or phrase from your opinion statement without repeating the whole thing.

To Go or Not to Go Make your final recommendation.

End with a Twist Leave readers with something to think about by relating the documentary to their lives in an unexpected or thought-provoking way.

YOUR TURN 6 Writing Your First Draft

Using the framework above as a guide, write the first draft of your review. Refer to the Writer's Model on the following page to see how one writer used the elements of the framework in a review.

This review of a documentary, which is a final draft, illustrates the framework on the previous page.

Documentary Scores High

On one level, *Hoop Dreams* is about poverty, social injustice, the sports machine, and basketball. On another, however, it is the story of William Gates and Arthur Agee, two African American boys from inner-city Chicago. Director Steve James's three-hour documentary records their incredible odyssey from ragged neighborhood courts to polished college floorboards in pursuit of NBA stardom. Yes, this film is important social commentary, but don't see it for that. See it because it is a moving, intimate portrait of two boys' struggle to fulfill their individual potential.

Hoop Dreams makes a significant contribution to our understanding of what life is actually like for promising young athletes. It does this by following the two teenagers for an amazing five years. James records their triumphs and failures, as well as the triumphs and failures of the society in which they live—from the decision of a wealthy white couple to pay William Gates's private school tuition to the government's decision to terminate eighteen-year-old Arthur Agee's benefits even though he is still in school. The events of the film lead viewers to one inescapable conclusion: If anyone outside their families cares what happens to William Gates or Arthur Agee, it is only because they can play basketball. Their talent is the only capital they have, and the film's suspense lies in whether or not the boys will be able to trade that talent for a better future. *Hoop Dreams* is an important film because it takes a steady, unflinching look at a reality most Americans prefer to avoid.

Perhaps this depiction of the stark realities of inner-city life accounts for the Academy of Motion Picture Arts and Sciences' surprising decision not to nominate the film for Best Documentary. From its premiere at the Sundance Film Festival, where it received the audience award, *Hoop Dreams* has won not only the hearts of viewers but also the praise of critics, who have included it on over one hundred "Ten Best" lists. Like its subjects, *Hoop Dreams* succeeds on its own merits as an important documentary.

In *Hoop Dreams*, importance and entertainment are not mutually exclusive but mutually reinforcing. The pleasure of watching the film—and it *is* a pleasure—is much like that of watching a

INTRODUCTION
Background information

Hook

Opinion statement
BODY
First criterion-based reason

Evidence

TIP You may need to give additional background in the body of your review. This paragraph gives background on critical response to *Hoop Dreams*.

Second criterion-based reason

(continued)

(continued)

Evidence

basketball game. It is life lived in real time, for real stakes, and no one knows how it will turn out. Director James's spare, factual narration—far less intrusive than that of most narrators—never comes between the viewer and the story, a technique that leaves viewers free to interpret events for themselves. The camera lens is the thinnest of boundaries between the viewer and the film's subjects, a group of ordinary people with the courage to reveal themselves and their struggle to James and, ultimately, to us.

Third criterion-based reason

Evidence

In truth, it takes real artistry to make a film that seems this artless. The film's power is in its restraint. From the minimal narration to the measured use of mood music to the editing, restraint is key. For instance, it would have been easy to dwell on Arthur's family's problems, but the single scene in which his largely absent father runs into Arthur on the basketball court is both unforgettable and understated. The viewer is also shown this restraint as Arthur triumphs on the court. There are no jumpy film edits or overpowering music; the simple shot of Arthur's upraised arms is more eloquent than any film technique the filmmaker might have added. The result of this exquisite restraint is a story with the power of real life, one that seems to tell itself.

CONCLUSION
Echo of opinion statement

Concluding thought

Final recommendation

Ultimately, *Hoop Dreams* is a record not of repression but of irrepressibility. Its heroes are heroes in the classic sense—human beings with extraordinary ability who overcome both external adversity and their own shortcomings. The fact that our society is responsible for much of the external adversity should certainly give us pause, but it is not the main point of the film. *Hoop Dreams* is not just social commentary, it is an experience. Experience it for yourself.

The following review of the documentary *Influenza 1918* was written by Shiven Patel, a student from DeLand, Florida. As you read, notice how he uses parenthetical citations to document his source for the factual background information he gives in the second paragraph. If you have included material from outside sources in your review, you will need to document those sources. For more about documenting sources, see page 268.

An Adventure into the Past

Influenza 1918 tells one of America's most tragic tales. It is the tale of a silent killer whose victims are more numerous than the sum of the victims of all of America's wars. This killer is the influenza virus, whose brutal effects throughout America are shown in *Influenza 1918*. Through firsthand accounts and documented events, director Robert Kenner exposes the harsh, depressing times during a disastrous period of American history. This well-constructed documentary takes viewers on a fascinating adventure into the past.

Hook

Opinion statement

The Influenza Epidemic of 1918, the most severe outbreak of the twentieth century, erupted because a new strain was introduced, one that had never been battled before. The first outbreak occurred in Camp Funston, Kansas, in early March, 1918. American troops are thought to have taken it with them to Europe. As the virus mutated into a more lethal strain, a second outbreak occurred nearly simultaneously in three different places—France, Sierra Leone, and Boston (Larson). This caused much more harm than the previous wave. From September 1918 through March 1919, tens of thousands of people died in the United States alone (Larson).

Background information

Influenza 1918 describes the conditions of that time by using black-and-white footage and presenting interviews of those who actually lived through the influenza. Elderly people tell their horrific stories and paint a clear, intimate picture of an arbitrary killer virus. The film reports that every American family lost at least one member, and the disease spread with savage rapidity. Masks and other devices were used, but as the survivors observed, "it was like trying to keep out dust using chicken wire." The

First criterion-based reason

Evidence

(continued)

(continued)

situation was hopeless; the reality was death, creating much dramatic tension. The documentary then focuses in on the American reaction to coping with the epidemic, which is a crucial part of American history. Getting through these troubled times while fighting World War I showed the strength of the American people.

Second criterion-based reason

The wide array of media used in the documentary is very impressive and effective in drawing in the viewer. Direct quotes from those in charge of dealing with the influenza, newspaper clippings, actual video footage, and other primary sources enhance this documentary. Director Robert Kenner creates a montage of tense, chilling events, including a direct account from a victim. Newspaper headlines screaming "417 Die of Influenza" demonstrate how grave the situation really was. The film teaches that October 1918 was the deadliest month in American history simply because of the wrath of the virus for which there was no cure. A feeling of hopelessness was created by the film, as health officials tried everything to combat the raging epidemic.

Evidence

Third criterion-based reason

The film builds to the climactic point, when the grip of influenza finally breaks. This occurs only because, as the film put it, "Influenza ran out of people to kill." Those still alive had acquired immunity to the virus. At this point, minimal narration sufficed because otherwise this simple statement would have been pointlessly repeated. This film ends with a heart-touching account and actual photos from the epidemic for dramatic emphasis. The background music complements the somber tone of the ending beautifully, conveying deep emotion and contributing a melancholy aura. The last words "Terrible things can happen, to anyone" leave the viewer with an ominous feeling.

Evidence

Echo of opinion statement

Influenza 1918 is an intimate view of an actual American experience. The trials and tribulations of the American people during this distressing period are an essential part of our history. The American people coped with death, despair, and hopelessness. The tale of overcoming this adversity is a tale that everyone should know. Experience this tragic event of our history by watching Influenza 1918.

Final recommendation

Works Cited

Larson, Erik. "The Flu Hunters." Time. 23 Feb. 1998. 10 Nov. 1999 < http://www.pathfinder.com/time/ magazine/1998/dom/980223/cover2.html>.

Revising

Evaluate and Revise Your Draft

Do a Double Take   To determine whether your review will persuade others, examine it from the point of view of your audience. Read your review at least twice—first for content and organization and then for style.

⟶ **First Reading: Content and Organization**   First, answer the evaluation questions, using the tips to locate trouble spots. Then, if necessary, use the revision techniques.

Review of a Documentary: Content and Organization Guidelines for Peer and Self-Evaluation

Evaluation Questions	▶ Tips	▶ Revision Techniques
❶ Does the introduction hook the reader?	▶ **Bracket** the "hook"—an intriguing or unexpected statement, question, or quotation. If there are no bracketed sentences, revise.	▶ **Add** an intriguing or unexpected statement, question, or quotation that will hook readers and make them want to read on.
❷ Does the introduction state the reviewer's overall opinion of the documentary? Is this statement persuasive?	▶ **Highlight** the opinion statement. **Circle** words that persuasively state the reviewer's overall opinion of the film. If there are no circled words in the highlighted statement, revise.	▶ **Elaborate** on the opinion statement by adding words, such as forceful verbs and vivid adjectives and adverbs, that state the reviewer's opinion persuasively.
❸ Does the reviewer give criteria-based reasons to support his or her opinion? Is each reason supported by evidence from the documentary?	▶ **Underline** each criterion-based reason. **Place a check mark over** each piece of evidence from the documentary— sights and sounds and other details that support the reasons. If there are fewer than three underlined sentences and six check marks, revise.	▶ **Add** or **elaborate** on criteria-based reasons and evidence from the documentary to support each evaluation. **Delete** any reasons for which you cannot find convincing evidence, and **replace** them with reasons for which evidence can be produced.
❹ Is the review organized effectively?	▶ **Number** the underlined reasons in order. Do the most persuasive reasons come first and last? Does the order make logical relationships between reasons clear? If not, revise.	▶ **Rearrange** your paragraphs to place the most persuasive reasons first and last or to order reasons according to another logical progression of ideas.
❺ Does the conclusion echo the reviewer's opinion and offer a concluding thought?	▶ **Highlight** the sentence in the conclusion that echoes the highlighted opinion statement in the introduction. **Draw a wavy line under** concluding thoughts. If both are not present, revise.	▶ **Add** a sentence that echoes the reviewer's opinion. **Add** a provocative or intriguing question or comment.

ONE WRITER'S REVISIONS   Here is how the writer of the review on page 355 used the content and organization guidelines to revise part of the review. Study the revisions, and then answer the questions that follow.

Elaborate

> *From the minimal narration to the measured use of mood music to the editing,*
> The film's power is in its restraint. ~~Restraint is the key.~~ For ⓛⓒ
>
> instance, it would have been easy to dwell on Arthur's family's
>
> *single scene in which his largely absent father runs into*
> problems, but the ~~film's treatment of this~~ is both unforgettable
> *⎿ Arthur on the basketball court*
>
> and understated.

Add

PEER REVIEW

Ask a classmate to read your review and to answer the following questions.

1. Which reason was most convincing and why? Which was least convincing and why?

2. Based on this review, would you want to see the documentary? Why or why not?

Analyzing the Revision Process

1. Why do you think the writer elaborated on the second sentence?

2. Does the addition of an example in the third sentence make the reviewer's evaluation more persuasive? Why or why not?

YOUR TURN 7   **Focusing on Content and Organization**

Use the guidelines on page 359 to evaluate and revise the content and organization of your review. Use the sample revisions above as a model.

Reference Note

For more about **eliminating clutter** from your sentences, see page 458.

▷ **Second Reading: Style**   Your audience's response to your review will depend in part on your style—on *how* you present your opinion. **Eliminating clutter** from your sentences will help ensure that you do not confuse, distract, or bore readers with unnecessary words.

Style Guidelines

Evaluation Question	▶ Tip	▶ Revision Technique
Are there any words or phrases that are unnecessary or that do not add meaning to the sentences?	▶ **Bracket** any words or phrases that seem unnecessary. If you can delete the bracketed words and phrases without changing the meanings of the sentences, revise.	▶ **Delete** words or phrases that do not add meaning to sentences. **Rearrange** words as necessary.

Eliminating Clutter

Just as listeners tune out when a speaker rambles on and on, readers' eyes glaze over when a writer clutters a piece with unnecessary words. Here are some suggestions for eliminating **clutter**—unnecessary words and phrases—from your writing.

■ **Do not hedge—avoid phrases such as *I think* and *in my opinion.* Simply state your opinion or thought.**

Cluttered In my opinion, the camera angles are innovative.

Concise The camera angles are innovative.

■ **Avoid redundancy.**

Cluttered That director is known for her original and unique approach.

Concise That director is known for her original approach.

■ **Avoid repeating words unless it is necessary for clarity or to create a certain rhetorical effect.**

Cluttered Of all the documentaries I have seen, this documentary was the most long-winded documentary I have seen.

Concise This documentary was the most long-winded I have seen.

■ **Avoid using unnecessary prepositional phrases.**

Cluttered The power of the film lies in its striking images.

Concise The film's power lies in its striking images.

ONE WRITER'S REVISIONS Here is how the writer of the model on page 355 followed the guidelines to eliminate clutter. Study the revisions below and on the next page and answer the questions that follow.

BEFORE REVISION

On one level, *Hoop Dreams* is about poverty, social injustice, the sports machine, and basketball. On another, however, [I think] it is the story of William Gates and Arthur Agee, two African American boys from [urban,] inner-city Chicago.

words and phrases that seem unnecessary are bracketed

AFTER REVISION

hedging phrase deleted

redundancy deleted

On one level, *Hoop Dreams* is about poverty, social injustice, the sports machine, and basketball. On another, however, it is the story of William Gates and Arthur Agee, two African American boys from inner-city Chicago.

Analyzing the Revision Process

1. How does deleting the phrase *I think* affect the second sentence?

2. Why was the word *urban* deleted?

 Eliminating Clutter

Using the style guidelines, revise the style of your review by eliminating clutter. Use the sample revisions as a model.

TIP If the documentary, the filmmaker, or the production company has a Web site, the site may include stills. If you do get a still from a Web site, make sure that you respect **copyright laws.** The rights to film stills are usually owned by the filmmaker or the company that produced the film. Look for a link on the Web site for information on how to request permission to reproduce a film still.

Designing Your Writing

Using Stills You may want to illustrate your review with a **still shot,** or photograph, from the documentary. Stills can be obtained by writing to request a publicity packet from the producers of the documentary. Stills should not be used only for decoration. Follow these guidelines for using a still shot that will support your review.

- **Choose a still of a scene mentioned in your review.**

- **Choose an image that reinforces one of your evaluations,** serving as additional evidence in support of your opinion. For example, the writer of the model on page 355 chose a still of Arthur Agee, his arms raised in triumph, to reinforce the idea that the director of *Hoop Dreams* does not use complicated film techniques where a simple image will do.

- **Place the still next to the description of the scene or the evaluation it illustrates.**

- **Choose a still that is self-explanatory**—one that readers who have not seen the documentary will understand.

- **If necessary, introduce the still in the text of your review.** Unless your review alludes to the still in a way that will be clear to readers, you will need to introduce it. Explain how the still supports or illustrates your point.

Proofread Your Review

A Smooth Read To ensure that readers can follow your train of thought, proofread your review carefully to correct derailing errors, such as sentence fragments. Work with a peer, if possible.

Reference Note

For more about **sentence fragments,** see page 431.

Grammar Link

Correcting Sentence Fragments

A **sentence** is a group of words that expresses a complete thought. If you punctuate a group of words that does not express a complete thought as if it were a sentence, you create a **sentence fragment.** Two types of sentence fragments are *phrase fragments* and *clause fragments.* A **phrase fragment** occurs when a phrase gets separated from the sentence with which it belongs. A **clause fragment** consists of a subordinate clause that, although it has a subject and a verb, does not express a complete thought. Here are some examples of phrase fragments and subordinate clause fragments.

Fragment	The film's soundtrack is great. **Featuring several famous musicians.** [participial phrase fragment]
Sentence	The film's soundtrack, featuring several famous musicians, is great.
Fragment	The film editor labored for hours. **To cut everything but the best footage.** [infinitive phrase fragment]
Sentence	The film editor labored for hours to cut everything but the best footage.
Fragment	**Since none of us had actually seen the film.** We hesitated to criticize it. [adverb clause fragment]

Sentence	Since none of us had actually seen the film, we hesitated to criticize it.

To correct phrase fragments and clause fragments, attach them to the independent clauses with which they belong.

PRACTICE

Some of the following items contain phrases or clauses that have been separated from the sentences with which they belong. On your own paper, correct each sentence fragment by attaching it to the independent clause. If the item includes only complete sentences, write *C,* for *correct.*

1. I have seen all of the director's work. It spans the last ten years.

2. He created the documentary. To chronicle the daily life of a Cherokee family.

3. Particularly struck by the film's extraordinary camera work. We nominated it for the award.

4. As a result of the footage of the horrifying pollution. Many protested to shut down the chemical plant.

5. Most inexcusable are all the scenes of sunflower fields. Because they confuse the film's message.

Publish Your Review

Don't Be Shy Try one or more of the following ideas for publishing your documentary review.

■ Submit your review to your school or community newspaper.

■ Get together with classmates, and make a bulletin board of student film reviews to be displayed in your school hall or cafeteria. The bulletin board could be updated as new films are released and could serve as an ongoing resource.

■ Read your review on a public radio or public-access television program.

■ Post your review on a Web site. You might consider a personal or class Web page, a Web page dedicated to film reviews, or the bulletin board of a Web site concerned with the topic of the documentary you reviewed. For example, if you reviewed a documentary about body image issues among teenaged girls, you might locate a Web site about dieting or eating disorders and post your review on its bulletin board.

PORTFOLIO

Reflect on Your Review

Hold up the Mirror Use the following questions to reflect on the choices you made in the process of writing your review. Write a short response to each question, and include your responses in your portfolio, along with the final draft of your review.

■ What did you learn about the evaluative process from writing this review?

■ Did your opinion of the documentary change as you worked on your review? If so, how did you adjust your review?

■ Do you think that the process of writing this review has made you a more critical viewer of documentaries or other media? Why or why not?

TIP Another way to reflect on your review is to discuss it with another reviewer, even a professional. Contact someone who writes reviews for a local newspaper and ask him or her about his or her reviewing and writing process. How are the reviewer's composition strategies similar to or different from the ones you used?

 Proofreading, Publishing, and Reflecting

Proofread your review carefully, looking especially for sentence fragments, and then publish it as widely as possible. Finally, reflect on the reviewing process by answering the questions above.

Connections to Life

Analyzing Television News

Mixed Messages Like documentaries, television news aims to inform viewers about their world. Most television news programs fall into one of two general categories.

■ **Nightly news shows** present brief reports on current local, national, and international events.

■ **Newsmagazines** air less frequently and feature stories about national and international events. The subject matter and approach of some newsmagazines is sensationalized—intended to shock or alarm viewers.

Many viewers assume that the sole **purpose** of news programs such as these is to inform. However, like documentaries, television news shows aim not only **to inform,** but also **to entertain,** in part because they must draw enough viewers to attract the financial support of advertisers. As a result, most news shows include a mix of **hard news** (stories meant primarily to inform) and **soft news** (stories meant primarily to entertain). The following chart lists some of the characteristics of hard and soft news.

Hard News	Soft News
May have serious consequences for many people—for example, a natural disaster, public policy decision, or military action.	**May affect only a few people**—for example, the rescue of a woman's border collie from a chasm.
Presents stories about current events and public affairs, focusing on factual, objective information.	**Presents human interest stories, focusing on the feelings and opinions of those involved and attempting to engage viewers' emotions.**
Presentation is often straightforward, with images and sound designed to convey information: • Accompanying images may be still photographs or live or filmed footage. • Images often include middle or long shots that show events from a distance. • Music is usually used only to open and close the program and to signal commercial breaks. • The tone of the narration, images, and any music is generally serious and unemotional.	**Presentation is often more elaborate, with images, sound, and narration designed to evoke emotion:** • Accompanying images are usually filmed footage. • Images often include close-ups that provide an intimate view of people and events. • Music may be used throughout to evoke viewers' emotions. • The tone of the narration, images, and any music may be lighthearted, sad, or comic.

A Critical Eye Critical viewers keep the dual purpose of television news in mind, analyzing how the need to attract viewers (and advertising dollars) affects the selection and presentation of information. In turn, they consider the ratio of hard to soft news.

Here is a chart created by one critical viewer to analyze three of the stories on one news show. Notice the detailed notes he makes about the characteristics of each story.

Story	Length	Characteristics—Hard or Soft?
a summit meeting on peace in the Middle East, held in Cairo	one minute	focus on a current event that could have serious consequences for many people; focus on facts rather than emotions; story narrated by news anchor; film of world leaders shaking hands—hard news
a cookbook published by local nursing home residents	three minutes	focus on people's feelings; close-ups of residents cooking and recounting memories about recipes; up-beat music played throughout—soft news
the addition of new city bus routes	two minutes	focus on a city service used by many people; focus on facts rather than emotions; story narrated by news anchor; map of new bus routes—hard news

Asking the Right Questions Use the following questions to help you determine whether a news story is meant primarily to inform or to entertain:

- What type of subject matter is the focus of the story? Does it affect many people? Does the subject matter appeal to viewers' emotions or to their intellects?

- What kinds of visual and audio elements are used? What is their purpose?

- Who is the source of the story? What do you think his or her intention was?

YOUR TURN 10 **Distinguishing Between Hard and Soft News**

With a classmate, choose a nightly news show and a newsmagazine to analyze. For each show, use the analysis questions to fill in a chart like the student example above. Then, use the data you gathered in your charts to answers these questions: What was the ratio of soft to hard news for each show? How do the two shows compare to one another? How does each affect your perceptions of the world? Are you surprised by your findings? Why or why not?

Creating an Investigative Documentary

ocumentaries investigate all sorts of subjects—from the hiring practices of corporations to the origins and implications of a new fashion trend. Despite the wide range of subject matter, however, **investigative documentaries** have one thing in common—they aim to explore, discover, and communicate. Rather than relying on someone else's research, the maker of an investigative documentary must explore unknown territory and come up with his or her own information and conclusions. In this section, you will explore a subject that intrigues you and create a ten- to fifteen-minute investigative documentary that communicates your discoveries to an audience.

WHAT'S AHEAD?

In this section, you will create an investigative documentary. You will also learn how to

- identify a subject and appropriate sources of information for an investigative documentary
- combine visual and audio elements
- solicit feedback

A Hot Topic

Curious? Makers of investigative documentaries often begin with a question—Why has the river suddenly become more polluted? What is life like for homeless teenagers? How do most couples meet? Is this different from how couples met twenty years ago?

What questions interest or even haunt you? If you haven't yet decided upon a subject to investigate, ask yourself the following questions.

- **What current community issue piques my interest?** (For example, why did the city council recently ban skateboarding in parking lots and how do those affected feel about this ordinance?)

- **Is there a career, cultural practice, fad, or hobby I would like to investigate?** (For example, why do people enjoy rock climbing?)

- **Is there an injustice in my community that I would like to expose?** (For example, why is the new landfill being located near a heavily populated, urban neighborhood?)

TIP Before you begin work, discuss your subject with your teacher. Ask whether it meets the criteria for the assignment. Invite your teacher to guide you toward a more practical or interesting aspect of the person, place, event, or situation you are investigating.

Is It Feasible? For practical reasons, not all subjects are appropriate for this assignment. The following criteria will help you choose a subject you can reasonably investigate in a ten- to fifteen-minute documentary. Make sure that your subject is

■ **readily accessible.** For example, exploring the child-rearing practices of Laplanders would require you to travel to Lapland to interview and tape Laplanders—a trip that might not be practicable.

■ **specific.** For example, you could not possibly do justice to the subject of seasonal workers in fifteen to twenty minutes. You could, however, focus on seasonal workers employed by a local theme park.

TIP You will also want to take an appropriate **tone,** or attitude toward your subject and toward your audience. For instance, you probably would not want to use a comical tone in a documentary on serious illnesses.

Playing to the Crowd

The Peanut Gallery As a documentarian, your **purpose** is to investigate a subject and then to inform your **audience** of the discoveries you made. In addition, however, you will want to present the results of your investigation in an engaging manner. To decide how best to inform and engage viewers, ask yourself the following questions. The sample answers show how the creator of an investigative documentary on layoffs at a local lumber mill responded to the questions.

Questions for Analyzing Audience	Sample Answers
Who will have a natural interest in my investigation? Who has been or will be either directly or indirectly affected by some aspect of the subject?	workers at the lumber mill; people who might want to get jobs there in the future (some of my classmates); everyone concerned about the town's economy
What aspect of my investigation might be most interesting to my prospective audience?	They probably wonder whether workers are being treated fairly and how they are affected. They might wonder how this will affect the town's economy.
What does my prospective audience already know about the subject? What background information will they need in order to understand my investigation?	They already know that the layoffs have occurred. In order to understand their significance, they will need to know that the lumber mill is one of the town's largest employers. They may also need to know some specifics, such as how many workers have been laid off.
What tone will best suit my subject and audience?	An objective, detached tone will probably work best.

A Grand Plan

Play Detective   Before you start videotaping, do some preliminary research. Talk to the people involved, visit locations, or read newspaper and magazine articles to become familiar with your subject. Write down the most important question(s) that you hope to answer in your documentary. Here is the overarching question one student hoped to answer in her investigative documentary:

> How are the massive layoffs at the lumber mill affecting our community and how will they affect it in the future?

Stay focused on one or two questions. Restricting the scope of your inquiry will help you conduct an effective investigation.

Go to the Source   What kind of investigation must you mount in order to answer the questions you have posed? To what sources of information will you turn? The answers to these questions will vary depending on the subject of your documentary. Here are some questions to help you choose appropriate sources, as well as one student's responses.

Questions	Sample Responses
People	
▪ **Who might be considered an expert or might have a strong opinion?**	▪ the owner of the Rocky Creek Lumber Mill; mill workers
▪ **Who is or will be affected?**	▪ Ruth McNeil, laid-off mill worker; local merchants
Factual Information	
▪ **Is relevant factual information (such as statistics, expert testimony, and data) available, and if so, where?**	▪ The Rocky Creek Chamber of Commerce has information about the mill's contribution to the local economy.
Personal Observation	
▪ **What have you seen or heard? Who could tell you more?**	▪ I have noticed that other local businesses are scaling back; there are also lots of "For Sale" signs around town. Local business people and real estate agents might be able to tell me more.

It's Elementary, My Dear Watson   Once you have thought about what question(s) your documentary will investigate and what sources you will go to for information, you will need to think about how you will convey the information you gather to your audience. For instance, you will probably want to interview people, but how will you present any factual information, such as data, that you collect? Creators of documentaries combine a variety of elements, both visual and auditory:

Reference Note

For more about conducting **interviews,** see page 133 and page 1025 in the Quick Reference Handbook.

- **Interviews**   In order to get to the bottom of things, good investigators usually ask a lot of questions. Brainstorm a list of interview questions related to your investigation. These questions should be open-ended—questions that evoke "yes" or "no" responses are both less interesting and less informative. Then, make up a list of the people who might be able to answer your questions. Prior to interviewing these people, ask their permission and establish a time and place to conduct the taping.

- **Taped events or action sequences**   Capture the action by videotaping events associated with your investigation. For example, if the laid-off mill workers were planning a protest march, the creator of the investigative documentary on that subject might want to tape the march.

- **Reenactments or dramatizations of events**   If it is impossible to tape the events themselves, consider recruiting a few peers to dramatize events on videotape. Just be sure to let your audience know that they are watching a dramatization.

- **Shots of places**   It may be important to give your audience a good idea of the setting of your investigation. For example, viewers of the documentary on mill layoffs would probably want to see shots of the mill and of the town.

- **Still shots of objects**   Perhaps an object is significant to your investigation; if so, tape it. For example, someone investigating the controversy surrounding a local statue would certainly want audiences to view the statue itself.

- **Background footage and background noise**   Background footage, sometimes known as "wallpaper" or "B-roll," can add visual interest while a narrator explains key ideas; and background noise, such as traffic sounds, can make scenes seem more realistic.

- **Music and sound effects**   These audio elements can be used to create a mood, to contribute to theme, or to communicate ideas. Be sure that music and sound effects are used for a specific purpose and in concert with other elements of your documentary.

- **Voice-over narration**   The voice of an off-camera speaker, or narrator, can be layered over any background sounds recorded at the time of taping. This narrator can explain and interpret the images shown. For your investigative documentary, you might let readers in on your investigative process by telling them the results of each stage of the investigation. Be careful, however, not to give too much away. Building suspense and allowing viewers to come to their own conclusions are good ways to keep your audience engaged. As a rule of thumb, say through narration only what you cannot show through specific, concrete images.

Piecing Together the Puzzle   Even though you will not be able to plan everything—after all, this is an *investigative* documentary—you will want to plan as many scenes as possible. This is especially true if you will be doing **in-camera editing**—editing your video by simply shooting only what you want to include in the finished documentary and in the order that you would like it to appear. Regardless of what editing method you will use, however, think carefully about which visual and audio elements to combine in each scene. Will you begin with an action sequence or an interview? Will you combine still shots with music, background noise, or voice-over narration? Here is how one student planned a few scenes.

Visual	Audio
Scene 1 —Ruth McNeil, laid-off mill worker, showing her car to a potential buyer	**Scene 1** —mood-setting music—Bing Crosby's recording of "Brother Can You Spare a Dime?" —narrator gives background information about mill layoffs
Scene 2 —shots of interview with Ruth McNeil at her kitchen table; shots of her house and family	**Scene 2** —interview with Ruth McNeil Questions to ask: How long did you work at the mill? How has being laid off affected your life? How was the layoff handled? What will you do now?

TIP   Makers of truly investigative documentaries don't know what surprises their explorations will yield. As your investigation progresses, you may discover a source of information that was unknown to you when you began or you may find that the plot is thicker than you first imagined. When this occurs, you should be prepared to change your plans and maybe even your mind.

Get It on Tape

Ready to Roll   Once you have planned all the scenes you can foresee, you are ready to begin taping. Here are a few basic camera angles you may want to use and brief explanations of the effects they create.

Camera Angle	Effect
High angle: camera above subject	subject appears smaller, less important
Low angle: camera below subject	subject appears larger, more important
Straight angle: camera level with subject	"realistic" perspective on subject

TIP   If you have access to editing equipment, tape at least twice as much footage as you will need to create your ten- to fifteen-minute documentary. That way, you can choose only the best footage to include in your videotape.

(continued)

(continued)

TIP To create smooth transitions between scenes, you can use voice-over narration to indicate transitions in time and place. For professional visual transitions, use the fade-in/fade-out function of the videocamera so that images gradually appear out of darkness (fade-in) or disappear into darkness (fade-out).

Camera Angle	Effect
Close-up: camera close to subject	shows details or reveals emotion
Extreme close-up: camera very close to subject	exaggerates features; makes subject appear ugly or menacing
Wide angle or long shot: camera far from subject	provides overview of setting or action scenes
Reaction shot: camera moves from interviewee to interviewer and back again	shows interviewer's reaction to what the interviewee says

Wrap It Up To leave viewers with a clear idea of the results of your investigation, shoot a concluding scene that ties up loose ends or identifies which questions remain unanswered.

Distribute Your Documentary and Gather Feedback

Opening Night Here are some ways to find an audience for your investigative video documentary.

- Submit your videotape to a local public-access television station.
- Stage a class film festival.
- Screen your documentary for groups interested in your subject.

An Applause Meter Prepare a **feedback questionnaire** for viewers. Afterwards, review the responses you get. If possible, use this feedback to revise your documentary. Then, write a brief reflection on how well your documentary conveyed your message and on what you learned from the process of making it. Here is a list of questions you might include in your questionnaire.

- What were the main questions posed by the documentary?
- What new insights into the subject did you gain?
- Were audio and visual elements combined effectively?

TIP As you reflect on the process of making your documentary, ask yourself how creating it has affected your perception of reality and of how reality is represented in the media. For example, did you discover anything about the power of the media to create a certain impression of a person, relationship, culture, or idea?

YOUR TURN 11 Creating an Investigative Documentary

Use the preceding guidelines to make, distribute, and solicit feedback on a ten- to fifteen-minute investigative documentary.

CHAPTER

8 *Choices*

Choose one of the following activities to complete.

▶ **CROSSING THE CURRICULUM: ART**

1. Art? Oscar Wilde once said, "Now art should never try to be popular. The public should try to make itself artistic." The problem is, few people agree on what is "artistic." With a small group of classmates, conduct a poll to determine what people value in a work of visual art. Each member of the group should talk to different people, preferably with different tastes and lifestyles. As a group, compare the answers you received. Are there any criteria on which people seem to agree? How do criteria differ? Why do you think criteria for evaluating art might vary so widely? Write a **collaborative report** and share it with an art or art history class at your school.

▶ **LITERATURE**

2. From Page to Screen Find and read several reviews of nonfiction books. Compare these reviews with reviews of documentary films. Do the book reviews use different criteria? How, exactly, do they vary? Write a **comparison-contrast essay** that analyzes the similarities and differences between the two types of reviews.

▶ **SPEAKING AND LISTENING**

3. If You Don't Have Something Good to Say . . . Write a **review** of a speech. Most libraries have recordings of famous speeches, or you could attend the meeting of a group, such as Toastmasters, whose members frequently make speeches. First, consider the criteria you will use to analyze, evaluate, and critique the speech. Remember to include criteria that relate not only to the text of the speech, but also to the delivery. Then, listen critically, focusing your attention on whether the speech meets your criteria.

▶ **CAREERS**

4. Review the Possibilities Write brief **reviews** of several different jobs. First, develop criteria for evaluation. What characteristics do you want in a job? Work that makes a difference? Prestige? A high salary? The opportunity to work with people? Then, evaluate whether each job meets your criteria. Share your criteria and your reviews with others. How do their ideas about the characteristics a job should have compare to the criteria you developed?

PORTFOLIO

Reading Workshop

Reading a Proposal
PAGE 376

Writing Workshop

Writing a Proposal
PAGE 387

Focus on Speaking and Listening

Conducting a Panel Discussion
PAGE 412

Every community has its problems. Every community also faces choices about how to address those problems. For example, suppose someone has donated a building to your city. Suggested uses for the building include turning it into a teen center, a health clinic, or a food bank. Which idea is best? Such a problem, especially if different groups must compete for existing funds and resources, compels citizens to search together for solutions.

Two kinds of thinking involved in recommending solutions to problems are first, **analysis,** or a clear-headed assessment of the problem and its potential solutions, and second, **persuasion,** an attempt to convince others to accept one solution as best. Think about it: When *you* begin to examine a problem, you may hit on more possible solutions than you will ultimately use. As you proceed to analyze the possible solutions, you begin to separate the ones that are more practical from those that are merely intriguing possibilities. Finally, with the best solution in hand, you are ready to persuade others of its merits, whether it is a solution for littered school hallways or for intolerance among your peers.

GO TO: go.hrw.com
KEYWORD: EOLang 12-9

YOUR TURN 1 Thinking About Proposals

In a small group, think about solutions to problems and how they are proposed. Where in everyday life would you come across a proposal? Who writes or gives speeches proposing solutions? Who reads and listens to proposals? Make a list of answers to each question, and share your ideas with other groups in your class.

Reading a Proposal

Picture these snapshots: an eagle feeding its young, a three-toed sloth hanging from a tree, a herd of gazelles bounding across an African plain. Chances are, you can visualize these images because you have previously seen photographs of wildlife. Photographers bring the wilderness to us in stunning color, but at what price? The following article, "Curbing Nature's Paparazzi," reveals a problem—the questionable methods used to obtain many of these wildlife photos—and recommends a solution.

WHAT'S AHEAD?

In this section, you will read an article and learn how to
- make generalizations
- analyze problem-solution structure

Preparing to Read

| READING SKILL

Making Generalizations   When you read or experience something new, you inevitably make **generalizations**—you combine the new information with what you already know to make broad judgments that apply to the world. Making generalizations is a way to give order to the information and the world around you. When you read about the world's most famous tightrope walker and combine what you have seen at the circus or on television with your own experience of trying to walk on a wire or on a balance beam, you may make the generalization that very few people have the balance and focus to perform this feat. As you read "Curbing Nature's Paparazzi" on the next page, see what generalizations you can make about the world of wildlife photographers.

| READING FOCUS

Problem-Solution Structure   Most proposals recommending solutions have similar structures. Readers expect to find certain information in certain places. For example, a recommendation or best solution will likely be found toward the end of a piece, after the problem has been explained. Graphically, problem-solution structure looks like this:

Problem	Background Information	Possible Solutions	Proposal of Best Solution

As you read the following article, note how the writer arranges information to convince you there is a problem before proposing a solution.

As you read this proposal to keep *paparazzi,* intrusive photographers, away from wildlife, jot down answers to the numbered active-reading questions.

from DOUBLETAKE

Curbing Nature's Paparazzi

by Bill McKibben

1   The art of wildlife photography employs quite a few people scattered around the country. Filmmakers supply hour upon hour of video for PBS, the major networks, and cable channels. Still photographers take pictures for magazines, calendars, books, and advertisements, and they market countless trips for amateurs and aspiring professionals, teaching them the tricks of the trade. Their images do a lot of good: From Flipper and Jacques Cousteau to the mountain lion nuzzling her kit on your latest mailing from an environmental group, they have helped change how we see the wild. I have seen neighbors of mine, who had no use for wolves, begin to melt during a slide show about the creatures. It is no great exaggeration to say that dolphin-safe tuna flows directly from the barrel of a camera, that without photographs there would be no Endangered Species Act.

1. What does this comment about photographs and the Endangered Species Act mean?

2   However, it is not a completely benign enterprise. In the wild, photographers often need to subtly harass wildlife to get their shots: to camp near watering holes, say, where their very presence may unnerve and scatter creatures. Worse, and less recognized, is a sort of conceptual problem. After a lifetime of exposure to nature shows and magazine photos, we arrive at the woods conditioned to expect splendor and are surprised when the parking lot does not contain a snarl of animals mating and killing one another. Because the only images we see are close-ups, we have lost much of our sense of the calm and quotidian[1] beauty of the natural world, of the fact that animals are usually preoccupied with hiding or wandering around looking for food.

2. What evidence here and in the next paragraph supports the idea that wildlife photographers harass animals?

3   There is something frankly disgraceful about the animal horror videos (*Fangs!*) marketed on late-night TV, and even about some of the shots you see in something as staid[2] as

---

1. **quotidian** (kwō•tid´ē•ən): everyday, ordinary
2. **staid:** respectable, serious

Natural History magazine. Here is an emerald boa eating a parrot—the odds, according to the photographers I talked to, were "jillions to one" that it was a wild shot. Indeed, the photographer who took it boasted to *People* magazine about how, in order to get other dramatic shots, he had spray-painted ferrets to convert them to the endangered blackfooted kind, and how he had hoisted tame and declawed jaguars into tree branches for good shots, and starved piranhas so that they would attack with great ferocity.

4   Even worse, perhaps, is the way the constant flow of images undercuts the sense that there is actually something wrong with the world. How can there really be a shortage of whooping cranes when you have seen a thousand images of them, seen ten times more images than there are actually whooping cranes left in the wild? We are rarely shown a photograph of the empty trees where there are no baboons anymore; whatever few baboons remain are dutifully pursued until they are captured on film, and even if all the captions are about their horrid plight, the essential message of the picture remains: baboons.

5   At this point we could—indeed we should—start talking about a new ethic.[3] People have tried, from time to time, to promulgate[4] ethics for most of the arts, and nature photography is no exception. Photographer Daniel Dancer, writing recently in *Wild Earth* magazine, suggested using photos for advocacy purposes—shooting the clear-cut next to the forest, for instance. One editor envisions sending a photographer out to document, say, the hour-by-hour life of a snake rather than a young grizzly striking poses at a game farm. Reading and talking to such thinkers, though, it is easy to find a note of resignation—the deep suspicion that such rhetoric is not going to affect very quickly or very profoundly the marketplace in which photographers operate.

6   "A big problem we see is an editor who says, 'I want this kind of picture,' and then the word gets out," says Chuck Jonkel of the Wildlife Film Festival. "Editors will say, 'Give us a picture of a caribou running full tilt, and we'll give you $1,700.' Someone's going to hire a helicopter and run the caribou relentlessly to get that $1,700. I don't blame the photographer for that—I blame the editors." If one photographer or editor falters, chances are that there will be another to take his place. Dancer offers the wise advice of Wendell Berry that "one must begin in one's own life the private solutions that can only in turn become public solutions." That is so. Nevertheless, my work on environmental issues has made me wary of com-

3. What effect does wildlife photography have on our perception of endangered species?

4. How do the editors and marketplace contribute to the problem?

---

3. ethic: a moral standard or value

4. promulgate (präm´əl•gāt´): proclaim as having the force of law

pletely private solutions, for the momentum of our various tragedies makes the slow conversion of small parts of the society insufficient. Aren't we ethically impelled to also try to imagine ways that such private solutions might turn into public and widespread practice?

7   It is precisely for that reason that wildlife photography interests me so much. It's a small enough world that, at least for purposes of argument, you could postulate[5] real changes. Suppose the eight or nine magazines that run most of the nature photos and the three or four top TV nature shows formed among them a cooperative, or clearinghouse, for wildlife images and announced that, up to a certain date, anyone could mail them as many slides or reels of film as they wished. *After that date they would not take any new submissions.* Then, when the editors of *Natural History* decided they needed some elephant photos, the staff of the cooperative agency could send over a wide array to choose from. For the fact is, there are already plenty of elephant photos in the world (when *Wildlife Conservation Magazine* was planning a piece on elephants a few years ago, its editors reviewed ten thousand slides). Since most of the competing magazines and TV shows would belong to the cooperative, commercial pressure might diminish; no one else would have a two-inch-away close-up of the golden tamarin monkey either.

8   If some member of the consortium had a good reason for needing a new picture—if there were a new species or a new behavior that needing illustrating, or someone was needed to accompany a scientific expedition—then the cooperative could assign a photographer, along with strict instructions about conduct: about, say, how far away to stay from the animals. These measures might solve some of the ethical problems surrounding the industry's treatment of animals. It is also possible that such a cooperative agency could eventually begin to deal with the larger questions—for instance, over time, it could cull from its stock extreme close-ups and other kinds of photos that miseducate viewers about the natural world. It is the kind of place where a new ethic might *adhere,* might grow into something powerful.

9   Imagining institutions allows you to test the strength of the ethic on which they are based against very real and practical objections. In this case, the most obvious drawback is that the cooperative would put photographers out of work or force them to find new subjects, for if the agency worked as planned, it would need very few new wildlife photos annually. This potential clearinghouse for wildlife photos would announce, in effect: "We've got enough images now;

5. What recommendation does the writer make for changing the business of wildlife photography? How would it help?

6. What are the possible drawbacks to the recommendation addressed in this and the following paragraph?

---

5. postulate: to assume without proof to be true, real, or necessary

we can recycle them more or less forever; please don't bother taking any more." Since negatives do not really degrade with use, that would be that. But this, we intuitively feel, is not fair. Who am I, or you, to tell someone else how he can or can't make a living?

10   It is an almost unknown thing in our society to say, "That's enough." It sounds especially heretical[6] in any creative endeavor. The word *censorship* rises unbidden to one's lips. Even if you can convince yourself that it is not really censorship (it's not the government, after all; it is no more than some magazine telling you that it will not print your story for whatever reason; it's editing), even so, it seems repressive. It *is* repressive. It's the imposition of a new taboo. Consumers are not supposed to have taboos; they are supposed to consume. And consume we do: not just goods and services but images, ideas, knowledge. Nothing is off-limits. So there is something a little creepy about saying, "We will be buying no new photos of wildebeests. We do not think it is a good idea to be taking them." Do we really want any new taboos?

11   As I have become more interested in environmental matters, I have thought a lot about these questions of restraint—about when one's curiosity or creative impulse can be bane as well as boon,[7] about whether there are

---

6. **heretical:** characteristic of any opinion opposed to the official or established views

7. **bane . . . boon:** the cause of harm or distress as well as benefit

places where taboos once more make sense. The answers are easier to see when the questions concern things, not ideas. Clearly, for instance, we would be better off environmentally if as a culture we frowned on automobiles, if we said that the freedom they afforded was not worth the cost in terms of global warming, suburban sprawl, and so forth.

However, the debate about limiting ideas is one we are incapable of having, because we operate under the assumption that the limitation of creativity is repellent. We take as a given that we should find out everything we can, develop everything we can, photograph and write about everything we can, and then let the marketplace decide what to do with it. By definition, therefore, if it sells, it is good. If we can clone animals, say, then we will; to suggest otherwise is to stand against not only free enterprise but also the free imagination. However, in our blind defense of these things that seem "right," we may be short-circuiting the process of thinking things through as a culture, leaving ourselves no way to entertain the possibility of restraint.

12

And yet self-restraint is a uniquely human capacity, belonging as exclusively to us as flight belongs to the birds. It is the one gift no other creature possesses—even as a possibility.

13

> **7.** Why do some oppose the limitation of "creativity"? What are the rewards of thinking about the "possibility of restraint"?

First Thoughts on Your Reading

Answering these questions on your own paper will help you to think more deeply about "Curbing Nature's Paparazzi."

1. Re-read the opening paragraph of the article. Why does the writer start with an overview of wildlife photography's accomplishments?

2. After reading this article, what general statement would you make about wildlife photographers?

3. What do you think of the solution proposed by the writer? Why do you think it will or will not work?

Making Generalizations

READING SKILL

More Than Just a Guess   A **generalization** is a type of inference, an educated guess about life or the world based on new information that you have combined with previous knowledge. You are making a generalization when you go beyond a specific situation—whether it is your latest math test or what one article said about whales—to form a judgment that applies generally to the world. These judgments become the ways we make sense of our complicated, ever changing experience; in turn, they form a scaffold on which we balance other new information. For example, suppose in an article about gray and humpback whales you find several examples of their intelligence. Based on the examples and your knowledge of other animals, you might generalize that whales are smarter than many other animals.

Making generalizations is not just an academic skill, but an important real-world skill that you probably use more often than you realize. Infants first communicate by crying. Often, when infants cry, they are picked up, talked to, changed, or fed. Soon they make a connection between crying and having their basic needs met. Infants then extend this activity to express other needs and wants—they might cry when they are bored or when they want a certain toy. You form generalizations about your reading in this same way: You find a common element between new knowledge and prior experience to formulate a general rule.

A word of caution: Beware of making **invalid generalizations,** which are constructed through faulty reasoning or inadequate information. To make **valid generalizations,** keep in mind the following points.

- **Use sufficient information.** Be sure you have enough information on which to base a generalization. One sentence in an article paired with one fuzzy memory probably is not enough information with which to build a sturdy generalization. After reading this article, for example, the generalization that all nature magazines use staged animal shots would be an invalid generalization.

TIP   Sometimes standardized reading tests ask you to make generalizations. When you make such generalizations, you should base your answers *only* on information in the reading passage.

- **Use relevant information.** Ask yourself if the details of your reading actually support your generalization. Re-reading will help you determine whether the details are relevant or whether you have twisted them out of context.

- **Use qualifying words.** When you make a generalization, you cannot ignore exceptions. Sometimes you can keep your generalization from becoming too broad by using qualifying words such as *many, most,* and *often.* Avoid words such as *always, everyone,* and *never*—remember that most generalizations do not apply in every situation.

TIP How can you spot a writer's generalizations in something you read? One way is to look for statements about categories of things or people. "Most communities have problems" is a generalization. Many generalizations use plural subjects, such as, "Often communities face this problem." The word *often,* in the previous sentence, also signals a generalization. Other words that may signal generalizations include *mostly, usually, probably,* and, of course, *generally* or *in general.*

THINKING IT THROUGH **Making Generalizations**

Read the following passage, and see how a student uses the steps below to make a valid generalization from the information in the passage.

> The woodpecker has a very hard bill that it uses to drill the bark of trees in search of insects. A small sooty-brown bird, the chimney swift often nests inside unused chimneys. Sporting a crest and long tail, the speedy roadrunner is often seen along highways in the Southwest. A builder of dome-shaped nests on the ground, the ovenbird is an American warbler.

▶ **STEP 1 Gather key details from the reading.** Woodpeckers peck at the bark of trees. Chimney swifts live in chimneys. Roadrunners run along roads. Ovenbirds build nests that look like ovens.

▶ **STEP 2 Think of something you know or have experienced that relates to what you have read.** Mourning doves live in my neighborhood. Their call sounds soft and sad.

▶ **STEP 3 Combine your prior knowledge with the text information. Use this combination as the basis for a generalization.** The habits of many birds have given rise to their names.

▶ **STEP 4 Evaluate your generalization. Is it valid? Use the bulleted list on pages 381–382 to test your generalization.** The information is sufficient and relevant because I've gathered several facts directly related to my statement. I have considered exceptions; my generalization includes a qualifying word, *many.*

Making Generalizations

Using the Thinking It Through steps on the previous page, make a generalization based on the third paragraph from "Curbing Nature's Paparazzi." Be prepared to explain your answer.

Problem-Solution Structure

READING FOCUS

The Bare Bones   When reading a proposal that recommends solutions, you will be able to comprehend the writer's ideas more quickly if you know that the proposal follows a fairly standard structure. Knowing what to look for allows you to grasp the problem being addressed and the solution the writer is proposing more readily. Many problem-solution essays, including "Curbing Nature's Paparazzi," use the following basic structure. (Note, however, that professional writers often vary the structure.)

A definition of the problem appears in the first few paragraphs.

The writer discusses different solutions or aspects of one solution; in turn, the writer addresses the advantages and disadvantages of each solution to convince readers of his or her reasoning.

Problem → **Background Information** → **Possible Solutions** → **Proposal of Best Solution**

Facts, expert opinions, examples, and descriptions support and demonstrate the problem.

The actual proposal can appear in the discussion of solutions or after other solutions have been discussed and cast aside. For maximum impact, many writers save it for last.

TIP   Except for the last item, the proposal itself, the structure above is similar to that found in an article which *describes* a problem and its solutions. The difference between a description and a proposal is in the **purpose** and the **point of view** of the writer. A proposal is usually written by someone who has a persuasive purpose as well as an informative one; thus, the writer is concerned about an issue and takes a compelling **tone.** In contrast, a description of a problem and its solutions has informing as its sole purpose. A descriptive article is often written by a journalist who does not have a personal interest in the problem and is merely reporting on it.

Copy and complete a graphic organizer like the one below to analyze the structure of "Curbing Nature's Paparazzi." Identify the paragraphs in which each part of the problem-solution structure is located, and write the numbers of the paragraphs in the space provided. (Remember to look for the paragraph numbers in the outside margins of the reading selection.) Write brief summaries of the parts of the article that belong in each box. As an example, the first box of this organizer has already been completed.

Problem (paragraphs __2__)
Photographers often misrepresent wildlife in their
photographs.
_____
_____

↓

Background Information (paragraphs ____)
_____
_____
_____
_____

↓

Solutions: Advantages/Disadvantages (paragraphs ____)
_____
_____
_____
_____

↓

Best Solution (paragraph ____)
_____
_____
_____
_____

Context Clues: Definitions/Restatements and Examples

When you encounter unfamiliar words in your reading, think of them not as obstacles to slow you but as problems to be analyzed and solved. To help you understand new words, use **context clues.** A common type of context clue, a **definition/restatement clue,** restates a word with a synonym or brief explanation (sometimes referred to as an *appositive).* Restatements are often introduced by words such as *that is, means, called,* and *which is.*

A heronry, a place for breeding herons, will open here next March.

These animals are phytophagous; **that is,** they feed on plants.

Another type of context clue is an **example.** An example concretely illustrates an unfamiliar word's meaning. Clue words that may introduce this type of context clue are *for example, such as,* and *for instance.* Look at the example context clue for *sympathetic* in the following sentence.

Some photographers are sympathetic to wildlife; **for instance,** they will not intrude on animals accompanied by their young.

THINKING IT THROUGH — Using Context Clues

Use the steps below to help you understand unfamiliar words, including the italicized word in the example below.

Films often do not show *quotidian* behavior—daily routines would be boring for the viewer.

1. Find other words in the sentence or passage that hint at, define, restate, or give an example of the new word. (Look for signals such as commas, dashes, or parentheses.) The dash is a clue that "daily routines" could be a restatement of "quotidian behavior."

2. Try replacing the unfamiliar word with a familiar word or phrase. Films often do not show daily routines.

3. Check the unfamiliar word in a dictionary. "Quotidian" means "daily" or "everyday."

PRACTICE

Use the steps above to figure out the definition of the following italicized words. Be prepared to explain your answers.

1. We wish wildlife photographers were always *benign,* never threatening the animals or habitats they photograph.

2. The treatment of animals is not always *ethical,* that is, not always in keeping with val-

ues many hold in common.

3. Such empty language, such *rhetoric,* will not affect the marketplace very much.

4. Let's *adhere* to a new policy—for example, stay firm in our support for banning certain types of photographs.

5. Controlling wildlife photography may seem *repressive*—just far too restrictive.

TEST TAKING

Answering Analogy Questions

Analogy questions on standardized tests are problems just waiting to be solved. An **analogy** is a comparison; it establishes a relationship between two words. In answering analogy questions on a standardized test, you must analyze the relationship between one pair of words, the **stem word pair,** in order to identify a second pair of words that has the most similar relationship. (Analogies are written and read in a certain way. Read the first example below like this: "*Hard drive* has the same relationship with *computer* as *step* has with *staircase*." The symbol : means "related to," while : : means "equal to.")

The examples below show four kinds of analogies that appear on standardized tests.

- **Part to Whole.** (One word is part of the other.)

  HARD DRIVE : COMPUTER : : step : staircase

- **Agent to Action.** (One word is the person or thing that performs the action described by the other word.)

  CHEF : COOK : : carpenter : build

- **Agent to Acted Upon.** (A person or thing is paired with another person or thing that it usually affects.)

  SINGER : AUDIENCE : : teacher : students

- **Adjective to Quality.** (An adjective is paired with a noun that names the quality that the adjective expresses.)

  WORRIED : ANXIETY : : jealous : envy

Here is an example of an analogy question:

1. CHAIN : BICYCLE : : _____

   A. engineer : train
   B. seat : airplane
   C. ship : boat
   D. piston : automobile
   E. buoyant : raft

THINKING IT THROUGH Answering Analogy Questions

Here is a three-step approach to help you answer analogy questions.

1. **Identify the relationship between the word stem pair:** CHAIN : BICYCLE = part to whole. Express this relationship in a short sentence: The chain is a part of a bicycle.

2. **Look for a similar relationship in each possible answer.** An engineer (**A**) is not part of a train. A seat is part of an airplane; **B** could be correct. A ship (**C**) is not part of a boat. A piston is part of an automobile; **D** could be correct. Buoyant (**E**) is not part of a raft.

3. **If there are two or more answers that fit the relationship, add details to your sentence that will help you define the relationship more fully.** For example, a chain is part of the operating mechanism of a bicycle. Whereas a seat is *not* part of the mechanism of an airplane, a piston *is* part of the mechanism of an automobile. **D** is the correct answer.

Writing a Proposal

"What in the world can we do about—?" You name it. The world is full of problems crying for solutions, problems like ozone depletion, urban decay, and juvenile crime. Every day scientists, politicians, experts, and citizens write to persuade others that they have discovered a workable solution to a problem. Some write because their occupations demand it; many write just because they are concerned.

At times only writing will do. Phone calls may carry some weight in a senator's office or on a customer relations hot line, but a letter shows you have taken the time to think carefully about an issue. The person on the receiving end is then more likely to take notice and take action.

This workshop is your chance to write about a problem that concerns you. It will be a public problem rather than a private one; and instead of a personal jotting or journal entry, you will write a structured essay aimed at convincing readers that your proposed solution will work. Your ideas on how to curb teen smoking or how to prepare high school students for the career world might provide an answer for someone who really needs one.

WHAT'S AHEAD?

In this workshop you will write an essay recommending a solution to a problem. You will also learn how to

- **define a problem**
- **analyze and evaluate possible solutions**
- **recognize either-or reasoning**
- **avoid overuse of passive voice**
- **punctuate adverb clauses**

Prewriting

Choose a Problem

So Many Problems, So Little Time   Your **purpose** for writing seems simple: Find the best solution to a problem, and then convince your readers that your solution is brilliant. In other words, your purpose is to persuade.

The first step in achieving that purpose is to choose a manageable problem—something neither too private nor too huge—to write about in a short paper. You cannot solve the problem of world hunger in a brief essay, but you might propose a specific way of getting food to hungry people in your city. The two following tips show you ways to discover a manageable topic.

- **Think about problems that people in your school or community share.** Often, current problems in your community can supply an occasion, or reason for writing, that will naturally interest readers. For example, during spring break what will working parents do about child care for their elementary school children? You might think of possible solutions—maybe a vacation day camp staffed by high school students or a temporary day-care program funded by the town.

- **Zero in on the local aspects of a national or international problem.** Instead of discussing water pollution in a general way, look up close and nearby. What can be done to remove the algae layer from the town lake to make it a healthier place for fish? Rather than arguing for worldwide economic change, you might focus on what to do with the ugly, abandoned power plant near downtown—maybe turning it into a career-training center for young people.

Brainstorm a list of problems you might like to take on, and select the one that interests you most. Starting where your interests lie will help you get involved in exploring the problem and its possible solutions.

Consider Occasion, Audience, and Tone

Everybody's an Expert   The **occasion** of your proposal is what prompts you to write—a problem that conerns you. Strive to maintain a balanced approach and avoid overly emotional language. Your **tone,** or your attitude toward your subject matter and your audience, should be formal yet sincere. As you try to persuade your readers, you want to convince them that you are addressing their concerns and have their best interests in mind. Analyze your audience with the questions below.

THINKING IT THROUGH   **Analyzing Audience**

▶ **What do my readers already know about this problem?** If most people are aware of the problem, but may not realize its serious impact on society, you will have to provide specific background. Show them that the problem affects not only individuals, but society in general.

▶ **What solution will my readers prefer?** If you believe they may prefer a solution you have rejected, you should explain in detail the pros and cons of that approach. Show how it lacks the advantages of your solution.

▶ **What kind of objections might my readers have to my solution?** If they will have doubts about how to implement your solution, you should provide convincing support that shows how the solution can be put into action.

► **What if my readers ask, "Who are *you*, anyway?"** You probably aren't a famous authority, so you need to establish your credibility. Show your readers that you have researched the problem thoroughly, weighed possible solutions fairly, and argued your case forcefully.

TIP No two members of your audience are likely to have the exact same biases, preferences, and objections. However, you can make an educated guess about the viewpoints they share. For example, an audience of students and teachers might think that a mandatory, national service program is a wonderful idea. For these readers, you might not need to defend the solution; you could move quickly to discussing implementation. However, an audience of business people might think that your solution would cost too much. You will have to persuade this audience that the need is great and your solution is worth the money.

Define the Problem

From the Ground Up   When you define a problem, you give it shape and clarify it for yourself. After all, you can't begin to solve a problem until you understand it. If you are having trouble defining a problem, use the strategies below.

THINKING IT THROUGH   **Defining Your Problem**

► **Describe the problem.** What is the problem, as precisely as you can state it? The stream that runs behind our school is putrid and filled with disgusting litter.

► **Tell more.** When did the problem start? What are its causes and effects? My mom remembers that thirty years ago people used to fish and swim in that stream. Now no one would dare. Wouldn't it be great if we could clean it up?

► **Compare and contrast.** How is this problem like other problems? How is it different? The problem of the polluted stream is just like the town lake problem—pollution. I wonder if it's like air pollution, too.

► **Evaluate the problem.** How serious is the problem, and why? What might happen if it is not solved? That polluted stream might become so toxic that everything in it dies. It might endanger childrens' health and my health, too.

TIP   An extended comparison is an **analogy,** a rhetorical device useful in persuasion. It often illustrates the problem in a way you and your readers can clearly understand.

Another way to define a problem is to ask the *5W-How?* questions (*who, what, when, where, why,* and *how*). Even if you can answer all your questions, you will probably need to do some research to find out why, for example, the trees behind the school are dying.

Reference Note

For more on **conducting research,** see page 248.

Explore Solutions

What's a Body to Do?   Now list all the possible solutions that occur to you. (You might also examine current and past attempts to solve the problem.) Then, use the questions below to examine the possible solutions to the problem. Notice how one student answered these questions while planning an essay recommending that all high school students be required to do some sort of work or service before or just after they graduate.

TIP Sometimes, exploring solutions collaboratively with other students leads you to valuable ideas you wouldn't have thought of yourself. If you do discuss solutions with other students, be sure to clearly express your own ideas and listen respectfully to the views of others.

Problem: Our society offers young people little help in making the transition from high school into the world of full-time work.

My Own Ideas

Can anything be done to solve or at least minimize the problem?	Yes, let's make sure every teenager participates in some type of work or service opportunity.
What is the easiest solution? the most difficult?	The easiest solution is a national program of mandatory community service. Every student would gain experience in some kind of job. This idea might also be the most difficult solution to implement because it would require such a huge bureaucracy.

Other People's Solutions

What other solutions are being—or have been—tried?	Possible solutions include summer jobs, internships, and community service opportunities, including the AmeriCorps program.
How well are these other solutions working?	These opportunities help teenagers gain work experience, but many do not participate.

KEY CONCEPT →

Take Off Your Blinders   Few solutions are perfect, but you need to choose the one that you think will work best. **Be sure to take an open-minded look at all solutions and avoid bias, an unexamined prejudice or preference.** For example, if the problem you care about is teen smoking, some possible solutions include education, advertising, and peer pressure. If you are an aspiring ad copywriter, you might focus only on anti-smoking ad campaigns, ignoring other possible solutions. Explore at least three different solutions by creating a chart like the one below. Fill in the first column yourself, and collaborate with a classmate or two to analyze the advantages and disadvantages of each possible solution.

Possible Solutions	Advantages	Disadvantages
Students work summer jobs.	They make money and get some work experience.	Summer jobs are too short. Not every teen works.
Some teenagers get internships.	They get some experience in fields that interest them.	Internships are highly competitive because there are so few. They are often given to insiders. Many interns may also perform, for a low wage, menial jobs unrelated to the field.
Teenagers work in community service programs (including the AmeriCorps program).	They learn about social problems firsthand.	Community service programs are rarely required by schools; not many students do community service.
National, mandatory service program requires teenagers to work in community service jobs.	Teenagers get all the advantages of other options. All teenagers participate. Their work experience may be more intense.	Such a program would be expensive to implement and would require political pressure to pass in Congress.

Evaluate Possible Solutions

Find the Winner   Now that you know the advantages and disadvantages of each proposed solution, which one will you recommend? As you answer the following questions, take notes and save them. They will be useful when you draft your essay.

■ **What is my primary objective?** Establishing a clear objective gives direction to your thinking. For the writer working on the problem of giving teenagers real-world work experience, the primary objective is to find a solution that will be available to all teenagers, not just to some.

■ **Will the solution work?** For each possible solution, think about the hard realities involved in making it happen. For example, who would have to approve a national program for mandatory community service for teenagers? How would the program be funded? Who would run it? Will the public support it?

Thinking about your solutions naturally leads you to develop criteria (standards of judgment) for evaluating possible solutions. To determine your criteria, think first about the boundaries within which you want your solution to operate. In other words, think about what your solution should and should not do. From these limits and goals you can create criteria. The student writing about a national service program used the following boundaries to determine criteria for solutions. The student also ranked the criteria in order of importance.

Boundaries	Criteria for a Good Solution	Rank
The solution should not exclude any teenagers.	Reaches out to all teenagers.	1
The solution should not be perceived as threatening existing programs or lowering their quality.	Makes use of or expands or at least does not impair existing programs.	3
It should give teenagers significant work experience.	Provides teenagers with more work experience than summer jobs or short-term internships.	2
Local efforts may not be enough to fulfill the solution.	Involves and serves communities at the state and local level.	4

The next step is to make a chart that shows how well each solution measures up against the criteria.

Possible Solutions	Criteria Met
Summer jobs; internships; community service (including the AmeriCorps program)	3, 4
A mandatory service program for all high school students	1, 2, 3, 4

TIP If no solution seems to meet all of your criteria, choose the one that meets the greatest number of criteria. Alternatively, you can assign points to your criteria based on order of importance. For example, if you have five criteria, give the most important one five points, the second most important four points, and so on. Then, add up the points for each possible solution and choose the one with the highest total as your proposed solution.

Plot the Steps

Your Mission—Should You Choose to Accept It Even the most brilliant solution does not fall automatically into place. You usually need to develop a plan, working toward a solution step by step. The following strategies and examples may help you flesh out your plan.

THINKING IT THROUGH **Planning the Steps to a Solution**

▶ **STEP 1 Review the prior knowledge you can bring to your plans.** You may know more than you think you do. *After considering the criteria and possible solutions, I realized that summer jobs, internships, and community service could all be preserved in a national service program.*

▶ **STEP 2 Anticipate possible problems.** *A mandatory, national service program would be expensive to establish and operate. How would it be funded? The program would need a broad support base, including the general public as well as members of Congress. To be successful, the program needs a system for registering and accounting for all teenagers.*

▶ **STEP 3 Figure out the order in which things need to be done.** *First, a public relations campaign might help convince people to consider the solution. Then, Congress would have to be willing to establish a national registration program to ensure all teenagers' participation. Last, and perhaps most important, funding would have to be provided.*

TIP When additional problems occur to you as you plan your solution, re-examine and revise your boundaries and criteria chart. For example, a mandatory national service program would affect families who need their teenagers' incomes. It would also affect other job programs that employ teenagers at minimum wage. Checking the example student's chart, however, confirms for her that the mandatory service program she has in mind should not threaten or impair existing programs. She will have to allow an exception for those teenagers who are needed by their families.

YOUR TURN 4 **Exploring a Problem and Its Solutions**

Explore your problem and solution. Be sure to
- carefully define the problem
- explore possible solutions to the problem
- analyze the advantages and disadvantages of each solution
- establish criteria to identify the best solution to the problem
- list and order the steps needed to implement your proposed solution

Identify the Thesis

A One-Sentence Combo To keep yourself on track, write a brief statement of your **thesis,** or main idea. Often in a problem-solution essay, the thesis may not appear in the first paragraph, especially if you include background information. Look in the third paragraph of the Writer's Model on page 399 for the following thesis, which combines the problem and the solution into a single sentence. Remember: The first version of your thesis statement may or may not end up as the thesis of your essay. However, it will help clarify your thinking as you continue planning your essay.

> problem
>
> Because society offers little guidance to teenagers when they make the transition from high school to the world beyond it,
>
> solution
>
> a national, mandatory service program should be implemented to guide young adults into the world of work.

Avoiding Either-Or Reasoning

You do not want to risk alienating your audience by presenting your solution as if it were the only workable option, so avoid **either-or reasoning.** Too many essayists assume that there is only one solution to a complicated problem—the brilliant one they favor. Either their solution is implemented or disaster will strike. This **logical fallacy** (error in thinking) ignores the fact that usually there are not just two possible (either this or this) outcomes. You can be reasonable and still persuade your readers that your solution is the best one.

To avoid *either-or* reasoning, don't exaggerate what will happen if your solution is not adopted. One way to do this is to avoid words like *never, always,* or *all.* Instead, use words like *many, some,* and *generally* to make statements more reasonable, and stick to specific outcomes. Look at the examples below.

Either-Or Statement: If voters do not approve the bond issue to build new schools, no one will ever want to move to this city.

More Reasonable Statement: If voters do not approve the bond issue to build new schools, classroom size will continue to increase, and some schools will have to go to double or triple shifts.

Reference Note

For more on **logical fallacies,** see page 309.

PRACTICE

Read each statement below and decide if it is an example of *either-or* thinking. If it is, on your own paper, revise the statement to make it more reasonable. If the statement does not need revision, write *C* for *Correct.*

1. All citizens must register and vote in every election, or our democracy will collapse.

2. If the schoolroom walls are not painted a calming green or blue, third-graders will never sit still for their lessons.

3. If space flights are discontinued, scientists will lose a valuable way to learn more about the universe.

4. If children are not given the right encouragement in their first five years, they will never be creative thinkers as adults.

5. All students should play sports at school; otherwise, they will never be physically fit.

6. Students who don't take all advanced classes in high school will never get into college.

7. People who wear the latest clothing fads are always the most popular students in school.

8. Unless our city and county governments can work together, we will not be able to control urban sprawl as effectively as we could if they cooperated.

9. Unless I stay up all night studying for my exam, I won't be able to pass the test.

10. Students should not be required to read five hundred pages of fiction outside of class, because they will never use literature in their careers.

Gather Support

KEY CONCEPT

Reference Note

For more on **citing sources,** see page 268.

Do the Legwork Do you have enough **evidence** to persuade your readers? **You need to demonstrate with details, facts, and examples that your proposed solution will work.** Here are some suggestions for gathering support for your solution.

- **Interview experts.** Go to the source. Find professionals working to solve your problem, and interview them. They will probably have facts you can use to support your solution. For example, if you are working on the problem of teen smoking, go to your city's health department and interview the person in charge of the anti-smoking campaign.

- **Study similar solutions.** If your solution is already in place somewhere else, observe it in action. You might visit a neighboring high school to see how opening the computer lab during evening hours solves the problem of inadequate computer facilities.

- **Research on the Internet.** Using keywords, look for a Web site devoted to your problem. If your solution addresses the local water pollution problem, look up *water pollution* and your state or city to find statistics on industrial waste in nearby streams. You might broaden your search nationally to find out what another community like yours is doing to keep its water clean.

Reference Note

For more on **evaluating sources,** see page 250.

- **Choose reliable sources.** To convince your readers, be sure to choose sources that are reliable. For example, find out the background of an author whose work you are citing. If you are researching on the Web, evaluate the source carefully for **accuracy, bias,** and **reliability.**

Once you have gathered a variety of support, jot a few notes about what you have found. Informal notes often help to refine your topic and clarify your ideas. Such notes may also help you see what still needs to be learned or researched before you begin writing your essay.

> **TIP** Vague statements and insubstantial support won't convince anyone. Your readers expect—and they deserve—specific, relevant evidence. Look at the two statements below. Which would *you* be more likely to accept?
>
> **Vague** Many students say they can never use the computers.
>
> **Precise** The log in the computer lab shows that 98 percent of the thirty-five computers are in constant use during school hours and that a daily average of twenty students sign a waiting list, confirming students' complaints that they cannot find a free computer.
>
> The first statement uses the terms *many* and *can never* without backing them up with numbers. The second statement gives a specific statistic from a reliable source.

Organize Your Information

A Place for Everything   You want your essay to provide information in a well-ordered way, showing a **logical progression,** so readers can follow your thinking. Your proposal should follow the traditional **problem-solution structure,** the organizational pattern that matches the order in which we typically think about problems and solutions. Look below at a graphic organizer that shows this structure.

TIP Logical progression means an order that makes sense, whether it is chronological order, order of importance, or any other order.

State Problem → Give Background Information → Briefly Discuss Advantages and Disadvantages of Other Solutions → Propose Best Solution

Because proposals can be quite complicated, you may find it necessary to use more than one type of organization within this larger structure. For example, individual sections might be organized chronologically, or in order of importance. The following chart shows how three basic types of organization may be used in an essay recommending a solution to a problem.

COMPUTER TIP

Some word-processing programs allow you to rearrange the order of the paragraphs in your essay. Number the paragraphs; then, select the paragraphs to reorder. Choose the sort function to rearrange them in ascending or descending order.

Types of Organization

Logical Order: Arrange ideas in logical groups. For example, in exploring Solution A, discuss disadvantages of Solution A, then advantages of Solution A; then, do the same for Solution B; and so on. Example: Solution A in an essay about urban sprawl could explain the advantages and disadvantages of zoning.

Chronological Order: Discuss the history of the problem in the sequence (time order) in which it developed. Discuss how to implement the proposed solution in the order the steps need to be done. Example: Reviewing the history of a local lake's pollution sets up the proposed solution.

Order of Importance: Proceed either from the most important point (a solution's major disadvantage, for example) to the least important or from the least important point to the most important. Example: An essay on improving student test scores might begin with the least important solution and end with the most important.

TIP Order of importance can often be used effectively in a section that presents the advantages and disadvantages of a specific solution.

YOUR TURN 5   Setting Up the Essay

As you complete the prewriting phase of your essay, remember to

- write a thesis statement that includes both problem and solution
- think about your audience and plan how you will convince them
- gather enough evidence to support your recommended solution
- organize your essay

Writing

Proposal of a Solution

Framework	**Directions and Explanations**

Introduction

- Get your readers interested in the problem right away.
- State the problem and provide background information.
- Include a clear thesis.

Grab Your Readers' Attention   A bold statement, question, quotation, fact, or statistic in the first sentence or two of your essay can make readers want to read more.

Establish the Problem   Briefly explain the problem your essay addresses: What are its causes, how serious is it, and what harm is it currently causing?

State Your Thesis   Use your prewriting thesis statement, or revise it to present a more forceful tone or to reflect new information from your research.

Body

- Briefly discuss potential solutions you have rejected.
- Persuade your readers to adopt your recommended solution.

Examine Possible Solutions   As you discuss why other solutions will not work, be sure to include their advantages as well as their disadvantages. (Including advantages shows readers that you are reasonable and unbiased.)

Focus on the Best Solution   Show why your solution is the best. Include

- a clear statement of your proposed solution
- convincing support (facts, examples, expert testimony)
- steps to implement your solution
- explanations to counter possible objections

Conclusion

- Restate your thesis, and possibly end with a call to action.

Wrap It Up   Summarize your proposal in a fresh way. You might leave your readers thinking about what the world will be like if your solution is (or is not) adopted. Tell readers what they can do to make your solution a reality.

 Writing a First Draft

Follow the framework above to write the first draft of your essay. Also, look at the Writer's Model on the following page.

A Writer's Model

The following Writer's Model, which is a final draft, closely follows the framework on page 398.

Mandatory Community Service for America's Youth: The Time Has Come

Graduation day—all high school students look forward to it. After a handshake, a diploma, tears, and laughter, high school is over. It is time to move on, to grow up. Many graduates go on to some type of higher education, some enter the work force, and others combine the two. A few will drift, trying to find their places in the world. Very few are totally prepared for the challenges that face them after graduation day.

Attention-grabbing introduction

The transition from high school to the "real" world is one of the most significant changes in a young person's life, yet our society offers little guidance in preparing students for this giant leap into maturity. Not being adequately prepared for work results in frustration for workers and high job turnover rates. Inadequate preparation for work can also cause unemployment for some young people; in turn, unemployment has an adverse impact on society as well as on the individuals themselves.

Statement of problem

Background/ seriousness of problem

High school graduates need better preparation for getting and holding a job. One step in this direction would be to make sure that every student has meaningful work experience either before or after graduation. Because the transition from high school to the world beyond is difficult, a national program of mandatory community service should be implemented to help guide young adults into the world of work.

Thesis statement

Some students already participate in summer jobs, internships, and community service programs. Drawbacks to these solutions, however, are many. The first two options often fail to provide extensive or substantive work experience. Summer jobs, by their very nature, are too short for students to learn very much about a field. Obtaining an internship is usually a highly competitive process, but those who land these plum positions often find that their work consists of getting coffee and photocopying memos. The third option, community service, affects too few teenagers. Relatively few schools require community service, and in those that do, teenagers usually serve for only several hours a week.

Disadvantages of existing solutions

A community service requirement, however, is still the most effective way to employ young people in an extended and mean-

Advantages of one existing solution/ Examples

(continued)

(continued)

ingful way. Students might work in hospitals, schools, and neighborhoods, or on environmental projects. They might plant trees in parks, help teach people to read, work in soup kitchens, or organize games and activities in child-care centers or senior citizen centers.

Factual support

More and more, United States citizens want youth to help with these vital services. Public-opinion polls consistently show that most Americans support a requirement for some type of community service. Young people can contribute to their communities by working in areas such as education, health care, and crime reduction. One innovative, ongoing national service program called AmeriCorps offers young adults a minimum-wage salary and college-tuition credit in exchange for full-time public service work. Although this program provides many benefits, it involves few young people—because it is not mandatory.

Proposal and advantages of recommended solution

On the other hand, a national program of mandatory community service will affect all students and directly benefit both young people and the country. For teens, one year in a national service program after graduation would provide an important and memorable life experience. Young adults going on to college would gain maturity and a perspective on life that goes beyond the four walls of a classroom. Those planning to go directly into the job market would learn valuable skills that will help them escape the dead-end trap of "no experience, no job; no job, no experience." Participants might even discover a field they want to study further as they are exposed to careers they might not have considered. Less tangibly but just as important, the country will benefit by having young people better understand the responsibilities and rewards of citizenship. They will expand their experience beyond their homes, communities, and cultures as they learn that serving others is part of being a mature citizen.

Expert testimony

Joseph Duffey, former chancellor of the University of Massachusetts at Amherst, summed up these advantages in a speech to the World Future Society:

> At its best, national service . . . offers young people a chance to grow and mature at a critical stage in their development that cannot be accomplished in the schoolhouse or the workplace. Youth Service—as opposed to all other kinds of service—can teach lessons that redound to personal success in work, as citizens of the community, and as examples to the generations that follow.

Duffey's observations confirm the importance that community

service has in developing the life skills and character that young people need as they face the challenges of their more mature years.

Of course, setting up a workable program will be difficult. Some may object that such a program infringes on teenagers' right to plan their own lives after high school. In reality citizens have many obligations that infringe on absolute control of their lives—school, for example, and military service during wartime. Society has deemed these things so valuable that, with certain exceptions, every citizen must participate. Also, any national service program would try to match student interest with the type of service to be performed. Others may argue that administering such a program would be too complicated and costly. Certain existing programs could be adapted to administer and fund a national community service program. Perhaps businesses, which would ultimately benefit the most from skilled workers, could be encouraged to help fund the program. In addition, consider that our military services spend a billion dollars a year trying to recruit new volunteers and another billion in reenlistment pay to keep them—yet they are still falling short of their recruitment targets. If teens were obligated to a year of national service, perhaps many would choose military service as a way of satisfying that obligation, even though their time commitment would be substantially longer. Teens might see the military's higher pay and benefits and extensive training as a good tradeoff for the longer service. Any money the military saved on recruiting and retaining personnel could be invested in the national service program.

Congress and concerned citizens will have to work extremely hard to get past the politics, opposition, and bureaucracy in order to approve the program. Once it has been approved, a national draft registration could be implemented for females as well as males to ensure that every young adult is identified. AmeriCorps could expand its National Civilian Community Corps, which is based on the Civilian Conservation Corps program of the 1930s. This expanded program might appeal to more young people because it would employ and train people in construction as well as service jobs.

The time for mandatory community service for all young people is now. You can do your part by writing to your United States senators and representative. Let them know that you support this program, and urge them to find a way to make it happen. Do you care about the future of our country and youth? Then act. It will be a national service.

First objection countered

Second objection countered

Steps to implement proposed solution

Summary of thesis/ Call to action

A Student's Model

The following excerpt is from an essay by Billie Jean Murray, a student at Moncks Corner High School in Moncks Corner, South Carolina. Notice how the she proposes solutions to a particular problem in her workplace.

A Recycling Plan for the Workplace

Attention-getting opener

Statement of problem

"What a waste!" I thought to myself, as I looked every day at the trash can next to my desk, overflowing with discarded paper. In the billing department of the electric company where I work, one hundred pounds of paper is discarded every week. Because I am conscious of the environmental problems with waste, this fact has bothered me. As cashiers in this department, my co-workers and I discussed the situation. We came up with a recycling alternative, based on several important criteria, to help the electric company to do its part to help the environment.

Thesis

Background information

First, we decided that any solution must meet three criteria. The recycling process must be convenient; it cannot interfere with the flow of business. The process must be affordable. Finally, the results of the process must be favorable and beneficial. With these criteria in mind, we brainstormed and came up with two recycling alternatives. For both alternatives, trash receptacles for paper would be placed at each workstation and would replace our usual trash cans.

First potential solution

In the first alternative, the paper would be picked up once a week after work by people from the recycling center. They would charge $10 a week for this service. The center would then pay us for the paper. The convenience of this alternative was appealing, but our calculations showed us that we would not break even. We asked several nearby businesses to use the electric company as their waste paper drop site and to share in the weekly pickup costs. No other business was interested, however, because none had the volume of waste paper that we did. After some debate, then, we rejected this proposal because of the cost of picking up the paper.

Reasons for rejection

402   Chapter 9   **Persuasion:** Recommending Solutions

Evaluate and Revise Your Essay

You Be the Judge Your revision process should include at least two readings. In the first reading, check that you have thoroughly treated and logically organized the content you set out to cover. Use the second reading to refine your sentence style.

First Reading: Content and Organization The guidelines that follow will help you make sure all the pieces of your proposal are in place. Respond to the questions on the left-hand side. Use the tips in the middle if you need help answering a question. If there is a problem with your paper, make the change on the right-hand side.

Proposal of a Solution: Content and Organization Guidelines for Peer and Self-Evaluation

Evaluation Questions	▶ Tips	▶ Revision Techniques
❶ Does the introduction clearly state the problem and give background information?	▶ **Draw two lines under** the statement of the problem. **Underline** the background information once. If you don't see both components, revise.	▶ **Add** a clear statement of the problem near the beginning of the paper. **Add** information about why the problem is worth solving.
❷ Does the thesis statement contain a proposed solution to the problem?	▶ **Put a check mark** by the thesis statement. **Put a double check mark** by the part of it that names the proposed solution. If you don't find any check marks, revise.	▶ **Add** a thesis statement giving the proposed solution. **Revise** the existing thesis statement to include a proposed solution.
❸ Does the essay include a brief discussion of other possible solutions?	▶ **Circle** sentences that explain other solutions. If you do not find any, revise.	▶ **Add** explanations of any solutions that you have rejected, including their advantages and disadvantages.
❹ Is the discussion of the recommended solution and the process for implementing it clear?	▶ **Bracket** sentences that explain the proposed solution. **Draw** a flowchart of the steps. If there are few bracketed sentences or if there are gaps in the order of the steps, revise.	▶ **Add** a sentence or two to explain the solution. **Elaborate** on details of the solution. **Reorder** steps or **add** missing steps. **Delete** any unnecessary steps.
❺ Are possible objections to the proposed solution discussed?	▶ **Put X's** in the margin where you discuss possible objections. If you have few or no X's, revise.	▶ **Add** sentences to acknowledge and counter objections.

ONE WRITER'S REVISIONS Here is how one writer used the guidelines to revise some sentences from the proposal that begins on page 399.

add

Once it has been approved,

A national draft registration could be implemented for females as well as males to ensure that every young adult is identified. Congress and concerned citizens will have to work

reorder

extremely hard to get past the politics, opposition, and

in order to approve the program

add

bureaucracy. AmeriCorps could expand its National Civilian Community Corps, which is based on the Civilian Conservation Corps program of the 1930s. This expanded program might

elaborate

appeal to more young people *because it would employ and*

train people in construction as well as service jobs.

Analyzing the Revision Process

1. Why do the additions to the sentences make them better?
2. How does reordering the sentences make the paragraph clearer?

PEER REVIEW

Ask a classmate to read your paper and answer the following questions.

1. What is the problem, and why is it important?
2. Did you find the proposed solution convincing? Why or why not?

YOUR TURN 7 **Focusing on Content and Organization**

Use the Content and Organization Guidelines to make the changes necessary to convey your message clearly.

TIP Forms of *be* **verbs:**

be	are
being	was
am	were
is	been

▶ **Second Reading: Style** In a proposal, your goal is to persuade your readers. Strong, clear language is essential. One way to achieve such language is by using **active voice** more often than passive voice. (Often you can identify passive voice by looking for *be* verbs.) Active voice not only gives your writing power and precision, but also keeps your readers interested. Passive voice, on the other hand, can make writing dull and lifeless, especially if it is overused. Use the following style guideline to evaluate and revise your verbs for active or passive voice.

Style Guideline

Evaluation Question	▶ Tip	▶ Revision Technique
Is passive voice overused?	▶ **Highlight** all *be* verbs or verb phrases. If the majority of verbs you have highlighted are in the passive voice, revise.	▶ **Replace** *be* verbs by revising unnecessary passive-voice verbs to active-voice verbs.

Active Voice

Are your verbs as forceful as possible? You will probably find that you have used a number of *be* verbs in your essay. *Be* verbs can signal an unnecessary use of the passive voice. **Voice** refers to the form of a verb showing whether the subject is acting (active) or is acted upon (passive).

Sentences

- A verb in the **active voice** expresses an action performed **by** its subject.
- A verb in the **passive voice** expresses an action done **to** its subject.

Active Voice	The students completed the project. [The subject (*students*) performs the action.]
Passive Voice	The project was completed by the students. [The subject (*project*) receives the action.]

ONE WRITER'S REVISIONS The following examples show how the writer of the proposal on page 399 revised one paragraph in the essay to eliminate the unnecessary use of *be* verbs.

TIP Sometimes passive voice is a good choice for writing, but overusing passive voice verbs makes it difficult for the reader to visualize actions or events because the actors are obscured. Active verbs make writing more concise and direct.

BEFORE REVISION

A community service requirement, however, is still the most effective way to employ young people in an extended and meaningful way. Students might be employed by hospitals, schools, or neighborhoods, or on environmental projects. Trees could be planted in parks, people could be taught to read, soup kitchens could be worked in, or games and activities in child-care centers or senior citizen centers could be organized.

There are six *be* verbs.

AFTER REVISION

A community service requirement, however, is still the most effective way to employ young people in an extended and meaningful way. Students might work in hospitals, schools, or neighborhoods, or on environmental projects. They might plant trees in parks, help teach people to read, work in soup kitchens, or organize games and activities in child-care centers or senior citizen centers.

Keep the *be* verb.

Change verb phrase.

Change the passive voice to active voice.

Analyzing the Revision Process

1. Why did the writer not eliminate all of the *be* verbs?
2. How do the writer's changes improve the paragraph?

 Focusing on Active Voice

Use the style guideline on page 405 to revise your essay's use of passive voice. Remember: When you use active voice, your writing usually becomes stronger and more direct.

Reference Note

For more information and practice on using **active voice,** see page 705.

Designing Your Writing

| COMPUTER TIP

Some word-processing programs have symbol fonts available in their pull-down menus. Experiment with the type-face, or font, options and use one appropriate to your pictograph.

Drawing a Pictograph One way to persuade your readers is to help them see important information. Graphs and charts allow writers to present information in a clear and concrete way. A **pictograph** is a special kind of bar graph that uses symbols instead of bars to represent quantities. Pictographs make your data visually interesting and memorable.

- **Choose a symbol** that is appropriate to your information. In the following graph, money bags represent hundreds of millions of dollars.
- **Draw the horizontal and vertical axes.** One axis should express the quantities you will show. The other should represent the measure you are using to compare quantities. The example shows hundreds of millions of dollars on the vertical axis and the two years that are compared on the horizontal axis.
- **Make sure the axes on the graph are equal** to one another—that is, the same length—so that your representation is not deceptive or unclear.

- **Label the axes of the graph.** Your information should be clear at a glance.

  To avoid misleading your readers, be sure to draw your pictograph accurately. Compare the two pictographs below. Both show funding for AmeriCorps in 1994 and 1999. The pictograph on the top distorts the 1999 increase by making the money bag in the right-hand column larger in height *and* width; the 1999 money bag covers a greater area than the 1994 money bag, thus exaggerating their difference. In the more accurate pictograph on the bottom, all of the money bags are the same size.

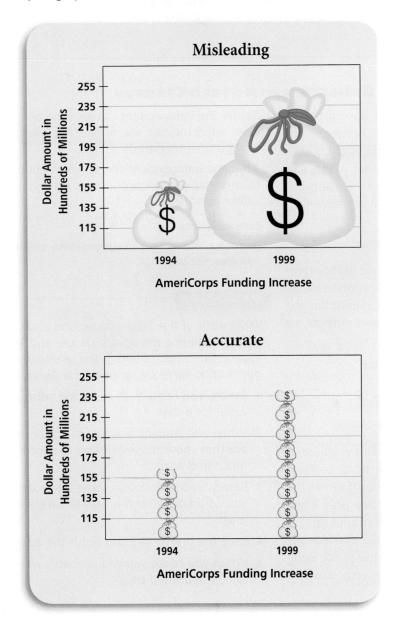

Reference Note

For more information about creating **bar graphs,** see page 974 in the Quick Reference Handbook.

Publishing

Proofread Your Essay

Reference Note

For more information on **proofreading,** see page 1081 in the Quick Reference Handbook.

Check and Double-check   After you have worked so hard to refine your proposed solution, you do not want any minor errors to mar the final product. Make sure your paper is free of errors in grammar, spelling, and punctuation. Commas seem like little things, but if one is missing in a sentence, readers may not follow the logic of a crucial sentence.

Grammar Link

Using Commas with Subordinate Adverb Clauses

Somewhere in your essay, you have probably tried to make the relationship between your problem and its solutions clearer by using subordinate clauses. (Remember that a subordinate clause does not express a complete thought and cannot stand alone as a sentence.)

Example:
Unless we act quickly, all of the turtles will die.

An **adverb clause** (like the one in the example) uses a **subordinating conjunction** to clarify the relationship between ideas. Subordinating conjunctions indicate time, cause, purpose, or condition.

time: after, as, before, until, when

cause: because, since, unless

purpose: so that

condition: although, if, though

When an adverb clause begins a sentence, the clause must be followed by a comma. However, when an adverb clause follows the independent clause, use a comma only when the meaning would be unclear without one.

The following examples are two equally correct ways of making the same point using the same words but with the adverb clause in two different positions.

Before the independent clause: If no one provides opportunities, young people's talents may go unappreciated.

After the independent clause: Young people's talents may go unappreciated if no one provides opportunities.

Reference Note

For more information on **subordinate adverb clauses,** see page 584.

PRACTICE

Write each of the following sentences on your paper, underline the adverb clause, and add appropriate punctuation. If the sentence is punctuated correctly, write a C for *Correct.*

1. Before you revise your paper set your draft aside for a day.

2. While one student saved each of her drafts, another chose to revise the same document again and again.

3. Because you might lose some information you could use later it is wise to save each draft.

4. Save the drafts until you finish the essay.

5. When you revise you will probably want to look at a printed copy.

Publish Your Essay

Extra! Extra!   Once you have submitted your essay to your teacher, consider publishing it in another way.

- Send your essay to friends or family who may care about the problem.

- If your problem and solution would be of interest to your peers, submit your essay to your school's student newspaper.

- Post your essay to an Internet newsgroup that focuses on the problem.

- Mail your essay to someone who can directly help solve the problem: a local official, your Congressional representative, or a community leader.

- Collaborate with a group of your classmates who may have chosen to write about problems and solutions similar to yours and stage a panel discussion based on your problem and solutions.

- Organize a bulletin board in your classroom or school hallway to inform other students about the problems and solutions your class has explored in their essays. Add visuals to your presentation as necessary.

- Collect problem-solution essays from other students in your class for a class resource booklet.

TIP   Before publishing your essay, check again to make sure it is legible and free of spelling and grammar errors.

Reflect on Your Essay

For Future Use   After setting your final draft aside for a day, return to it and read through it again, jotting down your responses to the following questions.

PORTFOLIO

- Did your choice of problem make your essay easy or difficult to write? Explain.

- What will you do differently when you write your next proposal?

- Do you think you convinced your readers that your proposed solution will work? Why or why not?

- How could you have made your proposal more convincing?

- What changes or refinements to your essay would be necessary before you could send it to a more specific audience, say a government official or a community group? Why would these changes be necessary?

YOUR TURN 9   Proofreading, Publishing, and Reflecting

Be sure to review the preceding proofreading and publishing steps. You might also use your answers to the above reflection questions to set goals for future essays.

Connections to Literature

Problems and Solutions in Literature

Pick up a newspaper or a magazine; turn on the TV. You can't miss nonfiction articles and documentaries about real-life problems. Novels, short stories, plays, and poems deal with problems, too. From *Beowulf* to *Macbeth*, from the novels of Charles Dickens to the stories of Katherine Mansfield, fictional characters struggle with problems (conflicts) that, in one way or another, get solved by the story's end.

It's Personal Broken hearts and bloody revenge—fictional conflicts are likely to involve personal feelings and powerful desires, like love, ambition, and greed. Often, fiction addresses personal conflicts more effectively and memorably than nonfiction. Shakespeare's *Macbeth*, for example, will probably outlast any nonfiction essay on the motives behind murder and the psychological effects of the crime.

What Are the Implications? Nonfiction writers state the problem as clearly as they can, but writers of fiction usually do not; they make you do the work by inferring the conflict. Once the conflict is clear, characters sometimes solve their problems, and sometimes they fail; sometimes there *is* no solution. In the poem "My Last Duchess," for instance,

Robert Browning implies the problem of jealousy and possessiveness. Evidence of the Duke's jealousy is given in lines 23–24:

> ". . . she liked whate'er
> She looked on, and her looks went
> everywhere."

The Duke thinks his wife greets everyone and every event with the same delight. He might have solved the problem by talking to her about her behavior, but the Duke rejects this solution. He chooses "Never to stoop" (line 43). The reader must then speculate about the Duke's ultimate solution.

Troubles Ahead Writers of proposals almost always want to find the best solution, but fiction writers, on the other hand, try to get their characters into trouble. Foolish choices, unfriendly fate, and doomed solutions often make for a memorable reading experience and a deeper understanding of human nature. In D. H. Lawrence's "The Rocking-Horse Winner," for example, the young boy's solution to his family's financial problems—his way of finding luck—works as a powerful, tragic symbol.

Analyze This To analyze problems and solutions in literature, look at these elements.

Elements	Definitions
plot	the series of related events that make up a story or drama
conflict	the problem between opposing forces, characters, or emotions (An *internal* conflict is a struggle within one character. In an *external* conflict, a character struggles against nature, society, or another character.)

complications	plot developments that intensify the conflict, build suspense, or create tension
climax	the turning point, or the moment of greatest suspense or emotional tension
resolution or denouement	ending—easing of tension; resolution of the conflict

You may not be able to identify the conflict in a modern short story. That is because modern writers often focus on the subtle psychology of characters or on details of ordinary lives, which have no clear-cut conflicts and resolutions. (For more on the elements of fiction, see Chapter 2.)

Use the questions in the left-hand column below to analyze conflicts in fiction. The right-hand column shows how one student answered the questions about D. H. Lawrence's "The Rocking-Horse Winner."

Questions	Example Answers
Identify the main **conflict.** What other conflicts can you identify?	There are conflicts at different levels in this story. The main conflict is between appearance and reality. The mother only appears to love her children; the family only appears to be wealthy.
What are the **complications**?	Desperation increases steadily through the story—the mother grows more desperate for money; the boy grows more desperate for love as he sees his efforts fall short of satisfying his mother.
How does the author create **suspense**?	There is suspense in the boy's increasingly frenzied rides on the rocking horse.
What is the story's **climax**?	The boy's final ride and his mother's discovery of his obsessive behavior make the climactic scene.
Was the **resolution** satisfying? Can you think of a better ending?	The resolution is not a happy one, but it is appropriate to the story.

YOUR TURN 10

Discussing Problems and Solutions in Literature

With a small group, choose a work of fiction that you have all read—one with a clear-cut conflict, or problem. Individually, re-read the work and take notes about the conflict and resolution. Then, meet in the group to discuss the work. Each participant should make a contribution relevant to the topic. Use the questions above as a springboard for the discussion. When you're done, summarize your discussion for the entire class. (Save your notes; you might use them for a future paper.)

Talk Listen

WHAT'S AHEAD?

In this section, you will learn how to

- **use a panel discussion format to examine problems and recommend solutions**
- **be an active panel participant**
- **be an active listener**

Conducting a Panel Discussion

Although many solutions to problems appear in written form, you have been using another way of finding solutions since early childhood—talking. In a **panel discussion,** three to six speakers discuss a topic, providing listeners with information and opinions and often trying to arrive at solutions to problems. For example, a city council might invite a panel of students, police, and youth workers to discuss solutions to the problem of graffiti on city signs and buildings. A board of education might ask a panel of teachers, students, and parents to discuss solutions to the problem of dropouts. To ensure that the process works, a panel discussion has a moderator. The other participants come prepared to talk about the topic. Usually, after the last speech, members of the audience ask questions and address comments to panel members.

Preparing for a Panel Discussion

If you are on a panel, use the following steps to prepare for a successful panel discussion.

- **Define the problem to be solved.** Restate the problem in your own words, so that you know exactly what you are planning to solve. (Often, the panel moderator will distribute a written description of the panel's purpose and goals.)

- **Analyze the problem.** Break the problem down into its parts to find places where solutions can be applied.

- **Identify possible solutions.** Propose several possible solutions. If the ground rules of the discussion permit, share ideas with fellow participants before the day of the presentation.

- **Evaluate the evidence.** Think about and, if necessary, research your solutions. Separate facts from opinions, and eliminate irrelevant information and unworkable solutions.

- **Organize your points.** To avoid omitting an important point during discussion, organize the main points and supporting evidence in a way that will be easy for you to use during the panel. You might use note cards with separate solutions as headings on each card. Underneath the headings, you might list your evidence, (facts, details, and quotations from experts) and notes about the solution's advantages and disadvantages.

Your Role as Participant

Throw Your Hat into the Ring   Participation in a panel discussion involves more than just stating your own case. You also must be prepared to listen to different ideas and provide feedback to other participants. In other words, you must be prepared for the give-and-take among panel members.

Being a Cooperative Speaker   When you are part of a panel, remember to show concern for the needs of others as well as your own needs.

- **Volume and Tone**   Speak loud enough to be heard by panel members and the audience. Be polite at all times.

- **Disagreeing**   If you disagree with another panel member's opinions or views, do it in a respectful and constructive way. Disagree with a person's solution, not with the person; ask a question that pinpoints a problem or difficulty with a proposed solution. Defend your own points with precise language and appropriate detail.

- **Interrupting**   Panel members rarely interrupt one another. However, you may interrupt to ask for clarification of a point or to refocus the discussion. Usually, the moderator will take care of these issues.

Being an Active Listener   Whether on the panel or in the audience, good listeners look for meaning, think about what they hear, and respond with both verbal and nonverbal signs. Use the following tips to become a better listener.

- **Think as you listen.** Focus on the speaker's main points, and concentrate on what he or she is saying rather than on what you will say next.

- **Apply what you hear to what you already know.** Relate the information to your own experience and knowledge by asking yourself, "Does that sound right to me? Do I accept that?"

- **Take notes.** Paraphrase, summarize, abbreviate, and focus on key words and main ideas.

- **Give the speaker feedback.** Use eye contact, or nod your head to show that you are listening. Ask relevant questions, or make appropriate comments when given the opportunity.

TIP   When you are on a panel, make sure that you offer meaningful and appropriate comments. Ask yourself:

- Does my remark relate to the problem or solution being discussed?

- Is my remark original—something that has not been said before?

- Does my remark help move the discussion forward?

Reference Note

For more on **active listening,** see page 1029 of the Quick Reference Handbook.

Your Role as Moderator

TIP Keep the discussion moving by preparing a list of questions and following it. When the group reaches consensus, or agreement, summarize that consensus for the audience.

Keep the Peace The success of a panel discussion depends upon every member's taking an active role. The leader, or moderator, has several responsibilities during the discussion itself.

- **Introduce the discussion.** Give a brief overview by presenting essential background information about the problem and discussing key terms related to the discussion.

- **Referee the discussion.** Make sure everyone has an equal chance to participate. Recognize speakers, and encourage participation from members who have not yet contributed. If things get tense between two speakers, defuse the situation by pointing out the shared goal of solving the problem.

- **Keep the discussion on track.** When participants digress, steer the conversation back to the main problem. Encourage politeness; try not to allow the discussion to bog down in interruptions and name-calling.

- **Conclude the discussion.** Summarize the major points made during the discussion. Give members a chance to comment on the summary and modify it.

Working the Q & A Conducting the question and answer session after the panelists have had their discussion is the moderator's hardest job. You are there to bridge the gap between the audience and the panelists. Use the following guidelines to keep the last part of the panel discussion focused on the problem and its solutions.

- **Limit speakers to asking questions.** Politely stop people who digress or who begin giving speeches rather than asking questions.

- **Call on people from all parts of the audience.** Avoid calling on only those in the middle of the audience or those seated in the front rows or those you know best. Give everyone a chance to ask a first question before calling on those with a second question.

- **Make sure panelists answer questions as briefly as possible.** Their conciseness will give more people a chance to ask questions.

TIP When you cannot answer a question during the Q & A session, offer to locate the information and provide it later.

YOUR TURN 11 Solving Problems in a Panel Discussion

Brainstorm a list of problems that exist in your school or community. Select one of them, and then follow the suggestions in this section to prepare and present a panel discussion on the problem and its solutions. During discussion, try to arrive at the best solution or combination of solutions. Note: Your teacher will let you know how many people will be on the panel and the time limitations for the presentation. He or she also may decide to assign a topic instead of letting you choose your own.

Choices

Choose one of the following activities to complete.

▶ **CAREERS**

1. Get a Job Suppose you have a skill that would solve a problem in your community, but there is no existing position for you to fill. For example, there are new computers at the local library, but not enough people know how to use them. You would like to offer after-school computer help. How will you go about convincing the library staff that they should create a position for you? Write a **proposal** in which you convince an employer that what you have to offer would solve a problem he or she may not even perceive.

▶ **ART AND LITERATURE**

2. Another Point of View Choose a literary work that interests you, and, in a series of **drawings,** illustrate the central problem (or problems) and the steps the main character takes to solve that problem. For example, if you choose *Beowulf,* think about how you would illustrate the steps Beowulf takes toward rescuing the Danes from Grendel and his mother. Illustrations might depict Beowulf battling the dragon, and, finally, restoring peace to Herot. Write a descriptive caption for each illustration.

▶ **VIEWING AND REPRESENTING**

3. Watch It Watch a television drama and notice how the characters react to conflict. List the central problem in the episode and any steps that the characters take to resolve it. Note any use of persuasive techniques. Then, in a **brief essay,** give your own personal evaluation of how the characters dealt with their problem. Include in your essay how you would have resolved the problem.

▶ **SPEAKING AND LISTENING**

4. Something to Talk About Take a poll of your classmates about a school-related problem, and listen carefully to their opinions. Go beyond simple yes or no answers, encouraging your classmates to elaborate their reasons, recommend solutions, and suggest steps for implementation. Create a plan for a **political campaign** based on the poll's results. Then, in a short **speech,** give your assessment of the results and present specific ideas about how you would implement a solution to the problem.

PORTFOLIO

Sentences and Paragraphs

10 | Writing Clear Sentences

internet connect

go.hrw.com

GO TO: go.hrw.com
KEYWORD: EOLang

Ways to Achieve Clarity

Have you ever stepped from a warm room into the surprisingly cold, crisp air outside? Did everything seem sharper, your mind suddenly alert and focused? Like the first cold snap of fall, clear writing also commands our attention. Clarity is essential in conveying information, whether your purpose is to explain the steam engine or to describe your new neighborhood. One of the best ways to bring clarity to your writing is to show the appropriate relationships between ideas. To do this, you must adjust and revise the structure of each sentence until it accurately communicates your message. *Coordinating* and *subordinating* ideas are two ways to sharpen and clarify your writing.

Coordinating Ideas

Ideas that are equally important—or that carry the same weight—in a sentence are called **coordinate** ideas. To show that ideas are coordinate, you link them with a coordinating conjunction, such as *and* or *but* or another connective. Sometimes the connective may simply be a punctuation mark, such as the semicolon in the second example that follows.

EXAMPLES The Pathfinder lander was sending back its first images of the surface of Mars, **and** everyone was focused on the television screens.

Matthew P. Golombek, "The Mars Pathfinder Mission," *Scientific American*

Crisp foods have to be loud in the upper register; foods which generate low-frequency rumblings are crunchy, or slurpy, but not crisp.

David Bodanis, *The Secret House*

The connective you use shows the relationship between the ideas. For example, *and* links similar ideas, while *but* links contrasting ideas. The following chart lists connecting words you can use to show *addition, contrast, choice,* and *result*.

Addition	Contrast	Choice	Result
also	but	either . . . or	accordingly
and	however	neither . . . nor	consequently
as well as	nevertheless		for
besides	still	nor	hence
both . . . and	yet	or	so
		otherwise	therefore
			thus

Reference Note

For more about **conjunctions,** see page 519.

When you use connectives to join words, phrases, or subordinate clauses (clauses that do not express complete thoughts), the result is a compound element in your sentence; these compound elements may be subjects, verbs, modifiers, or complements. When you use coordination to join complete thoughts, or independent clauses, the result is a compound sentence.

CONTRAST Elijah **slurped** his soup **but wiped** his mouth neatly afterward. [compound verb]

CHOICE **Either Regina or Bookie** will go to the movie with me. [compound subject]

ADDITION Basketball players are generally **tall, fit, and quick.** [compound predicate adjective]

RESULT **Mack's hair was uncombed;** consequently, **he looked too messy for the photo.** [compound sentence]

Be sure to choose a connective that shows the correct relationship between the linked ideas. Otherwise, your meaning will not be clear to your readers.

UNCLEAR   Nell looked for her wallet, and she couldn't find it anywhere.
CLEAR   Nell looked for her wallet, **but** she couldn't find it anywhere.
          [contrast]

UNCLEAR   Floss your teeth, yet you might get gum disease.
CLEAR   Floss your teeth; **otherwise,** you might get gum disease.
          [choice]

NOTE   When you use a coordinating conjunction to link independent clauses, put a comma before the conjunction unless the clauses are very short.

EXAMPLES   Vikram made peach cobbler, and he brought it to the picnic.

           Carly drove and Sandra slept.

When you use a conjunctive adverb to join independent clauses, put a semicolon before the adverb and a comma after it.

EXAMPLE   Francine studied hard for the driving exam; however, she overslept on the day of the test.

Reference Note

For more about **punctuating compound sentences,** see page 830.

Exercise 1 Using Appropriate Connectives

Complete each of the following sentences by deciding which connecting word(s) will best fit in the blank(s). Remember to use the correct punctuation with the connective you choose.

EXAMPLE   1. Princess Kaiulani was King Kalakaua's niece _____ Hawaii's last princess.

          1. *and*

1. Fourteen-year-old Kaiulani was quite young to travel long distances _____ she was sent to Great Britain from Hawaii anyway.
2. Kaiulani's family wanted to prepare her to assume the role of queen of Hawaii _____ Kaiulani was sent to Great Britain for a traditional education.
3. Kaiulani was halfway across the world from Hawaii _____ she managed to keep in touch with Hawaiian events through letters.
4. _____ friends _____ family members kept her informed of events in her homeland.

Princess Kaiulani

5. Kaiulani was glad to hear from her friends and family _____ she was unhappy to hear of increasing trouble with American business leaders known as *haoles* (pronounced *HOU-LEES*), or "foreigners."

6. These haoles wanted to annex Hawaii to the United States _____ Kaiulani's uncle considered them his enemies.

7. Many Hawaiians resisted annexation to the United States _____ in 1893, a group of powerful haoles overthrew the royal family _____ took control of the government.

8. In 1893, Kaiulani was still only a teenager _____ she acted decisively when she heard the news.

9. She went to New York in March 1893 _____ read a statement addressed "to the American People."

10. Kaiulani's persuasive statement gained the support of many Americans _____ the forces of annexation triumphed _____ in 1898, Hawaii was transferred to the United States.

King Kalakaua

Subordinating Ideas

Not all ideas are created equal. Sometimes, one idea in a sentence is more important than another, and you will want to downplay, or *subordinate,* the less important idea.

One way to subordinate an idea is to place it in a *subordinate clause.* Used as part of a sentence, the subordinate clause elaborates on the thought expressed in an independent clause.

EXAMPLES   Petra, **who is learning how to scuba dive,** took a trip to the coast.

Michael likes going to the coast **because the beaches are clean and uncrowded.**

The kinds of subordinate clauses you will use most often are *adverb clauses* and *adjective clauses.*

Adverb Clauses

An *adverb clause* modifies a verb, an adjective, or another adverb in a sentence. You introduce an adverb clause with a subordinating conjunction such as *although, after, because, if, when,* or *while.* The conjunction shows how the adverb clause relates to the main clause.

Reference Note

For more about the **types of subordinate clauses,** see page 577.

Usually, the conjunction shows a relationship of *time, cause or reason, purpose or result,* or *condition.*

TIME   At Bonanza Creek, **while our socks dried by the fire,** we fished for arctic grayling.

Barry Lopez, Crossing Open Ground

CAUSE OR REASON   **Because it is a direct reflection of the pressure and movement of the artist's hand across the surface of the painting,** brushwork is one of the most intimate links that we, as viewers, have with the artist's mind at work.

Dawson W. Carr and Mark Leonard, Looking at Paintings

PURPOSE OR RESULT   A synergy kicks in, **so that when you're finished, you drag yourself to the locker room in a state of euphoria, amazed at what you've done, completely drained.**

John Davidson, "Reach Your Peak," Self

CONDITION   He ran so hard that he could feel the sweat fly from his head and arms, **though it was winter and the air was filled with snow.**

N. Scott Momaday, House Made of Dawn

The following chart lists subordinating conjunctions you can use to show each kind of relationship.

Time	Cause	Purpose	Condition
after	as	in order that	although
as	because	so that	despite
before	even though	such that	if
since	since	that	provided that
until	unless		though
when	whereas		
whenever	while		
while			

Exercise 2 **Choosing Appropriate Subordinating Conjunctions**

Each of the following sentences is missing a subordinating conjunction. First, decide what the relationship is between the independent clause and the subordinate clause. Then, choose a subordinating conjunction that clearly shows that relationship.

1. _____ atmospheric scientists discovered a large hole in the ozone layer in the 1980s, people have been concerned about ozone depletion.
2. _____ scientists disagree about the exact cause of ozone depletion, many attribute the phenomenon to the effects of pollution.
3. Ozone depletion is a concern _____ ozone in the stratosphere protects the earth from the sun's harmful ultraviolet radiation.
4. _____ ultraviolet radiation is necessary to life on earth, overexposure to it is known to cause skin cancer among people and the destruction of many plant and animal species.
5. _____ the ozone layer is depleted, the risk of overexposure for humans and other species increases dramatically.
6. _____ scientists discovered the hole in the ozone layer, people feared that the hole would spread to other parts of the world.
7. Chlorofluorocarbons (CFCs) are believed by some to be responsible _____ these CFCs may break down ozone.
8. CFCs are released into the atmosphere _____ things such as aerosol spray cans, refrigerants, and other manufacturing products are used.
9. _____ there has been disagreement over the exact cause of ozone destruction, industrial countries took steps to reduce the use of CFCs during the 1980s and 1990s.
10. In 1994, Germany banned CFC production _____ depletion of the ozone layer might be prevented.

STYLE**TIP**

It is possible to use too many subordinate clauses in a sentence. Excessive subordination occurs when too many subordinate clauses are strung together. This type of sentence makes it difficult for the reader to keep track of the main idea of the independent clause.

Exercise 3 Revising Sentences by Inserting Adverb Clauses

Revise each of the following sentences by adding an adverb clause. Use a different subordinating conjunction for each sentence. (Note: Remember to add a comma if you place the clause at the sentence's beginning.)

EXAMPLE   1. Photography is a fun activity.

1. *Photography is a fun activity because it allows you to be creative.*

1. We tried to take some photographs outside.
2. We learned how to control the film's exposure to light.
3. You should try taking photographs of animals sometime.
4. Many schools offer courses in photography.
5. Some of the best photos I have taken were shot with an inexpensive camera.

HELP

You don't need to know anything about photography to revise the sentences for Exercise 3. Just use your imagination.

Adjective Clauses

You can also subordinate an idea by placing it in an **adjective clause,** a subordinate clause that modifies a noun or a pronoun in a sentence. An adjective clause usually begins with *who, whom, whose, which, that,* or *where.*

EXAMPLE   I propped myself against the brick wall of the schoolhouse, **where the school delinquent found me.**

Henry Louis Gates, Jr., "A Giant Step," *The New York Times*

Before you use an adjective clause in a sentence, you need to decide which idea in the sentence you want to subordinate. Suppose you wanted to combine these two ideas in one sentence:

Albert Einstein was born in 1879. He is considered one of the greatest scientists of the twentieth century.

If you wanted to emphasize that Einstein was born in 1879, you would put that information in an independent clause and the other information in an adjective clause.

Albert Einstein, **who is considered one of the greatest scientists of the twentieth century,** was born in 1879.

To emphasize that Einstein is considered one of the greatest scientists of the twentieth century, put his birth information in an adjective clause.

Albert Einstein, **who was born in 1879,** is considered one of the greatest scientists of the twentieth century.

Reference Note

For more about **combining sentences by subordinating ideas,** see page 447.

HELP

When completing Exercise 4, you may have to delete or add some words or change the word order.

Exercise 4 Subordinating Ideas by Using Adjective Clauses

Switch the emphasis on ideas in each of the following sentences. Emphasize the idea that is now in the subordinate clause and subordinate the idea that is now in the independent clause. Which version sounds better and clearer to you?

1. The term *baby boom,* which most people now recognize, refers to the generation born in the United States between the late 1940s and the early 1960s.
2. The previous generation, which had lived though the economic hardships of the 1930s and early 1940s, put off having children until the end of World War II.

3. These children, who are called baby boomers because of their generation, were born in the stable years following World War II.
4. Many of the baby boomers, who grew up during relatively peaceful and prosperous times, saw themselves as being very different from people in their parents' generation.
5. The baby boom generation, which is best known for rebelling against the previous generation's traditions, created a flourishing youth culture during the 1960s and 1970s.

Correcting Faulty Coordination

In everyday speech, we tend to be casual about stringing together ideas with *and*. In writing, though, it is essential to show clearly the relationships among ideas. If you use a coordinating conjunction to join ideas that are not coordinate, or equal, you end up with *faulty coordination.*

To avoid faulty coordination, check each compound sentence to see if the ideas are really equal in importance. If they are not, subordinate the less-important idea by placing it in a subordinate clause or a phrase. You may need to add, delete, or rearrange words in the sentence.

FAULTY   This male butterfly is distinguishable from females of its species, and its wings reflect ultraviolet light.

REVISED   **Because its wings reflect ultraviolet light,** this male butterfly is distinguishable from females of its species. [adverb clause]

FAULTY   Malaria is a serious infectious disease, and it can be transmitted to humans through mosquito bites.

REVISED   Malaria, **which can be transmitted to humans through mosquito bites,** is a serious infectious disease. [adjective clause]

FAULTY   The light was at the end of the pier, and it showed us how far we had walked.

REVISED   The light **at the end of the pier** showed us how far we had walked. [prepositional phrase]

FAULTY   Tama was the lifeguard on duty that day, and she saved the drowning child.

REVISED   Tama, **the lifeguard on duty that day,** saved the drowning child. [appositive phrase]

Butterfly under normal light

Butterfly under ultraviolet light

NOTE   After revising a sentence, re-read it within the context of the longer passage to make sure the relationship between ideas is accurately conveyed.

HELP

In Exercise 5, you may need to add or delete some words or change the punctuation.

Exercise 5 Revising Sentences by Correcting Faulty Coordination

Revise each of the following sentences by placing one of the ideas in a subordinate clause or in a phrase. Make sure each revised sentence shows the relationship between ideas that you think is most accurate.

1. Charlotte and Emily Brontë were sisters, and they both produced novels of enduring popularity and significance.
2. They lived in Yorkshire, and Yorkshire is a former county in England.
3. Yorkshire is now divided into three counties, and the area is on the North Sea.
4. Emily and Charlotte Brontë wrote novels, and the novels depict the complicated emotional lives of their characters.
5. Both authors drew upon the Yorkshire moors as a setting, and they wrote passionately about the landscape.

Using Parallel Structure

To create clarity and rhythm in a sentence, it is important to express similar ideas in similar grammatical forms. For example, pair an adjective with an adjective, a prepositional phrase with a prepositional phrase, and a noun clause with a noun clause. When you use the same grammatical form for similar ideas, you create *parallel structure.*

EXAMPLES   He had come to tell his brother **that power corrupts, that a man who fights for justice must himself be cleansed and purified, that love is greater than force.**

Alan Paton, *Cry, the Beloved Country*

Scribes were needed **to send messages, to convey news, to take down the king's orders, to register the laws. . . .**

Alberto Manguel, *A History of Reading*

He was the **weather-beaten, brown-faced, black-eyed** Cupid of the community.

Jovita González, "The Mail Carrier"

Remember to use parallel structure when you link coordinate ideas, as the following examples show.

FAULTY	Amanda's favorite forms of exercise are swimming and to run. [gerund paired with infinitive]
PARALLEL	Amanda's favorite forms of exercise are **swimming** and **running.** [gerund paired with gerund]

FAULTY	Derrick's editorial shows his knowledge and that he is passionate about the subject. [noun paired with noun clause]
PARALLEL	Derrick's editorial shows **that he is knowledgeable about the subject** and **that he is passionate about it.** [noun clause paired with noun clause]

Use parallel structure when you compare or contrast ideas.

FAULTY	Reading novels no longer interests me as much as to read poems. [gerund contrasted with infinitive]
PARALLEL	**Reading novels** no longer interests me as much as **reading poems.** [gerund contrasted with gerund]

FAULTY	In sports, enthusiasm is as important as that you have skill. [noun paired with noun clause]
PARALLEL	In sports, **enthusiasm** is as important as **skill.** [noun paired with noun]

Use parallel structure when you link ideas with correlative conjunctions (*both . . . and, either . . . or, neither . . . nor,* and *not only . . . but also).*

FAULTY	The medicine woman was revered not only for her healing abilities but also because she possessed wisdom. [prepositional phrase correlated with adverb clause]
PARALLEL	The medicine woman was revered not only **for her healing abilities** but also **for her wisdom.** [prepositional phrase correlated with prepositional phrase]

To avoid awkwardness and confusion, place correlative conjunctions directly before the parallel terms.

UNCLEAR	Shawna considered both pursuing careers in law and in journalism.
BETTER	Shawna considered pursuing careers **both** in law **and** in journalism.

UNCLEAR	Our choice of eight o'clock movies either was *Slime* or *Return of the Insect People.*
BETTER	Our choice of eight o'clock movies was **either** *Slime* **or** *Return of the Insect People.*

TIPS & TRICKS

To check for faulty parallelism in your writing, look for the words *and* and *or*. Then check on each side of these words to see that the items joined are parallel. If the two items on either side of *and* are not parallel, revise one of them.

FAULTY
She walked *proudly* <u>and</u> *in a big hurry.*

PARALLEL
She walked *proudly* <u>and</u> *swiftly.*

Creating sentences in which elements are parallel in form but not parallel in meaning is a common mistake. Remember that it is necessary to compare like, or similar, things. Comparing unlike things will not make sense to your readers.

Look at how the first example below compares two unlike things:

FAULTY
Arthur's pitching skills are better than the batting skills of Steve.

PARALLEL
Arthur's pitching skills are better than those of Steve.

When you create parallel structure, you often need to repeat an article, a preposition, or a pronoun before each of the parallel terms to make your meaning clear. Notice how the first version of each of the following sentences might be misread.

UNCLEAR   Before leaving the store, I talked with the clerk and manager.

BETTER   Before leaving the store, I talked with **the** clerk and **the** manager.

UNCLEAR   This Elvis biography reveals more about the era of the 1950s than the singer himself.

BETTER   This Elvis biography reveals more **about** the era of the 1950s than **about** the singer himself.

To clarify your meaning, you will often need to add a few words to the second part of a sentence that uses parallel structure.

UNCLEAR   I enjoyed the singing of the opera's soprano more than the tenor.

BETTER   I enjoyed the singing of the opera's soprano more than **that of** the tenor.

NOTE   For many writers, parallel structure is an important stylistic tool. Parallelism creates natural rhythm and flow in both prose and poetry. In the following stanza, notice that a string of parallel phrases follows the preposition *between*.

> On visiting days with aunts and uncles,
> I was shuttled back and forth—
> between Chavez bourgeois in the city
> and rural Lucero sheepherders,
> new cars and gleaming furniture
> and leather saddles and burlap sacks,
> noon football games and six packs of cokes
> and hoes, welfare cards and bottles of goat milk.
>
> Jimmy Santiago Baca, "Martín &
> Meditations on the South Valley"

When you use parallelism as a stylistic device in your own writing, revise by reading your work aloud, listening for a strong and consistent rhythm. If you cannot hear the rhythm of parallel statements, rework your sentences.

Some of the following sentences are unclear because they lack parallel structure. Revise each faulty sentence by putting parallel ideas into the same grammatical form. Add, delete, move, and replace words and punctuation as necessary. If a sentence is already in parallel form, write *C* for *correct*.

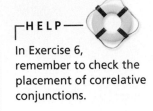

HELP

In Exercise 6, remember to check the placement of correlative conjunctions.

1. Kwame Nkrumah is known not only as the first prime minister of the African country Ghana but also because he led the country to independence from British rule.
2. Ghana interests many because it was called the Gold Coast by the British and then was the first of Britain's colonies to achieve independence after World War II.
3. Born in 1909, Nkrumah's educational influences included studying in the United States and that he was interested in Pan-Africanism.
4. After his study in the United States and attending a Pan-African conference in Great Britain in 1945, Nkrumah returned to the Gold Coast in 1947.
5. During the late 1940s, Nkrumah became the leader of the Gold Coast nationalist movement, not only through his organizing ability but also because he had great determination.
6. Nkrumah's goals were to gather wide popular support for the nationalist movement and gaining self-government apart from the British.
7. Nkrumah established the Convention People's Party, or CPP, in 1949 and led demonstrations and strikes in support of the cause.
8. Although the British jailed him, Nkrumah and the CPP were successful both popularly and as far as becoming major political forces.
9. Because of this pressure, the British both agreed to allow national elections and to grant a self-governing constitution in 1951.
10. Nkrumah's leadership led to CPP victory in the elections and that Britain granted the Gold Coast full self-government in 1957.

Review A **Revising Paragraphs for Clarity**

The following paragraphs are confusing because they contain faulty coordination and faulty parallelism. Using what you have learned, make each faulty sentence smoother and clearer. Remember to add, delete, or rearrange words and punctuation marks as necessary.

Sherman Alexie

Sherman Alexie is an American Indian of Spokane and Coeur d'Alene ancestry, and he writes powerfully about the experiences of American Indians. He is a prolific writer, and Alexie's writings include poetry, novels, short stories, essays, and screenplays. Alexie is known for his writing as well as producing and directing films based on his work. Alexie's depictions of American Indian life are sometimes grim, but the grittiness is often tempered by Alexie's wit and being humorous.

Alexie wrote and produced the movie <u>Smoke Signals</u>, and the film was released in 1998. <u>Smoke Signals</u> is the first Native American-produced, Native American-directed feature film written by an American Indian. The two lead characters in the film are American Indian men in their twenties who travel by bus across the country. One is sullen and angry, and he finds an outlet in playing basketball. The other one likes to tell long, involved stories and talking about his grandmother's frybread. These characters reflect Alexie's fresh and confident point of view and that he consciously works against the stereotypes of American Indians that have prevailed in our culture.

Alexie's portrayals of American Indians have won him acclaim from many critics, and they have also drawn reproach. Some people find Alexie's works dark, and they believe Alexie should write more optimistically about the life for American Indians. Alexie has said that he wants people to be provoked by what he writes and he seems comfortable with making people uncomfortable at times. As a talented and productive writer, who both enjoys critical success and a good fight, Alexie is likely to continue to shape the way we see contemporary American Indians.

Obstacles to Clarity

In this part of the chapter, you will learn how to check your writing for some common obstacles to clarity: *sentence fragments, run-on sentences,* and *unnecessary shifts.*

Sentence Fragments

A sentence expresses a complete thought. If you punctuate a part of a sentence as if it were a whole sentence, you create a *sentence fragment.* Fragments are usually confusing because the reader has to puzzle out the missing information.

FRAGMENT   In 1929, the global economy into a worldwide depression. [missing verb]

SENTENCE   In 1929, the global economy **collapsed** into a worldwide depression.

FRAGMENT   We observing the bacteria through a powerful microscope. [missing helping verb]

SENTENCE   We **were** observing the bacteria through a powerful microscope.

FRAGMENT   Photographed families who were victims of the Great Depression. [missing subject]

SENTENCE   **Dorothea Lange** photographed families who were victims of the Great Depression.

FRAGMENT   By closing the park to bicycle riders and skateboarders. [not a complete thought]

SENTENCE   **The city tried to cut down on accidents** by closing the park to bicycle riders and skateboarders.

Phrase Fragments

A *phrase* is a group of words that does not have a subject and a verb. When a phrase is separated from the sentence it belongs with, it becomes a *phrase fragment.*

FRAGMENT   I found my sister in the den. **Making origami swans out of blue and green paper.** [participial phrase fragment]

SENTENCE   I found my sister in the den making origami swans out of blue and green paper.

FRAGMENT   My sister is good at figuring out how to do things. **With very little instruction.** [prepositional phrase fragment]

SENTENCE   My sister is good at figuring out how to do things with very little instruction.

FRAGMENT   She just sits down and gives herself enough time. **To ensure her success.** [infinitive phrase fragment]

SENTENCE   She just sits down and gives herself enough time to ensure her success.

FRAGMENT	Later, my sister made me two beautiful objects. **An origami snail and a fish.** [appositive phrase fragment]
SENTENCE	Later, my sister made me two beautiful objects, an origami snail and a fish.

Subordinate Clause Fragments

A **subordinate clause** has a subject and a verb but does not express a complete thought. Unlike an independent clause, a subordinate clause cannot stand on its own as a sentence.

FRAGMENT	Sea urchins have long, moveable spines. **Which they use to push themselves across the ocean floor.** [adjective clause fragment]
SENTENCE	Sea urchins have long, moveable spines, which they use to push themselves across the ocean floor.

FRAGMENT	Sea urchins can also be eaten in sushi. **After they have been harvested from the sea and properly prepared.** [adverb clause fragment]
SENTENCE	Sea urchins can also be eaten in sushi, after they have been harvested from the sea and properly prepared.

Sea Urchin

NOTE A complete sentence is usually the clearest way to express a thought. However, experienced writers sometimes use fragments for stylistic effect. For example, in the following passage, notice how each fragment creates a precise image and how, grouped together, they recreate the rhythm of a child's day.

> There had been a fight about who was to be "It" next. It had been so fierce that their mother had emerged from her bath and made them change to another game. Then they had played another and another. Broken mulberries from the tree and eaten them. Helped the driver wash the car when their father returned from work. Helped the gardener water the beds till he roared at them and swore he would complain to their parents. The parents had come out, taken up their positions on the cane chairs. They had begun to play again, sing and chant. All this time no one had remembered Ravi. Having disappeared from the scene, he had disappeared from their minds. Clean.
>
> Anita Desai, "Games at Twilight"

You can use fragments occasionally in expressive and creative writing such as journal entries and short stories. For example, you might use fragments in dialogue to capture the natural sounds of your characters' speech. You can also use fragments in classified ads and other types of writing where an informal, shorthand style is appropriate. However, avoid fragments in informative writing such as research papers and reports. Because your readers expect formal, straightforward language in this type of writing, fragments may confuse your message.

Exercise 7 Revising to Eliminate Fragments

Some of the following items contain sentence fragments. Revise each item by combining any fragments with the adjoining sentences. Move or add words and punctuation marks as necessary. If the item is already correct, just write *C*.

1. Elizabeth Blackwell was born in 1821. And died in 1910.
2. In 1832, her parents immigrated with their eight children to New York. To escape an unpleasant social and political situation in Bristol, England.
3. Because of the financial plight of her family. Blackwell and her mother established a boarding school.
4. A friend of Blackwell's encouraged her to become a doctor. At first, Blackwell totally rejected this suggestion.
5. Eventually, Blackwell became interested in the idea of becoming a doctor. Leading her to investigate the possibility of a woman studying medicine.
6. She became even more determined to follow her friend's advice. After she was told that it would be impossible for a woman to become a doctor.
7. In 1847, Elizabeth Blackwell was granted admission to the Medical Institution of Geneva College. Which is today known as Hobart College.
8. She became the first woman in the United States to earn an M.D. degree. When she graduated in 1849 at the head of her class.
9. Elizabeth was not content with these honors. She spent the next two years doing graduate work in Europe.
10. In 1857, Elizabeth Blackwell established the New York Infirmary for Women and Children, a hospital staffed by women. She opened the hospital on May 12, the birthday of her friend Florence Nightingale.

Run-on Sentences

A **run-on sentence** is just the opposite of a fragment. It is made up of two complete sentences run together as if they were one sentence. Most run-ons are **comma splices**—two complete thoughts that have only a comma between them. Other run-ons, called **fused sentences,** have no punctuation between the two thoughts. The following examples show four ways to correct run-ons.

| RUN-ON | Naomi longed to make the basketball team, to achieve her goal, she practiced every afternoon. |
| CORRECT | Naomi longed make the basketball team**.** **To** achieve her goal, she practiced every afternoon. [two sentences] |

| RUN-ON | She tried different exercises, her skills showed no improvement. |
| CORRECT | She tried different exercises**,** **but** her skills showed no improvement. [compound sentence with comma and coordinating conjunction] |

| RUN-ON | Naomi worked hard, she was persistent. |
| CORRECT | Naomi worked hard**;** she was persistent. [compound sentence with semicolon] |

| RUN-ON | Her hard work paid off later she made the team. |
| CORRECT | Her hard work paid off**;** **later,** she made the team. [compound sentence with semicolon plus conjunctive adverb] |

Exercise 8 Revising Run-on Sentences

Revise each of the following run-ons by using one of the methods you have learned. Use each of the four methods at least once.

1. Exercise can increase the efficiency of your muscles, it can increase your muscles' strength and size.
2. Aerobic exercise helps your body supply oxygen to muscles, it increases the efficiency of the production of ATP, adenosine triphosphate.
3. ATP is a biological molecule scientists consider it the cell's fuel.
4. Some of the energy from food molecules is stored in ATP a steady supply of ATP is essential to cell functioning.
5. With aerobic exercise the heart pumps more efficiently, then the number of blood vessels in your muscles increases.

Unnecessary Shifts in Sentences

For clarity, it is usually best to keep the same subject and the same verb form throughout a sentence. Unnecessary shifts in subject, tense, or voice can make a sentence awkward to read.

Shifts in Subject

Note that sometimes, especially in short compound sentences, a shift in subject is necessary to express your intended meaning. In the following sentence, the shift in subject is natural.

NATURAL SHIFT   Jesse jumped off the swing, but no one caught him.

Most often, though, a shift in subject is awkward and unnecessary. In the following examples, notice that each sentence is much clearer when it has the same subject throughout.

AWKWARD   The Mullaneys have a new puppy, and the shelter is where they found it.

BETTER   **The Mullaneys** have a new puppy, and **they** found it at the shelter.

AWKWARD   All runners should be at the track by 7:00 so that you can pick up your registration forms.

BETTER   **All runners** should be at the track by 7:00 so that **they** can pick up their registration forms.

Shifts in Verb Tense and Voice

Unnecessarily changing verb tense or voice in midsentence can also create awkwardness and confusion. Stick to the tense and voice you start with unless you have a good reason for changing.

AWKWARD   Aldo talked about going to the North Pole, but then he goes to the Antarctic. [shift from past tense to present tense]

BETTER   Aldo **talked** about going to the North Pole, but then he **went** to the Antarctic. [past tense throughout]

AWKWARD   Volunteers made the dangerous journey after dark, but no wolves were encountered. [shift from active voice to passive voice]

BETTER   Volunteers **made** the dangerous journey after dark, but they **encountered** no wolves.

A shift in voice usually causes a shift in subject, too. Notice that in the awkward sentence in the last pair, the shift from active to passive voice results in a shift from the subject *volunteers* to the subject *wolves*.

TIPS & TRICKS

Often, the best way to correct a shift in subject and voice in a compound sentence is to create a compound verb. Just omit the second subject and place the second verb in the same voice as the first.

AWKWARD
   Julio Cortázar attended the University of Buenos Aires, and then literary translation work was done.

BETTER
   Julio Cortázar attended the University of Buenos Aires and then **did** literary translation work.

Reference Note

For more about **tense,** see page 692. For more about **active and passive voice,** see pages 405 and 705.

Exercise 9 Eliminating Unnecessary Shifts in Subject, Tense, and Voice

Most of the following sentences contain unnecessary shifts from one subject to another or from one verb to another. Revise each awkward sentence, adding, deleting, or rearranging words as necessary. If a sentence does not need to be revised, write *C* for *correct*.

1. Only four types of creatures have conquered the air, and this group is comprised of insects, pterosaurs, birds, and bats.
2. These flying animals share striking similarities, but major differences have also been found among them.
3. Birds possess feathers, and this unique feature is beneficial to birds.
4. Feathers are well-suited to flight and are easily replaceable.
5. Scientists think a creature called Archaeopteryx is the earliest known bird, and they estimated that it lived about 150 million years ago.
6. Archaeopteryx was roughly the size of a crow, and it has shared features with some of the smaller dinosaurs.
7. Archaeopteryx had teeth and a tail, and, unlike present-day birds, solid bones were also characteristic of the creature.
8. However, this creature possessed feathers, which dinosaurs do not have, and wishbones were also part of their skeletal structure.
9. Some biologists have called birds "feathered dinosaurs"; however, birds are classified in a separate class, *Aves*, by most biologists.
10. Within this class, there are 28 orders of birds and about 8,800 species.

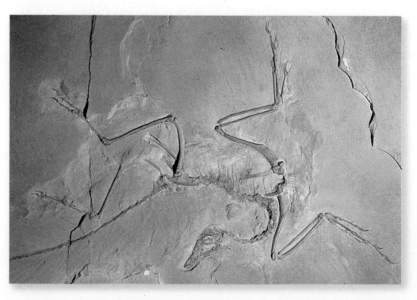

Fossil of Archaeopteryx

Fragments, run-ons, and unnecessary shifts in subject, tense, and voice make the following paragraphs awkward and unclear. Using the methods you have learned, revise the sentences to eliminate these obstacles to clarity. Notice how much smoother the paragraphs sound when you are finished.

Dorothy West began writing stories when she was seven, and several Boston Post prizes were won by her while she was a teenager. Opportunity published West's story "The Typewriter." Which later appeared in The Best Short Stories of 1926.

West born in Boston but eventually settled in New York City, there West met many writers of the Harlem Renaissance. Including Zora Neale Hurston and Langston Hughes. In the early 1930s, she founded Challenge, a magazine that published the works of young African American writers. Because many Harlem Renaissance writers were published in West's magazine, West is often considered a member of that group. However, her own writing published long after the height of the Harlem Renaissance movement. West stopped Challenge in 1937 and started a new, more political magazine named New Challenge later that same year it published the work of Richard Wright and Ralph Ellison.

After West's magazine ventures failed. She took a job as a welfare investigator in Harlem, she later joined the Federal Writers' Project. She became a contributor to the New York Daily News. Which published many of her stories. In 1945 West moved to Martha's Vineyard, where her novel The Living Is Easy was written.

Her most successful novel, The Wedding, was published in 1995, and West tells the story of a young woman of the Vineyard's black elite who marries a poor white jazz musician in The Wedding. West died in 1998. At the age of ninety-one.

Dorothy West

Combining Sentences

Combining for Variety

Have you ever found your mind drifting while reading, despite real efforts to concentrate? (Be honest.) Choppy sentences can make it hard to concentrate. Of course, a short, simple sentence is sometimes just the thing you want; short sentences can be used to create emphasis. If you use only short sentences, however, you probably will not hold your reader's attention for very long. Take a look at the following passage. Does its style help hold your attention, or do you find it hard to focus on the paragraph's meaning?

> The sinking of the <u>Titanic</u> was one of the worst maritime disasters in history. The <u>Titanic</u> was the largest ship of its time. It was the most luxurious ship of its time. The <u>Titanic</u> was on its maiden voyage. The ship struck an iceberg. The iceberg was located off the Grand Banks of Newfoundland. The accident happened on the night of April 14, 1912. The night was clear and cold. The <u>Titanic</u>'s hull had sixteen watertight compartments. The iceberg punctured five compartments. The ship sank in less than three hours.

When some of the sentences are combined to create longer, more varied ones, the passage sounds smoother and more interesting.

> The sinking of the <u>Titanic</u>, the largest and most luxurious ship of its time, was one of

the worst maritime disasters in history. On
the clear, cold night of April 14, 1912, the
ship, which was on its maiden voyage, struck
an iceberg off the Grand Banks of Newfound-
land. The iceberg punctured five of the sixteen watertight compartments in the ship's
hull, and the ship sank in less than three
hours.

Sentence-combining techniques can help you create balance,
rhythm, and precision in your writing. In this chapter, you will learn
several techniques for combining sentences to improve variety and style.

Inserting Words and Phrases

Sometimes, a sentence adds only a little information to a more important idea that appears before or after it. Instead of giving a small detail
a sentence of its own, you can insert that detail into another sentence
as a word or phrase. By combining the sentences, you eliminate extra
words and repeated ideas. (Notice, for example, how many words are
repeated in the four sentences printed below.)

FOUR SENTENCES   The surgeon considered doing the operation. The
                  operation would be simple. The surgeon was experi-
                  enced. She thought the operation would go smoothly.

ONE SENTENCE   **Thinking it would go smoothly,** the **experienced**
                  surgeon considered doing the **simple** operation.

                  or

                  The **experienced** surgeon considered doing the **sim-
                  ple** operation, **as she thought it would go
                  smoothly.**

Often, the words or phrases you are inserting can be placed in
several different ways. Just make sure your combined sentence sounds
clear and expresses the meaning you intend. Watch out for awkward,
confusing combinations like this one: *Thinking it would go smoothly,
the surgeon, who was experienced, considered doing the operation, which
would be simple.*

Single-Word Modifiers

Before you take a word from one sentence and insert it into another sentence, check to make sure the word can act as a modifier in the second sentence. You may need to change the word into an adverb or adjective before you insert it.

USING THE SAME FORM

ORIGINAL   Angela de Hoyos is a Mexican American poet. She is an award-winning poet.

COMBINED   Angela de Hoyos is an **award-winning** Mexican American poet.

ORIGINAL   De Hoyos has spoken out against racism and social oppression. She has spoken out publicly.

COMBINED   De Hoyos has spoken out **publicly** against racism and social oppression.

CHANGING THE FORM

ORIGINAL   She was involved in the revolution of the 1960s. It was a revolution of the culture.

COMBINED   She was involved in the **cultural** revolution of the 1960s.

ORIGINAL   In her poetry de Hoyos often explores themes through humor. The humor is based on irony.

COMBINED   In her poetry de Hoyos often explores themes through **ironic** humor.

Reference Note

For more about **prepositional phrases,** see page 554.

Prepositional Phrases

Usually, you can insert a prepositional phrase without any change in form.

ORIGINAL   Ole likes contemporary American films. He likes the ones with ensemble casts.

COMBINED   Ole likes contemporary American films **with ensemble casts.**

Sometimes you can change a part of one sentence into a prepositional phrase and then insert it into another sentence.

ORIGINAL   These movies make Ole weep. He cries tears of joy.

COMBINED   These movies make Ole weep **with tears of joy.**

Combining Sentences by Inserting Adjectives, Adverbs, and Prepositional Phrases

Combine each of the following groups of short sentences by inserting adjectives, adverbs, or prepositional phrases from the second and third sentences into the first sentence. Read your combined sentences aloud to make sure the meaning is clear.

EXAMPLE   1. Fungi make up one of the kingdoms of life. There are six kingdoms of life. Most fungi are multicellular organisms.

            1. *The mostly multicellular fungi make up one of the six kingdoms of life.*

1. Fungi secrete enzymes to get their food. The enzymes are digestive. Their food is organic.
2. The enzymes break down plant and animal matter. The matter is complex. The matter is broken into simple compounds.
3. You can find fungi growing on trees. These trees would be fallen. They would be on the forest floor.
4. The roots of most trees are surrounded by growing fungi. The fungi grow close to the roots. This association between roots and fungi is called a mycorrhiza.
5. You might find fungi, known as lichen. These fungi might be brown or brightly colored. You might find the fungi on rocks.

Participial Phrases

A *participial phrase* contains a participle and its modifiers and complements. Participial phrases act as adjectives in a sentence. They help develop concrete details that elaborate on a sentence's main idea and so can add interest to your writing.

EXAMPLE   Sometimes their mother sat in the room behind them, sewing, or **dressing their younger sister,** or **nursing the baby, Paul.**

James Baldwin, "The Rockpile"

Often, you can lift a participial phrase from one sentence and insert it directly into another sentence without a change in form.

ORIGINAL   Constance set out to conquer the wilds of Alaska. She set out armed with only a backpack and a strong will.

COMBINED   Constance, **armed with only a backpack and a strong will,** set out to conquer the wilds of Alaska.

HELP

In Exercise 1 you may need to change the forms of some words before you insert them.

Reference Note

For more about **participles** and **participial phrases,** see pages 558–559.

Sometimes you will need to change a verb into a participle before inserting the idea into another sentence.

ORIGINAL   Constance arrived in Alaska early in the morning. She gripped her guidebook and a photo of home.

COMBINED   Constance, **gripping her guidebook and a photo of home,** arrived in Alaska early in the morning.

NOTE Place a participial phrase beside the noun or pronoun you want it to modify. Otherwise, you may give your sentence a meaning you did not intend. Notice how the placement of the modifier makes a difference in the meaning of the following sentence.

MISPLACED   Buried inside her backpack, Constance tried to find the trail map.

CORRECT   Constance tried to find the trail map **buried inside her backpack.**

Absolute Phrases

An *absolute phrase* consists of (1) a participle or a participial phrase, (2) a noun or a pronoun that the participle or participial phrase modifies, and (3) any other modifiers of that noun or pronoun. The entire word group is used as an adverb to modify the independent clause of a sentence.

Absolute phrases express something about the time, cause, or circumstances of the action in the independent clause. Absolute phrases are easy to spot because they always contain a noun that is different from the subject of the independent clause. Using absolute phrases is another way to combine sentences.

ORIGINAL   The wind started gusting. Constance returned home.

COMBINED   **The wind gusting,** Constance returned home.

┌HELP──

When you change a verb form into a participle, you may also have to delete some words from a participial or absolute phrase to avoid an awkward combination. Remember to use correct punctuation in the combined sentence.

Exercise 2   Combining Sentences by Using Participial and Absolute Phrases

Combine each of the following pairs of sentences by reducing one sentence to a participial or an absolute phrase and inserting the phrase into the other sentence.

EXAMPLE   1. Marian Anderson demonstrated her love for music at an early age. She sang in the church choir.

             1. *Singing in the church choir, Marian Anderson demonstrated her love for music at an early age.*

1. Anderson traveled to Europe to study for a year when she was twenty-two. She was awarded a fellowship to do so.
2. European audiences received her warmly. Anderson became famous.
3. She returned to the United States for a recital in 1935. American opera lovers were eager to hear her.
4. Anderson sang on the steps of the Lincoln Memorial in protest on Easter morning of 1939. She had been banned from singing at Constitution Hall because she was black.
5. Seventy-five thousand people came to hear the Easter morning concert. They expressed their disapproval of the discriminatory treatment.

Appositive Phrases

An *appositive phrase* is made up of an appositive and its modifiers. Appositive phrases add detail by identifying or describing a noun or pronoun in a sentence. For clear meaning, insert an appositive phrase directly before or after the noun or pronoun it identifies or describes.

EXAMPLE   You can also imagine the enormous statue-filled gate that once dominated the place and marked the beginning of Watling Street, **the road that still takes you through London to the northwest of England.**

Benedict Nightingale, "The Garden of England," *Gourmet*

You can combine sentences in a variety of ways by using appositive phrases.

TWO SENTENCES   Isabella d'Este was a ruler of the Italian city-state Mantua during the Renaissance. She actively supported many great artists and writers of the time.

ONE SENTENCE   **A ruler of the Italian city-state Mantua during the Renaissance,** Isabella d'Este actively supported many great artists and writers of the time.

or

Isabella d'Este, **an active supporter of many great artists and writers of the time,** was a ruler of the Italian city-state Mantua during the Renaissance.

In the second combination, the verb *supported* was changed into the noun *supporter* to create the appositive phrase. Notice that each combination emphasizes a different idea.

Reference Note

For more about **punctuating appositive phrases** in sentences, see page 838.

NOTE   Set an appositive phrase off from the rest of the sentence with a comma—or two commas if you place the phrase in the middle of the sentence.

EXAMPLE   The town of Canterbury, **the ancient religious center of England,** attracted many pilgrims during the Middle Ages.

Exercise 3 Combining Sentences by Using Appositive Phrases

To combine the following pairs of sentences, turn one of the sentences into an appositive phrase and insert it into the other sentence. Be sure to check your punctuation.

EXAMPLE   1. Pierre Roux helped develop an antitoxin to combat diphtheria in 1894. He was a French bacteriologist.

1. *Pierre Roux, a French bacteriologist, helped develop an antitoxin to combat diphtheria in 1894.*

1. Diphtheria is a serious and highly infectious disease. Diphtheria particularly affects children.
2. Toxoids are harmless forms of diphtheria toxin. Toxoids have become more effective in treating the disease than the original antitoxin.
3. German measles is most common among teenagers and rarely affects babies. German measles is a contagious disease caused by a viral infection.
4. The virus that causes German measles was discovered and isolated in 1961. German measles is a disease that is also called rubella.
5. A vaccine for mumps was approved in 1967. Mumps is an infectious disease that attacks gland and nerve tissue.

Review A Combining Sentences

Combine some of the sentences in the following passage by using the methods you have learned. Use your judgment about which sentences to combine and how to combine them. When you are finished, the paragraphs should have a smoother, livelier style.

```
The surface of the planet Mars can be seen
through a telescope. The surface can be seen
from Earth. The planet is reddish in color. It
was named after the ancient Romans' red god of
war. Mars travels in an elliptical orbit. It
```

TIPS & TRICKS

When revising for style, first combine ideas that strike you as flowing together naturally. Then, read over the revised passage to see where else you can make changes to add variety to your work.

```
travels around the sun. It maintains a dis-
tance of at least 128 million miles from the
sun.
     Part of the planet's surface is covered
with craters. These craters were caused by
meteors. Mars also has canyons and gorges. The
gorges are deep. Such features seem to support
the view that large quantities of water once
flowed on the planet's surface. This is the
view of some scientists. Mars also has plains.
The plains are windblown. They are covered by
sand dunes and rocks. The rocks are jagged.
```

Coordinating Ideas

You can join equally important words, phrases, or clauses by using coordinating conjunctions (such as *and, but, or, for, yet*) or correlative conjunctions (such as *both . . . and, either . . . or, neither. . . nor*). When you combine sentences in this way, you will usually create a compound subject, a compound verb, a compound object, or a compound sentence.

ORIGINAL	Ella is an aikido expert. Sebastian is also an aikido expert.
COMBINED	**Both Ella and Sebastian** are aikido experts. [compound subject]

ORIGINAL	Many people who have fibromyalgia experience great pain. However, they lead active, productive lives.
COMBINED	Many people who have fibromyalgia **experience great pain yet lead active, productive lives.** [compound verb]

ORIGINAL	We saw the man on the moon. We also saw the meteor shower.
COMBINED	We saw **the man on the moon and the meteor shower.** [compound direct object]

ORIGINAL	Mrs. Granger gave Vinnie tickets to see the new exhibit at the museum. She gave me tickets, too.
COMBINED	Mrs. Granger gave **Vinnie and me** tickets to see the new exhibit at the museum. [compound indirect object]

ORIGINAL	Jaya ran to catch the train. She got there too late.
COMBINED	Jaya ran to catch the train, **but** she got there too late. [compound sentence]

Reference Note

For more about **coordination,** see page 418.

Reference Note

For a list of **conjunctive adverbs,** see page 589.

To form a compound sentence, you can also link independent clauses with a semicolon and a conjunctive adverb or with just a semicolon.

EXAMPLES   Winston had never made the smallest effort to verify his guess**; indeed,** there was no way of doing so.

George Orwell, *1984*

The mall is a common experience for the majority of American youth**;** they have probably been going there all their lives.

William Severini Kowinski, *The Malling of America*

Exercise 4 Combining Sentences by Coordinating Ideas

Combine each of the following pairs of sentences by creating a compound subject, a compound verb, a compound object, or a compound sentence. Make sure any connectives you use show the proper relationship between the ideas.

1. Between 1840 and 1850, Canton Province in China experienced severe economic problems. Large numbers of Chinese peasants emigrated to the United States.
2. During the 1850s, more than 41,000 Chinese made their way to this country. They joined the great gold rush of that time.
3. Most of these early Chinese immigrants found no gold. They found no reliable employment.
4. They came seeking prosperity. They found only hard work and discrimination.
5. The transcontinental railroad system was being built in the 1850s. Cheap labor was in great demand.
6. Ten thousand laborers built the Union Pacific railroad. Nine thousand of them were of Chinese descent.
7. The railroad builders of America initially favored Chinese immigration. The sentiment changed when the railroad system was finished.
8. In 1869, the tracks of the Central Pacific joined those of the Union Pacific in Ogden, Utah. Thousands of Chinese laborers were immediately out of work.
9. Most new immigrants in the nineteenth century lacked education. They possessed few skills.
10. Despite their hardships, many Chinese immigrants stayed in the United States. They began to make it their home.

Subordinating Ideas

When two related sentences contain ideas of unequal importance, you can combine the sentences by making the less important idea into a subordinate clause (an *adjective clause*, an *adverb clause*, or a *noun clause*). The use of subordination will help show the relationships between the ideas.

In the following sentences, notice how each subordinate clause begins with a connecting word that shows how the clause relates to the main idea.

EXAMPLES   Mustangs comprise a fascinating chapter in the story of the modern horse, **whose ancestors evolved here and then migrated over the Bering land bridge to Asia, Africa, and Europe.** [adjective clause]

Yva Mamatiuk, "Mustangs on the Move,"
Smithsonian

If birders can learn to distinguish dozens of characteristic songs and telegraphers could handle Morse code, we should be able to cope with a few simple electronic warbles and trills. [adverb clause]

James Gleick, "What the Beep Is Going On?"
The New York Times Magazine

Other studies along these lines have shown **that extroverts have greater pain tolerance than introverts.** [noun clause]

Atul Gawande, "The Pain Perplex,"
The New Yorker

Adjective Clauses

An ***adjective clause*** modifies a noun or pronoun and usually begins with *who, whose, which, where,* or *that.* To combine sentences by using an adjective clause, first decide which sentence you want to subordinate. Then, change that sentence into an adjective clause and insert it into the other sentence.

ORIGINAL   Mammals alone possess hair. Hair is really filaments made mainly of dead cells filled with protein.

COMBINED   Hair, **which mammals alone possess,** is really filaments made mainly of dead cells filled with protein.

ORIGINAL   Because hair is made of dead cells, I do not believe my friend Dante. He says it hurts when he gets his hair cut.

COMBINED   Because hair is made of dead cells, I do not believe my friend Dante, **who says it hurts when he gets his hair cut.**

Reference Note

For more about **subordination,** see page 577.

TIPS & TRICKS

Besides connecting the subordinate clause to the independent clause, subordinators explain relationships:

- To describe a person, use *who, whose*
- To describe a thing, use *which, that*
- To show why, use *as, since, because*
- To show how or where, use *if, how, as though*
- To show when, use *after, as, whenever, while*
- To show under what condition, use *although, if, though, unless*

Reference Note

For more about **adjective clauses,** see page 578.

Reference Note

For more about **punctuating adjective clauses,** see page 832.

STYLE TIP

When you combine sentences by using an adverb clause, make sure that the subordinating conjunction reflects the proper relationship between the ideas in the two clauses.

Reference Note

For more about **adverb clauses** and **subordinating conjunctions,** see pages 584 and 520.

NOTE Use a comma or commas to set off an adjective clause that is not essential to the meaning of the sentence.

ESSENTIAL	The computer **that is most reliable** is most likely to rank first in the survey.
NONESSENTIAL	That computer**, which Edgar just bought,** is fairly reliable.

Adverb Clauses

An *adverb clause* modifies a verb, an adjective, or an adverb in a sentence. To form an adverb clause, add a subordinating conjunction (such as *although, after, because, if, when, where,* or *while*) to the beginning of the sentence you want to subordinate. Then, attach the adverb clause to a related sentence. You may need to delete or replace some words to form a clause.

ORIGINAL	Carlos left the store. He could not find the CD he wanted.
COMBINED	Carlos left the store **because he could not find the CD he wanted.**

ORIGINAL	There may not be any racquetball courts open. In that case, we will go to the park and play tennis.
COMBINED	**If there are no racquetball courts open,** we will go to the park and play tennis.

Noun Clauses

A **noun clause** is a subordinate clause used as a noun. It usually begins with *that, what, whatever, why, whether, how, who, whom, whoever,* or *whomever.*

EXAMPLES **Whatever Mimi does** will have an impact on this situation. [noun clause as subject]

Many people do not realize **that Jim is a champion chess player.** [noun clause as direct object]

People were talking about **how Hugo ate twelve sandwiches.** [noun clause as object of a preposition]

Sometimes you can drop the introductory word, such as *that, whom,* or *which,* from a noun clause without any confusion.

EXAMPLE Irma told me [that] **I should get a haircut.**

You can combine sentences by turning one sentence into a noun clause and attaching it to the other sentence.

ORIGINAL   Cruciferous vegetables are good for your health. The magazine article explained the reason this is true.

COMBINED   The magazine article explained **why cruciferous vegetables are good for your health.**

ORIGINAL   Broccoli is a cruciferous vegetable. Vernon said he had heard this fact.

COMBINED   Vernon said he had heard **that broccoli is a cruciferous vegetable.**

Exercise 5 **Combining Sentences by Subordinating Ideas**

Combine each of the following pairs of sentences. Change one sentence into a subordinate clause, and attach the clause to the other sentence. Remember to choose connectives carefully, and check your combined sentences for correct punctuation.

┌HELP──
You may need to add, delete, or rearrange some words in Exercise 5.

1. Akira Kurasawa was Japan's most influential movie director. He died in 1998 at 88 years of age.
2. His first internationally known film was *Rashomon. Rashomon* portrays the same event from four different points of view.
3. Kurasawa's interests linked East and West. He was interested in Japanese folk tales, American westerns, and such authors as Shakespeare and Dostoyevsky.
4. Kurasawa's movie *Throne of Blood* is based on Shakespeare's *Macbeth.* One should not be surprised.
5. Early in his career, Kurasawa was interested in making beautiful films. Then he became more interested in realism.
6. Kurasawa wanted *Throne of Blood* to be realistic. Kurasawa required his lead actor to wear a protective vest so he could be shot with real arrows.
7. As a teenager, Kurasawa learned about film from his brother. His brother was a *benshi,* or silent film narrator.
8. In 1936, Kurasawa answered a movie studio advertisement for apprentice movie directors. He was desperate for money.

Akira Kurasawa and an actor on set (above); film still from Throne of Blood *(below).*

9. *Star Wars* was inspired by Kurasawa's movie *The Hidden Fortress*. *Star Wars* replaces the bickering peasants with bickering robots.
10. In *The Hidden Fortress,* the peasants help free a princess. *The Hidden Fortress* is an adventure film made in 1958.

Review B   Combining Sentences by Coordinating and Subordinating Ideas

Combine each of the following pairs of sentences by either coordinating or subordinating ideas. You may see more than one way to combine a sentence pair. If so, combine the sentences in the way that reads best to you.

EXAMPLE   1.   Japanese comic books are a multibillion dollar industry. Japanese comic books are called *manga.*

            1.   *Japanese comic books, which are called* manga, *are a multibillion dollar industry.*

1. *Manga* look like American comics. *Manga* have sequential panels and word balloons.
2. Modern *manga* are related to ancient illustrated scrolls. They are also related to ancient humorous woodblock prints.
3. The *manga* process has roots in American comics. In the 1920s, American comics were first translated into Japanese.
4. Early Japanese comic books really were books. They had as many pages as a novel and had hard covers.
5. After World War II, Osamu Tezuka became the major creator of *manga.* He was influenced by U.S. movie animation.
6. Tezuka expanded the story lines of *manga.* Tezuka's works are sometimes hundreds or thousands of pages long.
7. Tezuka made a comic book of the novel *Crime and Punishment.* The novel is by the Russian writer Feodor Dostoyevsky.
8. Today, *manga* first come out in magazines. The material in magazines is later collected and presented in book form.
9. Americans can find *manga* in translation. They can see cartoons based on *manga.*
10. Many readers think *manga* are like novels. Many people also think reading *manga* is like watching movies.

Review C   Revising a Passage by Combining Sentences

Using the methods you have learned, combine the short sentences in the following passage into longer sentences. In some cases you can

combine more than just two sentences. Your combined sentences should add variety and improve the style of the passage. Remember to check for correct punctuation when you have finished.

The western Roman Empire fell in A.D. 476. Much of this civilization persisted. One legacy of the Roman Empire lies in European languages. The Romance languages show this legacy. The Romance languages developed from Latin. Latin was the language of Rome. Romance languages include Italian, French, Spanish, Romanian, and Portuguese.

English developed from the Germanic languages. Some English also derives from Latin. This fact is in part a result of England's close association with France during Norman times. Some English words reveal Latin's influence. You can see Latin's influence in prefixes such as *pro-*. Many church words also come from Latin. The words *disciple, shrine,* and *bishop* are examples. Other English words including *veto* and *curriculum* come from Latin. These words come directly from Latin.

Another legacy of the Roman Empire is Roman architecture. Examples can be seen throughout southern Europe. Examples can also be seen in North Africa and Southwest Asia. Roman bridges are still used. Many of these bridges span rivers in France, Germany, and Spain. The Romans rebuilt the cities they conquered. They added their own city grid system. This grid system consisted of roads, baths, theaters, and a central forum.

The round arch and the vault are innovations of Roman architecture. They are the primary innovations. They are used in buildings and bridges even today. Roman buildings were often based on Greek models. The ruins of these buildings inspired later architects. Thomas Jefferson built his home in 1770. He named the home Monticello. Before Jefferson built Monticello he studied Roman architecture.

12 Improving Sentence Style

Revising for Variety

GO TO: go.hrw.com
KEYWORD: EOLang

No one likes to read dull writing—not your cousin in Chicago, not your chemistry teacher, and not your colleagues at work. Whether you are writing a personal letter, a report on ions, or a memo about time-saving techniques, a versatile writing style will help you convey your message with punch and pizazz.

As you learn to evaluate and revise your writing, you can develop an eye for sentence style. The next time you draft an essay, examine how your sentences fit together. Do they add up to lively, natural-sounding paragraphs? If your writing sounds dull, you probably need to vary the beginnings and the structures of some of your sentences.

Notice how the varied sentences below work together to form a smooth, effective passage.

> Beyond the stream, the river calmed into a long, wide pool. We stopped paddling for a time and turned to see the setting sun dye river and sky in crimson. Air and water seemed all one, of one color and translucence. The wind had died; a great stillness enveloped us. We rested together, drifting slowly backward through fiery waters, content simply to gaze as the red waters of the river slipped away into reddening skies, briefly obstructed by a dark silhouetted line of leafless trees on the far bank.
>
> Steve Faulkner, "Common Water,"
> *DoubleTake*

Varying Sentence Beginnings

Most sentences begin with a subject followed by a verb.

EXAMPLES   **Canoeing is** a popular activity.

                Some people prefer kayaking to canoeing.

While there is nothing wrong with this basic subject-verb pattern, it can begin to sound monotonous after a while. You can improve the style of your writing by beginning some sentences with introductory words, phrases, and clauses instead of with subjects. At the same time, you can make more effective connections between related sentences.

In each example below, the first version is clear. However, the second version brings the ideas into sharper focus by shifting the emphasis.

BLAND   Bernice won the sculpting contest. She told her best friend Emi as soon as she found out.

BETTER   Bernice won the sculpting contest. **As soon as she found out,** she told her best friend Emi.

BLAND   Emi was happy for Bernice. She told Ari the good news over the phone.

BETTER   Emi was happy for Bernice. **Over the phone,** she told Ari the good news.

Sometimes the best way to vary sentence beginnings is to reduce a short sentence to an introductory word, phrase, or clause and attach it to another sentence. This is where your sentence-combining skills come in handy.

BLAND   Emi kept Ari on the phone for an hour. She is talkative and sociable.

BETTER   **Talkative and sociable,** Emi kept Ari on the phone for an hour.

BLAND   Ari was excited to hear that Bernice had won. He wanted to congratulate her.

BETTER   **Excited to hear that Bernice had won,** Ari wanted to congratulate her.

NOTE Remember that there are many ways to combine sentences. In the second bland example above, another acceptable way to combine the two sentences would be *Ari was excited to hear that Bernice had won and wanted to congratulate her.*

Reference Note

For more about **combining sentences,** see page 444.

The following chart gives some examples of how to vary sentence beginnings.

A plant demonstrating phototropism.

Varying Sentence Beginnings	
Sentence Connectives	A tropism is a growth response in which the direction a plant grows is determined by a particular stimulus. **Consequently,** phototropisms are growth responses to light. The growth of a plant toward light is called positive phototropism. **However,** the growth of a plant's roots away from light is called negative phototropism.
Appositives and Appositive Phrases	Another example of this phenomenon, **gravitropism,** is the growth of a plant in response to gravity. **An example of positive gravitropism,** the downward growth of roots, occurs frequently.
Single-Word Modifiers	**Strangely,** some plants respond to touch. **Curly and green,** grapevines grow in response to touch and are therefore thigmotropic.
Phrase Modifiers	**From the window of my kitchen,** I can see many types of plants. **Looking closely,** I noticed that most of the plants were in need of water. **To address this problem,** I went outside and watered the plants.
Clause Modifiers	**Because I noticed the situation in time,** I was able to keep the plants from dying. **Although I am not the best gardener,** I am eager to learn more about plants.

NOTE Sentence connectives such as *and, but,* and *however* can help you make transitions between ideas. Usually, these connecting words link ideas within a sentence. Sometimes, though—especially in informal writing—they are used at the beginning of a sentence for variety and emphasis. For example, notice how the writer uses a sentence connective for emphasis in the following passage.

> It's crunch time for Julie Shama. Like thousands of high school seniors, she faces college-application deadlines in the next month. Julie's counselor at Brookline High, outside Boston, and her $300-a-session private college-application advisor are helpful. **But** they can't match the resources of the Internet.
>
> T. Trent Gegax, "www.Apply-Here.com," *Newsweek*

Use sentence connectives sparingly and carefully to begin sentences. When you use them, be sure that the connective shows the appropriate relationship between your ideas. Also, note that in formal writing it is best not to begin sentences with coordinating conjunctions such as *and* and *but*.

Exercise 1 Varying Sentence Beginnings

Revise each of the following sentences so that it begins with an appositive, an appositive phrase, a single-word modifier, a phrase modifier, or a clause modifier.

1. African Americans, many experiencing great hardships, played an important role during the Revolutionary War.
2. George Washington ordered at the beginning of the war that no African American soldiers could serve in the Continental Army.
3. The Continental Army's troops, poorly trained and prone to disease, were also few in number.
4. The British army also suffered a shortage of troops, and the British made plans to recruit African Americans into their army in 1775.
5. Washington ordered the Continental Army to enlist free blacks to counter this move.
6. Many African Americans served in units with European Americans, and others served in separate African American companies.
7. Most commanders of the all-black companies were white, and many of these commanders were reluctant to lead the groups at first.

The Granger Collection, New York

8. These commanders later changed their minds because of the notable courage of many African American troops.
9. African American soldiers, numbering about 5,000, helped win the Revolutionary War.
10. A few black soldiers received official recognition for their outstanding bravery, although many soldiers' heroic efforts went unacknowledged.

Varying Sentence Structure

Reference Note

For more information about the **four types of sentence structures,** see page 588.

When you revise your writing for style, it is not always enough to vary your sentence beginnings. It is also important to vary sentence structures by using a mix of simple, compound, complex, and sometimes compound-complex sentences.

Read the following short paragraph, which contains only simple sentences.

> Quasars are the brightest, most distant objects in the sky. For decades they have puzzled and intrigued astronomers. Quasars may hold important clues to the birth and formation of galaxies. Astronomers believe this. Astronomers first observed quasars in 1963. Since then, they have discovered over one thousand of these objects. With the help of two segmented-mirror telescopes in Hawaii, astronomers hope to discover the power source of quasars. According to some astronomers, giant black holes produce the energy.

Now, read the revised version of the paragraph. Notice how the writer has made the paragraph smoother by including a variety of sentence structures.

> Quasars are the brightest, most distant objects in the sky. For decades they have puzzled and intrigued astronomers, who believe quasars may hold important clues to the birth and formation of galaxies. Astronomers first observed quasars in 1963, and since then, they have discovered over one thousand of these objects. With the help of two segmented-mirror telescopes in Hawaii, astronomers hope to discover the power source of quasars, which some believe to be giant black holes.

Complex sentences do more than add variety to your writing. They also help bring your thoughts into focus by emphasizing main ideas and subordinating less important ones. For example, in the revised paragraph, notice how the complex sentence at the end establishes a clear connection between the last two ideas. The relative pronoun in the subordinate clause relates the information in that clause to *quasars,* the object of the preceding clause.

Reference Note

For more about **subordinating ideas in sentences,** see page 421.

Exercise 2 Varying Sentence Structure

The following paragraph contains too many simple sentences. Improve the paragraph by varying the structure of the sentences. You can add, delete, or rearrange words as needed.

```
     Kent is a county in southern England. It is
known as "the garden of England" because of its
lush and serene countryside. Sir Thomas Wyatt
wrote fondly about Kent. Wyatt introduced the
sonnet to England. Wyatt lists the unbearable
faults of other European countries in one poem.
He also praises the virtues of Kent in this
poem. Kent has lovely hills and fields, old vil-
lages, and abundant flowers in the spring. Kent
has these today just as it did in Wyatt's time.
The historic town of Canterbury lies in Kent.
Canterbury was made famous by Geoffrey Chaucer's
tales. A journey through Kent rewards the visi-
tor. The visitor enjoys history, as well as
robust food and beautiful country.
```

COMPUTER TIP

When you print out a draft to revise, use double- or triple-line spacing and wide margins to allow room for handwritten corrections. Then, when you are ready to print a final copy, remember to reset the spacing and margins.

Review A Varying Sentence Beginnings and Sentence Structure

Using what you have learned about varying sentence beginnings and sentence structure, revise the following paragraph for style. Add, delete, and rearrange words wherever necessary to make the sentences more varied.

```
     Extreme sports are growing increasingly
popular with television viewers. Extreme
sports are called extreme because they require
great physical agility and, often, risk.
Extreme sports include surfing, skateboarding,
snowboarding, and mountain biking, among other
sports. Traditional sports such as basketball,
```

STYLE   TIP

When revising for style, be careful to retain the meaning you wish to convey. After you have made revisions, remember to re-read what you have written aloud purely for sense.

football, and baseball used to dominate the
television ratings. Many athletes in traditional sports, with their big salaries and bad
attitudes, have alienated viewers. Some viewers think that extreme sports athletes take
their sports more seriously because they do
not participate in them just for money.
Extreme sports are especially popular with
young viewers. Television analysts say that
the traditional three-sport era may be over
for good.

┌TIPS┐ & ┌TRICKS┐

When revising for wordi-
ness, look for the following
two types of problems:

• Redundant Pairs—words
  that imply each other

EXAMPLES
  true facts

  future plans

• Redundant Categories—
  words that designate
  their general categories

EXAMPLES
  engineering field

  large in size

Revising to Reduce Wordiness

Which would you rather read: a ten-page essay on the health benefits of
broccoli or a one-or-two-paragraph statement on the subject? Skilled
writers make every word count, suiting length to purpose. Your writing
is most effective when it is clear, concise, and free of the clutter of unnecessary words. To avoid wordiness, keep these three points in mind.

• Use only the words you need to make your point.

• Avoid complicated words where simple ones will do.

• Do not repeat words unless it is absolutely necessary.

Sometimes you can fix a wordy sentence by taking out whole
groups of unnecessary words. At other times you can revise by reducing clauses to phrases and both clauses and phrases to single words.

Eliminating Unnecessary Words

The following paragraph is an example of wordy writing. Lines have
been drawn through the unnecessary words. First, read the paragraph
aloud, including the words that have been crossed out. Then, read the
shorter, more concise version. Notice the difference the revisions make
in the sound of the paragraph.

Anyone who has ever ~~in the course of his or
her life~~ searched the World Wide Web knows how
time-consuming the process ~~of searching~~ can
be. Although ~~helpful~~ search engines can aid
you in finding what you are looking for, often
the specific information you seek remains
elusive ~~and out of reach~~. At other times, a
search can ~~yield far too much information and~~

overload you with tens of thousands of irrelevant Web sites ~~that are not important to your~~
~~search. To address this problem,~~ in 1998,
researchers ~~working before the end of the~~
~~millennium,~~ developed a system called ARC,
which stands for automatic resource compiler,
in order to amend the situation. ARC ~~is a~~
~~technique that~~ analyzes how Internet documents
are linked to each other. Web pages are
~~categorized and~~ put into two separate types of
sites: "authorities" and "hubs." Authorities
~~are called such because they~~ are sites that
are cited by many other documents on the subject. Hubs are pages that link to a lot of
authorities. By categorizing sites, ARC helps
sort useful information from useless material
~~that will not help the searcher~~.

Following are more examples of how less can be more when it comes to sentences. Can you see other ways in which these sentences might be revised to reduce wordiness?

WORDY   Hiking in the wild, untamed, natural wilderness is, I believe, a great thing to do in my opinion.

BETTER   Hiking in the wilderness is, I believe, a great thing to do.

WORDY   From far away and at a great distance, you can see for miles, looking at huge, enormous mesas that fill the expanse of the sky.

BETTER   From far away, you can see mesas that fill the expanse of sky.

Exercise 3   Revising Wordy Sentences

Revise each of the following sentences to reduce wordiness. If a sentence is already concise, write *C*.

1. One of the many things that the poet William Shakespeare is known for is his sonnets.
2. In 1609, Shakespeare published his sonnets all together in one collection during the early seventeenth century.
3. Much mystery surrounds Shakespeare's sonnets, as many questions about the sonnets remain debated, discussed, and unresolved.
4. Among the conflicting theories lies the question of who the speaker in the sonnets who voices concerns really is.
5. Despite the controversy, however, most scholars agree that the son-nets are examples of extraordinary writing in the English language.

6. Another Shakespeare mystery involves uncertainty regarding his physical appearance.

7. Even though Shakespeare is famous throughout the world everywhere, no one can be sure about how he really looked in actual life.

8. From portraits of Shakespeare that have survived and withstood the passage of time, he appears to have been a slim man of slight build and average height.

9. Artists rendered Shakespeare with well-proportioned features and expressive eyes.

10. Although we may never learn more about Shakespeare the man himself, we can continue to learn and gain information about Shakespeare the writer by studying his magnificent works.

Exercise 4 Revising a Paragraph by Eliminating Unnecessary Words

Revise the following paragraph to make it more concise. Eliminate unnecessary words, keeping the original meaning of each sentence. You may need to change some verb forms, too.

Few athletes earn lasting reputations that endure in the record books and in the hearts of admirers. However, the accomplishments of athlete and Chicago Cubs baseball player Sammy Sosa will likely be remembered for a long and extensive time to come. It is true that in 1998 he broke the previous record for number of home runs in a season; he is now second only to Mark McGwire, who also broke the old record during the same season that Sosa broke the record. Sosa is also known as a compassionate, caring human being in his native Dominican Republic. Sosa grew up poor in his Dominican homeland and had to shine shoes to help his family. Now he invests in various businesses there, in order to create opportunities and positions for other poor and impoverished children.

Reducing Groups of Words

Writing concisely means using only as many words as you need. The following charts give examples of how you can trim away excess words from your writing.

| TIPS & TRICKS |

You do not want to delete words that clarify your meaning or add interest to your sentences. When considering whether or not to take out a word or phrase, ask yourself if the sentence would mean the same thing without it.

Clauses Reduced to Phrases	
Clause	**When Jessica was doing algebra equations in the library,** she forgot the time.
Participial Phrase	**Doing algebra equations in the library,** Jessica forgot the time.
Clause	Earlier in the day, she had decided **that she wanted to visit Davida after school.**
Infinitive Phrase	Earlier in the day, she had decided **to visit Davida after school.**
Clause	The problems **that were about applied algebra** took forever to complete.
Prepositional Phrase	The problems **about applied algebra** took forever to complete.
Clause	Davida's sisters, **one of whom is Sarah and the other Suzanne,** walked into the library.
Appositive Phrase	Davida's sisters, **Sarah and Suzanne,** walked into the library.

Clauses and Phrases Reduced to Single Words	
Clause	**The hat that belongs to Martin** is the nicest.
Word	**Martin's** hat is the nicest.
Clause	Martin is a person **who keeps up with fashion.**
Word	Martin is a **fashionable** person.
Phrase	**Cherishing his sneakers,** he cleans them nightly.
Word	He cleans his **cherished** sneakers nightly.
Phrase	He appraises other people's wardrobes **in an expert manner.**
Word	He appraises other people's wardrobes **expertly.**

Following is a list of concise, one-word replacements for some common wordy phrases.

Wordy	Simpler
at which time	when
by means of	by
due to the fact that	because, since
in spite of the fact that	although
in the event that	if
the fact is that	actually

Exercise 5 Revising Sentences Through Reduction

Reduce the italicized clauses and phrases in the following sentences by deleting, replacing, and rearranging words. Be sure to keep the original meaning of each sentence.

1. Movies were born in 1895, *at which time* two brothers *who were named Louis and Auguste Lumière* offered the first public screening in Paris.

2. That screening consisted of several one-minute film clips *that showed* workers *who were leaving* a factory and a baby *who was having* lunch.

3. Thomas Edison has also been cited as the inventor of movies *due to the fact that* he invented the Kinetoscope in 1889, *but the fact is that* his device could only be used by one viewer at a time.

4. *In America,* animation got its beginnings in 1906, *and the beginning of animated features, which are* full-length movies, *was in 1918.*

5. Animation has subjects *that can be seen as* both serious and comic, however, comedy seems *ideally and naturally* suited to animation.

6. The movies *that were produced first* had no sound, so actors *who acted in an expressive and physically agile manner, one of whom was Charlie Chaplin and another Buster Keaton,* became stars.

7. When sound was introduced *with success* in 1927, many movie directors thought it was *horrible and awful.*

8. Filmmakers *from the early era* preferred to make black-and-white movies; color seemed like *an extra, added annoyance and nuisance that audiences would find annoying.*

Charlie Chaplin.

9. Three-dimensional movies *that used three dimensions instead of two,* were *new, trendy, and popular* in the 1950s *when they had their heyday.*

10. *Now, showing daily* on *huge* screens as large as eight stories high *are* IMAX movies *that have as their basis* wide-screen technology.

Review B **Revising a Paragraph by Reducing Wordiness**

Revise the following wordy paragraph. Eliminate unnecessary words and reduce clauses and phrases to make the paragraph concise. You should be able to make at least five reductions.

As in the ancient cultures of Mesopotamia and Egypt that existed, early life in India developed in the basins of great rivers a long time ago. The first civilization to arise early on on the Indian subcontinent was located in the valley of the Indus River, which is in present-day Pakistan. The Indus Valley is a broad, vast plain bordered by desert, if you look eastward, and by mountains that rise up in the west. It resembles the valleys of other places such as those of the Nile, the Tigris, and the Euphrates, in terms of its geography. The land was arid, and people could clear it in order to settle it without too much difficulty. The Indus River flooded when mountain snows from the Himalayas melted and whenever monsoons, otherwise known as seasonal rainy winds, occurred as they did every year. Flooding of the river created the right conditions for agriculture to occur, which in turn fostered the situation which led to the growth of settlement in the area.

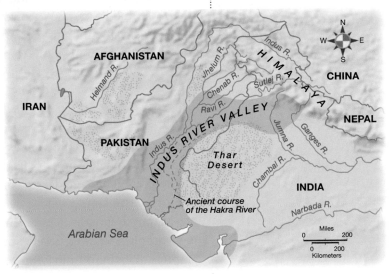

13 Understanding Paragraphs and Compositions

internet connect

**go.
hrw
.com**

GO TO: go.hrw.com
KEYWORD: EOLang

How Paragraphs and Compositions Fit Together

Imagine standing on top of a mountain, looking out over the thick forest below. What do you see? A wide ribbon of deep green—or that one tree that towers over the others? You have probably heard the saying about seeing the forest *or* seeing the trees. What about seeing both— the whole and its parts? When you write a composition, you do just that. You pay attention to the parts (the paragraphs), but you also keep the whole (the composition) in mind.

The Parts of a Paragraph

Paragraphs can be as different as oak trees are from pines. Some paragraphs are a single word; others run several pages. Their uses differ, too: to present a main idea, to connect one idea to another, to emphasize an idea, or simply to give the reader's eye a rest in long passages.

Many paragraphs in essays and other types of nonfiction, including workplace writing, develop one **main idea.** Each main-idea paragraph is often built from a **topic sentence, supporting sentences,** and a **clincher sentence.**

Parts of Paragraphs	
The Main Idea	▪ is the paragraph's central idea or focus
The Topic Sentence	▪ is an explicit statement of the main idea ▪ is often the first or second sentence in the paragraph ▪ can instead appear at the end of a paragraph to emphasize or summarize ▪ is not necessarily a dry statement—it can be lively and interesting

Supporting Sentences	▪ elaborate on the main idea; these sentences support, build, or prove the main idea
	▪ often use details of the following types:
	  sensory details: images of sight, sound, taste, smell, and texture
	  facts or statistics: details that can be proven true (a reader can check the accuracy). A statistic is a fact involving numbers.
	  examples: specific instances that illustrate a general idea
	  anecdotes: brief stories about people or events that illustrate a main idea

The Clincher Sentence	▪ may restate the topic sentence, summarize supporting details, offer a final thought, or help readers refocus on the main idea of a long paragraph ▪ is sometimes bold, colorful, or clever—a definite closing

STYLE TIP

To develop a good paragraph, you will often mix types of detail—for example, you may use strong sensory images and include impressive statistics.

STYLE TIP

Not every paragraph needs a clincher sentence. Use one for a strong or dramatic touch or for renewing a main idea in a lengthy or complicated paragraph.

NOTE Not every paragraph has, or needs, a topic sentence. In fiction, paragraphs rarely have topic sentences. Paragraphs presenting time sequences (how-to instructions or histories, for example) may also lack topic sentences—the steps or events themselves focus the reader's mind. Finally, a paragraph may imply, or suggest, its main idea without directly stating it in a topic sentence. In your school writing, however, topic sentences are a help: They keep *you* focused on each paragraph's topic.

Putting the Parts Together

You can clearly see the parts of a paragraph in the following example. Notice that its topic sentence expresses the paragraph's main idea and that the clincher sentence reemphasizes it.

William Caxton with a printing press.

Topic Sentence

Supporting Sentences

Clincher Sentence

The arrival of printing in England was to be of far more importance than any of the changes of ruler during the Wars of the Roses. Up until this time books had been copied out by hand by scribes in monasteries or other workshops, a long and laborious process. As a result books were rare and very costly. Printing by machine meant that they could be cheap and plentiful. The knowledge books contained could also be spread far wider, reaching new audiences, as more people than ever before learned to read. When William Caxton set up his printing presses in the precincts of Westminster Abbey in 1476, it was to be a landmark in the history of the English language and literature, daily life, and culture.

Sir Roy Strong, *The Story of Britain*

┌─HELP─
How do you find the main idea in a sequence paragraph with no topic sentence? One way is to summarize, in a single sentence, what is happening.

Exercise 1 Identifying the Parts of Paragraphs

Try identifying the parts of paragraphs. The following three paragraphs all have a main idea, but only two have topic sentences.

- Identify the two topic sentences.
- Write a topic sentence for the remaining paragraph.
- Identify the type of supporting details in each paragraph.
- Identify any clincher sentences.

1. Millions of years ago, a volcano built a mountain on the floor of the Atlantic. In eruption after eruption, it pushed up a great pile of volcanic rock, until it had accumulated a mass a hundred miles across at its base, reaching upward toward the surface of the sea. Finally its cone emerged as an island

with an area of about 200 square miles. Thousands of years passed, and thousands of thousands. Eventually the waves of the Atlantic cut down the cone and reduced it to a shoal—all of it, that is, but a small fragment which remained above water. This fragment we know as Bermuda.

Rachel L. Carson, The Sea Around Us

Aerial view of Bermuda.

2.   All waves, no matter how huge, start as rough spots—cats' paws—on the surface of the water. The cats' paws are filled with diamond-shaped ripples, called capillary waves, that are weaker than the surface tension of water and die out as soon as the wind stops. They give the wind some purchase on an otherwise glassy sea, and at winds over six knots, actual waves start to build. The harder the wind blows, the bigger the waves get and the more wind they are able to "catch." It's a feedback loop that has wave height rising exponentially with wind speed.

Sebastian Junger, The Perfect Storm

3.   In the 1950s, the American sneaker market saw the first of several "takeoffs." With families flocking to the suburbs, leisure time and sports participation on an upward slope, and the Baby Boom beginning to coalesce, sneakers—the word still meant canvas and rubber—were becoming the shoe of choice for American youth. As Jonathan Walford, curator of the Bata Shoe Museum in Toronto, observes, the sneaker was an integral part of the first distinctly marketed youth fashion and cultural movement in American history. As school dress codes began to relax, the sneaker also became acceptable for daily wear, although, he points out, "You would have had two pairs: one for school and one for gym class."

Tom Vanderbilt, The Sneaker Book

STYLE   TIP

While a single paragraph can stand alone, it is important to remember that most do not. Many of the sample paragraphs in this chapter were written as parts of longer works. Though their meaning and form are clear, the paragraphs are presented here outside of their larger context.

Qualities of Paragraphs

Think about trees again. Each type is so distinct: a pine with its needles and cones, a magnolia with its glossy leaves and huge blossoms. Yet while different, each is a pleasing whole. Paragraphs achieve this wholeness, too, through three major qualities: **unity, coherence,** and **elaboration.**

Unity

Unity means that all of a paragraph's supporting sentences really fit the main idea—no pine cones should poke out among the magnolia blooms. In other words, all of the supporting sentences must work together and stay on the topic. They must relate to the paragraph's main idea whether it is stated or implied (suggested). Unity, then, is achieved in one of three ways:

- All sentences relate to the main idea stated in the topic sentence.

- All sentences relate to an implied main idea.

- All sentences relate to a sequence of events. (In paragraphs like this, the main idea is often implied rather than stated.)

NOTE When a main idea is implied, you have to *infer* it from details within the paragraph. Here are two approaches to inferring:

- Ask yourself: "What is the topic of this paragraph—in a word or two?" Then, ask: "What is being said about this topic?"

- Decide the main idea of the paragraph's first sentence. Read the next sentence, and refine and adjust your idea. Do this with each sentence in the paragraph, continuing to refine as you read.

Coherence

When a paragraph has **coherence,** the ideas are arranged in a **logical progression,** or an order that makes sense so that the reader moves easily from one idea to another. The paragraph flows. It doesn't bounce readers around or befuddle them. You can create coherence in a paragraph by paying attention to

- **the order you use to arrange ideas**

- **the connections you make between ideas to show readers how they are related**

Building Coherence: Types of Order		
Order	**When to Use**	**How It Works**
Chronological	• to tell a story or relate an event • to explain a process • to show cause and effect	• presents events in the order they happen • shows how things change over time
Spatial	• to describe individual features • to create a complete visual picture	• arranges details by location in space—top to bottom, left to right, clockwise, near to far, center to edge, and so on
Order of Importance	• to inform • to persuade	• arranges ideas and details from most important to least or vice versa • places emphasis where the writer thinks it most effective
Logical	• to inform or to persuade, often by classifying: defining, dividing a subject into parts, or comparing and contrasting	• groups ideas or details together in ways that illustrate the relationships between them

COMPUTER TIP

One good use of the Cut and Paste function is trying out optional orders of details. Put an important detail first in a paragraph; then, move it to last. Which "reads" stronger? Also experiment with details of a spatial description. Is it clearer or more interesting to describe an interior detail before an exterior? Try it both ways.

NOTE As you become familiar with the types of order, you will find that they can overlap or can be used in combination. For example:

• To describe a person, you could move from head to toe, but you might want to start with an outstanding feature—like expressive hands. In other words, **order of importance** would guide your **spatial** description.

• To define early rock music, you might decide to explain how it is like and different from blues and country music. You would be using two **logical orders:** definition and comparison-contrast.

- To explain an effect, you might move **chronologically** from its causes. However, three simultaneous causes might produce a single effect. Is one cause more **important** than the others? For emphasis, you could discuss it first or last.

Building Coherence: Connecting Ideas	
Direct References	<ul><li>refer to a noun or pronoun used earlier in the paragraph</li><li>repeat a word used earlier</li><li>substitute synonyms for words used earlier</li></ul>
Transitional Expressions	<ul><li>compare ideas (*also, and, another, in the same way, just, like, likewise, moreover, similarly, too*)</li><li>contrast ideas (*although, but, however, in spite of, instead, nevertheless, on the other hand, still, yet*)</li><li>show cause and effect (*accordingly, as a result, because, consequently, for, since, so, so that, therefore*)</li><li>indicate time (*after, at last, before, early, eventually, first, later, next, then, thereafter, until, when, while*)</li><li>show place (*above, across, adjacent, behind, beside, beyond, down, here, in, near, over, there*)</li><li>show importance (*first, last, less significant, mainly, more important, to begin with*)</li></ul>

NOTE When you read, notice that the use of direct references keeps writing from being monotonous. By using synonyms and pronouns, writers avoid repeating key words over and over. Imagine a paragraph about dancer Savion Glover that used only his name—never words like *he, him, his, tap-dancer, star, performer.* Readers would certainly get "Savion Glover" overload.

Elaboration

In order to be coherent and unified, paragraphs need adequate content, or *elaboration*—the branches that fill out the bare trunk of a main idea. To **elaborate** is to refine, develop, or support an idea. The paragraph's **supporting sentences** do this important work, and they must do it fully. Supply skimpy elaboration, and readers may turn away from the best main idea. After all, readers need elaboration to be convinced, to see an image, or to carry out instructions. Always ask: "Have I said enough?"

Looking at the Qualities of Paragraphs

Read through the following paragraph about how flies maneuver when they can't see. Then re-read it, using the side notes and markings to examine its qualities. (Stars mark direct references; highlighting marks transitional expressions.) The paragraph is unified because all of its sentences relate to the main idea in the topic sentence. Notice that the writer orders ideas by showing the steps in a process. The ordering, direct references, and transitions all work together to create coherence, and the detail-rich supporting sentences provide plenty of elaboration.

> Because of its overspeeded vision, a fly has the problem that half of its* flying time—even with the kitchen light brightly on—is spent in what it* perceives as utter darkness. As any pilot knows, navigating in the dark is no easy task. The cruising fly* manages to get through its* cycles with the help of two gyrocompasses sticking out from behind its* wings. If it* accidentally yaws, pitches, rolls, or just gets dizzy when it* can't see anything, the gyros* inform the brain and a course correction is computed and sent along to the flight muscles. With all this* help, it* can easily work out where it* wants to go, and so the navigating fly* cruises into the living room and ascends up to the ceiling, there* to perform the most impressive feat of its* journey: landing upside down.
>
> David Bodanis, *The Secret House*

Topic Sentence

Supporting Sentences

Explanation of a Process

Clincher Sentence

Exercise 2 Improving the Qualities of Paragraphs

The ideas and facts in the following two paragraphs are not easy to follow. Rewrite each paragraph to improve its unity, coherence and elaboration. To rewrite, use the following hints.

- Identify the type of order that will work best for the paragraph and rearrange sentences to achieve that order.

- Eliminate sentences that are unrelated to the main idea.

- Add or revise direct references and transitions.

- Determine if the paragraphs are sufficiently elaborated. If not, add details.

1.   Serious bike riders concentrate on training and fitness, but serious bike riders know another key to making it through a long ride: nutrition. While riding for more than ninety minutes, you need to replenish the fuel for your muscles, but exactly what and when should you eat? Also eat *after* you ride, when the body is super-efficient at changing food into stored energy. The "what" is primarily carbohydrates. It can be an energy bar or carbohydrate-rich foods like fruit and bread. The "when" is before you feel you need it. Eat something about thirty minutes into the ride. That starts digestion. Two bananas or an energy bar every hour is about right. Pay attention to water, too. After riding, one banana or half a bagel will replenish expended energy.

2.   Whatever Stonehenge is, it is not a single structure built by one people. Most ancient is the outer ditch and earth bank—over 300 feet in diameter—encircling the whole site. Within the earth bank, Stonehenge's mysterious stones, or menhirs, make up four distinct groups. Some parts of Stonehenge, such as the Heelstone, clearly relate to the rising of the sun at midsummer. First, moving toward the center, is a circle of thirty sandstone blocks, known as sarsens, of huge proportions: Each is about 13 feet high, 6.5 feet wide, and 3 feet thick. The stones

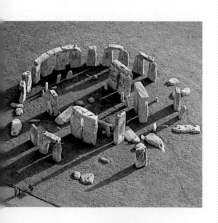

```
are topped by a continuous stone lintel.
A different set of ten similar stones (in
five pairs with lintels) is arranged in a
horseshoe shape. Before you get to that
set, a circle of smaller bluestone menhirs
was inserted at a later date. At the very
center of Stonehenge is a final circle or
ovoid, also of small bluestones. From pe-
rimeter to center, Stonehenge is a breath-
taking monument. The monument's building
and remodeling lasted 2,000 years.
```

Review A   **Analyzing Paragraphs**

With two or three classmates, find three nonfiction paragraphs to analyze. Look for paragraphs written for different purposes: to describe, to
inform, to persuade, and so on. Some possible sources are textbooks,
newspapers, popular magazines (look at articles, editorials, reviews,
and advertisements), CD liner notes, how-to books, and Web pages.
For each paragraph you select

- identify its main parts: topic, supporting, and clincher sentences
- analyze its qualities: unity, coherence (especially order), and
  elaboration

Uses of Paragraphs Within Compositions

The analogy that began this chapter compared the way paragraphs create a composition to the way trees create a forest. So far, you have been
studying individual trees. Now your focus will move to the forest—the
longer piece of writing, or **composition.** In compositions, a new paragraph marks a movement from one idea to another. When you write
your own compositions, you will usually begin a new paragraph for
one of the following reasons:

- to present a different part of your subject or another step in a
  process
- to introduce another type of support
- to jump forward or backward in time or to change location
- to indicate different experts or speakers (direct quotations)
- to make a transition or connection from one idea or subtopic
  to another

| STYLE | TIP |

Some paragraph indenta-
tions create a visual break
or rest, rather than marking a new idea or some
other shift. The new paragraph lets readers pause at
an appropriate place in a
lengthy thought or
description.

What Makes a Composition?

Paragraphs make compositions, as you have learned. Everything you know about effective paragraphs—their parts and qualities—still holds. Now, however, think about paragraphs serving the main idea of the *composition*. A **composition** is a typical nonfiction writing form; articles, essays, and reports (most of your school writing) are compositions.

Within compositions, paragraphs are usually arranged with a larger structure in mind. This structure consists of three parts: an **introduction,** a **body,** and a **conclusion.**

NOTE School assignments often ask you to write five-paragraph compositions, but that length is not a rule or a definition for a composition. Five paragraphs help ensure that you have proper form and enough elaboration. However, a composition written in school or at work could have fewer paragraphs or many more. What is important is thoroughly developing and supporting your main idea.

The Introduction

When you want to make a good first impression on someone, do you dress, speak, and act carefully? An **introduction** is your reader's first impression of your composition and its topic. It may be as short as one sentence or as long as several paragraphs, but it needs special care. An introduction should do three things:

- make readers pay attention (so they will read on)
- set the tone (humorous, friendly, critical, earnest, and so on)
- state the **thesis** (the thesis statement often, but not always, appears at the end of the introduction)

The Thesis Statement

Your thesis is not simply your topic, but what you want to say about it—your main idea. The expression of this main idea is the **thesis statement.** Your statement can be long or short, one sentence or more than one. Writing a thesis statement is always important because it helps guide and control your whole composition. All of the information or ideas your paper includes should support the thesis.

NOTE The *thesis statement* often appears in the introduction to present the composition's main idea or ideas right away. That position is a good strategy for school writing. However, experienced writers may put their thesis statements later in the composition (or article or essay). They may even imply a thesis, rather than stating it directly.

Hints for Writing and Using a Thesis Statement

1. **Develop your thesis statement from your prewriting notes.** You will gather many facts and details during prewriting. Look them over carefully, and ask yourself: "What do these details tell me about my topic? What will my point be in this paper?" Look for a unifying main idea.

2. **Avoid the following kinds of thesis statements:**

   - **Theses that are obvious,** such as "To play tennis, a person needs a racket, a tennis ball, and a tennis court." These kinds of statements don't need to be supported or defended.

   - **Theses that are blanket statements,** such as "Professional sports stars are always asking for better salaries." These statements, because they are all-inclusive, are almost impossible to support or defend.

3. **Include both your limited topic and your main idea about it.** A thesis statement ideally identifies two things: your topic *and* the specific main point (or points) you want to make about it. When you draft a thesis statement, check it by underlining your topic and circling your main idea about the topic.

   For example, think about this thesis statement: "Although computers put a universe of information in students' hands, their use in classrooms is not without problems." It clearly presents a limited topic *(computers in classrooms)* and a main idea *(computers are beneficial but also present problems).*

4. **Change or rewrite your thesis statement as you clarify and refine your ideas.** The first thesis statement you write may not be your last. You can rephrase it as you clarify your thoughts or if you have new ideas. Notice the difference between the thesis statements you have just read and this fuzzy, vague one: "There are good and bad things about computers in classrooms."

5. **Use your thesis statement as a guide.** Keep your thesis statement in front of you as you plan and write. Set aside ideas or details that do not support or develop it. Later, you might decide to revise your thesis statement to include these details. If not, discard them. Remember: Your composition should always support and develop the central idea expressed in your thesis statement.

STYLE TIP

You will see exceptions to the "limited topic plus main idea" statement. In a composition whose primary purpose is providing information, the thesis statement—for example, "Computers are now used widely in high school education"—may just announce a topic that the paper will then explain with facts and examples. However, even most reports contain an implied idea or position.

NOTE Your **working thesis statement** will probably be straight-forward; style is not the point during prewriting and drafting. A final thesis statement, though, does not have to be stiff or cumbersome; it may even be an attention-getting part of your introduction. During revision, think about style and reader interest. You will see the difference in the following preliminary and revised thesis statements.

PRELIMINARY   Many critics believe that the SAT does not measure critical thinking skills or students' true potential.

REVISED   In a yearly ritual, millions of high school students suffer the anguish of the SAT; many critics, however, believe the exam fails to measure students' critical thinking skills or their true potential.

Exercise 3   Analyzing Thesis Statements

Most of the following thesis statements have specific topics plus clear main ideas about these topics. Find the ones that present a topic, but not an idea. Then, rewrite them to make them more effective.

1. Common houseplants are one of the best ways to help reduce indoor air pollution.
2. Gwendolyn Brooks is a famous poet.
3. Despite a crippling motor neuron disease, British physicist Stephen Hawking has expanded our understanding of the universe.
4. In today's laboratories, robots carry out many precision tasks better than humans.
5. Despite the mysteriousness of dreams, some key concepts can help interpret their meanings.
6. Several U.S. astronauts have had some very close calls in space.
7. The speed of light is approximately 186,000 miles per second.
8. Country and western music has a varied past.
9. Sportsmanship is important.
10. People can gain several positive skills from viewing television.

The Structure of Introductions

In both formal and informal writing, introductions often have a similar structure. The writer "warms up" to the topic by moving from general information or comments to a more specific statement—frequently the thesis. Picture the structure as an inverted triangle. The flat top is the general beginning, and the bottom point *is* the point—the precisely stated idea your composition will explain or prove.

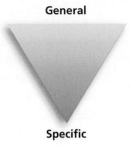

General

Specific

The following paragraph introduces a composition interpreting literature. Notice how the opening sentences offer broad information and ideas that grow more specific as the writer states the thesis in the final sentence. What is the paper's limited topic and main idea? (Notice that the introduction supplies other necessary information, such as the author's name and the title of the work.)

> Zora Neale Hurston (1891-1960) was more than a gifted novelist. She was also a perceptive student of her culture, an author of two notable books of folklore, and a member of the American Folklore Society and American Anthropological Society. Hurston's work as an anthropologist is, in fact, directly related to her creative writing. All her novels show not only her gift for story-telling, but also her interest in Southern folk customs. However, the connection is especially clear in the language and characters in her first novel, *Jonah's Gourd Vine*.

The next introduction, from a composition about the banding of wild birds, also ends with the thesis statement. Notice, however, that it features an attention-getting structure sometimes called the "But" or "However" introduction. In this kind of structure, the ideas seem to be going in one direction; then the writer changes the viewpoint. Here, the information in the opening sentences appears unsympathetic to banding, but the fifth sentence introduces another perspective, leading to the thesis in the last sentence. (Note that this introduction is different in another way: It "warms up" with quite specific details that capture interest.)

A banded bird.

Catching and banding birds can sound like a very bad business. Mist nets, the nylon mesh nets that catch smaller birds (even hummingbirds) were developed by the Japanese, who named them "suicide nets." Waterfowl are sometimes herded into corrals when they are molting, flightless, and helpless. At other times, they are drawn into an area with bait, when suddenly "cannon nets" are shot over the whole flock. These techniques may sound quite destructive, but catching and banding birds does not harm them. Banding is strictly regulated and, in fact, the procedure saves birds. Banding gives ornithologists vital information about migration, favored breeding areas, and ages within bird populations.

Techniques for Interesting Openers

Remember that an introduction should make readers pay attention. That is why some writers call a good opening a "hook": It grabs readers and does not let them go. Experienced writers have many techniques for writing openers that give their introductions impact. Here are several you can try. Each one is illustrated with a possible hook for a paper about dance companies that include performers who have physical disabilities.

1. **Start with a question.** An intriguing or challenging question immediately engages readers by making them think—and guess what will come next.

   > Why in the world would audiences want to see dancers who can't move their legs?

2. **Open with an anecdote, a "little story."** People like anecdotes, and you can use them to liven up many dry nonfiction topics. Anecdotes and extended examples draw readers in through humor, mystery, or simple human interest.

As a boy, Uli Schmitz had polio, leg braces, and a lot of friends. He kept up fine with his buddies by using braces and crutches—until a camping and hiking trip loomed. His friends saw a simple solution: Use a wheelchair. Uli wanted no part of it—a wheelchair would make him "*more* disabled." Still, a camping trip beckoned.... He tried the wheelchair. What he found was independence, pure and simple. The chair became his ally, his freedom—a liberation no one can doubt as Schmitz joyously skims across a stage with his partners in the Axis dance company.

3. **Begin with an unusual or startling fact, idea, or opinion.** The element of surprise can range from the merely unusual to the enlightening (a little-known fact) to the outrageous. All will pique interest. The following introduction opens with a bit of a shock.

Judy Smith gives audiences the opportunity to stare at people in wheelchairs. As she says, "They have permission to sit there and gawk for as long as they like." Smith started her company of dancers—composed of those with and without disabilities—because she wanted to move in new ways, but the effect on watchers is equally important. On the street, she says, people may look away from people in wheelchairs; onstage, they become riveting, individual performers.

4. **Address the reader directly.** Speak directly to readers, and you involve them at once. This technique is a good way to create an informal, friendly tone, though it can be used in other ways—even to provoke an "Ouch!" response. You will see the difference between these two examples.

You may think you don't want a ticket to a wheelchair dance concert. Catch a glimpse of the Light Motion dancers, three people balanced amazingly on one rolling chair, and you will think again.

> Do you think you are open-minded? Then why do you assume that people with disabilities can't dance?

5. **Simply state your thesis.** Often, a well-worded statement of the thesis or topic is interesting in itself.

> Dancers with disabilities are not injured dancers who need therapy; they are people who dance professionally, delight audiences, fulfill their own creativity, and show the world that *disability* does not mean "limitation."

6. **Begin with an interesting, vivid description.** Consider drawing readers right away into a word picture, whether a description of a place, person, object, or event. Use specific details, especially sensory ones.

> The curtain opens. In flickering streams of red and blue light, the four dancers enter in their sleek, painted unitards. Two pace stealthily to the eerie, synthesized music. Two roll, meet, clasp hands, and lock their streamlined wheelchairs in a giddy silver spin. Suddenly the two chairs shoot off to the right and left. Onto one wheelchair leap the two pacing dancers for a very wild ride. From the other wheelchair, a man lifts his muscled arms to catch a trapeze. At once he is floating above the stage, launched from his wheels into blue air.

7. **Take a stand on an issue.** In a persuasive essay, you may want to put your position up front. Make it a strong statement so that readers must focus on the issues (and are curious to see your support).

> Dancing companies that include dancers with disabilities are not just an interesting oddity. They show us something very wrong with our attitudes, our society, and our schools: the idea that only "normal" bodies can find expression and joy in movement.

8. **Open with a quotation.** Other people's words can be an excellent way to lead into your own. As you gather information, be alert to (and *record*) colorful or forceful or moving quotations.

> "Every body is perfect! Against the perfect body!" That heartfelt cry opens the Web site of Bilderwerfer, a company of disabled and nondisabled dancers who are dedicated to proving the point.

The techniques for writing openers overlap and can be combined. For example, an opening quotation may be a startling fact. An anecdote may use terrific sensory details. A direct address to the reader may be in the form of a question. Be creative—experiment.

NOTE Do not forget, as you try out openers, that **the hook and introduction set a tone for your composition.** Humor is a wonderful way to get attention, but you will not want to use it if the rest of the composition will be heavily serious, not light. A personal anecdote is engaging too, but not appropriate if your paper abruptly moves into an impersonal report of information. Always think about tone when you plan your opening. Remember the idea of first impressions: Will your paper deliver what you seem to promise?

Exercise 4 **Analyzing Introductions**

Read the following three introductions written by professional writers, and then answer the following questions about each one.

- Which of the techniques (on pages 478–481) does the writer use to open the introduction?

- Does the opener work well? Does it make you want to read the article? Why or why not?

- What is the tone of the introduction? What words or phrases show you how the writer feels about the topic?

- Does the structure of the introduction follow the patterns you learned about on pages 476–478? How? If not, how is it different?

- Which other technique might be an effective way to introduce this topic? Why?

1. Duane Johnson may have developed the world's cleanest motor oil. He is so sure of the safety of his product that he submits it to an unusual test: He eats it. "When I go to meetings and have an engine running on this stuff, I'll pull the dipstick out and lick it." Petroleum-based motor oils cause a significant amount of the pollution a car releases, says Johnson, an agronomist at Colorado State University. His motor oil, made from canola and other vegetable oils, not only produces no air pollution of its own but also cuts overall engine emissions by up to 30 percent.

"Edible Motor Oil," *Discover*

2. Many and varied are the faces of art, and together they reveal the basic urges and aspirations of humanity. The search for sights and sounds that delight the senses is only one of these many faces. The Cro-Magnon cave people in their vivid renderings of the animals that roamed the primeval forests were searching for the means of bringing their environment under control. The Mesopotamians constructed massive staged towers to reach upward into the abodes of their gods. The Egyptians built and embellished their tombs to provide for life beyond the grave. Minoan murals were painted to decorate their dwellings and delight the eye. The Greeks sought to find reality in the underlying mathematical and harmonic proportions of their temples and godlike figures. Throughout history, art holds up a mirror to humanity.

William Fleming, *Arts & Ideas*

Cro-Magnon cave painting of Bison.

3.   Pulsars, the dense spinning remnants of exploded stars, contain about the same mass as the sun crushed into a wad of neutrons less than ten miles wide. These stellar nuggets spin as much as several hundred times a second, a spin that astronomers have believed was inherited from the rotating core of the pulsar's exploded parent star. Recently, however, two astrophysicists proposed that the conventional explanation for what makes pulsars spin is probably wrong.

"Cosmic Kickball," *Discover*

The Body

The **body** of a composition develops the thesis statement. Each major point of the thesis is supported, or proved, in one or more paragraphs. In an effective body, these paragraphs have sufficient detail—and they work together. The body requires **emphasis, unity, coherence,** and **elaboration.**

NOTE   Before drafting the body of a composition, you should plan or outline your main points and the support that elaborates on them.

Reference Note

For information about making an **early plan** (also called a **rough outline**) or a **formal outline,** see page 1074 in the Quick Reference Handbook.

Emphasis

When you **emphasize** something, you stress it. In a composition, you can emphasize an idea by giving it extra space and attention. That is, you write more about one main point (or points) than others. You can also emphasize an idea by discussing it first or last. This means, before and during drafting, you need to decide what is most important in your composition. What is its meat?

Unity

Unity is the condition of being "one"—a whole. A composition has unity when all of the major points relate to the main idea in the thesis statement. Each paragraph states or implies a topic sentence that relates to the thesis. Each detail in the paragraph relates to the topic sentence.

Coherence

Coherence describes an orderly relationship. In a coherent composition, ideas are clearly connected. Readers get the sense that every sentence, every paragraph, flows smoothly and sensibly from one to the next. Two strategies for coherence are **direct references** and **transitions**.

Direct References   You use **direct references** naturally in writing: using *he* to refer to William Shakespeare; using *truck* in one sentence and *pickup* in another; repeating an important phrase. You improve coherence by paying attention to direct references and employing them purposefully.

1. Use pronouns to refer to nouns already used.
2. Use synonyms or slight rewordings of key words and ideas.
3. Repeat key words or phrases. In a composition, this repetition is a good way to link paragraphs. For example, you can repeat or rephrase a key word from the end of one paragraph at the beginning of the next.

Transitional References   You use **transitional expressions,** words and phrases such as *next, on the other hand, as an example, therefore*, and *most important,* to guide readers from one idea, sentence, or paragraph to the next. They show links in your thought and smooth the way for readers.

Elaboration

Elaboration is sufficiently detailed support. It is what fleshes out the bare bones of your thesis: examples, descriptions, expert opinions, reasons, evidence, personal experience, statistics—whatever type of information is relevant to your points and helpful to your readers. If the body of your composition is too "thin," your audience may not be interested in your topic and thesis or even understand them. They may not accept your argument or even be able to judge it. Make your body solid with detail.

NOTE   Both *what* you are writing about and *why* you are writing affect the kinds of information you use for support. For example, if you were writing a speech to persuade the school board to buy more computers for English classes, you would use different supporting details than if you were writing a first-person article for the school paper about the fun of writing with a computer.

Exercise 5   Analyzing Body Paragraphs

Read these body paragraphs from a popular book about male and female communication styles, and then:

STYLE   TIP

A paragraph can itself act as a transition. Sometimes as brief as a single sentence, such a paragraph is written to bridge the ideas in one paragraph with those in another.

TIPS & TRICKS

If your supporting details look skimpy, don't get tense. Instead, let your mind wander. Record your thoughts and associations in your favorite form: freewriting, brainstormed lists, clusters, even tape-recording. You can throw out wild ideas, but you will get usable ones, too.

- Explain what types of support the paragraphs use and whether each paragraph is unified. Is there enough elaboration of the main points? Why do you think so?
- Explain the order each paragraph uses (see page 469): chronological, spatial, order of importance, or logical.
- Identify nouns and their direct-reference pronouns, repeated words and synonyms, and transitional expressions. Note the links *between* paragraphs, too.

Who talks more, women or men? According to the stereotype, women talk too much. Linguist Jennifer Coates notes some proverbs:

A woman's tongue wags like a lamb's tail.

Foxes are all tail and women are all tongue.

The North Sea will sooner be found wanting in water than a woman be at a loss for words.

Throughout history, women have been punished for talking too much or in the wrong way. Linguist Connie Eble lists a variety of physical punishments used in Colonial America: Women were strapped to ducking stools and held underwater until they nearly drowned, put into the stocks with signs pinned to them, gagged, and silenced by a cleft stick applied to their tongues.

Though such institutionalized corporal punishments have given way to informal, often psychological ones, modern stereotypes are not much different from those expressed in the old proverbs. Women are believed to talk too much. Yet study after study finds that it is men who talk more—at meetings, in mixed-group discussions, and in classrooms where girls or young women sit next to boys or young men. For example, communications researchers Barbara and Gene Eakins tape-recorded and studied seven university faculty meetings. They found that, with one exception, men spoke more often and, without exception, spoke for a longer time. The men's turns ranged from 10.66 to 17.07 seconds, while the women's turns ranged from 3 to 10 seconds. In other words, the women's longest turns were still shorter than the men's shortest turns.

Deborah Tannen, *You Just Don't Understand*

The Conclusion

If you want readers to remember your essay, make an unmistakable exit. The **conclusion** of your composition should leave readers with a final thought and a sense of closure.

Techniques for Writing Conclusions

Here are helpful techniques for writing conclusions with examples for the topic of dancers with disabilities.

1. **Restate your thesis.** To be sure your main idea hits home, say it again in a different way. This example rephrases the thesis in introduction number five on page 480.

> No one who watches the dancers will ever again think that wheelchairs signify a defect or weakness. The dancers amaze and thrill audiences. You hear it in gasps, laughter, and thunderous applause. They are artists glorying in their creativity; you see it on their joyful faces.

2. **Close with a call to action or a recommendation.** Especially in persuasive essays and articles, writers ask readers to take action, or they offer a solution or recommendation. Any composition, though, may use these techniques to close in an active way. The first example is from a persuasive essay; the second is from an informative one.

> What our schools need are more opportunities for students with disabilities to try out physical activities they usually cannot. Call your school's coaches and tell them about "wheelchair dancing." Ask the principal to order a videotape about it. Get on the PTA and school board agendas and show the tape. Change attitudes, and change will happen.

> Don't wait for someone to offer you a ticket to the Light Motion dance company. Go directly to the box office, buy one, and get a good seat. You have never seen anything like it before—but I bet you will want to see it again.

STYLE TIP

For many essays, you can write a conclusion using the letters E.S.B. to help you think of what to say.

1. E. = first sentence **echoes** the thesis
2. S. = next sentence **summarizes** the key points
3. B. = last sentence **broadens** the scope of the topic

3. **Refer to your introduction.** Often writers make a satisfying close by coming full circle, back to their starting point. Re-read the first model in introduction number four on page 479 and then the second model in conclusion number two. Notice how the closing repeats the hook about a ticket.
4. **End with an appropriate quotation.** A quotation that sums up your main point or that is particularly striking can make a strong ending.

> Judy Smith knows that dancers with physical disabilities are different. They are not, however, alien. Here is what she believes happens when a person sits in a theater and really *sees* people with disabilities: You "become one of the gang on earth."

Other ways to conclude a composition include:

- summarizing your main points
- making a personal comment about your topic
- posing a dramatic question or challenge
- offering a final example of your main idea

Most important in any conclusion is tying your ideas together and leaving your readers with the thoughts and emotion you want.

NOTE In formal compositions, you will often be asked to conclude by restating your main points *and* your thesis. The shape of a formal conclusion is the *opposite* of the typical shape of a formal introduction, which moves from general to specific. In the conclusion, the writer moves from restating the paper's specific points to a more general statement of the main idea, or thesis. The structure looks like this:

Specific

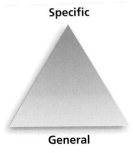

General

Exercise 6 Analyzing Conclusions

Work collaboratively with two or three classmates to find three professional conclusions that you like. Look in books, magazine articles, and
newspaper stories. Together, discuss and decide which techniques each
closing uses. Then, rewrite each closing, experimenting with different
techniques. (You might also rewrite the conclusion of the Writer's
Model beginning on the opposite page.)

Using a Basic Framework

The following chart is a framework for basic composition structure.
The Writer's Workshops in Part I of this book contain variations of this
structure, tailored to specific types of writing. Still, you will find that
most compositions follow this skeletal structure.

Framework for a Composition	
Introduction	• Engages the reader • Sets the tone • Presents the thesis statement
Body	• Gives the major points • Supports the major points with details
Conclusion	• Reinforces the main idea stated in the thesis • Ties the ideas together • Leaves the reader with a sense of closure

A Writer's Model

The following composition about computers in education includes the
thesis statement on page 475. You might want to use the composition
as a model for your own. (This writer includes interviews as support;
your paper might not.)

NOTE Students often wonder how many paragraphs they should
include in an essay. As this model shows, the number of body paragraphs is determined by the scope or breadth of your thesis. A narrow
thesis may have only two body paragraphs; a broad one may need many
more than three.

Computers and the Internet: The Classroom Goes Global

Seventeen-year-old Wyatt Pierce attends high school in a very small town in Oregon, but through classroom computers, he has access to a much wider world. He can browse through the online catalog of the state library, create a detailed map of his family's ranch, and even view live satellite pictures of the sun's explosive activity. Although computers put a universe of information in students' hands, their use in classrooms is not without problems.

Through Internet access, CD-ROMs, and software, computers make a difference in every subject students take, from math to science to English. In math classes, students use computers at every level from early arithmetic to the most advanced math. Interactive instruction "watches" students' attempts to solve math problems and gives them help when they need it. "Nice try. Why don't you try this?" is becoming a familiar computer refrain to students like Pierce. "I thought the computer feedback was a little stupid at first, but then came geometry, my downfall. Computers are *really* patient, which helps," he said.

In science classes, computers make possible "dry labs" where experiments and tests are carried out without physical contact with hazardous materials. They create three-dimensional physics problems, act as precise stopwatches, and allow animal dissection without animals. The Internet and World Wide Web also unfold undreamed of research opportunities, from National Science Foundation reports to consultation with university experts to real-time readings of data sent from the deep ocean.

(continued)

INTRODUCTION

Thesis statement

BODY
Major idea: Benefits of computers for studying subjects

Outside source: interview

STYLE TIP

The **title** of your composition is your first chance to grab your readers' attention. It should also point toward your main ideas. This means a clever title is good as long as it also indicates content and tone. Writers often start with a working title, which they revise when they finish the paper.

(continued)

In English classes, too, the Internet gives even remote school districts sophisticated research resources: the Library of Congress, faster inter-library loan, and online literary works. Word processing alone makes writing the dreaded essay a little easier to swallow. Students now write papers using electronic thesauruses, spellcheckers, dictionaries, and even grammar-and-style checkers. CD-ROMs also coordinate with traditional textbooks.

Major idea:
Benefits of
computers for
communication

The examples so far already hint at another classroom revolution courtesy of the Internet: communication. E-mail and chat rooms not only let students reach out to global pen pals but also to each other—twenty-four hours a day. The entire class can "listen" to and quiz a guest meteorology expert who lives across the country. The class can also hold a classroom discussion about *Hamlet* in which every student has a say, not just the confident students who always speak up. Wyatt Pierce likes being able to think and then comment: "Maybe I don't make my point in class, or maybe Sheila e-mails some weird but good idea. I can add to e-mail whenever I want." Also, teachers can have one-on-one conferences with students much more often. Sandra Sanchez, who teaches both English and computer literacy, even posts a newsletter for parents who have e-mail.

With computers and the Web, publishing is a reality, not just a classroom exercise. Papers, projects, and artwork can go online for all to see. Students also use desktop publishing systems to write and publish the school newspaper and to design the yearbook. Classes create their own Web pages—and receive feedback, even from foreign lands.

Major idea:
Problems with
classroom
computers

However, this unrestrained freedom is not all positive. Students who use the Internet must learn that the quality of its information is only as good as its contributors. If anyone can publish, viewers beware. Students must always evaluate sources and check accuracy.

Noneducational material is a concern, too, requiring teacher supervision and student limits. Sanchez now restricts e-mail and Net-surfing time. "Some students became obsessed with the technology. It is a great tool, but only a tool. I want their attention on what we're learning together," she said.

Outside source: interview

The "together" is important. Though computers aid communication and collaboration in some ways, they can also isolate. Many educators stress that human interaction is essential, in school as in life. Also, computers are not always best for learning. Math teachers, for example, worry that the computer becomes a crutch. Students need to be able to figure with paper and pencil and to measure a real, solid line.

At the same time, teachers who are locked out of our technological age are an issue, too. Most teachers have not grown up computer-literate; many even resist the technology. Until teachers are taught to guide students, computer "education" may be mostly gameplaying. Hardware cannot work miracles by itself.

That leads to a final problem: Cost. Computer equipment is expensive and quickly outdated. Big or rich school districts may have an unfair advantage over poor or small ones, which cannot afford the technology. Education should be equal opportunity.

CONCLUSION

No one doubts that computers in the classroom are here to stay. Concerns about their use are real but are minor compared with the enormous benefits. Sandra Sanchez sums up the advantages this way: "Computers are the most valuable tool to be introduced into the classroom over the last two hundred years. They don't just open doors into vast new worlds. They remove the walls."

Review B **Writing an Informative Composition**

Use the facts presented in note form below to write a brief composition. You may not use all of the information, and you may want to add additional information obtained through research or personal knowledge. Just be sure to keep your paper to a limited topic and to elaborate your main idea sufficiently.

Consult the sections of this chapter to develop a thesis statement and to draft the introduction, body, and conclusion. The framework on page 488 is a good checklist to begin the important work of revision. As you polish, continue to work on emphasis and coherence (direct references and transitions).

Hurricanes: Fascinating and Deadly

1. Hurricanes: of tropical origin; winds more than 74 miles/hour (64 knots); blow counterclockwise around center (in Southern Hemisphere, clockwise)
2. Necessary conditions: heat—thunderstorm plus ocean water more than 81°F plus high relative humidities in atmosphere (less cloud evaporation, more heat)
3. "Life cycle" from birth to death: cluster of thunderstorms, to tropical depression, to tropical storm, to hurricane—hurricanes can live up to three weeks
4. Break up rapidly over cold water or large land mass
5. Before satellites and radar, people knew little about weather just 60 miles offshore. Now meteorologists, satellites, and the Tropical Prediction Center can track storm's birth, give evacuation notice up to two days before hurricane hits
6. Hurricane hunters (since 1944): Keesler Air Force Base, Mississippi. Fly weather instruments right into storm, relay data
7. Hurricane Andrew 1992: 50 dead, $30 billion property damage
8. Danger: wind, torrential rain, flooding—important to heed warnings
9. Evacuation: plan place; take map (roads may close); don't drive through water; have rain gear on hand
10. Supply kit: first aid, canned food, water (3 gallons/person, 3 days), flashlight, radio, batteries
11. "Hurricane" (Atlantic & Eastern Pacific); "typhoon" (North Pacific & Philippines); "cyclones" (Indian Ocean & South Pacific)

12. Are named when still tropical storms. Since 1953, Tropical Prediction Center has listed names in advance for Atlantic & for Eastern Pacific—alphabetical; alternate female & male (2002: Arthur, Bertha, Cristobal, Dolly, etc.)
13. U.S. storms only 12% of worldwide tropical disturbances. Most? Western North Pacific, average is 25 typhoons/yr.
14. Hurricanes and tornadoes: hurricanes' lifetime measured in days, tornadoes in minutes
15. Hurricane Floyd 1999: caused major flooding in North Carolina, New Jersey, and Virginia

Satellite view of a hurricane.

PART 3

Grammar, Usage, and Mechanics

internet connect

go.
hrw.
.com

GO TO: go.hrw.com
KEYWORD: EOLang

Parts of Speech Overview
Identification and Function

Diagnostic Preview

A. Identifying Parts of Speech

For each of the following sentences, identify every word or word group that is the part of speech indicated in parentheses.

EXAMPLE   1. On September 8, 1998, Mark McGwire hit his sixty-second home run for the season, breaking Roger Maris's record. (*noun*)

         1. *September 8, 1998; Mark McGwire; home run; season; Roger Maris's; record*

1. If anyone calls me while I am out, will you please give whoever it is one of these two numbers? (*pronoun*)
2. Although she lost her sight and hearing during childhood, Helen Keller learned to communicate with other people. (*noun*)
3. As much as we all had wanted to eat at the new French restaurant, we could not afford the prices. (*conjunction*)
4. Inca artisans were quite expert; among the works they left behind are elaborate jewelry and colorful tapestries. (*adverb*)
5. The cat came screaming around the corner, scooted under the car, and seemed almost to fly up the tree. (*preposition*)
6. This clock chimes a delicate melody on the half-hour. (*adjective*)
7. Do you think that the weather will finally turn cool once this low-pressure system moves through the area? (*verb*)

8. I developed extremely painful shin splints when I jogged much farther than I usually do. (*adverb*)
9. Oh, how beautifully Kathleen Battle and Jessye Norman sang in their concert at Carnegie Hall! (*interjection*)
10. Neither the coach nor the team members offered excuses for the loss, for they had done their best. (*conjunction*)

B. Identifying Parts of Speech

Identify the part of speech of each italicized word in the following sentences.

EXAMPLE   1. *Although* I don't consider *myself* a chronic television viewer or an avid radio listener, I have *certainly* enjoyed my visit to the Museum of Television and Radio.

        1. *Although—conjunction; myself—pronoun; certainly—adverb*

11. When *it* opened in 1991, the Museum of Television and Radio became New York City's first new major museum *since* 1966.
12. The late William Paley, the *founder* of CBS, *established* the museum with contributions from the broadcasting industry.
13. The museum doesn't contain *everything* ever heard on radio or seen on TV, *for* many early programs were never copied, and some of those that were copied are missing or unplayable.
14. *Its* collection, however, is *quite* extensive: approximately twenty-five thousand TV programs, fifteen thousand radio shows, and ten thousand commercials.
15. *Whether* you want to hear Jack Benny in a comedy sketch from the 1930s *or* you wish to watch Billie Holiday in a live performance from the 1950s, you'll find the recording *here*.
16. In fact, the earliest material *dates* to 1920, *when* the nation's first radio station, KDKA in Pittsburgh, went on the air.
17. Modern *technology* provides *easy* access to most of the collection.
18. Simply answer a *few* questions and press a button *on* one of the computers that store the catalog.
19. *Instantly*, a museum worker, using the computer, signals special machines in the basement, *which* automatically load the tapes.
20. Often by the time you've made *yourself* comfortable in one of the console rooms, the tape is *ready* for you to enjoy.

The Noun

14a. A *noun* names a person, a place, a thing, or an idea.

Persons	carpenter, tourists, team, cousins, Faith Ringgold
Places	cities, theater, forest, neighborhood, Santa Fe
Things	merry-go-round, bricks, birds, horseshoe, Liberty Bell
Ideas	justice, creativity, self-control, opinions, Buddhism

┌─HELP─

Nouns can be classified as (1) common or proper, (2) concrete or abstract, (3) collective, and (4) compound.

Reference Note

For more information about **capitalizing proper nouns,** see page 792.

Common Nouns and Proper Nouns

A *common noun* names any one of a group of persons, places, things, or ideas. A *proper noun* names a particular person, place, thing, or idea. A common noun is not capitalized (except when it begins a sentence or is part of a title); a proper noun, however, is capitalized.

Common Nouns	Proper Nouns
woman	Queen Isabella, Wilma Mankiller, Judith Baca
nation	Egypt, Mexico, Vietnam, New Zealand
event	Pan American Games, French Revolution, Academy Awards, Boston Tea Party
holiday	Patriot's Day; Fourth of July; Martin Luther King, Jr., Day; Mardi Gras
language	Hebrew, Spanish, Bantu, Thai, Latin

Concrete Nouns and Abstract Nouns

A *concrete noun* names a person, place, or thing that can be perceived by one or more of the senses (sight, hearing, taste, touch, and smell). An *abstract noun* names an idea, a feeling, a quality, or a characteristic.

Concrete Nouns	sneeze, star, gravel, cinnamon, jack-o'-lantern, Beijing, Leaning Tower of Pisa, Sammy Sosa
Abstract Nouns	peace, civilization, honor, courage, citizenship, Victorianism, Manifest Destiny

Collective Nouns

The singular form of a *collective noun* names a group.

Collective Nouns	jury, band, family, class, flock, committee

Compound Nouns

A *compound noun* consists of two or more words that together name a person, a place, a thing, or an idea. The parts of a compound noun may be written as one word, as separate words, or as a hyphenated word.

One Word	stairway, bookcase, toenail, Newfoundland
Separate Words	lieutenant governor, ceiling fan, blue jay, Golden Gate Bridge
Hyphenated Word	sister-in-law, jack-of-all-trades, great-uncle, stick-in-the-mud

Reference Note

For information about **using verbs and pronouns that agree with collective nouns,** see pages 610 and 622.

┌─HELP─

If you are not sure how to write a compound noun, look it up in an up-to-date dictionary.

Exercise 1 Identifying and Classifying Nouns

Identify the nouns in each of the following sentences, and classify each noun as *proper* or *common* and as *concrete* or *abstract.*

EXAMPLE
1. In his report on the importance of religion in ancient Egypt, Joaquin wrote about the Great Sphinx and the Great Pyramid at Giza.

1. *report—common, concrete; importance—common, abstract; religion—common, abstract; Egypt—proper, concrete; Joaquin—proper, concrete; Great Sphinx— proper, concrete; Great Pyramid—proper, concrete; Giza—proper, concrete*

1. In one afternoon the crew repaired eleven helicopters.
2. Amalia Mesa-Bains and Michael Ríos are among the many Hispanic artists who launched their careers in San Francisco.
3. In Japan many homes have a place of honor in which the family displays a favorite scroll or a vase of flowers.
4. We purchased tomatoes, lettuce, and corn grown by local farmers.
5. Congress debated the merits of the bill but could not reach a consensus.
6. My goal is to visit every state in the United States.

7. Our family drove from our home in Kansas City to Chicago in our new van.

8. Her excellent record as treasurer convinced a majority of the students to vote for her for president.

9. Blunt honesty, quick wit, and fierce loyalty all characterize the protagonist of *The Adventures of Huckleberry Finn.*

10. The crowd roared as Chip sank the winning basket for the Falcons just before time ran out.

┌─HELP─
Not every sentence in Exercise 2 contains both compound nouns and collective nouns.

Exercise 2 Identifying and Classifying Nouns

Identify the compound nouns and collective nouns in the following sentences. Then, classify each as *common* or *proper* and as *concrete* or *abstract.*

EXAMPLE
1. After her class had viewed a filmstrip about some of the ancient Egyptians' engineering feats, which included the construction of the Great Pyramid, the teacher, Ms. Ng, displayed this snapshot.

1. *compound: filmstrip—common, concrete; Great Pyramid—proper, concrete; Ms. Ng—proper, concrete; snapshot—common, concrete*

collective: class—common, concrete

1. Did you do a double take when you saw this picture?

2. The juxtaposition of Egyptian landmarks with a seashore and a sign in Japanese writing is certainly an eye-opener.

3. Actually, the Sphinx and the pyramid are sand sculptures that a team of students from a high school in Japan built for the Kamakura Beach Carnival at Zaimokuza Beach.

4. Do you suppose the committee that judged the sculptures awarded the students' undertakings a prize?

5. The sightseers in front of the pyramid took a number of snapshots as keepsakes of the carnival.

6. Unlike the original Sphinx and Great Pyramid, which have stood for 4500 years, these sculptures will disappear with the first heavy rainstorm.

7. While the artists may use a variety of tools to carve and shape their creations, the final artwork consists of only two ingredients—sand and water.

8. Artists from around the world meet on beaches to see who can sculpt the most intricate and entertaining artwork made of sand.

9. Often, these sculptures illustrate stories or books, such as "Jack and the Beanstalk" and *Gulliver's Travels.*

10. One group built a sand castle that was over fifty-six feet tall.

The Pronoun

14b. A ***pronoun*** **takes the place of one or more nouns or pronouns.**

The word or word group that a pronoun stands for is called the *antecedent* of the pronoun.

EXAMPLES Jay enjoys hiking and camping; in fact, **they** are his two favorite pastimes. [The nouns *hiking* and *camping* are the antecedents of the pronoun *they.*]

One of the film projectors is broken. **It** is being repaired. [The pronoun *One* is the antecedent of the pronoun *It.*]

The students complained to the principal about the dress code. **They** wished **he** had consulted **them** about **it.** [The noun *students* is the antecedent of the pronouns *They* and *them;* the noun *principal* is the antecedent of the pronoun *he;* and the compound noun *dress code* is the antecedent of the pronoun *it.*]

Reference Note

For more information on **pronouns and their antecedents,** see pages 618 and 656.

HELP

Pronouns can be classified as (1) personal, (2) reflexive or intensive, (3) demonstrative, (4) interrogative, (5) relative, or (6) indefinite.

Reference Note

For more about the various forms of **personal pronouns,** see **Chapter 19: Using Pronouns Correctly.**

Personal Pronouns

A *personal pronoun* refers to the one(s) speaking (*first person*), the one(s) spoken to (*second person*), or the one(s) spoken about (*third person*).

	Singular	Plural
First Person	I, me, my, mine	we, us, our, ours
Second Person	you, your, yours	you, your, yours
Third Person	he, him, his, she, her, hers, it, its	they, them, their, theirs

EXAMPLES   If **I** give **you my** address, will **you** write to **me**?

We told **them** that **they** could go with **us**.

NOTE This textbook refers to the words *my, your, his, her, its, our,* and *their* as possessive pronouns. However, because they come before nouns and tell *which one* or *whose,* some authorities prefer to call these words adjectives. Follow your teacher's instructions regarding these possessive forms.

Reflexive and Intensive Pronouns

	Singular	Plural
First Person	myself	ourselves
Second Person	yourself	yourselves
Third Person	himself, herself, itself	themselves

A *reflexive pronoun* refers to the subject of a verb and functions as a complement or as the object of a preposition.

EXAMPLES   Mary excused **herself** from the table. [*Herself* is the direct object of *excused.*]

He said the mastermind was, in fact, **himself.** [*Himself* is a predicate nominative referring to the subject, *He.*]

They took extra biscuits for **themselves.** [*Themselves* is the object of the preposition *for.*]

┌HELP─

Do not use the nonstandard forms *hisself, theirself,* and *theirselves.* Use *himself* and *themselves* instead.

An *intensive pronoun* emphasizes its antecedent—a noun or another pronoun.

EXAMPLES   Joseph Vásquez **himself** wrote the script. [*Himself* emphasizes the subject, *Joseph Vásquez*, but has no grammatical function in the sentence.]

The final speech was given by Maya Angelou **herself.** [*Herself* emphasizes the object, *Maya Angelou*, but has no grammatical function in the sentence.]

Demonstrative Pronouns

A *demonstrative pronoun* points out a noun or another pronoun.

this	that	these	those

EXAMPLES   Is **this** the one you want?

That may be the only reasonable solution.

These or **those** are the pictures from our vacation.

Interrogative Pronouns

An *interrogative pronoun* introduces a question.

who	whom	whose	which	what

EXAMPLES   **What** is the capital of the Hawaiian Islands?

Whose is this red sweater?

To **whom** should I direct your call?

Relative Pronouns

A *relative pronoun* introduces a subordinate clause.

that	which	who	whom	whose

EXAMPLES   The college **that** I chose is in Texas.

The woman **who** chairs the committee is my aunt.

The birds, **which** usually have flown south by this time of the year, were still congregating in our backyard.

⌐ TIPS & TRICKS ⌐

If you are not sure whether a pronoun is reflexive or intensive, use this test: Read the sentence aloud, omitting the pronoun. If the basic meaning of the sentence stays the same, the pronoun is intensive. If the meaning changes, the pronoun is reflexive.

EXAMPLES
Mark repaired the car **himself.** [Without *himself*, the meaning stays the same. The pronoun is intensive.]

The children enjoyed **themselves** all morning. [Without *themselves*, the sentence doesn't make sense. The pronoun is reflexive.]

Reference Note

For more about **relative pronouns** and **subordinate clauses,** see page 579. For information on when to use **who** or **whom,** see page 646.

Reference Note

For more information about **indefinite pronouns,** see pages 603 and 619.

Indefinite Pronouns

An *indefinite pronoun* refers to a person, a place, a thing, or an idea that may or may not be specifically named. In other words, the pronoun may not have a specific antecedent.

EXAMPLES   **All** of the members have voted. [*All* refers to *members.*]

Does **everyone** favor a weekly meeting? [*Everyone* has no specific antecedent.]

The fallen tree provided homes for **several** of the creatures of the woods. [*Several* refers to *creatures.*]

Common Indefinite Pronouns				
all	both	few	nobody	several
another	each	many	none	some
any	either	more	no one	somebody
anybody	everybody	most	nothing	someone
anyone	everyone	much	one	something
anything	everything	neither	other	such

Pronoun or Adjective?

Many of the words that can be used as pronouns can also be used as adjectives.

EXAMPLES   **This** is the best baklava I have ever tasted. [*This* is a pronoun referring to *baklava,* the predicate nominative.]

This baklava is delicious. [*This* is an adjective modifying *baklava*.]

Which of the rooms is yours? [*Which* is a pronoun referring to *rooms,* the object of the preposition *of.*]

Which room is yours? [*Which* is an adjective modifying *room.*]

Exercise 3   Identifying Pronouns

Identify the pronouns in the following sentences.

EXAMPLE   1. Most of those who took the photography class learned a great deal about how they perceive their environment.

     1. *Most, those, who, they, their*

1. Last year my school gave two photography courses, neither of which had been offered before.
2. The course that I took dealt with the ways in which people perceive their environment.
3. Many of us block out much in our everyday surroundings.
4. You can demonstrate to yourselves how unaware of our surroundings nearly all of us are.
5. Which of you, on returning home from a trip, hasn't noticed how different all of the rooms look to you?
6. Some of your possessions may seem unfamiliar to you, and a few of them may appear quite peculiar.
7. Eventually the sensation fades, and your surroundings assume their usual background role.
8. Each of us can regain the ability to see freshly if we learn to make full use of our sense of sight.
9. We can train ourselves to perceive the objects as shapes instead of thinking about their functions.
10. As the French Impressionist painter Claude Monet remarked, we must forget the names of the things that we observe.

The Adjective

14c. An *adjective* modifies a noun or a pronoun.

To modify means "to describe" or "to make more definite." An adjective modifies a noun or a pronoun by telling *what kind, which one, how many,* or *how much.*

What Kind?	**ripening** apples	**happy** child
	Asian country	**up-to-date** look
Which One?	**this** book	**last** straw
	those girls	**next** step
How Many?	**two** students	**both** answers
	several choices	**many** people
How Much?	**one-half** cup	**enough** time
	more money	**less** trouble

HELP

To keep your readers from getting confused, always try to place pronouns near their antecedents—generally within the same sentence or in the next sentence.

CONFUSING
Please hand me the brushes. I also need some linseed oil. They are on the top shelf. [Does *They* refer to the brushes or to both the brushes and the linseed oil?]

CLEAR
Please hand me the **brushes. They** are on the top shelf. I also need some linseed oil. [Only the brushes are on the top shelf.]

TIPS & TRICKS

The phrase "these five interesting books" can help you remember the questions an adjective can answer: Which books? **These** books. How many books? **Five** books. What kind of books? **Interesting** books.

An adjective usually precedes the word it modifies.

EXAMPLE   The **tired** and **hungry** hikers straggled into camp.

Sometimes, for emphasis, an adjective follows the word it modifies.

EXAMPLE   The hikers, **tired** and **hungry,** straggled into camp.

An adjective that modifies the subject may appear in the predicate. Such an adjective is called a *predicate adjective.*

EXAMPLES   The hikers felt **tired** and **hungry.**

Tired and **hungry** were the hikers.

Articles

The most frequently used adjectives are *a, an,* and *the.* These words are called *articles.*

A and *an* are called *indefinite articles* because they refer to any member of a general group. *A* is used before words beginning with a consonant sound; *an* is used before words beginning with a vowel sound.

EXAMPLES   Felipe added **a** tomato and **an** avocado to the salad.

A European said, "It is **an** honor to be here with you." [*A* is used before *European* because *European* begins with a consonant sound. *An* is used before *honor* because the *h* in *honor* is not pronounced; *honor* is pronounced as though it began with a vowel.]

The is called the *definite article* because it refers to a specific person, place, thing, or idea.

EXAMPLE   We spent **the** hour discussing **the** revolution that began in 1791 in Haiti.

Adjective or Pronoun?

In different contexts, a word may be used as different parts of speech. For example, the following words may be used as adjectives and as pronouns.

all	either	much	some	those
another	few	neither	such	what
any	many	one	that	which
both	more	other	these	whose
each	most	several	this	

Reference Note

For more about **predicate adjectives,** see page 544. For guidelines on **using adjectives,** see Chapter 22.

┌HELP─

Remember that the sound, not the spelling, of a word determines which indefinite article to use before that word.

┌HELP─

In this book the words *my, your, his, her, its, our,* and *their,* which take the place of possessive nouns, are called possessive pronouns. Since they precede nouns and tell *which one* or *whose,* some teachers prefer to call these words possessive adjectives.

EXAMPLES
my job, **your** essay,

their plans

Follow your teacher's instructions in labeling these words.

Remember that an adjective *modifies* a noun or a pronoun and that a pronoun *takes the place of* a noun or another pronoun.

ADJECTIVE Ntozake Shange wrote **both** poems. [*Both* modifies the noun *poems.*]

PRONOUN Ntozake Shange wrote **both**. [*Both* takes the place of the noun *poems.*]

ADJECTIVE **These** books are overdue. [*These* modifies the noun *books.*]

PRONOUN **These** are overdue. [*These* takes the place of the noun *books.*]

ADJECTIVE **Several** ducks had dark green heads. [*Several* modifies the noun *ducks.*]

PRONOUN **Several** had dark green heads. [*Several* takes the place of the noun *ducks.*]

NOTE The words *this, that, these,* and *those* are called **demonstrative pronouns** when they take the place of nouns or other pronouns and are called **demonstrative adjectives** when they modify nouns or pronouns.

Reference Note

For more about **demonstrative pronouns,** see page 503.

HELP

Possessive forms of nouns, like possessive pronouns, are sometimes referred to as adjectives. Follow your teacher's instructions regarding these forms.

Adjective or Noun?

Most words that are used as nouns can also be used as adjectives.

Nouns	Adjectives
sofa	**sofa** cushion
hotel	**hotel** lobby
taco	**taco** salad
high school	**high school** senior
Marine Corps	**Marine Corps** cadet

An adjective that is formed from a proper noun, such as *Marine Corps* in the last example above, is called a **proper adjective.** Proper adjectives, like proper nouns, are capitalized.

NOTE Do not mistake part of a compound noun for an adjective. The entire word group is considered a noun.

COMPOUND NOUNS   paper clips, cable TV, time capsule, United States

HELP

If you are not sure if a word group is considered a compound noun or an adjective with a noun, consult a dictionary.

GRAMMAR

STYLE | TIP |

Using adjectives, especially those that appeal to the five senses—sight, hearing, touch, smell, and taste—can help you create vivid images. When describing nouns or pronouns, be as specific in your choices of adjectives as you can. For example, instead of using the adjective *red,* you might use an adjective that specifies a shade of red, such as *crimson, coral, magenta, maroon,* or *terra cotta.*

┌─HELP─

Two good
sources to use to find precise adjectives and other parts of speech (adverbs, nouns, and verbs) are a thesaurus and a dictionary. First, check a thesaurus for possible choices to use. Then, look up the words in a dictionary and compare their meanings so that you can decide which choice will convey the precise meaning you intend.

Exercise 4 **Identifying Adjectives and the Words They Modify**

Identify the adjectives and the words they modify in the following sentences. Do not include articles (*a, an,* and *the*).

EXAMPLE   1. I have read two fascinating books by the talented writer William Least Heat-Moon.

     1. *two—books; fascinating—books; talented—writer*

1. His first book, *Blue Highways,* chronicled a journey across the United States in 1978.
2. That book attracted many readers and made the national bestseller lists.
3. In *PrairyErth,* Heat-Moon narrows his focus to a single Kansas county.
4. The unusual title comes from the shorthand term scientists use for the unique soils of the central states.
5. Chase County lies in east-central Kansas.
6. It is, as Heat-Moon says, "the most easterly piece" of the West.
7. A county with a population of 3,013 may seem an unlikely location for an examination of the role humanity plays on this planet.
8. After all, the county has only two towns and a few villages.
9. In many ways, though, Kansas is a microcosm of America.
10. In this masterful prose, Chase County in turn reveals itself to be a microcosm of Kansas.

Review A **Identifying Nouns, Pronouns, and Adjectives**

Tell whether each italicized word or word group in the following sentences is used as a *noun,* a *pronoun,* or an *adjective.* If a word or word group is used as an adjective, give the word it modifies.

EXAMPLE   1. *Everyone* in class is writing a poem about an *American* pioneer.

     1. *Everyone—pronoun; American—adjective—pioneer*

1. Several students are writing *theirs* about people whose names are familiar to *many;* others have chosen people who they believe merit wider recognition.
2. After *much* thought, I have finally narrowed my choices to two *African American* women whom I admire.

3. Both of *these* women broke *new* ground in their fields—one in the performing arts and the other in the visual arts.

4. The fieldwork *that* Katherine Dunham (right) did as an anthropology student in the West Indies inspired her to incorporate elements of African and Caribbean folk culture into *modern dance.*

5. After touring the world for *several* decades, the dancer-choreographer founded the Katherine Dunham Children's Workshop, which she still directs, in *East St. Louis,* Illinois.

6. Tributes to Dunham continue to pour in, for *she* is considered a true *dance* innovator.

7. My other *potential* choice is Barbara Brandon, who in 1991 became the first African American woman cartoonist to achieve syndication in the *mainstream* press.

8. As you can see below, Brandon's *comic strip* depicts life from the *perspective* of an African American woman.

9. Brandon pictures only the heads and, occasionally, the hands of her characters, *all* of whom are women, because she believes that women's bodies are displayed enough in the *media.*

10. As *you* might guess, my final choice of a subject will not be an easy *one.*

The Verb

14d. A *verb* expresses action or a state of being.

Main Verbs and Helping Verbs

A *main verb* and one or more *helping verbs* (also called *auxiliary verbs*) make up a *verb phrase.*

┌HELP─
In this book, verbs are classified (1) as helping or main verbs, (2) as action or linking verbs, and (3) as transitive or intransitive verbs.

EXAMPLES   Daniel **has played.** [*Has* is the helping verb; *played* is the main verb.]

Simon **will be going.** [*Will* and *be* are the helping verbs; *going* is the main verb.]

Lynn **should have been working.** [*Should, have,* and *been* are the helping verbs; *working* is the main verb.]

Common Helping Verbs			
Forms of *Be*	am are be	been being is	was were
Forms of *Have*	had	has	have
Forms of *Do*	do	does	did
Modals	can could may	might must shall	should will would

Reference Note

For more about **modals,** see page 712.

A *modal* (or *modal auxillary*) is a helping verb that is joined with a main verb to express an attitude such as necessity or possibility.

EXAMPLES   We **must** win this game to reach the playoffs. [necessity]

Mr. Garza said that if we work hard enough on the play we are writing, we **may** get to perform it for the whole school. [possibility]

A helping verb may be separated from the main verb.

EXAMPLES   **Have** you **seen** Tom Stoppard's play *Rosencrantz and Guildenstern Are Dead*?

You **should** not **miss** it.

HELP

The word *not* and its contraction, *–n't,* are adverbs telling *to what extent;* neither is part of a verb phrase.

Action Verbs

An *action verb* expresses either physical or mental activity.

Physical	speak	sleep	carry	throw
Mental	think	imagine	dream	know

EXAMPLES   The horse **galloped** across the field.

The Colorado River **runs** through the Grand Canyon.

If the ball **touched** the line, the umpire **made** the right call.

Do you ever **wonder** what dogs **dream**?

Linking Verbs

A *linking verb* connects the subject to a word or word group that identifies or describes the subject. Such a word or word group is called a *subject complement.*

EXAMPLES   Wovoka **was** an influential Paiute prophet. [The subject complement *prophet* identifies the subject *Wovoka.*]

Marcy **looks** serious. [The subject complement *serious* describes the subject *Marcy.*]

Computers **were** once so large that they could fill a room but **are** now small enough, in some cases, to fit in a pocket. [The subject complements *large* and *small* describe the subject *Computers.*]

Reference Note

For more about **subject complements,** see page 543.

Common Linking Verbs			
Forms of *Be*			
am	be	will be	had been
is	can be	could be	shall have been
are	may be	should be	will have been
was	might be	would be	could have been
were	must be	has been	should have been
being	shall be	have been	would have been
Others			
appear	grow	seem	stay
become	look	smell	taste
feel	remain	sound	turn

TIPS & TRICKS

To determine whether a verb is a linking verb or an action verb, substitute a form of *be* or *seem.* If the sentence still makes sense, the verb is a linking verb.

LINKING
The fabric **felt** soft. [*The fabric was soft* makes sense.]

ACTION
I **felt** the fabric. [*I was the fabric* doesn't make sense.]

Some of the verbs listed as *Others* in the chart above can be used as either linking verbs or action verbs, depending on the context of the sentence.

LINKING   The alarm **sounded** shrill.
 ACTION   I **sounded** the alarm.

NOTE The forms of *be* are not always used as linking verbs. That is, they are sometimes used as state-of-being verbs but are not used to connect subjects to subject complements. In such cases, words that tell *where* or *when* are generally used to complete the meanings of the verb forms.

EXAMPLE   You **should have been** here yesterday. [*Here* tells *where*, and *yesterday* tells *when*.]

Transitive and Intransitive Verbs

A *transitive verb* has an *object*—a word or word group that tells who or what receives the action of the verb.

EXAMPLES   The rain **lashed** the windows. [The object *windows* receives the action of the verb *lashed*.]

We **closed** and **bolted** the shutters. [The object *shutters* receives the action of the verbs *closed* and *bolted*.]

An *intransitive verb* does not have an object.

EXAMPLES   The rain **fell.**

My cousin **arrived** yesterday.

Many English verbs can be either transitive or intransitive, depending on how they are used.

TRANSITIVE   The chorus **sang** patriotic songs. [The object *songs* receives the action of the verb *sang*.]
INTRANSITIVE   The chorus **sang** beautifully. [no object]

Like a one-word verb, a verb phrase may be classified as action or linking and as transitive or intransitive.

EXAMPLES   The actors **are practicing** their lines. [action, transitive]

The director **is meeting** with the stage crew. [action, intransitive]

Preparation for the opening night **has been** hectic! [linking, intransitive]

NOTE While action verbs may be transitive or intransitive, linking verbs and state-of-being verbs are always intransitive.

Reference Note

For more about **objects of verbs,** see page 539.

┌**HELP**──

Most dictionaries group the definitions of verbs according to whether the verbs are used transitively (*v.t.*) or intransitively (*v.i.*). If you use a dictionary to determine whether a verb is transitive or intransitive, be sure to check all of the definitions.

Exercise 5 Identifying and Classifying Verbs and Verb Phrases

Identify the verbs and verb phrases in the following sentences. Then, classify each verb or verb phrase as *linking* or *action*, and as *transitive* or *intransitive*.

EXAMPLE   1. The dark clouds did not make the day more pleasant.

          1. did make—action, transitive

1. When will Halley's Comet next appear?
2. A creosote bush in the Mojave Desert has lived for approximately twelve thousand years.
3. How many decimal places of pi can you name?
4. What is the purpose of the Electoral College?
5. You can remove chewing gum from clothing more easily if you first harden it with ice.
6. Mark Twain used a typewriter when he wrote *The Adventures of Tom Sawyer*.
7. You should be more careful, young man!
8. In 1997, Tiger Woods became the youngest winner of the Masters Tournament.
9. Have you been listening to the Shostakovich CD that I lent you?
10. The first Super Bowl was in 1967; the Green Bay Packers defeated the Kansas City Chiefs, 35 to 10.

HELP

Some sentences in Exercise 5 have more than one verb or verb phrase.

Exercise 6 Identifying and Classifying Verbs and Verb Phrases

Identify the verbs and verb phrases in the following sentences. Then, classify each verb or verb phrase as *linking* or *action*, and as *transitive* or *intransitive*.

EXAMPLES   1. I have never visited the Statue of Liberty.

          1. have visited—action, transitive

          2. It must be a truly amazing sight.

          2. must be—linking, intransitive

1. The Statue of Liberty, which has become a major American landmark, may be the most famous structure in the world.
2. It possesses a twofold appeal: It symbolizes human liberty, and it unfailingly awes the visitor by its colossal size.

HELP

Some sentences in Exercise 6 have more than one verb or verb phrase.

3. Moreover, it has withstood the continuous assaults of time and weather.

4. Frédéric Auguste Bartholdi designed the statue, and plans for the supporting framework came from the drawing board of Alexandre Gustave Eiffel.

5. The copper-plated statue has an intricate and strong iron framework that supports Liberty's familiar pose.

6. The statue was a gift from the people of France, but Americans paid the construction costs for the pedestal.

7. In newspaper editorials, Joseph Pulitzer persuaded the American people that they needed the statue.

8. The people agreed, and in 1886, the nation celebrated the dedication of the Statue of Liberty on what was at that time Bedloe's Island in Upper New York Bay.

9. Bartholdi modeled Liberty's face after his mother's features.

10. Those features have remained symbols of quiet determination.

The Adverb

14e. An **adverb** modifies a verb, an adjective, or another adverb.

An adverb tells *where, when, how,* or *to what extent* (*how much, how often,* or *how long*). Adverbs are most commonly used to modify verbs and verb phrases.

Adverbs may modify verbs.

EXAMPLES   Teresa spoke **eloquently.** [The adverb *eloquently* modifies the verb *spoke,* telling *how.*]

Have you heard this melody **before**? [The adverb *before* modifies the verb phrase *Have heard,* telling *when.*]

They searched **everywhere.** [The adverb *everywhere* modifies the verb *searched,* telling *where.*]

He had **not** read the contract **thoroughly.** [The adverbs *not* and *thoroughly* modify the verb phrase *had read,* telling *to what extent.*]

NOTE   The word *not* and its contraction, *–n't,* are adverbs telling *to what extent.*

"I've just read your latest book and found it fast moving and full of suspense and very well written. You're probably just the person who could clear up something that's been puzzling me for years, what's an adverb?"

© 1993 Sidney Harris.

Adverbs may modify adjectives.

EXAMPLES Phuong Vu is **quite** creative. [The adverb *quite* modifies the adjective *creative*, telling *to what extent*.]

This species is found on an **extremely** remote island. [The adverb *extremely* modifies the adjective *remote*, telling *to what extent*.]

Adverbs may modify other adverbs.

EXAMPLES Jackie Joyner-Kersee runs **remarkably** swiftly. [The adverb *remarkably* modifies the adverb *swiftly*, telling *to what extent*.]

It's **too** soon to know the results. [The adverb *too* modifies the adverb *soon*, telling *to what extent*.]

S T Y L E   T I P

The most frequently used adverbs are *too, so, really,* and *very.* In fact, these words are often overused. To make your speaking and writing more interesting, you can replace these adverbs with less common ones, such as *completely, especially,* or *quite.*

Noun or Adverb?

Some words that are often used as nouns may also be used as adverbs.

EXAMPLES My parents left **yesterday.** [The noun *yesterday* is used as an adverb telling *when*.]

They will return **home Saturday.** [The noun *home* is used as an adverb telling *where*. The noun *Saturday* is used as an adverb telling *when*.]

Reference Note

For more about **using adverbs,** see Chapter 22.

Exercise 7 **Identifying Adverbs and the Words They Modify**

Identify the adverbs and the words they modify in the following sentences.

EXAMPLE 1. I recently read an article about the American physicist Rosalyn Yalow.

1. *recently—read*

HELP

Some sentences in Exercise 7 contain more than one adverb.

1. Yalow helped develop an extremely sensitive biological technique.
2. Radioimmunoassay, which is now used in laboratories around the world, readily detects antibodies and hormones.
3. Yalow realized that anyone who proposes a distinctly new idea must always anticipate that it will not be widely accepted at first.
4. Most scientists do not leap excitedly from the bath crying "Eureka!" as people say Archimedes did.
5. Yalow and her colleague accidentally discovered radioimmunoassay while observing two patients.

Reference Note

For information about **adverbs used to join words or word groups,** see **relative adverbs** (page 579) and **conjunctive adverbs** (page 589).

6. After they carefully interpreted their observations, they arrived at their exciting discovery.

7. In 1977, although Yalow's collaborator had died, the Nobel Prize Committee awarded Yalow and two other researchers the undeniably prestigious Nobel Prize for medicine.

8. Radioimmunoassay ultimately became a basic diagnostic tool in very different areas of medicine.

9. According to Yalow, because people ordinarily resist change, the technique was not quickly accepted.

10. She believes that progress cannot be impeded forever and that good ideas are eventually accepted.

Review B Identifying Parts of Speech

Identify the part of speech of each italicized word in the following sentences. If the word is used as an adjective or an adverb, tell what word or words it modifies.

EXAMPLE   1. The *Mexican* artist Diego Rivera was a *remarkably* talented *muralist.*

1. *Mexican—adjective—artist*
   remarkably—adverb—talented
   muralist—noun

1. Diego Rivera is *chiefly* famous for his murals, but he was a prolific artist who *worked* in a wide variety of styles.

2. *This* landscape is an example of his early work; *it* was painted in 1904.

3. Rivera, *who* was born in Guanajuato, Mexico, in 1886, entered the San Carlos Academy of Fine Arts in Mexico City when he was *only* eleven.

4. In 1907, with the proceeds from his first *art* show, he made the *first* of several lengthy visits to Europe.

5. *There* he experimented with different approaches until he realized it was the fresco process, the art of painting on wet plaster, *that* best suited his artistic vision.

6. *Two* of Rivera's lifelong interests *were* machinery and Mexican history.

7. *His* murals in the former palace of *Hernán Cortés* in Cuernavaca, in the state of Morelos, depict the history of Morelos from before the conquest by Spain until after the Mexican Revolution of 1910.

8. *One* of the works *that* Rivera created in the United States was a series of twenty-seven murals that the Detroit Arts Commission asked him to paint on subjects related to Detroit and the general theme of industrialization.

9. Rivera was *controversial* in the United States because he included *political* themes in his work.

10. Ironically, capitalists sometimes attacked *him* for his affiliation with Communists, and Communists sometimes attacked him for accepting *commissions* from capitalists.

The Preposition

14f. A *preposition* shows the relationship of a noun or pronoun, called the *object of the preposition,* to another word.

Notice how changing the preposition in the following examples changes the relationship between the verb *swam* and the noun *raft.*

EXAMPLES   I swam **to** the raft.

I swam **from** the raft.

I swam **around** the raft.

I swam **past** the raft.

I swam **under** the raft.

Object of a Preposition

The *object of a preposition* is a noun, a pronoun, or a word group that functions as a noun; in most cases it follows a preposition. Together, the preposition, its object, and any modifiers of the object make a *prepositional phrase.*

EXAMPLES   Did you see Juanita **at the last game**?

The line starts **behind him.**

They played a new song **by Hootie and the Blowfish.**

HELP

As a preposition, the word *to* usually precedes a noun or a pronoun to form a prepositional phrase. Do not confuse a prepositional phrase with an *infinitive*—a verb form preceded by *to.*

PREPOSITIONAL PHRASES
to the lake   to them

INFINITIVES
to consider   to choose

Reference Note

For more information about **prepositional phrases,** see page 554. For more information about **infinitives,** see page 564.

The Preposition   **517**

Sometimes a preposition comes after its object. In formal writing and speaking situations, it is usually best to avoid using a preposition at the end of a sentence.

INFORMAL
The frescoes on the ceiling of the Sistine Chapel are perhaps the works that Michelangelo is most famous for.

FORMAL
The frescoes on the ceiling of the Sistine Chapel are perhaps the works **for which** Michelangelo is most famous.

Commonly Used Prepositions

about	beside	in	through
above	besides	inside	throughout
across	between	into	to
after	beyond	like	toward
against	but (meaning "except")	near	under
along		of	underneath
among	by	off	until
around	concerning	on	unto
at	down	out	up
before	during	outside	upon
behind	except	over	with
below	for	past	within
beneath	from	since	without

A preposition that consists of two or more words is called a *compound preposition.*

EXAMPLES   Alexandra has been accepted by several private colleges **in addition to** both state universities.

As of today, she hasn't made her final choice.

Commonly Used Compound Prepositions

according to	because of	in spite of
along with	by means of	instead of
apart from	in addition to	next to
aside from	in front of	on account of
as of	in place of	out of

Adverb or Preposition?

Some of the words that are commonly used as prepositions may also be used as adverbs. Keep in mind that an adverb is a modifier and that it does not have an object. Prepositions always have objects.

ADVERB   Jerry will meet you **outside** at noon. [*Outside* modifies *will meet.*]

PREPOSITION   I will meet you **outside** the library. [*Outside* introduces a prepositional phrase and has an object, *library.*]

Exercise 8 Completing Sentences by Adding Prepositional Phrases

Complete the following sentences by replacing each blank with a prepositional phrase.

EXAMPLE **1.** I found this information ———.

1. *I found this information on the Internet.*

1. Rob collects postcards ———.
2. ——— we collapsed.
3. We first heard the rumor ———.
4. ——— people had gathered to hear the concert.
5. I tiptoed ——— and listened quietly.
6. The deer darted quickly ——— and raced ———.
7. Everyone ——— applauded Branford Marsalis's solo.
8. Exhausted ———, the explorers pitched their tents ——— and planned the next day's work.
9. ——— the city council has voted to renovate the abandoned building ——— and turn it ———.
10. ——— I thought that something might have gone wrong ———.

The Conjunction

14g. A *conjunction* joins words or word groups.

Coordinating Conjunctions

A *coordinating conjunction* joins words or word groups that are used in the same way.

Coordinating Conjunctions						
and	but	for	nor	or	so	yet

EXAMPLES   In A.D. 711, the Berbers invaded **and** conquered Spain. [*And* joins two verbs.]

We missed the opening scene, **but** we enjoyed the rest of the play. [*But* joins two clauses.]

TIPS & TRICKS

You can remember the coordinating conjunctions as FANBOYS:

For
And
Nor
But
Or
Yet
So

Correlative Conjunctions

Correlative conjunctions are pairs of conjunctions that join words or word groups that are used in the same way.

Correlative Conjunctions		
both . . . and	either . . . or	whether . . . or
not only . . . but also	neither . . . nor	

EXAMPLES **Either** Fred **or** Manuela will bring music for the party. [*Either . . . or* joins two nouns.]

Not only did Garrett Morgan patent the first gas mask, **but** he **also** invented the automatic traffic signal. [*Not only . . . but also* joins two clauses.]

Subordinating Conjunctions

Reference Note

For more information about **subordinate clauses,** see page 577.

A *subordinating conjunction* begins a subordinate clause and connects it to an independent clause.

Commonly Used Subordinating Conjunctions			
after	because	since	until
although	before	so that	when
as	how	than	whenever
as if	if	that	where
as much as	in order that	though	wherever
as though	provided	unless	while

EXAMPLES Many American Indians are reluctant to reveal their traditional names for some places **because** the names have spiritual meanings.

I gasped **when** I saw the headline.

A subordinating conjunction may come at the beginning of a sentence instead of between the clauses it joins.

EXAMPLE **When** I saw the headline, I gasped.

NOTE Some words can be used either as prepositions or as subordinating conjunctions.

PREPOSITION	**After** the election, we celebrated.
SUBORDINATING CONJUNCTION	**After** we won the election, we celebrated.

Exercise 9 **Identifying and Classifying Conjunctions**

Identify the conjunctions in the following sentences, and tell whether each is a *coordinating conjunction*, a *correlative conjunction*, or a *subordinating conjunction*.

EXAMPLE
1. To avoid the traffic, Arturo and I left the stadium a few minutes before the game ended.

1. *and—coordinating conjunction; before—subordinating conjunction*

1. Our old car needs either a valve job or a new engine.
2. Can you tell me whether the express train will stop here or on the far platform?
3. Before you write your paper, you must submit an outline.
4. Would you prefer to go to Greece or Machu Picchu for the senior trip?
5. Workers here pay city, state, and federal taxes.
6. The exhibit of jade Olmec carvings is in either the main gallery or the museum's annex.
7. During the Tang dynasty (A.D. 618–906), China experienced not only a revival of Confucianism but also the development of Chinese schools of Buddhism.
8. Mi Kyung enjoyed the movie as much as Sarah did.
9. Have you decided whether you will take physics or economics?
10. While we are in Kwangju, Korea, we will visit a traditional celadon pottery studio.
11. Thomas Hardy found a publisher for his poetry only after he had published more than a dozen novels.
12. Dad said we can go mountain biking if we promise to be careful.
13. Not only did the movie feature scenes of the streets of Vienna, but it also included dialogue from a popular Austrian play.
14. I would like to be able to travel in time, for I want to see live dinosaurs.
15. José Martí, a hero of the Cuban rebellion against Spain, was both a revolutionary leader and a great poet.

16. Give these documents to the official so that he can process your passport application.
17. They say the prince is angry, yet he is smiling.
18. We can neither relax at home nor go ouside during the storm.
19. When Liberia was founded in 1821, thousands of free African Americans moved there.
20. Please turn down the stereo so that I can concentrate on my homework.

The Interjection

14h. An *interjection* expresses emotion and has no grammatical relation to the rest of the sentence.

Reference Note

For information about **punctuating interjections,** see page 821.

ah	oh	well	whew
yahoo	whoa	yeah	hooray
aha	alas	aw	oops
ow	hey	ouch	wow

An interjection is often set off from the rest of the sentence by an exclamation point or one or more commas. Exclamation points indicate strong emotion. Commas indicate mild emotion.

EXAMPLES   Hey! I think I know the answer!

Well, I thought I knew the answer.

I think that, aw, you two are the greatest.

Exercise 10 Completing Sentences by Adding Interjections

Complete the following conversation by replacing each blank with an appropriate interjection from the list above. Do not use any interjection more than twice.

EXAMPLE   [1] "_____ , Mom, please don't use the telephone now!" pleaded Mariana.

1. *Oh*

"[1] _____ , Mariana, why are you so edgy tonight?" Mrs. Montero asked her eighteen-year-old daughter.

"[2] _____ , Mom, don't you remember? Tonight's the night KHOP announces who won the drawing for a free car."

GRAMMAR

"[3] ____ , yes, how could I forget? You've been talking about it for months."

"[4] ____ , Mom, it's only been two weeks, and—wait, that's the phone; I'll get it. Hello? This is Mariana Montero. What? [5] ____ , are you kidding me? I did? Really?! [6] ____ , you're serious! [7] ____ ! That's incredible! When can I pick it up? Tonight? [8] ____ , that's great! I'll be there in twenty minutes! 'Bye—and thanks! [9] ____ , Mom, will you drive me? [10] ____ , just think: That's the last time you'll ever hear me say those words!"

Determining Parts of Speech

14i. The way a word is used in a sentence determines what part of speech the word is.

EXAMPLES This **plant** is native to North America. [noun]

We **plant** tomatoes every year. [verb]

Bacteria cause many **plant** diseases. [adjective]

Marisa led, and we followed **after.** [adverb]

We crossed the finish line **after** Marisa. [preposition]

We crossed it **after** all the other runners did, too. [conjunction]

This pillow is filled with **down** from geese. [noun]

I've always wanted a **down** pillow. [adjective]

Put it **down;** it's too expensive. [adverb]

We can find cheaper pillows at the store **down** the street. [preposition]

> **Review C** **Identifying Parts of Speech**

Identify the part of speech of each italicized word in the following sentences.

EXAMPLE 1. The first day *after* Christmas marks the *beginning* of the week-long *cultural* festival called Kwanzaa.

1. *after—preposition; beginning—noun; cultural—adjective*

1. Did you know that millions of African Americans celebrate a *uniquely* American holiday *that* has its roots in ancient Africa?

2. *Well,* they do; called Kwanzaa, which in Swahili means "the first fruits of the harvest," the holiday is observed *during* the week between Christmas and New Year's Day.

3. Kwanzaa isn't a religious holiday *or* a substitute for Christmas but a celebration of black Americans' rich cultural *heritage.*

4. The holiday, which was created in 1966 by Maulana Karenga of California State University in Long Beach, *synthesizes* elements from a variety of *African* harvest festivals.

5. Kwanzaa *focuses* on seven basic principles: unity, collective work and responsibility, self-determination, cooperative economics, purpose, *creativity,* and faith.

6. *Among* the symbols of the holiday are *a* straw mat for respect for tradition; an ear of corn for each child in the family; and a candle-holder with seven green, red, and black candles for the continent of Africa.

7. *Each* day during the week, family members light *one* of the candles and discuss one of the principles.

8. They *also* exchange simple gifts *that* reflect their heritage and eat foods from Africa and from the lands to which their ancestors traveled, such as the Caribbean and South America.

9. Some families strictly follow Karenga's original program for the holiday, *while* others *freely* adapt it.

10. In *some* communities families gather for concerts and *dance* performances.

Chapter Review

A. Identifying Parts of Speech

For each of the following sentences, identify each word that is the part of speech indicated in parentheses.

─HELP─

In the Chapter Review, do not identify articles as adjectives.

1. Whenever Anna started a new sculpture, she was usually not thinking of the time it would take to finish. (adverb)
2. Ms. Garcia decided to buy or lease a new computer because the speed and memory capacity of her old one were no longer satisfactory. (conjunction)
3. The film might be available on videotape, on a videodisc, or in some other form. (noun)
4. My mother's book of short stories, written when she was in college, was titled *New Yorkers* because of the stories' similarity in subject matter to James Joyce's stories in *Dubliners.* (preposition)
5. Only recently was my youngest sister, Jorena, allowed to ride her bicycle outside the yard. (verb)
6. In modern times, poets have usually used the term *elegy* to mean "a poem of lamentation for the dead." (noun)
7. This is just the book I wanted. (pronoun)
8. The word *atom* was first used by the ancient Greeks. (adverb)
9. In literature, a novel is not distinguished from other genres by its subject matter but is distinguished by its form and length. (conjunction)
10. Some Irish songs are comic songs, but others are patriotic songs, love songs, or laments. (adjective)
11. The mountain climber plants his flag in the snowbank on top of the mountain. (verb)
12. Will the plants in your garden survive the frost tonight? (noun)
13. As Anita walked along the river, a light rain was falling steadily. (preposition)
14. The dog trotted along with us as we jogged toward the light. (adverb)
15. After every issue had gone to press, the editor of the school paper gave a weekly party. (conjunction)

16. The coach and the football team reviewed the game videotapes weekly, on the day after each game. (adverb)

17. "Well!" exclaimed Ollie. "This is another fine mess!" (interjection)

18. Do you think this old pump will draw any water from the well? (noun)

19. Before he answered the question, he tried to remember just how high a falcon could fly. (conjunction)

20. Take the oregano from the high shelf above the stove, and sprinkle some in the stew before adding the thyme. (adjective)

B. Identifying Parts of Speech

Identify each italicized word in the following paragraphs as a *noun*, a *pronoun*, an *adjective*, a *verb*, an *adverb*, a *conjunction*, a *preposition*, or an *interjection*.

For less [21] *than* what you might pay to see a movie, [22] *you* can get to know yourself better. Simply purchase a [23] *blank* notebook and begin to keep a personal journal. You'll be amazed to see what you [24] *learn* [25] *about* yourself in just a short time.

Keeping a journal is [26] *easy*, [27] *for* there's only one rule: Date all of the entries. Writing four or five entries a week is a realistic goal; [28] *usually* your mood will determine the length of each entry. One type of entry is the [29] *daily* log, in which you record [30] *what* you did and how you felt on a particular day. Another is a [31] *list* of your favorite songs, movies, and poetry. [32] *Most* [33] *important* are [34] *those* entries that have nothing to do with your exterior life and, instead, [35] *reveal* your inner life: your dreams, your thoughts, your questions, your goals, and your feelings. [36] *Because* the journal is a personal book, which [37] *no one* else reads, it becomes a place where you're free to say [38] *anything* you want. Re-reading your entries [39] *later* will show you how you've changed.

If you're wondering [40] *whether* keeping a journal is worth the effort, [41] *yes*, it certainly is. According to one girl in [42] *Connecticut*, her journal is "the closest I've ever come to knowing [43] *myself*." The journal is an adventure [44] *in* self-awareness. [45] *Try* keeping one yourself.

Writing Application
Creating a Dictionary of New Words

The Parts of Speech   For a school project, you and your classmates have decided to create a dictionary of words that should exist but do not. What, for instance, do you call your former best friend or the feeling you have when a word is on the tip of your tongue but you can't quite remember it? Write a complete dictionary entry proposing a name for something that doesn't have a name or that you think could be more aptly named. Give the new word's derivation, use, meaning, and pronunciation.

Prewriting   Use observation, brainstorming, or freewriting to come up with situations, things, places, thoughts, feelings, and qualities that could benefit from a new word. Then, choose the one that appeals to you the most, and create a word for it. Next, think of the information you will need for your dictionary entry. How is your new word spelled and pronounced? What is its part of speech, and what other forms does it have? What is the word's derivation? definition(s)?

Writing   Refer to your prewriting notes often as you write your first draft. Do not be concerned about using complete sentences. Include an example sentence that gives the word in context.

Revising   As you re-read your dictionary entry, check to make sure that your organization and tone are appropriate for a dictionary entry. Make any changes that you think will improve your entry.

Publishing   Proofread your dictionary entry carefully. You and your classmates may want to gather all of your dictionary entries into a new-word dictionary, which could be photocopied for the entire class.

Reference Note

See "The Dictionary" in the Quick Reference Handbook for more information about the content and form of **dictionary entries.**

GRAMMAR

The Parts of a Sentence
Subject, Predicate, Complement

Diagnostic Preview

A. Identifying Subjects, Verbs, and Complements

Identify the italicized word or word group in each of the following sentences as a *subject*, a *verb*, a *direct object*, an *indirect object*, an *objective complement*, a *predicate nominative*, or a *predicate adjective*.

EXAMPLE   **1.** We *took* the shortest route.

           1. verb

1. Since she won the Pulitzer Prize in 1983, Alice Walker has become a famous *writer*.

2. In 1928, *Carlos Chávez* established the well-known Symphony Orchestra of Mexico.

3. The antique dresser *was* carefully *moved* to a protected corner of the showroom.

4. Margaret wants a *set* of leather luggage as a graduation present.

5. On Fajada Butte in northwestern New Mexico is an ancient Anasazi solar *calendar*.

6. The director gave my *grandfather* an interesting part in a play at the community theater.

7. Please *call* me at work immediately after you get home from school; it's urgent.
8. Exercising regularly and eating well keep me *energetic* despite my busy schedule.
9. My mother is much *taller* than any of her four sisters but not as tall as her brother.
10. Yesterday the girls' gymnastics team unanimously elected Ming Chin their *captain.*

B. Identifying Subjects, Verbs, and Complements

Identify each italicized word or word group in the following sentences as a *subject,* a *verb,* a *direct object,* an *indirect object,* an *objective complement,* a *predicate nominative,* or a *predicate adjective.*

EXAMPLE   1. In 1675, the Spanish friar Juan Paiva recorded the *rules* of a major sports contest between the Apalachee and the Timucuan peoples of North Florida.

     1. *direct object*

11. The arrival of a messenger in a raccoon costume was a *challenge* to a ballgame from the loser of the last game.
12. On acceptance of the challenge, *all* of the villagers traveled to meet their opponents.
13. In an all-night vigil before the game, elders of the host village interpreted their dreams and told the home *team* their predictions of the game's outcome.
14. Meanwhile, the visitors *made* a stew with rancid food, *mixed* it with decorative clays, and *painted* their bodies with the foul mixture to repel the other players.
15. On game day, a village leader started *play* by tossing out a small, hard ball to teams of forty to fifty players on each side.
16. Suddenly, eighty to one hundred men *were scrambling* for a ball only about an inch in diameter!
17. The goal post in the center of an empty field was a ten- to fifteen-foot *pole* with an eagle's nest on top.
18. Teams scored one *point* for each throw of the ball against the pole and two *points* for each basket.
19. When one team had scored eleven points, the game was *over.*
20. According to historians, these rules probably made the average game a one- to two-hour *contest.*

The Sentence

15a. A *sentence* is a word group that contains a subject and a verb and that expresses a complete thought.

A thought is complete when it makes sense by itself.

EXAMPLES   In many ways, the development of the microprocessor has revolutionized technology.

When did Mexico achieve independence from Spain?

How quickly this year has passed!

Stop! [The understood subject is *you*.]

A sentence should begin with a capital letter. The punctuation mark that follows a sentence depends on the purpose of the sentence.

Do not mistake a sentence fragment for a sentence. A *sentence fragment* is a group of words that is capitalized and punctuated as a sentence but that does not contain both a subject and a verb or does not express a complete thought.

Reference Note
For more about the **understood subject,** see page 535. For more about the **purposes of sentences,** see page 591. For more about **end marks,** see page 820.

SENTENCE FRAGMENT	Sponsors election-year debates. [This group of words does not contain a subject or express a complete thought.]
SENTENCE	The League of Women Voters sponsors election-year debates.
SENTENCE FRAGMENT	Students representing sixty-one historically black universities and colleges. [This group of words does not contain a verb or express a complete thought.]
SENTENCE	Students representing sixty-one historically black universities and colleges competed.
SENTENCE FRAGMENT	Because the graduation ceremony was rescheduled for June 20. [This group of words contains a subject and a verb but does not express a complete thought.]
SENTENCE	Because the graduation ceremony was rescheduled for June 20, my cousin Larry could attend after all.

Reference Note
For information about **correcting sentence fragments,** see page 431.

Exercise 1   Identifying and Revising Sentences and Sentence Fragments

Decide which of the following word groups are sentences and which are sentence fragments. If a word group is a sentence, add appropriate capitalization and punctuation. If a word group is a sentence fragment, revise the fragment by adding or deleting words to make it a sentence. Then, add appropriate capitalization and punctuation.

EXAMPLE 1. such as the Sioux, Cheyenne, and Comanche

       1. *American Indians, such as the Sioux, Cheyenne, and Comanche, were expert equestrians.*

1. here in the basement of the library lay stacks and stacks of dusty magazines, each a collector's prize
2. stretching in a seemingly endless blue expanse from the coast of Peru to the Great Barrier Reef
3. have you changed the drill bit
4. to estimate expenses accurately for the next three quarters of this fiscal year
5. when they swam under the boat and checked the hull
6. one of the only buildings from this period still in use today
7. an event held but once a year and eagerly anticipated by the population of this small rural county
8. take this as an example
9. covering the portrait's face with a few diagonal pink pastel strokes was the bold act of a creative genius
10. how surprised we all were at the news

The Subject and the Predicate

15b. Sentences consist of two basic parts: *subjects* and *predicates*. The *subject* is a word or word group that tells whom or what the sentence is about. The *predicate* is a word or word group that tells something about the subject.

Notice in the following examples that the subject may appear before or after the predicate or between parts of the predicate.

EXAMPLES

SUBJECT		PREDICATE
Rain		pelted the sailors.

SUBJECT		PREDICATE
Each of the amateur mimes		performed.

PREDICATE		SUBJECT
Away on the breeze sailed		the dry leaves.

PREDICATE		SUBJECT		PREDICATE
When did		Alex Haley		write *Roots*?

STYLE TIP

Sentence fragments are commonly used in casual conversation, in written dialogue, and in advertisements. In these situations, the context usually clarifies any confusion caused by the sentence fragment. In formal speaking and writing, however, it is best to use complete sentences for greater clarity.

The Simple Subject and the Complete Subject

15c. The *simple subject* is the main word or word group that tells whom or what the sentence is about.

The simple subject may be a noun, a pronoun, or a word group that functions as a noun. The *complete subject* consists of the simple subject and any word or word groups used to modify the simple subject.

SIMPLE SUBJECT	The **view** from the observatory on the top floor of the building is extraordinary.
COMPLETE SUBJECT	**The view from the observatory on the top floor of the building** is extraordinary.
SIMPLE SUBJECT	Lasting for eight days, **Hanukkah** celebrates the rededication of the temple in Jerusalem in 165 B.C.
COMPLETE SUBJECT	**Lasting for eight days, Hanukkah** celebrates the rededication of the temple in Jerusalem in 165 B.C.
SIMPLE SUBJECT	Was the **Memorial Coliseum** in Los Angeles filled to capacity?
COMPLETE SUBJECT	Was **the Memorial Coliseum in Los Angeles** filled to capacity?
SIMPLE SUBJECT	**Everyone** was very impatient for the feature to begin.
COMPLETE SUBJECT	**Everyone** was very impatient for the feature to begin. [The complete subject and the simple subject may be the same if no words modify the simple subject.]

NOTE A compound noun, such as *Memorial Coliseum,* may serve as a simple subject because it is considered a single name.

HELP

In this book, the term *subject* generally refers to the simple subject unless otherwise indicated.

Reference Note

For more information about **compound nouns,** see page 499.

Exercise 2 Identifying Complete Subjects and Simple Subjects

Identify each complete subject in the following sentences. Then, underline each simple subject.

EXAMPLE   1. The population of Abu Dhabi is one of the richest in the world.

1. *The population of Abu Dhabi*

1. Ravi Shankar was instrumental in popularizing Indian music in the West.

2. That dachshund was the only dog in the world with a taste for asparagus in hollandaise sauce.
3. Did he shoot, develop, print, and frame all these photographs?
4. Walking is a cheap, reliable, and healthful form of exercise.
5. A long line of ants was heading directly toward my lunch.
6. Few of the sailors aboard the *Caroline B* could claim a clear view of the strange sea creature.
7. Unfortunately, "Turkey in the Straw" occupied the sole slot on this young harmonica player's playlist.
8. I think of the remote control as my own personal property.
9. What a day the children in Ms. Gage's class had!
10. At the top of a very long flight of stairs and almost touching the roof were our seats.

The Simple Predicate and the Complete Predicate

15d. The *simple predicate,* or verb, is the main word or word group that tells something about the subject.

The simple predicate may be a one-word verb or a *verb phrase* (a main verb with one or more helping verbs). The *complete predicate* consists of the simple predicate and all of the words used to modify the simple predicate and to complete its meaning.

Reference Note

For more about **verbs** and **verb phrases,** see page 509.

| SIMPLE PREDICATE (VERB) | The victorious athletes **were surrounded** by admirers. |
| COMPLETE PREDICATE | The victorious athletes **were surrounded by admirers.** |

| SIMPLE PREDICATE (VERB) | In an hour-long press conference, the players graciously **answered** reporters' questions. |
| COMPLETE PREDICATE | **In an hour-long press conference,** the players **graciously answered reporters' questions.** |

| SIMPLE PREDICATE (VERB) | The crowd **surged.** |
| COMPLETE PREDICATE | The crowd **surged.** [The complete predicate and the simple predicate may be the same if no words modify or complete the meaning of the simple predicate.] |

NOTE In this book, the term *verb* generally refers to the simple predicate (a one-word verb or a verb phrase) unless otherwise indicated.

Identify each complete predicate in the following sentences. Then, underline each verb.

EXAMPLE   1. Will you be joining us for dinner tonight?

1. <u>Will be joining</u> us for dinner tonight

1. This new theory certainly does deserve consideration among the scientific community.
2. Debate about the voting district boundaries will be headline news.
3. Should the statistician have included these figures in the tally?
4. On the boardwalk, a glass blower was demonstrating her craft.
5. I will report to the registrar on July 22 at 8:00 A.M.
6. In the lower left-hand corner, a legend lists the symbols used on the map and their meanings.
7. When will the armadillo cross the solid white line?
8. The Ubangi River meanders through almost fifteen hundred miles of magnificent African country.
9. Under the circumstances, a pair of cutoffs and a t-shirt would not be in the best of taste.
10. Among the pine tree's dark and shining branches waited one very hungry owl.

The Compound Subject and the Compound Verb

15e. A *compound subject* consists of two or more subjects that are joined by a conjunction and that have the same verb.

The parts of a compound subject are usually joined by the conjunction *and* or *or.*

EXAMPLES   **Michelle** or **Chondra** will lead the petition drive.

Hokkaidō, Honshū, Shikoku, and **Kyūshū** are the four main islands of Japan.

When were **East Germany** and **West Germany** reunited?

15f. A *compound verb* consists of two or more verbs that are joined by a conjunction and that have the same subject.

The parts of a compound verb are usually joined by the conjunction *and, but,* or *or.*

TIPS & TRICKS

When you are identifying compound verbs, be sure to include all parts of any verb phrases.

EXAMPLE
Should we **wait** for Alex or **leave** a note for him?

EXAMPLES   Mary McLeod Bethune **founded** Bethune-Cookman
College and twice **served** as its president.

Gabrielle and Margaret **read** the book but **missed** the movie.

Would you rather **wash** the dishes or **dry** them?

Reference Note

For more about **simple sentences** and **compound sentences,** see page 588.

NOTE Do not mistake a simple sentence containing a compound subject or a compound verb, or both, for a compound sentence. In a compound sentence, the conjunction joins independent clauses.

EXAMPLES   **Anna** and **Lyle will sing** in the talent show. [simple sentence with a compound subject]

Anna and **Lyle will sing** and **dance** in the talent show. [simple sentence with a compound subject and compound verb]

Anna will sing, and **Lyle will dance** in the talent show. [compound sentence containing two complete clauses]

How to Find the Subject of a Sentence

To find the subject of a sentence, ask *Who?* or *What?* before the verb.

EXAMPLES   In the auditorium, friends and relatives of the graduates awaited the ceremony. [Who awaited? *Friends* and *relatives* awaited.]

Sharing the island of Hispaniola with Haiti is the Dominican Republic. [What is sharing? *Dominican Republic* is sharing.]

Here is the last history assignment for the week. [What is? *Assignment* is.]

There will be a meeting in the cafeteria immediately after school. [What will be? *Meeting* will be.]

Keep the following four guidelines in mind whenever you are trying to find the subject of a sentence.

- The subject in a sentence expressing a command or a request is always understood to be *you,* even if the word *you* does not appear in the sentence.

COMMAND   Always document the source of a direct quotation. [Who documents? *You* document.]

REQUEST   Please write soon. [Who writes? *You* write.]

If a command or a request contains a **noun of direct address**—a word naming the one or ones spoken to—the subject is still understood to be *you*.

EXAMPLES   Frances, [you] walk the dog.

[You] **Come** here, Bill.

• The subject of a sentence is never the object of a prepositional phrase.

EXAMPLES   A committee of students investigated the allegations. [Who investigated? *Committee* investigated. *Students* is the object of the preposition *of.*]

One of the parks in Austin, Texas, is named for the Mexican general Ignacio Seguín Zaragoza. [What is named? *One* is named. *Parks* is the object of the preposition *of. Austin, Texas* is the object of the preposition *in.*]

From the alley came the wail of a siren. [What came? *Wail* came. *Alley* is the object of the preposition *From. Siren* is the object of the preposition *of.*]

• The subject in a sentence expressing a question usually follows the verb or comes between the parts of a verb phrase.

EXAMPLES   Are these jeans on sale? [What are on sale? *Jeans* are.]

What year did Thurgood Marshall retire from the United States Supreme Court? [Who did retire? *Thurgood Marshall* did retire.]

Where are the children playing after school? [Who are playing? *Children* are playing.]

• The word *there* or *here* is almost never the subject of a sentence.

In the following examples, *there* and *here* are adverbs telling *where*.

EXAMPLES   There goes Rebecca. [Who goes? *Rebecca* goes.]

Here is your receipt. [What is? *Receipt* is.]

NOTE   The word *there* is not always an adverb. It may be used as an **expletive**—a word that fills out the structure of a sentence but does not add to the meaning.

EXAMPLE   There will be a special **broadcast** tonight at 11:30 P.M. [What will be? *Broadcast* will be.]

Reference Note

For more information about **prepositional phrases,** see pages 517 and 554.

TIPS & TRICKS

Turning a question into a statement will often help you find the subject of the question.

QUESTION
Have you tasted sushi?

STATEMENT
You have tasted sushi.
[Who has tasted? *You* have tasted.]

STYLE TIP

Expletives add no information to a sentence and can cause confusion about subject-verb agreement. You can improve your style by revising your sentences to eliminate unnecessary expletives.

ORIGINAL
There will be a special broadcast at 11:30 P.M.

REVISED
A special broadcast will air at 11:30 P.M.

Exercise 4 **Identifying Subjects and Verbs**

Identify each simple subject and verb in the following sentences.
Include all parts of any compound subjects and compound verbs and
all words in any verb phrases.

EXAMPLE   1. The miniature Japanese sculptures shown on this page
are called *netsuke.*

1. *subject—sculptures; verb—are called*

1. This exquisite art form originated as a practical solution to an
everyday problem.
2. During Japan's Tokugawa period (1603–1868), an integral part of
the traditional costume of the new merchant class was a set of
lacquerware boxes for medicines and spices.

3. The boxes were threaded onto the sash of the kimono and served
as pockets for the otherwise pocketless garment.
4. Originally just small, plain toggles of lightweight ivory or wood,
the *netsuke* held the boxes in place along the sash.
5. Under the feudal system then in effect, there were strict laws against
any display of wealth by persons below the rank of *samurai.*
6. However, many wealthy merchants wanted some obvious symbol
of their prosperity.
7. Over time, increasingly elaborate *netsuke* from the nation's finest
artisans became that symbol.

8. Eventually, the Japanese adopted Western clothing, with pockets.
9. As a result, both the small boxes and the *netsuke* became obsolete.
10. Today, collectors all over the world gladly pay large sums for specimens of these beautiful objects with humble origins.

Complements

15g. A *complement* is a word or word group that completes the meaning of a verb.

Some verbs do not need a complement to complete their meanings. Together, the subject and the verb express a complete thought.

EXAMPLES
    S V
    She won.

    V
    Look! [The understood subject is *you*.]

Often, however, a sentence requires one or more complements for the meaning of the verb to be complete.

             S   **V**
INCOMPLETE   Judith Baca created

             S   **V**   **C**
COMPLETE   Judith Baca created the **mural.**

             S **V**
INCOMPLETE   They mailed

             S **V**   **C**   **C**
COMPLETE   They mailed **me** the **information.**

             S   **V**
INCOMPLETE   The republics declared

             S   **V**   **C**   **C**
COMPLETE   The republics declared **themselves independent.**

             S   **V**
INCOMPLETE   Who in the world named

             S   **V**   **C**   **C**
COMPLETE   Who in the world named the **puppy Cerberus**?

TIPS & TRICKS

You can remember the difference in spelling between *complement* (the grammar term) and *compliment* (an expression of affection or respect) by remembering that a compl**e**ment compl**e**tes a sentence.

TIPS & TRICKS

Both independent and subordinate clauses contain subjects, verbs, and, sometimes, complements.

EXAMPLE
When **we attend hockey games,** my **sister** and **I cheer** loudly for our home team.

		S	V	
INCOMPLETE	Seiji Ozawa became			

	S	V	C
COMPLETE	Seiji Ozawa became a successful **conductor.**		

	S	V
INCOMPLETE	The horse seems	

	S	V	C
COMPLETE	The horse seems **skittish.**		

Nouns, pronouns, and adjectives may be complements. Be careful not to mistake an adverb for a complement.

ADVERB   Hatshepsut ruled **ably.** [The adverb *ably* modifies the verb *ruled,* telling *how* Hatshepsut ruled. The sentence does not contain a complement.]

COMPLEMENT   Hatshepsut ruled **Egypt** during the early fifteenth century B.C. [The noun *Egypt* completes the meaning of the verb *ruled.*]

The object of a prepositional phrase is not a complement.

OBJECT OF PREPOSITION   At first Hatshepsut ruled with her husband. [The noun *husband* is the object of the preposition *with.* The sentence does not contain a complement.]

Direct Objects and Indirect Objects

15h. A *direct object* is a complement that tells who or what receives the action of a verb or shows the result of the action.

A direct object may be a noun, a pronoun, or a word group that functions as a noun. To find a direct object, ask *Whom?* or *What?* after a transitive verb.

EXAMPLES   The employer interviewed several **applicants** for the job. [Interviewed whom? Applicants.]

Does a virus cause a common **cold**? [Cause what? Cold.]

I miss **you.** [Miss whom? You.]

They usually buy **whatever is on sale.** [Buy what? Whatever is on sale.]

Reference Note

For more about **adverbs,** see page 514.

Reference Note

For more information on **prepositional phrases,** see pages 517 and 554.

Reference Note

For more about **transitive verbs,** see page 512.

S T Y L E   T I P

For emphasis, a writer may place the direct object before the subject and the verb.

EXAMPLE

What an eerie **sound** we heard! [Heard what? Sound.]

Complements   **539**

A direct object may be compound.

EXAMPLES The team included **Bob** and **Ray**.

Did the car need **brakes, belts,** and a **battery**?

15i. An ***indirect object*** is a complement that often appears in sentences containing direct objects and that tells *to whom* or *to what* or *for whom* or *for what* the action of a transitive verb is done.

An indirect object may be a noun, a pronoun, or a word group that functions as a noun. To find an indirect object, ask *To whom?* or *To what?* or *For whom?* or *For what?* after a transitive verb.

EXAMPLES The Swedish Academy awarded **Octavio Paz** the 1990 Nobel Prize in literature. [Awarded the prize to whom? Octavio Paz.]

Julie's part-time work experience earned **her** a full-time position. [Earned the position for whom? Her.]

The teacher gives **whoever turns in the earliest paper a bonus.** [Gives a bonus to whom? Whoever turns in the earliest paper.]

NOTE Do not mistake an object of the preposition *to* or *for* for an indirect object.

| OBJECT OF PREPOSITION | Clarice wrote a letter to **me.** [The pronoun *me* is the object of the preposition *to.*] |
| INDIRECT OBJECT | Clarice wrote **me** a letter. |

An indirect object may be compound.

EXAMPLES Did the travel agent give **Aaron, Todd,** and **Steve** their itinerary?

That incident earned my **sister-in-law** and **me** our nicknames.

Exercise 5 Identifying Direct and Indirect Objects

Identify each direct object and indirect object in the following sentences.

EXAMPLE 1. An assistant showed the visitors the laser's interior design.

1. *visitors—indirect object; design—direct object*

1. The Rhind papyrus and the Golonishev papyrus provide proof that the decimal system was used by the ancient Egyptians.

GRAMMAR

┌HELP┐

Some transitive verbs that commonly take indirect objects are *ask, get, give, grant, hand, lend, offer, pay, send, teach, tell,* and *write.*

Reference Note

For more information about **prepositional phrases,** see pages 517 and 554.

┌TIPS & TRICKS┐

Remember that a sentence cannot have an indirect object unless the sentence has a direct object. Indirect objects usually come between the verb and the direct object.

┌HELP┐

Not every sentence in Exercise 5 has an indirect object.

---

2. Make me a graph of the results of your experiment.
3. Perhaps a neighbor would write you a recommendation.
4. That one small grapefruit tree gave us over ten bushels of fruit.
5. Some extinct dragonfly species had wingspans as long as 30 inches.
6. Tell Greg, Wesley, and Carol the story about your first day aboard the submarine.
7. A bland food, tofu quickly absorbs other flavors.
8. By the clear and bountiful waters of the Columbia River, thousands of Chinook Indians lived prosperous lives.
9. In fact, chefs will be serving ground gourmet worms in the near future.
10. Technology has always brought some people new opportunities and others an end to their way of life.

Objective Complements

15j. An ***objective complement*** is a complement that helps complete the meaning of a transitive verb by identifying or modifying the direct object.

An objective complement may be a noun, a pronoun, an adjective, or a word group that functions as a noun or an adjective.

EXAMPLES   France made Miles Davis a **knight** in the Legion of Honor. [The noun *knight* identifies the direct object *Miles Davis.*]

Mayor Thompson named Felicia **"Mayor for a Day."** [The word group *"Mayor for a Day"* identifies the direct object *Felicia.*]

Garfield considers the refrigerator **his.** [The possessive pronoun *his* modifies the direct object *refrigerator.*]

We have painted the new house **blue.** [The adjective *blue* modifies the direct object *house.*]

NOTE Only a few verbs take objective complements. These verbs are *consider, make,* and any verbs that can be replaced by *consider* or *make,* such as *appoint, believe, call, choose, color, cut, dye, elect, find, keep, name, paint, render,* and *sweep.*

EXAMPLES   The referee **called** [or *considered*] the line drive foul. [*Foul* is the objective complement.]

The Supreme Court's 1954 decision **rendered** [or *made*] the segregation of public schools unlawful. [*Unlawful* is the objective complement.]

TIPS & TRICKS

Remember that a sentence cannot have an objective complement unless the sentence has a direct object.

STYLE TIP

Objective complements generally come after the direct object, near the end of a clause. For emphasis, a writer may place the objective complement before the subject, verb, and direct object.

EXAMPLE

How **interesting** and **pleasant** the tour guide made our visit to the cliff dwellings! [The adjectives *interesting* and *pleasant* modify the direct object *visit*.]

An objective complement may be compound.

EXAMPLES   Did the stockholders elect Sara Gardner **president** and **chief executive officer**?

Lack of ventilation made the workroom **hot, stuffy,** and **uncomfortable.**

Exercise 6   **Identifying Direct Objects, Indirect Objects, and Objective Complements**

Identify each direct object, indirect object, and objective complement in the following sentences.

EXAMPLE   1. The photograph below shows an interactive television system.

     1. *system—direct object*

1. Recent advances in technology have made interactive television systems a reality.
2. The system shown below includes a remote-control converter box with a computer inside.
3. The computer gives viewers several on-screen options for the content of a program.

4. During a football game, for example, viewers can order different camera angles, alternative views, instant replays, or the scores of other games.
5. The computer records each response made by the viewer.
6. Viewers can also select exercise workouts suited to their needs and can tailor news and comedy shows to their interests.
7. Most viewers have found the new technology quite enjoyable.
8. In addition, advertisers consider it a boon to their business.
9. Viewers' responses give the advertisers valuable demographic data.
10. With that data, they can create commercials that target highly specific audiences.

Subject Complements

15k. A *subject complement* is a complement that identifies or modifies the subject of a linking verb.

Like other kinds of complements, the two kinds of subject complements—the *predicate nominative* and the *predicate adjective*—appear in the predicate.

(1) A *predicate nominative* identifies or refers to the subject of a linking verb.

A predicate nominative may be a noun, a pronoun, or a word group that functions as a noun.

EXAMPLES   Robert Hayden is my favorite **poet.** [The noun *poet* identifies the subject *Robert Hayden*.]

             Who are the people over there? [The pronoun *Who* refers to the subject *people*.]

             The object of the game is **to trap your opponent in a corner.** [The infinitive phrase *to trap your opponent in a corner* identifies the subject *object*.]

     A predicate nominative may be compound.

EXAMPLES   The four most populous states are **California, New York, Texas,** and **Florida.**

             The last people off the bus were **Julie** and **I.**

Reference Note

For more about **linking verbs,** see page 511.

| S T Y L E   T I P |

For emphasis, a writer may place the subject complement before the subject and the verb.

PREDICATE NOMINATIVE
What a truly amazing **coincidence** that is! [The noun *coincidence* identifies the subject *that*.]

PREDICATE ADJECTIVES
Hungry and **weary** were the refugees. [The adjectives *Hungry* and *weary* modify the subject *refugees*.]

(2) A *predicate adjective* is an adjective that is in the predicate and that modifies the subject of a linking verb.

EXAMPLES   Your lotus-blossom necklace is **lovely.** [The adjective *lovely* modifies the subject *necklace.*]

Does the cottage cheese smell **sour**? [The adjective *sour* modifies the subject *cottage cheese.*]

That small wood flute is **South American.** [The adjective *South American* modifies the subject *flute.*]

A predicate adjective may be compound.

EXAMPLES   Freedom is **precious** and **costly.**

Has the weather turned **cold, wet,** and **foggy**?

NOTE Do not assume that every adjective in the predicate is a predicate adjective. Keep in mind that a predicate adjective modifies the subject of a linking verb.

EXAMPLES   The epic hero Beowulf was **bold** and **courageous.** [The adjectives *bold* and *courageous* are predicate adjectives because they modify the subject *Beowulf.*]

The epic hero Beowulf was a bold and courageous warrior. [The adjectives *bold* and *courageous* are not predicate adjectives; they modify the predicate nominative *warrior,* not the subject *Beowulf.*]

Exercise 7 Identifying Predicate Nominatives and Predicate Adjectives

Identify the subject complement in each of the following sentences. Indicate whether the complement is a *predicate nominative* or a *predicate adjective.*

EXAMPLE   **1.** In Latvian mythology, Meness is the god of the moon and the protector of travelers and soldiers.

      1. god—predicate nominative; protector—predicate nominative

1. Do the strawberries on this vine look ripe to you?
2. The candidate's speech at last night's rally was brief but effective.
3. The villainous warrior became more ruthless and dictatorial.
4. On that day, thirteen colonies became one nation.
5. The dog grew restless and quiet just before the storm hit.

⌐ **TIPS** & **TRICKS** ⌐

When identifying kinds of complements, check first to see whether the verbs in the sentences are action or linking. Remember that only action verbs can take direct objects, indirect objects, and objective complements and that only linking verbs can take subject complements (predicate nominatives and predicate adjectives).

6. Pablo Casals was not only a brilliant cellist but also a sensitive conductor of orchestras.

7. The sea spray tasted extremely salty as it whipped over the bow and into my face.

8. How musty the rooms in this empty house smell!

9. Mark Russell is a popular political humorist.

10. Kicking Bear was a Sioux warrior, artist, and prophet.

11. In order to survive, young mountain goats must be quick and sure-footed.

12. He would remain a practicing physician and author for the rest of his life.

13. At that time, shiny chrome was the prime requirement on a brand-new automobile.

14. The capital of Colombia is the city of Bogotá.

15. Brushed by a careless visitor, a porcelain statue tilted dangerously but remained intact.

16. In one stroke, she would become the owner and president of her company's chief competitor.

17. Our Korean friends became avid fans of Italian food.

18. Can one be wealthy and free at the same time?

19. Wouldn't three days in Hawaii be magical and exciting?

20. Very sleek, very red, and incredibly powerful is Eric's dream car.

Review A Writing Complements

For each of the following sentences, write an appropriate complement.

EXAMPLE 1. All of a sudden, my dreams seemed _____.

1. *possible*

1. On the last warm day of the season, a group of first-graders played _____ on the sunny playground.

2. After years of small plays in small towns, the young actress became _____.

3. Why on earth did you paint your room _____?

4. The jungles of South America are _____ and _____.

5. Could we cook a _____ for dinner tonight?

6. However, the experience taught _____ a great deal about people.

7. My favorite book is _____.

8. Jamal, on a sudden inspiration, named his limestone sculpture _____, after his grandfather.

9. Strangely enough, her casual remark gave _____ a wonderful idea for an invention.
10. Back in those days, life in the Australian outback must have been _____.
11. To whom will the judges award the _____ at the banquet?
12. After decades of futile searching, the diligent archaeologist finally discovered _____, and all his theories were confirmed.
13. That painting by van Gogh is incredibly _____.
14. The pitcher threw _____ a nasty curveball.
15. I have finally made a decision; my least favorite movie of all time is _____.
16. Why do you never show _____ your poems?
17. Despite the wonderful performances by many of the others, the committee named Aaron _____.
18. How many _____ did Jarret score in last night's game?
19. Did the class really elect Janice _____?
20. Under intense heat and pressure, carbon can become _____.

Review B Identifying Subjects, Verbs, and Complements

Identify each subject, verb, and complement in the sentences in the following paragraphs. Indicate whether each complement is a *direct object*, an *indirect object*, an *objective complement*, a *predicate nominative*, or a *predicate adjective*.

EXAMPLE   [1] Arabesques are complex, elaborate designs of flowers, foliage, calligraphy, and geometric patterns.

1. *subject—Arabesques; verb—are; predicate nominative—designs*

[1] The arabesques from the fortress-palace of the Alhambra in Granada, Spain, and the ones from the king's palace in Fez, Morocco, illustrate a historic link between two cultures. [2] In A.D. 711, Arabs and Muslim Berbers from North Africa invaded and occupied Spain. [3] The Spanish gave them a name: the Moors.

[4] The Moors' encouragement of commerce made Spain's major cities wealthy. [5] Meanwhile, the Moors' patronage of art, literature, and science rendered the cities centers of learning for Christian, Jewish, and Muslim scholars.

[6] Through reconquest, parts of Spain became Christian again as early as 1085. [7] At the end of the fifteenth century, Granada remained

┌HELP─
Not every sentence in Review B has a complement.

the Moors' last stronghold. [8] In 1492, it too fell to the forces of Ferdinand V and Isabella I. [9] Spain expelled most of the Moors from the country. [10] Still, traces of their rich culture survive in the architecture, poetry, and music of Spain.

Review C Writing Sentences with Complements

Write your own sentences according to the following guidelines. In your sentences, underline the words you use as the italicized sentence parts. Use a variety of subjects, verbs, and complements in your sentences.

EXAMPLE   1. Write a sentence with an *indirect object* and a *direct object*.

1. The Lady of the Lake gave <u>Arthur</u> the <u>sword</u> known as Excalibur.

1. Write a sentence with a *compound subject*.
2. Write a sentence with a *compound verb*.
3. Write a sentence with a *direct object*.
4. Write a sentence with a *compound direct object*.
5. Write a sentence with an *indirect object* and a *direct object*.
6. Write a sentence with a *compound indirect object* and a *compound direct object*.

7. Write a sentence with a *predicate nominative*.
8. Write a sentence with a *compound predicate adjective*.
9. Write a sentence with a *direct object* and an *objective complement*.
10. Write a sentence with a *direct object* and a *compound objective complement*.

Seven Common Sentence Patterns

The subject and the verb produce one sentence pattern. The subject, the verb, and the various complements produce six other common sentence patterns.

S   V
Velma painted.

S   V   DO
Velma painted a landscape.

S   V   IO   DO
The judges gave Velma an award.

S   V   DO   OC (Noun)
They considered her landscape a masterpiece.

S   V   DO   OC (Adjective)
They called the painting brilliant.

S   V   PN
Velma has become a celebrity.

S V PA
She is famous.

Chapter Review

A. Identifying Sentences and Sentence Fragments

Identify each of the following word groups as a *sentence* or a *sentence fragment*.

1. Aren't the first ten amendments to the Constitution called the Bill of Rights?
2. Guaranteeing the people four basic freedoms.
3. Besides freedom of religion and freedom of the press, freedom of speech and of public assembly.
4. Most of the other amendments in the Bill of Rights are less sweeping than the First Amendment.
5. If the Third Amendment pertains specifically to the quartering of soldiers in private homes.

B. Identifying the Simple Subject and the Simple Predicate

Identify each simple subject and each simple predicate in the following sentences. Be sure to include all parts of a verb phrase and all parts of a compound subject or verb.

6. Garrett had become fluent in several languages.
7. Will you lend me some change for the telephone, please?
8. Leilani was unquestionably the best player on the team.
9. Down into the cave went the guide and the tourists.
10. The restaurant manager and his staff have never refused service to anyone.
11. Every student must complete his or her immunization card and return it to the office.
12. Is the elderly lady with the green hat Mrs. Daly?
13. This tiny room would be extremely uncomfortable to most people.
14. The National League playoff between the Philadelphia team and the Houston team was one of the most exciting in recent years.
15. Mimi has picked a kitten from the litter and will call him Mr. Alp.

C. Identifying Complements

Identify each complement in the following sentences as a *direct object,* an *indirect object,* a *predicate nominative,* or a *predicate adjective.*

16. They will send you an application if you write for one.

17. Is your dog male or female?

18. The doctor brought each of the nurses a cup of tea.

19. Roald Amundsen was the first man to reach the South Pole.

20. Does this photograph look old to you?

21. Many fugitive slaves found shelter with the Seminoles of Florida.

22. The water in the bay feels quite cold.

23. Cheryl gave me her paper to read.

24. The Great Wall of China is one of that nation's oldest structures.

25. Mr. Nickles divided the class into smaller sections.

26. The coach tossed Yolanda the soccer ball.

27. Please rinse your dishes and put them into the dishwasher.

28. Yesterday the mail carrier left me this letter from a bookstore.

29. Is Harrison Ford a more popular movie star than Mel Gibson?

30. The carrot bread smelled wonderful just after it came out of the oven.

D. Identifying Subjects, Verbs, and Complements

Identify the subject and verb in each sentence in the following paragraph. If a sentence has any complements, identify them as well, and indicate whether each is a *direct object,* an *indirect object,* an *objective complement,* a *predicate nominative,* or a *predicate adjective.*

[31] Along the coast of the Atlantic Ocean in Brooklyn, New York, lies Coney Island, a world-famous amusement park. [32] Until 1654, the island (now a peninsula) was the summer campground of the Canarsie and the Nyack peoples. [33] In that year, the Canarsie and the Nyack sold a group of Dutch settlers the island. [34] The Dutch named the island Konynen Eyland (Dutch for "rabbit island") because of the abundance of wild rabbits in the area. [35] In the 1820s, the island became popular as an ocean resort and throughout the nineteenth and early twentieth centuries grew increasingly lavish. [36] Among its many attractions were the mechanical horses and the 250-foot Parachute Jump of Steeplechase Park and the onion domes, minarets, and Japanese tea gardens of Luna Park. [37] Today, after years of neglect and a series of fires, the amusement area of this once-grand resort is

only a five-block strip between Surf Avenue and the eighty-foot-wide boardwalk along the ocean. [38] However, ten million people still visit Coney Island each year. [39] Now the founder of a restaurant chain is planning a major face lift for the area. [40] He holds the rights to the former site of Steeplechase Park and envisions the park spectacularly beautiful once again.

Writing Application
Using Sentence Variety in an Essay

Improving Sentence Style   You have been looking through a number of college brochures. At last, you have found a school that seems right for you and have decided to apply for admission. The admissions essay instructions are as follows: "In a short essay, tell about something that is important to you." Be sure to use a variety of subjects, verbs, and complements in your essay.

Prewriting   First, you'll need to decide on a topic for your essay. Brainstorm a list of issues, ideas, and activities that are important to you. Is playing music, writing fiction, or doing volunteer work a significant part of your life? Choose the most engaging topic from your list. Decide whether the tone of your essay will be serious or lighthearted. Jot down facts, details, and examples to help develop your topic.

Writing   You might start with a brief anecdote, a thoughtful question, or a surprising statement. Then, develop your topic with supporting examples, facts, and details. Sum up your ideas in a clincher paragraph.

Revising   Fine-tune the content, organization, and style of your essay. First, make sure that your thesis statement gives a clear focus to your essay. Then, make sure the body of your essay supports that thesis. Do your supporting paragraphs follow a clear, logical sequence? Next, evaluate the tone of your essay. Finally, check your sentence style. Have you varied the elements of your sentences to avoid a monotonous rhythm? Ask a friend to read your essay and give you suggestions.

Publishing   Check your writing carefully for errors in usage, spelling, and punctuation. Be sure that you've used only complete sentences. You may want to use the essay that you write for this assignment as part of an actual application packet.

16 | The Phrase
Kinds of Phrases and Their Functions

Diagnostic Preview

HELP

In Part A of the Diagnostic Preview, you do not need to identify separately a prepositional phrase that is part of a larger phrase.

A. Identifying Prepositional, Verbal, and Appositive Phrases

Identify the italicized phrase in each of the following sentences as a *prepositional phrase*, a *participial phrase*, a *gerund phrase*, an *infinitive phrase*, or an *appositive phrase*.

EXAMPLES 1. The sunlight shimmering *on the lake* was beautiful.
   1. prepositional phrase

   2. *Stretched out in a patch of sunlight,* the cat seemed to be grinning.
   2. participial phrase

1. Juanita likes *to draw caricatures of her friends.*
2. *Arriving late at school,* Bill went to the office to get a pass.
3. *Made in Ireland,* this kind of crystal is admired and collected throughout the world.
4. By *inventing the telephone,* Alexander Graham Bell assured himself a place in history.
5. Luciano Pavarotti, *the great Italian tenor,* received a hearty standing ovation at the end of his concert.
6. After the concert, we saw them *looking in vain for a taxi.*
7. Raúl has the talent *to sculpt and design beautiful objects.*
8. "It is a pleasure to be here with you today," remarked the mayor *at the beginning* of her talk.
9. A number of pioneer women kept diaries and journals *of their experiences* settling the American wilderness.
10. *To speak freely on almost any issue* is a right guaranteed to all U.S. citizens.

B. Identifying Prepositional, Verbal, and Appositive Phrases

Identify each italicized phrase in the following paragraph as a *preposi-tional phrase*, a *participial phrase*, a *gerund phrase*, an *infinitive phrase*, or an *appositive phrase*.

EXAMPLES **[1]** *For more than fifty years,* Thurgood Marshall worked **[2]** *to protect the rights of all people in the United States.*

   1. prepositional phrase

   2. infinitive phrase

HELP

In Part B of the Diagnostic Preview, you do not need to identify separately a prepositional phrase or a verbal phrase that is part of a larger phrase.

    [11] *Ranked at the top of his law school class,* Thurgood Marshall began law practice in Baltimore; and in 1936, he was selected **[12]** *to be a counsel for the National Association for the Advancement of Colored People.* From the start of his career, he believed strongly in **[13]** *using the U.S. Constitution to fight injustice.* **[14]** *Risking his life at times,* Marshall, **[15]** *the son of a schoolteacher,* won many civil rights cases **[16]** *before federal and state courts.* His arguments played an important role in **[17]** *convincing the Supreme Court that "separate but equal" educational facilities were unconstitutional.* **[18]** *During the Kennedy administration,* Marshall became a federal judge. **[19]** *After a two-year term* as U.S. solicitor general, he was nominated to the Supreme Court by President Lyndon Johnson. Marshall was the first African American **[20]** *to serve on the nation's highest court.*

What Is a Phrase?

16a. A *phrase* is a group of related words that is used as a single part of speech and that does not contain both a verb and its subject.

VERB PHRASE   have been waiting [no subject]

PREPOSITIONAL PHRASE   during the storm [no subject or verb]

INFINITIVE PHRASE   to run swiftly [no subject or verb]

NOTE A group of words that has both a subject and a verb is called a *clause.*

Reference Note
For more about **clauses,** see Chapter 17.

Prepositional Phrases

Reference Note

For more about **prepositions,** see page 517.

16b. A *prepositional phrase* includes a preposition, the object of the preposition, and any modifiers of that object.

EXAMPLES   Did officials **of the Smithsonian Institution** recently unveil plans **for a new museum**? [The compound noun *Smithsonian Institution* is the object of the preposition *of*. The noun *museum* is the object of the preposition *for*.]

        According to them, the National African-American Museum opened **in 1995.** [The pronoun *them* is the object of the compound preposition *According to*. The noun *1995* is the object of the preposition *in*.]

The object of a preposition may be compound.

EXAMPLE   Do you know the Greek myth about **Daedalus** and **Icarus**?

HI & LOIS reprinted with special permission of King Features Syndicate, Inc.

NOTE Be careful not to confuse a prepositional phrase beginning with *to* with an infinitive or infinitive phrase beginning with *to* (*to swim, to know, to see*). Remember, a preposition always has a noun or pronoun as an object.

Reference Note

For more about **infinitives,** see page 564.

The Adjective Phrase

16c. A prepositional phrase that modifies a noun or a pronoun is called an *adjective phrase.*

An adjective phrase tells *what kind* or *which one.*

EXAMPLE   One **of my friends** is making a film **about school.** [*Of my friends* modifies the pronoun *One*, telling *which one*. *About school* modifies the noun *film*, telling *what kind*.]

An adjective phrase almost always follows the word it modifies. That word may be the object of another preposition.

EXAMPLE   The film won't include all **of the students in our class.** [*Of the students* modifies the pronoun *all. In our class* modifies the noun *students,* which is the object of the preposition *of.*]

More than one adjective phrase may modify the same word.

EXAMPLE   Instead, it will relate the adventures **of five students at school** and **in their neighborhood.** [The three phrases *of five students, at school,* and *in their neighborhood* modify the noun *adventures.*]

NOTE   Sometimes an adjective phrase is combined with a noun to form a compound noun.

EXAMPLES   Helen of Troy   Meals on Wheels

              tug-of-war   jack-in-the-box

Exercise 1 Identifying Adjective Phrases and the Words They Modify

The following sentences contain adjective phrases. Identify each adjective phrase and the word it modifies.

EXAMPLE   1. If you are a rafting enthusiast, you might enjoy a trip to New Guinea, a large island in the East Indies.

1. *to New Guinea—trip; in the East Indies—island*

1. New Guinea rivers like the one shown are popular areas for rafting enthusiasts.
2. As you can see, a series of nearly continuous rapids crisscrosses jungles of primeval beauty.
3. The twenty-eight major rapids on the Tua River make it a course for rafters with experience and courage.
4. Brilliantly colored butterflies brighten the riverbanks, and the metallic whine of cicadas almost completely covers the roar of the river.
5. The banks are a chaos of tumbled boulders and uprooted trees.
6. Beautiful tropical forests along the way blanket the mountains above the river.

7. However, rafters don't have much chance for sightseeing.

8. They can't pay much attention to anything except the swirling water around their rafts.

9. Do you enjoy moments of high adventure?

10. Wouldn't you love a trip down this wild river in the South Pacific?

The Adverb Phrase

16d. A prepositional phrase that modifies a verb, an adjective, or an adverb is called an *adverb phrase*.

An adverb phrase tells *how, when, where, why,* or *to what extent* (*how much, how long,* or *how far*).

An adverb phrase may modify a verb.

EXAMPLE   **After the early 800s,** the Fujiwara family ruled **as regents in Japan for more than three hundred years.** [Each phrase modifies the verb *ruled. After the early 800s* tells *when, as regents* tells *how, in Japan* tells *where,* and *for more than three hundred years* tells *how long.*]

As the preceding example shows, more than one adverb phrase can modify the same word, and an adverb phrase, unlike an adjective phrase, often precedes the word it modifies.

An adverb phrase may modify an adjective.

EXAMPLE   Then the Minamoto, another family active **in court intrigues,** gained power. [*In court intrigues* modifies the adjective *active,* telling *how.*]

An adverb phrase may modify an adverb.

EXAMPLE   The Fujiwara had ruled too complacently **for their own good.** [*For their own good* modifies the adverb *complacently,* telling *how.*]

Exercise 2 **Identifying Adverb Phrases and the Words They Modify**

Each of the following sentences contains at least one adverb phrase. Identify each adverb phrase and the word or words it modifies.

EXAMPLE   1. From the map at right, you can clearly tell the function of the Panama Canal.

1. *From the map at right—can tell*

1. The canal, which is fifty-one miles long, links the Pacific Ocean to the Atlantic Ocean.
2. On the canal's elaborate series of locks, which raise and lower the water levels, ships can travel from ocean to ocean.
3. Construction of the canal, an engineering marvel, began in 1904 and continued until 1914.
4. Naturally, the builders faced many obstacles during the canal's construction.
5. Mosquitoes posed a major health risk throughout the area and had to be eliminated.
6. For the duration of the canal project, Dr. William C. Gorgas, an army surgeon, fought the mosquitoes.
7. With great efficiency, he drained swamps, fumigated buildings, and installed a pure water supply.
8. After the resignation of two chief engineers, President Theodore Roosevelt in 1907 appointed Army Lieutenant Colonel George W. Goethals chief engineer.
9. Goethals, active in all phases of canal construction, quickly gained the respect of workers.
10. This photograph shows some of the workers who dug through the mountains along the Isthmus of Panama.

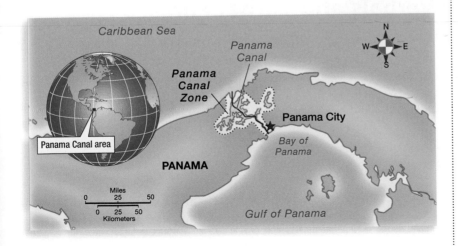

Identifying Adjective and Adverb Phrases

Identify each prepositional phrase in the following sentences. Then, tell whether it is an *adjective phrase* or an *adverb phrase*.

EXAMPLE **1.** The clay in bone china has actually been blended with bone ash.

1. *in bone china—adjective phrase; with bone ash—adverb phrase*

1. Tito, jump off and coil a line around that piling.
2. A large mirror reflected the light from the window.
3. Men in that part of the world commonly wear turbans, which protect their hair from sand.
4. Without a password, you cannot access the network.
5. Why do such small differences between people sometimes seem so large to the people themselves?
6. According to this source, the merger will take place later this week.
7. Hot corn bread muffins in the shape of fish tumbled out of the cast-iron pan.
8. Dozens of small framed photographs stood on the mantel over the fireplace.
9. Between the radiator and the engine, a large boa constrictor was taking a nap.
10. In England, the rear storage compartment of a car is called the "boot," not the "trunk."

Verbals and Verbal Phrases

A *verbal* is a verb form that is used as a noun, an adjective, or an adverb. The three kinds of verbals are the *participle*, the *gerund*, and the *infinitive*. A *verbal phrase* consists of a verbal and its modifiers and complements. The three kinds of verbal phrases are the *participial phrase*, the *gerund phrase*, and the *infinitive phrase*.

The Participle

16e. A *participle* is a verb form that can be used as an adjective.

Two kinds of participles are the *present participle* and the *past participle*.

(1) Present participles end in *–ing.*

EXAMPLES The **freezing** rain made the road slick. [*Freezing* modifies the noun *rain.*]

Bowing, the performers acknowledged the applause. [*Bowing* modifies the noun *performers.*]

Did I hear someone **knocking** on the door? [*Knocking* modifies the pronoun *someone.*]

(2) Most past participles end in *–d* **or** *–ed.* **Others are irregularly formed.**

EXAMPLES First prize was an **engraved** trophy. [*Engraved* modifies the noun *trophy.*]

The lab tested samples of water **taken** from wells in the area. [*Taken* modifies the noun *water.*]

Rested and relaxed, we returned to work. [Both *Rested* and *relaxed* modify the pronoun *we.*]

Reference Note
For lists of verbs that have **irregular past participles,** see page 674.

NOTE In addition to their present and past forms, participles have a *present perfect* form. This form adds *having* or *having been* to the past participle of a verb and indicates a completed action.

EXAMPLES **Having completed** his chores, Brian decided to join his friends playing soccer in the park.

Having been declared the winner, she called a press conference to thank her supporters.

Reference Note
For more about **present perfect participles,** see page 703.

The Participial Phrase

16f. A *participial phrase* consists of a participle and its modifiers and complements. The entire phrase is used as an adjective.

EXAMPLES **Grinning broadly,** Whoopi Goldberg accepted the award. [The participial phrase modifies the compound noun *Whoopi Goldberg.* The adverb *broadly* modifies the present participle *Grinning.*]

Proclaiming his innocence, the candidate vehemently denied the charges. [The participial phrase modifies the noun *candidate.* The noun *innocence* is the direct object of the present participle *Proclaiming.*]

HELP

Do not confuse a participle used as an adjective with a participle used as part of a verb phrase.

ADJECTIVE
The Hispanic Association of Colleges and Universities, **founded** in 1986, is based in San Antonio, Texas.

VERB PHRASE
The Hispanic Association of Colleges and Universities, which **was founded** in 1986, is based in San Antonio, Texas.

STYLE **TIP**

To prevent confusion, place participial phrases as close as possible to the words they modify.

MISPLACED
Stalking the squirrel, I saw the cat in the yard.

IMPROVED
I saw the cat **stalking the squirrel** in the yard.

Reference Note

For more about **misplaced participial phrases,** see page 744.

Puzzled by their behavior, I asked for an explanation. [The participial phrase modifies the pronoun *I*. The adverb phrase *by their behavior* modifies the past participle *Puzzled*.]

Zimbabwe, **formerly known as Rhodesia,** is in southern Africa. [The participial phrase modifies the noun *Zimbabwe*. The adverb *formerly* modifies the past participle *known*. The prepositional phrase *as Rhodesia* modifies the past participle *known*.]

Exercise 3 Identifying Participial Phrases and the Words They Modify

Each of the following sentences contains at least one participial phrase. Identify each participial phrase and the word or words it modifies.

EXAMPLE 1. Living far from the city, I developed an interest in nature at an early age.

1. *Living far from the city—I*

1. All of the students trying out for the soccer team have heard from the coach or her assistant.
2. Thanking us several times, the piano teacher returned the chairs borrowed for the recital.
3. Today's newspaper, printed last night, made no mention of the president's announcement.
4. Annoyed by the high prices, Mr. Sims has decided not to shop at that store anymore.
5. Addressing the senior class, the principal praised all of the students for their work on the cleanup campaign.
6. Having studied hard, Karen did well on both the Spanish test and the calculus quiz.
7. The movies showing at that theater are ones released before 1940.
8. Cheered by the crowd, our school's Special Olympics team rushed onto the field.
9. Looking through the catalog, Earl found a Cajun cookbook.
10. Smiling shyly, Lynn showed us the pictures she had taken.

The Absolute Phrase

An *absolute phrase* consists of (1) a participle or a participial phrase, (2) a noun or a pronoun that the participle or participial phrase modifies, and (3) any other modifiers of that noun or pronoun. The entire word group is used as an adverb to modify a clause in a sentence.

An absolute phrase has no grammatical connection to any word in the clause it modifies. Rather, the phrase, which tells *when, why,* or *how,* modifies the whole clause.

EXAMPLES   **Their car having been repaired,** the Pfeiffers continued their road trip. [The absolute phrase modifies the independent clause, telling *when* the Pfeiffers continued their road trip. The present perfect participle *having been repaired* modifies the noun *car.*]

Chris said that, **the weather being so fine,** he would prefer to go for a hike. [The absolute phrase modifies the subordinate clause, telling *why* Chris would prefer to go for a hike. The participial phrase *being so fine* modifies the noun *weather.*]

Wearily, the explorer trudged onward through the snow, **his loyal Alaskan malamute keeping pace at his side.** [The absolute phrase modifies the independent clause by telling *how* the explorer trudged onward through the snow. The participial phrase *keeping pace at his side* modifies the noun *Alaskan malamute.*]

Review B **Identifying Prepositional and Participial Phrases and the Words They Modify**

Identify each italicized phrase in the following sentences as a *prepositional phrase* or a *participial phrase.* Then, give the word or words each phrase modifies. If a participial phrase is part of an absolute phrase, write *absolute.*

EXAMPLE   [1] *Visiting friends in Los Angeles last year,* I became interested *in low-riders.*

    1. *participial—I; prepositional—interested*

[1] My friend Jorge told me that this unique form *of folk art* has been popular *for forty years or more.* [2] He said the term "low-rider" refers *to the automobile, its driver, and any passengers.* [3] *Making artistic statements with their automobiles,* many young men *in the Southwest* spend both time and money on their cars. [4] First, a car is lowered *by several methods* so that its chassis just skims the pavement. [5] *After the height adjustment,* the car is embellished *with exterior paint and trim work.* [6] *Decorated elaborately,* Jorge's car, *shown on the next page,* is a good example *of a low-rider.* [7] *Their cars finished and spotlessly clean,* riders drive slowly *through their communities.* [8] *Relaxing behind the*

HELP

In Review B, you do not need to identify separately a prepositional phrase that is part of a participial phrase.

steering wheel of his car, Jorge is proud when people admire the results *of his hard work.* **[9]** *On sunny days,* long caravans of low-riders may drive for hours *through the neighborhood.* **[10]** Low-riders in some cities have even formed clubs that work *with charitable organizations.*

The Gerund

Reference Note

For more about **subjects,** see page 531. For more about **direct and indirect objects,** see page 539. For more about **predicate nominatives,** see page 543. For more about **objects of a preposition,** see page 517.

16g. A *gerund* is a verb form ending in *–ing* that is used as a noun.

SUBJECT	**Photographing** animals requires great patience.
DIRECT OBJECT	Please stop **whispering.**
INDIRECT OBJECT	The team gave **passing** the ball their full attention.
PREDICATE NOMINATIVE	The issue is his **whining.**
OBJECT OF PREPOSITION	In **answering,** give specific examples.

Do not confuse a gerund with a present participle used as an adjective or as part of a verb phrase.

GERUND	I remember **driving** from Florida to Texas last fall. [direct object of the verb *remember*]
PRESENT PARTICIPLE	**Driving** on long road trips, we usually take turns behind the wheel. [adjective modifying the pronoun *we*]
PRESENT PARTICIPLE	We heard mostly country music on the radio while we were **driving.** [main verb in the verb phrase *were driving*]

GRAMMAR

NOTE Generally, a noun or a pronoun directly before a gerund should be in the possessive case.

EXAMPLES **Lee's** pitching won the game.

What did the teacher say about **your** missing the test yesterday?

The Gerund Phrase

16h. A *gerund phrase* consists of a gerund and its modifiers and complements. The entire phrase is used as a noun.

EXAMPLES **Managing the restaurant efficiently** required much hard work. [The gerund phrase is the subject of the verb *required*. The noun *restaurant* is the direct object of the gerund *Managing*. The adverb *efficiently* modifies *Managing*.]

My cousin enjoys **working as a lifeguard.** [The gerund phrase is the direct object of the verb *enjoys*. The adverb phrase *as a lifeguard* modifies the gerund *working*.]

Her greatest achievement was **winning three gold medals.** [The gerund phrase is a predicate nominative identifying the subject *achievement*. The noun *medals* is the direct object of the gerund *winning*.]

We were fined for **parking there.** [The gerund phrase is the object of the preposition *for*. The adverb *there* modifies the gerund *parking*.]

┌─ **TIPS** & **TRICKS** ─┐

If you're not sure whether an *–ing* word is a gerund or a participle, try this test. Substitute a pronoun for the *–ing* word. If the sentence still makes sense, the word is a gerund.

EXAMPLES
Swimming is good exercise. [It is good exercise. *It* makes sense in the sentence. *Swimming* is a gerund.]

We watched the dolphins swimming in circles. [We watched the dolphins it in circles. *It* does not make sense here. *Swimming* is a participle.]

Exercise 4 **Identifying Gerund Phrases and Their Functions**

Identify the gerund phrase in each of the following sentences, and tell whether it is used as a *subject*, a *predicate nominative*, a *direct object*, an *indirect object*, or an *object of a preposition*.

EXAMPLE 1. Learning to type has been one of my most practical accomplishments.

1. *Learning to type—subject*

1. Give traveling by rail a try.
2. Sylvia's method of making decisions reveals a great deal about her.
3. My grandparents enjoy practicing their square-dance routines.
4. Before making changes, please notify our secretary, Ms. Erikson.
5. Ms. Sanapaw finished writing her paper.

6. Producing a movie for Mr. Matsuyama's cinematography course requires organization and communication.

7. One habit that is very bad for teeth is chewing ice.

8. Dropping two cannonballs of different sizes from the Leaning Tower of Pisa may have proven to Galileo that falling objects travel at the same speed, whatever their masses.

9. Hector earns money on the weekends by giving guitar lessons.

10. My brother's singing in the shower early in the morning annoys me.

Review C **Identifying Gerunds and Participles**

For each of the following sentences, identify the italicized word as either a *gerund* or a *participle*.

EXAMPLE **1.** Isn't *shopping* becoming boring?

     1. gerund

1. The pilot leaned forward and lowered the flaps to twenty degrees in preparation for a *landing*.

2. Wait until proper weather conditions before *burning* leaves.

3. *Confusing* some listeners, the president's press secretary called the reporter by the wrong name.

4. The package was flown across the ocean, *arriving* at its destination in only a few hours.

5. *Saving* should be an important part of your budget.

6. Her favorite pastime was *diving* for Spanish doubloons.

7. What an *exhausting* day that was!

8. *Deciphering* the hieroglyphics, the professor realized that they were a fragment of a story.

9. We finished *gathering* firewood and returned to camp.

10. Carefully *following* instructions increases the likelihood of getting good results.

The Infinitive

16i. An *infinitive* is a verb form that can be used as a noun, an adjective, or an adverb. Most infinitives begin with *to*.

NOUNS   **To leave** now would be rude. [subject of *would be*]

           No one wants **to stay.** [direct object of *wants*]

           Her goal is **to win.** [predicate nominative identifying the subject *goal*]

ADJECTIVES	She is the candidate **to watch.** [adjective modifying the noun *candidate*]
	The one **to see** is the class president. [adjective modifying the pronoun *one*]
ADVERBS	We came **to cheer.** [adverb modifying the verb *came*]
	Is everybody ready **to go**? [adverb modifying the adjective *ready*]

NOTE In addition to the present form, infinitives have a ***present perfect*** form. This form adds *to have* to the past participle and *to have been* to the present or past participle and indicates completed action.

EXAMPLES **To have seen** him would have pleased Jerome.

Elsa was known **to have been chosen.**

Reference Note

For more about **present perfect infinitives,** see page 702.

The word *to*, the sign of the infinitive, is sometimes omitted.

EXAMPLES Let's [to] **wait** here.

The clowns made us [to] **laugh.**

Help me [to] **wash** the car.

The Infinitive Phrase

16j. An *infinitive phrase* consists of an infinitive and its modifiers and complements. The entire phrase can be used as a noun, an adjective, or an adverb.

NOUNS	**To get a medical degree** is her goal. [The infinitive phrase is the subject of the verb *is.* The noun *degree* is the direct object of the infinitive *To get.*]
	They promised **to return soon.** [The infinitive phrase is the direct object of the verb *promised.* The adverb *soon* modifies the infinitive *to return.*]
ADJECTIVE	We have time **to walk to the concert.** [The infinitive phrase modifies the noun *time.* The adverb phrase *to the concert* modifies the infinitive *to walk.*]
ADVERB	He is eager **to give Chris the award.** [The infinitive phrase modifies the adjective *eager.* The noun *Chris* is the indirect object of the infinitive *to give,* and the noun *award* is the direct object of *to give.*]

HELP

Do not confuse an infinitive with a prepositional phrase beginning with *to.* Remember that a preposition has a noun or a pronoun as an object.

INFINITIVES
to go
to forget
to graduate

PREPOSITIONAL PHRASES
to them
to the loud party
to everyone

NOTE   An infinitive may have a subject. An infinitive or infinitive phrase with a subject is called an *infinitive clause.*

EXAMPLES   Everyone expects **Guadalupe to win the election.** [*Guadalupe* is the subject of the infinitive *to win.* The entire infinitive clause is the direct object of the verb *expects.*]

We wanted **her to lead the discussion.** [*Her* is the subject of the infinitive *to lead.* The entire infinitive clause is the direct object of the verb *wanted.*]

I believe **them to be trustworthy.** [*Them* is the subject of the infinitive *to be.* The entire infinitive clause is the direct object of the verb *believe.*]

Notice in the examples above that the subjects of the verbs are in the nominative case and that the subjects of the infinitives are in the objective case.

STYLE   **TIP**

Placing words between the sign of the infinitive, *to,* and the verb results in a *split infinitive.* Generally, you should avoid using split infinitives in formal writing and speaking situations.

SPLIT
Most people should try to regularly have their blood pressure checked.

REVISED
Most people should try **to have** their blood pressure checked regularly.

Sometimes, however, you may need to use a split infinitive so that the meaning of the sentence is clear.

UNCLEAR
She expects her investment more than to triple by the year 2010.

CLEAR
She expects her investment **to more than triple** by the year 2010.

Exercise 5   **Identifying Infinitive Phrases and Their Functions**

Identify each infinitive phrase or infinitive clause in the following sentences as a *noun,* an *adjective,* or an *adverb.* If a phrase is used as a noun, tell whether it is the *subject,* the *direct object,* or the *predicate nominative.* If the phrase is used as a modifier, give the word it modifies.

EXAMPLE   1. I like to compose music for the guitar.

1. *to compose music for the guitar—noun, direct object*

1. To win an Olympic medal is the dream of every member of the women's ski team.
2. The candidate had the courage to speak on a controversial issue.
3. We went to Italy to see our grandparents.
4. The Latin and French clubs try to work together on projects.
5. Dr. Martin Luther King, Jr., believed that all U.S. citizens should be free to exercise their civil rights.
6. Louis Pasteur experimented for many years to discover a method for preventing rabies.
7. The ability to speak distinctly is an advantage in job interviews.
8. To open the box required a hammer and a crowbar.
9. Alana's hobby is to spend hours each day developing original computer programs.
10. Marvella, please help me learn about photography.

Review D Identifying Prepositional, Participial, Gerund, and Infinitive Phrases

Identify each numbered italicized word group in the following paragraph as a *prepositional phrase*, a *participial phrase*, a *gerund phrase*, or an *infinitive phrase*.

EXAMPLES   Vijay Amritraj first gained international attention for **[1]** *playing a world-class game of tennis,* and it almost seems that he has made a second career **[2]** *of taking on new challenges.*

1. gerund phrase
2. prepositional phrase

[1] *Being a famous tennis player* was not enough for Vijay Amritraj. For almost twenty years, Amritraj, [2] *born in Madras, India,* was a tennis superstar. [3] *Playing in the Wimbledon tournament for seventeen consecutive years,* he also led India to the Davis Cup finals in 1974 and 1987. Ranked the number-one player in Asia for fourteen years, he decided [4] *to branch out.* [5] *Along with his proficiency on the tennis court,* Amritraj added credits as a film actor by [6] *appearing in several TV and studio films,* including the fourth Star Trek movie. [7] *In recent years,* Amritraj, [8] *now living in California,* has become a movie producer, and he is still a leading tennis commentator for U.S. and Asian TV networks. [9] *To help U.S. media corporations enter the Indian marketplace,* he founded California-based First Serve Entertainment, which has become one of the leading multimedia companies [10] *working in Asia.*

┌─HELP─
In Review D, you do not need to identify separately a prepositional phrase, a verbal, or a verbal phrase that is part of a larger phrase.

Appositives and Appositive Phrases

16k. An *appositive* is a noun or a pronoun placed beside another noun or pronoun to identify or describe it.

An appositive usually follows the word it identifies or describes.

EXAMPLES   My cousin **María** is an accomplished violinist.

Riboflavin, a **vitamin,** is found in leafy vegetables.

For emphasis, however, an appositive may come at the beginning of a sentence.

EXAMPLE   **Mollusks,** both snails and clams, have shells.

16l. An *appositive phrase* consists of an appositive and its modifiers.

EXAMPLES   My brother's car, **a sporty red hatchback with bucket seats,** has over 100,000 miles on it.

    Mr. Hudson, **a member of the jury,** asked the judge a question.

An appositive phrase usually follows the word it describes or identifies but may precede it.

EXAMPLE   **Once a pagan feast,** Valentine's Day is now celebrated as a day of love.

Reference Note

For information on **how to punctuate appositives,** see page 838. For more about **the use of appositives,** see pages 443 and 642.

Exercise 6 Identifying Appositives and Appositive Phrases

Identify the appositive or appositive phrase in each of the following sentences.

EXAMPLE   1. The sapling, a variety of oak, will grow rather slowly.

    1. *a variety of oak*

1. The design, a complex pattern of interlocking knots, ran all the way around the door.
2. Look out; their cat, a Siamese, hates visitors.
3. Elsa is visiting her oldest brother, Joseph, in Ohio.
4. Dan's dog, a border collie, came running up to greet him.
5. A small animal, a hare, had been carved in the lid of the wooden chest over there.
6. One of only three in existence today, this folio remains in the possession of the British Museum.
7. "Have you ever read the poem 'Ozymandias'?" Sergio asked.
8. A gift from his grandfather, the silver-and-turquoise ring was never off his finger.
9. She wore a long, flowing gown tied with an *obi,* the traditional Japanese sash.
10. What I need is a job, an entry-level position with a good chance of advancement.

Review E Identifying Prepositional, Verbal, and Appositive Phrases

Identify each italicized phrase in the following paragraph as a *prepositional phrase*, a *participial phrase*, a *gerund phrase*, an *infinitive phrase*, or an *appositive phrase*.

EXAMPLES   Altamont Pass, **[1]** *located in northern California,* has become the topic of discussion **[2]** *among many energy entrepreneurs.*

1. participial phrase
2. prepositional phrase

Altamont Pass, [1] *an area of grassy hills* [2] *surrounding San Francisco Bay,* is producing a new cash crop. Energy entrepreneurs are hurrying [3] *to lease wind rights on acreage* [4] *throughout the Altamont.* One rancher owns several hundred acres [5] *dotted with tall white wind machines like the ones shown here.* [6] *Standing in rows on the wind-swept hills,* these machines work almost nonstop at [7] *producing electricity.* [8] *With any luck,* the wind-power industry may soon spread [9] *to other parts* of the country. The temperature differences [10] *between the cool coast and the hot valley* can create air surges [11] *funneling inland through natural gaps* [12] *like the Altamont.*

┌─**HELP**─

In Review E, you do not need to identify separately a prepositional or verbal phrase that is part of a larger phrase.

In 1997, wind energy [13] *from areas like this in California* produced enough electricity [14] *to light a city the size of San Francisco.* Electricity [15] *produced by these turbines* has the potential [16] *to provide 20 percent of the energy* [17] *needed by the world.* With developing countries, [18] *India and China, for example,* [19] *rapidly expanding their wind resources,* wind could produce over 18,000 megawatts more in the near future than it does today. Modern wind turbines may someday become as numerous [20] *in the United States* as windmills once were in the Netherlands.

Review F   Writing Sentences with Phrases

Write one sentence according to each of the following guidelines.

EXAMPLE   1. Use *into the wind* as an adverb phrase.
            1. *The plane took off into the wind to get more lift.*

1. Use *because of the rain* as an adverb phrase.
2. Use *from Puerto Rico* as an adjective phrase.
3. Use *running toward us* as a participial phrase.
4. Use *seen from a distance* as a participial phrase.
5. Use *building a fence* as a gerund phrase that is the object of a preposition.
6. Use *writing résumés* as a gerund phrase that is the subject of a verb.
7. Use *to dream* in an infinitive phrase that is the direct object of a verb.
8. Use *to sell* in an infinitive phrase that is a modifier.
9. Use *to study music* as an infinitive phrase that is a predicate nominative.
10. Use *our local newspaper* as an appositive phrase.

Chapter Review

A. Identifying Phrases

Identify the italicized phrase in each of the following sentences as a *prepositional phrase*, a *participial phrase*, a *gerund phrase*, an *infinitive phrase*, or an *appositive phrase*.

┌─HELP─
In the Chapter Review, you do not need to identify separately a prepositional phrase that is part of a larger phrase.

1. *Rolling up his shirt sleeves,* Tam prepared to chop wood for his fireplace.
2. Before we called in the others, we had decided *to discuss the matter thoroughly.*
3. *Seeing that opera* was an unforgettable experience.
4. The sentence *for the crime* was suspended.
5. Laura thought about *going away to college.*
6. The problem, *considered from this angle,* seems simple.
7. My suggestion was *to leave the baby with us.*
8. Her endurance was of great help to her in the marathon, *a twenty-six mile footrace.*
9. *In spite of its forbidding expression,* the bulldog is gentle with children.
10. I thought I saw a friend *in the audience.*

B. Identifying Phrases in a Paragraph

Identify each italicized phrase in the following paragraph as a *prepositional phrase*, a *participial phrase*, a *gerund phrase*, an *infinitive phrase*, or an *appositive phrase*.

[11] *Until the early years* of the twentieth century, the blacksmith's shop, or smithy, was a familiar part of the American scene. [12] The blacksmith's work included not only shoeing horses but also *making iron parts for wagons and carriages.* [13] A blacksmith was often expected *to repair a broken plow* or mend a broken frying pan. [14] Many blacksmiths provided a bench outside the front door of the smithy *for the convenience of the customers.* [15] A person waiting *to have a horse shod or a wagon fixed* could relax on the bench and chat with passersby. [16] In some communities, the blacksmith's bench came to serve as a center for the exchange of news, *a kind of substitute for a local newspaper.* [17] The

reason that most smithies went out of business in the early years of the twentieth century was not that the work *done by blacksmiths* had ceased to be important. [18] On the contrary, work with iron and steel became so important and so technical that a job often had to be given *to a specialist within the field.* [19] *Manufacturing a car* was a far more complicated task than making new metal parts for a wooden wagon. [20] Many men *trained in blacksmithing* decided to concentrate on the specialized aspect of the business that appealed to them most, some by opening hardware stores, others by going into the auto service industry.

C. Identifying Participial, Gerund, and Infinitive Phrases

Identify the participial, gerund, and infinitive phrases in the following sentences. For each participial phrase, give the word it modifies. For each gerund phrase, tell whether it is the *subject,* the *direct object,* or the *object of a preposition.* For each infinitive phrase, indicate whether it functions as a *noun,* an *adjective,* or an *adverb.*

21. My friend Alecca considered sending me a postcard from Rome.
22. My cousin, who is deaf, gives his full attention to ensuring that more television programs are close-captioned.
23. To learn about car repair, Herb is taking vocational courses.
24. To hurry home was my immediate goal.
25. Moving to the right, all of the drivers let the ambulance pass.

D. Identifying Phrases in a Paragraph

─HELP─
In Part D of the Chapter Review, you do not need to identify separately a prepositional phrase that is part of a larger phrase.

For each sentence in the following paragraph, identify the italicized phrase as an *adjective phrase,* an *adverb phrase,* a *participial phrase,* a *gerund phrase,* an *infinitive phrase,* or an *appositive phrase.*

[26] After a lively discussion in home economics class, Marcie wanted *to learn more about the history of fabrics, clothes, and clothing parts.* [27] One material *of special interest* to the entire class was Velcro. [28] In her research, Marcie discovered that the idea for Velcro is attributed to Georges de Mestral, *a Swiss hiker and engineer.* [29] *During an outing in the 1940s,* de Mestral started thinking about the burrs that stuck to his socks. [30] *Adapting the idea from nature,* de Mestral developed a pair of nylon tapes that fastened together. [31] The new material was called "Velcro," *a name that combines the French words for* velvet

(velours) *and* hook (crochet). **[32]** *Patented in 1955,* Velcro is widely used today instead of other fasteners, such as zippers. **[33]** However, zippers were once considered high-tech in the fashion industry, and *learning about these devices* was Marcie's next goal. **[34]** The zipper, she found out, was patented in 1893 *by Whitcomb Judson* of Chicago. **[35]** The public was reluctant to try the new fasteners until the United States military decided *to use zippers on some uniforms during World War I.*

Writing Application

Using Phrases in a Business Letter

Infinitive and Appositive Phrases   Every year your school holds a raffle to raise funds for special equipment and activities. As secretary of the student council, you have been asked to contact owners of local businesses and ask them to donate prizes for the raffle. Write a letter explaining the purpose of the raffle and persuading the business owners to donate their products or services. Include at least three infinitive phrases and two appositive phrases in your letter.

Prewriting   Invent specific information about the upcoming raffle, including when and where it is being held. Think about how you can convince business owners that they should donate prizes.

Writing   Begin your letter by clearly stating your purpose for writing. Then, give specific information about the raffle. Conclude by restating your request. Also, tell your reader whom to contact to make a donation.

Revising   Make sure that the form and the tone of your letter are appropriate for business correspondence. Be sure that you include at least three infinitive phrases and two appositive phrases.

Publishing   Errors in grammar, usage, spelling, and punctuation will not help your cause, so be sure to proofread carefully. Show your letter to two or three business owners in your area. Ask them if they find the letter effective. What changes would they suggest to make the letter more persuasive?

Reference Note

For more about writing **business letters,** see "Writing" in the Quick Reference Handbook.

The Clause
Independent and Subordinate Clauses, Sentence Structure

Diagnostic Preview

A. Identifying and Classifying Clauses

Identify the italicized clause in each of the following sentences as an *independent clause* or a *subordinate clause*. If a clause is subordinate, tell whether it is an *adjective clause*, an *adverb clause*, or a *noun clause*.

EXAMPLE   1. *While I was at the orthodontist's office,* Dr. Liu adjusted my retainer.

1. *subordinate clause—adverb clause*

1. *Tamara applied for the job last Monday,* and each day since then she has been waiting for a call from the company.
2. Serious hikers know *that a topographical map is often useful in unfamiliar territory.*
3. *The band played calypso and reggae music from the West Indies.*
4. Amelia Earhart, *who was the first woman to fly solo over both the Atlantic Ocean and the Pacific Ocean,* had great courage.
5. Mr. Benoit was the best coach at Northeast High School *even though he had become paraplegic after an auto accident.*
6. As you wait, concentrate on *what you have to do to win.*
7. Since last year Erin and Jim have been rotating household tasks; *as a result, each of them has become more understanding.*
8. *Renowned underwater explorer Jacques-Yves Cousteau was ten years old* when he made his first dive.

9. How was I ever going to get the parts of the engine put back together *before my father got home*?

10. The Vietnam Veterans Memorial, a black granite wall engraved with the names of those Americans *who died in the war in Vietnam,* was designed by Maya Ying Lin.

11. Tired after a long day in the summer sun, the lifeguard reported *that there had been no accidents.*

12. In high school, Lori Garcia set an all-city scoring record in basketball, and *she later went to college on a scholarship.*

13. Can you tell me *why there is still famine in parts of the world*?

14. After World War II, President Harry Truman authorized the Marshall Plan, *which was a program designed to speed economic recovery in Europe.*

15. Lawrence, who transferred to our school last month, is taller *than the other boys on the team.*

B. Classifying Sentences

Classify each of the following sentences first according to its structure and then according to its purpose.

EXAMPLE   **1.** Did you know that some of the best-preserved Anasazi dwellings are in Mesa Verde National Park in Colorado?

    1. complex—interrogative

16. *Anasazi* means "ancient ones," and that term accurately describes these cliff dwellers.

17. The Anasazi had a thriving culture around A.D. 1100.

18. They lived primarily in an area now called the Four Corners, where the states of New Mexico, Colorado, Utah, and Arizona converge.

19. These remarkable people built dwellings, some of which were several stories high, in the cliffs.

20. What unusual villages they created, and what views they had!

21. Don't assume, however, that this fascinating civilization lasted as long as the Mayan and Aztec civilizations did.

22. The Anasazi disappeared around A.D. 1300.

23. Do you know why they disappeared?

24. Nobody knows for sure, but anthropologists have several theories that may explain the disappearance.

25. A drought that lasted many years is one possibility, but the Anasazi may have been driven from their villages by enemies or by changes in climate.

What Is a Clause?

17a. A *clause* is a word group that contains a verb and its subject and that is used as a sentence or as part of a sentence.

                          V   S
EXAMPLES   where are you now

                        S   V
            after we won the game

Every clause has both a subject and a verb. Not every clause expresses a complete thought, however.

SENTENCE   A sitar is a stringed instrument that resembles a lute.

                      S   V
    CLAUSE   A sitar is a stringed instrument. [complete thought]

                      S   V
    CLAUSE   that resembles a lute [incomplete thought]

There are two basic kinds of clauses: the *independent clause* and the *subordinate clause.* Standing alone, an independent clause is a complete sentence. A subordinate clause, like a word or a phrase, acts as a single part of speech and by itself is not a complete sentence.

The Independent Clause

17b. An *independent* (or *main*) *clause* expresses a complete thought and can stand by itself as a sentence.

                            S   V
EXAMPLES   **The Mexican artist José Guadalupe Posada opposed the dictatorship of Porfirio Díaz.** [one independent clause]

                        S   V
            In his paintings, Posada attacked the Díaz regime, and

            S   V
            he made thousands of inexpensive prints of his work. [two independent clauses joined by *and*]

                        S   V   S   V
            Posada's art helped to stir the social unrest that led to the overthrow of Díaz in the revolution of 1910. [an independent clause combined with a subordinate clause]

The Subordinate Clause

17c. A *subordinate* (or *dependent*) *clause* does not express a complete thought and cannot stand by itself as a sentence.

EXAMPLES   whoever knows the song

which always pleases my mother

as we were singing

The meaning of a subordinate clause becomes clear only when the clause is combined with an independent clause.

       S   **V**
Whoever knows the song may join in.

                          S   **V**
We sang "We Shall Overcome," **which always pleases my mother.**

       S   **V**
As we were singing, we joined hands and formed a circle.

> **STYLE TIP**
>
> Subordinate clauses are often used by themselves in informal conversation when the speaker and the listener both understand the context. If the listener does not understand, he or she may interrupt and ask for clarification. However, in formal writing and speaking, the reader or listener does not have an opportunity to ask for clarification. Using complete sentences helps ensure that the reader or listener will understand your meaning.

Exercise 1 Identifying Independent and Subordinate Clauses

Identify the italicized word group in each of the following sentences as an *independent clause* or a *subordinate clause*.

EXAMPLE   **1.** *The inscriptions on the Rosetta stone,* which was found in 1799, *helped scholars learn more about ancient Egyptian hieroglyphics.*

                1. independent clause

> **HELP**
>
> Notice in the example for Exercise 1 that an independent clause may be divided by one or more subordinate clauses.

1. Egyptology is the branch of learning *that is concerned with the language and culture of ancient Egypt.*

2. *Until the Rosetta stone was discovered in 1799,* the ancient Egyptian language was an enigma to scholars.

3. A man named Bouchard, *who was a captain under Napoleon,* and some of Bouchard's men found the stone near Rosetta, a city near the mouth of the Nile.

4. As you can see in this photograph of the Rosetta stone, *it has three different kinds of writing inscribed on it.*

5. Because the same message was written on the stone in two kinds of Egyptian writing and in Greek script, *the stone provided the needed key for deciphering ancient Egyptian writings.*

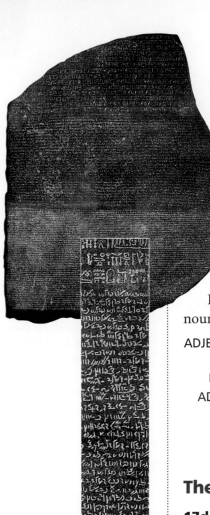

6. *When the Rosetta stone was found,* part of the hiero-glyphic portion was missing.

7. Scholars could easily read the Greek inscription, *which was nearly complete.*

8. *In 1816, Jean François Champollion and Thomas Young isolated several hieroglyphics* that they believed represented names.

9. *The message* that was inscribed on the stone *was not very exciting.*

10. Since the priests of Egypt were grateful for benefits from the king, *they were commemorating the crowning of Ptolemy V.*

Like a word or a phrase, a clause can be used as an adjective, a noun, or an adverb.

ADJECTIVE CLAUSE	We sang "We Shall Overcome," **which always pleases my mother.**
NOUN CLAUSE	**Whoever knows the song** may join in.
ADVERB CLAUSE	**As we were singing,** we joined hands and formed a circle.

The Adjective Clause

17d. An *adjective clause* is a subordinate clause that modifies a noun or a pronoun.

An adjective clause usually follows the word or words it modifies and tells *what kind* or *which one.*

EXAMPLES   The report **that Diego wrote** was on the Battle of the Little Bighorn. [The adjective clause modifies the noun *report.*]

The Cuban Cultural Heritage Walk, **which is located in Hialeah, Florida,** honors Cuban artists in exile. [The adjective clause modifies the compound noun *Cuban Cultural Heritage Walk.*]

Amanda is someone **whom I admire.** [The adjective clause modifies the pronoun *someone.*]

Mark Twain is the writer **whose books I have enjoyed the most.** [The adjective clause modifies the noun *writer.*]

Relative Pronouns

An adjective clause is usually introduced by a *relative pronoun*—a word that relates the clause to the word or words the clause modifies.

Common Relative Pronouns				
that	which	who	whom	whose

A relative pronoun has three functions.

(1) It refers to a preceding noun or pronoun—the antecedent.

(2) It connects the adjective clause with the rest of the sentence.

(3) It performs a function within its own clause by serving as a subject, a direct object, an indirect object, an object of a preposition, or a modifier in the adjective clause.

EXAMPLES   Mr. Mendoza is a good counselor **who never betrays a confidence.** [The relative pronoun *who* relates the adjective clause to the noun antecedent, *counselor,* and serves as the subject of the verb *betrays.*]

Have you practiced the speech **that you will give on Friday**? [The relative pronoun *that* relates the adjective clause to the noun antecedent, *speech,* and serves as the direct object of the verb *will give.*]

The mariachi band **in which I play** once performed for Governor Tommy Thompson. [The relative pronoun *which* relates the adjective clause to the noun antecedent, *band,* and serves as the object of the preposition *in.*]

Han-Ling is the one **whose essay took first place.** [The relative pronoun *whose* relates the adjective clause to the pronoun antecedent, *one,* and modifies the noun *essay* by showing possession.]

An adjective clause may be introduced by a relative adverb, such as *when* or *where.*

EXAMPLES   Dr. Martin Luther King, Jr., dreamed of the day **when freedom and justice would reign in the United States.** [The relative adverb *when* relates the adjective clause to the noun antecedent, *day,* and modifies *would reign.*]

The site **where Dr. King delivered his great "I Have a Dream" speech in 1963** is the Lincoln Memorial. [The relative adverb *where* relates the adjective clause to the noun antecedent, *site,* and modifies *delivered.*]

GRAMMAR

Reference Note

For information about **using *who* and *whom* correctly,** see page 646. For information about **using *who, that,* and *which* correctly,** see page 777.

Sometimes the relative pronoun or relative adverb is not expressed but is understood.

EXAMPLES   The vase **[that] my family brought from the Philippines** was made by my great-grandmother.

Do you remember the first time **[when] we met each other**?

Reference Note

For more about **punctuating nonessential clauses,** see page 832.

Depending on how it is used, an adjective clause is either essential or nonessential. An *essential clause* provides information that is necessary to the meaning of a sentence. A *nonessential clause* provides additional information that can be omitted without changing the basic meaning of a sentence. A nonessential clause is set off by commas.

ESSENTIAL   Students **who are auditioning for the school play** should meet in the auditorium at 4:15 P.M. [Omitting the adjective clause would change the basic meaning of the sentence.]

NONESSENTIAL   Liza Minnelli**, whose mother, Judy Garland, was best known for starring in *The Wizard of Oz*,** earned her own fame as a singer and actress. [The adjective clause gives extra information. Omitting the clause would not affect the basic meaning of the sentence.]

Exercise 2   Identifying Adjective Clauses and the Words They Modify

Each of the following sentences contains at least one adjective clause. Identify each adjective clause, and give the noun or pronoun that the adjective clause modifies. Be prepared to tell whether the relative pronoun or relative adverb is used as the *subject*, the *direct object*, the *object of a preposition*, or a *modifier* in the adjective clause.

—HELP—

In the example for Exercise 2, the relative pronoun *that* is used as a direct object in the adjective clause.

EXAMPLE   1.   Has the scientific information that the *Mariner* and *Pathfinder* space missions gathered about Mars increased readers' interest in science fiction books about the planet?

1.   *that the* Mariner *and* Pathfinder *space missions gathered about Mars—information*

1. The Mars of the nonscientist is a planet of the imagination, where an ancient civilization has left its mark and where maps blossom with romantic place names like Utopia and Elysium.
2. "Earthlings," who were awed by the planet's red glow in the evening sky, looked on Mars as a home for creatures who might someday cross cosmic barriers and visit planet Earth.

3. Such thinking was encouraged by an Italian astronomer, Giovanni V. Schiaparelli, who observed the planet through a telescope and saw a series of fine lines that crisscrossed its surface.

4. He called the lines *canali*, which is Italian for "channels"; this word was erroneously translated into English as "canals."

5. A planet where there are such canals would, of course, be inhabited by people who are capable of building not only canals but also cities that presumably sprang up at their intersections.

6. Percival Lowell, the astronomer who founded the Lowell Observatory in Flagstaff, Arizona, brought new life to old myths about life on Mars with nonscientific observations most astronomers disputed.

7. Lowell reported a total of more than four hundred Martian canals, of which a considerable number were discovered by his own team of astronomers.

8. One writer whose interest was drawn to Mars was Edgar Rice Burroughs, whom many people know as the creator of the Tarzan books.

9. In his Martian books, Burroughs recounts the adventures of John Carter, who could get to Mars by standing in a field and wishing.

10. Burroughs's best-known literary successor is Ray Bradbury, who wrote *The Martian Chronicles*, which was published in 1950.

The Noun Clause

17e. A *noun clause* is a subordinate clause that is used as a noun.

A noun clause may be used as a subject, a predicate nominative, a direct object, an indirect object, an object of a preposition, or an appositive.

SUBJECT	**How students can apply for college loans** was the speaker's topic.
PREDICATE NOMINATIVE	My suggestion is **that we all meet again tomorrow.**
DIRECT OBJECT	I wonder **whether Columbus was truly the first European to explore the Americas.**
INDIRECT OBJECT	Mrs. Romero offers **whoever completes additional assignments** extra credit.

Reference Note

For more about **subjects,** see page 531. For more about **predicate nominatives,** see page 543. For more about **direct objects** and **indirect objects,** see page 539. For more about **appositives,** see page 567.

TIPS & TRICKS

Do not mistake an adjective clause for a noun clause used as an appositive. An adjective clause *modifies* a noun or a pronoun. A noun clause used as an appositive *identifies* or *explains* the noun or pronoun beside it and can take the place of that noun or pronoun.

ADJECTIVE CLAUSE
The theory **that Copernicus proposed** was rejected by most other astronomers at the time. [The clause modifies the noun *theory.*]

NOUN CLAUSE
The theory **that the sun is the center of our solar system** was proposed by Copernicus. [The clause identifies the noun *theory.*]

Reference Note

For more about **introductory words in subordinate clauses,** see pages 579 and 585.

Reference Note

For more about **infinitive clauses,** see page 566.

| OBJECT OF A PREPOSITION | Write your research paper about **whomever you admire most.** |
| APPOSITIVE | Copernicus's theory **that the sun, not the earth, is the center of our solar system** was rejected at the time. |

Common Introductory Words for Noun Clauses		
how	whenever	who
if	where	whoever
that	wherever	whom
what	whether	whomever
whatever	which	whose
when	whichever	why

The word that introduces a noun clause may or may not serve a grammatical function in the noun clause.

EXAMPLES   Tawana will do well at **whatever she attempts.** [The word *whatever* introduces the noun clause and serves as the direct object of the verb *attempts.*]

Does Luís think **that Puerto Rico will become a state someday?** [The word *that* introduces the noun clause but does not serve a grammatical function in the clause.]

Sometimes the word that introduces a noun clause is not expressed but is understood.

EXAMPLES   I think **[that] I. M. Pei is one of the judges of the design contest.**

Did you know **[that] the actor James Earl Jones was once a pre-med student?**

NOTE Another type of noun clause is the infinitive clause. An ***infinitive clause*** consists of an infinitive with a subject, along with any modifiers and complements the infinitive has. The entire infinitive clause can function as the direct object of a verb.

EXAMPLE   Judy's father expected **her to finish her homework.** [The entire infinitive clause is the direct object of the verb *expected. Her* is the subject of the infinitive *to finish.* The infinitive *to finish* has a direct object, *homework.*]

Notice that the subject of an infinitive clause is in the objective case and that the infinitive takes the place of a main verb in the infinitive clause.

Exercise 3 Identifying Noun Clauses and Their Functions

Identify each noun clause in the following sentences, and tell whether it is a *subject*, a *direct object*, an *indirect object*, a *predicate nominative*, or an *object of a preposition*.

┌HELP┐

Some sentences in Exercise 3 contain more than one noun clause.

EXAMPLE   1. Do you know what the word *serendipity* means?

　　　　　　1. *what the word* serendipity *means*—direct object

1. My finances don't quite allow me to live in style; in fact, I'm completely broke!
2. Do you know what the referee says to the opponents at the start of a boxing match?
3. Through scientific research, psychologists have learned that everyone dreams during sleep.
4. Scientists disagree about why dinosaurs died out.
5. Sometimes I am amused and sometimes I am amazed by what I read in the newspaper's advice column.
6. What I like most about Harriet is that she never complains.
7. What the dancers Agnes de Mille and Martha Graham created was a new form of American dance.
8. Can you please tell me where the Museum of African Art is located and when it opens?
9. The radio station will give whoever can answer the next question one hundred dollars.
10. I don't know how they decided who would be the leader.

Review A Distinguishing Between Adjective and Noun Clauses

Identify the subordinate clause or clauses in each of the following sentences. Tell whether each subordinate clause is used as an *adjective* or a *noun*. Be prepared to tell what word each adjective clause modifies and whether each noun clause is a *subject*, a *predicate nominative*, a *direct object*, an *indirect object*, or an *object of a preposition*.

┌HELP┐

In the first example in Review A, the adjective clause modifies the pronoun *ones*. In the second example, the noun clause is the direct object of the verb *Did think*.

EXAMPLES   1. According to Dr. Athelstan Spilhaus, children are not the only ones who enjoy playing with toys.

　　　　　　1. *who enjoy playing with toys*—adjective

　　　　　　2. Did you think that only children enjoy playing with toys?

　　　　　　2. *that only children enjoy playing with toys*—noun

1. Dr. Spilhaus found that toys are not meant only for children.
2. Some of the toys that he collects are simply to be admired; his favorites are those that can be put into action.
3. Some of his collectibles are put into "intensive care," where he skillfully replaces parts that have been damaged or lost.
4. Dr. Spilhaus says that a toy is anything that gives us a chance to stop and refresh ourselves during our hectic lives.
5. I have read that many mechanical principles were first applied to playthings.
6. For example, the toy monkey shown here is activated by squeezing a rubber bulb that uses the same basic principle as the jackhammer that digs up our streets.
7. Only those who have lost touch with childhood question what a toy can be worth to a young boy or girl.
8. Ask someone who knows toys what their enchantment is worth.
9. What is appealing about some toys is that they can make us laugh.
10. Dr. Spilhaus, an oceanographer, admits he has sometimes been unable to distinguish between his work and his play.

The Adverb Clause

17f. An *adverb clause* is a subordinate clause that modifies a verb, an adjective, or an adverb.

An adverb clause tells *how, how much, when, where, why, to what extent,* or *under what conditions.*

EXAMPLES   The squirrel ran **as though it were being chased by a cat.** [The adverb clause modifies the verb *ran*, telling *how* it ran.]

Many Western artists were influenced by the Asian art they saw **while they were studying in Paris.** [The adverb clause modifies the verb *saw*, telling *when* the artists saw the art.]

Miriam Makeba attracts huge audiences **wherever she performs.** [The adverb clause modifies the verb *attracts*, telling *where* Miriam Makeba attracts huge audiences.]

Spain considered the conquest of Cuba essential **because the island is strategically located at the entrance to the Gulf of Mexico.** [The adverb clause modifies the verb *considered*, telling *why* Spain considered the conquest of Cuba essential.]

Davita likes instrumental music more **than she likes opera.**
[The adverb clause modifies the adverb *more*, telling *to what extent* Davita likes instrumental music.]

If you want to gain an understanding of American Indian culture, read *Voices of Our Ancestors* by Dhyani Ywahoo. [The adverb clause modifies the verb *read,* telling *under what conditions* you should read Ywahoo's book.]

NOTE An adverb clause that begins a sentence is followed by a comma.

EXAMPLE   When the weather starts getting cold, many animals grow heavier fur.

Reference Note
For more information about **punctuating adverb clauses,** see page 837.

Subordinating Conjunctions

An adverb clause is introduced by a *subordinating conjunction*—a word or word group that shows the relationship between the adverb clause and the word or words that the clause modifies.

Common Subordinating Conjunctions			
after	as though	since	when
although	because	so that	whenever
as	before	than	where
as if	if	though	wherever
as long as	in order that	unless	whether
as soon as	provided that	until	while

NOTE The words *after, as, before, since, until,* and *while* may also be used as prepositions.

CONJUNCTION   You must clean your room **before** you go to play basketball.

PREPOSITION   You must clean your room **before** dinner.

Reference Note
For more about **prepositions,** see page 517.

The Elliptical Clause

17g. Part of a clause may be left out when its meaning can be clearly understood in the context of the sentence. Such a clause is called an *elliptical clause.*

Most elliptical clauses are adverb clauses. In the examples on the following page, the words in brackets may be omitted because their meanings can be understood from the context.

EXAMPLES   Australia is smaller **than the other continents** [are small].

When [you are] **taking notes,** use your own words.

NOTE   Often the meaning of an elliptical clause depends on the form of the pronoun in it.

EXAMPLES   I like Anne as much as **she** [likes Anne].

I like Anne as much as [I like] **her.**

To be certain that you have expressed your meaning clearly, be sure to use the correct pronoun case when you write an elliptical clause.

Reference Note
For more about using the **correct forms of pronouns in elliptical clauses,** see page 643.

Exercise 4   **Identifying Adverb Clauses and the Words They Modify**

Identify the adverb clause in each of the following sentences. Give the word or words that the clause modifies. Be prepared to state whether the clause tells *how, how much, when, where, why, to what extent,* or *under what conditions.*

EXAMPLE   1.   After they had invited their friends to dinner, Lola Gómez and her father began preparing the meal.

1.   *After they had invited their friends to dinner—began*

1. Because it's one of their specialties, Lola and her father prepared a special treat of Cuban-style black beans.
2. After Lola had soaked a pound of black beans overnight, she drained them and covered them with fresh water to make the beans easier to digest.
3. Before she lit the stove, she added some chopped onion and green pepper, a bay leaf, cilantro leaves, oregano, and salt pork to the beans.
4. While the beans were simmering, Mr. Gómez prepared the *sofrito,* which is a characteristic ingredient in many Latin American dishes.
5. Whenever a recipe calls for *sofrito,* the cook finely chops some onion, green pepper, and garlic.
6. Then these vegetables are fried in a little oil until they are tender, and herbs and spices such as basil, cilantro, cumin, and black and white pepper are added.
7. As soon as the *sofrito* was ready, Mr. Gómez added it to the bean mixture.

┌HELP──

The adverb clause in the example for Exercise 4 tells *when* they began.

8. He then crushed some of the beans against the side of the pot so that the bean mixture would thicken.

9. When the mixture had thickened, Lola put in a blend of vinegar and sugar, which gives the beans that extra "tang."

10. No one at the dinner table was more eager than I to enjoy a large helping of the Gómezes' special black beans.

Review B **Identifying and Classifying Subordinate Clauses**

Identify the subordinate clause or clauses in each of the following sentences. Then, tell whether each subordinate clause is used as an *adjective*, a *noun*, or an *adverb*.

EXAMPLE   **1.** Many scholars were skeptical when their colleagues began applying computer science to the study of literature.

   1. when their colleagues began applying computer science to the study of literature—adverb

1. When a group of scholars first applied computer science to the study of literature, their colleagues expressed what can only be described as polite disbelief.

2. They asked what the computer could do.

3. Some scornful scholars argued that measuring the length of Hemingway's sentences was dreary enough when it was done without computers.

4. Would precise mathematical analyses of style determine whether the Earl of Oxford wrote Shakespeare's plays?

5. Initial studies made along these lines fueled controversy that raged for years.

6. Researchers now use computers whenever their projects involve such mechanical tasks as compiling an index or a bibliography.

7. Since ancient languages are now stored on computers, scholars can make analyses that shed light on etymology.

8. There are some features of literary works that computers can identify faster than human readers can.

9. Of course, today many students take advantage of computer technology when writing research papers about literature.

10. After they have written their first drafts, students may then revise their papers by using software programs that check spelling, grammar, and style.

┌ TIPS & TRICKS ┐

Some of the words that introduce adverb clauses may also introduce adjective clauses and noun clauses. To determine what type of clause the introductory word begins, look at how the clause is used in the sentence.

ADJECTIVE CLAUSE
The day **when we got our puppy** was a Friday. [The clause modifies the noun *day*.]

NOUN CLAUSE
Does Jimmy remember **when we got our puppy**? [The clause is the direct object of the verb *remember*.]

ADVERB CLAUSE
Our older dog sulked a little **when we got our puppy.** [The clause modifies the verb *sulked*.]

COMPUTER TIP

Because an adverb clause usually does not have a fixed location in a sentence, the writer must choose where to place the clause. The best place for it is usually a matter of personal taste and style, but often the placement is determined by the context.

If you use a computer, you can easily experiment with the placement of adverb clauses in sentences. Print out different versions of the sentence containing the adverb clause, along with the sentences that immediately precede and follow it. Read each version aloud to see how the placement of the clause affects the flow, rhythm, and overall meaning of the passage.

HELP

A colon or a dash may be used between two independent clauses when the second clause explains or restates the idea of the first clause.

EXAMPLES

The aardvark discovered that the old saying was true: The early bird does get the worm.

It was a difficult decision—one job included benefits, while the other offered flexible hours.

Sentences Classified According to Structure

17h. Depending on its structure, a sentence can be classified as simple, compound, complex, or compound-complex.

(1) A *simple sentence* contains one independent clause and no subordinate clauses.

A simple sentence may contain a compound subject, a compound verb, or both, and any number of phrases.

EXAMPLES   Great literature stirs the imagination.

Located on an island in Lake Texcoco, Tenochtitlán was the capital of the Aztec empire and may have had more than 100,000 inhabitants in the 1500s.

(2) A *compound sentence* contains two or more independent clauses and no subordinate clauses.

Independent clauses may be joined by a comma and a coordinating conjunction (*and, but, for, nor, or, so,* or *yet*), by a semicolon, or by a semicolon and a conjunctive adverb or transitional expression.

EXAMPLES   In 1528, the Spanish explored the area near present-day Tampa**, but** Europeans did not begin settling there until 1823. [two independent clauses joined by a comma and the coordinating conjunction *but*]

We could drive to San Antonio on the freeway**, or** we could take back roads to get there. [two indepedent clauses joined by a comma and the coordinating conjunction *or*]

The Aswan High Dam is on the Nile River in Egypt**;** it is one of the world's largest dams. [two independent clauses joined by a semicolon]

We should leave early**; otherwise,** we will miss our bus. [two independent clauses joined by a semicolon, the conjunctive adverb *otherwise,* and a comma]

Not all birds fly south for the winter**; for instance,** cardinals live in the northern states throughout the year. [two independent clauses joined by a semicolon, the transitional expression *for instance,* and a comma]

Reference Note
For more about **semicolons,** see page 850. For more about **dashes,** see page 878.

Common Conjunctive Adverbs		
also	incidentally	next
anyway	indeed	nonetheless
besides	instead	otherwise
consequently	likewise	still
finally	meanwhile	then
furthermore	moreover	therefore
however	nevertheless	thus

Common Transitional Expressions		
after all	even so	in fact
as a result	for example	in other words
at any rate	for instance	on the contrary
by the way	in addition	on the other hand

NOTE Do not confuse a simple sentence that has a compound subject, a compound verb, or both, with a compound sentence.

Reference Note
For more information about **compound subjects** and **compound verbs,** see page 534.

SIMPLE SENTENCE	The 1991 eruption of Mount Pinatubo destroyed many homes and led to the closing of Clark Air Base. [This sentence contains a compound verb.]
COMPOUND SENTENCE	The 1991 eruption of Mount Pinatubo destroyed many homes, and it led to the closing of Clark Air Base. [This sentence contains two independent clauses.]

(3) A *complex sentence* contains one independent clause and at least one subordinate clause.

EXAMPLES   Yiddish, which is a Germanic language, is now spoken by millions of people all over the world. [The independent clause is *Yiddish is now spoken by millions of people all over the world.* The subordinate clause is the adjective clause *which is a Germanic language.*]

After Napoleon Bonaparte was defeated at Waterloo, he was exiled to Saint Helena, where he died. [The independent clause is *he was exiled to Saint Helena.* One subordinate clause is the adverb clause *After Napoleon Bonaparte was defeated at Waterloo.* The adjective clause *where he died* is another subordinate clause.]

Whatever you can give will be very much appreciated. [The independent clause is *Whatever will be very much appreciated.* The subordinate clause is the noun clause *Whatever you can give.*]

(4) A *compound-complex sentence* contains two or more independent clauses and at least one subordinate clause.

EXAMPLES   The interest that you pay on a car loan will increase the cost of the car, so be sure to shop for the lowest interest rate. [The two independent clauses are *The interest will increase the cost of the car* and *be sure to shop for the lowest interest rate.* The subordinate clause is the adjective clause *that you pay on a car loan.*]

Hong Kong had been a crown colony of Britain since 1898; however, as my teacher explained, it reverted to China when the treaty expired in 1997. [The two independent clauses are *Hong Kong had been a crown colony of Britain since 1898* and *it reverted to China.* One subordinate clause is the adverb clause *as my teacher explained.* The adverb clause *when the treaty expired in 1997* is another subordinate clause.]

Exercise 5 **Classifying Sentences According to Structure**

Classify each of the following sentences as *simple, compound, complex,* or *compound-complex.*

EXAMPLE   **1.** H. J. (Henry Jackson) Lewis is generally regarded as the first African American political cartoonist.

   1. simple

1. During the late 1800s, H. J. Lewis drew political cartoons for *The Freeman,* which was the first illustrated African American newspaper.
2. Through his cartoons Lewis frequently criticized the U.S. government's racial policies; however, he also produced nonpolitical ink drawings, sketches, and chalk plates.
3. If you examine this self-portrait of Lewis, you can see evidence of his artistic versatility, and you can get a sense of the atmosphere in which he worked.
4. Lewis had to overcome many difficulties to achieve success as an artist, and parts of his life are shrouded in mystery.

S T Y L E   T I P

Although the use of short sentences is effective at times, overusing them will result in choppy writing. One way to avoid choppy sentences is to change some sentences into subordinate clauses. Furthermore, by using subordinate clauses, you can avoid the unnecessary repetition of words, such as *The blue whale* in the following example.

CHOPPY
The blue whale is the largest animal that has ever lived. The blue whale can grow up to one hundred feet long and weigh over two hundred metric tons.

SMOOTH
The blue whale, which can grow up to one hundred feet long and weigh over two hundred metric tons, is the largest animal that has ever lived.

5. Lewis was born into slavery in Mississippi, and he was blinded in one eye and badly burned when he was a toddler.

6. As a young man he worked at various menial jobs until a Little Rock newspaper artist taught him how to draw.

7. Lewis made sketches for archaeological studies in Arkansas, Mississippi, Tennessee, and Louisiana in 1882 and 1883.

8. The Smithsonian Institution now has most of these sketches; they include drawings of prehistoric Native American burial mounds.

9. Throughout his life, Lewis produced drawings for various publications.

10. Upon Lewis's death in 1891, *The Freeman,* the newspaper that had made him famous, praised his talent and mourned his loss.

Henry Jackson Lewis, *Self Portrait.* Courtesy of the DuSable Museum of African American History, Chicago, Illinois.

Sentences Classified According to Purpose

17i. Depending on its purpose, a sentence can be classified as declarative, imperative, interrogative, or exclamatory.

(1) A *declarative sentence* makes a statement and ends with a period.

EXAMPLE   Many homes are being made more accessible for people who have disabilities.

(2) An *imperative sentence* gives a command or makes a request. Most imperative sentences end with a period. A strong command ends with an exclamation point.

Sentences Classified According to Purpose   **591**

EXAMPLES   Please pay attention to the guest speaker. [request]

Listen to me. [command]

Stop what you're doing and listen! [strong command]

NOTE Imperative sentences always have the understood *you* as the subject.

(3) An ***interrogative sentence*** asks a question and ends with a question mark.

EXAMPLES   What is the name of the song you were singing?

Have you seen Alma at all today?

(4) An ***exclamatory sentence*** shows excitement or expresses strong feeling and ends with an exclamation point.

EXAMPLES   How happy you look!

What a surprise it is to see you here!

Exercise 6 Classifying Sentences According to Purpose

For each of the following sentences, identify its purpose as *declarative, imperative, interrogative,* or *exclamatory.* Then, supply the proper end mark.

EXAMPLE   **1.** Is soprano the highest range for a singing voice

           1. interrogative— ?

1. In Greek mythology, Pygmalion was a sculptor who fell in love with a statue; it was then transformed into a real woman
2. Will any baseball player ever surpass Hank Aaron's record of 755 career home runs
3. Write your report on Clara Barton, the nurse who founded the American Red Cross
4. Why, that's preposterous
5. Do you believe the claim that Archimedes shouted "Eureka!" when he realized that volume could be measured by the displacement of water
6. What beautiful designs these are

Reference Note

For more about the **understood subject,** see page 535.

S T Y L E   T I P

In dialogue and informal writing, statements may be used as questions and questions may be used to show strong emotion. In such cases, use the punctuation that indicates the tone you would use if you were speaking.

EXAMPLES

Rex came back yesterday? [declarative sentence structure with interrogative tone]

Ask Robin? [imperative sentence structure with interrogative tone]

How do you expect me to react?! [interrogative sentence structure with exclamatory tone]

In formal writing, however, you should use traditional sentence structure and punctuation to express your emotions and ideas clearly.

7. Stephen, please explain to the class the concept of a sonic boom

8. Vulcanization, the process that strengthens natural rubber, is named after the Roman god of fire, Vulcan

9. Why is an unlikely political candidate called a "dark horse"

10. The United States Constitution, written in 1787 and often considered the model of protection of individual rights, may have been based largely on the Magna Carta, which was signed by King John of England in 1215

Review C **Classifying Sentences According to Structure and Purpose**

Classify each of the following sentences first according to its structure and then according to its purpose.

EXAMPLE   1. Please read this article, which is about butterflies.

            1. *complex—imperative*

1. Are you aware that there is a huge worldwide demand for butterflies?

2. Millions are caught and sold each year to entomologists, museums, private collectors, and factories.

3. The plastic-encased butterflies that are used to decorate ornamental objects such as trays, tabletops, and screens are usually common varieties, many of which come from Taiwan, Korea, and Malaysia.

4. There is a difference, though, between collection practices in those countries and those used in Papua New Guinea.

5. Papua New Guinea, which was administered by Australia until 1975, has taken advantage of a growing interest in tropical butterflies.

6. Butterfly ranchers gather, raise, and market high-quality specimens, which are accompanied by scientific data.

7. Since biologists have not yet determined the life cycles of all of these butterflies, local villagers, because of their experience, have become the experts; as a result, butterfly ranching has improved the country's economy.

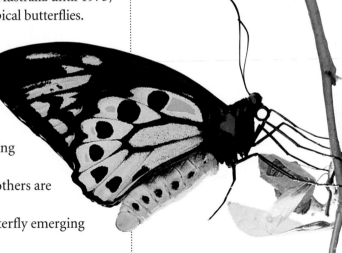

8. Some butterfly specimens are quite small, but others are larger than an adult human hand.

9. Look at the photograph, and you will see a butterfly emerging from a cocoon.

10. What rich, vibrant colors butterflies have!

COMPUTER TIP

Computers can help you get a better sense of your own sentence style. If you have access to style-checking software, run a style check on a few paragraphs of your writing.

The style checker will analyze your writing and will provide information such as the number of sentences per paragraph, the kinds of sentences, the average number of words per sentence, and the lengths of the longest and shortest sentences. If, for example, you discover that you tend to use only one or two sentence structures and that your sentences tend to be of similar length, you can focus your attention on revising sentences for greater variety.

Review D **Classifying Sentences**

Classify each of the following sentences first as *simple, compound, complex,* or *compound-complex* and then as *declarative, interrogative, imperative,* or *exclamatory.*

EXAMPLE   1. I have taken many interesting courses in high school, and one of my favorites is a course that Ms. Klein taught last year.

1. *compound-complex—declarative*

1. Have you discovered that imaginative teachers who are enthusiastic about their work can make school more enjoyable for their students?
2. Last year, when I took a social studies elective, Law and Order, I found myself looking forward to fourth period each day.
3. Our teacher, Ms. Klein, made our course more interesting by bringing the outside world into the classroom.
4. She had us watch the TV news and read the local newspaper, and she invited guest speakers who shared their experiences with us.
5. By the end of three months, the class had heard from a defense attorney, a prosecutor, and several local police officers; and we had interviewed an FBI agent.
6. Ms. Klein also invited four state representatives, and they talked to us about writing laws.
7. How hard it must be to write clear laws!
8. Ms. Klein set up a schedule of field trips, and she then took the classroom out into the world.
9. For example, on one of our trips, we visited the local jail; on another, when we observed a jury trial, we spoke personally with the judge.
10. I am glad that I was in Ms. Klein's Law and Order class, and I was very pleased when she was voted "Outstanding Educator of the Year."

Chapter Review

A. Identifying Independent and Subordinate Clauses

Identify the underlined word group in each of the following sentences as an *independent clause* or a *subordinate clause*.

1. Most film critics agree <u>that the most important member of a film crew is the director.</u>
2. <u>One director</u> who is known for his distinctive style <u>is the Japanese filmmaker Akira Kurosawa.</u>
3. Although he made contemporary dramas and gangster stories, <u>Kurosawa is perhaps best known for his epic action films about medieval Japan.</u>
4. <u>One such film is the action-packed *Seven Samurai*,</u> which may very well be Kurosawa's most popular film.
5. His other epics include *Throne of Blood* and *Ran*, <u>which are based on Shakespeare's plays *Macbeth* and *King Lear*,</u> respectively.

B. Identifying and Classifying Clauses

Identify the italicized word group in each of the following sentences as an *independent clause* or a *subordinate clause*. Then classify each subordinate clause as an *adjective clause*, an *adverb clause*, or a *noun clause*.

6. The violinist *whom I most enjoy hearing* is Itzhak Perlman.
7. Patricia put a pet flap in her back door *so that her cat, Tiger, could come in and go out by himself.*
8. *The pitcher read the catcher's signals,* and then she struck out the hitter with a fastball.
9. *Where the city will build the bridge* has still not been decided.
10. *When champion golfer Juan Rodríguez was a boy,* he worked on a sugar-cane plantation in Puerto Rico.
11. Here is the savings bond *that Dad gave me for graduation.*
12. *Because his artwork received wide recognition during his lifetime,* Pablo Picasso became famous and wealthy.
13. As we walked along the road, *we saw the wheat waving in the wind.*
14. The Kimbell Art Museum, *which was designed by architect Louis Kahn,* is one of the leading attractions in Fort Worth, Texas.

15. During the quiz bowl, *whoever rings the buzzer first* gets to answer the question.

16. After you put all the dishes in the dishwasher, *wipe off the kitchen counter with a clean sponge.*

17. *Ever since Jacob traveled to Chile,* he has been fascinated by the history of Latin America.

18. Tell me *if you see another raccoon in the backyard.*

19. *If you're interested in computers,* you ought to take Mr. Stefano's class.

20. Petra hopes *that the snow will be deep and solid enough for sledding.*

21. After we planted the tulip bulbs, *we had to wait through the winter for the tulips to appear.*

22. Mr. Chulski, *who served in the army thirty-five years ago,* can tell you what Vietnam was like in the 1960s.

23. This car is more fuel efficient *than the other ones.*

24. The playwright decided *that she preferred not to attend her play.*

25. Isn't that the writer *whose books are so popular?*

C. Classifying Sentences According to Structure and Purpose

Classify each sentence of the following paragraph as *simple, compound, complex,* or *compound-complex* and then as *declarative, interrogative, imperative,* or *exclamatory.*

[26] What simple beginnings great men and women often have! [27] Consider the life of the famed animator Walt Disney, for example. [28] Although he was born in Chicago in 1901, Disney grew up on a farm in Missouri. [29] Disney loved farm life, and he paid particular attention to the animals, which he sketched constantly. [30] Surely you're not surprised that his early drawings were of farm animals! [31] Where do you think he got his ideas for Mickey Mouse, Donald Duck, and the other Disney-animated animals that are now household names? [32] During his school years, Disney and a friend enjoyed acting; indeed, they even performed a short-lived comedy routine together. [33] How fortunate it is that Disney's main interest remained art! [34] He continued to doodle, and later he attended several art institutes where he learned not only about drawing anatomical figures but also about drawing cartoons. [35] Is it any wonder that one of Disney's first jobs was to draw farm animals for an advertising company?

Writing Application
Using a Variety of Sentences in an Interview

Sentence Purpose   For a class project, you are to interview someone employed in a field that interests you. Find out what kind of training the person needed for his or her job and what a typical day on the
job is like. If possible, arrange to visit the person's workplace. When you
write your interview, use end marks to reflect accurately your interviewee's tone and attitude.

Prewriting   First, brainstorm a list of interesting jobs. Choose the
one that most appeals to you, and find someone to interview who
works in that field. Next, write down a number of questions that you
might ask about the person's job. If you are planning to use a tape
recorder, be sure to get the person's permission before you begin
recording.

Writing   Begin with a brief paragraph introducing your interviewee
and telling the date and location of the interview. In writing the interview itself, you will need to record the interviewee's responses exactly.
As you write, use types of sentences that accurately reflect the speaker's
questions, exclamations, and tone.

Revising   Evaluate the written version of your interview for accuracy and clarity. Keep in mind the purpose of the interview—to gather
information about an interesting job. If you are lacking needed information, you may have to call your interviewee and conduct a brief
follow-up interview.

Publishing   Be sure that you have quoted the person exactly and
that your punctuation accurately reflects contractions, pauses, questions, and exclamations. Proofread your interview for any errors in
grammar, usage, and mechanics. You and your classmates may want to
collect the interviews in a booklet. Work together to write a brief introduction explaining the nature and purpose of the interviews. Also
include an acknowledgment page thanking each of the contributors.

Agreement
Subject and Verb, Pronoun and Antecedent

Diagnostic Preview

A. Proofreading for Subject-Verb Agreement and Pronoun-Antecedent Agreement

Most of the following sentences contain an error in agreement. If a sentence contains an error, identify the incorrect verb or pronoun and supply the correct form. If a sentence is already correct, write *C*.

EXAMPLE   1. Do you know where my binoculars is? I would like to take it with me on the nature hike.

     1. *is—are; it—them*

1. One of the South's most precious ecological treasures are the flatlands and estuary of Galveston Bay.
2. In September, the new teacher was delighted because her class were enthusiastic and cooperative.
3. One junior, as well as four seniors, have been invited to attend the Milford Youth Council next month.
4. The number of investors in companies that manufacture robots is large, and they are increasing daily.
5. Twenty miles are quite far for someone to walk without stopping and resting.
6. Neither Charlotte nor Tyrone answers the telephone on Saturdays.
7. Anyone earning such a small salary will occasionally have difficulty paying their bills.

8. You may be surprised to know that many a city dweller grows vegetables in a backyard garden.
9. A completed application, in addition to a full financial statement, are required of all students seeking college scholarships.
10. Every file cabinet, bookcase, and desk drawer have been stuffed with books and papers.
11. Don't the employees get bonuses for his or her work?
12. Where there's people and excitement, you're sure to find Kazuo and Yori.
13. Public relations and advertising is exciting but often stressful work.
14. Do you know whether the Netherlands are closer to Germany or to France?
15. Did you know that the city of Savannah, Georgia, has their own spectacular parade on Saint Patrick's Day?

B. Correcting Errors in Subject-Verb and Pronoun-Antecedent Agreement

Most of the sentences in the following paragraph contain errors in agreement. Identify each incorrect verb or pronoun, and give the correct form. If a sentence is already correct, write *C*.

EXAMPLE [1] Many a species are either endangered or threatened.

    1. *are—is*

[16] There's a number of people and programs making life safer for endangered and threatened animals. [17] For example, many a preservation effort have been directed at saving eagles. [18] What, you may ask, is the biggest threats to eagles? [19] Most of the danger comes from poachers and expanding civilization. [20] Fortunately, eagles are one of the world's most admired animals; in fact, it may be one of the most common symbols of freedom. [21] As a result, many governments have passed laws to protect eagles and their habitats. [22] The United States, for example, have created sanctuaries for bald eagles and golden eagles. [23] The Philippine eagle, which are the rarest of these magnificent birds, receives special protection on the Philippine island of Mindanao. [24] Ethiopia, as well as some other countries, has planted trees for their eagles to use as nesting places. [25] Anybody who wants to know more about these and other preservation programs for eagles should consult their local library or conservation club.

Number

Number is the form a word takes to indicate whether the word is singular or plural.

18a. A word that refers to one person, place, thing, or idea is *singular* in number. A word that refers to more than one is *plural* in number.

Singular	employer	theory	woman	that	either	it
Plural	employers	theories	women	those	both	they

Agreement of Subject and Verb

18b. A verb should agree in number with its subject.

(1) Singular subjects take singular verbs.

EXAMPLES   In her spare time, the art **student restores** old paintings.

He illustrates books for young readers.

Is the next lunar **eclipse** a full eclipse?

(2) Plural subjects take plural verbs.

EXAMPLES   In their spare time, the art **students restore** old paintings.

They illustrate books for young readers.

Are the next lunar **eclipses** full eclipses?

NOTE   A gerund phrase or an infinitive phrase used as a complete subject usually takes a singular verb. Do not be misled by any particular noun or pronoun in the phrase. The gerund or infinitive serves as a singular simple subject.

EXAMPLES   **Restoring old paintings occupies** much of her spare time. [The singular verb *occupies* is used because the gerund *Restoring*, not the noun *paintings*, is the subject of the verb.]

To illustrate books for young readers requires a vivid imagination. [The singular verb *requires* is used because the infinitive *To illustrate*, not the noun *books* or *readers*, is the subject of the verb.]

┌HELP─

Present-tense verbs, except *be* and *have*, add *–s* or *–es* when the subject is third-person singular. Present-tense verbs do not add *–s* or *–es* when the subject is a first-person pronoun (*I, we*), a second-person pronoun (*you*), or a third-person plural pronoun (*they*).

Reference Note

For more about **gerund phrases** and **infinitive phrases,** see page 563 and page 565. For information on **finding the subject,** see page 535.

In a verb phrase, the first helping verb agrees in number with the subject.

EXAMPLES The **Vietnam Veterans Memorial was designed** by Maya Lin. [singular subject and singular verb phrase]

The **Vietnam Veterans Memorial** and the **Civil Rights Memorial were designed** by Maya Lin. [plural subject and plural verb phrase]

Has he been studying since noon? [singular subject and singular verb phrase]

Have they been studying since noon? [plural subject and plural verb phrase]

Intervening Phrases and Clauses

18c. The number of a subject is not changed by a word in a phrase or a clause following the subject.

EXAMPLES The **short stories are** by various contemporary American Indian writers.

The **short stories** in this anthology **are** by various contemporary American Indian writers. [*Are* agrees with the subject *short stories,* not *anthology,* which is part of the prepositional phrase *in this anthology.*]

Edmonia Lewis was the first African American woman to achieve renown for her sculpture.

Edmonia Lewis, whose subjects included John Brown and Abraham Lincoln, **was** the first African American woman to achieve renown for her sculpture. [*Was* agrees with the subject *Edmonia Lewis,* not with any of the nouns in the adjective clause *whose subjects included John Brown and Abraham Lincoln.*]

NOTE Do not be misled by a phrase that begins with a compound preposition such as *along with, as well as, in addition to,* or *together with.* Such a phrase does not affect the number of a subject.

EXAMPLES The **man** in the next apartment, as well as the people across the hall, **has lived** in the building since the mid-1980s. [singular subject and singular verb]

The **people** across the hall, as well as the man in the next apartment, **have lived** in the building since the mid-1980s. [plural subject and plural verb]

Reference Note

For more about **verb phrases,** see page 509.

COMPUTER TIP

Some word-processing programs can find problems in subject-verb or pronoun-antecedent agreement. You can use such a program to search for errors when you proofread your writing. If you are not sure that an error found by the program is truly an error, check the rules in this textbook.

USAGE

18 a–c

┌HELP───
Remember that
the subject of a sentence
is never in a prepositional
phrase.

Exercise 1 **Identifying Subjects and Verbs That Agree in Number**

For each of the following sentences, identify the subject of the verb in parentheses. Then, choose the verb form that agrees in number with the subject.

EXAMPLE   1. The scientist, along with her two assistants, (*is, are*) working on a computer simulation of earthquake activity.

     1. *scientist; is*

1. The theory of plate tectonics (*has, have*) explained causes of earthquake activity throughout the world.
2. Enormous plates of rock (*is, are*) shifting constantly far beneath the earth's surface.
3. These movements, in addition to the pressure of molten rock, (*causes, cause*) the plates to collide.
4. The pressure of colliding plates (*forces, force*) the rock to bend until it breaks.
5. A ridge of these breaks (*is, are*) called a fault.
6. The cause of most earthquakes (*is, are*) the sudden release of stress along a fault.
7. The Richter scale, as well as other measurements, (*has, have*) been used to record the magnitude of earthquakes.
8. The tremors of the great San Francisco earthquake that occurred in 1906 (*was, were*) estimated to have measured 8.3 on the Richter scale.
9. California, with two major fault lines, (*has, have*) about ten times the world average of earthquake activity.
10. A map of the earth's plates, such as the one shown here, (*gives, give*) you a pretty good idea of why California has so many quakes.

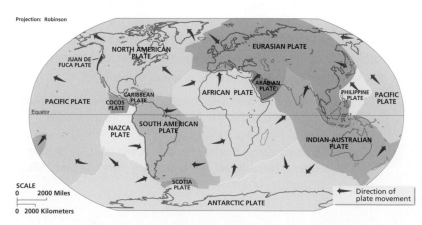

Indefinite Pronouns

18d. Some indefinite pronouns are singular, some are plural, and some can be singular or plural depending on how they are used.

(1) The following indefinite pronouns are singular: *anybody, anyone, anything, each, either, everybody, everyone, everything, neither, nobody, no one, nothing, one, somebody, someone,* and *something.*

EXAMPLES   **Is anyone** in the audience a medical doctor?

              Each of the boys **does** his own cooking.

              Either of these videos **is** suitable for a four-year-old.

(2) The following indefinite pronouns are plural: *both, few, many,* and *several.*

EXAMPLES   **Both** of the universities **offer** degrees in forestry.

              Few on the committee ever **miss** a meeting.

              Several of the students **have transferred.**

(3) The indefinite pronouns *all, any, more, most, none,* **and** *some* **may be singular or plural, depending on their meaning in a sentence.**

These pronouns are singular when they refer to singular words. They are plural when they refer to plural words.

EXAMPLES   **All** of the workout **seems** simple. [*All* refers to the singular noun *workout.*]

              All of the exercises **seem** simple. [*All* refers to the plural noun *exercises.*]

              Is any of the salad left? [*Any* refers to the singular noun *salad.*]

              Are any of the vegetables left? [*Any* refers to the plural noun *vegetables.*]

              More of the Senate **was** in favor of the highway funding bill than **was** against it. [*More* refers to the singular noun *Senate.*]

              More of the senators **were** in favor of the highway funding bill than **were** against it. [*More* refers to the plural noun *senators.*]

┌HELP┐

Some words that can be used as indefinite pronouns, such as *both, each,* and *some,* can also be used as adjectives. When such a word comes before the subject of a sentence, the verb agrees with the subject as it normally would.

EXAMPLE

An **astronaut dreams** of walking on Mars.

Each **astronaut dreams** of walking on Mars.

USAGE

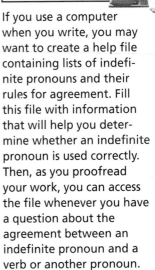

COMPUTER TIP

If you use a computer when you write, you may want to create a help file containing lists of indefinite pronouns and their rules for agreement. Fill this file with information that will help you determine whether an indefinite pronoun is used correctly. Then, as you proofread your work, you can access the file whenever you have a question about the agreement between an indefinite pronoun and a verb or another pronoun.

None of the deck **is** missing. [*None* refers to the singular noun *deck.*]

None of the cards **are** missing. [*None* refers to the plural noun *cards.*]

Exercise 2 Identifying Subjects and Verbs That Agree in Number

For each of the following sentences, identify the subject. Then, choose the verb form that agrees in number with the subject.

EXAMPLE   1. One of the most entertaining animated films I have seen (*is, are*) *Kiki's Delivery Service,* a movie crafted by the Japanese animator Hayao Miyazaki.

1. *One; is*

1. Each of the pictures (*was, were*) in a silver frame.
2. One of my friends (*play, plays*) the tuba.
3. All of our belongings (*is, are*) carefully unpacked.
4. Some of these rare books (*has, have*) leather covers.
5. None of the people in the theater (*was, were*) sitting in the first two rows.
6. More band members (*arrive, arrives*) early now that the bus schedules have changed.
7. A few in my class (*help, helps*) the coach set up the bleachers.
8. Both of the fund-raisers (*was, were*) successful.
9. Everybody living in Lewis Heights (*go, goes*) to George Washington Carver High School.
10. Each one of these computer games (*is, are*) on sale.

Exercise 3 Revising Subject-Verb Agreement in Sentences

Rewrite the following sentences according to the instructions in brackets after each sentence. Make any needed changes in the form of each verb.

EXAMPLE   1. Each of the contestants was confused by the question. [Change *Each* to *Several.*]

1. *Several of the contestants were confused by the question.*

1. All of the fruit has been picked. [Change *fruit* to *oranges.*]
2. Each of us was angry about the election. [Change *Each* to *Many.*]

3. Has anybody joined the choir lately? [Change *anybody* to *any of the new students.*]
4. The committee leaves today for Washington, D.C. [Add *representing the farmers* after *committee.*]
5. Our team is going to Austin for the debate tournament. [Add *Three members of* before *Our team.*]
6. Most of the classrooms were equipped with new microcomputers. [Change *Most* to *None.*]
7. The pitcher was disappointed by the head coach's decision. [Add *as well as the other players* after *pitcher.* Put a comma after *pitcher* and after *players.*]
8. Each one of the smoke detectors works well. [Change *Each one* to *All but two.*]
9. Both of them usually hope that things will turn out for the best. [Change *Both of them* to *Everyone.*]
10. Some of her plan has been adopted. [Change *plan* to *ideas.*]

Review A Proofreading Sentences for Subject-Verb Agreement

Most of the following sentences contain errors in subject-verb agreement. Identify each verb that does not agree with its subject, and give the correct form. If a sentence is already correct, write *C.*

EXAMPLE 1. The history of the Hawaiian Islands tell of some interesting rulers.

    1. tell—tells

1. One of the royal rulers of the Hawaiian Islands were Queen Liliuokalani, pictured here.
2. Of course, none of these rulers is more amazing than King Kamehameha I.
3. This powerful leader, together with his followers, are credited with uniting the numerous islands into a kingdom in 1795.
4. Kamehameha I, whose family ruled the islands until 1872, was sometimes called the Napoleon of the Pacific.

Agreement of Subject and Verb **605**

5. Few of his descendants was more influential than King Kamehameha III.

6. No one deny that he helped the common people by permitting them to own land and by issuing a democratic constitution.

7. The musical interests of Hawaii's last two royal rulers, King Kalakaua I and Queen Liliuokalani, are fascinating.

8. Both monarchs was known as songwriters.

9. The queen, whose regal bearing is evident in the photograph on the previous page, has several claims to fame.

10. One of these are having written the famous song *"Aloha Oe"* ("Farewell to Thee").

Compound Subjects

A *compound subject* consists of two or more subjects that are joined by a conjunction and that have the same verb.

18e. Subjects joined by *and* usually take a plural verb.

Reference Note

For more about **compound subjects,** see page 534.

EXAMPLES **Spanish** and **Quechua are** the official languages of Peru.

     Hannah and **Dot have been** friends for years.

NOTE Subjects joined by *and* may name only one person, place, thing, or idea. Such a compound subject takes a singular verb.

EXAMPLES My next-door **neighbor** and best **friend is** from Mexico. [one person]

     Macaroni and **cheese is** a popular main course. [one dish]

18f. Singular subjects joined by *or* or *nor* take a singular verb.

EXAMPLES A **jacket** or a **sweater is** warm enough for tonight.

     Neither the **coach** nor the **trainer knows** the umpire.

     Either **Soledad** or **Chen writes** the weekly editorial.

18g. When a singular subject and a plural subject are joined by *or* or *nor,* the verb agrees with the subject nearer the verb.

STYLE **TIP**

Sentences like the examples for Rule 18g can sound awkward. When possible, revise such sentences to avoid having a compound subject with both singular and plural elements.

EXAMPLE
Either the **singer is** off-key, or the **musicians are.**

EXAMPLES Either the **musicians** or the **singer is** off-key. [The singular subject, *singer,* is nearer the verb.]

     Either the **singer** or the **musicians are** off-key. [The plural subject, *musicians,* is nearer the verb.]

Exercise 4 **Identifying Verbs That Agree with Compound Subjects**

Choose the verb form in parentheses that correctly completes each of the following sentences.

EXAMPLE   1. A world atlas and an almanac (*is, are*) good sources of geographical information.

    1. *are*

1. Del Rio and San Antonio (*is, are*) two Texas cities that have names of Spanish origin.
2. My books and tennis racket barely (*fit, fits*) in the locker.
3. Either my cat or the raccoons always (*eat, eats*) all the food on the back steps by morning.
4. Together, that white blouse and this blue scarf (*makes, make*) a good combination.
5. Neither Mariah Carey nor Gloria Estefan, I believe, (*sing, sings*) that song.
6. Rhythm and blues (*have, has*) pockets of popularity all over the world today.
7. Either regular 3.5-inch disks or one of those high-density disks (*work, works*) on this new computer.
8. Cindy and her brother (*do, does*) yard work for many people in our neighborhood.
9. If you want a good, inexpensive car, both that sedan over there and this compact here (*run, runs*) well.
10. The owner and president of Clowns for Our Towns (*were, was*) a woman with a great sense of humor.

Review B **Correcting Errors in Subject-Verb Agreement**

Most of the following sentences contain verbs that do not agree with their subjects. If a verb does not agree with its subject, give the correct form of the verb. If a sentence is already correct, write *C*.

EXAMPLE   1. Either surface water or underground water are the source of a region's water supply.

    1. *are—is*

1. One of the most precious resources in the nation is water.
2. The abundance and the use of water varies greatly among the regions of the United States.

3. The water supply in every region come from either surface water or underground water.
4. Unfortunately, neither overuse nor contamination of our water supplies has stopped completely.
5. After years of study, the pollution of lakes, rivers, and streams continue to be a serious problem.
6. Lake Erie, as well as the Potomac River and the Cuyahoga River, have been saved by cleanup efforts.
7. As you can see in the picture on this page, Lake Erie, which is bounded by several large industrial cities, sparkle again.
8. Many in the government, in addition to environmentalists, are worried about the quality and abundance of ground water.
9. Aquifers, a source of ground water, is layers of rock, sand, and soil that hold water.
10. Billions of gallons of water is pumped out of the ground each day.
11. In some regions, drinking water for thousands of people come from aquifers.
12. Several recent studies of aquifers has revealed contamination to some degree.
13. The causes of contamination are varied.
14. Salt for melting ice on city streets cause pollution.
15. The chemicals that sometimes leak out of a sewer system or waste dump contaminates aquifers.
16. Some fertilizers and pesticides that are used widely all over the country also add pollutants to the water.
17. The extent of the damages from pollution are not known.
18. Another problem, according to scientists, is the uncontrolled use of water sources.
19. Ground water in some areas are being used faster than the supply can be renewed.
20. Each one of the fifty states have a stake in preserving sources of fresh water.

USAGE

Special Problems in Subject-Verb Agreement

18h. The contractions *don't* and *doesn't* should agree with their subjects.

Use *don't*, the contraction of *do not*, with all plural subjects and with the pronouns *I* and *you*. Use *doesn't*, the contraction of *does not*, with all singular subjects except the pronouns *I* and *you*. Avoid the common error of using *don't* for *doesn't*.

Reference Note

For more information about **contractions**, see page 872.

NONSTANDARD	He don't [do not] live here anymore.
STANDARD	**He doesn't** [does not] live here anymore.

NONSTANDARD	It don't [do not] look like rain.
STANDARD	**It doesn't** [does not] look like rain.

NONSTANDARD	Ruth don't [do not] know about the surprise party.
STANDARD	**Ruth doesn't** [does not] know about the surprise party.

18i. When the subject follows the verb, find the subject and make sure that the verb agrees with it.

The subject generally follows the verb in sentences that begin with *Here* or *There* and in questions.

EXAMPLES   Here **is** the **book** you reserved.
Here **are** the **books** you reserved.

There **was** a **detour** on the interstate.
There **were** no **detours** on the interstate.

When **is Passover** this year?
When **are Passover** and **Easter** this year?

NOTE   The contractions *here's, there's, when's,* and *where's* incorporate the verb *is*. Use such contractions only with subjects that are singular in meaning.

NONSTANDARD	When's your finals?
STANDARD	**When are** your **finals**?

NONSTANDARD	Here's your gloves.
STANDARD	**Here are** your **gloves.**
STANDARD	Here**'s** your **pair** of gloves.

TIPS & TRICKS

To find the subject when it follows the verb, rearrange the sentence to put the subject first.

EXAMPLE
The **book** you reserved **is** here.

STYLE TIP

Many people consider contractions informal. Therefore, it is generally best to avoid using contractions in formal speech and writing.

USAGE

Reference Note

For more about **collective nouns,** see page 499.

18j. A collective noun may be either singular or plural, depending on its meaning in a sentence.

The singular form of a *collective noun* names a group of persons or things.

Common Collective Nouns			
army	club	flock	squadron
assembly	committee	group	staff
audience	crowd	herd	swarm
band	family	jury	team
class	fleet	public	troop

A collective noun is

* singular when it refers to the group as a unit
* plural when it refers to the individual members or parts of the group

SINGULAR   The **class meets** Monday, Wednesday, and Friday. [The class meets as a unit.]

PLURAL   The **class** usually **bring** their calculators with them. [The members of the class bring separate calculators.]

SINGULAR   The **team has won** the semifinals. [The team won as a unit.]

PLURAL   The **team have voted** twenty-one to three to buy new uniforms. [The members of the team voted individually.]

SINGULAR   A **herd was stranded** by the flood. [The herd was stranded as a unit.]

PLURAL   The **herd were separated** by the rising waters. [The herd is thought of in terms of its individuals.]

18k. An expression of an amount (a measurement, a percentage, or a fraction, for example) may be singular or plural, depending on how it is used.

An expression of an amount is

* singular when the amount is thought of as a unit
* plural when the amount is thought of as separate parts

EXAMPLES   **Twenty-seven dollars is** all we have raised so far. [The amount refers to one unit.]

IT'S MALCOMB FROM OUTPOST FIVE, SIR...HE'S BEING OVERRUN!

....HE SAYS THE BULLETS IS FLYING EVERYWHERE

WHAT SHOULD HE DO?

WORK ON HIS SUBJECT AND VERB AGREEMENT.

CROCK reprinted with special permission of North America Syndicate, Inc.

Twenty-seven dollars were lying crumpled on the floor. [The amount refers to separate dollars.]

Eight hours is now the standard workday throughout the United States. [one unit]

Eight hours were set aside for that week-long miniseries about the Civil War. [separate hours]

A fraction or a percentage is

- singular when it refers to a singular word
- plural when it refers to a plural word

EXAMPLES   **Two thirds** of my works-cited page **has been typed.** [The fraction refers to the singular noun *page*.]

Two thirds of my citations **have been typed.** [The fraction refers to the plural noun *citations*.]

Forty-two percent of the senior class **is planning** to go to college. [The percentage refers to the singular noun *class*.]

Forty-two percent of the seniors **are planning** to go to college. [The percentage refers to the plural noun *seniors*.]

Expressions of measurement such as length, weight, capacity, and area are usually singular.

EXAMPLES   **Two and fifty-four hundredths centimeters equals** one inch.

Seven pounds was the baby's weight at birth.

Ninety miles is the distance between Florida and Cuba.

Reference Note

For information about when to **spell out numbers** and when to **use numerals,** see page 901.

Exercise 5   **Identifying Verbs That Agree in Number with Their Subjects**

Choose the word or word group in parentheses that correctly completes each of the following sentences.

EXAMPLE   **1.** (*Is, Are*) 2.2 pounds equivalent to 1 kilogram?

1. Is

1. Forty dollars (*is, are*) too much to pay for those jeans.
2. (*Where's, Where are*) my coat and boots?
3. There (*seems, seem*) to be something for everyone.

USAGE

4. The newspaper staff (*has, have*) turned in all their stories for the next edition.
5. One half of the receipts that we were looking for (*was, were*) found in a shoe box.
6. (*Here's, Here are*) the notes you took about the history and symbolism of Japanese pagodas.
7. Two thirds of the students (*intend, intends*) to go to trade school or college.
8. The orchestra (*specialize, specializes*) in the Big Band music of Count Basie and Duke Ellington.
9. Ninety percent of us (*think, thinks*) the college placement test was hard.
10. Fifty miles (*is, are*) a long way to drive to work every day.
11. (*When's, When are*) the moving truck coming?
12. Three quarters of the film (*takes, take*) place in India.
13. It just (*don't, doesn't*) matter, as far as I can tell.
14. In those days, thirty cents (*was, were*) good pay for an hour's work, young lady.
15. To our horror, we discovered that a swarm of wasps (*was, were*) nesting in the mulch.
16. Mom says that Reginald (*don't, doesn't*) have a blue backpack.
17. Yes, our family (*do, does*) spend Wednesday evening together whenever possible.
18. Three yards of fabric (*was, were*) all we needed for that futuristic costume, Mrs. Winter.
19. Surely 70 percent of the population (*knows, know*) that tune.
20. Dad, (*where's, where are*) the keys to the car?

18l. Some nouns that are plural in form take singular verbs.

The following nouns take singular verbs.

civics	gymnastics	mumps
economics	mathematics	news
electronics	measles	physics
genetics	molasses	summons

EXAMPLES   **Mumps is** usually more severe in adults than in children.

Economics was my mother's major in college.

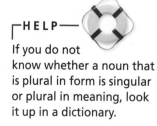

┌HELP─
If you do not know whether a noun that is plural in form is singular or plural in meaning, look it up in a dictionary.

However, some nouns that refer to single items take plural verbs.

binoculars	pliers	shears
eyeglasses	scissors	trousers

EXAMPLES   The **binoculars are** on the screened porch.

Have these **shears** ever **been sharpened**?

NOTE   Many nouns ending in *–ics,* such as *acoustics, athletics, ethics, politics,* and *tactics,* may be either singular or plural in meaning. Generally, such a noun takes a singular verb when it names a science, a system, or a skill. It takes a plural verb when it names qualities, operations, or activities.

EXAMPLES   Who said, **"Politics is** the art of the possible"?

Are your **politics** like those of your parents?

18m. Even when plural in form, the titles of creative works (such as books, songs, movies, or paintings) and the names of countries, cities, and organizations generally take singular verbs.

EXAMPLES   ***Dust Tracks on a Road* is** Zora Neale Hurston's autobiography.

***Vermilion Lotuses* was** among the paintings by the Chinese artist Chang Dai-chien exhibited at the Smithsonian Institution.

The **Netherlands borders** the North Sea and **exports** various chemical products.

Is Las Cruces where you spent your vacation?

The **Boy Scouts was founded** in 1908 in England.

NOTE   The names of some organizations may take either singular or plural verbs, depending on how the names are used. When the name refers to the organization as a unit, it takes a singular verb. When the name refers to the members of the organization, it takes a plural verb.

EXAMPLES   The **Veterans of Foreign Wars was founded** in 1899.
[The organization was founded in 1899.]

The **Veterans of Foreign Wars are leading** the parade.
[The members of the organization are leading the parade.]

TIPS & TRICKS

Some nouns that name games are singular if they refer to the game itself and plural if they refer to the pieces used in the game.

EXAMPLES
Checkers is an easy game to learn but hard to master.

Your **checkers are** going to get lost if you don't pick them up after the game.

HELP
Generally, geographical names (other than names of countries and cities) that are plural in form take plural verbs.

EXAMPLE
The **Rocky Mountains extend** from the central part of New Mexico to the northern part of Alaska.

USAGE

Reference Note

For more information on **predicate nominatives,** see page 543.

18n. A verb agrees with its subject but not necessarily with a predicate nominative.

EXAMPLES   Quick **reflexes are** one requirement for becoming an astronaut.

One **requirement** for becoming an astronaut **is** quick reflexes.

The **highlight** of the evening **was** the compositions by Quincy Jones.

The **compositions** by Quincy Jones **were** the highlight of the evening.

18o. Subjects preceded by *every* or *many a(n)* take singular verbs.

EXAMPLES   **Every takeoff** and **landing is cleared** with the tower.

Many a runner finishes a marathon long after the winner.

18p. When the relative pronoun *that, which,* or *who* is the subject of an adjective clause, the verb in the clause agrees with the word to which the relative pronoun refers.

EXAMPLES   San Juan, **which is** the capital of Puerto Rico, is a major tourist destination. [*Which* refers to the singular noun *San Juan.*]

I know some people **who own** a Christmas-tree farm. [*Who* refers to the plural noun *people.*]

NOTE   When the relative pronoun is preceded by *one of* + a plural word, it takes a plural verb. When it is preceded by *the only one of* + a plural word, it takes a singular verb.

EXAMPLES   Egypt is **one of the nations that border** the Red Sea. [The relative pronoun *that* takes the plural verb *border* because it refers to the plural noun *nations.*]

Quebec is **the only one of the Canadian provinces that has** a majority of French-speaking citizens. [The relative pronoun *that* takes the singular verb *has* because it refers to the singular pronoun *one.*]

HELP

In the expression *the number of, number* takes a singular verb. In the expression *a number of, number* takes a plural verb.

EXAMPLES

The number of volunteers **is** surprising.

A number of volunteers **are** signing up now.

Exercise 6 **Identifying Subjects and Verbs That Agree in Number with Their Subjects**

Choose the verb form in parentheses that correctly completes each of the following sentences.

EXAMPLE　　1. Mark Russell was one of the political humorists who
　　　　　　　(*was, were*) interviewed about the recent developments
　　　　　　　in Washington, D.C.

　　　　　1. *was*

1. Many a gymnast (*dreams, dream*) of winning a medal.
2. A number of unusual phenomena (*indicates, indicate*) a shift in the microclimate.
3. *Franny and Zooey* (*is, are*) my favorite book.
4. The Chicago Cubs is a team that (*rallies, rally*) in the late innings.
5. Civics (*is, are*) supposed to be his best subject.
6. The Society of Procrastinators (*has, have*) postponed its meeting.
7. The kitchen scissors (*was, were*) not on the counter when I looked there this morning.
8. That was one of those jokes that (*offends, offend*) everyone.
9. Every volunteer in the regional hospitals (*is, are*) being honored.
10. My favorite part of the movie (*was, were*) scenes in New York's Adirondack Mountains.
11. The tactics he used (*were, was*) very effective.
12. Roseanne's new eyeglasses (*looks, look*) nice.
13. They must be the children who (*were, was*) selling greeting cards.
14. When we walked into the American Legion Hall, "Sixteen Tons" (*were, was*) playing on the jukebox.
15. The only one of us who (*don't, doesn't*) plan to apply is Marcy.
16. (*Isn't, Aren't*) Barbados located just north of South America?
17. Allison's Imports (*trades, trade*) mostly in home accessories.
18. Every boy or girl (*needs, need*) a place to think and dream.
19. Ella Fitzgerald's songs (*was, were*) the best part of the show.
20. Ever since he dismantled a toaster in third grade, electronics (*have, has*) fascinated him.

Review C　Correcting Errors in Subject-Verb Agreement

Most of the sentences in the following paragraph contain verbs that do not agree with their subjects. Give the correct form of each verb that does not agree with its subject. If a sentence is already correct, write *C*.

EXAMPLE　　[1] Every year, many a tourist visit the White House.

　　　　　1. *visit—visits*

　　[1] The White House, which has been home to all U.S. presidents

since John Adams, is a national treasure. [2] The public, as you can see in this picture, likes to view the White House and grounds when visiting Washington, D.C. [3] How many people actually tours the White House each year? [4] One million are a conservative estimate. [5] There's more than 130 rooms in the White House. [6] Of course, a tourist don't get to see all the rooms. [7] In fact, only seven rooms, including the State Dining Room, is open to the public on the official tour. [8] Many a party have been given in the East Room, another large reception area. [9] The White House chefs, who works in two kitchens, sometimes prepare food for more than one hundred people in a single day. [10] The presence of recreational facilities, such as a movie theater and a bowling alley, in the White House surprises some visitors.

Review D Proofreading Sentences for Subject-Verb Agreement

Most of the following sentences contain errors in subject-verb agreement. Identify each verb that does not agree with its subject. Then, supply the correct form of the verb. If a sentence is already correct, write *C*.

EXAMPLE   1. This great book, called *Games of the World,* not only describe all kinds of games but also explain how to make and to play them.

   1. *describe—describes; explain—explains*

1. Although customs and languages differs across continents, people worldwide enjoy playing games.
2. The game of dominoes are a popular pastime throughout Europe and Latin America.
3. Many a player discover that winning a game of dominoes takes skill and strategy rather than luck.
4. One of the games that requires even more strategy than dominoes is chess.

5. Scholars believe that the earliest version of chess originated in India during the seventh century.
6. As chess became popular throughout Asia and Europe, its rules and appearance was transformed.
7. There's a number of skills a good chess player needs; among these are imagination, concentration, and foresight.
8. Like many other games, marbles require physical skills in addition to strategy and concentration.
9. Children all over the world, from the schoolyards of Israel to the sidewalks of Tahiti, enjoys "knuckling down outside the circle."
10. Don't the number of different games that can be played with marbles seem limitless?

Review E Revising Subject-Verb Agreement in Sentences

Rewrite each of the following sentences according to the directions given in brackets after each one. Make any needed changes in the forms of verbs.

EXAMPLE
1. A number of famous sports stars have made television commercials. [Change *A number of famous sports stars* to *Many a famous sports star.*]

1. *Many a famous sports star has made television commercials.*

1. The band holds its annual banquet in the school cafeteria. [Add *as well as many of the school's other organizations* after *band.* Put a comma after *band* and after *organizations.*]
2. Where is my book? [Add *and my pen* after *book.*]
3. Both of the candidates have promised to cut taxes. [Change *Both* to *Neither.*]
4. She writes neatly. [Add *is the only person in our group who* after *She.*]
5. Our basketball team has won the city championship. [Add *Neither our soccer team nor* at the beginning of the sentence.]
6. Nearly all people need at least one friend who is a good listener. [Change *all people* to *everyone.*]

7. A complete copy of your high school transcript is required by the state university. [After *transcript*, add *together with a completed application form and an autobiographical essay.* Put a comma after *transcript* and after *essay.*]
8. The tigers are growling ferociously. [At the beginning of the sentence, add *Either the lion or.*]
9. The movie screen is hard to see. [At the beginning of the sentence, add *The captions on.*]
10. A day in the library is all the time I will need to finish my research. [Change *A day* to *Two days.*]

Agreement of Pronoun and Antecedent

Reference Note

For more about **antecedents,** see page 501.

A pronoun usually refers to a noun or another pronoun. The word to which a pronoun refers is called its *antecedent.*

18q. A pronoun should agree in number, gender, and person with its antecedent.

(1) Singular pronouns refer to singular antecedents. Plural pronouns refer to plural antecedents.

EXAMPLES   **Arthur Mitchell** founded **his** own ballet company.

          Raccoons often dunk **their** food in water before eating.

(2) Some singular pronouns indicate gender.

The pronouns *he, him, his,* and *himself* refer to masculine antecedents. The pronouns *she, her, hers,* and *herself* refer to feminine antecedents. The pronouns *it, its,* and *itself* refer to antecedents that are neuter (neither masculine nor feminine).

EXAMPLES   **Rudolfo** stated **his** position clearly. [masculine]

          Maxine has already prepared **her** acceptance speech. [feminine]

          The **river** overflowed **its** banks. [neuter]

(3) *Person* indicates whether a pronoun refers to the one(s) speaking (*first person*), the one(s) spoken to (*second person*), or the one(s) spoken of (*third person*).

FIRST PERSON   I promised **myself** yesterday that **I** would clean **my** room today.

SECOND PERSON   Do **you** have **your** library card with **you**?

THIRD PERSON   **They** built **their** new house **themselves.**

18r. Some indefinite pronouns are singular, some are plural, and some can be either singular or plural, depending on how they are used in the sentence.

(1) Use a singular pronoun to refer to any of the following antecedents: *anybody, anyone, anything, each, either, everybody, everyone, everything, neither, nobody, no one, nothing, one, somebody, someone,* **or** *something.*

EXAMPLES   **Each** of the birds had staked out **its** own territory.

    Someone left a pair of shoes on the boys' locker room floor, and **he** had better pick them up before the coach sees them.

Indefinite pronouns do not indicate gender. Often a word in a phrase following such a pronoun indicates the gender of the pronoun.

EXAMPLES   **Each** of these **women** runs **her** own business.

    One of the **men** in the audience forgot **his** coat.

If the antecedent may be either masculine or feminine, use both the masculine and feminine pronouns to refer to it.

EXAMPLES   **Everyone** here knows how **he or she** can get help.

    Each of the participants in the contest paid **his or her** own entry fee.

In informal situations, plural pronouns are often used to refer to singular antecedents that can be either masculine or feminine.

INFORMAL   **Everybody** stayed late at the dance because **they** were enjoying **themselves.**

Such usage is becoming increasingly popular in writing. In fact, using a singular pronoun to refer to a singular antecedent that is clearly plural in meaning may be misleading in some cases.

MISLEADING   **Everybody** stayed late at the dance because **he or she** was enjoying **himself or herself.** [Since *Everybody* is clearly plural in meaning, the singular constructions *he or she* and *himself or herself,* though grammatically correct, are confusing.]

STYLE **TIP**

You can often avoid the awkward *his or her* construction by substituting an article (*a, an,* or *the*) for the construction or by using the plural forms of both the pronoun and its antecedent.

EXAMPLES

Each of the participants in the contest paid **an** entry fee.

All of the participants in the contest paid **their** own entry fees.

USAGE

Agreement of Pronoun and Antecedent   **619**

In formal situations, revise such sentences to make them both clear and grammatically correct.

EXAMPLE **All** of the students stayed late at the dance because **they** were enjoying **themselves.**

(2) Use a plural pronoun to refer to any of the following indefinite pronouns: *both, few, many,* **or** *several.*

EXAMPLES **Several** of the seniors discussed with the principal **their** ideas about forming another service club.

The judge met with **both** of the attorneys and **their** clients.

(3) Use a singular or a plural pronoun, depending on the meaning of the sentence, to refer to any of the following indefinite pronouns: *all, any, more, most, none,* **or** *some.*

SINGULAR I accidentally deleted **some** of the document. Is there a way that I can retrieve **it**? [*It* is used because *some* refers to the singular noun *document.*]

PLURAL I accidentally deleted **some** of the files. Is there a way that I can retrieve **them**? [*Them* is used because *some* refers to the plural noun *files.*]

18s. Use a plural pronoun to refer to two or more antecedents joined by *and.*

EXAMPLES **Hilda and Lupe** presented **their** reports.

After **Ethel, Jared, and Cam** ate lunch together, **they** went to **their** next class.

NOTE Antecedents joined by *and* that name only one person, place, thing, or idea take a singular pronoun.

EXAMPLE For my birthday dinner, Dad made **chicken and yellow rice**. He knows **it** is my favorite dish. [*Chicken and yellow rice* is a single dish.]

18t. Use a singular pronoun to refer to two or more singular antecedents joined by *or* or *nor.*

EXAMPLES Either **Paul or Diego** is willing to drive **his** car to the retreat in September.

Neither **Sue nor María** remembered to bring **her** vacation photos with **her.**

USAGE

┌HELP──

Some words that can be used as indefinite pronouns, such as *both, each,* and *some,* can also be used as adjectives. When such a word modifies a pronoun's antecedent, that pronoun and its antecedent should agree as they normally would.

EXAMPLE

Golfers dream of making **their** first hole in one.

Some **golfers** dream of making **their** first hole in one. [In both sentences, the pronoun *their* agrees with the antecedent *golfers.*]

Using a pronoun to refer to antecedents of different number may create an unclear or awkward sentence.

UNCLEAR   Neither the puppies nor our full-grown dog likes its new toys. [*Its* agrees with the nearest antecedent, *dog.* However, it is unclear whether all the animals were dissatisfied with their toys or all the animals were dissatisfied only with the full-grown dog's toys.]

UNCLEAR   Neither our full-grown dog nor the puppies like their new toys. [*Their* agrees with the nearest antecedent, *puppies.* However, it is unclear whether all the animals were dissatisfied with all of the new toys or all the animals were dissatisfied only with the puppies' toys.]

AWKWARD   Neither our full-grown dog nor the puppies like its or their new toys.

You should revise sentences to avoid unclear and awkward constructions like the ones above.

REVISED   Neither our full-grown dog nor the puppies like **the** new toys.
Our full-grown **dog** doesn't like **its** new toys, and the **puppies** do not like **theirs.**
None of the dogs like **their** new toys.

Exercise 7 Correcting Errors in Pronoun-Antecedent Agreement

Most of the following sentences contain pronouns that do not agree with their antecedents. If a pronoun does not agree with its antecedent, rewrite the sentence to correct the error. If a sentence is already correct, write *C.*

EXAMPLE   1. Each of the skiers waxed their skis every morning.

1. *Each of the skiers waxed his or her skis every morning.*

or

The skiers waxed their skis every morning.

1. Neither Elena nor Barbara made any errors on their test.
2. All of the senior citizens enjoyed their trip to Boston, where they walked the Freedom Trail.
3. Several of the reporters at the press conference asked her questions too quickly.
4. I believe that anybody should be free to express their opinion.
5. No one brought their camera to the party.

6. Both of the male soloists pronounced his words clearly.
7. Did any of the newborn kittens seem steady on its feet?
8. If anyone becomes lost while exploring Salt Lake City, they should use the street maps available from the tour guide.
9. As far as I could see, Ned and Dennis made a mistake while presenting his arguments during the debate.
10. Neither President Gerald Ford nor Vice President Nelson Rockefeller was elected to his high office.

Special Problems in Pronoun-Antecedent Agreement

18u. A collective noun may be either singular or plural, depending on how it is used.

A collective noun takes

- a singular pronoun when the noun refers to the group as a unit

- a plural pronoun when the noun refers to the individual members or parts of the group

SINGULAR   The tour **group** surprised **its** guide by presenting her with a lovely thank-you gift. [*Its* is used because the tour group as a unit surprised the guide.]

PLURAL   The guide surprised the tour **group** by presenting **them** with lovely souvenirs. [*Them* is used because the individual members of the tour group were presented with souvenirs.]

18v. An expression of an amount (a measurement, a percentage, or a fraction, for example) may take a singular or a plural pronoun, depending on how it is used.

An expression of an amount is

- singular when the amount is thought of as a unit

- plural when the amount is thought of as separate parts

EXAMPLES   That magazine costs **four dollars,** and I don't have **it.** [The amount refers to one unit.]

He had dropped **four dollars,** so I picked **them** up for him. [The amount refers to separate dollars.]

A fraction or a percentage is

- singular when it refers to a singular word

- plural when is refers to a plural word

Reference Note

For a list of **commonly used collective nouns,** see page 499.

Reference Note

For information about when to **spell out numbers** and when to **use numerals,** see page 901.

One third of the casserole is left, but **it** will be gone soon. [*One third* refers to *casserole*.]

One third of the bagels are left, but **they** will be gone soon. [*One third* refers to *bagels*.]

18w. Some nouns that are plural in form take singular pronouns.

The following nouns take singular pronouns.

civics	gymnastics	molasses
economics	linguistics	mumps
electronics	mathematics	news
genetics	measles	physics

EXAMPLE I am taking **physics** this year, and **it** is a very challenging course.

NOTE Many nouns ending in –*ics*, such as *acoustics, athletics, ethics, politics, statistics,* and *tactics,* may take either singular or plural pronouns. Generally, when such a noun names a science, a system, or a skill, the noun takes a singular pronoun. When the noun names qualities, activities, or individual items, the noun takes a plural pronoun.

SINGULAR Today, our government class discussed **ethics** and the role **it** has played in recent political campaigns.

PLURAL We believe that the candidate's **ethics** are beyond reproach; we have seen no evidence that would cause us to question **them.**

─HELP─

If you are not sure whether to use a singular or a plural pronoun to refer to an antecedent ending in –*ics,* look up the word in a dictionary.

However, a few nouns that refer to single items take plural pronouns.

binoculars	pants	shears
eyeglasses	pliers	shorts
Olympics	scissors	slacks

EXAMPLE The **pliers** are not in the toolbox. Have you seen **them**?

Even when plural in form, the titles of creative works (such as books, songs, movies, and paintings) and the names of countries, cities, and organizations generally take singular pronouns.

┌HELP┐

The names of some organizations, though plural in form, may take either singular or plural pronouns. When the name refers to the organization as a unit, use a singular pronoun. When the name refers to the members of the organization, use a plural pronoun.

SINGULAR
The **Bayview Rockets** won **its** first game of the season. [*Its* is used because the Bayview Rockets won as a unit.]

PLURAL
The **Bayview Rockets** left the field, waving **their** helmets high over **their** heads. [*Their* is used because the individual players were waving separate helmets over their heads.]

EXAMPLES
Have you ever watched **The X-Files**? I think I have seen every episode of **it.**

Sleeping Musicians was painted by Rufino Tamayo. **It** is one of his best-known works.

Situated in the Indian Ocean, **Seychelles** comprises about ninety islands; **its** three principal islands are Mahé, Praslin, and La Digue.

I don't know how many people live in **Grand Rapids,** but I do know that **it** is the second-largest city in Michigan.

Have you shopped at **Computers Unlimited**? **It** may have the software that you need.

18x. The gender and number of the relative pronoun *that, which,* or *who* is determined by the number of the word to which it refers—its antecedent.

SINGULAR
Wendy, **who** was elected president of the student council a few weeks ago, has already fulfilled most of **her** campaign promises. [*Who* refers to the singular, feminine noun *Wendy.* Therefore, the singular, feminine form *her* is used to agree with *Who.*]

PLURAL
The retainers **that** my orthodontist made for me have my name on **them.** [*That* refers to the plural, neuter noun *retainers.* Therefore, *them* is used to agree with *that.*]

Exercise 8 Proofreading for Errors in Pronoun-Antecedent Agreement

Most of the following sentences contain errors in pronoun-antecedent agreement. Write the incorrect pronoun and the correct form. If a sentence is already correct, write *C.*

EXAMPLE
1. If we had seventy dollars, they would be enough for that program.

1. *they—it*

1. The students who left his or her uniforms on the bus should report to the front hall.
2. The good scissors should be back next week; the repair shop is sharpening it.
3. No, two thirds of a tablespoon of oregano will be too much; they will make the pizza taste like lawn clippings.
4. In the summer, the team made Sarasota their home.

5. "The Stars and Stripes Forever" has been popular for decades, and they will probably continue to be a favorite.

6. *Drovers* will be on display in the library until Saturday, when they will join the sculpture exhibit at the university.

7. The news should be on in a few minutes; the game's overtime delayed them.

8. Does the band post its rehearsal schedule on the bulletin board?

9. Valencia Industries may provide wiring if they can meet our schedule.

10. Did you ask anyone who has finished their college applications to look over your personal essay?

Review F **Proofreading Sentences for Pronoun-Antecedent Agreement**

Most of the following sentences contain errors in pronoun-antecedent agreement. If a sentence contains an error in agreement, rewrite the sentence to correct the error. If a sentence is already correct, write *C.*

EXAMPLE   1. The band is practicing the selections that they will perform in the statewide competition.

 1. *The band is practicing the selections that it will perform in the statewide competition.*

1. Each of the men says that they will help deliver the gift packages to the families.

2. One of those cars has their own factory-installed stereo.

3. That factory has robots working on its assembly line.

4. Either Mrs. Wilson or Mrs. Kim will bring their camera.

5. Has either of the new students been assigned his or her locker?

6. Anyone who speaks a foreign language increases their chance for a high-paying job.

7. After you locate the Netherlands on the map, write the name of its capital.

8. No one in the crowd had noticed the pickpocket stealing their wallet.

9. Neither Jason nor Maggie bought their shoes until they went on sale.

10. Brenda and Charlene read her report about Rosa Parks and the civil rights movement.

11. The study of economics and their practical applications can last a lifetime.

12. Do you know someone who could lend me their community college catalog?

13. The jury will receive their instructions from the judge.
14. Red Feather Enterprises may award their million-dollar advertising campaign to us.
15. Three saxophone players and two trumpet players are waiting for his or her auditions.
16. Whom did the Confederate States of America make their president?
17. It was around then that the album *Rumours* soared through the airwaves as they became part of our pop history.
18. Nothing in the room was out of its place.
19. Awestruck by the final number, the audience remained in its seats, silent for a full minute.
20. Both of the artists had shown his or her work at the new gallery.

USAGE

Chapter Review

A. Choosing Verbs That Agree in Number with Their Subjects

Choose the correct verb form in parentheses in each of the following sentences.

1. *The Pickwick Papers* (*was, were*) Dickens's first published novel.
2. Neither Francisco nor Joe (*has, have*) called to order tickets yet.
3. (*Are, Is*) either one of them participating in the play?
4. There (*was, were*) a number of students in the hall.
5. Theodore or William always (*has, have*) a pocket calculator.
6. Either the guidance counselor or the principal (*is, are*) certain to know the answer to this question.
7. Here (*are, is*) the attendance figures for the current week.
8. Mathematics (*seem, seems*) more difficult than any of my other subjects.
9. Shelley is one of those poets who (*are, is*) almost certain to be represented in any anthology of English verse.
10. Seven dollars and fifty cents (*is, are*) too much to spend on lunch.
11. Either Carl or his parents (*was, were*) willing to leave early.
12. The Chess Club (*is, are*) Margaret Doyle, Robert Viapiano, Victor Mothersbaugh, and Judy Cheng-Cochran.
13. Every student and teacher in the school (*are, is*) contributing to the fund-raiser for the new library.
14. Jeremy and Chad (*don't, doesn't*) know the words to the song.
15. Ray, his brother Dave, Chrissy, and her brother Arthur (*is, are*) the Village Green Preservation Society.

B. Proofreading for Pronoun-Antecedent Errors

Each of the following sentences contains an error in pronoun-antecedent agreement. Identify each error, and then write the correct pronoun form.

16. One of the girls left their coat in my locker.
17. If anyone does not understand the directions, they should feel free to ask questions.

18. Did each person sign their name on the get-well card that we are sending to Frieda?

19. The band have been measured for its new uniforms.

20. Either Elena or Carla is driving their car to the picnic tomorrow.

21. Rock-and-roll is my father's favorite music; he has listened to them since he was a boy.

22. One of the repairmen left their toolbox in our kitchen.

23. Several actors in the play forgot his lines during the dress rehearsal.

24. Many an author has had trouble trying to get their books or stories accepted by publishers.

25. One of the girls fell down and cut their knee.

26. When Jamal and Dustin get through the snowstorm to the gas station, ask him to call us.

27. Neither Mimi nor Miriam believes that they will lose the spelling bee to the other.

28. After Jim used the scissors, he put it back in the kitchen drawer.

29. Each of the horses in the pasture had a white mark on their face.

30. Tanya is studying physics this semester, and she says she might major in them.

C. Proofreading a Paragraph for Subject-Verb Agreement and Pronoun-Antecedent Agreement

Each of the sentences in the following paragraph contains an error in agreement between subject and verb or between pronoun and antecedent. Identify each error, and then write the correct form.

[31] Most of us has some knowledge of the periods in European history known as the Middle Ages and the Renaissance. [32] Those times is the special interest of the Society for Creative Anachronism. [33] Members of this society take his or her pleasure in the study of the Middle Ages and the Renaissance. [34] Every member take a name and becomes a character appropriate to the society's historical period (A.D. 500 to A.D. 1500). [35] Popular characters in the society includes princes, princesses, lords, and ladies. [36] After joining, everyone is free to choose a new name and to re-create their favorite aspect of medieval or Renaissance life. [37] Many of the members pursue his or her own interests. [38] For example, some people enjoys costuming, armor making, calligraphy, and woodworking. [39] There is also some

members who compete in tournaments to become monarchs of the society's kingdoms. **[40]** If you want to learn more about such historical activities in your area, the society usually displays their brochures at Renaissance festivals.

Writing Application
Using Correct Agreement in a Letter

Subject-Verb Agreement A friend of yours is applying for a summer job as a camp counselor and has asked you to write a letter of recommendation. Write the letter of recommendation that you will send to the director of the summer camp. In your letter, follow the rules of formal, standard English and pay particular attention to subject-verb agreement.

Prewriting Take a few minutes to write down a list of your friend's positive qualities and outstanding abilities. Focus on traits that you think would make your friend a good camp counselor. Think of specific examples that illustrate the qualities you have listed.

Writing Begin your letter by introducing yourself and stating your purpose. Tell how long you have known the person you are recommending. Then, express your positive opinion of the person and his or her abilities. Be specific. You may want to give two or three brief examples to illustrate your friend's qualities, or you may want to tell one interesting anecdote that achieves the same result.

Revising Read through your letter once before you begin to revise it. Does it have the effect you want? Will it help your friend get the job? On a second reading, identify specific parts of the letter that need revising. Check to be sure you have followed the standard form for a business letter.

Publishing Be sure to proofread your letter carefully. When you check for errors in subject-verb agreement, take extra care with collective nouns, plural nouns, expressions of an amount, and relative pronouns. In pairs, conduct mock interviews with your classmates. The students playing the employer should ask questions about the letter of reference.

Reference Note

For more about **writing business letters,** see "Writing" in the Quick Reference Handbook.

USAGE

Using Pronouns Correctly

Case Forms of Pronouns; Special Pronoun Problems

Diagnostic Preview

A. Selecting Correct Forms of Pronouns

Choose the correct pronoun form in parentheses in each of the following sentences.

EXAMPLE   **1.** After a pause, I heard Mr. Karas say into the phone, "Yes, this is (*he, him*)."

        1. he

1. Last summer, my friend Megan and (*I, me*) worked in a factory that produces microchips for computers.

2. Before we began, we made a pact that (*we, us*) teenagers would show the adults that we were responsible workers.

3. For the first two weeks, everything ran smoothly because our supervisor, Mr. Karas, was a person (*who, whom*) we admired for being firm and just.

4. In fact, we were surprised by (*him, his*) showing interest in our progress and going out of his way to train us.

5. When Mr. Karas went on vacation, we doubted that his assistant, Ms. Sullivan, would be as firm as (*he, him*).

6. Our first mistake was in thinking that Mr. Karas and (*she, her*) would have different sets of standards.

7. We started giving (*us, ourselves*) ten extra minutes at lunch.

8. One afternoon, Ms. Sullivan walked up to us at our job stations and said, "Megan and Rick, until recently I had thought you were employees (*who, whom*) took pride in your work."

9. "If you continue to come back late," she said calmly, "we, Mr. Karas and (*I, me*), will be looking for two new trainees."

10. The experience has really taught (*we, us*) some valuable lessons.

11. First, (*us, our*) deliberately taking extra time at the break was wrong.

12. Second, we had let Mr. Karas down because it was (*he, him*) who had hired us, trained us, and trusted us.

13. Third, we had mistakenly presumed that Ms. Sullivan would not do her job as well as (*he, him*).

14. Fourth, we had let (*us, ourselves*) down by failing to do our best.

15. (*Who, Whom*) do you think became model employees?

B. Proofreading a Paragraph for Correct Pronoun Usage

Most of the sentences in the following paragraph contain errors in pronoun usage. Identify each error, and then give the correct pronoun form. If a sentence is already correct, write *C*.

EXAMPLE **[1]** Gaius Caesar Germanicus, whom perhaps is better known as Caligula, was emperor of Rome from A.D. 37 to A.D. 41.

1. *whom—who*

[**16**] Do you know whom Tiberius Claudius Drusus Nero Germanicus was? [**17**] Such a long, elegant name certainly seems fitting for a Roman emperor, and that is exactly what he was. [**18**] Us modern readers and television watchers, as well as historians, know him simply as Claudius. [**19**] Robert Graves wrote about he in the popular novel *I, Claudius*. [**20**] Claudius, whom had a severe speech impediment, lived from 10 B.C. to A.D. 54. [**21**] Him becoming emperor in A.D. 41 troubled many Romans because they thought that he was a fool and would be a weak ruler. [**22**] He had not been an important government figure during the reigns of emperors Tiberius and Caligula, but he outlived both of they. [**23**] Claudius was a more stable ruler than Caligula and accomplished more than him. [**24**] Claudius, who historians now generally praise, initiated many building programs, such as the huge Claudian Aqueduct. [**25**] In addition, many Roman civil and military accomplishments of the time are credited to himself.

Case

Case is the form that a noun or a pronoun takes to show its relationship to other words in a sentence. In English, there are three cases: *nominative, objective,* and *possessive.*

The form of a noun is the same in both the nominative case and the objective case. For example, a noun used as a subject (nominative case) will have the same form if used as an object (objective case).

NOMINATIVE CASE	The **ghost** of Banquo suddenly appeared. [subject]
OBJECTIVE CASE	Only Macbeth saw the **ghost.** [direct object]

A noun changes its form for the possessive case, usually by adding an apostrophe and an *s.*

POSSESSIVE CASE	What effect did the **ghost's** appearance have on Macbeth?

NOTE Some authorities prefer the term *subjective case* to *nominative case.* Follow your teacher's directions when labeling words in this case.

Reference Note

For more about **forming possessive nouns,** see page 869.

Case Forms of Personal Pronouns

Unlike nouns, most personal pronouns have three different forms, one for each case. The form a pronoun takes depends on its function in a sentence.

NOMINATIVE CASE	**We** enjoyed reading *Macbeth.* [subject]
OBJECTIVE CASE	Some of **us** had seen a performance of the play on PBS. [object of the preposition *of*]
POSSESSIVE CASE	**Our** next assignment is to read *Othello.*

Within each case, the forms of the personal pronouns indicate *number, person,* and *gender.*

- Number tells you whether the pronoun is singular or plural.

- Person tells you whether the pronoun refers to the one(s) speaking (***first person***), the one(s) spoken to (***second person***), or the one(s) spoken of (***third person***).

- Gender tells you whether the pronoun is masculine, feminine, or neuter (neither masculine nor feminine).

STYLE TIP

As a matter of courtesy, first-person pronouns are placed at the end of compound constructions.

EXAMPLES
Nan and **I** went to the opera.

My uncle Evander met Nan and **me** outside the theater.

Uncle Evander paid for Nan's ticket and **mine.**

USAGE

Personal Pronouns			
	Nominative Case	**Objective Case**	**Possessive Case**
Singular			
First Person	I	me	my, mine
Second Person	you	you	your, yours
Third Person	he, she, it	him, her, it	his, her, hers, its
	Nominative Case	**Objective Case**	**Possessive Case**
Plural			
First Person	we	us	our, ours
Second Person	you	you	your, yours
Third Person	they	them	their, theirs

Notice in the chart above that *you*, *it*, and *her* have the same forms for two cases and *her* has the same form for the objective and possessive cases. All other personal pronouns have different forms for each case. Notice also that only the third-person singular pronouns indicate gender.

MOTHER GOOSE & GRIMM © Tribune Media Services, Inc. All rights reserved. Reprinted with permission.

The Nominative Case

The personal pronouns in the nominative case—*I, you, he, she, it, we,* and *they*—are used as subjects of verbs and as predicate nominatives.

19a. The subject of a verb should be in the nominative case.

EXAMPLES   **They** are playing backgammon.

We think that **she** deserves the Most Valuable Player award.

STYLE   TIP

Use the neuter pronoun *it* when referring to an animal unless the gender of the animal is made clear by another word in the sentence.

EXAMPLES
The dog was barking because **its** food dish was empty. [The sentence does not indicate the dog's gender.]

The lioness watched the film crew warily from **her** resting spot in the shade of a tree. [The word *lioness* indicates that the animal is female.]

Josie's cat, Max, froze in **his** tracks when **he** heard the phone ring. [The name *Max* indicates that the animal is male.]

Reference Note
The personal pronouns in the nominative case may also be used as appositives. For more about **appositives,** see page 567.

Reference Note
For more about **subjects of verbs,** see page 531.

TIPS & TRICKS

To help you choose the correct pronoun form in a compound subject, try each form separately with the verb.

CHOICES
(*She, Her*) and (*I, me*) made the Aztec costumes for the pageant. [*She made* or *Her made*? *I made* or *me made*?]

ANSWER
She and **I** made the Aztec costumes for the pageant.

TIPS & TRICKS

As you can see, the predicate nominative and the subject of the verb both indicate the same individual(s). To help you choose the correct pronoun form to use as a predicate nominative, try each form as the subject of the verb.

CHOICES
The best clog dancers are (*they, them*). [*They are* or *them are* the best clog dancers? *They are.*]

ANSWER
The best clog dancers are **they.**

Reference Note

For more information on **predicate nominatives,** see page 543.

A compound subject may include a pronoun in combination with a noun or another pronoun.

EXAMPLES The twins and **they** will be giving a concert tonight.

You and **I** are in the same math class.

19b. A predicate nominative should be in the nominative case.

A *predicate nominative* is a word or word group in the predicate that refers to or identifies the subject. A pronoun used as a predicate nominative usually completes the meaning of a form of the linking verb *be: am, is, are, was, were, be, being,* or *been.*

EXAMPLES The first speaker will be **I.** [*I* completes the meaning of *will be* by identifying the subject *speaker.*]

The most polite person in class is **he.** [*He* completes the meaning of *is* by identifying the subject *person.*]

Like a subject, a predicate nominative may be compound, with a pronoun appearing in combination with a noun or another pronoun.

EXAMPLES The only seniors who volunteered were **Elia** and **I.** [*Elia* and *I* complete the meaning of *were* by identifying the subject *seniors.*]

The managers of the new Thai restaurant are **she** and **he.** [*She* and *he* complete the meaning of *are* by identifying the subject *managers.*]

Exercise 1 Using Pronouns in the Nominative Case

For each of the following sentences, give a personal pronoun that can be substituted for the word or words in brackets.

EXAMPLE 1. Carl and [*Sue Ann*] always seem to be happy.

1. *she*

1. Jorge and [*Mike*] are tied for third place.
2. [*Donna*] and her parents have moved to San Antonio.
3. [*First-person plural*] will take the exam on Friday.
4. Can it be [*those choir members*] in that picture?
5. Either Ellen or [*Sally*] will be in charge.
6. Jennifer and [*second-person singular*] will represent the class.
7. [*First-person plural*] earned our trophies.
8. Neither [*Carolyn*] nor Michele has change for the bus.
9. Did you know that Greg and [*first-person singular*] are leaving?

10. I am sure the ones on the dance floor were you and [*Ed*].
11. The designers of the set were Philip and [*first-person plural*].
12. One good practitioner of this laboratory technique is [*Marcus*].
13. Will our new team teachers be Mrs. Niari and [*Mr. Howard*]?
14. Believe it or not, [*those boys*] in the van over there are all my brothers.
15. In the whole school, the only students with pet iguanas are Betsy and [*first-person singular*].
16. With a little luck, the winners will be [*second-person plural*].
17. As usual, the first people in line for tickets were Terri and [*Paula*].
18. Kirara and [*first-person singular*] went to see the exhibit of Pakistani art.
19. The only volunteers are Aidan and [*third-person plural*].
20. Are Max and [*the Wilson twins*] on the list?

The Objective Case

The personal pronouns in the objective case—*me, you, him, her, it, us,* and *them*—are used as direct objects, as indirect objects, and as objects of prepositions.

19c. A direct object should be in the objective case.

A ***direct object*** completes the meaning of a transitive verb by telling *who* or *what* receives the action of the verb.

EXAMPLES   Carmen has invited **me**. [*Me* tells *whom* Carmen has invited.]

The kittens were asleep until the sudden noise woke **them**. [*Them* tells *what* the noise woke.]

A direct object may be compound.

EXAMPLES   My father drove my **friends** and **me** to the game.

Mr. Pascoe chose **him** and **her** for the leading roles.

19d. An indirect object should be in the objective case.

Indirect objects appear sometimes in sentences containing direct objects and tell *to whom* or *to what* or *for whom* or *for what* the action of a transitive verb is done.

EXAMPLES   His uncle bought **him** a poncho in Mexico. [*Him* tells *for whom* his uncle bought a poncho.]

Because the engine was running poorly, Uncle Theo gave **it** a tune-up. [*It* tells *to what* Uncle Theo gave a tune-up.]

STYLE   TIP

Expressions such as *It's me, This is her,* and *It was them* are examples of informal usage. Though common in everyday situations, such expressions should be avoided in formal speaking and writing.

USAGE

Reference Note

The personal pronouns in the objective case may also be used as appositives. For more about **appositives,** see page 567.

Reference Note

For more about **direct objects,** see page 539.

Reference Note

For more about **indirect objects,** see page 540.

Do not mistake
the object of a preposition
for an indirect object.

INDIRECT OBJECT
Dad bought me a
sandwich.

OBJECT OF A PREPOSITION
Dad bought a sandwich
for me. [*Me* is the object
of the preposition *for*.]

USAGE

TIPS & TRICKS

To help you choose the
correct pronoun form in a
compound direct object or
indirect object, try each
form separately with the
verb.

CHOICES
Celia showed (*he, him*)
and (*I, me*) photographs
of her vacation in Hawaii.
[*Showed he* or *showed
him*? *Showed I* or *showed
me*?]

ANSWER
Celia showed **him** and
me photographs of her
vacation in Hawaii.

An indirect object may be compound.

EXAMPLES   Aunt Marion sent my **brother** and **me** a letter from
Portugal.

Did you give **her** and **him** the message?

Exercise 2 Using Pronouns in the Objective Case

For each of the following sentences, write a personal pronoun
that can be substituted for the word or words in brackets.

EXAMPLES   1. I helped [*Rod*] and her with their projects.

1. *him*

2. Sonia and Molly sent [*first-person singular*] a get-well
card last week.

2. *me*

1. Did you tell the superintendent or [*Ms. Marshall*]?
2. Mrs. Hanks gave Josh and [*first-person plural*] the motivation we
needed.
3. Leave [*first-person plural*] alone for a while.
4. Carmen will be inviting both you and [*first-person singular*] to
the recital.
5. Did you see Lois or [*Andy*] today?
6. I sent the admissions director and [*her assistants*] a letter.
7. The coach chose Joan and [*Michelle and me*].
8. The principal should have notified [*Stephen*] and Gail.
9. Ron just passed Tina and [*first-person singular*] in the hall.
10. Please don't ask [*the athletes*] about today's game.
11. As during similar roundups, the old mustang easily evaded
[*third-person plural*].
12. Will you make [*Brenda*] a necklace out of those Chinese beads?
13. Georgia is giving Ted and [*first-person plural*] a ride to the
Renaissance Festival.
14. A sampan carried [*the spies*] across the busy river.
15. Did they mention Anthony or [*first-person singular*]?
16. Why did Mrs. Johnson assign Ricky and [*first-person singular*] an
extra report?
17. Tell [*Dad*] about your plan.
18. Who taught [*those paramedics*] the new emergency procedures?
19. Show Karen and [*Uncle Joseph*] the new trophy.
20. [*Carla*] and [*second-person singular*] I would never doubt.

Review A **Choosing Correct Forms of Personal Pronouns**

Choose the correct pronoun form in parentheses in each of the following sentences.

EXAMPLE   **1.** Paulo and (*her, she*) are my lab partners.

     1. she

1. The guests thanked Rita and (*she, her*).
2. Gloria and (*I, me*) are giving a report on the relationship between the Shoshone people and the Mormon settlers in the 1800s.
3. (*We, Us*) are learning about Hendrick Arnold, a scout who helped Texas win independence from Mexico.
4. What were you telling Chuck and (*we, us*) earlier?
5. Of course, I remember Monica and (*she, her*).
6. We knew the first guests to arrive would be (*they, them*).
7. Give (*we, us*) the message as soon as possible.
8. Jana and (*she, her*) are active members.
9. It is either you or (*he, him*) in the runoff against Jamie.
10. That's (*he, him*) standing on the corner.

Review B **Proofreading a Paragraph for Correct Pronoun Usage**

Most sentences in the following paragraph contain errors in pronoun usage. Identify each error, and then give the correct pronoun form. If a sentence is already correct, write *C*.

EXAMPLE   **[1]** Sarah and me are on the track team.

     1. me—I

[1] At the start of track season, our coach told Sarah and I the story of the famous sprinter Evelyn Ashford. [2] During high school, Ashford had started running races against the boys at lunchtime, and eventually she beat they. [3] The champion coach Pat Connolly recognized the young runner as a great talent when she saw Ashford race at the University of California at Los Angeles in 1976. [4] In 1983 and 1984, Ashford set records in the women's 100-meter dash, and her became the fastest woman in the world. [5] Our coach said that Ashford's speed—10.76 seconds for the 100-meter dash in 1984—amazed even he. [6] At the 1988 Olympic games, Ashford hoped that she could better her record time. [7] The other competitors knew that the runner to beat that year was her. [8] Ashford's talent, hard work,

and determination earned she a gold and a silver medal, but she set no new records at those games. **[9]** The athlete in the picture on the previous page is her running for the American team at the 1988 Olympics. **[10]** Don't you think she looks like a winner?

19e. An object of a preposition should be in the objective case.

A noun or pronoun (or a word group functioning as a noun) that follows a preposition is called the ***object of a preposition***. Together with any modifiers of the object, the preposition and its object make a ***prepositional phrase.***

EXAMPLES with **Joe**   before **her**   against **them**

above **him**   for **talking**   along with **you**
too much   and **me**

TIPS & TRICKS

An object of a preposition may be compound, as in the phrase *between you and me.* To help you determine the pronoun form to use in such a construction, try each form separately with the preposition.

CHOICES
Dwayne sat behind Norman and (*I, me*) at the jazz concert. [*Behind I or behind me?*]

ANSWER
Dwayne sat behind Norman and **me** at the jazz concert.

Reference Note

For more information about **prepositions,** see page 517. For more about **prepositional phrases,** see page 554.

Exercise 3 Choosing Pronouns Used as Objects of Prepositions

Choose the correct pronoun form in parentheses in each of the following sentences.

EXAMPLE   1. This letter is addressed to you and (*I, me*).

1. me

1. The chess team sent a challenge to Don and (*him, he*).
2. The two of (*we, us*) must discuss the schedule.
3. John went to the movie with Alice and (*them, they*).
4. I dedicated my poem to both Marcia and (*she, her*).
5. After Juanita and (*I, me*) come the twins.
6. The responsibility has fallen upon (*we, us*).
7. Were you sitting near Tony and (*she, her*)?
8. The matter is strictly between Ms. James and (*them, they*).
9. Consuelo has been asking about you and (*she, her*).
10. Will you draw a cartoon of (*we, us*) for me?
11. A fax from (*him, he*) just arrived.
12. Between you and (*I, me*), those hamburgers are the best I've ever had.
13. Did you make that coat for (*she, her*) or for yourself?
14. The hostess circulated among (*them, they*) and made introductions.
15. Don't you sit in front of Dave and (*him, he*) in chemistry?
16. Owners know that, at a show, dogs must stand quietly beside (*them, they*).
17. Everyone except Brandon and (*we, us*) had ridden on the subway.

USAGE

18. We aren't arguing against (*him, he*); we're arguing against his statements.
19. I've never met anyone like Rachel or (*she, her*) before.
20. Why does that macaw keep flying over and landing near Manny and (*I, me*)?

Review C **Choosing Correct Forms of Personal Pronouns**

For each of the following sentences, choose the correct pronoun form in parentheses. Then, tell how it is used in the sentence—as a *subject, predicate nominative, direct object, indirect object,* or *object of a preposition.*

EXAMPLE   1. Leave the pamphlets with Kim and (*he, him*).
          1. *him—object of a preposition*

1. The coach chose Darrell and (*he, him*).
2. Luckily, the Smiths and (*we, us*) got tickets to the concert.
3. I have not heard from Mark and (*she, her*) in ages.
4. It could be (*they, them*) across the street.
5. Ms. Grant, the Dodges, and (*she, her*) went to the Palos Verdes Peninsula for the day.
6. The mayor granted (*they, them*) an interview.
7. (*She, Her*) and Heather always sit in the last row.
8. Would you please stop bothering Simon and (*I, me*)?
9. Adele painted a picture for (*they, them*) and (*we, us*).
10. Jim Bob visited (*she, her*) and (*I, me*) in the hospital.

Review D **Proofreading a Paragraph for Correct Pronoun Usage**

Most of the sentences in the following paragraph contain errors in pronoun usage. Identify each error, and then give the correct pronoun form. If a sentence is already correct, write *C*.

EXAMPLE   [1] Mom showed Larry and I an old history book that she had found in the attic.
          1. *I—me*

[1] Looking through the book, Larry and me found the fascinating picture on the next page of four famous men. [2] Do you recognize any of they? [3] Of course, most of we are familiar with Thomas Edison and his inventions. [4] The man standing on the left is him. [5] Beside him on the old mill wheel are John Burroughs, Henry Ford, and Harvey Firestone. [6] Burroughs was an American naturalist and author; such

books as *Birds and Poets* and *Field and Study* were written by he. [7] Ford, as you probably know, gave us the Model T in 1908 and helped usher in the age of the automobile. [8] Standing next to he is Firestone, who was head of the world's largest rubber company. [9] It surprised Larry and I to see these four noted Americans together. [10] Wouldn't it have been great to meet and talk with they at the old mill?

Pictured above from left to right are Thomas Edison, John Burroughs, Henry Ford, and Harvey Firestone.

The Possessive Case

The personal pronouns in the possessive case—*my, mine, your, yours, his, her, hers, its, our, ours, their,* and *theirs*—are used to show ownership or possession.

19f. The possessive pronouns *mine, yours, his, hers, its, ours,* and *theirs* are used in the same ways that the pronouns in the nominative and objective cases are.

SUBJECT	**Mine** has a flat tire.
PREDICATE NOMINATIVE	This floppy disk is **hers.**
DIRECT OBJECT	We haven't received **ours** yet.
INDIRECT OBJECT	Do they give **theirs** a weekly allowance?
OBJECT OF PREPOSITION	My mother wants to talk to **yours.**

19g. The possessive pronouns *my, our, your, his, her, its,* and *their* are used to modify nouns and pronouns.

EXAMPLES   The subject of **my** report is the Inuit of Canada.

Her first novel was published in 1960.

Do you have **their** telephone number?

NOTE   In this book the words *my, our, your, his, her, its,* and *their* are called possessive pronouns. Some authorities prefer to call these words possessive adjectives because they are used to modify nouns. Follow your teacher's instructions when labeling these words.

19h. A noun or a pronoun preceding a gerund should be in the possessive case.

A *gerund* is a verb form that ends in –*ing* and functions as a noun. Since a gerund acts as a noun, the noun or pronoun that comes before it must be in the possessive case in order to modify the gerund.

EXAMPLES   John objected to his **sister's** using his new computer.
[*Sister's,* not *sister,* is used because John objected to the using, not to his sister.]

Their winning the Stanley Cup surprised us ice hockey fans.
[*Their,* instead of *them* or *they,* is used because the winning, not they, surprised us.]

NOTE   Do not confuse a gerund with a present participle, which also ends in –*ing*. A gerund serves as a noun, whereas a present participle serves as an adjective or as part of a verb phrase. A noun or a pronoun that is modified by a present participle does not need to be in the possessive case.

EXAMPLES   Suddenly, her Chihuahua started chasing a **boy** riding on a skateboard. [*Riding* is a participle that modifies the noun *boy.*]

All of the other children were impressed with the **boy's** riding. [*Riding* is a gerund modified by the possessive pronoun *boy's.*]

We heard **them** talking in the hallway. [*Talking* is a participle that modifies the pronoun *them.*]

Their talking in the hallway disturbed the class. [*Talking* is a gerund modified by the possessive pronoun *Their.*]

STYLE   TIP

The form of a noun or a pronoun before an –*ing* word often depends on the meaning you want to express. If you want to emphasize the –*ing* word, use the possessive form. If you want to emphasize the noun or pronoun preceding the –*ing* word, do not use the possessive form.

EXAMPLES
Can you imagine **my** singing? [emphasis on *singing*]

Can you imagine **me** singing? [emphasis on *me*]

Reference Note

For more about **gerunds,** see page 562. For more about **present participles,** see page 670.

Exercise 4 Using Possessive Pronouns

Complete each of the following sentences with an appropriate possessive pronoun.

EXAMPLE   1. _____ postponing the concert disappointed us fans.

         1. *Their*

1. I admire the work of Edmonia Lewis; _____ sculptures of famous people are outstanding.
2. His car looks great, but _____ is in better running condition.
3. Nathan is a dedicated student, but _____ winning the science contest was a surprise.
4. If you don't mind, I'd like to borrow _____.
5. _____ rescuing the kitten certainly was a humane act.
6. "Tell me about _____ rigging," the boat buyer asked the dealer.
7. "I hope _____ practicing drums isn't bothering you," I said.
8. "Thank you, _____ singing cheered us up," the residents of the hostel told the first-graders.
9. The skeptical executive asked, "Is this _____ recording?"
10. _____ playing the piano at such an early age astonished both her family and her teachers.

Special Pronoun Problems

Appositives

Reference Note

For more information about **appositives,** see page 567.

An ***appositive*** is a noun or a pronoun placed next to another noun or pronoun to identify or describe it.

19i. A pronoun used as an appositive should be in the same case as the word to which it refers.

EXAMPLES   Both teachers, Mr. Petrakis and **she,** have agreed to coach the academic team. [*Mr. Petrakis* and *she* identify the subject *teachers.* Since a subject of a verb is in the nominative case, an appositive identifying the subject is also in the nominative case.]

For two of the major roles in *Purlie Victorious,* the director chose us, Joel and **me.** [*Joel* and *me* identify the direct object *us.* Since the direct object is in the objective case, an appositive identifying *us* is also in the objective case.]

Exercise 5 **Selecting Pronouns to Use as Appositives**

For each of the following sentences, choose the correct pronoun form in parentheses.

EXAMPLE   1. Many of (*we, us*) seniors have part-time jobs.

1. *us*

1. On the first day of school, the bus driver greeted (*we, us*) students with a smile.
2. Owen said that, for the first time, the basketball team had elected co-captains, Mario and (*he, him*).
3. Two students, Angela and (*she, her*), toured the Frederick Douglass National Historic Site in Washington, D.C.
4. Should (*we, us*) members of the fitness club sponsor the next walk-a-thon?
5. The new mural in the cafeteria was painted by two seniors, Chad and (*he, him*).
6. The audience gave the comedians, Ken and (*she, her*), a standing ovation.
7. Mr. Webster awarded a special prize to his four best students, Tim and (*we, us*).
8. Who could have guessed that the winners would be our friends, Ms. Stein and (*he, him*)?
9. However, Grandma hadn't taught her two granddaughters, Lisa and (*I, me*), everything about candle making yet.
10. After the match, the reigning doubles champions remained the same team, Robin and (*I, me*).

Elliptical Constructions

An *elliptical construction* is a clause from which words have been omitted. The word *than* or *as* often begins an elliptical construction.

19j. A pronoun following *than* or *as* in an elliptical construction should be in the same case as it would be if the construction were completed.

ELLIPTICAL   The tenor sang louder **than he.**
COMPLETED   The tenor sang louder **than he sang.**

ELLIPTICAL   The accident hurt Tim as much **as her.**
COMPLETED   The accident hurt Tim as much **as the accident hurt her.**

┌HELP──

Sometimes the pronoun *we* or *us* is followed by a noun appositive. To determine which pronoun form to use, try each form without the noun appositive.

CHOICES
(*We, Us*) seniors are in charge of the paper drive. [*We are* or *Us are* in charge?]

ANSWER
We seniors are in charge of the paper drive.

CHOICES
Coach Klein talked to (*we, us*) players about sportsmanship. [*To we* or *to us*?]

ANSWER
Coach Klein talked to **us** players about sportsmanship.

USAGE

In an elliptical construction, the pronoun form determines the meaning of the construction. Therefore, you should be sure to use the pronoun form that expresses the meaning you intend. Notice how the meaning of each of the following sentences depends on the form of the pronoun in the elliptical construction.

EXAMPLES   I think I helped Macaulay more **than she.** [I think I helped Macaulay more *than she helped Macaulay.*]

               I think I helped Macaulay more **than her.** [I think I helped Macaulay more *than I helped her.*]

HELP

In several sentences in Exercise 6, either pronoun form may be correct, depending on how the elliptical clause is completed. In such cases, give both correct forms.

USAGE

Exercise 6   Selecting Pronouns for Elliptical Constructions

For each of the following sentences, add words to the elliptical clause to make its meaning clear. Include in the clause the correct pronoun form.

EXAMPLE   1. I don't know Brenda as well as (*she, her*).

       1. *as well as she knows Brenda*

               or

       as well as I know her

1. Have you and the rest of your family lived in this area as long as (*they, them*)?
2. Nolan has been working at that grocery store longer than (*he, him*).
3. I'm certain that Eva is shorter than (*I, me*) by at least four inches.
4. Surely they don't blame Taylor as much as (*we, us*).
5. The field trip next week will probably benefit Roger more than (*I, me*).
6. Can she really be six months older than (*I, me*)?
7. I understand him better than (*she, her*).
8. Do they play handball as often as (*we, us*)?
9. The results show that I do better on essay tests than (*he, him*).
10. Can Ms. Edwards tutor Paula as well as (*I, me*)?

Reflexive and Intensive Pronouns

Reflexive and intensive pronouns (sometimes called *compound personal pronouns*) have the same forms.

Reflexive and Intensive Pronouns

	Singular	Plural
First Person	myself	ourselves
Second Person	yourself	yourselves
Third Person	himself herself itself	themselves

A reflexive pronoun ends in *–self* or *–selves* and refers to the subject of the sentence or clause. A reflexive pronoun may serve as a direct object, an indirect object, an object of a preposition, or a predicate nominative.

DIRECT OBJECT	I can't believe I hurt **myself** laughing.
INDIRECT OBJECT	With part of the money from his first paycheck, Daniel bought **himself** a new CD.
OBJECT OF A PREPOSITION	Clarice and Sarah Jane should be proud of **themselves** for completing the project early.
PREDICATE NOMINATIVE	Sharon is not **herself** today.

An *intensive pronoun* emphasizes its antecedent and has no grammatical function in the sentence.

EXAMPLES   Simon **himself** developed both rolls of film. [*Himself* emphasizes *Simon.*]

Jorge and Kim installed the tape player **themselves.** [*Themselves* emphasizes *Jorge* and *Kim.*]

NOTE   The words *hisself, theirself,* and *theirselves* are nonstandard.

19k. A pronoun ending in *–self* or *–selves* should not be used in place of a personal pronoun.

Avoid using a pronoun ending in *–self* or *–selves* when there is no word that it can refer to or emphasize.

NONSTANDARD	Mariah and myself went to the rodeo.
STANDARD	Mariah and **I** went to the rodeo.

NONSTANDARD	I know I can depend on Katrina and yourself.
STANDARD	I know I can depend on Katrina and **you.**

TIPS & TRICKS

Unlike a reflexive pronoun, an intensive pronoun may be omitted from a sentence without significantly changing the sentence's meaning. To determine whether a pronoun is intensive or reflexive, try removing it from the sentence.

INTENSIVE
  Tamisha **herself** washed and waxed the car. [The sentence makes sense without the pronoun, so the pronoun is intensive.]

REFLEXIVE
  Tamisha washed and waxed the car by **herself.** [The sentence does not make sense without the pronoun, so the pronoun is reflexive.]

Do not be misled, however, by a reflexive pronoun used as an indirect object, which may be omitted from a sentence without a significant change in meaning.

EXAMPLE
  The children built **themselves** a treehouse. [The sentence still makes sense without the reflexive pronoun.]

USAGE

Reference Note

For more about **reflexive and intensive pronouns,** see page 644. For more about **hisself and theirselves,** see page 768.

Review E **Using Reflexive and Intensive Pronouns**

Complete each of the following sentences with an appropriate pronoun. Identify each pronoun you use as *reflexive* or *intensive*.

EXAMPLE   1. Diners at this restaurant serve _____ from a buffet.
          1. *themselves—reflexive*

1. Will the principal _____ preside at the academic awards ceremony?
2. After I ace the test, I will give _____ a pat on the back.
3. I bought _____ a Scottish kilt at the import store.
4. Mark and Ginger should be ashamed of _____ for forgetting your birthday.
5. Evelyn _____ raked the leaves in the front yard.
6. Probably, the person who was most surprised was Bill _____.
7. If you are hungry, you can fix _____ a sandwich.
8. "Can I do the experiment by _____ instead of with a partner?" she asked.
9. We promised that we would do all the carpentry work for the gazebo _____.
10. He remained true to _____ and his own values.

Who and Whom

Like most personal pronouns, the pronoun *who* (*whoever*) has three case forms.

Nominative	who	whoever
Objective	whom	whomever
Possessive	whose	whosever

Reference Note

For more information about **subordinate clauses,** see page 577.

These pronouns may be used to form questions and to introduce subordinate clauses.

NOTE   When *who, whom,* and *whose* are used to introduce adjective clauses, they are called **relative pronouns.**

In questions, *who* is used as a subject of a verb or as a predicate nominative. *Whom* is used as a direct object, an indirect object, or an object of a preposition.

NOMINATIVE	**Who** plays the part of Jack in the film *Titanic*? [*Who* is the subject of the verb *plays*.] **Who** could it be? [*Who* is a predicate nominative identifying the subject *it*.]
OBJECTIVE	**Whom** did Ella choose? [*Whom* is the direct object of the verb *did choose*.] With **whom** did Aaron Neville sing that ballad? [*Whom* is the object of the preposition *With*.] **Whom** did you ask the question? [*Whom* is the indirect object of the verb *did ask*.]

When choosing between *who* and *whom* in a subordinate clause, follow the steps shown in the following examples.

EXAMPLE	Nadine Gordimer, (*who, whom*) is famous for writing novels and short stories set in South Africa, won the Nobel Prize in literature in 1991.
STEP 1	Find the subordinate clause. In the sentence above, the subordinate clause is (*who, whom*) *is famous for writing novels and short stories set in South Africa.*
STEP 2	Decide how the pronoun is used in the clause—*subject, predicate nominative, direct object, indirect object,* or *object of a preposition.* In the example sentence, the pronoun serves as the subject of the verb *is.*
STEP 3	Determine the case for this use of the pronoun. A subject of a verb is in the nominative case.
STEP 4	Select the correct case form of the pronoun. The nominative form of the pronoun is *who.*
ANSWER	Nadine Gordimer, **who** is famous for writing novels and short stories set in South Africa, won the Nobel Prize in literature in 1991.

EXAMPLE	Harry Houdini, (*who, whom*) audiences adored, performed daring escape tricks.
STEP 1	The subordinate clause is (*who, whom*) *audiences adored.*
STEP 2	The pronoun serves as the direct object of the verb *adored.*
STEP 3	A direct object is in the objective case.
STEP 4	The objective form of the pronoun is *whom.*
ANSWER	Harry Houdini, **whom** audiences adored, performed daring escape tricks.

Remember that the case of a relative pronoun is not affected by any word outside the subordinate clause.

STYLE **TIP**

In informal situations, *who* is often used in place of *whom* to begin a question. In formal speaking and writing, however, the distinction between *who* and *whom* should be observed.

INFORMAL
Who did Jan call?

FORMAL
Whom did Jan call?
[direct object]

USAGE

TIPS & TRICKS

If you have trouble choosing between *who* and *whom* in a question, turn the question into a statement. What you end up with may not be a good sentence, but it may help you decide how the pronoun functions and which case form to use.

QUESTION
(*Who, Whom*) did Jan call?

STATEMENT
Jan did call (*who, whom*). [The pronoun is the direct object and should be in the objective case.]

CORRECT
Whom did Jan call?

EXAMPLE	A plaque will be given to (*whoever, whomever*) catches the most fish.
STEP 1	The subordinate clause is (*whoever, whomever*) *catches the most fish.*
STEP 2	The relative pronoun serves as the subject of the verb *catches,* not as the object of the preposition *to.* (The entire subordinate clause is the object of *to.*)
STEP 3	A subject of a verb is in the nominative case.
STEP 4	The nominative form of the relative pronoun is *whoever.*
ANSWER	A plaque will be given to **whoever** catches the most fish.

When choosing between *who* and *whom* to begin a question or a subordinate clause, do not be misled by an expression consisting of a subject and a verb, such as *I think, he feels,* or *they believe.* Select the pronoun form you would use if the expression were not in the sentence.

EXAMPLES   **Who** do you suppose will win the election? [*Who* is the subject of the clause *Who will win the election.*]

Roberta is the student **who** Mr. Hines thinks should be a chemist. [*Who* is the subject of the clause *who should be a chemist.*]

Exercise 7   Using *Who* and *Whom* Correctly

For each of the following sentences, choose the correct pronoun from the pair in parentheses. Then, tell how it is used in the subordinate clause—as a *subject, predicate nominative, direct object, indirect object,* or *object of a preposition.*

EXAMPLE   1. Can you tell me (*who, whom*) wrote *Bury My Heart at Wounded Knee?*

     1. *who—subject*

1. The two people (*who, whom*) I like most are Will and Rosa.
2. Someone called, but I don't know (*who, whom*) she was.
3. Be sure to talk to (*whoever, whomever*) she interviewed.
4. Several of the women (*who, whom*) had served on other committees were considered for the position.
5. I can't remember (*who, whom*) I asked that question.
6. Allen is the only person in school (*who, whom*) I think deserves the honor.

USAGE

7. I never found out (*who, whom*) the driver was.
8. Was he the person to (*who, whom*) this package belongs?
9. It does not matter (*who, whom*) wins, as long as you do your best.
10. Ralph Bunche was a man (*who, whom*) many people respected for helping to found the United Nations.

Review F Proofreading a Paragraph for Correct Pronoun Usage

Each sentence in the following paragraph contains an error in pronoun usage. Identify each error, and then give the pronoun form that is correct according to the rules of formal standard usage.

EXAMPLE   **[1]** Satoshi Yabuuchi is the artist whom created the sculptures shown below.

    1. whom—who

[1] Satoshi Yabuuchi is a modern Japanese sculptor whom works with wood. [2] Critics generally agree that few sculptors today are as inventive as him. [3] For example, look at some works by he, which are on this page. [4] Them are figures of children's heads representing the seven days of the week. [5] Working with simple tools, Yabuuchi created they out of cypress. [6] Whom do you think could resist these engaging faces? [7] As you can see, Yabuuchi's imagination and sense of humor are important to himself. [8] Other modern Japanese wood sculptors and him use techniques that date back more than 1,500 years. [9] Yabuuchi, whom was born in 1953, first studied European art but then became interested in wood carving and sculpture. [10] A number of works by himself also incorporate elements of American pop art.

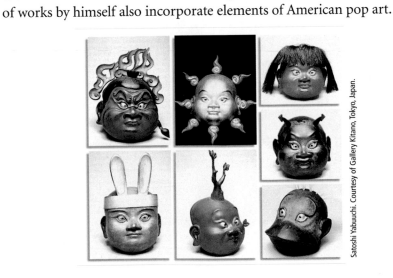

Satoshi Yabuuchi. Courtesy of Gallery Kitano, Tokyo, Japan.

Proofreading Sentences for Correct Pronoun Usage

Each of the following sentences contains an error in pronoun usage. Identify the error, and then give the pronoun form that is correct according to the rules of formal, standard usage.

EXAMPLE   1. Do you know whom won the women's 100-meter dash at the 2000 summer Olympic games?

      1. *whom—who*

1. "We sprinters are better than the ones on Central High's team," Phillip said, "so why aren't we doing better than them?"
2. Oscar, whom I believe is the most adventurous member of our family, is backpacking in the Appalachians.
3. Do you know who they gave the blue ribbon?
4. When Anna and I were young, us children loved to ride on the tractor with my father.
5. John and myself wish we could excel in both baseball and football, as Deion Sanders does.
6. Who did the teacher choose to give the first speech?
7. When Andrew and I study together, nobody else in our class does better than us.
8. Kyle was here looking for Josh and yourself.
9. When we heard that Ms. Cohen was going to retire, all three of we seniors felt sad.
10. The two people who you can always rely on are Dave and she.

STYLE   TIP

Do not make the mistake of trying to sound formal by using *whom* in all cases. In formal speech and writing, determine the function of the pronoun and use the correct form—*who* for nominative case, *whom* for objective case.

"Whom shall I say is calling, sir?"

Chapter Review

A. Selecting Correct Forms of Pronouns

For each of the following sentences, choose the correct pronoun form in parentheses.

1. Greg and (*I, myself*) both got our driver's licenses on the same day.
2. My uncle Bill, after (*who, whom*) I am named, worked in the Peace Corps for two years after he had finished college.
3. As we waited at the starting line, I knew in my heart that the race was really going to be between Ted and (*I, me*).
4. At the town meeting, Ellen McCarthy asked, "If (*we, us*) citizens don't vote, how can we expect the situation to change?"
5. I thought Manuel was in Kansas City; so when he walked into the restaurant, I could hardly believe it was (*he, him*).
6. "Does anyone dance better than (*she, her*)?" I wondered, as I watched the dancer on the stage.
7. (*Who, Whom*) can describe the different shapes of the Navajo hogans?
8. The patrol officer told her and (*I, me*) that the road was closed.
9. The coach watched (*me, my*) running and decided to tap me for the marathon team.
10. Although the tenor was handsome and funny, what the crowd appreciated most was (*him, his*) singing.

B. Proofreading Sentences for Correct Pronoun Forms

For each of the following sentences that contains an incorrect pronoun form, identify the error and then give the correct form. If a sentence is already correct, write *C*.

11. Losing the playoff game was an experience from which you and him have learned a valuable lesson.
12. Whom do you think made this mistake?
13. We knew about his giving her a birthday present.
14. I would like to know who you are voting for in the next election.

USAGE

15. They watched her and I playing a game of tennis.

16. Nobody remembered to bring paper plates except him and her.

17. The reporter asked him and I to meet her at the Riverside Restaurant.

18. Dolores is one person whom I am sure will be successful.

19. The prize will be awarded to whomever sells the most subscriptions.

20. Do you think I can play center on the basketball team even though I am shorter than him?

21. That is a matter about which you and her do not agree.

22. They respected Cornelius and I.

23. I had never met Gina and she before.

24. Sally and myself are planning to attend the weekend conference.

25. Was it Mr. Ross who they chose as their leader?

26. No one has worked harder than she.

27. Whom did you think it was on the phone?

28. We asked that Kara and him speak at the assembly.

29. No one knew who the woman in the mask could be.

30. I have already written to two of the women, she and Eva Dawson.

C. Proofreading a Paragraph for Correct Pronoun Usage

Most of the sentences in the following paragraph contain an error in pronoun usage. Identify each error, and then give the correct pronoun form. If a sentence is already correct, write *C*.

[31] Jim Henson's gifts to all of we puppet fans were some of the most beloved characters in show business—Kermit the Frog, Miss Piggy, and the Cookie Monster, to name a few. [32] You probably know that Henson was the puppeteer who created the Muppets. [33] In the history of television, few puppeteers have been as successful as him. [34] Henson's associate Frank Oz and himself operated many of the Muppets. [35] Whom do you think spoke for Kermit on *Sesame Street* and *The Muppet Show* and in such movies as *The Muppets Take Manhattan*? [36] As you may have guessed, us Kermit fans were listening to Henson's voice. [37] Kermit and him started performing together in 1956 when Henson introduced his frog to the audience

of the late-night TV show *Sam and Friends* in Washington, D.C.
[**38**] Henson, whom originally fashioned Kermit out of an old coat
and a split Ping-Pong ball, revolutionized puppetry. [**39**] Henson's ability to give each of his puppets a life of its own earned himself
international renown and many awards. [**40**] When Henson died in
1990, people throughout the world mourned his passing.

Writing Application
Using Pronouns in a Newspaper Article

Pronouns with Gerunds and Participles   Exam week is
approaching fast, and soon everyone will be busy studying for finals.
To help students cope with test anxiety, the editor of your school's
newspaper has decided to devote an entire issue to that subject. Write
an article to submit for publication in the paper. In your article, present some helpful tips for students studying for exams. Your article
may be humorous or serious. Use at least two pronouns preceding
gerunds and three pronouns preceding participles. Be sure to check
your writing for correct pronoun usage.

Prewriting   Brainstorm a list of strategies that have helped you
stay calm and collected through exams. If you wish, poll a number of
other students about their "survival" strategies. From your notes,
choose several of the most practical suggestions. Be sure to organize
your information in a rough outline.

Writing   Refer to your prewriting notes and outline as you write
your first draft. Begin with a lively, attention-grabbing opener.
Remember: You want to inform as well as to entertain the reader.

Revising   Ask a friend or classmate to read your article. Is it helpful
and interesting? Does it address the concerns of students preparing for
exams? If not, add, cut, and revise details. Be sure you have used at
least two gerunds and three participles preceded by pronouns.

Publishing   Read through your article once, checking for errors in
pronoun usage. Then, proofread for other errors in grammar, usage,
punctuation, and spelling. To publish your articles, you and your classmates may want to create a bulletin board display for your classroom
or for another area in your school.

20 Clear Reference
Pronouns and Antecedents

Diagnostic Preview

A. Correcting Faulty Pronoun References

Each of the following sentences contains at least one ambiguous, general, weak, or indefinite pronoun reference. Revise the sentences to correct each faulty pronoun reference.

EXAMPLE   **1.** On this train, they served meals without charge.

      1. *On this train, meals were served without charge.*

      or

      On this train, meals were included in the ticket price.

1. Golf wouldn't cost me quite so much if I didn't lose so many in the rough.

2. The radiator was leaking badly; it ran all over the garage floor.

3. In the log cabin, Ed checked the fuel supply; in those days this might mean the difference between life and death.

4. She overcame her hip injury, which doctors had said was nearly impossible.

5. Her spelling and sentence variety are not good, but most of it is due to carelessness.

6. Ruth saw Julie when she was in town last week.

7. In yesterday's editorial, it says that the mayor has failed to live up to his campaign promises.

8. The witness testified that she had seen the accused when she was eating dinner in the dining car, which convinced the jury that she had been on the train.

─ H E L P ─

Although some sentences in Part A may be correctly revised in more than one way, you need to give only one revision for each.

9. In Washington they are skeptical about the success of the new federal farm program.

10. The library does not have enough of the books in greatest demand by students writing research papers, which makes it difficult to find the information you need.

B. Revising Sentences to Correct Faulty Pronoun References

Revise the following sentences to correct each ambiguous, general, weak, or indefinite pronoun reference.

EXAMPLE **1.** I enjoy reading science fiction; the one I am reading now, *Contact,* was written by Carl Sagan.

1. *I enjoy reading science fiction; the novel I am reading now,* Contact, *was written by Carl Sagan.*

or

I enjoy reading science fiction novels such as the one I am reading now, Contact. *It was written by Carl Sagan.*

11. The scientist Carl Sagan wrote and lectured extensively about the possibility of life on other planets, which contributed to his appeal to the general public.

12. Johnny Carson liked Sagan's informal science lectures so much that he appeared many times on *The Tonight Show* after his first appearance in 1972.

13. Sagan came to be known around the world as an expert in the study of extraterrestrial life, even though he had never seen one.

14. In Daniel Cohen's book *Carl Sagan: Superstar Scientist,* it tells about Sagan's childhood in Brooklyn and about his early fascination with the stars and planets.

15. As a boy, Sagan discovered the genre of science fiction, and he read them regularly.

16. At the University of Chicago, they had a highly regarded astronomy department, so Sagan enrolled there in 1951.

17. Sagan served as a consultant for many of NASA's major programs, including the *Mariner, Viking,* and *Voyager* planetary expeditions; this resulted in such awards as the NASA Medal for Distinguished Public Service and the NASA Medal for Exceptional Scientific Achievement.

18. When my father saw Sagan on the popular television series *Cosmos,* he was greatly impressed.

HELP

Although some sentences in Part B may be correctly revised in more than one way, you need to give only one revision for each.

USAGE

19. Sagan's novel *Contact* explores a number of scientific and social issues that arise when extraterrestrial life makes contact with earthlings; of course, this made me want to read some of his nonfiction books.
20. Carl Sagan died on December 20, 1996, and it was six months before the movie version of *Contact* was released.

Pronouns and Their Antecedents

One cause of ambiguity in writing is the use of pronouns without clear antecedents. A pronoun generally has no definite meaning in itself. Its meaning is clear only when the reader knows to which word or word group the pronoun refers. This word or word group is called the *antecedent* of the pronoun.

20a. A pronoun should refer clearly to its antecedent.

In the following examples, arrows point from the pronouns to their antecedents.

EXAMPLES   Steven wanted to visit the Museum of Modern Art, but **it** had closed for the day.

Amy promised Jim **she** would help **him** clean the kitchen.

The Sanchezes have a new sailboat on **which they** intend to cruise to the Bahamas.

Handing Shina the novel, the librarian told **her,** "**This** won the Pulitzer Prize."

Often, a pronoun reference is unclear due to a lack of agreement between a pronoun and its antecedent.

UNCLEAR   Eli is always thinking about computers. It seems to be his only interest.

CLEAR   Eli is always thinking about computers. **They** seem to be his only interest.

UNCLEAR   You should learn how to use several different Internet search engines. It can make research much easier.

CLEAR   You should learn how to use several different Internet search engines. **They** can make research much easier.

Reference Note

For more information about **pronouns and antecedents,** see page 501.

Reference Note

For more about **agreement between pronouns and their antecedents,** see page 618.

USAGE

Ambiguous Reference

20b. Avoid an *ambiguous reference,* which occurs when any one of two or more words could be a pronoun's antecedent.

A simple way to correct some ambiguous pronoun references is to replace the pronoun with an appropriate noun.

AMBIGUOUS   The partnership between Jones and Potter ended when he withdrew the firm's money from the bank and flew to Brazil. [To whom does *he* refer: *Jones* or *Potter*?]

CLEAR   The partnership between Jones and Potter ended when **Jones** withdrew the firm's money from the bank and flew to Brazil.

CLEAR   The partnership between Jones and Potter ended when **Potter** withdrew the firm's money from the bank and flew to Brazil.

If replacing the pronoun with a noun results in awkward repetition, rephrase the sentence to eliminate the ambiguous pronoun reference.

AMBIGUOUS   The mayor appointed Ms. Vásquez chairperson of the committee because she was convinced of the need for an environmental study. [To whom does *she* refer: *mayor* or *Ms. Vásquez*?]

CLEAR   Convinced of the need for an environmental study, the mayor appointed Ms. Vásquez chairperson of the committee.

CLEAR   Because Ms. Vásquez was convinced of the need for an environmental study, the mayor appointed her chairperson of the committee.

Exercise 1   Correcting Ambiguous Pronoun References

Revise each of the following sentences to correct the ambiguous pronoun reference.

EXAMPLE   1. As soon as Lucinda arrived with Gwen, we asked her to tell us about the trip to the Yukon.

1. *As soon as Lucinda arrived with Gwen, we asked Lucinda to tell us about the trip to the Yukon.*

or

As soon as Lucinda arrived with Gwen, we asked Gwen to tell us about the trip to the Yukon.

┌─HELP─

Although some sentences in Exercise 1 may be correctly revised in more than one way, you need to give only one revision for each.

1. Dad dropped Tom off, and then he went to class.
2. One of the passengers told the bus driver that she didn't know the route very well.
3. Right after the accountant sent in a report to the treasurer, he became very much alarmed.
4. After the sergeant reported to the lieutenant, he informed the captain of the situation.
5. We separated the jars from the bottles and washed them.
6. This lever controls the conveyor belt; it's broken, and I want you to get it fixed.
7. Leta offered Molly a bowl of plantain porridge, which she thoroughly enjoyed.
8. That cord shouldn't be tangled around the leg of a chair where people can trip and break it and hurt themselves.
9. While the musicians were talking to some of the dancers, they were called onstage.
10. Set the first reel next to the second one and make sure its case isn't cracked.

General Reference

20c. Avoid a *general reference,* which is the use of a pronoun that refers to a general idea rather than to a specific antecedent.

The pronouns that are most commonly used in general references are *it, that, this,* and *which.* To correct a general pronoun reference, either replace the pronoun with an appropriate noun or rephrase the sentence.

GENERAL   Great ships were moving slowly up the harbor; tugs and ferryboats scurried in and out among them; here and there a white cabin cruiser sliced through the blue water under the suspension bridge. It was thrilling to a young farmer. [*It* has no specific antecedent.]

CLEAR   Great ships were moving slowly up the harbor; tugs and ferryboats scurried in and out among them; here and there a white cabin cruiser sliced through the blue water under the suspension bridge. **The sight** was thrilling to a young farmer.

GENERAL   In her act Mariana told jokes, did impersonations, and sang comic songs. This amused her audience. [*This* has no specific antecedent.]

CLEAR   Mariana **amused her audience by** telling jokes, doing impersonations, and singing comic songs.

GENERAL	More than half of the elm trees along the street had to be cut down, which was unfortunate. [*Which* has no specific antecedent.]
CLEAR	That more than half of the elm trees along the street had to be cut down was unfortunate.
CLEAR	Unfortunately, more than half of the elm trees along the street had to be cut down.

Exercise 2 Revising Sentences to Correct General Pronoun References

Revise the following sentences to correct each general pronoun reference.

EXAMPLE
1. Carla was declared the winner of the debate, which didn't surprise me.

1. *That Carla was declared the winner of the debate didn't surprise me.*

or

The debate, which Carla won, didn't surprise me.

1. In the 1800s, Spanish-language newspapers sprang up throughout the Southwest. This helped many Mexican Americans maintain ties to their culture.
2. Clarissa's four-year-old sister brought a frog inside and let it loose, which made Clarissa shriek.
3. I enjoyed the author's style and the types of characters she wrote about. It made me want to read her other books.
4. Rabbi Meyer came to the house daily, from which a sturdy friendship grew.
5. A great deal of effort went into planning that expedition, hiring the right people, and anticipating every emergency, which accounts for the success of the undertaking.
6. Much songbird habitat in North America is rapidly being destroyed, and this greatly concerns ornithologists.
7. The children were asleep, all the chores were done, and the house was clean. It was almost shocking to the young parents.
8. Complex operations can be performed with a single click. Please remember that when you program your trackball buttons.
9. A sailboat with a tall mast was moving toward the bridge. That caused the bridge to open and traffic to stop.
10. Last night in the mountains, it started to snow heavily. This made a lot of skiers, including me, quite happy.

USAGE

┌HELP────
Although some sentences in Exercise 2 may be correctly revised in more than one way, you need to give only one revision for each.

┌HELP───

Some sentences
in Review A may be revised
in more than one way. You
may find it helpful to read
all of the sentences before
you begin to revise them.
Context may make it easier
to identify the antecedents
for some of the pronouns.

Review A **Correcting Ambiguous and General Pronoun References**

Revise the following sentences to correct all ambiguous and general pronoun references.

EXAMPLE   1. After Maximilian was defeated by Juárez in 1867, he was reelected president of Mexico.

1. After Maximilian was defeated by Juárez in 1867, Juárez was reelected president of Mexico.

1. Benito Pablo Juárez was a liberal reformer and president of Mexico during the 1860s and early 1870s, and he helped mold Mexico into a nation. That established Juárez as Mexico's foremost national hero.

2. Juárez, of Zapotec ancestry, was a serious, hard-working man, which is suggested in this photograph.

3. A professor who obviously had researched Juárez's life described his childhood in Oaxaca, his interest in law and social reforms, and his military successes. This kept the students' attention.

4. One of the students told the professor that he hoped he would write a biography of Juárez someday.

5. Juárez, a state governor in 1855, and General Santa Anna were on opposing sides, and he was exiled.

6. Juárez later returned to Mexico and joined the revolution to overthrow Santa Anna, who had seized control of the government. It was a brave and risky endeavor.

7. France installed Maximilian as emperor of Mexico in 1864, and Juárez moved his capital from Mexico City, but he was not popular.

8. Maximilian's government collapsed in 1867, which opened the way for Juárez to be reelected president.

9. Juárez was interested in education and helped to establish free public schools in Mexico. This, of course, had a major impact on Mexico's people.

10. José de la Cruz Porfirio Díaz overthrew Juárez's successor and governed Mexico longer than any other person. It was certainly a contrast to Juárez's government.

Weak Reference

20d. Avoid a *weak reference,* which occurs when a pronoun refers to an antecedent that has been suggested but not expressed.

To correct a weak pronoun reference, either replace the pronoun with an appropriate noun or give the pronoun a clear antecedent.

WEAK   The people want honest public servants, but many voters think that is not a virtue of any of the candidates. [The antecedent of *that* is not expressed.]

CLEAR   The people want honest public servants, but many voters think that **honesty** is not a virtue of any of the candidates.

WEAK   We spent the entire day on a fishing boat, but we didn't catch a single one. [The antecedent of *one* is not expressed.]

CLEAR   We spent the entire day on a fishing boat, but we didn't catch a single **fish.**

CLEAR   We spent the entire day on a fishing boat, trying to catch **some fish,** but we didn't catch a single **one.**

USAGE

Exercise 3 Revising Sentences to Correct Weak Pronoun References

Revise each of the following sentences to correct the weak pronoun reference.

EXAMPLE   1. We went to the card shop but did not buy any.

        1. *We went to the card shop but did not buy any cards.*

                    or

        We went shopping for cards but did not buy any.

┌HELP──

Although some sentences in Exercise 3 may be correctly revised in more than one way, you need to give only one revision for each.

1. I take many photographs with my camera and consider it an enjoyable hobby.
2. Being neighborly is important because you may need their help someday in an emergency.
3. Nguyen has become a virtuoso violinist, but he has never owned a valuable one.
4. Luis is highly intelligent, but he hides it from people he doesn't know well.
5. Our guide said the Pueblo village was well worth seeing, but it would take three hours.
6. Evan wanted to be like the public speakers who seem so relaxed, but he rarely got the chance to do any.

7. The sisters traveled to their family's ancestral land, hoping to meet some.

8. Even though the roommates spent two-and-a-half hours at the laundry room, they didn't finish it all.

9. I'd love antique collecting, but I can't afford them.

10. Prospective students must fill out a college admission form if they want to get into one.

Indefinite Reference

20e. Avoid an *indefinite reference*—the use of a pronoun that refers to no particular person or thing and that is unnecessary to the structure and meaning of a sentence.

The pronouns that commonly cause indefinite references are *you*, *it*, and *they*. To correct an indefinite reference, rephrase the sentence, eliminating the unnecessary pronoun.

INDEFINITE   In some countries, you do not dare express your political views openly. [*You* and *your* do not refer to any specific person.]

CLEAR   In some countries, **people** do not dare express **their** political views openly.

INDEFINITE   In the magazine article, it describes the aftermath of the eruption of Mount Pinatubo. [*It* does not refer to any specific thing.]

CLEAR   **The magazine article describes** the aftermath of the eruption of Mount Pinatubo.

INDEFINITE   Each summer in Cherokee, North Carolina, they present the historical drama *Unto These Hills* outdoors. [*They* does not clearly refer to any specific group.]

CLEAR   Each summer in Cherokee, North Carolina, **the historical drama *Unto These Hills* is presented** outdoors.

Exercise 4   Revising Sentences to Correct Indefinite Pronoun References

Revise each of the following sentences to correct the indefinite pronoun references.

EXAMPLE   1. In the newsmagazine, it profiles each of the presidential candidates.

       1. *The newsmagazine profiles each of the presidential candidates.*

STYLE TIP

The indefinite use of *it* in familiar expressions such as *it is raining, it seems,* and *it is late* is acceptable.

COMPUTER TIP

You can use a word processor's search function to locate all occurrences of the pronoun *it* in a piece of your writing. Every time the pronoun appears, check its reference carefully. Is the reference clear, or is it general or indefinite? You can use the same procedure to check your use of the pronouns *this, that, which, such, they,* and *you.*

1. In many households in India, they serve a flat, pancakelike bread called a *chapati*.
2. In large cities you often don't feel comfortable calling the mayor about problems.
3. In the newspaper article, it calls this presidential election the closest race in many years.
4. Each summer in Round Top, Texas, they have an international music festival that is extremely popular.
5. In the telephone book, it lists only five music stores in the city.
6. Underneath the headline, it read, "Related story on page 12."
7. Only about six feet from shore, it drops off about twenty feet.
8. During much of the colonial period in New England, you were supposed to obey strict regulations governing Sabbath activities.
9. After the age of ten, you just don't do certain things.
10. Throughout the book, it uses expressions unique to Maine.

DRABBLE reprinted by permission of
United Feature Syndicate, Inc.

┌─HELP───
Although some
sentences in Review B
may be correctly revised
in more than one way,
you need to give only
one revision for each.

| Link to  Literature |

Review B **Revising Sentences to Correct Weak and Indefinite Pronoun References**

Revise the following sentences to correct weak pronoun references and indefinite pronoun references.

EXAMPLE   1. Many writers create fictional stories about overcoming great odds, but I prefer it when they are real people.

1. *Many writers create fictional stories about overcoming great odds, but I prefer stories about real people.*

1. The Irish author Christy Brown (1932–1981) was extremely talented, but he had to overcome great physical challenges for it to be recognized.
2. In Brown's autobiography, *My Left Foot,* it tells about his lifelong struggle with a debilitating illness.
3. In some biographies, you don't become emotionally involved, but Brown's autobiography is very personal.
4. Brown had a disorder they call cerebral palsy, which is a type of brain damage leading to lack of muscle control.
5. In most cases of cerebral palsy, you cannot determine the cause of the damage, which occurs before or shortly after birth.
6. In the book, they explain how Brown learned to write and type with his only functioning limb—his left foot.
7. Brown married in 1972, and her help contributed to Brown's improved muscular control.
8. Brown excelled as a writer, but locating them in libraries and bookstores in the United States is sometimes difficult.
9. Brown was acclaimed as a poet as well as a novelist, but many people have never read one.
10. In the card catalog it lists these books by Brown: *My Left Foot, Down All the Days, A Shadow on Summer,* and *Wild Grow the Lilies.*

Chapter Review

A. Correcting Ambiguous and General References

Most of the following sentences contain ambiguous or general references. Revise each faulty sentence. If a sentence is already correct, write *C*.

1. Margaret e-mailed Gretchen about the interesting Web pages she had seen at the Web site of the British Broadcasting Corporation (BBC).

2. The BBC had asked two British writers, Malcolm Bradbury and J. G. Ballard, each to name the ten greatest writers of the last one thousand years, which resulted in the Web page that Margaret saw.

3. Gretchen read Bradbury's list; she found it surprising.

4. Bradbury's number-one writer, for example, was not Shakespeare, but Dante, which Gretchen did not expect.

5. Ballard also had Shakespeare on his list, where he was number one.

6. Only Shakespeare and Miguel Cervantes, the author of *Don Quixote*, were on both lists, which also surprised Gretchen.

7. While Cervantes is on both lists, Gretchen noticed that Ballard ranked him higher than Bradbury did.

8. Malcolm Bradbury provides more commentary with his list than J. G. Ballard does, perhaps because he is an English professor.

9. Ballard mentions four twentieth-century writers, Franz Kafka, Joseph Heller, George Orwell, and Aldous Huxley, which is different from Bradbury, who mentions only one, James Joyce.

10. "Jane Austen is the only woman on either list," Margaret wrote to Gretchen, "and she appeared only on Bradbury's list."

B. Correcting Weak and Indefinite References

Most of the following sentences contain weak and indefinite pronoun references. Revise each faulty sentence. If a sentence is already correct, write *C*.

11. In San Antonio they have the Alamodome, one of the largest domed stadiums in the world.

12. Keith finds bird-watching most exciting when he actually sees one.

13. I spent several hours at the library, but I didn't bring any home.

14. Aunt Dee enjoys reading the works of Raymond Chandler, who is a mystery novelist.

15. I decided to request information on how you become a member of the Peace Corps.

16. How many meteors did you see last night? Wasn't it spectacular?

17. In the documentary on television last night, they told the story of Lewis and Clark's expedition.

18. My father taught at a small college in Michigan for twenty-five years, and it was the best job he ever had.

19. We have been listening to a collection of English poetry on tape, but I haven't decided yet which one is my favorite.

20. Ileana has read so much it is hard for her to remember them all.

C. Revising Sentences to Correct Faulty Pronoun References

Revise the following sentences to correct ambiguous, general, weak, and indefinite pronoun references.

21. Dana is afraid of large dogs, but she doesn't let it show.

22. In Washington, D.C., they have a subway system that is modern and efficient.

23. James saw Michael Jordan play basketball when he was ten years old.

24. My cousins showed a video and several photos of their travels in Puerto Rico, which made me want to go there.

25. Beth wanted Laura to see the movie because she is a fan of Lou Diamond Phillips.

D. Revising Sentences to Correct Faulty Pronoun References

Revise the following sentences to correct ambiguous, general, weak, and indefinite pronoun references.

26. In the city library, they have a videotape about Martha Washington's early life and first marriage to a wealthy Virginia planter.

27. After Aaron Burr played matchmaker for Dolley Payne Todd and James Madison, he married Dolley.

28. Abigail Adams is the only woman who was the wife of one president and mother of another, which is an interesting bit of First Lady trivia.

29. Julia Tyler supported her husband John Tyler's causes, especially the annexation of Texas, and that gave him strength.

30. In one book I read, it says that people accused Mary Todd Lincoln, who was from Kentucky, of opposing the Union, but she actually was a strong Unionist.

Writing Application

Using Pronouns Correctly in a Letter

Clear Pronoun Reference   A famous Hollywood producer wants to make British literature more accessible to high school students. As a result, he is sponsoring a "Be a Movie Director" contest. To enter, you have to write a letter explaining your idea for a movie version of a story, poem, or play that you have read in English class. Tell which actors you would cast in your movie and what music you would want for the soundtrack. Include at least ten pronouns in your sentences. Be sure that every pronoun has a clear antecedent.

Prewriting   Start by choosing the work for which you want to create a movie. Then, list some ideas for three or four scenes in your movie. Next to each scene idea, list the actors you would use in that scene and describe the action.

Writing   As you write, make the sequence of events clear. Make the spatial relationships clear, too, telling where the cast members should be located in each scene. Remember that the producer will need to have a clear picture of what you want, and you have only words with which to paint that picture for him. Be sure to use the proper form for a business letter.

Revising   Check your rough draft to be sure that your explanation is clear. Have a classmate read your letter, looking for unclear uses of the pronouns *it, this, that,* and *which.* Revise any unclear references.

Publishing   Proofread your letter for any errors in grammar, usage, and mechanics. Collect the letters written by the other members of your class, and make a chart showing which works would be made into movies, who the cast members would be, and what music would be included.

Reference Note
For more about **writing business letters,** see "Writing" in the Quick Reference Handbook.

Using Verbs Correctly

Principal Parts, Tense, Voice, Mood

Diagnostic Preview

A. Proofreading Sentences for Verb Usage

Reference Note

For more about **formal, standard English,** see page 756.

Most of the following sentences contain awkward, informal, or incorrect verb usage. If a sentence has an awkward, informal, or incorrect usage, revise the sentence, using the verb form that is correct according to the rules of formal, standard English. If a sentence is already correct, write *C*.

EXAMPLE 1. Oh no, I think I have broke my watch.
           1. *Oh no, I think I have broken my watch.*

1. They were setting on the bench and feeding the ducks.
2. She brung her brother when she came over to visit our family last Saturday evening.
3. When we saw the group perform, Julia, the lead vocalist, just broke her contract with a big recording company.
4. Mrs. Ames was pleased that when the driver's test was taken by her son, he passed easily.
5. The shoppers laid down their purchases carefully.
6. We cheered when the movie finally begun.

7. If we had the chance, we would have stopped by your house before we went to the concert.

8. They hoped to interview the astronauts.

9. On vacation they plan to have gone deep-sea fishing.

10. Yesterday I swum in the Millers' new pool.

11. The rate of inflation has raised steadily.

12. When they returned to the scene, they discovered that the weapon was taken.

13. When I enter college, my parents will be married thirty years.

14. We would have preferred to have eaten Chinese food.

15. If I was Anne, I would ask for a promotion and a raise.

B. Proofreading for Correct Verb Usage

Most of the sentences in the following paragraph contain awkward, informal, or incorrect verb usage. Revise the sentences, using appropriate verb forms. If a sentence is already correct, write *C*.

EXAMPLE **[1]** How to use an abacus to do arithmetic problems was shown to my classmates and me by our second-grade teacher, Ms. Atchison.

1. *Our second-grade teacher, Ms. Atchison, showed my classmates and me how to use an abacus to solve arithmetic problems.*

[16] When you were a child, you might have played with an abacus as though it was a toy. [17] A teacher may have told you that the abacus was a device for counting—for adding and subtracting. [18] If you would have spent the time, you might have learned to calculate on this simple device. [19] An abacus consists of a series of bars on which beads have slid. [20] Because the abacus has been widely used for hundreds of years, many forms have been taken by it. [21] For example, on a Chinese abacus you move beads toward a crossbar to add a sum, while other types of abacuses did not even have crossbars. [22] Mastering the appropriate technique, operators calculate quickly and accurately. [23] In fact, on any number of occasions, people using abacuses have beated people using calculators in speed trials. [24] Consequently, an abacus sits beside many tradespeople all over Asia, just as it has did for centuries. [25] A century from now, the abacus will probably have remained practical, rugged, portable, fast, accurate, and comparatively inexpensive.

Reference Note
Depending on how they are used, verbs may be classified as **transitive verbs** or **intransitive verbs,** as **action verbs** or **linking verbs,** and as **main verbs** or **helping verbs.** For a discussion of these different kinds of verbs, see page 509.

HELP

The words *is* and *have* are included in some charts in this chapter because the present participle and the past participle forms require helping verbs (forms of *be* and *have*) to form tenses.

TIPS & TRICKS

Sometimes the helping verb is not obvious. It may appear as part of a contraction.

EXAMPLES

He**'s** buying a new hat.

We**'ve** already finished.

Pay close attention to contractions so that you can be certain you are using the appropriate verb forms.

The Principal Parts of a Verb

21a. The *principal parts* of a verb are the *base form*, the *present participle*, the *past*, and the *past participle*. All other verb forms are derived from these principal parts.

Base Form	Present Participle	Past	Past Participle
live	[is] living	lived	[have] lived
talk	[is] talking	talked	[have] talked
run	[is] running	ran	[have] run
rise	[is] rising	rose	[have] risen
hit	[is] hitting	hit	[have] hit

All verbs form the present participle in the same way: by adding *–ing* to the base form. Not all verbs form the past and past participle in the same way, however. The way in which a verb forms its past and past participle determines whether the verb is classified as *regular* or *irregular*.

NOTE Some teachers refer to the base form as the *infinitive*. Follow your teacher's directions in labeling this verb form.

Regular Verbs

21b. A *regular verb* forms its past and past participle by adding *–d* or *–ed* to its base form.

Base Form	Present Participle	Past	Past Participle
care	[is] caring	cared	[have] cared
remove	[is] removing	removed	[have] removed
fix	[is] fixing	fixed	[have] fixed
suppose	[is] supposing	supposed	[have] supposed
match	[is] matching	matched	[have] matched
offer	[is] offering	offered	[have] offered
stay	[is] staying	stayed	[have] stayed
push	[is] pushing	pushed	[have] pushed

Reference Note

For information on **spelling rules,** see Chapter 28.

NOTE Most regular verbs that end in *e* drop the *e* before adding *–ing* or *–ed*. Some regular verbs double the final consonant before adding *–ing* or *–ed*.

EXAMPLES   use   **us**ing   **us**ed

            plan   **plann**ing   **plann**ed

A few regular verbs have alternative past and past participle forms ending in *–t.*

Base Form	Present Participle	Past	Past Participle
burn	[is] burning	burned *or* burnt	[have] burned *or* burnt
dream	[is] dreaming	dreamed *or* dreamt	[have] dreamed *or* dreamt
leap	[is] leaping	leaped *or* leapt	[have] leaped *or* leapt

NOTE The regular verbs *deal* and *mean* always form the past and past participle by adding *–t: dealt, [have] dealt; meant, [have] meant.*

When forming the past and past participle of regular verbs, do not make the common mistake of leaving off the *–d* or *–ed* ending. Pay particular attention to the forms of the verbs *ask, attack, drown, prejudice, risk, suppose,* and *use.*

NONSTANDARD   We use to live in Bakersfield.
STANDARD   We **used** to live in Bakersfield.

NONSTANDARD   I was suppose to be home by now.
STANDARD   I was **supposed** to be home by now.

Reference Note

For information on **standard and non-standard English,** see page 756.

SALLY FORTH reprinted with special permission of King Features Syndicate, Inc.

Most of the following sentences contain errors in the use of past or past participle forms of verbs. If a verb form is incorrect, give the correct form. If a sentence is already correct, write *C*.

EXAMPLES 　　1.　Weren't these parts order over two months ago?

　　　　　　　 1.　ordered

　　　　　　　2.　Alec and Maribel are suppose to meet at the museum.

　　　　　　　 2.　supposed

1. Before them stretch the great Kalahari Desert.
2. Once, centuries ago, tens of thousands of men, women, and children had populate this ancient city.
3. Actually, I meant to do that.
4. You use to work for Mr. Hall's lawn service.
5. Those magnificent examples of Native American pottery were etch with a traditional design.
6. Before arriving in Santa Fe, the wagon train had survive every sort of hardship.
7. A month-long national advertising blitz had successfully popularize this unlikely product.
8. Hadn't she check the gas gauge?
9. Oh, no, you were suppose to answer questions on both sides of the test!
10. After a week of constant effort and attention, Nicole finally tame the little parrot.

Irregular Verbs

21c. An *irregular verb* forms its past and past participle in some way other than by adding *–d* or *–ed* to its base form.

An irregular verb forms its past and past participle in one of these ways:

- changing vowels

Base Form	Past	Past Participle
sing	sang	[have] sung

- changing consonants

Base Form	Past	Past Participle
lend	lent	[have] lent

- changing vowels and consonants

Base Form	Past	Past Participle
buy	bought	[have] bought

- making no change

Base Form	Past	Past Participle
cost	cost	[have] cost

When forming the past and past participle of irregular verbs, avoid these common errors:

- Do not use the past form with a helping verb.

NONSTANDARD	I have sang in the Alexander Hamilton High School chorus for three years.
STANDARD	I **sang** in the Alexander Hamilton High School chorus for three years.

- Do not use the past participle form without a helping verb.

NONSTANDARD	I sung three solos this year.
STANDARD	I **have sung** three solos this year.

- Do not add *d*, *ed*, or *t* to the base form.

NONSTANDARD	This cassette costed only $6.95.
STANDARD	This cassette **cost** only $6.95.

NOTE If you are not sure about the principal parts of a verb, look up the verb in a dictionary. Generally, entries for irregular verbs list the principal parts. If the principal parts are not listed, the verb is a regular verb.

USAGE

STYLE TIP

Some irregular verbs have two correct past or past participle forms. However, these forms are not always interchangeable.

EXAMPLES
Judy **shone** the lantern into the woods. [*Shined* would also be correct.]

Al **shined** his shoes. [*Shone* would be incorrect in this usage.]

If you are unsure about which past participle form to use, look up the word in an up-to-date dictionary.

Common Irregular Verbs

Group I: Each of these irregular verbs has the same form for its past and past participle.

Base Form	Present Participle	Past	Past Participle
bind	[is] binding	bound	[have] bound
bring	[is] bringing	brought	[have] brought
build	[is] building	built	[have] built
buy	[is] buying	bought	[have] bought
catch	[is] catching	caught	[have] caught
creep	[is] creeping	crept	[have] crept
feel	[is] feeling	felt	[have] felt
fight	[is] fighting	fought	[have] fought
find	[is] finding	found	[have] found
fling	[is] flinging	flung	[have] flung
have	[is] having	had	[have] had
hear	[is] hearing	heard	[have] heard
hold	[is] holding	held	[have] held
keep	[is] keeping	kept	[have] kept
lay	[is] laying	laid	[have] laid
lead	[is] leading	led	[have] led
leave	[is] leaving	left	[have] left
lend	[is] lending	lent	[have] lent
lose	[is] losing	lost	[have] lost
make	[is] making	made	[have] made
meet	[is] meeting	met	[have] met
pay	[is] paying	paid	[have] paid
say	[is] saying	said	[have] said
seek	[is] seeking	sought	[have] sought
sell	[is] selling	sold	[have] sold
send	[is] sending	sent	[have] sent
sit	[is] sitting	sat	[have] sat
spend	[is] spending	spent	[have] spent
spin	[is] spinning	spun	[have] spun
stand	[is] standing	stood	[have] stood
sting	[is] stinging	stung	[have] stung
swing	[is] swinging	swung	[have] swung

Common Irregular Verbs

Group I: Each of these irregular verbs has the same form for its past and past participle.

Base Form	Present Participle	Past	Past Participle
teach	[is] teaching	taught	[have] taught
tell	[is] telling	told	[have] told
think	[is] thinking	thought	[have] thought
win	[is] winning	won	[have] won

Exercise 2 **Using the Past and Past Participle Forms of Irregular Verbs Correctly**

Most of the following sentences contain errors in the use of the past or past participle forms of irregular verbs. If a verb form is incorrect, give the correct form. If a sentence is already correct, write *C*.

EXAMPLE 1. Uncle Octavio brung all of us souvenirs of his visit to Costa Rica.

      1. brought

1. Before the festival last Sunday, the Conchero dancers had meet behind the church to practice.
2. By some unlucky chance, I winned the door prize—a full-grown leghorn rooster.
3. The accomplishments of Maggie Lena Walker, the first female bank president in the United States, layed a firm financial foundation for the African American community of Richmond, Virginia.
4. The macaw, happy to see its owner, standed at the door of its cage and shrieked excitedly.
5. After a few hesitant steps, we swinged into the rhythm of the fox trot.
6. For all those years, the old man had keeped the dogeared photograph of his childhood home in Hawaii.
7. While in Arizona, Uncle Arthur boughten a magnificent storm-pattern Navajo rug by Shirley Tsinnie.
8. How could you have spended all of your weekly allowance before Saturday afternoon!
9. A green velvet ribbon binded the large white box that was on the dining room table.
10. The cool skin of the chameleon feeled dry, not wet.
11. She lost her hat when a gust of wind blew it into the lake.

12. No one said a word as the host spinned the big yellow arrow to determine who would take the first turn.
13. Haven't you sayed enough?
14. On the front porch that very afternoon, the two second-graders had fighted furiously over the only blue crayon.
15. In modern China, Qiu Jin leaded the way for women's emancipation.
16. Have you selled the mare with three white feet and a white mane?
17. My father taught me to save some money—even just a few dollars—each month.
18. I seeked my fortune in a faraway country.
19. We should have sat in the shade of a towering oak tree on the university's front lawn.
20. That colorful painting by the Haitian artist Euguerrand Gourgue lended a cheery touch to the room.

Exercise 3 Using the Past and Past Participle Forms of Irregular Verbs Correctly

Complete each of the following sentences, using the correct past or past participle form of the italicized verb.

EXAMPLE   1. *tell*   Mr. Paz _____ us about the early Spanish explorers who searched for gold in the Americas.

   1. *told*

1. *seek*   Spanish explorers had _____ gold in the Americas.
2. *find*   The gold they _____, however, was in golden ears of corn.
3. *leave*   Spanish ships _____ carrying the precious kernels to Europe.
4. *bring*   The holds of the ships _____ a cheap, new food source into a land of recurrent famine.
5. *lead*   A diet of corn _____ many of the world's poor to suffer from pellagra, a disease of the stomach, mind, and skin.
6. *build*   The peoples of Mexico and Central America, however, had _____ healthy bodies on a steady diet of corn.
7. *make*   When the people of Mexico and Central America _____ tortillas, they added some lime or ashes to the dough.
8. *stand*   Then, after the mixture of corn, water, and lime or ashes had _____ for a few hours, the tortillas were cooked.
9. *have*   Heated, this alkali solution _____ the ability to release not only corn's niacin but also its protein and calcium.
10. *lose*   In European and African methods of preparation, corn had unfortunately _____ much of its nutrient value.

Common Irregular Verbs

Group II: Most of these irregular verbs have different forms for the past and past participle.

┌HELP───

Several of these verbs have alternate past or past participle forms.

Base Form	Present Participle	Past	Past Participle
arise	[is] arising	arose	[have] arisen
be	[is] being	was, were	[have] been
bear	[is] bearing	bore	[have] borne *or* born
beat	[is] beating	beat	[have] beaten *or* beat
become	[is] becoming	became	[have] become
begin	[is] beginning	began	[have] begun
bite	[is] biting	bit	[have] bitten *or* bit
blow	[is] blowing	blown	[have] blown
break	[is] breaking	broke	[have] broken
choose	[is] choosing	chose	[have] chosen
come	[is] coming	came	[have] come
dive	[is] diving	dove *or* dived	[have] dived
do	[is] doing	did	[have] done
draw	[is] drawing	drew	[have] drawn
drink	[is] drinking	drank	[have] drunk
drive	[is] driving	drove	[have] driven
eat	[is] eating	ate	[have] eaten
fall	[is] falling	fell	[have] fallen
fly	[is] flying	flew	[have] flown
forbid	[is] forbidding	forbade *or* forbad	[have] forbidden *or* forbid
forget	[is] forgetting	forgot	[have] forgotten *or* forgot
forgive	[is] forgiving	forgave	[have] forgiven
forsake	[is] forsaking	forsook	[have] forsaken
freeze	[is] freezing	froze	[have] frozen
get	[is] getting	got	[have] gotten *or* got
give	[is] giving	gave	[have] given

(continued)

USAGE

(continued)

Common Irregular Verbs

Group II: Most of these irregular verbs have different forms for the past and past participle.

Base Form	Present Participle	Past	Past Participle
go	[is] going	went	[have] gone
grow	[is] growing	grew	[have] grown
hide	[is] hiding	hid	[have] hidden *or* hid
know	[is] knowing	knew	[have] known
lie	[is] lying	lay	[have] lain
ride	[is] riding	rode	[have] ridden
ring	[is] ringing	rang	[have] rung
rise	[is] rising	rose	[have] risen
run	[is] running	ran	[have] run
see	[is] seeing	saw	[have] seen
shake	[is] shaking	shook	[have] shaken
show	[is] showing	showed	[have] shown or showed
shrink	[is] shrinking	shrank *or* shrunk	[have] shrunk
sing	[is] singing	sang	[have] sung
sink	[is] sinking	sank *or* sunk	[have] sunk
slay	[is] slaying	slew	[have] slain
speak	[is] speaking	spoke	[have] spoken
spring	[is] springing	sprang *or* sprung	[have] sprung
steal	[is] stealing	stole	[have] stolen
strike	[is] striking	struck	[have] struck *or* stricken
strive	[is] striving	strove *or* strived	[have] striven *or* strived
swear	[is] swearing	swore	[have] sworn
swim	[is] swimming	swam	[have] swum
take	[is] taking	took	[have] taken

Common Irregular Verbs

Group II: Most of these irregular verbs have different forms for the past and past participle.

Base Form	Present Participle	Past	Past Participle
tear	[is] tearing	tore	[have] torn
throw	[is] throwing	threw	[have] thrown
wake	[is] waking	woke *or* waked	[have] waked *or* woken
wear	[is] wearing	wore	[have] worn
weave	[is] weaving	wove *or* weaved	[have] woven *or* weaved
write	[is] writing	wrote	[have] written

Exercise 4 Using the Past and Past Participle Forms of Irregular Verbs Correctly

Choose the correct one of the two verb forms in parentheses in each of the following sentences.

EXAMPLE 1. Bantu languages, which are (*spoke, spoken*) by many Africans, have an interesting history.

1. *spoken*

1. Years ago in Africa, Bantu languages had no alphabet, and no one (*wrote, written*) in these languages.
2. In fact, the musical quality of many African languages (*gived, gave*) them an intricacy unsuitable for written alphabets.
3. Consequently, drums (*sung, sang*) these languages throughout equatorial and southern Africa, and the drum songs acted as a kind of musical writing.
4. According to Janheinz Jahn, the use of drums (*arose, arisen*) for communication at a distance.
5. Just as you learned to read using the alphabet, young Africans learned to "read" the different sounds of the drums and (*knew, known*) the meanings of these sounds in combinations.
6. The wide acoustic range of drums like the Yorubas' *dundun* (*gived, gave*) quick and easy access to a complex language.
7. By varying tone, pitch, and modulation, a skillful drummer (*striven, strove*) to re-create the sounds of his language.

8. With this meaningful music, he (*wove, woven*) the news of the day into an informative report.
9. At the speed of sound, his warnings, invitations, and other messages (*flew, flown*) over miles of jungle and plain.
10. With drum scripts that had been (*beated, beaten*) for decades, he sent information to interested listeners.
11. Many of the scripts eventually (*became, become*) classic epics.
12. Drummers were not just musicians; they (*been, were*) also teachers and historians.
13. Through them, generations of young Africans (*drank, drunk*) in the history of their ancestors.
14. When European missionaries came to Africa, however, they (*forbidden, forbade*) the playing of drums.
15. Their prohibitions (*struck, stricken*) severely at the hearts of many African cultures.
16. Today, through disuse, almost all of the old drum scripts have been (*forgotted, forgotten*).
17. Some scholars have (*did, done*) their best to record many of the remaining scripts.
18. Sadly, many listeners have not (*spoke, spoken*) Bantu in their whole lives; consequently, even verbal translations of the drum songs are meaningless to many Bantu people.
19. Has the power of the drums (*went, gone*)?
20. Like so much other ancient knowledge and wisdom, this marvelous system of communication has largely been (*forsaken, forsook*).

Exercise 5 Using the Past and Past Participle Forms of Irregular Verbs Correctly

Most of the following sentences contain incorrect past or past participle forms of irregular verbs. If a verb form is incorrect, give the correct form. If a sentence is already correct, write *C*.

EXAMPLE 1. By the time Beowulf arrives, the monster Grendel has slew many of King Hrothgar's warriors.
1. *slain*

1. She should not have drew a beard on that poster.
2. Benjamin Franklin may have gotten many of his ideas for the structure of our government from his observations of the League of the Iroquois.
3. Why would you think someone had stole your notebook?
4. Frank said, "I have ran too far to turn back now."

5. Dwayne has growed two inches taller than his older brother, the all-state basketball player.
6. After the discoveries made in the tomb of Tutankhamen, other ancient treasures seemed to Joseph to have shrank in significance.
7. The noise from the party woke the neighborhood.
8. I seen that movie several times, but I would be happy to see it again.
9. Who in the world throwed out all my old baseball cards?
10. They have frozen a peck of green beans for next winter.
11. Henry done his best yesterday, and it was enough.
12. In the courtroom the young man sworn to give truthful testimony.
13. Jesse Owens's spectacular run at the 1936 Olympic games shaked the world.
14. Have you ever dove from the high board at the swimming pool?
15. As we huddled in the corner, thunder crashed and wind blowed the candles out.
16. I guess we should have chose seats closer to the stage.
17. Why have they tore up the newspapers?
18. The coach said, "I think we have began to wear them down."
19. He always rid the bus to school, even if his parents offered to drive him.
20. Has the bell for third period rung yet?

Review A **Proofreading for Correct Verb Forms**

Find and correct any errors in verb forms in each sentence in the following paragraphs. If a sentence is already correct, write *C*.

EXAMPLE   **[1]** Part of an Apache ceremony called Sunrise Ceremonial is shone in the photograph here.

    1. shown

[1] Many cultures have not forsaked their traditional ceremonies that mark the significant stages in a person's life. [2] For instance, when an Apache girl has came of age, she sometimes receives a Sunrise Ceremonial. [3] Through this ceremony, the young woman is forever separated from her girlhood and lead into womanhood. [4] Everything in the ceremony is suppose to remind the young woman of the deep spiritual meaning of her life. [5] Perhaps part of that meaning can be founded in the glad hearts of her many friends and family members who come to participate in the ceremony.

[6] Not long ago, Carla, the young woman in the photograph on the previous page, and her mother seeked the blessings of a traditional Sunrise Ceremonial. [7] Complex preparations had began months in advance. [8] During the winter Carla's mother choose a campsite where Carla, her family, and her friends would live for two weeks according to the ways of their ancestors. [9] The crucial choice of godparents for the young woman also had been maked by Carla's mother. [10] Not surprisingly, she chose a couple who had kept to the traditional Apache way of life. [11] By summer Carla's mother and godparents had built enough shelters at the campsite to house at least eight families.

[12] During Carla's ceremonial, many traditional songs were sang. [13] The two cows that had been slew for the feasting were eaten. [14] In addition, Carla and her family gave the gifts they had brung to the godparents and other friends. [15] Young women used to dance all night, and Carla danced for six hours at a time. [16] Then she standed for endless hours in the burning sun. [17] Through it all, she worn a hot, heavy buckskin dress. [18] Surely, these tests of self-discipline taught Carla and everyone who attend the ceremony about the endurance and strength that a woman needs to live as a proper Apache. [19] Finally, after offering a blessing, a medicine man gived Carla a cane, a reminder that she will not always be young. [20] In her old age, when the cane has became her constant companion, it will, no doubt, remind her of the strength of her youth.

Common Irregular Verbs

Group III: Each of these irregular verbs has the same form for its base form, past, and past participle.

Base Form	Present Participle	Past	Past Participle
burst	[is] bursting	burst	[have] burst
cost	[is] costing	cost	[have] cost
cut	[is] cutting	cut	[have] cut
hit	[is] hitting	hit	[have] hit
hurt	[is] hurting	hurt	[have] hurt
let	[is] letting	let	[have] let
put	[is] putting	put	[have] put
read	[is] reading	read	[have] read
set	[is] setting	set	[have] set
spread	[is] spreading	spread	[have] spread

Exercise 6 **Using the Past and Past Participle Forms of Irregular Verbs Correctly**

Most of the following sentences contain incorrect past or past participle forms of irregular verbs. If a verb form is incorrect, give the correct form. If a sentence is already correct, write *C*.

EXAMPLE 1. In the fourteenth century a plague known as Black Death spreaded throughout Europe and Asia.

 1. *spread*

1. During the freeze last March, the water pipes at school bursted.
2. My jaw hurted after the orthodontist adjusted my braces.
3. Yesterday evening, I had just putted dinner on the table when the phone rang.
4. Shaka Zulu led his warriors into battle, and soon news of Shaka's victory had spreaded throughout Zululand.
5. Have you ever cutted out a pattern before?
6. Have you read the assignment yet?
7. After art class, Jeremy, Mr. Fitzcarraldo, and I setted our pottery out in the sun to dry.
8. The drought hitted the spring crops hard.
9. One chance remark costed her the election.
10. Wisely, Francisca Henrique de Ribera letted the Andean people treat her malaria attack with cinchona bark, from which the medicinal ingredient quinine is extracted.
11. Have you ever hit a ball out of the park?
12. News of the new state-of-the-art computers spreaded quickly through the high school.
13. Yikes, Timmy, you've cutted a hole right in the middle of the lace tablecloth!
14. Shouldn't you have setted those forks on the other side of the plate?
15. Wow! That big house on the hill must have costed a fortune to design and build.
16. Of course, Eric and I putted the slides back in the drawer, Mr. Stevens.
17. Have you letted those puppies out of the laundry room?
18. Overnight, the daffodil bulbs planted last fall had bursted into vivid bloom.
19. This book by Amy Tan was so good that I readed the whole thing last night.
20. No, those horseshoe nails haven't hurted a horse yet.

Most of the sentences in the following paragraphs contain errors in verb usage. If a verb form is incorrect, give the correct form. If a sentence is already correct, write *C*.

EXAMPLE [1] The early European and Asian explorers of the Americas taked home with them many foods indigenous to North and South America.

1. *took*

[1] Now that you have read the map shown on the next page, are you surprised by where these food products originated? [2] Perhaps you have ate some of these foods. [3] Many food products have became vital, even characteristic, parts of their adopted nations. [4] Consequently, most people have forgotten that key ingredients, such as tomato sauce on pizza, originated in the Americas.

[5] Reports from early explorers putted cooks all over Europe into a creative frenzy. [6] As soon as the explorers returned home, dozens of strange and exotic foods become available to Europeans. [7] Some of the foods that the explorers taked home include sweet potatoes, white potatoes, corn, peppers, tomatoes, avocados, vanilla, maple sugar, chocolate, peanuts, all sorts of beans (kidney, lima, snap, string, butter, pole, and navy), and a host of other welcome additions to a chef's pantry. [8] So many new spices, fruits, vegetables, meats, and grains hitted the market that this period in history can be called a "Food Revolution."

[9] In these unfamiliar foods, many peoples also founded new hope. [10] For example, the Chinese use to experience severe famine. [11] Countless people losed their lives when rice crops failed. [12] However, with the introduction of the sweet potato, an alternative to rice arisen. [13] Sweet potatoes cost little and did well in poor soil. [14] Soon, cooks had putted sweet potato flour into Chinese dumplings, noodles, and many other dishes. [15] Because of the continuing popularity of the sweet potato in China, Chinese farmers have growed more sweet potatoes than farmers in any other country.

[16] Famine often had struck Europe, too, because of poor weather conditions. [17] For Europeans, their salvation lain in the Andean potato. [18] With harvest after harvest of potatoes, Europeans fighted famine and also created a whole new menu. [19] In soups, stews, pancakes, and pies, the potato lended its substance and nutrition to a host

of European dishes. [20] Who in the time of Columbus could have dreamt of the vast variety of American food sources or of the vital roles they would play in the world's fight against famine?

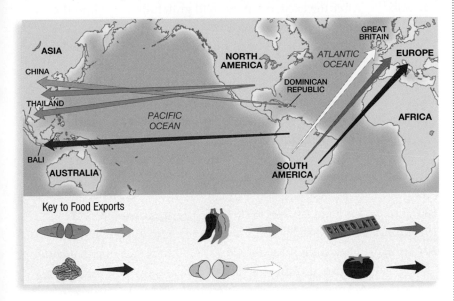

Review C **Using the Past and Past Participle Forms of Verbs Correctly**

For each of the following sentences, write the correct past or past participle form of the given italicized verb.

EXAMPLE   1. *know*   A sport called baggataway was first played by North American Indians; today, the sport is _____ as lacrosse.

         1. known

1. *steal*   While the children were asleep, their father _____ into their room to kiss them good night.
2. *let*   After breakfast I _____ the cat outside.
3. *visit*   Many Cheyenne, Arapaho, Shoshone, Blackfoot, Crow, and Sioux have _____ the Bighorn Medicine Wheel in Wyoming, a ceremonial site for perhaps two thousand years.
4. *fling*   Joyfully, he _____ his cap into the air.
5. *sting*   Where had the bee _____ her?
6. *win*   The baby's trusting smile _____ our hearts.
7. *think*   At last, I had _____ of the perfect present for Amy.
8. *bear*   We _____ his rudeness for only a few minutes.

9. *swim*   The frantic cat _____ desperately to the shore.
10. *blow*   Even before the whistle had _____, they had seen the train coming across the bridge.
11. *sink*   After the excitement, we had gratefully _____ into the plush velvet chairs to wait.
12. *hide*   Someone _____ one of my birthday presents at the back of the top shelf in a kitchen cabinet.
13. *set*   That afternoon, we hurriedly _____ the table for the party.
14. *lie*   During World War II, the success of England's military blood bank _____ in the capable hands of Dr. Charles Drew.
15. *hold*   Only that morning, I had _____ the tiny bird in my hands.
16. *bite*   Sharks _____ the whale but did not badly injure it.
17. *lead*   Boadicea, a queen in ancient Britain, _____ her people in a revolt against the Romans.
18. *cut*   He had _____ his ties to his native country.
19. *throw* That horse has _____ everybody who has tried to ride it.
20. *break* The death of Mao Zedong _____ the rigid rule that had governed China for many years and opened the way for somewhat greater freedom for the Chinese people.

Review D Proofreading for Correct Verb Forms and Usage

Most of the sentences in the following paragraphs contain at least one error in the use of verbs. If a verb form is incorrect, give the correct form. If a sentence is already correct, write *C*.

EXAMPLE   [1] From my aunt I learned a great deal about the use of lacquer, a substance that is drawed from certain trees of the cashew family.

1. *drawn*

[1] For over thirty years, my aunt has had a lacquerware plate similar to the one in the picture on the next page. [2] When I been a child, she displayed the plate on a low table in her living room in Tacoma, Washington. [3] Naturally, she forbidded me to touch her prized plate, and I respected her wish. [4] One day, however, my younger brother runned through the living room. [5] As he zoomed past the table, his foot accidentally hitted the leg. [6] In the blink of an eye, my aunt's beautiful plate falled and spinned wildly on the floor. [7] After that, the plate, which was miraculously unbroken, sitted on the top shelf of my aunt's china closet.

[**8**] Ever since I first expressed an interest in lacquerware, my aunt has told me more and more about its history and production. [**9**] People have maked lacquerware since around 300 B.C. [**10**] The art begun in China and later spreaded to Japan and then to the Western world. [**11**] To protect their trade, the tappers of lacquer in ancient China keeped their valuable knowledge of lacquer production secret. [**12**] Now we know that they drew the sap from lacquer trees, filtered it, and dried it to a thick, syrupy consistency. [**13**] Then they selled it to artists for its beauty and for its waterproofing ability.

[**14**] In the finer pieces of lacquerware, like this one, an artist may have spread some two hundred coats of lacquer over the plate. [**15**] For each coat, a thin film of lacquer was applied and then was leaved to dry thoroughly. [**16**] Consequently, the whole lacquering process sometimes taked as long as a year to complete. [**17**] Then, when the artist had choosed a design, the carving began. [**18**] Would you have devote a year's work to such an intricate design? [**19**] What confidence these artists must have feeled! [**20**] My aunt bought her plate years ago for only a few dollars; now, it has brought offers of many, many times the price that she payed.

Song-Yuan Dynasties (13th century). Tray, brown and red lacquer with gilt background. Height, 1 in.; diameter, 9 in. B83M9. The Avery Brundage Collection. Asian Art Museum of San Francisco.

Six Troublesome Verbs

Lie and Lay

The verb *lie* means "to rest," "to recline," or "to be in a certain place."
Lie does not take a direct object. The verb *lay* means "to put [something] in a place." *Lay* generally takes a direct object.

Base Form	Present Participle	Past	Past Participle
lie	[is] lying	lay	[have] lain
lay	[is] laying	laid	[have] laid

STYLE ✏ **TIP**

The verb *lie* can also mean "to tell an untruth." Used in this way, *lie* still does not take an object. The past participle forms of this meaning of *lie* are *lied* and [have] *lied*.

EXAMPLE
You should never **lie** on an application.

EXAMPLES A napkin **is lying** on each diner's plate. [no direct object]

The servers **are laying** a napkin on each diner's plate.
[*Napkin* is the direct object of *are laying.*]

The seed **lay** on the ground. [no direct object]

We **laid** seed on the ground for the wild birds. [*Seed* is the direct object of *laid.*]

The issues **have lain** before the voters. [no direct object]

The state legislators **have laid** the issues before the voters.
[*Issues* is the direct object of *have laid.*]

Exercise 7   Choosing the Forms of *Lie* and *Lay*

Choose the correct verb form in parentheses in each of the following sentences.

EXAMPLE 1. On your desk are (*lying, laying*) several letters that
require your signature, Ms. Carmichael.

1. *lying*

1. If you are sick, you should be (*lying, laying*) down.
2. They (*lay, laid*) the heavy crate on the handcart.
3. Lucia's mother has been (*lying, laying*) the canvas out to dry.
4. Amy (*lay, laid*) down for a while.
5. (*Lie, Lay*) down and rest for a minute.
6. She had just (*lain, laid*) down when the doorbell rang.
7. They (*lay, laid*) their plans before the committee.
8. The calf (*lay, laid*) on a pile of straw.
9. Kiyoshi has just (*lain, laid*) his paintbrush down.
10. Please (*lie, lay*) all of those blankets down here.

Sit and Set

The verb *sit* means "to be in a seated, upright position" or "to be in a place." *Sit* seldom takes a direct object. The verb *set* means "to put [something] in a place." *Set* generally takes a direct object.

Base Form	Present Participle	Past	Past Participle
sit	[is] sitting	sat	[have] sat
set	[is] setting	set	[have] set

EXAMPLES   Who **is sitting** next to the hearth? [no direct object]

Who **is setting** the chair next to the hearth? [*Chair* is the direct object of *is setting.*]

Where **should** we **sit**? [no direct object]

Where **should** we **set** the groceries? [*Groceries* is the direct object of *should set.*]

We **sat** near the end zone during last night's game. [no direct object]

We **set** the giant papier-mâché football near the end zone during last night's game. [*Football* is the direct object of *set.*]

Exercise 8 Choosing the Forms of *Sit* and *Set*

Choose the correct verb form in parentheses in each of the following sentences.

EXAMPLE   1. (*Sit, Set*) this box of diskettes on her computer desk, please.

1. *Set*

1. After he had struck out, Pete (*sat, set*) on the bench.
2. Part of San Francisco's Chinatown (*sits, sets*) on an incline that overlooks San Francisco Bay.
3. Where were the packages (*sitting, setting*) this morning?
4. We had (*sat, set*) the new cushions on the Adirondack chairs.
5. In Japan people often (*sit, set*) on tatami instead of chairs.
6. They were (*sitting, setting*) placemats on the table.
7. Have you (*sat, set*) here long, Aaron?
8. We have (*sat, set*) down our packs and gotten out our map.
9. Mr. Carr told me to (*sit, set*) the equipment on his desk.
10. I may never know who (*sat, set*) on my glasses.

USAGE

STYLE TIP

The verb *raise* has definitions other than the one given here. Another common definition is "to grow" or "to bring to maturity."

EXAMPLES
They **raise** sorghum.

She **raised** two foster children.

Notice that both of these uses take an object.

Rise and *Raise*

The verb *rise* means "to go up" or "to get up." *Rise* does not take a direct object. The verb *raise* means "to lift up" or "to cause [something] to rise." *Raise* generally takes a direct object.

Base Form	Present Participle	Past	Past Participle
rise	[is] rising	rose	[have] risen
raise	[is] raising	raised	[have] raised

EXAMPLES   One by one, the students' hands **were rising.** [no direct object]

One by one, the students were **raising** their hands. [*Hands* is the direct object of *were raising.*]

Una **rose** and then walked to the front of the classroom. [no direct object]

Una **raised** her eyebrows and then walked to the front of the classroom. [*Eyebrows* is the direct object of *raised.*]

The number of women who work outside the home **has risen** steadily during the past decade. [no direct object]

Has working outside the home **raised** their economic status? [*Status* is the direct object of *Has raised.*]

Exercise 9 Choosing the Forms of *Rise* and *Raise*

Choose the correct verb form in parentheses in each of the following sentences.

EXAMPLE   1. The financial planner predicted, "In the near future, interest rates will not (*rise, raise*); they may decline."

1. *rise*

1. Air bubbles have been (*rising, raising*) to the surface.
2. Increasing the import duty had (*risen, raised*) retail prices.
3. The speaker (*rose, raised*) from her chair and took the microphone.
4. The star has (*risen, raised*) in the east.
5. The rooster (*rises, raises*) early.
6. Before and during the Revolutionary War, many colonists worked hard to (*rise, raise*) public sentiment against King George III.

7. Hot-air balloons can (*rise, raise*) because they contain heated air, which is less dense than the surrounding air.
8. At the tribal council meeting, someone (*rose, raised*) the issue of land ownership within reservation boundaries.
9. Taylor is (*rising, raising*) the fallen child to her feet.
10. To make traditional challah, braid the bread dough after it has (*risen, raised*) for an hour.

Review E　Choosing the Forms of *Lie* and *Lay, Sit* and *Set,* and *Rise* and *Raise*

Choose the correct verb form in parentheses in each of the following sentences.

EXAMPLE　　**1.** The snapshots of our trip to Kenya are (*lying, laying*) on top of the photo album.

　　　　　　1. lying

1. All week that box has (*lain, laid*) unopened on the desk.
2. We had (*rose, raised*) our hats to salute the astronauts.
3. The fawn (*lay, laid*) motionless in the underbrush.
4. Our applications were (*lying, laying*) in front of the file.
5. Would you like to (*sit, set*) with us at the powwow?
6. Yesterday I (*sat, set*) the telephone book on this table.
7. Where have you (*laid, lain*) your glasses?
8. Kathy sang as she (*lay, laid*) the baby in the crib.
9. Please (*rise, raise*) if you have a question.
10. Last night's victory really (*rose, raised*) the team's confidence.
11. Our potbellied pig, Oscar, often (*lies, lays*) in my lap when I watch TV.
12. Fred should (*lie, lay*) on his side to stop snoring.
13. After the fire, the museum curator (*sat, set*) on the curb and wept.
14. Tempers (*rose, raised*) as the debate progressed.
15. In Washington, D.C., we will (*lie, lay*) flowers at the Vietnam Veterans Memorial.
16. Mrs. Nasser (*sat, set*) the tabbouleh and the kibbe next to other traditional Lebanese foods.
17. He has (*sit, set*) the pie on the ledge.
18. Billows of dust had (*risen, raised*) from the field.
19. Haven't they (*sat, set*) down yet?
20. You should (*lie, lay*) on a padded surface to do exercises.

Tense

21d. The *tense* of a verb indicates the time of the action or of the state of being expressed by the verb.

Reference Note

For information about **conjugating verbs in the passive voice,** see page 706. For more information about **active and passive voice,** see page 705.

Listing all the forms of a verb according to tense is called *conjugating* a verb. The tenses are formed from the verb's principal parts. Verbs in English have the six tenses shown on the following time line:

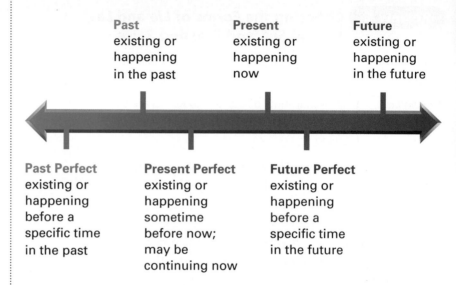

Past
existing or happening in the past

Present
existing or happening now

Future
existing or happening in the future

Past Perfect
existing or happening before a specific time in the past

Present Perfect
existing or happening sometime before now; may be continuing now

Future Perfect
existing or happening before a specific time in the future

Conjugation of the Verb *Give*	
Present Tense	
Singular	*Plural*
I give	we give
you give	you give
he, she, it gives	they give
Past Tense	
Singular	*Plural*
I gave	we gave
you gave	you gave
he, she, it gave	they gave

USAGE

Conjugation of the Verb *Give*

Future Tense

Singular	*Plural*
I will (shall) give	we will (shall) give
you will (shall) give	you will (shall) give
he, she, it will (shall) give	they will (shall) give

Present Perfect Tense

Singular	*Plural*
I have given	we have given
you have given	you have given
he, she, it has given	they have given

Past Perfect Tense

Singular	*Plural*
I had given	we had given
you had given	you had given
he, she, it had given	they had given

Future Perfect Tense

Singular	*Plural*
I will (shall) have given	we will (shall) have given
you will (shall) have given	you will (shall) have given
he, she, it will (shall) have given	they will (shall) have given

| STYLE   TIP |

Traditionally, the helping verbs *shall* and *will* were used quite differently. Now, however, *shall* can be used almost interchangeably with *will*.

The Progressive Form

Each tense has an additional form called the **progressive form,** which expresses continuing action or state of being. In each tense the progressive form consists of the appropriate tense of *be* plus the present participle of a verb.

PRESENT PROGRESSIVE	am, is, are giving
PAST PROGRESSIVE	was, were giving
FUTURE PROGRESSIVE	will (shall) be giving
PRESENT PERFECT PROGRESSIVE	has been, have been giving
PAST PERFECT PROGRESSIVE	had been giving
FUTURE PERFECT PROGRESSIVE	will (shall) have been giving

The Emphatic Form

Only the present and the past tenses have another form, called the **emphatic form,** which shows emphasis. In the present tense the emphatic form consists of *do* or *does* plus the base form of a verb. In the past tense the emphatic form consists of *did* plus the base form of a verb.

PRESENT EMPHATIC   I **do** not **intend** to give up on our team.

Although the grass is green, the front lawn **does need** watering.

PAST EMPHATIC   The explorers suffered many hardships, yet they **did** finally **reach** their destination.

She **did** not **say** what they thought she had said.

The Verb *Be*

The conjugation of the verb *be* is different from that of any other verb. The progressive form of *be* is rarely used in any tenses other than the present and past tenses, and not one of the tenses of *be* has an emphatic form.

Conjugation of the Verb *Be*	
Present Tense	
Singular	*Plural*
I am	we are
you are	you are
he, she, it is	they are
Present Progressive: am, are, is being	
Past Tense	
Singular	*Plural*
I am	we were
you were	you were
he, she, it is	they were
Past Progressive: was, were being	

STYLE TIP

The emphatic form is also used in questions and negative statements. These uses do not place special emphasis on the verb.

QUESTION
Do you **know** who wrote that?

NEGATIVE STATEMENT
They **do**n't **have** the answer.

HELP

The emphatic form is not a separate tense but is another form of each of the present and past tenses.

Conjugation of the Verb *Be*	
Future Tense	
Singular	*Plural*
I will (shall) be	we will (shall) be
you will (shall) be	you will (shall) be
he, she, it will (shall) be	they will (shall) be
Present Perfect Tense	
Singular	*Plural*
I have been	we have been
you have been	you have been
he, she, it has been	they have been
Past Perfect Tense	
Singular	*Plural*
I had been	we had been
you had been	you had been
he, she, it had been	they had been
Future Perfect Tense	
Singular	*Plural*
I will (shall) have been	we will (shall) have been
you will (shall) have been	you will (shall) have been
he, she, it will (shall) have been	they will (shall) have been

The Uses of the Tenses

21e. Each of the six tenses has its own uses.

(1) The *present tense* expresses an action or a state of being that is occurring now, at the present time.

EXAMPLES   Deborah, Ashley, and Brendan **wait** patiently for the bus. [present]

Deborah, Ashley, and Brendan **are waiting** patiently for the bus. [present progressive]

Deborah, Ashley, and Brendan **do wait** patiently for the bus. [present emphatic]

The present tense is also used

- to show a customary or habitual action or state of being
- to state a general truth—something that is always true
- to summarize the plot or subject matter of a literary work (such use is called the *literary present*)
- to make a historical event seem current (such use is called the *historical present*)
- to express future time

EXAMPLES After school I **wash** the breakfast dishes and **start** supper. [customary actions]

In the Northern Hemisphere the summer solstice **occurs** when the sun is at its northernmost position each year. [general truth]

Countee Cullen **uses** traditional verse forms such as the epigram and the sonnet to explore African American themes. [literary present]

In 1520 Ferdinand Magellan **rounds** the southern tip of South America and **names** the ocean that **lies** before him the Pacific Ocean. [historical present]

The movie that **opens** tomorrow **runs** through next week. [future time]

(2) The *past tense* expresses an action or a state of being that occurred in the past and did not continue into the present.

EXAMPLES I **stayed** at the library until closing time. [past]

I **was researching** the life and times of Timothy Thomas Fortune, an early civil rights advocate in the 1800s. [past progressive]

My research **did provide** me with enough information for my paper on Fortune. [past emphatic]

(3) The *future tense* expresses an action or a state of being that will occur. The future tense is formed with the helping verb *will* or *shall* and the base form of a verb.

EXAMPLES I **will attend** the Writer's Workshop at the University of Iowa in the fall. [future]

I **will be attending** the Writer's Workshop at the University of Iowa in the fall. [future progressive]

┌HELP─

A past action or state of being may also be shown in another way.

EXAMPLE
She **used to collect** stamps.

Used to typically expresses habitual action in the past.

NOTE A future action or state of being may also be expressed by using

- the present tense of *be* with *going to* and the base form of a verb

EXAMPLE My aunt and uncle **are going to visit** the Philippines next year.

- the present tense of *be* with *about to* and the base form of a verb

EXAMPLE Mr. Campos **is about to open** the time capsule in front of the whole school.

- the present tense of a verb with a word or word group that expresses future time

EXAMPLE Finals **begin next Monday.**

(4) The *present perfect tense* expresses an action or a state of being that occurred at some indefinite time in the past. The present perfect tense is formed with the helping verb *have* or *has* and the past participle of a verb.

EXAMPLES I **have written** to the governor, but I **have** not **received** a reply. [present perfect]

Who **has been playing** my cassettes? [present perfect progressive]

NOTE Avoid the use of the present perfect tense to express a specific time in the past. Instead, use the past tense.

NONSTANDARD *Prairie Schooner* has published a new short story by Louise Erdrich last month.

STANDARD *Prairie Schooner* **published** a new short story by Louise Erdrich last month.

The present perfect tense is also used to express an action or a state of being that began in the past and that continues into the present.

EXAMPLES Over one thousand United States communities **have joined** the International Sister City program. [present perfect]

The program **has been pairing** cities in the United States with cities in other nations since 1956. [present perfect progressive]

Reference Note

For information about using **past perfect** in "if" clauses, see page 701, Rule 21g.

(5) The *past perfect tense* expresses an action or a state of being that ended before some other past action or state of being. The past perfect tense is formed with the helping verb *had* and the past participle of a verb.

EXAMPLES I finally remembered where I **had seen** a copy of Rufino Tamayo's mural *Nature and the Artist.* [past perfect—The seeing occurred before the remembering.]

I **had been looking** through dozens of old magazines before I finally remembered to check the latest issue of *Smithsonian.* [past perfect progressive—The looking occurred before the remembering.]

(6) The *future perfect tense* expresses an action or a state of being that will end before some other action or state of being. The future perfect tense is formed with the helping verbs *will have* or *shall have* and the past participle of a verb.

EXAMPLES By the time the bus arrives, we **will have waited** for an hour. [future perfect—The waiting will occur before the arrival of the bus.]

By then, we **will have been waiting** for two hours. [future perfect progressive—The waiting will occur before the time indicated by *then.*]

Exercise 10 Understanding the Uses of the Six Tenses

Identify the tenses of the verbs in each of the following pairs of sentences. Also tell whether the verbs are in the progressive or emphatic form. Be prepared to explain how these differences in tense affect the meanings of the sentences.

EXAMPLE   1. a. Why had she gone to the theater?
   b. Why has she been going to the theater?

1. a. *past perfect tense*
   b. *present perfect progressive tense*

1. **a.** Margo lived in Brazil for eight years.
   b. Margo has lived in Brazil for eight years.
2. **a.** How many home runs did Sammy Sosa hit this season?
   b. How many home runs has Sammy Sosa hit this season?
3. **a.** Have the directions been explained clearly?
   b. Had the directions been explained clearly?

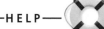

HELP

In the example in Exercise 10, the past perfect is used in the first sentence to show action that was completed in the past, while the second sentence uses present perfect progressive to show action that is continuing into the present.

USAGE

4. a. Was she driving?

   b. Had she been driving?

5. a. As of June 30, they will have raised taxes twice this year.

   b. As of June 30, they will be raising taxes for the second time this year.

6. a. Our team is producing the whole film ourselves.

   b. Our team will be producing the whole film ourselves.

7. a. People do like these science fiction films.

   b. People did like these science fiction films.

8. a. Uncle Jed lived in Abilene for sixty years.

   b. Uncle Jed has lived in Abilene for sixty years.

9. a. The game has been on for an hour.

   b. The game was on for an hour.

10. a. His quail eggs will have hatched by Saturday.

    b. His quail eggs will be hatching by Saturday.

Exercise 11 **Understanding the Uses of the Six Tenses**

Identify which sentence in each of the following pairs of sentences most clearly expresses the meaning given. Be prepared to name the tense(s) used in each sentence and to tell whether the verbs are in the progressive or emphatic form.

EXAMPLE   **1.** *Meaning:* The Yeary family no longer lives in Anchorage.

         a. The Yeary family lived in Anchorage for years.

         b. The Yeary family has lived in Anchorage for years.

      1. a

1. *Meaning:* John still works for Mr. Porzio.

   a. John had worked for Mr. Porzio for a year.

   b. John has worked for Mr. Porzio for a year.

2. *Meaning:* Ann Rosine could be on her way to Worcester right now or could be going in the future.

   a. Ann Rosine is moving to Worcester, Massachusetts.

   b. Ann Rosine will be moving to Worcester, Massachusetts.

3. *Meaning:* Jaime is still studying physics.

   a. Jaime has been studying physics since last summer.

   b. Jaime studied physics last summer.

4. *Meaning:* Alison takes a bus to work on a regular basis.

   a. Alison will be taking the bus to work.

   b. Alison takes the bus to work.

┌─**HELP**─

In the example in Exercise 11, the first sentence uses the past tense, while the second sentence uses the present perfect tense.

5. *Meaning:* Joe has not yet reached the school.
   a. Joe is riding his bike to school today.
   b. Joe rode his bike to school today.
6. *Meaning:* The opening of the shop will occur before September 8.
   a. On September 8, the shop will open.
   b. On September 8, the shop will have opened.
7. *Meaning:* Aunt Nell is currently photographing Alaskan wildflowers.
   a. Aunt Nell is photographing Alaskan wildflowers.
   b. Aunt Nell photographs Alaskan wildflowers.
8. *Meaning:* I no longer enjoy ice skating every winter.
   a. I did enjoy ice skating every winter.
   b. I do enjoy ice skating every winter.
9. *Meaning:* My brother is no longer practicing piano.
   a. My brother has been practicing piano all day.
   b. My brother had been practicing piano all day.
10. *Meaning:* Ray was a bank officer at the age of twenty-four.
    a. When Ray turned twenty-five, he had been promoted to the position of bank officer.
    b. When Ray turned twenty-five, he was promoted to the position of bank officer.

Special Problems in the Use of Tenses

Sequence of Tenses

21f. Use tense forms correctly to show relationships between verbs in a sentence.

(1) When describing events that occur at the same time, use verbs in the same tense.

EXAMPLES   The bell **rings,** and the classroom **empties.** [present tense]

The bell **rang,** and the classroom **emptied.** [past tense]

(2) When describing events that occur at different times, use verbs in different tenses to show the order of events.

EXAMPLES   I **play** football now, but I **played** basketball in junior high. [Because I am playing football now, the present tense form *play* is correct. My playing basketball occurred in the past and did not continue into the present; therefore, the past tense form *played* is correct.]

Sabrena **mentioned** that she **had invited** some of her neighbors to the party. [Because Sabrena made the statement in the past, the past tense form *mentioned* is correct. She invited the neighbors before she made the statement; therefore, the past perfect form *had invited* is correct.]

The tense you use depends on the meaning you want to express.

EXAMPLES   I **believe** they **own** the Flamingo Cafe. [Both verbs are in the present tense to indicate both actions are occurring now.]

I **believe** they **owned** the Flamingo Cafe. [The change in the tense of the second verb implies that they no longer own the Flamingo Cafe.]

Joan **said** that she **worked** at the textile mill last year. [Both verbs are in the past tense to indicate that both actions no longer occur.]

Joan **said** that she **will work** at the textile mill next year. [The change in the tense of the second verb implies that Joan did not work at the textile mill when she made the statement but that she planned to work there.]

21g. Do not use *would have* in an "if" clause that expresses the earlier of two past actions. Use the past perfect tense.

NONSTANDARD   If he would have taken more time, he would have won.
STANDARD   If he **had taken** more time, he would have won.

NONSTANDARD   I would not have been late if I would have had a watch.
STANDARD   I would not have been late if I **had had** a watch.

Exercise 12 Using Tenses Correctly

Each of the following sentences contains an error in the use of tenses. Revise each sentence to correct the error.

EXAMPLE   1. Frida not only wrote the story but also has illustrated it.

     1. *Frida not only wrote the story but also illustrated it.*

or

Frida not only has written the story but also has illustrated it.

1. Pam appreciated the old saying that every cloud had a silver lining.
2. By the time we graduate in June, Ms. Vargas will be teaching Spanish for twenty-four years.
3. Although Denny's skill was demonstrated during the season, he was not chosen to play in the all-star game.

⌐HELP—
Although two answers are given for the example in Exercise 12, you need to give only one answer for each sentence.

USAGE

4. If they would have called sooner, we would have given them a ride.

5. When Jeremy got to the dentist after school, his tooth already stopped hurting.

6. The company hired Ms. Littmann because she lived for many years in Japan.

7. By the time I presented my report before the special committee, the members have already studied several other reports on nuclear-waste disposal.

8. Mr. Frey already complained to the neighbors many times before he called the police.

9. By then I will receive my first paycheck.

10. If she forgot the directions, we could have been lost.

11. Hiram R. Revels, the first African American to be elected United States senator, has been a minister and teacher before he entered into politics.

12. If they had enough money, they could have taken a taxi to the opening of that new musical.

13. As I thought about our argument, I was sure that you lost your temper first.

14. Next Saturday is a very important anniversary for Mai's family; they will be living in the United States for exactly one year.

15. When we reviewed the videotapes of the game, we saw that the other team committed the foul.

16. The clerk remembered that the manager has ordered the new shipment last Tuesday.

17. How could I have forgotten that the sun rose in the east?

18. We estimate that when we are in our forties, we will be working more than twenty years.

19. If Gary would have read the ad more carefully, he could have saved more than fifty dollars on his new camera.

20. J. D. would have done much better on the art history exam if he reviewed the chapter on Aztec stonework.

The Present Infinitive and the Present Perfect Infinitive

Present Infinitive	Present Perfect Infinitive
to be	to have been
to discover	to have discovered

21h. The *present infinitive* expresses an action or a state of being that follows another action or state of being.

EXAMPLES   Charlotte had expected **to go** with us to the state fair. [The action expressed by *to go* follows the action expressed by *had expected.*]

Charlotte had planned **to ask** her boss for time off. [The action expressed by *to ask* follows the action expressed by *had planned.*]

21i. The *present perfect infinitive* expresses an action or a state of being that precedes another action or state of being.

EXAMPLES   My little brother pretended **to have read** my diary. [The action expressed by *to have read* precedes the action expressed by *pretended.*]

I would like **to have gone** to the new movie with you and your brother and sister. [The action expressed by *to have gone* precedes the action expressed by *would like.*]

Reference Note

For more information about **infinitives,** see page 564.

The Present Participle, the Past Participle, and the Present Perfect Participle

Present Participle	Past Participle	Present Perfect Participle
being	been	having been
discovering	discovered	having discovered

21j. When used as a verbal, the *present participle* or *past participle* expresses an action or a state of being that occurs at the same time as another action or state of being.

EXAMPLES   **Receiving** word of their freedom in June 1865, former slaves in Texas created the Juneteenth holiday. [The action expressed by *Receiving* occurs at the same time as the action expressed by *created.*]

Gathered at my grandmother's house, my family celebrated Juneteenth this year. [The state of being expressed by *Gathered* occurs at the same time as the action expressed by *celebrated.*]

Thrown at over ninety miles per hour, the baseball flew past the batter before he could swing. [The action expressed by *Thrown* occurs at the same time as the action expressed by *flew.*]

Reference Note

For more information about **participles used as verbals,** see page 558.

21k. When used as a verbal, the *present perfect participle* expresses an action or a state of being that precedes another action or state of being.

EXAMPLES   **Having missed** the midterm exam, I took a makeup test.
[The action expressed by *Having missed* precedes the action expressed by *took.*]

Having been accepted by several colleges, Rosa chose one.
[The action expressed by *Having been accepted* precedes the action expressed by *chose.*]

Exercise 13 Using Tenses Correctly

Each of the following sentences contains an error in the use of verb forms. Identify the error, and then give the correct form of the verb.

EXAMPLE   1. Finishing his research, Simon began writing his report on the Seneca chief Kaiiontwa'ko.

      1. *Finishing—Having finished*

⌐HELP⌐

Although some sentences in Exercise 13 can be correctly revised in more than one way, you need to give only one revision for each item.

1. Spending three hours on a review of chemistry, we then worked on irregular French verbs.
2. Standing in line for more than two hours, Vicky finally got tickets to the Trisha Yearwood concert.
3. To have written about Pueblo ceremonies, I would have to do more research at the library.
4. Flying from Missouri to California before, we remembered to set our watches back.
5. We wanted to have avoided any controversy about the new rules for packaging dairy products.
6. Having attempted to travel across the African continent, the explorers encountered vast deserts, dense rain forests, and tall mountains.
7. Through the centuries, arctic peoples learned to have survived in a harsh environment.
8. They were hoping to have had a multiple-choice test in history instead of an essay exam.
9. If you want to go shopping, I would have driven you to the mall with Neil.
10. Tutankhamen, Helen of Troy, and Shakespeare are the three people I would have most liked to have met.

Active Voice and Passive Voice

21l. *Voice* is the form a transitive verb takes to indicate whether the subject of the verb performs or receives the action.

Transitive verbs may be in the *active voice* or the *passive voice.* When the subject of a verb performs the action, the verb is in the **active voice.** When the subject receives the action, the verb is in the **passive voice.**

As the following examples show, verbs in the active voice take direct objects, and verbs in the passive voice do not.

ACTIVE VOICE   Mark Riley **anchors** the news. [*News* is the direct object.]
PASSIVE VOICE   The news **is anchored** by Mark Riley. [no direct object]

ACTIVE VOICE   The firefighters **have extinguished** the blazing fire. [*Fire* is the direct object.]
PASSIVE VOICE   The blazing fire **has been extinguished** by the fire-fighters. [no direct object]
PASSIVE VOICE   The fire **has been extinguished.** [no direct object]

From the preceding examples, you can see how an active construction can become a passive construction.

- The direct object of the verb in the active voice becomes the subject of the verb in the passive voice.

- The subject of the verb in the active voice may become an object of a prepositional phrase beginning with *by.* (As the last example shows, this prepositional phrase is not always included.)

The Retained Object

A verb in the active voice often has an indirect object as well as a direct object. When such a verb is put into the passive voice, either object can become the subject. The other object then serves as a complement called a **retained object.**

             S   V   IO   DO
ACTIVE VOICE   Mrs. Platero gives each new employee a tour of the plant.

             S   V   RO
PASSIVE VOICE   Each new employee is given a tour of the plant by Mrs. Platero.

             S   V   RO
PASSIVE VOICE   A tour of the plant is given each new employee by Mrs. Platero.

Reference Note

For more about **transitive verbs,** see page 512.

USAGE

A verb in the passive voice always includes a form of *be* and the past participle of a verb. The form of *be* and the helping verb, if any, indicate the tense of the verb phrase.

Reference Note

For the **conjugation of give in the active voice,** see page 692.

—HELP—

The progressive forms of the passive voice exist for the future, present perfect, past perfect, and future perfect tenses. However, the forms are not shown in the chart because the use of *been* with *being* is extremely awkward. *Give,* for example, in the passive future perfect progressive is *will (shall) have been being given.*

Conjugation of the Verb *Give* in the Passive Voice	
Present Tense	
Singular	*Plural*
I am given	we are given
you are given	you are given
he, she, it is given	they are given
Present Progressive: am, are, is being given	
Past Tense	
Singular	*Plural*
I was given	we were given
you were given	you were given
he, she, it is was given	they were given
Past Progressive: was, were being given	
Future Tense	
Singular	*Plural*
I will (shall) be given	we will (shall) be given
you will (shall) be given	you will (shall) be given
he, she, it will (shall) be given	they will (shall) be given
Present Perfect Tense	
Singular	*Plural*
I have been given	we have been given
you have been given	you have been given
he, she, it has been given	they have been given
Past Perfect Tense	
Singular	*Plural*
I had been given	we had been given
you had been given	you had been given
he, she, it had been given	they had been given

Conjugation of the Verb *Give* in the Passive Voice	
Future Perfect Tense	
Singular	*Plural*
I will (shall) have been given	we will (shall) have been given
you will (shall) have been given	you will (shall) have been given
he, she, it will (shall) have been given	they will (shall) have been given

The Uses of the Passive Voice

21m. Use the passive voice sparingly.

Choosing between the active voice and the passive voice is a matter of style, not correctness. In general, however, the passive voice is less direct, less forceful, and less concise than the active voice. In fact, the passive voice may produce an awkward effect.

AWKWARD PASSIVE	The event was completed when a triple somersault was done by Mario.
ACTIVE	Mario **completed** the event by doing a triple somersault.

A string of passive-voice verbs is particularly awkward.

STRING OF PASSIVES	I was invited by Ms. Long to visit her animal shelter. Rows of cages had been placed along two sides of a large storage shed. Dozens of cats, dogs, hamsters, and guinea pigs were held in the cages. In one corner of the noisy building, a scrawny brown puppy was being hand-fed by an assistant. I was told by Ms. Long that so many unwanted pets had been brought to her by people that homes could not be found for all of them. It was agreed by us that the responsibility of owning a pet should be understood by people before one is bought.
ACTIVE	Ms. Long **invited** me to visit her animal shelter. She **had placed** rows of cages along two sides of a large storage shed. The cages **held** dozens of cats, dogs, hamsters, and guinea pigs. In one corner of the noisy building, an assistant **was hand-feeding** a scrawny brown puppy. Ms. Long told me that people **had brought** her so many unwanted pets that she **could** not **find** homes for all of them. We **agreed** that people **should understand** the responsibility of owning a pet before they **buy** one.

USAGE

HELP

The active voice is preferable in the example in Exercise 14 because it makes the sentence more direct and forceful.

Passive voice constructions are not always awkward. In fact, the passive voice is useful in the following situations:

- when you do not know who performed the action

EXAMPLE   All of the tickets **had been sold** weeks before the concert.

- when you do not want to reveal the performer of the action

EXAMPLE   Mistakes **were made.**

- when you want to emphasize the receiver of the action rather than the performer

EXAMPLES   Lasers **are used** in industry, communications, and medicine.

Aretha Franklin **has been emulated** by many singers.

Exercise 14   Revising Sentences in the Passive Voice

Revise the following sentences by changing verbs from the passive voice to the active voice wherever you think the changes are desirable. If you think the passive voice is preferable, write *C*. For each verb, be prepared to explain why you think the active or passive voice is preferable.

EXAMPLE   1. An interesting legend about the origin of the kachinas was told to us by one of the participants in the Hopi ceremonial dance.

1. *One of the participants in the Hopi ceremonial dance told us an interesting legend about the origin of the kachinas.*

1. After all of the new computers had been installed by the service representatives, a training session was given to us by them.
2. If the children had been enchanted by Mr. Wright's tales before, they would be even more enthralled by his new story of a fantasy kingdom on the moon.
3. A meeting was held by the area homeowners to discuss the landfill project that had been proposed by the city council.
4. The value of storytelling is explained in an ancient Seneca myth.
5. While the decorations are being created by Clarence, the buffet will be prepared by Edna.
6. Potatoes had been cultivated in South America for more than twenty centuries before they were grown in Europe.
7. The 1539 expedition of Francisco Vásquez de Coronado was guided by Estevanico, a well-known black explorer.

8. The chapters on constitutional amendments, which had been assigned to us last week by Mrs. Robinson, were reviewed by us before the test.
9. Shinae Chun is admired and respected by her colleagues.
10. If the practicality of home robots had been demonstrated by Mike Smith, his request for funding would not have been rejected by the review committee.

Mood

Mood is the form a verb takes to indicate the attitude of the person using the verb. Verbs may be in one of three moods: *indicative*, *imperative*, or *subjunctive*.

21n. The *indicative mood* expresses a fact, an opinion, or a question.

EXAMPLES   Heitor Villa-Lobos **was** a composer who **became** known for his use of Brazilian folk music.

Isabel Allende **is** a gifted writer.

Can you **tell** me when the United States **entered** World War I?

21o. The *imperative mood* expresses a direct command or a request.

A verb in the imperative mood has only one form. That form is the same as the verb's base form.

EXAMPLES   **Tell** me when the United States entered World War I.

Please **pass** the salsa.

21p. The *subjunctive mood* expresses a suggestion, a necessity, a condition contrary to fact, or a wish.

Only the present and past tenses have distinctive forms in the subjunctive mood.

Notice in the following partial conjugation of *be* how the present tense and the past tense in the subjunctive mood differ from those in the indicative mood.

Reference Note

For more information about **conjugating verbs,** see pages 692 and 694.

Present Indicative		Present Subjunctive	
Singular	**Plural**	**Singular**	**Plural**
I am	we are	[that] I be	[that] we be
you are	you are	[that] you be	[that] you be
he, she, it is	they are	[that] he, she, it be	[that] they be

Past Indicative		Past Subjunctive	
Singular	**Plural**	**Singular**	**Plural**
I was	we were	[if] I were	[if] we were
you were	you were	[if] you were	[if] you were
he, she, it was	they were	[if] he, she, it were	[if] they were

┌HELP─

The use of *that* and *if* in the chart is explained in Rules 21p(1) and 21p(2).

The present subjunctive form of a verb is the same as the base form of the verb. *Be* is the only verb whose past subjunctive form is different from its past indicative form.

(1) The *present subjunctive* expresses a suggestion or necessity.

The verb in a subordinate clause beginning with *that* is usually in the subjunctive mood when a word in the independent clause indicates a suggestion (such as *ask, request, suggest,* or *recommend*) or a necessity (such as *necessary* or *essential*).

EXAMPLES   We recommended that Marva Collins **be invited** to speak at the assembly tomorrow.

The students have urged that John **be reinstated.**

I move that the committee **adjourn.**

It is essential that she **have** a chance to compete in the state debating finals.

(2) The *past subjunctive* expresses a condition contrary to fact or expresses a wish.

A clause beginning with *if, as if,* or *as though* often expresses a condition contrary to fact—something that is not true. In such a clause, use the past subjunctive.

┌STYLE   TIP┐

Although the use of the subjunctive is declining in informal situations, you should use it in formal writing and speech.

USAGE

EXAMPLES   If I **were** you, I'd be pleased.

                    If she **were** careful, she would make fewer errors.

                    My friend Doris teases me as though she **were** my sister.

Similarly, use the past subjunctive to express a wish.

EXAMPLES   I wish I **were** on a Caribbean island.

                    Jaime wishes that his mother **weren't** feeling ill.

Exercise 15 Using the Subjunctive Mood Correctly

For each of the following sentences, identify the mood of the italicized verb as *indicative, imperative,* or *subjunctive.*

EXAMPLE   1. If I *were* as talented an actor as you, I would try out for the lead in the play.

                    1. *subjunctive*

1. Willis had insisted that every employee *be* invited to the company's Juneteenth picnic.
2. Felicia, *sit* closer to the table, please.
3. Did you hear that Tanya's mother *is* the new deputy fire chief?
4. Having struck out again, Katie moaned, "I wish I *were* a better hitter!"
5. *Are* you and your brother excited about seeing your grandparents?
6. If you want to join the league, *sign* up before the end of school.
7. "I wish this book *were* a little shorter," sighed Sabrena as she turned to page 378.
8. Please *wait* here while I get the rest of my books.
9. I wish I *were* able to go to the sneak preview of the new Spike Lee movie, but I have to work.
10. "This time next year, I *will be* in college," Takala said.

Modals

21q. A modal is a helping (auxiliary) verb that is joined with a main verb to express an attitude toward the action or state of being of the main verb.

(1) The modals *can* and *could* are used to express ability.

EXAMPLES   **Can** you **swim**?

I **could** not **move** my computer desk.

(2) The modal *may* is used to express permission or possibility.

EXAMPLES   **May** I **drive** your car? [permission]

I **may have put** my library card in my locker before I came to class. [possibility]

(3) The modal *might*, like *may*, is used to express a possibility.

Often, the possibility expressed by *might* is less likely than the possibility expressed by *may*.

EXAMPLE   I **might have put** my library card in my locker before I came to class, but I doubt it.

(4) The modal *must* is used most often to express a requirement. Sometimes *must* is used to express an explanation.

EXAMPLES   First, we **must obtain** our principal's permission to hold the fund-raiser in the school cafeteria. [requirement]

My aunt Rowena said, "You **must have** a green thumb, for all of your plants are healthy and beautiful." [explanation]

(5) The modal *ought* is used to express an obligation or a likelihood.

EXAMPLES   We **ought to reserve** judgment until we have examined all of the evidence. [obligation]

The soccer game **ought to be** over by 6:00 P.M. [likelihood]

(6) The modals *shall* and *will* are used to express future time.

EXAMPLES   I **will** [or **shall**] **graduate** from high school this June.

Where **will** the graduation ceremony **be held**?

USAGE

(7) The modal *should* is used to express a recommendation, an obligation, or a possibility.

EXAMPLES   You **should visit** each campus again before deciding which university to attend. [recommendation]

I see now that I **should have asked** before borrowing the book. [obligation]

Should you **decide** to accept the other job offer, please let me know. [possibility]

(8) The modal *would* is used to express the conditional form of a verb.

A conditional verb form usually appears in an independent clause that is joined with an "*if*" clause. The "*if*" clause explains *under what condition(s)* the action or state of being of the conditional verb takes place.

EXAMPLE   If it had continued to rain, we **would have canceled** the outdoor concert.

Would is used also to express future time in a subordinate clause when the main verb in the independent clause is in the past tense.

EXAMPLE   Janetta wrote in her e-mail message that she **would call** me tonight at nine o'clock.

Additionally, *would* is used to express an action that was repeated in the past, a polite request, or an invitation.

EXAMPLES   I remember that each year, usually in February, our school **would hold** a winter carnival. [action repeated in the past]

Would you please **take** these letters to the post office for me? [polite request]

Would you **accompany** me to the picnic? [invitation]

Reference Note

For more about **helping (auxiliary) verbs** and **main verbs,** see page 509.

Exercise 16 Writing Appropriate Modals

For each of the following sentences, supply an appropriate modal.

EXAMPLE   **1.** If no one objects, I _____ tell the council what our decision is.

    1. will

1. One of the amazing things about Lord Byron is the way he _____ write both romantic love poems and biting satire.

┌HELP─

Although more than one response may be possible for each item in Exercise 16, you need to give only one answer for each.

2. Because you asked so politely, you _____ choose the subject of your report first.

3. "_____ I call you when it's over?" asked Deanna.

4. If this weather continues, we _____ have snow on the field during the finals.

5. "You really _____ read that story by Isak Dinesen!" Jerome urged.

6. _____ you ask Ms. Gibson about the assembly on Friday?

7. While the sun is still shining, you _____ wash your parents' car.

8. Without Yoshi's help, we _____ not finish this on time.

9. If you have time, we _____ listen to the new Brandy album.

10. After using that brand of computer, I _____ highly recommend it to all my friends.

Review F **Proofreading Sentences for Errors in the Form and Use of Verbs**

Each of the following sentences contains awkward, informal, or incorrect verb usage. Revise each sentence according to the rules of formal, standard English.

EXAMPLE   **1.** Keisha said that if she was the President, she would veto the bill.

1. *was—were*

1. If we would have checked, we would have known the library was closed.

2. The movie was especially liked by Kira and her brother because of the beautiful nature photography.

3. If I was Luís, I wouldn't have argued with the umpire.

4. Cindy retraced her steps and found the cafe at which she left her credit card.

5. Did Kadonna realize that *hurricane* and *typhoon* were two names for the the same phenomenon?

6. As he slowly turned the key, the door suddenly swings wide open.

7. Last week, the school newspaper has printed Kim's story.

8. Winning the medal, she revised her practice schedule and gave herself more free time.

9. By the time the next presidential election comes up, I will be in the United States for six years.

10. Mr. Washington wanted to have shown them his collection of African sculptures, but he was suddenly called away on business.

11. Ladies and gentlemen of the jury, I demand that this innocent man is acquitted.
12. She would have volunteer for the project, but she already had too much to do.
13. If you are tired, why don't you lay down for a while before dinner.
14. Yes, I use to baby-sit them years ago.
15. To have celebrated the victory, the team met at a local pizza parlor.
16. Do you mean that the letter was setting right there in plain sight the whole time?
17. I realized suddenly that I had tore up the directions that I needed.
18. As we watched, the eagle spread its wings and raised into the sky.
19. In only an hour, he had wrote almost eight pages.
20. If you would have been watching the clock, you would have been on time.

Review G **Proofreading Paragraphs for Errors in the Form and Use of Verbs**

Most of the sentences in the following paragraphs contain awkward, informal, or incorrect verb usage. Revise each such sentence according to the rules of formal, standard English. If a sentence is already correct, write C.

EXAMPLE   [1] Every time I have performed this experiment, the outcome amazed me.

1. *Every time I have performed this experiment, the outcome has amazed me.*

or

Every time I performed this experiment, the outcome amazed me.

[1] Have you ever seen a band of light shimmering over a hot road, as though a pool of water was lying just ahead? [2] Mirages have been just one of many types of optical illusions that will fool the average observer.

[3] The simple illustration shown on the next page will allow you to have experienced another kind of illusion. [4] In a few minutes the flying bird will be returned to its cage by you. [5] However, to do so, it is essential that you are calm and give the experiment your full attention. [6] Fix your stare on the bird for a minute or two, and then focus on the white space in the center of the cage next to the bird. [7] Having stared at the white space, you will, at the same time, see the bird

appear. [8] When the bird appears, you will probably have noticed something strange—its feathers will be green and purple. [9] Although you have no longer been looking at the bird, its image (or, rather, its afterimage) has remained on your retina. [10] The afterimage is composed of colors opposite to the bird's original red and yellow colors.

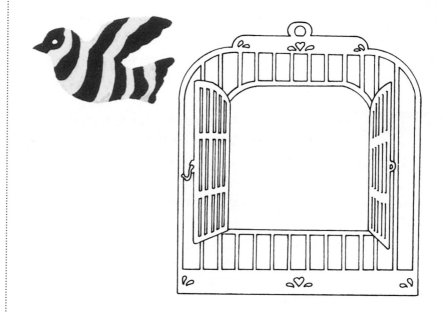

Chapter Review

A. Using the Past and Past Participle Forms of Verbs Correctly

For each of the following sentences, write the correct form of the italicized verb in parentheses.

1. The lion had silently (*creep*) up behind its prey.

2. The outfielder has (*catch*) the ball in the tip of his glove.

3. She (*fling*) open the door and raced out of the house.

4. Candida has always (*beat*) me at tennis.

5. She (*tear*) her coat while she was climbing over the fence.

B. Choosing the Forms of *Lie* and *Lay, Sit* and *Set,* and *Rise* and *Raise*

Choose the correct verb form in parentheses in each of the following sentences.

6. What time did you (*set, sit*) down to start your report?

7. The exhausted wrestler could not (*rise, raise*) himself from the mat.

8. In a hurry to go to work, I couldn't remember where I had (*laid, lain*) my keys.

9. Malcolm (*sat, set*) his new computer on the desk.

10. Whenever Joan reads, her puppy (*lies, lays*) down at her feet.

C. Using Tenses Correctly

Each of the following sentences contains an error in the use of tenses. Identify the error, and then give the correct form of the verb.

11. By the time we get to the concert, the orchestra will be playing for half an hour.

12. If Benito would have done his homework after school, he would have been allowed to go to the play last night.

13. Sophie did not want to go to the movie because she already saw it twice.

14. Mrs. Gleason had hoped to have been here today.

15. Did you know that the solar system included asteroids and comets as well as planets and moons?

D. Revising Sentences in the Passive Voice

Revise the following sentences by changing verbs from the passive voice to the active voice wherever you think the changes are appropriate. If you think the passive voice is preferable for a sentence, write *C.*

16. Clearer skies were hoped for by us that spring, so that the snow would be melted by the sun.

17. The missing painting was replaced in the middle of the night.

18. The novel *As I Lay Dying* was written by William Faulkner when he was working as a night watchman.

19. Special effects are often used to create excitement in Hollywood blockbusters.

20. The results of the aptitude test were told to us by the principal.

E. Identifying Indicative, Imperative, and Subjunctive Mood

For each of the following sentences, identify the mood of the italicized verb or verb phrase as *indicative, imperative,* or *subjunctive.*

21. *Send* a thank-you note to anyone who gives you a gift.

22. Tollie asked that her suggestion *be reconsidered.*

23. *Be* quiet while I'm talking.

24. Karen spoke to her brother as though she *were* his mother.

25. The brown color of the leaves showed that they *were* about to fall.

F. Revising Sentences in a Paragraph by Correcting Verb Forms

Identify each incorrect verb form in the following paragraph. Then, write the correct form.

[26] For at least five thousand years, people been eating popcorn. [27] If you are like most of them, you probably falled in love with popcorn when you were a child. [28] The ancient Aztecs thought so highly of popcorn that they even use to wear it around their necks. [29] Centuries ago adult American Indians probably remember

popcorn as a source of delight and excitement in their childhoods. [30] After all, at that time popcorn was often simply throwed into a fire or roasted on a stick. [31] What a stir there must have been among the children when the kernels began to have popped clear of the fire! [32] Like children today, they probably would not be too bothered by the sand or dirt that the popcorn has picked up. [33] Still, these early popcorn lovers were not plagued by duds, which can have broken your teeth and which were the scourge of the popcorn industry until the 1950s. [34] That was when Orville Redenbacher and Charles Bowman successfully growed a variety of corn that did not have as many duds. [35] When the big popcorn manufacturers rejected the new corn, Redenbacher started his own company, and as you probably know, he had experienced phenomenal success.

Writing Application
Using Standard Verb Forms in a Paragraph

Irregular Verbs   The editor of your school's yearbook is planning a seniors-only feature. Interested seniors may submit one-paragraph descriptions of school events that have helped to make this year memorable. Write a paragraph to submit for publication. In your paragraph, include at least five irregular verbs. Be sure to use the correct past and past participle forms of verbs.

Prewriting   Make a list of memorable events in which a number of students participated during the school year. From your list, choose the event that you remember most vividly, and note what made the event special.

Writing   Describe the event, capturing the mood it inspired in your school. Include sensory details to hold the reader's interest. Take extra care with the past and past participle forms of verbs.

Revising   Ask a classmate who took part in the event to read your paragraph. Add, cut, and revise details as necessary to improve your description. Be sure that you have used at least five irregular verbs.

Publishing   Proofread your paragraph, checking for errors in grammar, usage, spelling, and punctuation. To publish your descriptions, you and your classmates can compile them in a mini-yearbook. You may want to include photographs or drawings to accompany the descriptions.

Reference Note
For more information about **irregular verbs,** see page 672.

Using Modifiers Correctly

Forms and Uses of Adjectives and Adverbs; Comparison

Diagnostic Preview

A. Using Modifiers Correctly

Most of the following sentences contain errors in the use of modifiers and comparisons. Rewrite each incorrect sentence to correct the error. If a sentence is already correct, write *C*.

EXAMPLE   **1.** Of my three brothers and sisters, my sister Giselle has the better sense of humor.

         1. Of my three brothers and sisters, my sister Giselle has the best sense of humor.

1. Which is widest, the Mississippi River or the Colorado River?

2. When the temperature reached 103 degrees in August, hotter than any day that year, the board of health warned people not to go outdoors unless they absolutely had to do so.

3. That is the most palest shade of blue I have ever seen.

4. Because the drummer played bad, the band's rhythm was thrown off.

5. Pointing to the two glasses partially filled with water, the magician asked, "Which glass contains the least water?"

6. When you dress for job interviews, you should wear the styles and colors of clothing that look attractively on you.

7. If Mark keeps moving that slowly, he'll never get home before dark.

8. Has Thomas been saving money regular for his trip to the Yucatán this year?

9. Philadelphia and Atlantic City are the largest cities near my home, and Philadelphia is the closest of the two.

10. Although they can't play their guitars very good, they sell many CDs.

11. "Nurse López, I feel remarkably well today, better than I have ever felt before," said Mr. Parker.

12. "Sharon, you have been working harder than anyone here," I said.

13. My brother William became the strongest player on the local wheelchair-basketball team.

14. You can adjust the control on the television set to make the picture a little less brighter.

15. The cheese smells badly but tastes good.

B. Selecting Modifiers to Complete Sentences

For each sentence in the following paragraph, select the correct modifier from the pair given in parentheses.

EXAMPLE   **[1]** The skilled house movers dismantled the beautiful Victorian mansion (*careful, carefully*).

       1. *carefully*

[16] It's (*real, really*) amazing what house movers can accomplish! [17] The (*most, more*) interesting house-moving feat that I have ever heard of involved the Queen Anne Mansion in Eureka Springs, Arkansas. [18] Built in 1891, the three-story home, with a tower and wrap-around porch, was moved (*efficient, efficiently*) from Carthage, Missouri. [19] Crews worked (*speedy, speedily*) to dismantle the mansion. [20] They used special tools and worked (*careful, carefully*) to cut and pry the building apart. [21] The contractor had planned (*well, good*) for the move to Eureka Springs. [22] It was the (*bigger, biggest*) move ever seen in that area, requiring thirty-seven long flatbed trucks and three storage vans. [23] The new owners looked on (*happy, happily*) as workers reassembled the mansion's more than two thousand exterior stones, its wooden walls and floors, its hand-beveled windows, and its central oak staircase. [24] The restored Victorian mansion, which is open for tours, has a more unusual history than (*any other, any*) house in the city. [25] It now looks (*impressive, impressively*), set atop a hill near downtown Eureka Springs.

Forms of Modifiers

A *modifier* is a word or word group that makes the meaning of another word or word group more specific. The two kinds of modifiers are *adjectives* and *adverbs*.

One-Word Modifiers

Adjectives

Reference Note

For more information about **adjectives,** see page 505. For more about **adverbs,** see page 514.

22a. An *adjective* makes the meaning of a noun or a pronoun more specific.

EXAMPLES	**perfect** score	**eager** participant	**Irish** accent
	clear water	**last** one	**falling** snow

Adverbs

22b. An *adverb* makes the meaning of a verb, an adjective, or another adverb more specific.

EXAMPLES	walks **briskly**	ran **very quickly**
	completely innocent	**not** lonesome

Adjective or Adverb?

Most modifiers with an *–ly* ending are used as adverbs. Many adverbs, in fact, are formed by adding *–ly* to adjectives.

Adjectives	usual	calm	brief
	absurd	appropriate	sad
Adverbs	usual**ly**	calm**ly**	brief**ly**
	absurd**ly**	appropriate**ly**	sad**ly**

However, some modifiers ending in *–ly* are used as adjectives.

EXAMPLES   **monthly** budget   **early** indication   **likely** outcome

A few modifiers have the same form whether they are used as adjectives or as adverbs.

Adjectives	a **fast** train	a **little** sleep	an **early** start
Adverbs	moves **fast**	slept **little**	starting **early**

Phrases Used as Modifiers

Like one-word modifiers, phrases can also be used as adjectives and adverbs.

EXAMPLES   I prefer this time **of the year.** [The prepositional phrase *of the year* acts as an adjective that modifies the noun *time.*]

Falling from the very top of the tree, the leaf seemed to take hours to float to the ground. [The participial phrase *Falling from the very top of the tree* acts as an adjective that modifies the noun *leaf.*]

Drive especially carefully **on wet roads.** [The prepositional phrase *on wet roads* acts as an adverb that modifies the verb *Drive.*]

You will have to climb to the top of that hill **to see what is happening on the other side.** [The infinitive phrase *to see what is happening on the other side* acts as an adverb that modifies the verb *climb.*]

Reference Note

For more about **phrases,** see page 553.

Reference Note

For information about **dangling and misplaced modifiers,** see pages 744 and 746.

Clauses Used as Modifiers

Like words and phrases, clauses can also be used as modifiers.

EXAMPLES   Guglielmo Marconi helped develop wireless telegraphy, **which we now know as radio.** [The adjective clause *which we now know as radio* modifies the noun *telegraphy.*]

Before he became famous for such feats as sending a message across the Atlantic Ocean, Marconi worked in his father's attic, sending signals across the room. [The adverb clause *Before he became famous for such feats as sending a message across the Atlantic Ocean* modifies the verb *worked.*]

Reference Note

For more about **clauses,** see page 576.

Exercise 1   Identifying Adjectives and Adverbs

For each of the following sentences, tell whether the italicized word or word group functions as an *adjective* or an *adverb*.

EXAMPLE   **1.** The girl with the *brown* hair is a new student.

1. *adjective*

1. How many birds would you guess are sitting in the *tallest* tree?
2. The chipmunk quickly disappeared into a hole *in the ground.*
3. The kite soared *majestically* over the treetops.
4. Stephan always has *more* homework than his brother.

5. *Since he left the White House in 1981,* Jimmy Carter has stayed active internationally as an unofficial diplomat and domestically as a spokesperson for Habitat for Humanity.
6. *On quiet, moonlit nights,* Jason likes to go for long walks.
7. Sarah's paper airplane stayed in the air *longer* than anyone else's in her class.
8. Photosynthesis, *which converts carbon dioxide and water into sugar and oxygen,* is the process plants use to turn solar energy into energy they can use.
9. The *annual* wildflower blooms are later than usual this year.
10. *Although they are not as blind as some people think,* many types of bats rely more on smell or sound than on sight to find their way around.

Uses of Modifiers

22c. Use an adjective to modify the subject of a linking verb.

Reference Note

For more about **predicate adjectives,** see page 544.

The most common linking verbs are the forms of *be: am, is, are, was, were, be, been,* and *being.* A linking verb often connects the subject to a *predicate adjective*—an adjective that is in the predicate and that modifies the subject.

EXAMPLES   The company's training program is **rigorous.**

The baby soon became **tired** and **cranky.**

22d. Use an adverb to modify an action verb.

An action verb is often modified by an adverb—a word that explains *how, when, where,* or *to what extent* the action is performed.

EXAMPLES   The world's population is increasing **rapidly.**

The astronaut spoke **enthusiastically** about her successful mission in space.

Some verbs may be used as linking verbs or as action verbs.

EXAMPLES   Carlos looked **happy.** [*Looked* is a linking verb. Notice that the modifier following it, *happy,* is an adjective.]

Carlos looked **happily** at his latest design. [*Looked* is an action verb. Notice that the modifier following it, *happily,* is an adverb.]

USAGE

Exercise 2 Selecting Modifiers to Complete Sentences

Reference Note

For more information about **linking verbs** and **action verbs,** see page 510.

Select the correct modifier from the pair in parentheses in each of the following sentences.

EXAMPLE 1. The pizza you are baking smells (*delicious, deliciously*).

1. *delicious*

1. The sled's runners glided (*smooth, smoothly*) over the ice and packed snow of the trail.
2. The weather outside looks (*miserable, miserably*).
3. Neka embroidered the rain-bird symbol (*perfect, perfectly*), checking each stitch as she worked.
4. Do you think the official explanation of the budget cut sounds (*incredible, incredibly*)?
5. Why was she looking (*suspicious, suspiciously*) at me?
6. This apple tastes (*peculiar, peculiarly*) to me.
7. Mike smiled (*proud, proudly*) when he told us about his West African heritage.
8. Dawn goes jogging (*regular, regularly*).
9. He disappeared (*silent, silently*) into the underbrush.
10. The conference room smelled (*stuffy, stuffily*).
11. With the proper care and conditions, these flowers will grow (*rapid, rapidly*).
12. Still, we remain (*confident, confidently*) that there will be a solution to these problems.
13. The young architect's design for the apartment complex was (*simple, simply*) and efficient.
14. His model engine ran (*rapid, rapidly*) at first but soon ran down.
15. Although we reassured Alexandra about her solo, she remained (*nervous, nervously*).
16. Doesn't this cashmere coat feel (*soft, softly*) to you?
17. An open can of paint tilted (*precarious, precariously*) at the top of the ladder.
18. The six spaniel puppies grew (*bold, boldly*) in the company of their mother.
19. She's only six, but she dances (*beautiful, beautifully*) and already has an audition for a commercial.
20. A good chemist must be (*careful, carefully*) with materials and containers used at work.

TIPS & TRICKS

To determine whether to use an adjective or an adverb after a verb, replace the verb with the appropriate form of the linking verb *seem.* If the form of *seem* makes sense in the sentence, the original verb is being used as a linking verb, which calls for an adjective. If the form of *seem* is absurd in the sentence, the original verb is being used as an action verb, which calls for an adverb.

EXAMPLES
Carlos looked happy. [Since *Carlos seemed happy* makes sense, *looked* is being used as a linking verb and calls for the adjective *happy.*]

Carlos looked happily at his latest design. [Since *Carlos seemed happily at his latest design* is absurd, *looked* is being used as an action verb and calls for the adverb *happily.*]

For each sentence in the following paragraph, select the correct modifier from the pair given in parentheses.

EXAMPLE   [1] Debbie Allen is an (*incredible, incredibly*) talented performer and choreographer.

1. *incredibly*

[1] In the picture to the left, Debbie Allen dances quite (*energetic, energetically*) in a scene from the TV series *Fame.* [2] You might say that fame itself looks (*comfortable, comfortably*) on her. [3] Allen, who grew up in Houston, Texas, has danced (*regular, regularly*) since the age of three. [4] She attended the Houston Ballet School, graduated from Howard University, and then headed (*confident, confidently*) to New York City. [5] On Broadway she was (*triumphant, triumphantly*) in revivals of the musicals *West Side Story* and *Sweet Charity.* [6] Later, she (*successful, successfully*) choreographed *Fame* and won two Emmy Awards for her work on that show. [7] Allen looks (*natural, naturally*) in a producer's chair, too, and worked with Steven Spielberg and Colin Wilson to produce the film *Amistad.* [8] Through the years, she has worked (*diligent, diligently*) and has battled racism and sexism to succeed. [9] Never one to accept second best, Allen has risen (*steady, steadily*) to the top in her profession. [10] In interviews Debbie Allen seems (*proud, proudly*) of her achievements but also ready for new challenges.

Eight Troublesome Modifiers

Bad and *Badly*

Bad is an adjective. *Badly* is an adverb. In standard English, only the adjective form should follow a sense verb, such as *feel, look, sound, taste,* or *smell,* or other linking verb.

NONSTANDARD   This leftover chicken smells badly.
STANDARD   This leftover chicken smells **bad.**

The expression *feel badly* is common in informal situations, but you should use *feel bad* in formal speaking and writing.

INFORMAL   The boys feel badly about forgetting your birthday.
FORMAL   The boys feel **bad** about forgetting your birthday.

Good and *Well*

Good is an adjective. *Well* may be used as an adjective or an adverb. Avoid using *good* to modify an action verb. Instead, use *well* as an adverb meaning "capably" or "satisfactorily."

NONSTANDARD   The track team did good at the meet.
   STANDARD   The track team did **well** at the meet.

Feel good and *feel well* mean different things. *Feel good* means "to feel happy or pleased." *Feel well* means "to feel healthy."

EXAMPLES   Helping pick up litter in our neighborhood makes me feel **good.**

             Chris had to leave because she didn't feel **well.**

Real and *Really*

Real is an adjective. *Really* is an adverb meaning "actually" or "truly." Although *real* is often used as an adverb meaning "very" in informal situations, avoid this use in formal speaking and writing.

INFORMAL   Your new car is real nice.
   FORMAL   Your new car is **really** nice.

Slow and *Slowly*

Slow is used as both an adjective and an adverb. *Slowly* is used as an adverb. In most adverb uses, it is better to use *slowly* than to use *slow.*

EXAMPLES   Jorge sat at the intersection watching the **slow** progress of the train.

             Jorge sat at the intersection as the train **slowly** rolled past.

STYLE   **TIP**

Well is also used as an adjective meaning "suitable, proper, right" or "in satisfactory condition."

EXAMPLES
It is **well** you arrived when you did.

All is **well** with us.

STYLE   **TIP**

The expressions *drive slow* and *go slow* are common in informal situations. In formal speaking and writing, however, use *drive slowly* and *go slowly.*

USAGE

> **Exercise 4** **Revising Sentences to Correct Errors in the Use of Troublesome Modifiers**

Most of the following sentences contain errors in the standard, formal use of modifiers. Identify each incorrect modifier, and then give the correct form. If the sentence is already correct, write *C.*

EXAMPLE   **1.** After a long rehearsal, the dance troupe performed quite good.

         1. good—well

 1. After she had lost the election, Bernadette felt very bad.
 2. Charlotte seemed real happy about getting an A on her history test.

3. Ms. Stein is a good teacher who prepares her lessons well.
4. Some shades of blue and green go good together.
5. "Life can't be treating you all that bad," I told Walker as we sat down at the lunch table.
6. "I'm positive I did good on that test," Edward confidently remarked to his friends.
7. Since the Turkish candy halvah is very sweet, it should be served in small pieces and eaten slow.
8. Everyone wondered whether the stone he had found in his backyard was a real diamond.
9. "Remember to speak slow when you give your speech," Mr. Wells advised the nervous candidate.
10. Chen tried to teach me to use chopsticks, but the lesson didn't go very good.
11. Yuck! That burnt milk smells badly!
12. The plot wasn't much, but the actors were good.
13. Wakame may be seaweed, but I am told it tastes quite well in many Japanese dishes.
14. Don't worry; almost everybody plays bad when they start learning a new sport.
15. Doesn't the train seem slowly to you?
16. Actually, once you see it, the solution is real easy.
17. Wow! Is that a real saber-toothed tiger jaw?
18. No, adult raccoons certainly do not make well pets.
19. Their weather reports are always well.
20. Go slow at first until you get used to the course.

Review A Determining the Correct Use of Modifiers

Each of the following sentences contains an italicized modifier. First, identify the word that each modifier describes. If the modifier is incorrect according to the rules of standard, formal usage, give the correct form. If the modifier is already correct, write *C*.

EXAMPLE   1. Something sounds *strangely* next door.

     1. *something—strange*

1. The players did *good* in the fourth quarter.
2. The bread dough rose too *rapid*.
3. We walked *slowly* on the icy sidewalk.

4. Sam feels *badly* about forgetting to meet us.
5. She sounded very *angrily* on the phone.
6. These new jeans do not fit me *good* at all.
7. Rita answered the questions *precisely*.
8. Fortunately, no one was hurt *bad* in the accident.
9. Mr. Tate's company can do the job *efficiently*.
10. The judge rapped her gavel *sharp* to restore order.

Review B Proofreading for Correct Use of Modifiers

Most of the sentences in the following paragraph contain errors in the standard, formal use of modifiers. Identify each incorrect modifier, and then give the correct form. If a sentence is already correct, write *C*.

EXAMPLE: [1] Country and western music is rooted firm in the traditional music of the American South.

1. *firm—firmly*

[1] The popularity of country and western music (C & W) has grown rapid in the past thirty-five years. [2] In fact, many radio stations all over the nation are playing C & W exclusive. [3] Nowadays, country music appeals to fans of near all ages and occupations. [4] For example, one modern American president, George Bush, officially declared his fondness for country music when he attended the Country Music Awards ceremony. [5] Top country stars, such as Clint Black, Reba McEntire, and Garth Brooks, not only have best-selling albums but play to increasing large numbers of fans. [6] In the photo on the left, for example, Garth Brooks looks ecstatically as he acknowledges his fans' enthusiastic applause. [7] Many C & W performers, such as Brooks, are known for their real successful music videos. [8] Some country singers feel badly about the problems in the United States and have started taking stands on social issues. [9] Others do really good singing songs on the traditional country themes of love and heartache. [10] Veteran performer Loretta Lynn, country music's own "Coal Miner's Daughter," is shown on the right singing movingly before an admiring crowd.

© 1999 Troy Waynynen.

Comparison of Modifiers

22e. Modifiers change form to show comparison.

There are three degrees of comparison: *positive, comparative,* and *superlative.*

	Positive	Comparative	Superlative
Adjectives	big	bigger	biggest
	eager	more eager	most eager
	good	better	best
	late	later	latest
Adverbs	swiftly	more swiftly	most swiftly
	well	better	best

Regular Comparison

(1) Most one-syllable modifiers form the comparative degree by adding *–er* and the superlative degree by adding *–est*.

Positive	Comparative	Superlative
neat	neat**er**	neat**est**
warm	warm**er**	warm**est**
fast	fast**er**	fast**est**
strong	strong**er**	strong**est**

(2) Two-syllable modifiers may form the comparative degree by adding *–er* and the superlative degree by adding *–est,* or they may form the comparative degree by using *more* and the superlative degree by using *most*.

Positive	Comparative	Superlative
gentle	gentl**er**	gentl**est**
lively	lively**ier**	lively**iest**
agile	**more** agile	**most** agile
clearly	**more** clearly	**most** clearly

┌HELP─
A dictionary will tell you when a word forms its comparative or superlative form in some way other than just by adding *–er* or *–est* or *more* or *most*. Be sure to look in a dictionary if you are not sure whether a word has irregular comparative or superlative forms. A dictionary will also tell you if you need to double a final consonant (or otherwise change the spelling of a word) before adding *–er* or *–est*.

┌STYLE   TIP┐
Most two-syllable modifiers can form their comparative and their superlative forms either way. If adding *–er* or *–est* makes a word sound awkward, use *more* or *most* instead.

USAGE

(3) Modifiers that have three or more syllables form the comparative degree by using *more* and the superlative degree by using *most*.

Positive	Comparative	Superlative
expensive	**more** expensive	**most** expensive
delightful	**more** delightful	**most** delightful
poetically	**more** poetically	**most** poetically

(4) To show a decrease in the qualities they express, modifiers form the comparative degree by using *less* and the superlative degree by using *least*.

Positive	Comparative	Superlative
weak	**less** weak	**least** weak
useful	**less** useful	**least** useful
urgently	**less** urgently	**least** urgently

Irregular Comparison

The comparative and superlative degrees of some modifiers are not formed by the usual methods.

Positive	Comparative	Superlative
bad	worse	worst
ill	worse	worst
good	better	best
well	better	best
many	more	most
much	more	most
far	farther/further	farthest/furthest
little	less	least

NOTE The word *little* also has regular comparative and superlative forms: *littler, littlest*. These forms are used to describe physical size (the **littlest** kitten). The forms *less* and *least* are used to describe an amount (**less** rain). An alternative comparative form, *lesser,* is usually used to describe importance (the **lesser** infraction).

┌ S T Y L E ╱ T I P ┐

In formal English the words *farther* and *farthest* are used to compare physical distance; the words *further* and *furthest* are used to compare amounts, degrees, and abstract concepts.

EXAMPLES
Kiyoshi walked **farther** than any other senior in the walkathon.

The defendant told his attorney, "The witness's testimony could not have been **further** from the truth."

─HELP─
If you are
unsure how to spell the
forms of any of the words
in Exercise 5, look the
words up in a dictionary.

Exercise 5 Writing the Comparative and Superlative Forms of Modifiers

Give the comparative forms and the superlative forms of each of the following modifiers.

EXAMPLE　　1.　brave

　　　　　　　1.　braver, less brave; bravest, least brave

1. tiny	**10.** abruptly	**19.** magnificent
2. ill	**11.** quickly	**20.** politely
3. wistful	**12.** easy	**21.** agile
4. modest	**13.** cold	**22.** placidly
5. curious	**14.** glorious	**23.** precisely
6. proudly	**15.** fiercely	**24.** misty
7. thin	**16.** bad	**25.** colorful
8. good	**17.** jealous	
9. gently	**18.** sour	

┌S T Y L E　　　　T I P┐

In informal situations, the
superlative degree is sometimes used to emphasize
the comparison of only two
things. Avoid such use of
the superlative degree in
formal speaking and
writing.

INFORMAL
　Which park did you enjoy
　most, Yellowstone or Hot
　Springs?

FORMAL
　Which park did you enjoy
　more, Yellowstone or Hot
　Springs?

The superlative degree is
also used to compare two
things in some idiomatic
expressions.

EXAMPLE
　Put your best foot
　forward.

Uses of Comparative Forms and Superlative Forms

22f. Use the comparative degree when comparing two things. Use the superlative degree when comparing more than two things.

COMPARATIVE　　Both Laura and Justin wrote about the development of the Swahili culture, but Laura's paper was **longer.** [comparison of two papers]

　　　　　　　　After listening to both candidates, we concluded that Ms. García was the **more highly** qualified. [comparison of two candidates]

SUPERLATIVE　　Of the four major river-valley cultures that arose long ago in Africa and Asia, the Huang He was probably the **most fully** isolated from the others. [comparison of four civilizations]

　　　　　　　　I bought this model of car because it gets the **best** mileage. [comparison of many models]

22g. Include the word *other* or *else* when you are comparing one member of a group with the rest of the group.

Keep in mind that the original member is a part of the group. You must use *other* or *else* to avoid an illogical comparison of one thing with itself.

ILLOGICAL	Diamond, a crystalline form of carbon, is harder than any mineral in the world. [Diamond is one of the minerals of the world. Logically, the diamond cannot be harder than itself.]
LOGICAL	Diamond, a crystalline form of carbon, is harder than any **other** mineral in the world.

ILLOGICAL	Pete has won more races than anyone in his club. [Pete is a member of his club. Logically, he cannot have won more races than himself.]
LOGICAL	Pete has won more races than anyone **else** in his club.

22h. Avoid using double comparisons.

A **double comparison** is the result of using two comparative forms (usually –er and more) or using two superlative forms (usually –est and most) to modify the same word.

NONSTANDARD	Alice is a more faster swimmer than you.
STANDARD	Alice is a **faster** swimmer than you.

NONSTANDARD	What is the name of the most brightest star in the sky?
STANDARD	What is the name of the **brightest** star in the sky?

Exercise 6 Using the Comparative and Superlative Forms of Modifiers

Most of the following sentences contain errors in the use of comparisons and comparative and superlative forms. Rewrite each incorrect sentence to correct the error. If a sentence is already correct, write C.

EXAMPLE   1. Is that your most highest grade?
           1. *Is that your highest grade?*

1. Colleen thought nothing could be as bad as the sleet, wind, and snow; but when the ice storm hit, she said, "This is even worser!"
2. Both twins, Holly and Julie, have brown eyes, but Holly's are darkest.
3. In each graduating class, the valedictorian is the student whose academic average is higher than that of any senior.
4. Thomas Jefferson is sometimes regarded as the more important statesman in United States history.
5. To gain a more better understanding of the problems in the Middle East, people should learn more about the history of that region.
6. Suzanne made the mistake of buying less paint than she needed for the small room.

7. Performing better than all the gymnasts, Mary Lou Retton was the first American woman to win an Olympic gold medal in her sport.
8. Which of the two flavors do you like best?
9. Dividing the remaining pumpkin pie in two, Felicia gave me the largest portion.
10. My friend Juan says that Houston, Texas, is more interesting and more exciting than any city in that state.

Clear Comparisons

22i. Be sure comparisons are clear.

When making comparisons, clearly indicate what items you are comparing.

ILLOGICAL	Deciding after the auditions that Julia's characterization of Lady Macbeth was more compelling than Rita, the director offered Julia the role. [The sentence makes an illogical comparison between a characterization and Rita.]
LOGICAL	Deciding after the auditions that Julia's characterization of Lady Macbeth was more compelling than **Rita's [characterization],** the director offered Julia the role. [The sentence logically compares Julia's characterization with Rita's characterization.]
ILLOGICAL	The wingspread of the wandering albatross is greater than any other bird. [The sentence makes an illogical comparison between a wingspread and a bird.]
LOGICAL	The wingspread of the wandering albatross is greater than **that of** any other bird. [By including *that,* which stands for *wingspread,* the sentence logically compares the wingspread of the wandering albatross with the wingspread of any other bird. Notice that using *that* instead of *wingspread* prevents unnecessary repetition.]

Use a complete comparison if there is any chance that an incomplete, or elliptical, one could be misunderstood.

UNCLEAR	We have known Chen a great deal longer than Anzu. [The comparison is unclear because the elliptical construction *than Anzu* may be completed in more than one way.]
CLEAR	We have known Chen a great deal longer **than we have known Anzu.**
CLEAR	We have known Chen a great deal longer longer **than Anzu has known her.**

Reference Note

For more about **elliptical constructions,** see page 585.

USAGE

UNCLEAR	Ms. Vasquez offered me a better job than anyone else.
CLEAR	Ms. Vasquez offered me a better job **than she offered anyone else.**
CLEAR	Ms. Vasquez offered me a better job **than anyone else offered me.**

Include all of the words necessary to complete a *compound comparison,* which uses both the positive and the comparative degrees of a modifier. Avoid the common error of omitting the second *as* in the positive degree.

| NONSTANDARD | This year's soccer team is playing as well, if not better than, last year's team. |
| STANDARD | This year's soccer team is playing **as well as,** if not better than, last year's team. |

Absolute Adjectives

Some adjectives have no comparative or superlative forms; they do not vary in degree. Such adjectives are called *absolute adjectives.* In formal situations, avoid using absolute adjectives in comparative constructions.

Common Absolute Adjectives		
complete	equal	perfect
correct	eternal	round
dead	full	square
empty	impossible	true
endless	infinite	unique

INFORMAL	Smiling, Mr. Martin told me, "I have heard many excuses, but I must say that yours is more unique than most."
FORMAL	Smiling, Mr. Martin told me, "I have heard many excuses, but I must say that yours is **unique.**"
FORMAL	Smiling, Mr. Martin told me, "I have heard many excuses, but I must say that yours is **more ingenious** than most."

INFORMAL	Don't you agree that Brentwood Park is the most perfect place to have the senior-class picnic?
FORMAL	Don't you agree that Brentwood Park is the **perfect** place to have the senior-class picnic?
FORMAL	Don't you agree that Brentwood Park is the **most suitable** place to have the senior-class picnic?

TIPS & TRICKS

To make sure a sentence contains all of the words necessary for a compound comparison, try creating a sentence using each part of the comparison separately.

EXAMPLES

This year's soccer team is playing **as well as** last year's team.

This year's soccer team is playing **better than** last year's team.

USAGE

Throughout the years, the rules regarding absolute adjectives have changed, becoming alternately more and less strict. Current usage increasingly allows comparisons of absolute adjectives. One historical precedent for this usage occurs in the preamble to the Constitution of the United States of America.

*We the People of the United States, in order to form a **more perfect** Union, establish Justice, insure domestic Tranquility, provide for the common defense, promote the general Welfare, and secure the Blessings of Liberty to ourselves and our Posterity, do ordain and establish this Constitution for the United States of America.*

Follow your teacher's instructions regarding the use of absolute adjectives.

HELP

Some sentences in Exercise 7 may be correctly revised in more than one way. You need to give only one revision for each sentence.

An absolute adjective may be used in comparison if the adjective is accompanied by *more nearly* or *most nearly*.

NONSTANDARD	Ben's responses to survey questions were more complete than anyone else's.
STANDARD	Ben's responses to the survey questions were **more nearly complete** than anyone else's.
NONSTANDARD	Scientists said that the diamond had the most perfect crystalline structure they had ever seen.
STANDARD	Scientists said that the diamond had the **most nearly perfect** crystalline structure they had ever seen.

Exercise 7 **Correcting Unclear and Illogical Comparisons**

Most of the following sentences contain unclear or illogical comparisons. Rewrite each sentence, following the rules of formal, standard usage and making sure the comparisons are clear. If a sentence is already correct, write *C*.

EXAMPLE   1. Of all the creatures on earth, the platypus is one of the most unique.

1. *Of all the creatures on earth, the platypus is one of the most unusual.*

or

Of all the creatures on earth, the platypus is unique.

1. Sarah's test scores arrived by mail two weeks sooner than Jesse.
2. Which one of these is more complete?
3. Bryan amazed even himself by swimming as far, if not farther than, anyone at the school had ever swum before.
4. Some historians say that Lincoln's accomplishments in such a relatively short time far exceed any other president.
5. Shirley's design for the set of the next musical was obviously more practical than Ruben.
6. Luisa sees movies much more often than her friend Sandra.
7. Ernesto enjoyed the literature of the Romantic Period as much as, if not more than, the literature of the Renaissance.
8. Hercules had to perform twelve labors, each of which was more impossible than the previous one.
9. Katherine agrees with the literary critics who call Sonnet 18 Shakespeare's most perfect poem.
10. Jason's bike is even lighter than Daniel's.

Review C Using Modifiers Correctly

Most of the following sentences contain errors in the use of comparisons and modifiers. Rewrite each incorrect sentence to correct the error. If a sentence is already correct, write *C*.

EXAMPLE   1. Which of the two teams has won the most games?
           1. *Which of the two teams has won more games?*

1. I am least prepared to take the test than you.
2. Jim speaks Portuguese more fluently than any person in his class.
3. You cheered more often than anyone at the concert.
4. Mr. Brown is many pounds more heavier than I.
5. We thought Patti was the most talented of all the actors in the community play.
6. The picture looks much more clearer on this television set than on that one.
7. I read the shorter of the three books for my report.
8. I have narrowed my choices to two colleges, and I want to visit them to see which I like best.
9. She was less determined to win than her sister was.
10. Modeling her mother's silk kimono, Toshi seemed even more gracefuller than usual.

Review D Proofreading for Correct Use of Modifiers

Most of the sentences in the following paragraph contain errors in the standard, formal use of comparisons and modifiers. Identify each error, and then give the correct form. If a sentence is already correct, write *C*.

EXAMPLE   [1] Moviegoers who have enjoyed George Lucas's *Star Wars* trilogy may also find Akira Kurosawa's samurai films real appealing, especially *The Hidden Fortress,* which inspired Lucas's trilogy.
           1. *real—really*

[1] Of all the world's movie directors, Akira Kurosawa of Japan is considered one of the greater. [2] He is certainly better known in the United States than any Japanese director. [3] In addition to directing, the multitalented Kurosawa edited and wrote many of his films. [4] Acclaimed by critics, his films not only look beautifully but also contain serious moral themes. [5] Among the most popular of his dozens of films is *Ran,* which blends Shakespeare's *King Lear* with a Japanese folk tale. [6] Kurosawa made his version of the story more

USAGE

unique by creating a conflict between a father and three sons instead of three daughters. [7] That conflict is real apparent in the scene below from *Ran*. [8] Moviegoers in the United States also enjoyed Kurosawa's film *Dersu Uzala*, which won an Academy Award for bestest foreign film. [9] The stark scenery in that film certainly shows how fiercely the Siberian wilderness can be. [10] If you have the chance to see these two films, you can decide which one you like best.

Chapter Review

A. Selecting Modifiers to Complete Sentences

For each of the following sentences, select the correct modifier from the pair given in parentheses.

1. The rainstorm hit the town (*sudden, suddenly*).

2. Cindy looked (*cheerful, cheerfully*) before beginning her solo.

3. Carry the flag (*proud, proudly*) in the parade.

4. The tabletop felt (*smooth, smoothly*) after we had sanded it.

5. Lynea wrapped the package (*careful, carefully*).

B. Revising Sentences to Correct Errors in the Use of Troublesome Modifiers

Most of the following sentences contain at least one error in the standard, formal use of modifiers. Identify each incorrect modifier, and then give the correct form. If the sentence is already correct, write *C*.

6. Was anyone hurt bad in the train derailment?

7. The conductor was real happy with the choir's performance.

8. Larry does not play the tuba well, but he is a good drummer.

9. When you're really hungry, the lunch line always seems to move too slow.

10. The baby behaved real good on the long car trip.

C. Using Modifiers Correctly

Most of the following sentences contain errors in the use of comparisons and modifiers. Rewrite each incorrect sentence to correct the error. If a sentence is already correct, write *C*.

11. Which city is largest, Wichita or Topeka?

12. My cat Mr. Alp is smarter than all the cats I own.

13. That was the most wonderfullest day of my life.

14. My mother has worked in the real estate business more longer than my father has.

15. Lara is obviously the best qualified of the two candidates.

USAGE

16. Stephen King has probably sold more books than any other writer of his generation.
17. Of the two themes that I wrote, this one is most coherent.
18. Ms. Harrington's comments were more useful than Mr. Karswell's.
19. Of the three sisters, Leora is the better singer.
20. My brother Roger knows more about German history than anyone in our family.

D. Correcting Unclear and Nonstandard Comparisons

Most of the following sentences contain unclear or informal comparisons. Rewrite each sentence, following the rules of standard, formal English and making sure the comparisons are clear. If a sentence is already correct, write *C*.

21. My father's photos of our trip to the Grand Canyon arrived by mail a week before my uncle.
22. Keith's list of the birds of Washtenaw County is more complete than Nick's list.
23. We have been acquainted with Carlyle longer than Robert.
24. I know the songs of John Lennon better than I know the songs of anyone.
25. What you are asking me to do is extremely impossible.

E. Proofreading a Paragraph for Correct Use of Modifiers

Most of the sentences in the following paragraph contain errors in standard, formal use of modifiers. Rewrite the paragraph to correct the errors. If a sentence is already correct, write *C*.

[26] Making a pot on a potter's wheel, or "throwing" a pot, is more relaxing than any artistic activity I know. [27] I feel peacefully as the wheel spins and I shape the ball of clay with my fingers. [28] Sometimes I plan what to make, but other times a pot takes shape slow, almost by itself. [29] To me, kneading the clay to get rid of air bubbles is the more difficult of the dozen or so steps in throwing a pot. [30] The real exciting part is pulling up on the clay to form a cone and then pressing a hole in

the center. **[31]** To prevent the pot from becoming lopsided, I have to work steady and keep the wheel spinning. **[32]** I'm happiest while gently pressing the clay and forming the walls of a pot. **[33]** This stage is more pleasant than any stage because I can daydream as my fingers seem to do the work almost automatically. **[34]** Most of the time, though, I have to concentrate careful to try to make a perfect pot. **[35]** I usually don't feel too badly if a pot doesn't turn out right the first time; part of the fun is starting over.

Writing Application

Using Comparisons in a Consumer's Guide

Comparative and Superlative Forms   You and your classmates have decided to compile a consumer's guide to some products available in your community. Choose a product, and write a paragraph comparing at least three different choices for the product and telling which you think is best. Include at least three comparative and two superlative forms of modifiers.

Prewriting   Write down notes on at least three brands, judging the quality, effectiveness, and cost of each. Using your notes and a set of criteria, compare the brands. You may wish to look in some reliable consumer guides to see the criteria their evaluators use.

Writing   Begin by identifying the type of product you are evaluating and the brands on which you will focus. Then, write a detailed comparison of the brands, rating them on quality and cost. Give specific, objective reasons for your opinions.

Revising   Ask a classmate to read your draft. Have you evaluated each brand thoroughly? Have you stated your opinions and reasons clearly? Be sure that you have used at least three comparative and two superlative forms of modifiers.

Publishing   Check your writing for errors in grammar, usage, punctuation, and spelling. Pay special attention to modifiers, and revise any double comparisons. You and your classmates may wish to compile the evaluations into a booklet, which can serve as a handy reference.

Placement of Modifiers

Misplaced and Dangling Modifiers

Diagnostic Preview

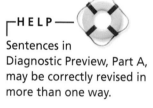
A. Revising Sentences by Correcting Faulty Modifiers

The following sentences contain misplaced and dangling modifiers. Revise each sentence so that its meaning is clear and correct.

EXAMPLE   1. We bought a gadget from a vendor at the flea market that was guaranteed to reduce gas consumption in our car by ten percent.

        1. From a vendor at the flea market, we bought a gadget that was guaranteed to reduce gas consumption in our car by ten percent.

1. Preferring the mountains rather than the nearby seashore, the Adirondacks were chosen as our vacation spot.
2. After working in Washington, D.C., for more than twenty years, the methods of lobbyists were familiar.
3. This bank approves car loans to qualified individuals of any size.
4. Because they were untamed, the signs warned that the animals were dangerous.
5. One can see more than a hundred lakes flying at an altitude of several thousand feet.
6. Jack bought a book of shorthand lessons along with his new word processor, which he read and studied diligently.

7. The people in line only had to stand out in the cold for a few minutes.
8. We followed several routes that early Spanish explorers took on vacation last year.
9. Salvador said after the game the head referee had explained his unpopular decision to the two team captains.
10. Rounding a sharp curve on El Camino del Rio on the way to Big Bend, a detour sign warned of danger.

B. Revising Sentences by Correcting Faulty Modifiers

The following sentences contain misplaced and dangling modifiers. Revise each sentence so that its meaning is clear and correct.

EXAMPLE   1. We saw Agatha Christie's play *The Mousetrap* last year in London, which has been running since 1952.

     1. *Last year in London, we saw Agatha Christie's play* The Mousetrap, *which has been running since 1952.*

┌HELP─
Sentences in Diagnostic Preview, Part B, may be correctly revised in more than one way.

11. Among popular mystery writers, the works of Agatha Christie continue to lead sales.
12. Phoebe said during the summer Karl is planning to read all of Christie's books about the Belgian detective Hercule Poirot.
13. Famous as the world's longest running play, audiences have enjoyed Christie's *The Mousetrap* for over forty years.
14. Concluding the play, the audience is always told by the cast not to give away the surprise ending.
15. After reading all of Christie's works, our library received a number of requests for books by another great mystery writer, Dorothy L. Sayers.
16. When in junior high school, Mom bought me my first Sayers mystery novel.
17. Named Lord Peter Wimsey, there are few criminal investigators who rival Sayers' amateur detective.
18. After reading a detective story by Ngaio (pronounced Ny-o) Marsh, New Zealand became an interest of mine.
19. Reading Marsh's *Died in the Wool* for the third time, it is still one of my favorites.
20. Fond of mysteries, novels such as *Devices and Desires* by the British author P. D. James keep Ben spellbound.

Link to Literature

USAGE

Misplaced Modifiers

A modifying word, phrase, or clause that seems to modify the wrong word or word group in a sentence is a *misplaced modifier.*

23a. Avoid using misplaced modifiers.

To correct a misplaced modifier, place the modifying word, phrase, or clause as close as possible to the word or words you intend to modify.

MISPLACED	We plan to go to the antique auto show that we read about in the paper tomorrow. [Did we do the planning before reading the paper?]
CLEAR	**Tomorrow,** we plan to go to the antique auto show that we read about in the paper.
MISPLACED	I finished reading the book that Alice Walker wrote about Langston Hughes during spring break. [Did Alice Walker write the book about Langston Hughes during spring break?]
CLEAR	**During spring break** I finished reading the book that Alice Walker wrote about Langston Hughes.
MISPLACED	The thief tried to run away from the police officer abandoning the stolen car and dashing into the woods. [Was the police officer abandoning the stolen car and dashing into the woods?]
CLEAR	**Abandoning the stolen car and dashing into the woods,** the thief tried to run away from the police officer.
MISPLACED	Each actor needs to affect a British accent that auditions for the role of Professor Higgins. [Does a British accent audition for the role?]
CLEAR	Each actor **that auditions for the role of Professor Higgins** needs to affect a British accent.
MISPLACED	My nephew told me that he wanted to become an astronaut and fly to the moon when he was six years old. [Could my nephew become an astronaut at the age of six and fly to the moon?]
CLEAR	**When he was six years old,** my nephew told me that he wanted to become an astronaut and fly to the moon.

Squinting Modifiers

23b. Avoid misplacing a modifying word, phrase, or clause so that it seems to modify either of two words.

Such a misplaced modifier is often called a *squinting,* or *two-way,* modifier.

MISPLACED	Mary said during rehearsal Lori acted nervous. [Did Mary say this about Lori during rehearsal, or did Lori act nervous during rehearsal?]
CLEAR	**During rehearsal** Mary said Lori acted nervous.
CLEAR	Mary said Lori acted nervous **during rehearsal.**

MISPLACED	Tell Marco before he goes to his karate class I want to see him. [Do I want to see him before he goes, or do I want you to tell him before he goes?]
CLEAR	**Before he goes to his karate class,** tell Marco I want to see him.
CLEAR	Tell Marco I want to see him **before he goes to his karate class.**

Exercise 1   Revising Sentences by Correcting Misplaced Modifiers

The following sentences contain misplaced modifiers. Revise each sentence so that its meaning is clear and correct.

EXAMPLE   1. Recently vetoed by the president, Congress is amending the tax bill.

     1. Congress is amending the tax bill recently vetoed by the president.

1. Captain Andre Callioux was one of many heroic African American soldiers during the Civil War that fought in the Union Army.
2. Rolling slowly down the alley, the bowler watched the straightest ball he had ever thrown.
3. One of our observers sighted a plane through binoculars that she could not identify.
4. The causeway has a drawbridge to permit the passage of large fishing boats from which all fishing is prohibited.
5. Please tell Terry when he gets home from the mall Mom wants him to make dinner.
6. At Tuesday's meeting, the mayor discussed the enormous cost of draining Buskill Swamp with city council members.
7. According to the hieroglyphics, the mummy had nearly been buried for four thousand years.
8. Li Hua inherited that antique fan from her great-aunt that has a mother-of-pearl handle.

STYLE **TIP**

Be sure to place modifiers correctly to show clearly the meaning you intend.

EXAMPLES

Only Mr. Reyes sees the essays. [Mr. Reyes, not anybody else, sees the essays.]

Mr. Reyes **only** sees the essays. [Mr. Reyes sees the essays; he does not mark them.]

Mr. Reyes sees **only** the essays. [Mr. Reyes does not see anything else.]

HELP

Sentences in Exercise 1 may be correctly revised in more than one way.

9. Ms. Steinberg, the explorer, described her trips through the jungle in our social studies class.
10. Uncle Jim said after reading all the consumer guides and asking his friends for advice he would decide what kind of personal computer to buy.

Dangling Modifiers

A modifying word, phrase, or clause that does not clearly and sensibly modify any word or word group in a sentence is a *dangling modifier.*

23c. Avoid using dangling modifiers.

To correct a dangling modifer, add or replace words to make the meaning of the sentence clear.

Reference Note

For more about **modifying phrases and clauses,** see Chapter 16 and Chapter 17.

DANGLING	Foggy, we couldn't see eight feet in front of us. [Were we foggy?]
CORRECT	**In the fog,** we couldn't see eight feet in front of us.
CORRECT	We couldn't see eight feet in front of us **in the foggy weather.**
DANGLING	After reading the article "Keeping America Beautiful," a recycling program was organized in their neighborhood. [Who read the article?]
CLEAR	**After reading the article "Keeping America Beautiful," Luís and Gabrielle** organized a recycling program in their neighborhood.
CLEAR	**After Luís and Gabrielle read the article "Keeping America Beautiful,"** they organized a recycling program in their neighborhood.
DANGLING	To win the election, your support will be needed. [Is your support trying to win the election?]
CLEAR	**To win the election, I** will need your support.
CLEAR	**If I am to win the election,** your support will be needed.
DANGLING	Convicted of stealing a loaf of bread for his sister's seven starving children, Jean Valjean's sentence was five years in prison. [Was Jean Valjean's sentence convicted?]
CLEAR	**Convicted of stealing a loaf of bread for his sister's seven starving children, Jean Valjean** was sentenced to five years in prison.
CLEAR	**Jean Valjean was convicted of stealing a loaf of bread for his sister's seven starving children** and was sentenced to five years in prison.

Possessive nouns and pronouns act as adjectives and therefore cannot be modified by adjectives. Adjective phrases and clauses that seem to modify possessive nouns or pronouns are considered dangling modifiers. The most common way to correct such dangling modifiers is to reword the sentence to avoid using the possessive form.

DANGLING	Having chopped off the Green Knight's head, Gawain's part of the bargain must be fulfilled.
CLEAR	Having chopped off the Green Knight's head, **Gawain** must fulfill his part of the bargain.
DANGLING	Washing them repeatedly, Lady Macbeth's hands still appear bloody.
CLEAR	Washing her hands repeatedly, **Lady Macbeth** still sees blood on them.

Exercise 2 **Revising Sentences by Correcting Dangling Modifiers**

The following sentences contain dangling modifiers. Revise each sentence so that its meaning is clear and correct.

EXAMPLE 1. Before moving to San Angelo, Miami had been their home.

1. *Before they moved to San Angelo, Miami had been their home.*

1. Listening to his grandfather's stories, it was amazing to learn that several of their ancestors had worked with the Underground Railroad.
2. Architecturally striking, everyone is quite impressed by the new building's size and elegance.
3. When selecting a college, a number of factors should be carefully considered.
4. While talking with some friends of mine, the topic of careers in dentistry came up.
5. After searching all over the bookstore, Amy Tan's novel was found in the "Bestseller" section.
6. When using a word processor, the spellchecker should not be relied on to proofread.
7. After working in the fields all day, little energy was left for social activities.
8. To understand many of the allusions in modern literature, Greek and Roman mythology is essential.

STYLE TIP

A dangling modifier often occurs when a sentence is in the passive voice. Rewriting sentences in the active voice not only eliminates many dangling modifiers but also makes your writing more interesting and lively.

PASSIVE VOICE
Having just waxed the car, a trip to the fair was planned. [*Having just waxed the car* is a dangling modifier.]

ACTIVE VOICE
Having just waxed the car, **I** planned a trip to the fair. [*Having just waxed the car* modifies *I.*]

Reference Note

For more about **active voice** and **passive voice,** see page 705.

USAGE

9. Thirsty and weary, the oasis was a welcome sight.
10. Riding in the glass-bottomed boat, hundreds of beautiful tropical fish could be seen.

> **Review A** **Revising Sentences by Correcting Faulty Modifiers**

The following sentences contain misplaced and dangling modifiers. Revise each sentence so that its meaning is clear and correct.

EXAMPLES
1. Candace told me at the conference Leora gave a very interesting presentation about solar eclipses.

1. *At the conference, Candace told me Leora gave a very interesting presentation about solar eclipses.*

or

1. *Candace told me Leora gave a very interesting presentation about solar eclipses at the conference.*

2. After hiking across the South Downs from Eastbourne to Brighton, Jim's boots were battered and scratched.

2. *After Jim hiked across the South Downs from Eastbourne to Brighton, his boots were battered and scratched.*

1. Having left the box cutter in the drawer under the front counter, the boxes of new science fiction and fantasy books in the back room were difficult for the librarian to open.
2. Elected to serve the people of her state in Congress for the next two years, the new representative's term began with a difficult vote about taxes.
3. To get his students ready for the coming semester, the Latin teacher asked his class to read the versions of Homer's *Iliad* and *Odyssey* translated by Robert Fagles over Christmas break.
4. Aiming the giant radio telescope at the distant star in the constellation of Cassiopeia, the astronomer's hope was that it would quickly detect signs of extraterrestrial intelligence.
5. He wanted to see the scary new film that was advertised on television and in the newspaper before anybody else saw it.
6. Aunt Alice told us after talking to a friend who knew quite a bit about automobiles and trucks she had decided to buy a new car with air conditioning, automatic transmission, and a sun roof.
7. To enjoy ancient Chinese poetry, even in translation, an understanding of Chinese history and of the poetic tradition in China is helpful.

8. The university's planetological survey team discovered a large asteroid with the enormous new reflecting telescope in the Andes that no one had ever catalogued or even seen before.

9. The champion bicyclist in the Tour de France tried to break away from the other bicyclists pedaling harder and faster than anyone else.

10. Having hidden the silver, Nostromo's reputation was made as the man who rescued the country from the rebels.

Review B **Revising Sentences by Correcting Faulty Modifiers**

The sentences in the following paragraph contain misplaced and dangling modifiers. Revise each sentence so that its meaning is clear and correct.

EXAMPLE **[1]** Using the map shown on the next page, it is easy to identify the homelands of many American Indians.

1. *Using the map shown on the next page, a person can easily identify the homelands of many American Indians.*

[1] I found a fascinating book at the library book sale that includes a map showing where American Indians traditionally lived. [2] You can see the homelands of the major Plains peoples looking

The Granger Collection, New York

at the map. [3] The size of the Great Plains especially surprised me, extending farther north and south than I had thought. [4] While thumbing through the book, a picture of a Sioux encampment caught my attention. [5] Living much of the year in villages, farming was the main activity of most of these peoples. [6] However, I read during the summer they hunted buffalo. [7] Hunting for survival instead of sport, fewer buffalo were killed by them than were killed by European settlers. [8] Characterized by a strong sense of independence, a form of democracy was practiced by the Plains peoples. [9] To make key decisions, votes were cast at council meetings. [10] I'm going to find out more about such peoples as the Crow and Cheyenne, having read this fascinating book about the peoples of the Plains.

23

Chapter Review

A. Revising Sentences by Correcting Misplaced and Dangling Modifiers

The following sentences contain misplaced and dangling modifiers. Revise each sentence so that its meaning will be clear on first reading.

┌HELP──

Sentences in the Chapter Review may be correctly revised in more than one way.

1. The Kovaks gave a toy robot to one of their children with a square glass head and flashing red eyes.
2. Pounding the piano keys with all her might, the chords of the prelude resounded through the concert hall.
3. We saw a herd of sheep on the way to our hotel in Wales.
4. To succeed in college, a great deal of time must be spent studying.
5. Dipped in yogurt, many people love fresh strawberries.
6. When only five years old, Dad took me camping on the Fort Apache Reservation in Arizona.
7. While trying to get ready for school, the doorbell rang suddenly.
8. Elaine told Joanne after the first act the drama gets more exciting.
9. By putting money aside regularly, a small savings account will grow steadily larger.
10. A tarantula bit one of the dockworkers that had a hairy, huge body as big as a man's hand.

B. Revising Sentences by Correcting Misplaced and Dangling Modifiers

The following sentences contain misplaced and dangling modifiers. Revise each sentence so that its meaning will be clear on first reading.

11. Jody said on Saturday Fred should go to the classic car show.
12. Seeing a red 1928 Hispano-Suiza motorcar, his family's minivan seemed bulky and drab to Rick.
13. The Volkswagen Beetle remains one of the world's most popular cars first made in Germany in 1938.
14. Captivated by the Italian sports cars, the 1938 Alfa Romeo impressed Mark.
15. Mr. Reynolds showed a Model T Ford to his daughter that came off the assembly line in 1924.

USAGE

16. Would you please tell Thelma after lunch Mary plans to watch the documentary about the history of U.S. motorcars?

17. To keep a classic car in excellent condition, much money and patience often are needed.

18. I got a chance to ride in a 1914 Rolls-Royce Continental that the Arnolds had restored during the parade.

19. After writing a report about classic luxury motorcars, the 1940 Packard and 1938 Lagonda De Ville were of special interest to me.

20. Looking at the various exhibits, it is easy to see why very early cars were called horseless carriages.

C. Revising Sentences by Correcting Misplaced and Dangling Modifiers

The following sentences contain misplaced and dangling modifiers. Revise each sentence so that its meaning will be clear on first reading.

21. Jorie wrote a report about the Battle of Gettysburg during Christmas vacation.

22. Mom said after dinner my brother and I should wash the dishes.

23. Repeating the chorus an octave higher, the song was performed brilliantly.

24. Jim told Mimi during the holidays they would go to the ice-skating show.

25. Every player needs to prove her ability to the coach who wants to make the team.

26. With her clearly defined stripes, Jo thinks her cat's coloring is prettier than that of her friend's cat.

27. Having learned to heel, fetch, and sit, the dog's training was done.

28. After seeing the film, an argument nearly broke out between Ernesto and Claudia about what the message was.

29. Before Thanksgiving dinner, Alejandro discussed the proper method of stuffing a turkey with his mother.

30. Anxious about this morning's history test, thoughts raced through my head, and sleep did not come easily.

31. Remember to tell the equipment manager before the game the coach wants to see him.

32. Blowing steadily off the ocean, we had a difficult time walking into the wind.

33. Having learned the facts about Dutch elm disease, a program to save the trees was formulated by the members of the neighborhood association.

34. Professor Dellamorte said throughout class some students were not taking notes.

35. Whistling through the trees and between the buildings, the wind's force scattered loose trash in the street.

Writing Application
Using Modifiers in a News Report

Correct Placement of Modifers   Scientists have just discovered an entirely new life form in the Florida Everglades. You have been assigned the job of reporting the news to the public. You will need to describe not only the new creature but also the environment in which it was found and the methods used to find it.

Prewriting   First, you will need to decide what your creature is and what made it so difficult to discover for so long. Then, you will need to decide the conditions in which your creature lives. Finally, decide how the scientists made the discovery. You may wish to research recent discoveries to find out how actual scientists work.

Writing   Begin with a brief paragraph describing the new creature. Explain what makes this creature so different from previously known species. Then, give the details about how and where the creature lives and how it was discovered. You will need to use vivid modifiers to attract and keep your readers' attention.

Revising   Evaluate the written version of your article for believability and clarity. Remember that this information is entirely new and potentially confusing, so you will need to make sure your modifiers are placed carefully.

Publishing   Proofread your work for errors in grammar, spelling, and punctuation. You and your classmates may want to collect the fictional news reports in a booklet about recent discoveries. Add illustrations of the different creatures you have described. Work together to write an introduction explaining the nature of the scientific discovery.

A Glossary of Usage
Common Usage Problems

Diagnostic Preview

A. Correcting Errors in Usage

Most of the following sentences contain errors in the use of standard, formal English. If a sentence contains an error, revise the sentence. If a sentence is already correct, write *C*.

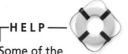

┌─ H E L P ─

Some of the sentences in the Diagnostic Preview, Part A, may be revised in more than one way. You need to give only one revision for each sentence.

EXAMPLE
  1. I was surprised to learn that Roberto's parents are wealthy; he doesn't act like he's rich.

  1. *I was surprised to learn that Roberto's parents are wealthy; he doesn't act as if he's rich.*

1. Please enclose a copy of your birth certificate, and we will try and return the document to you as soon as possible.
2. You hadn't ought to be so careless with your new watch.
3. The Student Council's arguments had little affect on the faculty's vote on the new dress code for school dances.
4. Theo don't care what others think; he has the courage to say what he believes.
5. Tricia, Angelo, Candace, and myself have tickets to the White Sox game next Saturday.
6. Whenever I feel sad, I can't hardly wait to talk with my friend Marcus, who always cheers me up.
7. Arthur Fiedler he made the Boston Pops' concerts popular with millions of people all over America.

8. The reason we're so late is because our car battery was dead.
9. We didn't know whether the light was a phenomena of nature or a UFO.
10. I had never seen this kind of insect before.
11. Because Eula made a mistake when she dropped the film cartridge in the camera, none of her pictures could be developed.
12. Being as we haven't seen Tim since he moved to New Mexico, we plan to visit him very soon.
13. She asked Tom whether he would be going to the dance, and he says, "Maybe I'll go, and maybe I won't."
14. Where was Beth at last night when we went to the game?
15. Our teacher said we done a creditable job on our project.

B. Correcting Errors in Usage

Each of the sentences in the following paragraph contains an error in the use of standard, formal English. Identify and correct each error.

EXAMPLE   **[1]** The number of versions of the Cinderella story are quite surprising.

1. *The number . . . are—The number . . . is*

[16] There are hardly no tales in the world that are as popular as the story of Cinderella. [17] Almost everywheres, people tell some version of this folk tale. [18] The reason for the story's popularity is probably because its themes of love and wealth appeal universally. [19] However, each culture adopts the tale by changing the heroine's name and other details. [20] Data collected by folklorists indicates that almost seven hundred versions of the Cinderella story exist. [21] In the English version, Cinderella is granted a wish by her fairy godmother; in Scotland, Rashin Coatie wishes on a dead calf's bones; and in Italy, it is a magic date tree who grants Zezolla's wish. [22] In the Chinese version, perhaps the oldest Cinderella story, the main character is Yeh-Shen, who is prosecuted by her stepmother. [23] In this here version, the stepmother, notorious for her cruelty, gives Yeh-Shen the dangerous task of drawing water from very deep wells. [24] As in other Cinderella stories, a slipper drops off of Yeh-Shen's foot on her way back from a festival. [25] The endings of all the stories are the same— the mistreated heroine, no matter what type name she has, finds love and happiness with the man who searches for the owner of the slipper.

Reference Note

For information about **words often confused,** such as *already* and *all ready,* see page 904.

USAGE

About the Glossary

This chapter provides a compact glossary of English usage. A *glossary* is an alphabetical list of special terms or expressions with definitions, explanations, and examples. You will notice that some examples in this glossary are labeled *nonstandard, standard, formal,* or *informal.* The label *nonstandard* identifies usage that does not follow the guidelines of standard English usage and is suitable only in the most casual speaking situations and in writing that attempts to re-create casual speech. The label *standard* identifies usage that is grammatically correct and appropriate in formal and informal situations. The label *formal* identifies language that is appropriate in serious speaking and writing situations (such as in speeches and in compositions for school). The label *informal* indicates standard usage common in conversation and in everyday writing such as personal letters. In doing the exercises in this chapter, be sure to use only standard English.

The following are examples of formal and informal English.

Formal	Informal
angry	steamed
unpleasant	yucky
agreeable	cool
very impressive	totally awesome
accelerate	step on it
request	put in for
in serious trouble	up a creek

Reference Note

For more information about **articles,** see page 506.

a, an   These *indefinite articles* refer to one of the members of a general group. Use *a* before words beginning with a consonant sound. Use *an* before words beginning with a vowel sound.

EXAMPLES   It was **an** honor and **a** surprise to receive **an** award last night for my work as **a** hospital volunteer. [The *h* in *honor* is silent; therefore, the word begins with a vowel sound. The *h* in *hospital* is not silent; therefore, the word begins with a consonant sound.]

The report of **a** unicorn came from **an** unnamed source. [The word *unicorn* begins with a consonant sound. The word *unnamed* begins with a vowel sound.]

accept, except *Accept* is a verb meaning "to receive." *Except* may be a verb or a preposition. As a verb, *except* means "to leave out." As a preposition, *except* means "excluding."

EXAMPLES   Did you **accept** the gift?

Does the new census **except** homeless people? [verb]

We were busy every night **except** Tuesday. [preposition]

adapt, adopt *Adapt* means "to change or adjust something in order to make it fit or to make it suitable." *Adopt* means "to take something and make it one's own."

EXAMPLES   The play was **adapted** from a popular book.

My aunt and uncle in New York **adopted** a nine-year-old boy from Guatemala.

affect, effect *Affect* is a verb meaning "to influence." *Effect* may be used as a verb or a noun. As a verb, *effect* means "to bring about [a desired result]" or "to accomplish." As a noun, *effect* means "the result [of an action]."

EXAMPLES   Try not to let unkind remarks **affect** you.

The board **effected** drastic changes in the budget. [verb]

The **effects** of the hurricane were evident. [noun]

ain't *Ain't* is nonstandard. Avoid *ain't* in formal speaking and in all writing other than dialogue.

all ready, already   See page 904.

all right *All right* means "satisfactory," "unhurt," "safe," "correct," or, as a reply to a question or to preface a remark, "yes." Although some dictionaries include *alright* as an optional spelling, it has not become standard usage.

EXAMPLES   The firefighters found that everyone in the building was **all right.**

All right, you may go to the movie, but be sure to be home by ten o'clock.

all together, altogether   See page 904.

Reference Note

For information about **writing dialogue,** see page 72.

USAGE

all the farther, all the faster   These expressions are used informally in some parts of the United States. In formal situations, use *as far as* or *as fast as*.

INFORMAL   Thirty miles per hour was all the faster the first airplane could travel.

FORMAL   Thirty miles per hour was **as fast as** the first airplane could travel.

allusion, illusion   An *allusion* is an indirect reference to something. An *illusion* is a mistaken idea or a misleading appearance.

EXAMPLES   Amy Tan's writings include numerous **allusions** to Chinese folklore and mythology.

At one time, many people shared the **illusion** that the earth was flat.

The movie's special effects created the **illusion** of space travel.

a lot   Always write the expression *a lot* as two words. In informal situations, *a lot* may be used as a noun meaning "a large number or amount" or "a great deal" or as an adverb meaning "a great deal" or "very much." Avoid using *a lot* in formal situations.

INFORMAL   I have a lot of homework to do tonight. [noun]
FORMAL   I have **a great deal** of homework to do tonight.

INFORMAL   The final exam was a lot easier than I had expected. [adverb]
FORMAL   The final exam was **much** easier than I had expected.

alumni, alumnae   *Alumni* (ə • lum´• nī) is the plural of *alumnus* (a male graduate). *Alumnae* (ə • lum´• nē) is the plural of *alumna* (a female graduate). Considered as a group, the graduates of a coeducational school are referred to as *alumni*.

EXAMPLES   Both men are **alumni** of Harvard University.

All of my sisters are **alumnae** of Hollins College.

My parents went to their **alumni** reunion.

NOTE   In informal usage, the graduates of a women's college may be called *alumni*. In formal situations, however, the form *alumnae* should be used.

among   See **between, among.**

amount, number Use *amount* to refer to a singular word. Use *number* to refer to a plural word.

EXAMPLES The **amount** of research on stress has increased. [*Amount* refers to the singular word *research*.]

A large **number** of studies have been conducted. [*Number* refers to the plural word *studies*.]

and etc. *Etc.* is an abbreviation of the Latin words *et cetera*, which mean "and others" or "and so forth." Since *and* is part of the definition of *etc.*, using *and* with *etc.* is redundant.

EXAMPLE This unit discusses writers associated with the Harlem Renaissance: Countee Cullen, Langston Hughes, Zora Neale Hurston, **etc.** [not *and etc.*]

anyways, anywheres Omit the final *s* from these words and others like them (*everywheres, nowheres, somewheres*).

EXAMPLE I couldn't find my keys **anywhere** [not *anywheres*]; I looked **everywhere** [not *everywheres*], but they were **nowhere** [not *nowheres*] in the house.

as See **like, as.**

as if See **like, as if, as though.**

as though See **like, as if, as though.**

assure, ensure, insure *Assure* means "to state with confidence" or "to promise." *Ensure* means "to make certain." *Insure* means "to protect against loss."

EXAMPLES Marion **assured** me that she would bring the book with her.

I **ensured** that Bret had his lunch before I left.

Chris **insured** her car against damage and theft.

at Avoid using *at* after a construction beginning with *where*.

NONSTANDARD Where do most Navajo live at now?
STANDARD **Where** do most Navajo live now?

a while, awhile The noun *while*, often preceded by the article *a*, means "a period of time." *Awhile* is an adverb meaning "for a short time."

EXAMPLES For **a while** Delia was the band's lead vocalist. [noun]

They lived **awhile** in Dallas before settling in Chicago. [adverb]

STYLE TIP

Many style guides advise against using *etc.* in formal writing. Whenever possible, revise your sentences to avoid using *etc.*

ORIGINAL
Shelley uses rhyme, alliteration, onomatopoeia, etc., to create sound images that complement his visual images.

REVISED
Shelley uses sound devices **such as** rhyme, alliteration, and onomatopoeia to create sound images that complement his visual images.

USAGE

For each of the following sentences, choose the correct word or words in parentheses.

EXAMPLE 1. After practicing law for (*a while, awhile*), Mr. Milano decided that he would rather be a teacher.

1. *a while*

1. Some pets (*ain't, aren't*) suited for life in a small apartment.
2. I own a large (*number, amount*) of campaign buttons.
3. During my travels in Mexico, I met (*a lot, alot*) of Canadian students in Jalisco.
4. Everyone I know likes peanut butter (*accept, except*) you.
5. One line appears to be longer because the drawing is an optical (*allusion, illusion*).
6. Do you know whether or not Anderson Boulevard will be turned into (*a, an*) one-way street?
7. The research committee's job is to analyze the possible long-term (*affects, effects*) of acid rain on European forests.
8. Four hundred miles is (*all the farther, as far as*) this car will go on one tank of gas.
9. Were any crops (*affected, effected*) by this year's dry spell?
10. The expression "lock, stock, and barrel" is an (*allusion, illusion*) to the parts of a flintlock rifle.
11. What (*affect, effect*) will new telecommunications options have on your future?
12. We've ordered balloons, streamers, paper napkins, paper cups, (*and etc., etc.*)
13. On behalf of Miss West, I am honored to (*accept, except*) this award.
14. A vast (*amount, number*) of this mineral may well be buried under the ocean floor.
15. The animal shelter has plenty of cats that you could (*adopt, adapt*).
16. Where are the Canary Islands (*located, located at*)?
17. That's all right; I was going to the mall (*anyway, anyways*).
18. Is everything (*allright, all right*) here, Tony?
19. Several of the (*alumni, alumnus*) have donated money for the new scoreboard.
20. For centuries, scholars have been fascinated by the pyramids, mummies, and scrolls of ancient Egypt, but new discoveries and techniques (*assure, ensure*) that the search for their secrets will continue for a long time.

Exercise 2 Identifying Correct Usage

For each sentence in the following paragraphs, choose the correct word or words in parentheses.

EXAMPLE **[1]** By developing, marketing, and selling shampoos, lotions, oils, (*and etc., etc.*), Madame C. J. Walker became a successful businesswoman.

    1. etc.

[1] At one time, the name Madame C. J. Walker was known by black women just about (*everywhere, everywheres*) in America and Europe. [2] Walker's likeness, which you can see in this photo of her driving a car, was familiar, too, because it appeared on each of the huge (*amount, number*) of packages of beauty products that she manufactured. [3] For eighteen years, Walker washed clothes for a living, but she never believed people who said she had gone (*all the farther, as far as*) a black woman could go in business. [4] Eventually, she invested in a sizable (*number, amount*) of oils, shampoos, and lotions and began experimenting with them in her washtub. [5] When she was done, Walker had a formula that softened hair; later, she would patent (*an, a*) hair-straightening comb that gave users soft, manageable coiffures. [6] The public, however, was reluctant to (*accept, except*) Walker's new products, and she had to go door-to-door to sell her system of hair care. [7] The success of her dynamic personal demonstrations enabled Walker to purchase (*a, an*) office. [8] Before long, her offices, laboratory, manufacturing plant, (*and etc., etc.*) took

up a city block, and thousands of Walker's sales representatives canvassed the United States and Europe, where the performer Josephine Baker used the Walker method.

[9] A pioneer in the development, sales, and marketing of cosmetics, Madame Walker insisted that her salespeople (*adopt, adapt*) a strict program of hygiene, a requirement that later became part of state cosmetology laws. [10] As a wealthy older woman, she did not forget her years of poverty and toil, and many (*alumnae, alumnus*) of Tuskegee Institute and Palmer Memorial Institute have been grateful for the scholarships that Walker funded for young women.

bad, badly   See page 726.

because   In formal situations, do not use the construction *reason . . . because.* Instead, use *reason . . . that.*

INFORMAL   The reason I'm late is because my car had a flat tire.

FORMAL   The reason I'm late is **that** my car had a flat tire. [This sentence can also be revised to make the statement more direct: *I'm late because my car had a flat tire.*]

being as, being that   Avoid using either of these expressions for *since* or *because.*

EXAMPLE   **Because** [not *Being as*] Elena lived in Mexico until she was almost eight years old, she can speak fluent Spanish.

beside, besides   *Beside* is a preposition meaning "by the side of" or "next to." *Besides* may be used as a preposition or an adverb. As a preposition, *besides* means "in addition to" or "except." As an adverb, *besides* means "moreover."

EXAMPLES   Who sits **beside** you in English class?

Besides my homework, I still have chores to do. [preposition]

This soup is cold; **besides,** I didn't order it. [adverb]

between, among   Use *between* when referring to only two items or when referring to more than two items when each is being discussed in relation to each of the others individually.

EXAMPLES   The final chess match was **between** Anne and Lisa.

Do you know when the borders **between** the northwestern states were drawn?   [*Between* is used because each border lies between two states.]

Use *among* when you are referring to more than two items and are not considering each item separately in relation to each of the others.

EXAMPLE   He decided **among** thousands of qualified applicants.

borrow, lend   *Borrow* means "to take [something] temporarily." *Lend* means "to give [something] temporarily." Its principal parts are *lend, (is) lending, lent, (have) lent.*

EXAMPLES   May I **borrow** your tennis racket?

Will you **lend** me your tennis racket?

STYLE   TIP

Using *borrow* to mean *lend* is nonstandard. *Loan,* which is a noun in formal English, is sometimes used in place of the verb *lend* in informal situations.

NONSTANDARD
Will you borrow me a couple of dollars?

INFORMAL
Will you loan me a couple of dollars?

FORMAL
Will you **lend** me a couple of dollars?

bring, take   *Bring* means "to come carrying something." *Take* means "to go carrying something."

EXAMPLES   When you come to my house tonight, please **bring** your collection of Black Heritage postage stamps.

Please **take** the recycling bin out to the curb.

bust, busted   Do not use these words as verbs in formal situations. Use a form of *break* or *burst* or *catch* or *arrest,* depending on the meaning.

EXAMPLES   How were your glasses **broken** [not *busted*]?

My car's radiator hose **burst** [not *busted*].

Roxanne **caught** [not *busted*] her little sister reading her diary.

Have the police **arrested** [not *busted*] anyone for that car theft?

but, only   See **The Double Negative,** page 780.

can, may   See page 712.

can't hardly, can't scarcely   See **The Double Negative,** page 780.

could of   See **of.**

credible, creditable, credulous   *Credible* means "believable." *Creditable* means "praiseworthy." *Credulous* means "inclined to believe too readily."

EXAMPLES   The children gave a **credible** excuse for being late.

Her quick thinking and competent action were **creditable.**

The **credulous** listeners thought that the Martians really had invaded Earth.

data   *Data* is the plural form of the Latin *datum.* In standard, informal English, *data* is frequently used as a collective noun, with singular pronouns and verbs. In formal usage, *data* takes plural pronouns and verbs.

INFORMAL   As soon as the census data was published, it was challenged by several scientists.

FORMAL   As soon as the census **data were** published, **they** were challenged by several scientists.

discover, invent *Discover* means "to learn of the existence of [something]." *Invent* means "to bring [something new] into existence."

EXAMPLES Engineers **discovered** oil deposits in Michigan.

Sequoyah **invented** a written Cherokee language based on the spoken Cherokee language.

done *Done* is the past participle of *do*. When used as a main verb, *done* requires a helping, or auxiliary, verb. Avoid using *done* for *did*, which does not require an auxiliary verb.

NONSTANDARD We done all of our chores today.
STANDARD We **have done** all of our chores today.
STANDARD We **did** all of our chores today.

don't, doesn't *Don't* is the contraction of *do not*. *Doesn't* is the contraction of *does not*. Use *doesn't*, not *don't*, with singular subjects except *I* and *you*.

EXAMPLES Franklin **doesn't** [not *don't*] often complain.

Our local grocery store **doesn't** [not *don't*] carry mangoes.

effect See **affect, effect.**

emigrate, immigrate *Emigrate* means "to leave a country or a region to settle elsewhere." *Immigrate* means "to come into a country or a region to settle there."

EXAMPLES The war forced people to **emigrate** from their homeland.

Marie's grandparents **immigrated** to the United States.

ensure See **assure, ensure, insure.**

etc. See **and etc.**

everywheres See **anyways, anywheres.**

except See **accept, except.**

famous, notorious *Famous* means "widely known." *Notorious* means "widely but unfavorably known."

EXAMPLES Gloria Steinem is a **famous** leader of the women's movement in the United States.

Al Capone was a **notorious** gangster in the 1920s.

farther See **all the farther, all the faster.**

fewer, less Use *fewer,* which tells "how many," to modify a plural noun. Use *less,* which tells "how much," to modify a singular noun.

EXAMPLES   I worked **fewer** hours this week than last week.

               I worked **less** time this week than last week.

good, well See page 727.

Exercise 3 Identifying Correct Usage

For each of the following sentences, choose the correct word or word group in parentheses.

EXAMPLE   **1.** I'm surprised that this cookbook (*doesn't, don't*) include a recipe for the Middle Eastern dish *baba ghanouj.*

          1. doesn't

  1. (*Being that, Because*) Eric is shy, he doesn't say much.
  2. When the car finally broke down, they had only thirteen dollars (*between, among*) the six of them.
  3. (*Beside, Besides*) coordinating our volunteer work, our club sponsors an annual ski trip.
  4. Please (*bring, take*) your guitar when you come to my party.
  5. Jon is so (*credulous, credible, creditable*) that he believed Barbara's outrageous story.
  6. They sold (*fewer, less*) new cars than used cars.
  7. In what year was the automobile (*invented, discovered*)?
  8. Their reason for being late to the rehearsal was (*because, that*) they missed their bus.
  9. Did Carla (*bring, take*) her camera on her trip to Panama?
10. This is a picture of me (*beside, besides*) our pony.
11. All the film critics praised his (*creditable, credulous*) performance in his most recent movie.
12. They (*done, did*) well in the playoffs.
13. Angie forgot to (*bring, take*) her homework assignment when she went to school this morning.
14. We divided the tasks (*among, between*) the four of us.
15. Please (*lend, borrow*) me five dollars; I'll pay you back tomorrow.
16. Lupe's family (*emigrated, immigrated*) from the Philippines when she was nine years old.
17. I had (*fewer, less*) cavities than my sister.

18. Alan Shepard, Jr., became (*famous, notorious*) as the first American in space.

19. Kristine decided to (*invent, discover*) a computer game of her own.

20. Cold weather (*don't, doesn't*) bother him very much.

Exercise 4 Correcting Errors in Usage

Most of the following sentences contain errors in the use of standard, formal English. If a sentence contains an error, revise the sentence. If a sentence is already correct, write *C*.

EXAMPLE **1.** We excepted the telegram nervously.

1. *We accepted the telegram nervously.*

1. Frank has less hobbies than his friend.

2. Being as Bernard Malamud is my favorite writer, I was excited to find one of his novels on sale at my local bookstore.

3. Would you please take this monstrosity out of here?

4. I think someone busted the culprits.

5. One of the main reasons for the widespread concern for eagles is because many are dying from lead poisoning.

6. The manager divided the work between the four of us.

7. The Chinese ballet dancer immigrated from his homeland to find creative freedom.

8. Have any of you did your research for your report yet?

9. To prepare her report, Judy used current data that were published by the Department of the Treasury.

10. Roy told me that he don't care, but I know that he does.

Review A Correcting Errors in Usage

Most of the sentences in the following paragraphs contain errors in the use of standard, formal English. Revise each sentence that contains an error. If a sentence is already correct, write *C*.

EXAMPLE **[1]** Do you know where the notorious painting on the next page was discovered at?

1. *Do you know where the notorious painting on the next page was discovered?*

[1] One of the most powerful works of art anywheres, the bull shown here was painted some fifteen thousand years ago in Lascaux, France. [2] The painting remained hidden until 1940, when a dog named Robot darted down a hole and the four young men following him

accidentally invented these marvelous cave paintings. [3] According to one of these boys, Marcel Ravidat, it was he who painstakingly enlarged the hole and wriggled down into the now notorious caverns. [4] With only a weak light to guide him, he soon tripped and fell; luckily, his flashlight was not busted. [5] When Ravidat aimed the light at the walls, an herd of animal figures leapt into view. [6] As the other boys joined him, the sight of the giant bulls, cows, elk, stags, and etc., filled the young men with joy and wonder, prompting them to celebrate with a wild dance. [7] With difficulty, the boys got out of the cavern, promising to return and admonishing each other, "Don't tell anyone about this!"

[8] When they left home the next day, the boys brought a stronger light with them. [9] They investigated the cave excitedly until they found a passage that was so deep and dark that no one accept Ravidat would enter it. [10] Using a rope, the boys lowered him down the dangerous vertical passage all the farther he could go. [11] At the bottom, Ravidat hardly knew where he was at, but gradually he began to explore this new area. [12] Soon, a picture of a human body with a bird's head appeared, and though it spanned less feet than the great bulls, it was just as awesome. [13] One by one, the other boys came down to glimpse the image of the strange creature, which is shown being knocked over by a bison. [14] This eerie figure effected the boys; instead of feeling triumphant, they were left shaken and pale.

The Granger Collection, New York.

[15] For Ravidat and his friends, these days were sometimes frightening beside being joyous and exciting. [16] Quite possibly, the artists who done the paintings hoped to instill these very emotions in viewers long ago. [17] Despite all the data that has been collected about the age and meaning of the paintings, much about them remains uncertain. [18] Some scientists believe that the purpose of the paintings was to initiate young hunters; others think that the paintings were a form of magic meant to increase the amount of game animals; but most scientists do agree that the paintings were considered sacred and were kept secret. [19] The reason they have survived for so long is because they were hidden away in dark caves, protected from light and kept at a constant humidity. [20] Being as modern-day tourists have introduced destructive microorganisms into the Lascaux caverns, the caves are now, unfortunately, closed to the public.

had of See **of.**

had ought, hadn't ought Do not use *had* or *hadn't* with *ought.*

NONSTANDARD	You had ought to be more patient.
STANDARD	You **ought** to be more patient.

NONSTANDARD	I hadn't ought to spend any more money on Jason's birthday party.
STANDARD	I **ought not** to spend any more money on Jason's birthday party.

hardly See **The Double Negative,** page 780.

he, she, it, they Avoid using a pronoun along with its antecedent as the subject of a verb. Such an error is sometimes called a *double subject.*

NONSTANDARD	Faith Ringgold, who was featured in a one-woman show, she designs remarkable story quilts.
STANDARD	Faith Ringgold, who was featured in a one-woman show, designs remarkable story quilts.

hisself, theirself, theirselves Avoid using these nonstandard words for *himself* and *themselves.*

EXAMPLE	Lou built the shed **himself** [not *hisself*].

hopefully *Hopefully* is an adverb meaning "in a hopeful manner."

EXAMPLE	We waited **hopefully** for the announcement of the election results last night.

illusion See **allusion, illusion.**

immigrate See **emigrate, immigrate.**

imply, infer *Imply* means "to suggest something indirectly." *Infer* means "to interpret" or "to draw as a conclusion."

EXAMPLES	Mayor Hanson **implied** during yesterday's press conference that she would run for reelection.
	I **inferred** from the mayor's comments that she would run for reelection.

in, into *In* means "within." *Into* means "from the outside to the inside." In formal situations, avoid using *in* for *into.*

STYLE	TIP

Some authorities do not approve of the use of "hopefully" to mean "it is to be hoped." Therefore, it is generally best to avoid using "hopefully" in this sense in formal speech and writing.

INFORMAL
Hopefully, the election results will be announced soon.

FORMAL
I hope the election results will be announced soon.

INFORMAL	Feeling nervous, Jim opened the door and walked in the personnel office.
FORMAL	Feeling nervous, Jim opened the door and walked **into** the personnel office.

insure See **assure, ensure, insure.**

invent See **discover, invent.**

it See **he, she, it, they.**

its, it's See page 907.

kind(s), sort(s), type(s) With the singular form of each of these nouns, use *this* or *that*. With the plural form, use *these* or *those*.

EXAMPLES **This kind** of package is recyclable, but **those kinds** are not.

These types of examples are helpful.

kind of, sort of In formal situations, avoid using *kind of* or *sort of* for the adverb *somewhat* or *rather*.

INFORMAL	You look kind of nervous.
FORMAL	You look **rather** [or **somewhat**] nervous.

kind of a(n), sort of a(n) In formal situations, omit the *a(n)*.

INFORMAL	What kind of a car is that?
FORMAL	What **kind of** car is that?

learn, teach *Learn* means "to gain knowledge." *Teach* means "to provide with knowledge."

EXAMPLE If you will **teach** me how to play the guitar, I will **learn** some traditional Mexican folk songs.

leave, let *Leave* means "to go away." *Let* means "to permit" or "to allow." Do not use *leave* for *let*.

EXAMPLES **Let** [not *Leave*] us finish our dinner.

I knew I shouldn't have **let** [not *left*] them borrow my car.

lend See **borrow, lend.**

less See **fewer, less.**

liable See **likely, liable.**

lie, lay See pages 688.

Reference Note

| For more information about **subordinate clauses,** see page 577.

like, as In formal situations, do not use *like* for the conjunction *as* to introduce a subordinate clause.

INFORMAL   The plan to win the election worked like they had thought it would.

FORMAL   The plan to win the election worked **as** they had thought it would.

like, as if, as though In formal situations, avoid using *like* for the conjunction *as if* or *as though* to introduce a subordinate clause.

INFORMAL   I feel like I have the flu.

FORMAL   I feel **as if** [or **as though**] I have the flu.

likely, liable In informal situations, *likely* and *liable* are interchangeable. However, in formal situations, use *likely* to express simple probability and *liable* to express probability with potential harm or misfortune.

EXAMPLES   Ginny is **likely** to arrive any minute.

The children playing in the abandoned building are **liable** to get hurt.

Liable is also used to mean "responsible" or "answerable."

EXAMPLES   The Smiths are **liable** for the damages that their dog has caused.

literally, figuratively *Literally* means "following the letter" or "in a strict sense." *Figuratively* means "metaphorically" or "not literally."

EXAMPLES   I was **literally** hopping mad—jumping up and down and hollering at the broken computer.

Figuratively speaking, I was paralyzed, each day a little less able to act decisively.

may See page 712.

might of, must of See **of.**

myself, ourselves Avoid using pronouns ending in –*self* or –*selves* (reflexive and intensive pronouns) in place of personal pronouns.

EXAMPLES   Amy and **I** [not *myself*] appreciate your help.

Could you do a favor for Wanda and **us** [not *ourselves*]?

Reference Note

| For more about **personal pronouns and reflexive and intensive pronouns,** see page 644.

USAGE

Correcting Errors in Usage

For each of the following sentences, choose the word or word group in parentheses that is correct according to the rules of standard, formal English.

EXAMPLE   1.   What (*kind of a, kind of*) computer did you buy?

            1.   *kind of*

1. In his address to Congress, the president (*implied, inferred*) that an economic reversal might occur soon.
2. When you have time, will you (*learn, teach*) me to sew?
3. He slipped on the wet deck and fell (*in, into*) the water.
4. We (*ought, had ought*) to have asked Allison for the recipe.
5. You look (*like, as if*) you've just seen a ghost!
6. Doyle and (*I, myself*) worked together on this project.
7. You (*ought, had ought*) to have asked me; I would have told you.
8. Have you been changing the oil (*as, like*) you're supposed to do?
9. (*Leave, Let*) them stay if they don't want to go with us.
10. Her recordings are (*liable, likely*) to become classics.
11. As for Ted and (*myself, me*), we're going to the dance.
12. This (*kind of a, kind of*) figure decorates many Navajo rugs.
13. (*Figuratively, Literally*) then, the singer was catapulted to fame.
14. From the evidence, we may (*imply, infer*) the presence of a much older civilization.
15. Mr. Hashem had an assignment for Emilio and (*ourselves, us*).
16. The new mare (*had, she had*) a foal this morning, a paint filly.
17. Glasses like these (*had ought, ought*) to be washed by hand.
18. Those (*kind, kinds*) of cats have bobtails.
19. I checked the meter daily, (*like, as*) I was instructed to do.
20. Did you hear that Tom got (*himself, hisself*) a new job?

Exercise 6   **Correcting Errors in Usage**

Each sentence in the following paragraph contains an error in the use of standard, formal English. Revise each sentence to correct the error.

EXAMPLE   **[1]** Leave me explain the painting technique called pointillism.

            1.   *Let me explain the painting technique called pointillism.*

     [1] Georges Seurat he spent his short career studying the mysteries of light, color, and the human eye. **[2]** One of the results of his study is

USAGE

this painting, which is composed of thousands, perhaps millions, of kind of small dots. [3] This sort of a technique is called pointillism; the name is derived from the small points of color on the canvas. [4] Rather than mix paint theirselves, artists using this technique let the viewer's eyes blend the colors. [5] Seen from a certain distance, the small points of color flow together and become solid, like the pixels on a computer screen or the dots of a printed photograph do. [6] In fact, some critics believe that observations of modern printed photographs learned Seurat all about pointillism. [7] However, these critics had ought to examine Seurat's painting more closely. [8] Unlike some of his contemporaries, Seurat was interested in photographic technology; however, the dots that make up his paintings are rather large, and obviously these type of points are not meant to appear completely solid. [9] If you go to a museum to see one of these kind of paintings, estimate the diagonal length of the picture and then step back about three times that distance. [10] From this viewpoint, a pointillist painting is liable to flicker or shimmer with the very vibrancy of life itself.

Georges Seurat (French, 1859–1891), *A Sunday on La Grand Jatte* (1884–86). Oil on canvas (207.5 cm × 308 cm). Helen Birch Bartlett Memorial Collection, 1926.224. Photograph © 1996, The Art Institute of Chicago. All rights reserved.

Most of the following sentences contain errors in the use of standard, formal English. If a sentence contains an error, revise the sentence. If a sentence is already correct, write *C*.

EXAMPLE   1. Hopefully, the working conditions in the factory will continue to improve.

            1. *We hope the working conditions in the factory will continue to improve.*

1. The magician dazzled us with flawless allusions.
2. The cat jumped from the chair and leaped in my arms.
3. The children helped theirselves to more vegetable curry.
4. Your room looks like it's been hit by a tornado.
5. What can you infer from the refrain in the poem "Sympathy"?
6. You hadn't ought to complain so much.
7. Jane and myself are the editors of our yearbook.
8. What sort of a CD player does Margaret plan to buy with her Christmas bonus?
9. I asked my boss whether he would let me have the day off.
10. Some people they're always making a fuss about nothing.

nauseated, nauseous   Informally, *nauseated* and *nauseous* are often used interchangeably. In formal English, however, *nauseated* means "sick," while *nauseous* means "disgusting" or "sickening."

EXAMPLES   After riding the roller coaster, the child became **nauseated**.

            The chemical reaction gave off a **nauseous** odor.

no, nobody, none, no one, not, nothing, nowhere
See **The Double Negative,** page 780.

nor   See **or, nor.**

notorious   See **famous, notorious.**

nowheres   See **anyways, anywheres.**

number   See **amount, number.**

number of   Use a singular verb after the expression *the number of.* Use a plural verb after the expression *a number of.*

EXAMPLES   **The number of** candidates **was** surprising.
            A **number of** candidates **were nominated**.

of *Of* is a preposition. Do not use *of* in place of *have* after verbs such as *could, should, would, might, must,* and *ought* [*to*]. Also, do not use *had of* for *had.*

NONSTANDARD	You could of told me that you were hungry.
STANDARD	You **could have** told me that you were hungry.
NONSTANDARD	You ought to of seen the look on his face.
STANDARD	You **ought to have** seen the look on his face.
NONSTANDARD	If Amy had of heard that the party was casual, she wouldn't of worn that dressy outfit.
STANDARD	If Amy **had** heard that the party was casual, she **wouldn't have** worn that dressy outfit.

Avoid using *of* after other prepositions such as *inside, off,* or *outside.*

EXAMPLE   Leslie turned **off** [not *off of*] the parkway.

off, off of Do not use *off* or *off of* for *from.*

NONSTANDARD	I got some good advice off that mechanic.
STANDARD	I got some good advice **from** that mechanic.

or, nor Use *or* with *either;* use *nor* with *neither.*

EXAMPLES   **Either** Jennifer **or** Gloria will bring the book.

Neither Gwen **nor** Lily has been absent this term.

ought See **had ought, hadn't ought.**

ought to of See **of.**

persecute, prosecute *Persecute* means "to attack or annoy someone constantly." *Prosecute* means "to bring legal action against someone for unlawful behavior."

EXAMPLES   The dictator **persecuted** those who opposed him.

The district attorney **prosecuted** the person caught looting.

phenomena *Phenomena* is the plural form of *phenomenon.* Do not use *phenomena* as a singular noun.

PLURAL	We have been studying those **phenomena** of nature, which are quite rare.
SINGULAR	We have been studying that **phenomenon** of nature, which is quite rare.

reason . . . because   See **because.**

Reverend, Honorable   Do not use either of these titles before a person's last name alone. Also, be sure to use the word *the* before the title.

| NONSTANDARD | My grandfather remembers meeting both Reverend King and the Honorable Inouye. |
| STANDARD | My grandfather remembers meeting both **the Reverend** Martin Luther King, Jr. [or **the Reverend Dr. King**] and **the Honorable** Daniel K. Inouye [or **the Honorable Mr. Inouye,** or **the Honorable Sen. Inouye**]. |

rise, raise   See page 690.

say   Do not use *say* or *says* after a past-tense verb. Use *said.*

| NONSTANDARD | Then she glared at me and says, "Where have you been?" |
| STANDARD | Then she glared at me and **said,** "Where have you been?" |

scarcely   See **The Double Negative,** page 780.

she   See **he, she, it, they.**

should of   See **of.**

sit, set   See page 689.

slow, slowly   See page 727.

some, somewhat   In formal situations, avoid using *some* to mean "to some extent." Use *somewhat.*

| INFORMAL | Tensions between the nations began to ease some. |
| FORMAL | Tensions between the nations began to ease **somewhat.** |

somewheres   See **anyways, anywheres.**

sort(s)   See **kind(s), sort(s), type(s)** and **kind of a, sort of a.**

sort of   See **kind of, sort of.**

supposed to, used to   When writing the past form of *suppose* or *use,* especially before the word *to,* be sure to add the *–d* ending.

| EXAMPLES | Desmond is **supposed to** [not *suppose to*] be in charge of the props for the senior play. |
| | I **used to** [not *use to*] work part time at that store. |

take   See **bring, take.**

teach   See **learn, teach.**

Reference Note

For information about forming the **past tense of regular verbs,** see page 670.

USAGE

Reference Note

For information about **subordinating conjunctions,** see page 520. For information on **adverbs,** see page 514.

than, then   *Than* is a subordinating conjunction used in comparisons. *Then* is an adverb telling *when*.

EXAMPLES   Tyrone is more studious **than** I am.

Take your diploma in your left hand, and shake hands with the principal; **then** leave the stage, and return to your seat.

that   See **who, which, that.**

their, there, they're   See page 911.

theirself, theirselves   See **hisself, theirself, theirselves.**

them   Do not use *them* as an adjective. Use *those*.

EXAMPLE   Have you seen **those** [not *them*] murals by Judith Baca at the art museum?

they   See **he, she, it, they.**

this here, that there   Avoid using *here* or *there* after the demonstrative adjective *this* or *that*.

EXAMPLE   **This** [not *This here*] magazine has an article about the Japanese koto player Kazue Sawai.

this, that, these, those   See **kind(s), sort(s), type(s).**

try and, try to   Use *try to*, not *try and*.

EXAMPLE   Did anyone **try to** [not *try and*] help Ted?

type(s)   See **kind(s), sort(s), type(s).**

type, type of   Avoid using *type* as an adjective. Add *of* after *type*.

NONSTANDARD   That's the type job I'd like to have.
STANDARD   That's the **type of** job I'd like to have.

used to   See **supposed to, used to.**

ways   Use *way*, not *ways*, when referring to distance.

EXAMPLE   At dusk we were still a long **way** [not *ways*] from home.

well, good   See page 727.

what   Use *that*, not *what*, to introduce an adjective clause.

EXAMPLE   The song **that** [not *what*] Annie has chosen to sing in the talent show is "Anytime You Need a Friend."

USAGE

when, where   Unless you are defining a time or place, do not use *when* or *where* to begin a definition.

STANDARD	Two o'clock is **when** we will have the next meeting.
STANDARD	This is **where** the new high school will be built.

NONSTANDARD	A hurricane is when a tropical cyclone has winds of 74 miles (118 kilometers) per hour or greater.
STANDARD	A hurricane is **a tropical cyclone that has winds of 74 miles (118 kilometers) per hour or greater.**

NONSTANDARD	An implosion is where something bursts inward.
STANDARD	An implosion is **an inward burst.**

where   Do not use *where* for *that*.

EXAMPLE   I read **that** [not *where*] the Smithsonian Institution has sixteen museums and galleries.

where . . . at   See **at.**

who's, whose   See page 912.

who, which, that   *Who* refers to persons only. *Which* refers to things only. *That* may refer to either persons or things.

EXAMPLES   Shah Jahan was the Indian ruler **who** [*or* **that**] built the Taj Mahal. [The antecedent is *ruler,* a person.]

The monument, **which** is a tomb, is near the city of Agra. [The antecedent is *monument,* a thing.]

It is a building **that** is much admired for its beautiful architecture. [The antecedent is *building,* a thing.]

who, whom   See page 646.

would of   See **of.**

your, you're   See page 912.

Exercise 7   Correcting Errors in Usage

Most of the sentences on the following page contain errors in the use of standard, formal English. If a sentence contains an error, revise the sentence. If a sentence is already correct, write *C.*

EXAMPLE   **1.** Can you name all of the American astronauts which have walked on the surface of the moon?

    1. Can you name all of the American astronauts who have walked on the surface of the moon?

USAGE

┌HELP─
Some sentences in Exercise 7 may be correctly revised in more than one way. You need to give only one revision for each sentence.

1. I was suppose to meet Jade here.
2. Backlighting is when the main source of light is placed in back of the subject being photographed.
3. Why don't you borrow some change off of Rhoda?
4. A number of unusual themes has already been proposed for the senior prom.
5. Neither Chico or Robert has any albums by Tish Hinojosa.
6. Sharon turned to me and says, "Did you see the beautiful sari that woman was wearing?"
7. You should of seen the premiere last night.
8. The aurora borealis is a spectacular phenomena of nature.
9. We stayed up to watch the late-night horror movie, which wasn't worth the loss of sleep.
10. It's a long ways to Memphis from Denver.
11. This sort inscription is common in the Mayan records.
12. Deleting files will help some with the space problem on your hard drive.
13. After some discussion, the district attorney decided not to persecute.
14. The smell of sour milk makes some people nauseous.
15. Take this here hose around to the back, and water the lawn.
16. Did you read where the new highway will bypass the town?
17. Many household cleansers are poisons what should be handled with caution.
18. Is Sudan bigger then Ethiopia, Nathan?
19. These phenomena have attracted astronomers' attention for decades.
20. She had long wanted to meet the woman which had done so much to register voters.

Exercise 8 Correcting Errors in Usage

Most of the sentences in the following paragraphs contain errors in the use of standard, formal English. If a sentence contains an error, revise the sentence. If a sentence is already correct, write *C*.

EXAMPLE   [1] I wish you could of gone with us on our trip to Alaska.

      1. *I wish you could have gone with us on our trip to Alaska.*

[1] Several years ago, I accompanied Reverend Alan Kemp and his wife, Angela, on a sightseeing trip to Alaska in July. [2] On our flight to Fairbanks, we saw a double rainbow—a marvelous phenomena that we felt was a lucky sign. [3] At the hotel, we began to plan what we would do the next day, but the number of possibilities were huge, and we

didn't know where to start. [4] Finally, we decided that we would neither stay in our rooms or eat dinner at the hotel; instead, we would go for a drive that evening. [5] As we headed for the car, I noticed on a poster where the World Eskimo-Indian Olympics were being held that very day. [6] "Doesn't this here event sound like fun?" I asked, showing Mrs. Kemp the advertisement for the games.

[7] The Kemps agreed, and as soon as we arrived at the fairgrounds, we introduced ourselves to a woman named Mrs. McBride. [8] She was a friendly woman which was happy to tell us about the games. [9] I was surprised some by the many different events that had been scheduled. [10] These games included tests of skill, such as the notorious Alaskan high kick, and tests of strength, such as drop-the-bomb.

[11] The Alaskan high kick is where a person sitting on the ground tries to kick a ball suspended in midair. [12] An event requiring exceptional balance, the Alaskan high kick is an example of the type skills that were traditionally developed by Alaska's native peoples. [13] The drop-the-bomb competition begins when three men lift another man off of the ground. [14] The man, who is held by his wrists and ankles, must remain perfectly horizontal while them three other men carry him. [15] The contestant who is carried the longest ways without sagging wins the event.

[16] As Mrs. McBride finished describing the games, she smiled and says, "This is the thirty-first year we've held these Eskimo Olympic games." [17] Than she proudly pointed out Cecelia Chanerak, who was sailing through the air during the blanket toss. [18] This event is when a group of people stretch out a hide blanket and throw a man or a woman as high as possible; the winner is whoever soars the highest and keeps the best balance. [19] I must confess that I got a bit nauseous watching people fly up so far in the air, but I managed to snap a picture anyway. [20] That there day was one of the best of our trip, and when I got back home, I eagerly described the Eskimo-Indian Olympics to my family and friends.

The Double Negative

A **double negative** is a construction in which two or more negative words are used to express a single negative idea.

Common Negative Words		
barely	never	not (–n't)
but (meaning "only")	no	nothing
	nobody	nowhere
hardly	none	only
neither	no one	scarcely

NONSTANDARD She has never missed none of the reunions.
STANDARD She has **never** missed **any** of the reunions.
STANDARD She has missed **none** of the reunions.

NONSTANDARD I have not said nothing about your plans.
STANDARD I have **not** said **anything** about your plans.
STANDARD I have said **nothing** about your plans.

WINTHROP reprinted by permission of Newspaper Enterprise Association, Inc.

NOTE Avoid the common error of using *–n't*, the contraction of *not*, with another negative word, such as *barely, hardly,* or *scarcely.*

NONSTANDARD I can't hardly see anything in this fog.
STANDARD I can **hardly** see anything in this fog.

NONSTANDARD Our lunch break was so short that we didn't scarcely have time to eat.
STANDARD Our lunch break was so short that we **scarcely** had time to eat.

The words *but* and *only* are considered negative words when they are used as adverbs meaning "no more than." In such cases, the use of another negative word with *but* or *only* is considered informal.

INFORMAL   I don't have but one pair of dress shoes.
  FORMAL   I have **but** one pair of dress shoes.
  FORMAL   I have **only** one pair of dress shoes.

Exercise 9 Identifying Correct Usage

For each of the following sentences, choose the correct word from the pair given in parentheses.

EXAMPLE   1. The club doesn't have (*any, no*) funds left in its treasury.
           1. *any*

1. Benjamin will never get (*nowhere, anywhere*) until he starts believing in himself.
2. Luís (*can, can't*) hardly keep from being proud of you.
3. I was so sleepy that I (*could, couldn't*) hardly keep my eyes open.
4. The detectives (*haven't, have*) no clues in the case.
5. There (*is, isn't*) no good reason for your being late.
6. We hadn't (*ever, never*) tasted papaya before.
7. Neither of them wants (*nothing, anything*) to do with the prank you're planning.
8. We (*had, hadn't*) but one choice to make.
9. The candidates (*have, haven't*) only three minutes each to state their positions.
10. The manager insisted that there wasn't (*any, no*) reason for making the customers wait so long.
11. We didn't see (*anybody, nobody*) there, so we came home.
12. By the time those boys were through, there (*wasn't, was*) barely enough tuna salad left for a sandwich.
13. I wouldn't go (*nowhere, anywhere*) wearing that outfit.
14. Wouldn't (*any, none*) of those shoes suit you?
15. There shouldn't be (*no one, anyone*) here who doesn't have a solid background in experimental design.
16. Aren't you (*ever, never*) going to be ready to go?
17. Nothing we did made (*no, any*) difference.
18. They (*weren't, were*) finding scarcely any traces of copper in that mine.
19. There (*was, wasn't*) no way I was riding in that contraption.
20. Do not touch (*nothing, anything*) on my desk!

USAGE

Nonsexist Language

Nonsexist language is language that applies to people in general, both male and female. For example, the nonsexist terms *humanity*, *human beings*, and *people* can substitute for the gender-specific term *mankind*.

In the past, many skills and occupations were generally closed to either men or women. Expressions like *seamstress*, *stewardess*, and *mailman* reflect those limitations. Since most jobs can now be held by both men and women, language is adjusting to reflect this change.

When you are referring generally to people, use nonsexist expressions rather than gender-specific ones. Following are some widely used nonsexist terms that you can use to replace the older, gender-specific ones.

Gender-Specific	Nonsexist
businessman	executive, businessperson
chairman	chairperson, chair
deliveryman	delivery person
fireman	firefighter
foreman	supervisor
housewife	homemaker
mailman	mail carrier
mankind	humankind, people
man-made	synthetic, manufactured
manpower	workers, human resources
May the best man win!	May the best person win!
policeman	police officer
salesman	salesperson, salesclerk
seamstress	needleworker
steward, stewardess	flight attendant
waiter, waitress	server
watchman	security guard

If the antecedent of a pronoun may be either masculine or feminine, use both masculine and feminine pronouns to refer to it.

EXAMPLES   **Anyone** who wants to purchase a class T-shirt must bring **his or her** money to Room 307 by Friday.

Any **student** may bring the money with **him or her** to Room 307.

Often, you can avoid the awkward *his or her* construction (or the alternative *his/her*) by substituting an article (*a, an,* or *the*) for the construction. You can also rephrase the sentence, using the plural forms of both the pronoun and its antecedent.

EXAMPLES   Any **student** who wants to purchase a class T-shirt must bring **the** money to Room 307 by Friday.

All **students** who want to purchase a class T-shirt must bring **their** money to Room 307 by Friday.

STYLE   TIP

Avoid using the awkward expressions *s/he* and *wo/man*.

Exercise 10 Using Nonsexist Language

Rewrite each of the following sentences to avoid using gender-specific terms and awkward expressions.

EXAMPLE   1. Many parking garages hire watchmen to deter thieves.

1. *Many parking garages hire security guards to deter thieves.*

1. More and more man-made objects are littering outer space.
2. The Boston Marathon got underway to cries of "May the best man win!"
3. Being a foreman in a factory must be a tough job.
4. The lobby of the office tower was full of businessmen arriving for appointments.
5. One problem the team faced was a shortage of manpower.
6. Anyone who wants to audition for the play must be sure that s/he can memorize long passages of dialogue.
7. In the last century or so, fewer and fewer women have chosen to become seamstresses.
8. The airline we took to Mexico had very courteous stewardesses.
9. There was a fascinating TV program last night about a day in the life of a fireman.
10. Dr. Zaharias has told her close associates that she is interested in becoming chairman of the department.

Review C Correcting Errors in Usage

Most of the following sentences contain errors in the use of standard, formal English. If a sentence contains an error, revise the sentence. If a sentence is already correct, write *C*.

EXAMPLE   1. An allegory is where a story's characters and events symbolize abstract ideas or moral principles.

1. *An allegory is a story in which the characters and events symbolize abstract ideas or moral principles.*

1. The professor made an illusion to Ralph Ellison's novel *Invisible Man*.
2. We had to adapt the stage lighting for the rock concert.
3. The organization helped a large amount of Asian refugees find work.
4. Where did you stay at over Thanksgiving?
5. Everyone except Tim has excepted the invitation.
6. Among the two performers, I prefer Keb' Mo'.
7. The data on acid rain is not complete.
8. My parents immigrated from Cuba before I was born.
9. Have you ever read about the nurse Florence Nightingale, who is notorious for having modernized the nursing profession?
10. Were you credulous enough to believe the fortuneteller?
11. My sister she attends Iowa State University.
12. We implied from Rudy's comment that the movie was dull.
13. The Coopers grew all the vegetables theirselves.
14. I had ought to spend more time with my friends.
15. He has been the catcher every inning so far, and he is beginning to look kind of tired.
16. Ms. Robinson learned me all I know about botany.
17. I think I just busted my watch, Marilyn.
18. At the assembly yesterday, the Honorable John Murphy encouraged students to register to vote as soon as they turn eighteen.
19. A number of suggestions have been submitted to the prom decorations committee.
20. There were four freshmen which made the basketball team.

Chapter Review

A. Identifying Correct Usage

For each of the following sentences, choose the correct word or words in parentheses. Base your answers on the rules of standard, formal usage.

1. We (*can't hardly, can't*) help feeling proud of our team.
2. The lifeguard dived (*into, in*) the water to rescue the child.
3. Did we do (*alright, all right*), Coach Garcia?
4. (*Being as, Being that, Because*) he was a good actor, he got the lead role in the play.
5. You are (*likely, liable*) to go far if you apply yourself.
6. We hiked a long (*way, ways*) before we found a suitable campsite.
7. The rescuers looked (*like, as if, as*) they had not slept.
8. There are (*less, fewer*) students in the senior class this year.
9. (*Those kinds of, That kind of a, This kind of*) movie is fun.
10. We (*hadn't ought, ought not*) to spill any of this paint on the floor.
11. The temperature has warmed (*some, somewhat*).
12. Please (*bring, take*) this report to Mr. Benson when you go.
13. The audience was deeply (*affected, effected*) by her speech.
14. We (*could have, could of, should of*) done a better job.
15. Kim's letter (*implied, inferred*) that she would be paying us a visit soon.
16. We received a large (*amount, number*) of offers.
17. Ana has done a very (*credible, creditable, credulous*) job.
18. Liev was (*suppose to, supposed to*) bring his pictures of Bali.
19. Do you remember borrowing a dollar (*off, off of, from*) me?
20. The first speaker will be (*Reverend Jackson, the Reverend Jackson, the Reverend Edward Jackson*).

B. Correcting Errors in Usage

Most of the sentences on the following page contain errors in the use of standard, formal English. If a sentence contains an error, revise the sentence. If a sentence is already correct, write *C*.

USAGE

21. After the play, Shirley acted like she were a movie star.

22. Do you know where the tape is at?

23. The other waiters and I divide the tips evenly between ourselves.

24. When the bill came, I realized that I hadn't scarcely any money.

25. Accept for Carlos and Glenn, everyone went to the fair.

26. The reason he left is that he felt tired.

27. Hasina and I are effected differently by the same song.

28. Take your dog with you when you come over to my house.

29. Could you try and help me move this table?

30. Both of Emily's grandmothers emigrated here in the 1940s.

31. We were kind of disappointed with the results.

32. Beside Ted and Ann, who else knows?

33. Doesn't a hot summer day make you long for an ice-cold drink?

34. My aunt Beverly, who was born in 1949, she served in the army.

35. The repair will take awhile.

36. Both tires busted when the bicycle rolled over the broken glass.

37. In his speech, Mr. Marlowe made an illusion to Shakespeare.

38. Finally, the gangster was successfully prosecuted for tax evasion.

39. After that the director says to me, "Just stay in the chariot, Chuck. I'll make sure you win the race."

40. Tony and myself are responsible for clearing the brush.

C. Identifying Correct Usage

For each sentence in the following paragraph, choose the correct word or words in parentheses.

[41] Even during ancient times, people (*which, who*) were sweltering in the heat found ways to cool off. [42] Around 3000 B.C., the Egyptians beat the heat when they (*discovered, invented*) the cooling effect of evaporation. [43] The Egyptians poured water into shallow trays made of clay; (*than, then*) they put the trays on a layer of straw. [44] As the temperature dropped during the night, the (*water it, water*) quickly evaporated and formed a thin layer of ice, which was eagerly gathered early the next morning. [45] Because more ice forms in very dry air, the (*amount, number*) of ice depended on the dryness of the air.

[46] A thousand years later, wealthy Babylonians would use the (*effects, affects*) of evaporation to cool their homes. [47] At twilight, they had the exterior walls and interior floors doused with water; as it evaporated from these surfaces, the houses cooled down (*some, somewhat*). [48] In ancient India, the same (*type, type of*) system was adapted for home cooling. [49] Wet grass mats hung in windward windows were (*liable, likely*) to create a considerable drop in temperature inside the house—as much as thirty degrees. [50] To maintain cooling, either someone kept the mats wet during the nights, or (*a, an*) reservoir over the windows slowly dripped water onto the mats.

Writing Application
Using Standard English in a Story

Standard and Nonstandard English   Recently you heard about a strange, inspiring, or funny experience. You have decided to write a fictional narrative based on the event. You may use nonstandard English in dialogue, but be sure to write the rest of the story in standard English.

Prewriting   Think about something strange, inspiring, or funny that happened to you or to someone you know. Decide on the setting, the characters, and the point of view of the story. Finally, create a brief plot outline.

Writing   Using your prewriting notes, write a draft of your story. Expand on your original ideas by inventing vivid details.

Revising   Read your story aloud to friends and ask them to tell you which part held their interest and which parts did not. Revise accordingly.

Publishing   Be sure to use the **Glossary of Usage** to help you correct unintentional nonstandard usages. Then, proofread your story for errors in grammar, usage, spelling, and punctuation. Be sure that you have placed quotation marks around dialogue. You and your classmates may wish to collect all of the class's stories in a booklet and add illustrations or photographs.

Reference Note
For information about **developing a short-story plot,** see Chapter 2.

Reference Note
For more about **using quotation marks,** see page 859.

USAGE

Capitalization
Standard Uses of Capital Letters

Diagnostic Preview

A. Using Standard Capitalization

Many of the following sentences contain at least one error in capitalization. For each error, write the correct form of the word. If a sentence is already correct, write *C*.

EXAMPLE   **1.** Manolo Cruz will be attending Stanford university in the Fall.

        1. University, fall

1. I am studying russian, English, and Art this Semester.
2. Go north for two Streets and then turn east on Central Avenue.
3. In U.S. History, only one person, Gerald R. Ford, has held the nation's highest office without being elected president or Vice President.
4. Last summer I enjoyed reading *To Kill A Mockingbird*, a novel by the southern writer Harper Lee.
5. I have fished from the sea wall on the shore of lake Pontchartrain.
6. The first American woman in space, Sally Ride, was a member of the crew aboard the space shuttle *challenger*, launched from cape Canaveral, Florida, on June 18, 1983.
7. The Mountain Ranges in the West offer a variety of hiking experiences for those who love the outdoors.
8. Local representatives from the democratic party and the republican party worked together to increase voter registration.

9. Because Michael's letter was addressed to 730 Lexington Place instead of to 730 Lexington Court, it was delayed.
10. The United States' political and economic interests are closely tied to those of its northern neighbor, Canada, and to those of its southern neighbors, Mexico and the central American countries.

B. Proofreading Paragraphs for Correct Capitalization

Proofread the following paragraphs. Write the words that are incorrectly capitalized, changing capital letters to lowercase letters and lowercase letters to capital letters where necessary. If a sentence is already correct, write *C*.

EXAMPLE   [1] Chattanooga, Tennessee, is the seat of Hamilton county.

        1. *County*

[11] Chattanooga, on the Georgia border in Southeast Tennessee, is building its future by inviting visitors to explore its past. [12] The city has been welcoming tourists since at least 1866, when an ad in the *Chattanooga Times* invited people from the north to visit with the assurance that the Ku Klux Klan had no power in Chattanooga. [13] Today a multimillion-dollar plaza on the banks of the Tennessee river marks the city's original site, a landing established about 1815 by a trader named john Ross. [14] exhibits throughout the plaza depict the city's history, including the 1838 forced removal of the Cherokee to the area now known as Oklahoma. [15] Ross, who was himself part Cherokee and who vehemently protested the removal, led that tragic journey, which became known as the trail of Tears.

[16] Chattanooga's Terminal Station on Market Street, now a hotel, was a stop for the *Chattanooga Choo Choo*, the first train to provide passenger service between the north and the south. [17] Chattanooga's status as a rail center made the City strategically important to both sides during the Civil War. [18] As the junction point for railroads to Atlanta, Memphis, Nashville, and Knoxville, Chattanooga provided a vital link for the movement of confederate troops and equipment. [19] In fact, the struggle for control of the railroads in the fall of 1863 led to a series of battles that took place in and around the city and that may have determined the outcome of the war. [20] It was general William Tecumseh Sherman's victory in the last of those confrontations, the Battle of Missionary Ridge on November 24–25, that cleared the way for his devastating march through Georgia to the Sea.

Using Capital Letters Correctly

In your reading, you may notice variations in the use of capital letters. Most writers, however, follow the rules presented in this chapter. In your own writing, following these rules will help you communicate clearly with the widest possible audience.

25a. Capitalize the first word of every sentence.

EXAMPLES   **R**eading the article, I learned about the Blessingway and other traditional Navajo ceremonies.

          What is the formula for converting degrees Celsius to degrees Fahrenheit?

(1) Capitalize the first word of a sentence following a colon.

EXAMPLE   We have one important recommendation: **I**n light of the statistics, four-way stop signs should be installed.

(2) Capitalize the first word of a resolution following the word *Resolved.*

EXAMPLE   Resolved: **T**hat government support of the arts be increased.

(3) Capitalize the first word of a quoted sentence.

The first word of a quoted sentence should begin with a capital letter, whether or not the quotation comes at the beginning of your sentence.

EXAMPLE   In one of his essays, Sir Francis Bacon wrote, "**S**ome books are to be tasted, others to be swallowed, and some few to be chewed and digested."

When quoting only part of a sentence, capitalize the first word of the quotation if the person you are quoting capitalized it or it is the first word of your sentence.

EXAMPLES   To which books do you think Bacon was referring when he wrote "**s**ome few [are] to be chewed and digested"?

          "**S**ome few to be chewed and digested" refers to books that should be read carefully and studied.

NOTE   Capitalize the first word of a sentence fragment used in dialogue.

EXAMPLE   When I asked Julia how many of Sir Francis Bacon's essays she had read, she replied, "**F**our of them."

STYLE   TIP

Do not capitalize the first word of a list following a colon unless it would be capitalized otherwise.

EXAMPLES

Bring the following items to practice every day: **r**acquet, court shoes, towels.

In this unit, we will be reading the following poets: **M**arlowe, Raleigh, and the metaphysical poets.

Reference Note

For more about **capitalizing** and **punctuating direct quotations,** see page 859.

Traditionally, the first word in each line of a poem is capitalized.

EXAMPLE

He clasps the crag with crooked hands;
Close to the sun in lonely lands,
Ringed with the azure world, he stands.

The wrinkled sea beneath him crawls;
He watches from his mountain walls,
And like a thunderbolt he falls.

Alfred, Lord Tennyson, "The Eagle"

For reasons of style, however, some writers do not follow this rule.

EXAMPLE

The art of losing isn't hard to master;
so many things seem filled with the intent
to be lost that their loss is no disaster.

Elizabeth Bishop, "One Art"

When quoting from another writer's work, always use capital letters as the writer does.

(4) Capitalize the first word of a statement or question inserted without quotation marks into a sentence.

EXAMPLE   My question is, **W**ill this action solve the problem?

25b. Capitalize the pronoun _I_ and the interjection _O_.

The interjection _O_ is usually used only for invocations and is followed by the name of the person or thing being addressed. Do not confuse _O_ with the common interjection _oh,_ which is generally not capitalized and which is usually set off with punctuation.

EXAMPLES   Where could **I** have put my book report?

Rejoice in the Lord, **O** ye righteous!

He was driving, **oh,** about thirty-five miles an hour.

25c. Capitalize the first word in both the salutation and the closing of a letter.

EXAMPLES   **D**ear Ms. Wong: **S**incerely yours,

My dear Caroline,   **B**est regards,

Dear **P**rincipal **C**uneo:

Reference Note

For more about **writing letters,** see "Writing" in the Quick Reference Handbook. For more about **punctuating salutations and closings,** see pages 842 and 854.

Reference Note

For more about **common and proper nouns,** see page 498.

25d. Capitalize proper nouns and proper adjectives.

A *common noun* names any one of a group of persons, places, things, or ideas. A *proper noun* names a particular person, place, thing, or idea. A *proper adjective* is formed from a proper noun.

Common nouns are capitalized only if they begin a sentence (also, in most cases, a line of poetry), begin a direct quotation, or are part of a title.

Common Nouns	Proper Nouns	Proper Adjectives
a king	King Arthur	Arthurian legend
a country	Thailand	Thai restaurant
a city	Moscow	Muscovite voters
a people	Algonquians	Algonquian customs
a religion	Buddhism	Buddhist shrine

In proper nouns made up of two or more words, do not capitalize

- articles (*a, an, the*)

- short prepositions (those with fewer than five letters, such as *at, of, for, with*)

- coordinating conjunctions (*and, but, for, nor, or, so, yet*)

EXAMPLES   International Union **f**or **t**he Conservation **o**f Nature **a**nd Natural Resources

Gulf **o**f Oman

Alfred **t**he Great

NOTE   Some proper nouns and proper adjectives have lost their capital letters after long usage.

EXAMPLES   a **c**ardigan (sweater)   **c**hina (dishes)

                morocco leather   **w**atts

Others may be written with or without capital letters.

EXAMPLES   **R**oman (**r**oman) numerals   **V**enetian (**v**enetian) blinds

                plaster of **P**aris (**p**aris)   **G**othic (**g**othic) style

HELP

If you are not sure whether to capitalize a word, look it up in an up-to-date dictionary.

(1) Capitalize the names of persons and animals. Capitalize initials in names and abbreviations that either precede or follow names.

Persons	Marco **M**artínez	**D**r. **L**ee **T**seng
	St. **F**rancis of **A**ssisi	**C**. **S**. **L**ewis
	Christina **Y**oungblood	**J**amaal **J**ohnson, **J**r.
Animals	**B**abe	**P**olly
	Wishbone	**M**orris the **C**at
	Trigger	**M**r. **E**d

NOTE Some names may contain more than one capital letter. If you are not sure about the spelling of a name, check with the person or consult a reference source.

EXAMPLES
De **L**a **T**our   **V**on **R**yan   **M**orning **S**tar
de la **T**our   von **R**yan   **M**orningstar

La **F**ontaine   **D**upont   **M**ac**K**enzie
Lafontaine   du **P**ont   **M**ackenzie

(2) Capitalize geographical names.

Type of Name	Examples	
Towns and Cities	**C**ampbellsville	**P**igeon **F**orge
	Stratford-on-**A**von	**S**an **J**uan
Counties, Townships, and Parishes	**M**aricopa **C**ounty	**O**rleans **P**arish
	Concord **T**ownship	**L**awrence **T**ownship
States and Provinces	**A**laska	**S**outh **C**arolina
	Manitoba	**D**istrict of **C**olumbia
Regions	the **S**outh	**W**estern **H**emisphere
	Great **P**lains	the **P**acific **R**im

NOTE Words such as *north, eastern,* and *southwestern* are not capitalized when they indicate direction.

EXAMPLE flying **s**outh for the winter

Reference Note
For more information about **capitalizing abbreviations such as** *Dr.* **and** *Jr.,* see page 824.

COMPUTER TIP

The range of correct spellings of personal names can challenge even the best computer spellchecker. One way to avoid this problem is to customize your spellchecker. If your software allows, add to it any frequently used names that you have difficulty spelling or capitalizing correctly.

Reference Note
The abbreviations of the names of states are capitalized. For more about **using and punctuating state abbreviations,** see page 825.

Reference Note

In addresses, abbreviations such as *St., Blvd., Ave., Dr., Ct.,* and *Ln.* are capitalized. For more information about **abbreviations,** see page 823.

TIPS & TRICKS

Avoid including the type of geographical name, such as *mountain, desert,* or *river,* as part of the proper noun if the proper noun already indicates the type of name.

EXAMPLES

Fujiyama or **Mount Fuji** [not *Mount Fujiyama,* because *yama* is Japanese for "mountain"]

Sahara [not *Sahara Desert,* because *sahara* is Arabic for "desert"]

Rio Grande [not *Rio Grande River,* because *rio* is Spanish for "river"]

HELP

If you are not sure about the spelling or capitalization of a geographical name, check in a dictionary or an encyclopedia.

Type of Name	Examples	
Countries	**Z**imbabwe	**S**audi **A**rabia
Continents	**A**ntarctica	**N**orth **A**merica
Islands	**I**sle of **W**ight	**S**olomon **I**slands
Mountains	**M**ount **S**t. **H**elens	**S**ierra **M**adre
	Pobeda **P**eak	**S**ugarloaf **M**ountain
Bodies of Water	**A**rctic **O**cean	**A**mazon **R**iver
	Lake **H**uron	**P**ersian **G**ulf
	Dead **S**ea	**G**uanabara **B**ay
Parks and Forests	**L**ake **C**lark **N**ational **P**ark	**O**uachita **N**ational **F**orest
Roads, Streets, and Highways	**R**oute 66	**R**aintree **R**oad
	Interstate 10	**B**luegrass **P**arkway
	Quail **B**riar **D**rive	**F**ifth **A**venue
	East **T**hird **S**treet	**G**ulf-to-**B**ay **B**oulevard
Other Geographical Names	**P**ainted **D**esert	**K**eweenaw **P**eninsula
	Palo **D**uro **C**anyon	**D**ismal **S**wamp
	Longhorn **C**averns	**S**hip **R**ock

NOTE The second word in a hyphenated street number begins with a lowercase letter.

EXAMPLE   Twenty-**s**econd Street

A word such as *city, lake, park,* or *street* is capitalized only when it is part of a proper noun.

Common Nouns	Proper Nouns
in the **c**ity	in **S**ioux **C**ity
near the **l**ake	near **L**ake **O**keechobee
through the **p**ark	through **M**esa **V**erde **N**ational **P**ark
on the next **s**treet	on **D**unbar **S**treet

Exercise 1　Identifying Correct Uses of Capitalization

For each of the following pairs of items, select the letter of the item that is correctly capitalized.

EXAMPLES　　**1. a.** the gulf of Mexico
　　　　　　　　b. the Gulf of Mexico

　　　　　　1. b

　　　　　　2. a. Yours truly,
　　　　　　b. yours truly,

　　　　　　2. a

1. a. the Nile river
　　b. the Nile River

2. a. She said, "Tell me, too."
　　b. She said, "tell me, too."

3. a. Bering strait
　　b. Bering Strait

4. a. Fifty-Second Street
　　b. Fifty-second Street

5. a. a German movie
　　b. a german movie

6. a. Charles Adams, Jr.
　　b. Charles Adams, jr.

7. a. New Jersey Turnpike
　　b. New Jersey turnpike

8. a. cedar rapids, Iowa
　　b. Cedar Rapids, Iowa

9. a. a United States Citizen
　　b. a United States citizen

10. a. Los Angeles
　　　County highways
　　b. Los Angeles
　　　County Highways

11. a. east of the river
　　b. East of the river

12. a. the Iberian peninsula
　　b. the Iberian Peninsula

13. a. people of the Far East
　　b. people of the far east

14. a. a cat named Banjo
　　b. a cat named banjo

15. a. an Irish setter
　　b. an Irish Setter

16. a. Billy The Kid
　　b. Billy the Kid

17. a. We heard him say he was
　　　"pleased to be here."
　　b. We heard him say he was
　　　"Pleased to be here."

18. a. dear Mr. Faust:
　　b. Dear Mr. Faust:

19. a. Give me, oh, ten or so.
　　b. Give me, Oh, ten or so.

20. a. the grand Canyon
　　b. the Grand Canyon

21. a. Follow me!
　　b. follow me!

22. a. The problem is, How do we
　　　fund the project?
　　b. The problem is, how do we
　　　fund the project?

23. a. Jake and i planted several
　　　trees.
　　b. Jake and I planted several
　　　trees.

24. a. a Shakespearean actor
　　b. a shakespearean actor

25. a. Resolved: That educational
　　　funding should be increased.
　　b. Resolved: that educational
　　　funding should be increased.

Exercise 2 Capitalizing Words and Names Correctly

Write each of the following items, using capital letters where they are needed.

EXAMPLE   **1.** horseshoe mountain

          1. Horseshoe Mountain

1. cook county

2. an african village on the atlantic

3. four miles south of route 10

4. ranching in the south

5. forty-ninth street

6. olympic national park

7. a city like new orleans, louisiana

8. along the mississippi river

9. coffee from colombia

10. st. paul, minnesota

11. new zealand

12. boats on the coral sea

13. lake Placid

14. Hear us, o mighty ruler!

15. Carson city

16. a pacific island

17. Here's a clue: the answer is round.

18. the great lakes

19. a cottage on the isle of man

20. Angel falls, Venezuela

(3) Capitalize the names of organizations, teams, institutions, and government bodies.

Type of Name	Examples	
Organizations	National Collegiate Athletic Association League of Women Voters Humane Society of Austin National Forensic League	
Teams	Detroit Red Wings Seattle Seahawks	San Antonio Spurs Oak Ridge Rangers
Institutions	Beverly Hills High School Catawba Valley Technical College Smithsonian Institution Massachusetts General Hospital	
Government Bodies	House of Representatives Federal Aviation Administration Department of Commerce Peace Corps	

Reference Note

For more about **punctuating abbreviations,** see page 823.

NOTE The names of some organizations and government bodies are often abbreviated as a series of capital letters.

EXAMPLES   **N**ational **O**rganization for **W**omen   **NOW**

Federal **C**ommunications **C**ommission   **FCC**

Generally, the letters in such abbreviations are not followed by periods. If you are not sure whether an abbreviation requires periods, look it up in an up-to-date dictionary or other reliable source.

Do not capitalize a word such as *association, school, hospital,* or *department* unless it is part of a proper noun.

Common Nouns	Proper Nouns
a member of the **a**ssociation	**A**merican **M**edical **A**ssociation
a nearby **h**igh **s**chool	**W**ebster **H**igh **S**chool
at the **h**ospital	**G**ates **M**emorial **H**ospital
working in the **d**epartment	**D**epartment of **T**ransportation

"After working all day on my MBA, I hop into my BMW and race home to watch PBS on my VCR—OK?"

© 1990; reprinted courtesy of Bunny Hoest and Parade magazine.

NOTE Do not capitalize words such as *democratic, republican,* and *socialist* when they refer to principles or forms of government. Capitalize such words only when they refer to the political parties.

EXAMPLES a **d**emocratic policy   the **D**emocratic **P**arty (*or* **p**arty)

(4) Capitalize the names of historical events and periods, special events, and holidays and other calendar items.

Type of Name	Examples	
Historical Events and Periods	**V**ietnam **W**ar **R**enaissance	**A**merican **R**evolution **B**ronze **A**ge
Special Events	**S**uper **B**owl **S**pecial **O**lympics	the **B**oston **M**arathon **C**onference on **W**orld **H**unger
Holidays and Other Calendar Items	**L**abor **D**ay **M**onday **D**ecember	**P**residents' **D**ay **F**ourth of **J**uly **H**ispanic **H**eritage **M**onth

NOTE Do not capitalize the name of a season unless the season is being personified or is being used as part of a proper noun.

EXAMPLES an early **w**inter

"O wild West Wind, thou breath of **A**utumn's being, . . ."
                              Percy Bysshe Shelley, "Ode to the West Wind"

the **S**uncoast **S**ummer **F**estival

(5) Capitalize the names of nationalities, races, and peoples.

EXAMPLES   **A**sian   **H**ispanic   **O**jibwa

            Zulu   **N**orse   **A**frican **A**merican

            Caucasian   **A**ztec   **S**wedish

(6) Capitalize the names of religions and their followers, holy days and celebrations, holy writings, and specific deities.

Type of Name	Examples	
Religions and Followers	**C**hristianity	**C**onfucian
	Judaism	**M**ethodist
	Hinduism	**T**aoist
Holy Days and Celebrations	**C**hristmas	**R**amadan
	Purim	**R**osh **H**ashana
Holy Writings	**T**orah	**N**ew **T**estament
	Veda	**T**ao **T**e **C**hing
Specific Deities	**A**llah	**Y**ahweh
	God	**B**rahma

The words *god* and *goddess* are not capitalized when they refer to deities of ancient mythology. However, the names of specific mythological gods and goddesses are capitalized.

EXAMPLE   Cassandra could foretell the future but was condemned by the **g**od **A**pollo never to be believed.

NOTE Some writers always capitalize pronouns that refer to a deity. Other writers capitalize such pronouns only if necessary to prevent confusion.

EXAMPLE   The priest asked God to bring peace to **H**is people. [The capitalization of *His* shows that the pronoun refers to God, not the priest.]

(7) Capitalize the names of businesses and the brand names of business products.

Type of Name	Examples
Businesses	**P**rocter & **G**amble **C**ompany®
	International **B**usiness **M**achines®
	Southwest **A**irlines®
	Uptown **D**iscount **S**hoe **S**tore
Business Products	**P**olaroid® camera
	Xerox® copier
	Nintendo® video game
	Jif® peanut butter

Notice that a common noun that follows a brand name is not capitalized, but the name of a trademarked product is capitalized.

EXAMPLES   Nintendo **v**ideo **g**ame   Nintendo **G**ameboy

(8) Capitalize the names of ships, trains, aircraft, spacecraft, and other vehicles.

Type of Name	Examples	
Ships	*Merrimac*	*Cunard Princess*
Trains	*Orient Express*	*North Coast Limited*
Aircraft	*Spirit of St. Louis*	*Air Force One*
Spacecraft	*Atlantis*	*Saturn 5*

Reference Note
For more about the **use of italics,** see page 856.

NOTE   Notice above that the names of individual ships, trains, aircraft, and spacecraft are not only capitalized but also italicized. The names of the make and the model of a vehicle, though, are capitalized but not italicized.

EXAMPLES   **H**onda **A**ccord   **F**ord **E**xplorer

(9) Capitalize the names of buildings and other structures.

EXAMPLES   **S**hubert **T**heatre   **G**olden **G**ate **B**ridge

Plaza **H**otel   **L**eaning **T**ower of **P**isa

Hoover **D**am   **H**adrian's **W**all

(10) Capitalize the names of monuments, memorials, and awards.

Type of Name	Examples	
Monuments	**M**ontezuma **C**astle	**S**tatue of **L**iberty
Memorials	**L**incoln **M**emorial	**C**ivil **R**ights **M**emorial
Awards	**A**cademy **A**ward	**P**ulitzer **P**rize

Reference Note
For more about **common nouns and proper nouns,** see page 498.

NOTE   Do not capitalize a word such as *building, monument,* or *award* unless it is part of a proper noun.

MECHANICS

(11) Capitalize the names of planets, stars, constellations, and other heavenly bodies.

Type of Name	Examples	
Planets	Neptune	Mercury
Stars	Sirius	the North Star
Constellations	Cassiopeia	Canis Major

NOTE Generally, the words *sun* and *moon* are not capitalized. The word *earth* is not capitalized unless it is used along with the name of another heavenly body that is capitalized.

EXAMPLES   gazing at the **s**un, **m**oon, and stars

below the surface of the **e**arth

the distance between **V**enus and **E**arth

25e. Do not capitalize the names of school subjects, except course names that include a number and the names of language classes.

EXAMPLES   **art**   **a**lgebra   **c**hemistry

Art 102   **A**lgebra I   **C**hemistry II

English   **S**panish   **G**erman

NOTE Generally, a singular noun identified by a number or letter is capitalized.

EXAMPLES   **R**oom 31   **F**igure B   **S**chool **D**istrict 18   **C**hapter 4

However, the word *page* is usually not capitalized when followed by a number or letter, nor is a plural noun followed by two or more numbers or letters capitalized.

EXAMPLE   Look at **f**igures A and B on **p**age 327.

Do not capitalize the class name *senior, junior, sophomore,* or *freshman* unless it is part of a proper noun.

EXAMPLES   The **j**uniors and the **s**eniors will hold their talent show on May 4.

The **J**unior-**S**enior Revue will be held on May 4.

Exercise 3 — Capitalizing Words Correctly

Write the following items, using capital letters correctly. If an item is already correct, write *C*.

EXAMPLE   1.   earth science I

              1.   *Earth Science I*

1. itawamba junior college
2. a hotel across town
3. central high school
4. the world series
5. medal of freedom
6. a ford ranger
7. winter blizzard
8. the barclay hotel
9. trigonometry
10. physics I
11. labor day
12. history class
13. ibm computer
14. senior career day
15. bureau of the census
16. *zephyr* (train)
17. the crusades
18. She is a junior.
19. newport athletic club
20. the rings of saturn
21. a methodist minister
22. one saturday in October
23. Chinese families
24. the industrial revolution
25. a trophy for the Johnson High School wildcats

Review A — Proofreading a Paragraph for Correct Capitalization

Proofread the following paragraph. Write each word that is incorrectly capitalized, changing capital letters to lowercase letters and lowercase letters to capital letters where necessary. If a sentence is already correct, write *C*.

EXAMPLE   [1] Only well-educated, highly skilled candidates are chosen as mission specialists with Today's National Aeronautics and Space administration (NASA).

              1.   *today's, Administration*

[1] A physician who speaks four languages and is trained in modern dance, dr. Mae Jemison (right) is one of NASA's most sought-after speakers. [2] Jemison, the first African american female astronaut, grew up in Chicago and won a scholarship to Stanford university in California. [3] At Stanford she turned her attention to chemical engineering and African and african American studies. [4] Later, while earning her Medical degree at Cornell University in Ithaca, new York, she worked at a refugee camp in Thailand. [5] After obtaining her degree, she served in the Peace corps in the African nations of Sierra

leone and Liberia. [6] Jemison joined NASA in 1987 while working as a general practitioner and attending graduate Engineering classes in Los angeles. [7] With her first spaceflight on *Endeavor* in the Fall of 1992, she sought to bring people "A view of the space program they may not [otherwise] get." [8] As the United States gets closer to completing a space station and sending crews to the Moon and to Mars, the number of mission specialists is expected to increase dramatically. [9] As a result, more opportunities will be available to all candidates who excel in research, science, and engineering. [10] "everyone has skills and talents," Jemison emphasizes, "and no one has a lock on scientific ability or physical ability."

25f. Capitalize titles.

(1) Capitalize a person's title when the title comes before the person's name.

EXAMPLES   **C**aptain Valdés   **J**ustice O'Connor

               Senator Inouye   **P**resident White Feather

Generally, do not capitalize a title used alone or following a person's name.

EXAMPLES   the **c**aptain of the ship

               every **j**ustice of the U.S. Supreme Court

               Daniel Inouye, a **s**enator from Hawaii

               Uta White Feather, the class **p**resident

For clarity or special emphasis, however, you may capitalize a title used alone or following a person's name. In addition, a few titles are always capitalized. If you are unsure of whether to capitalize a title, look it up in a current dictionary.

EXAMPLES   Both the **P**resident and the **V**ice **P**resident met with the **P**rime **M**inister of Israel.

               The **S**urgeon **G**eneral addressed the assembly.

Generally, capitalize a title when using it alone in direct address.

EXAMPLES   Goodbye, **P**rofessor.

Thank you, **S**ir [or *sir*].

NOTE   Do not capitalize prefixes such as *ex–,* suffixes such as *–elect,* or the words *former* or *late* when using them with titles.

EXAMPLES   the governor-**e**lect

ex-President Carter

former Prime Minister Thatcher

the **l**ate Senator Humphrey

(2) Capitalize a word showing a family relationship when the word is used before or in place of a person's name, unless the word is preceded by a possessive.

EXAMPLES   **U**ncle Juan   **C**ousin Denisa   **G**randpa

my **a**unt Eunice   Jay's **c**ousin Ramón   your **m**other

(3) Capitalize the first and last words and all important words in titles and subtitles.

Unimportant words in a title include

- articles (*a, an, the*)

- short prepositions (those with fewer than five letters, such as *in, of, to, for, from, with*)

- coordinating conjunctions (*and, but, for, nor, or, so, yet*)

Reference Note

For more about **articles,** see page 506. For more about **prepositions,** see page 517. For more about **coordinating conjunctions,** see page 519.

Type of Title	Examples
Books	*A Portrait of the Artist as a Young Man* *Modern Poetry: American and British*
Chapters and Other Parts of Books	"The 1920s: A Turbulent Decade" "Glossary of Usage"
Periodicals	*The San Diego Tribune* *People Weekly*

MECHANICS

Type of Title	Examples
Poems	"**O**de on a **G**recian **U**rn" **I A**m **J**oaquín
Short Stories	"**T**he **O**ld **M**an at the **B**ridge" "**T**he **T**rain from **R**hodesia"
Plays	**T**he **M**erchant of **V**enice **A L**and **B**eyond the **R**iver
Historical Documents	**D**eclaration of **I**ndependence **M**agna **C**arta
Movies	**I**t's a **W**onderful **L**ife **A**ir **B**ud: **G**olden **R**eceiver
Radio and TV Series	**B**illboard's **T**op 40 **C**ountdown **T**he **T**onight **S**how
Videos and Video Games	**L**eonard **B**ernstein: **R**eaching for the **N**ote **A**steroids
Computer Programs and Games	**I**nfopedia 2.0 **T**om **C**lancy's **R**ainbow **S**ix
Comic Strips	**H**i and **L**ois **D**ennis the **M**enace
Works of Art	**N**ike of **S**amothrace [sculpture] **I** and the **V**illage [painting]
Musical Compositions	**R**agtime **D**ance "**T**he **S**ky **I**s **C**rying"
Audiotapes and CDs	**G**ershwin's **S**ongbook **T**hese **A**re **S**pecial **T**imes

NOTE Capitalize an article (*a, an,* or *the*) in a title or subtitle only if the article is the first word of the official title or subtitle. The official title can usually be found in the table of contents or in the masthead, the section of a periodical that lists the publisher, the editor, the owner, and other information.

EXAMPLES   **t**he *Science Digest*   ***T**he Spectator*   ***A** Farewell to Arms*

Exercise 4 Capitalizing Titles Correctly

Write each of the following items, using capital and lowercase letters where they are needed. If an item is already correct, write *C*.

EXAMPLE   1. governor Nellie Tayloe Ross

   1. *Governor Nellie Tayloe Ross*

1. captain Ahab
2. *guernica* (painting)
3. a Sergeant in an army
4. the club president
5. aunt Betty
6. senator Campbell
7. mayor Fulton of Nashville
8. *down and out in paris and london* (book title)
9. *All In the Family* (television series)
10. Rabbi Klein, a military chaplain
11. former president Jimmy Carter
12. the leader of a brass band
13. Ms. Solomon, the center director
14. mayor-elect Marc Morial
15. the bill of rights
16. your Aunt Shirley
17. the *Los Angeles times*
18. duties of a Legislator
19. former Golf Champion Annika Sörenstam
20. "the world is too much with us" (poem)
21. a recipe in *Family Circle* (magazine)
22. "All summer in a day" (short story)
23. "The Monsters are Due On Maple Street" (television episode)
24. *The Life and times of Rosie The Riveter* (film)
25. Please come in, doctor.

Review B Capitalizing Words Correctly

For each of the following sentences, correctly write the words that should be capitalized.

EXAMPLE   1. My best friend, alonzo, played the part of petruchio in the senior class's production of shakespeare's comedy *the taming of the shrew.*

   1. *Alonzo, Petruchio, Shakespeare's,* The Taming, Shrew

1. In their english classes this term, the juniors have read *o pioneers!*, a novel written by willa cather about swedish immigrants in the state of nebraska.

2. A recent report from the secretary of labor includes the following statement: "most of the new jobs in the next decade will be in service fields."

3. According to professor De La Rey, the first poems of Alfred, lord Tennyson's *idylls of the king* were published in 1859, the same year as the publication of Charles Darwin's *the origin of species,* George Eliot's *adam bede,* and Charles Dickens's *a tale of two cities.*

4. In "canto I" the poet Ezra Pound describes an ominous sea voyage to one of the same mythical lands visited by the hero Odysseus in the *Odyssey,* an epic by the greek poet Homer.

5. Speaking to a reporter from the *County Clarion,* coach Sheila Smith explained the debate team's latest resolution, which read, in part, "Resolved: that we will win all of our debates next year."

6. In ancient egypt the people worshiped many gods equally until the sun god Ra became the principal deity.

7. Dr. Bruce Jackson, jr., the principal of the high school, formerly taught mathematics I classes and an introductory class in computer science offered to sophomores and juniors.

8. From the St. Croix island national monument in Maine to the Huleia wildlife refuge in Hawaii, public lands managed by the federal government, including the military, equal a large percentage of the nation's total acreage.

9. Suzanne o'Rourke, the president of the jogging club, has an exercise route that takes her three times a week through Myers park, down Carriage street, and then back west to Dean avenue.

10. The will of the swedish industrialist and inventor of dynamite, Alfred Nobel, established the Nobel prize to honor those who have done great service for the world in the areas of literature, medicine, physics, chemistry, and peace; a prize in economics was added in 1969.

11. Calvin Peete, the first african american to succeed on the professional golf tour, earned hundreds of thousands of dollars at events like the greater milwaukee open and walked away with awards like the vardon trophy.

12. did corporal Myers receive a radio transmission from squad 5?

13. While cousin Marty and I were at the Capital theater seeing *Mr. Smith goes to Washington* at the Frank Capra festival, we saw Mayor Balard and his wife.

14. Although Paula Gunn Allen is sioux, scottish, and lebanese, she grew up around the pueblo indian culture; later, she made a career of her fascination with her native american heritage by writing, among other things, *Studies in american indian Literature.*

15. That their living room was decorated in the victorian style was a little strange considering that a Packard Bell computer was under a lace cover and the ruffled curtains over the front window concealed a view of a military base full of jets and helicopters.

16. Around the world, jewish people observe yom kippur, during which they remember and fast in reparation for their failings.

17. The treaty of Versailles simultaneously put an end to world war I and inaugurated the league of nations.

18. The voting rights act of 1965 ensured the registration of many voters by outlawing literacy tests and other unfair practices.

19. It's a good thing that doctor Daniel Hale Williams III decided not to become a shoemaker as his father had planned; otherwise, open-heart surgery might not have gotten its start in 1893, and the Provident hospital and medical center, where so many African American interns and nurses trained, might not have been built.

20. Commanded by general Dwight D. Eisenhower, the Allies mounted the multifaceted attack known as the normandy invasion.

Review C Proofreading Paragraphs for Correct Capitalization

Proofread the following paragraphs, and change capital letters to lowercase letters and lowercase letters to capital letters as necessary. If a sentence is already correct, write *C.*

EXAMPLE [1] An intriguing museum in Western Oklahoma celebrates the diversity and vitality of American Indian Culture.

1. *western, culture*

[1] The Southern Plains Indian Museum on Highway 62, East of Anadarko, Oklahoma, was founded in 1947. [2] Administered by the Indian arts and crafts board, an agency of the U.S. department of the Interior, the museum showcases the creative achievements of the Kiowa, Comanche, Kiowa-Apache, Southern Cheyenne, Southern Arapaho, Wichita, Caddo, Delaware, and Ft. Sill Apache. [3] A display of authentically detailed traditional costumes highlights the Museum's permanent

collection. [4] Also on permanent display are four dioramas and a mural by the nationally renowned Artist and sculptor Allen Houser, a Ft. Sill Apache; these exhibits illustrate the traditional social and ceremonial customs of the region's peoples. [5] The museum also offers changing exhibits of contemporary arts and crafts, including painting, beadwork, metalwork, and featherwork.

[6] These displays, as well as frequent one-person shows and demonstrations, are held in cooperation with the Oklahoma Indian Arts and Crafts cooperative, an independent business owned and operated by American indian artists and craftworkers. [7] The Cooperative operates the museum's gift shop and certifies the authenticity of all products sold there. [8] One special attraction during the Summer is a display on the museum grounds of full-scale tepees, like these, painted by contemporary artists. [9] Another attraction is the week-long American Indian Expo held each August at the Caddo county Fairgrounds adjacent to the museum. [10] The largest gathering of native American peoples in the State of Oklahoma, the exposition features dance contests, a pageant, horse races, and parades.

Abbreviations

An *abbreviation* is a shortened form of a word or phrase.

25g. Generally, abbreviations are capitalized if the words that they stand for are capitalized.

Personal Names

Abbreviate given names only if the person is most commonly known by the abbreviated form of the name. Capitalize initials.

EXAMPLES **W.E.B.** DuBois   **T. S.** Eliot   **D. H.** Lawrence

NOTE   Leave a space between two initials, but not between three or more.

Reference Note

For information on **forming the plurals of abbreviations,** see page 873.

Titles

Abbreviate and capitalize social titles whether used before the full name or before the last name alone.

EXAMPLES   **Mr.** Jon Ferguson   **Sra.** (Señora) Santiago

Sr. (Señor) Aguilar   **Ms.** Cohen

Mrs. Douglass   **Dr.** Jefferson

You may abbreviate civil and military titles used before full names or before initials and last names. Spell them out before last names alone. Capitalize the title whether or not it is abbreviated.

EXAMPLES   **Sen.** Joseph Biden   **Senator** Biden

Prof. I. B. Haro   **Professor** Haro

Gen. George Patton   **General** Patton

Abbreviate and capitalize titles and academic degrees that follow proper names.

EXAMPLES   Cuba Gooding, **Jr.**   Sara Kincaid, **M.D.**

Lon Chaney, **Sr.**   Rafael Castillo, **D.V.M.**

Giselle Richard, **D.D.S.**   Kuri Asato, **Ph.D.**

MECHANICS

NOTE Do not include the titles *Mr., Mrs., Ms., Sr., Sra.,* or *Dr.* when you use a title or degree after a name.

EXAMPLE **Dr.** Joanna Wilde *or* Joanna Wilde, **M.D.** [not *Dr. Joanna Wilde, M.D.*]

Agencies and Organizations

An *acronym* is a word formed from the first (or first few) letters of a series of words. Acronyms are usually capitalized and written without periods. After spelling out the first use of the names of agencies, organizations, and other things commonly known by their acronyms, abbreviate these names.

EXAMPLE My cousin applied for a job with the **Internal Revenue Service (IRS).** She said that working for the **IRS** would allow her to use the math skills she has worked so hard to develop.

HUD	Department of Housing and Urban Development
OPEC	Organization of Petroleum Exporting Countries
ACLU	American Civil Liberties Union
PBS	Public Broadcasting Service
MDOT	Michigan Department of Transportation
JAG	judge advocate general
MVP	most valuable player
VCR	videocassette recorder
HMO	health maintenance organization

STYLE TIP

Many common abbreviations are capitalized though the spelled-out words are not. If you are not sure whether to capitalize an abbreviation, look it up in a current dictionary.

STYLE TIP

A few acronyms, such as *radar, laser,* and *sonar,* are now considered common nouns. They do not need to be spelled out on first use and are no longer capitalized. When you are not sure whether an acronym should be capitalized, look it up in a current dictionary.

MECHANICS

Geographical Terms

In regular text, spell out names of states and other political units whether they stand alone or follow other geographical terms. Abbreviate them in tables, notes, and bibliographies. Generally, you should use the same capitalization rules for the abbreviations as you use for the full words.

MECHANICS

TEXT	Edgar Allan Poe spent his early years in Richmond, Virginia, and Boston, Massachusetts.
	On their tour of the United Kingdom, they visited Belfast, the capital of Northern Ireland.

TABLE

Liverpool, **U.K.**	Santa Fe, **N. Mex.**
Vancouver, **B.C.**	Columbia, **N.C.**

FOOTNOTE   ³Clemens's letters, literary manuscripts, and scrapbooks are kept at the Univ. of **Calif.,** Berkeley.

BIBLIOGRAPHY ENTRY   "The Last Honest Man." Editorial. *Ledger-Tribune* [Tucson, **Ariz.**] 29 Mar. 1997:30.

In regular text, spell out every word in an address. Such words are generally abbreviated in letter and envelope addresses and may be abbreviated in tables and notes.

TEXT   They live at 4726 South Oak Street.

Send the package to Wharton Court, Suite 101, San Diego, California.

ENVELOPE   4726 **S.** Oak **St.**

TABLE

Wharton **Ct.**	San Diego, **Calif.**

NOTE   Two-letter state abbreviations without periods are used only when the ZIP Code is included.

EXAMPLE   Wilmington, **DE** 19899-8962

Time

Abbreviate the two most frequently used era designations, *A.D.* and *B.C.* The abbreviation *A.D.* stands for the Latin phrase *anno Domini,* meaning "in the year of the Lord." It is used with dates in the Christian era. When used with a specific year, *A.D.* precedes the number. When used with the name of a century, it follows the name.

EXAMPLES   The Middle Ages is usually considered to have begun in Britain in **A.D.** 1066, with the Norman Conquest.

The fifteenth century **A.D.** saw the beginnings of the Renaissance in England.

The abbreviation *B.C.*, which stands for *before Christ*, is used for dates before the Christian era. It follows either a specific year number or the name of a century.

EXAMPLES   The Roman poet Virgil was born in 70 **B.C.**

Tutankhamen ruled Egypt for a short time during the fourteenth century **B.C.**

In regular text, spell out the names of months and days whether they appear alone or in dates. Both types of names may be abbreviated in tables, notes, and bibliographies.

TEXT   The project is due on Thursday, March 14.

NOTE   **Thurs. Mar.** 14

BIBLIOGRAPHY   "The Last Honest Man." Editorial. *Ledger-Tribune*
ENTRY   [Tucson, Ariz.] 29 **Mar.** 1997:30.

Abbreviate the designations for the two halves of the day measured by clock time. The abbreviation *A.M.* stands for the Latin phrase *ante meridiem*, meaning "before noon." The abbreviation *P.M.* stands for *post meridiem*, meaning "after noon." Both abbreviations follow the numerals designating the specific time.

EXAMPLES   The alarm goes off at 8:00 **A.M.**

By 5:30 **P.M.**, Sandy has completed most of her work for the day.

Units of Measurement

In regular text, spell out the names of units of measurement whether they stand alone or follow a spelled-out number or a numeral. Such names may be abbreviated in tables and notes when they follow a numeral. Most abbreviations for units of measurement are not capitalized.

TEXT   In town, the speed limit is generally twenty-five **miles per hour** [not *mph*].

The tent measured ten **feet** [not *ft*] by twelve.

TABLE

1 **tsp** salt	2 **tbsp** oil	26° **F**
6 **ft** 1 **in.**	6 **oz** lemon juice	5 **mph**

STYLE   **TIP**

In your reading, you may come across the abbreviations *C.E.* and *B.C.E.* These abbreviations stand for *Common Era* and *Before Common Era*. These abbreviations are sometimes used in place of *A.D.* and *B.C.*, respectively, and are used after the date.

EXAMPLES
The Saxon king Egbert ruled England from 829 to 839 **C.E.**

Hannibal and his elephants entered Italy in 218 **B.C.E.**

STYLE   **TIP**

Do not use *A.M.* or *P.M.* with numbers spelled out as words or as substitutes for the words *morning*, *afternoon*, or *evening*.

EXAMPLES
The rally will begin at **8:00 A.M.** (or **eight o'clock in the morning**) Sunday [not *eight A.M.*].

Her letter vividly describes the fog on an **evening** [not *on a P.M.*] in London.

MECHANICS

As the examples on the preceding page show, the abbreviations of most units of measurement do not include periods. To prevent confusion with the word *in,* however, writers should include a period in the abbreviation of *inch* or *inches* (*in.*).

Exercise 5 Using Abbreviations and Correct Capitalization

For the following sentences, correct any errors in the use of abbreviations and capitalization. If a sentence is already correct, write *C.*

EXAMPLE   1. Dad was born in new london, WI.

              1. *New London, Wisconsin*

1. Tomorrow, the lecture begins at 10:30 A.M.
2. Julius Caesar started the Roman Civil War by crossing a small river, the Rubicon, in B.C. 49.
3. The Hundred Years' War between England and France began in A.D. the fourteenth century.
4. Lake Michigan, the largest body of fresh water in the United States, touches four states: MI, IN, IL, and WI.
5. Sandy has moved from elm st. to Sycamore avenue.
6. Have you asked ms. Pellitier about the results?
7. The blueprint says "32 FT by 60 FT."
8. My father still has not figured out how to set the clock on the new v.c.r.
9. The guest speaker will be Juanita Acosta, Ph.D.
10. Please call gen. Rogers tomorrow.

Chapter Review

A. Identifying Correct Uses of Capitalization

For each of the following pairs of items, select the letter of the item that is correctly capitalized.

1. **a.** Battle of the Coral sea
   b. Battle of the Coral Sea
2. **a.** my uncle Francis
   b. my Uncle Francis
3. **a.** Maytag washer and dryer
   b. Maytag Washer and Dryer
4. **a.** Hearken to me, o Israel!
   b. Hearken to me, O Israel!
5. **a.** the Nobel prize
   b. the Nobel Prize
6. **a.** Dear Ms. Evans,
   b. dear ms. evans,
7. **a.** English, Math I, Science
   b. English, Math I, science
8. **a.** a chinese elm tree
   b. a Chinese elm tree
9. **a.** live in Buffalo County
   b. live in Buffalo county
10. **a.** Davis High School in Alton
    b. Davis high school in Alton
11. **a.** in honor of Arbor Day
    b. in honor of Arbor day
12. **a.** the train known as the *city of New Orleans*
    b. the train known as the *City of New Orleans*
13. **a.** took courses in English, Spanish, and chemistry
    b. took courses in English, Spanish, and Chemistry
14. **a.** the islamic sacred month called Ramadan
    b. the Islamic sacred month called Ramadan
15. **a.** at the intersection of Sixth avenue and Market street
    b. at the intersection of Sixth Avenue and Market Street
16. **a.** a trip to Yosemite National Park
    b. a trip to Yosemite national park

17. **a.** the Roosevelt hotel in New York city
    b. the Roosevelt Hotel in New York City
18. **a.** enjoyed Toni Morrison's novel *the Bluest Eye*
    b. enjoyed Toni Morrison's novel *The Bluest Eye*
19. **a.** a visit to the world Trade Center
    b. a visit to the World Trade Center
20. **a.** the moons of Jupiter
    b. the Moons of Jupiter

B. Identifying and Correcting Errors in Capitalization

Most of the following items contain one or two errors in capitalization. Correct each error, using capital letters and lowercase letters where they are necessary.

21. Father's day is observed on the third Sunday in June.
22. For years uncle Wyatt was in the Mesa Garden club.
23. I work in a Drugstore on Breakstone Parkway.
24. When we traveled on the Continent of europe, we especially enjoyed seeing the Swiss Alps.
25. Resolved: that freedom of speech is the foundation of our liberty.
26. Booker T. Washington, an African American educational leader in the late 1800s, wrote *Up from slavery*.
27. The Western High school volleyball team is playing the championship game tonight in Davis gymnasium.
28. The local Post Office is being remodeled by Teller Construction.
29. The revolutionary war was fought in North America more than two centuries ago.
30. Ms. Li is now a Professor of music at Lawson College.
31. sincerely yours,
    Fouad Hussein, m.d.
32. Is the British museum on Great Russell street in London?
33. The Saint Angelica choir performed there on Friday.
34. She said, "that is easy."
35. In 1998, senator John Glenn participated in a Nasa mission.

C. Using Abbreviations and Correct Capitalization

For the following sentences, correct any errors in the use of abbreviations and capitalization.

36. I read that the second millennium began in 1001 A.D.

37. My father was born in Woodland, MI, on Sept. 13, 1958.

38. Try to remember the following: the rental truck cannot be driven any faster than 55 mph.

39. After the Civil war, General Ulysses s. Grant became the eighteenth president of the United States.

40. I believe the vcr was shipped on August 23 from San diego, CA.

Writing Application
Using Capital Letters in a Letter

Standard Capitalization   Write a letter to the school librarian, recommending five books, periodicals, or videocassettes. Briefly describe each one, telling why you think it would be a worthwhile addition to the library. Be sure to use correct capitalization.

Prewriting   Write down a list of novels, biographies, newspapers, literary journals, educational videocassettes, and other materials that you think would be helpful additions to the library. Choose five titles from your list. Note whether each is a book, a periodical, or a videocassette. Briefly describe the subject matter of each.

Writing   Use your notes to help you write your first draft. Give clear, specific information about each suggested item to convince the librarian to acquire it.

Revising   Read your draft critically. Is your letter persuasive? Does it follow the proper form for a business letter? Be sure that all of your information is accurate and complete.

Publishing   Make sure you have spelled each title correctly, followed the rules of standard capitalization, and italicized each title or enclosed it in quotation marks correctly. Be sure you have corrected any errors in grammar, usage, spelling, and punctuation. Show your letter to the school librarian. Ask him or her what is most effective in the letter and what could be improved to make it more persuasive.

Reference Note

For more about **writing business letters,** see "Writing" in the Quick Reference Handbook.

Reference Note

For more about **using italics and quotation marks,** see pages 856 and 859.

MECHANICS

Punctuation
End Marks and Commas

Diagnostic Preview

A. Correcting Punctuation Errors in Sentences

Rewrite the following sentences, adding, deleting, or changing periods, question marks, exclamation points, and commas as necessary.

EXAMPLE   1. My best friend has moved to 9782, Revere Avenue, New York NY 10465-2879

          1. My best friend has moved to 9782 Revere Avenue, New York, NY 10465-2879.

1. Marilyn and Antonio who both work at a nearby child-care center greatly enjoy inventing, and playing games with the children.
2. Unfolding the solar panels placing satellites into orbit and conducting medical experiments had kept the space shuttle crew busy
3. Because we had to rekindle the fire twice our cookout was delayed
4. Well if you apply to all eight colleges Paul you will pay a sizable sum in application fees
5. "It is my pleasure to introduce Vernon K Foster Jr. who has recently returned from a visit to Nairobi Kenya," said Adele Peters the president of our school's Student Foreign Exchange League
6. The diplomats both educated at American University in Washington DC. were assigned posts in Athens Greece and Nicosia Cyprus.
7. "The house is on fire" shouted my father. "Everyone get out of here right now".
8. On the far wall to the right of the entrance you will see a striking oil painting done in matte black, ash white, and neutral gray.

9. Studying *Beowulf* for the first time the class particularly enjoyed Grendel the grim gruesome monster

10. The treasurer's report did I believe make it clear that the senior class has been very successful in its fund-raising activities this year.

11. Interrupting his friends Philip asked, "Are you ready to leave".

12. We spent the morning cleaning the basement and sorting boxes and in the afternoon we rode our bikes along lovely country roads.

13. My sister's class decided to hold its first class reunion on July 4 2010 at the Bollingbroke Hotel in San Francisco California

14. Using hyperbole the store claimed in a colorful full-page newspaper ad that it would be having the "World's Most Spectacular Labor Day Sale."

15. When they went to the prom did Martha wear a lavender gown with blue satin ribbons and did George wear a light gray tuxedo

B. Correcting Errors in the Use of End Marks and Commas in a Paragraph

Rewrite the following paragraph, adding, deleting, or changing any end marks and commas to correct the numbered word groups that are incorrectly punctuated.

EXAMPLE   [1] In looking through a United States atlas have you ever been tempted to use it, as a menu to create a meal of places named for foods.

        1. *In looking through a United States atlas, have you ever been tempted to use it as a menu to create a meal of places named for foods?*

[16] For an appetizer, that will take the edge off your family's hunger, without filling them up why not serve a relish tray assembled from Pickleville in Utah, Olive in Montana, and Pepperton in Georgia, along with Rolls from Arizona and Indiana and Butters from North Carolina [17] You might follow that opener with a salad made with Tomato from Mississippi and dressed with Mayo from Maryland, Thousand Island from New York, or French from New Mexico, or Wyoming. [18] Seafood-loving families won't be disappointed for you can find Whitefish in Montana, Salmon in Idaho, Haddock in Georgia and Trout in Louisiana. [19] Families that enjoy red meat can savor selections from Rib Lake in Wisconsin, Lambs Junction in South Carolina, Rabbithash in Kentucky, or indeed Beef Island in the Virgin Islands. [20] If your family prefers poultry on the other hand, consider

MECHANICS

Chicken from Alaska, or Duck or Turkey from North Carolina
[21] You'll want to serve some vegetables too so choose your family's favorites from Corn in Oklahoma, Bean City in Florida, Greens in Kansas and Michigan, and Pea Patch Island in Delaware. [22] For a delicious nourishing side dish look no further than Noodle in Texas, Rice in Minnesota or Virginia, or Wild Rice in North Dakota.
[23] Milk River in Montana, Goodwater in Alabama, and Tea in South Dakota will remind you to include a beverage or two [24] Round out your satisfying meal with Oranges, which you'll find in both California and Vermont, and Almonds from Alabama and Wisconsin [25] When your little brother raves about the meal, but complains about having to do the dishes, simply suggest that he get out the atlas and see how far it is to Soap Lake, Washington.

End Marks

An *end mark*—a period, a question mark, or an exclamation point — is used to indicate the purpose of a sentence. A period is also used at the end of many abbreviations.

Sentences

26a. A statement (or declarative sentence) is followed by a period.

EXAMPLES   Mexico City is the home of the Ballet Folklórico.

My words are like the stars that never change.
Chief Seattle, "Speech of Chief Seattle"

26b. A question (or interrogative sentence) is followed by a question mark.

EXAMPLES   When will Terrell prepare the wild rice?

Have you read Lorraine Hansberry's *To Be Young, Gifted, and Black*?

(1) Do not use a question mark after a declarative sentence containing an indirect question.

INDIRECT   Mariana wants to know when Junko Tabei climbed
QUESTION   Mount Everest.
QUESTION   In what year did Junko Tabei climb Mount Everest?

Reference Note
For information on how sentences are **classified according to purpose,** see page 591.

MECHANICS

(2) In informal writing, a polite request in question form may be followed by either a question mark or a period.

EXAMPLE   Would you please return these books and videotapes to the media center**?**

or

Would you please return these books and videotapes to the media center**.**

In formal writing, an interrogative sentence should always be followed by a question mark.

(3) A question mark should be placed inside the closing quotation marks when the quotation itself is a question. Otherwise, it should be placed outside the closing quotation marks.

EXAMPLES   Cara asked, "Did Scott Joplin compose the opera *Treemonisha***?"** [The quotation is a question.]

Do you agree with the Spanish proverb "Whoever gossips to you will gossip about you**"?** [The entire sentence, not the quotation, is a question.]

26c. An exclamation (or exclamatory sentence) is followed by an exclamation point.

EXAMPLES   What a talented artist Frida Kahlo was**!**

I can't stand that noise**!**

(1) An interjection at the beginning of a sentence is generally followed by a comma or an exclamation point.

EXAMPLES   Ah**,** there you are!

Ah**!** There you are! [Notice that an exclamation point may be used after a single word as well as after a sentence.]

(2) An exclamation point should be placed inside the closing quotation marks when the quotation itself is an exclamation. Otherwise, it should be placed outside the closing quotation marks.

EXAMPLES   "What a good movie that was**!"** exclaimed Natalie as she left the theater. [The quotation is an exclamation.]

How quickly she said, "I'll take it**"!** [The entire sentence, not the quotation, is an exclamation.]

Reference Note

For more about the **placement of end marks with closing quotation marks,** see page 861.

STYLE TIP

In informal writing and dialogue, almost any mark of punctuation can be used after an interjection, depending on the meaning of the sentence.

EXAMPLES
"Hmm**.** You might be right after all, Geraldo," Angelo mused.

"Well**?** What's your answer?" inquired Sarah.

"Hey—I mean, Sir—can you help me?" asked Kris.

"Wow **. . .** that's incredible!" Judi exclaimed.

Reference Note

For information on **dashes** and **ellipsis points,** see pages 878 and 865.

MECHANICS

26d. A request or a command (or imperative sentence) is followed by either a period or an exclamation point.

A request or a mild command is generally followed by a period. A strong command is generally followed by an exclamation point.

EXAMPLES   Please write me a letter. [request]

                  Turn to page 126. [mild command]

                  Hold that line! [strong command]

HI & LOIS reprinted with special permission of King Features Syndicate, Inc.

STYLE   **TIP**

Do not overuse exclamation points. Use an exclamation point only when the expression is obviously emphatic.

When they are used too frequently, exclamation points lose their effect.

OVERUSED
Last Sunday, we went tubing! In some places, the rapids got very rough! By the time we landed, we were all thoroughly soaked!

IMPROVED
Last Sunday, we went tubing. In some places, the rapids got very rough. By the time we landed, we were all thoroughly soaked!

MECHANICS

Exercise 1   Correcting a Passage by Adding End Marks

Many periods and all exclamation points and question marks have been omitted from the following passage. Write each word that should be followed by an end mark, add the appropriate end mark, and as needed, capitalize the first word of the sentence following the end mark. For any quotation requiring an end mark, include the closing quotation marks to show the proper placement of the end mark.

EXAMPLES   **[1]** Dr. Lynn Block, director of research for the Larson Soap Company, looked at her appointment book

        1. book.

        [2] "oh, no" she groaned

        2. "Oh, no!"; groaned.

[1] Today she must conduct interviews to hire a new secretary [2] she thought, "How nerve-racking it is when an applicant is unprepared" [3] nonetheless, she was ready for the 9:00 A.M. interview [4] At 9:35 A.M., the receptionist ushered in the late arrival [5] "Oh, dear," thought Dr. Block as she surveyed the young man's torn jeans, unironed T-shirt, and shaggy hair [6] to questions about his qualifications, the young man answered only yes or no instead of mentioning

specific details, and he did not apologize for his lateness [7] "Well," Dr. Block puzzled, "this person has much experience and good typing skills, but he certainly doesn't seem to want the job"

[8] The next applicant, Ms. Smith, entered wearing a professional tool belt with carpentry tools around her waist [9] she said, "I'm so sorry to disturb you [10] I'm interested in the maintenance position being advertised [11] I must have taken a wrong turn when I got off the elevator"

[12] "I'll say" exclaimed Dr. Block [13] she directed the woman to the maintenance office on the other side of the building and wished her luck [14] To herself, she mused, "Whew at this rate, I may never get a secretary" [15] By then, the next interviewee had arrived—on time [16] Dr. Block wondered, "Now what" [17] Looking up to see a neatly dressed young man, she asked, "Are you sure you're in the right place [18] it's been a highly unusual morning so far"

[19] he replied, "Oh, yes, I'm applying for the secretarial position" [20] he gave brief, helpful explanations and asked appropriate questions about the job. [21] About his career plans, he said, "I would someday like to be an office manager [22] I like office work and believe good management is vital to a smooth operation"

[23] "You're right about that" exclaimed Dr. Block. [24] After the interview ended, Dr. Block pondered her choices [25] she thought, "Well, he doesn't have as much experience or quite as high a typing rate as the first interviewee, but I know whom I'm going to hire"

Abbreviations

26e. Many abbreviations are followed by a period.

An **abbreviation** is a shortened form of a word or phrase. Notice how periods are used with abbreviations in the following examples.

Personal Names

Abbreviate given names only if the person is most commonly known by the abbreviated form of the name.

EXAMPLES   Ida **B.** Wells   **E. M.** Forster   **W.E.B.** DuBois

              F. Scott Fitzgerald   Harry **S.** Truman   **M.F.K.** Fisher

NOTE Leave a space between two such initials, but not between three or more.

MECHANICS

┌ STYLE   TIP ┐

Sometimes (most often in dialogue), a writer will use more than one end mark to express intense emotion or a combination of emotions.

EXAMPLES
More and more loudly, the team's fans cheered, "We're number one**!!**" [intense emotion]

"You had to pay how much**?!**" Steven exclaimed. [combination of curiosity and surprise]

Using such double end punctuation is acceptable in most informal writing. However, in formal writing, you should use only one end mark.

┌HELP┐

If a statement ends with an abbreviation, do not use an additional period as an end mark. However, do use a question mark or an exclamation point if one is needed.

EXAMPLES
The new president is Daniel Franklin, **Jr.**

Is the new president Daniel Franklin, **Jr.?**

STYLE TIP

Only a few abbreviations are appropriate in the text of a formal paper written for a general audience. In tables, notes, and bibliographies, abbreviations are used more freely in order to save space.

STYLE TIP

Roman numerals that follow a proper name do not end with periods. Also, they are not separated from the name by a comma.

EXAMPLES
Davis Love **III**

Pope John Paul **II**

STYLE TIP

A few acronyms, such as *radar, laser,* and *sonar,* are now considered common nouns. They do not need to be spelled out on first use and are no longer capitalized. When you are not sure whether an acronym should be capitalized, check a recent dictionary.

Titles

Abbreviate social titles whether used before the full name or before the last name alone.

| EXAMPLES | **Mr.** John Kelley | **Mrs.** Rachel Draper | **Ms.** Young |
| | **Sr.** (Señor) Reyes | **Sra.** (Señora) Jiménez | **Dr.** Jefferson |

You may abbreviate civil and military titles used before full names or before initials and last names. Spell them out before last names used alone.

EXAMPLES	**Gen.** H. Norman Schwarzkopf	**General** Schwarzkopf
	Sen. Daniel K. Akaka	**Senator** Akaka
	Prof. Samuel Isaacharoff	**Professor** Isaacharoff

Abbreviate titles and academic degrees that follow proper names.

EXAMPLES   Marco Lopez, **Jr.**   Jeremy Stone, **M.D.**

NOTE Do not include the titles *Mr., Mrs., Ms.,* or *Dr.* when you use a title or degree after a name.

EXAMPLE   Dr. Jeremy Stone *or* Jeremy Stone, **M.D.** [not *Dr. Jeremy Stone, M.D.*]

Agencies, Organizations, and Acronyms

After spelling out the first use of the names of agencies and organizations, abbreviate these names.

EXAMPLE   Janelle was researching the International Monetary Fund and learned that the United Nations created the **IMF** to promote international economic cooperation.

An **acronym** is a word formed from the first (or first few) letters of a series of words. Notice that acronyms are written without periods.

ADA American Dental Association	**OAS** Organization of American States
PRI Public Radio International	**HUD** Department of Housing and Urban Development
ERIC Educational Resources Information Center	**CPB** Corporation for Public Broadcasting

Geographical Terms

In regular text, spell out names of states and other political units whether they stand alone or follow other geographical terms. Abbreviate them in tables, notes, and bibliographies.

TEXT   Rudyard Kipling was born in Bombay, India, and was educated in England.

Our tour included stops in Olympia, Washington; Salem, Oregon; and Sacramento, California.

CHART

Mumbai, Ind.	Sacramento, Calif.
London, U.K.	Piedras Negras, Mex.

FOOTNOTE   [3] The Stanford University Libraries in Stanford, Calif., hold a special collection of Irish literature.

BIBLIOGRAPHY   Johansen, Bruce. Forgotten Founders. Boston,
ENTRY   Mass.: The Harvard Common Press, 1982.

NOTE Include the traditional abbreviation for the District of Columbia, *D.C.*, with the city name *Washington* to distinguish it from the state of Washington.

In regular text, spell out every word in an address. Such words may be abbreviated in letter and envelope addresses as well as in tables and notes.

TEXT   Our new house is located at 1492 Columbia Avenue, Fort Myers, Florida.

For more information, write us at Park Drive in Laredo, Texas.

ENVELOPE   1492 Columbia Ave.
Fort Myers, **FL** 33906

TABLE

Park Dr.	Laredo, Tex.
Columbia Ave.	Durham, N.C.

NOTE Two-letter state abbreviations without periods are used only when the ZIP Code is included.

EXAMPLE   Yorba Linda, **CA 92886**

Reference Note
For information on **capitalizing geographical terms,** see page 793.

STYLE TIP

In your reading, you may see the abbreviations *B.C.E.* (Before the Common Era) and *C.E.* (Common Era). These abbreviations should be placed after the year.

EXAMPLES
The city of Rome was founded in 753 **B.C.E.**

Genghis Khan began his conquest of Asia in the late twelfth century **C.E.**

COMPUTER TIP

Publishers usually print time abbreviations as small capitals—uppercase letters that are slightly smaller than standard uppercase letters. Your word processor may offer small capitals as a style option. If it does not, or if you are writing by hand, you may use either uppercase or lowercase letters for time abbreviations, as long as you are consistent.

Time

Abbreviate the two most frequently used era designations, *A.D.* and *B.C.* The abbreviation *A.D.* stands for the Latin phrase *anno Domini*, meaning "in the year of the Lord." It is used with dates in the Christian era. When used with a specific year number, *A.D.* precedes the number. When used with the name of a century, it follows the name.

EXAMPLES
Attila the Hun began his reign in **A.D.** 433.

The first books printed from wood blocks were produced in China in the tenth century **A.D.**

The abbreviation *B.C.*, which stands for "before Christ," is used for dates before the Christian era. It follows either a specific year number or the name of a century.

EXAMPLES
In 55 **B.C.**, Julius Caesar invaded Britain.

The first Olympic games were held in Greece during the eighth century **B.C.**

In regular text, spell out the names of months and days whether they appear alone or in dates. Both types of names may be abbreviated in tables, notes, and bibliographies.

TEXT   The convention will begin Thursday, February 4, in the Civic Center.

NOTE   Thurs**.**, Feb**.** 4

Abbreviate the designations for the two halves of the day measured by clock time. The abbreviation *A.M.* stands for the Latin phrase *ante meridiem*, meaning "before noon." The abbreviation *P.M.* stands for *post meridiem*, meaning "after noon." Both abbreviations follow the numerals designating the specific time.

EXAMPLES
The meeting will pause for lunch at 11:30 **A.M.**

The video must be returned by 10:00 **P.M.** tomorrow.

Units of Measurement

Abbreviations for units of measurement are usually written without periods. However, do use a period with the abbreviation for inch (*in*__.__) to prevent confusing it with the word *in*.

EXAMPLES   mm, kg, ml, tsp, doz, yd, ft, lb

In regular text, spell out the names of units of measurement whether they stand alone or follow a spelled-out number or a numeral. Such names may be abbreviated in tables and notes when they follow a numeral.

TEXT   The speed limit in the mall's parking lot is five **miles per hour** [not *mph*].

She wanted a rug that was at least five **feet** [not *ft*] by seven.

TABLE

2 **tsp** pepper	47° **C**
8 **ft** 2 **in.**	6 **oz** shredded cheese

Exercise 2   **Using Abbreviations**

Rewrite the following sentences, correcting errors in the standard, formal use of abbreviations.

EXAMPLE   1. The next stop for the train is Cincinnati, OH.

         1. *Cincinnati, Ohio.*

1. The bus is leaving at 7:30 A.M. in the morning.
2. Scientists found enough clues to date the artifact B.C. 1124.
3. Shakespeare's first play was produced sometime before 1592 A.D.
4. In 1975, Jim Sparks of Visalia, CA, set a record by sitting in a tree for almost sixty-two days.
5. The race would begin on Franklin St. and finish on Euclid Ave.
6. I'll be there at 7:00 A.M..
7. Dr. Sylvia Irving, DVM, was a guest for career day.
8. Marshall refused to trade his Ken Griffey, Junior, rookie card.
9. Very few of the residents have forgotten the time when Moses Hazard Robinson, III, passed through their town.
10. A. Lincoln was the sixteenth president of the United States.

Commas

Items in a Series

26f. Use commas to separate items in a series.

EXAMPLES   She had been a correspondent for the wire service in London, Paris, Rome, and Madrid. [words in a series]

STYLE   TIP

Do not use *A.M.* or *P.M.* with numbers spelled out as words or as substitutes for the words *morning, afternoon,* or *evening.*

EXAMPLE
The parade began at **9:00 A.M.** (or **nine o'clock in the morning**) Friday [not *nine A.M. Friday*].

Also, do not use the words *morning, afternoon,* or *evening* with numerals followed by *A.M.* or *P.M.*

INCORRECT
The results should be in by 2:30 P.M. in the afternoon.

CORRECT
The results should be in by **2:30 P.M.** (or **two-thirty in the afternoon.**)

MECHANICS

STYLE ✎ TIP

Words customarily used in pairs, such as *bag and baggage, law and order,* and *macaroni and cheese,* are set off as one item in a series.

EXAMPLE

For supper they served a tossed salad, **spaghetti and meatballs,** garlic bread, milk, and fruit.

STYLE ✎ TIP

A comma before the conjunction in a series of three or more items is not incorrect. If you have any doubt about the clarity of the sentence without the comma, add the comma.

Reference Note

For more information about punctuating **nouns of direct address,** see page 838.

Reference Note

For more about **using semicolons to separate independent clauses,** see page 850.

I studied for the test on the way to school, during homeroom, and in study hall. [phrases in a series]

The reporter wanted to know who I was, where I went to school, and how I felt about getting my driver's license. [clauses in a series]

NOTE Do not use a comma before the first item or after the final item in a series.

INCORRECT   The students in auto mechanics class learned, to replace the spark plugs, to check the fluid levels, and to change the oil, in several makes of cars.

CORRECT   The students in auto mechanics class learned to replace the spark plugs, to check the fluid levels, and to change the oil in several makes of cars.

When *and, or,* or *nor* joins the last two items in a series, writers sometimes omit the comma before the conjunction if the comma is not needed to make the meaning of the sentence clear.

CLEAR   Soccer, basketball and lacrosse are my favorite sports. [The meaning of the sentence is clear without a comma before the conjunction *and.*]

UNCLEAR   Joetta, Lucia and Ben are rehearsing a scene from the musical *Grease.* [The meaning of the sentence is unclear: Are three people rehearsing a scene, or is Joetta being addressed?]

CLEAR   Joetta, Lucia, and Ben are rehearsing a scene from the musical *Grease.* [The sentence clearly states that all three people are rehearsing a scene.]

CLEAR   Lucia and Ben are rehearsing a scene from the musical *Grease,* Joetta. [The sentence clearly indicates that Joetta is being addressed. *Joetta* is a noun of direct address.]

If all the items in a series are joined by *and, or,* or *nor,* do not use commas to separate them.

EXAMPLE   Derrick **and** Han **and** Jina will represent the senior class.

Short independent clauses in a series may be separated by commas.

EXAMPLE   I came, I saw, I conquered.

Long independent clauses separated by commas can be difficult to read. To make the break between clauses more distinct, use semicolons instead of commas.

26g. Use a comma to separate two or more adjectives preceding a noun.

EXAMPLES   Katherine Dunham is a creative, talented dancer and choreographer.

Did you see that boring, silly, worthless movie?

Do not use a comma before the final adjective in a series if the adjective is thought of as part of the noun.

EXAMPLES   Lawanda hung colorful, delicate Chinese lanterns around the patio. [*Chinese lanterns* is regarded as a compound noun.]

It was a crisp, clear fall day. [*Fall day* is considered one item.]

NOTE A word that modifies one of the adjectives in a series is an adverb, not another adjective. Do not separate the adverb from the adjective with a comma.

EXAMPLE   Why did he wear a **bright red** cap?

Exercise 3 Correcting Sentences by Adding Commas

For each of the following sentences, write each word that should be followed by a comma, and place a comma after it. If a sentence is already correct, write *C*.

EXAMPLE   1. The firefighters arrived promptly extinguished the blaze and returned to the station.

        1. *promptly, blaze,*

1. She is a bright charming woman.
2. Albert Cunningham prepared a tossed green salad ham and cheese sandwiches and iced tea.
3. Armando sang danced and juggled in the talent show.
4. My parents always ask me where I'm going who will be there and when I'll be home.
5. Should we go to the mall or to the park or to Yoko's house?
6. Study this ancient complex pattern for any thematic repetitions from right to left.
7. That station airs jazz rock-and-roll rhythm and blues, and just about everything else.
8. Wouldn't a light blue-green color look nice on the wall in the new family room?

MECHANICS

TIPS & TRICKS

You can use two tests to determine whether an adjective and a noun form a unit.

TEST 1:
Insert the word *and* between the adjectives. If *and* fits sensibly between the adjectives, use a comma.

EXAMPLE
It was a crisp, clear fall day. [*And* would fit logically between the first two adjectives (*crisp* and *clear*) but not between *clear* and *fall*.]

TEST 2:
Change the order of the adjectives. If the order of the adjectives can be reversed sensibly, use a comma. [*Clear, crisp day* makes sense, but *fall, crisp day* and *fall, clear day* do not.]

9. My little sister said, "I want a book and a puzzle and a doll and a big sand castle and a rocket ship and a puppy and a cell phone for my birthday."
10. There was confetti on the floor in our hair on every stick of furniture and even under the sofa.

Independent Clauses

26h. Use a comma before a coordinating conjunction (*and*, *but*, *for*, *nor*, *or*, *so*, or *yet*) when it joins independent clauses.

EXAMPLES   The sky looks clear, yet rain has been forecast.

I saw a performance of August Wilson's *Fences*, and now I am eager to read his other plays.

NOTE   Always use a comma before *for, so,* or *yet* joining independent clauses. The comma is sometimes omitted before *and, but, or,* or *nor* when the independent clauses are very short and the meaning of the sentence is clear without the comma.

CLEAR   We didn't enjoy the film but you might.

UNCLEAR   I will work with Emma and Josh will help Madison.
CLEAR   I will work with Emma, and Josh will help Madison.

Do not confuse a compound sentence with a simple sentence that contains a compound verb.

COMPOUND SENTENCE   Ashley and I looked everywhere for the sheet music, but we couldn't find it. [two independent clauses]

SIMPLE SENTENCE   Ashley and I looked everywhere for the sheet music but couldn't find it. [one independent clause with a compound verb]

Also, keep in mind that compound subjects and compound objects are not separated by commas unless they are made up of three or more items.

EXAMPLES   When you begin a project and when you finish it are closely related. [two subordinate clauses serving as a compound subject]

Dave planned to watch both the Super Bowl and the Pro Bowl. [two compound nouns serving as a compound object]

STYLE TIP

It is not incorrect to use a comma before a coordinating conjunction separating independent clauses. If you are not sure that the meaning of the sentence would be clear without a comma, use a comma.

Reference Note

For more information about **compound subjects** and **compound verbs,** see page 534. For information about **compound sentences,** see page 588.

MECHANICS

My Three Sons, I Love Lucy, and *The Dick Van Dyke Show* are all considered television classics. [compound subject made up of three items]

Exercise 4 Correcting Sentences by Adding Commas

For each of the following sentences, write the word that should be followed by a comma, and place a comma after it. If a sentence is already correct, write *C*.

EXAMPLE   1. My aunt Rosa used to be a flight attendant but now she owns and manages a travel agency.

      1. *attendant,*

1. Are you busy Friday night or would you like to go to the movies?
2. I'm eating dinner now but will call you back as soon as I finish.
3. Don't forget to take your history book home this weekend for the test is Monday.
4. The recipes in *Spirit of the Harvest: North American Indian Cooking* are adapted for modern cooks yet the ingredients listed are all traditional.
5. Quilting is a practical folk art and it is also a relaxing and enjoyable pastime.
6. We shivered and clutched our jackets close for the wind had picked up, and the sea had grown troubled and crashed against the rocks by the cliff.
7. The Yaqui of Mexico have always maintained their social organization so their traditions have remained largely intact to this day.
8. They did not go to sleep nor did they stop talking till dawn that first night in the college dorm.
9. Back in 1865, Maria Mitchell had the distinction of being a professor of astronomy and of becoming the first U.S. woman in the American Academy of Arts and Sciences.
10. A tiger slept in the shade under dense green leaves yet her cubs were busy investigating several large beetles.

Review A Correcting Errors in the Use of Commas in a Paragraph

Rewrite the paragraph on the following page, adding or deleting commas in order to correct sentences that are incorrectly punctuated. If a sentence is already correct, write *C*.

EXAMPLE   [1] Do you know what the second-largest, Russian city is?

EXAMPLE   [1] Do you know what the second-largest, Russian city is?
1. *Do you know what the second-largest Russian city is?*

[1] In 1697, Czar Peter I of Russia toured western Europe, liked what he saw and determined to remodel his nation along Western lines. [2] Six years later, he decreed that an entirely, new city be built at the eastern end of the Gulf of Finland on land that had recently been controlled by Sweden. [3] Peter hired leading Russian French, and Italian architects to create a city with planned squares, wide avenues, and extensive parks, and gardens. [4] He named the city St. Petersburg, and in 1712 moved the capital there from Moscow. [5] The German name of the capital was kept for two centuries, but in 1914 was

Russianized to *Petrograd* by Czar Nicholas II. [6] Three years later, the city witnessed both the abdication of Nicholas, and the return from exile of the Russian Marxist revolutionary V. I. Lenin. [7] Petrograd served as the first capital of Soviet Russia after the Communist Revolution of 1917 but lost that status to Moscow early the following year. [8] Then, in 1924, the Second Congress of the Soviets of the U.S.S.R. changed the city's name to Leningrad to honor the recently, deceased Lenin. [9] Further name changes seemed unlikely once the Communist system became firmly entrenched. [10] In 1991, however, the Russian people went to the polls, repudiated the name Leningrad and reclaimed their beautiful historic city's original name—St. Petersburg.

Nonessential Elements

26i. Use commas to set off nonessential subordinate clauses and nonessential participial phrases.

A **nonessential** (or **nonrestrictive**) clause or participial phrase contains information that is not necessary to the meaning of the sentence.

Reference Note

For more information about **subordinate clauses**, see page 577. For more about **participial phrases**, see page 559.

MECHANICS

NONESSENTIAL CLAUSES	Carla Harris**, who was offered scholarships to three different colleges,** will go to Vassar in the fall.
	The word *telethon***, which is a combination of the words *television* and *marathon*,** is an example of a portmanteau word.
NONESSENTIAL PHRASES	Antonio**, following his grandmother's recipe,** prepared *arroz con pollo* for his cooking class.
	Frightened by the thunder, both of the kittens jumped into my lap.

Each nonessential clause or phrase in the examples above can be omitted without changing the main idea expressed in the rest of the sentence.

EXAMPLES	Carla Harris will go to Vassar in the fall.
	The word *telethon* is an example of a portmanteau word.
	Antonio prepared *arroz con pollo* for his cooking class.
	Both of the kittens jumped into my lap.

An ***essential*** (or ***restrictive***) subordinate clause or participial phrase is not set off by commas because it contains information that is necessary to the meaning of the sentence.

ESSENTIAL CLAUSES	Carla Harris is the only senior **who was offered scholarships to three different colleges.**
	Mercury is the planet **that is closest to the sun.**
ESSENTIAL PHRASES	Any student **wanting to learn about the new reference database** should sign up in the library by Friday.
	The lines **cited at the beginning and the end of the speech** are from Omar Khayyám's *Rubáiyát*.

Notice below how the omission of the essential clause or phrase affects the main idea of each example above.

EXAMPLES	Carla Harris is the only senior.
	Mercury is the planet.
	Any student should sign up in the library by Friday.
	The lines are from Omar Khayyám's *Rubáiyát*.

TIPS & TRICKS

A subordinate clause or a participial phrase that tells *which one(s) of two or more* is generally essential. Furthermore, a subordinate clause beginning with *that* and modifying a noun or pronoun is generally essential. A subordinate clause or a participial phrase that modifies a proper noun is generally nonessential.

MECHANICS

Some subordinate clauses and participial phrases may be either essential or nonessential. The presence or absence of commas tells the reader how the clause or phrase relates to the main idea of the sentence.

ESSENTIAL   Dave took his problem to the librarian **who is an authority on children's literature.** [The library has more than one librarian, but only one is an authority on children's literature.]

NONESSENTIAL   Dave took his problem to the librarian**,** **who is an authority on children's literature.** [The library has only one librarian.]

ESSENTIAL   The squirrel **with its bushy tail twitching** was nibbling on an acorn. [More than one squirrel was visible, but only one had its tail twitching.]

NONESSENTIAL   The squirrel**,** **with its bushy tail twitching,** was nibbling on an acorn. [Only one squirrel was in view.]

Exercise 5 Identifying Essential and Nonessential Subordinate Clauses and Participial Phrases

In each of the following sentences, identify the italicized clause or phrase as *essential* or *nonessential*. Add commas where they are needed, or write *no comma needed*.

EXAMPLES   1. Do you know the name of the actor *who provides the voice for the title character in the new animated film*?

1. *essential—no comma needed*

2. Sisyphus *who had been a greedy king of Corinth* was doomed to push a heavy stone uphill, only to have it always roll down again.

2. *nonessential—Sisyphus, Corinth,*

1. Employees *who always have a ready smile* make the job seem easier.
2. Toni Morrison has been widely praised for her novel Beloved *which is one of my favorite books.*
3. Tortellini *that is filled with garden vegetables* is one of Eduardo's favorite meals.
4. People *who are overly nervous* may not make good drivers.
5. The Federal Reserve System *serving as the central bank of the United States* monitors money and credit growth.
6. Cities *that seem alike* may require a closer look.
7. Lake Chad *covering an area of about six thousand square miles* is West Africa's largest body of water.

MECHANICS

8. Human adults *whose development has been studied and recorded over time* continue to mature, usually in predictable stages, after the age of eighteen.

9. That law *which may have met a real need one hundred years ago* should be repealed or rewritten to deal with today's situation.

10. The Suez Canal *extending more than a hundred miles* links the Mediterranean Sea and the Red Sea.

Review B **Correcting Errors in the Use of Commas in a Paragraph**

Rewrite the following paragraph, adding or deleting commas to correct sentences that are incorrectly punctuated. If a sentence is already correct, write *C*.

EXAMPLE   [1] Rona asked me when the Old, Spanish Days fiesta is.

            1. *Rona asked me when the Old Spanish Days fiesta is.*

[1] Each August, visitors are welcomed to the Old Spanish Days fiesta which is sponsored by the city of Santa Barbara in California. [2] The festival, lasting five days, attracts nearly half a million people. [3] It honors the Spaniards, who colonized the area, beginning in the early 1700s. [4] The festivities start on Wednesday with blessings and singing and dancing at *La Fiesta Pequeña* which is Spanish for "Little Festival," outside Mission Santa Barbara on East Los Olivos and Laguna streets. [5] This mission founded in 1786 is one of the best preserved of the twenty-one missions, that the Spanish established in California between 1769 and 1823. [6] Costumed dancers and colorful floats enliven Thursday's *Desfile Histórico* ("Historic Parade"), which recounts how the Spanish conquistador Sebastian Vizcaino sailed into the nearby bay in 1602 why he named the bay Santa Barbara and what drew settlers to the area. [7] A free, variety show that begins later in the day and continues nightly features Spanish flamenco dancers and Mexican folkloric dancers like those, pictured here. [8] On the weekend, artists and craftworkers set up booths along Cabrillo Boulevard and State

Street, and sell handmade items. [9] Fiesta-goers needn't go hungry for authentic Latin foods such as tortas tacos enchiladas flautas and tamales are sold in the two open-air markets. [10] What an eventful fun-filled five days Old Spanish Days provides!

Introductory Elements

26j. Use a comma after certain introductory elements.

(1) Use a comma after *yes, no,* or any mild exclamation such as *well* or *why* at the beginning of a sentence.

EXAMPLES   **Yes,** you are welcome to join us.

Well, what do you think?

Why, the whole story sounds suspicious!

(2) Use a comma after an introductory participle or participial phrase.

EXAMPLES   **Beaten,** I shook hands with my opponent and walked off the court.

Proofreading my report, I saw that I had written *gorilla,* instead of *guerrilla,* before the word *warfare.*

Almost hidden by the dense brush, the tiny rabbit sat absolutely still.

NOTE   Do not confuse a gerund phrase used as the subject of a sentence with an introductory participial phrase.

GERUND PHRASE   **Planting the Japanese quinces along the fence** took several hours.

PARTICIPIAL PHRASE   **Planting the Japanese quinces along the fence,** I stepped on a mound of fire ants.

(3) Use a comma after two or more introductory prepositional phrases or after one long introductory prepositional phrase.

EXAMPLES   **In the park near my house,** a music festival will take place this weekend.

Near the beginning of the trail, the scout leader found an overturned canoe.

On the day when the last autumn leaf finally fell, I packed my bags.

⎡TIPS⎤ & ⎡TRICKS⎤

Be sure that an introductory participial phrase modifies the subject of the sentence; otherwise, the phrase is probably misplaced or dangling.

MISPLACED
Burrowing under the fence, Mr. O'Brien startled an armadillo opening the gate to his backyard.

REVISED
Opening the gate to his backyard, Mr. O'Brien startled an armadillo burrowing under the fence.

Reference Note
For more information about **correcting misplaced or dangling modifiers,** see page 744.

Reference Note
For more information about **gerund phrases** and **participial phrases,** see pages 563 and 559.

NOTE A single short introductory prepositional phrase does not require a comma unless the phrase is parenthetical or unless the sentence is confusing or awkward without the comma.

EXAMPLES **During spring break** we're going camping in the mountains. [clear without comma]

By the way, you're late. [The comma is needed because the phrase is parenthetical.]

From Laura, Lee had borrowed a sleeping bag and a flashlight. [The comma is needed to avoid reading "Laura Lee."]

Reference Note

For more information about **parenthetical expressions,** see page 839.

(4) Use a comma after an introductory adverb clause.

An introductory adverb clause may appear at the beginning of a sentence or before any independent clause in the sentence.

EXAMPLES **While the orchestra tuned their instruments,** the stagehands checked the curtain.

My friends came over, and **as soon as we finished eating,** we cleared the table for a game of mah-jongg.

Reference Note

For more about **adverb clauses,** see page 584.

Exercise 6 **Correcting Sentences by Adding Commas**

For each of the following sentences, write the word that should be followed by a comma, and place a comma after it.

EXAMPLE 1. On your trip to Washington, D.C., last summer did you visit either the Library of Congress or the Folger Shakespeare Library?

1. *summer,*

1. When they had finished playing the musicians moved their instruments offstage to make room for the dancers.
2. By the end of the second day of school nearly all of the students seemed to have found their assigned classrooms, teachers, and lockers.
3. Oh I meant to ask Gloria whether she had watched the Chinese New Year parade.
4. In the second half of the third quarter Johnson caught a twenty-yard pass and raced into the end zone.
5. After a lengthy discussion of the options the committee voted to reject both of the themes proposed for the prom and to seek fresh ideas.

6. Following the example of ancestors who had served in the Revolutionary War Susie King served in the Civil War as a nurse.
7. Just as I came into the house the phone rang.
8. Yes we will be happy to refund your money.
9. To Linda Ramón sent a video of his family in Puerto Rico.
10. Having taken the prerequisite course Jason registered for the advanced section.

Interrupters

26k. Use commas to set off an expression that interrupts a sentence.

(1) Use commas to set off nonessential appositives and appositive phrases.

An *appositive* is a noun or a pronoun placed beside another noun or pronoun to identify or describe it. An *appositive phrase* consists of an appositive and its modifiers.

A *nonessential* (or *nonrestrictive*) appositive or appositive phrase provides information that is unnecessary to the meaning of the sentence. In other words, the basic meaning of the sentence is the same, with or without the appositive or appositive phrase.

EXAMPLES   An interview with Florence Cohen, **the well-known landscape architect,** will appear in the *Herald*.

Sipa, **a game similar to volleyball,** is a popular sport in the Philippines.

An *essential* (or *restrictive*) appositive adds information that makes the noun or pronoun it identifies or describes more specific. In other words, without the appositive, the sentence loses necessary information or changes meaning. Therefore, an essential appositive should not be set off by commas.

EXAMPLES   We are studying the works by the landscape artist **Fernando Amorsolo.**

James Baldwin wrote the novel ***Go Tell It on the Mountain.***

(2) Words used in direct address are set off by commas.

A *noun of direct address* is a word that names the person or persons being spoken to.

┌ TIPS ┐ & ┌ TRICKS ┐

Generally, an appositive or appositive phrase that identifies or describes a proper noun is nonessential; an appositive or appositive phrase that tells *which one(s) of two or more* is essential.

NONESSENTIAL
An interview with Florence Cohen, **the well-known landscape architect,** will appear in the *Herald*.

ESSENTIAL
An interview with the well-known landscape architect **Florence Cohen** will appear in the *Herald*.

Reference Note
For more information about **appositives** and **appositive phrases,** see page 567.

MECHANICS

EXAMPLES   Will you explain to the class, **Lena,** how you solved the
last problem?

Dexter, please help your brother set the table.

You seem upset, **my friend.**

(3) Parenthetical expressions are set off by commas.

A *parenthetical expression* is a side remark that adds information or
shows a relationship between ideas.

Commonly Used Parenthetical Expressions		
after all	I believe	naturally
at any rate	incidentally	nevertheless
by the way	in fact	of course
consequently	in general	on the contrary
for example	in the first place	on the other hand
for instance	meanwhile	that is
however	moreover	therefore

EXAMPLES   The train heading toward Edinburgh will, **I am sure,**
be on time today.

On the contrary, exercise is relaxing.

Jameson was the first of the senior students to solve the
puzzle, **naturally.**

Some of these expressions are not always parenthetical. When an
expression is not used parenthetically, it is not set off by commas.

EXAMPLES   My grandfather, **by the way,** created these colorful sand
paintings. [parenthetical, meaning "incidentally"]

We could see **by the way** Melinda worked that she wanted
to do her best. [not parenthetical, meaning "by the manner
in which"]

NOTE   A contrasting expression introduced by *not* is parenthetical and
should be set off by commas.

EXAMPLE   Frank Robinson, **not Jackie Robinson,** was the first African
American to manage a major-league baseball team.

MECHANICS

Reference Note

Some parenthetical
expressions, such as
*consequently, however,
moreover,* and *therefore,*
are **conjunctive
adverbs.** See page 850.

Reference Note

Parentheses and **dashes**
are sometimes used to set
off parenthetical expres-
sions. See page 878.

Exercise 7 Correcting Sentences by Adding Commas

For the following sentences, write each word that should be followed by a comma, and place a comma after it. If a sentence is already correct, write *C*.

EXAMPLE 1. My take-home pay at any rate is less than yours.
  1. *pay, rate,*

1. The Red Sea not the Black Sea separates Northeast Africa and the Arabian Peninsula.
2. My father's youngest sister Pilar is an architect in New Orleans.
3. The future of course is largely in your hands.
4. Certainly well-nourished babies have a better chance of surviving infancy Thomas.
5. Call Felipe as soon as you can Hope.
6. A rose window by the way resembles an open rose.
7. The Chiricahua Apache leader Geronimo took part in President Theodore Roosevelt's inaugural procession in 1901.
8. In college however students usually arrange their own schedules.
9. Alex Haley the author of *Roots* attributed his interest in writing to stories his grandmother and great-aunts told.
10. I believe the fairy tale "Cinderella" originated in ninth-century China.

Review C Correcting Sentences by Adding Commas

For each of the following sentences, write each word that should be followed by a comma, and place a comma after it. If a sentence is already correct, write *C*.

EXAMPLE 1. The students read William Shakespeare's *Hamlet* watched the most recent film adaptation of the play and discussed the similarities and differences between the two.
  1. *Hamlet, play,*

1. If you give us your application now our office will process it before the deadline which is this afternoon.
2. The plot of that book a murder mystery is far too complicated in my opinion.
3. Ancient Mayan ruins tropical rain forests and beautiful mountains are just a few of the beautiful sights I saw in Guatemala where my cousins live.

4. Please understand friends that as much as I would like to I cannot be at the picnic the game and the track meet all at the same time.

5. The people riding in the front seat of the roller coaster were the ones who screamed the loudest.

6. Hiroshi whom you met last night is an exchange student from Kyoto a large city in Japan.

7. Looking for economical transportation Harry who had never bought a car before nervously investigated all of the possibilities at Country Motors.

8. Before you start putting that jigsaw puzzle together Rosa make sure that all of it will fit on the table.

9. When Jamie had finished the chicken and salad were all gone; the beans carrots and potatoes however had been left untouched.

10. In my opinion *My Fair Lady* not *Breakfast at Tiffany's* is Audrey Hepburn's best movie.

| COMPUTER TIP

If you use a computer, you may want to create a file of the parenthetical expressions listed on page 839. Refer to this file as you proofread your writing, and be sure that you have punctuated these expressions correctly. Use the search function to speed up your proofreading. The computer will search for and highlight each occurrence of whatever expression you select.

Conventional Uses

26I. Use commas in certain conventional situations.

(1) Use commas to separate items in dates and addresses.

EXAMPLES   Hawaii achieved statehood on August 21, 1959, and became the fiftieth state. [Notice that a comma separates the final item in a date (*1959*) from the words that follow it.]

Write to me at 423 Twentieth Street, Salt Lake City, UT 84101-0423, after the first of May. [Notice that a comma separates the final item in an address (*84101-0423*) from the words that follow it.]

Do not use a comma to separate

• the month from the date

EXAMPLE   We began rehearsals on **June 20.**

• the date from the month when the date is given before the month

EXAMPLE   After many years of foreign rule, the Philippines became an independent nation on **4 July 1946.**

• the month from the year when no date is given

EXAMPLE   Did a severe storm hit Luzon in **October 1999**?

MECHANICS

- a house number from a street name

EXAMPLE   Their address is **531 Belmont Avenue,** St. Louis, MO
53308-3150.

- a state code from a ZIP Code

EXAMPLE   Is 1208 Elmhurst Drive, Seattle, **WA 43211-8614,** the correct
address?

- items joined by prepositions

EXAMPLE   Joanna lives **at 301 Green Street in San Diego.**

Reference Note

Use a **colon** after the
salutation of a business
letter. For more about
colons, see page 853. For
more about the differ-
ences between **personal
letters** and **business letters,** see "Writing" in the
Quick Reference
Handbook.

**(2) Use a comma after the salutation of a personal letter and after
the closing of any letter.**

EXAMPLES   Dear Angela,   Sincerely yours,

**(3) Use a comma to set off a title, such as *Jr., Sr.,* or *Ph.D.,* that
follows a person's name.**

EXAMPLES   Peter Grundel, Jr.   Lorraine Henson, Ph.D.

NOTE   Within a sentence, a comma appears both before and after a
title following a person's name.

EXAMPLE   Hazel Sellers, M.D., will be the guest speaker.

Unnecessary Commas

26m. Do not use unnecessary commas.

Too many commas can be as confusing as too few. Use a comma only
when a rule requires one or when the meaning of the sentence would
be unclear without one.

CONFUSING   Amy, and I put a videocassette, and a fashion catalog in the
time capsule.

CLEAR   Amy and I put a videocassette and a fashion catalog in the
time capsule.

Exercise 8 Using Commas Correctly

Write the following sentences and word groups, adding and deleting
commas where needed.

EXAMPLE   1. On our road trip from Durham North Carolina to Salt
              Lake City Utah we traveled through twelve states.

          1. On our road trip from Durham, North Carolina, to Salt
              Lake City, Utah, we traveled through twelve states.

1. Mr. Boyd still talks about the "blue moon" of March, 1998.
2. Sammy Davis, Jr. was one of the stars in that musical.
3. Our new apartment at 310 Columbia Avenue Fort Wayne Indiana
   is comfortable; however, I wish we were still living at 2125 West
   Third Street in Omaha Nebraska.
4. Did you and Maureen know that Jay Carson Sr. arranged the benefit concert and helped with the financing?
5. In the summer of 1936, the library staff at the *Tribune* began
   recording copies of every issue from October 14 1858 up to the
   most recent one.
6. Dear Aunt Judy
7. That restaurant can be found at 2904 Barton Avenue, in Austin.
8. Yours truly
9. My mother's diploma is dated 29 May, 1980.
10. Are you certain you addressed it to 4900 Elm Street, Kansas City
    MO 64112-1278?

Review D Correcting Errors in the Use of Commas in a Paragraph

Rewrite the following paragraph, adding, deleting, or changing any
commas to correct each sentence that is incorrectly punctuated. If a
sentence is already correct, write *C*.

EXAMPLE   [1] The Japan America Theatre is the performing arts stage
              of the Japanese American Cultural and Community
              Center in Los Angeles California.

          1. The Japan America Theatre is the performing arts stage
              of the Japanese American Cultural and Community
              Center in Los Angeles, California.

[1] Since it opened in 1984 the theater has won worldwide acclaim
for the quality and scope of its productions. [2] Those productions range
from all-male casts (such as the one shown on the next page) performing works in the sixteenth-century Grand Kabuki tradition to U.S. pre-
mieres of contemporary works by leading Japanese choreographers.
[3] The theater doesn't just book productions; it works closely with the
artists, whom it presents. [4] In fact according to the managing director
for programs between 60 and 70 percent of the theater's presentations

MECHANICS

are developed in partnership with the artists. [5] In 1988, for example the theater staged the first, Broadway-style Japanese musical, *Utamoro: The Musical* which is Tako Izumi's story of the eighteenth-century woodcut artist Utamoro. [6] In order to make the work more accessible to American audiences, the Los Angeles production pared down the slang from the Tokyo version, emphasized movement and gesture more, and provided narration, and supertitles in English. [7] It also used more elaborate costumes, wigs, and masks, to convey the splendor of the Edo period. [8] Recognizing that outstanding art transcends national boundaries the theater features performing artists of all nationalities. [9] In recent years, for example, both New York City's Theater of the Open Eye and the Los Angeles Chamber Ballet have performed there. [10] In addition a few years ago the Indian sitar player Ravi Shankar working with American musicians created a composition incorporating classical Japanese instruments into an Indian musical form.

Chapter Review

A. Using Periods, Question Marks, and Exclamation Points

Rewrite the following sentences, adding, deleting, or changing punctuation as necessary.

1. The Andromeda Galaxy is the galaxy closest to the Milky Way
2. Paolo wants to know what you are bringing to the party?
3. Yes That was a spectacular touchdown
4. Mr Simon Clark, Jr, would like to speak to you.
5. "Have you ever seen *The Wizard of Oz*" asked Tasha? "What a wonderful movie it is"!
6. Didn't Dr Sanchez used to work for NATO.
7. The women's rights activist Anna Howard Shaw grew up near Big Rapids, Michigan
8. Look out for that car
9. Who first said "A penny saved is a penny earned?"
10. We will meet you in front of the school at 8:00 AM. tomorrow

B. Correcting Sentences by Adding or Deleting Commas

Most of the following sentences contain errors in the use of commas. Write the word preceding each error, and add or delete punctuation to correct the error. If a sentence is already correct, write *C*.

11. We asked our class advisor who had several suggestions.
12. Randy please lend me some paper tape and paint.
13. It was a raw, blustery, night when Kahlil met me in Edgewater.
14. After she listened to the players' strategy the coach nodded.
15. Yes our second composition assignment is due tomorrow.
16. My theory, unfortunately, was disproved by new research.
17. Salim who was born on Friday September, 13 1985 has never been superstitious about the number thirteen.
18. That our candidate was fighting a losing battle for political office, was evident to most of the campaign staff.

19. I had worked with her at the resort for three summers, and I admired her determination to put herself through college.

20. John Buse the president of our class asked me to sell tickets for the benefit concert.

C. Correcting Errors in the Use of Periods, Question Marks, Exclamation Points, and Commas in Sentences

Add, delete, or change punctuation to correct any of the following sentences that contain punctuation errors. If a sentence is already correct, write *C*.

21. Mr Stanton will you please give me a reference.

22. Ouch Watch where you're going

23. Hoping to meet Oprah Winfrey we got tickets to a taping of her show.

24. My niece P J will celebrate her twenty-first birthday tomorrow

25. Mom or Dad or Uncle Paul will cook dinner tonight.

D. Correcting Errors in the Use of Commas in Paragraphs

Add or delete commas in the following paragraphs to correct sentences that are incorrectly punctuated. If a sentence is already correct, write *C*.

[26] Sports medicine is a branch of medicine concerned with preventing and treating injuries, suffered during participation in sports. [27] Initially practiced by doctors working with professional sports teams, the practice of sports medicine has grown rapidly as interest in amateur sports and physical-fitness programs has increased. [28] One ailment that doctors, who specialize in sports medicine, frequently encounter is tendinitis the inflammation of a tendon. [29] Tendons are the tough fibrous inelastic tissues that connect muscles to bones or other body parts. [30] Tennis elbow is a form of tendinitis caused by straining the tendons, that attach the muscles of the lower arm at the elbow.

[31] You don't have to be active in sports to benefit from advances in sports medicine for those advances are now being applied in the workplace. [32] Repetitive strain injury (RSI) a disorder caused by tendinitis can afflict anyone, whose job requires performing the same motion hundreds or even thousands of times a day. [33] In fact RSI strikes workers as varied as meat packers, word processors fruit pickers supermarket checkout clerks and musicians. [34] Because permanent

disability can set in if RSI is left untreated physicians are teaming up with ergonomists scientists who adapt working conditions or the work itself to prevent injuries. **[35]** Employers, are finding that preventive measures are a sound investment not a waste of money, paying for themselves many times over in increased productivity reduced turnover and lower medical costs.

Writing Application
Using Commas in Instructions

Commas for Clarity   You and some friends are planning to study together for an important final exam. To make the study sessions more interesting, you have decided to create a game using the information to be covered on the exam. As you write the instructions for playing the game, include at least five adverb clauses. Be sure to use commas correctly.

Prewriting   First, write down several ideas for a game based on one of your school subjects. Then, decide which idea you want to develop. What are the rules of the game? Take notes for your instructions. Arrange the information in an easy-to-follow order.

Writing   Begin by giving a brief, general description of the game. Then, give complete step-by-step instructions for playing the game. Be sure to explain the game clearly so that a reader can easily learn to play it from your instructions.

Revising   To help you evaluate your instructions, ask a friend to read them. Can your friend follow the instructions easily? As you revise, try to combine sentences to make the instructions more concise. Be sure you have used at least five adverb clauses.

Publishing   Read your instructions for errors in grammar, usage, punctuation, and spelling. Pay special attention to your use of commas with introductory elements, interrupters, and items in a series. You may want to publish your game by distributing the instructions to your classmates so they can use the game as a study tool.

MECHANICS

Reference Note
For more information about **sentence combining,** see Chapter 11. For more information about **adverb clauses,** see page 584.

Punctuation
Other Marks of Punctuation

Diagnostic Preview

A. Proofreading Sentences for Correct Punctuation

Each of the following sentences contains at least one error in the use of semicolons, colons, dashes, parentheses, ellipsis points, brackets, italics (underlining), quotation marks, apostrophes, or hyphens. Rewrite each sentence, punctuating it correctly.

EXAMPLE
1. Why did you wait until the last minute? asked my friend Tanya when I told her my problem.

1. *"Why did you wait until the last minute?" asked my friend Tanya when I told her my problem.*

1. When I read The Hobbit, my favorite chapter was the one in which Bilbo meets Gollum.
2. Among the members of the Fine Arts Commission who met in New York City were some very talented people Diane Keaton, actress Paul McCartney, musician Paul Taylor, choreographer and Lee Krasner, artist.
3. My brothers and sisters and I have been encouraged to be self reliant since we were children.
4. The rapid spread of the bacterial infection see the time line and the map below posed a grave puzzle to the medical experts.
5. We're going to win this championship! said the soccer coach to the newspaper sportswriter.
6. Paulette sent in her application before the deadline however, she neglected to put a stamp on the envelope.
7. Finally, his mother said "Well . . . . . . I guess it will be okay."

8. "The packages sitting over there are your's," said Tamala.

9. Although the contract had not been renewed, the oil company made a delivery the customers complained when they received the bill.

10. The mayor elect met for two hours yesterday afternoon with members of the Allentown Youth Council see the picture on page 17.

11. At Book Lore the bookstore where I work we sold twenty seven copies of that book in one day.

12. Ill never forget the first time I read Walt Whitmans poem Song of Myself said Megan it made me think about self-acceptance in a new way.

13. Within the next three week's, new television stations will begin broadcasting from the following cities Kalamazoo, Michigan, Salinas, California and Fairbanks, Alaska.

14. Helena knew the day would be less than perfect when she heard herself saying Don't forget to dot your ts and cross your is.

15. In 1813, Governor Claiborne offered a reward for the capture of Jean Laffitte (Laffitte 1780?–1826 was a pirate who in 1814 fought for the U.S. at the battle of New Orleans).

B. Proofreading a Paragraph for Correct Punctuation

Rewrite the following paragraph, punctuating each sentence correctly.

EXAMPLE   [1] A list of composers of extraordinary talent and I am sure most of you will agree would include Mozart, Bach, Beethoven, and Chopin.

1. *A list of composers of extraordinary talent—and I am sure most of you will agree—would include Mozart, Bach, Beethoven, and Chopin.*

[16] When you hear the word *composer,* you probably think of the world renowned musical masters of long ago Mozart, Bach, Beethoven, and Chopin, among others. [17] However, you dont really have to think that far back the twentieth century also has produced some outstanding talents. [18] Youll probably recognize at least one of these modern composers George Gershwin, Benjamin Britten, Leonard Bernstein, Richard Rodgers, or Paul McCartney. [19] Yes, McCartney and other rock musicians have produced many memorable compositions for example, McCartney and his long time composing partner John Lennon gave us such popular ballads as Yesterday and Michelle. [20] Richard Rodgers worked with the lyricist Oscar Hammerstein II on many projects including the following musical plays Oklahoma, South Pacific, The King and I, and The Sound of Music. [21] Leonard

Bernstein, too, was involved in many musical productions, but perhaps his most famous is West Side Story. [22] Both Bernstein and Rodgers are known primarily for their Broadway musicals however, much of their music is popular outside the theater. [23] Benjamin Britten, on the other hand, is often ranked as Englands greatest technical composer his difficult operas, such as Death in Venice, are performed only by highly skilled musicians and vocalists. [24] George Gershwin 1898–1937 was one of Americas finest and best loved composers. [25] He wrote the opera Porgy and Bess, which contains the all time classic song Summertime.

Semicolons

Reference Note

For information on **clauses,** see page 574.

27a. Use a semicolon between independent clauses that are closely related in thought and are not joined by a coordinating conjunction *(and, but, for, nor, or, so, or yet)*.

EXAMPLES   "No man is an island entire of itself**;** every man is a piece of the continent, a part of the main."

John Donne, "Meditation 17"

Three candidates have filed for the new commission seat**;** all of them have experience in public office.

Do not use a semicolon to join independent clauses unless there is a close relationship between the main ideas of the clauses.

INCORRECT   Madagascar is a small nation made up of several islands; for many years, scientists have studied this country because of its unusual wildlife.

CORRECT   Madagascar is a small nation made up of several islands**.** For many years, scientists have studied this country because of its unusual wildlife.

Reference Note

For more information on **conjunctive adverbs** and **transitional expressions,** see page 589.

27b. Use a semicolon between independent clauses joined by a conjunctive adverb or a transitional expression.

A *conjunctive adverb* or a *transitional expression* indicates the relationship between the independent clauses that it joins.

EXAMPLES   The speech was long and repetitious**; consequently,** people in the audience began fidgeting in their seats and whispering among themselves.

"To excel the past we must not allow ourselves to lose contact with it**;** **on the contrary,** we must feel it under our feet because we raised ourselves upon it."

José Ortega y Gasset, "In Search of Goethe
from Within, Letter to a German"

Commonly Used Conjunctive Adverbs		
accordingly	however	moreover
besides	indeed	nevertheless
consequently	instead	otherwise
furthermore	meanwhile	therefore

Commonly Used Transitional Expressions		
as a result	for instance	on the contrary
for example	in fact	that is

When a conjunctive adverb or a transitional expression is used between independent clauses, it is preceded by a semicolon and followed by a comma.

EXAMPLES   The leaders of the two nations saw no hope for a settlement**;** **however,** they were willing to meet again.

The leaders of the two nations saw no hope for a settlement**;** **on the other hand,** they were willing to meet again.

When used within a clause, a conjunctive adverb or a transitional expression is set off by commas.

EXAMPLES   The leaders of the two nations saw no hope for a settlement**;** they were willing**,** **however,** to meet again.

The leaders of the two nations saw no hope for a settlement**;** they were**,** **on the other hand,** willing to meet again.

27c. You may need to use a semicolon (rather than a comma) before a coordinating conjunction to join independent clauses that contain commas.

EXAMPLE   Stephen Foster wrote many songs**,** including "Oh! Susanna," "Camptown Races**,**" and "Beautiful Dreamer"**;** **but,** as I recall**,** he is best remembered for "My Old Kentucky Home."

When the independent clauses contain only one or two commas, the semicolon may not be needed. However, a semicolon is required when a sentence would be confusing without a semicolon.

MECHANICS

27d. Use a semicolon between items in a series if the items contain commas.

EXAMPLES   Winners in the competition were Alina Murphy, first place; Jeff Bates, second place; and Eduardo Davis, third place.

On our trip to South America, we visited Santiago, Chile; Bogotá, Colombia; and Lima, Peru.

Exercise 1   Correcting Sentences by Adding Semicolons

Rewrite the following sentences, using semicolons where they are needed.

EXAMPLE   1. An allegory is a story in which the characters, settings, and events stand for abstract or moral concepts one of the best-known allegories is *The Pilgrim's Progress* by John Bunyan.

1. *An allegory is a story in which the characters, settings, and events stand for abstract or moral concepts; one of the best-known allegories is* The Pilgrim's Progress *by John Bunyan.*

1. Performers in the show were Tony Fleming, trumpet and trombone Donna Lee Bryant, clarinet and saxophone and Phyllis Ward, drums and steel guitar.
2. The first Alaskans most likely traveled to North America from Asia around twenty thousand years ago they may have been following caribou herds.
3. The new republic at once began increasing production and distribution of goods furthermore, it also appealed to other nations for financial assistance.
4. I bought my father several gifts, including a book, a shirt, and a battery charger, but, to my dismay, I couldn't find a present for my sister.
5. Our dates of birth are as follows: September 27, 1969, September 2, 1957, October 27, 1967, and March 27, 1960.
6. Some scientists believe that once, long ago, all the earth's land was joined into one continent that continent is known as Pangaea.
7. Savannas, which are valuable grasslands, may be found in tropical or subtropical climates and, I believe, they are known variously as prairies, veldts, pampas, and chaparrals.
8. The expression "gung-ho," which is used to describe an exceptionally hard worker, was originally Chinese U.S. troops made it their motto during World War II.

9. She bought a shirt, $19.98, jeans, $34.79, and socks, $3.98.

10. Louise has already been working on that spreadsheet for hours however, we need to change the format.

Colons

27e. Use a colon to mean "note what follows."

(1) Use a colon before a list of items, especially after expressions like *as follows* and *the following*.

EXAMPLES   The volumes in Edward Brathwaite's autobiographical trilogy are as follows**:** *Rights of Passage, Masks,* and *Islands.*

Central America comprises seven countries**:** Belize, Costa Rica, El Salvador, Guatemala, Honduras, Nicaragua, and Panama.

NOTE Do not use a colon before a list that serves as a complement or an object of a preposition.

INCORRECT   We collected: blankets, canned goods, and clothing.

CORRECT   We collected blankets, canned goods, and clothing. [The list is the direct object of the verb *collected*.]

INCORRECT   The concert included performances by: Placido Domingo, Luciano Pavarotti, and José Carreras.

CORRECT   The concert included performances by Placido Domingo, Luciano Pavarotti, and José Carreras. [The list is the object of the preposition *by*.]

(2) Use a colon before a long, formal statement or quotation.

EXAMPLE   The Gettysburg Address, delivered by President Lincoln during the American Civil War, begins with these words**:** "Four score and seven years ago our fathers brought forth on this continent a new nation, conceived in liberty, and dedicated to the proposition that all men are created equal."

Reference Note

For more information on **using long quotations,** see page 862.

(3) Use a colon between independent clauses when the second clause explains or restates the idea of the first.

EXAMPLES   Those hanging lamps are the most popular kind**:** They are inexpensive, available in many colors, and easy to install.

"A cutting word is worse than a bowstring**:** A cut may heal, but the cut of the tongue does not."

African proverb

MECHANICS

The first word of a sentence following a colon is capitalized.

EXAMPLES   Luisa felt a great sense of accomplishment**:** **S**he had successfully developed and printed her first roll of film.

It was a poor lunch**:** **T**he paper sack held a soggy sandwich, a
bruised banana, and a few pieces of limp celery.

27f. Use a colon in certain conventional situations.

(1) Use a colon between the hour and the minute.

EXAMPLES   8**:**00 A.M.   9**:**30 in the evening

**(2) Use a colon between a chapter and verse in referring to
passages from the Bible.**

EXAMPLES   Proverbs 3**:**3   Ecclesiastes 3**:**1–8

(3) Use a colon between a title and subtitle.

EXAMPLES   "Ghosts and Voices**:** Writing from Obsession" [article]

*Middlemarch***:** *A Study of Provincial Life* [novel]

*Billie Holiday***:** *The Golden Years* [recording]

(4) Use a colon after the salutation of a business letter.

EXAMPLES   Dear Ms. Ayala**:**   To Whom It May Concern**:**

Dear Sir or Madam**:**   Dear Editor**:**

Use a comma after the salutation of a personal letter.

EXAMPLE   Dear Grandma and Grandpa**,**

Reference Note

For information on
writing business letters
and **personal letters,** see
"Writing" in the Quick
Reference Handbook.

Exercise 2   Using Colons Correctly

Rewrite the following items, adding colons where they are needed.

EXAMPLE   1.   Your assignment is to read the following poems "Ode on
a Grecian Urn," "Ode to a Nightingale," and "Ode to the
West Wind."

       1.   *Your assignment is to read the following poems:* "Ode
on a Grecian Urn," "Ode to a Nightingale," *and* "Ode to
the West Wind."

   1. For a more thorough discussion of the woman who was pharaoh
of Egypt, read *Hatchepsut The Female Pharaoh.*

2. Two of my favorite stories from the Bible are the story of the battle between David and Goliath in I Samuel 17 4–58 and the story of the good Samaritan in Luke 10 25–37.

3. Groups of art students, all going to see Egyptian, Assyrian, and Greek exhibits, boarded the buses at 8 30 A.M. and arrived at the museum at 10 00 A.M.

4. She revised her report three times She looked first at the content, then considered organization, and then read the report for style.

5. Our local paper is divided into the following five sections news, features, business, sports, and classified advertising.

6. Not surprisingly, my mom, who was a big fan of *Star Trek* during the '60s, regularly watched *Star Trek The Next Generation* in the '90s.

7. The chairperson rose and read the mission statement "We dedicate ourselves to the education of young people and commit ourselves to providing them with every opportunity to prepare for tomorrow's world."

8. So far, I've lived in three places Phoenix, Arizona; Williamsburg, Pennsylvania; and Sarasota, Florida.

9. Your reading assignment is as follows pages 217–232, pages 275–302, and pages 335–410.

10. Dear Sir or Madam

Review A — Correcting Paragraphs by Adding Semicolons and Colons

Rewrite the following paragraphs, adding semicolons and colons where they are needed.

EXAMPLE [1] Arthur Mitchell was more than a talented ballet dancer He was a pioneer in the world of ballet.

1. Arthur Mitchell was more than a talented ballet dancer: He was a pioneer in the world of ballet.

[1] Arthur Mitchell blazed new trails in the world of ballet He became the first African American male dancer to become a permanent member of a major ballet company, the New York City Ballet, and he founded the Dance Theatre of Harlem. [2] As a young man, Mitchell studied tap dance, modern dance, and ballet at a special high school for the performing arts the challenges of ballet especially appealed to him. [3] After graduation from high school in 1952, Mitchell enrolled in the School of American Ballet, part of the New York City Ballet however, he continued performing modern dance with other companies.

[4] Mitchell's fine technique and commanding style, evident in the photograph at left, were impressive consequently, he was invited to join the New York City Ballet in 1955. [5] Director George Balanchine admired Mitchell's talent as a result, Balanchine choreographed dances for Mitchell and cast him in many leading roles. [6] Among the New York City Ballet productions featuring Mitchell were these *Agon, Arcade, The Nutcracker,* and *Creation of the World.* [7] The company was often criticized for showcasing an African American dancer nevertheless, Balanchine remained adamant in his support for Mitchell.

[8] During his years with the New York City Ballet, Mitchell broke racial barriers, received much praise on foreign tours, and helped organize ballet companies in many countries and in 1968 Mitchell decided to form his own ballet company and school, which became the Dance Theatre of Harlem. [9] The ballet company quickly established a name for itself in fact, it is acclaimed throughout the world. [10] Critics and audiences have responded enthusiastically to such productions as the following *Creole Giselle, Fancy Free,* and *Firebird.*

Italics (Underlining)

Italics are printed characters that slant to the right. To indicate italics in handwritten or typewritten work, use underlining.

PRINTED   *The Once and Future King* was written by T. H. White.

TYPED   <u>The Once and Future King</u> was written by T. H. White.

27g. **Use italics (underlining) for titles and subtitles of books, plays, long poems, periodicals, works of art, films, radio and television series, long musical works and recordings, videos, video and computer games, and comic strips.**

Type of Title	Examples
Books	*Blue Highways: A Journey into America* *Wuthering Heights*
Plays	*The King and I* *Barefoot in the Park*
Long Poems	*I Am Joaquín* *The Song of Roland*

| COMPUTER TIP

If you use a personal computer, you may be able to set words in italics. Most word-processing software and many printers can produce italic type.

Type of Title	Examples
Periodicals	*San Diego Tribune*
	The New Yorker
Works of Art	*Nocturne in Black and Gold: The Falling Rocket*
	The Thinker
Films	*Hank Aaron: Chasing the Dream*
	The Maltese Falcon
Radio and TV Series	*The Lone Ranger*
	Seinfeld
Long Musical Works and Recordings	*Appalachian Spring*
	La Bohème
	Miracles: The Holiday Album
Videos	*How to Get Fit Fast*
	Animal Bloopers
Video and Computer Games	*Madden Football 99*
	Escape Velocity
Comic Strips	*Jump Start*
	Doonesbury

The titles of poems that are long enough to be published as separate volumes should be italicized. Such poems are usually divided into titled or numbered sections, such as cantos, parts, or books. The titles of these sections should be enclosed in quotation marks.

EXAMPLES   *The Faerie Queene*   "Canto IV"

the *Iliad*   "Book I"

NOTE The articles *a, an,* and *the* before a title are italicized and capitalized only if the article is part of the official title.

EXAMPLES   I found some good ideas in several back issues of **the** *Chicago Tribune* and ***The*** *Wall Street Journal.*

Jason did not immediately understand that Swift's ***A*** *Modest Proposal* was a satire.

STYLE TIP

On the cover page or title page of a paper of your own, do not use italics for your paper's title. However, if your title contains a title that belongs in italics, you will need to use italics for that part of the title.

EXAMPLES
Shakespeare's Tragic Heroines [contains no title that belongs in italics]

Cordelia in *King Lear:* A Daughter's Love [contains a title that belongs in italics]

Be creative when giving your paper a title. Avoid using the title of another work as the complete title of your paper.

MECHANICS

Reference Note

For information about **titles** that are not italicized but are **enclosed in quotation marks,** see page 863.

HELP

The official title of a periodical can usually be found in the masthead, the section of the newspaper or magazine that lists the publisher, the editor, the owner, and other information about the periodical.

STYLE   TIP

When words that should
be italicized appear in a
sentence that is already
italicized, use roman letters
for those words to contrast
them with the rest of the
italicized sentence.

EXAMPLE

(*Note: The class will have
finished reading* Othello
*before beginning the
research project.*)

HELP

If you are not
sure whether to italicize a
foreign word, look it up in
an up-to-date dictionary.

Do not use italics for titles of religious texts or of legal or
historical documents.

RELIGIOUS TEXTS	New Testament
	Veda
LEGAL OR HISTORICAL DOCUMENTS	Treaty of Medicine Lodge
	Declaration of Independence

**27h. Use italics (underlining) for the names of trains, ships,
aircraft, and spacecraft.**

Type of Title	Examples	
Trains, Ships	*Orient Express*	*Queen Mary*
Aircraft	*Enola Gay*	*Hindenburg*
Spacecraft	*Atlantis*	*Skylab 1*

**27i. Use italics (underlining) for words, letters, symbols, and
numerals referred to as such and for foreign words that have not
been adopted into English.**

EXAMPLES   The most common word in English is ***the;*** the letters used
most frequently are ***e*** and ***t;*** and the numerals most often
confused are ***7*** and ***9.***

The symbol **&** means "and."

The Latin phrase ***ad astra per aspera*** means "to the stars
through difficulties."

Exercise 3 **Correcting Sentences by Adding
Underlining**

Rewrite the following sentences, underlining each word or word group
that should be italicized.

EXAMPLE   1. Didn't Joseph Conrad write the novel Heart of Darkness?

1. *Didn't Joseph Conrad write the novel <u>Heart of Darkness</u>?*

1. Is the Pietà the only work Michelangelo ever signed?
2. For my birthday I received a print of Rousseau's The Jungle and a
tape of the soundtrack for the musical Cats.
3. Die dulci fruere means "Have a nice day" in Latin, according to the
book Latin for All Occasions by Henry Beard.

4. Chris Burke, who was born with Down's syndrome, became a successful actor in the TV series Life Goes On.

5. Frank Capra, a Sicilian immigrant, made such film classics as It's a Wonderful Life and Mr. Smith Goes to Washington.

6. Try to vary your transitional expressions; I counted five so's on this page alone.

7. Mr. Lawrence, do you have the latest copy of Popular Mechanics?

8. Out of necessity, the USSR developed the world's foremost icebreaker technology; the Soviet ship Arktika was the first surface vessel to reach the North Pole.

9. Last summer, Dad and Uncle Jim built an ultralight airplane that they call Firefly.

10. Whenever I try to write &'s, I end up writing cursive S's.

Quotation Marks

27j. Use quotation marks to enclose a *direct quotation*—a person's exact words.

Be sure to place quotation marks both before and after a person's exact words.

EXAMPLES   Eleanor Roosevelt said, "No one can make you feel inferior without your consent."

"People are trapped in history and history is trapped in them," wrote the author James Baldwin in *Notes of a Native Son*.

Do not use quotation marks to enclose an *indirect quotation*—a rewording of a direct quotation.

DIRECT QUOTATION   Natalie said, "My favorite singer is Whitney Houston."

INDIRECT QUOTATION   Natalie said that her favorite singer is Whitney Houston.

(1) A direct quotation generally begins with a capital letter.

EXAMPLE   In *Up from Slavery,* Booker T. Washington writes, "**S**uccess is to be measured not so much by the position that one has reached in life as by the obstacles which he has overcome while trying to succeed."

MECHANICS

When writing only a part of a quoted sentence, do not begin the quotation with a capital letter unless the person you are quoting capitalized it or it is the first word in your sentence.

EXAMPLES   A film critic has called the movie "**a** futile attempt by the director to trade on his reputation as a creator of blockbusters."

I'm sure the expression she used in her essay was "**L**affite's exile."

"**M**y all-time favorite dish" was how Martha described the entree.

(2) When a quoted sentence is interrupted by an expression that identifies the speaker, the second part of the quotation begins with a lowercase letter.

EXAMPLE   "When we do the best that we can," explained Helen Keller, "**w**e never know what miracle is wrought in our life, or in the life of another." [Notice that each part of the divided quotation is enclosed in quotation marks.]

When the second part of a divided quotation is a new sentence, it begins with a capital letter.

EXAMPLE   "Please don't open the door!" Albert shouted. "**W**e're developing film."

NOTE   When a direct quotation of two or more sentences is not divided, only one set of quotation marks is used.

EXAMPLE   "Please don't open the door! We're developing film!" Albert shouted.

(3) A direct quotation is set off from the rest of the sentence by a comma, a question mark, or an exclamation point, but not by a period.

EXAMPLES   "For tomorrow, please read the article about the Sherpas of Nepal**,**" requested Ms. Estevan.

"Who do you think is the current president of the Philippines**?**" asked Nathan.

"The Wildcats have upset the Rockets**!**" exclaimed the sportscaster.

NOTE Do not set off a quotation that is clearly an integral part of the sentence you are writing. Generally, such a quotation is a word or phrase that would require no pause before or after it.

EXAMPLE In his speech, Enrique said that "one for all and all for one" is the key to a successful club.

(4) When used with quotation marks, other marks of punctuation are placed according to the following rules:

- Commas and periods are placed inside closing quotation marks.

EXAMPLE "Generosity," said Nathaniel Hawthorne, "is the flower of justice."

- Semicolons and colons are placed outside closing quotation marks.

EXAMPLES "Eva," my grandmother said, "you should keep up with your chores"; then she reminded me to vacuum.

Gail Sloan described the following as "deserted-island reading": *An Encyclopedia of World History,* the complete works of Shakespeare, and *Robinson Crusoe.*

- Question marks and exclamation points are placed inside closing quotation marks if the quotation is a question or an exclamation. Otherwise, they are placed outside.

EXAMPLES The teacher asked me, "Where did you find this information about José Rizal?"

Someone behind me shouted, "Watch out!"

Did Franklin Roosevelt say, "The only thing we have to fear is fear itself"?

How proud and happy Colleen was when her supervisor told her, "You deserve a raise"!

NOTE In a sentence that ends with a quotation, only one end mark is necessary.

INCORRECT Have you ever asked yourself, "Where will I be ten years from now?"?

CORRECT Have you ever asked yourself, "Where will I be ten years from now?"

(5) When writing dialogue, begin a new paragraph every time the speaker changes, and enclose each speaker's words in quotation marks.

EXAMPLE   "Don't stand chattering to yourself like that," Humpty Dumpty said, looking at her for the first time, "but tell me your name and business."

"My *name* is Alice, but—"

"It's a stupid name enough!" Humpty Dumpty interrupted impatiently. "What does it mean?"

"*Must* a name mean something?" Alice asked doubtfully.

"Of course it must," Humpty Dumpty said with a short laugh: " *My* name means the shape I am—and a good handsome shape it is, too. With a name like yours, you might be any shape, almost."

Lewis Carroll, *Through the Looking-Glass*

(6) When quoting a passage that consists of more than one paragraph, place quotation marks at the beginning of each paragraph and at the end of only the last paragraph in the passage.

EXAMPLE   "The engine cuts again, and then catches, and each time it spurts to life I climb as high as I can get, and then it splutters and stops and I glide once more toward the water, to rise again and descend again, like a hunting sea bird.

"I find the land. Visibility is perfect now and I see land forty or fifty miles ahead. If I am on my course, that will be Cape Breton. Minute after minute goes by. The minutes almost materialize; they pass before my eyes like links in a long slow-moving chain, and each time the engine cuts, I see a broken link in the chain and catch my breath until it passes."

Beryl Markham, *West with the Night*

A long passage quoted from a published source is often set off from the rest of the text. According to some style guides, the entire passage should be indented. When a passage is set off in this way, no quotation marks are necessary to indicate that it is a quotation. However, if there are quotation marks in the passage, be sure to include them.

EXAMPLE   Markham uses vivid imagery and intense verbs to draw the reader into the action. These techniques are clearly displayed in the following passage:

The engine cuts again, and then catches, and each time it spurts to

life I climb as high as I can get, and
then it splutters and stops and I glide
once more toward the water, to rise
again and descend again, like a hunting
sea bird.

   I find the land. Visibility is perfect now and I see land forty or fifty
miles ahead. If I am on my course, that
will be Cape Breton. Minute after
minute goes by. The minutes almost
materialize; they pass before my eyes
like links in a long slow-moving chain,
and each time the engine cuts, I see a
broken link in the chain and catch my
breath until it passes.

(7) Use single quotation marks to enclose a quotation within a quotation.

EXAMPLES   Mrs. Winters said, "Cristina, please tell us what you think Alexander Pope meant when he said, 'To err is human, to forgive divine.'" [Notice that the period is placed inside the single quotation mark.]

Mrs. Winters asked, "Do you think the moral of the story could be 'To err is human, to forgive divine'?" [Notice that the question mark is placed between the single quotation mark and the double quotation marks because only Mrs. Winters' words, not Pope's, are a question.]

How did Cristina respond when Mrs. Winters said "Please explain what Alexander Pope meant when he said, 'To err is human, to forgive divine'"? [Notice that the question mark is placed outside of both the single and double quotation marks because the whole sentence, not the words of Mrs. Winters or of Pope, is a question.]

NOTE   Be sure to reproduce quoted material as it appears in the original. If the original contains an error, write *sic* in brackets directly after the error to indicate that you have not made the error.

EXAMPLE   The drama critic continued, "In Act III, the young soldier must chose [*sic*] between equally disagreeable alternatives."

27k. Use quotation marks to enclose titles (including subtitles) of short works, such as short stories, short poems, essays, articles and other parts of periodicals, songs, episodes of radio and television series, and chapters and other parts of books.

Reference Note
For information on using **brackets,** see page 879.

Reference Note
For examples of **titles that are italicized,** see page 856.

Generally, do not use quotation marks for the title of a paper you are writing. However, if your title contains a title that belongs in quotation marks, you should use quotation marks for that part of your title.

EXAMPLES

King Arthur: Real or Mythical? [contains no title that belongs in quotation marks]

"Do Not Go Gentle into That Good Night": An Analysis of a Villanelle [contains a title that belongs in quotation marks]

Be creative when giving your paper a title. Avoid using the title of another work as the complete title of your own work.

Avoid using slang words in formal speaking and writing whenever possible. When using technical terms, be sure to explain their meanings. If you are not sure whether a word is appropriate or its meaning is clear, consult an up-to-date dictionary. If the dictionary labels a word *slang* or *colloquial,* it probably is inappropriate in formal speaking and writing.

Type of Title	Examples
Short Stories	"Raymond's Run" "Chee's Daughter" "The Necklace" "A Worn Path"
Short Poems	"My Mother Pieced Quilts" "The Eagle: A Fragment"
Essays	"A Child's Christmas in Wales" "Old English: Where English Came From"
Articles and Other Parts of Periodicals	"How to Choose a Career" "Water: Not as Cheap as You Think"
Songs	"We Are the World" "The Star-Spangled Banner"
Episodes of Radio and Television Series	"The All-Night Listener: A Mystery" "Secret of the Dead Sea Scrolls"
Chapters and Other Parts of Books	"The War in the Persian Gulf" "Biology: The Study of Life"

27l. Use quotation marks to enclose slang words, invented words, technical terms, dictionary definitions of words, and any expressions that are unusual in standard English.

EXAMPLES   In the drama club's latest production, Dylan plays the role of Lyndon, a "nerd."

The running of the bulls through the streets (one might say "bullevards") of Pamplona, Spain, is an annual event.

What do you mean by "looping" the computer instructions?

The name *Arkansas* is derived from the Sioux word for "downstream people."

What do Southerners mean when they say they are "fixing to" do something?

Exercise 4 **Correcting Sentences by Adding Quotation Marks, Other Punctuation Marks, and Capitalization**

Revise the following sentences, correctly using quotation marks, other marks of punctuation, and capitalization.

EXAMPLE   1. Jim asked have you read James Alan McPherson's story
                Why I Like Country Music.

            1. *Jim asked, "Have you read James Alan McPherson's story
                'Why I Like Country Music'?"*

1. How many of you Mrs. Martínez asked have studied a foreign language for more than two years.
2. Nice try, Donna was what the coach said.
3. We should have started our homework earlier said Beth we have answered only three questions so far.
4. Where have you been she asked.
5. It is said that someone once asked Bernard Shaw how old he was, and he answered I'm as old as my tongue and a few years older than my teeth.
6. Can you please tell me asked Mrs. Ross how many syllables are in a haiku?
7. Was it Elizabeth Barrett Browning asked Lani who wrote the poem Cry of the Children?
8. My baby brother calls elephants elephanuts.
9. Would you let us hand in our research papers next week, Ms. Lewis we asked none of the books we need are in the library.
10. Alice whispered thank you for lending me the article Is There Life on Other Planets?

Ellipsis Points

27m. Use ellipsis points to mark omissions from quoted material and pauses in a written passage.

ORIGINAL   At Lincoln, making us into Americans did not mean scrubbing away what made us originally foreign. The teachers called us as our parents did, or as close as they could pronounce our names in Spanish or Japanese. No one was ever scolded or punished for speaking in his native tongue on the playground. Matti told the class about his mother's down quilt, which she had made in Italy with the fine feathers of a thousand geese. Encarnación acted out how boys learned to fish in the Philippines. I astounded the third grade with the story of my travels on a stagecoach, which nobody else in the class had seen except in the museum at Sutter's Fort. After a visit to the Crocker Art Gallery and its collection of heroic paintings of the golden age of California, someone showed a silk scroll with a Chinese painting. Miss Hopley herself had a way of expressing wonder over these matters before a class, her eyes wide open until they popped slightly. It was easy for

When using ellipsis points, be sure to leave a space before, between, and after the points.

me to feel that becoming a proud American, as she said we should, did not mean feeling ashamed of being a Mexican.

Ernesto Galarza, *Barrio Boy*

(1) When you omit words from the middle of a sentence, use three spaced ellipsis points.

EXAMPLE   In his autobiography, Galarza recalls, "It was easy for me to feel that becoming a proud American . . . did not mean feeling ashamed of being a Mexican."

(2) When you omit words at the beginning of a sentence within a quoted passage, keep the previous sentence's end punctuation and follow it with the points of ellipsis.

EXAMPLE   Galarza remembers that his teachers encouraged him and his classmates to share stories about their families and backgrounds: "Matti told the class about his mother's down quilt, which she had made in Italy with the fine feathers of a thousand geese. Encarnación acted out how boys learned to fish in the Philippines. I astounded the third grade with the story of my travels on a stagecoach, which nobody else in the class had seen except in the museum at Sutter's Fort. . . . [S]omeone showed a silk scroll with a Chinese painting."

Notice in the above example that the *s* beginning *someone* has been capitalized because it begins the sentence following the ellipsis points. Brackets are used around the *S* to show that *someone* was not capitalized in the original passage.

(3) When you omit words at the end of a sentence within a quoted passage, keep the sentence's end punctuation and follow it with the points of ellipsis.

EXAMPLE   Miss Hopley herself had a way of expressing wonder over these matters before a class. . . . It was easy for me to feel that becoming a proud American, as she said we should, did not mean feeling ashamed of being a Mexican.

(4) When you omit one or more complete sentences from a quoted passage, keep the previous sentence's end punctuation and follow it with the points of ellipsis.

EXAMPLE   About Lincoln School, Galarza writes, "At Lincoln, making us into Americans did not mean scrubbing away what made us originally foreign. . . . It was easy for me to feel that becoming a proud American, as she [the principal] said we should, did not mean feeling ashamed of being a Mexican."

Reference Note

For information on using **brackets,** see page 879.

HELP

If you omit words from a quoted passage, be absolutely certain that you are not changing the meaning of the passage.

MISLEADING
"I astounded the class with the story of my travels on a stagecoach . . . in the museum at Sutter's Fort." [Galarza did not say or mean that he had traveled on a stagecoach in a museum.]

If you have any doubt about whether your omission changes the meaning, do not omit anything.

MECHANICS

Notice in the previous example that the words *the principal* are included to identify *she*. The words are enclosed in brackets to show that they have been inserted into the quotation and are not the words of the writer.

(5) To show that a full line or more of poetry has been omitted, use an entire line of spaced periods.

ORIGINAL   I dream of Hanoi:
Co-ngu Road
ten years of separation
the way back sliced by a frontier of hatred.
I want to bury the past
to burn the future
still I yearn
still I fear
those endless nights
waiting for dawn.

Nguyen Thi Vinh, "Thoughts of Hanoi"

WITH OMISSION   I dream of Hanoi:

. . . .

ten years of separation

. . . .

still I yearn
still I fear
those endless nights
waiting for dawn.

STYLE   **TIP**

Notice in the example to the left that the line of spaced periods is as long as the line of poetry above it.

MECHANICS

(6) Use three spaced ellipsis points (. . .) to indicate a pause in written dialogue.

EXAMPLE   "Well, . . . I don't know what to say," Sarah answered.

Exercise 5   **Using Ellipsis Points Correctly**

Rewrite the following passages, omitting the italicized parts and using ellipsis points to punctuate each omission correctly.

EXAMPLE   1. This thief during the last months had broken into the sheepfolds of the neighborhood like a wolf, *had killed and dragged away his prey like a wolf,* and like a wolf had left no trace after him.

Isak Dinesen, "The Ring"

    1. *This thief during the last months had broken into the sheepfolds of the neighborhood like a wolf . . . and like a wolf had left no trace after him.*

HELP

You may keep or omit internal sentence punctuation, such as commas, depending on whether that punctuation is necessary to the meaning of the sentence with the omission.

1. It was nearly the time of full moon, and *on this account, though the sky was lined with a uniform sheet of dripping cloud,* ordinary objects out of doors were readily visible.

Thomas Hardy, "The Three Strangers"

2. The old native stood, *breath blowing out the skin between his ribs, feet tense,* balanced in the sand, smiling and shaking his head.

Nadine Gordimer, "The Train from Rhodesia"

3. In the world's broad field of battle,
   In the bivouac of Life,
   Be not like dumb, driven cattle!
   Be a hero in the strife!

Henry Wadsworth Longfellow,
"A Psalm of Life"

4. Remember, I am not recording the vision of a madman. *The sun does not more certainly shine in the heavens, than that which I now affirm is true. Some miracle might have produced it, yet the stages of the discovery were distinct and probable.* After days and nights of incredible labor and fatigue, I succeeded in discovering the cause of generation and life; nay, more, I became myself capable of bestowing animation upon lifeless matter.

Mary Shelley, *Frankenstein*

5. When the lights went on, little boys like a bevy of flies assembled around the lamppost for gossip and stories. *Elsewhere in a similar manner men gathered to throw dice or cut cards or simply to talk.* The spectacle repeated itself at each crossing where there was a street lamp ringed to a post.

George Lamming, *In the Castle of My Skin*

Apostrophes

Possessive Case

The **possessive case** of a noun or a pronoun shows ownership or possession.

EXAMPLES   Alice Walker's poetry   Crowfoot's family

                the students' suggestions   five dollars' worth

                your opinion   my grandparents

27n. Use an apostrophe to form the possessive of nouns and indefinite pronouns.

(1) To form the possessive of most singular nouns, add an apostrophe and an *s*.

EXAMPLES   the senator's comments   Charles's grades

              tennis racquet's size   player's turn

NOTE When forming the possessive of a singular noun ending in an *s* sound, add only an apostrophe if the noun has two or more syllables and if the addition of an apostrophe and an *s* would make the noun awkward to pronounce. Otherwise, add an apostrophe and an *s*.

EXAMPLES   for goodness' sake

            Achilles' battles

            the Netherlands' exports

(2) To form the possessive of a plural noun ending in *s*, add only an apostrophe.

EXAMPLES   the girls' team   the Millses' backyard

              the winners' trophy   the governors' conference

    The few plural nouns that do not end in *s* form the possessive by adding an apostrophe and an *s*.

EXAMPLES   those sheep's wool   children's playground

NOTE Generally, you should not use an apostrophe and an *s* to form the plural of a noun.

INCORRECT   Two of the novel's that Jean Rhys wrote are *Wide Sargasso Sea* and *Voyage in the Dark.*

CORRECT   Two of the **novels** that Jean Rhys wrote are *Wide Sargasso Sea* and *Voyage in the Dark.*

(3) Do not use an apostrophe with possessive personal pronouns or with the possessive pronoun *whose*.

INCORRECT   We thought the top score was her's.
CORRECT   We thought the top score was **hers.**

INCORRECT   I have witnessed democracy at it's best.
CORRECT   I have witnessed democracy at **its** best.

Reference Note

For information about using **apostrophes to form plurals of numerals, letters, symbols, and words used as such,** see page 873.

MECHANICS

| | INCORRECT | Who's notebook is this? |
| | CORRECT | **Whose** notebook is this? |

Reference Note

For information about how to distinguish the **possessive pronouns** *your, their, theirs, its,* and *whose* from the **contractions** *you're, they're, there's, it's,* and *who's,* see pages 907, 911, and 912.

Possessive Personal Pronouns					
First Person	my	mine	our	ours	
Second Person	your	yours			
Third Person	his	her	hers	its	their	theirs

(4) To form the possessive of an indefinite pronoun, add an apostrophe and an s.

EXAMPLES **No one's** contribution was overlooked.

She consented to **everybody's** request for a class meeting.

Reference Note

For a list of **indefinite pronouns,** see page 504.

NOTE For the expressions *anyone else* and *somebody else,* the correct possessives are *anyone else's* and *somebody else's.*

(5) Generally, in compound words, in names of organizations and businesses, and in word groups showing joint possession, only the last word is possessive in form.

EXAMPLES father-in-law's hobby

the Economic and Social Council's members

Lewis and Clark's expedition

Reference Note

For information on **compound nouns,** see page 499.

When a possessive pronoun is part of a word group showing joint possession, each noun in the word group is also possessive.

EXAMPLE **Lusita's, Joshua's,** and **my** report

Reference Note

For information on **acronyms,** see page 824.

NOTE The possessive of an acronym is formed by adding an apostrophe and an *s.*

EXAMPLES NATO's membership   NBC's prime-time programs

(6) Form the possessive of each noun in a word group showing individual possession of similar items.

EXAMPLE **Maria Bethania's** and **Aster Aweke's** albums

MECHANICS

(7) Use an apostrophe to form the possessives of words that indicate time, such as *minute, hour, day, week, month,* **and** *year,* **and of those that indicate an amount in cents or dollars.**

EXAMPLES   a **minute's** work   five **minutes'** work

                a **day's** rest   three **days'** rest

                one **cent's** worth   five **cents'** worth

"Sorry, but I'm going to have to issue you a summons for reckless grammar and driving without an apostrophe."

STYLE   TIP

If a possessive form sounds awkward to you, use a phrase beginning with *of* or *for* instead.

AWKWARD
  my sister's best friend's photograph

IMPROVED
  a photograph of my sister's best friend

Exercise 6 Forming Possessive Nouns and Pronouns

Each of the following groups of words expresses a possessive relationship by means of a prepositional phrase. Revise each word group so that a possessive noun or pronoun expresses the same relationship.

EXAMPLE   1. a vacation of two weeks

            1. a two weeks' vacation

1. hats of the firefighters
2. dressing room of the star
3. job of my sister-in-law
4. character of a person
5. business of Jorge and her
6. speech of the mayor-elect
7. a pause of a moment
8. owner of the Doberman pinscher
9. highlights of the film
10. kimonos of the women
11. costumes of the matadors
12. worth of four dollars
13. admission prices for adults and children
14. prize of Ralph Bunche
15. sides of it
16. trip of Maria and Cam
17. a wait of an hour
18. responsibility of everyone
19. CD of the group Depression Glass
20. the charter of the Organization of American States

MECHANICS

Contractions

27o. Use an apostrophe to show where letters, numerals, or words have been omitted in a contraction.

A *contraction* is a shortened form of a word, word group, or numeral in which an apostrophe takes the place of all the letters, words, or numerals that are omitted.

EXAMPLES

I am . . . . I'm	they had . . . . they'd
he has . . . . he's	where is . . . . where's
let us . . . . let's	we are . . . . we're
of the clock . . . . . . o'clock	we have . . . . we've
1950s . . . . '50s	you will . . . . .you'll

The word *not* can be shortened to *n't* and added to a verb, usually without any change in the spelling of the verb.

EXAMPLES

is not . . . . isn't	has not . . . . hasn't
does not . . . . doesn't	should not . . . . . .shouldn't
do not . . . . don't	were not . . . . weren't
was not . . . . wasn't	had not . . . . hadn't
have not . . . . haven't	would not . . . . . . wouldn't

EXCEPTIONS

will not . . . . won't	cannot . . . . can't

Do not confuse contractions with possessive pronouns.

Contractions	Possessive Pronouns
It's [*It is*] time to go.	**Its** diameter is almost 2,290 kilometers.
It's [*It has*] been snowing since noon.	
Who's [*Who is*] the captain?	**Whose** umbrella is this?
Who's [*Who has*] been using the computer?	
You're [*You are*] late.	**Your** skates are in the attic.
They're [*They are*] in the gym.	We are learning about **their** customs.
There's [*There is*] only one left.	This equipment is **theirs**.

Plurals

27p. Use an apostrophe and an *s* to form the plurals of all lower-case letters, of some capital letters, of numerals, of symbols, and of words referred to as words.

EXAMPLES   *Hawaii* ends with two *i*'s. [Without the apostrophe, the plural of *i* would spell *is*.]

Not many names begin with *U*'s, but the names of my oldest sister's favorite bands do—U2 and UB40. [Without the apostrophe, the plural of *U* would spell *Us*.]

Jeremy's *No want to*'s are just a sign that he's a normal two-year-old.

Make sure your *1*'s do not look like your *7*'s.

Writers sometimes add only an *s* to form the plurals of such items—except lowercase letters—if the plural forms cannot be misread.

EXAMPLE   Most of his grades this term are **Cs.**

Be sure to use apostrophes consistently.

EXAMPLE   The printed *T*'s look like *I*'s. [Without the apostrophe, the plural of *I* would spell *Is*. The apostrophe in the plural of *T* is included for consistency.]

NOTE To form the plurals of abbreviations that end with a period, add an apostrophe and an *s*.

EXAMPLES   Ph.D.'s   M.A.'s

To form the plurals of abbreviations not followed by periods, add either an apostrophe and an *s* or just *s*.

EXAMPLES   VCR's *or* VCRs   CD's *or* CDs

Reference Note

For more information about forming the **plurals of abbreviations,** see page 900.

> **Exercise 7** **Proofreading for the Correct Uses of the Apostrophe**

Write the following phrases and sentences, adding apostrophes where they are needed. If an item is already correct, write *C*.

EXAMPLE   **1.** Hes sure those are *us*.

1. *He's sure those are* u*'s*.

1. Its a pagoda, isn't it?
2. shouldnt be disrespectful
3. How many CPAs are here?
4. sand in its gears

5. Shes wearing a sari, Im sure.
6. If he lets you, youll go, too.
7. His choices were the same as hers.
8. Lets see whats going on.
9. I've found its no help.
10. could've fainted
11. Whats its title?
12. Your handwritten *win*s look like *urn*s.
13. the tornadoes of 99
14. Whos on the bicycle?
15. How many *um*s did you hear?
16. How many *i*s are there in *Mississippi*?
17. Did the *Titanic* send out *SOS*s?
18. His grades in French are all As.
19. Are these *l*s or *I*s?
20. Its lost its shine.
21. Back in 77, disco was popular.
22. Yes, weve called everyone.
23. Of course, youre invited!
24. Doesnt he have two Ph.D.s?
25. Cross these *t*s.

Hyphens

27q. Use a hyphen to divide a word at the end of a line.

When dividing a word at the end of a line, remember the following rules:

- Do not divide a one-syllable word.

INCORRECT   Alicia chose to write her report about the pli-ght of the homeless.

CORRECT   Alicia chose to write her report about the plight of the homeless.

- Divide a word only between syllables.

INCORRECT   Isn't Ethan running for student council presid-ent this year?

CORRECT   Isn't Ethan running for student council presi-dent this year?

NOTE   Generally, if a word of more than one syllable contains double consonants, you may divide the word between those consonants.

EXAMPLES   swi**m-m**ing   sy**l-l**able

Similarly, as a rule, you may divide a word with an affix (prefix or suffix) between the affix and the base word or root.

EXAMPLES   pre-heat [prefix]

allow-ance [suffix]

MECHANICS

┌─HELP─
When you are not sure about how to divide a word, look it up in a current dictionary.

Reference Note

For more about **prefixes, suffixes, base words, and roots,** see "Reading and Vocabulary" in the Quick Reference Handbook.

• Divide an already hyphenated word at the hyphen.

| INCORRECT | Hirohito was the emperor of Japan for six-ty-three years. |
| CORRECT | Hirohito was the emperor of Japan for sixty-three years. |

• Do not divide a word so that one letter stands alone.

INCORRECT	Proofreading my report, I saw that I had o-mitted an important quotation.
CORRECT	Proofreading my report, I saw that I had omitted an important quotation.
CORRECT	Proofreading my report, I saw that I had omit-ted an important quotation.

27r. Use a hyphen with compound numbers from *twenty-one* to *ninety-nine* and with fractions used as modifiers.

EXAMPLES **forty-two** applicants

about **three-fourths** empty [*Three-fourths* is an adverb modifying *empty.*]

a **two-thirds** majority [Here, *two-thirds* is an adjective modifying *majority.*]

two thirds of the voters [Here, *two thirds* is not a modifier. *Thirds* is a noun modified by the adjective *two* and the prepositional phrase *of the voters.*]

27s. Hyphenate a compound adjective when it precedes the word it modifies.

EXAMPLES a **well-liked** author   an author who is **well liked**

a **world-renowned** composer   a composer who is **world renowned**

the **less-appreciated** services   the services that are **less appreciated**

NOTE Some compound adjectives are always hyphenated whether they precede or follow the words they modify.

EXAMPLE a **well-balanced** meal   a meal that is **well-balanced**

If you are unsure about whether a compound adjective is usually hyphenated, look up the word in a current dictionary.

MECHANICS

STYLE TIP

The prefix *half–* often requires a hyphen, as in *half-life, half-moon,* and *half-truth.* However, sometimes *half* is used without a hyphen, either as a part of a single word (*halftone, halfway, halfback*) or as a separate word (*half shell, half pint, half note*). If you are not sure how to spell a word containing *half,* look up the word in a current dictionary.

Do not use a hyphen if one of the modifiers preceding a noun is an adverb ending in –*ly*.

EXAMPLE a **highly polished** surface

27t. Use a hyphen with the prefixes *ex–*, *self–*, *all–*, and *great–*; with the suffixes *–elect* and *–free*; and with all prefixes before a proper noun or proper adjective.

EXAMPLES **ex-**mayor president-**elect** **non-**European

self-control mayor-**elect** **anti-**fascist

all-star fat-**free** **pro-**Canadian

great-grandson sugar-**free** **Pan-**American

27u. Use a hyphen to prevent confusion or awkwardness.

EXAMPLES re-**collect** [prevents confusion with *recollect*]

de-**icer** [avoids the awkwardness of *deicer*]

Exercise 8 **Using Hyphens**

Rewrite the following groups of words, adding hyphens where they are needed and correcting any incorrect uses of hyphens. If a word group is already correct, write *C*.

EXAMPLE 1. a self cleaning oven

1. *a self-cleaning oven*

1. almost two thirds full
2. preColumbian artifact
3. well spoken individual
4. a highly motivated employee
5. antiimperialism
6. burrowing under the gro-und
7. a new form of tran-sportation
8. stepped into the aren-a
9. one hundred fifty five years
10. three fourths of the crowd at the fair

11. recreation of a historical event
12. building an adob-e house
13. part time job
14. one fourth completed
15. greatgrandfather
16. since she's a doctor of o-ptometry
17. treasurer elect
18. a singer who is world famous
19. an antiinflammatory ointment
20. a dictionary that is up to date

Reference Note

For more about adding **prefixes** and **suffixes** to words, see page 892.

S T Y L E T I P

Although you may see a variety of spellings for some words (*reelect*, *re-elect*), the preferred style is to make most pre-fixes not listed in Rule 27t part of single, unhyphen-ated words.

EXAMPLES
biannual reevaluate

semiarid miniseries

COMPUTER TIP

Some software programs can evaluate your writing for common errors in the use of punctuation marks. Such programs can help you proofread your writ-ing, but remember that they cannot find every error. You should still proofread your work carefully.

MECHANICS

Review B **Correcting Paragraphs by Adding Italics (Underlining), Quotation Marks, Ellipsis Points, Apostrophes, and Hyphens**

Rewrite the following paragraphs, adding italics (underlining), quotation marks, ellipsis points, apostrophes, and hyphens where they are needed.

EXAMPLES
[1] This is one of Georgia O'Keeffes paintings, isnt it, Anthony? asked Darla.

1. "This is one of Georgia O'Keeffe's paintings, isn't it, Anthony?" asked Darla.

[2] Anthony said Youve been studying, havent you?

2. Anthony said, "You've been studying, haven't you?"

[1] "This painting, Cow's Skull: Red, White, and Blue, really intrigues me; Im sure its extremely symbolic, Darla said. [2] What do you think of it?"

[3] Youve asked the right person, replied Anthony, because Georgia O'Keeffe is one of my favorite painters. [4] One biography of her, which is simply titled Georgia O'Keeffe, tells how shed collect horses and cows skulls in New Mexico and then paint pictures of them. [5] This well known work, which she painted in 1931, is symbolic; the paintings colors represent O'Keeffe's pro American feelings.

[6] "I like this photograph of O'Keeffe, too, Darla added. [7] Dont you think she looks extremely self reliant and self assured?"

[8] "Well, . . thats probably an understatement, chuckled Anthony. [9] O'Keeffe, who was born in Wisconsin in 1887, developed her own independent style in art and life. [10] Shes best known for her abstract paintings, especially the ones of flowers and of New Mexico desert scenes, such as her painting Ranchos Church—Taos.

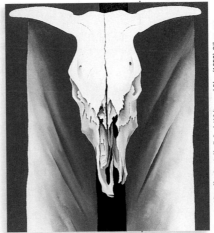

Georgia O'Keeffe, *Cow's Skull: Red, White, and Blue* (1952) Oil on canvas, 39½" x 35 ⅞". The Metropolitan Museum of Art, The Alfred Stieglitz Collection (52.203). Photograph © 1994 The Metropolitan Museum of Art.

Laura Gilpin, *Georgia O'Keeffe* (1953). Saf. neg. (P 1979.230.4297). © 1981, Laura Gilpin Collection, Amon Carter Museum, Fort Worth, Texas.

Dashes

Sometimes a word, phrase, or sentence is used parenthetically; that is, it breaks into the main thought of a sentence. Most parenthetical elements are set off by commas or by parentheses.

EXAMPLES Jorge, **however,** had already finished his work.

    Karina's idea **(that we each work on a separate part of the project)** made sense to all of us.

Sometimes, though, such elements call for a sharper separation from the rest of the sentence. In such cases, dashes are used.

27v. Use a dash to indicate an abrupt break in thought or speech.

EXAMPLES The director of the film—I can't recall his name—said that there would be a sequel.

    The truth is—and you probably already know this—we can't finish the project on time.

27w. Use a dash to mean *namely, in other words,* or *that is* before an explanation.

EXAMPLES It was a close call—the sudden gust of wind pushed the helicopter to within inches of the power line.

    Early Native American civilizations—the Mayan, the Incan, and the Aztec—relied on farming for their livelihood.

Parentheses

27x. Use parentheses to enclose informative or explanatory material of minor importance.

EXAMPLES The late Representative Barbara Jordan **(Texas)** was on that committee.

    The length of the Mekong River is 4,186 kilometers **(about 2,600 miles).**

Be sure that the material within parentheses can be omitted without losing important information or changing the basic meaning or structure of the sentence.

INCORRECT Tina had been shopping (in that store) most of her life.
     [The idea in parentheses is important to the meaning of the sentence.]

| COMPUTER TIP

Many computer programs are capable of setting dashes. If your computer program does not set dashes, type two hyphens to represent a dash. Do not leave a space before, between, or after the hyphens. When you write a dash by hand, use an unbroken line about as long as two hyphens.

MECHANICS

CORRECT   Tina had been shopping in that store **(Mr. Dan's)** most of
her life.

A sentence enclosed in parentheses may fall within another sentence or may stand by itself.

(1) A parenthetical sentence that falls within another sentence

- should not begin with a capital letter unless it begins with a word that should be capitalized
- should not end with a period but may end with a question mark or an exclamation point

EXAMPLES   The largest island of the Solomon Islands **(see the map on page 453)** is Guadalcanal.

I hope I persuaded Alex **(is he a senior?)** to help us.

(2) A parenthetical sentence that stands by itself

- should begin with a capital letter
- should end with a period, a question mark, or an exclamation point before the closing parenthesis

EXAMPLES   The largest island of the Solomon Islands is Guadalcanal. **(See the map on page 453.)**

Alex asked me if he could help us. **(What do you think I said?)**

NOTE   When parenthetical material falls within a sentence, punctuation should not come before the opening parenthesis but may follow the closing parenthesis.

INCORRECT   According to this article about Grandma Moses,
(1860–1961) she began to paint in her seventies.

CORRECT   According to this article about Grandma Moses
(1860–1961), she began to paint in her seventies.

Brackets

27y. Use brackets to enclose an explanation within quoted or parenthetical material.

EXAMPLES   Ms. Grayson was quoted as saying in her acceptance speech:
"I am honored by this **[the award]**, and I would like to share the recognition with those who made my work possible."

MECHANICS

By a vote of 5 to 4, the Supreme Court overturned the lower court's ruling. (See page 149 **[Diagram A]** for a chronology of the case.)

Use brackets and the Latin word *sic* to indicate that an error existed in the original version of a quoted passage.

EXAMPLE   As one critic has said, "The publication of 'The Raven' in 1846 **[sic]** ensured Poe's lasting literary fame but did little for his immediate financial needs." [The publication date should be 1845, but the critic being quoted used the wrong year.]

Reference Note

For information on **italicizing foreign words and phrases,** see page 858.

Exercise 9 Correcting Sentences by Adding Dashes, Parentheses, and Brackets

Rewrite each of the following sentences, adding or replacing dashes, parentheses, and brackets as needed.

EXAMPLE   1. One of the most prolific writers of England's Victorian Period most of the nineteenth century was Charles Dickens.

1. One of the most prolific writers of England's Victorian Period (most of the nineteenth century) was Charles Dickens.

1. Dr. Percy Lavon Julian, who was born in Montgomery, Alabama, is noted for developing helpful drugs from this surprised me, too soybeans.
2. My cousin Matthew my father's brother's son plans to open an aerobics and yoga center on the north side of town.
3. Some offspring of famous performers Michael Douglas, Liza Minnelli, Jeff and Beau Bridges, and Jane Fonda, for example have established distinguished careers for themselves.
4. Christine was quoted as saying in her valedictory speech: "We seniors are not at an ending but a beginning, and it graduation marks an exciting time of change in our lives."
5. For the new course on government and society, students are required to analyze the nonfiction writings of Ayn Rand 1905–1982 and to read her novel *Anthem.*
6. The parenthetical annotation said, "(please direct your attention to Figure C (page 764))."
7. Babysitters in my neighborhood all quake at the very mention of one name Tanyisha.

8. "Wait until you meet Annie oh, Annie, there you are," said Tom.
9. At this time, the power of Carthage see Appendix III on page 579 rivaled that of Rome.
10. The word *pants* derives from the name of a character called Pantaloon an old man in the commedia dell'arte whose preference for the garment became well known.

Review C **Proofreading a Paragraph for Correct Punctuation**

Rewrite the following paragraph, inserting end marks, semicolons, dashes, parentheses, apostrophes, and hyphens where they are needed. If a sentence is already correct, write *C*.

EXAMPLE [1] Jim Thorpe 1888–1953 was named our nations most outstanding athlete for the first half of the twentieth century.

1. *Jim Thorpe (1888–1953) was named our nation's most outstanding athlete for the first half of the twentieth century.*

[1] As you can see in the picture at right, Jim Thorpe his American Indian name was Wa-tho-huck looked exactly like what he was a strong athlete. [2] No discussion of Americas outstanding sports figures would be complete without reference to Thorpe, who in 1950 was voted the greatest athlete of the centurys first half. [3] He achieved unique feats in football, track, and baseball and, as I read recently, his strength and speed are legendary. [4] Born of Irish, French, and Native American heritage and reared in Prague, Oklahoma, Thorpe began earning honors early in his life. [5] He was an all American halfback for two years while playing for a local school and broke all previous records in winning the gold medals for the pentathlon and the decathlon at the 1912 Olympic Games, where he was hailed as the greatest athlete in the world. [6] Because hed already begun playing professional baseball, however, he was forced to return his medals a year later. [7] (They were restored in 1982 posthumously) [8] Thorpe spent six outstanding years in professional baseball, but he became best known as a football player who could do everything well run, pass, catch, punt, and more. [9] He played professional football for more than ten years. [10] In 1969, sixteen years after his death and on the National Football Leagues fiftieth birthday, Thorpe was named to footballs all time all professional team.

MECHANICS

Rewrite the following dialogue, adding commas, semicolons, quotation marks, apostrophes, and capital letters where they are needed. If a sentence is already correct, write *C*.

EXAMPLE   [1] Roger thought to himself I think that Ms. Zimsky will be pleased with these business letters.

1. *Roger thought to himself, "I think that Ms. Zimsky will be pleased with these business letters."*

[1] Feeling proud of himself, Roger Morton sat back for a moment.

[2] Have you finished those sample business letters yet asked Ms. Zimsky, the typing teacher.

[3] Yes Roger replied. [4] I think Ive improved the format, too. [5] See how much space Ive saved on each page!

[6] Ms. Zimsky glanced down. [7] These arent done the way they are in the book. [8] Just do them that way for now. [9] You need to finish this chapter today, or youll be far behind. [10] Theres no time to talk about format.

[11] Embarrassed and tired, Roger later told his friend Annette about the incident.

[12] Your problem she explained isnt that you improved the letters its that you didn't get Ms. Zimskys permission first. [13] I learned that any time you want to change a procedure, no matter how great an improvement the change will make, you should first talk your idea over with the person who will need to approve it. [14] Try discussing your suggestions again when Ms. Zimsky has more time.

[15] Roger went back to the typing classroom after school, and Ms. Zimsky listened to his ideas.

[16] Oh, I see what youre doing she said. [17] Its really a very good idea in fact, I'd like you to share it with the whole class tomorrow. [18] See you then, Roger.

[19] See you tomorrow said Roger and thanks for listening, Ms. Zimsky. [20] If I think of any other improvements, Ill be sure to discuss them with you first.

MECHANICS

Chapter Review

A. Using Semicolons and Colons Correctly

Most of the following sentences have either a comma or no mark of punctuation at all where a semicolon or a colon should be used. Write the word preceding each error, and add the semicolon or colon. If a sentence is already correct, write *C*.

⌐HELP—

Some sentences in Part A of the Chapter Review contain more than one error.

1. William Faulkner is remembered today for such novels as *Light in August, The Sound and the Fury,* and *As I Lay Dying,* but, as I remember, during his lifetime he cowrote screenplays, including the scripts for *The Big Sleep, To Have and Have Not,* and *Land of the Pharaohs.*

2. My grandparents were born and raised in a little town in the south of France, however, they speak English with only a slight accent.

3. Several people contributed to the book Dr. Newman, who did the research, Ms. Lewis, who provided the photographs, and Mr. Jung, who wrote the introduction.

4. The town has four landmarks: the town hall, the Baptist church, Butler Memorial Library, and the Sheraton House.

5. Some people can play musical instruments by ear without formal training, others need years of lessons and practice to play an instrument well.

6. He was tired and greatly in need of a warm place to rest, nevertheless, he refused to ask anyone for help.

7. The finalists for the Northwestern States Debating Team were from American Falls, Idaho, Medicine Bow, Wyoming, and Sunburst, Montana.

8. Stella has the following annoying habits, entering my room without knocking and borrowing my things without asking.

9. Juanita went home right after softball practice, she was expecting an important phone call.

10. I have applied for the following jobs delivery person for a greenhouse, dishwasher at a restaurant, clerk at a drugstore, and packer at a supermarket.

B. Using Italics, Quotation Marks, and Ellipsis Points Correctly

Rewrite each of the following sentences, correctly using underlining (italics), quotation marks, and ellipses. Be careful to show the correct position of quotation marks in relation to other punctuation.

11. Do not rush into anything, Leroy warned, that you are not willing to finish.

12. Marguerita said that An Apology for Idlers, by Robert Louis Stevenson, is one of her favorite essays.

13. Emily asked, Have you ever used the word ineluctable or ineffable in a sentence?

14. In his novel Moby-Dick, said Professor Donadio, Herman Melville writes about life on the whaling ship Pequod.

15. Did you know that the word Texas comes from the Caddo language?

16. I would like to read the magazine Computer Digest, Phoebe said, because I want to understand more of the technical terms that are related to computers.

17. I do not like that dress Wanda sighed. However, I will wear it to please my mother.

18. Well Kelly hesitated, and then said, I suppose I could have done a better job.

19. We will be rehearsing The Long Christmas Dinner for two more weeks, replied the drama coach.

20. Then, a boy standing across the street yelled, Are you hurt? David told the reporter.

C. Using Apostrophes, Hyphens, Dashes, Parentheses, and Brackets Correctly

Rewrite the following sentences, adding apostrophes, hyphens, dashes, parentheses, and brackets where needed.

21. Everyone this means you, too, Carla needs to rest for twenty five minutes before we continue the hike.

22. After a minutes consideration, Mark realized that there were as many *ss* as *is* in Mississippi.

23. The shops plainly marked sale tags showed a one third discount on seasonal gift items.

24. We enjoyed Glendas and Maraya's speeches more than anyone elses at the assembly.

25. My sister-in-laws reaction to her new computer's user friendly features was relief.

26. The grain companies vice presidents met recently to discuss marketing strategies for Europe. See the article on page 3 of the Business Section.

27. Cant you tell me which bicycle is Victors and which one is hers?

28. One of the measures of distance in astronomy is the light-year, which is the distance light travels in a vacuum in a year about 5,880,000,000,000 miles.

29. I think Poe (Edgar Allan Poe 1809–1849) wrote the first modern detective story.

30. The results of our survey are and let me be absolutely clear about this rather distressing for the company's long term prospects.

D. Proofreading Sentences for Correct Punctuation

The following sentences contain errors in the use of semicolons, colons, dashes, parentheses, brackets, italics (underlining), quotation marks, apostrophes, and hyphens. Rewrite the sentences, correcting each error.

31. Traffic was stopped for the citys Martin Luther King, Jr., Day parade consequently, a massive traffic jam developed.

32. One of my favorite Biblical passages is the story of Jesus and the Samaritan woman in John 4;5–42.

33. Since Bethany visited Europe last summer, she has been using foreign expressions such as bonjour and arrivederci.

34. "How long will it take for these three rolls of film to be developed"? I asked.

35. Our English class agrees that the short story The Rockpile by James Baldwin 1924–1987 is one of the best we have ever read.

36. Please turn up the radio Id like to hear the governor elects speech.

37. The confusion occurred because I thought that the briefcase was your's, not Dorothy's.

38. Very successful people, whether they excel in politics, the arts, or sports, are expert at self motivation.

39. We might and, according to the tour schedule, should have a free afternoon in Rome, the first city on the tour.

40. The newspaper quoted Mr. Bowen as saying, "People who take it Introduction to Auto Mechanics usually are glad they did".

E. Proofreading Paragraphs for Correct Punctuation

Rewrite the following paragraphs, adding, changing, or deleting semi-colons, colons, italics (underlining), quotation marks, apostrophes, hyphens, dashes, and parentheses as needed.

[41] The National Museum of American History formerly the National Museum of History and Technology is a fascinating place its part of the Smithsonian Institution in Washington, D.C. [42] You may ask I know I did what makes the museum so fascinating. [43] The museum offers changing displays on various themes represented by extremely-diverse artifacts of the United State's culture. [44] When we visited the three story building, we saw the actual flag that inspired Francis Scott Key to write The Star Spangled Banner and a pair of ruby slippers that Judy Garland wore in the film The Wizard of Oz. [45] Another crowd pleaser was the museums collection of First Ladies gowns. [46] Children shouldnt miss the Hands-On History Room they can explore our history and culture there in well planned, creative ways.

[47] We spent all day looking for such cultural keepsakes as the Fonzs jacket from the television show Happy Days however, there were also many scientific and technological displays to see. [48] One of these displays the Foucault Pendulum was almost impossible to overlook upon entering the building. [49] Some of the other scientific treasures were: Henry Fords Model T, our country's oldest working steam engine, cotton gins, and Samuel Morses telegraph. [50] We also allowed time for such interesting displays as the National Philatelic Collection, which was especially popular with stamp collectors like my dad, a country store post office, which came from a West Virginia town, and a variety of other wonderful exhibits.

Writing Application

Using Apostrophes in a Report

Using Correct Punctuation   In biology class you have learned that a *community* is a group of living things that forms a system of production, consumption, and decomposition. Now your biology teacher wants you to observe a community and write a report on your findings. Here is your assignment:

- Identify a community of organisms, and form a hypothesis about how the organisms interact.

- Observe their interactions for at least ten minutes a day for several days in a row.

- Take notes on your observations.

- Decide whether the data you collect support your hypothesis.

- Write your hypothesis, observations, and conclusions in a brief report. (Be sure to use apostrophes correctly to form the possessive case of nouns and pronouns.)

Prewriting   Choose a community that you can observe easily. Record the date and time of each observation. After you have completed your observations, review your notes carefully. What tentative conclusions can you draw about how the community functions?

Writing   Write a draft of your report. State your hypothesis, present your observations, state your conclusions, and then explain how your conclusions differ from or support your hypothesis. Finally, write your report in formal English appropriate for scientific writing.

Revising   Check your draft against your notes. Do your conclusions follow clearly from your observations? Revise your report as necessary.

Publishing   Proofread your report for errors in grammar, usage, spelling, and punctuation. You may want to attach your report to poster board and illustrate it with photographs or drawings. With your teacher's permission, display your poster in the classroom.

Reference Note

For information on **formal English,** see page 756.

Spelling
Improving Your Spelling

Diagnostic Preview

Proofreading Sentences for Correct Spelling

Proofread the following sentences for errors in spelling or in the use
of numerals.

EXAMPLE   1. The 3 mooses were startled by the plain roaring overhead.

            1. *three, moose, plane*

1. After the 17th boxcar past us, we knew we were in for a wait.
2. Oh, no, one of the mice must have hoped out of the cage somehow.
3. A half dozen loafs of raisin bread sat cooling on the kitchen counter; surly no one could be expected to resist just a little piece.
4. For the 5th time, the band's conductor raised his arms and said, "All together now."
5. Keep your personnel property safely locked in a drawer.
6. In my opinion, this issue could be resolved in a series of breif meetings.
7. Surely, your consceince will guide you through this situation.
8. Chris makes toyes that are truely clever.
9. These cloths that you made for us to wear in the play look quite authentic.
10. Whose next in line for tickets?
11. Be sure to complement Justin on his new glasses.

12. 1 of the miners refused to waist a moment and quickly filled cart after cart with coal.

13. Of course, Isaac and his friends will be their.

14. Its almost time for the first hard frost of the season.

15. The plows were working hard to keep the roads clear, but the snow was falling to fast.

16. The principal of osmosis can be difficult to comprehend.

17. The corn is ready, but the tomatos are not sliced yet.

18. Why do some lowercase *a*s look almost like upside-down *e*s?

19. I've never known friendlier people then your cousins.

20. As you probably all ready have discovered, sometimes an ilogical solution works best.

21. The parade will procede as planned.

22. Who said that the only sure things in life are death and taxs?

23. Are they going to the movie altogether?

24. The morale of the story is that you shouldn't judge a book by its cover.

25. Didn't the Davis' order 72 8-foot sections of fence?

Good Spelling Habits

Using the following techniques will improve your spelling.

1. Pronounce words carefully.

EXAMPLES   ath•let•ic [*not* a•the•let•ic]

soph•o•more [*not* soph•more]

jew•el•ry [*not* jew•le•ry]

2. Spell by syllables. A *syllable* is a word part that can be pronounced as one uninterrupted sound.

EXAMPLES   prob•a•bly [three syllables]

dip•lo•ma•tic [four syllables]

co•in•ci•den•tal [five syllables]

3. Use a dictionary. Do not guess about correct spelling. Look up any words you are unsure of how to spell. Using a dictionary to check the spelling of one word may help you spell other words. For example, by checking the spelling of *criticism*, you will see that the word ends in *–ism*, not *–isim*. Learning this spelling may help you spell other words ending in *–ism*, such as *patriotism*, *skepticism*, and *socialism*.

┌HELP──

If you are not sure how to pronounce a word, look in a dictionary. In the dictionary, you will usually find the pronunciation given in parentheses after the word. The information in parentheses will show you the sounds used, the syllable breaks, and any accented syllables. A guide to the pronunciation symbols is usually found at the front of the dictionary.

STYLE TIP

Becoming a careful speller takes a little practice, but the results are certainly worth the effort. Because readers constantly base assumptions about writers on their writing, looking good on paper is important.

If, for example, a written passage contains misspellings, a reader may suspect that the writer was careless about other information in the passage. By correcting misspelled words, the writer helps to focus the reader's attention on what is being said.

4. **Proofread for careless spelling errors.** Always re-read what you have written so that you can eliminate careless spelling errors, such as typos (*trail* for *trial*), missing letters (*goverment* for *government*), and the misuse of words that sound the same (*except* for *accept*).

5. **Keep a spelling notebook.** Divide each page into four columns.

COLUMN 1	Write correctly any word you find troublesome.
COLUMN 2	Write the word again, dividing it into syllables and marking the stressed syllable(s). (You may need to use a dictionary.)
COLUMN 3	Write the word again, circling the part(s) causing you trouble.
COLUMN 4	Jot down any comments that will help you remember the correct spelling.

Correct Spelling	Syllables and Accents	Trouble Spot	Comments
emperor	em´•per•or	emper(or)	Pronounce clearly.
awfully	aw´•ful•ly	awfu(ll)y	Study rule 28e.

NOTE In some names, diacritical marks (marks that show pronunciation) are as essential to correct spelling as the letters themselves. If you are not sure about the spelling of a name, check with the person who has that name or consult a reference source.

EXAMPLES   François   d'Alembert   Muñoz   Lemaître

Janáček   Dalén   Fu'ād   Rölvaag

Exercise 1   Spelling Words by Syllables

Without using a dictionary, divide each of the following words into syllables, inserting a hyphen between syllables. Be sure that the division of each word includes all the letters of the word. When you have finished, use a dictionary to check your work.

EXAMPLE   1. evacuate

1. *e-vac-u-ate*

1. annotate
2. similar
3. library
4. surprise
5. privilege
6. disastrous
7. quiet
8. embarrassing
9. perspiration
10. boundary
11. candidate
12. equipment
13. recognize
14. business
15. representative
16. entrance
17. accidentally
18. mischievous
19. government
20. unnecessary
21. establishment
22. unnerving
23. attempt
24. happiness
25. modern

Spelling Rules

ie and *ei*

28a. Write *ie* when the sound is long *e*, except after *c*.

EXAMPLES	th**ie**f	bel**ie**ve	c**ei**ling	rec**ei**ve	dec**ei**ve
EXCEPTIONS	s**ei**ze	**ei**ther	l**ei**sure	n**ei**ther	prot**ei**n

28b. Write *ei* when the sound is not long *e*, especially when the sound is long *a*.

EXAMPLES	forf**ei**t	n**ei**ghbor	fr**ei**ght	h**ei**ght	w**ei**gh
EXCEPTIONS	anc**ie**nt	consc**ie**nce	misch**ie**f	fr**ie**nd	rev**ie**w

COMPUTER TIP

Spellchecking software programs can help you proofread your writing. Even the best spellcheckers are not foolproof, however. Some accept British spellings, obsolete words, archaic spellings. Most accept words that are spelled correctly but are used incorrectly (such as *compliment* for *complement*). Always double-check your writing to make sure that your spelling is error-free.

B.C. by Johnny Hart. By permission of Johnny Hart and Creators Syndicate.

┌─HELP─

Different dictionaries show variations in spelling in different ways. To understand your dictionary's presentation of such variations, check the guide that explains how to use the book (usually found in the front).

When you look up the spelling of a word, make sure that its use is not limited by a label such as *British* or *chiefly British* (*flavour* for *flavor*), *obsolete* (*vail* for *veil*), or *archaic* (*spake* for *spoke*). In general, optional spellings that are not labeled, such as *cargos/ cargoes*, are equally correct.

NOTE Rules 28a and 28b apply only when the *i* and the *e* are in the same syllable.

Exercise 2) Spelling *ie* and *ei* Words

Spell each of the following words correctly by supplying *ie* or *ei*.

EXAMPLE   **1.** f . . . ld

        1. field

1. for . . . gn	**11.** counterf . . . t	**21.** sold . . . r
2. br . . . f	**12.** ach . . . ve	**22.** h . . . r
3. rel . . . ve	**13.** handkerch . . . f	**23.** sh . . . ld
4. s . . . ge	**14.** perc . . . ve	**24.** s . . . ze
5. v . . . l	**15.** conc . . . ve	**25.** c . . . ling
6. n . . . ce	**16.** . . . ther	
7. sl . . . gh	**17.** rec . . . pt	
8. gr . . . f	**18.** bel . . . f	
9. p . . . ce	**19.** f . . . nd	
10. retr . . . ve	**20.** ch . . . f	

–cede, –ceed, and –sede

28c. The only English word that ends in *–sede* **is** *supersede*. **The only words ending in** *–ceed* **are** *exceed, proceed,* **and** *succeed.* **Most other words with this sound end in** *–cede.*

EXAMPLES   ac**cede**   con**cede**   inter**cede**

                  pre**cede**   re**cede**   se**cede**

Adding Prefixes

A *prefix* is a letter or group of letters added to the beginning of a word to create a new word that has a different meaning.

Reference Note

For a list of **common prefixes,** see page 1010.

28d. When adding a prefix, do not change the spelling of the original word.

EXAMPLES	a + moral = a**moral**	il + legal = il**legal**
	mis + spell = mis**spell**	in + elegant = in**elegant**
	re + print = re**print**	im + movable = im**movable**
	over + rule = over**rule**	un + necessary = un**necessary**

Adding Suffixes

A *suffix* is a letter or group of letters added to the end of a word to create a new word with a different meaning.

28e. When adding the suffix *–ness* or *–ly,* do not change the spelling of the original word.

Reference Note

For a list of **common suffixes,** see page 1011.

EXAMPLES	mean + ness = **mean**ness	royal + ly = **royal**ly
	open + ness = **open**ness	social + ly = **social**ly
	dry + ness = **dry**ness	sly + ly = **sly**ly

EXCEPTIONS For most words that have two or more syllables and end in *y,* change the *y* to *i* before adding *–ness* or *–ly:*

	heavy + ness = heav**iness**	steady + ly = stead**ily**
	happy + ness = happ**iness**	busy + ly = bus**ily**
	empty + ness = empt**iness**	easy + ly = eas**ily**

Exercise 3   Spelling Words with Prefixes and Suffixes

Spell correctly each of the following words, adding the prefix or suffix given.

EXAMPLES   **1.** un + known

1. *unknown*

2. happy + ness

2. *happiness*

1. over + rate
2. habitual + ly
3. green + ness
4. im + material
5. dis + appoint
6. mis + apprehend
7. practical + ly
8. un + abated
9. un + natural
10. silly + ness
11. il + legible
12. in + appropriate
13. dis + appear
14. mis + step
15. re + construct
16. in + animate
17. dis + similar
18. keen + ness
19. un + avoidable
20. merry + ly
21. dry + ness
22. actual + ly
23. happy + ly
24. safe + ly
25. thin + ness

MECHANICS

28f. Drop the final silent *e* before adding a suffix that begins with a vowel.

EXAMPLES	care + ing = **car**ing	use + able = **us**able
	active + ity = **activ**ity	large + er = **larg**er

EXCEPTIONS   1. Keep the final silent *e* in most words ending in *ce* or *ge* before a suffix that begins with *a* or *o*: notic**eable**; courag**eous**. Sometimes the *e* becomes *i*, as in *spacious* and *gracious.*

                2. To avoid confusion with other words, keep the final silent *e* in some words: *dyeing* and *dying, singeing* and *singing.*

                3. mile + age = mileage

NOTE When adding *–ing* to words that end in *ie,* drop the *e* and change the *i* to *y.*

EXAMPLE	lie + ing = l**ying**	tie + ing = t**ying**

28g. Keep the final silent *e* before adding a suffix that begins with a consonant.

EXAMPLES	use + less = us**eless**	care + ful = car**eful**
	nine + ty = nin**ety**	amuse + ment = amus**ement**
EXCEPTIONS	nine + th = nin**th**	argue + ment = argu**ment**
	true + ly = tru**ly**	awe + ful = aw**ful**

NOTE Certain words that end with a silent *e* can drop or keep the final *e* when a suffix is added. Either spelling is acceptable.

EXAMPLES	acknowledge + ment = acknowledg**ment** *or*
	acknowledg**ement**
	judge + ment = judg**ment** *or* judg**ement**

28h. For words ending in *y* preceded by a consonant, change the *y* to *i* before adding any suffix that does not begin with *i.*

EXAMPLES	funny + er = funn**ier**	twenty + eth = twent**ieth**
	reply + ed = repl**ied**	reply + ing = repl**ying**

NOTE Some one-syllable words do not follow Rule 28h.

EXAMPLES	dry + ness = dry**ness**	shy + ly = shy**ly**

28i. For words ending in *y* preceded by a vowel, keep the *y* when adding a suffix.

EXAMPLES   gray + est = gra**yest**   convey + ing = conve**ying**

                    pay + ment = pa**yment**   employ + ed = emplo**yed**

EXCEPTIONS   lay—la**id**   pay—pa**id**   say—sa**id**   day—da**ily**

28j. Double the final consonant before adding a suffix that begins with a vowel if the word both (1) has only one syllable or has the accent on the final syllable and (2) ends in a single consonant preceded by a single vowel.

EXAMPLES   slim + er = sli**mmer**   prefer + ing = prefe**rring**

                    excel + ed = exce**lled**   forget + able = forge**ttable**

Do not double the final consonant unless the word satisfies both of the conditions.

EXAMPLES   benefit + ed = benefi**ted** [*Benefit* ends in a single consonant preceded by a single vowel but does not have the accent on the final syllable.]

                    select + ing = selec**ting** [*Select* has the accent on the final syllable but does not end in a single consonant.]

When a word satisfies both conditions but the addition of the suffix causes the accent to shift, do not double the final consonant.

EXAMPLES   refer + ence = refe**rence** [*Refer* has the accent on the final syllable, but *reference* has the accent on the first syllable.]

                    prefer + able = prefe**rable** [*Prefer* has the accent on the final syllable, but *preferable* has the accent on the first syllable.]

EXCEPTIONS   excel—exce**llent,** exce**llence,** exce**llency**

NOTE   The final consonant of some words may or may not be doubled. Either spelling is acceptable.

EXAMPLES   cancel + ed = cance**led** *or* cance**lled**
                    travel + ing = trave**ling** *or* trave**lling**
                    program + er = progra**mer** *or* progra**mmer**

If you are not sure whether you should double the final consonant, consult a dictionary.

Exercise 4　Spelling Words with Suffixes

Spell each of the following words, adding the suffix given.

EXAMPLE　　**1.** swim + ing

　　　　　　　1. swimming

1. defer + ed

2. defer + ence

3. hope + ing

4. approve + al

5. discover + er

6. safe + ty

7. prepare + ing

8. obey + ing

9. spicy + er

10. propel + ing

11. desire + ed

12. control + ed

13. hope + less

14. green + er

15. due + ly

16. run + ing

17. singe + ing

18. remote + est

19. tie + ing

20. red + est

21. day + ly

22. chose + en

23. defy + ance

24. courage + ous

25. employ + able

Review A　Proofreading a Paragraph to Correct Misspelled Words

┌HELP┐

No proper nouns in Review A are misspelled.

Proofread the following paragraph, correcting any misspelled words. If all the words in a sentence are already spelled correctly, write *C*.

EXAMPLE　　**[1]** Accordding to legend, Jean-Jacques Dessalines created the Haitian flag by removeing the white panel from the French flag.

　　　　　　　1. According, removing

　　[1] When news of the French Revolution reached the colony of Saint Domingue on the Caribbean island of Hispaniola, the African slaves and the freed islanders of mixxed ancestry rebeled against the French colonists. **[2]** Uniting the two rebel groups, the man shown here, General François Dominique Toussaint-L'Ouverture, conquerred the entire island and abolished slavery in 1802. **[3]** The next year, however, Toussaint was siezed by the French and deported to France, where he dyed a prisoner. **[4]** General Jean-Jacques Dessalines then declared the island independent and renamed it Haiti. **[5]** Declaring himself emperor, Dessalines ordered that a fortress, the Citadelle, and a series of smaller fortresses be built to prevent the Europeans from reestablishing power on the island. **[6]** Dessalines' breif reign lasted until 1806, when he was assassinated in an uprising believed to have been ploted by his cheif rival, General Henri Christophe. **[7]** Christophe, unable to control the legislature, in 1807 set up a separate state in northern Haiti and had himself crowned Henri I, King of Haiti. **[8]** Convinced that imposing structures such as the Citadelle shown here would boost his nation's stature, Christophe launched an extensive building program carried out by forced labor. **[9]** Hospitals and schools sprang up, and work on the Citadelle progressed steadily, but eventualy the people rebeled. **[10]** In 1820, having sufferred a series of strokes, Christophe, the last of the revolution's three great generals, took his own life.

Forming the Plurals of Nouns

28k. **Remembering the following rules will help you spell the plural forms of nouns.**

(1) For most nouns, add *s*.

SINGULAR	artist	song	lake	flower	muscle	Wilson
PLURAL	artist**s**	song**s**	lake**s**	flower**s**	muscle**s**	Wilson**s**

(2) For nouns ending in *s, x, z, ch,* or *sh*, add *es*.

SINGULAR	dress	box	waltz	birch	bush	Ruíz
PLURAL	dress**es**	box**es**	waltz**es**	birch**es**	bush**es**	Ruíz**es**

> **NOTE** Some one-syllable words ending in *z* double the final consonant when forming plurals.
>
> EXAMPLES   quiz—qui**zz**es   fez—fe**zz**es

(3) For nouns ending in *y* preceded by a vowel, add *s*.

SINGULAR	monkey	journey	essay	decoy	alley	Friday
PLURAL	monkey**s**	journey**s**	essay**s**	decoy**s**	alley**s**	Friday**s**

(4) For nouns ending in *y* preceded by a consonant, change the *y* to *i* and add *es*.

SINGULAR	fly	enemy	lady	trophy	ally	theory
PLURAL	fl**ies**	enem**ies**	lad**ies**	troph**ies**	all**ies**	theor**ies**

For most proper nouns, add *s*.

EXAMPLES   Brady—Brady**s**   Mallory—Mallory**s**

(5) For some nouns ending in *f* or *fe*, add *s*. For others, change the *f* or *fe* to *v* and add *es*.

SINGULAR	roof	chief	carafe	knife	loaf
PLURAL	roof**s**	chief**s**	carafe**s**	kni**ves**	loa**ves**

For proper nouns, add *s*.

EXAMPLES   Cardiff—Cardiff**s**   Wolfe—Wolfe**s**

(6) For nouns ending in *o* preceded by a vowel, add *s*.

SINGULAR	radio	studio	cameo	stereo	igloo	Matsuo
PLURAL	radio**s**	studio**s**	cameo**s**	stereo**s**	igloo**s**	Matsuo**s**

(7) For many nouns ending in *o* preceded by a consonant, add *es*.

SINGULAR	tomato	potato	hero	veto	torpedo	echo
PLURAL	tomato**es**	potato**es**	hero**es**	veto**es**	torpedo**es**	echo**es**

For some common nouns, especially those referring to music, and for most proper nouns, add *s*.

SINGULAR	burrito	silo	photo	piano	soprano	Yamamoto
PLURAL	burrito**s**	silo**s**	photo**s**	piano**s**	soprano**s**	Yamamoto**s**

NOTE   For some nouns ending in *o* preceded by a consonant, you may add either *s* or *es*.

SINGULAR	motto	tornado	mosquito	zero	banjo
PLURAL	motto**s**	tornado**s**	mosquito**s**	zero**s**	banjo**s**
	or	*or*	*or*	*or*	*or*
	motto**es**	tornado**es**	mosquito**es**	zero**es**	banjo**es**

If you are in doubt about the plural form of a noun ending in *o*, check the spelling in a dictionary.

(8) The plurals of a few nouns are formed irregularly.

SINGULAR	mouse	woman	tooth	foot	child
PLURAL	m**ice**	wom**en**	t**ee**th	f**ee**t	child**ren**

(9) For a few nouns, the singular and the plural forms are the same.

SINGULAR AND PLURAL	sheep	deer	species	trout
	moose	aircraft	Chinese	Sioux

(10) For most compound nouns, form the plural of only the last word of the compound.

SINGULAR	bookshelf	two-year-old	seat belt	baby sitter
PLURAL	bookshel**ves**	two-year-old**s**	seat belt**s**	baby sitter**s**

(11) For compound nouns in which one of the words is modified by the other word or words, form the plural of the noun modified.

SINGULAR	sister-in-law	runner-up	passer-by	senior citizen
PLURAL	sister**s**-in-law	runner**s**-up	passer**s**-by	senior citizen**s**

NOTE Some compound nouns have two acceptable plural forms.

SINGULAR	attorney general	court-martial	notary public
PLURAL	attorney general**s**	court-martial**s**	notary public**s**
	or	*or*	*or*
	attorney**s** general	court**s**-martial	notarie**s** public

HELP

Check an up-to-date dictionary whenever you are in doubt about the plural form of a compound noun.

(12) For some nouns borrowed from other languages, the plural is formed as in the original language.

SINGULAR	alumnus [male]	alumna [female]	phenomenon
PLURAL	alumn**i** [male]	alumn**ae** [female]	phenomen**a**

NOTE When referring to graduates of both genders, use *alumni*.

STYLE **TIP**

Some people use *phenomenons* as an alternative plural form, but this spelling has not become accepted in standard, formal English.

MECHANICS

A few nouns borrowed from other languages have two acceptable plural forms. For each of the following nouns, the plural form preferred in English is given first.

SINGULAR	index	stigma	formula	cactus	seraph
PLURAL	index**es**	stigma**s**	formula**s**	cactus**es**	seraph**s**
	or	*or*	*or*	*or*	*or*
	ind**ices**	stigma**ta**	formul**ae**	cact**i**	seraph**im**

(13) To form the plurals of numerals, most uppercase letters, symbols, and most words referred to as words, add an *s* or both an apostrophe and an *s*.

SINGULAR	5	1990	*B*	+	*and*
PLURAL	5**s**	1990**s**	*B***s**	+**s**	*and***s**
	or	*or*	*or*	*or*	*or*
	5**'s**	1990**'s**	*B***'s**	+**'s**	*and***'s**

Reference Note

For information on **using italics with words, letters, and numerals referred to as such,** see page 858.

TIPS & TRICKS

It is not incorrect to add both an apostrophe and an *s* to form the plurals of numerals, letters, symbols, and words referred to as words. Therefore, if you have any doubt about whether or not to use the apostrophe, use it.

Reference Note

For more information about **forming the plurals of numerals, letters, symbols, and words referred to as words,** see page 873.

To prevent confusion, add both an apostrophe and an *s* to form the plural of all lowercase letters, certain uppercase letters, and some words referred to as words.

EXAMPLES   The word *Philippines* contains three **p's** and three **i's**. [Both letters are lowercase.]

Most of her grades are **A's**. [Without an apostrophe the plural of *A* could be confused with the word *As*.]

In the last paragraph of your story, I can't tell which woman the **her's** refer to. [Without an apostrophe the plural of *her* could be confused with the possessive pronoun *hers*.]

Exercise 5 Spelling the Plural Forms of Nouns

Spell the plural form of each of the following nouns.

EXAMPLE   1. alto

1. *altos*

1. turkey	**11.** fly	**21.** *I*
2. sheep	**12.** soprano	**22.** passer-by
3. hairdo	**13.** poncho	**23.** alumnus
4. aircraft	**14.** shelf	**24.** hero
5. *but*	**15.** #	**25.** medium
6. video	**16.** editor in chief	
7. *6*	**17.** spoonful	
8. belief	**18.** twelfth-grader	
9. embargo	**19.** Gomez	
10. fox	**20.** goose	

HELP

To form the plural of an abbreviation that includes periods, add both an apostrophe and an *s*. To form the plural of an abbreviation that does not include periods, add both an apostrophe and an *s*, or add only an *s*.

EXAMPLES
Ph.D.—Ph.D.'s
CD—CD's *or* CDs

Review B Explaining the Spellings of Words

By referring to the rules on the preceding pages, explain the spelling of each of the following words.

EXAMPLE   1. living

1. *Drop the final silent* e *before adding a suffix that begins with a vowel.*

1. misstate	**4.** ladies	**7.** occurred	**9.** roofs
2. stubbornness	**5.** alumnae	**8.** writing	**10.** weigh
3. peaceable	**6.** niece		

Writing Numbers

28l. Spell out a *cardinal number*—a number that states how many—if it can be expressed in one or two words. Otherwise, use numerals.

EXAMPLES **thirteen** seniors   **forty-four** days   **one hundred** books

313 seniors   **344** days   **1,100** books

> NOTE Generally, you should not spell out some numbers and use numerals for others in the same context. If numerals are required for any of the numbers, use numerals for all of the numbers.

INCONSISTENT The Congress of the United States is composed of one hundred senators and 435 representatives.

CONSISTENT The Congress of the United States is composed of **100** senators and **435** representatives.

However, to distinguish between numbers that appear beside each other but that count different things, spell out one number and use numerals for the other.

EXAMPLES We bought **seven 15**-pound sacks of birdseed.

or

We bought **7 fifteen**-pound sacks of birdseed.

28m. Spell out a number that begins a sentence.

EXAMPLE **Four hundred twenty-one** students participated in the contest.

If a number appears awkward when spelled out, revise the sentence so that it does not begin with the number.

AWKWARD Two hundred twenty-three thousand six hundred thirty-one votes were cast in the election.

IMPROVED In the election, **223,631** votes were cast.

28n. Spell out an *ordinal number*—a number that expresses order.

EXAMPLES Junko Tabei, the **first** [not *1st*] woman who climbed Mount Everest, was born in Japan in 1939.

Of the fifty states, Tennessee ranks **thirty-fourth** [not *34th*] in total land area.

Reference Note

For information about **hyphenating compound numbers,** see page 875.

| STYLE | TIP |

For large round numbers, you may use words, numerals, or a combination of words and numerals.

EXAMPLES
thirty trillion dollars *or* **30 trillion** dollars

10,800,000 people *or* **10.8 million** people

MECHANICS

28o. Use numerals to express numbers in conventional situations.

Type of Number	Examples		
Identification Numbers	Room 12 Channel 4	pages 246–315 State Road 541	Model 19-A lines 3–19
Measurements, Statistics	72 degrees 14 percent	$6\frac{1}{2}$ yards 84 years old	32.7 ounces ratio of 6 to 1
Dates	July 4, 1776 1200 B.C.		A.D. 2000
Addresses	345 Lexington Drive Tampa, FL 33628-4533		Route 6 P.O. Box 105
Times of Day	8:20 P.M. 7:35 A.M.		4:00 EST

NOTE Spell out a number used with *o'clock.*

EXAMPLE **ten** [not *10*] o'clock

Exercise 6 Using Numbers in Sentences

Each of the following sentences contains at least one error in the use of numbers. Revise each sentence to correct the error(s).

EXAMPLE 1. In the bottom of the 9th inning, the Wildcats scored 7 runs and won the playoff.

1. *In the bottom of the ninth inning, the Wildcats scored seven runs and won the playoff.*

1. When you go to Washington, D.C., visit the Frederick Douglass National Historic Site, which is located at One Thousand Four Hundred Eleven W Street SE.
2. Since he was 15, my brother's 1st choice as a college major has been computer science, and his second choice has been mathematics.
3. 590 people attended the play on opening night, September fourth, setting an attendance record for the community theater.
4. Did you realize that ninety-seven percent of the earth's water supply is salt water?
5. According to the chart on page three, only fifty-one of the company's 360 products are sold in this region.
6. That summer they sailed approximately 70 miles along the Carolina coastline.
7. Please get fifty two-inch nails and a new claw hammer, Rita.

8. There's plenty of time; the show doesn't start until 9 o'clock.

9. It was only a 3rd-place ribbon, but I had never even placed before.

10. Fully seventy-five percent of the sample were tested without problems.

Review C **Proofreading Paragraphs to Correct Misspelled Words and Errors in the Use of Numbers**

Proofread the following paragraphs, correcting any misspelled words or errors in the use of numbers.

EXAMPLE   **[1]** 5 days ago, members of my family joined in a lovly birthday celebration for my great-auntes.

1. *Five; lovely; great-aunts*

┌HELP─
All of the
proper nouns in Review C
are spelled correctly.

[1] Last Saturday my grandmother's twin sisters, Aunt Maeve and Aunt Margaret, celebrated their sixtyeth birthdays in an enormous family gathering at La Vista Park. [2] Since I am almost 16 years old and have my learnner's permit, Mom let me drive to the park. [3] My aunts and uncles on Mom's side of the family were there with their husbands and wifes. [4] 6 of my cousins, all but Erin, whom I had been especially hoping to see, attended the celebration. [5] Unfortunately, the flights from Chicago, where Erin goes to nursing school, had been canceled because it had snowed heavyly that night. [6] Although I missed Erin, I enjoyed visiting with many of the 85 friends and family members who had come to the cel-ebration. [7] Aunt Maeve and Aunt Margaret had insisted that birthday gifts were unecessary, but this time they were overruled. [8] You could tell that they were truely stunned when they opened the gift and found plane tickets to Dublin, Ireland, which is where they were born. [9] Mom and her sisters had chiped in to buy them a 2-week vacation. [10] Everyone had such a good time that we have already started planing for Aunt Maeve and Aunt Margaret's 61st birthday party on May fourth, 2002.

Reference Note

If there is a word that you cannot find in the list of words often confused, refer to Chapter 24 or look up the word in a dictionary.

Reference Note

For more information about using **all right,** see page 757.

┌HELP─

Notice that both *born* and *borne* are past participles of *to bear*. The definition you mean determines the spelling you should use.

Words Often Confused

all ready	[adjective] *all prepared*
	Give the signal when you are *all ready.*
already	[adverb] *previously*
	I had *already* read several articles about the customs of the Micmac people of Canada.
all right	[adjective] *satisfactory;* [adverb] *satisfactorily*
	I did *all right* on the quiz.
	[Although the spelling *alright* is in some dictionaries, it has not become standard usage.]
all together	[adverb] *in unison;* [adjective] *in the same place*
	Please sing *all together,* now.
	We were *all together* for the holidays.
altogether	[adverb] *entirely*
	Her reaction was *altogether* unexpected.
altar	[noun] *a table or stand at which religious rites are performed*
	The priest was standing beside the *altar.*
alter	[verb] *to change*
	If we are late, we will *alter* our plans.
assure	[verb] *to make certain by removing doubt or suspense; to promise*
	Did she *assure* you that the problem would be resolved by tomorrow?
ensure	[verb] *to make certain by protecting; to guarantee*
	Doesn't the First Amendment *ensure* U.S. citizens the freedom of speech?
insure	[verb] *to arrange for monetary payment in case of loss, accident, or death*
	Did you speak to an insurance agent to see what the cost to *insure* both vehicles would be?
born	[verb, past participle of *bear*] *given birth*
	Where was Zora Neale Hurston *born?*
borne	[verb, past participle of *bear*] *carried; endured*
	The people there have *borne* many hardships.

brake	[verb] *to slow down or stop;* [noun] *a device for slowing down or stopping* Remember to *brake* cautiously on wet roads. The report concluded that a defective *brake* caused the accident.
break	[verb] *to cause to come apart; to shatter;* [noun] *a fracture* Try not to *break* any dishes as you clear the table tonight. The doctor says that the X-ray shows a *break* in your left fibula.
capital	[adjective or noun; spelling used in all cases except when referring to a building in which a legislature meets] Washington, D.C., has been the *capital* of the United States since 1791. [*city*] Do you think they have enough *capital* to start their business? [*wealth*] In most states, first degree murder is a *capital* offense. [*punishable by death*] That idea is *capital.* [*of major importance*] Proofread your work to be sure that every sentence begins with a *capital* letter. [*uppercase*]
capitol	[noun] *a building in which a legislature meets* [capitalized when it refers to a building for a national legislature] The *capitol* faces a park. On our visit to Washington, D.C., we toured the *Capitol.*
choose	[verb, rhymes with *shoes*] Did you *choose* the movie for today?
chose	[verb, past tense of *choose,* rhymes with *shows*] Who *chose* the movie yesterday?
clothes	[noun] *wearing apparel* Should these *clothes* be dry-cleaned, or can I put them in the washing machine?
cloths	[noun] *pieces of fabric* Use these *cloths* to dust the furniture.

TIPS & TRICKS

To remember the spelling of *capitol,* use this sentence: The capit**o**l has a d**o**me.

MECHANICS

From the choices in parentheses, select the correct word or words for each of the following sentences.

EXAMPLE   1. He writes poetry with no (*capital, capitol*) letters.

       1. *capital*

1. Mother was (*all together, altogether*) too surprised to protest.
2. (*All right, Alright*), I'll wrap the package now.
3. What was the Supreme Court decision on (*capital, capitol*) punishment?
4. Did you (*chose, choose*) the green one?
5. We polished the car with (*cloths, clothes*).
6. They will (*altar, alter*) the building to suit tenants.
7. How have we (*born, borne*) such disrespect?
8. For how much did you (*assure, ensure, insure*) the jewels, sir?
9. If you (*brake, break*) a window, you will pay for it.
10. Are the sandwiches (*already, all ready*) prepared?

coarse	[adjective] *rough; crude* This fabric is as *coarse* as burlap.
course	[noun] *path of action; part of a meal; series of studies;* [also used after *of* to mean *naturally* or *certainly*] What *course* should I follow to find a job? Soup was the first *course*. I am taking a *course* in creative writing. Of *course*, I'll help you set the table.
complement	[noun] *something that makes whole or complete;* [verb] *to make whole or complete* The *complement* of a 50° angle is a 40° angle. [The two angles complete a 90° angle.] Her part of this job *complements* mine. [Together the parts complete the job.]
compliment	[noun] *praise; a courteous act or expression;* [verb] *to express praise or respect* Thank you for the *compliment*. The tennis coach *complimented* me on my backhand.

TIPS & TRICKS

You can remember the difference in spelling between *complement* (something that completes) and *compliment* (an expression of affection or respect) by remembering that a complement completes a sentence.

consul	[noun] *a person appointed by a government to serve its citizens in a foreign country*
	The American *consul* helped us during our visit.
council	[noun] *a group gathered to accomplish a job*
	The *council* met to vote on the proposal.
councilor	[noun] *a member of a council*
	Did each *councilor* vote in favor of the proposal?
counsel	[noun] *advice;* [verb] *to advise*
	I accepted the wise *counsel* of Ms. Ariyoshi.
	Ms. Ariyoshi had *counseled* me to take Algebra II.
counselor	[noun] *one who gives advice*
	Ms. Ariyoshi is my guidance *counselor.*
desert	[noun, pronounced des'•ert] *a dry region*
	The Sahara is the world's largest *desert.*
desert	[verb, pronounced de•sert'] *to leave or abandon*
	She would never *desert* her friends.
dessert	[noun, pronounced des•sert'] *the sweet, final course of a meal*
	For *dessert* we had strawberry yogurt.
formally	[adverb] *in a proper or dignified manner, according to strict rules*
	The Nobel Prizes are *formally* presented on December 10.
formerly	[adverb] *previously; in the past*
	Katherine Ortega was *formerly* the U.S. treasurer.
its	[possessive form of *it*] *belonging to it*
	The community is proud of *its* school system.
it's	[contraction of *it is* or *it has*]
	It's a symbol of peace.
	It's been a long time since your last visit.
later	[adjective or adverb] *more late*
	We will send the package at a *later* time.
	I will help you *later.*
latter	[adjective] *the second of two*
	When given the choice of a volleyball or a tennis racket, I chose the *latter.*

(continued)

┌─HELP─────

The adjective *latter* is often used as the opposite of *former* to indicate which of two items is being discussed. In the example to the left, *latter* means *tennis racket,* as opposed to *volleyball,* which would be the *former.*

(continued)

lead	[verb, pronounced "leed"] *to go first; to guide*
	Who will *lead* the parade?
led	[verb, past form of *lead*]
	She *led* the team to victory.
lead	[noun, pronounced "led"] *a heavy metal; graphite in a pencil*
	The alchemist truly believed that he would one day transform *lead* into gold.
	I bought new *leads* for my mechanical pencil.

Exercise 8 **Distinguishing Between Words Often Confused**

From the choices in parentheses, select the correct word for each of the following sentences.

EXAMPLE **1.** We decided to make baklava for (*desert, dessert*).

    1. dessert

1. These supplies will (*complement, compliment*) those that you already have.
2. How long will it take Art to cross the (*dessert, desert*)?
3. Why does he use such (*course, coarse*) language?
4. I do not enjoy parties conducted as (*formally, formerly*) as this one.
5. We are not sure which (*course, coarse*) to follow.
6. Are you sure (*its, it's*) not too late?
7. I worked last summer as a camp (*councilor, counselor*).
8. He spoke to both the mayor and the school superintendent, and the (*later, latter*) was more helpful.
9. Last season, Albert (*lead, led*) the team to a championship.
10. Our (*consul, counsel*) in China has returned to Washington.

loose	[adjective, rhymes with *noose*] *free; not close together; not firmly fastened*
	The *loose* chickens roamed the barnyard.
	They stumbled in the *loose* sand.
	Some of the shingles on the roof are *loose*.
lose	[verb, rhymes with *shoes*] *to suffer loss of*
	When did you *lose* your books?

MECHANICS

miner	[noun] *a worker in a mine*
	Her father is a coal *miner*.
minor	[noun] *a person under legal age;* [adjective] *less important*
	A *minor* cannot vote in local, state, or federal elections.
	They raised only *minor* objections.
moral	[adjective] *good; virtuous;* [noun] *a lesson of conduct*
	His conduct throughout the situation showed him to be a *moral* person.
	The class understood the *moral* of the story.
morale	[noun] *spirit; mental condition*
	The victory boosted the team's *morale*.
passed	[verb, past form of *pass*] *went beyond*
	The red car *passed* me at the finish line.
past	[noun] *time gone by;* [adjective] *of a former time;* [preposition] *beyond*
	To understand the present, you need to study the *past*.
	For some people, *past* events are much more interesting than present ones.
	After you drive *past* the shopping mall, turn right at the first traffic light.
peace	[noun] *calmness* (as opposed to *war* or *strife*)
	Doesn't everyone prefer *peace* to war?
piece	[noun] *a part of something*
	I fed the dog a boneless *piece* of turkey as a special treat.
personal	[adjective] *individual; private*
	The celebrity declined to answer any *personal* questions.
personnel	[noun] *a group of people employed in the same work or service*
	The *personnel* of the company ranged in age from sixteen to sixty-four.

(continued)

TIPS & TRICKS

Here is a way to remember the difference between *peace* and *piece*. You eat a p**ie**ce of p**ie.**

MECHANICS

(continued)

plain	[adjective] *not fancy; clear;* [noun] *an area of flat land*
	The tourist cabin was small and *plain* but quite comfortable.
	Our problem is *plain* to see.
	The *plain* stretched before them for miles.
plane	[noun] *a flat surface; a wood-working tool; an airplane*
	Geometry is the study of imaginary flat surfaces, or *planes.*
	The carpenter used a *plane* to smooth the edge of the board.
	Waiting for the fog to lift, the *plane* circled the airport for an hour.
principal	[noun] *the head of a school;* [adjective] *main or most important*
	Jorge's mom, Mrs. Pacheco, is the assistant *principal* at our school.
	The *principal* cause of accidents is carelessness.
principle	[noun] *a rule of conduct; a fact or a general truth*
	The plaintiff accused the defendant of having no *principles.*
	We have been studying many of the *principles* of aerodynamics.
quiet	[adjective] *still; silent*
	The library is usually *quiet,* but it wasn't today.
quite	[adverb] *completely; rather; very*
	I had *quite* forgotten her advice.
	Angela's report on the lifestyle of the Amish was *quite* interesting.

TIPS & TRICKS

Here is an easy way to remember the difference between *principal* and *principle.* The princi**pal** is your **pal.**

Exercise 9 Distinguishing Between Words Often Confused

From the choices in parentheses, select the correct word for each of the following sentences.

EXAMPLE   **1.** The jigsaw puzzle consisted of more than one thousand (*peaces, pieces*).

   1. pieces

1. All three nations signed a (*peace, piece*) treaty to end the long-standing conflict.
2. Do these printed instructions seem (*plain, plane*) to you?
3. This store's sales (*personal, personnel*) have been very helpful every time I've shopped here.
4. The (*principal, principle*) underlying solar energy is not difficult to understand.
5. If you (*loose, lose*) your concentration, you might (*loose, lose*) the tennis match.
6. What are the (*principal, principle*) parts of the verb *shrink*?
7. Mrs. Wilson insists that students remain absolutely (*quiet, quite*) during study period.
8. Does every fable have a (*moral, morale*)?
9. On my way to school every day, I always walk (*passed, past*) the bakery.
10. Now that he is officially no longer a (*miner, minor*), he can vote in the upcoming election.

stationary	[adjective] *in a fixed position*
	Is that a new *stationary* bicycle in the gym?
stationery	[noun] *writing paper*
	I received a box of *stationery* at Christmas.
than	[conjunction used for comparisons]
	Jupiter is larger *than* any other planet in our solar system.
then	[adverb] *at that time; next*
	First, make an outline; *then,* write the composition according to the outline.
their	[possessive form of *they*] *belonging to them*
	The performers made *their* own costumes.
there	[adverb] *at that place;* [expletive used to begin a sentence]
	We were *there* at two o'clock.
	There were four of us in the final round of competition.
they're	[contraction of *they are*]
	They're going with us to the jazz festival.

(continued)

Reference Note

For more about **expletives,** see page 536.

TIPS & TRICKS

Here is an easy way to remember the difference between *stationary* and *stationery.* You write a lett**er** on station**er**y.

MECHANICS

(continued)

to	[preposition; part of the infinitive form of a verb] Are you going *to* Puerto Rico this summer? My father showed me how *to* prepare sushi.
too	[adverb] *also; more than enough* Lamont is a senior, *too.* It is *too* late to go now.
two	[adjective] *totaling one plus one;* [noun] *the number between one and three* We had only *two* dollars. *Two* of my favorite singers are Whitney Houston and Sheryl Crow.
waist	[noun] *the midsection of the body* She wore a colorful obi around her *waist.*
waste	[noun] *unused material;* [verb] *to squander* Pollution can be caused by industrial *wastes.* Don't *waste* your time.
who's	[contraction of *who is* or *who has*] *Who's* in charge of the recycling program? *Who's* been using my computer?
whose	[possessive form of *who*] *belonging to whom* *Whose* castanets are these?
your	[possessive form of *you*] *belonging to you* Wasn't that *your* cue?
you're	[contraction of *you are*] *You're* a true friend.

Exercise 10 Distinguishing Between Words Often Confused

From the choices in parentheses, select the correct word for each of the following sentences.

EXAMPLE   1. (*Who's, Whose*) the captain of the team?

1. *Who's*

1. They had neglected to close (*there, their*) lockers.
2. I wanted to go to camp, (*to, two, too*).
3. Tie the rope around your (*waist, waste*).

4. The platform, we discovered, was (*stationary, stationery*).
5. No one could remember (*whose, who's*) name had been drawn first.
6. As soon as (*their, they're*) printed, we will ship the books.
7. Write your letters on business (*stationery, stationary*).
8. (*Your, You're*) lucky to have such a good job.
9. I cannot do any more (*than, then*) I have done.
10. I was surprised at (*you're, your*) attitude.

Review D **Distinguishing Between Words Often Confused**

From the choices in parentheses, select the correct word or words for each of the following sentences.

EXAMPLE 1. Which math (*coarse, course*) are you taking?

    1. *course*

1. Columbia is the (*capital, capitol*) of South Carolina.
2. Aaron, have you discussed this problem with your guidance (*councilor, counselor*)?
3. The amount of vegetation in the (*dessert, desert*) surprised us.
4. My companion (*lead, led*) me down a dark passage.
5. We were (*all ready, already*) to start before dawn.
6. Try not to (*lose, loose*) your keys.
7. Each success helps to build (*moral, morale*).
8. Members of the (*counsel, council*) are elected annually.
9. My red scarf (*complements, compliments*) my outfit.
10. The peace-keeping mission was accomplished without loss of (*personal, personnel*).
11. Do not (*altar, alter*) any part of the contract.
12. The wheels screamed as the train's engineer hit the (*brakes, breaks*).
13. She doesn't just design her own (*stationary, stationery*); she makes the paper.
14. (*Who's, Whose*) books are these on the kitchen counter?
15. I thought the word problems on this test would be hard, but (*they're, their, there*) easy.
16. Will *x* be greater (*than, then*) *y* in this equation?
17. Discuss the (*principal, principle*) historical events in Africa during the twelfth century.
18. Suddenly, four boys on skateboards zoomed (*passed, past*) us.
19. The compressor has been delivered, but (*it's, its*) installation has been delayed.
20. You may use the potter's wheel now, if (*you're, your*) interested.

Review E **Proofreading Paragraphs to Correct Misspelled Words**

Proofread the following paragraphs, correcting all of the misspelled or incorrectly used words or numerals.

EXAMPLE   [1] We spent this passed weekend in San Francisco.

1. *past*

[1] Many of the more than 100,000 Hispanics who live in San Francisco make they're homes in the Mission District. [2] They come from many different countries, of coarse, but altogether they've created one of San Francisco's most inviting areas. [3] Comprising twenty square blocks on the city's south side, the district takes it's name from the mission founded in 1771 by the Franciscan missionary Junípero Serra.

[4] The whitewashed adobe mission is formerly named Mission San Francisco de Asís, but its popularly known as Mission Dolores after the name of a nearby stream. [5] One of the few structures that survived the devastating earthquake of 1906, it's beleived to be the oldest intact building in the city. [6] Its gilded alter was among the most ornate in the twenty-one Spanish missions Fray Junípero founded in what is now California. [7] The basilica, the grander church next door too the original mission, was demolished in the 1906 earthquake but was latter rebuilt. [8] Nestled between the to buildings, a small park invites visitors to spend a quite moment resting before exploring further.

[9] Even the most unobservant visitor can't fail to notice the striking outdoor murals, like the one here, which brighten walls throughout the neighborhood; all together, their are 45 of these murals. [10] Its not surprising that quiet a few well-known Hispanic artists, including Amalia Mesa-Bains, Enrique Chagoya, and to many others to list here, launched they're careers there.

Chapter Review

A. Proofreading Sentences for Correct Spelling

Proofread the following sentences for errors in spelling or the use of numbers.

1. "Have you ever wondered what would happen," asked the philosopher, "if an irresistible force met an imovable object?"
2. The space shuttle took off at exactly nine twenty-seven A.M. on Thursday.
3. Ken and Teresa finally resolved their arguement about sports by agreeing to disagree.
4. Who was the funnyest comedian we saw on television last night—Whoopi Goldberg, Billy Crystal, or Robin Williams?
5. 400 readers wrote to the newspaper to praise its coverage of the recent flood.

B. Spelling the Plural Form of Nouns

Spell the plural form of each of the following nouns.

6. query
7. valley
8. leaf
9. spacecraft
10. toothbrush

11. quantum
12. father-in-law
13. Smith
14. *but*
15. burrito

C. Distinguishing Between Words Often Confused

In each of the following sentences, write the correct word or words in parentheses.

16. Having been (*stationary, stationery*) for quite a while, the mannequin in the shop window suddenly blinked and looked right at me.
17. Have you (*all ready, already*) picked up your graduation invitations?
18. Because of the storms, the (*plain, plane*) waited on the runway for an hour before being cleared for take-off.

19. If our company is to meet these deadlines, management will need to add (*personal, personnel*).

20. Yesterday there was an unexpected (*break, brake*) in the transmission of satellite signals.

21. Alec hopes to have enough (*capital, capitol*) to invest in his friends' auto parts business this spring.

22. (*Its, It's*) true that the Rosetta Stone was the key to understanding Egyptian hieroglyphics.

23. Coach Russell wants to know (*whose, who's*) truck is blocking the entrance to the playing field.

24. Only one (*counselor, councilor*) voted against the mass transit plan during the meeting of the city's leaders Tuesday night.

25. Mr. Davidson is the (*principal, principle*) of our school and our school's only algebra teacher.

26. I think this video is a little longer (*then, than*) the one we watched last night.

27. I think *The Hobbit* is an entertaining novel in itself, not just a (*complement, compliment*) to *The Lord of the Rings*.

28. Will the family be (*all together, altogether*) for Aunt Minnie's birthday?

29. This policy (*ensures, insures*) that your family will be taken care of in case you become seriously ill.

30. The concert last night was (*quite, quiet*) loud, don't you think?

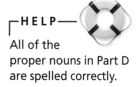

HELP

All of the proper nouns in Part D are spelled correctly.

D. Proofreading a Paragraph to Correct Misspelled Words and Errors in the Use of Numbers

Identify the spelling errors and errors in the use of numbers in the following paragraph. Then, write the correct spellings and numbers.

[31] For more than one hundred sixty years, women have been working on the railroad. [32] Women have exceled in all kinds of railroad work, from domestic service jobs to engineering and executive jobs. [33] Before radioes were used by railroads, telegraph operators were essential to railway safety. [34] Ella Campbell, a young telegraph operator at a Pennsylvania depot, prevented a collision between a westbound frieght train and an eastbound passenger train. [35] In the nineteenth century, female railroad workers usualy were telegraph operators, or

MECHANICS

"ops." [**36**] Historians beleive that Ida Hewitt of West Virginia was the first female locomotive engineer in the United States. [**37**] Before 1900, she was emploied, like her father, by the Calico Railroad. [**38**] One of the 1st women to be president of a railroad company was Sarah Clark. [**39**] Clark was nameed president of the Nevada County Narrow Gauge in 1901. [**40**] An estimated 27,000 women work for the railroads today, and many are succeding in a variety of important jobs.

Writing Application

Using Correct Spelling in an Application Letter

Spelling Words   Imagine the best job you could have. Then, write the letter of application that will get you that job. The letter should be short—no longer than two paragraphs—and should be as clear as possible. In your letter use ten words from the spelling list on page 918.

Prewriting   Start by making a list of five jobs that might interest you. Do some research in specialist publications or on the Internet on the major requirements of your dream job so that you can use professional terms authoritatively in your letter. Once you have drawn up a list of dream jobs, choose one job and freewrite about it. Write down as many details as you can to describe the job, its responsibilities, and where you see the job taking you in the future.

Writing   Use your freewriting notes to help you write the first draft of your letter. You may want to begin your letter by stating how you learned of the job opening. Then, go on to explain how your training and experience make you suited for this particular job.

Revising   Ask a classmate to play the part of a personnel officer, and read your letter to him or her. Rearrange or cut details to make the letter more effective.

Publishing   Be sure that all words are spelled correctly. Proofread your letter for any errors in grammar, usage, and mechanics. With your teacher's approval, you might suggest a contest among your classmates to determine which students get their dream jobs. Post the completed letters on the class bulletin board or Web page, and follow up with the announcement of the successful applicants.

300 Spelling Words

The following list contains three hundred words that are commonly misspelled.

abundant
academically
accelerator
accessible
accidentally
acclimated
accommodation
accompaniment
accomplishment
accuracy
acknowledge
acquaintance
adequately
admission
admittance
adolescence
advantageous
advertisement
aerial
allege
allegiance
alliance
allotting
annihilate
anonymous
apologetically
apparatus
apparent
arrangement
atheistic
atmosphere
attendance
awfully

background
ballet
bankruptcy
barbarian

beggar
beneficial
bibliography
biscuit
blasphemy
boulevard
buffet
bureaucrat
burial
business

calculation
camouflage
capable
capitalism
carburetor
caricature
catastrophe
cellar
cemetery
changeable
chassis
Christianity
circumstantial
colossal
commercial
communist
competition
complexion
conceivable
connoisseur
conscientious
consciousness
consistency
controlling
controversy
courtesy

cruelty
curriculum

deceitful
decision
definitely
descendant
desirable
despair
desperately
detrimental
devastation
devise
dilemma
diligence
disagreement
disastrous
disciple
discrimination
dissatisfied

ecstasy
efficiency
embarrassment
emperor
emphasize
endeavor
enormous
entertainment
enthusiastically
entrance
environment
especially
espionage
exercise
exhaustion
exhibition
expensive

familiarize
fascination
fascism
feminine
financier
fission
forfeit
fulfill
fundamentally

galaxy
gauge
government
grammatically
guaranteed
guidance

harassment
hereditary
hindrance
horizontal
hygiene
hypocrisy

ideally
immediate
incidentally
independent
indispensable
inevitable
inexperienced
influential
ingenious
initiative
innocent
institution
intellectual
interference
irrelevant

irresistible
irritating

kerosene

laborious
larynx
license
liquor
livelihood
luxurious

magistrate
magnificence
maintenance
malicious
manageable
maneuver
marriageable
martyrdom
materialism
meadow
mediocre
melancholy
melodious
metaphor
miniature
mischievous
misspelled
mortgage
mosquito
municipal
mysterious

naive
necessary
neurotic
noticeable
nucleus
nuisance
nutritious

obedience

occasionally
occurrence
omitting
opportunity
orchestra
outrageous

pageant
pamphlet
paralysis
parliament
pastime
peasant
pedestal
penicillin
perceive
permanent
permissible
persistent
perspiration
petition
phenomenon
physician
picnicking
playwright
pneumonia
politician
precede
presence
prestige
presumption
prevalent
privilege
probably
procedure
propaganda
prophesy
psychoanalysis
pursue

quietly

rebellion
receive
recommendation
recruit
reference
referred
refrigerator
rehearsal
relieve
reminiscent
representative
responsibility
restaurant

safety
seize
separation
sergeant
siege
significance
souvenir
specimen
sponsor
statistics
straight
strategic
stubbornness
succeed
succession
summed
superintendent
supersede
suppress
surprise
surroundings
susceptible
symbolic
symmetrical
synonymous

tariff
temperament

temperature
tendency
theoretical
tolerance
tomorrow
tortoise
traffic
tragedy
transcend
transparent
tried
twelfth
tyranny

undoubtedly
universal
unmistakable
unnatural
unnecessary
unscrupulous

vaccine
vacuum
variation
vaudeville
vegetable
vehicle
vengeance
versatile
vigilance
villain
vinegar
visage

welcome
whisper
whistle
withhold

yacht
yawn
yield

Correcting Common Errors

Key Language Skills Review

This chapter reviews key skills and concepts that pose special problems for writers.

- **Sentence Fragments and Run-on Sentences**
- **Subject-Verb and Pronoun-Antecedent Agreement**
- **Pronoun Forms and Clear Pronoun Reference**
- **Verb Forms**
- **Comparison of Modifiers**
- **Misplaced and Dangling Modifiers**
- **Standard Usage**
- **Capitalization**
- **Punctuation—End Marks, Commas, Semicolons, Colons, Quotation Marks, and Apostrophes**
- **Spelling**

Most of the exercises in this chapter follow the same format as the exercises found throughout the grammar, usage, and mechanics sections of this book. You will notice, however, that two sets of review exercises are presented in standardized test formats. These exercises are designed to provide you with practice not only in solving usage and mechanics problems but also in dealing with such problems on standardized tests.

Exercise 1 Identifying and Correcting Sentence Fragments

Reference Note

For information on correcting **sentence fragments,** see page 431.

For each of the following word groups, identify and revise each sentence fragment to make it a complete sentence. If a word group is already a complete sentence, write *C*.

EXAMPLE   **1.** Since the invention of plastic.

        1. Since the invention of plastic, technology has come a long way.

1. Frances Perkins who, in 1933, was the first woman to serve as a Cabinet member.
2. Pausing before he answered their question about his experimental method.
3. The perfect symmetry of the room imparted a certain serenity to those who entered it.
4. Within a small box that had been hidden in the chimney of the old cottage that had stood unchanged since the Civil War.
5. The boy in the striped shirt playing guitar under the oak trees on the quadrangle between the buildings.
6. Spanning a chasm this wide required a new engineering solution and new technology.
7. That first expedition to venture so far into the Arctic.
8. Her all-consuming goal to become an astronaut.
9. Surprising to no one who knew him.
10. Quechua, the ancient Incan language that is still used widely in the Andes of South America.

Exercise 2 Identifying and Revising Run-on Sentences

Reference Note

For information about correcting **run-on sentences,** see page 434.

Most of the word groups on the following page are run-on sentences. Revise each run-on sentence to make it at least one complete sentence. If a word group is already correct, write *C*.

EXAMPLE   **1.** Many varieties of fish inhabit this coral reef a number of them are vividly colored.

        1. Many varieties of fish inhabit this coral reef, and a number of them are vividly colored.

                  or

        Many varieties of fish inhabit this coral reef. A number of them are vividly colored.

┌HELP─

Although the example in Exercise 2 gives two possible answers, you need to give only one for each item.

COMMON ERRORS

1. I don't know how he does that trick I'd like to find out.
2. Cedar panels lined all four walls of the room, they had been fashioned from trees that grew right there on the property.
3. Luckily, Mr. Hawkins is a skilled metalworker, so he made another part, the line was up and running in less than two hours.
4. A cold, wicked wind blew through the dark trees, and the horses stamped nervously in the stables.
5. An accomplished actress, Ida Lupino was Hollywood's only female director for some time, she also worked as a writer and producer.
6. Take these to the supervisor he's expecting them.
7. Act Three begins with a complete reversal of fortunes notice the parallels between the two families.
8. A ridge of mountains rose before them, yet they pressed on, for winter was near.
9. The stones of the ancient fortress had been placed with extraordinary precision; the archaeologist realized that the masonry was more sophisticated than she had thought.
10. Kofi Atta Annan assumed the office of secretary general of the United Nations in 1997, prior to that time he had held many positions at the United Nations.

Reference Note

For information on correcting **sentence fragments** and **run-on sentences,** see pages 431 and 434.

Exercise 3 Identifying and Correcting Sentence Fragments and Run-on Sentences

Each numbered item below is a sentence fragment, a run-on sentence, or a complete sentence. First, identify the item by writing *F* for a sentence fragment, *R* for a run-on sentence, or *S* for a complete sentence. Then, rewrite each sentence fragment or run-on sentence to make at least one complete sentence.

EXAMPLE   1. Rice and potatoes, two food staples of the world.

    1. *F—Rice and potatoes are two food staples of the world.*

1. Enjoying a bounty harvested from the orchards on the coast.
2. Domestic canaries are usually yellow, they may be bright orange if red peppers are part of their diet.
3. One of the fastest runners and usually the winner in races.
4. Because the fertile land in the river valley had never been farmed before.
5. To go home was all Dorothy wanted.
6. The huge gears had long ago become rusty, they groaned as the blades of the windmill turned.

7. After twenty years had passed, he no longer recognized the prince.
8. An old oak grew there, it had survived being struck by lightning.
9. The Black Hills are in southwestern South Dakota, southeast of the Black Hills are the Badlands.
10. Calamity Jane, born in 1852 near Princeton, Missouri, about whom many wild stories are told.

Exercise 4 Revising Sentence Fragments and Run-on Sentences in a Paragraph

The paragraph below contains complete sentences, sentence fragments, and run-on sentences. Rewrite the paragraph to correct each sentence fragment and run-on sentence.

EXAMPLE   **[1]** Sculptors in Benin create extremely detailed statues, they use the lost-wax process of bronze casting to do so.

1. *Using the lost-wax process of bronze casting, sculptors in Benin create extremely detailed statues.*

[1] To begin the process, a sculptor forms a core figure from loamy soil and water, after the figure has dried, the sculptor coats it with beeswax. [2] Which is quite easy to shape. [3] The sculptor can then add details to the wax figure. [4] With knives and modeling tools. [5] When the design is complete, it must be sealed, the sculptor presses a smooth coating of soil all over the beeswax and then leaves the figure to dry. [6] After applying three such layers. [7] The sculptor heats the sealed figure in a hot fire, and all of the wax melts and runs out of a channel formed in the base. [8] Creating a hollow mold, which is buried upside down. [9] Next, the sculptor heats bronze until it liquefies, pouring molten bronze into the upside-down mold, the sculptor fills the hollow area left by the "lost" wax. [10] Once the mold is cool, the sculptor breaks it with a hammer, to complete the process, the sculptor cleans and polishes the finished bronze figure.

Reference Note

For information on correcting **sentence fragments** and **run-on sentences,** see pages 431 and 434.

Exercise 5 Choosing Verbs That Agree in Number with Their Subjects

Choose the verb in parentheses that correctly completes each of the sentences on the following page.

EXAMPLE   **1.** (*Has, Have*) you or your sister ever been in a play?

1. *Have*

Reference Note

For information on **subject-verb agreement,** see page 600.

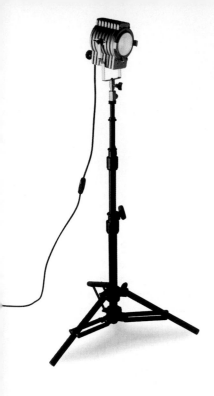

1. My friend and I (*takes, take*) English literature every semester.
2. Charles Dickens's *Great Expectations* (*is, are*) the novel that we are studying now.
3. Our class, fortunate enough to have several talented drama students, (*plans, plan*) to dramatize Dickens's novel.
4. We hope that raising funds (*don't, doesn't*) prove very difficult.
5. Do you think four dollars (*is, are*) too much for an advance ticket?
6. We're going to see whether the PTA (*has, have*) any resources available for a project like this.
7. Hawkins Lumber and Tools (*has, have*) promised to donate some building supplies.
8. One thing we've learned in producing this play is that economics (*needs, need*) to be considered carefully.
9. Even scissors (*costs, cost*) three dollars apiece, and we need six pairs.
10. All the students and adults helping to put on the show (*has, have*) been working to make the production well worth the time and resources our class and community have been investing in it.
11. The director and production consultant for the set designers (*is, are*) Teresa Gonzales, who is a senior.
12. (*Don't, Doesn't*) she have a brother with the Little Theater who might loan us some sound equipment?
13. (*There's, There are*) still openings for the stage crew.
14. All of the roles (*has, have*) been assigned, but we might be able to put you in the chorus.
15. Many of the costumes (*is, are*) just our everyday street clothes.
16. (*Here's, Here are*) the bluejeans and work shirt Pip will wear.
17. Several of the costumes (*was, were*) borrowed from our teacher.
18. Jimmy and James, who are writing the lyrics for all the songs, (*don't, doesn't*) have them finished yet.
19. Neither the actors nor the director (*knows, know*) what the audience's reaction to a twenty-first century *Great Expectations* will be.
20. The goal of every member of the team (*has, have*) two parts—happy memories and pride in a job well done.

Exercise 6 Correcting Errors in Subject-Verb Agreement

Most of the following sentences contain verbs that do not agree with their subjects. Identify each verb that does not agree with its subject, and give the correct form of the verb. If a sentence is already correct, write *C*.

Reference Note

For information on **subject-verb agreement,** see page 600.

COMMON ERRORS

EXAMPLE   1. Don't he want to go to the Renaissance Fair?

　　　　　1. *Don't—Doesn't*

1. Admission to most movie theaters now cost more than one hundred times the price of attending a nickelodeon movie theater in 1905.
2. The Schomburg collection of books and other materials about Africa and Africans are owned by the New York Public Library.
3. Pilot-training programs incorporating virtual-reality technology have recently been improved.
4. The writers and painters of the Pre-Raphaelite Brotherhood was determined to reform English art.
5. The red doors along the hallway open into classrooms.
6. A number of brightly colored fish swims among the coral and kelp.
7. Mr. Blake said that *Elemental Odes* contain many of Pablo Neruda's most eloquent poems.
8. The class president or the members of the French Club usually announces the results of the election at the assembly.
9. Each of the men know my uncle Louis.
10. There are among many cultures all over the world a great respect for the elderly.

Exercise 7 Correcting Errors in Pronoun-Antecedent Agreement

The following sentences contain errors in pronoun-antecedent agreement. If a pronoun does not agree with its antecedent, rewrite the sentence to correct the error.

EXAMPLE   1. Jim Gatacre founded the Handicapped Scuba Association (HSA), which opened their doors in 1981.

　　　　　1. *Jim Gatacre founded the Handicapped Scuba Association (HSA), which opened its doors in 1981.*

1. Currently, more than a dozen diver-certification agencies exist, and each one makes sure that their divers meet rigorous standards.
2. In addition to getting regular certification, all HSA students and instructors agree to make sure his or her dives meet HSA standards.
3. HSA has set these standards to help ensure that their members have safe and rewarding dives.
4. Everyone who becomes certified through HSA learns to plan dives according to the level of assistance that they require from team members.
5. No one, not even a Level A diver, goes on their dives alone.

─HELP─

In Exercise 7, you may need to revise the wording, especially in sentences that are awkward or misleading.

Reference Note

For information on **pronoun-antecedent agreement,** see page 618.

COMMON ERRORS

6. Additionally, Level B and Level C divers are required to take extra precautions; for example, he or she must always be part of a three-person team.
7. A Level C diver always has a trained Rescue Diver as one of their team members.
8. However, neither instructors nor students are required by law to make his or her dives in accordance with those standards.
9. Every diver must have great control over their movements.
10. Most people who have had physical therapy know how to focus his or her effort and attention; this ability can be of great importance in disorienting underwater environments.

HELP

In Exercise 8, you may need to revise the wording, especially in sentences that are awkward or misleading. Although two revisions are shown in the example, you need to give only one for each sentence.

Reference Note

For information on **pronoun-antecedent agreement,** see page 618.

Exercise 8 Correcting Errors in Pronoun-Antecedent Agreement

Most of the following sentences contain errors in pronoun-antecedent agreement. If a pronoun does not agree with its antecedent, rewrite the sentence to correct the error. If a sentence is already correct, write *C*.

EXAMPLE
1. Ellen is organizing our senior class picnic, and she needs somebody to bring their grill.

1. *Ellen is organizing our senior class picnic, and she needs somebody to bring his or her grill.*

    or

    Ellen is organizing our senior class picnic, and she needs somebody to bring a grill.

1. Nobody wanted to be left out, so they all called Ellen and volunteered to help with the preparations.
2. Everyone wants to do their part to make the class picnic a success.
3. Michael or Don has offered to spend their afternoon today planning the schedule and assigning the teams for the volleyball tournament.
4. Ellen is bringing a stereo, and each of the Mullaney girls will bring their favorite CDs.
5. All of the members of the Art Club said that he or she will help make a banner for the occasion.
6. Mr. Johnston and Miss Sidney say that he or she both can chaperon our picnic.
7. By the way, the parks commission has already given their permission.
8. If anybody wants to play music, they are welcome to bring an instrument.

9. All seven drivers will be at the school by 10:30 A.M. this Saturday to pick up their passengers.

10. I heard that anyone in the senior class can attend and bring their friends, too.

Reference Note

For information on **pronoun-antecedent agreement,** see page 618.

Exercise 9 **Correcting Errors in Pronoun-Antecedent Agreement**

Most of the following sentences contain pronouns that do not agree with their antecedents. Identify and correct each pronoun that does not agree with its antecedent. If a sentence is already correct, write *C*.

EXAMPLE   **1.** A number of students here plan to make computer animation his or her career.

        1. his or her—their

1. Be sure to review the statistics; it revealed some interesting trends.

2. After the short meeting, the staff returned to its offices.

3. Not only has the price of binoculars dropped, but technology has improved it as well.

4. You'll need to take ethics; the summer session at the community college offers them this year.

5. A jury summons is a serious obligation, and it should not be ignored.

6. Yes, I read *The Three Musketeers* years ago and remember them quite well.

7. Many a young person learns their full potential in the armed services.

8. She left the pliers downstairs; it should still be there.

9. If anyone has lost a backpack, they must go to Ms. Kasmarski's room to claim it.

10. The number of applications has risen for two years, and they may do so again this year.

Exercise 10 **Correcting Errors in the Use of Pronouns**

Most of the sentences on the following page contain errors in the use of pronoun forms. Identify and correct each error. If a sentence is already correct, write *C*.

EXAMPLE   **1.** John is going to let me know when Greg and him are planning to go hiking in Big Bend National Park.

        1. him—he

Reference Note

For information on **using pronouns correctly,** see Chapter 19.

COMMON ERRORS

1. Did he say that the guest of honor at the banquet will be seated near Ann and I?
2. Which members of the chorus, besides they, do you want to invite to the auditions?
3. In the story, the butler arrives at the worst possible moment and asks, "Pardon, Madame, are you expecting Mr. Forster? It is him at the door."
4. When large drops began to pelt Christy and I, we ran for cover.
5. Mrs. Blair gave Richard and him several fifty-cent pieces to take with them.
6. Did Scott remember to write down directions for her and I, or should we remind him?
7. Donna sent her and we postcards from Moscow.
8. Was it them who arranged the interview with her?
9. Here's a picture of she and they standing in front of the entrance to the New Orleans World's Fair.
10. Us soloists need another practice session before we have the dress rehearsal.
11. To whom should we assign the research?
12. Mr. Laughlin gave Mother and we a tour of the museum grounds and the special exhibit.
13. Didn't Fran and her do their report on the rise and fall of the Ottoman Empire?
14. Wow! Who taught Linda and she how to mix tracks?
15. Yes, my brother and me are great admirers of Isaac Stern's violin technique.
16. Will the cancellation affect yourself at all?
17. Nobody, not even those politicians on television, can give a speech better than her.
18. I suspect that, in any debate between Danielle and she, Shannon would always win.
19. Let the victory go to those whom have met the challenge.
20. No, it's not for you, old pal; I'm fixing this tuna fish and tomato sandwich for me.

Exercise 11 Revising Sentences to Correct Faulty Pronoun References

Rewrite the following sentences to correct each ambiguous, general, weak, or indefinite pronoun reference.

Reference Note

For information on **clear reference,** see Chapter 20.

EXAMPLE　　1. Kaitlin gave Lynda the photographs just before she went to lunch.

　　　　　　1. *Just before Kaitlin went to lunch, she gave Lynda the photographs.*

　　　　　　　　　　　　　or

　　　　　　Just before Lynda went to lunch, Kaitlin gave her the photographs.

1. Although the delegates discussed the issues, it didn't settle anything, and no agreement was reached.
2. Jonathan likes watching archaeological films and hopes to become one someday.
3. The singing was so loud that they were heard three blocks away.
4. In this article, it describes the Genroku Era in Japan.
5. When my mom and Aunt Lil spend the afternoon baking, they usually let us have some.
6. Reporters mobbed the jurors until the police led them away.
7. In A.D. 900 in Europe, you usually never travelled more than ten miles from your birthplace.
8. Amber spoke with Mrs. Davison about her plans for the summer.
9. Last Saturday, we pulled weeds in the garden, but it took longer than we had planned.
10. Clowns were performing acrobatics on the median, and that slowed traffic all morning.

Exercise 12 Rewriting Sentences to Correct Faulty Pronoun References

Rewrite the following sentences to correct each ambiguous, general, weak, or indefinite pronoun reference.

EXAMPLE　　1. Good roads promote communication and trade. This was well understood by many ancient peoples.

　　　　　　1. *Many ancient peoples understood well that good roads promote communication and trade.*

　　　　　　　　　　　　　or

　　　　　　That good roads promote communication and trade was well understood by many ancient peoples.

1. In the Roman Empire, they had some 50,000 miles of road connecting the distant points of their domain.
2. Some of these roads, which once stretched from Scotland to North Africa, can still be seen, and this is a testament to the skill of the builders.

─HELP─

Although the example in Exercise 11 shows two revisions, you need to give only one for each sentence.

─HELP─

Although the example in Exercise 12 shows two revisions, you need to give only one for each item.

Reference Note

For information about **clear reference,** see Chapter 20.

COMMON ERRORS

3. As the Romans discovered, sound foundations and good drainage are critical features of a good roadway. It ensures longevity.
4. Without drainage, water collects on a road, which causes the surface to deteriorate and creates hazards for travelers.
5. The Roman roads were constructed to bear heavy chariot and cart traffic, but in the Incan civilization, they did not use such vehicles.
6. One of the most famous Incan roads ran more than 2,200 miles along the coast, while another snaked along the Andes, which tied together their far-flung empire.
7. In relays, Incan runners would cover distances of up to 1,200 miles, which sometimes took as few as five days.
8. In various civilizations, roads paved with stone slabs withstood much wear from wheeled carts and wagons, and they are still sometimes used.
9. Improperly designed roads are soon marred by puddles and ruts, and this causes travelers much inconvenience.
10. Layers of sand, gravel, and concrete used in modern road construction help make its foundation strong and stable.

Exercise 13 Using Past and Past Participle Forms of Irregular Verbs Correctly

Reference Note

For information on **using verbs correctly,** see Chapter 21.

For each of the following sentences, fill in the correct past or past participle form of the italicized verb.

EXAMPLE   1. *bind*   Libraries existed long before books were printed and _____.

1. *bound*

1. *hold*   Ancient libraries in Mesopotamia and Egypt _____ collections of inscribed clay tablets and papyrus scrolls.
2. *see*   The Alexandrians, whose library was famous, _____ the rival library at Pergamum as a threat to their prestige.
3. *forbid*   Therefore, the Alexandrians _____ the export of any papyrus to Pergamum.
4. *make*   The citizens of Pergamum substituted parchment, which they _____ from dried animal skins, for the papyrus.
5. *lose*   The world _____ a great storehouse of knowledge when the library at Alexandria was destroyed in 47 B.C.
6. *keep*   One of the greatest manuscript collections in the Americas was _____ at Maní, in what is now Mexico.

COMMON ERRORS

7. *leave*   Unfortunately, most of the manuscripts at Maní were burned; today, only three are _____.

8. *write*   Prior to the invention of the printing press, monks copied by hand what scholars had _____.

9. *strike*   Before they _____ Monte Cassino monastery by air in 1944, the Allied forces warned the monks, thereby giving them the chance to protect manuscripts at the monastery.

10. *tell*   My grandmother, who has seen the manuscripts at Monte Cassino, has _____ me that they are very ornate.

Exercise 14   Correcting Errors in the Use of Past and Past Participle Verb Forms

Identify the incorrect verb form in each of the following sentences, and then provide the correct verb form.

EXAMPLE   1. The brothers had ran all the way to the ballpark before they found out that the game had been canceled.

   1. *ran—run*

Reference Note

For information on **using verbs correctly,** see Chapter 21.

1. The snow that fell in early spring had froze the blossoms.
2. He beared his burdens with such great dignity that the emperor finally forgave him.
3. His terrier has stole a dog biscuit and has run out the door.
4. The tomb had laid undisturbed for centuries before the archaeologist found it.
5. After she won the first race, she done her best to win the next two.
6. Have they sprang the trap and caught the thief yet?
7. The goldfish they bought at the fair swum round and round in its new home.
8. I met Mr. Russell last fall when he teached math at my brother's middle school.
9. Before the sun had rose, we had already driven many miles toward Ontario.
10. Someone set on my sunglasses, which were lying on the couch.
11. The expedition had came in search of gold but found something far more valuable.
12. I don't know why, but that cat has never hurted my little brother's hamster; in fact, the two seem to be friends.
13. Alberto must have rode by that store a hundred times without noticing it.

COMMON ERRORS

14. Is that the same movie you seen in Mexico last summer?
15. Who cutted this wonderful design in the stencil?
16. His friends and he were sure they had did everything they could to help the Pakistani exchange student feel at home.
17. Have you and your opponent already finished your match and gave the results to the officials?
18. Yes, I have already took Spanish II.
19. "Aw," she answered, "it was a draw, so nobody winned."
20. Just then, a first-grader holding up a purple Easter egg yelled that she had finded one.

Reference Note

For information on **using verbs correctly,** see Chapter 21.

Exercise 15 Correcting Errors in the Use of Past and Past Participle Verb Forms

Identify the incorrect verb form in each of the following sentences, and then provide the correct form.

EXAMPLE 1. By the time the Spanish come to the desert country of the Southwest, the Navajo had already been living there for at least a hundred years.

1. come—came

1. The Navajo learned to weave from the Pueblo people, many of whom had chose to live with the Navajo in northern New Mexico.
2. The Spanish, Navajo, and Pueblo cultures influenced one another, but each one also kept its own traditions.
3. The Spanish had brung with them a breed of sheep, the churro, which thrived in the high deserts of New Mexico.
4. Woven from the wool of these sheep, the Navajo blanket was often wore as a robe.

COMMON ERRORS

5. Wide blankets, known as chief's blankets, could also be lain on the ground and used as rugs.
6. While we often think of blankets as ordinary household items, these blankets were greatly valued and sometimes costed as much as twenty horses.
7. Since the mid-1800s, the Navajo have maked weaving a major commercial enterprise.
8. The Navajo drawed on new markets for designs and soon found ways to incorporate trains, flags, and other elements into their traditional designs.
9. In the last century and a half, the market for these useful and durable blankets has growed rapidly.
10. Many Navajo blankets and rugs are buyed by art lovers, crafts-people, and others who particularly admire things that have both beauty and utility.

Exercise 16 Revising a Paragraph for Consistent and Logical Use of Tenses

Reference Note

For information on **using tenses consistently,** see page 700.

The verb tenses in the following paragraph are not used consistently and logically. Rewrite the paragraph to correct errors in the use of tense.

EXAMPLE   [1] The name *Haiti* came from the Arawak word *Ayiti,* which means "land of high mountains."

1. The name Haiti *comes from the Arawak word* Ayiti, *which means "land of high mountains."*

[1] Haiti's natural resources—ranging from mahogany forests and Caribbean coral reefs to mountain slopes where farmers grow coffee and cacao—have been remarkably diverse. [2] Today, Haiti's environment has been under serious threat. [3] Only 10 percent of Haiti's once lush forests were remaining. [4] Similarly, waters that will have been teeming with fish no longer yielded rich catches. [5] However, efforts were now underway to protect and restore Haiti's lands and waters. [6] For instance, several groups had supported the creation of a marine conservation park at Les Arcadins Bank. [7] Also, fine-mesh nets that will harvest young fish before they have reproduced had already been outlawed. [8] Fishing boats were working in deeper waters now so that fish can grow and spawn in shallow waters. [9] Schoolchildren were being taught about the value of the forests and waters. [10] These efforts and others, it is hoped, will have helped to conserve and restore Haiti's natural resources.

COMMON ERRORS

Reference Note

For information on **using verbs correctly,** see Chapter 21.

Exercise 17 Using Tenses Correctly

Each of the following sentences contains an error in the use of tenses. Rewrite the sentences to correct the errors.

EXAMPLE   1. Once the rain stopped, we had a picnic.
1. *Once the rain had stopped, we had a picnic.*

1. The project would have been more profitable if they would have consulted the experts.
2. While I sand one board, Kathy stained the other.
3. While having walked through the park, Debra saw a nest of red squirrels near the ranger station.
4. If you would have asked me, I would have helped you.
5. Even though we already have tickets, we waited in line for almost an hour just to enter the arena.
6. My mom and I just finished painting the boat when the rain started to fall.
7. Because fire ants' stings were painful, we were especially careful to avoid ant mounds when we worked in the yard yesterday.
8. Reading the novel last year, I am eagerly awaiting the film version.
9. Detectives examined the evidence left at the crime scene and decided that the butler hasn't committed the crime.
10. On the first of next month, Nelson's Deli on First Street will be open for forty years.

Exercise 18 Using Modifiers and Comparisons Correctly

Reference Note

For information on **using modifiers correctly,** see Chapter 22.

Some of the following sentences contain errors in the standard, formal use of modifiers. Revise each incorrect sentence to correct the error. If a sentence is already correct, write *C*.

EXAMPLE   1. Of the McDonald twins, Jessica is the best basketball player.
1. *Of the McDonald twins, Jessica is the better basketball player.*

1. Try to be carefuller the next time you stack dishes in the sink.
2. For almost two days, the sea had been more calmer than the captain had thought it would be.
3. Which is least expensive—the tall vase or the music box?
4. After watching the litter awhile, we chose the more playful one of the three kittens.

5. The speech you gave today was better than any I've heard this week.
6. My stepsister thinks it's real easy to put together a jigsaw puzzle.
7. Is this the most narrowest stretch of the trail?
8. Joshua usually finishes his worksheets faster than anyone in his math class.
9. We tried green lampshades, but I like the warm look of the red ones better.
10. During the dinner hour, a number of our customers prefer lighting that is less brighter.
11. Everybody knows that Scott is better than anyone at identifying bacteria.
12. Of Jorge Luis Borges, Gabriel García Márquez, and Pablo Neruda, I like Borges better.
13. Let's move more closer to the stage; I can't understand what they're saying.
14. Keep going; the cabin's just a little more farther down this road.
15. The weather forecasters said driving conditions would be more worse today, but, thank goodness, they were wrong.
16. At last, it was official—Maria was a faster runner than any other girl in town.
17. The plan sounds badly to me; do you think it will work as they hope it will?
18. Seemingly from out of nowhere floated the beautifulest flute music.
19. Which of the two do you like best—the Persian rug or the Chinese one?
20. I didn't know you could speak Italian so good.

Exercise 19 — Revising Sentences to Correct Misplaced Modifiers and Dangling Modifiers

Each of the sentences on the following page contains a misplaced or dangling modifier. Revise each sentence so that its meaning is clear and correct.

EXAMPLE

1. When training animals, firm and consistent commands should be used.

1. *When training animals, a person should use firm and consistent commands.*

or

A person who is training animals should use firm and consistent commands.

Reference Note

For information on the **correct placement of modifiers,** see Chapter 23.

HELP

Although the example in Exercise 19 shows two revisions, you need to give only one for each sentence.

1. Having seen the video before, it didn't seem very exciting.
2. We saw a flock of geese on the way to the mall in San Jose.
3. Looking down from the thirtieth story, even buses seemed small.
4. To discuss this issue adequately, several meetings have been scheduled.
5. The train sped past the van pulling twelve boxcars.
6. While recording in the studio, absolute silence is required of bystanders.
7. To assign priorities, your goals must be clear.
8. Your idea is more practical even than mine.
9. While performing a routine safety check, a leak was found in the duct.
10. Growing at a remarkable rate, the fence around the backyard was soon covered with ivy.

Exercise 20 Revising Sentences to Correct Misplaced Modifiers and Dangling Modifiers

Each of the following sentences contains a misplaced or dangling modifier. Revise each sentence so that its meaning is clear and correct.

EXAMPLE   1. There was only one glitch in this computer program that we could find.

           1. *There was only one glitch that we could find in this computer program.*

1. Mr. Smith's class watched a movie about how electricity was first used last week.
2. According to our debate schedule, your rebuttal will only be limited to three minutes.
3. Practicing for the piano recital, the out-of-tune key was very bothersome.
4. When conducting an experiment, precise notes should be kept.
5. The boom swung wildly over the crowd hanging from the crane at the top of the building.
6. Mrs. Chamberlin said on Thursday my assignment is due.
7. While pondering how to proceed, my neighbor's advice came to mind.
8. You should only dial 911 in an emergency.
9. Having studied all week, the test was easy for me.
10. The ranger told us not to feed the bears before we drove into the park.

COMMON ERRORS

Reference Note

For information about correct **placement of modifiers,** see Chapter 23.

Exercise 21 Correcting Errors in Usage

Most of the following sentences contain an error in usage. If a sentence contains an error, revise the sentence. If a sentence is already correct, write *C*.

EXAMPLE
1. Where were you at when I called?
1. *Where were you when I called?*

1. There are less ingredients in this recipe than you think there are.
2. Being as you have studied programming, could you help us install the new software?
3. I did good on the quiz because I've been paying attention in class.
4. We had ought to take a map with us.
5. Several dinosaur skeletons have been discovered besides the river near here.
6. A team of three screenwriters will adapt the novel for a three-part television miniseries.
7. Douglas is more skillful at flying model airplanes then John is.
8. No one yet knows how the World Wide Web will ultimately effect our culture.
9. Many a traveler has been fooled by the type of allusion commonly known as a mirage.
10. Few stores specialize in these kind of programs.

Reference Note
For information about **common usage errors,** see Chapter 24.

Exercise 22 Correcting Errors in Usage

Each of the following sentences contains an error in usage. Rewrite each sentence to correct the error.

EXAMPLE
1. Both French and Spanish are understood in Andorra, an European country between France and Spain.
1. *Both French and Spanish are understood in Andorra, a European country between France and Spain.*

1. I read where the settlement that became St. Paul, Minnesota, used to be known as "Pig's Eye," which was the nickname of Pierre Parrant, the settlement's founder.
2. The reason ice floats on water is because water expands and becomes less dense as it freezes.
3. Rita implied from Avi's letter that he had decided to stay somewhere in Montana for the summer.
4. Between the thirty theories, there were only three that gave credible explanations for those phenomena.

Reference Note
For information about **common usage errors,** see Chapter 24.

COMMON ERRORS

5. Lisa and myself were just wondering when the scholarship committee would begin accepting applications.
6. A number of penguins dove off of the huge chunk of floating ice.
7. Like Mr. Faust indicated, the eruption of Mount Vesuvius covered the city of Pompeii not with lava but with ashes.
8. Amy said that less people visit the gallery on Thursdays than on Fridays.
9. Neither the first or the last person in line knew when the tickets were supposed to go on sale.
10. Joey ought to of written the address on the notepad beside the phone.

Exercise 23 Correcting Errors in Usage

Each of the following sentences contains an error in usage. Identify and correct each error.

EXAMPLE   1. Has that phenomena ever been explained?

            1. *phenomena—phenomenon*

1. Then, right after both of us had lost our passports, Erin says, "I just knew this would happen."
2. Richard looked everywheres for Maria and Laura and then asked the information clerk to page them.
3. A number of trout was feeding on the minnows under the lights at the end of the pier.
4. Simone and myself will narrate the tale while Nicole and Peter present it in pantomime.
5. Be careful that you don't bust that mirror.
6. The mechanic told my brother Tim that we had ought to change the oil every three thousand miles.
7. The papers must of blown off the table.
8. If you go to the library tomorrow afternoon, will you bring these videotapes back for me?
9. The reason Jackson Street is closed to vehicles is because a parade will be passing there soon.
10. Where was the Hope diamond found at?

Exercise 24 Correcting Double Negatives and Other Errors in Usage

Rewrite the sentences on the following page, eliminating the double negatives and other errors in usage.

Reference Note

For information about **common usage errors,** see Chapter 24.

Reference Note

For information about **common usage errors,** see Chapter 24.

COMMON ERRORS

EXAMPLE   1. Megan doesn't want no more mashed potatoes.

1. *Megan doesn't want any more mashed potatoes.*

1. You can't never tell what will happen.
2. I still haven't had a chance to see none of this summer's block-buster movies yet.
3. The travelers walked a long ways to reach their destination.
4. We looked all over, but neither my books nor my papers were nowhere in the library.
5. After working outside all morning in the wind and rain, he isn't feeling good.
6. Mr. Lee hadn't hardly started class before the bell rang for a fire drill.
7. The power outage couldn't of lasted longer than a minute or so.
8. I did well on every test accept this last one.
9. Were you in the kitchen when the china teapot fell off of the counter?
10. None of the clerks remembered nothing about our order.

BORN LOSER reprinted by permission of Newspaper Enterprise Association, Inc.

Grammar and Usage Test: Section 1

DIRECTIONS   Read the paragraph below. For each numbered blank, select the word or group of words that best completes the sentence. Indicate your response by shading in the appropriate oval on your answer sheet.

EXAMPLE   Have you ever wondered __(1)__ systems for classifying fingerprints?

> **1.** **(A)** who discovered the first
> **(B)** whom discovered the first
> **(C)** who invented the first
> **(D)** whom invented the first
> **(E)** who first invented the

ANSWER   1.   Ⓐ   Ⓑ   **Ⓒ**   Ⓓ   Ⓔ

Fingerprinting __(1)__ a significant role in investigative work ever since the late nineteenth century, when Sir Francis Galton, a British anthropologist, determined that __(2)__ identical fingerprints. Building upon the research of Galton, Juan Vucetich of Argentina and Sir Edward R. Henry of Great Britain __(3)__ fingerprint classification systems during the 1890s. Fingerprints are one of the __(4)__ of identification because a person's fingerprints are unlikely to change during __(5)__ lifetime. Thus, when working to solve crimes, __(6)__ find fingerprints that identify people and place them at crime scenes. Sometimes such fingerprints are clearly visible, but other times __(7)__ cannot be seen. Most latent, or hidden, fingerprints __(8)__ detected until they have been covered with colored powder or special chemicals. Moreover, there are some types of latent fingerprints __(9)__ with a laser beam. Fingerprints, which are also used to identify victims of tragedies such as fires and plane crashes, __(10)__ to be an invaluable tool for more than a century.

---

1. **(A)** has played
   (B) played
   (C) plays
   (D) had played
   (E) will have played

2. **(A)** no two people never have
   (B) people they never have
   (C) two people don't have no
   (D) no two people don't have
   (E) no two people have

3. **(A)** introduced his
   (B) introduced their
   (C) were introducing his
   (D) had introduced their
   (E) have introduced their

4. **(A)** more useful type
   (B) usefuller types
   (C) most usefullest types
   (D) most useful types
   (E) usefullest types

5. (A) his or her
   (B) her
   (C) there
   (D) their
   (E) they're

6. (A) investigators they try and
   (B) investigators try and
   (C) investigators try to
   (D) investigators they try to
   (E) those investigators try to

7. (A) they
   (B) no fingerprints
   (C) these here fingerprints
   (D) these kind of fingerprints
   (E) those type of fingerprints

8. (A) can't hardly be
   (B) can't in no way be
   (C) can hardly be
   (D) they can't hardly be
   (E) can't scarcely be

9. (A) that only can be seen
   (B) that can be seen only
   (C) what can be seen only
   (D) only that can be seen
   (E) what can only be seen

10. (A) has proven
   (B) proves
   (C) will have proven
   (D) proved
   (E) have proven

Grammar and Usage Test: Section 2

DIRECTIONS In the following sentences, either part or all of each sentence is underlined. Using the rules of standard, formal English, choose the answer that most clearly expresses the meaning of the sentence. If there is no error, choose *A*. Indicate your response by shading in the appropriate oval on your answer sheet.

EXAMPLE **1.** Gail told Wendy that the tryout had gone so <u>well that she was sure she got</u> the part of Emily in *Our Town*.

   (A) well that she was sure she got
   (B) good that she was sure Wendy had got
   (C) well that she was sure Wendy had got
   (D) well that Wendy was sure she had got
   (E) good that Gail was sure she had got

ANSWER **1.** A B C D E

1. On the other side of <u>these here mountains lie</u> some of the richest farmland in the world.

   (A) these here mountains lie
   (B) these mountains lie
   (C) these mountains lies
   (D) these mountains lay
   (E) these mountains lays

2. The myelin sheath which surrounds nerve cells and helps to speed up nerve impulses.

    (A) The myelin sheath which surrounds nerve cells and helps to speed up nerve impulses.

    (B) The myelin sheath surrounding nerve cells, which helps to speed up nerve impulses.

    (C) The myelin sheath which surrounding nerve cells and helping to speed up nerve impulses.

    (D) The myelin sheath, which surrounds nerve cells, helps to speed up nerve impulses.

    (E) Helping speed up nerve impulses, the myelin sheath surrounding nerve cells.

3. Arnie carves soapstone beautifully; he plans to give them to his friends.

    (A) them

    (B) these

    (C) carvings

    (D) it

    (E) ones

4. Beaming proudly, a medal hung around her neck at the ceremony.

    (A) Beaming proudly, a medal hung around her neck at the ceremony.

    (B) At the ceremony, a medal hung around her neck, beaming proudly.

    (C) At the ceremony, she wore a medal around her neck beaming proudly.

    (D) Beaming proudly, she wore a medal around her neck at the ceremony.

    (E) Beaming proudly at the ceremony, a medal hung around her neck.

5. The contract between him and them is quite complex.

    (A) between him and them

    (B) between him and they

    (C) between he and them

    (D) among him and them

    (E) among he and they

6. I can't hardly believe that less people than we had predicted turned out for today's carnival.

    (A) I can't hardly believe that less people than

    (B) I can hardly believe that fewer people then

    (C) I can hardly believe that less people then

    (D) I can't hardly believe that fewer people than

    (E) I can hardly believe that fewer people than

7. In 1824, I read that a fifteen-year-old student who was blind, Louis Braille, developed a system of reading that used raised dots.

   (**A**) In 1824, I read that a fifteen-year-old student who was blind, Louis Braille, developed a system of reading that used raised dots.

   (**B**) I read in 1824 that a fifteen-year-old student who was blind, Louis Braille, developed a system of reading that used raised dots.

   (**C**) I read that in 1824 a fifteen-year-old student who was blind, Louis Braille, developed a system of reading that used raised dots.

   (**D**) I read that Louis Braille, a fifteen-year-old student who was blind in 1824, developed a system of reading that used raised dots.

   (**E**) I read that a fifteen-year-old student who was blind, Louis Braille, developed a system of reading that used raised dots in 1824.

8. In golf, a "mulligan" is when a player is given a free shot after having made a poor shot.

   (**A**) when a player is given a free shot after having made

   (**B**) where a player is given a free shot after having made

   (**C**) when a player is given a free shot after he or she has made

   (**D**) a free shot given to a player after he or she has made

   (**E**) that a player is given a free shot after having made

9. Skimming through the magazine, there were two articles I found for my report on Marcus Garvey.

   (**A**) Skimming through the magazine, there were two articles I found for my report on Marcus Garvey.

   (**B**) While skimming through the magazine, there were two articles I found for my report on Marcus Garvey.

   (**C**) Skimming through the magazine, I found two articles for my report on Marcus Garvey.

   (**D**) I found two articles for my report on Marcus Garvey skimming through the magazine.

   (**E**) Two articles for my report on Marcus Garvey were found skimming through the magazine.

10. Each of the athletes in the Olympics wore their nation's jersey.

   (**A**) Each of the athletes in the Olympics wore their

   (**B**) Each of the athletes in the Olympics wore his or her

   (**C**) Every athlete in the Olympics wore their

   (**D**) All of the athletes in the Olympics wore their

   (**E**) All of the athletes in the Olympics wore his or her

Reference Note

For information on **capitalization,** see Chapter 25.

Exercise 25 **Using Standard Capitalization**

For each of the following items, correct any errors in capitalization by changing lowercase letters to capital letters or capital letters to lowercase letters as necessary. If an item is already correct, write *C*.

EXAMPLE 1. tests in Physics, history IV, and spanish

1. *tests in physics, History IV, and Spanish*

1. business in latin America
2. the middle ages
3. a book called *Everyday life of The Aztecs*
4. on Lake Texcoco
5. the north American Free Trade Agreement
6. American broadcasting company, inc.
7. my uncle Matthew
8. Carol Williams, m.d.
9. ancient toltec peoples
10. the sinai peninsula
11. the university of Michigan
12. the organization habitat for humanity
13. dr. j. s. ramírez, jr.
14. a roman catholic church
15. East of the Jordan River
16. the Nobel Prize
17. at aunt Susan's house
18. queen Elizabeth I
19. 87 Thirty-Third street
20. a Bakery in New York city
21. the Capital theater
22. Harley-davidson motorcycles
23. Benjamin Franklin high school
24. travis county
25. my irish setter

Reference Note

For information on **using commas,** see page 827.

Exercise 26 **Correcting Errors in the Use of Commas**

For each of the following sentences, add or delete commas to correct each error in the use of commas. If a sentence is already correct, write *C*.

EXAMPLE 1. Wearing a gorilla suit Joe put aside his stage fright, and stepped into the spotlight.

1. *Wearing a gorilla suit, Joe put aside his stage fright and stepped into the spotlight.*

1. Thunder clapped lightning flashed and rain pounded the roof.
2. Lewis having read the book was especially eager to see the film adaptation.
3. The conference Mr. Cherensky will focus on technological advances in medicine.
4. Scheduled to employ some 1,200 people the factories will open in Dayton Ohio and Phoenix Arizona.
5. Copies of the videotape have been sent to Michael Tan M.D. and Cindy Lowe Ph.D.
6. Yes we still need people to play the roles of Diana, and Pan, and Apollo in next month's production.
7. Actually John Adams not Thomas Jefferson was the second president of the United States.
8. Hey, have you read about the African American leader Malcolm X?
9. Robert Penn Warren who was a poet, novelist, and essayist was the first official U.S. poet laureate.
10. That is one of the oldest most valuable paintings in the collection I believe.

Exercise 27 **Correcting Errors in the Use of Commas**

Rewrite the following sentences, adding or deleting commas as necessary.

EXAMPLE   1. "Wow" said Ms. Gage "just listen to those, African drummers!"

　　　　　　1. *"Wow," said Ms. Gage, "just listen to those African drummers!"*

1. The oldest musical instrument the drum is a percussion instrument.
2. Of the musical instruments that have come from Africa percussion instruments are probably the most common.
3. Percussion instruments those that are tapped shaken or struck, include drums bells and xylophones.
4. The banjo which was brought to this country from Africa is a modified percussion instrument.
5. Although, the banjo is generally considered a string instrument its body is actually a small drum with a tightly stretched skin on one side.
6. Maurice have you noticed that African drums have many different shapes, and sizes?
7. Drums are often shaped like cones or cylinders and some such as ceremonial drums are decorated with complex fanciful carvings.

Reference Note

For information on **using commas,** see page 827.

8. Reserved for special occasions ceremonial drums, can be quite elaborate.
9. Drums can be made from hollow logs cooking pots tin cans or even oil drums.
10. The steel drum which is a 55-gallon oil drum that has been carefully tuned to produce a full range of notes was invented on the islands of Trinidad and Tobago in the 1930s.

Exercise 28 **Correcting Sentences by Adding Semicolons and Colons**

Reference Note

For information about **semicolons and colons,** see page 850.

Rewrite the following sentences, replacing commas with semicolons and colons and adding semicolons and colons as necessary.

EXAMPLE
1. The house is in need of very few cosmetic repairs, furthermore, the foundation is sound.

1. *The house is in need of very few cosmetic repairs; furthermore, the foundation is sound.*

1. Three books sat on Ethan's desk his journal, a dictionary, and a copy of *Middlemarch A Study of Provincial Life.*
2. Leather car seats require upkeep for instance, they should be cleaned regularly and kept out of direct sunlight.
3. The prizes are as follows first prize, $500, second prize, $200, and third prize, $100.
4. This setback doesn't mean that the project is over, on the contrary, we'll be reorganizing it and redoubling our efforts.
5. Here are our next reading assignments pages 51–67, pages 110–130, and pages 185–200.
6. Baby-sitting can be profitable and enjoyable, however, it entails a great deal of responsibility.
7. The following students should report to the front office Kyle Werner, Brian Weber, and Amanda Lawrence.
8. The unconscious mind is said to contain all the forgotten experiences of a person's lifetime psychologists are seeking ways to tap that knowledge.
9. Performances will be given in several major cities, Atlanta, Georgia, Orlando, Florida, San Francisco, California, and Seattle, Washington.
10. One of Shakespeare's best-known soliloquies includes these three lines, "Tomorrow, and tomorrow, and tomorrow / Creeps in this petty pace from day to day, / To the last syllable of recorded time."

Proofreading a Dialogue for Correct Punctuation and Capitalization

Rewrite the following dialogue, adding or deleting paragraph indents, commas, end marks, and quotation marks where necessary. You may also need to replace some lowercase letters with capital letters.

EXAMPLE   **[1]** Hey, Annie, look at this sari my aunt brought me from India" Irene said.

      1.   *"Hey, Annie, look at this sari my aunt brought me from India," Irene said.*

Reference Note

For information on **quotation marks,** see page 859.

[**1**] "Wow, how do you put it on? Annie asked." [**2**] "You just wrap it around yourself and put the end over your shoulder," Irene answered.

[**3**] "It's beautiful! Annie declared. What was your aunt doing in India"?

[**4**] "She's a professor, and she's studying ancient Hindu texts and manuscripts." "She translated some of her favorite passages and wrote them in a little book for me".

[**5**] Annie said, "Oh, how nice of her! [**6**] "Yes, it was Irene replied "she also brought back a number of other interesting things—earrings, wooden carvings, clothes, and recipes." [**7**] "I'd love to see them." Annie remarked.

[**8**] Sure, Irene said, tonight she's going to teach me to cook a whole Indian dinner.

Have you ever had Indian food? [**9**] "No" Annie answered.

[**10**] "Well, stay for dinner tonight! You can help us cook and eat!

Exercise 30 **Proofreading for the Correct Use of Quotation Marks, Other Marks of Punctuation, and Capitalization**

Rewrite each of the following sentences, correcting any error in the use of quotation marks, capitalization, commas, or end marks.

EXAMPLE   1.   "Since it's sunny, she said Let's take a walk."

      1.   *"Since it's sunny," she said, "let's take a walk."*

Reference Note

For information on **using quotation marks,** see page 859. For information on **capitalization,** see Chapter 25.

1. Did the flight attendant just say, "This is the last call for passengers boarding Flight 304?"
2. "Next week's story," Ms. Sorvino said "Will be "The Ring."
3. Mr. Keith posted Christine's latest essay, Reading for Life, outside the classroom.

COMMON ERRORS

4. What are 'green bytes' in a computer file?

5. "Are you really going to write music for Robert Frost's poem "Fire and Ice"? Paul asked.

6. Didn't he say that "There will be a test this Friday"?

7. Jethro always called the swimming pool behind his house the 'cement pond.'

8. Yesterday's review called the novel "immature;" however, I think the novel is fresh and spontaneous.

9. Jonathan asked me whether I knew the lyrics to the second verse of America the Beautiful.

10. The next chapter, Healthy Teeth and Gums, details basic dental hygiene.

Exercise 31 Using Apostrophes Correctly

Rewrite the following word groups and sentences, adding or deleting an apostrophe to correct each error. If an item is already correct, write *C*.

EXAMPLE   1. a boys' trousers

         1. *a boy's trousers*

1. Angelas room
2. mices' exercise wheel
3. Our's are here, but yours' are missing.
4. anybody's suggestion
5. somebody elses turn
6. her two brothers-in-laws dogs
7. Theres the bell!
8. Susie's and Bill's haircuts
9. both gymnasts routines
10. Dont say *can't* to me!
11. Dot your *i*s so that they don't look like *l*s.
12. Its six o clock.
13. Youre right again.
14. Were ready to go!
15. Whos next on the tryout list?
16. Youd need two Ph.D.s to program these VCRs!
17. twenty-five cents worth
18. a friend of theirs'
19. Lisa and Tom's uniforms
20. The blouse is her's.

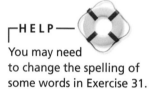

┌HELP─

You may need to change the spelling of some words in Exercise 31.

Reference Note

For information on **apostrophes,** see page 868.

21. the runner's-up prize
22. Mom's and Dad's car
23. Aren't those womens shoes on sale?
24. Greg and Paul's lab table
25. two weeks time

Exercise 32 Proofreading Sentences to Correct Misspelled Words

Reference Note

For information on **spelling,** see Chapter 28.

Rewrite the following sentences, correcting any misspelled words or incorrectly used numerals. If a sentence contains no errors, write *C*.

EXAMPLE   1. Do you have a reciept for the loafs of bread?

        1. *receipt, loaves*

1. If you are still mispelling many words, study your spelling rules more carefuly.
2. With 3 of the bookshelfs almost complete, our job was nearly finished.
3. "Julia has always exceled at math," her mother replyed.
4. How many solos will there be in tonight's recital?
5. Dishs filled with appetizeing foods of all kinds covered the banquet table.
6. The Welchs looked at several stereoes and chose the one with the bigest speakers.
7. Approximatly half of the precincts have already reported election results.
8. My uncle Bill is the editor in cheif of the local newspaper.
9. "Ladys and gentlemen," the speaker said, "we have a tie for 3rd place!"
10. Let's cook five or six potatos to serve with the sea trouts Timothy caught.
11. Companies must give satisfaction to those few disatisfied customers that they have.
12. They had made a couragous decision, but it created numerous political difficulties.
13. His opponent failed to appear and forfieted the race.
14. The soft yellow glow from the oil lamp made us look forward to expereincing another power failure.
15. Two soldeirs stood at attention beside the guard house.

16. As we watched, a family of dolphins began swiming around a school of mullet.
17. Be carful; you can easily miss the turn to State Road 13.
18. Does that expression actually mean "sieze the day"?
19. These oxen have been trained to pull a plow.
20. "I have already payed, though," insisted the moviegoer who had stepped outside to turn his car's headlights off and was now trying to return to his seat in the theater.

Reference Note

For information on **words often confused,** see page 904.

Exercise 33 **Distinguishing Between Words Often Confused**

Choose the correct word from the choices in parentheses in the following sentences.

EXAMPLE   1. Yesterday we borrowed (*their, they're*) bicycles to go to the movies.

1. *their*

1. The (*principals, principles*) of calculus are generally more difficult to master than those of algebra.
2. I have (*already, all ready*) told them that we are ready to go.
3. (*Your, You're*) performance in the play was terrific!
4. In order to obtain water, a mesquite tree in a (*desert, dessert*) may extend its roots more than 250 feet into the ground.
5. Rather (*then, than*) read a report, they're going to give a live demonstration.
6. Can you tell me (*who's, whose*) in charge of personnel?
7. Do you expect that the team will break the record for this (*coarse, course*)?
8. The scout leader carefully (*lead, led*) our troop to the top of the mountain.
9. Have you decided (*weather, whether*) you're going to the gym?
10. We must have (*past, passed*) twenty motels before we found one with a "Vacancy" sign.
11. Leave your completed application with the receptionist at the front desk in the (*personal, personnel*) office.
12. A sign above the delicate glass figurines read, "If you (*brake, break*) it, you buy it."
13. Before them stretched a great (*plane, plain*) dotted with gazelles.
14. Don't (*waist, waste*) time; our flight leaves in fifteen minutes.

15. Somehow the sash became (*loose, lose*) and, right in the middle of my big scene, the curtain dropped and almost knocked me over.

16. Would you care for a (*peace, piece*) of this mandarin orange?

17. Oh, Uncle Jim and the others are still getting (*their, there, they're*) luggage.

18. Except for the rippling of the water over the rocks, all nature was (*quiet, quite*) that summer afternoon.

19. I can't decide between the convertible and the compact, although the (*later, latter*) would cost less to maintain.

20. The hawk turned (*its, it's*) keen eyes toward the perch swimming just below the surface.

Mechanics Test: Section 1

DIRECTIONS Each of the following sentences contains an underlined group of words. Choose the answer that shows the correct capitalization, punctuation, and spelling of the underlined part. If there is no error, choose answer E (*Correct as is*). Indicate your response by shading in the appropriate oval on your answer sheet.

EXAMPLE   1. The nearest mailbox is on <u>Twenty-First Street</u>.

        (A) Twenty-first street

        (B) Twenty first Street

        (C) Twenty First Street

        (D) Twenty-first Street

        (E) Correct as is

ANSWER   1.

1. Have you ever been to my <u>brother-in-laws repair shop, Gus's Garage?</u>

    (A) brothers-in-law's repair shop, Gus's garage

    (B) brother-in-laws repair shop, Gus' Garage

    (C) brother in law's repair shop, Gus' garage

    (D) brother-in-law's repair shop, Gus's Garage

    (E) Correct as is

2. Please read the next <u>chapter *Filing Your Income Tax.*</u>

    (A) chapter, *Filing your Income Tax.*

    (B) chapter "Filing Your Income Tax."

    (C) chapter, "Filing your Income Tax."

    (D) chapter, "Filing Your Income Tax."

    (E) Correct as is

3. Volunteers should <u>bring: hammers,</u> wrenches, and screwdrivers.

    (A) bring hammers,

    (B) bring—hammers,

    (C) bring; hammers,

    (D) bring, hammers,

    (E) Correct as is

4. Mrs. Hendrix <u>said that "The Chemistry II exam will be next Wednesday."</u>

    (A) said, "The Chemistry II exam will be next wednesday."

    (B) said that the Chemistry II exam will be next Wednesday.

    (C) said that the chemistry II exam will be next Wednesday.

    (D) said that "The chemistry II exam will be next Wednesday."

    (E) Correct as is

5. "Next, we will visit the Moody Museum of Art." said Mr. Singh.

   (A) Museum Of Art,"
   (B) Museum of Art"
   (C) Museum of Art,"
   (D) Museum of Art",
   (E) Correct as is

6. "I don't want to hear any *if*'s, *and*'s, or *but*'s," my Aunt Marjorie said to my cousin and me.

   (A) *if*'s, *and*'s, or *but*'s," my aunt Marjorie
   (B) *if*'s *and*'s or *but*'s," my Aunt Marjorie
   (C) *if*s', *and*s', or *but*s'," my aunt Marjorie
   (D) *if*s, *and*s, or *but*s" my Aunt Marjorie
   (E) Correct as is

7. Honeybees live and work together, however, the majority of the world's bees are solitary.

   (A) together, however the
   (B) together; however, the
   (C) together however, the
   (D) together; however the
   (E) Correct as is

8. "Did you see," asked Tom, "the television movie Gulliver's Travels?"

   (A) movie "Gulliver's Travels"?
   (B) movie *Gulliver's Travels*?"
   (C) movie, "Gulliver's Travels,"?
   (D) movie, *Gulliver's Travels*?
   (E) Correct as is

9. The state of Michigan borders all of the Great Lakes except lake Ontario.

   (A) Great lakes except lake Ontario
   (B) great lakes except Lake Ontario
   (C) great Lakes except lake Ontario
   (D) Great Lakes except Lake Ontario
   (E) Correct as is

10. More than nine million people live in Mexico City one of the largest cities in the world.

   (A) More then 9 million people live in Mexico City, one
   (B) More than 9 million people live in Mexico city one
   (C) More than nine million people live in Mexico City, one
   (D) More then nine million people live in Mexico City, one
   (E) Correct as is

Mechanics Test: Section 2

DIRECTIONS Each numbered item below contains an underlined group of words. Choose the answer that shows the correct capitalization, punctuation, and spelling of the underlined part. If there is no error, choose answer E (*Correct as is*). Indicate your response by shading in the appropriate oval on your answer sheet.

EXAMPLE   [1] St. Paul MN, 55101

1. **(A)** St. Paul MN 55101
    (B) St. Paul, MN 55101
    (C) St. Paul Minn. 55101
    (D) St. Paul, Minnesota, 55101
    (E) Correct as is

ANSWER   1.   Ⓐ   Ⓑ   Ⓒ   Ⓓ   Ⓔ

---

[1] April 7. 2001

Ms. Luisa Gibson
Amalgamated Automation, Inc.
[2] 8723 Forty-Third Street

St. Paul, MN 55101

[3] Dear Ms. Gibson

We would like to thank you for coming to speak to our chapter of the Future Businesspeople [4] club and for sharing your guidelines on [5] principals of good business management. At our meeting the [6] week after your talk, we had a very, lively discussion about the information you had given us. It is always helpful for our group to hear from [7] someone who has already succeded in doing what we hope to accomplish. We especially appreciated your insights concerning [8] government agencies and their regulations regarding business practices. We are looking forward to seeing you again at the upcoming Small Business Association Summer Conference at [9] the Leicester hotel and, of course, would be happy to have you speak to our chapter in the future.

[10] Yours sincerely,

Alfonso Santiago

Alfonso Santiago
President, Future Businesspeople Club

COMMON ERRORS

1. **(A)** April Seventh 2001
   (B) April 7th, 2001
   (C) April, 7 2001
   (D) April 7, 2001
   (E) Correct as is

2. **(A)** 8723 Forty-third Street
   (B) 8723 Forty third Street
   (C) 8723 Forty Third Street
   (D) 8723 Fortythird Street
   (E) Correct as is

3. **(A)** Dear Ms. Gibson:
   (B) Dear Ms. Gibson,
   (C) Dear Ms Gibson:
   (D) Dear Ms Gibson,
   (E) Correct as is

4. **(A)** club and for sharing you're
   (B) Club and for sharing you're
   (C) club and for shareing your
   (D) Club and for sharing your
   (E) Correct as is

5. **(A)** principals of good business managment
   (B) principles of good business management
   (C) principals of good busyness management
   (D) principles of good business managment
   (E) Correct as is

6. **(A)** week after your talk we had a very lively
   (B) week after your talk we had a very, lively
   (C) week after your talk, we had a very lively
   (D) week after your talk, we had a very livly
   (E) Correct as is

7. **(A)** someone who has all ready suceded
   (B) someone who has all ready succeeded
   (C) someone, who has already suceded
   (D) someone who has already succeeded
   (E) Correct as is

8. **(A)** goverment agencies and they're
   (B) goverment agencys and their
   (C) government agencies and they're
   (D) government agencys and their
   (E) Correct as is

9. **(A)** The Leicester hotel and, of course
   (B) the Leicester Hotel and, of coarse,
   (C) the Leicester Hotel and, of course,
   (D) the Leicester hotel and, of coarse,
   (E) Correct as is

10. **(A)** Your's sincerely:
    (B) Yours' sincerely,
    (C) Yours sincerely:
    (D) Yours sincerly,
    (E) Correct as is

PART 4

Quick Reference Handbook

The Dictionary

Information About Words

Types of Dictionaries

A dictionary is a record of the ways in which words are used. In a dictionary, you can find the meaning and spelling of a word as well as the way the meaning changes in different contexts. Most dictionaries tell how a word should be pronounced and how it changes its spelling or meaning as it is used for different parts of speech. Some dictionaries also provide information about the history of a word and list its synonyms and antonyms. Different types of dictionaries provide various kinds of information—as well as different degrees of detail—about the words they contain. When you need information about a word, you will likely turn to one of the kinds of dictionaries listed on the next two pages.

Abridged   An *abridged,* or *college, dictionary* is the most common type of dictionary. (The word *abridged* means "shortened" or "con-

densed"; an abridged dictionary contains *most* of the words people use or encounter in writing and reading.) Abridged dictionaries offer basic information about each entry word, including spelling, parts of speech, definitions, pronunciation, and etymology or word source. Generally they also contain sections that list commonly used abbreviations, weights and measures, and rules for grammar and punctuation. One advantage of abridged dictionaries is that they are updated frequently, so they are a reliable indicator of the most current meanings of words.

Online   *Online dictionaries* are accessible on the Internet, and may be abridged, unabridged, or specialized. You can often search for a word in this type of dictionary by entering not only the word itself, but also the word's part of speech or etymology. Some online dictionaries have audio features that allow you to hear a word's pronunciation. Some sites will also offer you more than the print versions of their dictionaries; for instance, they may offer interactive word games, descriptions of how words are selected for their books, and interesting histories of how the English language has developed. You can usually find links to online dictionaries under the reference section of several search engines' subject catalogs. (See also **World Wide Web, Searching** on page 992.)

Specialized   *Specialized dictionaries* include only entries that relate to a specific subject or field. For example, you can find specialized dictionaries for terms used in science, medicine, literature, sports, or art. Some specialized dictionaries contain words and definitions not ordinarily found in general dictionaries, such as idioms and slang words.

Other specialized dictionaries contain ordinary words that have been grouped together for a particular purpose. A *thesaurus,* or *synonymy,* is one example of this kind of dictionary. Thesauri group together synonyms (words of similar meanings) and antonyms (words of opposite meanings). Thesauri do not usually arrange entries in an alphabetical order, so you will commonly find an index of words to help guide you. Other examples of specialized dictionaries include crossword puzzle dictionaries, which group together words that have the same number of letters and have the same letter combinations in the same places, and foreign language dictionaries, which contain foreign words and phrases, conjugations of irregular verbs, and rules of grammar and punctuation.

Unabridged   An *unabridged dictionary* is the most comprehensive source for finding information about a word in the English language. Unabridged dictionaries offer thousands of word entries, including words that are rarely used. The information they give about their entry words is usually more complete than the information found in abridged or specialized dictionaries. The largest unabridged English dictionary is the *Oxford English Dictionary,* or the *OED,* as it is often called. The current edition of the *OED* contains over 50,000 entries and consists of many volumes. It identifies the approximate date when a word was introduced into the English language, defines its meaning, and includes a quotation from a contemporary source to show how the word was used at that time. The *OED* also traces how a word's spelling and meaning have changed since the word first appeared in the English language. Since the *OED* focuses more attention on word histories than current meanings, it is generally not consulted for ordinary reference purposes. It is very useful, however, when a reader needs to figure out the meaning of a word in an older book.

Unlike the *OED,* other unabridged dictionaries take the form of a single, large volume. *Webster's Third New International Dictionary* is one well-known, single-volume unabridged dictionary. It is called international because it contains words from many English-speaking cultures. Most of its entries, however, are in current use in the United States. Another well-known unabridged dictionary is the *Random House Dictionary of the English Language.*

Dictionary Entry

A *dictionary entry* begins with a boldface word and then gives information about it. The entry on the following page for the word *empty* is from an abridged (college) dictionary. The parts of the entry are labeled; an explanation follows.

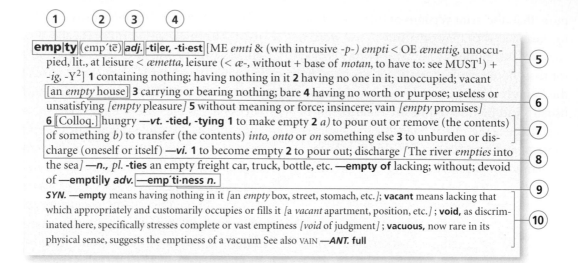

The labeled dictionary entry reads:

①②③④

emp|ty (emp′tē) *adj.* **-ti|er, -ti·est** [ME *emti* & (with intrusive *-p-*) *empti* < OE *æmettig*, unoccupied, lit., at leisure < *æmetta*, leisure (< *æ-*, without + base of *motan*, to have to: see MUST¹) + *-ig*, -Y²] **1** containing nothing; having nothing in it **2** having no one in it; unoccupied; vacant [an *empty* house] **3** carrying or bearing nothing; bare **4** having no worth or purpose; useless or unsatisfying [empty pleasure] **5** without meaning or force; insincere; vain [empty promises] **6** [Colloq.] hungry —*vt.* **-tied, -ty·ing 1** to make empty **2** *a*) to pour out or remove (the contents) of something *b*) to transfer (the contents) *into, onto* or *on* something else **3** to unburden or discharge (oneself or itself) —*vi.* **1** to become empty **2** to pour out; discharge [The river *empties* into the sea] —*n., pl.* **-ties** an empty freight car, truck, bottle, etc. —**empty of** lacking; without; devoid of —**empti|ly** *adv.* —**emp′ti·ness** *n.*

SYN. —**empty** means having nothing in it [an *empty* box, street, stomach, etc.]; **vacant** means lacking that which appropriately and customarily occupies or fills it [a *vacant* apartment, position, etc.]; **void,** as discriminated here, specifically stresses complete or vast emptiness [*void* of judgment]; **vacuous,** now rare in its physical sense, suggests the emptiness of a vacuum See also VAIN —**ANT. full**

⑤⑥⑦⑧⑨⑩

1. **Entry word.** The boldface entry word shows how the word is spelled and divided into syllables. The entry word may also show the word's capitalization and most common alternate spellings.

2. **Pronunciation.** A word's pronunciation is shown by diacritical marks and phonetic respellings. (A pronunciation key, often found in the inside front cover, explains the sounds represented by these symbols.) Accent marks indicate which syllables receive greater stress.

3. **Part-of-speech labels.** These labels (usually abbreviated) show how the entry word is to be used in a sentence. Because some words may be used as more than one part of speech, a part-of-speech label is given in front of each numbered (or lettered) series of definitions.

4. **Other forms.** Spellings may be shown for other forms of the word. These may include complete or partial spellings of irregular comparison forms of adjectives and adverbs, a variety of verb tenses, or plural forms of nouns.

5. **Etymology.** The *etymology* is a word's origin and history. Many word entries explain how a word (or its parts) came into English, tracing it from its earliest known form and indicating the language from which it came. If the etymology contains an asterisk (*), then the word is believed to have derived from a base word in the hypothetical Indo-European language.

6. **Examples.** Phrases or sentences may show how the word is used in context.

7. **Definitions.** If there are multiple meanings, definitions are numbered or lettered. Most dictionaries arrange definitions in the order of frequency of their current use, with the most frequent definitions appearing first. Other dictionaries, like the *OED*, arrange definitions according to their appearance in the English language, with the earliest definitions appearing first. Consult the introduction to your dictionary to see which method of organization it follows.

8. **Special usage labels.** These labels (such as *archaic, colloquial, British,* or *Law)* identify words that are used in special ways or in

QUICK REFERENCE HANDBOOK

certain fields or situations. Every dictionary will have a key for the labels it uses.

9. **Related word forms.** These forms are variations of the entry word, usually created by adding suffixes or prefixes.

10. **Synonyms and antonyms.** Synonyms or antonyms appear at the end of some word entries. In some cases synonyms will be included in the list of definitions, printed in capital letters.

Although not illustrated in the entry on the previous page, many dictionary entries give additional information specific to that entry.

■ **Homographs**   Words that are spelled alike but have different meanings usually are listed as separate entry words, often with superscript numbers (flue[1], flue[2]).

■ **Illustrations**   Pictures and diagrams help to clarify difficult concepts.

■ **Subentries**   Phrases that use the main entry word may appear as subentries underneath the main word. "Meet halfway," for example, is a subentry of the word *halfway.*

Other Parts of a Dictionary

You will also find the following parts in most dictionaries:

■ **Abbreviations**   Many dictionaries include a chart of common *abbreviations,* including those for government agencies, weights, measurements, and the names of states or geographical regions.

■ **Biographical and Geographical Entries** Many dictionaries include a special section of entries for famous people, including writers, politicians, scientists, inventors, and explorers. (In other dictionaries, these entries are alphabetized along with word entries.) The entries briefly identify the person's profession, coun-

try of origin, and birth and death dates. The geographical section lists most of the major cities in the world and includes the pronunciation of the place name and the size of the population. Some may also list the individual countries' capitals and land areas.

■ **Colleges and Universities**   Some dictionaries list many of the colleges and universities in the United States; some include Canadian universities, too. An entry may tell the college's location, the date of its establishment, and the number of students enrolled at the time of publication.

■ **Copyright Date**   The *copyright date* (on the back of the title page) tells when a dictionary was published. Use the most up-to-date edition you can find to be sure that it includes new words and new meanings of old words.

■ **Guide to the Dictionary**   Most dictionaries begin with several pages that explain how the information is organized and what the abbreviations and labels mean.

■ **Index**   Some dictionaries have an *index,* which indicates where you may find the dictionary features listed here, including the pronunciation key, the pages dedicated to word entries, and the biographical and geographical entries.

■ **Pronunciation Key**   A *pronunciation key* appears at the front (inside front cover) and also often at the bottom of each page or pair of pages within the dictionary.

■ **Scholarly Essays**   The *scholarly essays* written by language experts provide information about various subjects, such as the history and growth of the English language and etymology. You may also find essays describing how a new edition differs from the previous one, and how the dictionary was researched and prepared.

Document Design

Manuscript Style

Not all documents are designed on a computer—or even need to be. Most teachers only require a neat and legible manuscript from you. The following chart provides guidelines for preparing papers on a typewriter, on a computer, or by hand. (See also **Writing** on page 1063.)

Guidelines for Submitting Papers

1. Use only one side of a sheet of paper.

2. Write in blue or black ink, or type your paper.

3. If you write by hand, do not skip lines, unless your teacher directs you to do otherwise. If you type, double-space the lines.

4. Leave one-inch margins at the top, sides, and bottom of each page.

5. Indent the first line of each paragraph (about five letter spaces).

6. Number all the pages except the first

page. Place the number in the upper right-hand corner of the page.

7. Keep all pages neat and clean. You may make a few corrections with correction fluid. If you have several errors on a page and the page is difficult to read, write out or type the page again.

8. Follow your teacher's instructions for placing your name, the date, your class, and the title of your paper. Your teacher may also request that information be placed on a separate title page. Here are samples of both formats.

Name
Course
Teacher
Date

Title

Title

Name
Course
Teacher
Date

Desktop Publishing

Page Design or Layout

Whether created with computer software or pasted up by hand, page design should always combine text (words), images, and graphics to communicate a message and to attract readers' attention. The following section explains some key concepts for designing professional-looking pages, whether you use a high-tech or low-tech approach.

Alignment   *Alignment* refers to how the lines of text are arranged on a page. A block of text may be aligned at the left, at the right, centered, or justified.

- **Left aligned**   *Left-aligned* text is set so each line begins on the left margin. It is easiest to read because your eye has been trained to jump back to the left margin at the end of each line. The quote below is left aligned.

  EXAMPLE
  A people without history is like
  the wind on the buffalo grass.
  —Sioux saying

- **Right aligned**   Text that is *right aligned* ends flush with the right margin. Since right-aligned text is not easy to read, it is usually reserved for special purposes, such as presenting pull-quotes and poetry. (*See also* **Pull-quote** on page 966.)

  EXAMPLE

  To the person who seizes
  two things,
  One always slips from his grasp.
  —Swahili proverb

- **Center aligned**   *Center-aligned,* or *centered,* text is set in the middle of the page. It is frequently seen on posters, advertisements, and invitations.

  EXAMPLE

  Please come to a
  graduation party at Milo's house
  June 15th at 7:00 P.M.
  R.S.V.P. 555-5430

- **Justified alignment**   *Justified* means that both ends of several lines of text are flush with the margin, forming a straight edge. To make sure lines are the same length, extra spaces are added between words, as necessary.

  EXAMPLE
  This above all: to thine own self be true,
  And it must follow, as the night the day,
  Thou canst not then be false to any man.
  — William Shakespeare, *Hamlet,* Act I

- **Ragged alignment**   *Ragged* means that the lines of the text do not create a straight edge on both sides. Usually the right-hand side of the text is ragged in alignment, but in some cases (like the poetry below) both sides of the text are ragged.

  EXAMPLE
  My heart leaps up when I behold
      A rainbow in the sky:
  So was it when my life began;
  So is it now I am a man; . . .
  —William Wordsworth, "My Heart Leaps Up"

Bullets   A *bullet* (·) is a symbol used to attract readers' attention to important information.

Usually bullets are used to break information into lists so it is easier to read and remember. When using bulleted lists, keep in mind the following tips.

1. Always indent your bulleted list from the body of the text.
2. Use plain bullets in formal documents. In informal writing, such as journal entries, you can use decorative symbols (for example, Δ, ◊, §, ∞, and *).
3. Make sure that the items in your list are grammatically parallel. For example, use all verb phrases or all noun phrases.

Callouts   A *callout* is a line or phrase of text that describes some aspect of a graphic image. An arrow or line usually connects the callout to the illustration. Notice how callouts identify various parts of the following illustration.

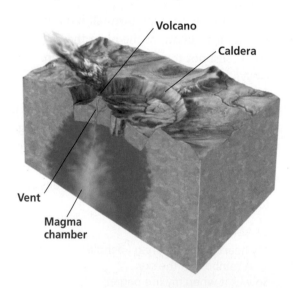

Volcano
Caldera
Vent
Magma chamber

Columns, or blocks of text   Text is printed in *columns* or *blocks*. When you create a document, you can vary the number of columns on a page and also the column width.

A newsletter or magazine, for example, may have a multicolumn (two- or sometimes three-column) format; a report is almost always single column. If a block of text does not run a whole column, it may be set off by a rule line at the bottom. The text in posters, advertisements, and fliers is usually set in short blocks, separated by white space. This enables readers to read quickly. (See also **Rule lines** on page 967.)

Contrast   *Contrast* refers to the balance of light and dark areas on a page. Dark areas contain blocks of text or graphics. Light areas have little type or graphics. A page with high contrast, or a balance of light and dark areas, is easier to read than a page with low contrast, such as one filled mostly with light areas or mostly with text and images. (See also pages 968 and 971.)

Emphasis   *Emphasis* is the way writers attract readers' attention to the most important information on a page. For example, visual cues (such as color, capital letters, boldface or italic fonts, and large type) draw readers' attention to the most important story on the front page of a newspaper. Graphics are also used to attract and direct readers' attention.

Graphics   A *graphic* is a diagram, chart, illustration, or graph that is used to convey information visually. Short sections of text that serve a visual function—such as headings, subheadings, titles, headers, and footers—may also be considered graphics. (See also **Graphics** on page 970, **Headers and footers** and **Headings and subheadings** on the next page.)

Gray page   A *gray page* contains text but few or no graphics to show how information on the page is organized. As a result, it is more difficult to read and comprehend material on a gray page than material on a page that uses some graphics. Today, many publications avoid gray pages in favor of a page layout that balances text and graphics. (See also **Contrast** on the previous page.)

Grid lines   *Grid lines* are intersecting vertical and horizontal lines that indicate margins and alignment and divide a page into sections or columns. They do not appear in a printed document; they are only visible when the document is laid out on a computer screen. (When documents are created by hand, grid lines are used to plan the appearance of a document.) Grid lines help writers and designers align similar design elements (headings, subheadings, text, indented lists, and paragraphs, for example) consistently at the same line or point on a page.

Gutters   A *gutter* is the margin of space between the printed area and the binding (or fold) of a book or document. A gutter may also refer to the space between two columns on a page.

Headers and footers   *Headers* appear in the top margin of each page; *footers* appear in the bottom margin. Use one or the other, not both. The header or footer may include the following information:

- the name of the **author**
- the name of the **publication**
- chapter or section **titles**
- the **date** of the publication
- **page numbers** (in many publications the first page is not numbered; the second page begins with *2*)

Headings and subheadings   *Headings* and *subheadings* (also called *heads* and *subheads*) are lines of text that break up a page of text and give readers information about the text's content and organization.

- **Headings**   A *heading* functions as a title or headline; it lets readers know what an article, book, or chapter is about. Headings are often set in large bold type, sometimes in all capital letters. To contrast the headings from the text, you may use a different typeface from the body of the text.

- **Subheadings**   A *subheading* links the heading and the text. It gives additional information about a particular section of the text. For contrast and emphasis, it may be set in boldface or italic type or in a different font from the rest of the text. Sometimes subheads are "run in" at the beginning of a line of text; usually they are set on a separate line.

EXAMPLE

Tornadoes: What They Are and What To Do———heading

How Tornadoes Form———subheading

Tornadoes are dark, twisting,———text
funnel-shaped clouds with
violent winds. Where they
touch down on the earth . . .

Indentation   An *indentation* is the space skipped over from the left margin to indicate the beginning of a new paragraph. The standard paragraph indentation for formal writing is one-half inch. If you are keyboarding your text on a computer, set a two-space tab for indenting every paragraph. If you are typing or writing your paper by hand, indent each paragraph five character spaces.

Line length   *Line length* is the number of characters (letters, spaces between words, and punctuation marks) a line contains. You determine line length by setting the left and right margins. Line length is measured not in inches, but in **characters** (the letters, spaces between words, and punctuation marks) in a line of text. The lines in this paragraph, for example, contain on the average forty-six (46) characters. The line length for a document necessarily varies according to the size of type: the bigger the type, the fewer characters per line. In general, limit line length to nine or ten words or about sixty-five (65) characters across a single-column, $8\frac{1}{2}" \times 11"$ document. Longer lines are difficult to read; very short lines may be annoying in a long text.

Margins   *Margins* are the space that surrounds the text on a page, whether the text is typewritten, computer processed, or handwritten. Most word-processing programs automatically set side margins at one and one-quarter inches and top and bottom margins at one inch. You can adjust these default margins to suit your purpose. If your teacher recommends a different set of measurements for margins, be sure to use them instead. (See also **White space** on page 967.)

Publishing Methods   There are two basic ways to publish a document—either on a computer or by hand. You can produce clear and creative documents using either method.

- **Computer software**   Computers have changed the way books and magazines are designed. Before computers, designers created layouts, or designs, for each page by cutting up *galleys* (long proofs of printed text); arranging blocks of text, illustrations, head-

ings, and captions on each page layout; and then carefully pasting everything down. Today all these steps can be done easily on a computer with page-making software and word-processing programs. If you have access to high-tech software and a scanner (for graphics), consult manuals or get expert advice on how to use them.

- **Cut-and-tape method**   You do not need expensive equipment to publish a creative, polished newsletter or document. Begin by typing the body of the text on a typewriter or computer, and print the text.

  - Then, make a grid (see **Grid lines** on page 965) in dark lines and tape the grid on a flat surface. For every page of text, place a blank sheet of paper over the grid; the grid lines should show through.
  - Cut out the blocks of text you've printed from your computer or typed on a typewriter, and place them in columns or blocks on the blank sheet of paper. Follow the grid lines, and tape the blocks neatly (or use rubber cement) onto the blank page.
  - Draw or photocopy graphics, cut them out, and tape them neatly in place.
  - Tape down headings and titles, using either computer type or press-on letters.
  - Photocopy each page. If the photocopy shows lines at the tape edges, use a special white-out fluid for photocopies to cover these lines. Then, photocopy the page again.

Pull-Quotes   A *pull-quote* is a brief quotation "pulled out" from a text and set in the margin to catch the reader's interest and attention. Pull-quotes should be short and concise. Often they are set in larger, bolder type than regular text and are usually boxed.

> Here am I asking why women did not write poetry in the Elizabethan age, and I am not sure how they were educated; whether they were taught to write; whether they had sitting rooms to themselves; how many women had children before they were twenty-one; what, in short, they did from eight in the morning till eight at night.
>
> *Here am I asking why women did not write poetry in the Elizabethan age . . .*
> *—Virginia Woolf*

Rule lines *Rule lines,* or *rules,* are lines used to create visual effects on a page. You can use boxes and horizontal or vertical rules to set off blocks of text. Rule lines occasionally separate text from headlines and captions—an old-fashioned look. They also may separate columns or draw the reader's eye to something on a page.

Titles and Subtitles The name of an entire book, article, or essay is called the *title.* A *subtitle* is generally longer than the title and gives more specific information about the text. Sometimes subtitles are set in a smaller typeface and attached to a title by a colon. Sometimes titles, with or without their subtitles, appear alone on the title page at the beginning of a book.

Familiar Quotations
A Collection of Passages, Phrases, and Proverbs Traced to Their Sources in Ancient and Modern Literature

Visuals Like *graphics,* *visuals* are pictures, charts, drawings, diagrams, or artwork that convey information. (See also **Graphics** on page 964 and **Types of Graphics** on page 973.)

White space *White space* is the blank area on a page—the area without any text or graphics. The margins, the *gutter* (the white space between two pages in a bound book or between columns on a page), and the spaces above and below graphics and headings provide white space. A page with a lot of white space seems open and inviting, and is much easier to read than a page crammed with text.

Typography

Typography refers to the letters and markings used in printing and publishing. When the first printing press was created over five hundred years ago, letters of movable type were cut out of wood. Fortunately, the development of computer technology has made it much easier to print letters in many different styles and sizes. The following section provides basic information about working with type.

Capital letters *Capital* (or *uppercase*) *letters* are generally used to begin a new sentence or idea. Since they draw readers' attention, capital letters can be used in several ways to create emphasis in a document.

- **Initial caps** An *initial cap* calls attention to the first word of a first paragraph in a book, chapter, article, or essay. Initial caps date back to a convention followed by monks who illuminated, or illustrated, medieval manuscripts. To attract readers' attention, they enlarged the first letter of each chapter or section and transformed it into a colorful drawing. Today initial caps are not colorful drawings but larger-than-usual letters at the beginning of a text; they often serve as visual cues that a new section or chapter is beginning. Generally, there are two kinds of initial caps: **drop caps** (shown below), which descend below the line of text, and **stickup caps,** which rise above the line of text. Some computer software packages may use only one of these terms for the command that lets you design initial caps in a variety of ways.

EXAMPLE

I t was the best of times, it was the worst of times. . . .

■ **Headings or titles**   To create contrast or emphasis without changing typeface, set headings and titles in all capital letters.

HEAT WAVE STIFLES NORTHEAST
ANOTHER CELEBRITY SEEKS PUBLIC OFFICE

■ **Small caps**   **Small caps** are uppercase letters that are reduced in size. Traditionally they are used in abbreviations of time (4:00 P.M. and A.D. 1066) or, sometimes, for the names of organizations (EEC or MADD).

NOTE   Long lines of capital letters are difficult to read. Use capital letters for contrast or emphasis, but avoid typing long sections of text in all caps.

Captions   **Captions** are lines of text that explain the meaning of a graphic and connect it to the text. They normally appear below or beside photographs and drawings. Captions should be concise, accurate, and interesting so they will attract readers to the text and give them an idea of what they should expect to read there. Captions are often set two point sizes smaller than the rest of the text or italicized in type of the same size.

Contrast   In type, **contrast** refers to the visual effect of using more than one font in a document. In most formal writing, it is stand-ard to use only two different fonts—one for the body of the text and one for headings and sub-headings. Documents designed with more than two fonts can be difficult to read.

Font   A **font** is a complete set of characters (including letters, numbers, and punctuation marks) in a particular size and design. (Usually, the term *typeface* and *font* are used interchange-ably, although those in the printing industry make a distinction between the two terms.) Computer technology has created more than ten thousand fonts, more than any single soft-ware package can include. Writers and designers choose fonts that fit the subject matter of their projects and are easy to read.

Font, Categories of   Each font has a name and a unique appearance. Fonts can be classified into three categories: *serif, sans serif,* and *decorative.*

■ **Decorative, or script**   The elaborately designed characters of **decorative** fonts often convey a distinct mood or feeling. They are used in small doses for an artistic effect, but they are too difficult to read as regular text. In script fonts, the letters touch each other, as they do in handwriting. They are frequently used in wedding invitations and graduation announcements.

EXAMPLE
Zapf Chancery, *Linoscript,* and **San Marco** are decorative fonts.

■ **Sans serif**   **Sans serif** means "without serifs, or strokes," so characters in sans serif fonts are formed by neat straight lines, with no small strokes at the ends of letters. Sans serif fonts work well as headings and subheadings, pull-quotes, and captions because they have clean edges and are fairly easy to read.

EXAMPLE

Helvetica, Franklin Gothic, and Futura are sans serif typefaces.

■ **Serif**   Letters in serif fonts have little strokes (*serifs*) attached at each end. These little strokes, modeled on the connectors between characters in handwriting, help guide the readers' eyes from letter to letter and word to word. Serif fonts were the first fonts designed for printing books, and they are still used to set long texts.

EXAMPLE

Palatino, Century Schoolbook, and Times are all serif typefaces.

NOTE   If you choose to mix fonts on a page to create contrast, be sure not to use more than one from each category. Too many fonts can confuse readers.

Font size or point size   The size of type in a document is called the *font size* or *point size*. Every font comes in many different sizes, which are determined by measuring a sample of type (a capital letter) against a scale of seventy-two points (there are seventy-two points to an inch). Type size ranges from tiny two-point type to very large seventy-two point type; in computer word-processing programs, the smallest point size is eight point. Many textbooks use twelve-point type. Captions are usually set in nine- to eleven-point type. Headings and headlines may range anywhere from eighteen to forty-eight points.

EXAMPLES

Experimenting
28 point type

Gradually we became familiar with different fonts.
9 point type

Font, Styles of   In addition to the various categories of fonts, there are also different styles. Using such styles can provide emphasis and contrast to your regular font. **Boldface** or ***boldface italic***, for example, can be used to highlight new and important concepts. *Italics* are often used to set the titles of books, plays, or poems and to make foreign words stand out in a sentence. Many elaborate styles are available on computer software, but the most common differences between font styles are between *roman* (meaning, in this case, "not slanted") and italic, or between capital letters and lowercase letters. Both roman and italic fonts are demonstrated in the following examples. (See also **Font, Categories of** on page 968.)

EXAMPLES

roman boldface	roman shadow font
roman outline font	r o m a n e x p a n d e d
roman underscored	roman lowercase letters
roman condensed	ROMAN CAPITALS
italic lowercase	*ITALIC CAPITALS*
italic boldface	

NOTE   If you decide to use different font styles in your document, be sure not to use too many. Too many changes in style can distract readers. Also, be consistent in how you use italics or boldface.

Knockout type   *Knockout,* or *reversed, type* is light type set within a dark background. It can be very hard to read, so use it sparingly. You might try using knockout type in a heading or title.

EXAMPLE

Here is type set in knockout, or reversed, type.

Leading, or line spacing   *Leading* (rhymes with *sledding*), or *line spacing,* is the white space between lines of text—a very important part of page design. Without leading, lines of type would be so close together that paragraphs would be unreadable. Most word processors and typewriters allow you to adjust the amount of line spacing to single-, double-, or even triple-space measurements. In formal documents, it is standard to use double-spacing to allow room for handwritten edits and comments. Remember also to add some leading above and below headings and subheadings. Usually, at least a line and a half of space is left above a head; a smaller amount comes below.

Legibility   *Legibility* refers to the ease with which a reader can decipher a short section of text like a headline or cross reference. Clear typefaces and simple fonts in readable sizes make a text more legible.

Lowercase   *Lowercase* type is all of the letters in a font that are not capitals. These letters are called lowercase because when type was set by hand, printers kept these letters in the lower case on the shelf—below the upper case where they kept the capital letters. Lowercase letters are characterized by *ascenders* (rising strokes, as in the letters *k* and *t*) and *descenders* (dropping strokes, as in the letters *q* and *y*). (See also **Capital letters** on page 967 and **Readability** below.)

Readability   *Readability* measures the ease with which a reader can read long sections of text. You can make your documents readable by choosing simple fonts in a clear size (at least ten points). Use white space generously to give pages high contrast, and place graphics close to the text that introduces them. (See also **Typography** on page 967 and **Font** on page 968.)

Graphics

In any document, important information may be communicated in graphics as well as in text. Graphics have several different purposes:

- to display data or information
- to explain a process
- to illustrate how something looks, works, or is organized
- to show trends or relationships over time.

As you select graphics, consider how well they support the text that appears on the page. Graphics should help readers understand the text better, not give the reader unrelated—and therefore confusing—information to absorb. (See also **Graphics** on page 964.)

Arrangement and Design

The challenge of designing a document is to place all the components—the text and graphics—in such a way that they create a sense of balance and order. Keep the following elements in mind as you incorporate graphics into a document.

Accessibility   *Accessibility* refers to the ease with which readers can find information in a document. Bulleted lists, headers, headings, footers, and subheadings all improve the accessibility of a document.

Accuracy   Readers must be able to trust that the facts shown in your graphics and visuals are *accurate,* or true. If you are reproducing a graphic from another source, do not change the images or data in any way and be sure to cite the source. If you are creating an original graphic, be sure to acknowledge the source of your information in small type right below the graphic. (For examples, see **Tables** on page 973 and **Graphs** on page 974.)

Color   Use *color* to attract the reader's attention, highlight a piece of information, indicate that certain items on a page belong together, and show the organization of the parts of a document or page.

- **Choosing color**   Keep the following tips in mind when choosing colors.
  1. **Use colors for emphasis, but sparingly for text.** Text may look nice in color, but readers may find it difficult to read. They may also have trouble comprehending and remembering it.
  2. **Use colors in pairs or schemes, if possible.** Color schemes provide contrast. A single color on a black and white page may look out of place.
  3. **Choose colors that complement each other.** Colors that appear opposite each other on the color wheel are always complementary.
  4. **Use warm colors (such as red and orange) sparingly.** These colors appear to expand or jump off the page.
  5. **Use cool colors (such as blue and green) as background.** Because of their calming effect, blue and green will not compete with your text.

- **Color wheel**   The *color wheel* is a tool that shows the relationships colors have to one another. The primary colors are yellow, red, and blue; all other colors are the result of combining these colors or mixing them with white or black. If you want to work with two colors, choose two that are directly opposite each other on the color wheel. To create a

color scheme, choose three complementary colors, one from each of the primary color families. Be sure that they are equidistant from each other on the color wheel.

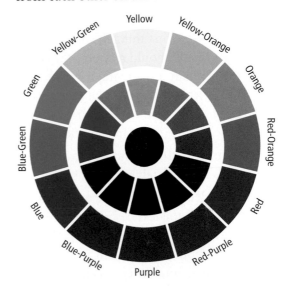

Contrast   *Contrast* is the difference, sometimes striking, between the visual elements of your document. Create contrast by using different kinds of visual cues. For example, graphics may be boxed (surrounded by thin rule lines) or separated from the text with several lines of white space. Use type for contrast, too. Set important terms in boldface type or in bulleted lists, and set chart titles in boldface or capital letters. Use color in charts, graphs, and tables so readers can easily distinguish columns or items of information. For example, in a table you could identify each row or column in a different color to make the information stand out. Contrast makes it easier for a reader to understand your graphic and remember its content. (See also **Contrast** on pages 964 and 968.)

Emphasis   Graphics provide *emphasis* on a page—in other words, they attract a reader's attention. Visual cues (such as color, capital letters, boldface or italic fonts, and large type) draw readers' attention to the most important parts of a graphic.

Focus   *Focus* refers to the center of attention in a graphic—the first thing the reader sees. The focus of a graphic should reinforce the content in the text. Usually a photograph or drawing depicts a subject as seen through the eyes of the photographer or artist. For each graphic you plan to use, ask the following questions:

- **Is the subject clear?** Choose a graphic whose subject is immediately recognizable.

- **Is the subject shown at the angle you intend?** Does the text describe the subject as enormous? tall? tiny? Be sure the graphic is drawn or photographed from an angle that reinforces the mental image created by the text.

- **Does the graphic include any distracting details?** Crop (or trim) the graphic; zoom in on the main subject and get rid of distracting details.

- **Does the graphic show all relevant parts of the subject, or are some hidden from view?** Check to see if parts of the subject are hidden. If so, choose a graphic taken from a different angle or point of view.

- **Are labels or captions needed?** Make sure they can be easily read. Remember, though, that too many labels make a graphic hard to understand. Limit yourself to about five labels. If the graphic needs more, look for a better, simpler graphic.

(For more on **point of view, angle,** and **cropping of graphics,** see pages 1051–1062.)

Font and Font size   Captions and labels for graphics should be small, around nine and a half to eleven points. They may be set in the same font as the text type, but smaller or in italics. You may also set labels and captions in a different font to create contrast. (See also **Labels and Captions** below.)

Integration   Graphics should be *integrated;* that is, they should fit well into the text. Ideally, the text refers to a graphic just before it appears, directs the reader's attention to it, and briefly identifies its content. You may choose to put some types of graphics (such as large graphs, charts, and diagrams) on a separate page following the text reference.

Labels and Captions   Many graphics need labels or captions. *Labels* identify the various parts of charts, tables, and diagrams. They may appear within the body of the graphic, or they may be treated as **callouts** and attached to the graphic by a thin rule line. *Captions* are usually sentences that describe or explain a diagram or an illustration. Most captions appear directly under the graphic, but they are sometimes placed to the right or left side. If you choose not to italicize captions, set them in a type at least two point sizes smaller than the text type. (See also **Font** on page 968, **Font Size** on page 969, **Captions** on page 968, and **Callouts** on page 964.)

Organization   *Organization* refers to the way text and graphics are positioned on a page. In general, words and images that deal with the same subject should be grouped together. To show that certain text and graphics are related, use visual clues such as headings and subheadings, similar fonts, color, and rule lines. (See also **Integration** above.)

Voice   Like words, graphics convey a writer's personal way of talking to the reader, known as *voice.* The voice of the graphics and text in a document should always reinforce one another.

Cartoons are appropriate graphics for a text with a light or humorous voice; clear, simple photographs are better for a text about a serious situation. (See also page 1083.)

Types of Graphics

Many types of graphics are useful for communicating information quickly and effectively. As you will see below, some are especially suited for particular kinds of information.

Charts   A *chart* shows relationships among ideas or data. Three types of charts you are likely to use are *flow charts*, *pie charts*, and *tables*.

■ **Flow charts**   *Flow charts* demonstrate a sequence of events or steps. They set each event or step in a box and use arrows to help readers follow the direction of movement. Flow charts are usually read left to right or top to bottom.

EXAMPLE

Total Eclipse of the Sun

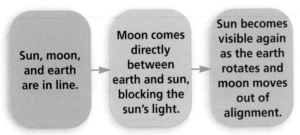

■ **Pie charts**   *Pie charts* show the relationships among parts and a whole. Like any pie, they are made up of slices, or wedges, which are arranged in a way that lets readers compare them to each other. Usually each wedge includes a label and percentage to show how it relates to the whole pie. The largest wedge

usually appears at the top of the pie, and the other wedges are arranged clockwise, in descending order according to size.

EXAMPLE

How Energy Is Used Worldwide

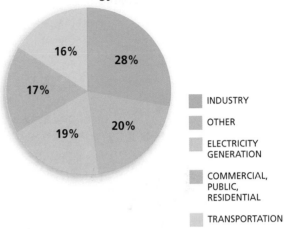

■ **Tables**   *Tables,* or simple charts, organize information in horizontal and vertical grids. The categories of information in the table are listed above and along the left-hand side of the grid. Tables need to be clearly organized so their information can be easily interpreted by the reader. (See also **Tables** on page 1004.)

EXAMPLE

Earliest Known Major Comets		
Name of comet	First recorded sighting	Orbital period (in years)
Halley's comet	240 B.C.	76
Comet Tempel-Tuttle	A.D. 1366	33
Biela's comet	1772	6.6
Encke's comet	1786	3.3
Comet Swift-Tuttle	1862	120 (approximately)

Source: *Webster's New World Encyclopedia*

Diagrams   *Diagrams* use symbols, such as circles and arrows, or pictures to give instructions, show a process, or compare abstract ideas. They tend to be simple images, showing only the important details a person needs to know in order to understand the subject.

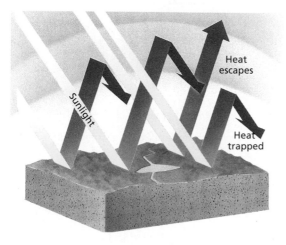

Sunlight
Heat escapes
Heat trapped

Graphs   *Graphs* present information in a way that allows readers to see the "big picture" at a glance. A graph can either show a comparison of quantities or reveal changes or trends over time. Notice that in the line and bar graphs that follow, the horizontal axis indicates time and the vertical axis indicates quantities.

EXAMPLES
Line Graph

Percentage of Population Using Cell Phones United States

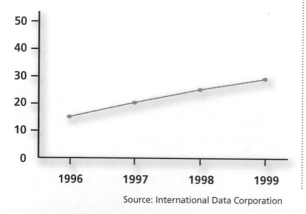

Source: International Data Corporation

Bar Graph

Wireless Phone Subscribers United States

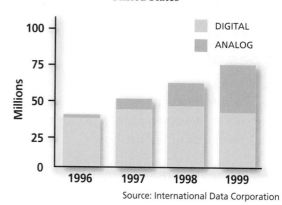

DIGITAL
ANALOG

Source: International Data Corporation

Illustrations   Photographs, drawings, and other kinds of art are *illustrations* that may show readers what something or someone looks like or how something works.

Earth's three compositional layers

Storyboards   A *storyboard* shows the sequence of events in a story. Generally, storyboards are used to map out the scenes and shots in a film or video. Note that a complete storyboard consists of two parts: drawings of scenes, which appear inside the boxes, and text that describes the scenes, which appears beneath the boxes.

Dissolve to Goldilocks entering the house. Camera dollies in, from long shot to close up, to focus on Goldilocks looking curious.

Cut to shot of three chairs, in graduated sizes. Goldilocks should be just sitting down in the smallest chair, which will break as soon as she settles in it.

Camera pans down table, left to right, showing three bowls of cereal. Slow pan reveals Goldilocks, smiling while she eats some delicious-looking cereal.

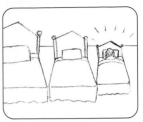

Fade in to show three beds. Camera dollies in to show Goldilocks fast asleep in the smallest bed.

Time lines   A time line shows historical events in the order they occurred. Usually, the horizontal axis, or line, of a graph shows the dates or time period, and events which correspond to these dates are identified above or below the horizontal line. Some time lines include drawings and photos above certain dates on the line.

EXAMPLE

Life of Dr. Martin Luther King, Jr.

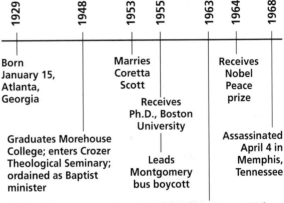

| 1929 | 1948 | 1953 | 1955 | 1963 | 1964 | 1968 |

Born January 15, Atlanta, Georgia

Marries Coretta Scott

Receives Nobel Peace prize

Receives Ph.D., Boston University

Graduates Morehouse College; enters Crozer Theological Seminary; ordained as Baptist minister

Leads Montgomery bus boycott

Assassinated April 4 in Memphis, Tennessee

Organizes August 28th civil rights march on Washington; "I Have a Dream" speech

The History of English: Origins and Uses

History of English

The first appearance of the English language in writing occurred about thirteen hundred years ago, but the language was spoken long before that. The English language of a thousand years ago is so different from the language we speak today that it is almost like a foreign tongue. There is, however, some continuity across the ages. The history of the English language may be divided into four major periods: *Pre-English, Old English, Middle English,* and *Modern English.* The following time line shows approximately when English moved from one period to the next and when other languages influenced the development of English. It also indicates how the number of English speakers has grown over the centuries.

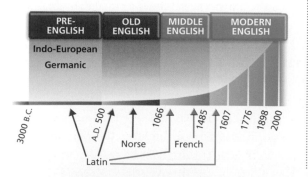

Pre-English

About five thousand years ago, migrating peoples in Asia Minor and southeast Europe spoke a language that became the ancestor of English and many other languages but of which no record exists. We call that parent language *Proto-Indo-European* because most of the languages of Europe, as well as many of those spoken in India and Iran, descended from it. (*Proto–* means "first," or "earliest.") As people migrated from their original homelands and settled in various parts of the Indo-European area, they developed their own *dialects,* or ways of speaking. One group of these migrating people, composed of three tribes—the Jutes, the Angles, and the Saxons—settled in northern Europe, along the coast of the North Sea. They spoke a version of Proto-Indo-European we call *Germanic,* from which Modern English is descended.

The *Anglo-Saxons,* as these tribes were collectively known, eventually came into contact with Latin-speaking Romans in southern Europe. From the Romans, the Anglo-Saxons adopted many words into their language. For example, the Latin words for *wine (vinum), cheese (caseus), pepper (piper), kettle (catillus),* and *sack (saccus),* among many others, made their way into the language of the Anglo-Saxons. Words, such as these, that one language borrows from another are called **loanwords.** The following chart shows the origins of some present-day English words.

Old English

History   Beginning around A.D. 450, the Angles, Saxons, and Jutes began invading Britain, taking over land that had been settled much earlier by the Celts, then colonized for centuries by the Romans. The separate dialects these tribes spoke eventually blended into one language—*Old English,* sometimes called *Anglo-Saxon.* (The words *English* and *England* come from *Englaland,* or "land of the Angles.") Later, Latin-speaking missionaries came to the island to convert the Anglo-Saxons to Christianity. Many Latin words associated with religion and other things came into English during this time. The following chart shows some of these Latin words and the changes they underwent on their way to Modern English.

Latin	Old English	Modern English
presbyter	preost	priest
apostolus	apostol	apostle
schola	scol	school

In the ninth to the eleventh centuries, Viking invaders from Scandinavia invaded Britain. Many of these Norse invaders then settled in Britain, introducing words from their language into Old English. For example, Norse provided English with such words as *give, skin, take, want,* and *window* and the pronouns *they, their,* and *them.*

Relationship to Modern English   The English spoken by the Anglo-Saxons was very different from Modern English, so different that you would not recognize it. The Anglo-Saxons used sounds that have been lost over time, as in their word *cniht,* which meant "boy" but has evolved into the Modern English word *knight.* In Old English, *cniht* had an initial hard *c* or *k* sound, which we continue to spell although we do not pronounce it.

Written English was different, too. When Anglo-Saxons wrote at all, the alphabet they used was an angular-looking system of characters called *runes.* Later, the Irish monks who first converted the Anglo–Saxons to Christianity taught them to write a rounded form of letters called *insular hand.*

Old English also differed from Modern English in that it had word endings, or **inflections,** to show the grammatical function of certain words—nouns, pronouns, adjectives, and verbs—in a sentence. The grammatical function of Old English nouns was also indicated by one of the many different forms of the definite article (*the* in Modern English) that preceded it. In Old English, the order of the words in a sentence did not mean as much as these inflections and definite articles. The following two Old English sentences illustrate the way inflections and definite articles worked. (The letter þ in the examples is an Old English letter that does not exist in Modern English. It has been replaced by *th* and is called *thorn.*) The Modern

English meanings of the sentences are given in parentheses.

Sē cyning þone guman andwyrde.
(The king answered the man.)
Þone cyning sē guma andwyrde.
(The man answered the king.)

In the first sentence, the Old English word for *the* is written as *sē* to tell us that *king (cyning)* is the subject and as *þone* to tell us that *man (guman)* is the direct object. The opposite is true of the second sentence. In the first sentence, *guman* is spelled with the *an* inflection to tell us it is the direct object. In the second, it is spelled with the *a* inflection to tell us it is the subject.

As the English language changed over the centuries, most of the inflections and the forms of the definite article were dropped. However we still have a few inflections that we use everyday in writing and speaking. For example, *s, es,* and *'s* indicate plurals and possessives, and *ed* indicates the past tense of regular verbs. Moreover, many of our most familiar, everyday words have been used by English speakers since the origin of the English language. The following chart shows the Old English and Modern English forms of several everyday words.

Old English	Modern English
finger	finger
fōt	foot
broþor	brother
hnutu	nut
hlaf (meaning "bread")	loaf
tūn (meaning "enclosed place")	town

Middle English

In 1066, the Normans, a French-speaking group of Norse who had settled earlier in France and adopted the French language, invaded and conquered England. For the next two centuries, the important languages of the country were French and Latin. The affairs of government, business, education, literature, and law were conducted in these languages rather than in English. At this time, many English words were replaced with French and Latin vocabulary. *Army, court, government, literature, mirror,* and *service* are a few French loanwords, for example. Here are some other French and Latin loanwords that entered English in the Middle English period.

French	Modern English	Latin	Modern English
cité	city	mercurius	mercury
contrée	country	scriba	scribe
juge	judge	sub poena	subpoena
libraire	library	("under penalty")	

Despite the importance of French and Latin, English, by now evolved into **Middle English,** was still the language of the common people. It did not die out under French rule, primarily because the English-speaking commoners outnumbered the French-speaking rulers. Another reason that English did not vanish was that the French-speaking rulers in England gradually lost contact with French culture and language. As a result, in the fourteenth century, English was once again recognized as the national language of England. By this time, however, it looked a great deal more like the English spoken today.

Modern English (1500–Present)

Despite the Scandinavian and Norman invasions of England, the Anglo-Saxons in England were relatively isolated and protected for nearly 1,200 years. Most of the Anglo-Saxons were illiterate. They had no need to read or write because books were not available to them.

Around 1475, however, the availability of books began to change when William Caxton published the first English book on a printing press in Belgium. Two years later, he began publishing books in England. Books, which previously had been hand copied and affordable only to the rich, became more available to the masses. This mass production of books resulted in an increase in literacy, which helped to standardize the English language and make universal education possible.

Shortly after the introduction of the printing press into England, the adventurous English began to explore the world. From the sixteenth century to the nineteenth century, English merchants, explorers, and settlers spread English to other parts of the globe. Englishmen settled in North America, first in 1607 at Jamestown, Virginia, and then thirteen years later at Plymouth, Massachusetts. Later, English settlers and traders traveled to virtually every part of the globe, including Canada, the Caribbean, India, Australia, New Zealand, and South Africa. English language and culture would permanently influence the native languages and cultures of all these places. In turn, the English travelers' interaction with other cultures brought many new loanwords into English. For example, the word *alligator* came from Spanish via Latin, *pariah* from Tamil, *caravan* from Persian, and *knapsack* from Dutch.

American English

English settlers in the North American colonies in the seventeenth and eighteenth centuries changed their language by necessity, eventually creating a new version of the language—**American English**. Separated from their homeland by an ocean and confronted by a land entirely new and different to them, the new Americans developed a variety of English clearly distinguishable from its British parent.

One of the many problems faced by English settlers in North America was to describe things and experiences never before seen or described by an English speaker. Often, they had to borrow words from the American Indians or to invent new words for new objects or situations. For example, to describe a nocturnal animal with a ringed, bushy tail and black marks around its eyes that made it look like a bandit wearing a mask, they adopted the Algonquian name for the creature, *ärähkun*, which the settlers imitated as *raccoon*.

With the signing of the Declaration of Independence in 1776 and the successful revolution that followed, the differentiation of American English from British English was greatly accelerated. The citizens of the new United States of America set about building a new nation, a new literature, and a new variety of the English language.

By the late nineteenth century, Americans began to turn their attention to other parts of the world. As the United States became an increasingly powerful influence in world affairs, the influence of American English on other varieties of English and on other languages around the world also increased. Other languages have had a corresponding effect on American English.

English: An International Language

In the contemporary world, English has three types of speakers. Most or much of the populations of the United States, Canada, the United Kingdom, Ireland, Australia, New Zealand, South Africa, Jamaica, and a number of other countries speak English as their native language.

Others use English as a second language. India, for example, has two official languages—Hindi and English—and many regional dialects, some totally unrelated to Hindi. Non-Hindi speakers often prefer English to Hindi for official business. No other language is used more as a first or second language than English.

Some people use English occasionally or for special purposes. It is the principal language of international commerce, communication, transportation, entertainment, science, technology, and scholarship all over the globe. A tour conductor in Spain speaks to a translator for a Japanese tour group in English, their only common language. The Japanese translator then speaks to the Japanese group in their own language. A Thai pilot speaks to an air traffic controller in the Netherlands in English. In total, about 500 million people use English fluently. About another 250 million use it with less fluency.

With so many people using English in so many places around the world, it is inevitable that new varieties and uses of the language will develop. Some people think that because of such new varieties, English will break up into a number of different and mutually incomprehensible languages. That is exactly what happened to Latin some 1,500 years ago when Italian, Spanish, French, Portuguese, Romanian, and other Romance languages began to develop out of local dialects of Latin.

Today, however, circumstances are different. All languages change constantly. They must in order to adapt to changes in human knowledge and society. Still, an international variety of the language is also developing. Because those who use that international variety communicate frequently with each other, it will stay relatively uniform, influencing the local varieties so that they do not turn into separate languages. What we are likely to see in the future is an international English that is pretty much the same all over the earth. Many local subvarieties of English will flourish, but they will be related to the central international variety as planets are to the sun.

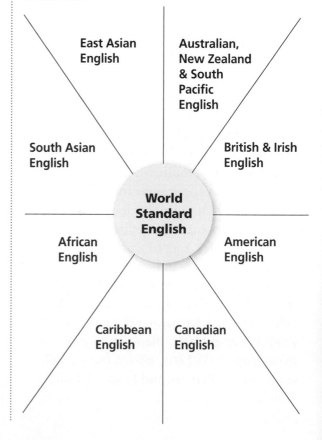

East Asian English

Australian, New Zealand & South Pacific English

South Asian English

British & Irish English

World Standard English

African English

American English

Caribbean English

Canadian English

Varieties of International English

American and British English are the two major varieties of English. Together they account for the vast majority of native English speakers. American and British English differ to some degree in pronunciation and accent. There are also differences in informal and specialized vocabulary. Because there are no significant differences in grammar, however, Americans and Britons have very little difficulty understanding each other in writing and not much difficulty in understanding each other's speech.

Here are some differences in word choices between British and American English.

British	American
beetroot	beet
biscuit	cracker or cookie
block of flats	apartment building
drawing pin	thumbtack
fiddle	swindle, cheat
hire (a car)	rent (a car)
mash	mashed potatoes
polling day	election day
rota	duty roster, work schedule
sister	nurse
toffee-nosed	snobbish, stuck-up
zip	zipper

Other varieties of international English have their own distinctive characteristics. Americans have "barbecues," but Australians have "barbies." When a New Zealander buys "kitset furniture," he or she knows that the furniture is "ready to assemble."

Varieties of American English

Dialects of American English

Like all languages, American English has many distinct versions of speech, called **dialects**. Each dialect has unique features of grammar, vocabulary, and pronunciation. Everyone uses a dialect, and these language variations can communicate much about us—our home locality, education, gender, and age, for example.

Ethnic Dialects   *Ethnic dialects* are the speech patterns of particular communities that have preserved some of their ethnic heritage. Most people who have come to the United States have brought language characteristics of their original homeland. For example, English, Dutch, Welsh, French, Spanish, Scandinavian, German, Yiddish, Polish, Czech, Italian, Greek, Armenian, Chinese, Japanese, Korean, and Vietnamese have all influenced American English.

The two most prominent ethnic dialects in the United States are the African American and Hispanic dialects. The African American dialect unites some features of West African languages, some features of early Southern United States speech, and other usages developed by speakers of the dialect themselves. Hispanic English includes Mexican-influenced English in the Southwest, Cuban-influenced English in Florida, and Puerto Rican-influenced English in New York City and Puerto Rico. Of course, not all African Americans or Hispanic Americans use the ethnic dialect associated with their groups, and some features of these dialects turn up in other speech communities, too. The boundaries of ethnic dialects, like those of regional dialects, are fluid and ever-changing.

Regional Dialects   *Regional dialects* are based on four major geographic regions shown in the map below. The dialects of these four areas translate into the following categories: **the Northern, the Midland, the Southern,** and **the Western.** (Eastern New England is labeled to indicate where colonists first introduced the language.)Remember, however, that not everyone in a region speaks the dialect of that region, just as all members of a particular ethnic group do not speak the same way.

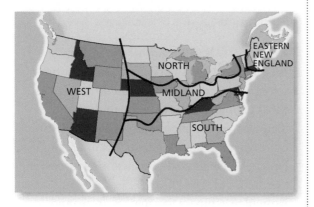

Within each of the major regions, there are also local dialects. Bostonians talk differently from New Yorkers; Charlestonians talk differently from New Orleanians. Furthermore, Northern Midland dialects often differ slightly from Southern Midland dialects, as shown in the chart at the bottom of the page. The chart shows some of the distinctive features of pronunciation, vocabulary, and grammar that distinguish a few regional dialects. (According to linguists, the Western dialect is still developing and is not yet as well-defined as other regional dialects; one clear difference is the tendency to pronounce words like *cot* and *caught* the same way.)

Standard English   *Standard English* is the most useful and the most widely used variety of English. Unlike other dialects, it is not limited to a particular place or ethnic group. Because it is commonly understood, people from many different regions and cultures can communicate with one another clearly. In the United States, standard English is usually more a matter of writing than of speech. Standard English is especially appropriate for communicating with a general audience and with anyone outside a familiar circle of family and friends. People are expected to use standard English in most school and business situations. Standard English is also the written and spoken language of public affairs and education, of publications and television, of science and technology, and of

Features of Regional Dialects				
	Northern	**Northern Midland**	**Southern Midland**	**Southern**
Pronunciation	"greassy" "hahg" "pahked cah"	"greassy" "hahg" or hog parked car	"greazy" hog parked car	"greazy" "hawg" "pawked caw"
Word Choice	burlap bag or gunnysack pail	burlap bag bucket	burlap bag bucket	burlap bag or croker sack bucket
Grammar	quarter of/to you, youse	quarter to you	quarter til you, you'uns	quarter til/to you, y'all

business and government. This textbook presents and illustrates many of the rules and guidelines for using standard English. To identify the differences between standard English and other varieties of English, this book uses the labels *standard* and *nonstandard*. *Nonstandard* does not mean "wrong" language. It means "language that is inappropriate in situations where standard English is expected."

- **Formal English,** Like formal dress and formal manners, *formal English* is for special occasions, such as writing serious papers and reports or speaking at formal occasions. The sentence structure of formal English is often longer and more complex; word choice is precise, sometimes specialized; spelling is conventional and does not include contractions; and the tone is serious and dignified.

- **Informal English** Everyday English is called *informal English.* Used for writing personal letters, journal entries, and many newspaper and magazine articles, informal English has a short and easy sentence structure and simple and ordinary word choices. Informal English often includes contractions, colloquialisms, slang, and a conversational tone.

  - *Colloquialisms* are the informal words and phrases of conversational language. If you say that the home team "bit the dust" in last night's basketball game, you are using a colloquialism. If you tell a friend that you "couldn't care less" about new fashions, you are using a colloquialism. Colloquialisms bring flavor and color to everyday speech and a friendly, conversational tone to writing. They also have a place in expressive and creative writing. Many colloquialisms are figures of speech, or idioms, that are not meant to be taken literally.

    EXAMPLES   When I told my friends where I was working, they thought I was **a couple of bricks shy of a load**.
    When the car stalled for the sixth time, I knew something was **out of whack**.

  - *Slang* is newly coined language or old words used in unconventional ways. Often a special language used by a specific group of people, such as students, musicians, or military personnel, slang is sometimes an indication of identification with a particular group. Closely related to this type of slang is *argot,* the made-up language of a secretive social group. Cockney slang, which probably originated from an argot, features words that rhyme with the words they represent. For example, *apples and pears* means "stairs" and *I suppose* means "nose."

    Some slang words have been around for centuries—for example, the slang word *lousy* dates back to the 1600s. However, most slang is short-lived. It rides a crest of popularity and then is quickly replaced.

    EXAMPLES
    chill out—relax
    bummer—disappointment
    awesome—very good
    lame—weak, pathetic
    zone out—relax

    Slang is considered highly informal and is inappropriate in most kinds of writing. However, like colloquial language, slang sometimes has a place in expressive and creative writing. In fictional dialogue, slang can make characters sound like real people.

The Library/ Media Center

Using Print and Electronic Sources

The library or media center in your school or community contains a wide variety of print and electronic sources to help you find and use information. *Print sources* include books, periodicals (newspapers, magazines, and journals), and special forms (such as microforms or vertical files). *Electronic sources* include CD-ROMs, the Internet, and online databases.

Call Number   A *call number* is the unique code of numbers or letters assigned to a book in a library. The call number reveals how a book has been classified and where it is located in the library. Libraries use either the Dewey decimal system or the Library of Congress system to classify their books. (See also *Card Catalog* on the next page.)

- **Dewey Decimal System**   The *Dewey decimal system* groups nonfiction books and

some works of literature according to ten general subject areas, such as science and history. Each general subject area is then subdivided into more specific categories. For example, the numbers 630–639 indicate the specific subject of Agriculture, which is grouped within the broader subject area of Technology and Applied Science (numbers 600–699).

- **Library of Congress System**   The *Library of Congress system* uses call numbers that begin with letters to identify subject categories. The first letter always shows the book's general category (P = Language and Literature, for example). The second letter identifies the subcategory (R = English Literature). Your library's reference desk will have a complete list of codes for Library of Congress categories.

Card Catalog   A *card catalog* is a collection of alphabetically arranged index cards that contain information about the books in a particular library. Every book has both a *title card* and an *author card*. A nonfiction book also has a *subject card,* which indexes the book by its subject. Each card contains most of the following information:

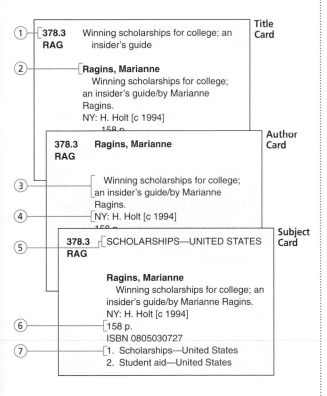

1. the **call number** assigned to the book by either the Dewey decimal or the Library of Congress classification system
2. the **author's full name**, last name first
3. the full **title** and **subtitle** of the book
4. the **place** and **date** of **publication**
5. the general **subject** of the book; a subject card shows specific headings
6. a **physical description** of the book—its size and number of pages, and whether it is illustrated

7. **cross-references** to other headings or related topics under which a book is listed

In many libraries, card catalogs no longer exist in drawers; they have been converted to electronic or online formats. (See also *Online Card Catalog* on page 986.)

CD-ROMs   A *CD-ROM* (*C*ompact *D*isk *R*ead *O*nly *M*emory) is a compact disk that holds visual as well as audio information. The data, which has been encoded digitally, can only be accessed by a computer with a CD-ROM drive. A single CD-ROM may contain more than 250,000 pages of printed text. Reference works (such as encyclopedias, dictionaries, and indexes) on CD-ROM contain the same text as the print versions but have the advantage of search capabilities, interactive graphics, and audio. (See also the **Reference Sources** chart on page 988.)

Internet   The *Internet* consists of a global network of computers. It enables users to access information from another computer or a network of computers anywhere in the world. Research scientists created the Internet in the late 1960s to share their data electronically, and today the Internet has expanded far beyond scientific data to include almost every topic. Anyone who has access to a computer with a modem (at home, at school, at work, or in a library) can use the Internet. There are many ways to view material on the Internet, including FTP (File Transfer Protocol), Gopher, and Telnet. *World Wide Web browsers* provide access to files and documents, news and discussion groups, bulletin boards, e-mail, and the *World Wide Web,* which you are most likely to use when you do research online. (See also **World Wide Web** on page 990.)

Microforms Instead of taking up space with back issues of newspapers and magazines, libraries use *microforms* to store photographically reduced newspapers and magazines. The two most common kinds of microforms are *microfilm* (a roll or reel of film) and *microfiche* (images stored on a card or sheet). Special machines enlarge the reduced pages for viewing, and some allow you to print copies of microform pages.

Online Card Catalog An *online card catalog* is an electronic or computerized version of the card catalog. The online catalog can locate information quickly and may tell you if a book you are looking for is checked out or is located at another library. To use an online catalog, type a book's *title, author,* or *subject*. You may also type *keywords* related to the title or subject. The catalog will retrieve information about one or more books to match your request. Here is an online catalog entry for a book on space.

Online
Full Record

CALL NUMBER:	629.477/Stine
AUTHOR:	Stine, G. Harry (George Harry), 1928–
TITLE:	Living in space: a handbook for work & exploration beyond the earth's atmosphere
EDITION:	1st ed.
PUBLISHER:	New York : M. Evans and Company, 1997
DESCRIPTION:	248 p. : ill.
NOTES 1:	Includes index.
SUBJECT 1:	Life support systems (Space environment)
SUBJECT 2:	Space colonization.
ISBN:	0871318415

Online Databases An *online database* is a contained system of electronic information that may be accessed only by computer. Many online databases, created by businesses or organizations, are available on a subscription-only basis and must be accessed with a private password; sometimes, however, subscription-based databases may be available for use in a library. One example is LEXIS-NEXIS, which allows you to search for topics and information in more than a million magazine and newspaper articles. In addition, many public databases, such as those of the U.S. Census Bureau (www.census.gov), are available on the World Wide Web at no charge.

Online Sources Any information that you access by using a computer comes from an *online source*. Computers that are online are equipped with modems that are able to communicate with each other over telecommunication lines, such as telephone lines and fiber-optic cables, and via satellite. When computers are linked, they form a *network,* such as the World Wide Web.

Radio, Television, and Film *Radio* and *television* provide news coverage and other kinds of information. Newscasts, newsmagazines, and documentaries are regular features of these media. Descriptive listings of radio and television programs often appear in newspapers and, in some cases, on the Internet. Documentaries and educational materials are also available on film and video. You can find indexes of educational films and videos, such as *The Video Source Book* (Gale Research, 1998), at libraries and in bookstores. Be sure to check descriptions of content and ratings when you are deciding which film or video to view. (See also **Critical Viewing** on page 1055 and **Listening** on page 1029.)

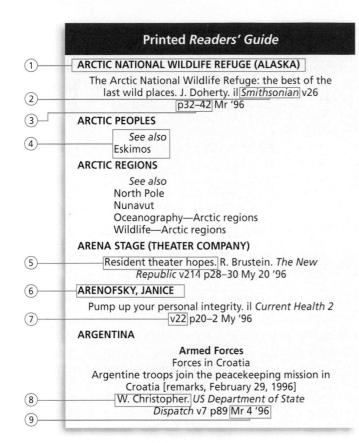

Printed *Readers' Guide*

① **ARCTIC NATIONAL WILDLIFE REFUGE (ALASKA)**
The Arctic National Wildlife Refuge: the best of the
last wild places. J. Doherty. il *Smithsonian* v26
p32–42 Mr '96
②

③ **ARCTIC PEOPLES**
See also
④ Eskimos

ARCTIC REGIONS
See also
North Pole
Nunavut
Oceanography—Arctic regions
Wildlife—Arctic regions

ARENA STAGE (THEATER COMPANY)
⑤ Resident theater hopes. R. Brustein. *The New
Republic* v214 p28–30 My 20 '96

⑥ **ARENOFSKY, JANICE**
Pump up your personal integrity. il *Current Health 2*
⑦ v22 p20–2 My '96

ARGENTINA
Armed Forces
Forces in Croatia
Argentine troops join the peacekeeping mission in
Croatia [remarks, February 29, 1996]
⑧ W. Christopher. *US Department of State
Dispatch* v7 p89 Mr 4 '96
⑨

① **Subject entry**

② **Name of periodical**

③ **Page reference**

④ **Subject cross-reference**

⑤ **Title of article**

⑥ **Author entry**

⑦ **Volume number of periodical**

⑧ **Author of article**

⑨ **Date of periodical**

Readers' Guide to Periodical Literature

The ***Readers' Guide to Periodical Literature***
indexes articles, poems, and stories from more
than two hundred magazines and journals.
Paperback editions of the Readers' Guide
appear throughout the year. Each issue covers
materials published in the previous two to four
weeks. At the end of the year, the paperback editions are bound into one hardcover volume.
The *Readers' Guide* lists articles alphabetically
by author and by subject but not by title (see
sample entry above). The *Reader's Guide* also
gives cross-references, indicated by the words
see and *see also*. A key at the front of the *Readers'
Guide* explains abbreviations used in the entries.

In some libraries, you can find an online
version of the *Readers' Guide*. To use the online
version, enter a keyword or phrase into the
computer. From the search results, choose the
records which suit your purpose. A researcher
selected the sample record below when his
search phrase—*Arctic National Wildlife
Refuge*—yielded seventy-seven articles.

Online

Readers' Guide Record

AUTHOR: Doherty, Jim
TITLE: The Arctic National Wildlife
Refuge: the best of the last
wild places
SOURCE: Smithsonian v. 26 (Mar. '96)
p. 32-41 il.
DATE: 1996
RECORD TYPE: art
CONTENTS: feature article
SUBJECT: Arctic National Wildlife
Refuge (Alaska)

Recorded Materials *Recorded materials* such as *audiocassettes* of short stories by renowned authors or *videotapes* of film versions of famous novels or plays are available in many libraries. Such materials can be useful as primary sources, or as additional research.

Reference Books *Reference books* (such as encyclopedias, dictionaries, thesauri, indexes, books of quotations, atlases, and almanacs) contain specialized information. The information is usually organized in a logical way, such as alphabetically, chronologically, or by category. In every library, you will find a separate section of reference books which cannot be checked out; this section is called the *reference section.*

Reference Sources You can use many different kinds of *reference sources* to find specific information. The chart below identifies and describes some common reference sources; it also provides both print and electronic examples.

Reference Sources		
Types of Reference Sources	Description	Examples
ALMANACS	Up-to-date information about current events, facts, statistics, and dates	• *The World Almanac and Book of Facts* • *The 20th Century Video Almanac* (CD-ROM)
ATLASES (CURRENT)	Maps and geographical information	• *Hammond Atlas of the World* • *Microsoft Encarta World Atlas* (CD-ROM)
ATLASES (HISTORICAL)	Maps and graphic representations of significant historical events and changes	• *The American Heritage Pictorial Atlas of United States History* • *Rand McNally Atlas of World History* • *Small Blue Planet: Time City Flashback Atlas* (CD-ROM)
BIOGRAPHICAL REFERENCES (GENERAL)	Information about birth, nationality, and major accomplishments of prominent people. Biographical indexes tell where to find books and periodicals with information about specific prominent people.	• *Who's Who: An Annual Biographical Dictionary* • *Dictionary of American Biography*
BIOGRAPHICAL REFERENCES (SPECIALIZED)	Information about people noted for accomplishments in a specific field or for membership in a specific group	• *Contemporary Black Biography* • *Who's Who of American Women* • *The Multimedia Encyclopedia of the American Indian* (CD-ROM)

Types of Reference Sources	Description	Examples
BOOKS OF QUOTATIONS	Famous quotations indexed or grouped together by subject	• The Oxford University Press *Dictionary of Quotations* • *Bartlett's Familiar Quotations* (CD-ROM) • Flesch's *New Book of Unusual Quotations*
BOOKS OF SYNONYMS	Lists of exact or more interesting words to express ideas	• *Roget's International Thesaurus* • *Oxford Thesaurus on CD-ROM* • *The New Roget's Thesaurus: In Dictionary Form*
CAREER GUIDES	Information about occupations in various industries, including job descriptions, projected figures for employment for specific occupations, and job-related educational requirements	• *Encyclopedia of Careers and Vocational Guidance* (CD-ROM) • *Dictionary of Occupational Titles* • *Occupational Outlook Handbook* • *Career Opportunities Series* • *Guide to Federal Jobs*
COLLEGE REFERENCE SOURCES	Detailed information on finding and applying to colleges, universities, and vocational schools	• *Barron's Profiles of American Colleges* (CD-ROM) • *College Admissions Data Handbook* • *Technical, Trade, and Business School Data Handbook*
CURRENT EVENT RESOURCES	Current information on many subjects such as business, global issues, health, and the environment	• *Social Issues Resources Series* (SIRS) (posters, databases, and volumes of articles from newspapers, magazines, and U.S. government publications)
ENCYCLOPEDIAS	Articles of general information arranged alphabetically by subject in several volumes	• *The World Book Encyclopedia* • *Compton's Interactive Encyclopedia* (CD-ROM) • *The Random House Electronic Encyclopedia*
INDEXES	Provides information as a guide to articles in periodicals and other information sources	• *The New York Times Ondisc* • Cumulative Index to *the National Geographic Magazine* • *Social Sciences Index*

(continued)

QUICK REFERENCE HANDBOOK

Reference Sources		
Types of Reference Sources	Description	Examples
LITERARY REFERENCE	Information about where to locate various works of literature; information about authors and about individual literary works, such as plot summaries and book reviews	• *Contemporary Literary Criticism* • *Gale's Literary Index* (CD-ROM) • *The Oxford Companion to American Literature* • *Dictionary of Literary Biography* • *Contemporary Authors on CD-ROM*
SPECIAL REFERENCES FOR SPECIFIC SUBJECTS	Information on specific subjects or of interest to researchers in specific fields.	• *The Encyclopedia of Religion* • *International Encyclopedia of the Social Sciences* • *Facts on File* • *The Sports Encyclopedia* • *History of Music CD-ROMs*
STYLE AND WRITING MANUALS	Information about proper writing style and preparation of research papers	• *MLA Handbook for Writers of Research Papers* • *The Chicago Manual of Style* • *Harbrace College Handbook* (CD-ROM)

Vertical File   A *vertical file* is a special file cabinet that contains folders of various up-to-date materials, such as pamphlets, newspaper clippings, and photographs. These materials are usually organized by subject or alphabetically.

World Wide Web   (*WWW* or the *Web*) The *World Wide Web* is one part of the Internet. It is a huge network of connected, or linked, documents that may contain text, graphics, visuals, sounds, and video. Each document (known as a *Web site* or *Web page*) has its own address, or *URL.* These documents are connected by *hyperlinks,* underlined or color-coded text that provides a link to another section within the document (*internal link*) or another site altogether (*external link*). While you are viewing a Web page, you can click on a hyperlink, and a new Web site will appear on the computer screen. In order to use the World Wide Web, you must have access to a computer with a modem and *browser* software.

World Wide Web, Key Terms   The following terms will help you understand the workings of the World Wide Web.

■ **Browser**   A *browser* is a software application that allows you to find and access information on the Web. Using a browser, or *browsing,* allows you to explore, read, save, and download documents, images, sounds, and videos from Web pages. (See also *Web Site* on the next page.)

■ **Domain**   A *domain* is the name of a computer or server on the Internet from which you may access information. Every Web address specifies a domain, or particular computer. (See also *URL* on the next page.)

- **Home Page**   A *home page* is the first screen or page of a Web site. On a home page, you can usually find the name of the person or organization that created the site, an index or table of contents for the site, and hyperlinks to related sites. (See also *Web Site* on this page.)

- **Hyperlink**   A *hyperlink,* or *link,* is a specially coded word or image that, when clicked, allows you to move from one Web site to another. On a computer screen, hyperlinks are usually underlined and printed in a contrasting color; sometimes they may appear as shaded "buttons." (See also *Hypertext Markup Language* below.)

- **Hypertext**   *Hypertext* is a system that allows a user to find and open related files and documents on the Web without having to quit or close the original file. It allows you to move from one document to another via hyperlinks.

- **HyperText Markup Language (HTML)**   *HyperText Markup Language* is the language computer programmers use to create sites on the World Wide Web or to publish on the Web. You do not have to know this language to use the Web.

- **HyperText Transfer Protocol (HTTP)**   *HyperText Transfer Protocol* is the language, or set of communication rules, used by browser software to connect to different sites or documents on the World Wide Web. Again, you do not have to know this language to use the Web.

- **Search Engine**   A *search engine* is a specific tool used to find specific information on the Web. Search engines search a variety of sites looking for keywords that you supply. (See also *World Wide Web*, *Searching* on page 992.)

- **URL (Uniform Resource Locator)**   Every document or Web page has a *URL*, or address, which includes words, abbreviations, numbers, and punctuation. The URL shown below will connect you to information on documentary films that are broadcast on the Public Broadcasting Service (PBS). The parts of the address are explained below.

    1   2   3

http://www.pbs.org/arts/pov

1. The *protocol,* or how the site is formatted.

2. The *domain name.* Domain names have at least two parts. The part in the middle is the name of the company, institution, or other organization. The part on the right is a general domain. Here are the abbreviations of the most common general domains. (See also *domain* on page 990.)

Common Domains on the World Wide Web	
com	commercial
edu	educational
gov	governmental
net	administrative
org	nonprofit organization

3. The *subdirectory name* that shows where the piece of information that you want is stored. (Each word following a slash requests a narrower search into the site.) Not all addresses have this part.

- **Web Site (or Web Page)**   A *Web site* or *Web page* is a document or location on the Web that is linked to other locations on the Web. A site may contain several Web pages. The example Web site on the next page is about *spelunking,* or exploring caves.

1. **Toolbar** The buttons on the toolbar allow you to connect to other Web sites, search, print out information, and see or hide images.

2. **Location window** This box shows the URL, or address, of the Web site you are observing.

3. **Content area** The area of the screen where the text, images, hyperlinks, and other parts of a Web page appear.

4. **Hyperlinks** Clicking on these coded words allows you to access Web sites. Internal hyperlinks send you to different parts of this site; external hyperlinks send you to other addresses (or URLs).

5. **Scroll Bar** Clicking the arrows at the ends of this bar scrolls the page horizontally. There is also a vertical scroll bar on the side. Some sites also have a message area below the horizontal scroll bar. If you let your cursor rest on a hyperlink, the link's address will appear in this space.

World Wide Web, Plagiarism

To present the ideas or work of another person as your own is *plagiarism*. Because downloading or copying information from the World Wide Web is such a simple process, plagiarism of electronic material has become a serious matter. It is essential that you treat any information you find on the World Wide Web as if it were from a copyrighted (printed or published) source. You should always acknowledge (or cite) the source of your information. (See page 275 for examples of **citations of online sources**.)

World Wide Web, Searching

You can search for information on the World Wide Web in three ways: by using *direct address, search engines,* and *subject catalogs.* Each type of search has certain benefits and drawbacks. Unless you know specifically what you are looking for on the Web, it is a good idea to use a combination of all three types of searches,

which most search services allow. Here is more information about each type of search.

- **Direct Address** The quickest way to access a Web site is to type in the Web site's *direct address,* or URL, in the location box. The address you type in must be exact, down to uppercase and lowercase letters and punctuation.

- **Search Engines** *Search Engines* are really databases that contain information about the millions of sites on the Web. They are compiled automatically by computer programs called *robots.* Through *search engines* you can search indexes' databases for specific information. (See also **World Wide Web** on page 990, and **World Wide Web, Using Search Engines** on the next page.)

- **Subject Catalogs** A *subject catalog* is really an elaborate table of contents that organizes information from Web sites into broad categories, such as *Education* and *Entertainment*. (Subject categories are organized by human beings, not computer programs, as is the case with search engines.) Each category in a subject catalog is broken down into many subcategories, which in turn are divided into even narrower sub-subcategories. You search a subject catalog by narrowing from general topics to specific ones.

World Wide Web, Using Search Engines

Search engines allow you to search for Web sites by using keywords or phrases. Search engines also allow you to refine your searches. The fol-lowing methods will make your searches more efficient.

- **Keyword Search**   A *keyword search* calls up Web sites that contain specific words or phrases. To do a keyword search, type a keyword or words into the space provided on the search engine screen. Then press the Return key or the Search or Find button. The search engine analyzes the Web sites in its database to find those that match the keywords you requested. The search results appear as a list with the most useful sites at the top of the list, and other sites listed in descending order of relevance. Most search engines give each site

Refining a Keyword Search	
Tip	**How It Works**
Replace general terms with specific ones.	A key word that is common or has multiple meanings will result in irrelevant matches.
	EXAMPLE If you are interested in Shakespeare's play, enter *Julius Caesar* instead of just *Caesar*.
Use quotation marks.	By placing your keywords or phrases in quotation marks, you are directing the search engine to find sites that use the words exactly as you have typed them.
	EXAMPLE Enter "Julius Caesar" to find sites about both the play and the Roman emperor rather than sites about any Julius or any Caesar.
Use *and* and *not*.	Narrow your search by putting the word *and* between your keywords. The search engine will find only Web sites that contain all words connected by *and*.
	EXAMPLE For sites about the Roman emperor, enter "Gaius Julius Caesar" AND "Roman emperor"
	Use *not* between keywords to make sure the search engine does not pull up sites about similar but unrelated topics.
	EXAMPLE Enter "Shakespeare's Julius Caesar" NOT "Gaius Julius Caesar" for sites about Shakespeare's play.
Use *or*.	To broaden your search, use *or* to let the search engine know that you would accept sites containing any of your keywords.
	EXAMPLE If you want sites that discuss either Shakespeare's play or Prokofiev's ballet music, enter "Shakespeare's play Romeo and Juliet" OR "Prokofiev's ballet music Romeo and Juliet"

on the list a percentage or rank number to indicate how well the site matches your request.

■ **Refining a Keyword Search** Search engines may list hundreds or thousands of Web sites that contain your keywords, in which case you should *refine,* or narrow, your search. The chart on the previous page suggests some strategies for refining a search. Remember, however, that each search engine's commands may be slightly different from those in the chart. Consult the Help section of your search engine to find out its specific commands.

World Wide Web, Web Site Evaluation

Since the Web is not monitored for accuracy as most publications are, you must carefully evaluate any information you find on it. The following questions will help you to *evaluate* how reliable a Web site is.

Evaluating a Web Site	
Questions to Ask	**Why You Should Ask**
Who created or sponsored this Web site?	The Web site's creator or sponsor, usually identified on the home page, controls all of the information on the Web site. The most accurate, reliable, and unbiased information can be found on Web sites that are affiliated with reputable organizations, such as universities, government agencies, museums, and national news organizations. The addresses for these Web sites usually belong in the *edu, gov,* or *org* networks.
What is the purpose of the Web site?	People and groups have various reasons for publishing on the Web, such as to provide information, to market a product, or to promote a cause. Determining the site's purpose will help you to assess its reliability.
Does the Web site offer adequate coverage of your subject?	If the site contains a type and depth of coverage not available elsewhere, being online is probably worth your time. Otherwise, you might want to refer to alternative reference sources.
When was the page first posted and is it frequently updated?	This information usually appears at the end of a home page along with the creator's e-mail address. To judge whether information is up-to-date, check the site's copyright notice and the date of the most recent update.
What other Web pages is the site linked to?	Looking at the hyperlinks on a Web site can help you determine how accurate and reliable the source is. A site that has links to other reputable Web sites is likely to contain accurate information.
Does the Web site present information objectively?	Look for strong language and one-sided statements of opinion, both common signs of bias. An objective site presents the facts and gives equal time to both sides of a controversial issue.
Is the Web site well designed?	A well-designed Web site has legible type, clear graphics, and working links; it is easy to search and navigate. Its written content should be clear and follow the conventions of standard English (spelling, punctuation, capitalization, and grammar).

Reading and Vocabulary

Reading

Skills and Strategies

The following skills and strategies can help you to become a more effective reader.

Author's Purpose and Point of View, Determining
Every author has a reason, or *purpose,* for writing. For instance, an author might write to inform, to persuade, to express something, or to entertain. Every author also has a *point of view*, or attitude toward his or her subject. Considering the author's purpose and point of view will make you a more effective, critical reader of any text. Generally, an author's purpose will not be directly stated; you will have to infer it from evidence in the text. (See also page 297.)

EXAMPLE   When American citizens turn eighteen, they are given one of the most important responsibilities of citizenship—voting. Far too many young people opt out, saying that voting has nothing to do with their lives. Voting is the foundation of democracy in the United States. Register now, and cast your ballot in every election. Your vote counts!

Author's purpose: to persuade young people to register and to vote in elections

Author's point of view: Voting is an important responsibility because it is the foundation of democracy in the United States.

Cause-Effect Relationships, Analyzing
In a *cause-effect relationship,* one thing leads to, or causes, another. To analyze cause-effect relationships as you read, ask questions like *Why?* and *What are the effects?* and look for cause-effect clue words like *because, consequently,* and *therefore.* (See also pages 144–145 and **Clue Words** on the next page.)

EXAMPLE   Scientists are attempting to determine how much of the recent global warming is due to humans and how much is natural. Sulfate aerosols and waste industrial gases are the most significant human factors; airborne particles emitted during volcanic eruptions and changes in solar radiation are natural causes. Scientists predict long-range effects of continued global warming such as a rise in sea levels that will engulf shorelines and severe climactic changes.

Analysis: Both human and natural factors *cause* global warming. Some predicted *effects* of global warming are a rise in sea levels and climactic changes.

Clue Words				
Cause-effect	Chronological Order	Comparison-contrast	Listing	Problem-solution
as a result	after	although	also	as a result
because	before	as well as	for example	nevertheless
consequently	finally	but	for instance	therefore
if . . . then	first	either . . . or	in fact	this led to
nevertheless	not long after	however	more important	thus
since	now	not only . . . but also	most important	
so that	second	on the other hand	to begin with	
therefore	then	similarly	firstly	
this led to	when	unless	secondly	
thus	while	yet		

Clue Words, Using   Writers use transitional words and phrases, or *clue words,* like the ones in the chart above to connect ideas and describe the relationships between ideas. Transitional words and phrases provide clues to understanding these relationships as well as the text's overall structure. (See also **Text Structures** on page 1000.)

Drawing conclusions   A *conclusion* is an opinion or judgment you form by combining information in a text with information you already know. As you read, you analyze and interpret the information in the text. You then connect that information to your prior knowledge and experiences and draw a conclusion about the text. A valid conclusion is one firmly grounded in textual evidence. An invalid conclusion is not consistent with the evidence presented in the text. (See also page 254.)

EXAMPLE   Six o'clock and it's already bright outside. At least it won't be dark until almost nine—time enough to get home from work, grab some dinner, and mow the seriously out-of-control grass.

Conclusion: The days are long; it must be summer.

Fact and Opinion, Distinguishing   A *fact* is a piece of information that can be verified by testing, personal experience, or reliable sources, while an *opinion* is a personal belief or attitude that cannot be proven true or false. Only opinions that are supported with factual evidence are considered **valid.** (See also page 337.)

EXAMPLE

Fact: Derek Walcott, a Caribbean poet, won the 1992 Nobel Prize in literature. [Reference works support this as a true statement.]

Opinion: Derek Walcott is the best contemporary poet. [This is one writer's judgment or belief; the statement cannot be proven to be true or false.]

Generalizations, Forming   A *generalization* combines textual information with prior knowledge to draw a conclusion not only about the text but also about the world in general. (See also page 381.)

EXAMPLE   Poison ivy, poison oak, and poison sumac contain a sap that causes a severe, itchy, blistering rash in most people who come in direct contact with these plants. The rash may last for two weeks. You can also get the rash by touching pets, clothing, gardening tools, or sports equipment that has been contaminated by the poisonous sap.

Generalization: Everyone should learn to recognize poison ivy, poison oak, and poison sumac and try to avoid direct and indirect contact with these plants.

Implied Main Idea, Identifying
Writers do not always state their main ideas directly. As a result, readers must be able to analyze and interpret details to identify main ideas that are *implied*, or expressed indirectly. (See also page 103, and **Making Inferences** and **Stated Main Idea** in this section.)

EXAMPLE   All of the different types of yoga share three features: a series of postures and stretches, breathing exercises, and relaxation meditations. Yoga does not aim to build muscles and increase strength as weightlifting does, nor does it aim to give a cardiovascular workout as aerobic exercise does, although it can do both of these things. Yoga aims to make the mind more peaceful.

Implied main idea: Unlike other forms of exercise, yoga aims to benefit the mind as well as the body.

Making Inferences
When you *make inferences* about a text, you read between the lines, making educated guesses about ideas the text does not state directly. These guesses are "educated" because they are based on information in the text combined with prior knowledge.

EXAMPLE   Nicolaus Copernicus, a sixteenth-century Polish astronomer, completely reversed the commonly held view of the universe. In 1543, just before he died, he published a scientific treatise postulating that the earth revolves around the sun. This revolutionary idea literally turned the universe topsy-turvy, setting the stage for modern astronomy.

Inference: Before Copernicus, people believed that the earth was the center of the universe—that the sun revolved around the earth.

Paraphrasing
When you *paraphrase,* you restate in your own words the information and ideas in a text. Paraphrasing is a good way to check your comprehension of a complex poem or prose passage—if you are able to paraphrase it, you probably understand it. Unlike a summary, a paraphrase is often the same length as the original text. (See the chart on page 189 for paraphrasing guidelines.) Here are the first eight lines of William Shakespeare's "Sonnet 25," followed by a paraphrase.

EXAMPLE

Let those who are in favor with their stars
Of public honor and proud titles boast,
Whilst I, whom fortune of such triumph bars,
Unlooked for joy in that I honor most.
Great princes' favorites their fair leaves spread
But as the marigold at the sun's eye,
And in themselves their pride lies burièd,
For at a frown they in their glory die....

Paraphrase: Let some boast of their fame and recognition; the speaker has neither. Instead, the speaker has a quiet joy in something he values above all else. Those popular at court enjoy only temporary regard; they have no pride and self-respect. Without noble favor, they wither and die—as a marigold does without sunlight.

Persuasive Techniques, Analyzing
An author uses *persuasive techniques* to convince readers to think or act in a certain way. Persuasive techniques include logical, ethical, and emotional appeals. As you read persuasive writing, analyze and evaluate the persuasive techniques. Is the writer's argument grounded in logical appeals—reasons and evidence? Emotional and ethical appeals add persuasive force to an argument, but they should never be

a substitute for logical reasoning. (See also page 117.)

EXAMPLE   Before graduating from elementary school, all students should pass a test demonstrating that they can swim well. Such a test could help prevent deaths by drowning. Last year, fourteen young children drowned and another six nearly drowned. How many more children have to die before we do the right thing?

Analysis: The first sentence states an opinion. The second sentence states a reason, and the third sentence gives evidence. Together these sentences form a logical appeal. The fourth sentence includes both an emotional and an ethical appeal.

Précis   When you write a *précis,* you summarize a text, including only its main ideas. Here are some guidelines for writing a précis.

- **Be brief.**   Don't paraphrase. A précis is usually less than a third of the length of the original text, while a paraphrase is often the same length.

- **Include only main ideas.**   Omit details and descriptions.

- **Use your own wording.**   Do not copy phrases or sentences from the original.

- **Be faithful to the author's ideas and tone.**   Do not change or add to the ideas in the original text and try to retain its tone—whether it be formal, ironic, or comic.

Predicting   When you make a prediction about a text, you combine information from earlier in that text with your prior knowledge to make an educated guess about what will happen next.

EXAMPLE   Ashley was only thirty minutes late for her job interview. After all, it wasn't as if she were actually working there yet. Chewing bubble gum always calmed her, and she had purposely worn her favorite old jeans so she wouldn't feel nervous. She blew a large bubble just as her prospective employer greeted her. Prediction: Ashley will not get the job.

Problem-Solution Relationships, Analyzing

When authors write about a problem, they usually also discuss one or more possible solutions. When you read a problem-solution essay, analyze the problem under discussion by asking the following questions.

- What is the problem?
- Who is affected by the problem?
- What are the causes and effects of the problem?

Analyze and evaluate proposed solutions by asking

- What are the advantages and disadvantages of each proposed solution?
- Are there any other possible solutions?

EXAMPLE   Three schools have not met the higher academic standards mandated by the state legislature. As a result, these schools will not receive funding. Several solutions to this problem have been proposed. Additional teachers will be hired to reduce class size to twenty-eight students or fewer. Expert teachers will assess textbooks to choose those that seem most effective for helping schools meet the new standards. Finally, a committee is organizing an after-school tutoring program that will be staffed by trained volunteers—parents, college students, and senior citizens.

Analysis: *What is the problem?* Three schools have not met the new academic standards mandated by the legislature. *Who is affected by the problem?* School staff, students, and parents. *What are the effects of the problem?* Schools that do not meet the requirements will lose funding. *What are the advantages and disadvantages of each proposed solution?* Each solution is likely to be effective. The first (more teachers) will cost the most. The second will also cost a lot of money, and teachers will have to learn how to use the new textbooks. The third solution won't cost money but will take lots of time and effort to organize. *Are there any other possible solutions?* Raising teachers' salaries might attract and retain more experienced teachers.

Reading Log, Using a   A *reading log* is a notebook (or section of a notebook) in which you write about your reading. As you read, jot down comments and questions, make connections to your experiences and past reading, and note important passages. A reading log may also contain your prereading and postreading responses to the text. Since every reader has different opinions, experiences, and interests, your reading log will be unique.

Reading Rate, Adjusting   *Reading rate* is the speed at which you read a text. Whether you read quickly or slowly depends on a combination of three things: your purpose for reading, the difficulty of the text, and your prior knowledge of the text's content. The following chart shows you how to adjust your reading rate.

SQ3R   *SQ3R* is a popular reading-study strategy. *SQ3R* stands for the following five steps in the reading process.

S   *Survey* the entire text. Look briefly at each page. Read all titles, headings, subheadings, and boldface and italicized terms. Look at illustrations, charts, outlines, and summaries.

Q   *Question* yourself. List questions you should be able to answer after you finish reading. Look at any questions provided at the end of a selection.

R   *Read* the material carefully. Think of answers to your questions as you read.

R   *Recite* (say aloud or to yourself) in your own words the answer to each question you identified earlier.

R   *Review* the material by re-reading quickly, looking over questions, and recalling the answers.

Reading Rates According to Purpose		
Reading Rate	**Purpose**	**Example**
Scanning—reading very quickly	To find a specific detail	You are looking for the date of a specific battle.
Skimming—reading fairly quickly, looking primarily at headings, subheadings, boldface terms, and graphics	To get an overview or review the main points of a text	You are reviewing several chapters of a history textbook to study for a test.
Reading for mastery	Reading slowly to understand and remember	In anticipation of a class discussion the next day, you are reading a section of a text for the first time.
Reading for enjoyment	Reading at whatever speed you find most comfortable	You are reading a novel or a magazine article.

Stated Main Idea and Supporting Details, Identifying

The *main idea* is the focus of or key idea in a piece of writing. A stated main idea often appears as a topic sentence of a paragraph or as a thesis statement in the introduction or conclusion of a longer piece of writing. *Supporting details* support or explain the main idea. Note: A stated main idea is also called an *explicit main idea.* (See also **Implied Main Idea** on page 997.)

EXAMPLE   Household chemicals are dangerous and should be used with care. Glue-dissolving solutions, paint thinner, and other solvents give off toxic fumes. These solutions should only be used in well-ventilated rooms. Some common household cleaners, such as chlorine and ammonia, also give off fumes and are especially harmful when they are used in combination with each other.

Stated main idea: Household chemicals are dangerous and should be used with care.

Supporting details: Many solvents and some common cleaners give off toxic fumes and should be used only in well-ventilated rooms.

Summarizing

A *summary* is a brief restatement in your own words of the main points of a selection or passage. When you **summarize,** you present only the key ideas, omitting unnecessary details. (See also page 238.)

EXAMPLE   In Mexico, printmaking has had a long and venerable history as a popular art form. Giovanni Paolo, an Italian artist, set up the first printing press in North America in Mexico City in 1539. A printmaking school was founded there in 1781 by Jeronimo Antonio Gil. Two years later students began studying printmaking as one of the "three noble arts" (sculpture, painting, and printmaking) at the new art school in Mexico City. Popular printmakers, such as José Guadalupe Posada, Leopoldo Mendez, Diego

Rivera, and José Clemente Orozco, have eloquently depicted life in Mexico.

Summary: By 1781, printmaking had become a popular art form in Mexico. Artists began to study printmaking and to use prints to depict life in Mexico.

Text Structures, Analyzing

A *text structure* is a pattern a writer uses to organize ideas or events. Writers often use one of five patterns of organization—*cause-effect, chronological order, comparison-contrast, listing,* and *problem-solution.* As you read, you can use the following strategies to analyze a text structure:

1. **Identify the main idea of the text.** A stated main idea may include clue words that signal a particular pattern of organization. (See also **Clue Words** on page 996.)

2. **Study the text for other important ideas and the relationships among them.** Think about how the ideas connect, and look for clue words or an obvious pattern of organization.

3. **Remember that a writer might use a single organizational pattern or combine two or more patterns.** Often a text has an overall pattern but different patterns within sections or paragraphs.

4. **Create a graphic organizer to map the relationships among the ideas.** The five common text structures, or organizational patterns, are illustrated on the next two pages.
   - *Cause-effect* shows the relationship between each cause and each effect. One type of cause-effect pattern is the *causal chain.* In a causal chain, one thing leads to the next, and so on, as in the following example, which explains what causes a rainbow. (For more on causal chains, see page 148.)

Causal chain

Light rain or fog on sunny day

↓

Light refracted as it enters drop of water in air

↓

Light reflected from drop's opposite side

↓

Light again refracted as it leaves drop of water and enters observer's eye

↓

Observer sees rainbow, an arc of 180 degrees opposite the sun.

- *Chronological order* shows the sequence of events. (See also page 469.) The sequence chain in the right hand column above shows part of the plot of the epic *Beowulf*.

Sequence chain

The monster Grendel goes on a killing spree in Herot.

↓

Beowulf hears of the carnage and goes to Herot to help the Danes.

↓

Unferth challenges Beowulf to spend the night in the hall, waiting for Grendel.

↓

Grendel goes to Herot, where Beowulf waits.

↓

Beowulf fights and slays Grendel.

- *Comparison-contrast* points out likenesses, differences, or both. (See also page 105.) The following Venn diagram compares and contrasts the Italian (Petrarchan) sonnet with the English (Shakespearean) sonnet. (See also **Venn diagram** on page 1073.)

Venn Diagram

Differences	Similarities	Differences
Italian Sonnet		English Sonnet

Italian Sonnet (Differences)
- 2 sections (octave and sextet)
- most common rhyme scheme: *abbaabba cdecde*
- also called "Petrarchan," for Francis Petrarch

Similarities
- 14-line poem
- regular rhyme scheme
- usually iambic pentameter

English Sonnet (Differences)
- 3 quatrains plus final 2-line couplet
- most common rhyme scheme: *abab cdcd efef gg*
- also called "Shakespearean," for William Shakespeare

- **_Listing_** presents material grouped according to certain criteria, such as size, location, or importance. The following example lists the five highest North American mountains according to size.

EXAMPLE

Mount McKinley, Alaska–20,320 feet
Mount Logan, Yukon–19,850 feet
Mount Orizaba, Mexico–18,700 feet
Mount St. Elias, Alaska and Canada–18,008 feet
Popocatépetl (volcano), Mexico–17,887 feet

- **_Problem-solution_** identifies at least one problem, discusses one or more possible or already implemented solutions to each problem, and predicts or explains the results of the solutions. (See also page 383.) The following chart shows a problem-solution analysis of a neighborhood traffic problem.

Transitional Words and Phrases, Using

Transitional words and phrases create coherence in a text by describing how ideas and details are related. As you read, use such transitions to help you understand these relationships as well as the overall text structure. (See also **Text Structures** on page 1000 and **Transitional Expressions** on page 470.)

Graphics, Interpreting

Graphics can be used to organize and display information, to explain a process, to describe relationships among things, or to illustrate. Begin by reading any sentences, titles, captions, labels, or legends that explain the graphic and relate it to the text. The most common graphics are _charts_, _diagrams_, _graphs_, _tables_, and _time lines_.

Problem-Solution Chart

Problem

- What is the problem?

- Automobile traffic on N.E. 10th Avenue is heavy. Many drivers speed and run stop signs.

- Whom does the problem affect?
- Pedestrians (including schoolchildren) and drivers.

- What are the effects of the problem?
- There were six accidents in two months; two children were injured by a driver who ran a stop sign.

Solutions implemented

- Post police officers along N.E. 10th Avenue to ticket speeding drivers and drivers who run stop signs.
- Add three temporary stop signs on N.E. 10th Avenue.

Outcomes of Solutions

- Many tickets have been given. Traffic slows when police are visible; speeding resumes when police are not visible.
- Fewer cars use N.E. 10th Avenue, and they must travel more slowly. Only local traffic remains.

Final results

The additional stop signs were made permanent.

Traffic volume has decreased significantly. No accidents reported in the last six months.

Charts *Charts* show relationships among ideas or data. Two types of charts you are likely to find in your reading are flowcharts and pie charts.

■ **Flowcharts** *Flowcharts* often use geometric shapes linked by arrows to show the sequence of events in a process. When reading this type of chart, keep in mind that the direction of the flow is always from left to right or from top to bottom. The following flowchart shows how sound is heard.

EXAMPLE

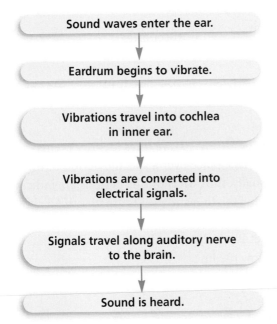

Sound waves enter the ear.

↓

Eardrum begins to vibrate.

↓

Vibrations travel into cochlea in inner ear.

↓

Vibrations are converted into electrical signals.

↓

Signals travel along auditory nerve to the brain.

↓

Sound is heard.

■ **Pie charts** *Pie charts* show the relationships of the parts of a whole to each other. The emphasis in a pie chart is always on the proportions of the sections; when percentages are given, they total one hundred percent. Pie charts may be "exploded" (one slice pulled away from the others), and your eye naturally will be drawn to the exploded piece. When reading a pie chart, be sure that you understand what each section represents. Labels may be found inside the sections of the pie, or there may be a color-coded legend beside it. The following pie chart shows the results of a survey of 140 seniors at Brantley High School.

EXAMPLE

After-Graduation Plans of 140 Seniors at Brantley High School

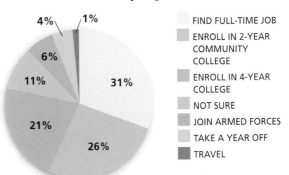

4% 1% 6% 11% 31% 21% 26%

- FIND FULL-TIME JOB
- ENROLL IN 2-YEAR COMMUNITY COLLEGE
- ENROLL IN 4-YEAR COLLEGE
- NOT SURE
- JOIN ARMED FORCES
- TAKE A YEAR OFF
- TRAVEL

Diagrams *Diagrams* use symbols or drawings to show the appearance of something or to show a process. (A ***Venn diagram***, for example, uses intersecting circles to compare two ideas or things. See page 1001.) The following diagram shows the effect of both temperature and pressure on the formation of magma.

EXAMPLE

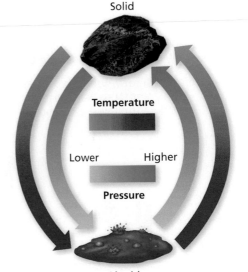

Solid

Temperature

Lower   Higher

Pressure

Liquid

Graphs   *Line and bar graphs* show how one variable changes in relation to another. Typically, the horizontal axis in a line or bar graph indicates points in time, and the vertical axis shows quantities. When reading graphs, check to see that the axis that shows quantity (usually the vertical axis) begins at zero. If it does not, the ratios suggested by the graph may be misleading.

EXAMPLES

Line Graph

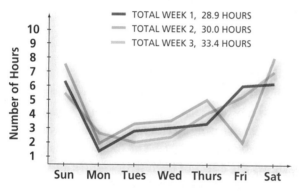

Source: Survey of 172 4th graders at Sabal Palm Elementary School

Bar Graph

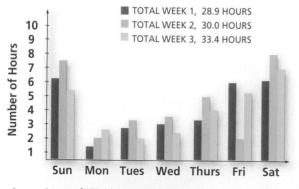

Source: Survey of 172 4th graders at Sabal Palm Elementary School

Tables   *Tables* are lists of related data arranged in rows and columns. A table does not interpret its data; you must draw your own conclusions.

EXAMPLE

Students Currently Enrolled in Volunteer Program		
Number of students	Type of volunteer work	Average hours per week
3	visit children's ward of hospital	2.5
12	tutor after school	4
2	visit elderly in nursing home	2

Time lines   *Time lines* identify events that take place over a specific period of time. Usually, time divisions or periods are indicated below the line and events are identified above it. The following time line tracing the life of the poet Byron lists the dates above and events below the line.

EXAMPLE

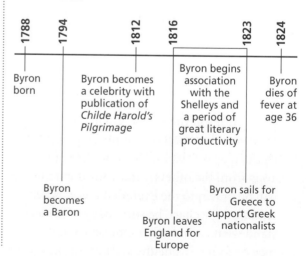

Reading Graphics Critically

Because graphics are presentations of concentrated information, you should always read them with a critical eye. Be careful not to be too quick in your analysis of the information presented. Keep in mind the following tips.

1. **Read the title, labels, and legend** of any graphic before analyzing the data. A *title* identifies the subject or main idea of the graphic. *Labels* identify and give meaning to the information shown in the graphic. A *legend* identifies special symbols, color-coding, scales, or other features you need in order to read the graphic; it appears as a small box placed near the body.

2. **Draw your own conclusions about the data,** and compare them to those of the writer. If they are different, ask yourself why.

3. **Think about what information is *not* included** in the graphic. Often, important information is left out because it does not match the author's conclusions. If you find that to be the case, you must question all of the author's conclusions.

4. **Watch out for optical illusions in graphs.** For example, bar graphs and pie charts that are shown in three dimensions are easily misread because some sections look more dense than others.

5. **Look for manipulated data** by making sure that the horizontal axis of any graph indicates time, not amount. Also, make sure that the axes of a graph or sections of a pie chart are clearly labeled and consistently marked.

6. **Look for the source.** The *source* is a citation; it identifies where the information contained in the graphic was obtained and how current it is. Knowing the source helps you evaluate the accuracy of the graphic.

Vocabulary

Context Clues   Often the meaning of an unfamiliar word is revealed by its *context*—the words, phrases, and sentences that surround it. The following chart shows five types of context clues and an example of each. The vocabulary words are printed in italics and the clue word or words are boldface. (See also pages 150 and 385.)

Context Clues
Definition and Restatement: Words or phrases that define the unfamiliar word or restate it in more familiar language. EXAMPLE Her poem crackled with *alliteration,* **the repetition of initial consonant sounds**.
Example: A word that illustrates the unfamiliar word's meaning. EXAMPLE Lewis Carroll coined the term *portmanteau words* to describe words such as **"smog."**
Synonym: A word that is similar in meaning to an unfamiliar word. EXAMPLE The ascetics considered any comfort *superfluous,* or **unnecessary.**
Antonym: A word that is opposite in meaning to an unfamiliar word. EXAMPLE The symphony's *dissonant,* rather than **harmonious,** sounds conveyed the chaos and horror of war.
Cause and Effect: A word or phrase related to the unfamiliar word by cause or effect. EXAMPLE **Because he rebelled against convention,** Byron is seen as an *iconoclast.*

Word Bank   Keeping a *word bank*—a list of new words you encounter in your reading, listening, and viewing—can help to build your vocabulary just as a savings account might help to build your wealth. Each time you encounter a new word, enter it into your word bank— usually a separate notebook or a computer file. Be sure to check a dictionary to make sure you understand the meaning and use of each new word.

Word Formations   New words, or *neologisms,* are constantly added to the English language to name or describe new ideas, inventions, products, and so on. The most common way new words are formed is by combining words or word parts. Prefixes and suffixes are usually added to a *base word,* or a word *root,* to make a new word. Sometimes, however, two base words can be combined (with or without a hyphen) to make a new word. The table below shows the most common ways new words are formed. (See also **Word Parts** on page 1009.)

Word Meanings   A word's meaning can change depending on the time, the place, and the situation in which it is used. Use the following definitions and examples to help you make sure that your words convey the meaning that you intend.

- **Analogies**   An *analogy* is a kind of comparison that points out the similarities between two seemingly unlike things. In an analogy question, you are asked to analyze the relationship between one pair of words in order to identify a second pair of words that are related in the same way. Analogy questions measure your knowledge of vocabulary as well as your ability to identify relationships and patterns between words. (See page 386 for more about completing analogy questions.)

  EXAMPLE
  1. THERMOMETER : TEMPERATURE :: __D__
  A. snow : cold   **C.** barrel : rain
  B. speedometer: car   **D.** ruler : length

- **Clichés**   A *cliché* is a tired expression. Often clichés are figures of speech—metaphors, similes, or personifications—that have become hackneyed, weak, and boring through overuse.

Word Formations		
Process	**Description**	**Examples**
Combining	Combining two base words to make a compound or combining a word with a prefix or suffix	doorway, high-rise, unfold, wonderful
Shortening	Omitting part of an original word to shorten it or to change it to another part of speech	telephone > phone burglar > burgle nuclear > nuke
Blending	Shortening and combining two words	breakfast + lunch = brunch smoke + fog = smog
Shifting	Changing the meaning or usage of a word	host (n.) > host (v.) farm (n.) > farm (v.)

EXAMPLES   stubborn as a mule, fresh as a daisy, bone-dry, crystal clear

When you write, avoid clichés; try instead to think of fresh, new ways of expressing your ideas.

■ **Denotation and Connotation**   The *denotation* of a word is the meaning or meanings given in a dictionary. Many words also have *connotations,* the emotions and associations a word may suggest. Because connotations often stir people's feelings, they can have powerful effects on a listener or reader. Word connotations often contribute to the tone of a text, revealing the writer's attitude toward the subject.

EXAMPLE   The words *unique* and *strange* have similar denotations; both mean "unusual" or "extraordinary." However, *unique* has positive connotations, suggesting a desirable difference, while *strange* has negative connotations, suggesting an undesirable or even sinister difference.

■ **Euphemisms**   A *euphemism* is an indirect, agreeable-sounding word or phrase used in place of a direct word or phrase that might offend people. Sometimes euphemisms are actually used to mislead—to hide the truth or misrepresent the facts.

Euphemism	More Direct Term
passed away	died
previously owned vehicle	used car
additional revenues	higher taxes
refuse management facility	garbage dump
sanitary engineer	garbage collector

■ **Figurative language**   *Figurative language* describes one thing in terms of another and is not meant to be taken literally. By comparing unlike things, the writer helps the reader see something familiar in a new way. The following chart gives definitions and examples of three common types of figurative language.

Types of Figurative Language

A *simile* compares two things using a connective word, such as *like, as,* or *than.*
EXAMPLE
"My heart is like a singing bird . . ."
—Christina Rossetti

A *metaphor* equates two things without using a connective word.
EXAMPLE
"All the world's a stage . . ."
—William Shakespeare

Personification gives human characteristics to something nonhuman.
EXAMPLE
"The sullen wind was soon awake, / It tore the elm-tops down for spite . . ."
—Robert Browning

■ **Gobbledygook**   Wordy, puffed-up language is sometimes referred to as *gobbledygook.* It is characterized by long, complicated words and sentences, and it obscures rather than clarifies meaning. Often intended to impress readers, gobbledygook usually does the opposite.

EXAMPLE
Gobbledygook: A plethora of culinary specialists has a deleterious effect upon the quality of purées, consommés, and other soluble pabula.
Translation: Too many cooks spoil the broth.

■ **Idioms**   *Idioms* are colloquial expressions that are not meant to be understood literally. They make no sense when translated word for word into another language.

EXAMPLES

Josie *fell head over heels for* Ryan.

Harold *went out on a limb* and promised to *clean up his act.*

■ **Jargon**   *Jargon* is the specialized vocabulary of a particular profession, occupation, hobby, or field of study. Avoid using jargon unless you are sure that your audience will understand the terms. It is a good idea to define or explain briefly any unfamiliar jargon terms.

EXAMPLES

Sailing	**fox:** several ropes twisted together
Aviation	**check the runway:** to fly at high speed with wheels up just above an airstrip
Film	**cut:** to stop filming
Psychology	**constellation:** several thoughts having a relationship to one another and centered on one idea

■ **Loaded words**   Words and phrases that have strong connotations, either positive or negative, are called **loaded words.** Because loaded words appeal to emotions, writers and speakers often use them to persuade. Loaded language may also indicate bias or propaganda. In the following sentences, the loaded words are underscored.

EXAMPLES

Drive the new *Paloma*—the marriage of European elegance and Yankee ingenuity.

Senator Whatshisname stands for home, hearth, and good, old-fashioned values.

■ **Multiple meanings**   Many English words have more than one meaning. When you use

a dictionary to find a word's meaning, look at all the definitions given and keep in mind the context in which you read or heard the word. Then, try the various definitions in that context until you find the one that fits.

EXAMPLE   Because I do not have any *mace,* I left out the teaspoon of mace the recipe said was optional. (The third definition below fits best in this context.)

mace (mās) *n.* **1.** a heavy, medieval war club, often with a spiked metal head **2.** a staff used as a symbol of authority by certain officials **3.** a spice, usually ground, made from the outer covering of the nutmeg

■ **Nonsexist language**   *Nonsexist language* is language that applies to people in general, both male and female. Unless you are referring specifically to someone of a particular gender, language that applies to both genders is more accurate and more appropriate.

   Here are some examples of nonsexist language that can be used when gender-specific language is not appropriate.

EXAMPLE

Gender-Specific	Nonsexist
businessman	businessperson
chairman	chairperson
stewardess	flight attendant
housewife	homemaker
fireman	firefighter

■ **Tired words**   A *tired word* has been used so often and so carelessly that it is vague and almost meaningless. Instead of using tired words, choose lively, specific words that give an exact, vivid description of your subject.

EXAMPLES   bad, great, cute, really, nice

Word Origins Every word has a history, or *origin*—how it came into the English language. A *dictionary etymology,* usually in brackets following the entry word, traces a word's origin and history. The following etymology indicates that the English word *amateur* came from French (Fr) and Latin (L). The abbreviation *pp.* stands for "past participle"; the symbol < means "comes from."

EXAMPLE **amateur** [Fr < L *amator,* lover < pp. of *amare,* to love]

Word Parts Most English words, like *legible* and *misfortune,* can be divided into **word parts.**

The three types of word parts are ***roots, prefixes,*** and ***suffixes.*** Knowing the meanings of word parts can help you determine the meanings of many unfamiliar words.

- **Roots** The *root* is the foundation on which a word is built. The root carries the word's core meaning, and it is the part to which prefixes and suffixes are added. The following chart includes some common roots, their meanings, and examples of words that contain the roots. (See also pages 242 and 341.)

Commonly Used Roots		
Roots	**Meanings**	**Examples**
Greek		
–astr(o)–	star	astronaut, astronomy
–bio–	life	biosphere, biology
–chrom–	color	polychromatic
–dem–	people	democracy
–graph–	write, writing	graphologist, graphic
–log–, –logy–	study, word	epilogue, ecology
–phil–	like, love	bibliophile
–phono–	sound	symphony, cacophony
–zo–	life, animal	zoological, zoophobia
Latin		
–aud–, –audi–	hear	audition, auditory
–ben–, –bene–	good	benefactor, benevolent
–cent–	hundred	percent, century
–cogn–	know	incognito, cognate
–duc–, –duct–	draw, lead	introduce, induce
–loc–	place	local, circumlocution
–magn–	large, grand	magnify, magnanimous
–man–	hand	maneuver, mandate
–mater–, –matr–	mother	maternity, matrilineal

(continued)

QUICK REFERENCE HANDBOOK

Commonly Used Roots

Roots	Meanings	Examples
–mor–, –mort–	death	immortal, mortuary
–omni–	all	omnipotent
–pater–, –patr–	father	patriot, paternity
–prim–	early, first	primordial, primer
–solv–	loosen, accomplish	absolve, dissolve
–spir–	breath	spirit, conspire
–uni–	one	unison, unification
–vid–, –vis–	see	videotape, visualize

■ **Prefixes** A *prefix* is a word part that is added to the beginning of a root. The word that is created from a prefix and a root combines the meanings of both. The chart below includes some common prefixes, their meanings, and examples of words that contain the prefixes. (See also page 194.)

Commonly Used Prefixes

Prefixes	Meanings	Examples
Greek		
a–	lacking, without	amoral, atypical
anti–	against, opposing	antibody, antisocial
dia–	through, across	diagram, dialectic
hyper–	excessive	hyperactive, hyperbole
hypo–	under, below	hypodermic
mon–, mono–	one	monarchy, monocle
neo–	new	neonatal, neoclassical
para–	beside, beyond	parallel, paramilitary
peri–	around	periscope, peripheral
psych–, psycho–	mind	psychoanalysis, psyche
syn–, sym–, syl–, sys–	together, with	synchronize, sympathy, syllable, system
Latin and French		
ab–	from, away	abduct, abhor
contra–	against	contrast, contraband
de–	away, from, off	depart, deflate
e–, ef–, ex–	away, from, out	eject, efface, expiration
inter–	among, between	intersect, interval
intra–	within	intravenous

Commonly Used Prefixes

Prefixes	Meanings	Examples
per–	through	permeate, persist
post–	after, following	postpone, postscript
pre–	before	predict, predisposition
pro–	forward, favoring	propel, promise
re–	back, backward, again	revoke, recede, recur
retro–	back, backward	retroactive, retrospective
semi–	partly, half	semisweet, semiprecious
ultra–	beyond, excessively	ultrasonic, ultramodern
Old English		
be–	around, treat as	begrime, befriend
for–	away, off, from	forbid, forsake
mis–	badly, not, wrongly	misfire, misspell
over–	above, excessively	oversee, overdo
un–	not, reverse of	untrue, unfold

■ **Suffixes** A *suffix* is a word part that is added to the end of a root. Often, adding or changing a suffix changes both a word's meaning and its part of speech, as in *labor*, a noun or verb, and *laborious*, an adjective. The following chart includes some common suffixes, their meanings, and examples of each. (See also page 194.)

Commonly Used Suffixes

Suffixes	Meanings	Examples
Greek, Latin, and French		
Nouns		
–ance, –ence	act, condition	radiance, excellence
–cy	state, condition	advocacy, redundancy
–er, –or	doer, action	banker, inheritor
–ism	act, doctrine, manner	criticism, ostracism
–tude	quality, state	attitude, fortitude
–ty, –y	quality, state, action	subtlety, reality
–ure	act, result, means	pleasure, measure
Adjectives		
–able, –ible	able, likely	likable, legible

(continued)

Commonly Used Suffixes

Suffixes	Meanings	Examples
–ate	having, characteristic of	desperate, irate
–esque	in the style of, like	arabesque, statuesque
–fic	making, causing	horrific, scientific
–ous	marked by, given to	glorious, laborious
Verbs		
–ate	become, cause to be	punctuate, alleviate
–esce	become, grow, continue	coalesce, effervesce
–fy	make, cause to have	magnify, falsify
–ize	make, cause to be	energize, agonize
Old English		
Nouns		
–dom	state, rank, condition	officialdom, martyrdom
–hood	state, condition	likelihood, childhood
–ness	quality, state	kindness, craziness
Adjectives		
–en	made of, like	golden, frozen
–ful	full of, marked by	restful, wonderful
–less	lacking, without	fearless, restless
–some	apt to, showing	irksome, handsome
–ward	in the direction of	upward, skyward
Verbs		
–en	cause to be, become	strengthen, lighten

Words to Learn The three hundred words in the list below may be used as the basis of your vocabulary study this year. Make it a habit to learn unfamiliar words from this list.

aberration
abeyance
abject
abnegation
abscond
absolve

abstruse
acrimonious
adjudge
adjure
admonish
adroit

affront
allay
amorphous
anachronism
anarchy
antipathy
antipodes
apostasy
artifice
ascetic
ascribe
aspersion

assiduous
assimilate
atrophy
augury
auspices
avarice
aver

banal
bauble
bellicose
biennial

blazon
bode
bravado
broach
bullion
burgeoning
burnish

cadaverous
cajole
calumny
candor
capitulate
capricious
captivate
caricature
cessation
charlatan
chastise
chauvinism
chicanery
choleric
circumvent
civility
clandestine
coerce
cognizant
colloquy
commensurate
commiserate
commodious
conciliate
configuration
connoisseur
consign
consternation
contingency
copious
corollary
corroborate
cosmopolitan

dearth
decorum
deduce

demagogue
denizen
deplore
desist
despot
detriment
devoid
differentiate
dirge
discrepancy
discursive
disparity
distraught
diurnal
doggerel
dogma
duress

effusion
elegy
elicit
elocution
emaciate
emanate
empirical
engender
enigma
ennui
epitome
equanimity
equivocal
erudite
esoteric
espouse
ethereal
ethnology
etymology
eulogy
euphemism
euphony
evanescent
exhilaration
exhort
expatriate
expound

extant
extenuate
extol
extort
extraneous
extricate

facetious
facile
farcical
feign
fervid
festoon
fiasco
finesse
fissure
foible
foment
fortuitous
fresco
frugal

gambol
gauntlet
germane
glib
gratuitous
gregarious
guffaw
guile

hackneyed
harbinger
herculean
hiatus
homily
homogeneous
humdrum
hyperbole

idiosyncrasy
ignominy
illicit
immutable
impair
impassive

impeccable
implicit
incarcerate
incognito
inconsequential
incorrigible
indigent
indulgent
inexorable
infringe
iniquity
inordinate
inscrutable
intercede
introvert
inundate
inveigle
iridescent
irrevocable

lampoon
litigation
longevity
loquacious
ludicrous
lugubrious

magnanimous
maim
malign
malinger
maudlin
menial
mercurial
mesmerism
mete
misnomer
mollify
moot
mottled
mundane
munificent

nadir
nebulous
nefarious

nemesis
nettle
nondescript
nonentity

obnoxious
obsequious
officious
omniscient
opulence
ostensible

pallor
paragon
parsimonious
patrimony
pecuniary
perfidious
pervade
pestilence
phlegmatic
poignant
precocious
precursor
predispose

prevaricate
primordial
proffer
profuse
progeny
prognosis
promontory
promulgate
propensity
propitious
proponent
propriety
prosaic
protégé
pseudonym
punctilious
purloin

quell
querulous
quiescent

rampant
rancor
recant

refute
regimen
remonstrate
remuneration
renounce
repository
reprisal
repudiate
retaliate
reticent
retroactive
retrospect
revile

sagacity
salient
sanguine
scathing
scrupulous
scurrilous
sedentary
seraphic
solicitous
sonorous
specious

strident
subjugate
subversion
sumptuous
sundry

taciturn
temerity
tenable
tenuous
tenure
terra firma
testimonial
treatise
truism

usury

vantage point
venal
venerate
vestige
vindicate
virulent
vociferous
voluminous

Speaking and Listening

Speaking

Most of the speaking that you do is informal conversation with family, friends, classmates, teachers, and co-workers. Sometimes, however, you are asked to speak on formal occasions. This type of speaking requires careful preparation, planning, and delivery. The following sections discuss various strategies and techniques that will make you a more effective speaker in any kind of situation—formal or informal.

Debate

Debate is an ancient means of decision making. Both the Greeks and the Romans engaged in debate. In the United States today, debate is an important ingredient of modern democracy. Debate occurs continually in legislative bodies, courtrooms, and election campaigns all over the country. A formal debate involves two teams who publicly discuss a controversial topic in a systematic way. The topic under discussion is called the *proposition.* The *affirmative team* argues that the proposition should be accepted or adopted and presents proof to establish its case. The *negative team,* the opposing team,

argues that the proposition should be rejected. The negative team must refute the affirmative case by defending the status quo (the present situation) or by presenting a counterplan.

Features of a Debate   All debates share the following features: They deal with a proposition; they follow certain rules of etiquette; and they are judged by officials.

- **Debate Proposition**   The central issue in a debate is a ***proposition*** that is phrased as a resolution and limited to a specific idea. A debate proposition deals with an issue that is actually debatable—one on which reasonable people disagree—so that both teams have an equal chance to build a winning case. The proposition should be clearly expressed in language that debaters and the audience can understand. In an actual debate, debaters often do not get to choose whether they argue the *affirmative* (for the proposition) or *negative* (against the proposition) and must be prepared to argue either side.

Debate Propositions		
Type	**Definition**	**Example**
Proposition of value	States the value of a person, place, or thing	Resolved: That the American system of education offers learning opportunities to all citizens.
Proposition of policy	Determines what action should be taken	Resolved: That some form of compulsory public service should be required of all citizens.

NOTE Another type of proposition is the proposition of fact, which makes a statement about the truth or falsity of what has happened in the past, what is happening presently, or what will happen in the future. The proposition of fact occurs most often in courts of law, not in debate.

■ **Debate Etiquette** An important aspect of debate is the etiquette, or courteous behavior, required of debaters. Debaters refer to each other formally and politely in such terms as "the first affirmative speaker," "my opponent," or "my colleague." Personal attacks and sarcasm are not allowed. Deliberately misquoting or trying to distract or disturb the opposing team is also unacceptable. A debate must be won—or lost—solely on the strength of the debaters' arguments and delivery.

■ **Debate Officials** A chairperson often presides during a debate. A debater may appeal to the chairperson if he or she believes that any debating procedures or time limits have been violated by the opposing team. The most common method of determining the winner of a debate is by the decision of three (or sometimes fewer) appointed judges. Judges base their decision not on their personal views on the proposition, but on the performance of the debaters and on the merits of the arguments. Occasionally, an audience may vote to determine the winning team.

Formats of Debate Most debates are divided into two parts. In the first part, both teams make *constructive speeches* in which they do two things: First, they present their arguments for or against the proposition; second, they try to refute, or disprove, their opponents' arguments. After a brief intermission, both teams make *rebuttal speeches,* in which they reply to damaging arguments raised by the opposing team and restate their own main arguments. Specific time limits are assigned for each speech, although these limits vary depending on the type of debate.

■ **Traditional, or Formal, Debate** This debate format has two speakers on a team. One team argues the affirmative position on a proposition of policy; the other argues the negative position. Each debater speaks twice within set time limits. (Each debater has a designation: the affirmative team members are 1A and 2A; the negative team members are 1N and 2N.) The chart on the next page shows the speaking order and time limits of a typical traditional, or formal, debate.

The Traditional Debate

1. Constructive speeches (10 minutes each speaker)
   a. First affirmative (1A)
   b. First negative (1N)
   c. Second affirmative (2A)
   d. Second negative (2N)

2. Rebuttal speeches (5 minutes each speaker)
   a. First negative (1N)
   b. First affirmative (1A)
   c. Second negative (2N)
   d. Second affirmative (2A)

2. Rebuttal speeches
   a. First negative (1N)   5 minutes
   b. First affirmative (1A)   5 minutes
   c. Second negative (2N)   5 minutes
   d. Second affirmative (2A)   5 minutes

- **Cross-examination Debate**   This type of debate also has two affirmative speakers (designated as 1A and 2A) and two negative speakers (1N and 2N). In a *cross-examination debate,* debaters can question opponents immediately after each constructive speech. During this cross-examination period, a speaker can clarify issues and point out weaknesses in an opponent's position. The following chart shows the speaking order and typical time limits in a cross-examination debate. Times may vary.

The Cross-Examination Debate

Order of Speakers	Typical Time Limit
1. Constructive speeches	
a. First affirmative (IA)	8 minutes
b. Cross-examination by 2N	3 minutes
c. First negative (1N)	8 minutes
d. Cross-examination by 1A	3 minutes
e. Second affirmative (2A)	8 minutes
f. Cross examination by 1N	3 minutes
g. Second negative (2N)	8 minutes
h. Cross-examination by 2A	3 minutes

- **Lincoln-Douglas Debate**   A *Lincoln-Douglas debate* has only one affirmative speaker and one negative speaker. In this format (named for the 1858 debates between Abraham Lincoln and Stephen A. Douglas, rival candidates for senator from Illinois) the speakers debate a proposition of value. The affirmative speaker argues that the proposition is a true and worthy statement; the negative speaker argues the opposite. This type of debate encourages the logical analysis of abstract concepts. As part of their argument, Lincoln-Douglas debaters often quote famous writers and thinkers.

Lincoln-Douglas Debate

Speaker	Time Limits
Affirmative	6-minute constructive speech
Negative	3-minute questioning of the affirmative
Negative	7-minute constructive speech and refutation
Affirmative	3-minute questioning of the negative
Affirmative	4-minute rebuttal speech
Negative	6-minute rebuttal speech and summary
Affirmative	3-minute rebuttal speech and summary

Preparing for a Debate   A debate requires careful preparation. Use the following steps to research the proposition and plan a strategy for the debate.

1. **Research the proposition thoroughly.** Refer to books, newspapers, magazines, and the Internet to glean accurate, unbiased, and up-to-date information. Record on notecards the facts and other kinds of evidence that you find. Be sure to evaluate your sources. (See also the **Evaluating Web Sites** chart on page 994.)

2. **Identify specific issues.** The *issues* in a debate are the specific differences between the affirmative and the negative positions. Every debatable proposition rests on several issues. For instance, in a debate in which the affirmative is arguing for a curfew law that keeps teenagers at home at night, issues might include the causes of crime, the reasons for car accidents involving teens, the importance of nighttime teen activities to the local economy, and so on.

3. **Plan your arguments.** List the most significant arguments you have for supporting your side of the proposition and the most important arguments you think your opponents will use. To refute your opposition, think of ways to attack the opposition's arguments.

4. **Support your arguments.** Using the information gathered during your research, identify evidence (examples, quotations, statistics, expert opinions, analogies, and logic) that supports your arguments. Also, find evidence to refute arguments your opponents are likely to use.

5. **Build a brief.** A *brief* is an outline for a debate. It is like a formal outline for an argumentative essay. The affirmative side in a debate creates a brief that contains a logical arrangement of all the arguments needed to prove the proposition, as well as the evidence

necessary to support its arguments. The negative side creates a brief to disprove the proposition.

Excerpt of a Brief: Opposing Arguments

Resolved: That people under the age of eighteen should be required to be inside their homes between 11 P.M. and 5 A.M. unless they are accompanied by a parent or guardian.

Affirmative

I. A curfew would decrease the number of crimes committed by teenagers.
   A. Some crimes involving teenagers (vandalism, robbery, and crimes involving gangs) occur late at night.
   B. In 1996, the first year after a curfew was put into place in New Orleans, the city experienced a 27 percent drop in teen crimes at night, a 42 percent drop in auto thefts, and a 33 percent drop in armed robberies.

II. A curfew would benefit children who are not likely to commit crimes.
   A. Children who are out late at night without supervision are at risk for becoming victims of crime, including violent crime.
   B. A curfew law will help children be better rested for school.

III. A curfew may slightly restrict children's rights, but it is for their own protection and the good of society.
   A. A curfew law is similar to laws that prevent people under eighteen from buying cigarettes and people under twenty-one from buying alcohol.
   B. Many parents cannot control their own children, and the government therefore needs to intervene.
   C. The law will promote parental responsibility because parents will be more aware of their children's activities; families will spend more time together.

Excerpt of a Brief: Opposing Arguments

Negative

I. A curfew does not prevent crime, and teenagers will violate the curfew and lose respect for the law.
   A. There is no evidence that curfews work: Youth crime has gone down in New York City, where there is no curfew; in San Francisco, youth crime went down after a curfew was repealed.
   B. Since many teenagers will disregard a curfew, teens will be more likely to think that breaking the law is acceptable.

II. Enforcing a curfew will use resources that are better spent on protecting society.
   A. Police should be spending their time investigating crimes and pursuing serious criminals.
   B. Curfew violators will have to be processed by the police and the justice system; the government will have to spend money to fight lawsuits challenging the curfew.

III. A curfew for everyone under eighteen hurts a large group because of the misbehavior of a few.
   A. Most teenagers are law-abiding and should not be punished by having their freedom of movement restricted when they have done nothing wrong.
   B. Parents, not the government, should have the right to supervise their children, to control curfews, and to permit late-night activities for mature teens.
   C. Local business owners will be harmed by a curfew because teenagers will not be at the movies, getting pizza, and so on after a certain hour.

■ **Refuting Opposing Arguments**   In addition to building a strong case for or against the proposition, each team must argue against its opponents' case. To refute, or attack, your opponents' arguments, you should

1. state clearly the arguments you are going to refute.
2. tell the audience how you plan to refute the argument.
3. present proof (logical reasoning, facts, statistics, quotations, and other supporting data or evidence) to refute the argument.
4. explain how the proof you have presented effectively refutes your opponents' arguments.

■ **Building a Rebuttal**   A *rebuttal* is a restatement or rebuilding of your case. During this part of the debate, each side gets a chance to repair or rebuild the arguments that have been attacked by the opposing team. An effective rebuttal should

1. restate your original arguments.
2. state your position on the issues your opponents have attacked.
3. present proof that supports your arguments.
4. point out any weaknesses in your opponents' arguments.
5. summarize your original evidence, and present any additional evidence you have gathered that supports your position.

Formal Speaking Occasions

In school and at work, you will be asked to participate in several kinds of formal speaking occasions: delivering formal speeches, participating in formal group discussions, conducting interviews, and being the subject of an interview. Each of these types of formal speaking requires more preparation than an informal speaking occasion.

General Purposes for Giving a Speech		
General Purpose for Speech	Purpose	Examples
Informative Speeches	To present new information to an audience, or to provide a new view of old information	• Lecture • News broadcast • Orientation • Instruction
Persuasive Speeches	To change the audience's attitude or belief, or to move an audience to action	• Campaign speech • Advertisement • Debate
Speeches for Special Occasions	To entertain or amuse an audience or to acknowledge a special reason for the audience's presence	• After-dinner speech • Anecdote • Oral interpretation of a piece of literature • Graduation speech • Speech at a memorial service

Formal Speeches   Formal speeches do not just happen; like essays, book reports, and research papers, they require time and thoughtful preparation. The process of preparing a formal speech is similar to the process of writing a paper. Use the following steps to prepare a formal speech.

1. **Recognize Task**   A formal speech is a *task* you must perform because of your position or circumstances. For example, a teacher assigns a speech; as a student, your task is to fulfill the requirements of the assignment. Your graduating class is giving your school an electronic bulletin board; as class president, your task is to plan, write, and deliver a speech commemorating the occasion.

2. **Identify Purpose**   Begin the process of preparing a speech by identifying the purpose of your speech. Your general *purpose* is the overall intent of your speech—most often to inform or to persuade an audience. Common purposes and some examples of

each purpose are described in the chart at the top of this page.

3. **Select a Topic**   If you can choose your own topic, be sure to select one that interests you and that you think will interest your audience. Consider the following questions.
   - *What is the occasion of your speech?* Are you speaking to members of the student government to propose a peer mediation program? Are you speaking to members of the chamber of commerce to inform them of changes at your school? Will the topic you are considering fit the occasion, or context?
   - *How much time will you have to speak?* Can you limit your topic so that you can cover it effectively in the time allowed?

4. **Analyze the Audience**   As you plan your speech and limit your topic, you will also need to consider the needs and interests of your audience. The following chart provides some questions and strategies for adapting material to a particular audience.

Analyzing Your Audience

Questions about audience	Evaluation	Your speech should include
Who are the people in your audience?	• Mostly younger than you • Mostly older than you	• Simple language, short sentences, age-specific examples, and clear explanations • A respectful tone, general examples that people will understand, no slang or jargon
What does the audience already know about the topic?	• Very little • A little • A good deal	• Basic background or details to inform your listeners • Some background • A more advanced discussion that focuses on little-known issues or aspects of the topic
How interested will the audience be in your topic?	• Very interested • Somewhat interested • Uninterested	• Details about the topic to maintain the audience's interest • A discussion of aspects that are most interesting to the audience • Material that persuades the audience that the topic is important

5. **Gather Material and Organize Content**
The next steps in preparing your speech are to research your topic and to organize your notes. (See also **The Library/Media Center** on page 984, **taking notes** on page 1036, and **preparing outlines** on page 1074.)

6. **Write the Speech** When you write your speech, you must consider three things: the structure or composition of your speech, the language you use, and the way that you involve your audience in your material. The following chart provides some basic guidelines.

Features of a Formal Speech

Language

The language you use should be appropriate for your audience.
1. Use formal, standard English.

2. Use technical terms sparingly, and be sure to define them.
3. Avoid slang, jargon, and euphemisms in your speech.
(See also pages 982 and 1083.)

Audience Involvement

It is important to remember that written English sounds different when it is read aloud. Make your speech more listener-friendly by doing the following.
1. Use personal pronouns. For example, say "you may think" or "we believe" instead of "one may think" or "people believe."
2. Ask rhetorical questions (questions not meant to be answered but asked only for effect) instead of making statements. For example, instead of stating a fact or statistic about voter turnout in presidential elections, ask "Can you guess what percentage of the nation's registered voters cast a ballot in the last presidential election?"

Methods of Delivering a Speech

Method	Advantages	Disadvantages
Manuscript speech (read to audience word for word from a prepared script)	Provides exact words you wish to say; less chance of errors or omissions	Does not permit audience feedback; tends to be dull for audience
Memorized speech (memorized word for word from a written script)	Gives speaker freedom to move around and look at the audience	May not sound natural; requires much practice and memorization; risk of forgetting speech
Extemporaneous speech (outlined and carefully prepared, but not memorized; speech notes often used)	Sounds natural; allows speaker to respond to audience in a natural, less formal manner	Requires practice and preparation

7. **Determine Your Method of Delivery** The chart above describes three basic methods of delivering a speech, as well as the advantages and disadvantages of each.

When you deliver a formal speech to a live audience, the extemporaneous method is usually the most effective. To prepare an extemporaneous speech, first organize your ideas by writing a complete outline. Then, prepare notecards that you will refer to as you present your speech. Use the following guidelines for your notecards.

Guidelines for Extemporaneous Speech Notecards

1. Put only one key idea on each notecard, perhaps with a brief example or detail.
2. Make a separate notecard for material you plan to read word for word, such as a quotation, a series of dates, or a list of statistics.
3. Make a separate notecard to indicate when you should pause to show a visual (for example, a chart, diagram, graph, illustration, or model).
4. Arrange your completed cards in order, and number them.

8. **Rehearse the Speech** You will give a better and more convincing presentation if you rehearse your speech. You can try one or more **rehearsal strategies.** You can practice by yourself in front of a full-length mirror, marking word groupings, pauses, and voice inflections on your written speech or notes. You can also get a friend to listen to your speech and suggest ways to improve it. Another excellent rehearsal strategy is to videotape and watch rehearsals; use **feedback** from yourself and others to improve your speech.

Remember that an audience judges a speech not only by the ideas you present, but also on the basis of certain **nonverbal** and **verbal signals** you use in delivering your speech.

■ *Nonverbal Signals* In addition to communicating with words, you communicate with nonverbal signals, like those described in the chart on the next page. Use the appropriate nonverbal signals when you deliver your speech.

Communicating with Nonverbal Signals

Nonverbal signals	Tips and Effects
Eye contact	To communicate your honesty and sincerity, look directly into the eyes of as many audience members as you can. Eye contact makes an audience feel as if you are speaking *with* them individually rather than lecturing to them as a group.
Facial expression	Vary your facial expression (smiling, frowning, raising an eyebrow, and so on) to reveal your feelings and attitude. A facial expression can enhance (or may even take the place of) a verbal message.
Gestures	Do not stand like a statue. For emphasis, make relaxed and natural gestures with your head, hands, or arms. You might nod or shake your head, indicate size or shape with your hands, pound the podium, or point with your index finger.
Posture	To convey an air of confidence, stand erect and look alert.

- *Verbal Signals*   Use your voice expressively when you deliver a speech. The following verbal signals will help you communicate your message to an audience.

Communicating with Verbal Signals

Verbal signals	Tips and Effects
Diction (the clarity of your pronunciation)	Always speak clearly and carefully so that your listeners can understand you.
Emphasis (the stress put on a word or phrase)	Emphasize important words and phrases. If you were arguing that Internet access should be available to everyone, you might emphasize two key phrases: *equal opportunity* and *access to information.*
Pause (small silences in your speech)	Use pauses to suggest what is important. Occasional pauses also help listeners catch up with your thinking.
Pitch (how high or low your voice sounds)	When you are nervous, the pitch of your voice tends to rise, so take a deep breath and relax before you speak. Avoid a monotone. Use the natural rise and fall of your voice to emphasize your ideas.
Rate (the speed at which you talk)	Normal, conversational speed is about 120 to 160 words per minute. When delivering a speech, speak more slowly than normal so that listeners can follow your ideas easily.
Volume (the loudness of your voice)	Speak loudly when giving a speech; your audience appreciates the extra volume. Be sure to ask listeners if they can hear you before you begin.

9. **Deliver the Speech**   Feeling nervous before delivering a speech is normal. However, it is important for you not to allow nervousness to affect your delivery. Here are some suggestions that can help.

- **Be prepared.** You can keep nervousness to a minimum by being organized and very familiar with your speech notes and audiovisual devices.
- **Focus on your purpose for speaking.** Concentrate on what you want your listeners to feel, believe, or do as a result of your speech.
- **Pay attention to audience feedback.** Every audience is different and will react differently. Pay attention to the messages the audience sends you. Are people alert or yawning? Are they nodding in agreement or shaking their heads no? Depending on audience feedback, you might need to adjust your pace, use more emphatic gestures, or speak more loudly to keep their attention.

10. **Use Audiovisual Devices (if appropriate)**
Audiovisual devices can clarify or enhance your presentation. Depending on the circumstances, you might use audio or video recordings, short films or filmstrips, slides, charts, graphs, illustrations, and diagrams. Use the following questions to determine if your presentation can benefit from the use of one or more audiovisual devices.

- **Will audiovisual devices help clarify a point?** You can easily explain some ideas with just words; other ideas benefit from visual clarification. Using a chart or a poster may save you time and help the audience follow your ideas.
- **Will using audiovisual devices make an idea more memorable?** Do not overload your presentation with audiovisual devices. Decide which points in your speech are important enough to warrant audio or visual emphasis, or both.

- **Will using audiovisual devices distract the audience while you are speaking?** Any audiovisual device you are considering should be essential to your talk but not so engaging that it replaces you as the focus of your audience's attention.

Make sure that your media materials are audible, visible, and legible to your audience. Audio materials should be cued up and ready to play. Visuals should be large enough to read or see. (See also **Document Design** on page 962.)

Group Discussion   A *formal group discussion* takes place when members of a group meet regularly to discuss issues of importance to the entire group. In their meetings, formal groups usually follow an established set of rules known as *parliamentary procedure.* The basic principles of parliamentary procedure, outlined below, protect the rights of individual group members and also provide a system for dealing with issues that come before the group.

1. The majority decides.
2. The minority has the right to be heard.
3. Decisions are made by voting.
4. Only one issue is decided at a time.
5. Everyone is assured of the chance to be heard and has the right to vote.
6. All votes are counted as equal.
7. All sides of an issue are debated.

The best source for information about parliamentary procedure is a book by Henry Robert called *Robert's Rules of Order, Revised.* The order of business and the procedures for the discussion of business presented on the next page come from this book.

Order of Business

A formal meeting usually follows the standard order of business suggested in *Robert's Rules of Order:*

1. Call to order: The chairperson says, "The meeting will come to order."

2. Reading and approval of the minutes: The chairperson says, "The secretary (or recorder) will read the minutes from our previous meeting." The secretary reads the minutes, and the chairperson asks the group, "Are there any additions or corrections to the minutes?" The minutes are then approved, or they are corrected and then approved.

3. Officers' reports: The chairperson calls for a report from other officers who need to report. The chairperson says, for example, "Will the treasurer please give us a report?"

4. Committee reports: The chairperson may ask the presiding officer of each standing committee to report to the group.

5. Old business: Following the committee reports, any issues that were not fully resolved at the last meeting may be discussed. The chairperson asks the group, "Is there any old business to be discussed?"

6. New business: Any new issue that has not been previously discussed may now be addressed (introduced, discussed, and decided).

7. Announcements: The chairperson may ask the members, "Are there any announcements?"

8. Adjournment: The chairperson ends the meeting, saying, "The meeting is now adjourned."

Procedures for Discussion of Business

1. A member introduces a motion (proposal) for discussion by saying, "I move that . . ."

2. Another member must second the motion by saying, "I second the motion."

3. A motion that is seconded may be discussed by the group. A motion that is not seconded cannot be discussed.

4. Other members may move to amend the motion under consideration; to postpone, limit, or extend debate or discussion; or to refer the motion to a committee for further research.

5. After discussion, the group votes on the motion. The chairperson usually only votes to break a tie.

(See also **Informal Group Discussions** on page 1028.)

Interviewing   An *interview* is a communication situation in which one person, the *interviewer*, gathers ideas or information from another person, the *interviewee*. You are the interviewer when you ask another person a series of questions to gather firsthand information for a research paper or a newspaper article or to ascertain a potential employee's qualifications. You are the interviewee when a potential employer or a college admissions officer asks you questions about yourself.

- **Conducting an Interview**   Successful interviews require careful and thoughtful preparation. The chart on the next page gives you suggestions for planning and conducting an interview.

(See also **Listening in an Interview** on page 1033.)

Conducting an Interview	
Preparing for the Interview	• Make arrangements well in advance. Set a convenient time for the interviewee. • Prepare a list of questions. The questions should be open-ended, requiring more than *yes* or *no* answers. (For example, "Tell me what it was like when you arrived in . . .") Arrange the questions in a logical order.
Participating in the Interview	• Arrive on time, and be polite and patient. • Ask the interviewee's permission to take notes or use a tape recorder. • Always be tactful and courteous. Avoid any kind of argument. Remember the interview was granted at your request. • Listen carefully. Ask follow-up questions if you do not understand an answer or if you think you need more information.
Following up on the Interview	• Review your notes to refresh your memory, and then make a summary of the material you have gathered. • Send a thank-you note expressing your appreciation for the interview.

■ **Interviewing for a Job**   Being thoroughly prepared can relieve some of the anxiety of a job interview. The following chart suggests strategies for successful interviewing.

How to Interview for a Position

1. Arrange an appointment. Write a business letter of application in which you request an interview for the job. If you are granted an interview, be prompt for your appointment.

2. Bring a résumé. If you have not already submitted a résumé, bring one with you and give it to the interviewer. (See also **résumé** on page 1080.)

3. Look your best. Be neat and well-groomed. Wear appropriate clothing.

4. Answer questions clearly and honestly. Answer the interviewer's questions accurately. Add any additional information that might convince the interviewer that you are the right person for the job.

5. Ask questions. Job applicants often ask questions about work hours, salary, and chances for advancement. By your questions, show that you know something about the company or business and that you would welcome the chance to be part of it.

6. Be prepared to be tested. The employer may require you to take tests to demonstrate your skills, intelligence, or personality.

7. Follow up the interview. After the interview, write a short thank-you note. Tell the interviewer that you appreciated the opportunity for the interview and that you look forward to hearing from the company in the near future.

Informal Speaking Occasions

Most of the communication that you do is informal—asking for and sharing information in a casual situation. Informal speaking situations allow you personal and up-close contact, unlike formal speaking situations, in which you are usually at a distance from your audience. The following chart describes some common informal speaking situations, which tend to be social or informational in nature.

Informal Speaking Situations

Situation	Purpose	Preparation and Presentation
Critique	To give criticism in a constructive manner (School or business situation)	Think about the effect you want to achieve. Clearly state the problem and the solution. Praise things the person does well. Speak truthfully and positively.
Directions	To explain how to get to a particular place (Informational situation)	Choose the easiest route. Divide the route into logical steps. Use precise terms that are accurate or visual (e.g., "Turn east"). If necessary, draw a map. Repeat any steps if the listener is confused.
Impromptu speech	To speak for five minutes on a particular topic without any previous preparation (Informational situation)	If you choose the topic, think of one that is appropriate for your audience and the occasion. Think of an attention-getting opener, a main idea with supporting details. Speak clearly in a confident voice. Adopt a tone that is appropriate for the topic.
Instructions	To give information on how to do a particular task (Informational situation)	Divide the information into clear, logical steps. Give the steps in order. Use transitions such as *first, second, next,* and *finally.* Make sure your listener understands.
Introduction	To introduce yourself or another person to a person or group (Social situation)	Take the initiative, and introduce yourself if no one else does. When introducing another person, identify the person by name. When introducing another person, mention first the name of • the person with higher status • the older person • the person you know better
Telephone conversation	To communicate via telephone (Social situation)	Call people at appropriate times of day. Identify yourself, and state the reason for your call. Be polite and patient. Limit your call to an appropriate length.

Informal Group Discussions An *informal group discussion* is one that takes place when a group is small enough to allow everyone to participate. Informal group discussions have no formal rules or procedures. In some groups, the discussion follows an *agenda,* a prepared order of topics, set by the chairperson. In other groups, the agenda is established by a preliminary discussion and agreed upon by the group. To be effective, informal group discussions require that each participant play a role and take on certain responsibilities. The first of the following charts shows typical purposes for informal group discussions. The second chart lists the responsibilities of group members, the chairperson, and the secretary or recorder.

Purposes for Informal Group Discussion

- to brainstorm and share ideas
- to learn cooperatively
- to make a decision, evaluation, or recommendation
- to make plans
- to negotiate agreements
- to resolve conflicts
- to solve a problem

Group Members' Responsibilities

All Group Members

1. To make relevant contributions to the discussion.

2. Cooperate with other members, and respond appropriately to others' opinions and suggestions.

3. Stick to the subject under discussion.

4. Ask clear questions for a variety of purposes.

The Chairperson

1. Announces the topic, and explains the agenda.

2. Follows the agenda, keeping the discussion on the topics to be considered.

3. Encourages participation by each member.

4. Avoids disagreements by being objective and settling conflicts or confusions fairly.

The Group Secretary or Recorder

1. Makes notes of significant information or actions.

2. Prepares a final report. Often, this report is a record of the group's discussion for use at the next group meeting

Oral Interpretation

In an *oral interpretation,* you present your interpretation of a work of literature to a group of listeners. Both you and your listeners benefit from an oral interpretation. You learn more about the work of literature as you prepare to interpret it. Your performance of the work makes it more meaningful to your listeners.

When presenting your interpretation, you use both acting and speaking skills—vocal techniques, facial expressions, body language, and gestures—to express the overall meaning of the literary work. Use the following strategies to create an oral interpretation.

1. Find and cut material. It is easier to select material for an oral interpretation if you have a specific purpose and audience in mind. A practical consideration is the length of time allotted for your presentation. Props and costumes are not usually used for oral interpretation; instead, the audience relies on its imagination. You may present the full text of one or more short poems or an excerpt from a longer work. Most oral interpretations, however, use an abbreviated version, or **cutting,** of a work of fiction, nonfiction, a long poem, or a play. Use the following guidelines to make a cutting of your work.

- Follow the story line in chronological order.
- Delete tag lines, such as *he responded grumpily.* Instead, use these clues to tell you how to say a character's words.
- Delete passages that do not contribute to the overall effect or general impression you intend to create.

2. **Prepare the reading script.** Type the cutting (double-spaced) and mark your reading script to guide your presentation. For example, you might underline words you wish to emphasize or mark a slash (/) to indicate where you will pause. In the margins, note tone of voice and emotions you want to convey—*sheepishly* or *wistfully,* for example.

3. **Rehearse your interpretation.** Try out several different interpretations (readings) until you find the one you think most effectively expresses the meaning of your selection. Be sure to pronounce words clearly. You can vary your voice and body language to portray different speakers and to reveal their character traits. Use gestures, body language, and your voice to emphasize meaning.

4. **Deliver your presentation.** Write a brief introduction, mentioning the title and the author of your work. Your introduction may also tell something about the author, set the scene, and give some background details. If you are doing an excerpt from a play, for example, you might give some details about events that have already taken place.

Listening

Listening is much more than just hearing a speaker's words. Listening requires that you play an active role in the communication process. As an active listener, you receive both verbal and nonverbal messages from a speaker. You construct meanings for those messages and then respond to those meanings.

Basics of the Listening Process

Listening is an indispensable part of the communication process. Like reading and writing, effective listening involves a process. The stages in the listening process are explained below.

The Three Stages of the Listening Process

Before you listen

- **Be physically and mentally prepared.** You should be physically comfortable and free from thoughts that will interfere with your ability to focus on the speaker's words.

- **Determine your purpose for listening.** Are you listening to be informed? to provide support or understanding? to receive directions or instructions? to be entertained? Identifying your purpose for listening sets you up as an active listener.

- **Add to your prior knowledge of the speaker and the subject.** Do some research or brainstorm with others to gain knowledge about the speaker and the subject. The information you gain will improve your ability to understand and evaluate what the speaker says.

- **Keep an open mind.** Set aside any biases, prejudices, or preconceived notions you may have about the speaker or the topic of the speech. Reserve your judgments until after you listen to what the speaker has to say.

(continued)

The Three Stages of the Listening Process

As you listen

- **Make connections to your prior knowledge and experience.** Relate what the speaker is saying to what you already know—from experiences, books and magazines, television, school, and so on.

- **Think of questions you would like to ask the speaker.** After a speech, you may be able to ask the speaker to clarify a point or expand upon an idea. Even if you cannot, thinking of questions as you listen helps you to focus on the speaker's message.

- **Based on what a speaker has said, guess what the speaker will say next.** If you are wrong, try to determine what misled you.

- **Find meaning behind what the speaker says directly.** Make inferences about the speaker's attitudes, opinions, biases. Pay attention to what the speaker does not say.

After you listen

- **Discuss the speaker and the speaker's message.** Get together with others to exchange ideas about the speaker's message, and to agree or disagree about the speaker's opinions. Discuss how the speaker's messages relate to what you have experienced, observed, and read.

- **Write a summary and evaluation.** Writing about a presentation while it is still fresh in your mind can help you clarify and solidify your thoughts and opinions.

Evaluating Yourself as a Listener

How good a listener are you? Understanding what a speaker is saying is as much your responsibility as the speaker's. To evaluate yourself as a listener, measure your listening habits against the characteristics of effective listeners.

Characteristics of an Effective Listener

A good listener should

- be mentally and physically prepared to focus on the speaker's message

- be able to ignore distracting behavior by the speaker or members of the audience

- focus on the speaker throughout the presentation

- follow the organization of the speaker's presentation

- distinguish between facts and opinions

- think of questions to ask the speaker

- determine the speaker's main idea and primary supporting details

- withhold judgment until the presentation is over

- listen for any bias or prejudice expressed by the speaker

- reflect upon the presentation after it is over

- discuss the presentation with others

- ask questions if given the opportunity

- write a summary or evaluation of the presentation

Four Types of Listening

The four basic types of listening are *appreciative*, *critical*, *comprehensive*, and *empathic* listening. Associated with these types of listening are various purposes or reasons for listening.

Appreciative (or Aesthetic) Listening

When you do this type of listening, your purpose is to enjoy. You may, for example, listen to someone read a story or a poem. Use the following strategies to make this type of listening experience more rewarding.

1. **Before you listen, recall your prior knowledge about the work, the genre, and the author.** You may have read the work or other works by the same author. To what literary *genre,* or type, does the work belong? Recall the literary elements (such as conflict, imagery, character, figurative language, sound effects) that are basic to this type of literature. Make predictions about what the work will be like.

2. **While you listen, identify and analyze the effects of artistic elements within the work.** Think about how characters are developed. Identify specific images in the work. Are they effective appeals to your senses? Listen for sound devices such as rhyme and alliteration. How do they affect the rhythm of the text? Listen for figurative language. Are the figures of speech appropriate and effective?

3. **After you listen, discuss the presentation with others and evaluate it.** Were your predictions correct? Can you figure out why any were incorrect? Which literary or artistic elements were most important? Evaluate the speaker's clarity, body language, and voice. Write what you liked and disliked about the presentation and why.

Critical Listening When you listen critically, you try to understand, analyze, and evaluate a speaker's message. Critical listening is one of the most important kinds of listening you do. You use critical listening skills in school, in the workplace, and with media messages. Use the strategies in the following chart to analyze and evaluate media presentations as well as live presentations.

How to Listen Critically	
What to do	**What to listen for**
Identify the speaker's purpose.	Does the speaker make clear why he or she is giving the speech?
Distinguish between facts and opinions.	Does the speaker make statements with which you agree or disagree? Ask yourself why you disagree. (Such statements are opinions. An *opinion* is a belief or a judgment about something that cannot be proved. A *fact* is a statement that can be proved true.)
Identify main ideas.	What are the most important points? Listen for clue words or phrases, such as *major, main,* and *most important.*
Identify significant or supporting details.	What dates, names, or facts does the speaker use to support the main points of the speech? What kinds of examples or explanations support the main ideas?
Identify the order of organization.	What kind of order does the speaker use to present the information—time sequence, spatial order, order of importance, or logical order?
Listen to detect bias.	Is the speaker *biased*, or prejudiced, toward one point of view? Does the speaker use stereotypes? Does the speaker use all-inclusive words such as *never* or *always*? Does the speaker acknowledge other points of view?

(continued)

How to Listen Critically	
What to do	**What to listen for**
Evaluate the speaker's credibility.	Is the speaker an authority on the subject? Does the speaker refer to his or her sources of information? Are sources respectable or credible such as newspaper and journal articles or reference materials?
Note comparisons and contrasts.	Are some details compared or contrasted with others?
Predict outcomes and draw conclusions.	What can you reasonably conclude from the facts and evidence presented in the speech?
Look for logic.	Does the speaker build the arguments in a logical way? Does the speaker use false logic such as hasty generalization, false cause and effect, or circular reasoning?
Look for emotional appeals.	Does the speaker use the bandwagon appeal? the glittering generality? snob appeal? plain-folks appeal? the veiled threat?
Understand cause and effect.	Do some events described by the speaker relate to or affect others? Does the speaker make logical connections between causes and effects?

Comprehensive Listening When you listen to understand the content of a message, you are engaged in *comprehensive listening,* or listening to comprehend. Most of the listening you do in school is of this type, listening for information or instructions.

■ **Listening for Information** You may be listening to a group of college representatives talking about undergraduate programs at their schools, or you may be listening to representatives from different businesses talking about job prospects with their companies. The following strategies are helpful when you listen to acquire information.

1. **The LQ2R Method** This listening strategy takes its name from its four steps.

   L Listen carefully to material as it is being presented.

   Q Question yourself as you listen. Mentally, or in your notes, make a list of questions as they occur to you.

   R Recite in your own words the information as it is being presented. Summarize the material in your mind.

   R Review the entire presentation. Restate or reemphasize the major points.

2. **Note Taking** Listen with a pen or pencil in your hand. An effective way to keep track of a speaker's ideas is to take notes. Do not try to write down everything the speaker says. Instead, jot down the speaker's main points and supporting details. You might add your own thoughts, questions, and comments as you listen or after the speaker finishes. (See also **Study Skills** on page 1035.)

- **Listening to Instructions** Have you ever gotten lost listening to instructions? Because instructions are usually made up of a series of steps, you can easily misunderstand them or remember them incorrectly. The following strategies can help you make sense of instructions.

1. **Listen for the order of the steps.** Listen for words (such as *first, second, next, then,* and *last*) that tell you when one step ends and the next one begins.

2. **Identify the number of steps in the process.** Whenever instructions are long or complicated, take notes. Do not hesitate to ask for clarification or for the speaker to slow down as you take notes.

3. **Visualize each step.** Imagine yourself actually performing each step. Try to get a mental image of what you should be doing at every step in the process.

4. **Review the steps.** When the speaker is finished, be sure you understand the process from beginning to end. Ask questions if you are unsure.

NOTE Often, you listen for information to answer the basic *5W-How?* questions—*Who? What? When? Where? Why?* and *How?* For example, when you take a message on the telephone, you listen for details such as these: *Who* is calling? *What* is the message? *Where* and *when* can the caller be reached? *How* may you help the caller?

Empathic (or Reflective) Listening

This is the kind of listening you do when you listen to a friend or show someone your understanding and respect. You demonstrate your empathy by your facial expressions and body language as well as your verbal responses to the speaker. Here are some strategies to use.

- Do much more listening than talking.
- Show genuine warmth and concern.
- Paraphrase what the speaker says to show your understanding.
- Respond to the speaker's feelings rather than analyzing the facts.
- Keep your opinions to yourself.

Special Listening Situations

Some listening situations, like **interviews** and **group discussions,** require that you participate as a speaker as well as a listener.

Listening in an Interview You are both speaker and listener during an interview. You can use the following listening techniques when you are the interviewer (the person doing the interview) or the interviewee (the person being interviewed). In addition to the strategies recommended in "Conducting an Interview" and "Interviewing for a Job" in the Speaking portion of this section, there are some special listening techniques you can use to make the most of an interview.

- **As interviewer**

1. **When you ask a question, listen to the complete answer.** Be courteous and patient as your interviewee answers. Be thinking of related follow-up questions as he or she responds.

2. **Respect the interviewee's opinions, even if you do not agree.** You may state your disagreement politely *only* if your comment will prompt the interviewee to clarify, expand, or provide support for a statement or claim. Do not express your disagreement if it is likely to upset your interviewee and disrupt the interview.

3. **Monitor your nonverbal communication.** Make sure that your nonverbal reactions,

such as your facial expressions and your gestures, reflect a respectful tone. Maintain good eye contact, nod to show understanding, and smile to indicate your interest.

4. **Always thank the interviewee at the end of your interview.**

■ **As interviewee**

1. **Listen to the interviewer's complete question before answering.** If you start answering before the interviewer finishes asking a question, you might answer a completely different question from what the interviewer intended to ask.

2. **Answer the question.** Stick to the point the interviewer is addressing. Do not simply ignore a question and respond with something totally off track.

Listening in a Group Discussion Your role as listener in a group discussion is quite different from that of a listener in a large audience.

In a group discussion, you are listening in order to respond to others' comments and questions. Use the following tips to listen effectively in a group discussion.

■ **Use nonverbal signals.** To show that you are paying attention, sit up, look attentively at each speaker, and nod to register agreement or understanding.

■ **Show respect for the other group members.** Pay attention and do not interrupt. Refrain from making comments or jokes while others are speaking or listening.

■ **Focus on the speaker.** Concentrate on what the speaker is saying, not on what you intend to say.

■ **Take notes.** Write each speaker's main points, as well as your questions or comments.

■ **Be recognized.** Raise your hand and be recognized before you speak.

Studying and Test Taking

Study Skills and Strategies

You study to do well on tests and get good grades, but you also study for more general purposes: to understand and remember information that you may need later. (See also **Test-Taking Skills and Strategies** on page 1039 and **Reading and Vocabulary** on page 995.)

Making a Study Plan

To make the most effective use of your study time, follow these suggestions.

1. **Know your assignments.** Record all assignments and due dates in a special notebook or planner. Make sure you understand what you are expected to do or know.

2. **Make a plan.** Break large assignments (such as writing a research paper) into steps and then decide the order in which they need to be done. Decide how much time it will take to finish each step and set a deadline for each one.

3. **Concentrate.** Set aside a regular time and place strictly for studying. Can you study more efficiently alone or with a study partner? Discover the study habits that work best for you and then stick with them.

Organizing and Remembering Information

The following strategies and techniques will help you to organize and remember information you need to know for school or for work.

Classifying   *Classification* is a method of organizing items by arranging them into categories or groups. You use classification when you decide how details fit together; when you group items, you are identifying the relationships or patterns among them.

> EXAMPLE   What characteristic do each of the following people have in common?
>
> Robert Browning; Elizabeth Barrett Browning; Matthew Arnold; Alfred, Lord Tennyson; William Wordsworth; Samuel Taylor Coleridge
>
> **Answer:** They were all British poets who lived during the nineteenth century.

You also use classifying when you identify patterns. For example, look at the relationship between the numbers in the following sequence.

EXAMPLE

| What is the next number in the sequence below? |
| 48   53   43   58   38   <u>?</u> |

Answer: To the first number (48), *5* is added to produce 53. From this number, *10* is subtracted to produce 43. Then, *15* is added to produce 58. The pattern is to add, then subtract, by increments of five. Therefore, to produce the next number in the series, you should add *25* to produce *63*.

Graphic Organizers

Graphic organizers such as diagrams, charts, and tables summarize information in a visual form, making the information easier to understand and remember. You may find it useful to adapt readings or class notes to a chart, map, or diagram. (See **Graphic Organizers** on page 1071.)

Memorization

You are more likely to remember important information if you memorize material frequently in short sessions. Use the following guidelines to help improve your memory skills.

How to Memorize

1. Summarize the information. Outline or condense information found in a textbook chapter. List dates, names, and places.

2. Rehearse the material in several different ways. For example, write notes, and read them silently. Then, listen as you read the notes aloud. You might tape-record and play back material you are memorizing.

3. Use memory games. Form a word or acronym from the first letters of key terms. Make up a rhyme or associate the information with a particularly vivid mental image.

Notes on Reading or Lectures

Taking careful *notes* while you are reading or listening to a lecture will help you to organize and remember information for later when you are studying or writing research papers. Keep the following guidelines in mind as you take notes.

How to Take Study Notes

1. Recognize and record main points. In a lecture, listen for *key words and phrases* such as *major* or *most important*. In a textbook, look for chapter headings, subheadings, lists, charts, and time lines.

2. Summarize what you hear or read. Use abbreviations and condense information about main ideas. As you take notes, indent supporting points under main ideas.

3. Note important examples. A few vivid examples can help you recall main ideas. Jotting the word *detritus* in your notes, for instance, along with a sketch of decaying leaves, will help you remember that *detritus* refers to disintegrating material.

Look closely at the following student notes. The details about various scientists are all grouped together under a single heading that reminds a reader of the main idea.

Major Figures of the Scientific Revolution

- Nicolaus Copernicus (1473–1543), Polish, wrote <u>On the Revolutions of the Heavenly Spheres</u>; proposed sun as center of universe; ideas controversial
- Galileo Galilei (1564–1642), Italian, first to use telescope; described universe using mathematics
- Isaac Newton (1642–1727), English, wrote <u>Mathematical Principles of Natural Philosophy</u>; theory: universe a machine with regular laws (replaced by Einstein's theory of relativity)

Outlines An *outline* helps you organize information by grouping main ideas and details in a way that shows their relationship to each other and their relative importance. (See also **Outlines** on page 1074.)

Paraphrasing A *paraphrase* is a restatement of someone else's ideas in your own words. Paraphrasing can help you understand the meaning of a complex poem or prose passage. A paraphrase is longer than a *summary* (see below) because a paraphrase includes not only main ideas, but also important details. Since a paraphrase is roughly the same length as the original, paraphrasing is seldom used for long passages. (See also **Paraphrasing** on pages 189 and 997.)

SQ3R *SQ3R* stands for *Survey, Question, Read, Recite,* and *Review.* SQ3R is a 5-step strategy designed to help you study a book or textbook. (See also **SQ3R** on page 999.)

Summarizing *Summarizing* is restating the main ideas of a text or lecture in condensed form. A summary can help you understand the basic meaning of a selection you are studying. Writing a summary also helps you think critically; you have to analyze the material, identify the important ideas, and eliminate less significant details. (See also **Summarizing** on pages 238 and 1000.)

Writing a Précis When you write a précis, you shorten a piece of writing (such as a reading passage, a chapter, an article, or a report) to its bare essentials. A précis is shorter than a summary. In writing a précis, use the conventions described in the following chart.

How to Write a Précis

1. Be brief. A précis is seldom more than a third as long as the material you are summarizing, often less than a third.

2. Do not paraphrase. If you merely reword each sentence, you will wind up with as much material as the original.

3. Stick to key points. Cut details, descriptions, examples, and repetition.

4. Use your own words. Do not just take phrases or sentences from the original.

5. Be faithful to the author's points and views. Do not add your own ideas or comments. Do not use the expressions "the author says" or "the passage means."

Here is a sample reading passage. A précis follows the chart on the next page.

Sample Passage

What is particularly strange about the current passivity regarding travel is that not so very long ago the reverse was considered to be the norm; once upon a time, flying was a highly participatory activity—as was automobile driving. As recently as the middle of the twentieth century, the driver of an ordinary car expected to be intimately involved with the event of driving by means of direct access to the steering wheel, brakes, transmission, and the outside environment. Since then, however, the automobile driver has given up any direct involvement with his or her vehicle in favor of power controls, automatic transmissions, on-board computerized readouts, and sealed-in passenger interiors. Nowadays, only the most adventurous people insist on direct participation in the act of driving by means of sports cars, the last vestige of the old ways. (136 words)

Common Errors in Précis Writing

Type of Error	Example
Précis uses phrases taken directly from original.	Until about the 1950s, travel by air or auto was a <u>highly participatory activity</u>.
Précis misses the point of the original or emphasizes unimportant points.	Makers of modern vehicles have really <u>improved many models</u> by adding devices <u>that make driving much less complicated</u>.
Writer of précis injects own ideas.	Today, however, almost all cars insulate their drivers, and <u>that detachment decreases the full enjoyment of travel</u>.

Sample Précis

Until about the 1950s, airplane and automobile drivers interacted directly with their vehicles and surroundings. Today, however, almost all cars insulate drivers from direct contact with their machinery and the environment. Only the boldest of adventurers demand hands-on driving, still found in driving sports cars. (45 words)

When you write a précis, avoid the errors listed in the chart above. Examples in the right-hand column refer to the sample passage on page 1037.

Writing to Learn   Writing is a valuable study tool. Writing helps you to clarify your thoughts, analyze and recall information, and plan your work. Here are some ways you can use writing when you study.

Writing to Learn

Type of Writing	How it Helps	Example
Freewriting	To focus your thoughts and identify key ideas	Write notes on the Industrial Revolution before writing an essay on the topic.
Autobiographical Notes	To help you examine the meaning of important events in your life	Record your impressions of a visit to a prospective college.
Diaries	To recall your impressions and express your feelings	Write your thoughts and opinions about issues raised during class or in a reading passage.
Journals and Learning Logs	To record observations, descriptions, solutions, and questions	Write down each step in the process of doing research or conducting an experiment.
	To present a problem, analyze it, and propose a solution	Write about a community problem and propose a solution.

Test-Taking Skills and Strategies

Classroom Tests   The typical *classroom test* measures your ability to use important academic skills or to show your knowledge of specific academic subjects. Classroom tests often combine several types of test questions and scoring methods. For example, you might take a test with thirty completion items worth two points each and two essay questions worth twenty points each. The best way to prepare for a classroom test is to be sure you are familiar with the assigned material or to practice the skill to be tested until you are proficient at it. If you review and use the study skills outlined in the preceding section, you can generally improve your performance on classroom tests. It is also useful to be familiar with the kinds of questions that typically appear on classroom tests.

Essay Questions   An *essay question* is intended to measure your ability to express your understanding of selected material in an organized, written form. Writing an essay for a test requires both critical thinking and writing skills. A well-written essay answer must be a complete response to the question asked and must contain a sufficient amount of information to demonstrate thorough knowledge of the material. To study for an essay test, use the following guidelines:

- Read carefully the text on which you are being tested. Take notes on the major ideas and important examples.
- Use your reading notes to make an outline. If you are studying a science or history text, identify main points and important details.

For a literary text, take notes on plot, character, theme, and other literary elements.

- Make up several possible essay questions and prepare an answer to each question.
- Evaluate and revise your practice answers. Check your notes and textbook to make sure your answers are accurate.

For strategies on how to answer essay questions during a test, take a look at the following chart.

How to Answer Essay Questions

1. Scan the test questions. If you have a choice between several items, pick those you can answer best. Plan how much time to spend on each answer; then, stay on schedule.

2. Read the question carefully. Note that there may be several parts to the question.

3. Pay attention to important terms in the questions. Pay attention to each key verb and identify the tasks that you need to accomplish in your essay.

4. Take a moment to use prewriting strategies. Make notes or a simple outline on scratch paper to help you plan your response.

5. Evaluate and revise as you write. You will not be able to redraft your whole essay, but you can edit to strengthen it. Be sure to leave yourself some time to proofread for spelling, punctuation, and grammatical errors.

Essay questions ask you to perform specific tasks, each of which is indicated in the question with a verb. Become familiar with these tasks by reviewing the verbs commonly used in essay questions and the kinds of information they require. The chart on the next page will help you.

Key Verbs That Appear in Essay Questions

Key Verb	Task	Sample Question
Analyze	Take something apart to see how each part works.	Analyze the process of amending the U.S. Constitution.
Argue	Take a viewpoint on an issue and give reasons to support this opinion.	Argue whether or not students who fail a class should repeat it.
Compare or Contrast	Point out likenesses or differences.	Compare Mel Gibson and Laurence Olivier in *Hamlet.* Contrast the processes of fission and fusion.
Define	Give specific details that make something unique.	Define the term *gouache* as an artistic medium.
Demonstrate, Illustrate, Present, Show	Provide examples to support a point.	Demonstrate the advantages of using a word processor.
Describe	Give a picture in words.	Describe the storm scene in *King Lear.*
Discuss	Examine in detail.	Discuss the end of the Soviet Union.
Explain	Give reasons.	Explain gravity.
Identify	Point out specific persons, places, things, or characteristics.	Identify the major political figures in the Watergate scandal.
Interpret	Give the meaning or significance of something.	Interpret the meaning of the Monroe Doctrine in terms of American foreign policy.
List, Outline, Trace	Give all steps in order or all details about a subject.	List the events leading to the invasion of Kuwait by Iraq.
Summarize	Give a brief overview of the main points.	Summarize the plot of Bernard Shaw's *Pygmalion.*

There are endless varieties of essay questions, but all good answers contain the same qualities:

- The main idea is presented early and clearly.
- The essay is well organized.
- The supporting points are specific and tied to the main idea.
- The sentences are complete and well written.
- There are no distracting errors in spelling, punctuation, or grammar.

Matching Questions
Matching questions ask you to match up the items on two lists.

EXAMPLE

Directions: Match each literary work with its author. Write the letter of the title in the space preceding the author's name.

_E_	**1.** George Eliot	**A.**	"The Convergence of the Twain"
_C_	**2.** John Keats	**B.**	*Mrs. Dalloway*
_D_	**3.** William Blake	**C.**	"To Autumn"
_A_	**4.** Thomas Hardy	**D.**	"The Tyger"
_B_	**5.** Virginia Woolf	**E.**	*Silas Marner*

How to Answer Matching Questions

1. Read the directions carefully. Some answers may be used more than once.

2. Scan the columns and match items you know first. Then, take a few minutes to evaluate the answers about which you are less sure.

3. Complete the matching process. If any items remain unmatched, make your best guess.

Multiple-Choice Questions
To answer multiple-choice questions, you must select a correct answer from among a number of choices.

EXAMPLE

1. Which of the following events did *not* take place in 1948?

  A. Israel is declared a nation.

  B. Indian leader Mohandas K. Gandhi is assassinated.

  C. Fidel Castro becomes premier of Cuba.

  D. Harry S. Truman is elected president of the United States.

How to Answer Multiple-Choice Questions

1. Read the initial statement carefully. Make sure you understand the statement completely before examining your answer choices.

2. Always look for qualifiers, such as *not, always,* or *never.* Qualifiers limit, or affect, the answer in an important way. In the preceding example, if you do not notice the word *not,* you might choose an event that *did* happen in 1948 and answer incorrectly.

3. Read all of the answers before making a choice. Some answers combine two or more choices, such as "Both A and B" or "All of the above."

4. Narrow your choices by eliminating answers you know are incorrect. Often at least one choice is clearly wrong, while others may be somewhat related to the correct answer. If you already know that Gandhi was assassinated in 1948, and you are looking for the event that did *not* happen in 1948, you can easily rule out Answer B.

5. From the remaining choices, select the answer that makes the most sense. In this example, *C* is the correct answer; Castro did not become premier of Cuba until 1959.

Short-Answer Questions
Short-answer questions ask you to explain what you know about a subject in a brief, written response. Most of the time, short-answer questions require a specific answer of one or two sentences. Some fill-in-the-blank questions—or maps or diagrams that you are supposed to label—can be answered with one or a few words.

EXAMPLE

1. Briefly describe how Samuel Johnson used actual quotations from books to write his *Dictionary of the English Language*.

1. Samuel Johnson examined thousands of books and marked quotations of words in context. He wrote his definitions based on the way words were actually used in context and also included the quoted passages, arranged in chronological order, in his dictionary entries.

True/False Questions

True/False questions ask you to decide whether a given statement is true or false.

EXAMPLE

1. T (F) The meanings of all current English words had been standardized at least 100 years before Samuel Johnson undertook to write his *Dictionary*.

How to Answer True/False Questions

1. Read the statement carefully.

2. Check for qualifiers. Words such as *always, all, none,* or *never* qualify or limit a statement's meaning and may even make a statement untrue.

3. Choose an answer based on the following principles:

- If any part of the statement is false, the entire statement is false.
- A statement is true only if it is completely and always true.

Standardized Tests

On **standardized tests,** your score is evaluated according to a standard or norm compiled from the scores of a great number of other students who have taken the same test. Standardized tests required by a specific school district or by your particular state, such as the *Scholastic Assessment Test (SAT)* and the *American College Testing*

Program (ACT), are also given to students across the entire United States. The two basic types of standardized tests are described in the following chart.

Types of Standardized Tests

Aptitude (or Reasoning) Tests

- intended to assess basic skills or reasoning abilities that are needed in various general areas of higher-level study
- often cover material you have learned during many years of study (such as verbal expression and critical-thinking skills)

Achievement (or Academic Subject) Tests

- intended to measure knowledge of specific subjects (such as history, literature, sciences, mathematics, or foreign languages)
- some achievement tests are used to obtain college credit and placement

To help you prepare for both kinds of tests, keep in mind the three tips in the following chart:

How to Prepare for a Standardized Test

1. Learn what specific abilities will be tested and what kind of questions will be asked. Test makers often distribute information booklets. It often helps to practice with these or with published study guides.

2. Know what materials you will need. You may need to bring specific materials to the testing center, such as your official test registration card, number 2 pencils, or lined paper for writing an essay.

3. Determine how the test is evaluated. If there is no penalty for wrong answers, make your best guess on all questions possible. If wrong answers are penalized, make guesses only if you are fairly sure of the correct answer.

Analogy Questions *Analogy questions* require you to analyze the relationship between a pair of words (called the **stem pair**) and to identify a second pair of words that has the same relationship. These questions measure your command of vocabulary as well as your ability to identify word patterns and relationships. Analogy questions usually appear on standardized tests in multiple-choice form. (Be sure to note the symbols used in analogy questions; the symbol : means "is related to," and :: means "is equivalent to.")

> EXAMPLE
> **Directions:** Write the letter of the pair of words that completes the analogy.
> THERMOMETER : TEMPERATURE :: _____
> **A.** speedometer : car
> **B.** snow : cold
> **C.** barrel : rain
> **D.** ruler : length

Sometimes analogy questions are written as fill-in-the-blank questions, in which you provide the missing item.

> EXAMPLE
> **Directions:** Complete the following analogy.
> INSOLVENT : BANKRUPT :: loquacious :
> _talkative_

How to Answer Analogy Questions

1. Analyze the first pair of words and identify the relationship between them. In the first example, a *thermometer* is an instrument used to measure temperature. (For more about types of relationships in analogies, see the **Types of Analogies** chart on page 1044.)

2. Express the analogy in sentence or question form. The analogy in the first example can be expressed as, "A *thermometer* is used to measure *temperature,* just as a _____ is used to measure

_____." Then, fill the blank with each pair of words provided to see which makes sense.

3. Find the best available choice to complete the analogy. If you are given multiple choices, select the pair of words that has the same type of relationship as the first pair given in the question. If you must fill in the blank to complete an analogy, you are usually given one word of the second pair of words. You need to supply a word that gives the second pair of words the same relationship as the first pair.

Here are some additional strategies for solving analogy questions.

- **Consider the parts of speech.** Some words may be used as more than one part of speech. If you cannot unlock the relationship in the analogy, it may help to determine if one of the words can be another part of speech.

- **Familiarize yourself with the types of analogy relationships.** Become familiar with the types of analogies typically found on standardized tests. (See the **Types of Analogies** chart on page 1044.)

- **Remember that it is the relationship between the words that is important, not the meanings of the individual words.** Look again at the example provided above the "How to Answer Analogy Questions" chart. *Insolvent* and *loquacious* have nothing in common; but the relationship between *insolvent* and *bankrupt* is the same as the one between *loquacious* and *talkative. Bankrupt* is a synonym for *insolvent,* and *talkative* is a synonym for *loquacious.*

Many different relationships can be represented in analogy questions. Examples of the most common relationships are shown in the chart on the following page.

Types of Analogies

Type	Example	Solution
Action to Performer or **Performer to Action**	COOKING : CHEF :: shaving : barber	*Cooking* is performed by a *chef,* just as *shaving* is performed by a *barber.*
Antonyms or **Synonyms**	SERENE : AGITATED :: determined : hesitant	*Serene* is the opposite of *agitated,* just as *determined* is the opposite of *hesitant.*
Cause or **Effect**	MATCH : IGNITION :: flood : destruction	A *match* causes *ignition,* just as a *flood* causes *destruction.*
Characteristic	SPENDTHRIFT : EXTRAVAGANT :: optimist : hopeful	A *spendthrift* is always *extravagant,* just as an *optimist* is always *hopeful.*
Classification	IRON : MINERAL :: neon : gas	*Iron* belongs to the category of *minerals,* just as *neon* belongs to the category of *gases.*
Degree	TERROR : FEAR :: condemnation : disapproval	*Terror* is an extreme form of *fear,* just as a *condemnation* is an extreme type of *disapproval.*
Measure	DECIBEL : VOLUME :: meter : length	A *decibel* is a unit used to measure *volume,* just as a *meter* is a unit used to measure *length.*
Part to Whole or **Whole to Part**	TALON : HAWK :: tentacle : octopus	A *talon* is a part of a *hawk,* just as a *tentacle* is a part of an *octopus.*
Place	GRAND CANYON NATIONAL PARK : ARIZONA :: Mt. Rainier : Washington	*Grand Canyon National Park* is in *Arizona,* just as *Mt. Rainier* is in *Washington.*
Time Sequence	ACORN : OAK :: caterpillar : butterfly	An *oak* grows from an *acorn,* just as a *butterfly* grows from a *caterpillar.*
Use	JEWELRY : ADORNMENT :: umbrella : protection	*Jewelry* is used for *adornment,* just as an *umbrella* is used for *protection.*

Critical-Reading Questions   Standardized tests may contain questions that measure your ability to analyze and interpret a piece of writing. These *critical-reading questions* (sometimes called *on-demand reading questions*) require you to analyze the meaning, purpose, and organization of a reading passage. In addition, these questions may require you to evaluate how effectively the passage conveys the meaning intended by the writer.

Critical-reading questions focus on either a particular approach to the passage or an element within it. The following chart shows types of critical-reading questions and the actions you must take to answer them. For more information and practice with any of the bulleted elements indicated, see the pages referred to in parentheses after each item.

Critical-Reading Test Questions

Rhetorical Strategy Questions (or Evaluation Questions) You analyze and evaluate the effectiveness of specific techniques used by the author of a reading passage. Test items often cover identification of

- the author's intended audience
- the author's opinion (page 337)
- the author's purpose
- the author's tone or point of view (page 297)
- the author's strategies of development

(See also page 342.)

Interpretation Questions (or Inference Questions) You draw conclusions or make inferences about the meaning of information presented in a reading passage. These test items often cover identification of

- ambiguities in information
- conclusions or inferences based on given material (page 997)
- specific conclusions or inferences that can be drawn about the author or the topic of a passage (page 996)

(See also page 66.)

Organization Questions (or Main Idea and Detail Questions) You identify the organizational techniques used by the author of a reading passage. These test items often cover identification of

- the author's use of particular writing strategies
- the main idea of a passage (page 243)
- specific supporting details (page 108)
- techniques used to conclude the passage (pages 486 and 1069)
- transitional devices that make the passage coherent (pages 469 and 484)

Style Questions (or Tone Questions) You analyze a passage to evaluate the author's use of style. These test questions often cover identification of

- the author's intended audience
- the author's style
- the author's voice and tone

(See also page 300.)

Synthesis Questions You show your understanding of how each part of a passage fits together into a whole. These test items often cover interpretation of

- the cumulative meaning of details in a passage
- techniques used to unify details (page 468)

Vocabulary-in-Context Questions You infer the meaning of an unfamiliar word by using context clues.

(See also page 27.)

Here is a typical reading passage, followed by sample test questions.

During the period from 1660 through 1800, Great Britain became convinced of its place as the world's leader. Beginning with the restoration of Charles II to the throne, this period in England's history is best described as a period of authority.

(continued)

(continued)

Language itself became submitted to rules during this period. This need to "fix" the English language is best illustrated in the making of *The Dictionary of the English Language* by Samuel Johnson. Guides to the English language had been in existence before Johnson began his project in 1746. These, however, were often little more than lists of hard words. When definitions of common words were supplied, they were often unhelpful. For example, a "horse" was defined in an early dictionary as "a beast well known."

Johnson changed all that, but the task was not an easy one. Renting a house at 17 Gough Square, Johnson began working in the worst of conditions. Supported only by installments from his publisher, Johnson worked on the *Dictionary* with five assistants. Compared to the French Academy's dictionary, which took forty workers fifty-five years to complete (1639–1694), Johnson's dictionary was completed by very few people very quickly.

Balanced on a chair with only three legs, Johnson sat propped against a wall in a room scattered with books. Johnson would read widely from these books, mark quotations illustrating the use of a particular word, and give the books to his assistants so that they could copy the passages on slips of paper. These slips were then pasted in eighty large notebooks under the key words that Johnson had selected. "Fixing" the word by this method, Johnson could record a word's usage and its definition. To help the reader of the *Dictionary* gain a sense of the history of the word, Johnson also arranged the passages chronologically.

How many passages were used? According to Johnson's modern biographer Walter Jackson Bate, the original total number could have been over 240,000. How many words were defined by the lexicographer? Over 40,000 words appeared in two folio volumes in April of 1755. Did Johnson fully understand the enormous task he was undertaking when he began? As he told his contemporary biographer James Boswell, "I knew very well what I was undertaking—and very well how to do it—and have done it very well."

Sample Critical-Reading Questions

1. According to the passage, in which order (from earliest to latest) did the following events occur?
  I. Johnson published his *Dictionary.*
  II. The French Academy's dictionary was published.
  III. Johnson rented a house at 17 Gough Square.
  IV. Charles II was restored to the throne.

  A. II, III, IV, I
  B. IV, II, III, I
  C. IV, I, II, III
  D. IV, III, II, I

[This is an organization question. It requires you to identify the time sequence of these events and to arrange them in the correct historical time order.]

2. Shortly before the publication of the *Dictionary,* Johnson wrote a famous letter to the noble and wealthy Lord Chesterfield, who had been Johnson's sponsor during the project. The following lines are an excerpt from that letter.

Seven years, my Lord, have passed since I waited in your outward rooms,

Sample Critical-Reading Questions

or was repulsed from your door; during which time I have been pushing on my work through difficulties, of which it is useless to complain, and have brought it, at last, to the verge of publication, without one act of assistance, one word of encouragement, or one smile of favor. Such treatment I did not expect, for I never had a Patron before. . . .

You could assume that Johnson is critical of

(A.) the lack of assistance from Chesterfield.
B. the conditions under which he had to work.
C. royalty.
D. patrons.

[This is an evaluation question. It requires you to recognize the main point of the original passage and to analyze the second passage to identify which of these main points fits with Johnson's complaint.]

3. The word *fixing* in paragraph four is best taken to mean

A. repairing.
B. correcting.
(C.) standardizing.
D. augmenting.

[This is an interpretation question. You are asked to examine the context of the word noted in order to explain its meaning in the passage.]

4. It can be inferred from the description of Samuel Johnson that he was a man who

(A.) represented the eighteenth century.
B. worked inconsistently.
C. never worked under impoverished conditions.
D. was jealous and petty.

[This is an inference question; the question also asks you to *synthesize* the meaning of the passage as a whole. After reading in the passage about the details of the eighteenth-century preoccupation with standardization,

you can conclude that Johnson's attempt to standardize English was in keeping with the times in which he lived.]

5. The word *lexicographer* in paragraph five means

(A.) a maker of dictionaries.
B. a biographer.
C. a scholar.
D. a harmless fellow.

[This is a vocabulary-in-context question. It requires you to examine the context of the passage in which the word appears in order to determine the appropriate definition.]

6. Readers of the reading passage are likely to describe it as

A. informal
B. confessional
(C.) historical
D. biographical

[This is a style question. You analyze the way the passage is written to determine the type of writing it represents.]

Multiple-Choice Questions   Many of the questions you encounter on standardized tests will be *multiple-choice questions* similar to those you have seen on classroom tests. Usually, the multiple-choice questions on a standardized test will vary in difficulty, often starting out easy and becoming progressively more challenging. Since all questions are probably worth the same number of points, be sure to answer all the easy questions first, and then come back to work on the more difficult ones. Keep track of time—you don't want to spend too much time on any single question or get into a situation where time constraints lead you to make careless mistakes. (See also **Multiple-Choice Questions** on page 1041.)

On-Demand Writing Prompts   *On-demand writing prompts,* like essay questions, require you to write several paragraphs in a limited amount of time. The key difference between on-demand writing prompts and essay questions is that you cannot study beforehand for an on-demand writing test. On-demand writing prompts require you to write an essay (either persuasive, informative, or descriptive) in response to a broad question that is often related to your experience. Such questions are the core of many statewide writing tests.

EXAMPLE

Many schools across the country require students to perform a specified number of hours of community service in order to graduate from high school. Students' volunteer work must be approved and verified by a school guidance counselor or other school employee in charge of the program. Write a persuasive essay in which you argue for or against such a requirement.

Another kind of on-demand writing prompt, found on placement tests, asks you to demonstrate your knowledge of a specific subject area. For example, the prompt on a placement test for English might require you to know certain novels or plays and to show that you understand literary elements and their role in a piece of literature.

EXAMPLE

Select a literary work in which setting plays an important role. In a well-organized essay, describe how different aspects of the setting contribute to the overall tone or message of the work. Avoid plot summary. Do not base your essay on a movie, television program, or any other adaptation of a work.

How to Respond to an On-Demand Writing Prompt

1. Read the question carefully and determine what it is asking. Key verbs will tell you whether your answer should be persuasive, informative, or descriptive. (See also **Key Verbs That Appear in Essay Questions** on page 1040.) Also, determine how long your response must be.

2. Use prewriting strategies to plan your answer. Brainstorm, jot down notes, or make a rough outline of what you want to say in your answer. Take the time to plan your answer—identifying your main ideas and supporting details—before you start writing. (For more on **prewriting strategies,** see pages 1077–1080.)

3. Follow your plan and be sure your points do not stray from your controlling idea. In other words, make sure you address the prompt.

4. Evaluate and revise your answer as you write. Make sure that your answer has a topic sentence, supporting details, transitions between ideas, and a clear conclusion.

NOTE Although you cannot study for the content of an on-demand writing test, you can still prepare yourself by becoming familiar with the types of writing required by on-demand writing prompts. Find out if your school library or counselor has a collection of tests administered at your school in the past. Practice answering the questions, using a timer to help you get used to the time constraints.

Reasoning or Logic Questions

Reasoning or logic questions (sometimes called *sentence completion questions*) measure your ability to recognize certain kinds of relationships. To answer these questions, you need to analyze a sentence or a brief passage and fill in one or more blanks with the most appropriate word or words from among the choices given.

EXAMPLE

Since Samuel Johnson's huge task was so _____, he never did receive fair _____ for completing the *Dictionary*.

A. minimal . . . criticism
B. herculean . . . remuneration
C. banal . . . recognition
D. equivocal . . . compensation

How to Answer Reasoning or Logic Questions

1. Be sure that you understand the instructions. Reasoning or logic questions are usually multiple choice. Determine how you are to mark your answer.

2. Analyze the meaning implied in the question. The question suggests a cause-and-effect relationship between the degree of difficulty of Johnson's task and his not receiving a fair "something."

3. Try out each pair of words in the sentence. Remember that *both* words must make perfect sense. The second word in answer D (*compensation*) could be the right one, but the first word (*equivocal*) makes no sense in the context of the sentence.

Verbal-Expression Questions

Standardized tests of verbal expression measure your ability to understand the meaning expressed in written passages and to judge the grammatical correctness or clarity of written expression. The chart below indicates different types of verbal-expression questions. For more information about any of the grammar, usage, and mechanics items listed, see the pages referred to in parentheses after each item.

Types of Verbal-Expression Questions

Grammar Questions   You demonstrate your knowledge of standard grammar and usage rules. These test items often cover correct use of

- principal parts of verbs (page 670)
- pronouns (page 630)
- subject-verb agreement (page 600)

Punctuation Questions   You identify use of correct punctuation. These test items often cover correct use of

- apostrophes, hyphens, dashes, and parentheses (pages 868, 874, and 878)
- end marks and commas (pages 820 and 827)
- quotation marks (page 859)
- semicolons and colons (pages 850 and 853)

Sentence-Structure Questions   You demonstrate knowledge of what is (and what is not) a complete sentence. These test items often cover

- combining sentences (page 438)
- fragments and run-ons (page 922)
- modifiers (page 934)
- parallel structure (page 426)
- transitional words (page 484)
- verb tense (page 933)

Revision-in-Context Questions   You show appropriate revision of a part of or an entire composition. These test items often cover correct use of

- arranging ideas (page 469)
- composition structure (page 464)
- tone (page 1083)
- unity and coherence (page 468)

Multiple-choice verbal-expression questions are usually not presented as isolated questions. Instead, they appear in the context of a reading passage. You are given a sample passage, usually a long paragraph, with several words and phrases underlined and numbered. Then you are given a series of test items related to the passage. For each item, you are expected to select the answer that best expresses the meaning, is grammatically correct, or is consistent with the style and tone of the passage. The chart on page 1050 describes the two most common types of verbal-expression test items. A typical verbal expression passage with sample questions follows the chart.

Most Common Types of Verbal-Expression Test Items

"NO CHANGE" Items
- give a list of suggested revisions for under-lined, numbered portions of a passage
- always contain one "NO CHANGE" choice (often printed in capital letters); this means that indicated part is correct as is

Critical-Thinking Items
- ask you to analyze and evaluate the passage as a whole
- ask you to make inferences about portions of a passage as related to the whole

Everyone has fears. Young children are often terrified of being left alone in the dark, trembling in their beds at night. With a slightly queasy stomach—a(1) passenger momentarily grips the seat arms as the huge jet lumbers up the runway for takeoff. A high school student is faced with a three-minute speech in front of classmates. She feels weak-kneed and dry-mouthed as the moment approaches. These fears are normal; everyone has them, or is in danger of suffering such fears,(2) at some time. For most people, however, the moment passes and so do(3) the fear and its accompanying physical reactions. The child grows older and becomes less afraid of the dark; the traveler continues to fly; the student survives the speech.

Sample Verbal-Expression Questions

1. A. NO CHANGE
   B. stomach, a
   C. stomach. A
   D. stomach; a

[This is a question about punctuation. It requires you to know which mark of punctuation is appropriate here.]

2. Which of the following is the best revision of the portion of the passage indicated by the number 2?
   A. fears to be similar to them,
   B. everyone feels fears like these,
   C. might have them,
   D. fears like them—

[This is a revision-in-context question. It requires you to use revision skills to choose the answer that best expresses the idea in the passage.]

3. A. NO CHANGE
   B. did
   C. does
   D. would do

[This is a question about grammar. It requires you to know the correct subject-verb agreement and consistency of verb tense.]

4. If the fourth and fifth sentences were combined into one sentence, how might it begin?
   A. A high school student has been faced with a three-minute speech, but. . . .
   B. A high school student in front of class-mates feels. . . .
   C. When a high school student is faced with a three-minute speech in front of classmates, she feels. . . .
   D. When a high school student feels weak-kneed and dry-mouthed, then she. . . .

[This is a question about sentence structure. It requires you to know how to combine sentences effectively.]

Viewing and Representing

Media Terms

Because media messages, such as advertisements, television programs, music videos, and movies, are a constant part of life, it is important to be able to understand, interpret, analyze, evaluate, and create media messages. The terms defined below refer to many different areas of media communication, including television and film production, advertising, and journalism. The terms are grouped into three lists: **electronic media terms** (below), **general media terms** (page 1055), and **print media terms** (page 1060). (Terms relating to the Internet and the World Wide Web can be found in the **Library/Media Center** section on page 984; terms relating to the use of type and graphics can be found in **Document Design** on page 962.)

Electronic Media Terms

Advertising   (See **Advertising** on page 1060.)

Affiliate   An *affiliate* is a privately owned, local television or radio station that presents the programming of a national network. (See also **Network** on page 1053.)

Animation   *Animation* is the film art of making drawings appear to move. An animated film may combine drawing, painting, sculpture, or other visual arts. Animators take film or video pictures of a scene at a rate of twenty-four frames per second, making small changes as they go. When viewed, the frames create the illusion of movement. Animation is used in many different types of media messages, including advertising and cartoons. (See also **Advertising** on page 1060.)

Broadcasting   *Broadcasting* means using airwaves to send television or radio content over a wide area of potential viewers or listeners. **Commercial broadcasting** is for profit. Advertisers pay broadcasters for airtime in which to persuade the audience to buy their products or services. **Public broadcasting** is not-for-profit. In the United States, the Public Broadcasting Service (PBS) has more than three hundred affiliates, or member stations. The service is funded mostly by the federal government, corporations, and individual viewers and listeners. (See also **Affiliate** on this page.)

Byline (See **Byline** on page 1060.)

Cable Television *Cable television* is a method of distributing TV signals using cables and wiring instead of airwaves to bring messages into people's homes. There are two principal types of cable TV companies. Some companies *create* original programming in the form of channels or networks, such as all-sports networks or all-movie channels. Other companies *distribute* packages, or groups, of many different channels into homes.

Camera Angle The *camera angle* refers to the angle at which a camera is set when it is pointed at its subject. The angle may be low, high, or tilted. The effect of a low angle is to make the subject look tall and powerful. The high angle makes the subject look small. The tilt angle may suggest that the subject is not balanced.

Camera Shots A *camera shot* is what the viewer sees in a movie or video. A film or video needs many shots in order to create a scene or story. Below are the most common shots used in film production.

- **Close-up shot** A *close-up shot* is a shot of only the subject, usually a person's face.
- **Extreme close-up shot** An *extreme close-up shot* is a very close shot, usually of only part of a person's face or part of the subject.
- **Medium shot** A *medium shot* is a shot that shows the subject, usually a person from the waist up, and perhaps some of the background.
- **Long shot** A *long shot* is a shot that shows a scene from far away, usually to establish the setting of a scene.
- **Reaction shot** A *reaction shot* is a view of the subject's face used to show the subject's reaction to the events in the scene.

- **Reverse angle shot** A *reverse angle shot* is a view of the opposite side of a subject or of another person in the scene.

Channel A *channel* is the means by which a message is communicated. For example, if you are communicating verbally (such as by talking), the channel is sound waves. If you communicate nonverbally (for instance, by gestures, expressions, or sounds such as clapping), the channel is waves of light, sound waves, or the sense of touch. In television and radio, a channel is a fixed band of frequencies used for the transmitting of television or radio broadcasts. (See also **Medium** and **Message** on page 1061.)

Copy (See **Copy** on page 1060.)

Credits *Credits* refer to the list of names of people who worked to produce a program. This list usually appears at the end of a television program, film, or video.

Demographics (See **Demographics** on page 1060.)

Digital Editing (See **Digital Editing** on page 1060.)

Docudrama *Docudrama* is a type of documentary that blends elements of both documentary and drama to explore an actual historical, political, or social event. For example, docudramas may use actors and scripted dialogue to re-create historical events.

Documentary *Documentary* is a genre of film and television programming which uses language, sounds, and imagery to provide an interpretation of real-life events. Although documentaries attempt to relate factual information, they may show only one producer's perceptions or point of view. Documentaries often have informative, persuasive, and artistic purposes.

Drama   *Drama* is an art form that tells a story through the speech and actions of the characters in the story. Most dramas use actors who impersonate the characters. Some dramas are performed in a theater, while others are presented on film.

Editor   (See **Editor** on page 1060.)

Electronic Media   The term *electronic media* refers to the forms of mass media products that are available to consumers through some type of electronic technology, such as a computer or a television. Electronic media products can be found on the Internet, on the radio, and on television.

Feature News   (See **Feature News** on page 1060.)

Hard News   (See **Hard News** on page 1061.)

In-Camera Editing   *In-camera editing* refers to any editing that is performed through the operation of a video or film camera and not by the cutting and shaping of an editor. The shots and scenes remain in the sequence in which they were filmed by the camera operator. In-camera editing is an effective method of creating video when editing equipment is unavailable or when editing is too time-consuming. To create an effective work using in-camera editing, a great deal of preproduction planning is required, including storyboards and a com-

plete shot list. In most cameras, sound can be added after the images have been shot.

Internet   The *Internet* is a global network of computers. With the Internet, a computer user may access information from another computer or a network of computers anywhere in the world. The Internet may be used by almost anyone who has a computer equipped with a modem.

Lead   (See **Lead** on page 1061.)

Marketing   (See **Marketing** on page 1061.)

Medium   (See **Medium** on page 1061.)

Message   (See **Message** on page 1061.)

Multimedia Presentation   A *multimedia presentation* is any presentation that involves two or more forms of media. For example, when you give an oral presentation including visuals (such as artwork, charts, or graphs), you are giving a multimedia presentation, one medium being your voice, the other being the visuals you use to support your presentation. A multimedia presentation that involves the use of presentation software or Web sites is sometimes called a **technology presentation**.

Network   A *network* is a company that obtains and distributes programming to affiliated local stations or cable systems. Networks are not TV stations, but nearly 85 percent of all TV stations are affiliated with a network. Examples of networks include CBS, ABC, NBC, FOX, and WB. Each local station is responsible for its own programming, but a station that is affiliated with a network receives morning news programs, talk shows, soap operas, national news programs, situation comedies, dramas, and late-night programming. The networks provide the programs free to stations in exchange for the right to sell advertising. (See also **Affiliate** on page 1051.)

Nielsen Rating *Nielsen rating* refers to the ratings system invented by the A. C. Nielsen Company, one of the largest marketing research companies in the United States. Nielsen ratings gather information about household television viewing choices from a sample of five thousand households selected to represent the population as a whole. Using a device called a people-meter, the firm gathers and later distributes information, including the program watched, who was watching it, and the amount of time each viewer spent watching. Nielsen ratings are used to measure a program's popularity and to pinpoint target audiences for shows. Advertisers make decisions about buying airtime for their commercials during specific shows, and these decisions are based in part on Nielsen ratings.

News (See **News** on page 1061.)

Newsmagazine (See **Newsmagazine** on page 1061.)

Photography (See **Photography** on page 1062.)

Political Advertising (See **Political Advertising** on page 1062.)

Producer A *producer* is the person responsible for overseeing the creation of a movie or television or radio program. He or she is responsible for the following tasks:

■ developing the overall message

■ finding appropriate materials

■ organizing a crew or staff

■ finding and budgeting funding

■ keeping the production on a timetable

Public Access *Public access* refers to the channels on a cable TV system that are set aside for use by the public to create a variety of programs. These channels are often controlled by education officials or government leaders.

Public Relations (See **Public Relations** on page 1062.)

Ratings *Ratings* refers to the system of categorizing films, TV programs, or video games according to whether the content is appropriate for people of different ages. Ratings help adults and children evaluate the content of a message before viewing. (See also **Nielsen Rating** on this page.)

Reality TV *Reality television* is the presentation of actual video footage taken by amateurs with police monitors and by surveillance cameras. Usually the footage is highly edited, but because reality TV is presented as an eyewitness account, people tend to find it believable.

Reporter (See **Reporter** on page 1062.)

Script A *script* is the text or words of a film or TV or radio show. The format for film and TV scripts often includes information about the images to be shown. The script for news broadcasts is called *copy*. (See also **Copy** on page 1060.)

Sequencing *Sequencing* is the order in which scenes or images appear in a narrative. In TV, film, and video, sequencing is enhanced in the editing process, in which scenes, usually filmed separately and in different locations, are spliced, or joined, together to create a sense of flow or sequence.

Soft News   (See **Soft News** on page 1062.)

Source   (See **Source** on page 1062.)

Sponsorship   A *sponsorship* takes place when a business gives money to support a TV or radio program in return for airtime. Sponsorship is different from advertising because in sponsorship, a company's name is acknowledged, but usually the product is not promoted. Even though public broadcasting does not include commercials, it may include sponsors' names and slogans. (See also **Broadcasting** on page 1051.)

Storyboard   A *storyboard* is a visual script, or series of drawings, that indicates the appearance and order of shots and scenes in a script as well as audio and visual cues. (For an example of a **Storyboard**, see page 91.)

Target Audience   (See **Target Audience** on page 1062.)

Text   (See **Text** on page 1062.)

General Media Terms

Audience   An *audience* is a group of receivers of a media message. Audiences may receive a message by listening, reading, or viewing. The audience is important to mass media business, since advertisers pay to reach specific audiences when they place ads in the media. Audiences are often identified by specific characteristics, or demographics. (See also **Demographics** on page 1060.)

Authority   *Authority* refers to the believability of a message. When a message seems believable because it comes from a trustworthy and knowledgeable individual, the message has authority. For example, a message about the ozone layer would have more authority coming from a scientist than from a non-scientist. (See also **Credibility** below and **Source** on page 1062.)

Bias   A *bias* is a negative connotation of point of view. An editorial writer with a bias may present only one side of an issue or ignore information that does not support his or her position. (See also **Point of View** on page 1059.)

Communicator   A *communicator* is a person involved in the act of sharing messages with others. The communicator is the person who sends the message to the audience. The receiver takes on the role of communicator when he or she returns the message.

Credibility   *Credibility* is the willingness to believe in a person or to trust what a person says and does. Credibility is not a characteristic of a speaker. It is a perception that exists in the mind of a listener or viewer. (See also **Authority** above.)

Critical Viewing   *Critical viewing* is the ability to use critical thinking skills to view, question, analyze, and understand issues presented in visual media, including photography, film, and TV. Critical viewers use **media literacy** concepts to access, analyze, evaluate, and communicate media messages. On the next page are five key concepts of media literacy and some questions to help you evaluate media messages.

Media Concepts	Evaluation Questions
1. All messages are made by someone. Every message sent out by the media is written, edited, selected, illustrated, or composed by someone or by a group of individuals. Writers, photographers, artists, illustrators, and TV and radio producers all make decisions about which elements (words, images, sounds) to include in a media message, which ones to leave out, and how to arrange and sequence the chosen elements. Knowing how media messages are constructed will help you better interpret the meaning of a message.	Ask yourself: "What words, images, or sounds are used to create the message?" and "What words, images, or sounds may have been left out of the message?"
2. Media messages are not reality. Media messages are *representations* **of reality that in turn shape people's ideas of the world.** Fictional stories in the media can seem realistic if characters act in ways that seem authentic, but, of course, the stories are not real. Even an eyewitness news account of a flood can seem real, but it usually reflects only one person's point of view, filtered through a TV camera and carefully edited down to a few images and words. Media messages can never perfectly match the complexity of the real world. Every media message also affects the way you think about the world. It is important that you judge the accuracy of media messages and whether or not you think the messages reflect reality.	Ask yourself: "What is the point of view or experience of the message maker?" and "How does this message affect the way I think about a particular topic or idea?"
3. Each person interprets media messages differently. Your interpretation of a media message is based on your knowledge of the world in which you live. You can use your prior knowledge and experience to examine the many different stylistic features of a message and to evaluate the message within its context.	Ask yourself: "How does the message make me feel?" or "What does the message make me think of?"
4. People have a wide range of purposes for creating media messages. People create and share messages for many reasons, but making money is one of the most important reasons that message making is so important in modern culture. When people have political purposes, they use messages to gain power or authority over others. Understanding how messages operate in terms of their economic, political, social, and aesthetic purposes will help you better understand the context of a work.	Ask yourself: "Who created the message and why?" or "Is the producer's purpose to inform, to influence, to present ideas, to make money, to gain power, or to express ideas?"
5. Each mass medium—from TV to the newspaper to the Internet—has unique characteristics. Media messages come in different forms. A media producer makes choices about which kinds of media are most appropriate to convey a particular message. For example, TV news favors messages that are immediate and visual, while news photographs favor messages that have an emotional component. Knowing how the medium shapes the message will help you understand why its creator used certain elements and why the message makes you feel the way it does.	Ask yourself: "Through what medium is the message delivered?" and "How does the form affect the message?"

Decoding *Decoding* is the making of meaning from verbal and nonverbal signals. For example, audiences decode symbols, such as words and pictures, when they watch TV or read a newspaper.

Deconstruction *Deconstruction* is the process of analyzing, or taking apart, the pieces of a media message to understand its meaning. The process of deconstruction involves looking at both what is stated, such as the words and images contained in an advertisement, and what is not directly stated, including elements of the historical, economic, and political context in which the ad was created.

Feedback *Feedback* is a response from an audience to the sender of a message. It can be immediate or delayed. Applause, booing, and asking questions are typical forms of **immediate feedback** from an audience. Writing a letter to the editor to respond to a newspaper editorial and filling out a questionnaire on a Web page are forms of **delayed feedback.**

Formula A *formula* is an established or conventional model or approach. In television and film, it refers to a typical combination of characters or presentation of material. Crime movies, for example, often chronicle a criminal's rise to power and subsequent fall to failure.

Genre A *genre* is a category of artistic forms or of media products that share **conventions,** or commonly accepted ways of presenting messages. For example, TV talk shows usually show a host interviewing celebrities in front of a live audience. Each genre has a particular audience and conventions. The chart below contains examples of some common genres of film and television.

Genre Categories: Film and Television	
Genre	**Explanation**
Action-Adventure	Action adventure programming offers the viewer excitement, suspense, and escape. Most action adventure films or TV shows feature the hero in a series of physical feats, fights, and chases, sometimes in unusual settings or exotic locations.
Comedy	Comedies give viewers the opportunity to laugh and feel comforted by a happy ending. Most comedies show the ludicrous in human behavior and affairs. Comedies allow audiences to laugh at the mistakes and misfortunes of people a little less smart or less secure than themselves. A **situation comedy** is a television format that involves stories about a regular set of characters in either a home or work setting. Situation comedies involve humor and focus on life's ordinary problems and solutions.
Fantasy	A fantasy features improbable and impossible characters and events. Fantasies create an unreal world in which the laws of physics and biology do not apply. Fantasies satisfy the audience's desire for highly imaginative storytelling.
Farce	A farce is a type of comedy that features exaggerated characters in exaggerated situations to evoke laughter. Farces often feature absurdly funny plots, physical action including slapstick, and ridiculous character types.

(continued)

Genre Categories: Film and Television

Genre	Explanation
Horror	Works of horror seek to cause fright and even terror in viewers. Horror offers the audience the chance to experience extreme feelings of revulsion, disgust, and fear as entertainment, since viewers sit comfortably and safely while watching. Horror often deals with anything that unsettles, disturbs, and threatens us— including violence, death, the unknown, and even science and outer space.
Parody	Parodies are humorous imitations (and often exaggerations) of another work or group of works. Some parodies are good-natured, while others are satirical.
Romance	Romance is about love relationships. The love relationship is usually presented in a positive, emotional, and sometimes sentimental manner.
Romantic Comedy	Romantic comedies show comic misunderstandings, obstacles, and difficulties in love relationships. Romantic comedies usually have happy endings.
Science Fiction	Science fiction is a subgroup of the fantasy genre. Often science fiction offers the viewer a futuristic vision of life based on some elements of contemporary society. Science fiction stories often involve space exploration and alien encounters.
Slapstick	Slapstick refers to any comic action that involves an aggressive or violent action as a source of humor.
Soap Opera	A soap opera is a genre of television programming that uses a serial structure: each daily program continues an ongoing story. Soap operas feature sentimental, romantic, melodramatic, and escapist events among a group of related characters.

Interpretation *Interpretation* is the process of creating meaning from exposure to a message through reading, viewing, or listening. People's interpretations of messages differ, depending on their life experiences, backgrounds, and points of view.

Media Law Various government structures, laws, and policies regulate access, content, delivery, and use of the mass media. For example, the *First Amendment* to the Constitution forbids Congress to set up or in any way pass laws limiting speech or the press. *Copyright law* protects the rights of authors and other media owners against the unauthorized publishing, reproduction, and selling of their works. *Censorship* is any governmental attempt to suppress or con-

trol people's access to media messages. Some censorship, however, may be used to protect citizens against damage to reputation (*libel*) or against invasions of privacy.

News Values *News values* are the set of criteria journalists use to determine whether information is newsworthy, which include

- **timeliness:** events or issues that are happening now
- **conflict:** unresolved events or issues that are interesting to the public
- **novelty:** stories that contain unique, interesting elements
- **relevance:** stories that are of interest to local readers

- **human interest:** stories that touch people's emotions
- **prominence:** stories about celebrities, politicians, or other noteworthy people
- **impact:** stories that make a difference in people's lives

Newsworthiness *Newsworthiness* is the quality of an event that is worthy of being reported in a newspaper or news broadcast. An event must be of interest or importance to the public in order to be considered newsworthy. (See also **News Values** on page 1058.)

Omission An *omission* is what is left out of a media message. All messages are selective and incomplete. For example, some advertisements omit information about the cost or the negative side effects of their products. Some news photographs show only the speakers at an event, omitting images of the event's audience and its size. Noticing what is not included in a message helps to identify the author's point of view. (See also **Point of View** below.)

Point of View *Point of view* can refer to the position or view of the person reporting a story or telling a tale in the mass media. Point of view is also a literary concept which can be used to interpret mass media texts ranging from docudramas to newspaper editorials. In the electronic media, point of view can be indicated by the type of narration used or by the type of camera shot used. There are many possible points of view.

Propaganda *Propaganda* is any form of communication that uses persuasive techniques to reach a mass audience. Propaganda was originally defined as the spreading of biased ideas and opinions through lies and deception. This definition gave the concept of propaganda a negative connotation. However, as scholars began to study the topic in the 1940s, they came to realize that propaganda was everywhere. Over time, the concept of propaganda has lost some of its negative connotation. Propaganda is now thought of as the communication of a point of view with the goal of having audience members come to voluntarily accept this position as one of their beliefs. Advertising is one of the major forms of propaganda. (See also **Advertising** on page 1060.)

Purpose The *purpose* of a media message is what its sender or creator intends to achieve. Usually, the purpose of a message is to inform, to educate, to persuade, to entertain, to express oneself, or to make money. A message may have a primary and a secondary purpose at the same time.

Sensationalism *Sensationalism* is the media's use or portrayal of material that is intended to generate curiosity, fear, or other strong responses. The material can be exaggerated or shocking in content. Content that refers to romance, death, children, or animals is often sensational. (See also **Reality TV** on page 1054 and **Tabloid** on page 1062.)

Stereotypes *Stereotypes* are generalized beliefs based on misinformation or insufficient evidence about an entire group of individuals. A stereotype, for example, would be that all people over age sixty-five are retired. (For more on **Stereotypes,** see page 88.)

Visual Literacy *Visual literacy* is a person's awareness of how meaning is communicated through visual media, including the use of color, line, shape, and texture.

Print Media Terms

Advertising   *Advertising* is the use of images or text to promote or sell a product, service, image, or idea to a wide audience. Advertising is a marketing technique that is designed to persuade an audience. Typical advertising formats include print advertisements in newspapers and magazines, billboards, radio and television commercials, and electronic banners on the World Wide Web. (See also **Marketing** on page 1061 and **Sponsorship** on page 1055.)

Byline   A *byline* is the name of the reporter or writer of a report published in a newspaper or magazine or presented on television or radio.

Circulation   *Circulation* is a measurement of the size of the audience for print media. It includes the total number of copies of a publication, such as a newspaper, that is delivered to subscribers, newsstands, and vendors.

Copy   *Copy* is the text in a media message.

Cross Promotion   *Cross promotion* is a marketing technique used when images or information about a product are advertised alongside a different product. For example, film companies often promote their new movies by licensing certain images to fast food companies.

Demographics   *Demographics* are the characteristics that define a particular audience. They include gender, age, educational background, cultural heritage, and income. Advertisers use demographics to target certain audiences. For example, advertisers know that many people eat snacks while they watch movies, so they will advertise snacks at the beginning of a movie or a video.

Digital Editing   *Digital editing* is the use of computer technology to alter or change an image before it is presented to an audience.

Photo editors often edit out distracting elements—such as telephone wires or shadows—from photo illustrations. However, large-scale digital editing of hard-news photographs is thought to be an unethical practice.

Editor   An *editor* supervises reporters. Editors decide what news stories will appear in print media or in broadcasting. They also check facts for accuracy and correct errors. (See also **News Values** on page 1058.)

Elements of Design   *Elements of Design* give meaning to visual representations in the following ways. (See also **Document Design** on page 962.)

- **Color**   creates mood and can also designate areas of space by separating and emphasizing parts of a visual.

- **Line**   determines the direction and speed of the viewer's eye movement. For example, curvy lines suggest gracefulness.

- **Shape**   emphasizes elements in the visual, adds interest, and communicates concepts. For example, a square represents solidness; a circle, completeness.

- **Texture**   appeals to a viewer's sense of touch. For example, a grainy visual suggests roughness.

Feature News   *Feature news,* also called soft news, refers to news stories whose primary purpose is to entertain. Feature stories usually are not timely. Stories about celebrities and ordinary people, places, animals, events, and products are considered feature news because they generate sympathy, curiosity, or amazement in viewers, readers, or listeners. An example of feature news would be a story about the mayor's vacation trip. (See also **Hard News** on the next page and **Soft News** on page 1062.)

Font   A *font* is a style of lettering used for printing text. There are many different typefaces and fonts used for different types of media messages in books, in magazines, on billboards, and on television. Different fonts can create certain non-verbal messages by making a message look more important or humorous, or silly by the shape of the letters used. (For more on **Fonts,** see page 968.)

Hard News   *Hard news* refers to fact-based reporting of breaking news stories. Hard news answers the basic *5W-How?* questions about timely subjects, such as national and international politics, economics, social issues, the environment, and scientific discoveries. An example of hard news would be a story reporting the discovery of a cure for a disease. (See also **Feature News** on page 1060 and **Soft News** on page 1062.)

Headline   A *headline* is the title of a newspaper or magazine article, usually set in large or bold type. It has two purposes: to inform the reader of the content of the article and to get the reader's attention.

Information Graphics   *Information graphics* are facts, data, or other information that has been translated into a visual form to communicate facts to readers in an attractive, understandable way. Types of information graphics include charts, maps, graphs, and special information designs. (For more on **Graphics,** see page 973.)

Lead   A *lead* is the introduction to a newspaper article or a broadcast report. It ranges from one sentence to several paragraphs in length. A lead contains information that motivates a reader or viewer to continue reading the story. A lead usually contains the major facts of a story. A lead may also describe a curious or unusual situation to attract reader or viewer attention.

Marketing   *Marketing* is the process of moving goods or services from the producer to the consumer. It includes identifying consumer wants or needs; designing, packaging, and pricing the product; and arranging for locations where the product will be sold. Marketing also includes promoting the product to a target audience through advertising or other means. (See also **Advertising** on page 1060.)

Medium   The *medium* of a message is the form in which it is presented or distributed, including film, video, radio, television, the Internet, and print. (The plural of medium is *media*.)

Message   A *message* is a combination of symbols that is communicated to one or more people. Messages are created by people who use symbols, including language, gestures, images, sounds, and electronic forms. Media messages are communicated through various mass media. (See also **Medium** above.)

News   *News* is the presentation of current information that will interest or affect an audience. Local news is produced by local newspapers and radio and TV stations, which use their own equipment, reporters, and resources. The focus of local news is information that affects a small audience with regional interests. National news is produced by large newspapers and radio and TV stations. Because their resources are greater, national news organizations may cover more national and world issues or events.

Newsmagazine   A *newsmagazine* is a weekly, biweekly, monthly, or bimonthly printed journal that focuses on news issues. On TV, a newsmagazine is a news program divided into several news segments or stories.

Photography   *Photography* is a process of making pictures by using cameras to record patterns of light and images on film or on computer disks. Photography is both an art form and a major component of the mass media; it is used in making still photographs and motion pictures. People sometimes think that "a photograph never lies," but a photograph, like all media messages, is selective and incomplete. Photographers use a wide range of techniques to communicate their points of view, including the framing and composition of an image and the use of filters or digital editing. (See also **Digital Editing** on page 1060 and **Point of View** on page 1059.)

Political Advertising   *Political advertising* is the use of the mass media to persuade listeners and viewers about a political candidate's ideas or opinions. Political candidates who use advertising must use techniques similar to those used to sell products. Their messages must be simple and attention-getting. (See also **Advertising** on page 1060.)

Print Media   *Print media* refers to the hard copies of mass media products that are printed on paper to be read or looked at by consumers. Examples of print media are newspapers, magazines, pamphlets, and fliers.

Public Relations   A *public relations* department in a company is responsible for shaping and responding to public opinion about the company's products, services, image, or individual staff. A public relations department acts as a go-between for the company, the mass media, and the public. Public relations

departments write press releases to try to persuade the mass media to report on their issues in a favorable light. (See also **Marketing** on page 1061.)

Reporter   A *reporter* is a journalist who is responsible for gathering information. Reporters gather information and work with editors to create TV and print news. (See also **Editor** on page 1060.)

Soft News   *Soft news,* or feature news, is the presentation of general interest material, such as celebrities and sports, in a news format. Soft news is designed to entertain readers or viewers. (See also **Feature News** on page 1060 and **Hard News** on page 1061.)

Source   A *source* is the person who first supplies information or ideas that are then shared with others. Journalists rely on sources for the information they report and select individuals that they believe are credible and have authority. (See also **Authority** on page 1055.)

Tabloid   A *tabloid* is a publication with a newspaper format that provides sensational news items and photographs. Tabloids are highly dependent on stories and photographs of media celebrities. Tabloid producers often admit that the stories they report are either false or exaggerations of the truth.

Target Audience   A *target audience* is a segment of the population for which a product or presentation is designed. (See also **Demographics** on page 1060.)

Text   *Text* refers to the symbols used to create a message, such as a book, a magazine article, or a TV show.

Writing

Skills, Structures, and Techniques

Good writing takes practice, but it also requires a knowledge of the basic conventions and strategies of writing. Use the following ideas and information to become a more effective writer.

Business Letters The purpose of a *business letter* is to take action in a business-related matter, such as requesting information or applying to a college or for a job. In many types of jobs, you will be expected to write business letters to colleagues and to customers. Business letters should always follow the correct format, use formal, standard English, and clearly provide all necessary information.

- **Parts of a business letter** A business letter has six parts, which are arranged on the

Guidelines for Business Letters

Write or type the letter on plain, unlined 8" x 11" paper.

Type the letter single-spaced, or write it neatly and legibly in black or blue ink. Proofread carefully for typing errors and misspellings; avoid cross outs, smudges, and inkblots.

Center the letter with equal margins on the sides and at the top and bottom. Follow standard business letter form—either block or semi-block (see the next page).

Use only one side of the paper. If your letter does not fit on one page, leave a one-inch margin at the bottom of the first page and continue the letter (with at least two lines of the body) onto the second page.

Use formal, standard English. Avoid slang, contractions, and most abbreviations. Use a polite, respectful, professional tone.

Include all necessary information, and get to the point quickly. Make sure your reader knows exactly why you are writing and what you want. When appropriate, enclose copies of relevant documents.

page in either the block or modified block form. In **block form**, all six parts begin at the left margin; the paragraphs in the body of the letter are *not* indented. In **modified block form**, the heading, closing, and handwritten and typed signature begin a little to the right of the center of the page. All of the other parts begin at the left margin; paragraphs in the body of the letter are indented.

Block Form

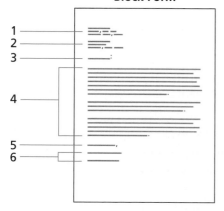

Modified Block Form

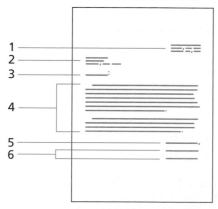

1. The **heading** usually has three lines:
   - your street address (Note: Your name does not appear in the heading.)
   - your city, state, and ZIP Code
   - the date you are writing the letter
2. The **inside address** gives the name, title, and complete address of the person to whom you are writing. If you are writing to a specific person, use a courtesy title (such as *Mr., Miss,* or *Ms.*) or a professional title (such as *Dr.* or *Professor*) in front of the person's name. If you know the person's business title, write the title (such as *Editor* or *Admissions Officer*) on a separate line after the name. If you do not know the name of a specific person, address your letter to the appropriate department (such as *Financial Aid Office* or *Customer Service Department*).

3. The **salutation,** or greeting, is always followed by a colon. Write *Dear,* a courtesy title or professional title, and the person's last name. If you don't know the name of a specific person, you can use a general salutation (such as *Dear Sir or Madam*). You can also use a department or position title, with or without the word *Dear.*

4. The **body** is the main part of your letter, the part that contains your message. If the body contains two or more paragraphs, leave a blank line between them.

5. The **closing,** or ending, should be courteous and should be followed by a comma. *Yours truly, Sincerely,* and *Sincerely yours* are appropriate business letter closings. Capitalize only the first letter of the closing.

6. Write your complete **signature** in ink below the closing. Under your handwritten signature, type or print your full name. If you have a title (such as *Editor* or *Student Council Secretary*), type or print your title on a separate line below your name.

> **NOTE** If you are including enclosures with your letter, such as a résumé, brochure, or writing sample, leave two blanks after the signature. Then, type "Encl." or "Enclosure"; many people often also type the type of item or items they are enclosing—*Encl. brochure,* for example.

- **Types of business letters** Guidelines for the four most common types of business letters follow.

1. **Appreciation or commendation letters** In an *appreciation* or *commendation letter*, you express your thanks to a person, a group, or an organization. You may also write to say you are pleased with a specific product or service. Such letters are most effective when they explain clearly why you are pleased.

2. **Complaint and adjustment letters** A *complaint* or *adjustment letter* reports an error or states that you have not received satisfactory services or products. First, provide all the necessary information (date, item number, and price). Then, tell exactly why you are displeased and what you want the company to do. Always use a calm and courteous tone. Here is an example.

```
                         8511 Callo Ct.
                         Pueblo, CO 81005
                         July 7, 2001

Customer Service Department
Haley Clothing Co.
535 7th Ave.
Orange, CA 92667

Dear Sir or Madam:

     On May 25, I sent an order to
you that included requests for
several items of clothing,
including two red T-shirts, No.
86, size 36, @ $10.00. When the
shipment arrived, I found that
these shirts were missing.

     I assume that this was merely
an oversight and would appreciate
your sending the two shirts as
soon as possible.

                    Sincerely,
                    Dwayne Patterson
                    Dwayne Patterson
```

3. **Letter of Application** A *letter of application,* or a cover letter, introduces you to a prospective employer or to a selection committee. Sometimes your qualifications for a position are judged by the strength of your letter of application. The following chart lists several suggestions for writing a letter of application.

Guidelines for Letters of Application

1. Identify the job or position for which you are applying and mention how you heard about it.

2. Depending on the position you are applying for, you might mention the following:
- your grade in school
- your grade-point average
- your experience, activities, awards, or honors
- your personal qualities
- the date or time you are available for the position

3. Always offer to provide references. Your references should include two or three responsible adults (usually not relatives) who have agreed to recommend you. Be prepared to supply their addresses and telephone numbers.

NOTE Some of the information you include in a letter of application may also be covered in your résumé or on the form you enclose with your letter. Always ask your references for permission to use them as references *before* you list them in a letter of application, on your résumé, or on the form you enclose. (See also **Résumés** on page 1080.)

A model letter of application follows on page 1066. Notice in the last paragraph, the writer indicates when and how the prospective employer may establish further contact.

```
4974 King Terrace
Rockford, IL 61103
June 8, 2001

Mr. Lyle Walzell
Walzell and Reid Architecture
96 Manor Drive
Rockford, IL 61104

Dear Mr. Walzell:

Please consider me an applicant
for the position of summer intern
advertised in Sunday's Sentinel.

I am a graduate of Lincoln High
School. In addition to college
preparatory courses with emphasis
on math, I have taken courses in
art history, mechanical drawing,
and computer science. I will be
entering Illinois Institute of
Technology this fall, and I plan
to major in architecture.

Last summer I worked at The
Drawing Board, where I made
requested changes to mechanical
drawings and created a computer
file of stock home plans. I also
was given an opportunity to
work with the artists producing
computer-assisted designs.

I believe my education and summer
work experience qualify me for
the summer intern position. My
résumé, which includes refer-
ences, is enclosed. Please call
me at 555-9263 to set an appoint-
ment for an interview. I am home
after 4:30 on weekdays. I look
forward to hearing from you.

Sincerely,

Marty Castellano

Marty Castellano

Enclosure
```

4. **Request and order letters**   A *request letter* asks for information or for someone's time or services. If you are requesting information or a form, enclose a self-addressed, stamped envelope. Be sure to write well in advance of when you need the information. An *order letter* requests something specific, such as a free brochure or an item in a catalog. You must provide *all* of the information needed (size, color, price, quantity) for someone to fill your order. Here are the body and closing of a sample request letter.

```
    I am a senior in high school
and am interested in applying for
admission to your university's
undergraduate program.

    I would like to know more
about the courses you offer in
sociology, my area of interest.
Please send me your general
catalog.

                  Sincerely yours,

                  Greg Nolanski

                  Greg Nolanski
```

Composition   A *composition* (sometimes called an *essay*) is a longer piece of writing comprised of paragraphs. A composition usually has three main parts: *introduction*, *body*, and *conclusion*. Each part serves a specific function, and all work together to communicate the writer's ideas, which are summarized in the *thesis*. For more about the **parts of compositions**, see page 474.

■ **Introduction**   A typical *introduction* begins with an attention-grabbing device, followed by some general information. The introduction then moves to more specific information and ends with the thesis statement. The following graphic may help you visualize the organization of a typical introduction.

Introduction

General

Specific (Thesis)

In just one or two paragraphs, the introduction must do three things:

1. **Catch the readers' attention.** The introduction should intrigue readers so that they want to read the whole composition.
2. **Set the tone.** The *tone*—formal or informal, humorous or serious, analytical or critical—communicates how you feel about your topic and also suggests how you want your readers to respond.
3. **Present the thesis.** The most important sentence in the introduction is the *thesis statement,* which states your paper's main idea and direction.

The chart below suggests several strategies to introduce an essay on a community service requirement for graduation.

(See also page 474.)

■ **Thesis statement**   A *thesis statement* is a sentence or two in the introduction that announces your limited topic and expresses your main idea about it. A thesis statement is sometimes called a *controlling idea* because it actually controls what goes into your paper;

Strategies for Introductions	Examples
Begin with an anecdote or example.	It is Monday afternoon, and Anna Williams, ninety-two and nearly blind, knows that at four o'clock, her doorbell will ring. Lisa M., a perky senior at Webster High, will arrive to read Anna her mail, chat about the news, and paint Anna's fingernails.
Begin with a startling fact or statistic; or adopt an unusual position or perspective.	During the two years that she has been volunteering with the Key Club, Lisa M. has acquired three new grandmothers and four grandfathers. "They're really wonderful people," Lisa brags, "and I never would have met any of them if I hadn't been a volunteer."
Use an appropriate quotation.	"The seventeenth-century English poet John Donne wrote, 'No man is an island,'" said Ms. Elena Ramirez, advisor to the high school Key Club. "Key Club members learn just that during their yearlong volunteer projects. It is important that every student has a chance to help others."
Start with background information.	Through the centuries and in all countries, individuals and organizations have given their time and money to help others. Helping others has always been strictly voluntary. For the past ten years, however, many school boards around the country have required community service for high school graduation.
Begin with a simple statement of your thesis.	The Board of Education is considering a new policy requiring that all high school seniors volunteer 40 hours of community service in order to graduate. This new policy should be adopted.

everything must support that thesis statement. Look at the chart at the bottom of this page; it suggests strategies for writing a thesis statement. (For more about **thesis statements,** see page 476.)

- **Body**   The *body* of a composition states and develops its main points, each of which supports the thesis statement. Use the following guidelines as you develop the body.

  1. **Think of every paragraph as a unit.** Each paragraph expresses a main idea, often stated directly as a *topic sentence*. Within the paragraph, elaborate the main idea with a variety of specific supporting details —facts, statistics, examples, anecdotes, quotations, sensory details, and so on.

2. **Aim for *coherence*.** Arrange your ideas in a way that will help your readers follow your thinking. Depending on your topic and your purpose, you may choose to arrange information in **order of importance, spatial order, logical order,** or **chronological order.** (See also page 468.)

3. **Stick to the point.** Your composition should have *unity*. Eliminate any sentence or detail that does not support a paragraph's main idea. Eliminate also any paragraph that does not directly support your thesis.

4. **Connect ideas.** Use direct references and transitional expressions (such as *for example, therefore, as a result*) to show the relationship between sentences or ideas. (See also **body paragraphs** on page 483.)

Strategies for Thesis Statements	Examples
Review the facts and details in your prewriting notes and begin thinking about how they fit together. Identify the main or unifying idea. If you are writing a persuasive essay, clearly state your opinion.	Your prewriting notes contain arguments for and against the proposal requiring seniors to volunteer for a specific number of hours. You decide that you support this proposal. Your thesis might read: *The Board of Education should pass the proposal making forty hours of community service a requirement for high school graduation.*
Check your thesis statement by asking both of the following questions: What is my topic? What am I saying about my topic?	Topic: *new proposal to make forty hours of volunteering a requirement for seniors* Main idea: *I believe this proposal should be passed.*
Be clear and specific. Sharpen your focus and present a definite, focused idea.	Add more information to the thesis to make it more specific: *The proposed new policy making 40 hours of community service a requirement for high school graduation should be passed. It will help students appreciate their community and increase their empathy for individuals outside their own family units.*
Evaluate your thesis with your audience in mind. Will readers care what you are saying about your topic?	*My audience is my classmates, who will be directly affected by the proposed policy. They will definitely be interested in my topic.*

■ **Conclusion** The *conclusion*, or final part of your paper, often begins with a specific statement, such as a restatement of the thesis, and moves to general information. The graphic at right may help you visualize this organization.

Conclusion

Specific

General

Remember, your conclusion should accomplish two tasks:

1. **Wind things up.** A definite ending gives readers a sense of completeness.
2. **Say it again.** Reinforce your main idea by bringing your readers back to the thesis.

Try one of the following strategies for writing an effective conclusion. (See also page 486.)

Strategies for Conclusions	Examples
Restate your main idea.	I strongly believe in teens' volunteering—in helping those who need help—and I support the Board of Education's proposal to make forty hours of community service a requirement for high school graduation.
Summarize your main points.	The proposed new program requiring forty hours of community service in order to graduate will, I believe, enhance students' appreciation of their community and also increase their sense of caring for others beyond their limited world of family and friends. For these reasons, I believe the policy should be put into effect.
Close with a final idea or example.	At the end of their senior year, a group of students published a journal about the volunteer work they had done. All looked back at their experiences as extremely positive. They learned a lot about living in the real world, they said—lessons they would never have been able to learn on their own or in school.
End with a comment on the topic (a thoughtful observation, a personal reaction, or a look to the future).	Of more than one hundred students surveyed recently, more than half say they already do regular volunteer work through religious or civic organizations. They tutor after school, lead sports leagues, visit hospitals and nursing homes, help elderly shut-ins. The proposed new program will engage all students in the "volunteering habit" and will make our community a better place to live.
Call on your readers to take action.	The school board meets next Wednesday at five o'clock to vote on the proposed new policy. Whatever your opinion is, attend the meeting and sign up to speak on the issue.
Refer to your introduction.	Lisa M. and her adopted "grandparents" speak enthusiastically of the benefits of a volunteer program for all high school students. "They need us," Lisa says, "and we can learn so much from them."

E-mail   *Electronic mail*, or *e-mail*, is correspondence sent by computer rather than through your local post office. Informal content and format are acceptable when you write to someone you know well or send comments to a newsgroup or chat group. However, when you send e-mail for business or research purposes, follow the guidelines listed at the bottom of this page. Your message should be formal, polite, and to the point—like a mini-business letter. Online etiquette, or "Netiquette," stresses the importance of good manners in cyberspace.

Envelopes   Write addresses legibly in blue or black ballpoint ink, or type them. Place your complete return address in the top left-hand corner of the envelope. Center on the envelope the name and address of the person who will receive the letter. On a business letter, the addressee's name, title, and address should exactly match the inside address. Use the two-letter state postal code on the envelope—NM rather than New Mexico—and include the correct ZIP Code.

Forms   Use the following strategies to help you fill out any form accurately and completely.

- Read the instructions and the entire form carefully before you start writing.

Guidelines for E-mails for Business and Research

- Keep your message brief and to the point—no more than one full screen of text. Scrolling through long e-mail messages is tedious.

- Use bulleted lists and indentation to make the message easy to read. Bulleted lists are especially helpful if you are raising more than one question or point.

- Use standard English, and proofread carefully to check spelling, grammar, and punctuation.

- Include a salutation (such as *Dear Dr. Knopp).* End with a closing (such as *Sincerely* or *Thank you)* followed by your full name.

- Be polite, and thank the person in advance for his or her time and attention. Being rude in an e-mail is called *flaming*. Flaming often backfires because there is always the chance that your angry message could be forwarded to someone you didn't intend to see it.

- Avoid using all capital letters, which is called *shouting*. If you want to emphasize an important word or term, place an asterisk (*) on either side of the word or term.

- Never use *emoticons* in a business e-mail. These are combinations of symbols that, when you tilt your head to the left, look like faces and suggest feelings. For example, the emoticon :-) suggests laughter or "I'm just kidding."

- Check the recipient's address to make sure that you are sending appropriate messages to the right people. Once you hit the Send button, you can't retrieve an e-mail message.

- Fill in the subject line to give your receiver a clear idea of the content of your message. Some people and organizations receive many messages daily; providing a subject will help the receiver identify the importance of the message.

- Do not forward e-mail without asking the original sender for permission.

- Type neatly or print legibly. Unless pencil is specified, type or print information in either blue or black ballpoint pen.

- Proofread your completed form and correct any spelling, grammar, punctuation, or factual errors.

- Keep the form neat and clean. Avoid cross outs.

- Be sure you have given all information requested on the form. If a question does not apply to you, write *N/A* or *not applicable* instead of leaving the space blank.

- Submit the form to the correct person, or mail it to the correct address.

Application for College Admission

Personal Information

Last name <u>Yee</u>   First <u>Elizabeth</u> Middle <u>Marie</u>
Phone <u>(617) 555-6929</u>
Weight <u>110</u>   Height <u>5' 2"</u>   Birthdate <u>7/10/81</u>
Address <u>812 Ashland Drive, Newton, MA 02161</u>

Academic Information

List high school attended

Name   City, State, Zip   Dates   Principal/Head
<u>Newton H. S. Newton, MA 02165 9/95–now Dr. Albert Souza</u>
Prizes, honors, awards <u>Science Fair prize, '96, '97</u>
Rank in high school graduating class <u>6th in class of 612</u>
Possible major <u>Chemistry</u> Career goal <u>Medical Research</u>

Extracurricular Activities

List school, community, and church activities

Activity   Achievements
<u>Piano Accompanist</u> <u>Accompanied choir for 4 years,</u>
<u>for school</u>   <u>toured New England, Feb. '97</u>
<u>Volunteer Coordi-</u>   <u>Coordinated student volunteers</u>
<u>nator at Elmwood</u>   <u>at placement home for children</u>
<u>Children's Home</u>   <u>waiting for foster care</u>

Other activities, hobbies, interests <u>Reading; Music (piano</u>
<u>lessons for 11 years); Computers and computer pro-</u>
<u>gramming; Hiking; Pets; Baby-sitting</u>

Which two books that you read during the past year most impressed you? List title and author. <u>Things Fall Apart</u>
<u>by Chinua Achebe; Sense and Sensibility by Jane Austen</u>

THE INFORMATION ON THIS APPLICATION IS TRUE AND COMPLETE

Date <u>1/10/2000</u> Signature <u>Elizabeth M. Yee</u>

Graphic organizers A *graphic organizer* is a visual that helps you "see" what you are thinking. You can use graphic organizers to find a subject to write about, to gather information, and to organize your information.

- **Charts** By breaking a subject into its logical parts, you can organize the details you have gathered. A *chart* allows you to summarize important information and arrange it into categories so that you (and readers) can easily understand it. In the following chart, the writer describes a healthy diet. (The writer's sources are the U.S. Department of Agriculture and the U.S. Department of Health and Human Services.)

A Healthy Diet		
Food Groups	**Daily Servings**	**Serving Size**
Grains	6–11	1 slice of bread 1 ounce ready-to-eat cereal $\frac{1}{2}$ cup cooked cereal, rice, or pasta
Vegetables	3–5	1 cup of raw, leafy vegetables $\frac{1}{2}$ cup of other vegetables—cooked or chopped raw 1 cup of vegetable juice
Fruits	2–4	1 medium apple, banana, orange $\frac{1}{2}$ cup chopped, cooked, or canned fruit 1 cup of fruit juice
Dairy	2–3	1 cup of milk or yogurt

(continued)

A Healthy Diet		
Food Groups	**Daily Servings**	**Serving Size**
		$1\frac{1}{2}$ ounces of natural cheese 2 ounces of processed cheese
Meat or beans	2–3	2–3 ounces cooked lean meat, poultry, or fish $\frac{1}{2}$ cup of cooked dry beans or 1 egg (counts as 1 ounce of lean meat) 2 T. peanut butter or $\frac{1}{2}$ cup nuts (counts as 1 ounce of lean meat)

- **Clustering** See **Prewriting Techniques,** page 1078.

- **Mapping** See **Prewriting Techniques,** page 1079.

- **Sequence chain** A **sequence chain** is a diagram that helps the reader understand the order in which actions must take place. Sequence chains are especially useful in explaining a process because they help the reader visualize each step from beginning to end. In the following example, the writer uses a sequence chain to show each step in the process of completing word analogy questions, such as the following:

HOT: COLD :: BARREN: _____
a. humid   b. arid   c. leafy   d. fertile

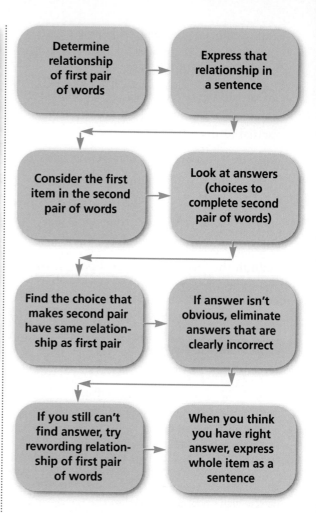

Incidentally, the correct answer is D. See also **Flowchart** on page 973.

- **Time line** A *time line* organizes historical information chronologically on a horizontal line so that readers can easily see a sequence of events from earliest to latest. Time lines are read from left to right, with the earliest event at the far left and the most recent event at the far right. The example on the next page shows some important U.S. historic and literary events from 1865 to 1876. (See also **Time lines** on page 975.)

U.S. Historic and Literary Events 1865–1876

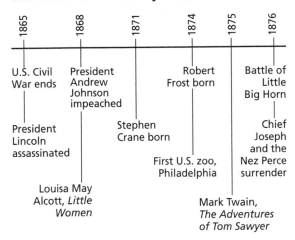

1865	1868	1871	1874	1875	1876
U.S. Civil War ends	President Andrew Johnson impeached		Robert Frost born		Battle of Little Big Horn
President Lincoln assassinated		Stephen Crane born			Chief Joseph and the Nez Perce surrender
			First U.S. zoo, Philadelphia		
	Louisa May Alcott, *Little Women*		Mark Twain, *The Adventures of Tom Sawyer*		

- **Venn diagram** A Venn diagram compares and contrasts two subjects by means of two intersecting circles. The following Venn diagram compares and contrasts two gases, hydrogen and helium.

Different   **Alike**   **Different**

Hydrogen   **Helium**

- symbol H
- extremely flammable
- reacts readily with other elements

- chemical element
- colorless gas
- lighter than air
- common element in universe

- symbol He
- not flammable (used for balloons)
- inert gas (does not combine with other elements)

Informal or Personal Letters Unlike business letters, personal letters (also called *social letters*) are less formal. They tend to be written by hand rather than typed, and they follow a modified block form, without the inside address. (See **Business Letters,** page 1063.) There are three common types of informal or personal letters.

- **Invitations** An informal *invitation* should provide all the specific information about the planned event, including the time, place, occasion, and any other details guests should know.

- **Letters of regret** If you have been invited somewhere and are unable to go, it is polite to send a *letter of regret.* A written reply is particularly appropriate if you have received an invitation with the letters *RSVP* (the French abbreviation for *please reply*).

- **Thank-you letters** A *thank-you letter* lets the recipient know that you appreciate the time, effort, or expense he or she spent on your behalf. The most effective thank-you letters go beyond simply saying "thank you"; they tell how a person's gift or efforts were particularly helpful or appreciated.

Manuscript Form The appearance of a composition is always important. Follow these guidelines to create papers with a clean, professional look.

Guidelines for Manuscript Form

Use only one side of a sheet of paper.

Write in blue or black ink, or type.

If you write by hand, don't skip lines. If you type, double-space the lines.

Leave margins of about one inch at the top, sides, and bottom of a page.

Indent the first line of each paragraph.

(continued)

Guidelines for Manuscript Form

Number all pages except the first page. Place the number in the upper right-hand corner.

All pages should be neat and clean. You may make a few corrections with correction fluid.

Follow your teacher's instructions for placing your name, the date, your class, and the title of your paper.

Memos   A memorandum, or *memo*, is a standard form of communication in many businesses. Memos are concise messages, generally covering only one topic. For example, an employee might send a memo to a supervisor reporting on the status of a project, or a supervisor might send a brief summary of discussions and decisions made in a meeting. Memos should provide all essential information—*who, what, when, where, why,* and *how*— and get quickly to the point. They should also be written in formal standard English. Many businesses use e-mail for memos because of the speed of communication and ease of record keeping. When writing a memo, refer to the guidelines that follow the example below.

```
DATE:     January 17, 2001
   TO:    Shipping Department
          Staff
FROM:     Ella Jones, Shipping
          Manager, Ext. 7890
   CC:    Chet Park, Director,
          Distribution
SUBJECT:  Missed shipping dates

There will be a meeting
Wednesday, January 24, from 2:00
to 3:00 P.M., in Room 3A to dis-
cuss missed shipping dates.
Please bring any ideas you have
regarding this subject.
```

Memo Guidelines

Use the words *DATE, TO, FROM,* and *SUBJECT* to guide you as you write your memo.

State your request clearly and briefly.

If you are asking for action and information, include a deadline.

Include your phone number so the recipient can call you if there are any questions.

Send a copy (CC) of the memo to those who need to know about the meeting or event but do not need to attend. The abbreviation CC stands for "carbon copy," a once-popular method of making copies by placing carbon paper between sheets of paper in a typewriter.

Messages   Taking a *message* involves listening to information and then communicating it to someone else. When writing a message, keep in mind the 5 "W" questions:

Who left the message and for **whom**?
What is the message?
When was the message written (date and time)?
Where can the sender be reached, if necessary?
Why is the message important?

Outlines   An *outline* is a plan for the body of a composition—a way of grouping and organizing information to show the relationships among ideas. Writers create outlines as a guide for organizing and presenting ideas clearly and logically. Outlines may be either *formal* (topic or sentence outlines) or *informal* (early plans).

■ **Formal outlines**   A *formal outline* is a highly structured, clearly labeled list of the essay's contents. It uses letters (capital and lowercase) and numbers (roman and Arabic) to indicate the level of importance of headings.

Topic outlines use words and phrases for each item, while *sentence outlines* use complete sentences. Formal outlines may be used for planning, but they are more often written after the essay is complete, providing an overview or summary for the reader. Here is a portion of a formal outline about preventing Lyme disease.

Title: Preventing Lyme Disease
Thesis statement: A new vaccine helps protect against Lyme disease, but people must still take other precautions.
  I. Lyme disease (background information)
  A. How people get it
  B. Where people get it
  C. Typical course of illness
 II. How to prevent
  A. New vaccine
    1. How it works
    2. Possible problems
       a. Not effective in everyone
       b. Needs booster shots
       c. Not tested for elderly and children
  B. Other preventive measures
    1. Clothing
       a. Long sleeves
       b. Light-colored pants, tucked into socks
       c. Tick repellent on clothing and skin
    2. Check skin for deer ticks
       a. After walking in wooded area
       b. What deer tick looks like
       c. Remove deer tick with tweezers
III. What to do
  A. Check for bull's-eye shaped red rash
  B. Get to doctor quickly

■ **Informal outlines or early plans** An *informal outline*, which does not have a set form, will help you organize your notes. To begin sorting facts and details from your notes into related groups, ask yourself the following questions.

- Which facts and details seem to belong together?
- What do they have in common?
- Which items do not seem to fit anywhere?

Then, give each group of related details a heading that reveals what they have in common. Here is a partial informal outline for a composition on Lyme disease.

BACKGROUND INFORMATION ON LYME DISEASE
↑
how people get Lyme disease, details of the illness
_____
PREVENTIVE MEASURES (ONE TYPE)
↑
long sleeves, light-colored pants, tucked into socks

Next, arrange your information in a way that you think will make the most sense to your readers: *chronological order, spatial order, logical order,* or *order of importance.* (See pages 468–470.) Check your early plan by asking: "Are the groupings logical?" "Is the order of ideas understandable?"

Paragraphs A *paragraph*—the primary building block in a composition—is a group of sentences that presents and supports a main idea. Within a composition, most paragraphs will be of one major type; however, any composition may have more than one type of paragraph. The four types of paragraphs (descriptive, expository, narrative, and persuasive) have different purposes.

- **Descriptive Paragraphs** A *descriptive paragraph* helps readers *visualize* your subject, whether it is a person, an object, or a scene. Descriptive paragraphs often use spatial order and almost always contain sensory details (sight, sound, smell, touch, taste). Here is a descriptive paragraph.

Sensory details

The ground was hard, the air was still, my road was lonely: I walked fast till I got warm, and then I walked slowly to enjoy and to analyze the species of pleasure brooding for me in the hour and situation. It was three o'clock; the church bell tolled as I passed under the belfry: the charm of the hour lay in its approaching dimness, in the low-gliding and pale-beaming sun. I was a mile from Thornfield, in a lane noted for wild roses in summer, for nuts and blackberries in autumn, and even now possessing a few coral treasures in hips and haws, but whose best winter delight lay in its utter solitude and leafless repose. If a breath of air stirred, it made no sound here; for there was not a holly, not an evergreen to rustle, and the stripped hawthorn and hazel bushes were as still as the white worn stones which cause-wayed the middle of the path. Far and wide, on each side, there were only fields, where no cattle now browsed; and the little brown birds, which stirred occasionally in the hedge, looked like single russet leaves that had forgotten to drop.

Charlotte Brontë, *Jane Eyre*

- **Expository Paragraphs** An *expository paragraph* explains or informs, usually by presenting information in logical order. The following expository paragraph gives information about the history of weather science during the 1950s and 1960s.

The fifties and sixties were years of unreal optimism about weather forecasting. Newspapers and magazines were filled with hope for weather science, not just for prediction but for modification and control. Two technologies were maturing together, the digital computer and the space satellite. An international program was being prepared to take advantage of them, the Global Atmosphere Research Program. There was an idea that human society would free itself from weather's turmoil and become its master instead of its victim. Geodesic domes would cover cornfields. Airplanes would seed the clouds. Scientists would learn how to make rain and how to stop it.

James Gleick, *Chaos: Making a New Science*

- **Narrative Paragraphs** A *narrative paragraph,* which tells a story or illustrates an event or a series of events, is usually organized in chronological order. Narrative paragraphs occur in both fiction and nonfiction. The following example tells what happened immediately after the series of volcanic eruptions that destroyed the island of Krakatau on August 27, 1883. Notice that this paragraph also gives information.

1

2

3

4

5

6

   As the island collapsed into the subterranean chamber emptied by the eruption, the sea rushed in to fill the newly formed caldera. A column of magma, rock, and ash rose 5 kilometers into the air, then fell earthward, thrusting the sea outward in a tsunami 40 meters in height. The great tidal waves, resembling black hills when first sighted on the horizon, fell upon the shores of Java and Sumatra, washing away entire towns and killing 40,000 people. The segments traversing the channels and reaching the open air continued on as spreading waves around the world. The waves were still a meter high when they came ashore in Ceylon, now Sri Lanka, where they drowned one person, their last casualty. Thirty-two hours after the explosion, they rolled in to Le Havre, France, reduced at last to centimeter-high swells.

   Edward O. Wilson,
   The Diversity of Life

■ **Persuasive Paragraphs**   A *persuasive paragraph* expresses or supports a writer's *opinion* about a particular subject. The purpose of a persuasive paragraph is to convince readers to share the writer's opinion or to take action. Writers of persuasive paragraphs usually use order of importance or logical order to organize their ideas. In the following paragraph, the writer writes persuasively about a controversial topic—requiring school uniforms in public schools as a means to combat crime.

   Uniforms' effectiveness in deterring school crime is well documented. Far from robbing students of their individuality, uniforms reinforce their identity and identify them both in and out of school. Uniforms establish equality with peers, curbing the distinction between rich or poor and the need to make class a fashion show rather than an educational experience. To safeguard creativity and individual schools' identities, each school will choose its own uniform. School is a place to learn, not to show off. School uniforms are an effective tool to achieve this.

   Demetrio Perez, Jr.,
   The Miami Herald

Prewriting Techniques   Use the following techniques to find a topic to write about and also to gather information and details about a topic. You may try using several at a time, and you may find that you prefer some techniques more than others.

■ **Asking the *5W-How?* questions**   Try asking yourself the six basic questions that reporters try to answer in the first paragraph of a newspaper article: *Who? What? When? Where? Why? How?*

EXAMPLES
Who are the groups with the highest voter turnout in the last election?
What can be done to get more people to vote?
When is the best time to register to vote?
Where can people register to vote?
Why do so many registered voters not vote?
How can we get more young people to register and vote?

- **Asking "What if? Questions"** In searching for a topic to write about, turn on your creativity by asking yourself "What if" questions about a variety of topics.

EXAMPLES

What if Great Britain had won the Revolutionary War?

What if there were no gravity on earth?

What if the mayor and all of the city council members were high school students?

What if college were totally free and everyone could go?

- **Brainstorming** Brainstorming is a useful way to narrow a general topic or to gather details about a topic. With a group or by yourself, write down a general topic, and then list every idea about that topic that pops into your mind. (If you work as a group, it's helpful to have just one person jotting down notes.) Work as quickly as you can without stopping to evaluate your ideas. Keep going until you run out of ideas. The following example shows how one writer brainstormed cluster notes on the topic of music.

EXAMPLE

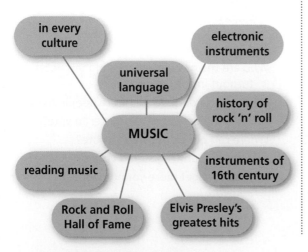

- **Chaining** This technique uses questions and answers to help you make connections between ideas. It is a way to build new ideas from existing ones and often helps you to see subjects in a totally new light. Here are the steps for chaining.
  1. The first link in the chain is a question.
  2. The answer to that question becomes the next link.
  3. The third link is a question prompted by the answer in step 2. This process continues until you hit upon the ideas you want.

- **Clustering** Like brainstorming, clustering (also called *webbing*) helps you generate ideas. First, write a topic in the middle of your paper. Circle the topic. Then, in the space around the topic, write whatever related ideas occur to you. Draw circles around the new ideas and add lines to connect them to the original subject. Continue to branch off as necessary. Let your mind wander, and continue to draw circles and lines to show connections among ideas.

EXAMPLE

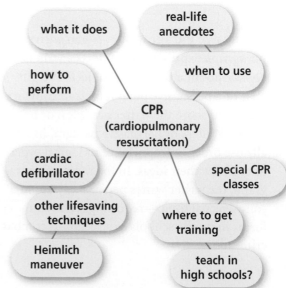

- **Cubing**   Imagine a cube that has one of the following suggestions written on each of its six sides: *Describe it. Compare it. Associate it. Analyze it. Apply it. Argue for or against it.* A good way to explore a topic is to write for three minutes in response to each of these suggestions on the sides of the cube.

EXAMPLE

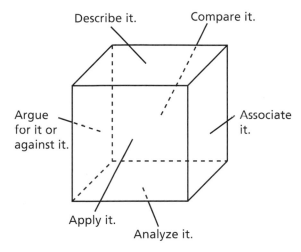

EXAMPLE
IMPRESSIONISM

Describe it. *Impressionism* refers to a school of painting that started in France at the end of the nineteenth century. Impressionists tried to capture light and color in broad brushstrokes. They often painted outdoor scenes and everyday objects. Impressionists held their first exhibit in Paris in 1874.

- **Freewriting**   To *freewrite*, think of a subject or word that interests you, and write about it for three to five minutes. Write whatever pops into your head, and just keep writing. Do not worry about complete sentences or proper punctuation. If you become stuck, keep writing the last word until you think of something new to write.

- **Listening with a Focus**   You can gather information and topic ideas by listening to radio and television programs, audiotapes and videotapes, and live speeches and performances. If you can locate an expert in a subject that interests you, try to arrange a personal or telephone interview. Prepare for listening by writing down your topic and brainstorming what you already know about it. Then, list some questions about your topic that you would like to have answered. These questions will help focus your listening. Listen carefully to see if you can hear the answers to your questions, and take notes. (As you take notes, remember that you don't need to write down every word you hear; use phrases and abbreviations, and underline key points.)

- **Mapping**   *Mapping,* which resembles clustering, is useful for organizing ideas and seeing whether you have enough support for each main idea. Notice how the following map groups main and supporting ideas.

■ **Pentad**   Investigate a topic by imagining a five-pointed star with one of the following questions on each point: *What is happening? Who is causing it to happen? How is it being done? Where and when is it happening? Why is it happening?* After answering each question, determine a focus: Which points did you write the most about, and is there some relationship between those points? This focus will probably lead to your thesis statement. The pentad prewriting technique is especially useful when you are writing about literature.

EXAMPLE

What is happening?
Paul tries to get money to silence the house's cries for money.

Why is it happening?
Paul desperately tries to make his mother happy but can't.

Who is causing it to happen?
Paul's mother is never satisfied with the money she has, so Paul tries to get more.

Story: "The Rocking-Horse Winner" by D. H. Lawrence

Where and when is it happening?
Somewhere in England in a house in a good neighborhood during racing season.

How is it being done?
Paul rides his rocking horse until he knows the name of a winning racehorse.

■ **Reading with a focus**   You can get ideas for writing by reading books, newspapers, magazines, or browsing the World Wide Web. When you read to find information about a topic, don't read everything. Use a book's index and table of contents to see if it contains relevant information. Skim the material, searching only for information about your topic. When you find relevant information, slow down, read carefully, and take notes.

■ **Using your five senses**   Observe your subject directly if you can. Gather details that appeal to all five senses: sight, hearing, smell, taste, and touch.

■ **Visualizing**   When you *visualize,* you create mental images of something in your "mind's eye." As you visualize a scene, try to use your other senses as well.

EXAMPLE

I'm crouched down with my cousin in a field of dried cornstalks. Even though the air is very warm, my rain-soaked shorts and T-shirt feel icy on my skin. We're both scared as lightning crashes nearby—way too close for comfort. Huge claps of thunder set my eardrums ringing. I peer through dense sheets of rain at the stand of old oaks a little way ahead of us. The trees look like tempting shelter, but we know better. In an electrical storm, be the lowest thing you can be.

■ **Writer's notebook or journal**   Use a separate notebook or file folder to record your experiences, thoughts, feelings, opinions, questions. Add things you like or things that intrigue you, such as poems, songs, cartoons, and newspaper articles. Try to write in your notebook daily, and date your entries. Look back at your entries to gather writing ideas.

Résumés   A *résumé* summarizes your skills, education, achievements, and work experience. Prepare a résumé to use when you apply for a job or when you seek admission to a college or special program. Most prospective employers want you to fax or mail a résumé before they schedule an interview. Notice how clearly the following model résumé organizes information about the writer with the most recent work experience listed first.

```
                Sarah Planco                        September 1999:
          13200 Hartsook Street                     Organizer of Pet Fair
          Grass Valley, CA 91103                    Martin Luther King
            (818) 981-9023                          Elementary School
          Email: splanco@ISP.net                    June-August 1999:
                                                     Stock clerk, Pet Network
Objective  Part-time job in veteri-                  store, Grass Valley, CA
           narian's clinic
                                           Extra-        Vice president, student
Education  Grass Valley High School,       curricular    government
           Grass Valley, California        Activities    Editor, yearbook
           Presently in 12th grade;                      Member, 4-H Club and
           3.5 grade-point average                       Science Club
           Advanced Placement class        Achieve-      Blue ribbon, Science
           in Biology                      ments         Fair 2000
Qualifi-   Familiarity with and                          Leadership award—10th
cations    love for all kinds of                         grade
           pets and farm animals           References
           Experience working with         Dr. Mary Ellen Wells, Principal
           animals in pet shop and         Grass Valley High School
           animal shelter                  Grass Valley, CA 94901
           Excellent people skills         (818) 555-1195
           Fluent in Spanish               Mr. Tom McGee, Director
Work       June 1998 to present:           Grass Valley Animal Shelter
Experience Volunteer,Grass Valley          Grass Valley, CA 94901
           Animal Shelter                  (818) 555-0643
```

Revising and Proofreading Symbols

When you are revising and proofreading a draft, you can use the following symbols to indicate changes to correct in your final version.

Symbols for Revising and Proofreading

Symbol	Example	Meaning of Symbol
≡	805 Linden avenue	Capitalize a lowercase letter.
/	the First of May	Lowercase a capital letter.
∧	one ∧my friends (of)	Insert a missing word, letter, or punctuation mark.
∧	appeer (a)	Change a letter.
⌐‾	at the beginning (lake)	Replace a word.
℘	Give me a a number	Leave out a word, letter, or punctuation mark.
⌒	a misstake	Leave out and close up.
⌣	a touch down	Close up space.
∽	beleive	Change the order of letters.
(tr)	He walked ⟨slowly⟩ forward.	Transfer the circled words. (Write *tr* in nearby margin.)

(continued)

Symbols for Revising and Proofreading

Symbol	Example	Meaning of Symbol
¶	¶ "Yes," she answered.	Begin a new paragraph.
⊙	Follow me⊙	Add a period.
⋀	Oh⋀not now!	Add a comma.
#	upper/atmosphere	Add a space.
⊙	the following items⊙	Add a colon.
⋀	Columbus, Ohio⋀Orlando, Florida; and Seattle, Washington	Add a semicolon.
=	one=third portion	Add a hyphen.
⋁	Juan⋁s idea	Add an apostrophe.
stet	A faster method	Keep the crossed-out material. (Write *stet* in nearby margin.)

Technical Documents *Technical documents* are documents that provide specific information or directions for a particular audience. Technical documents—such as manuals, handbooks, bylaws, or minutes of meetings—use precise language, a formal tone, and a clear, straightforward style. Usually technical documents have some of the following purposes:

1. to report information and convey ideas logically and correctly

2. to offer detailed and accurate specifications

3. to include scenarios, definitions, and examples to aid comprehension

4. to anticipate readers' problems, mistakes, and misunderstandings

The following example of a technical document is a set of minutes recorded by a student for an important class discussion. Notice that the date, class, teacher, and the members absent are listed as part of the record keeping. The action items list the people, their responsibilities, and the date due. The class discussion is summarized in the highlights, with one or two example comments noted. In general, minutes do not record in chronological order everything that might have been said in a meeting.

November 29, 1999

Minutes of Class Discussion:
November 29, 1999
Third Period, Business Management
Viewing and Discussing Customer
Return Scenes

Teacher: Ms. Avis Sturdivant
Members Present: Entire class except Travis Montgomery, Lucinda Olsen, and Fiona McShane

Action Items:

1. Ms. Sturdivant asked students to choose a partner and prepare to role-play a customer-service scene. They could use one of the three introduced in the video seen at our last class meeting, or they could choose one of their own.

2. Each student was instructed to pick one of the return scenes enacted today and prepare to give a three- to-four minute summary. This summary will help absent students understand the role of these scenes.

(continued)

(continued)

3. Mercedes Rivera was appointed to take minutes for our next class (November 30, 1999).

Overview of Class Discussion
The following are the key points presented by Ms. Sturdivant, following our viewing of the video and the class role-playing scenes.

1. Deal with customers without putting decisions off to a manager.
2. Be courteous and conciliatory toward the customer, regardless of the customer's attitude.
3. Present the store's policy as reasonable and fair.

Discussion
Thad Bonjuorno's Comment: He suggested that sometimes clerks think that a store's return policy is more important than the customer. He observed that store clerks should be willing to work with customers until they are happy. He used the example of a local store's return policy for after-holiday sales.

Sarita Tejas's Comment: She disagreed. As a part-time clerk in a local store, she has observed a number of customer attitudes. She insisted that a store's return policy should be followed because it protects the store and the clerk. If the clerks start making exceptions to the rule, the store stands to lose money, and the clerk may be held accountable. She felt that stores are moneymaking businesses and need to protect their revenues.

Submitted by: Jefferson Chang, Secretary for the Day

Tone   Words carry feeling as well as meaning. *Tone,* your attitude toward your topic or readers, comes through in the choice of words and details and even in the rhythm of your sentences.

■ **Choice of Details**   The *details* you choose to include in your essay indicate what is important to you. For example, providing statistics on a subject lets readers know you are serious about your topic and want to be objective. On the other hand, providing details from personal experiences creates a more intimate tone.

■ **Sentence Length**   The *length* and *structure* of the sentences in your writing also influences your tone. Long, complex sentences let readers know that you are writing formally about a serious subject. Shorter sentences may indicate a conversational attitude.

■ **Word Choice**   Your *word choice* indicates your attitude toward your subject and your relationship with your audience. For example, if you are serious about your topic, you can use formal language to express that attitude. On the other hand, informal language, which includes contractions and colloquialisms, suggests a more friendly, personal tone.

Remember that your tone should always be suitable for the *occasion,* or reason, for your writing. Often you write to fulfill assignments for school, but you may also write to communicate with friends who have moved away or to give advice to someone younger than you are.

Transitions   *Transitions,* or *transitional expressions,* are words and phrases that help readers see how ideas and details are related. (See also page 470.)

Voice   *Voice* is really the unique sound and rhythm of a writer's language—a writer's personal way of speaking to a reader that is unlike anyone else's. Voice gives a ring of authority and honesty to writing. Unless you are aiming for some special effect, your voice should sound like yourself—natural and clear.

Grammar at a Glance

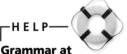

┌HELP┐

Grammar at a Glance is an alphabetical list of special terms and expressions with examples and references to further information. When you encounter a grammar or usage problem in the revising or proofreading stage of your writing, look for help in this section first. You may find all you need to know right here. If you need more information, **Grammar at a Glance** will show you where in the book to turn for a more complete explanation. If you do not find what you are looking for in **Grammar at a Glance,** turn to the index on page 1112.

abbreviation An abbreviation is a shortened form of a word or a phrase.

■ **capitalization of** (See page 810.)

TITLES USED WITH NAMES	**M**s.	**G**ov.	**S**r.	**M.B.A.**
KINDS OF ORGANIZATIONS	**C**o.	**I**nc.	**A**ssn.	**C**orp.
PARTS OF ADDRESSES	**B**lvd.	**A**ve.	**H**wy.	**P.O. B**ox
NAMES OF STATES	[without ZIP Codes]		**Tex.**	**A**la.
			Ind.	**N. D**ak.
	[with ZIP Codes]		**TX**	**AL**
			IN	**ND**
TIMES	**A.M.**	**P.M.**	**B.C.**	**A.D.**

■ **punctuation of** (See page 823.)

WITH PERIODS	(See preceding examples.)			
WITHOUT PERIODS	PC	FM	GPA	VISTA
	DC (**D.C.** without ZIP Code)			
	ml	kb	lb	mph mm
	[Exception: inch = in.]			

action verb An action verb expresses physical or mental activity. (See page 510.)

EXAMPLES   Every day, Eleanor **works** in the garden.

I **remember** most of my lines.

active voice Active voice is the voice a verb is in when it expresses an action done by its subject. (See page 705. See also **voice.**)

EXAMPLE   We **planted** the oak next to the fence.

adjective An adjective modifies a noun or a pronoun. (See page 505.)

EXAMPLE   **The sturdy** horse showed **no** signs of tiring.

adjective clause An adjective clause is a subordinate clause that modifies a noun or a pronoun. (See page 578.)

EXAMPLE   The school **that outperformed us** was our old rival.

adjective phrase A prepositional phrase that modifies a noun or a pronoun is called an adjective phrase. (See page 554.)

EXAMPLE   Airbags **in cars** can be lifesavers.

adverb An adverb modifies a verb, an adjective, or another adverb. (See page 514.)

EXAMPLE   I thought **quickly** before I gave my name.

adverb clause An adverb clause is a subordinate clause that modifies a verb, an adjective, or an adverb. (See page 584.)

EXAMPLE   **After she comes home,** Katya is frequently too tired to go out.

adverb phrase A prepositional phrase that modifies a verb, an adjective, or an adverb is called an adverb phrase. (See page 556.)

EXAMPLE   **Until the last possible moment,** the judges kept us guessing.

agreement Agreement is the correspondence, or match, between grammatical forms. Grammatical forms agree when they have the same number, gender, and person.

- **of pronouns and antecedents** (See page 618.)

SINGULAR   At the winter carnival, **Trenton** won first prize for **his** ice sculpture.

PLURAL   At the winter carnival, the Duarte **twins** won first prize for **their** ice sculpture.

SINGULAR   To go on the field trip, **each** of the students must return **his or her** permission slip to Mr. Wilkins by Friday.

PLURAL   To go on the field trip, **all** of the students must return **their** permission slips to Mr. Wilkins by Friday.

SINGULAR	**Neither Ling nor Soledad** has indicated what **her** major field of study in college will be.
PLURAL	**Both Ling and Soledad** have indicated what **their** major fields of study in college will be.

■ **of subjects and verbs** (See page 600.)

SINGULAR	The yearbook **editor is working** hard to meet the publisher's deadline.
SINGULAR	The yearbook **editor,** as well as the other staff members, **is working** hard to meet the publisher's deadline.
PLURAL	The yearbook staff **members are working** hard to meet the publisher's deadline.
PLURAL	The yearbook staff **members,** especially the editor, **are working** hard to meet the publisher's deadline.

SINGULAR	**Each** of these garden tools **belongs** to my neighbor.
PLURAL	**All** of these garden tools **belong** to my neighbor.

SINGULAR	**Lauren or Amanda** usually **goes** snorkeling with me.
PLURAL	**Lauren and Amanda** usually **go** snorkeling with me.

SINGULAR	Here **is** a **snapshot** of the winners of the salsa dance contest.
PLURAL	Here **are** some **snapshots** of the winners of the salsa dance contest.

SINGULAR	**Two days is** not enough time to complete the project.
PLURAL	**Two days** in January **are** national holidays.

SINGULAR	*Gulliver's Travels* **includes** a satirical look at Great Britain's political system.
PLURAL	Gulliver's **travels include** voyages to Lilliput and Brobdingnag.

SINGULAR	One possible side **effect** of the medication **is** headaches.
PLURAL	**Headaches are** one possible side effect of the medication.

SINGULAR	Kelly is one freshman **who plays** on the varsity team.
PLURAL	Kelly is one of the freshmen **who play** on the varsity team.
SINGULAR	Kelly is the only one of the freshmen **who plays** on the varsity team.

ambiguous reference Ambiguous reference occurs when a pronoun incorrectly refers to either of two antecedents. (See page 657.)

AMBIGUOUS	A tortoise is different from a turtle only in that it lives on land, not in water.
CLEAR	A tortoise is different from a turtle only in that a tortoise lives on land, not in water.

antecedent An antecedent is the word or words that a pronoun stands for. (See page 501.)

EXAMPLE   **Mr. Haynes** sent the **winners** the photos **he** had taken of **them.** [*Mr. Haynes* is the antecedent of *he*. *Winners* is the antecedent of *them*.]

apostrophe

- **to form contractions** (See page 872. See also **contractions.**)
  EXAMPLES   isn't   they'll   let's   '01

- **to form plurals of numerals, symbols, and words referred to as words** (See page 873.)
  EXAMPLES   *a*'s, *e*'s, *i*'s, *o*'s, and *u*'s   *A*'s, *I*'s, and *U*'s [*but Zs or Z*'*s and Qs or Q*'*s*]

  1600's [*or* 1600s]   SUV's [*or* SUVs]

  %'s, +'s, and ='s   using &'s for *and*'s [*or using &s for ands*]

- **to show possession** (See page 868.)
  EXAMPLES   the doctor's office
  the doctors' offices
  children's rights
  someone's eyeglasses
  my mother's and father's birthdays
  my mother and father's wedding anniversary
  one month's [*or four weeks*'] allowance

appositive An appositive is a noun or a pronoun placed beside another noun or pronoun to identify or explain it. (See page 567.)

EXAMPLE   Bernard, an aspiring **artist,** wants to study in New York.

appositive phrase An appositive phrase consists of an appositive and its modifiers. (See page 568.)

EXAMPLE   Anthony, **our track-and-field star,** has been awarded a scholarship.

article The articles, *a, an,* and *the,* are the most frequently used adjectives. (See page 506.)

EXAMPLE   **A** sudden gust of wind and **an** ominous rumbling in **the** distance were **the** first signs of **an** impending storm.

bad, badly (See page 726.)

NONSTANDARD   This chicken soup tastes badly.
STANDARD   This chicken soup tastes **bad.**

base form The base form, or infinitive, is one of the four principal parts of a verb. (See page 670.)

EXAMPLE   We heard Suzi **sing** the national anthem before last night's game.

brackets (See page 879.)

EXAMPLES   Ms. Kwan explained the Yoruban proverb "A river does not flow so far that it forgets its source" by rewriting it as follows: "A river **[**person**]** does not flow **[**travel**]** so far that it **[**he or she**]** forgets its source **[**his or her roots**]**."

The first director of the Environmental Protection Agency (EPA **[**1970**]**) was William Ruckelshaus.

capitalization

- **of abbreviations and acronyms** (See page 810. See also **abbreviations.**)

- **of first words** (See page 790.)
  EXAMPLES   **I**n Greek mythology, Nike is the goddess of victory.

  Mr. Tyler asked, "**D**id you know that the human body has 206 bones and 650 muscles?"

  Dear Dr. Nunez:

  Best regards,

- **of proper nouns and proper adjectives** (See page 792.)

Proper Noun	Common Noun
Gen. **H. N**orman **S**chwarzkopf	leader
Edward the **C**onfessor	king

Proper Noun	Common Noun
North **A**merica	continent
New **Z**ealand	country
Grenada **C**ounty	county
Tsinghai **P**rovince	province
Kauai	island
Chang **R**iver	body of water
Lamotte **P**eak	mountain
Klondike **G**old **R**ush **N**ational **H**istorical **P**ark	park
Argonne **F**orest	forest
Altamira	caves
Black **R**ock **D**esert	desert
Southwest	region
traveling **s**outhwest	direction
Twenty-**n**inth **S**treet	street
Republican **P**arty (or **p**arty)	political party
Operation **D**esert **S**torm	historical event
Stone **A**ge	historical period
the **S**pecial **O**lympics	special event
Bastille **D**ay	holiday
February	calendar item
Quiché **M**ayas	people
Hinduism	religion
Mormon	religious follower
God [*but* the Egyptian **g**od **R**a]	deity
Epiphany	holy day
Talmud	sacred writing
Casa **G**rande **R**uins **N**ational **M**onument	monument
Water **T**ower **P**lace	building
Bollingen **P**rize in **P**oetry	award
Pluto	planet
Vega	star
Crux, or **S**outhern **C**ross	constellation
Lady of the Lake	ship
Galileo	spacecraft
Computer **S**cience **II** (*but* **c**omputer **s**cience)	school subject

■ **of titles** (See page 803.)

EXAMPLES   **G**overnor Benjamin Cayetano [preceding a name]

Benjamin Cayetano, the **g**overnor of Hawaii [following a name]

Welcome, **G**overnor. [direct address]

Uncle Cesare [*but* my **u**ncle Cesare]

*Baseball: **A**n **I**llustrated **H**istory* [book]

*I'll **M**ake **M**e a **W**orld: **A** **C**entury of **A**frican-American **A**rts* [TV program]

*The **T**hinker* [sculpture]

*Riders to the **S**ea* [musical composition]

"**B**ye **B**ye **L**ove" [song]

"**T**he **T**rain from **R**hodesia" [short story]

"**S**pring and **F**all: **T**o a **Y**oung **C**hild" [poem]

*Consumers **D**igest* [magazine]

the *Star-**L**edger* [newspaper]

Doonesbury [comic strip]

case of pronouns Case is the form a pronoun takes to show how the pronoun is used in a sentence. (See page 632.)

NOMINATIVE   Terrell and **she** were named the athletes of the year.

The first and second runners-up were Dylan and **he,** respectively.

Both guest speakers, Mr. Jimenez and **she,** inspired their listeners with confidence.

We seniors met with the class sponsors to discuss the plans for Grad Night.

The last person **who** speaks to Prince Hamlet is Horatio.

Do you know **who** the chaperons will be?

I don't see Elise as often as **he.** [meaning *as often as he sees Elise*]

OBJECTIVE   The helpful theater usher led **us** back to our seats.

Aunt Helen gave **me** a video camera for graduation.

Who won the jujitsu match between Aaron and **him**?

The band dedicated its last song to the prom's king and queen, Miguel and **her.**

As the principal handed **us** graduates our diplomas, she shook our hands and congratulated us.

A conversation with my great-uncle inspired **me** to chart my ancestry.

The last person to **whom** Prince Hamlet speaks is Horatio.

Among the members of the Ballets Russes dance company was Vaslav Nijinsky, **whom** many regard as the most talented dancer of the twentieth century.

I don't see Elise as often as **him.** [meaning *as often as I see him*]

POSSESSIVE   **Your** poems are more imaginative than **mine** are.

Their winning the Pulitzer Prize in investigative reporting came as no surprise to their colleagues.

clause A clause is a group of words that contains a verb and its subject and that is used as a sentence or as part of a sentence. (See page 576.)

                            S   **V**

INDEPENDENT CLAUSE   Irv went to a Chinese restaurant for the first time last night

                            S   **V**

SUBORDINATE CLAUSE   because Kris really enjoys Renaissance music and theater

colon (See page 853.)

■ **before lists**

EXAMPLES   On our cross-country road trip to see my parents in Seattle, we traveled through seven states: Oklahoma, Kansas, Colorado, Wyoming, Idaho, Oregon, and Washington.

Some of the sites we visited along the way are as follows: Cherokee Cultural Center, Oklahoma; John Brown's cabin at Osawatomie, Kansas; and Mount Saint Helens, Washington.

■ **in conventional situations**

EXAMPLES   12:15 P.M.

Luke 10:25–27

Bulfinch's Mythology: The Age of Fable, The Age of Chivalry, Legends of Charlemagne

"First Aid: Principles and Practices"

Dear Mrs. Komachi:

comma (See page 827.)

- **in a series**

  EXAMPLES   Among the species of flightless birds are the emu, ostrich, rhea, and penguin.

                  Gina's hobbies include designing greeting cards on her computer, collecting coins, and piecing quilts.

- **in compound sentences**

  EXAMPLES   Dr. Mariano Azuela wrote several novels, but his most famous is *The Underdogs,* a novel about the revolution in Mexico during the early part of the twentieth century.

                  Marta and I have not completed our woodworking project, and the deadline is Friday.

- **with nonessential phrases and clauses**

  EXAMPLES   Seeking fame, Gilgamesh travels with Enkidu to the cedar forest.

                  West Side Story, **which was written almost four hundred years later,** is based on Shakespeare's *Romeo and Juliet.*

- **with introductory elements**

  EXAMPLES   In the summer of 1994, Dr. Chiaki Naito-Mukai became the first Japanese woman to travel in space.

                  As my lab partner performed the chemistry experiment, I recorded the steps of the procedure.

- **with interrupters**

  EXAMPLES   The best program on television, in my opinion, is *Nova.*

                  Did you know that some foods we call vegetables, such as tomatoes and lima beans, are actually fruits?

- **in conventional situations**

  EXAMPLES   On Saturday, October 7, 2000, they drove to West Lafayette, Indiana, to visit the campus of Purdue University.

                  They mailed the letter to Dean of Admissions, Purdue University, West Lafayette, Indiana 47907-1080, on 5 February 2000.

comma splice A comma splice is a run-on sentence in which only a comma separates two independent clauses. (See page 434. See also **fused sentence, run-on sentence.**)

COMMA SPLICE	A haiku is a three-line poem that consists of seventeen syllables, the first and third lines contain five syllables each, the second line has seven.
REVISED	A haiku is a three-line poem that consists of seventeen syllables**;** the first and third lines contain five syllables each**, and** the second line has seven.
REVISED	A haiku is a three-line poem that consists of seventeen syllables**.** **T**he first and third lines contain five syllables each**;** the second line has seven.

comparison of modifiers (See page 730.)

■ **comparison of adjectives and adverbs**

Positive	Comparative	Superlative
dark	dark**er**	dark**est**
busy	bus**ier**	bus**iest**
imaginative	**more** imaginative	**most** imaginative
cautiously	**less** cautiously	**least** cautiously
far	**farther/further**	**farthest/furthest**
good/well	**better**	**best**

■ **comparing two**

EXAMPLES   This brand of orange juice tastes **tangier** than the brand we normally drink.

The team played **more aggressively** in the second half than in the first half.

■ **comparing more than two**

EXAMPLES   Weighing about three hundred pounds, the ostrich is the **largest** bird.

Of all of the species of birds that can swim, the penguin can propel itself underwater **most easily.**

complement A complement is a word or word group that completes the meaning of a verb. (See page 538. See also **direct object, indirect object, predicate nominative,** and **predicate adjective.**)

EXAMPLES   Tony gave **Suzanne** a **ring.**

It's not a dull **movie,** but it is **long.**

complex sentence A complex sentence has one independent clause and at least one subordinate clause. (See page 589.)

EXAMPLES   My friend Kishi, who draws cartoons for the school newspaper, wants to become a professional animator.

When the school holds its annual Shakespeare Festival on April 23, the drama classes will perform excerpts from some of the plays by the honored dramatist.

compound-complex sentence A compound-complex sentence has two or more independent clauses and at least one subordinate clause. (See page 590.)

EXAMPLES   Marcie had no difficulty downloading the article, but when she tried to e-mail it to her friend Will, who had requested it, her computer shut down.

When you are in Pittsburgh next summer, you should visit The Carnegie Museum of Art; it has impressive exhibits of American Indian and pre-Columbian artwork.

compound sentence A compound sentence has two or more independent clauses but no subordinate clauses. (See page 588.)

EXAMPLES   The horse was the first animal to be featured on a United States postage stamp; the two-cent stamp was issued in 1869.

Last summer, John worked two jobs to earn money for his college expenses; during the day, he caddied at a local golf course and at night bagged groceries at a nearby supermarket.

conjunction A conjunction joins words or groups of words. (See page 519.)

EXAMPLES   I am taking civics **and** art.

Shelley wants to **either** grow vegetables **or** raise pigs.

Sign the guest book **before** you go inside.

contraction A contraction is a shortened form of a word, a numeral, or a group of words. Apostrophes in contractions indicate where letters or numerals have been omitted. (See page 872. See also **apostrophe.**)

EXAMPLES   She'd [she had *or* she would]   there's [there is *or* there has]

who's [who is *or* who has]   it's [it is *or* it has]

haven't [have not]   they're [they are]

can't [cannot]   won't [will not]

'14–'18 war [1914–1918 war]   o'clock [of the clock]

dangling modifier A dangling modifier is a modifying word, phrase, or clause that does not clearly and sensibly modify a word or a word group in a sentence. (See page 746.)

DANGLING   Using deductive reasoning, the mystery was solved. [Who was using deductive reasoning?]

REVISED   Using deductive reasoning, **the detective** solved the mystery.

dash (See page 878.)

EXAMPLE   Among the pen names used by the Brontë sisters—Anne, Charlotte, and Emily—were Acton Bell, Currer Bell, and Ellis Bell, respectively.

declarative sentence A declarative sentence makes a statement and is followed by a period. (See page 591.)

EXAMPLE   The two countries with the highest life expectancy are Japan and Iceland**.**

direct object A direct object is a word or word group that receives the action of the verb or shows the result of the action. A direct object answers the question *Whom?* or *What?* after a transitive verb. (See page 539.)

EXAMPLE   Sandra bought **sunglasses.**

double comparison A double comparison is the nonstandard use of two comparative forms (usually *more* and *–er*) or two superlative forms (usually *most* and *–est*) to express comparison. In standard usage, the single comparative form is correct. (See page 733.)

NONSTANDARD   In classical mythology, was Hercules more stronger than Atlas?

STANDARD   In classical mythology, was Hercules **stronger** than Atlas?

double negative A double negative is the nonstandard use of two or more negative words to express a single negative idea. (See page 780.)

| NONSTANDARD | Sitting at the back of the theater, I couldn't barely hear the actors' dialogue. |
| STANDARD | Sitting at the back of the theater, I **could barely** hear the actors' dialogue. |

NONSTANDARD	Our library doesn't have no copies of August Wilson's most recent play.
STANDARD	Our library **doesn't have any** copies of August Wilson's most recent play.
STANDARD	Our library **has no** copies of August Wilson's most recent play.

double subject A double subject occurs when an unnecessary pronoun is used after the subject of a sentence.

| NONSTANDARD | The oystercatcher it's a large shorebird that feeds mainly on bivalve mollusks, such as oysters. |
| STANDARD | **The oystercatcher** is a large shorebird that feeds mainly on bivalve mollusks, such as oysters. |

elliptical construction An elliptical construction is a clause from which words have been omitted. (See page 643.)

| EXAMPLE | Joel is much taller **than his brothers** [are tall]. |

end marks (See page 820.)

■ **with sentences**

EXAMPLES	Weather permitting, the powwow will be held on the first Saturday in June**.**
	What is the difference between an endangered species and a threatened species**?**
	Bravo**!** What a heartfelt performance that was**!**
	Please tell us another story, Aunt Frida**.**

■ **with abbreviations** (See **abbreviations.**)

| EXAMPLES | In that movie, Tom Hanks portrays Commander James A. Lovell, Jr**.** |
| | In that movie, doesn't Tom Hanks portray Commander James A. Lovell, Jr**.?** |

essential clause/essential phrase An essential, or restrictive, clause or phrase is necessary to the meaning of a sentence; it is not set off by commas. (See page 833.)

EXAMPLES   The person **who left a bag in the library** can claim it at the office. [essential clause]

The man **wearing a bowler hat** is my grandfather. [essential phrase]

exclamation point (See **end marks.**)

exclamatory sentence An exclamatory sentence expresses strong feeling and is followed by an exclamation point. (See page 592.)

EXAMPLE   What a beautiful sunset that is**!**

faulty coordination Faulty coordination occurs when unequal ideas are presented as though they were coordinate. Usually, the clauses are strung together with coordinating conjunctions like *and* or *but*. (See page 425.)

FAULTY   Daedalus warned Icarus to avoid flying too high, for the sun would melt the wax, causing the wings to fall off, but before they had flown very far, Icarus soared too close to the sun, and as his father had warned, the wax melted, and the wings dropped off, and Icarus fell into the sea and drowned.

REVISED   Dadealus warned Icarus to avoid flying too high because the sun would melt the wax, causing the wings to fall off. Before they had flown very far, however, Icarus soared too close to the sun. As his father had warned, the wax melted, the wings dropped off, and Icarus fell into the sea and drowned.

fragment (See **sentence fragment.**)

fused sentence A fused sentence is a run-on sentence in which no punctuation separates independent clauses. (See page 434. See also **comma splice, run-on sentence.**)

FUSED   The Vietnam Veterans Memorial in Washington, D.C., was built in the early 1980s the Civil Rights Memorial in Montgomery, Alabama, was constructed only a few years later both monuments had been designed by Maya Ying Lin.

REVISED   The Vietnam Veterans Memorial in Washington, D.C., was built in the early 1980s**, and** the Civil Rights Memorial in Montgomery, Alabama, was constructed only a few years later**;** both monuments had been designed by Maya Ying Lin.

F

QUICK REFERENCE HANDBOOK

REVISED	The Vietnam Veterans Memorial in Washington, D.C., was built in the early 1980s; the Civil Rights Memorial in Montgomery, Alabama, was constructed only a few years later. Both monuments had been designed by Maya Ying Lin.

general reference A general reference is the incorrect use of a pronoun to refer to a general idea rather than to a specific noun. (See page 658.)

GENERAL	Yolanda, the team's star player, has been sidelined by a wrist injury. That may be the reason for her teammates' low morale. [To what does *That* refer?]
REVISED	That Yolanda, the team's star player, has been sidelined by a wrist injury may be the reason for her teammates' low morale.

gerund A gerund is a verb form ending in *–ing* that is used as a noun. (See page 562.)

EXAMPLE	**Smoking** is prohibited on all commercial domestic flights.

gerund phrase A gerund phrase consists of a gerund and any modifiers and complements it has. (See page 563.)

EXAMPLE	On weekends, Alberto enjoys **sending his friends e-mail.**

good, well (See page 727.)

EXAMPLES	To say that Pete Sampras is a **good** tennis player is an understatement.
	To say that Pete Sampras plays tennis **well** [not *good*] is an understatement.

hyphen (See page 874.)

■ **to divide words**

EXAMPLE	Seeing the patches of daffodils dotting the hill-side reminded me of a Wordsworth poem.

■ **in compound numbers**

EXAMPLE	By the time you graduate, will you have earned twenty-four credits?

■ **with prefixes and suffixes**

EXAMPLES	The grand opening of the new shopping mall is scheduled for mid-October.
	Janet handed the gavel to the president-elect.

imperative mood The imperative mood is used to express a direct command or request. (See page 709.)

EXAMPLES **Put** that magazine down!

Read what the sign says.

imperative sentence An imperative sentence gives a command or makes a request and is followed by either a period or an exclamation point. (See page 591.)

EXAMPLES List the first six presidents**.**

Be quiet**!**

indefinite reference An indefinite reference is the incorrect use of the pronoun *you, it,* or *they* to refer to no particular person or thing. (See page 662.)

INDEFINITE In this book they state that *The Mahabharata* is the longest poem ever written.

REVISED This book states that *The Mahabharata* is the longest poem ever written.

independent clause An independent, or main, clause expresses a complete thought and can stand by itself as a sentence. (See page 576.)

EXAMPLE **Egypt is an African nation,** but **it is an Arabic nation as well**.

indicative mood The indicative mood is used to express a fact, an opinion, or a question. (See page 709.)

EXAMPLES Flann O'Brien **was** the pen name of an Irish writer and journalist.

Jacques Villeneuve **is** a Canadian race-car driver.

Don't you **live** next door to the Sandovals?

indirect object An indirect object is a noun, pronoun, or word group that sometimes appears in sentences containing direct objects. An indirect object tells *to whom* or *to what* (or *for whom* or *for what*) the action of a transitive verb is done. Indirect objects generally precede direct objects. (See page 540.)

EXAMPLE Lucy cooked **us** dinner.

infinitive An infinitive is a verb form, usually preceded by *to*, that is used as a noun, an adjective, or an adverb. (See page 564.)

EXAMPLES   Would you like **to dance**?

              The casserole is ready **to go** into the oven.

infinitive phrase An infinitive phrase consists of an infinitive and any modifiers and complements it has. (See page 565.)

EXAMPLE   Aunt Usha, I would like **to introduce my fiancé.**

interjection An interjection expresses emotion and has no grammatical relation to the rest of the sentence. (See page 522.)

EXAMPLE   **Wow!** There goes another one!

interrogative sentence An interrogative sentence asks a question and is followed by a question mark. (See page 592.)

EXAMPLE   Are you Stephen Welch of Austin, Texas**?**

intransitive verb An intransitive verb is a verb that does not take an object. (See page 512.)

EXAMPLE   Arthur **called,** but no one **answered.**

irregular verb An irregular verb is a verb that forms its past and past participle in some way other than by adding *–d* or *–ed* to the base form. (See page 672. See also **regular verb.**)

Base Form	Present Participle	Past	Past Participle
arise	[is] arising	arose	[have] arisen
be	[is] being	was, were	[have] been
become	[is] becoming	became	[have] become
cost	[is] costing	cost	[have] cost
freeze	[is] freezing	froze	[have] frozen
lead	[is] leading	led	[have] led
meet	[is] meeting	met	[have] met
seek	[is] seeking	sought	[have] sought
spread	[is] spreading	spread	[have] spread

italics (See page 856.)

- **for titles**

  EXAMPLES   *A Portrait of the Artist as a Young Man* [book]

                   People Weekly [periodical]

                   Duke Ellington: Reminiscing in Tempo [film]

                   Thor's Fight with the Giants [work of art]

                   Pomp and Circumstance [long musical composition]

- **for words, letters, and symbols referred to as such and for foreign words**

  EXAMPLES   I had made two spelling errors in my report: I had added *i* after *l* in **similar** and had omitted *i* after *l* in **familiar.**

                   Many epic poems begin **in medias res,** that is, "in the middle of the action."

its, it's (See page 907.)

EXAMPLES   **Its** [California's] nickname is the Golden State.

                 In land area **it's** [it is] the third-largest state in the Union.

                 It's [It has] been a state since 1850.

lie, lay (See page 688.)

EXAMPLES   As soon as he came home from school, Terence went to his room and **lay** down. [past tense of *lie*]

                 As soon as he came home from school, Terence **laid** his book bag down, took out his report card, and showed it to his father. [past tense of *lay*]

linking verb A linking verb connects its subject with a word that identifies or describes the subject. (See page 511.)

EXAMPLE   Brasilia **is** the capital of Brazil.

misplaced modifier A misplaced modifier is a word, phrase, or clause that seems to modify the wrong word or words in a sentence. (See page 744.)

MISPLACED   Written by Zeami Motokiyo, a videotaped performance of the Noh drama *Atsumori* inspired the drama club to write and produce a play in the style of the famous Japanese play-wright. [Was the performance written by Zeami Motokiyo?]

REVISED   A videotaped performance of the Noh drama *Atsumori*, **written by Zeami Motokiyo,** inspired the drama club to write and produce a play in the style of the famous Japanese playwright.

modifier A modifier is a word or word group that makes the meaning of another word or word group more specific. (See page 722.)

EXAMPLE   Forster **quickly** asked his **important** question.

mood Mood is the form a verb takes to indicate the attitude of the person using the verb. (See page 709. See also **imperative mood, indicative mood,** and **subjunctive mood.**)

nonessential clause/nonessential phrase A nonessential, or nonrestrictive, clause or phrase adds information not necessary to the main idea in the sentence and is set off by commas. (See page 832.)

EXAMPLES   The lakeside hotel, **which was built in 1900,** is being renovated. [nonessential clause]

Juan and Howard, **the team's co-captains,** walked to the middle of the field. [nonessential phrase]

noun A noun names a person, place, thing, or idea. (See page 498.)

EXAMPLES   The **study** of **subjects** such as **geography** and **chemistry** helps us to learn about the **world.**

Alsace is a **region** of **France.**

noun clause A noun clause is a subordinate clause used as a noun. (See page 581.)

EXAMPLE   The main message of Ms. Pinckney's talk was **that we should always be punctual.**

number Number is the form a word takes to indicate whether the word is singular or plural. (See page 600.)

SINGULAR	chair	she	knife	child
PLURAL	chairs	they	knives	children

objective complement An objective complement is a word or word group that helps complete the meaning of a transitive verb by identifying or modifying the direct object. (See page 541.)

EXAMPLE   Sandy called her grandfather a **hero.**

object of a preposition An object of a preposition is the noun or pronoun that ends a prepositional phrase. (See page 554.)

EXAMPLE   He complained about **Minna.**

parallel structure Parallel structure is the use of the same grammatical forms or structures to balance related ideas in a sentence. (See page 426.)

NONPARALLEL   Each day, I reserve time for engaging in a forty-minute aerobic workout and to write in my journal.

PARALLEL   Each day, I reserve time **for engaging in a forty-minute aerobic workout** and **for writing in my journal.** [two prepositional phrases]

PARALLEL   Each day, I reserve time **to engage in a forty-minute aerobic workout** and **to write in my journal.** [two infinitive phrases]

parentheses (See page 878.)

EXAMPLES   The three small bones in the middle ear of a human **(**see diagram A**)** are the malleus **(**hammer**)**, incus **(**anvil**)**, and stapes **(**stirrup**)**.

The three small bones in the middle ear of a human are the malleus **(**hammer**)**, incus **(**anvil**)**, and stapes **(**stirrup**)**. **(**See diagram A**.)**

participial phrase A participial phrase consists of a participle and any complements and modifiers it has. (See page 559.)

EXAMPLE   The dog, **straining at the leash,** obviously wanted to go for a walk.

participle A participle is a verb form that can be used as an adjective. (See page 558.)

EXAMPLE   The painting depicts a calm landscape and **billowing** clouds.

passive voice The passive voice is the voice a verb is in when it expresses an action done to its subject. (See page 705. See also **voice.**)

EXAMPLE   Finally, Uncle Ed **was given** a promotion.

period (See **end marks.**)

phrase A phrase is a group of related words that does not contain both a verb and its subject and that is used as a single part of speech. (See page 553.)

EXAMPLES   Ahmed Nasr, **one of the Egyptian Embassy's attachés, will discuss** the excavations **in the Valley of the Kings.** [*One of the Egyptian Embassy's attachés* is an appositive phrase. *Will discuss* is a verb phrase. *In the Valley of the Kings* is a prepositional phrase.]

Telling the truth is the best way **to stay out of trouble.** [*Telling the truth* is a gerund phrase. *To stay out of trouble* is an infinitive phrase.]

Perching on a nearby branch, the bird sang a beautiful tune. [*Perching on a nearby branch* is a participial phrase.]

predicate The predicate is the part of a sentence that says something about the subject. (See page 533.)

EXAMPLE   **All his life,** he **wanted to walk along the Seine.**

predicate adjective A predicate adjective is an adjective that completes the meaning of a linking verb and modifies the subject of the verb. (See page 544.)

EXAMPLE   Grandma looked **rested** and **healthy.**

predicate nominative A predicate nominative is a noun or pronoun that completes the meaning of a linking verb and that identifies or refers to the subject of the verb. (See page 543.)

EXAMPLE   Joel is a **guitarist.**

prefix A prefix is a word part that is added before a base word or root. (See page 892.)

EXAMPLES   un + harmed = **un**harmed   im + proper = **im**proper mis + spoke = **mis**spoke   re + invest = **re**invest

mid + March = **mid**-March   ex + coach = **ex**-coach

self + addressed =   pre + Columbian =
    self-addressed   **pre**-Columbian

preposition A preposition shows the relationship of a noun or a
pronoun to some other word in a sentence. (See page 517.)

EXAMPLE   *A Tale **of** Two Cities,* **by** Charles Dickens, is a novel **about**
    the French Revolution.

prepositional phrase A prepositional phrase includes a preposition, its object (a noun or a pronoun), and any modifiers of that object.
(See page 554.)

EXAMPLE   **During class,** the teacher made us practice **for the exam.**

pronoun A pronoun is used in place of one or more nouns or pronouns. (See page 501.)

EXAMPLES   Paula left Mike alone, so as to give **him** more time.

    Eric and Carla promised **they** would come to the party.

    Everyone should get **himself** or **herself** a plate and a fork.

question mark (See **end marks.**)

quotation marks (See page 859.)

- **for direct quotations**
  EXAMPLE   "When using statistics in your writing," said Mr. Torres,
      "you need to check more than one reliable source."

- **with other marks of punctuation** (See also preceding example.)
  EXAMPLES   "In that year," said Marlena, "the Commonwealth of
      Independent States was formed."

      The teacher asked, "Which poem by Dylan Thomas
      ends 'Rage, rage against the dying of the light'?"

- **for titles**
  EXAMPLES   "The Japanese Quince" [short story]
      "Do Not Go Gentle into That Good Night" [short poem]
      "Blowin' in the Wind" [song]

regular verb A regular verb is a verb that forms its past and past participle by adding *d* or *ed* to the base form. (See page 670. See also **irregular verb.**)

Base Form	Present Participle	Past	Past Participle
ask	[is] asking	asked	[have] asked
drown	[is] drowning	drowned	[have] drowned
perceive	[is] perceiving	perceived	[have] perceived
risk	[is] risking	risked	[have] risked
suppose	[is] supposing	supposed	[have] supposed
use	[is] using	used	[have] used

rise, raise (See page 690.)

EXAMPLES   The price of a movie ticket is expected to **rise.**

The legislators are voting on whether to **raise** the minimum wage.

run-on sentence A run-on sentence is two or more complete sentences run together as one. (See page 434. See also **comma splice** and **fused sentence.**)

RUN-ON   Frank Trilby and Benny O'Hara were a pair of Chicago detectives in the 1930s who specialized in tracking down those responsible for gangland executions, they made their name in a notorious case known as "The Navy Pier Slaying."

REVISED   Frank Trilby and Benny O'Hara were a pair of Chicago detectives in the 1930s who specialized in tracking down those responsible for gangland executions; they made their name in a notorious case known as "The Navy Pier Slaying."

REVISED   Frank Trilby and Benny O'Hara were a pair of Chicago detectives in the 1930s who specialized in tracking down those responsible for gangland executions. They made their name in a notorious case known as "The Navy Pier Slaying."

semicolon (See page 850.)

■ **in compound sentences with no conjunction**

EXAMPLE   The five-day forecast calls for unseasonably warm weather; daytime temperatures are expected to rise above seventy degrees Fahrenheit.

- **in compound sentences with conjunctive adverbs or transitional expressions**

  EXAMPLE This story is written in the omniscient point of view; **that is,** the thoughts and actions of all of the characters are revealed to the reader by an all-knowing narrator who is not part of the story.

- **between items in a series when the items contain commas**

  EXAMPLE The senior-class reading list includes *The Book of Songs,* an anthology of early Chinese poetry; *Panchatantra,* a collection of fables from India; and *Oedipus Rex,* a play by the Greek tragedian Sophocles.

sentence A sentence is a group of words that contains a subject and a verb and expresses a complete thought. (See page 530.)

       S   V

EXAMPLE **Rain falls** mostly on the central plains.

sentence fragment A sentence fragment is a group of words that is punctuated as if it were a complete sentence but that does not contain both a subject and a verb or that does not express a complete thought. (See page 530.)

FRAGMENT Which is the growing of plants in solutions rather than in soils.

SENTENCE The horticulturist explained the benefits of hydroponic gardening, which is the growing of plants in solutions rather than in soils.

FRAGMENT Because she had left school early for her orthodontist appointment.

SENTENCE Because she had left school early for her orthodontist appointment, Karen missed the pop quiz in her algebra class.

simple sentence A simple sentence has one independent clause and no subordinate clauses. (See page 588.)

EXAMPLES May Francine and I have your mother's recipe for tabouli salad?

This magazine features an article about the Paiute writer and interpreter Thoc-me-tony, perhaps better known as Sarah Winnemucca.

sit, set (See page 689.)

EXAMPLES   Tamisha **sat** in the rocking chair, gently cradling her newly adopted Australian terrier puppy. [past tense of *sit*]

Emilia, who **set** this box of office supplies on the credenza? [past tense of *set*]

slow, slowly (See page 727.)

EXAMPLES   "**Slow** drivers can be as much of a menace on the road as fast drivers," said Erwin.

Dr. Emmet spoke very **slowly,** with a pronounced accent.

subject The subject tells whom or what a sentence is about. (See page 531.)

EXAMPLES   **Mr. Papastratos** proudly presided over the inauguration of his new restaurant.

Its **specialties** include moussaka, dolmades, and *keftedes.*

subject complement A subject complement is a word or word group that completes the meaning of a linking verb and identifies or describes the subject. (See page 543. See also **predicate nominative** and **predicate adjective.**)

EXAMPLES   Maurice's aunt is a college **administrator.**

The effect was **dramatic.**

subjunctive mood The subjunctive mood is used to express a suggestion, a necessity, a condition contrary to fact, or a wish. (See page 709.)

EXAMPLES   Ms. Chen recommended that Gloria **audition** for the leading role. [suggestion]

If I **were** you, I would have a skilled mechanic inspect the used car before I would consider buying it. [condition contrary to fact]

subordinate clause A subordinate, or dependent, clause does not express a complete thought and cannot stand alone as a sentence. (See page 577. See also **noun clause, adjective clause,** and **adverb clause.**)

EXAMPLE   **While we walk,** can we talk?

suffix A suffix is a word part that is added after a base word or root. (See page 893.)

EXAMPLES
habitual + ly = habitual**ly**	easy + ly = easi**ly**
polite + ness = polite**ness**	survey + or = survey**or**
believe + able = believ**able**	manage + able = manage**able**
plan + ing = plann**ing**	sugar + free = sugar-**free**

tense of verbs The tense of a verb indicates the state of being or time of the action expressed by the verb. (See page 692.)

Present Tense

I choose	we choose
you choose	you choose
he, she, it chooses	they choose

Past Tense

I chose	we chose
you chose	you chose
he, she, it chose	they chose

Future Tense

I will (shall) choose	we will (shall) choose
you will (shall) choose	you will (shall) choose
he, she, it will (shall) choose	they will (shall) choose

Present Perfect Tense

I have chosen	we have chosen
you have chosen	you have chosen
he, she, it has chosen	they have chosen

Past Perfect Tense

I had chosen	we had chosen
you had chosen	you had chosen
he, she, it had chosen	they had chosen

Future Perfect Tense

I will (shall) have chosen	we will (shall) have chosen
you will (shall) have chosen	you will (shall) have chosen
he, she, it will (shall) have chosen	they will (shall) have chosen

transitive verb A transitive verb is an action verb that takes an object. (See page 512.)

EXAMPLE Jack, my poodle, **fetches** any ball as eagerly as a retriever would.

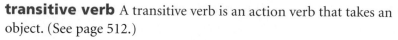

verb A verb expresses an action or a state of being. (See page 509.)

EXAMPLES My cousin Ignacio **traveled** from the Arctic Circle to the Bay of Biscay.

Where **is** the Bay of Biscay?

verbal A verbal is a form of a verb used as a noun, an adjective, or an adverb. (See page 558. See also **gerund, infinitive,** and **participle.**)

EXAMPLES **Laughing** and **waving,** the president sat down. [participles]

Hard work will help you **to succeed.** [infinitive]

Make **saving** money a priority. [gerund]

verbal phrase A verbal phrase consists of a verbal and its modifiers and complements. (See page 558. See also **gerund phrase, infinitive phrase,** and **participial phrase.**)

EXAMPLES **Schooled in ancient Celtic traditions,** the shanachie, or Irish storyteller, also sometimes learns **to sing folk songs.** [participial phrase/infinitive phrase]

Brian will never forget **swimming in the ocean.** [gerund phrase]

verb phrase A verb phrase consists of a main verb and at least one helping verb. (See page 509.)

EXAMPLES I **am sailing** across the bay.

Have you ever **been** to Peru?

voice Voice is the form a transitive verb takes to indicate whether the subject of the verb performs or receives the action. (See page 705.)

ACTIVE VOICE Percy Spencer **invented** the microwave oven in 1947.
PASSIVE VOICE The microwave oven **was invented** by Percy Spencer in 1947.

weak reference A weak reference is the incorrect use of a pronoun to refer to an antecedent that has not been expressed. (See page 661.)

WEAK   Stephen King is a prolific writer; many of them have been made into films. [To what does *them* refer?]

REVISED   Stephen King is a prolific writer; many of his **novels** have been made into films.

well (See *good, well.*)

who, whom (See page 646.)

EXAMPLES   Family members, friends, and teachers are only a few of the people **who** play influential roles in our lives.

Advertisers, journalists, celebrities, and other people **whom** we have never met influence our lives every day, too.

wordiness Wordiness is the use of more words than necessary or of fancy words where simple ones will do. (See page 458.)

WORDY   At the present time, I am currently reading a biography that chronicles the life of W.E.B. DuBois, who was an African American educator and writer who helped to cofound the National Association for the Advancement of Colored People (NAACP) in the year 1909.

REVISED   Currently, I am reading a biography of W.E.B. DuBois, an African American educator and writer who cofounded the National Association for the Advancement of Colored People (NAACP) in 1909.

cross-examination debate, 1017
debate proposition, 1015–16
etiquette for, 1016
features of, 1015–16
formal debate, 1016–17
formats of, 1016–17
Lincoln-Douglas debate, 1017
negative team, 1019
officials for, 1016
preparing for, 1017–18
proposition of policy and, 1016
proposition of value and, 1016
rebuttal speeches, 1019
refuting opposing arguments, 1019
Declarative sentences, 591, 820, 1095
Decoding, 1057
Deconstruction, 1057
Deduction, definition of, 159
Definite articles, 506
Definitions. *See also* Dictionaries; Vocabulary.
 context clues as, 385
 in dictionaries, 960
 for dramatic reading, 225
Democratic process, media influencing, 110
Demographics, definition of, 1060
Demonstrative pronouns, 503, 507
Denotations
 dramatic reading and, 225
 understanding denotations, 299
Dependent clauses. *See* Subordinate clauses.
Depth, of media coverage, 114, 115
Desai, Anita, 432
Descriptive details. *See also* Details.
 in introductions to compositions, 480
 in reflective essay, 33
Descriptive paragraphs, 1076
Desert, dessert, 907
Designing your writing. *See* Document design.
Desktop publishing, page layout, 963–67
Detail questions, 108
Details
 choosing details, 1083
 as conveying theme, 33
 descriptive details, 33
 evaluating film version of drama and, 223
 interpreting and analyzing, 6
 narrative details, 33
 recalling details for reflective essay, 33
 sensory details, 33
 strategies for gathering, 33
 supporting details from literary sources, 182, 191–93
Dewey decimal classification system, 984
Diagrams, 974, 1003
Dialects, 976, 981–82
Dialogue. *See also* Direct quotations.
 in ballads, 173

dialogue tags, 34, 44
 punctuating correctly, 44
 punctuation of, 862
 showing versus telling and, 34
 stilted dialogue, 72
 as ungrammatical, 72
 writing dramatic scenes and, 218
 writing effective dialogue, 72
Diction, for speeches, 1023
Dictionaries. *See also* Library/media center; Sources; Vocabulary.
 abbreviations in, 961
 antonyms and, 961
 biographical and geographical entries, 961
 definitions in, 960
 entry word and, 959–60
 etymology and, 960, 1009
 examples in, 960
 geographical material, 961
 part-of-speech labels in, 960
 principal parts of verbs and, 673
 pronunciation and, 960
 related word forms and, 961
 special usage labels and, 960–61
 as spelling aids, 889
 synonyms and, 961
 types of, 958–59
 using dictionary to research word origins, 26
Diderot, Denis, 3
Digital editing, definition of, 1060
Dinesen, Isak, 867
Direct address, noun of, 536, 838–39
Direct characterization, definition of, 63
Directions, giving and receiving, 1027, 1033
Direct objects
 compound direct object, 540
 definition of, 539, 635, 1095
 placement of, 539
 pronouns as, 635
Direct quotations. *See also* Dialogue.
 capitalization and, 44, 790–91, 859–60
 integrating into text, 211–12
 punctuation of, 44, 859–63
Direct references, definition of, 470
Discover, invent, 764
Discussions. *See* Group discussions.
Dive, **principal parts of,** 677
Divided quotation, 860
Do
 as helping verb, 510
 principal parts of, 677
Docudramas, 344, 1052
Documentaries
 audio elements of, 346
 comparison-contrast essay on nonfiction book and documentary of same subject, 373
 criteria for evaluating, 332, 339–40

O

ACKNOWLEDGMENTS

For permission to reprint copyrighted material, grateful acknowledgment is made to the following sources:

American Historical Association: From review by Ellen Carol Dubois of *The Civil War*, produced by Ken Burns and Ric Burns from *American Historical Review*. Copyright © 1991 by American Historical Association.

The Asia Society: "Thoughts of Hanoi" by Nguyen Thi Vinh, translated by Nguyen Ngoc Bich from *A Thousand Years of Vietnamese Poetry*. Copyright © 1975 by The Asia Society.

Discover Magazine: From "Edible Motor Oil" by Fenella Saunders from *Discover*, August 1998. Copyright © 1998 by Fenella Saunders. From "Cosmic Kickball" by Jeffrey Winters from *Discover*, August 1998. Copyright © 1998 by Jeffrey Winters.

Farrar, Straus & Giroux, Inc.: From "One Art" from *The Complete Poems 1927-1979* by Elizabeth Bishop. Copyright © 1979, 1983 by Alice Helen Methfessel.

Steve Faulkner: From "Common Water" by Steve Faulkner from *DoubleTake*, Winter 1998. Copyright © 1998 by Steve Faulkner.

Kevin Featherly: From "TV's Threat Gets Bigger on the Web: How the TV Networks are Competing with Papers" by Kevin Featherly from *mediainfo.com Magazine*, November 1998. Copyright © 1998 by Kevin Featherly.

Fromm International Publishing Corporation, New York: From "William Caxton: Printer" from *The Story of Britain* by Sir Roy Strong. Copyright © 1996 by Oman Productions Ltd. Originally published in the United Kingdom by Hutchinson, in association with Julia McRae, London, 1996. All rights reserved under International and Pan-American Copyright Convention.

Harcourt, Inc.: From "Onward into the Past" from *Art & Ideas*, Ninth Edition, by Bill Fleming. Copyright © 1995 by Harcourt Brace & Company.

Harvard University Press: From "Krakatau" from *The Diversity of Life* by E. O. Wilson. Copyright © 1992 by E. O. Wilson.

George Lamming: From *In the Castle of My Skin* by George Lamming. Copyright © 1970 by Longman Group Limited. Published by Schocken Books Inc.

Macmillan General Reference, a division of IDG Consumer Reference, part of IDG Books Worldwide, Inc.: Entry "empty" from *Webster's New World College Dictionary*, Fourth Edition, Michael Agnes, Editor-in-Chief. Copyright © 1999 by Simon & Schuster, Inc.

Carol Mann Agency: From "Late Afternoon" from *The Secret House: 24 Hours in the Strange and Unexpected World in Which We Spend Our Nights and Days* by David Bodanis. Copyright © 1986 by David Bodanis. All rights reserved.

Bill McKibben: Adapted from "Curbing Nature's Paparazzi" by Bill McKibben from *DoubleTake*, Fall 1997. Copyright © 1997 by Bill McKibben.

William Morrow & Company, Inc. a division of HarperCollins Publishers, Inc.: From "Put Down That Paper and Talk to Me!" from *You Just Don't Understand: Woman and Men in Conversation* by Deborah Tannen, Ph.D. Copyright © 1990 by Deborah Tannen, Ph.D.

NASA: "Earth Observatory," from *NASA*, online, June 11, 1999. Available http://earthobservatory.nasa.gov.

National Wildlife Federation: "The Value of Autumn Leaves" by Richard Busch from *National Wildlife*, vol. 36, no. 6, October/November 1998. Copyright © 1998 by National Wildlife Federation.

New Directions Publishing Corp.: From *Martín and Meditations on the South Valley* by Jimmy Santiago Baca. Copyright © 1987 by Jimmy Santiago Baca.

The New Press, 450 W 41 St., New York, NY 10036: From *The Sneaker Book: Anatomy of an Industry and an Icon* by Tom Vanderbilt. Copyright © 1998 by Tom Vanderbilt.

Newsweek, Inc.: From "www.Apply-Here.com" by T. Trent Gegax from *Newsweek*, October 19, 1998. Copyright © 1998 by Newsweek, Inc. All rights reserved. "My Turn: Homegrown Varieties" by Russell A. Mittermeier from *Newsweek*, August 11, 1997. Copyright © 1997 by Newsweek, Inc. All rights reserved.

North Point Press, a division of Farrar, Straus & Giroux, Inc.: From *West with the Night* by Beryl Markham. Copyright © 1942, 1983 by Beryl Markham.

W. W. Norton & Company: From "Graveyard of the Atlantic" from *The Perfect Storm: A True Story of Men Against the Sea* by Sebastian Junger. Copyright © 1997 by Sebastian Junger.

Oxford University Press, Inc.: From *The Sea Around Us* by Rachel Carson. Copyright 1950, 1951, ©1961 by Rachel Carson; copyright renewed © 1979 by Roger Christie.

Peter Pauper Press, Inc.: From a Mauritanian proverb from *African Proverbs,* compiled by Charlotte and Wolf Leslau. Copyright © 1962, 1985 by Peter Pauper Press, Inc.

Penguin, a division of Penguin Putnam Inc.: From "Reading Shadows" from *A History of Reading* by Alberto Manguel. Copyright © 1996 by Alberto Manguel.

The Pennsylvania State University Press: From "Beyond the Verbal in Pygmalion" by Richard Hornby from *Shaw's Plays in Performance,* edited by Daniel Leary. Copyright © 1983 by The Pennsylvania State University, University Park.

Demetrio Perez, Jr.: From "School uniforms have been proven beneficial" by Demetrio Perez, Jr., from *The Miami Herald,* March 24, 1997, p. 12A. Copyright © 1997 by Demetrio Perez, Jr.

Random House, Inc.: "My Mother's Blue Bowl" from *Anything We Love Can Be Saved* by Alice Walker. Copyright © 1997 by Alice Walker.

Anita Desai, c/o Rogers, Coleridge & White Ltd., 20 Powis Mews, London W11 1JN: From "Games at Twilight" from *Games at Twilight and Other Stories* by Anita Desai. Copyright © 1978 by Anita Desai.

University of Notre Dame Press: From *Barrio Boy* by Ernesto Galarza. Copyright © 1971 by University of Notre Dame Press.

University of Pennsylvania Press: From *Jane Austen and the Province of Womenhood* by Alison G. Sulloway. Copyright © 1989 by the University of Pennsylvania Press.

Viking Penguin, a division of Penguin Putnam, Inc.: From "The Rocking-Horse Winner" from *Complete Short Stories of D. H. Lawrence.* Copyright 1933 by the Estate of D. H. Lawrence; copyright renewed © 1961 by Angelo Ravagli and C. M. Weekly, Executors of the Estate of Frieda Lawrence.

SOURCES CITED:

From *Chaos: Making a New Science* by James Gleick. Published by Penguin Books, a division of Penguin Putnam, Inc., New York, 1987.

Abbreviations used: (tl)top left, (tc)top center, (tr)top right, (l)left, (lc)left center, (c)center, (rc)right center, (r)right, (bl)bottom left, (bc)bottom center, (br)bottom right.

COVER: Scott Van Osdol/HRW Photo.

TABLE OF CONTENTS: Page viii (tr), *Noya + Bill Brandt with Self Portrait (Although They Were Watching This Picture Being Made) Pembroke Studios London 8th May 1982, 1982,* Composite Polaroid, 24 1/2" x 24 1/2". © David Hockney; viii (br), Paul Vismara/The Stock Illustration Source, Inc.; ix, Paul Vismara/The Stock Illustration Source, Inc.; x, *Family of Robot: Grandfather* by Nam June Paik, 1986. Robert J. Shiffler Collection. Photo courtesy of the Carl Solway Gallery. Photo by Cal Kowal.; xi, Johnny Autery/Peter Menzel Photography; xii, Paul Davis; xiii, American Library Services; xv, Brown Brothers; xvii, Reuters/Dwight Andrews/Archive Photos; xviii, Fred McConnaughey/Photo Researchers, Inc.; xix, Lawrence Migdale/Photo Researchers, Inc.; xx, Photo Edit; xxi, Bill Aron/Photo Edit; xxii, Tony Duffy/Allsport; xxiii, The Lowe Art Museum, The University of Miami/SuperStock; xxiv, Corbis Images; xxv, David R. Frazier Photolibrary; xxvi, SuperStock; xxvii, The Lowe Art Museum, The University of Miami/SuperStock; xxviii; Royal Ontario Museum, Toronto Canada/HRW Photo Research Library; xxix, NASA; xx, Walter Bibikow/FPG International.

PART OPENERS: Page xxiv, 1, 416, 417, 494, 495, 956, 957, Dave Cutler/The Stock Illustration Source, Inc.

CHAPTER 1: Page 16, *Noya + Bill Brandt with Self Portrait (Although They Were Watching This Picture Being Made) Pembroke Studios London 8th May 1982, 1982,* Composite Polaroid, 24 1/2" x 24 1/2". © David Hockney; 43, © Jake Rajas / Photonica; 54 (tl), Victoria Smith/HRW Photo; 54 (cl) ©1997 Radlund & Associates for Artville; 54 (l), Michelle Bridwell/Frontera Fotos.

CHAPTER 2: Page 56, Paul Vismara/The Stock Illustration Source, Inc.

CHAPTER 3: Page 94, *Family of Robot: Grandfather* by Nam June Paik, 1986. Robert J. Shiffler Collection. Photo courtesy of the Carl Solway Gallery. Photo by Cal Kowal.; 128, NASA.

CHAPTER 4: Page 138, Johnny Autery/Peter Menzel Photography; 141, Image Copyright ©2001 PhotoDisc, Inc.; 142, Whit Bronaugh.

CHAPTER 5: Page 180, Paul Davis.

CHAPTER 6: Page 288, American Library Services; 292, Luiz C. Marigo /Peter Arnold, Inc.

CHAPTER 8: Page 330, Brown Brothers; 356, Fine Line/Shooting Star International.

CHAPTER 9: Page 374, Paul Schulenburg/The Stock Illustration Source, Inc.; 377, Image Copyright ©2001 PhotoDisc, Inc.

CHAPTER 10: Page 420, Culver Pictures, Inc.; 421, Corbis-Bettmann; 425 (cr) (br), Gary Retherford/Photo Researchers, Inc.; 430, Photofest; 432, Fred McConnaughey/Photo Researchers, Inc.; 436, Sinclair Stammers/Science Photo Library; 437, The Gamma Liaison Network.

CHAPTER 11: Page 439, Ed Carlin/Archive Photos; 441, Larry West/FPG International; 443, Corbis/Bettmann-UPI; 445, NASA/Peter Arnold, Inc.; 449 (cr) (br), Photofest; 451, Steve Vidler/Nawrocki Stock Photo.

CHAPTER 12: Page 454, Runk/Schoenberger/Grant Heilman Photography; 456, The Stock Market; 460, Reuters/Dwight Andrews/Archive Photos; 462, Photofest.

CHAPTER 13: Page 466, CORBIS; 467, CORBIS/Karen Huntt Mason; 470, Michael Daniel; 472, Lawrence Migdale/Photo Researchers, Inc.; 477, Culver Pictures, Inc.; 478, David Weintraub/Photo Researchers, Inc.; 479, Photo by Amy Snyder; 480, StageImage; 482, Tom McHugh/Photo Researchers, Inc.; 493, NOAA/Science Photo Library/Photo Researchers, Inc.

CHAPTER 14: Page 500, AP/Wide World Photos; 509, FPG International; 514 (tr), Bill Aron/Photo Edit; 524, John Pinderhughes/The Stock Market.

CHAPTER 15: Page 537 (cl) (cr), The Lowe Art Museum, The University of Miami/SuperStock; 542, Michael Newman/PhotoEdit; 547 (tl) (tr), Bruno Barbey/Magnum Photos.

CHAPTER 16: Page 555, David Austen /Woodfin Camp & Associates; 557, Everett/CSU Archives; 562, Josef Armendariz/HRW Photo; 567, Sygma Paris; 569, Georgia Lowell/Photo Researchers, Inc.

CHAPTER 17: Page 578, British Museum, London/Art Resource, NY; 581, Corbis Images; 584, Courtesy of Dr. Athelstian Spilhaus; 586, Image Copyright ©2001 Photodisc, Inc. 593, Corbis Images.

CHAPTER 18: Page 605, George Rinhart/Corbis-Bettmann; 608, SuperStock; 616, Walter Bibikow/FPG International; 617, Granitsas/The Image Works.

CHAPTER 19: Page 637, Tony Duffy/Allsport; 640, CORBIS/Baldwin H. Ward.

CHAPTER 20: Page 660, Stock Montage, Inc.

CHAPTER 21: Page 676, Corbis Images; 679, Michel Garnier-Explorer/Photo Researchers, Inc.; 681, Fred Hirschmann.

CHAPTER 22: Page 726, Everett Collection; 729 (cr), Archive Photos; 738, The Kobal Collection.

CHAPTER 24: Page 761, Schomburg Center for Research in Black Culture/The New York Public Library/Astor, Lenox and Tilden Foundations; 779, Lawrence Migdale.

CHAPTER 25: Page 803, NASA; 809, Stan Byers.

ILLUSTRATION CREDITS